THE
SOUND AND THE FURY

BY WILLIAM FAULKNER

William Faulkner
Los Angeles, Cal
26 May 1932

I put my living guts into this.

NEW YORK
JONATHAN CAPE AND HARRISON SMITH

The Sound and the Fury (A6c).

Carl Petersen

EACH IN ITS ORDERED PLACE:

A Faulkner Collector's Notebook

Ardis, Ann Arbor

For the Memory of IJA ADLER

Contents

Photographs

    Jacket photograph by Martin J. Dain. (Copyright
      © 1963. All rights reserved.)
    Frontispiece—*The Sound and the Fury* (A6c) 2
    Soldiers' Pay (A2b) 22
    Dedication page of A3a 26
    Mosquitoes manuscript fragment (A4a) 28
    Jacket (A4b) 30
    Jacket (A4c). Probably the scarcest of
      Faulkner jackets. 30

FOREWORD

This bibliographic notebook is assembled in celebration of twenty-five years of collecting Faulkner following the excitement and delight of my discovery of *As I Lay Dying.*

An author collection is usually formed because the books, the letters, the relics give the collector a sense of closer approach to the intents, the techniques, and the talents of the author. One collects a particular writer because that writer's art evokes in the collector positive personal responses that may be esthetically informed or may involve simple curiosity or even a kind of greed. Whatever the combination of motivations, Faulkner is the writer who has for me made the chase pleasurable.

Securing collectible Faulkner items is always gratifying. However, much of the satisfaction of collecting has come from the people involved in the pursuit. I am grateful to friends who tried never to be bored by my enthusiasm, to bookdealers who offered the scarce and ephemeral often out of mutual pleasure rather than the prospect of substantial profit, and to those people whose lives had intersected Faulkner's life and who were willing to share their experiences.

Certain individuals have been particularly influential and helpful in molding this collection: Professor Howard P. Vincent, who introduced me to *As I Lay Dying* in 1949 and had the grace not to stifle my enthusiasm as I searched for other, out of print, titles; Captain and Mrs. Louis Henry Cohn, who welcomed me to their book shop in 1951, though I was an Army Private of small means, and shared their taste and intelligence in ways that can never be forgotten; Linton Massey, who in 1959 convinced me that, while books are the foundation of a collection, the real fun was in pursuing the unusual; James B. Meriwether, who taught me the value of order and first suggested this catalogue; and Carvel Collins, who challenged my imagination during late evening sessions enhanced by the company and hospitality of his wife, Ann.

In preparing this book I used information on edition sizes and publication dates supplied by Professor Meriwether and he has my thanks. Much gratitude is owed Robert and Christine Liska for helping me move through the difficulties of what I hope will prove a useful index. The sources of various of the photographs are indicated in the captions but I want to acknowledge here the generous cooperation of Tony Buttitta, "Colonel" J. R. Cofield, and Martin Dain. The majority of the photographs illustrating textual descriptions are the product of the talents and patience of Arthur England to whom I am indebted. Finally, I am especially grateful to Jill Faulkner Summers for granting permission to reproduce certain documents from her father's hand.

(Note: The text of this volume was completed before the death of that respected bookman, Linton R. Massey. All references to him remain as they were written.)

INTRODUCTION

In the August 15, 1931 issue of *Publisher's Weekly* there is a Faulkner checklist prepared by Merle Johnson (entry 1931.17 below). The list includes an announcement of a complete bibliography being prepared by Evelyn Harter and Kenneth Godfrey, both of whom were employed by Cape and Smith, Faulkner's publisher, each possessing an enthusiasm for Faulkner's work beyond manufacturing and selling his books. Shortly after Johnson's announcement appeared, Paul Romaine, who together with Harry Schwartz constituted Milwaukee's Casanova Booksellers, wrote Godfrey to say he was doing a Faulkner bibliography and hoped they would not conflict. Romaine and Schwartz had published a Faulkner checklist (1931.30) and went on to publish a collection of some of Faulkner's early material in *Salmagundi* (A11). The house of Cape and Smith became successively Harrison Smith, Inc. and Smith and Haas. Ultimately there was no bibliographic conflict because there was no bibliography from either source; many good intentions went unrealized in the Depression.

The first published Faulkner bibliographic study of some seriousness was Aubrey Starke's "An American Comedy" in *The Colophon,* Number 19, published in 1934 (1934.7). In 1942 Robert Daniel put together a Faulkner exhibit at Yale; the catalogue was a useful publication (1942.10). In 1956 Richard Archer gave dimension to the task facing Faulkner's potential bibliographers in *Papers of the Bibliographical Society of America* (1956.4). A major exhibit at Princeton in 1957 resulted in the richly informative checklist and catalogues prepared by James B. Meriwether (1957.4, 1960.8, 1961.13). A checklist by another compiler in a book collector's magazine (1964.2) was so distorted as to be worthless. Auction and dealers' catalogues have contained individually useful pieces of information but are often of dubious accuracy. In 1968 the University Press of Virginia issued Linton Massey's listing of the

University of Virginia's Faulkner holdings in a handsome volume. Devoted mostly to the splendid collection formed by Massey, *"Man Working"* (1968.12) is handicapped by an unfortunate arrangement of material.

The present volume is an attempt to usefully list in one place the sum of a single collection and the direction taken in its assembly. I would be pleased if it suggested to younger collectors the varieties of collecting available to an orderly acquisitiveness. Or, more accurately, that some orderliness can be superimposed after the acquisitiveness has gotten out of hand. In short, this is a personal book, but it borrows unashamedly from the work of others where others affirm my own notions of bibliographic arrangement. I continue to look forward to a definitive bibliography.

Extent of Listing

The collection includes material relating to every aspect of Faulkner's literary career from novelist and short story writer to essayist and screenplay writer. The listing thus includes books, magazines, pamphlets, broadsides, press releases, photographs and drawings, clippings, phonograph records, posters, telegrams, and theater programs. At an elevated level of rarity are manuscript leaves, letters, and inscribed books. All books may be assumed first editions unless otherwise designated. Initial listings of short stories, poems, and essays may be assumed first appearances of these pieces.

The final third of the listings is secondary in nature, devoted to background and critical material.

Everything listed is in the collection. Not everything in the collection is listed. No personal correspondence concerning formation of the collection is included in these entries. Duplicate items are not listed unless the second copy differs in some significant aspect. Not listed is that mass of clippings of tertiary interest analyzing material written about Faulkner. Nor are there listings of all the book reviews pointing up Faulkner's influence in the first novels of new writers. These omissions are justified. Of course there are no listings for items which exist only outside the collection. Examples of the missing include *Ole Miss* yearbooks, out-of-series copies of limited editions (there were very many), yet more binding variants of the first edition of *Go Down, Moses,* and—among the secondary material—important critical essays. Some of these omissions are regretted.

General Arrangement

All material falls within the categories defined by the Table of Contents. I have tried to eliminate duplicate listings for a single publication; nevertheless a few occur. Cross references are used only when they appear to have immediate value. The index is intended as the principal guide.

Books

Books by Faulkner (Category A) are listed in three groups for each title: American editions, other English language editions, and foreign editions. Within the first two groups the listings are as close to chronological as possible. For the third classification I have placed the foreign first editions in chronological order. When two or more countries are represented by a translation in a particular year the copies are listed for that year in alphabetical order by name of country using the American spelling. (Swiss editions often precede German because identical translations published in these two countries have normally been published in Zurich a short time before Stuttgart.) Once a title appears for a country subsequent issues from the same nation are immediately listed in chronological order.

Binding Colors

Generally, where binding, endpaper, and top edge stain colors are noted, color names are chosen to conform to common acceptance. However, the problems created by the multiple bindings of the second printing of *Pylon* and the first printing of *Go Down, Moses* are best solved by resorting to a special method of designation. I have chosen to use code numbers and names from the Container Corporation of America *Color Harmony Manual,* Fourth Edition (Chicago: 1958). The binding colors in these two cases are thus coded CCA4- followed by the color number and name from the *Manual* closest to the color of the unfaded binding.

Other Primary Categories

In all Faulkner categories other than books (B through L), listings are chronological by first appearance. If there are reprints they are immediately listed after the first appearance chronologically without regard to nation of source. Thus foreign and American appearances are interspersed, and in a few instances where the initial appearance was in a foreign publication the listing reflects that fact.

Poetry Appendix

In listing certain of Faulkner's poems in their initial appearances in periodicals, as reprinted in poetry anthologies, and (in several cases) as sections of *A Green Bough* I felt the need of an added organizational device. This I have tried to provide by means of the publication chart inserted at the end of this volume. This appendix does not reflect the revisions affecting some of this verse, but it does show that several of these poems have done double and triple duty.

Secondary Material

The last portion of this volume consists of material about Faulkner or relating to his background. These items are listed by year of publication or appearance. Within each year periodicals are in chronological order and precede books alphabetized by author or editor. Books entirely about Faulkner precede those only partially concerned with him or his work. The arrangement by year of publication gives a sense of the volume and type of attention paid Faulkner at any point during his life and in the period since his death.

Reviews of Faulkner Books

Among the secondary listings are groups of reviews that appeared as each new Faulkner title was published. Because so many reviews exist as clippings long since removed from the publication in which they were printed, I have had to decide to omit some or list all even if complete attribution may sometimes be lacking. I have chosen the latter approach, attesting to their existence, though not always their source.

The following source abbreviations have been used in listing reviews:

ChiDn	Chicago *Daily News*
ChiDT	Chicago *Daily Tribune*
ChiSTMB	Chicago Sunday *Tribune Magazine of Books*
ChiSunS-T	Chicago Sunday *Sun-Times*
NR	*New Republic*
NYr	*New Yorker*
NYHT	New York *Herald Tribune*
NYHTBR	New York *Herald Tribune Book Review*
NYS	New York *Sun*
NYT	New York *Times*

NYTBR	New York *Times Book Review*
NYTel	New York *Telegram*
NYW	New York *World*
NYW-T	New York *World-Telegram*
NYW-T&S	New York *World-Telegram & Sun*
SR	*Saturday Review*
SRL	*Saturday Review of Literature*
TLS	*Times Literary Supplement* (London)

"Each in Its Ordered Place"

In a number of instances individual items or whole groups seemed equally appropriate to two or more locations. Whenever such a dilemma had to be resolved my listing choice was prompted by the desire to avoid duplicate entries and was rationalized by the intended value of the index.

The reader may feel some entries are positioned in an arbitrary fashion, and that is perhaps correct. A chosen location may even be argued as illogical. If, however, the choice seems to betray that borrowed Faulkner phrase, "each in its ordered place," I refer the reader to the use of the phrase in the context of *The Sound and the Fury*. Like many qualities in Faulkner's work, irony is not in short supply. And, of course, rereading *The Sound and the Fury* is worth anyone's time.

EACH IN ITS ORDERED PLACE:

A Faulkner Collector's Notebook

PRIMARY MATERIAL

SECTION A: BOOKS

.

To

Sherwood and Elizabeth Anderson

Bill Faulkner
17 March 1926

SOLDIERS' PAY

Soldiers' Pay (A2b).

A1a **The Marble Faun.**
Boston: The Four Seas Company, (December 15) 1924.
Green boards, printed labels on front and spine. 51 pp. Preface by
Phil Stone. Lacks jacket in which it was issued. However, also lacks
any sign of the humidity damage common to many copies that spent
several years in the Gulf area.

This volume of verse exists in an unknown, but small, quantity.
Weighing first book attraction with known rarity of Faulkner's limited
editions, current prices might imply barely 100 surviving copies.

A1b **The Marble Faun** and **A Green Bough.**
New York: Random House, 1965.
"First Random House Edition." Bound as a single volume, Faulkner's
two poetry titles are reproduced photographically from the original
editions of 1924 and 1933 respectively.

◆

A2a **Soldiers' Pay.**
New York: Boni and Liveright, (February 25) 1926.
Dark blue cloth stamped in yellow. Top edges stained yellow. Blue
and white endpapers. With jacket. 319 pp.

Faulkner's first novel was recommended for publication by Sherwood Anderson, for which gesture Faulkner frequently and publicly
expressed his gratitude.

Robert W. Daniel's *A Catalogue of the Writings of William
Faulkner* (1942.10) mentions 2500 copies of the first printing.

A2b **Soldiers' Pay.**
Another copy, without jacket. Above the half-title is inscribed:

> *To*
> *Sherwood and Elizabeth Anderson*
> *Bill Faulkner*
> *17 March 1926*

A2c **Soldiers' Pay.**
New York: Horace Liveright. "Third Printing, April, 1931."
The blue-on-blue jacket on this copy is totally different from the
first printing jacket, is marked "Third Printing," and has reviews of
the book quoted on the back.

Horace Liveright was the successor firm to Boni and Liveright.

A2d **Soldiers' Pay.**
Garden City: The Sun Dial Press, 1937.
"Hampton Court Edition." With jacket.

A2e **Soldiers' Pay.**
New York: The New American Library. "First Printing, December,

1951." Signet Book 887. Paperback.

A2f   **Soldiers' Pay.**
Another copy of Signet Book 887: "Third Printing, June, 1952."

A2g   **Soldiers' Pay.**
New York: The New American Library. "First Printing, September, 1968." Signet Modern Classic CQ411. Paperback. With an Afterword by Robie Macauley.

A2h   **Soldiers' Pay.**
New York: Liveright Paperbound Edition, 1970.

Other English Language Printings:

A2i   **Soldiers' Pay.**
London: Chatto and Windus, (June 20) 1930.
Green cloth stamped in gold. Top edges stained green. With jacket. 326 pp. Preface by Richard Hughes.
      James B. Meriwether has determined there were 2000 copies in the first printing.

A2j   **Soldiers' Pay.**
Harmondsworth: Penguin Books, 1938. Penguin paperback 125.

A2k   **Soldiers' Pay.**
Harmondsworth: Penguin, 1964.
Reprint of the previous paperback with the cover incorrectly marked: **Soldier's Pay.**

Translations:

A2l   **Monnaie de singe.**
Grenoble: Arthaud, 1948.
(Series: Univers Particuliers.) Trans. Maxime Gaucher. Wrappers. No. 56 of a limitation of 300 copies.

A2m   **Monnaie de Singe.**
Another copy of the 1948 edition. Trade issue (no limitation). Inscribed by Gaucher, the translator.

A2n   **Monnaie de Singe.**
Paris and Bruge: Swedish Academy and Nobel Foundation, 1969. A deluxe large paper volume in boards: *La Collection des Prix Nobel de Littérature.* Presumably the Gaucher translation.

A2o   **La paga de los soldados.**
Buenos Aires: Schapire, 1953
Trans. Francisco Gurza. Wrappers.

A2p   **La paga del soldato.**
Milan: Garzanti, 1953.
(Series: R. M. G.) Trans. Massimo Alvaro. Boards.

A2q   **La paga del soldato.**
Milan: Garzanti, 1966.
(Series: I rossi e i blu.) Contents of the 1953 edition. Wrappers.

A2r   **La paga de los soldados.**
Barcelona: Caralt, 1954.
(Series: Gigante.) Translator's name not given. Boards.

A2s   **Heisha no moratta hoshu.**
Tokyo: Jiji Tsushinsha, 1956.
Trans. Ichiro Nishizaki. Wrappers.

A2t   **Soldatenlohn.**
Hamburg: Rowohlt, 1958.
(Series: rororo, No. 260.) Trans. Susanna Rademacher. Wrappers.

A2u   **Soldatens lön.**
Stockholm: Bonniers, 1962.
Trans. Gunnar Barklund. Boards.

A2v   **Soldatens Løn**
Copenhagen: Forlaget Fremad, 1965.
(Series: FFB, No. 129.) Trans. Hagmund Hansen. Boards.

A2w   **Żołnierska Zapłata.**
Warsaw: Państwowy Instytut Wydawniczy, 1965.
(Series: KIK.) Trans. Zofia Kierszys. Wrappers.

◆

Sherwood Anderson & Other Famous Creoles: A Gallery of Contemporary New Orleans.
New Orleans: The Pelican Bookshop Press, (December 16) 1926.
52 unnumbered pp.

This book of caricatures by William Spratling is included in the listing as a Faulkner book because he "arranged" it; and the text, save for the captions, consists entirely of his introduction.

According to Daniel, 400 copies were printed at one time and all copies marked: "...THE FIRST EDITION LIMITED TO 250 NUMBERED

Ave et Cave
per Ars ad Artis

To

ALL THE ARTFUL AND CRAFTY
ONES OF THE FRENCH QUARTER

*and to Elizabeth & Sherwood
Anderson to whom this
copy is inscribed with affection.*

W S Spratling

Dec. 20th, 1926

Dedication of A3a.

COPIES OF WHICH THIS IS NUMBER . . ." On 150 copies a label was pasted over the limitation stating: "SECOND ISSUE 150 COPIES JANUARY 1927." Forty to fifty copies were bound in decorative boards, with various of the illustrations hand tinted by Spratling. The numbering started with these copies and proceeded through the plain copies to terminate at 250, the remainder receiving the "Second issue" label.

A3a **Sherwood Anderson & Other Famous Creoles: A Gallery of Contemporary New Orleans.**
Copy in buff paper boards overprinted in orange and green. Deep green label on cover. Frontispiece tinted.

There is neither label nor number on limitation page, but dedication page bears an inscription. After the printed: "TO ALL THE ARTFUL AND CRAFTY ONES OF THE FRENCH QUARTER" is added, "and to Elizabeth & Sherwood Anderson to whom this copy is inscribed with affection. W. P. Spratling   Dec. 20th, 1926."

A3b **Sherwood Anderson & Other Famous Creoles: A Gallery of Contemporary New Orleans.**
Another Copy.
Bright green covered boards with deep red label on cover. Second issue label.

A3c **Sherwood Anderson & Other Famous Creoles: A Gallery of Contemporary New Orleans.**
Another copy.
Bright green covered boards with pale green label on cover. Second issue label. Poorly opened and badly scuffed.

A3d "**Sherwood Anderson & Other Famous Creoles,** by William Spratling and William Faulkner—A Facsimile." In *Texas Quarterly,* IX (Spring 1966), pp. 41-96.

Though a periodical, included here with the books because the content of the original edition is included complete. In turn a hardbound issue followed the periodical appearance.

Also in the same issue of the *Quarterly:* "Chronicle of a Friendship: William Faulkner in New Orleans," by William Spratling, pp. 34-40, and "William Spratling's Mexican World," by Robert David Duncan, pp. 97-104.

A3e "**Sherwood Anderson & Other Famous Creoles,** by William Spratling and William Faulkner—A Facsimile."
Another copy of the *Texas Quarterly,* in which the widow of one of the men caricatured has noted under several illustrations those who were dead by 1967. In some cases she has added the date of death.

It was Fairchild had found David, a hump, in Jackson Park one afternoon, and he lying on his stomach reading a dog-eared book. David's eyes were calm and gray, his body was young and splendid; he had done a little of everything and had just completed a voyage as messman on a freighter, and Fairchild had set Mr. Maurier to take him on as steward to the crew. The book turned out to be a western novel by Zane Grey.

That morning, David came up on deck and was a quiet tatternless mien. It was soon the world, untroubled, moved through the valley companionway to the o

A page from the original manuscript of "Mosquitoes" which does not appear in the published novel. (If it does, find it!) Given by the author's friend

Bee Wasson

to his friend
Earle F. Walbridge
Aug. 4, 19*7.

Mosquitoes manuscript fragment (A4a).

A3f   **Sherwood Anderson & Other Famous Creoles.**
        Austin: University of Texas Press, 1967.
            This hardbound volume also reprints the Spratling and Duncan
        articles from the *Texas Quarterly*.

♦

A4a   **Mosquitoes.**
        Holograph manuscript fragment of approximately 120 words.
        Discarded by Faulkner. The characters remain in the published novel;
        the plot incident does not.

A4b   **Mosquitoes.**
        New York: Boni and Liveright, (April 30) 1927.
        Dark blue cloth stamped in yellow. Top edges stained yellow. Blue
        and white endpapers. With jacket of red on green featuring mosquito
        design. 349 pp.
            Faulkner's second and final book for this publisher. Daniel
        says 3047 copies.

A4c   **Mosquitoes.**
        Another copy of the first printing in an alternate jacket. The jacket
        design, in red, blue and black, is a cartoon representation of four
        card players aboard a yacht. Otherwise, the matter on the spine,
        back and flaps is the same as on the mosquito motif jacket, though
        the printing is in the altered colors. Publisher is noted on the jacket
        as Boni & Liveright.

A4d   **Mosquitoes.**
        "Second printing, September, 1931." Without jacket. Inscribed on
        the front endpaper by Faulkner with his own recollection of the
        text of the James Joyce poem, "Watching the Needleboats at San
        Sabba."

A4e   **Mosquitoes.**
        Another copy of the first printing with a jacket perhaps belonging
        to the second printing. The jacket features the card players design,
        but the publisher is now identified as Horace Liveright, Inc.
        Sanctuary is mentioned on the front flap. Printed price is $2.50.

A4f   **Mosquitoes.**
        New York: Liveright Publishing Corporation, no date.
        (Publication some time later than 1931.)
        Purplish blue cloth stamped in orange. Endpapers and top edges
        plain. Card players jacket with *Mosquitoes* blurb restricted to front
        flap and a printed price of $3.00.

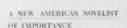

Jacket (A4b).

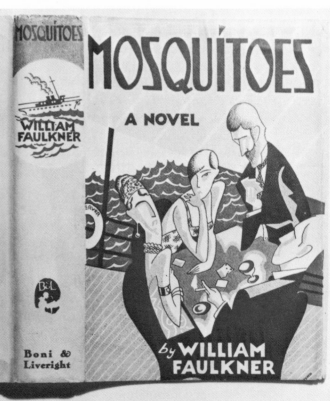

Jacket (A4c). Probably the scarcest
of Faulkner jackets.

SOLDIERS' PAY

BY WILLIAM FAULKNER

"We have read a great many novels that portrayed the disillusioned veteran's conflict with the unfamiliar life of restored peace, but, in our opinion, for originality of design and beauty of writing, this book stands alone among them. Pathos, sacrifice, heroism, a magical beauty are here in abundance."

—*N. Y. Evening Post.*

"A deft hand has woven this narrative of mixed and frustrated emotions and has set it down with hard intelligence as well as consummate pity. The book rings true."

—*N. Y. Times.*

"Like it or hate it, the after-war period is here in SOLDIERS' PAY. To put it in a word, this seems to be one of the books that will be worth reading a few years from now, when most of its mates on the spring list of best fiction are meditating dustily on inaccessible shelves."

—*Baltimore Sun.*

"His book seems to be a rich compound of imagination, observation and experience. In an isolated world of Faulkner's own making, shadows having the reality of men grope through a maze complex enough to be at once pitiful and comic, passionate, tormenting and strange."

—*Louis Kronenberger, in The Literary Digest.*

LIVERIGHT

MOSQUITOES

MOSQUITOES

A NOVEL

by WILLIAM FAULKNER

A4g   **Mosquitoes.**
        Garden City: The Sun Dial Press, 1937.

A4h   **Mosquitoes.**
        New York: Avon Books, (1942?).
        A paperback, number 12 in the "Avon pocket-size Book" series.
        Perhaps a first issue in this format; the advertised list of titles on a
        page near the back goes only through number 12.

A4i   **Mosquitoes.**
        Another copy of the Avon edition. With ads through number 19.

A4j   **Mosquitoes.**
        New issue by Liveright, no printing date, but shows copyright
        renewal in 1955. Deep blue cloth stamped in gold. Card game jacket,
        with most printed matter changed from previous issues of the jacket.
        No printed price.

A4k   **Mosquitoes.**
        New York: Dell Publishing Company, n. d. (after 1950)
        Paperback: Dell Book 708. Price 25 cents.

A4l   **Mosquitoes.**
        "New Dell Edition: First Printing - May, 1962."
        Number S38. Price 60 cents.

        Other English Language Printings:

A4m   **Mosquitoes.**
        London: Chatto and Windus, (October) 1964.
        Gray-brown boards (imitation cloth), spine stamped in gold. Jacket
        designed by E. R. Bartelt. 288 pp.

        Translations:

A4n   **Moustiques.**
        Paris: Editions de Minuit, 1948.
        Trans. Jean Dubramet. Intro. Raymond Queneau. Wrappers.
        Number 28 of a limitation of 50 copies.

A4o   **Moustiques.**
        Another copy of the 1948 edition. Wrappers.
        Number 156 of a limitation of 150 copies (numbered 51
        through 200).

A4p **Moustiques.**
Paris: Union Generale d'Editions, 1963.
(Series: Collection 10-18, No. 101/102.) Contents of the 1948
edition. Wrappers.

A4q **Mosquitoes.**
Buenos Aires: Siglo Veinte, 1956.
Trans. Jeronimo Cordoba. Wrappers.

A4r **Zanzare.**
Milan: Mondadori, 1957.
(Series: Medusa, No. 399.) Trans. Giulio De Angelis. Boards.

A4s **Mosquitos.**
Barcelona: Caralt, 1959.
(Series: Gigante.) Trans. Domingo Manfredi. Boards.

A4t **Moskitos.**
Hamburg: Rowohlt, 1960.
(Series: rororo, No. 384.) Trans. Richard K. Flesch. Wrappers.

◆

A5a **Sartoris.**
New York: Harcourt, Brace and Company, (January 31) 1929.
Black cloth stamped in red. Top edges stained red. With jacket
designed by Arthur Hawkins, Jr. 380 pp.
The only Faulkner title published by Harcourt, Brace. Daniel
says 1998 copies.

A5b **Sartoris.**
Another copy, with jacket. Signed "William Faulkner" on endpaper facing title page.

A5c **Sartoris.**
New York: Grosset & Dunlap, 1933.
Yellow cloth stamped in purple. Top edges purple.

A5d **Sartoris.**
New York: Harcourt, Brace. "reissued, 1951."
Gray-green cloth, stamped in red. With jacket mentioning Nobel Prize.

A5e **Sartoris.**
New York: The New American Library, "First Printing, July, 1953."
Signet Giant S1032. Paperback. Introduction by Robert Cantwell.

A5f   **Sartoris.**
Another copy. "Second Printing, September, 1958."
Now Signet Book D1614.

A5g   **Sartoris.**
New York: Random House.
Shows copyright renewal of 1956, but advertisements on the jacket
indicate 1961 appearance. This is the earliest issue after Random
House had acquired rights from Harcourt, Brace.

A5h   **Sartoris.**
New York: The New American Library, "Sixth Printing, May, 1964."
This is the first printing as Signet Classic CT226, and it has an after-
word by Lawrance Thompson, as well as the foreword by Robert
Cantwell.

Other English Language Printings:

A5i   **Sartoris.**
London: Chatto and Windus, (February 18) 1932.
Blue cloth stamped in gold. Top edges gray-blue. With jacket. 379 pp.
    Four pages of ads between last page of text and colophon.
    Meriwether: 2000 copies.

A5j   **Sartoris.**
Another copy of the English first printing. Tan cloth stamped in red.
Top edges unstained. With jacket bearing "Cheap Edition" label
priced at 4s. 6d. There are no ads.

Translations:

A5k   **Sartoris.**
Paris: Gallimard, 1937.
(Series: *nrf.*) Trans. R. N. Raimbault and H. Delgove. Wrappers.
    S. P. copy, signed by both translators.

A5l   **Sartoris.**
Milan: Jandi Sapi, 1946.
(Series: Le Najadi, Vol. 17.) Trans. Filiberto Storoni. Wrappers.

A5m   **Sartoris.**
Milan: Garzanti, 1955.
(Series: R.M.G.) Trans. Maria Stella Ferrari. Boards.

A5n   **Sartoris.**
Buenos Aires: Schapire, 1953.
Trans. Francisco Gurza. Wrappers.

A5o   **Sartoris.**
Stockholm: Bonniers, 1955.
Trans. Th. Warburton. Wrappers.

A5p   **Sartoris.**
Lisbon: Ulisseia, 1958.
(No. 27 in the publisher's series.) Trans. Carlos Vieira. Wrappers.
Includes a translation of the Robert Cantwell introduction to the
Signet edition.

A5q   **Sartoris.**
Warsaw: Państwowy Instytut Wydawniczy, 1960.
Trans. Kalina Wojciechowska. Wrappers.

A5r   **Sartoris.**
Hamburg: Rowohlt, 1961.
"1.-5 Tausend." Trans. Hermann Stresau. Boards.

◆

A6a   **The Sound and the Fury.**
Advance copy. Consists of a stitched, but unbound copy of the first
printing laid into an early state of the dust jacket. Though the jacket
resembles that of the first edition, it lacks all printed matter on the
back and flaps.
     A damaged copy with three leaves missing constituting pages
137 through 142. The jacket has been repaired.

A6b   **The Sound and the Fury.**
New York: Jonathan Cape and Harrison Smith, (October 7) 1929.
Black, white and gray paper covered boards. White cloth spine
stamped in black. Top edges stained blue-gray. Endpapers match
cover. With jacket featuring adaptation of Käthe Kollwitz theme,
"Woman and Death." 401 pp.
     Daniel says 1789 copies. Cape and Smith sales records show that
about 1500 copies had been sold by the time *Sanctuary* was published
in February, 1931.
     Faulkner often called this his favorite work because its composi-
tion had caused him the greatest agony.

A6c   **The Sound and the Fury.**
Another copy of the first edition with jacket.
Beneath the title is inscribed:

> *William Faulkner*
> *Los Angeles Calif*
> *26 May 1932*
> *I put my living guts into this*

A6d   **The Sound and the Fury.**
Another copy.
"Second Printing February 1931." Top edges deep gray. With jacket identical to that on the first printing.

A6e   **The Sound and the Fury** with **As I Lay Dying**
New York: The Modern Library, (December 20) 1946.
"First Modern Library Edition, 1946." With jacket. Number 187.
   The appendix, "1699-1945 The Compsons," from the Viking *Portable Faulkner* appears here, slightly revised, as a foreword to *The Sound and the Fury*.

A6f   **The Sound and the Fury** with **As I Lay Dying.**
Modern Library Paperback, P 6 (December 30, 1954).
   Probably not the first issue in this format: the back cover advertisements run through P 34.

A6g   **The Sound and the Fury.**
Modern Library Paperback, P 6. Shows copyright renewal of 1956.
   Here the novel appears alone, though the Compson foreword has been retained.

A6h   **The Sound and the Fury.**
New York: The New American Library, "First Printing, March, 1959."
Signet Book D1628. Paperback. 50 cents. "Printed in the United States of America."

A6i   **The Sound and the Fury.**
New York: The New American Library, "First Printing, April, 1959."
Signet Book D1628. Paperback. 60 cents. "Printed in Canada."

A6j   **The Sound and the Fury.**
New York: Vintage Books. Probably 1963.
Vintage V-5. The Compson foreword has again assumed the appendix position it initially held in the Viking *Portable Faulkner*.
   After Alfred Knopf became associated with Random House, Vintage (paperback) Books replaced Modern Library Paperbacks.

A6k   **The Sound and the Fury.**
New York: The Modern Library, 1966.
ML 187. Includes the Compson appendix. With jacket.

A6l   **The Sound and the Fury.**
New York: Random House, (March) 1966.
This, like the two preceeding issues, was reproduced photographically from a copy of the original edition of 1929. It is, however, more "authentic" in that it does not include the 1946 appendix. With the white jacket of the Random House "uniform" edition.

A6m   **The Sound and the Fury.**
New York: Modern Library College Editions, (1967?).
T 94. One of a series of paperbacks generally available in college bookstores. With the appendix.

A6n   **The Sound and the Fury.**
New York: Random House, 1970.
Red cloth stamped in gold. Ochre endpapers. Literary Guild edition. 249 pp.
       Issued as part of a special four-volume Faulkner offering by the Literary Guild. The other titles selected: *As I Lay Dying, Sanctuary, Light in August.* The format is uniform and all were issued without jackets.

A6o   **"The Sisters."**
100 Modern Poems, ed. Seldon Rodman. New York: Pellegrini & Cudahy, 1949. pp. 75-77. An excerpt from *The Sound and the Fury.*
       The title indicates the editor's confusion of the gender of the male Quentin in conversation with his sister, Caddy.

Other English Language Printings:

A6p   **The Sound and the Fury.**
London: Chatto and Windus, (April 16) 1931.
Black cloth stamped in red. Top edges red. With jacket. 321 pp. Introduction by Richard Hughes.
       Meriwether: 2000 copies.

A6q   **The Sound and the Fury.**
London: Landsborough, (1959). Four Square paperback 116.

A6r   **The Sound and the Fury.**
Harmondsworth: Penguin, (1964). Paperback, No. 2087.

Translations:

A6s   **Le bruit et la fureur.**
Paris: Gallimard, 1938.
(Series: *nrf,* Du monde entier, Vol. XXXIV.) Trans. and preface
Maurice E. Coindreau. Wrappers.
     Number 60 of a limitation of 70 copies. (This is one of 20
copies *hors commerce,* and it is signed by the translator.)

A6t   **Le Bruit et la fureur.**
Paris: Gallimard, 1959.
(Series: Livre de Poche, No. 501/502.) Contents of the 1938
edition. Wrappers.

A6u   **Le bruit et la fureur.**
Paris: Gallimard, (1963?).
(Series: Collection Soleil, No. 114.) Contents of the 1938
edition. Boards.
     Number 2412 of a limitation of 4100 copies.

A6v   **Le bruit et la fureur.**
Paris: Gallimard, 1972.
(Series: folio, No. 162.) Contents of the 1938 edition. Wrappers.

A6w   **El sonido y la furia.**
Buenos Aires: Futuro, 1947.
Trans. Floreal Mazia. Wrappers.

A6x   **Schall und Wahn.**
Zurich: Fretz & Wasmuth, 1956.
Trans. Helmut M. Braem and Elisabeth Kaiser. Boards.

A6y   **Schall und Wahn.**
Stuttgart: Scherz & Goverts, 1956.
The Braem-Kaiser translation. Boards.

A6z   **Schall und Wahn.**
Munich: Kindler, 1964.
(Series: Kindler Taschenbücher, No. 35.) The Braem-Kaiser
translation. Wrappers.

A6aa   **Krik i bijes.**
Zagreb: Naprijed, 1958.
Includes the *Portable Faulkner* Appendix. Croatian translation and
lengthy introduction by Stjepan Krešić. Boards.

A6bb   **Khasm va Hyahu.**
        Tehran: N. I. L., 1960.
        Trans. Bahman Shalavar. Persian text. Boards.

A6cc   **O Som e a Furia.**
        Lisbon: Portugalia, ca. 1960.
        (Series: Os Romances Universais, No. 22.) Trans. Mario Henrique
        Leiria and H. Santos Carvalho. Preface Luis de Sousa Rebelo.
        Wrappers.

A6dd   **(The Sound and the Fury).**
        Beirut: Dar el-Ilm Lil-Malayeen, 1963.
        Trans. Jabra I. Jabra. Arabic text. Wrappers.

A6ee   **Stormen och vreden.**
        Stockholm: Bonniers, 1964.
        Trans. Gunnar Barklund. Boards.

A6ff   **Ääni ja vimma.**
        Helsinki: Tammi, 1965.
        Trans. Kai Kaila. Boards. The Finnish text begins with the Comp-
        son appendix.

A6gg   **Hibiki to ikari.**
        Tokyo: Fuzanbo, 1969.
        (Series: Faulkner Zenshu, Vol. 5.) Trans. Masaji Onoe.
            (See listing under *Requiem for a Nun,* 1951 novel edition, for
        a note on this series.)

                                    ◆

A7a   **As I Lay Dying.**
        New York: Jonathan Cape and Harrison Smith, (October 6) 1930.
        Beige cloth stamped in dark brown on front and spine. Endpapers
        beige, similar to color of binding cloth. 254 pp. With jacket.
            The binding stamping on this copy is thrust upward enough
        that the tops of the letters on the spine touch the top of the bind-
        ing, while on the front a fraction of the top of each letter is
        missing.
            Top edges stained dark brown. Initial "I" on page 11 is
        dropped from proper alignment.

A7b   **As I Lay Dying.**
        Another copy.
        Stamping on front and spine is properly positioned. However, the

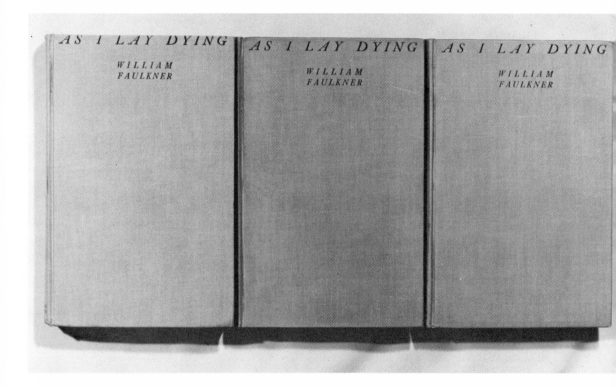

Bindings (l. to r.) of A7a, A7b, A7c.

serif at the top of the word "I" stamped on the front is missing. Top edges dark brown. "I" on page 11 is dropped. With jacket.

A7c   **As I Lay Dying.**
Another copy.
Stamping on front and spine is complete and undamaged. Top edges dark brown. "I" on page 11 is dropped. With jacket.

A7d   **As I Lay Dying.**
Another copy.
Stamping on front and spine complete and undamaged. Top edges light brown. "I" on page 11 is dropped. With jacket.

A7e   **As I Lay Dying.**
Another copy.
Stamping on front and spine complete and undamaged. Top edges light brown. "I" on page 11 is properly aligned. With jacket.
    Above five copies all represent the first printing, of which Daniel says there were a total of 2522 copies. By February, 1931 1150 had been sold.

A7f   **As I Lay Dying.**
New York: Harrison Smith & Robert Haas, "Second Printing, January, 1933."

A7g   **As I Lay Dying.**
For joint Modern Library and Modern Library Paperback appearances with *The Sound and the Fury,* see listings A6e-f.

A7h   **As I Lay Dying.**
New York: Random House, (February) 1964.
Reset edition. With the white uniform edition jacket.

A7i   **As I Lay Dying.**
New York: Vintage Books, "First Vintage Edition, March, 1964." Paperback, V-254. The reset text.

A7j   **As I Lay Dying.**
New York: The Modern Library, "First Modern Library Edition, February, 1967." Again, the reset text of 1964. ML 378. With jacket.

A7k   **As I Lay Dying.**
New York: Random House, 1970.
Red cloth stamped in gold. Ochre endpapers. Literary Guild edition. 182 pp.

A7l   **As I Lay Dying.**
London: Chatto and Windus, (September 26) 1935.
Blue cloth stamped in white. Top edges stained blue. With jacket.
248 pp.
  Meriwether: 1500 copies.

A7m   **As I Lay Dying.**
Harmondsworth: Penguin, 1963. Paperback, No. 1940.

Translations:

A7n   **Tandis que j'agonise.**
Paris: Gallimard, 1934.
(Series: *nrf,* Du monde entier, Vol. XV.) Trans. Maurice E. Coindreau.
Preface by Valery Larbaud. Wrappers.
  Number H. C. S. P. 40 of a limitation of 60 copies.

A7o   **Tandis que j'agonise.**
Another copy in the Du monde entier format. Wrappers.
Number 110 of a limitation of 150 copies.

A7p   **Tandis que j'agonise.**
Paris: Jean Boisseau, 1946.
The Coindreau translation. Engraved illustrations by Courtin.
Unsewn gatherings laid into wrappers, boxed.
Number 22 of a limitation of 25 copies, with an extra set of
illustrations.

A7q   **Tandis que j'agonise.**
Another copy of the Boisseau edition.
Number 40 of a limitation of 175 copies (numbered 26 through
200).

A7r   **Tandis que j'agonise.**
Paris: Gallimard, (1966?).
(Series: Collection Soleil, No. 190.) Contents of the 1934
Gallimard edition. Boards.
Number 2478 of a limitation of 3100 copies.

A7s   **"Addie."**
All världens Berättare, II (May 1946), pp. 62-66. Trans. Jöran Mjöberg;
the "Addie" section only. In Swedish.

A7t   **Mientros yo agonizo.**
Buenos Aires: Santiago Rueda, 1952.
Trans. and preface Max Dickmann. Wrappers.

A7u   **Kun tein kuolemaa.**
Helsinki: Tammi, 1952.
Trans. and preface Alex. Matson. Boards.

A7v   **I min sidste time.**
Copenhagen: Carit Andersen, n.d. (1954?).
(Series: Den nye Karat.) Trans. Gunnar Juel Jørgensen. Wrappers.

A7w   **Mientras agonizo.**
Madrid: Aguilar, 1954.
Trans. Agustin Caballero Robredo and Arturo del Hoyo. Wrappers.

A7x   **Uitvart in Mississippi.**
Amsterdam: Bezige Bij, 1955.
(Series: Bijenreeks.) Trans. Apie Prins and John Vandenbergh. Limp boards.

A7y   **Mentre Morivo.**
Milan: Mondadori, 1958.
(Series: Medusa, No. 397.) Trans. Giulio De Angelis. Boards.

A7z   **Als ich im Sterben lag.**
Zurich: Fretz & Wasmuth, 1961.
Trans. Albert Hess and Peter Schünemann. Boards.

A7aa   **Als ich im Sterben lag.**
Stuttgart: Goverts, 1961.
The Hess-Schünemann translation. Boards.

A7bb   **Als ich im Sterben lag.**
N. p. (Berlin?): Suhrkamp, "Erstes bis siebtes Tausend dieser Ausgabe 1963." (Series: Bibliothek Suhrkamp, No. 103.) The Hess-Schünemann translation. Boards.

A7cc   **Když jsem umírala.**
Prague: Odeon, 1967.
(Series: Světová Četba, No. 388.) Trans. Jiři Valja. Introduction Josef Škvorecký. Wrappers.

A7dd   **Na Minha Morte.**
Lisbon: Livros do Brasil, n. d.
(Series: Miniatura, No. 156.) Trans. Alfredo Margarido. Wrappers.

◆

A8a   **Sanctuary.**
        Uncorrected proof (unbound long sheets) of the original version.

A8b   **Sanctuary.**
        New York: Jonathan Cape and Harrison Smith, (February 9) 1931.
        Magenta boards. Gray cloth spine stamped in magenta. Endpapers
        are a magenta design on gray paper. With jacket. 380 pp.
            Top edges on this and the following four copies are stained deep
        gray to black.

A8c   **Sanctuary.**
        Another copy. "Second Printing, February, 1931." Endpapers solid
        magenta.

A8d   **Sanctuary.**
        Another copy. "Third Printing, February, 1931." Endpapers
        solid magenta.

A8e   **Sanctuary.**
        Another copy. "Fifth Printing, April, 1931." Endpapers solid
        magenta.

A8f   **Sanctuary.**
        Another copy. "Sixth Printing, July, 1931." Plain white endpapers.

A8g   **Sanctuary.**
        New York: The Modern Library, (March 25) 1932.
        Blue cloth limp covers stamped in gold. Top edges dark blue-gray.
        With jacket. Number 61.
            This and the following three copies have 380 pages, plus a two-
        page Faulkner introduction in its initial appearance. All four copies
        indicate "First Modern Library Edition 1932."

A8h   **Sanctuary.**
        Another copy. Green cloth. Top edges green. With jacket.

A8i   **Sanctuary.**
        Another copy. Tile red cloth. Top edges tile red.

A8j   **Sanctuary.**
        Another copy. Dark brown cloth. Top edges dark brown. With jacket.
        The jacket drawing for the original format of the Modern Library *Sanc-
        tuary* was by Jacob Burck.

A8k   **Sanctuary.**
New York: The Modern Library, 1940.
Green cloth stiff covers, stamped in red and gold. Top edges stained
red. With jacket designed by E. McKnight Kauffer. Introduction extending over four pages. A new Modern Library format; this volume
is still Number 61 in the series.

A8l   **Sanctuary.**
New York: Grosset and Dunlap, ca. 1946.
With jacket.

A8m   **Sanctuary.**
New York: Penguin Books, "First Penguin Books Edition, April, 1947"
Number 632. Paperback.
    This was the first of the postwar Faulkner paperback reprints.

A8n   **Sanctuary.**
New York: The New American Library, "Twelfth Printing, March,
1950." Signet Book 632.
    The New American Library Signet label was the successor to
American Penguin paperbacks. There is no indication of price on
these books as the twenty-five cent figure was generally assumed.

A8o   **Sanctuary** and **Requiem for a Nun.**
New York: The New American Library, "First Joint Printing, March,
1954." Signet Book S1079.   35 cents.

A8p   **Sanctuary.**
New York: Random House, (August) 1962.
A reset edition, produced with Faulkner's cooperation, and appearing
shortly after his death. With the uniform white jacket.

A8q   **Sanctuary.**
New York: Vintage Books, "First Vintage Books Edition, February,
1967." Vintage V-381. The reset text of the 1962 Random House
edition.

A8r   **Sanctuary.**
New York: The New American Library, "First Printing, September,
1968." Signet Modern Classic CQ413. With an introduction by Allen
Tate.

A8s   **Sanctuary.**
New York: Random House, 1970.
Red cloth stamped in gold. Ochre endpapers. Literary Guild edition.
250 pp.

A8t   "The Bordello."
        Taken at the Flood, ed. Ann Watkins. New York: Harper, 1946, pp.
        142-48. Excerpt from *Sanctuary.*

        Other English Language Printings:

A8u   **Sanctuary.**
        London: Chatto and Windus, (September 10) 1931.
        Wine-red cloth stamped in gold. Top edges stained gray. With jacket.
        316 pp.
                This issue contains four pages of ads.
                Meriwether: 2000 copies.

A8v   **Sanctuary.**
        Another copy of the English first printing. Bright red cloth stamped
        in black. Top edges unstained. With jacket. There are no ads.

A8w   **Sanctuary.**
        Harmondsworth: Penguin, 1955.
        Penguin paperback 899. The first printing in this format had appeared
        in 1953.

A8x   **Sanctuary.**
        Paris: Crosby Continental Editions, 1932.
        In English. Wrappers.
                This copy bears the bookplate of Harry and Caresse Crosby.

        Translations:

A8y   **Sanctuaire.**
        Paris: Gallimard, 1933.
        (Series: *nrf,* Du monde entier, Vol. XIII.) Trans. R. N. Raimbault
        and Henri Delgove. Preface Andre Malraux. Wrappers.
        Number 41 of a limitation of 150 copies.

A8z   **Sanctuaire.**
            Paris: Gallimard, 1958.
            (Series: Livre de Poche, No. 362/363.) Contents of the 1933
            edition. Wrappers.

A8aa   **Sanctuaire.**
            Paris: Gallimard, (1963?).
            (Series: Collection Soleil, No. 113.) Contents of the 1933 edition.
            Boards. Number 176 of a limitation of 4100 copies.

Sanctuary in translation.

A8bb   **Sanctuaire.**
Paris: Gallimard, 1972.
(Series: folio, No. 231.) Contents of the 1933 edition. Wrappers.

A8cc   **Sanctuaire** and **Tandis que j'agonise** (excerpts).
L'érotisme dans la littérature étrangère (Vol. I: Anglo-Saxon
Literature), ed. and intro. René Varin. Lyon: Lutecia, ca. 1948.
Includes four brief excerpts from the first title (pp. 74-88) and
one from the second (pp. 89-98).

A8dd   **Santuario.**
Madrid: Espasa-Calpe, 1934.
(Series: Hechos Sociales, No. 7.) Trans. Lino Novás Calvo. Preface
Antonio Marichalar. Wrappers.

A8ee   **Det allerhelligste.**
Copenhagen: Athenaeum, 1942.
Trans. Sven Møller Kristensen. Wrappers.

A8ff   **Santuario.**
Milan: Jandi Sapi, 1943.
(Series: Le Najadi, Vol. I.) Trans. Aldo Scagnetti. Wrappers.

A8gg   **Santuario.**
Milan: Mondadori, 1958.
(Series: Medusa, No. 411.) Trans. and Intro. Paola Ojetti
Zamattio. Boards.

A8hh   **Santuario.**
Milan: Mondadori, 1958.
(Series: Il Ponte, No. 9.) Same translation, third edition in this
format. Boards.

A8ii   **Santuario.**
Buenos Aires: Espasa-Calpe, 1945.
(Series: Austral, No. 493.) Trans. Lino Novás Calvo. Preface Antonio
Marichalar. Wrappers.

A8jj   **Santuario.**
Sao Paulo: Instituto Progresso, 1948.
(Series: Oceano, No. 12.) Trans. Ligia Junqueira Smith. Boards.

A8kk   **Grijze Zomer.**
The Hague: Oisterwijk, 1951.
Trans. John van Keulen. Boards.

A8ll   **Grijze Zomer.**
Another copy of the van Keulen translation; fourth printing,
with an introduction by the translator.

A8mm **Det aller helligste.**
Oslo: Gyldendal Norsk, 1951.
Trans. Leo Strøm. Foreword Sigurd Hoel. Includes a translation of
Faulkner's Modern Library introduction. Boards.

A8nn **Det allra heligaste.**
Stockholm: Bonniers, 1951.
Trans. Mårten Edlund. Boards.

A8oo **Die Freistatt.**
Zurich: Artemis, 1951.
Trans. Herberth E. Herlitschka. Boards. Includes German translation
of the Modern Library introduction.

A8pp **Die Freistatt.**
Frankfurt: Goldene Vlies, n. d. (1955?).
(Series: Ullstein Buch, No. 87). The Herlitschka translation, including
Faulkner's introduction. Wrappers.

A8qq **Die Freistatt.**
Another copy of the Ullstein paperback, 1960.

A8rr **Svetilište.**
Novi Sad; Bratstvo jedinstvo, 1953.
Serbian trans. Milica Mihajlović. Boards.

A8ss **Azyl.**
Warsaw: Państwowy Instytut Wydawniczy, 1957.
Trans. Zofia Kierszys. Wrappers.

A8tt **Santuário.**
Lisbon: Minerva, (1958?)
(Series: Minerva, No. 299.) Trans. Marília de Vasconcelos. Wrappers.

A8uu **Sanctuaire.**
Lausanne: Guilde de Livre, 1965.
In a "limited" edition of 8000 copies; this copy stamped *"d'Auteur."*
A Swiss edition with the contents of the 1933 Paris edition. Boards.

◆

A9a **These 13.**
New York: Jonathan Cape and Harrison Smith, (September 21) 1931.
Blue cloth covers. Gray cloth spine stamped in red. Endpapers are a
blue design on gray paper, in this case a dark blue design. With jacket
designed by Arthur Hawkins, Jr. 358 pp.

[49]

Misprinted *These 13* copyright page (A9e).

This short story collection contains in their first appearance: "Victory," "All the Dead Pilots," "Crevasse," "A Justice," "Mistral," "Divorce in Naples," and "Carcassonne." Titles which had previously appeared were: "Ad Astra," "Red Leaves," "A Rose for Emily," "Hair," "That Evening Sun," and "Dry September."

A9b   **These 13.**
Another copy. The endpaper design is a deeper blue than the previous copy.

A9c   **These 13.**
Another copy. The endpaper design is in medium blue.

A9d   **These 13.**
Limited, signed issue of 299 copies. Silver beige cloth covers. Tile red cloth spine stamped in silver. Top edges silver. Gray endpapers. With tissue wrapper.

The term "Large paper edition," often misused, has meaning in this instance: both the paper weight and the page size are greater than for the regular trade issue. It is likely that the limited issue precedes the trade issue, as the page numbers in the limited issue are italicized and enclosed in brackets, while the brackets are removed and the type is Roman in three successive printings of the trade issue.

The limitation page, as in most Faulkner limited editions, is tipped in. This is copy number 106.

A9e   **These 13.**
Loose title/limitation leaf.
A leaf with the sides reversed in printing error; the tip-in edge thus appears incorrectly on the right as the title page is observed. Numbered (184) and signed by Faulkner.

A9f   **These 13.**
Another copy of the trade issue. "Second Printing, September, 1931." Binding and top edges resemble first printing, but endpapers are plain.

A9g   **These 13.**
Another copy. "Third Printing, October, 1931." Endpapers are again figured, as in the first printing.

Other English Language Printings:

A9h   **These Thirteen.**
London: Chatto and Windus, (September 21) 1933.

Blue cloth stamped in gold. Top edges stained green. With jacket.
357 pp.   Contents the same as the American *These 13*.
Meriwether: 1500 copies.

Translations:

A9i   **Treize histoires.**
Paris: Gallimard, 1939.
(Series: *nrf.*) Translators: R.-N. Raimbault, Ch.-P. Vorce, M.-E.
Coindreau. Preface Raimbault. Wrappers.
S.P. copy, inscribed by Raimbault.

A9j   **Victoria y otros relatos.**
Buenos Aires: Corinto, 1944.
Trans. Jose Blaya Lozano. Wrappers.
Omits "Carcassonne"; includes an introduction by "Los
Editores."

A9k   **Questi tredici.**
Turin: Lattes, 1948.
Trans. and intro. Francesco Lo Bue. Wrappers.

A9l   **Estos trece.**
Buenos Aires: Losada, 1956.
Trans. Aurora Bernardez. Wrappers.

A9m   **Korera 13 pen.**
Tokyo: Fuzanbo, 1968.
(Series: Faulkner Zenshu, Vol. 8.) Trans. Nobuyuki Hayashi.

♦

A10a   **Idyll in the Desert.**
New York: Random House, (December 10) 1931.
Red marbled paper on boards; label printed in red and black on front.
Limited, signed edition of 400 copies. 17 pp.
The only publication of this story, and Faulkner's first Random
House book. With laid in advance brochure announcing publication
for December 15, "at $3.50 per copy"; lacking order coupon. Copy
number 203.

A10b   **Idyll in the Desert.**
Another copy. On the limitation page where the copy number would
normally be inscribed is the penciled phrase "Printer's Copy." Beneath

With Tony Buttitta, 1931 (L6).
Courtesy Tony Buttitta.

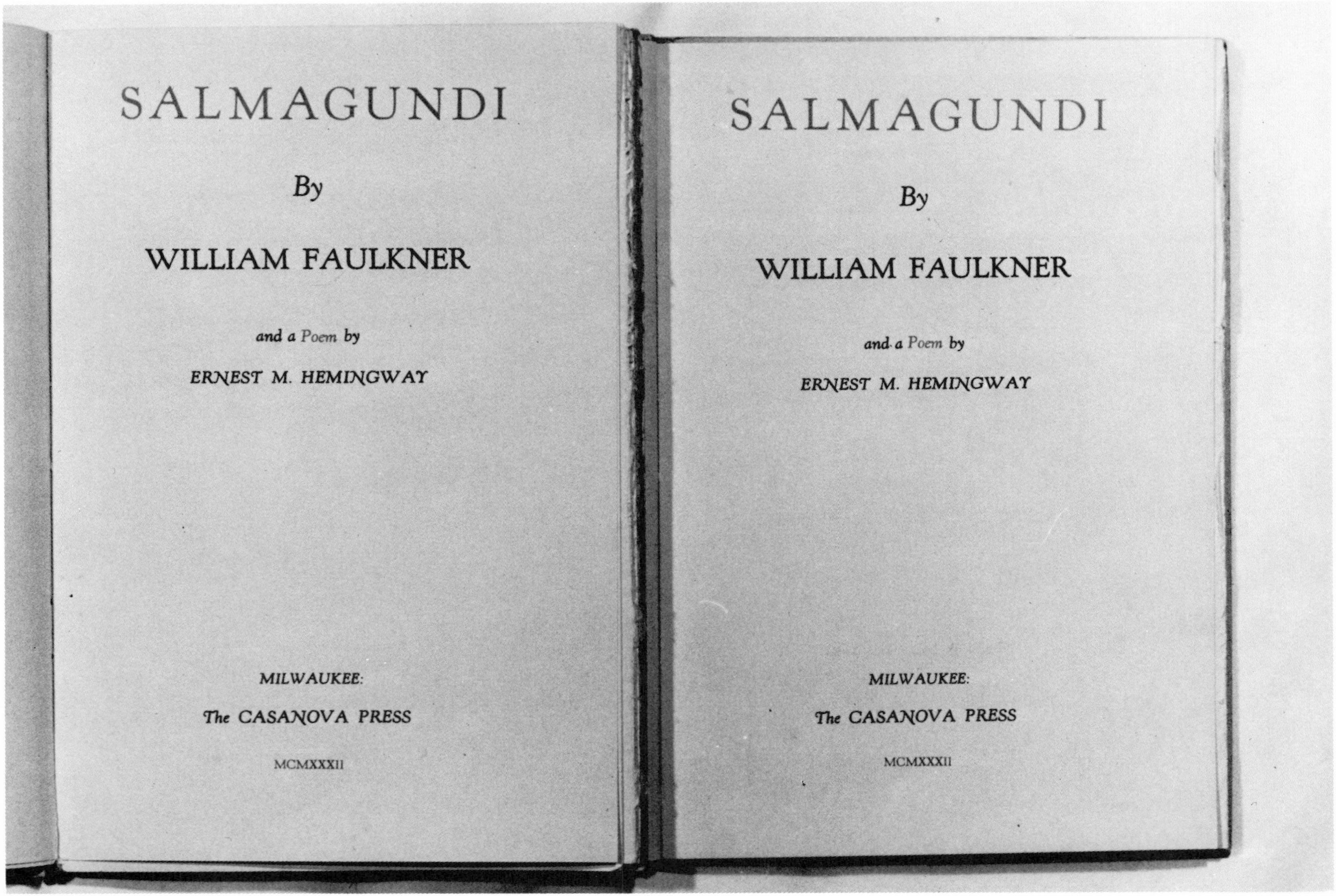

SALMAGUNDI

By

WILLIAM FAULKNER

and a Poem by

ERNEST M. HEMINGWAY

MILWAUKEE:

The CASANOVA PRESS

MCMXXXII

SALMAGUNDI

By

WILLIAM FAULKNER

and a Poem by

ERNEST M. HEMINGWAY

MILWAUKEE:

The CASANOVA PRESS

MCMXXXII

A11c on left; one of 26 copies.
A11a on right

the colophon in the same handwriting is the comment in ink, "This 'Printer's Copy' was mine. It was designed by me, John S. Fass." Fass was the designer for Harbor Press.

♦

A11a   **Salmagundi.**
Milwaukee: The Casanova Press, (April 30) 1932.
("and a poem by Ernest M. Hemingway")
Ribbed tan wrappers printed in black and red. Limited edition of 525 copies. 53 pp. With burgundy box.

Contains prose pieces: "New Orleans," "On Criticism," "Verse Old and Nascent: A Pilgrimage," and the poems: "The Faun," "Dying Gladiator," "Portrait," "The Lilacs," and "L'Apres-Midi d'un Faune"; all reprinted from periodical appearances. (The Hemingway poem, "Ultimately," is on the back cover.)

With advance brochure ("March 15, 1932 at $3.00 per copy.") Copy number 87.

A11b   **Salmagundi.**
Another copy, with box.
Inscribed by Paul Romaine, who designed the book and was half of the Casanova Press. Copy number 158.

In these two copies the pages are trimmed uniformly on three sides, and are centered, top to bottom, within the wrappers.

A11c   **Salmagundi.**
Another copy.
In the first 26 copies the pages were thrust upward and trimmed at the top flush with the wrappers. The bottoms of the pages are of un-even length, but all are shorter than the wrappers. This is such a copy, number 10, in box.

♦

A12a   **Miss Zilphia Gant.**
Dallas: The Book Club of Texas, (June 27) 1932.
Reddish brown cloth stamped in gold. 29 pp. With tissue wrapper.
Preface by Henry Nash Smith.

This short story was distributed to members of the Texas Book Club in an edition of 300 numbered copies and never reprinted in this country. Copy number 197.

Translation:

A12b **La pallida Zilphia Gant.**
Milan: Saggiatore, 1959.
(Series: Biblioteca delle Silerchie, Vol. 9.) Trans. and intro. Fernanda
Pivano. Boards.

♦

A13a **Light in August.**
New York: Harrison Smith and Robert Haas, (October 6) 1932.
Coarse tan cloth stamped in orange on front, and blue and orange on
spine. Top edges stained orange. 480 pp. With printed jacket designed
by Arthur Hawkins, Jr. Lacks tissue over-wrapper.
    A contemporary clipping says the publisher printed 8500 copies
in the first printing and that there would be 2500 copies in the second
printing.
    Merle Johnson's discovery of the error on page 340 was unfor-
tunate in that it created a point that is pointless: the "Jefferson"
reading recurs in several subsequent printings.

A13b **Light in August.**
Another copy. "Fourth Printing." Exterior resembles first printing,
but stamping is in blue only.

A13c **Light in August.**
Another copy marked "Fourth Printing." Internally the same as the
previous copy, including the imprint of Harrison Smith & Robert
Haas on the title page. Pale green cloth stamped in deep green; top
edges unstained. The spine identifies the publisher as Random House.
    Obviously fourth printing sheets bound after 1936 when Ran-
dom House became Faulkner's publisher.

A13d **Light in August.**
Norfolk (Conn.): New Directions, 1947.
Reprint in the Modern Readers Series. Dark green cloth, spine stamped
in gold. A photographic reproduction from the original 1932 text.
With the jacket designed by Lustig and Barrows.

A13e **Light in August.**
New York: The Modern Library, "First Modern Library Edition, 1950."
Number 88. With jacket. Includes an introduction by Richard Rovere.

A13f **Light in August.**
A later Modern Library issue, perhaps 1961. ML 88. The Rovere

introduction has been dropped. With the white jacket, at this point becoming standard for Modern Library and Random House reprints of Faulkner.

A13g **Light in August.**
New York: Modern Library College Editions, ca. 1965.
Wrappers in beige and pale blue. Text of the two previous Modern Library issues. T 68.

A13h **Light in August.**
New York: Random House, 1967.
A new issue using a text photographically reproduced from a copy of the first printing. With white jacket.

A13i **Light in August.**
A later issue in the Modern Library College Editions series, probably 1967. Deep blue and white wrappers. The text of the 1967 Random House edition. Includes an introduction by Cleanth Brooks.

A13j **Light in August.**
New York: Random House, 1970.
Red cloth stamped in gold. Ochre endpapers. Literary Guild edition. 378 pp.

A13k **Light in August.**
New York: Vintage Books, "First Vintage Books Edition, January 1972." Vintage V-189. The first edition text, photographically reproduced.

A13l **"Percy Grimm."**
The World Within, ed. Mary Louise Aswell, intro. and notes Frederic Wertham. New York: Whittlesey House (McGraw-Hill), (1947), pp. 356-370. The excerpt from *Light in August* used by Malcolm Cowley in *The Portable Faulkner.*

A13m **"Joe Christmas."**
A Little Treasury of American Prose, ed. George Mayberry. New York: Scribner's, 1949. pp. 807-826. An excerpt from *Light in August.*

Other English Language Printings:

A13n **Light in August.**
London: Chatto and Windus, (January 26) 1933.
Brick red cloth stamped in gold. Top edges reddish brown. With jacket. 480 pp. Meriwether: 2500 copies.

A13w (tabloid format) with A13u.

A13o **Light in August**
London: Chatto and Windus, 1941. The Pelham Library.

A13p **Light in August.**
Harmondsworth: Penguin, 1960.
Paperback, No. 1433.

Translations:

A13q **Mørk August.**
Oslo: Gyldendal Norsk, 1934.
Trans. Sigurd Hoel. Boards.

A13r **Lumière d'Août.**
Paris: Gallimard, 1935.
(Series: *nrf.)* Trans. and intro. Maurice E. Coindreau. Wrappers.
S.P. copy, signed by the translator.

A13s **Lumière d'Août.**
Paris: Gallimard, 1961.
(Series: Livre de Poche, No 753/754/755.) Contents of the
1935 edition. Wrappers.

A13t **Lumière d'Août.**
Paris: Gallimard, (1965?).
(Series: Collection Soleil, No. 152.) Contents of the 1935 edition.
Boards. Number 430 of a limitation of 3100 copies.

A13u **Licht im August.**
Berlin: Rowohlt, 1935.
"1.-3. Tausend." Trans. Franz Fein. Boards.

A13v **Licht im August.**
Stuttgart, Hamburg, Baden-Baden: Rowohlt, 1949.
"1.-5. Tausend." This version of the Fein translation was issued
in boards and published by Rowohlt at Stuttgart in January 1949.

A13w **Licht im August.**
Hamburg, Stuttgart: Rowohlt, 1949.
The Fein translation issued in the format of a tabloid newspaper
by Rowohlt at Hamburg, May 1949.

A13x **Licht im August.**
Hamburg: Rowohlt, 1955.
(Series: Bucher der Neunzehn, No. 13.) Fein translation. Boards.

A13y   **Licht im August.**
Berlin: Volk & Welt, 1957.
The Fein translation. Boards.

A13z   **Srpnové Svetlo.**
Prague: Nakladatelské druzstvo Máje, 1936.
(Series: Standard Library anglo-americká knihovna.) Trans. Vilém
Werner. Boards.

A13aa **Luce d'Agosto.**
Milan: Mondadori, 1939.
(Series: Medusa, No 98.) Trans. Elio Vittorini. Wrappers.

A13bb   **Luce d'Agosto.**
Milan: Mondadori, 1954.
(Series: Biblioteca Contemporanea Mondadori, No. 13.) Same
translation. Boards.

A13cc   **Luce d'Agosto.**
Milan: Mondadori, 1968.
(Series: Il Bosco, No. 190.) Same translation. Wrappers.

A13dd **Luz de Agosto.**
Buenos Aires: SUR, 1942.
Trans. Pedro Lecuona. Wrappers, rebound in leather.

A13ee **Ljus i augusti.**
Stockholm: Bonniers, 1944.
Trans. Erik Lindegren. Wrappers.

A13ff **Lys i August.**
Copenhagen: Athenaeum, 1946.
Trans. and foreword Sven Møller Kristensen. Rebound.

A13gg **Luz de Agosto.**
Porto Alegre: Globo, 1948.
(Series: Nobel, No. G22.) Trans. Berenice Xavier. Wrappers.

A13hh **Svetloba v Avgustu.**
Ljubljana: Cankarjeva zalozba, 1952.
Slovene trans. Mira Mihelić. Boards.

A13ii **Światłość w Sierpniu.**
Warsaw: Czytelnik, 1959.
Trans. Maciej Słomczyński. Boards.

A13jj   **Megszületik Augusztusban.**
Budapest: Szépirodalmi Könyvkiadó, 1965.
(Series: Olcsó Könyvtar.) Trans. György Déri, afterword Mihály
Sükösd. Two volume edition in wrappers.

A13kk   **Llum d'Agost.**
Barcelona: Edicions 62, 1965.
(Series: El Balanci, No. 4.) Trans. Manuel de Pedrolo. Boards.

A13ll   **Luz de Agosto.**
Lisbon: Livros do Brasil, n. d.
(Series: Dois Mundos, No. 58.) Trans. Armando Ferreira. Wrappers.

A13mm   **Liekehtivä elokuu.**
Helsinki: Tammi, 1968.
Trans. Kai Kaila. Boards.

A13nn   **Hachigatsu no hikari.**
Tokyo: Fuzanbo, 1968.
(Series: Faulkner Zenshu, Vol. 9.) Trans. Shizuo Suyama.

◆

A14a   **A Green Bough.**
New York: Harrison Smith and Robert Haas, (April 20) 1933.
Green cloth; front blind stamped, spine gold stamped. With dust
jacket featuring Lynd Ward engraving. 67 pp.
      This second (and final) book of Faulkner's poetry contains
forty-four numbered poems, of which fourteen had appeared
previously, wholly or in part.

A14b   **A Green Bough.**
Limited, signed issue of 360 copies. Tan cloth stamped in black on
front and spine. Two Lynd Ward labels on front. Copy number 274.

A14c   **"William Faulkner."**
Mississippi Verse, ed. Alice James. Chapel Hill: University of North
Carolina Press, 1934, pp. 31-34.
      Reprints seven poems from *A Green Bough.* Titles (and corres-
ponding numbers in *A Green Bough)* are: "Mirror of Youth" (XVI),
"The Courtesan Is Dead" (XXXV), "Green Is the Water" (XIX),
"If There Be Grief" (XLIV), "Here He Stands" (XX), "Boy and
Eagle" (XVIII), and "Mother and Child" (XXXIV).

A14d   "Poèmes."
           La table ronde, No. 6 (June 1946), pp. 97-109.
           No translator given; the French texts differ from those in *Le rameau*
           vert. The numbering in that book for the six poems included here is
           I, II, VI, XV, XXIV, and XXXIV.
                Number 502 of a limitation of 2000 copies (numbered 151
           through 2150).

A14e   **Le rameau vert.**
           Paris: Gallimard, 1955.
           (Series: *nrf.* Du monde entier, Vol. CLII.) Trans. R. N. Raimbault.
           Wrappers. The English text is faced by the French translation
           throughout.
                Number 37 of a limitation of 86 copies.

A14f   **Le rameau vert.**
           Another copy of the 1955 Du monde entier edition. Boards.
           Binding designed by Mario Prassinos.
                Number 166 of a limitation of 550 copies (numbered 81
           through 630).

A14g   **Ein grüner Zweig.**
           Zurich: Fretz & Wasmuth, 1957.
           Trans., selection and afterword Hans Hennecke. Boards. Facing
           German and English texts of 25 poems of the original 44, omitting
           I, II, VII, VIII, XI, XIII through XVI, XXII, XXIII, XXVI, XXVII,
           XXIX, XXXI, XXXVI, XXXVIII, XLII, XLIII.

A14h   **Ein grüner Zweig.**
           Stuttgart: Goverts, 1957.
           Text of the Hennecke translation. Boards.

A14i   **"and let" and "look, cynthia."**
           Documenta poetica, ed., trans. Hans Rudolf Hilty. Munich: Kindler,
           1962, pp. 230-33. English and German texts of Poems IV and
           XXXII.

◆

A15a   **Doctor Martino and Other Stories.**
           New York: Harrison Smith and Robert Haas, (April 16) 1934.
           Deep blue cloth stamped in gold. Top edges stained yellow. With
           jacket designed by Arthur Hawkins, Jr. 371 pp.

The short stories in this collection making their initial appearance are: "Black Music" and "Leg." The remainder had appeared previously: "Doctor Martino," "Fox Hunt," "The Hound," "Death Drag," "There Was a Queen," "Smoke," "Turn About," "Beyond," "Wash," "Elly," "Mountain Victory," and "Honor."

Publisher's slip laid in requesting no review appearances before April 16.

A15b   **Doctor Martino and Other Stories.**
Limited, signed issue of 360 copies. Black and deep red cloth stamped in gold. Top edges stained black. With tissue wrapper. Copy number 104.

Other English Language Printings:

A15c   **Doctor Martino and other stories.**
London: Chatto and Windus, (September) 1934.
Red-orange cloth stamped in gold. Top edges red. With jacket.
371 pp. Contents same as the American edition.
    Meriwether: 1500 copies.

A15d   **The Collected Works of William Faulkner.**
Dr Martino and Other Stories.
London: Chatto and Windus, 1965.
    The contents are the same as the 1959 *Collected Short Stories* edition: "The Hound" and "Smoke" have been replaced by "Barn Burning" and "Lo!"

Translations:

A15e   **Le docteur Martino et autres histoires.**
Paris: Gallimard, 1948.
(Series: *nrf,* Du monde entier, Vol. LXXII.) Trans. R.-N. Raimbault and Ch.-P. Vorce. Wrappers. Number CXI of a limitation of 210 copies.

A15f   **Le docteur Martino et autres histoires.**
    Another copy of the 1948 *nrf* edition. Boards. Binding designed by Mario Prassinos. Number 115 of a limitation of 1040 copies.

A15g   **Il dottor Martino.**
Milan: Mondadori, 1968.
(Series: Medusa, No. 528.) Trans. Giorgio Monicelli and Attilio

Landi. Boards. Contains only: "Barn Burning," "Elly," "Turna-bout," "Honor," "Doctor Martino," "Beyond," "Black Music," "The Leg," and "The Hound."

A15h   **Ishi Matino hoka.**
Tokyo: Fuzanbo, 1971.
(Series: Faulkner Zenshu, Vol. 10.) Trans. Motoo Takigawa.

◆

A16a   **Pylon.**
Advance copy in wrappers. The printed wrappers are formed by a pasted-on first-printing jacket folded at the edge and trimmed top and bottom to be flush with the pages on all sides.

A16b   **Pylon.**
New York: Harrison Smith and Robert Haas, (March 25) 1935. (Copyright page says "First Printing, February, 1935.") Blue cloth with horizontal black band. Stamped in gold. Top edges stained black. With jacket designed by Maurer, on unglazed paper. 315 pp.

A16c   **Pylon.**
Limited, signed issue of 310 copies. Front and back covered with silver paper, front stamped in blue. Corners and spine in blue cloth. Spine stamped in silver. Top edges silver. In gray box with paper labels on front and spine of box.
   A facsimile of page 58 of the manuscript, folded, is tipped in before the title page. Copy number 272.

A16d   **Pylon.**
Trade issue, "Second Printing, March, 1935."
This and the next six copies of this printing are identical except for the binding cloth. All are stamped in black on the spine. Top edges unstained. The jacket is the first printing design, but on glazed paper and has different printed matter on the front flap; the back and back flap are blank. The jacket is present on each of the seven copies. This copy: Cedar cloth, CCA4-6 le.

A16e   **Pylon.**
Another copy: Redwood cloth, CCA4-6 ne.

A16f   **Pylon.**
Another copy: Bright red cloth, CCA4-7½ pa.

A16g   **Pylon.**
Another copy: Medium blue cloth, CCA4-15 le.

A16h   **Pylon.**
            Another copy: Turquoise blue cloth, CCA4-17 ic.

A16i   **Pylon.**
            Another copy: Mint green cloth, CCA4-22 gc.

A16j   **Pylon.**
            Another copy: Bayberry green cloth, CCA4-22 ig.

A16k   **Pylon.**
            New York: The New American Library, "First Printing, April, 1951."
            Signet Book 863. Paperback.

A16l   **Pylon.**
            Another copy. "Second Printing, January, 1958." Now Signet Book
            S1485. Covers promote the film adaptation, *The Tarnished Angels,*
            released the same month.

A16m   **Pylon.**
            New York: Random House, 1965.
            Text reproduced photographically from a copy of the first printing.
            With uniform edition white jacket.

A16n   **Pylon.**
            New York: The Modern Library, "First Modern Library Edition,
            September, 1967." Text as in the previous Random House edition.
            ML 380. With jacket.

A16o   **Pylon.**
            New York: The New American Library, "First Printing, September,
            1968." Signet Modern Classic CQ 415. With an introduction by
            Reynolds Price.

            Other English Language Printings:

A16p   **Pylon.**
            London: Chatto and Windus, (March 25) 1935.
            Bright red cloth stamped in white. Top edges unstained. With jacket.
            318 pp.   Possibly this is not a first issue: Meriwether mentions a
            browner cloth and rose stained top edges. 2900 copies.

A16q   **Pylon.**
            London: John Lehmann, 1950.
            The Holiday Library.

A16r   **Pylon.**
London: Chatto and Windus, 1954.
The New Phoenix Library, No. 27.

A16s   **The Collected Works of William Faulkner.**
Pylon.
London: Chatto and Windus, 1967.

A16t   **Pylon.**
Hamburg: Albatross, 1935.
Albatross paperback 293. In English.

Translations:

A16u   Wendemarke.
Berlin: Rowohlt, n. d. (1936?).
Trans. Georg Goyert. Boards.

A16v   **Wendemarke.**
Hamburg: Rowohlt, 1951.
(Series: rororo, No. 21.) Goyert translation. Wrappers.

A16w   **Oggi si vola.**
Milan: Mondadori, 1937.
(Series: Medusa, No. 81.) Trans. & intro. Lorenzo Gigli. Wrappers.

A16x   **Oggi si vola.**
Another copy, second edition, 1947.
The Gigli introduction has been dropped. Wrappers.

A16y   **Oggi si vola.**
Milan: Mondadori, 1966.
(Series: Gli Oscar, Vol. 46.) Trans. Lorenzo Gigli. Wrappers.

A16z   **Pylone.**
Paris: Gallimard, 1946.
(Series: *nrf,* Du monde entier, Vol. XLIX.) Trans. R. N. Raimbault
and G. Louis-Rousselet. Wrappers. Number LVIII of a limitation of
105 copies.

A16aa   **Pylone.**
Another copy of the 1946 *nrf* edition. Boards. Binding designed
by Mario Prassinos. Number 880 of a limitation of 1040 copies.

A16bb **Trekanten.**
Copenhagen: Winther, n. d. (1952?).
Trans. Peter Toubro. Wrappers.

A16cc **Sora no yuwaku.**
Toyko: Dabiddosha, 1954.
Trans. Kenzo Ohashi. Wrappers.

A16dd **Hyōshikito.**
Toyko: Fuzanbo, 1971.
(Series: Faulkner Zenshu, Vol. 11.) Trans. Shoji Gotoh.

A16ee **Luftcirkus.**
Stockholm: Bonniers, 1961.
Trans. Gun and Nils A. Bengtsson. Wrappers.

A16ff **Pylon.**
Barcelona: Plaza & Janes, 1962.
(Series: Libro Plaza, No. 289.) Trans. Julio Fernandez-Yanez.
Wrappers.

A16gg **Punkt zwrotny.**
Warsaw: Państwowy Instytut Wydawniczy, 1967.
Trans. Zofia Kierszys. Wrappers.

♦

A17a **Absalom, Absalom!**
Salesman's dummy. Externally resembles the trade issue, though
the top edges are unstained and the covers are limp. Internally it
differs in many ways, containing only ten pages of printed text
(from Chapter II) with the map on the reverse of pages 3 and 4.
The remainder of the volume consists of blank leaves.

A17b **"Work in Progress: Absalom, Absalom!"**
American Mercury, XXXVIII (August 1936), pp. 466-474.

A17c **Absalom, Absalom!**
New York: Random House, (October 26) 1936.
Black cloth stamped in red and gold. Top edges red. With jacket.
384 pp.
Tipped in facing page 384 is a two-color folding map of Jeffer-
son and Yoknapatawpha County, reproduced from a drawing by
Faulkner.

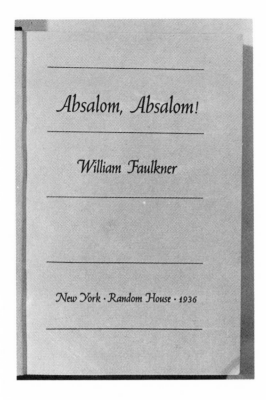

Upper: Salesman's dummy (A17a).
Lower: Published book (A17c).

A17d   **Absalom, Absalom!**
Limited, signed issue of 300 copies. White paper-covered boards
printed in a green and gold pattern. Green cloth spine stamped in gold.
Top edges gold. Copy number 50.

A17e   **Absalom, Absalom!**
New York: The Modern Library, "First Modern Library Edition 1951."
Introduction by Harvey Breit. Number 271. With jacket.
    The Yoknapatawpha County map present is a redrawn variant of
the Faulkner map in the 1936 first edition.

A17f   **Absalom, Absalom!**
A later printing of the Modern Library edition. 1962 can be inferred
from the jacket advertisements. Though the jacket still lists the Harvey
Breit introduction, it has been dropped.

A17g   **Absalom, Absalom!**
New York: Random House, (March) 1966.
Another of the Random House texts reproduced photographically
from a copy of the original edition, with the usual white jacket.

A17h   **Absalom, Absalom!**
New York: Modern Library College Editions, ca. 1967.
Gray and white wrappers, printed in black. T 78.

A17i   **Absalom, Absalom!**
New York: Vintage Books, "First Vintage Books Edition August
1972." A paperback. V-780.

Other English Language Printings:

A17j   **Absalom, Absalom!**
London: Chatto and Windus, (February 11) 1937.
Pale beige cloth stamped in red and black. Top edges stained brick red.
With "jacket" consisting of a glassine wrapper with glued-on printed
paper flaps. 384 pp.
    Sheets were printed in the United States.
    Meriwether: 1750 copies.

A17k   **The Collected Works of William Faulkner.**
        Absalom, Absalom!
London: Chatto and Windus, 1965.
    All volumes in the *Collected Works* series have a uniform jacket
designed by John Woodcock.

Translations:

A17l **Absalom, Absalom!**
Berlin: Rowohlt, n. d. (1938?).
"1.-3. Tausend." Trans. Hermann Stresau. Boards.

A17m **¡Absalón, Absalón!**
Buenos Aires: Emece, 1950.
(Series: Grandes Novelistas.) Trans. Beatriz Florencia Nelson. Boards.

A17n **Absalon! Absalon!**
Paris: Gallimard, 1953.
(Series: *nrf,* Du monde entier, Vol. CXXXV.) Trans. R.-N. Raimbault
and Ch. P. Vorce. Wrappers. Number 19 of a limitation of 87 copies.

A17o **Assalonne, Assalonne!**
Milan: Mondadori, 1954.
(Series: Il Ponte, No. 34.) Trans. Glauco Cambon. Boards.

A17p **Absalomie, Absalomie...**
Warsaw: Państwowy Instyut Wydawniczy, 1959.
(Series: Powiesci XX Wieku.) Trans. Zofia Kierszys. Afterword Ewa
Zycieńska. Boards.

A17q **Absolone, Absolone!**
Prague: Mladá fronta, 1966.
Trans. and afterword Jiři Valja. Boards.

A17r **Absarom, Absarom.**
Tokyo: Fuzanbo, 1968.
(Series: Faulkner Zenshu, Vol. 12.) Trans. Kichinosuke Ohashi.

A17s **Absalom, Absalom!**
Stockholm: Bonniers, 1969.
Trans. Gunnar Barklund. Wrappers.

◆

A18a **The Unvanquished.**
New York: Random House, (February 15) 1938.
Gray cloth. The cover is stamped with two figures in deep red within
a midnight blue wreath. The spine is stamped in rust and black. Top
edges stained reddish brown. Drawings by Edward Shenton. With
jacket. 293 pp.
    A novel though the first six chapters are revised versions of

previously published short stories. The chapters are headed "Ambuscade," "Retreat," "Raid," "Riposte in Tertio," "Vendée," "Skirmish at Sartoris," and "An Odor of Verbena."

A18b **The Unvanquished.**
Another copy. Top edges stained red. Inscribed in pencil on the title page:

> *William Faulkner*
> *New York*
> *6 Oct 1938*

A18c **The Unvanquished.**
Limited, signed issue of 250 copies. White paper covered boards printed in a wine red and gold pattern. Wine red cloth spine stamped in gold. Top edges gold. Copy number 154.

A January 14, 1938, newspaper account said the "special edition of 250 copies, signed by the author, will precede the regular edition."

A18d **The Unvanquished.**
Another copy of the trade issue. "Second Printing." Gray cloth. Figures on cover in medium blue within a deep red wreath. Spine stamped in rust and medium blue. Top edges deep red.

A18e **The Unvanquished.**
New York: The New American Library, "First Printing, December, 1952." Signet Book 977. Paperback.

A18f **The Unvanquished.**
New York: The New American Library, "Second Printing, October, 1958." Signet Book D1616. 50 cents.

A18g **The Unvanquished.**
New York: The New American Library, "First Signet Classics Edition, August, 1959." Signet Classic CD9. With a foreword by Carvel Collins.

A18h **The Unvanquished.**
New York: Random House, 1965.
Text and illustrations photographically reproduced from the first edition. With white jacket.

A18i **The Unvanquished.**
New York: Vintage Books, "First Vintage Books Edition, September, 1966." Paperback. V-351. Text of the previous Random House issue.

Other English Language Printings:

A18j   **The Unvanquished.**
        London: Chatto and Windus, (May 12) 1938.
        Pale blue cloth printed and decorated in black so that some of the
        printing on front and spine is pale blue against the black background.
        Top edges deep maroon. No jacket. (Considering the decorated bind-
        ing, is it possible there was no jacket for this title?) The Shenton
        drawings are not used. 319 pp.
              Meriwether: 1750 copies.

A18k   **The Unvanquished.**
        Harmondsworth: Penguin, 1955.
        Paperback, No. 1058.

A18l   **The Collected Works of William Faulkner.**
        The Unvanquished.
        London: Chatto and Windus, 1967.
        Photographically reproduced from the original American edition; the
        Shenton drawings are therefore included.

A18m   **The Unvanquished.**
        Berlin: Velhagen & Klasing, n. d. (1957?)
        In English; No. 22 in a series of teaching aids. Excerpted from sections
        I, III, IV of the book. Foreword and notes in German. Wrappers.

        Translations:

A18n   **De Familie Sartoris.**
        Haarlem: Spaarnestad, (1938?).
        (Series: Kennemer, No. 12.) Translator's name not given. Includes the
        Edward Shenton illustrations. Boards.

A18o   **Gli invitti.**
        Milan: Mondadori, 1948.
        (Series: Medusa, No. 221.) Trans. Alberto Marmont. Wrappers.

A18p   **De obesegrade.**
        Stockholm: Folket i Bilds, 1948.
        Trans. Håkan Norlén. Intro. Thorsten Jonsson. Boards.

A18q   **L'invaincu.**
        Paris: Gallimard, 1949.
        (Series: *nrf,* Du monde entier, Vol. LXXXIII.) Trans. R. N. Raimbault
        and Ch.-P. Vorce. Wrappers. Number CXLVII of a limitation of 205
        copies.

A18r   **L'invaincu.**
Another copy of the 1949 Gallimard edition. Boards. Binding designed by Mario Prassinos. Number 896 of a limitation of 1050 copies.

A18s   **Los invictos.**
Barcelona: Caralt, 1951.
(Series: Gigante.) Trans. Alberto Vilá de Avilés. Boards.

A18t   **Die Unbesiegten.**
Zurich: Fretz & Wasmuth, 1954.
Trans. and preface Erich Franzen. Boards.

A18u   **Die Unbesiegten.**
Stuttgart: Scherz & Goverts, 1954.
The Franzen translation. Boards.

A18v   **Die Unbesiegten.**
Frankfurt: Fischer, 1957.
(No. 159 in the paperback series.) The Franzen translation.

A18w   **Taskhir nā Pazir.**
Tehran: Amīr Kabīr, 1956.
Trans. Parvīz Dāriūsh. (Persian text.) Boards.

A18x   **Nepřemoženi.**
Prague: Naše vojsko, 1958.
(Series: Knihovna Vojáka, No. 8.) Trans. Josef Schwarz. Wrappers.

A18y   **Os Invencidos.**
Lisbon: Minerva, 1960.
(Series: Minerva, No. 356.) Trans. Abel Marques Ribeiro. Wrappers.

A18z   **Niepokonane.**
Warsaw: Państwowy Instytut Wydawniczy, 1961.
Trans. Ewa Zycieńska. Wrappers.

◆

A19a   **The Wild Palms.**
Advance copy in wrappers. The wrappers are devised of the first edition dust jacket trimmed flush with the pages.

A19b   **The Wild Palms.**
New York: Random House, (January 19) 1939.

Advance copies in wrappers: A6a,
A16a, and A19a.

Tan cloth, stamped in gold and green on front and spine. Top edges stained green. With jacket. 339 pp.

A19c **The Wild Palms.**
Another copy. Differs from the last in that the spine is stamped in brown and green while the front stamping is still gold and green.

A19d **The Wild Palms.**
Limited, signed issue of 250 copies. Paper covered boards in wood pattern. Wine red cloth spine stamped in gold. Top edges gold. Copy number 185.

A19e **The Wild Palms.**
Another copy of the trade issue: "Fourth Printing." Front and spine stamped in gold and green. Inscribed by Faulkner, 1951.

A19f **The Wild Palms.**
New York: Penguin Books, "First Penguin Books Edition, January, 1948." Number 659. Paperback.
Reprints only the chapters designated "Wild Palms" in the original edition.

A19g **The Wild Palms.**
Another copy of the previous paperback, marked "Penguin Signet Books" and "659A" on the cover. The verso of the title page is undated and indicates: "Published as a SIGNET BOOK and Reprinted by Arrangement with The Ajax Library."

A19h **The Old Man.**
New York: The New American Library, "First Printing, November, 1948." Number 692. Paperback.
Reprints only the chapters designated "Old Man" in the original edition.

A19i **The Wild Palms and The Old Man.**
New York: The New American Library, "First Joint Printing, September, 1954." Signet Giant S1148. 35 cents.
Includes both paperback texts, all of the first followed by all of the second, rather than the interspersed chapters of the original edition.

A19j **The Old Man.**
Ten Modern Short Novels, ed. Leo Hamalian and Edmond L. Volpe, New York: Putnam's, 1958. pp. 479-555.

A19k **The Wild Palms and The Old Man.**
Another copy of the joint Signet paperback: "Second Printing, February,

1959." Signet D1643. 50 cents.

Again, the two texts are printed separately.

A19l **The Wild Palms.**
New York: Vintage Books, "First Vintage Edition, September, 1964."
Vintage V-262.

A19m **The Wild Palms.**
New York: The New American Library, "First Printing, September, 1968." Signet Modern Classic CQ414. With an introduction by R. V. Cassill.

The first Signet printing to put the chapters back into the order intended by Faulkner.

Other English Language Printings:

A19n **The Wild Palms.**
London: Chatto and Windus, (March 16) 1939.
Coarse weave white and blue cloth across upper third lettered on spine in green; green cloth across remainder lettered on spine in white. A dark green line is stamped across binding where the two fabrics meet. Top edges stained green. With jacket. 315 pp. Meriwether: 2000 copies.

A19o **The Wild Palms.**
Stockholm: Continental Book Company, 1945.
Zephyr paperback 68. In English.

A19p **The Wild Palms.**
Another copy of the Zephyr edition, 1947.

Translations:

A19q **De vilde palmer.**
Copenhagen: Atheneum, 1939.
Trans. Niels Haislund and Sven Møller Kristensen. Wrappers.

A19r **Las palmeras salvajes.**
Buenos Aires: Sudamericana, 1940.
Trans. Jorge Luis Borges. Boards, perhaps rebound.

A19s **Yasei no jonetsu.**
Tokyo: Hibiya Shuppansha, 1950.

Trans. Yasuo Okubo. Boards.

A19t **Yasei no.**
Tokyo: Fuzanbo, 1968.
(Series: Faulkner Zenshu, Vol. 14.) Trans. Kenzi Inoue.

A19u **Palmiers sauvages.**
Les Temps Modernes.
 No. 63 (January 1951), pp. 1153-1192.
 No. 64 (February 1951), pp. 1442-1472.
 No. 65 (March 1951), pp. 1623-1653.
 No. 66 (April 1951), pp. 1826-1854.
 No. 67 (May 1951), pp. 1990-2027.
Trans. M.-E. Coindreau.
 "Wild Palms" chapters in French translation.

A19v **Les palmiers sauvages.**
Paris: Gallimard, 1952.
(Series: *nrf*, Du monde entier, Vol. CXV.) Trans. and preface
M.-E. Coindreau. Wrappers. Number 16 of a limitation of 107
copies.

A19w **Palme selvagge.**
Milan: Mondadori, 1956.
(Series: Medusa, No. 364.) Trans. Bruno Fonzi. Boards.

A19x **Wilde Palmen und Der Strom.**
Zurich: Fretz & Wasmuth, 1957.
Trans. Helmut M. Braem and Elisabeth Kaiser. Boards. Includes a
translation of an interview comment made by Faulkner in 1956 concerning the alternation of chapters.

A19y **Wilde Palmen und Der Strom.**
Stuttgart: Scherz & Goverts, 1957.
The Braem-Kaiser translation. Boards.

A19z **Der Strom.**
Frankfurt: Fischer, 1961.
(No. 425 in the paperback series.) The Braem-Kaiser translation
of the "Old Man" sections.

A19aa **Wilde Palmen.**
N. p. (Berlin?): Suhrkamp, "Erstes bis fünftes Tausend dieser
Ausgabe 1962." (Series: Bibliothek Suhrkamp, No. 80.) Braem-
Kaiser translation of the "Wild Palms" sections only. Boards.

A19bb **Ya-sang ui jung-yul.**
Seoul: Sum moon Kag, 1958
Trans. Sung Hoon Park. Wrappers.

A19cc **Dzikie palmy / Stary.**
Warsaw: Czytelnik, 1958.
Trans. and afterword Kalina Wojciechowska. Boards.
All the chapters of one story are followed by all the chapters of the other.

A19dd **Divje palme.**
Ljubljana: Državna založba Slovenije, 1959.
Slovene trans. Herbert Grün. Boards.

A19ee **Divoké palmy.**
Prague: Mladá fronta, 1960.
Trans. and afterword Jiří Valja. Boards.

A19ff **Palmeiras Bravas.**
Lisbon: Portugália, ca. 1960.
(Series: O Livro de Balso, No. 19-20.) Trans. Jorge de Sena, with preface and notes by the translator. "Wild Palms" sections only.

A19gg **O Homem e o Rio.**
Lisbon: Portugália, ca. 1960.
(Series: O Livro de Balso, No. 1.) Trans. Luis de Sousa Rebelo, with preface by the translator. "Old Man" sections only.

◆

A20a **The Hamlet.**
New York: Random House, (April 1) 1940.
Black cloth stamped in gold and red. Top edges stained red. With jacket designed by Salter. 421 pp.
Back of jacket bears advertisements for other Random House titles.

A20b **The Hamlet.**
Another copy. Identical to the last except that back of jacket features reviews of *The Hamlet*.

A20c **The Hamlet.**
Limited, signed edition of 250 copies. Light green paper-covered boards. Dark green cloth corners and spine. Spine stamped in gold. Top edges gold. Copy number 17.

A20d The Hamlet.
Another copy of the trade issue. "Second Printing."

A20e The Hamlet.
Another copy of the trade issue. No printing designated; advertisements on back of jacket would imply 1948. Dark red cloth stamped in gold and pale blue.

A20f The Hamlet.
Modern Library Paperback, P 18, March 20, 1956.
Front wrapper red and white, printed in black.
   Probably the first issue in this format; advertisements on back cover run only to volume P 19.

A20g The Hamlet.
Another copy of the Modern Library paperback. Front wrapper blue and white, printed in black.
   Later issue of A20f; advertisements run through volume P 44.

**A20h The Hamlet.
The Long Hot Summer.**
New York: The New American Library, "First Printing, March, 1958."
   Book Three of *The Hamlet* ("The Long Summer") reprinted in time for the release of the film adaptation, *The Long Hot Summer.*

A20i The Hamlet
New York: Random House, 1964.
"Third Edition 1964: First Printing." With tissue wrapper.
   First printing as part of the boxed Snopes trilogy.

Other English Language Printings:

A20j The Hamlet.
London: Chatto and Windus, (September 12) 1940.
Yellow cloth stamped on spine in green. Top edges stained yellow. With jacket. 333 pp. Meriwether: 2000 copies.

Translations:

A20k El villorrio.
Buenos Aires: Futuro, 1947.
Trans. Raquel W. de Ortiz. Wrappers.

A20l   **El villorrio.**
Barcelona: Caralt, 1953.
(Series: Gigante.) Trans. J. Napoletano Torre and P. Carbó Amiguet.
Boards.

A20m **Scheckige Mustangs.**
Wiesbaden: Insel-Verlag, 1956.
(Series: Insel-Bücherei, No. 623.) Trans. Kurt Alboldt. Boards.
"Spotted Horses" as revised for *The Hamlet.*

A20n **Das Dorf.**
Zurich: Fretz & Wasmuth, 1957.
Trans. Helmut M. Braem and Elisabeth Kaiser. Boards.

A20o **Das Dorf.**
Stuttgart: Goverts, 1957.
The Braem-Kaiser translation. Boards.

A20p   **Scheckige Mustangs.**
Stuttgart: Manus, 1965.
Folio edition in boards, illustrated by Gunter Bohmer. Boxed.
Text in the Braem-Kaiser translation.
      Number 16 in a limited edition of 200 copies. With extra
lithographs signed by the artist, four black and white, one tinted.

A20q **Le hameau.**
Paris: Gallimard, 1959.
(Series: *nrf,* Du monde entier, Vol. CCXIII.) Trans. René Hilleret.
Wrappers. Number 2 of a limitation of 66 copies.

A20r **"Eula"**
La Nouvelle Revue Francais, No. 84 (December 1959), pp. 1035-59.
Chapter Two, Part 1 of the "Eula" section of *The Hamlet.*

A20s **El villorio.**
Buenos Aires: Fabril, 1961.
(Series: mirasol, No. 67.) Trans. Santos Merino. Paper-covered boards.

A20t **A Aldeia.**
Lisbon: Arcadia, n. d.
(Series: Encontro, No. 37.) Trans. Jorge Sampaio. Boards.

A20u **Byn.**
Stockholm: Bonniers, 1965.
Trans. Gunnar Barklund. Boards.

A20v **Kyla**

Helsinki: Tammi, 1972.
Trans. Kai Kaila. Boards.

◆

A21a   **Go Down, Moses.**
Three sheets of discarded typescript, each with text on both sides.
One page is headed "GO DOWN, MOSES"; it and another sheet contain early drafts of material found on pages 369, 370, 372, and 373
of the published book as well as material deleted from publication.
The third sheet has brief passages on each side from "Was," pages
7 and 8 in the book. It is on this sheet that Faulkner has inscribed in
pencil: *"To Dan Brennan / William Faulkner / July 19, 1940 / Oxford,
Miss."*

A21b   **Go   Down, Moses and Other Stories.**
New York: Random House, (May 11) 1942.
Black cloth stamped in gold and red. Top edges stained red. With
jacket. 383 pp.
      Not all the first printing sheets were immediately bound,
but this is presumably the first state of the binding.
      Faulkner intended this as a novel, though it includes material pre-
viously (or concurrently) published as individual stories. The sections
are entitled "Was," "The Fire and the Hearth," "Pantaloon in Black,"
"The Old People," "The Bear," "Delta Autumn," and "Go Down,
Moses." Generally these sections are considerably rewritten from
previously published short stories bearing the same titles.

A21c   **Go Down, Moses and Other Stories.**
Limited, signed issue of 100 copies. Salmon paper covered boards.
Brick red cloth corners and spine. Spine stamped in gold. Top edges
gold. Copy number 57.
      Published at a time when Faulkner's career was not at its peak,
this was the smallest limitation of any Faulkner title.

A21d   **Go Down, Moses and Other Stories.**
Another copy of the first printing. This and the following four copies
were bound in whatever cloth the publisher found available during a
period of wartime shortages. All are stamped in lettuce green; none
have staining of top edges.
      This copy: Tile red cloth, CCA4-5 ne.

A21e   **Go Down, Moses and Other Stories.**
Another copy. Cherry red cloth, CCA4-7 nc.

[81]

GO DOWN, MOSES

On that bright hot July morning, the same xind
bright hot wind which shook the mulberry leaves just outside the
window blew into the office too, contriving a semblance of coolness
of what was merely motion..

The face was black, young, smooth, impenetra-
ble, sophisticated; the eyes were inscrutable, indomitable and
tired and they knew too much. The negroid hair had been treated
                                                      neat-
until it covered the skull like a cap, in a single ixxquaxadxridged
curve that had the appearance of having been lacquered, the part
trimmed out with a razor. He wore a sports garment, shirt and
trousers matching and cut from fawn-colored flannel and they had
cost too much, axixtxix tax droped too much, with too many pleats,
and he half lay on the ix steel cot in the steel cubicle just outside which for twenty hours now an armed guard had stood. smoking
         in a voice consistently and carefully not a Southern voice
a cigarette and answering/the questions of the spectacled young
 white man who sat on the steel stool opposite, the broad census-
taker's portfolio open upon his knees:

"Carothers Edmonds Beauchamp. 25. Born in the
country near Jefferson, Mississippi.

Typescript page from A21a.

A21f **Go Down, Moses and Other Stories.**
Another copy. Ivory cloth, CCA4-2 db.

A21g **Go Down, Moses and Other Stories.**
Another copy. Dutch blue cloth, CCA4-13 lc. With jacket.

A21h **Go Down, Moses and Other Stories.**
Another copy. Midnight blue cloth, CCA4-13 pn. With jacket.

A21i **Go Down, Moses.**
Another copy of the trade edition, "Second Printing," probably
1948. With jacket.
    In this and subsequent printings *"and Other Stories"* has been
removed from the title page and does not appear on the redesigned
jacket.

A21j **Go Down, Moses.**
New York: The Modern Library, "First Modern Library Edition, 1955."
With jacket. Number 175.

A21k **Go Down, Moses.**
New York: Vintage Books, "First Vintage Books Edition, April 1973."
Vintage V-884.

Other English Language Printings:

A21l **Go Down, Moses and Other Stories.**
London: Chatto and Windus, (October 8) 1942.
Dark green cloth stamped in white on spine. With jacket. 268 pp.
Meriwether: 2500 copies.

A21m **Go Down, Moses.**
Harmondsworth: Penguin, 1960. Paperback, No. 1434.

Translations:

A21n **Scendi, Mosè.**
Milan: Mondadori, 1947.
(Series: Medusa, No. 186.) Trans. Edoardo Bizzarri. Wrappers.

A21o **"Der Bär."**
Der Monat.
        No. 29 (February 1951), pp. 510-528.
        No. 30 (March 1951), pp. 603-631.

No. 31 (April 1951), pp. 58-84.
The five-part *(Go Down, Moses)* version of "The Bear."

A21p **Das verworfene Erbe.**
Zurich: Fretz & Wasmuth, 1953.
Trans. and foreword Hermann Stresau. Boards.
Includes a McCaslin genealogy, omits "Pantaloon in Black."

A21q   **Jagdgluck.**
Zurich: Arche, 1956.
(Series: Kleinen Bücher, no. 233.) German translation of "Was"
with an afterword by the translator, Elisabeth Schnack. Boards.

A21r **Das verworfene Erbe.**
Stuttgart and Hamburg: Scherz & Goverts, 1953.
The Stresau translation with the same addition and omission as the
Zurich edition. Boards.

A21s   **Der Bär.**
Frankfurt: Forum, n. d. (1955?).
(Series: Forum-Taschenbücher, No. 19.) Again, the Stresau trans-
lation of the five-part version. Wrappers.

A21t   **Der Bär.**
Berlin: Suhrkamp, "Erstes bis fünftes Tausend 1960."
(Series: Bibliothek Suhrkamp, No. 56.) Trans. Hermann Stresau.
Boards. Five-part version of "The Bear."

A21u **Medved.**
Novi Sad: Matica srpska, 1954.
Serbian trans. Aleksandar Nejgebauer. Wrappers. The five-part version
of "The Bear."

A21v **Descends, Moïse.**
Paris: Gallimard, 1955.
(Series: *nrf,* Du monde entier.) Trans. R.-N. Raimbault. Wrappers.
Number 36 of a limitation of 76 copies.

A21w **¡Desciende, Moises!**
Barcelona: Caralt, 1955.
(Series: Gigante.) Trans. and preface Ana-María de Foronda. Boards.

A21x **Bjørnen.**
Copenhagen: Gyldendal, 1957.
(Series: Gyldendals Nye Serie, No. 23.) Trans. and foreword Ole Storm.
Copy in boards, copy in wrappers. Danish translation of five-part version
of "The Bear."

A21y **Het Oude Volk.**
　　　 Delft: W. Gaade, 1957.
　　　 Trans. and preface Hans Edinga. Boards. Dutch translations of "The Old People" and "Go Down, Moses."

A21z **A medve.**
　　　 Budapest: Európa Könyvkiadó, (1959?).
　　　 (Series: Modern Könyvtar, No. 11.) Trans. János Viktor. Wrappers. Five-part version of "The Bear" with translator's afterword and Mc-Caslin genealogy.

A21aa **Zstap, Mojzeszu.**
　　　 Warsaw: Państwowy Instytut Wydawniczy, 1968.
　　　 Trans. Zofia Kierszys. Wrappers.

A21bb **Ike Mōze yo.**
　　　 Tokyo: Fuzanbo, 1973.
　　　 (Series: Faulkner Zenshu, Vol. 16.) Trans. Kenzaburo Ohashi.

◆

A22　 **A Rose for Emily and Other Stories.**
　　　 New York: Editions for the Armed Services, (April, 1945).
　　　 Wrappers. Series title 825. 225 pp.
　　　　　 One of a series of paperback books available at no charge to servicemen overseas. Contains: "A Rose for Emily," "The Hound," "Turn About," "That Evening Sun," "Dry September," "Delta Autumn," "Barn Burning," and "An Odor of Verbena." Foreword by Saxe Commins.

◆

A23a　 **The Portable Faulkner.**
　　　 New York: The Viking Press, (April 29) 1946.
　　　 Edited, with introduction and notes, by Malcolm Cowley. First appearance of Appendix: "1699-1945. The Compsons." Includes reprints of the short stories "A Justice," "Red Leaves," "Was," "Wash," "The Bear," "That Evening Sun," "Ad Astra," "A Rose for Emily," "Death Drag," "Delta Autumn," as well as sections from *The Wild Palms, Absalom, Absalom!, The Unvanquished, The Hamlet, The Sound and the Fury, Sanctuary, Light in August.* Also present on the endpapers is another variant of Faulkner's Yoknapatawpha County

[85]

map, the third since the first edition of *Absalom, Absalom!* With jacket. 756 pp.

Signed on the title page by Malcolm Cowley.

A23b   **The Indispensable Faulkner.**
New York: The Book Society, 1950.
The content is identical to that of *The Portable Faulkner.* With tissue wrapper and gray-blue box.

A23c   **The Portable Faulkner.**
In wrappers, title page: "1961," verso: "Seventh Printing (X P) November 1960."

A23d   **The Portable Faulkner.**
Same format as the previous but in library (hard) binding. "Seventeenth Printing September 1966."

A23e   **The Portable Faulkner.**
Revised and Expanded Edition, 1967. Wrappers.
Drops the "Wedding in the Rain" section from *Absalom, Absalom!* and adds two sections from *Requiem for a Nun*–"The Courthouse" and "The Jail"–as well as the text of the Nobel Address.

A23f   **The Portable Faulkner.**
Another copy of the revised edition. In library binding.

A23g   **The Portable Faulkner.**
Autograph postcard signed from Malcolm Cowley.
"The revised *Portable* is about 20,000 words longer than the original."

Translation:

A23h   **664 pagine di William Faulkner.**
Milan: Saggiatore, 1959.
(Series: La Cultura, Vol. III.) Trans. Edoardo Bizzarri, Augusto Dauphine, Alberto Marmont, Cesare Pavese, Fernanda Pivano, Elio Vittorini. Boards.

The Portable Faulkner plus two excerpts from *Requiem for a Nun.*

◆

A24a **Intruder in the Dust.**
Uncorrected proof, stapled in blue paper covers. "For advance readers."

A24b **Intruder in the Dust.**
New York: Random House, (September 27) 1948.
Black cloth stamped in blue and gold. Top edges stained blue. With jacket designed by E. McKnight Kauffer. 247 pp.
    Faulkner's first novel in six years.

A24c **Intruder in the Dust.**
Another copy, signed "William Faulkner," in ink on the title page. With jacket.

A24d **Intruder in the Dust.**
Another copy, much used. Pasted in at every possible white space at the front and back are accounts from the *Oxford Eagle* of the filming of the motion picture adaptation. Also pasted in is Bosley Crowther's *New York Times* review. This copy belonged to an Oxford, Mississippi neighbor of Faulkner.

A24e **Intruder in the Dust.**
New York: The New American Library, "First Printing, September, 1949." Signet Book 743. Paperback.
    The photograph on the back cover by Walter Sanders identified as William Faulkner, is actually of John Faulkner, William's brother.

A24f **Intruder in the Dust.**
Another copy, "Seventh Printing, March, 1958."
Signet Book S1511. 35 cents.

A24g **Intruder in the Dust.**
New York: The Modern Library, 1964.
With white jacket. ML 351.
    The only Faulkner novel in this reprint series that was never imprinted "First Modern Library Edition."

A24h **Intruder in the Dust.**
New York: Modern Library College Editions, ca. 1967.
Green and white wrappers, printed in black. T 88.

A24i **Intruder in the Dust.**
New York: Vintage Books, "First Vintage Books Edition, August 1972." A paperback. V-792.

Other English Language Printings:

A24j   **Intruder in the Dust.**
London: Chatto and Windus, (September 29) 1949.
Blue cloth stamped on spine in gold. Top edges blue-green. With
jacket designed by Sydney Greenwood. 247 pp.
    Meriwether: 2000 copies.

A24k   **Intruder in the Dust.**
Harmondsworth: Penguin, 1960. Paperback No. 1432.

A24l   **"Intruder in the Dust (extract)."**
Readings in American Literature, No. 5, ed. Sabina Jedraszko.
Warsaw: Państwowe Wydawnictwo Naukowe, 1961, pp. 80-88.
Part of an English language teaching aid for language and literature
students; reprints the last few pages of the original American edition.

Translations:

A24m   **Ubuden gaest i støvet.**
Copenhagen: Aschehoug, 1950.
Trans. Mogens Boisen. Wrappers.

A24n   **Inkräktare i stoftet.**
Stockholm: Bonniers, 1950.
Trans. Th. Warburton. Not a first: "Tredje-femte tusendet." Boards.

A24o   **Intruso en el polvo.**
Buenos Aires: Losada, 1951.
Trans. Aída Aisenson. Wrappers.

A24p   **Non si fruga nella polvere.**
Milan: Mondadori, 1951.
(Series: Medusa, No. 284.) Trans. and intro. Fernanda Pivano. Boards.

A24q   **Bojo eno chinnyusha.**
Tokyo: Hayakawa Shobo, 1951.
Trans. Shozo Kato. Wrappers.

A24r   **Bochi e no shinnyusha.**
Tokyo: Fuzanbo, 1969.
(Series: Faulkner Zenshu, Vol. 17.) Trans. Kenzo Suzuki.

A24s   **Griff in den Staub.**
Zurich: Fretz & Wasmuth, 1951.
Trans. Harry Kahn. Boards.

A24t **Griff in den Staub.**
Stuttgart and Hamburg: Scherz & Goverts, 1951.
The Kahn translation. Boards.

A24u **Griff in den Staub.**
Darmstadt: Goldene Vlies, n. d. (1954?).
(Series: Burgers Taschenbuch, No. 36.) The Kahn translation.
Wrappers.

A24v **L'intrus.**
Paris: Gallimard, 1952.
(Series: *nrf,* Du monde entier, Vol. CXVII.) Trans. R.-N. Raimbault.
Wrappers. Number 30 of a limitation of 131 copies.

A24w **L'intrus.**
Another copy of the 1952 Gallimard edition. Boards. Binding
designed by Mario Prassinos. Number 941 of a limitation of 1050
copies (numbered 126 through 1175).

A24x **O mundo não perdoa.**
Lisbon: Publicacões Europa-America, 1952.
Trans. Antonio de Sousa. Wrappers.

A24y **O mundo não perdoa.**
Another copy of the Lisbon edition, second printing, 1954.
Wrappers.

A24z **Intruz.**
Warsaw: Czytelnik, 1961.
Trans. Ewa Zycieńska. Boards.

♦

A25a **Knight's Gambit.**
Uncorrected proof, tied in blue paper covers. "For advance readers."

A25b **Knight's Gambit.**
New York: Random House, (November 7) 1949.
Red cloth stamped in gold and black. Top edges stained deep gray
blue. With jacket designed by E. McKnight Kauffer. 246 pp.
  Six "detective" stories written around the character Gavin Stevens.
The title story appears for the first time. The other stories are: "Smoke,"
"Monk," "Hand upon the Waters," "Tomorrow," and "An Error in
Chemistry."
  One of the Faulkner titles in which "First Printing" (or a variant)

does not appear on the verso of the first edition title page.

A25c **Knight's Gambit.**
New York: The New American Library, "First Printing, December, 1950." Signet Book 825. Paperback.

A25d **Knight's Gambit.**
Another copy, "Third Printing, June, 1956." Signet Book 1315.

Other English Language Printings:

A25e **Knight's Gambit.**
London: Chatto and Windus, (April 16) 1951.
Blue cloth lettered in gold on spine. Top edges stained gray. With jacket designed by Lynton Lamb. 218 pp. Contents same as the American edition.
    Meriwether: 4000 copies.

Translations:

A25f **Gambito de caballo.**
Buenos Aires: Emecé, 1951.
Trans. Lucrecia Moreno de Sáenz. Wrappers.

A25g **Le gambit du cavalier.**
Paris: Gallimard, 1951.
(Series: *nrf,* Du monde entier, Vol. CIX.) Trans. Andre du Bouchet. Wrappers. Number 18 of a limitation of 129 copies.

A25h **Kishi no kansei.**
Tokyo: Yukeisha, 1951.
Trans. Yasuo Okubo. Boards.

A25i **Høje Ret!**
Copenhagen: Wangel, 1952.
Trans. Georgjedde *(sic).*

A25j **Duman.**
Istanbul: Varlik Yayinevi, 1952.
(Series: Varlik Yayinlari, No. 52.) Trans. Talât Halman. Wrappers. *Knight's Gambit* lacking the title story.

A25k **Duman.**
Another copy. 1963 edition with translator's foreword.

A25l **Konjički gambit.**
Belgrade: Prosveta, 1954.
Serbian trans. Božidar Marković with an afterword. Wrappers. Contains only the story "Knight's Gambit."

A25m **Kapnos kai alla diégémata.**
Athens: Eklekta, n. d. (c. 1956?).
Trans., intro. Bas. L. Kazantzés. Wrappers. Contains only: "Smoke," "Tomorrow," "Knight's Gambit," and "Hand upon the Waters."

A25n **Dukhān wa quisas ukhrā.**
Beirut: Dār al-Kitāb, 1957.
Trans. and preface Ādil Hāmid (Arabic text). Wrappers. Contains: "Smoke," "Monk," "Hand upon the Waters," "Tomorrow," "An Error in Chemistry."

A25o **Der Springer greift an.**
Zurich: Fretz & Wasmuth, 1962.
Trans. Elisabeth Schnack. Boards.

A25p **Gambit.**
Warsaw: Państwowy Instytut Wydawniczy, 1963.
Trans. Zofia Kierszys. Wrappers.

◆

A26a **Collected Stories of William Faulkner.**
New York: Random House, (August 21) 1950.
Gray cloth, spine stamped in blue and gold. Top edges stained deep gray-blue. With jacket. 900 pp.
    Forty-two stories in reprint appearances: "Barn Burning," "Shingles for the Lord," "The Tall Men," "A Bear Hunt," "Two Soldiers," "Shall Not Perish," "A Rose for Emily," "Hair," "Centaur in Brass," "Dry September," "Death Drag," "Elly," "Uncle Willy," "Mule in the Yard," "That Will Be Fine," "That Evening Sun," "Red Leaves," "A Justice," "A Courtship," "Lo!," "Ad Astra," "Victory," "Crevasse," "Turnabout," "All the Dead Pilots," "Wash," "Honor," "Dr. Martino," "Fox Hunt," "Pennsylvania Station," "Artist at Home," "The Brooch," "My Grandmother Millard," "Golden Land," "There Was a Queen," "Mountain Victory," "Beyond," "Black Music," "The Leg," "Mistral," "Divorce in Naples," "Carcassonne."

A26b **Collected Stories of William Faulkner.**
Another copy, with top edges unstained. The lower right-hand corner of the back cover is blind-stamped in the manner of book club

editions. With jacket. Corner is clipped from front jacket flap.

Other English Language Printings:

A26c   **Collected Stories of William Faulkner.**
London: Chatto and Windus, (October 18) 1951.
Blue cloth stamped in gold on spine. Top edges gray-blue. With jacket.
900 pp. Sheets were printed in the United States. Contents same as
the American edition.
    Meriwether: 1526 copies.

A26d   **The Collected Short Stories of William Faulkner. Volume I, Uncle
Willy and Other Stories.**
London: Chatto and Windus, (March 24) 1958.
Blue cloth stamped in gold on spine. With jacket. 320 pp.
    Contents: "Shingles for the Lord," "The Tall Men," "A Bear
Hunt," "Two Soldiers," "Shall Not Perish," "Centaur in Brass," "Un-
cle Willy," "Mule in the Yard," "That Will Be Fine," "A Courtship,"
"Pennsylvania Station," "Artist at Home," "The Brooch," "My
Grandmother Millard and General Bedford Forrest and The Battle
of Harrykin Creek," "Golden Land."
    Meriwether: 6000 copies.

A26e   **The Collected Short Stories of William Faulkner. Volume II, These
Thirteen.**
London: Chatto and Windus, (September 18) 1958.
Blue cloth stamped in gold on spine. With jacket. 272 pp.
Contents the same as the English edition of 1933 and the American
first edition of *These 13* of 1931.

A26f   **The Collected Short Stories of William Faulkner. Volume III,
Dr Martino and Other Stories.**
London: Chatto and Windus, (February 5) 1959.
Blue cloth stamped in gold on spine. With jacket. 320 pp.
    Contents: "Barn Burning," "Death Drag," "Elly," "Lo!,"
"Turnabout," "Wash," "Honor," "Dr. Martino," "Fox Hunt,"
"There Was a Queen," "Mountain Victory," "Beyond," "Black
Music," "The Leg."

Translations:

A26g   **Opowiadania.**
Warsaw: Państwowy Instytut Wydawniczy, 1958.
Trans. Zofia Kierszys, Jan Zakrzewski, Ewa Zycieńska. Two volumes.
Wrappers. Volume I contains the first three sections (twenty stories)

of the original American edition, Volume 2 the remaining three sections (twenty-two stories).

A26h **Erzählungen II.**
Zurich: Frezt & Wasmuth, 1966.
Trans. Elisabeth Schnack. Boards. Contains the stories in sections three and four of the American edition of *Collected Stories.*

Other Short Story Collections

A26i **Selected Short Stories of William Faulkner.**
New York: The Modern Library, ("First Printing") 1962.
ML 324. With jacket. A selection of stories in reprint: "Barn Burning," "Two Soldiers," "A Rose for Emily," "Dry September," "That Evening Sun," "Red Leaves," "Lo!," "Turnabout," "Honor," "There Was a Queen," "Mountain Victory," "Beyond," and "Race at Morning."

Other English Language Editions:

A26j **A Rose for Emily.**
Tokyo: Nan'un-do, 1956.
In English. Ed. Naotaro Takiguchi and Masao Takahashi. Wrappers. Contains: "A Rose for Emily," "Shall Not Perish," "That Evening Sun," and "Crevasse."

Other Foreign Language Editions:

A26k **William Faulkner.**
Coimbra (Portugal): Atlantida, 1948.
Edited and translated by Victor Palla. Wrappers. Includes: "That Evening Sun," "Elly," "The Old People," "The Bear" (short version), "Delta Autumn," "Two Soldiers," and a long preface by the translator.

A26l **Abendsonne.**
Munich: Piper, 1956.
Trans. Erich Franzen. Boards. Contains: "That Evening Sun," "Red Leaves," "Dry September."

A26m **Emily no bara; Ryoken.**
Tokyo: Eihosha, 1956.

Trans. Masao Takahashi and Kichinosuke Ohashi. Wrappers. Contains: "A Rose for Emily," "Crevasse," "The Hound," "Pantaloon in Black," and "Eula."

A26n **Doktor Martino.**
Istanbul: Yenilik Yayinevi, 1956.
(Series: Yenilik Yayinlari, No. 21.) Trans. Bilge Karasu. Wrappers. Contains: "Go Down, Moses," "Elly," "Carcassonne," "Doctor Martino."

A26o **Victorie.**
Bucharest: Editura de stat pentru literatura si arta, 1957.
Trans. Margareta Sterian with a publisher's foreword. Wrappers. Contains: "Victory," "Dry September," "A Rose for Emily," "Red Leaves," "A Justice."

A26p **Růže pro Emilii.**
Prague: Státni nakladatelstvi krásné literatury, 1958.
(Series: Soudobá Svetová Próza, No. 80.) Boards. Contains: "Lo!," "Mountain Victory," "Barn Burning," "A Rose for Emily," "A Bear Hunt," "The Brooch," "Golden Land," "Ad Astra," "Victory," trans. Zdeněk Urbánek. "Wash," "That Will Be Fine," "That Evening Sun," "Dry September," "Elly," "Pennsylvania Station," "Crevasse," "Turnabout," "The Tall Men," "Two Soldiers," "Shall Not Perish," trans. Josef Schwarz. Afterword Vítezslav Kocourek.

A26q **Meine Grossmutter Millard und die Schlacht am Harrykin-Bach; Schwarzer Harlekin.**
Stuttgart: Reclam, 1958.
(Series: Universal-Bibliothek, No. 8221.) Wrappers. Contains: "My Grandmother Millard and General Bedford Forrest and the Battle of Harrykin Creek," trans. Elisabeth Schnack, "Pantaloon in Black," trans. Hermann Stresau, and an afterword by Helmut M. Braem.

A26r **Sem' rasskazov.**
Moscow: Izdatel'stvo inostrannoi literatury, 1958.
Afterword by I. Kashkin. Wrappers. Contains: "Barn Burning," "A Justice," trans. I. Kashkin; "Red Leaves," "That Evening Sun," trans. O. Kholmskaya; "Smoke," trans. R. Rait-Kovaleva; "Percy Grimm," (from *Light in August*), trans. M. Bekker; "Victory," trans. M. Bogoslovskaya.

A26s **Kirmizi Yapraklar.**
Istanbul: Atac Kitabevi, 1959.
Trans. Ülkü Tamer. Wrappers. Contains the Nobel Prize address and "That Evening Sun," "Dry September," "Red Leaves," "A Justice."

A26t   **Faulkner Tampenshu.**
Tokyo: Shincho-sha, 1960.
Trans. Naotaro Tatsunokuchi. Wrappers. Contains: "Jealousy," "A Rose for Emily," "Dry September," "That Evening Sun," "Barn Burning," "Wash."

A26u   **Czerwone liście. (Red Leaves.)**
Warsaw: Państwowy Instytut Wydawniczy, 1963.
(Series: Biblioteka Powszechna.) Wrappers. Contains: "The Tall Men," "Two Soldiers," "A Rose for Emily," "Dry September," "That Evening Sun," trans. Jan Zakrzewski; "Red Leaves," "Turnabout," "Wash," "Pennsylvania Station," trans. Zofia Kierszys; "Mountain Victory," "Mistral," trans. Ewa Życieńska.

A26v   **Ümberpöörd.**
Tallinn: Kirjastus Perioodika, 1965.
(Series: "Loomingu" Raamatukogu, No. 14.) Estonian translation by Valda Raud. Wrappers. Contains: "Two Soldiers," "Honor," "That Will Be Fine," "Turnabout."

A26w   **Histoires diverses.**
Paris: Gallimard, 1967.
(Series: *nrf,* Du monde entier, Vol. CDLXVI.) Wrappers. Duplicates no American title and contains: "Barn Burning," "Shingles for the Lord," "Two Soldiers," "Centaur in Brass," "Uncle Willy," "Mule in the Yard," "That Will Be Fine," "A Courtship," "Lo!," "Pennsylvania Station," "Artist at Home," "The Brooch," "My Grandmother Millard..." trans. R.-N. Raimbault; "The Tall Men," "A Bear Hunt," "Shall Not Perish," "Golden Land," trans. Celine Zins.
Number 6 of a limitation of 42 copies.

A26x   **Histoires diverses.**
Another copy of the above edition (A26w), wrappers. Regular first French edition, unnumbered.

A26y   **Durrer September.**
Zurich: Diogenes, 1968.
"1.-6. Tausend." Trans. and afterword Elisabeth Schnack. Boards. Contains: "Barn Burning," "Two Soldiers," "Shall Not Perish," "A Rose for Emily," "Dry September," "A Justice," "Crevasse," "There Was a Queen," "Carcassonne."

A26z   **Karhu ja muita novelleja.**
Helsinki: Tammi, 1969.
Nine stories. Boards. Contains: "Wash," "Pantaloon in Black," "The Bear," trans. Kai Kaila; "Red Leaves," "Dry September," "A Justice,"

trans. Paavo Lehtonen. "That Evening Sun," "Barn Burning," trans. Jouko Linturi; "A Rose for Emily," trans. Marketta Ormala.

♦

A27a **Notes on a Horsethief.**
Greenville, Mississippi: The Levee Press, November 1950.
(Copyright date is February 1, 1951.) Green cloth stamped in silver on front and spine. End-papers pale green with deep green drawings. Decorations by Elizabeth Calvert. Limited, signed edition of 975 copies. 71 pp.
       Issued without a jacket. Copy number 580.

A27b **Notes on a Horsethief.**
Another copy. Inscribed to a California friend on the title page. Inscribed again, rather than numbered, on the limitation page. Full signature on limitation page, "Bill" on title page.

A27c **"Notes on a Horsethief."**
Vogue, CXXIV (July 1954), pp. 46-51, 101-107.

A27d **"Notes on a Horsethief."**
Perspectives U. S. A., No. 9 (Autumn 1954), 24-59.

♦

A28a **"A Name for the City."**
Harper's Magazine, CCI (October 1950), pp. 200-202, 204, 206, 208, 210, 212-214.
       An early version of the introduction to Act I of *Requiem for a Nun.*

A28b **Requiem for a Nun.**
New York: Random House, (September 27) 1951.
Pale green cloth covers; spine black cloth stamped in gold. Top edges dark gray. With jacket designed by E. McKnight Kauffer. 286 pp.
       A novel in the form of a three act play, with each act introduced by a narrative section. The sections bear titles, as: Act I, "The Courthouse (A Name for the City)"; Act II, "The Golden Dome (Beginning Was the Word)"; Act III, "The Jail (Nor Even Yet Quite Relinguish)."
       The verso of the first edition title page does not bear any indication of first printing.

A28c **Requiem for a Nun.**
Limited, signed issue of 750 copies. Front and back are covered

with multi-colored marbled paper. Corners and spine are black cloth. Top edges medium gray. Gray endpapers. Copy number 66.

A28d   **"A Name for the City."**
Prize Stories of 1951: The O. Henry Awards, ed. Herschel Brickell. Garden City, Doubleday, 1951, pp. 98-115. The *Harper's* version.

A28e   **"The Jail."**
Partisan Review, XVIII (September-October 1951), pp. 496-515, 598-608.
     Introduction to Act III of *Requiem for a Nun.*

Other English Language Printings:

A28f   **Requiem for a Nun.**
London: Chatto and Windus, (February 9) 1953.
Pale blue cloth stamped in gold on spine. With jacket designed by Paul Hogarth. 251 pp.
     Meriwether: 5500 copies.

A28g   **Requiem for a Nun.**
Harmondsworth: Penguin, 1960. Paperback, No. 1435.

A28h   **The Collected Works of William Faulkner.**
Requiem for a Nun.
London: Chatto and Windus, 1965.

Translations:

A28i   **Réquiem para una mujer.**
Buenos Aires: Emecé, 1952.
Trans. Jorge Zalamea. Wrappers.

A28j   **Requiem para una mujer.**
Buenos Aires: Emece, 1962. (Fourth printing.)
Trans. Jorge Zalamea. Wrappers.

A28k   **Själamässa för en nunna.**
Stockholm: Bonniers, 1952.
Trans. Mårten Edlund. Wrappers.

A28l   **Requiem per una monica.**

Milan: Mondadori, 1955.
(Series: Medusa, No. 347.) Trans. Fernanda Pivano. Boards.

A28m   **Requiem per una monica.**
Milan: Mondadori, 1964.
(Series: Il Bosco, Vol. 145.) The Pivano translation. Wrappers.

A28n   **Requiem für eine Nonne.**
Zurich: Fretz and Wasmuth, 1956.
Trans. Robert Schnorr. Boards.

A28o   **Requiem für eine Nonne.**
Stuttgart: Goverts, 1956.
The Schnorr translation. Boards. Not a first printing; jacket ads imply 1958.

A28p   **Requiem für eine Nonne.**
Berlin: Deutsche Buch-Gemeinschaft, 1961.
The Schnorr translation. Boards.

A28q   **Requiem pour une nonne.**
Paris: Gallimard, 1957.
(Series: *nrf,* Du monde entier, Vol. CLXXX.) Trans. M. E. Coindreau. Preface Albert Camus. Wrappers. Number 67 of 77 copies.

A28r   **Requiem por uma Freira.**
Lisbon: Gleba, 1958.
(Series: Folio.) Trans. and preface Luis de Sousa Rebelo. Plastic. Number 332 of a limitation of 1500 copies.

A28s   **Amaso eno chinkonka.**
Tokyo: Fuzanbo, 1967.
(Series: Faulkner Zenshu, Vol. 19.) Trans. Katsuzo Sakata.
     This was the first volume issued in this series of Japanese translations. Scheduled to run to twenty-five volumes, the series is issued in uniform, boxed format.

◆

A29a   **Mirrors of Chartres Street.**
Minneapolis: Faulkner Studies, (November 30) 1953.
Tan cloth, spine stamped in red. Introduction by William Van O'Connor; illustrated by Mary Demopoulos. With jacket bearing photograph by Clell Mize. Limited edition of 1000 copies. 93 pp.
     The first of the volumes reprinting, with varying degrees of

accuracy, the sketches Faulkner did in 1925 for the New Orleans *Times-Picayune*. Eleven appear in this collection: "Mirrors of Chartres Street," "Damon and Pythias Unlimited," "Home," "Cheest!," "Out of Nazareth," "The Kingdom of God," "The Rosary," "The Cobbler," "Chance," "Sunset," and "The Kid Learns."

Copy number 150.

A29b **Mirrors of Chartres Street.**
Another copy.
Bound in gray cloth stamped in red and black. On the certificate of limitation page there is, hand lettered in ink: "This is no. 6 of a press overrun bound by Allan Campbell Minneapolis Sept 1957."

◆

A30a **The Faulkner Reader.**
New York: Random House, (April 1) 1954.
Blue cloth stamped in gold and black. Top edges stained red. With jacket featuring Henri Cartier-Bresson photograph. 682 pp.

Contains a foreword by the author in its first appearance and the following reprint material: The Nobel Prize Address, *The Sound and the Fury*, "The Bear" (from *Go Down, Moses*), "Old Man" (from *The Wild Palms*), "Spotted Horses" (from *The Hamlet*), "A Rose for Emily," "Barn Burning," "Dry September," "That Evening Sun," "Turnabout," "Shingles for the Lord," "A Justice," "Wash," "An Odor of Verbena" (from *The Unvanquished*), "Percy Grimm" (from *Light in August*), and "The Courthouse" (from *Requiem for a Nun*).

The verso of the title page of the first edition does not mention first printing.

This copy has "Review Copy" slip laid in.

A30b **The Faulkner Reader.**
Another copy.
Top edges unstained. Blind stamp at lower right of back cover, characteristic of book club editions. Front flap indicates a "Book Dividend" of the Book-of-the-Month Club.

A30c **The Faulkner Reader.**
New York: The Modern Library, "First Modern Library Giant Edition, 1959." G 82. With jacket adapted from Random House edition jacket.

◆

Other prose collections, mostly fiction:

A30d **Three Famous Short Novels.**
New York: Random House, 1958.
Modern Library Paperback, P36. Contains "Spotted Horses," "Old Man," and "The Bear."
　　　Exterior printing that is colored is in green; perhaps first issue as the advertisements on back cover run only to P39.

A30e **Three Famous Short Novels.**
Another copy.
Exterior printing that is colored is red; advertisements on back cover run through P50.

A30f **Twelve American Writers.**
Ed. William M. Gibson and George Arms. New York: Macmillan, 1962.
Includes "The Kingdom of God," "A Louisiana Sheep Ranch" (from *Mosquitoes)*, "Dry September," "That Evening Sun," "Carcassonne," "Barn Burning," "The Bear" (short version), "Shingles for the Lord," the Nobel Acceptance Speech, "Sherwood Anderson: An Appreciation," and an extract from the Jean Stein interview.

A30g **Nobel Prize Library: Faulkner O'Neill Steinbeck.**
New York: Gregory and CRM, 1971.
Includes the Nobel Acceptance Speech, "A Rose for Emily," and *As I Lay Dying.* Also, "The Life and Works of William Faulkner," by Joseph Blotner.

A30h **Some Modern Writers.**
Ed. Robert Scholes. New York: Oxford, 1971.
Includes the Foreword to *The Faulkner Reader,* the Nobel Acceptance Speech, "Sunset," "Dry September," and "The Old People."

Other English Language Printings:

A30i **Faulkner's County: Tales of Yoknapatawpha County.**
London: Chatto and Windus, (July 11) 1955.
Green cloth with brown ground on portion of spine, stamped in gold on spine. With jacket. 494 pp.
　　　Contains the following reprint material: The Nobel Prize Address, *As I Lay Dying,* "The Bear" (from *Go Down, Moses)*, "Spotted Horses" (from *The Hamlet)*, "A Rose for Emily," "Barn

Burning," "Dry September," "That Evening Sun," "Turnabout,"
"Shingles for the Lord," "A Justice," "Wash," "Percy Grimm" (from
Light in August), and "The Courthouse" (Act I and its narrative intro-
duction from *Requiem for a Nun).*
Meriwether: 5000 copies.

A30j **The Best of Faulkner.**
London: Reprint Society.
Reprints contents of *Faulkner's County.*

Translated Prose Collections:

A30k **Jefferson, Mississippi.**
Paris: Club du meilleur livre (by arrangement with Gallimard), 1956.
Ed. and intro. Michel Mohrt. Boards.
    Contains: Trans. M. E. Coindreau: "A Name for the City" from
Requiem for a Nun, "That Evening Sun." "Dilsey" and the Appendix
from *The Sound and the Fury*, "A Rose for Emily," "Dry September";
trans. R.-N. Raimbault: An excerpt from *Absalom, Absalom!*, "The
Bear" from *Go Down, Moses*; trans. Raimbault and Ch.-P. Vorce:
"Wash," "An Odor of Verbena" from *The Unvanquished,* "All the
Dead Pilots," "There Was a Queen," "A Justice"; trans. Raimbault and
H. Delgove: Four excerpts from *Sartoris.* Map and illustrations by
Jacques Noel.
    Number 1524 of a limitation of 5500.

A30l **Obras escogidas. Vol. I**
Madrid: Aguilar, 1956.
Intro. Agustín Caballero. Contains: Trans. Agustín Caballero and Arturo del Hoyo: *As I Lay Dying*; trans. Julio Fernández Yánez: *Pylon*;
trans. Alberto Vilá de Avilés: *The Unvanquished*; trans. J. Napoletano
and P. Carbó: *The Hamlet*; trans. Ana M. de Foronda: *Go Down,
Moses.*

A30m **Gendai Amerika bungaku zenshu.**
Tokyo: Arechi Shuppansha, 1958.
(Series: Collection of Contemporary American Literature, No. 8.)
Trans. Junzaburo Nishiwaki, et. al. Boards. Contains *Absalom, Absa-
lom!,*" "The Bear," "A Rose for Emily," "That Evening Sun."

A30n **Shino tokoni yo kotawannte.**
Tokyo: Takami Shobo, 1959.
(Series: Collection of Modern Western Literature, Vol. 61.) Trans.

Masami Nishikawa. Boards.

    Contains *As I Lay Dying, Pylon,* "Mississippi," as well as Hemingway's *A Farewell to Arms.*

A30o   **I Negri e gli Indiani.**
Milan: Mondadori, 1960.
(Series: Tutte le opere di William Faulkner, Vol. II.) Ed. and intro. Fernanda-Pivano.
    Contains: Trans. Edoardo Bizzarri: *Go Down, Moses;* Trans. Fernanda Pivano: *Intruder in the Dust,* "Red Leaves," "A Justice"; Trans. Magda De Cristofaro Maldini: "Lo!," "A Courtship"; Trans. Giorgio Monicelli: "Race at Morning."

A30p   **I piantatori e i poveri bianchi. / Le donne del Sud.**
Milan: Mondadori, 1961.
(Series: Tutte le opere di William Faulkner, Vol. III-IV.) Ed. and introductions Fernanda Pivano.
    Contains: Trans. Glauco Cambon: *Absalom, Absalom!;* Trans. Fernanda Pivano: "Wash," "Ad Astra"; Trans. Giorgio Monicelli: "Mountain Victory," "My Grandmother Millard...," "All the Dead Pilots," "There Was a Queen"; Trans. Alberto Marmont: *The Un-Vanquished.*

A30q   **La famiglia Stevens.**
Milan: Mondadori, 1963.
(Series: Tutte le opere di William Faulkner, Vol. VI.) Ed. and intro. Fernanda Pivano.
    Contains: Trans. Giorgio Monicelli: *Sanctuary;* trans. Fernanda Pivano: *Requiem for a Nun* (novel); trans. Elena Vivante: *Knight's Gambit.*

◆

A31a   **A Fable.**
New York: Random House, (August 2) 1954.
Maroon cloth. Cover blind stamped and stamped in black; spine stamped in beige and silver. Top edges blue-gray. Blue-gray endpapers. With jacket designed by Riki Levinson. 437 pp.
    Faulkner is known to have done at least one sketch suggestion for the jacket design.

A31b   **A Fable.**
Limited, signed issue of 1000 copies.
Dark blue cloth stamped in white and blue on cover; stamped in white and gold on spine. Top edges stained midnight blue. Blue-gray endpapers.

With tissue jacket; boxed in blue-gray box with wraparound paper label. Copy number 463.

A31c   **A Fable.**
Another copy of the trade issue. With "Review Copy" slip laid in.

A31d   **A Fable.**
New York: The Modern Library, "First Modern Library Edition, September, 1966."
With white jacket.

A31e   **A Fable.**
New York: The New American Library, "First Printing, September, 1968."
Signet Modern Classic CY 412. Paperback. Introduction by Michael Novak.

A31f   **A Fable.**
A Great Books Reader II.
Chicago: Great Books Foundation, 1957, pp. 69-70.
A very brief excerpt. Contains also a slightly abbreviated version of the Nobel Address, pp. 39-40.

Other English Language Printings:

A31g   **A Fable.**
London: Chatto and Windus, (June 9) 1955.
Red cloth stamped on spine in gold. With jacket designed by Lynton Lamb. 391 pp.
      Meriwether: 13,160 copies.

Translations:

A31h   **Una fabula.**
Mexico City: Cumbre, 1955.
Trans. Antonio Ribera. Preface Agustí Bartra. Boards.
      This and the next two volumes have identical content and similar format.

A31i   **Una fabula.**
Barcelona: Exito, 1955.

Trans. Antonio Ribera. Preface Agustín Bartra. Boards. (Bartra's name suffers a sea change.)

A31j **Una fabula.**
Buenos Aires: Jackson, 1956.
Trans. Antonio Ribera. Preface Agustí Bartra. Boards.

A31k **Eine Legende.**
Zurich: Fretz and Wasmuth, 1955.
Trans. Kurt Heinrich Hansen. Boards.

A31l **Eine Legende.**
Stuttgart: Scherz and Goverts, 1955.
The Hansen translation. Boards.

A31m **Uma fábula.**
São Paulo: Mérito, 1956.
Trans. Olívia Krähenbühl. Boards.

A31n **Una fabula.**
Santiago de Chile: Circulo Literario, 1956.
Again, the Antonio Ribera translation with the preface by Agustí Bartra, in boards.

A31o **Parabole.**
Paris: Gallimard, 1958.
(Series: *nrf,* Du monde entier, Vol. CXCI.) Trans. R.-N. Raimbault. Wrappers.
    Number 19 of a limitation of 76 copies.

A31p **Guwa.**
Tokyo: Iwanami, 1960.
Trans. Tomoji Abe. Wrappers.

◆

A32a **New Orleans Sketches.**
Tokyo, Japan: The Hokuseido Press, (April 1) 1955.
Dark blue cloth stamped in gold. With pale blue jacket printed in black. 134 pp.
    Thirteen of Faulkner's 1925 *Times-Picayune* sketches are reprinted in this Japanese volume. The eleven that had appeared in the United States in *Mirrors of Chartres Street* in 1953 are joined by "Jealousy" and "Episode." Prior to this volume these two sketches had appeared in *Faulkner Studies,* III (Winter 1954), pp. 46-53.

[104]

A32b   **New Orleans Sketches.**
Another copy.
Pink mottled wrappers.

A32c   **New Orleans Sketches.**
Another copy.
Tan mottled wrappers with publisher's device on cover.

A32d   **Jealousy and Episode: Two Stories by William Faulkner.**
Minneapolis: Faulkner Studies, (September 1) 1955.
Orange-tan cloth stamped in black. Issued without a jacket. Limited edition of 500 copies. 9 pp.
Reprints two of Faulkner's 1925 *Times-Picayune* sketches.

For original *Times-Picayune* publication dates of all sixteen Faulkner sketches see the Rutgers University Press edition of *New Orleans Sketches,* edited by Carvel Collins (A32f).

A32e   **New Orleans Sketches.**
Typescript of Carvel Collins' contribution together with first and second proof of the full text.
Each version shows considerable handwritten notation as the Faulkner sketches are closely corrected by Collins while his own material undergoes progressive revision.

A32f   **New Orleans Sketches.**
New Brunswick, N. J.: Rutgers University Press, 1958.
Light brown paper covered boards. Maroon spine stamped in gold. Beige endpapers. With jacket. 223pp.
The first collection of the 1925 *Times-Picayune* sketches to reprint all sixteen pieces, and to use the most authoritative possible text. Carvel Collins' introduction gives the background and circumstances of original publication.
These sketches are preceded by eleven very short pieces under the title "New Orleans," reprinted from the *Double Dealer,* VII (January-February 1925).
All dates of the *Times-Picayune* sketches are Sundays as the pieces were all in the Sunday magazine section: "Mirrors of Chartres Street" (February 8), "Damon and Pythias Unlimited" (February 15), "Home," (February 22), "Jealousy" (March 1), "Cheest" (April 5), "Out of Nazareth" (April 12), "The Kingdom of God" (April 26), "The Rosary" (May 3), "The Cobbler" (May 10), "Chance " (May 17), "Sunset" (May 24), "The Kid Learns" (May 31), "The Liar" (July 26), "Episode" (August 16), "Country Mice" (September 20), and

"Yo Ho and Two Bottles of Rum" (September 27).

A32g **"The Kid Learns."**
Anthology of Best Short-Short Stories, Volume 7, ed. Robert Ober-first. New York: Frederick Fell, 1959. pp. 78-81.

A32h **New Orleans Sketches.**
New York: Grove Press, "First Evergreen Edition 1961."
A paperback.

A32i **"The Kid Learns."**
Gamma, I (No. 2, 1963), pp. 45-49.

A32j **"The Liar."**
The Saint Magazine Reader, ed. Leslie Charteris and Hans Santesson. Garden City: Doubleday, 1966. pp. 99-108.

A32k **New Orleans Sketches.**
New York: Random House, 1968.
Dark blue cloth stamped in orange and gold on the cover, and orange, gold, and yellow on the spine. Top edges red. With jacket designed by Anita Karl. 139 pp.

A new edition of the collection originally published by Rutgers University Press in 1958. An additional piece by Faulkner, "Sherwood Anderson," is included as an appendix. This critical essay is reprinted from the Dallas, Texas, *Morning News* of April 26, 1925.

Carvel Collins' introduction has been revised from the earlier edition.

A32l **"Sunset."**
The Sea-Green Horse, ed. Barbara Howes and Gregory Jay Smith. New York: Macmillan, 1970. pp. 260-267.

The editors are mother and son; the stories intended for teenage readers.

Other English Language Printings:

A32m **New Orleans Sketches.**
London: Sidgwick and Jackson, 1959.
Tan boards (imitation cloth), spine stamped in gold. With jacket. 223 pp.

Text of the 1958 Rutgers edition, including Carvel Collins' introduction.

A32n   **New Orleans Sketches.**
Another copy of the 1959 London edition.
Dark blue boards (imitation cloth). With jacket.

A32o   **New Orleans Sketches.**
London: Brown, Watson. Digit paperback R 442.
The Rutgers text.

A32p   **"Sunset" and "The Kid Learns."**
Lilliput, XLIV (March 1959), pp. 26-31.
English magazine appearance.

A32q   **New Orleans Sketches.**
London: Chatto and Windus, 1968.
Green boards (imitation cloth), spine stamped in gold. With jacket.
139 pp.
    Text identical to that of the 1968 Random House edition.

Translations:

A32r   "Episod."
All världens Berättare, XI (November 1955), pp. 35-37. Trans.
Brita Eijde.

A32s   **New Orleans.**
Milan: Saggiatore, 1959.
(Series: Biblioteca delle Silerchie, Vol. 27.) Trans. Cesare Salmaggi.
Boards. Contains a very brief version of Carvel Collins' introduction
and only six of the sketches: "Out of Nazareth," "The Kingdom of
God," "The Kid Learns," "The Liar," "Country Mice," "Yo Ho and
Two Bottles of Rum."

A32t   "Il bambino impara." ("The Kid Learns.")
Il meglio della fantascienza, ed. Franco Enna.
Milan: Longanesi, 1967.
(Series: Il meglio, Vol. 22.) Trans. Arianna Livenzev.

A32u   **New Orleans: Skizzen und Erzählungen.**
Zurich: Fretz and Wasmuth, 1962.
Trans. Arno Schmidt. Boards. German translation of the Rutgers
edition.

A32v   **New Orleans: Skizzen und Erzählungen.**

Stuttgart: Govarts, 1962.
The Schmidt translation. Boards.

A32w   **New Orleans: Skizzen und Erzahlungen.**
Munich: Deutscher Taschenbuch, 1964.
(Series: dtv, No. 30.) The Schmidt translation. Wrappers.

◆

A33a   **Big Woods.**
New York: Random House, (October 14) 1955.
Green cloth stamped in gold and black. Top edges stained green.
Beige endpapers. Decorations by Edward Shenton. With jacket designed
by Miriam Woods. 198 pp. with supplementary material on unnumbered
pages.
    Contains four short stories ("The Bear," "The Old People," "A
Bear Hunt," "Race at Morning"), four brief narrative passages interspersed with the stories, and an epilogue. All the material had appeared
previously; part was revised for appearance here to achieve a tonal
continuity.

Translations:

A33b   **Wielki las.**
Warsaw: Panstwowy Instytut Wydawniczy, 1962.
Trans. Zofia Kierszys and Jan Zakrzewski. Wrappers.

A33c   **Der grosse Wald.**
Zurich: Fretz and Wasmuth, 1964.
Trans. Hermann Stresau and Elisabeth Schnack. Boards.

◆

A34a   **The Town.**
New York: Random House, (May 1) 1957.
Wine red cloth stamped in gray and gold. Top edges blue-gray.
Threaded gray endpapers. With jacket designed by Push Pin Studios.
371 pp.
    On page 327, in error, line 10 repeats line 8.
    Jacket has "5/57" printed on lower right corner of front flap;
this is not printed on jackets of the orange or beige binding variants.
    The second novel in the *Snopes* trilogy; *The Hamlet,* published
in 1940, having been the first.

Dedication: "To Phil Stone / He did half the laughing for thirty years." (Compare with A34l.)

A34b   **The Town.**
Another copy; without jacket.
Inscribed on the front endpaper to a former administrator of the University of Mississippi, and signed:

> *William Faulkner*
> *Charlottesville, Va*
> *9 May 1957*

A34c   **The Town.**
Limited, signed issue of 450 copies.
Tan cloth stamped in gold. Top edges stained red. Mottled tan end-papers. With acetate jacket.
  Page 327 contains the error of the trade issue.
  Copy number 385.

A34d   **The Town.**
Another copy of the trade issue.
Deep orange cloth stamped in black and green. Top edges green. Endpapers plain. With jacket.
  In this binding variant, as well as in the one that follows, the error is present on page 327.

A34e   **The Town.**
Another copy of the trade issue.
Gray beige cloth stamped in black and green. Top edges unstained; endpapers plain. Upper right corner of front jacket flap has been clipped off.

A34f   **The Town.**
Another copy of the trade issue in red cloth with blue-gray top edges and gray endpapers. "Second Printing." With jacket imprinted $3.95; a bookseller's sticker increases price to $4.75.
  The error on page 327 is corrected.

A34g   **The Town.**
Another copy of the trade issue in orange cloth with top edges green. "Second Printing."
  The error is still present on page 327.

A34h   **The Town.**
New York: Vintage Books, "First Vintage Edition, January, 1961." Vintage V-184.

A34i   **The Town.**
New York: Random House, 1964.
"Fourth Printing." With tissue wrapper.
First printing as part of the boxed *Snopes* trilogy.

A34j   **"The Waifs."**
Saturday Evening Post, CCXXIX (May 4, 1957), pp. 26-27, 116, 118,
120. Extract from *The Town.*

A34k   **"The Waifs."**
The Saturday Evening Post *Stories: 1957.* New York: Random House,
(April) 1958, pp. 18-28.

Other English Language Printings:

A34l   **The Town.**
London: Chatto and Windus, (January 30) 1958.
Dull orange boards (imitation cloth) stamped in gold on spine. With
jacket designed by Dick Hart. 319 pp.
Dedication reads: "To Phil Stone / He did the laughing for thirty
years."
Meriwether: 10,000 copies.

A34m   **"The Waifs."**
The Saturday Evening Post *Stories: Volume Four.*
London: Elek Books, (1958), pp. 18-28.

Translations:

A34n   **Staden.**
Stockholm: Bonniers, 1958.
Trans. Pelle Fritz-Crone. Wrappers.

A34o   **Die Stadt.**
Zurich: Fretz and Wasmuth, 1958.
Trans. Elisabeth Schnack. Boards.

A34p   **Die Stadt.**
Stuttgart: Goverts, 1958.
The Schnack translation. Boards.

A34q   **Grad.**

Zagreb: Mladost, 1959.
Croatian trans. and afterword by Branko Brusar. Wrappers.

A34r **En la ciudad.**
Barcelona: Plaza and Janes, 1960.
Trans. Ramon Hernandez. Boards. Includes a brief introduction to
the author and the book.

A34s **La città.**
Milan: Mondadori, 1961.
(Series: Medusa, No. 454.) Trans. Giorgio Monicelli and Bruno Tasso.
Boards.

A34t **La ville.**
Paris: Gallimard, 1962.
(Series: *nrf,* Du monde entier, Vol. CCC.) Trans. J. and L. Breant.
Wrappers.
> Number 13 of a limitation of 66 copies.

A34u **La ville.**
Another copy of the 1962 *nrf* edition; wrappers. Regular first
French edition, unnumbered.

A34v **La ville.**
Paris: Gallimard, (1963?).
(Series: Collection Soleil, No. 112.) The Breant translation.
Boards.
> Number 2626 of a limitation of 4100 copies.

A34w **Machi.**
Tokyo: Fuzanbo, 1969.
(Series: Faulkner Zenshu, Vol. 21.) Trans. Hiroshi Hayakawa.

♦

A35a **Requiem for a Nun: A Play from the novel by William Faulkner
adapted to the stage by Ruth Ford.**
New York: Random House, (January 30) 1959.
Gray vinyl "cloth" covered boards stamped in gold and black; photograph pasted on front cover. Top edges golden yellow. Illustrated with
photographs of the London production by Antony Armstrong Jones.
With jacket uniform to the Random House Play series. 105 pp.
> The narrative sections of of the novel have been removed and
the remainder revised for dramatic unity.

REQUIEM FÜR EINE NONNE
(REQUIEM FOR A NUN)

von

William Faulkner
Deutsch von Robert Schnorr

Alle Rechte, insbesondere das der Übersetzung vorbehalten.

Dieses unverkäufliche Manuskript darf nur auf Grund eines besonderen s c h r i f t l i c h e n Vertrages mit dem Verlag verwertet, insbesondere vervielfältigt oder sonst irgendwie entgeltlich oder unentgeltlich weitergegeben werden. Eine Verletzung dieser Verpflichtung hat die zivil- und strafrechtlichen Folgen, insbesondere des Urheberrechtes.

Donnerstag, den 10. November 1955:

Deutsche Erstaufführung

Requiem für eine Nonne

von William Faulkner

Deutsch von Robert Schnorr

Inszenierung: Erwin Piscator
Bühnenbilder und Kostüme: Franz Mertz
Musikalische Einrichtung: Herbert Baumann

Der Richter	Franz Weber
Nancy Mannigoe	Eva Buhat
Der Gerichtsdiener	Max Grothusen
Temple Stevens, geb. Drake	Joana Maria Gorvin
Clark Stevens, ihr Mann	Siegmar Schneider
Gavin Stevens, der Verteidiger	Wilhelm Borchert
Der Gouverneur	Robert Müller
Pete	Klaus Kammer
Der Gefängniswärter	Eduard Wandrey

Kleinere Pause nach dem 3. Bild · Größere Pause nach dem 6. Bild

Inspizient: Hans Naundorf · Technische Leitung: Ferdinand Ohm
Beleuchtung: Willy Sommer

SCHILLER-THEATER

PEER GYNT
VON HENRIK IBSEN · DEUTSCH VON CHRISTIAN MORGENSTERN
Inszenierung: Heinrich Koch · Bühnenbilder und Kostüme: Ita Maximowna
Musik von Edvard Grieg, bearbeitet von Enno Dugend

DAS KALTE LICHT
DRAMA IN DREI AKTEN VON CARL ZUCKMAYER
Inszenierung: Boleslaw Barlog · Bühnenbilder und Kostüme: Wilhelm Reinking

DON CARLOS
EIN DRAMATISCHES GEDICHT VON FRIEDRICH SCHILLER
Inszenierung: Gustav-Rudolf Sellner
Bühnenbilder und Kostüme: Franz Mertz

NATHAN DER WEISE
EIN DRAMATISCHES GEDICHT VON GOTTHOLD EPHRAIM LESSING
Regie: Karl Heinz Stroux · Bühnenbilder und Kostüme: Jean Pierre Ponnelle

KRIEG UND FRIEDEN
EIN ROMAN VON LEO TOLSTOI, FÜR DIE BÜHNE NACHERZÄHLT VON
ALFRED NEUMANN / ERWIN PISCATOR / GUNTRAM PRUFER
Regie: Erwin Piscator · Bild: H. W. Lenneweit · Musik: Boris Blacher

DIE MEUTEREI AUF DER CAINE
EIN STÜCK IN ZWEI AKTEN VON HERMAN WOUK · DEUTSCH VON FRANZ HOLLERING
Inszenierung: Boleslaw Barlog · Bühnenbilder: Wilhelm Reinking

FAUST I.
VON JOHANN WOLFGANG GOETHE
Inszenierung: Boleslaw Barlog · Bühnenbilder und Kostüme: Jörg Zimmermann
Choreographie: Harald Kreutzberg · Musik: Kurt Heuser

Freitag, den 18. November 1955, zum ersten Male:
PROFESSOR BERNHARDI
KOMÖDIE IN FÜNF AKTEN VON ARTHUR SCHNITZLER
Inszenierung: Heinrich Schnitzler · Bühnenbilder und Kostüme: H. W. Lenneweit
Deutsch · P. Wagner · Ferman · Graf · Hellmer · Sattler · A. Schröder · Fiedler
Genest · Siedel · Buecheler · Staas · Miedel · Schott · Bluhm · Meissner · Ledinek
Noorden · Peters · Krüger · Bechmann · Goetzke

Den täglichen Spielplan erfahren Sie auch unter der Rufnummer 256
im Fernsprech-Sonderdienst

Requiem: German script (A35c) and
playbill (A35f).

A35b   **Requiem for a Nun.**
The Best Plays of 1958-1959, ed. Louis Kronenberger. New York: Dodd, Mead, 1959, pp. 189-208.
    In the *Burns Mantle Yearbook* series; the script is condensed.

A35c   **Requiem für eine Nonne.**
Frankfurt: Fischer, n. d. (1955?).
German translation by Robert Schnorr in an acting copy reproduced from typewritten matter. Apparently not for general distribution. Horizontal format, wrappers.

A35d   **"Faulkner 'Requiem' Click In a Preem at Zurich."**
Clipping from *Variety* of October 26, 1955 concerning world premiere.

A35e   **Requiem für eine Nonne.**
Program for the Schauspielhaus, Zurich, season of 1956/1957.
In this theater a year earlier *Requiem* had received its world premiere performance. As usual in German productions of this play, the Robert Schnorr version.

A35f   **Requiem für eine Nonne.**
Program for the Schlosspark-Theater in Berlin, season of 1955/56.
Laid in leaflet indicates opening night performance of November 10, 1955. German production is the Robert Schnorr version.

A35g   **Requiem für eine Nonne.**
Program for the Volkstheater, Vienna.
First Austrian production, Vienna Festival Week, 1956. The Robert Schnorr version.

A35h   **Requiem pour une nonne.**
Paris: Gallimard, 1956.
(Series: *nrf,* Le manteau d'arlequin.) French adaptation for the theater by Albert Camus. Wrappers.
    Number 79 of a limitation of 85 copies (designated 11 through 85 and G through P).
    Precedes the Faulkner-Ford stage adaptation.

A35i   **Requiem pour une nonne.**
Program for the Paris production at the Mathurins-Marcel Herrand Theatre; laid in leaflet indicates March 1957.
    The French version in the Albert Camus adaptation had received its initial performances at this theater the preceding September.

Royal Court Theatre

Sloane Square S.W.1

English Stage Company

6ᴅ.

Requiem For a Nun

by

William Faulkner

First produced at the Royal Court Theatre
Tuesday, November 26th, 1957

London playbill (A35m).

A35j   **Requiem pour une nonne.**
L'Avant-Scene, No. 407.
Text of the Camus version issued in a periodical format to coincide
with a Comédie de l'Ouest production of January 31, 1968.

A35k   **Réquiem para una reclusa.**
Buenos Aires: SUR, 1957.
Spanish translation of the Camus version by Victoria Ocampo.
Wrappers.

A35l   **Requiem por una Mujer.**
Program for the Spanish production by the Compania Lope de
Vega.
    The Camus version has been translated into Spanish by Jose
Lopez Rubio.

A35m **Requiem for a Nun.**
Program of the Royal Court Theatre in London where the first English
production was given on November 26, 1957. Signed by Ruth Ford and
Zachary Scott.

A35n **Messe for en Skøge.**
Program for the Danish production at the Det ny Teater in Copenhagen,
season of 1957-58. Translation by H. C. Branner.

A35o **Oracao para uma negra.**
Rio de Janeiro: AGIR, 1958.
Trans. Guilherme Figueiredo; from the Camus adaptation. Wrappers.

A35p **Requiem for a Nun.**
Playbill of the John Golden Theatre in New York for the American
premiere performance of January 30, 1959. Credit page signed by
Ruth Ford and Zachary Scott. Laid in is a program leaflet for preview
performances.

A35q **Requiem pour une nonne.**
Program for the Brussels production at the Theatre Royal des Galeries,
October 1959. Albert Camus version.

◆

A36a **The Mansion.**
"Uncorrected proof" spiral bound in blue paper covers. For advance
readers.

A36b **The Mansion.**
New York: Random House, (November 13) 1959.
Blue cloth stamped in gray and gold. Top edges stained yellow. Blue
endpapers. With jacket featuring, on the back, a photograph by Ralph
R. Thompson. 436 pp.
　　The third novel in the *Snopes* trilogy.

A36c **The Mansion.**
Limited, signed issue of 500 copies.
Black cloth stamped in gold. Top edges blue. Mottled deep blue end-
papers. With acetate jacket. Copy number 100.

A36d **"Mink Snopes."**
Esquire, LII (December 1959), pp. 226-30, 247-50, 252-64.
Long excerpt from *The Mansion.*

A36e **The Mansion.**
New York: Random House, "Second Printing."

A36f **The Mansion.**
New York: Vintage Books, "First Vintage Edition, September, 1965."
Vintage V-282.

A36g **The Mansion.**
New York: Random House, 1964. "Third Printing."
With tissue wrapper.
　　First printing as part of the boxed *Snopes* trilogy. The three
volumes are in a magenta box with a gold and red paper label on one
side.

Other English Language Printings:

A36h **The Mansion.**
London: Chatto and Windus, (January 12) 1961.
Dull orange boards (imitation cloth), spine stamped in gold. Top edges
stained orange. With jacket designed by John Woodcock. 399 pp.

A36i **The Mansion.**
London: Reprint Society, 1962.

Translations:

A36j **Das Haus.**
Zurich: Fretz and Wasmuth, 1960.
Trans. Elisabeth Schnack. Boards.

A36k **Das Haus.**
Stuttgart: Goverts, 1960.
The Schnack translation. Boards.

A36l **Le domaine.**
Paris: Gallimard, 1962.
(Series: *nrf,* Du monde entier, Vol. CCLXXXIII.) Trans. Rene
Hilleret. Wrappers.
> Number 44 of a limitation of 66 copies.

A36m **Le domaine.**
Another copy of the 1962 *nrf* edition.
Wrappers. Regular first French edition, unnumbered.

A36n **Mink.**
Prague: Státní nakladatelství krásné literatury a umeni, 1963.
Trans. and afterword Jiří Valja. Wrappers. Translation of the first
third of *The Mansion.*

A36o **Il palazzo.**
Turin: Frassinelli, 1963.
Trans. Luciano Bianciardi. Boards.

A36p **Huset.**
Helsingfors: Holger Schildts, 1966.
(Swedish text, printed in Sweden by Bonniers.) Trans. Gunnar
Barklund. Wrappers.

A36q **Yakata.**
Tokyo: Fuzanbo, 1967.
(Series: Faulkner Zenshu, Vol. 22.) Trans. Masao Takahashi.

◆

A37a **The Reivers.**
"Advance proofs" in unbound long sheets.

A37b **"Hell Creek Crossing."**
Saturday Evening Post, CCXXXV (March 31, 1962), pp. 22-25.
Illustration by James Lewicki. Prepublication extract from *The
Reivers.*

A37c   "The Education of Lucius Priest."
Esquire, LVII (May 1962), pp. 109-110, 112, 113, 114, 116. Pre-publication excerpt from *The Reivers*.

A37d   **The Reivers: A Reminiscence.**
New York: Random House, (June 4) 1962.
Red cloth stamped in orange and gold. Top edges stained red. Ochre endpapers. With jacket designed by Milton Glaser featuring, on the back, a photograph by Phyllis Cerf. 305 pp.
     Faulkner's last novel was published shortly before his death, July 6, 1962.

A37e   **The Reivers.**
Limited, signed issue of 500 copies.
Burgundy cloth stamped in gold. Top edges red. Mottled olive endpapers. With acetate jacket. Copy number 300.

A37f   **The Reivers.**
A "copy" of the trade edition, about half as thick as a normal copy. Red cloth, the spine stamped in silver. The top edges and endpapers are plain. A true reivers copy: a pirated edition printed in Taiwan by photographic reproduction of a copy of the first American printing. The paper is much thinner than that used in the American edition. Complete with similarly pirated dust jacket, so carefully reproduced from the original as to include the statement: "Printed in U. S. A."

A37g   **The Reivers.**
Another copy of the trade issue, marked "First Printing" on copyright page.
Lower right corner of back cover bears imprint of square blind stamp. With jacket indicating "Book-of-the-Month Club Selection."

A37h   **The Reivers.**
Another copy of the trade issue, marked "W" on copyright page.
Lower right corner of back cover bears imprint of circular blind stamp. With jacket indicating "Book-of-the-Month Club Selection."

A37i   **The Reivers.**
New York: Vintage Books, "First Vintage Edition, September 1966." Vintage V-339.

A37j   **The Reivers.**
New York: The New American Library, "First Printing, October, 1969."
Signet Book Q 4033. Paperback.

A37k **The Reivers.**
London: Chatto and Windus, 1962.
Blue boards (imitation cloth), spine stamped in gold. With jacket
designed by John Woodcock. 284 pp.

Translations:

A37l **Os Desgarrados.**
Rio de Janeiro: Editora Civilizacao Brasileira, 1963.
(Series: Biblioteca do Leitor Moderno, No. 32.) Trans. Breno Silveira.
Wrappers.

A37m **I saccheggiatori.**
Milan: Mondadori, 1963.
(Series: Medusa, No. 478.)
Trans. Giorgio Monicelli. Boards.

A37n **Los rateros.**
Barcelona: Plaza and Janes, 1963.
Trans. Jorge Ferrer-Vidal Turull. Boards.

A37o **Tre rövare.**
Stockholm: Bonniers, 1963.
Trans. Gunnar Barklund. Wrappers.

A37p **Die Spitzbuben.**
Zurich: Fretz and Wasmuth, 1963.
Trans. Elisabeth Schnack. Boards.

A37q **Die Spitzbuben.**
Stuttgart: Goverts, 1963.
The Schnack translation. Boards.

A37r **Les larrons.**
Paris: Gallimard, 1964.
(Series: *nrf,* Du monde entier, Vol. CCCXLI.) Trans. Maurice-Edgar
Coindreau and Raymond Girard. Preface Girard. Wrappers.
Number 40 of a limitation of 67 copies.

A37s **Les larrons.**
Another copy of the 1964 *nrf* edition.

Wrappers. Regular first French edition, unnumbered.

A37t   **Les larrons.**
Paris: Gallimard, (1965?).
(Series: Collection Soleil, No. 149.) Contents of the 1964 edition.
Boards.
     Number 88 of a limitation of 3100 copies.

A37u **Os Ratoneiros.**
Lisbon: Portugália, 1964.
(Series: Contemporanea, No. 56.) Trans. and preface Manuel Barbosa.
Wrappers.

A37v **Pobertove.**
Prague: Státní nakladatelství krásné a uměni, 1965.
Trans. and afterword Jiří Valja. Boards.

A37w **Zsiványok.**
Budapest: Európa Könyvkiadö, 1965.
Trans. László Szíjgyártó. Boards.

A37x **Rosvot.**
Helsinki: Tammi, 1966.
Trans. Kai Kaila. Boards.

A37y **Koniokrady.**
Warsaw: Czytelnik, 1966.
Trans. Anna Przedpelska-Trzeciakowska. Boards.

◆

A38a **Faulkner's University Pieces.**
Tokyo: Kenkyusha Limited, 1962.
Blue cloth, spine stamped in gold. With jacket. 114 pp.
     Contains material by Faulkner published in outlets associated
with the University of Mississippi during the period of 1917 to 1925.
Included are several drawings done for *Ole Miss* annuals as well as for
the student humor magazine, *The Scream.* Also reprinted from *Ole
Miss* annuals are the poems "To a Co-ed" and "Nocturne."
     The bulk of the material was originally published in the student
newspaper, *The Mississippian.* Included are the poems: "Cathay,"
"Sapphics," "After Fifty Years," "Une Ballade des Femmes Perdues,"
"Naiads' Song," "Fantoches," "Clair de Lune," "Streets," "A Poplar,"
"A Clymene," "Study," "Alma Mater," and "Co-education at Ole
Miss." Short stories are "Landing in Luck" and "The Hill." Under the

general title "Books and Things" are reviews of W. A. Percy's *In April Once*, Conrad Aiken's *Turns and Movies*, and *Aria da Capo* by Edna St. Vincent Millay. Under the same heading are essays entitled: "American Drama: Eugene O'Neill," "American Drama: Inhibitions," and "Joseph Hergesheimer."

The compilation and introductory essay are by Carvel Collins.

A38b **William Faulkner: Early Prose and Poetry.**
"Uncorrected Advance Proof" spiral bound in pale blue covers.

A38c **William Faulkner: Early Prose and Poetry.**
Boston: Little, Brown, 1962.
Light gray cloth. Cover blind stamped, spine stamped in maroon. With jacket designed by Chermayeff & Geismar Associates. 134 pp.

An American edition of *Faulkner's University Pieces,* somewhat expanded from the Japanese publication. Added are three poems published in the *Double Dealer* during 1922 and 1925, "Portrait," "Dying Gladiator," and "The Faun," as well as two critical essays published in the same New Orleans magazine during 1925: "On Criticism" and "Verse Old and Nascent: A Pilgrimage." (All five of these pieces had been reprinted in 1932 in *Salmagundi*.) Also new to this American edition is Faulkner's poem "L'Apres-Midi d'un Faune," which had appeared in two separate periodicals in 1919.

A38d **William Faulkner: Early Prose and Poetry.**
Another copy. Atlantic-Little Brown Paperback, LB 1.

Other English Language Printings:

A38e **William Faulkner: Early Prose and Poetry.**
Advance copy of the London edition in wrappers.

A38f **William Faulkner: Early Prose and Poetry.**
London: Jonathan Cape, (October) 1963.
Green boards (imitation cloth), spine stamped in gold. Top edges blue-black. With jacket featuring Faulkner drawings. 134 pp. Contents the same as the American edition.

Translations:

A38g **Proses, poesies et essais critiques de jeunesse.**
Paris: Gallimard, 1966.

Trans. and preface Henri Thomas. Wrappers.
Number 1417 of a limitation of 1500 copies.

A38h   **Proses, poesies et essais critiques de jeunesse.**
Another copy: wrappers.
Number 1563 of a limitation of 150 copies *hors commerce* numbered 1501 through 1650.

◆

A39a   **Essays, Speeches and Public Letters.**
New York: Random House, (January 7) 1966.
Dark blue cloth stamped in red and gold. Top edges stained red. Gray endpapers. With jacket. 233 pp.
Reprints most of Faulkner's published non-fiction prose, covering the period from 1926 to 1962. Edited by James B. Meriwether.

Other English Language Printings:

A39b   **Essays, Speeches and Public Letters.**
London: Chatto and Windus, (January) 1967.
Turquoise boards (imitation cloth), spine stamped in gold. With jacket. 233 pp. Text identical to that of the American edition.

Translation:

A39c   **Essais, discours et lettres ouvertes.**
Paris: Gallimard, 1969.
(Series: *nrf*, Du monde entier, Vol. DXLV.) Trans. J. and L. Bréant. Wrappers.
Number 1 of a limitation of 42 copies.

◆

A40a   **The Wishing Tree.**
"Uncorrected proofs" in pale blue covers with a single corner fastener. For advance readers.

A40b   **"The Wishing Tree."**
Saturday Evening Post, CCXL (April 8, 1967), pp. 48-53, 57-58, 60-63. Illustrated by Jerry Pinkney. The complete text of the book.

A40c   **The Wishing Tree.**
New York: Random House, (April 11) 1967.
Blue cloth. Stamped on the cover in green, on the spine in gold. Top
edges yellow. Illustrated by Don Bolognese, with jacket by the same
artist. 81 pp.

Faulkner's only children's book, posthumously published, consisting of a fantasy written many years earlier for private circulation.

The verso of the title page states "First Printing," and the front
jacket is marked "$3.95" at the top and "4/67" at the bottom. The
lettering on the jacket spine is in black and white.

A40d   **The Wishing Tree.**
Limited issue of 500 copies.
Ochre cloth stamped in gold. Top edges stained light blue with endpapers of similar shade. With plain olive jacket printed in green on
spine; copy number handwritten on jacket spine. Decorated green box;
spine on box printed in white.

Copy number 353.

A40e   **The Wishing Tree.**
Another copy of the trade issue, with blind stamp at lower right of
back cover indicating book club edition.

Verso of title page does not indicate first printing. Front jacket
flap is clipped at top and bears no date at bottom. Jacket spine is lettered in white and blue.

Translations:

A40f   **"L'Arbre aux Souhaits."**
La Nouvelle Revue Francaise, No. 180 (December 1967), pp. 995-
1022. Trans. M. E. Coindreau.

The full text in French; the periodical appearance actually preceded the book format by more than a year.

A40g   **L'arbre aux souhaits.**
Paris: Gallimard, 1969.
(Series: *nrf,* Du monde entier, Vol. DXLVI.) Trans. M.-E. Coin-
dreau. Wrappers.

Number 4 of a limitation of 41 copies.

A40h   **L'arbre aux souhaits.**

Another copy of the 1969 *nrf* edition; wrappers.
Regular first French edition, unnumbered.

◆

A41a **Flags in the Dust.**
New York: Random House, (August) 1973.
Mustard yellow cloth stamped in deep gold on cover, silver on spine.
Top edges russet brown. Mustard yellow endpapers. With jacket designed by Anita Karl. 370 pp.

The "original" version of *Sartoris* (A5); edited and with an introduction by Douglas Day.

A41b **Flags in the Dust.**
New York: Vintage Books, "First Vintage Books Edition, October 1974." V-239. Includes the Day introduction.

SECTION B: SHORT STORIES

Bla   "A Rose for Emily."
       Forum, LXXXIII (April 1930), 233-238. Drawings by Weldon Bailey.

Blb   **"A Rose for Emily."**
       Creeps by Night, selected by Dashiell Hammett (New York:
       John Day, 1931), 15-32.

Blc   **"Une rose pour Emily."**
       Commerce, No. 29 (Winter 1932), 111-137. Trans. Maurice Ed-
       gar Coindreau.
           Number 1114 of a limitation of 2900 copies. This copy is
       inscribed by the translator.

Bld   **"A Rose for Emily."**
       Golden Book, XV (March 1932), 223-228.

Ble   **"A Rose for Emily."**
       The Bedside Book of Famous American Stories, ed. Angus Bur-
       rel and Bennett A. Cerf (New York: Random House, 1936),
       1122-1129.

Blf   **"A Rose for Emily."**
       The Bedside Tales, ed. Peter Arno (New York: Wm. Penn Pub-
       lishing, 1945), 560-569.

Blg   **"A Rose for Emily."**
       The Golden Argosy, ed. Van H. Cartmell and Charles Grayson
       (New York: Dial, 1947), 167-174.

Blh   **"A Rose for Emily."** (Condensed.)
       History and Anthology of American Literature, ed. Leighton B.
       Brown and Takashi Kawatsu (Tokyo: Hokuseido, 1952), 357-
       361. Boards. Text in English.
           The butchered story is preceded by a preface of concentrated
       inaccuracy.

Bli   **"A Rose for Emily."**
       Modern American Short Stories (Second Series) (Tokyo: Ken-
       yusha, n. d.), 57-72. (Pocket English Series, No. 161). English
       text. Wrappers.

Blj   **"Uma rosa para Emily."**
       Obras primas do conto Norte Americano (São Paulo: Martins,
       1958), 331-342. Probably the Dutra translation listed below.

B1k   **"Uma rosa para Emily."**
Contos Norte-americanos (Rio de Janeiro: Biblioteca Universal Popular, 1963), 224-236. Trans. Lia Corrêa Dutra.

B1l   **"A Rose for Emily."**
Chance International, I (No. 2), 65-67. Undated (c. 1965?), men's magazine published in Australia.

B2a   **"Honor."**
American Mercury, XX (July 1930), 268-274.

B2b   **"Honor."**
American Mercury, LXIII (October 1946), 485-493.

B2c   **"Honor."**
Hi-Life, I (November 1958), 20-23, 63, 64.

B3a   **"Thrift."**
Saturday Evening Post, CCIII (September 6, 1930), 16-17, 78, 82. Illustrated by Albin Henning.

B3b   **"Thrift."**
O. Henry Memorial Award Prize Stories of 1931, ed. Blanche Colton Williams (Garden City: Doubleday, Doran, 1931), 153-169.
        This copy, probably the regular trade edition, is black cloth stamped in silver, top edges green, and has the publisher's device on the title page in green. Copyright page: "First edition."

B3c   *O. Henry Memorial Award Prize Stories of 1931.*
Another copy, green cloth stamped in black, top edges plain. Title page publisher's device in black, beneath it: "Text Edition." Copyright page: "First Edition."

B4a   **"Red Leaves."**
Saturday Evening Post, CCIII (October 25, 1930), 6-7, 54, 56, 58, 60, 62, 64. Illustrated by W. H. D. Koerner.

B4b   **"Red Leaves."**
Eight Great American Short Novels (New York: Berkley, [April] 1963), 222-243. Paperback.

B4c   **"Folhas Vermelhas."**

Perspectivas dos Estados Unidos (Lisbon: Portugalia, n. d.), 117-148. (Series: Antologias Universais Varia, No. 1.) Wrappers. Trans. Jorge de Sena.

B4d   **"Red Leaves."**
The Black Experience, ed. Francis E. Kearns (New York: Viking, 1970), 419-443.

B5a   **"Dry September."**
Scribner's Magazine, LXXXIX (January 1931), 49-56.

B5b   **"Septembre ardent."**
La Nouvelle Revue Francaise, No. 220 (January 1932), 49-65. Trans. M. E. Coindreau.

B5c   **"Dry September."**
A Study of the Short Story, ed. Henry Seidel Canby and Alfred Dashiell (New York: Henry Holt, 1935), 333-348. With historical and introductory material by the editors.

B5d   **"Dry September."**
Short Stories of Distinction, ed. Walter Hendricks (Chicago: Packard, 1939), 217-231.

B5e   **"Dry September."**
Strange Barriers (New York: Lion, [October] 1955), 7-18. Paperback.

B5f   **"Dry September."**
The Edge of the Chair, ed. Joan Kahn (New York: Harper & Row, 1967), 409-420.

B5g   **"Dry September."**
Stories in Black and White, ed. Eva H. Kissin (Philadelphia: Lippincott, 1970), 108-122.

B6a   **"That Evening Sun Go Down."**
American Mercury, XXII (March 1931), 257-267.

B6b   **"That Evening Sun Go Down."**
The Best Short Stories of 1931 and the Yearbook of the American Short Story, ed. Edward J. O'Brien (New York: Dodd, Mead, 1931), 104-121.

B6c   **"That Evening Sun."**
Modern American Prose, ed. Carl Van Doren (New York: Literary Guild, 1934), 672-686.

B6d   **"That Evening Sun."**
A Southern Harvest, ed. Robert Penn Warren (Boston: Houghton Mifflin, 1937), 177-194.

B6e   **"That Evening Sun."**
50 Best American Short Stories, 1915-1939, ed. Edward J. O'Brien (Boston: Houghton Mifflin, 1939), 413-433.

B6f   **"That Evening Sun."**
50 Best American Short Stories 1915-1939, ed. Edward J. O'Brien (New York: Literary Guild of America, 1939), 413-433.

B6g   **"That Evening Sun Go Down."**
Contemporary Southern Prose, ed. Richard Croom Beatty and William Perry Fidler (Boston: D. C. Heath, 1940), 405-422.

B6h   **"That Evening Sun Go Down."**
This Is My Best, ed. Whit Burnett (New York: Dial Press, 1942), 522-538. Also includes a letter to Mr. Burnett.

B6i   **"That Evening Sun Go Down."**
The Pocket Book of Modern American Short Stories (New York: Pocket Books [October] 1943), 225-246. Paperback.

B6j   **"That Evening Sun Go Down."**
The American Mercury *Reader*, ed. Lawrence E. Spivak and Charles Angoff (Philadelphia: Blakiston, 1944), 70-81.

B6k   **"That Evening Sun."**
50 Great Short Stories (New York: Bantam, [August] 1952), 473-493. Paperback.

B6l   **"Aksam günesi batarken."**
Bes Amerikan hikâyesi (Istanbul: Varlik Yayinevi, 1952), 57-79. Trans., ed., and brief comments on the five writers included, Orhan Azizoğlu.

B6m   **"Naar solen gaar ned."**
Moderne Amerikanske noveller, ed. Ole Storm (Copenhagen: Thaning & Appel, 1954), 21-40. Trans. Sven Møller Kristensen.

B6n   "Słońce zachodzi."
18 Wspoeczesnych Opowiadan Amerykanskich (Warsaw: Iskry, 1957), 216-239. Trans. Jan Zakrzewski.

B6o   **"That Evening Sun."**
Great Stories by Nobel Prize Winners, ed. Leo Hamalian and Edmond L. Volpe (New York: Noonday [paperback], 1959), 264-283.

B6p   **"Solnedgång."**
24 Nobelpristagare, ed. Mårten Edlund (Stockholm: Folket i Bilds, 1960), 243-266. The Faulkner story is one of those translated by the editor.

B6q   **"That Evening Sun."**
Two and Twenty, ed. Ralph H. Singleton (New York: St. Martin's Press, 1962), 195-214.

B7a   **"Ad Astra."**
American Caravan IV (New York: The Macaulay Company, [March 27] 1931), 164-181. Edited by Alfred Kreymborg, Lewis Mumford, and Paul Rosenfeld. With jacket.

B8a   **"Hair."**
American Mercury, XXIII (May 1931), 53-61.

B9a   **"Spotted Horses."**
Scribner's Magazine, LXXXIX (June 1931), 585-597.

B9b   **"Spotted Horses."**
Editor's Choice, ed. Alfred Dashiell (New York: Putnam's, 1934), 133-153.

B9c   **"Spotted Horses."**
The House of Fiction, ed. Caroline Gordon and Allen Tate (New York: Scribner's, 1950), 489-531.

B10a   **"The Hound."**
Harper's Magazine, CLXIII (August 1931), 266-274.

B10b   **"The Hound."**

This Generation, ed. George K. Anderson and Eda Lou Walton. (Chicago: Scott, Foresman, 1939), 792-799. A college text with the story introduced by the usual biographical essay.

B10c   **"The Hound."**
Ellery Queen's Mystery Magazine, V (January 1944), 51-62.

B10d   **"Le chien."**
La table ronde, No. 2 (April 1945), 107-129. Trans. R. N. Raimbault.
      Number 94 of a limitation of 150 copies.

B10e   **"The Hound."**
A Treasury of Short Stories, ed. Bernardine Kielty (New York: Simon and Schuster, 1947), 804-812.

B10f   **"The Hound."**
The American Literary Record, ed. Willard Thorp, Carlos Baker, James K. Folsom, Merle Curti (Chicago: Lippincott, 1961), 869-875. A college text.

B11a   **"Fox Hunt."**
Harper's Magazine, CLXIII (September 1931), 392-402.

B11b   **"Fox Hunt."**
The PL Book of Modern American Short Stories, ed. Nicholas Moore (London: Editions Poetry London, 1945), 22-38.

B11c   **"Chasse au renard."**
Courtes histoires Américaines (Paris: Corrêa, 1948), 141-164. Trans. R.-N. Raimbault. French edition of *The PL Book of Modern American Short Stories.*

B12a   **"All the Dead Pilots."**
(A9)   *These 13* (published September 21, 1931), 81-109.

B13a   **"Carcassonne."**
(A9)   *These 13* (published September 21, 1931), 352-358.

B13b   **"Carcassonne."**
Bonniers Litterära Magasin, XIX (December 1950), 731-733. Trans. Erik Lindegren.
      Also contains: Åke Runnquist, brief commentary on Faulkner winning Nobel Prize, 724. Åke Janzon, article on Faulkner's

career, 734-739.

B13c   **"Carcassonne."**
Dude, I (March 1957), 6-7, 59.

B14a **"Crevasse."**
(A9)   *These 13* (published September 21, 1931), 110-123.

B15a **"Divorce in Naples."**
(A9)   *These 13* (published September 21, 1931), 330-351.

B15b   **"Divorce in Naples."**
Gent, I (June 1957), 6-11, 65, 66.

B16a **"A Justice."**
(A9)   *These 13* (published September 21, 1931), 183-207.

B16b   **"A Justice."**
Perspectives U. S. A., Pilot Issue (January 1952), 29-45.
    Also includes: William Faulkner, "I Decline to Accept the End of Man," 5-6. Malcolm Cowley, "William Faulkner and Yoknapatawpha County," 7-27.

B17a **"Mistral."**
(A9)   *These 13* (published September 21, 1931), 283-329.

B18a **"Victory."**
(A9)   *These 13* (published September 21, 1931), 3-49.

B19a **"Doctor Martino."**
Harper's Magazine, CLXIII (November 1931), 733-743.

B20a **Idyll in the Desert.**
(A10) (Published December 10, 1931.)

B21a **"Death-Drag."**

Scribner's Magazine, XCI (January 1932), 34-42.

B22a   **"Centaur in Brass."**
American Mercury, XXV (February 1932), 200-210.

B22b   **"Le centaure de bronze."**
Les oeuvres Libres, No. 182 (July 1961), 3-26. Trans. R.-N. Raimbault.

B23a   **"Once Aboard the Lugger."**
Contempo, I (February 1, 1932), 1, 4.

B23b   **"Once Aboard the Lugger."**
Lillabulero, I (Spring 1967), 20-23. Also reprinted from 1932
and 1933 issues of *Contempo* are the poems "April," 24; "Winter is Gone," 25; "Visions in Spring," 26-27; "I Will Not Weep
for Youth," 28; and "A Child Looks from His Window," 29.

B24a   **"Lizards in Jamshyd's Courtyard."**
Saturday Evening Post, CCIV (February 27, 1932), 12-13, 52, 57.
Illustrated by J. Clinton Shepherd.

B25a   **"Turn About."**
Saturday Evening Post, CCIV (March 5, 1932), 6-7, 75, 76, 81, 83.
Illustrated by Albin Henning.

B25b   **"Turn About."**
O. Henry Memorial Award Stories of 1932, ed. Blanche Colton
Williams (Garden City: Doubleday, Doran, 1932), 165-192.

B25c   **"Turn About."**
Stories for Men, ed. Charles Grayson (New York: Garden City
Publishing, 1938), 191-218.

B25d   **"Turn About."**
More Stories to Remember, Volume II, ed. Thomas B. Costain
and John Beecroft (Garden City: Doubleday, 1958), 96-117.

B25e   **"Turnabout."**
Great Flying Stories (New York: Dell [July] 1958), 13-43.
Paperback.

B26a   "Smoke."
         Harper's Magazine, CLXIV (April 1932), 562-578.

B26b   "Smoke."
             The Best Short Stories of 1932 and the Yearbook of the Ameri-
             can Short Story, ed. Edward J. O'Brien (New York: Dodd, Mead,
             1932), 108-133.

B26c   "Smoke."
             The Best Short Stories of 1932 II: American, ed. Edward J.
             O'Brien (London: Cape, 1932), 133-160.

B26d   "Smoke."
             Golden Book, XXI (April 1935), 304-321.

B26e   "Smoke."
             Ellery Queen's Mystery Magazine, X (October 1947), 50-71.

B27a   **Miss Zilphia Gant.**
(A12)   Published June 27, 1932.

B28a   **"A Mountain Victory."**
         Saturday Evening Post, CCV (December 3, 1932), 6-7, 39, 42, 44, 45,
         46. Illustrated by Albin Henning.

B28b   **Sieg in den Bergen.**
             Munich: Langen & Müller, 1956. "1.-5. Tausend." (Series:
             Kleine Geschenkbücher, No. 53.) Trans., afterword, Hans Hen-
             necke. Boards.

B29a   **"There Was a Queen."**
         Scribner's Magazine, XCIII (January 1933), 10-16.

B29b   **"Il était une Reine."**
             La Nouvelle Revue Francaise, No. 239 (August 1933), 213-233.
             Trans. M. E. Coindreau.

B30a   **"Artist at Home."**
         Story, III (August 1933), 27-41.

B30b   **"Artist at Home."**

Story in America, 1933-1934, ed. Whit Burnett and Martha Foley (New York: Vanguard Press, 1934), 236-250.

B31a   "Beyond."
Harper's Magazine, CLXVII (September 1933), 394-403.

B31b   "Beyond."
The Best Short Stories: 1934 and the Yearbook of the American Short Story, ed. Edward J. O'Brien (Boston and New York: Houghton Mifflin, 1934), 91-104.

B31c   "Au-Dela."
Fontaine, IX (May 1946), 711-728. Trans. R.-N. Raimbault.

B32a   "Elly."
Story, IV (February 1934), 3-15.

B32b   "Elly."
Daughters of Eve (New York: Berkley, [November] 1956), 24-38. Paperback.

B33a   "Pennsylvania Station."
American Mercury, XXXI (February 1934), 166-174.

B33b   "Pennsylvania Station."
Amerika erzahlt, ed. Heinz Politzer (Frankfurt: Fischer, 1958). No. 209 in paperback series. German translation by Kurt Heinrich Hansen.

B34a   "Wash."
Harper's Magazine, CLXVIII (February 1934), 258-266.

B34b   "Wash."
O. Henry Memorial Award Prize Stories of 1934, ed. Harry Hansen (Garden City: Doubleday, Doran, 1934), 143-157.

B34c   "Wash."
L'Arbalete, No. 9 (Autumn 1944), 125-136. Trans. R.-N. Raimbault.
      Number 1229 of a limitation of 2150 copies.

B35a **"A Bear Hunt."**
Saturday Evening Post, CCVI (February 10, 1934), 8-9, 74, 76. Illustrated by George Brehm.

B36a **"Black Music."**
(A15) *Doctor Martino* (published April 16, 1934), 263-290.

B37a **"Leg."**
(A15) *Doctor Martino* (published April 16, 1934), 291-314.

B38a **"Mule in the Yard."**
Scribner's Magazine, XCVI (August 1934), 65-70. Decorations by Edward Shenton.

B39a **"Ambuscade."**
Saturday Evening Post, CCVII (September 29, 1934), 12-13, 80, 81. Illustrated by F. R. Gruger.

B39b **"Hinterhalt."**
Der Monat, No. 72 (September 1954), 548-562. German translation by Erich Franzen.

B40a **"Retreat."**
Saturday Evening Post, CCVII (October 13, 1934), 16-17, 82, 84, 85, 87, 89. Illustrated by F. R. Gruger.

B41a **"Lo!"**
Story, V (November 1934), 5-21.

B41b **"Lo!"**
The Best Short Stories of 1935 and the Yearbook of the American Short Story, ed. Edward J. O'Brien (Boston and New York: Houghton Mifflin, 1935), 150-167.
    Inscribed by the editor at Chicago, October 20, 1935.

B42a **"Raid."**
Saturday Evening Post, CCVII (November 3, 1934), 18-19, 72, 73, 75, 77, 78. Illustrated by F. R. Gruger.

B43a **"Skirmish at Sartoris."**
Scribner's Magazine, XCVII (April 1935), 193-200. Decorations by Edward Shenton.

B44a **"Golden Land."**
American Mercury, XXXV (May 1935), 1-14.

B44b **"Terra Dourado."**
A Respeito de uma pecadora (Sao Paulo: Exposicão do Livro, n. d.), 94-110. Trans. Rudy Margherito and Guarany Gallo, from the American paperback, *Concerning a Woman of Sin*.

B45a **"That Will Be Fine."**
American Mercury, XXXV (July 1935), 264-276.

B45b **"That Will Be Fine."**
The Best Short Stories: 1936 and the Yearbook of the American Short Story, ed. Edward J. O'Brien (Boston and New York: Houghton Mifflin, 1936), 87-105.

B45c **"Sería espléndido."**
SUR, No. 75 (December 1940), 70-92. Published in Buenos Aires.

B45d **"That Will Be Fine."**
Crazy Mixed-Up Kids (New York: Berkley, [November] 1955), 17-36. Paperback.

B46a **"Uncle Willy."**
American Mercury, XXXVI (October 1935), 156-168.

B47a **"Lion."**
Harper's Magazine, CLXXII (December 1935), 67-77.

B47b **"Lion."**
O. Henry Memorial Award Prize Stories of 1936, ed. Harry Hansen (Garden City: Doubleday, Doran, 1936), 171-191.

B48a **"The Brooch."**
Scribner's Magazine, XCIX (January 1936), 7-12. Decorations by Edward Shenton.

"Two Dollar Wife" (B49a).

B49a   **"Two Dollar Wife."**
College Life, XVIII (Winter 1936), 8-11, 85, 86, 88, 90. Illustrations by Louis Luboff.

B50a   **"Fool About a Horse."**
Scribner's Magazine, C (August 1936), 80-86. Decorations by Edward Shenton.

B50b   **"Fool About a Horse."**
The Best Short Stories: 1937 and the Yearbook of the American Short Story, ed. Edward J. O'Brien (Boston and New York: Houghton Mifflin, 1937), 38-54.
      Review copy slip laid in; publication date, May 25, 1937.

B51a   **"The Unvanquished."**
Saturday Evening Post, CCIX (November 14, 1936), 12-13, 121, 122, 124, 126, 128, 130. Illustrated by F. R. Gruger.

B52a   **"Vendée."**
Saturday Evening Post, CCIX (December 5, 1936), 16-17, 86, 87, 90, 92, 93, 94. Illustrated by F. R. Gruger.

B53a   **"Monk."**
Scribner's Magazine, CI (May 1937), 16-24. Drawings by Howard Cook.

B53b   **"Monk."**
The Literature of Crime, ed. Ellery Queen (Boston: Little, Brown, 1950), 127-143.

B53c   **"Monk."**
Süddeutsche Zeitung, Saturday/Sunday, 14/15 July 1962. German translation by Elisabeth Schnack.

B54a   **"Barn Burning."**
Harper's Magazine, CLXXIX (June 1939), 86-96.

B54b   **"Barn Burning."**
O. Henry Memorial Award Prize Stories of 1939, ed. Harry Hansen (New York: Doubleday, Doran, 1939), 3-29.

B54c   **"Barn Burning."**
The Pocket Book of O. Henry Prize Stories (New York: Pocket
Books, "1st Printing September, 1947"), 384-406. Paperback.

B54d   **"Barn Burning."**
*First-Prize Stories 1919-1966 from the O. Henry Memorial
Awards*, intro. Harry Hansen (Garden City: Doubleday, 1966),
318-333.
     Also contains "A Courtship," 439-452.

B54e   **"Barn Burning."**
The Loners, ed. L. M. Schulman (New York: Macmillan, 1970),
86-109.

B55a   **"Hand Upon the Waters."**
Saturday Evening Post, CCXII (November 4, 1939), 14-15, 75, 76,
78, 79. Illustrated by Floyd Davis.

B55b   **"Hand Upon the Waters."**
*The Best Short Stories 1940 and The Yearbook of the American
Short Story*, ed. Edward J. O'Brien (Boston: Houghton Mifflin,
1940), 65-81.

B55c   **"Hand Upon the Waters."**
O. Henry Memorial Award Prize Stories of 1940, ed. Harry Hansen (New York: Doubleday, Doran, 1940), 97-116.

B56a   **"A Point of Law."**
Collier's, CV (June 22, 1940), 20-21, 30, 32. Illustrated by William
Meade Prince.

B57a   **"The Old People."**
Harper's Magazine, CLXXXI (September 1940), 418-425.

B57b   **"The Old People."**
O. Henry Memorial Award Prize Stories of 1941, ed. Herschel
Brickell (Garden City: Doubleday, Doran, 1941), 155-169.

B57c   *O. Henry Memorial Award Prize Stories of 1941*. Another copy
(New York: Book League of America, 1941).

B57d   **"The Old People."**

The Story: A Critical Anthology, ed. Mark Schorer (New York: Prentice-Hall, 1950), 397-418.

B57e   **"Gens de jadis."**
Les oeuvres Libres, No. 115 (December 1955), 3-28. Trans. R.-N. Raimbault.

B58a   **"Pantaloon in Black."**
Harper's Magazine, CLXXXI (October 1940), 503-513.

B58b   **"Bouffonnerie noire."**
Les oeuvres Livres, No. 112 (September 1955), 3-28. Trans. R.-N. Raimbault.

B58c   **"Pantaloon in Black."**
An Introduction to Literature: Fiction, ed. Theodore Gross and Norman Kelvin (New York: Random House, 1967), 281-297. Paperback; introduction by the editors on 273-279.

B58d   **"Pantaloon in Black."**
Poetry, Drama, Fiction: An Introduction to Literature, ed. Edmond L. Volpe, Marvin Magalaner, Theodore Gross, and Norman Kelvin (New York: Random House, 1967), 771-787. Same format and introduction (763-769) as the preceding volume.

B59a   **"Gold Is Not Always."**
Atlantic Monthly, CLXVI (November 1940), 563-570.

B59b   **"Gold Is Not Always."**
The Best Short Stories 1941 and The Yearbook of the American Short Story, ed. Edward J. O'Brien (Boston: Houghton Mifflin, 1941), 83-96.

B59c   **"Ikke altid Guld."**
Hele Vejen rundt, ed. and trans. Gerhard Madsen (Copenhagen: Branner, 1943), 54-71.

B60a   **"Tomorrow."**
Saturday Evening Post, CCXIII (November 23, 1940), 22-23, 32, 35, 37, 38, 39. Illustrated by Floyd Davis.

B60b   **"I morgon."**

Bonniers Litterära Magasin, XIX (January 1950), 16-25. Trans. Mårten Edlund.

B60c   **"Tomorrow."**
Fiction Goes to Court, ed. Albert P. Blaustein (New York: Henry Holt, 1954), 169-185.

B61a   **"Go Down, Moses."**
Colliers, CVII (January 25, 1941), 19-20, 45, 46. Illustrated by George Howe.

B61b   **"İn, Musa, İn..."**
Yenīlīk, VIII (April 1956), 71-88. Turkish trans. Bilge Karasu.

B61c   **"Go Down, Moses."**
Modern Short Stories, ed. Jim Hunter (London: Faber and Faber, 1964), 184-197.

B62a   **"The Tall Men."**
Saturday Evening Post, CCXIII (May 31, 1941), 14-15, 95, 96, 98, 99. Illustrated by F. R. Gruger.

B63a   **"Two Soldiers."**
Saturday Evening Post, CCXIV (March 28, 1942), 9-11, 35, 36, 38, 40. Illustrated by Harold Von Schmidt.

B63b   **"Two Soldiers."**
O. Henry Memorial Award Prize Stories of 1942, ed. Herschel Brickell (New York: Literary Guild of America, 1942), 139-158.

B63c   **"Two Soldiers."**
The Pocket Book of America (New York: Pocket Books, [September] 1942), 77-96. Paperback.

B63d   **"Two Soldiers."**
Time to Be Young, ed. Whit Burnett (Philadelphia and New York: Lippincott, 1945), 252-265.

B63e   **"Two Soldiers."**
The Avon Annual 1945: 18 Great Modern Stories (New York: Avon, 1945), 94-106. Paperback.

B63f   "Two Soldiers."
Stories for Tonight (New York: Avon, 1955), 7-21. Paperback.

B63g   "Two Soldiers."
The Best Short Stories of World War II, ed. Charles A. Fenton
(New York: Viking, 1957), 27-44.

B63h   "Zwei Soldaten."
Reader's Digest Auswahl Bücher (No. 8). (Stuttgart: Beste, 1957),
151-168. Trans. Kurt Alboldt.

B63i   "Two Soldiers."
The Golden Shore, ed. William Peden (New York: Platt & Munk,
1967), 85-105.

B64a   "The Bear."
Saturday Evening Post, CCXIV (May 9, 1942), 30-31, 74, 76, 77.
Illustrated by Edward Shenton.

B64b   "The Bear."
*The Best American Short Stories 1943 and The Yearbook of the
American Short Story*, ed. Martha Foley (Boston: Houghton
Mifflin, 1943), 70-86.

B64c   *The Best American Short Stories 1943.* Another copy (Cleveland: World, Forum Books Edition, "First Printing October
1944.")

B64d   "The Bear."
The College Omnibus, 7th Edition, ed. Leonard F. Dean (New
York: Harcourt, Brace, 1951), 457-467.
          Also contains the Nobel Address.

B64e   "An Insignificant Fyce Baits a Bear."
Life, XXXIX (November 14, 1955), 194. Brief excerpts from
"The Bear." With wood engraving by Bernard Brussel-Smith.

B64f   The Bear
(Paderborn: Schoningh, 1958).
A much condensed version in English; No. 134 in a series published in Germany as English language teaching aids. With notes
and explanation in German by Alex Niederstenbruch. Pamphlet.

B64g   The Bear.

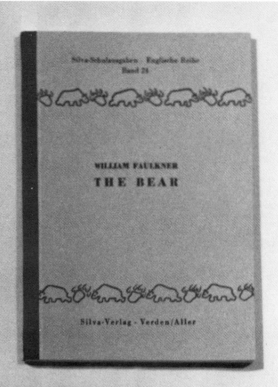

English language teaching aids for
German students (B64f, B64g, A18m).

(Verden/Aller: Silva, 1959).
In English; No. 24 in a series of teaching aids. Four part version with introduction and notation in English by Paul Fussell. Wrappers.

B64h   **Björnen.**
(Stockholm: Raben & Sjogren, 1959). Trans. and intro. Olov Jonason. Boards.

B64i   **"O Urso."**
Mestres do Moderno Conto Americano (Lisbon: Portugalia, n. d.), 253-272 (Series: Antologias Universais Conto, No. 9.) Wrappers. Trans. Cabral do Nascimento; short version.

B65a   **"Delta Autumn."**
Story, XX (May-June 1942), pp. 46-55.

B65b   **"Delta Autumn."**
The Story Pocket Book (New York: Pocket Books, [December] 1944), pp. 168-184. Paperback.

B65c   **"Delta Autumn."**
A New Southern Harvest (New York: Bantam, [January] 1957), pp. 1-20. Paperback.

B66a   **"Shingles for the Lord."**
Saturday Evening Post, CCXV (February 13, 1943), pp. 14-15, 68, 70, 71. Illustrated by Floyd Davis.

B67a   **"My Grandmother Millard and General Bedford Forrest and the Battle of Harrykin Creek."**
Story, XXII (March-April 1943), pp. 68-86.

B67b   **"My Grandmother Millard and General Bedford Forrest and the Battle of Harrykin Creek."**
Story: The Fiction of the Forties, ed. Whit Burnett and Hallie Burnett (New York: Dutton, 1949), pp. 235-263.

B68a   **"L'Apres-midi d'une Vache."**
Fontaine, 27-28 (June-July 1943), pp. 66-81. This special issue of *Fontaine* devoted to American writing was published in Algiers. The

French translation of the Faulkner story, and an introductory note, are by Maurice Edgar Coindreau. This copy inscribed by M. Coindreau.

B68b   **"L'Apres-midi d'une Vache."**
Ecrivains et Poetes des Etats-Unis (Paris: Fontaine, 1945), pp. 68-81. A reprint of the Algiers issue of 1943.

B68c   **"Afternoon of a Cow."**
Furioso, II (Summer 1947), pp. 5-17. First English language publication.
  Also contains "Notes on Mr. Faulkner," by Reed Whittemore, pp. 18-25.

B69a   **"Shall Not Perish."**
Story, XXIII (July-August 1943), pp. 40-47.

B70a   **"An Error in Chemistry."**
Ellery Queen's Mystery Magazine, VII (June 1946), pp. 5-19.

B70b   **"An Error in Chemistry."**
The Queen's Awards, 1946, ed. Ellery Queen (Boston: Little, Brown, 1946), pp. 25-42.
  Contains Vincent Starrett's bookplate and signature. Inscribed by "Ellery Queen" (Frederic Dannay).

B71a   **"A Courtship."**
Sewanee Review, LVI (Autumn 1948), pp. 634-653.

B71b   **"A Courtship."**
Prize Stories of 1949: The O. Henry Awards, ed. Herschel Brickell (Garden City: Doubleday, 1949), pp. 1-16.

B71c   **"A Courtship."**
Great Tales of the Deep South (New York: Lion Library, [July] 1955), pp. 40-54. Paperback.

B71d   **"A Courtship."**
Craft and Vision: The Best Fiction from The Sewanee Review, ed. Andrew Lytle (New York: Delacorte, 1971), pp. 62-77.

  "A Courtship."

See also B54d.

B72a   **"Sepulture South: Gaslight."**
Harper's Bazaar, LXXXVIII (December 1954), pp. 84-85, 140, 141.

B72b   **"Sepulture Sud."**
La Nouvelle Revue Francaise, No. 159 (March 1966), pp. 568-576. Trans. Michel Gresset.

B73a   **"Race at Morning."**
Saturday Evening Post, CCXXVII (March 5, 1955), pp. 26-27, 103, 104, 106. Illustrated by Ray Prohaska.

B73b   **"Race at Morning."**
The Saturday Evening Post *Stories: 1955* (New York: Random House, [April] 1956), pp. 3-20.

B73c   **"Ritt i morgonväkten."**
Bonniers Litterära Magasin, XXIV (December 1955), pp. 784-794. Trans. Birgitta Hammar.

B73d   **"Race at Morning."**
Prize Stories 1956: The O. Henry Awards, ed. Paul Engle and Hansford Martin (Garden City: Doubleday, 1956), pp. 178-193.

B73e   **"Chasse matinale."**
Les vingt meilleures: Nouvelles Americaines, ed. and intr. Alain Bosquet (Paris: Editions Seghers, 1957), pp. 335-353. Trans. R. N. Raimbault. Boards. Printed in Belgium.

B74a   **"By the People."**
Mademoiselle, XLI (October 1955), pp. 86-89, 130-139. Drawings by Jean Watts.

B74b   **"By the People."**
Prize Stories 1957: The O. Henry Awards, ed. Paul Engle and Constance Urdang (Garden City: Doubleday, 1957), pp. 121-140.

B74c   **"By the People."**
40 Best Stories from Mademoiselle 1935-1960, ed. Cyrilly Abels and Margarita G. Smith (New York: Harper, 1960), pp. 263-282.

B75a   **"Mr. Acarius."**
Saturday Evening Post, CCXXXVIII (October 9, 1965), pp. 26-31.
Illustrated by George Giusti.

B75b   **"Mr. Acarius."**
*The Best American Short Stories 1966 and the Yearbook of the
American Short Story,* ed. Martha Foley and David Burnett
(Boston: Houghton Mifflin, 1966), pp. 69-82.

SECTION C: VERSE

C1a   **"L'Apres-Midi d'un Faune."**
New Republic, XX (August 6, 1919), 24.

C2a   **"Portrait."**
Double Dealer, III (June 1922), 337.

C3a   **"Dying Gladiator."**
Double Dealer, VII (January-February 1925), 85.

C4a   **"The Faun."**
Double Dealer, VII (April 1925), 148.

C5a   **"The Lilacs."**
Double Dealer, VII (June 1925), 185-187.

C5b   **"The Lilacs."**
Anthology of Magazine Verse for 1925 and Yearbook of American Poetry, ed. William Stanley Braithwaite (Boston: B. J. Brimmer, 1925), 115-118.

C5c   **"The Lilacs."**
Anthology of Magazine Verse for 1958, ed. William Stanley Braithwaite (New York: Schulte, 1959). The Faulkner poem is in the special section: *Anthology of Poems from the Seventeen Previously Published Braithwaite Anthologies,* ed. Margaret Haley Carpenter, 275-278.

C6a   **"I Will Not Weep for Youth."**
Contempo, I (February 1, 1932), 1.

C7a   **"Knew I Love Once."**
Contempo, I (February 1, 1932), 1.

C8a   **"Twilight."**
Contempo, I (February 1, 1932), 1.

C9a   "To A Virgin."
        Contempo, I (February 1, 1932), 2.

C10a   "Winter is Gone."
        Contempo, I (February 1, 1932), 2.

C11a   "My Epitaph."
        Contempo, I (February 1, 1932), 2.

C12a   *An Anthology of the Younger Poets.*
(C6-C11) (Philadelphia: Centaur Press, 1932). Edited by Oliver Wells. With tissue wrapper.

      Includes, as the Faulkner contribution, the six preceding poems from the February 1, 1932 issue of *Contempo.* Does not include the three other Faulkner poems in the same issue. Pp. 122-126.

C12b   *An Anthology of the Younger Poets.*
        Another copy; number 97 of an issue limited to 500 copies.

C13a   "Visions in Spring."
        Contempo, I (February 1, 1932), 1.

C14a   "Spring."
        Contempo, I (February 1, 1932), 2.

C15a   "April."
        Contempo, I (February 1, 1932), 2.

C16a   "A Child Looks from His Window."
        Contempo, II (May 25, 1932), 3.

C17a   **This Earth.**
        (New York: Equinox, [December] 1932). Tan wrappers, printed in brown. Drawings by Albert Heckman. 8 pp.

      This somewhat revised version of the poem, "My Epitaph," was one of four pamphlets published by the Equinox Press in time for the

1932 Christmas trade. The others were Clement Moore's "A Visit from St. Nicholas;" Thomas Mann's "A Christmas Poem," English "arrangement" by Henry Hart, wood engravings by Lynd Ward; and a poem by Conrad Aiken, illustrated by John P. Heins. Each sold for twenty-five cents.

C18a   **"The Flowers That Died."**
Contempo, III (June 25, 1933), 1.

C19a   **"The Race's Splendor."**
New Republic, LXXIV (April 12, 1933), 253.

C19b   **"The Race's Splendor."**
New Republic, CXXXI (November 22, 1954), 82. The magazine's 40th anniversary issue.

C20a   **"Night Piece."**
New Republic, LXXIV (April 12, 1933), 253.

C21a   **"Gray the Day."**
New Republic, LXXIV (April 12, 1933), 253.

C22a   **"Over the World's Rim."**
New Republic, LXXIV (April 12, 1933), 253.

C23a   **"The Ship of Night."**
New Republic, LXXIV (April 19, 1933), 272.

C24a   **"Man Comes, Man Goes."**
New Republic, LXXIV (May 3, 1933), 338.

C24b   **"Man Comes, Man Goes."**
The New Republic Anthology: 1915-1935, ed Groff Conklin (New York: Dodge Publishing, 1936), 451.
    First issue with beige cloth stamped in red and black, top edges red.

SECTION D: ESSAYS AND SPEECHES

D1a   For the essay, "Literature and War," written 1924 or 1925, see
       Mississippi Quarterly, XXVI (Summer 1973), 388. (1973.2)

D2a   "On Criticism."
       Double Dealer, VII (January-February 1925), 83-84.

D3a   "New Orleans."
       Double Dealer, VII (January-February 1925), 83-84.

D4a   "Verse Old and Nascent: A Pilgrimage."
       Double Dealer, VII (April 1925), 129-131.

D4b   "Poésie ancienne, Poésie à naitre."
           La Nouvelle Revue Francaise, No. 151 (July 1965), 188-192.
           Trans. Henri Thomas.

D5a   "Sherwood Anderson."
       Dallas Morning News (April 26, 1925), Part III, 7. (Facsimile copy.)

D6a   Brief extract from an autobiographical reminiscence, written approx-
       imately 1930. *Yale University Library Gazette,* XXIX (October
       1954), 69-70. (1954.34)

D7a   "William Faulkner's Essay on the Composition of *Sartoris." Yale
       University Library Gazette,* XLVII (January 1973), 121-124. With
       editing and an introduction by Joseph Blotner. Published here for
       the first time, the essay was apparently written around 1931.

D8a   "Beyond the Talking."
       New Republic, LXVII (May 20, 1931), 23-24. Review of Erich Maria
       Remarque's *The Road Back.*

D9a   *Boy.* A Novel by James Hanley (New York: Knopf, 1932). First
       American edition. On the rear jacket flap is a favorable comment by
       Faulkner on Hanley's earlier *Men in Darkness.*

REDUCE

Figures molded, unsightly rolls of fat removed, beauty and health regained through Swedish massage, pine needle oil sulphus and vapor baths. Positive results! Healthatorium at Nineteenth Century Club. 7-3203.

I WILL not be responsible for any bills made or debts contracted or notes or checks signed by Mrs. William Faulkner or Mrs. Estelle Oldham Faulkner.

WILLIAM FAULKNER
Oxford, Miss.

FREE! Stomach ulcers, gas pains, indigestion relieved quick. Get free sample doctor's prescription, Udga, at Moseley-Robinson, Pantaze and White Way Dru' Stores.

Disclaimer-of-debt notice (D12a).

Faulkner Says Of Great Prize:
Not For Me, But For My Work

By The Associated Press

STOCKHOLM, Dec. 10.—The text of Nobel Prize Winner William Faulkner's acceptance speech at a state banquet in the Stockholm City Hall Sunday night:

I feel that this award was not made to me as a man but to my work—a life's work in the agony and sweat of the human spirit, not for glory but to make out of the material of the human spirit something which was not there before. So this award is only mine in trust. It will not be hard to find a dedication for the money part of it commensurate with the purpose and the significance of its origin, but I would like to do the same with the acclaim, too, by using this fine moment as a pinnacle from which I might be listened to by the young man or young woman already dedicated to the same anguish and sweat who will some day stand here where I am standing.

Our Tragedy Today

Our tragedy today is a general and universal physical fear so long sustained by now that we can even bear it. There are no longer problems of the spirit. There is only the question: When will I be blown up?

Because of this, the young man or woman writing today has forgotten the problems of the human heart in conflict with itself, which alone can make good writing because only that is worth writing about, worth the agony and the sweat.

He must learn them again, he must teach himself that the basest of all things is to be afraid, and teaching himself that forget it forever, leaving no room in his workshop for anything but the old verities and truths of the heart, the old universal truths lacking which any story is ephemeral and doomed —love and honor and pity and pride and compassion and sacrifice. Until he does so, he labors under a curse. He writes not of love but of lust, of defeats in which nobody loses anything of value, of victories without hope and, worst of all, without pity or compassion. His griefs grieve on no universal bones, leaving no scars. He writes not of the heart but of the gland.

'Don't Believe In End of Man'

Until he relearns these things, he will write as though he stood among and watched the end of man.

I do not believe in the end of man. It is easy enough to say that man is immortal simply because he will endure: that when the last ding-dong of doom has clanged and faded from the last worthless rock hanging tideless in the last red and dying evening, that even then there will still be one more sound: that of his puny inexhaustabel voice still talking.

I believe more than this. I believe man will not merely endure, he will prevail. He is immortal, not because he alone among creatures has an inexhaustible voice, but because he has a soul, a spirit capable of commission and sacrifice and endurance. The poet's, the writer's duty is to write about these things, it is his privilege to help man endure by lifting his heart, by reminding him of courage and honor and hope and pride and compassion and pity. The poet's voice need not merely be the record of man, it can be one of the props to help him endure and prevail.

First publication of Nobel Prize
Address (D16a).

D10a   "An Introduction for *The Sound and the Fury*," ed. James B. Meriwether. *Southern Review,* VIII New Series (October 1972), 705-710. The Faulkner text dates from 1933.

D10b   James B. Meriwether. "Faulkner, Lost and Found." With Faulkner's introduction for *The Sound and the Fury. New York Times Book Review,* (November 5, 1972), 6, 7. The Faulkner text appears concurrently with publication in the *Southern Review.*

D10c   For another version of this introduction, see *Mississippi Quarterly,* XXVI (Summer 1973), 410-415. (1973.2)

D11a   "Folklore of the Air."
American Mercury, XXXVI (November 1935), 370-372. Review of Jimmy Collins' *Test Pilot.*

D12a   Disclaimer-of-debt advertisement.
Classified "Personals" advertisement in the Memphis *Commercial Appeal,* June 24, 1936.

D13a   "A Prefatory Note by Faulkner for the Compson Appendix."
American Literature, XLIII (May 1971), 281-284. An article by James B. Meriwether quoting Faulkner's two paragraph note. The note, published here for the first time, was apparently written in early 1946.

D14a   "His Name Was Pete."
Oxford *Eagle* (August 15, 1946), 1. (Facsimile copy.)

D15a   "To the Voters of Oxford."
The "beer broadside" printed in Oxford, Mississippi, shortly before the letter on legalization of beer sales that appeared in the Oxford *Eagle* of September 14, 1950, E20a.

D16a   Nobel Prize Address (Stockholm, December 10, 1950).
"Faulkner Says of Great Prize: Not for Me, But for My Work."
Memphis *Commercial Appeal,* December 11, 1950.
     In the early publications of this address the text has slight differences from the eventual text that has so often been reprinted. A

key phrase in the early state is: "I do not believe in the end of man."

D16b Nobel Prize Address.
"Faulkner Speaks; Accepts Nobel Prize in Stockholm." Oxford *Eagle,* December 14, 1950.

D16c Nobel Prize Address.
Les Prix Nobel en 1950.
Stockholm, Imprimerie Royale, P. A. Norstedt & Soner, 1951.
White wrappers printed in red. Official publication of the Nobel Committee. The text, 71-72, is in the first state.

D16d Nobel Prize Address.
"I Decline to Accept the End of Man."
New York *Herald Tribune Book Review* (January 14, 1951), 5.
Probably the first publication with the changed phrasing (here used as the title).

D16e Nobel Prize Address.
Saturday Review, XXXIV (February 3, 1951), 4-5. Also a comment by Harrison Smith, 18.

D16f Nobel Prize Address.
The College Omnibus, 7th Edition, ed. Leonard F. Dean (New York: Harcourt, Brace [February] 1951). Probably the first book appearance. The Address is on two unnumbered sides of a leaf between the Preface and the main text; it is not listed in the table of contents. Also contains "The Bear."

D16g Nobel Prize Address.
The Nobel Prize Speech.
(New York: Spiral Press, March 1951). Pamphlet. Beige wrappers printed in red and black. "Fifteen hundred copies of this Address were printed..."

D16h *The Nobel Prize Speech.*
Another copy. "Two thousand five hundred copies have been printed..."

D16i *The Nobel Prize Speech.*
Another copy. "Three thousand five hundred copies have been printed..."

D16j   Nobel Prize Address.
"Faulkner's Credo."
A. D. II (Spring 1951), 64-65.

D16k   Nobel Prize Address.
William Faulkner on Receiving the Nobel Prize (New York:
Hunterdon Press, April 1951). Pamphlet. Blue wrappers. Limited
to 200 copies. With mailing envelope.

D16l   "Nobel Prize Acceptance Speech." *The Writer,* LXIV (June 1951),
180.

D16m   "Nobel Prize Award Speech."
Saturday Review *Reader.* (New York: Bantam, [September]
1951), 67-69. Paperback.

D16n   Nobel Prize Address.
"William Faulkner's Speech of Acceptance upon the award of
the Nobel Prize for Literature, delivered in Stockholm 10th
December, 1950 " (London: Chatto & Windus, December 1951).
Pamphlet.

D16o   "Nobelpristale."
(Copenhagen: Aschehoug, 1951). Trans. Kay Nielsen. Pamphlet
limited to 1300 copies.

D16p   *I Decline to Accept the End of Man.*
(Rochester, N.Y.: Press of the Good Mountain, [1951?].)
[Date of speech is incorrectly indicated as December 14, 1950.]
Large pamphlet published in an edition of 100 copies by the
Hand Composition Laboratory of the Rochester Institute of
Technology.

D16q   "I Decline to Accept the End of Man."
Perspectives U. S. A., No. 1 (Fall 1952), 9-10. Also includes a
review of *Requiem for a Nun,* Albert J. Guerard, pp. 171-172.

D16r   "Je me refuse à admettre la fin de l'homme."
Profils, No. 1 (October 1952), 239-240. The French language
edition of *Perspectives U. S. A.*

D16s   "...Der junge Mensch, der heute schreibt..." *Lyrik der Welt,* ed.
Reinhard Jaspert (Berlin: Safari, 1953), 389-391. Truncated
translation by Donata Helmrich-Hardt.

D16t   "Predominio espiritual do homen."
Transicao Literaria nos. EE. UU., no date (1960?), 3. Published in Portuguese by the United States Information Service for distribution at the U. S. Embassy in Rio de Janeiro.

D17a   Statement to the press on the Willie McGee case, March 26, 1951.
Memphis *Commercial Appeal* (March 27, 1951). (Facsimile copy.)

D18a   Commencement Address: University High School (Oxford, Mississippi, May 28, 1951). "Never Be Afraid." *Harvard Advocate,* CXXXV (November 1951).

D18b   "Var aldrig rädda!"
Bonniers Litterära Magasin, XXI (March 1952), 165-166.
Translator's name not given.

D18c   Commencement Address: University High School.
"An Address." *Middle South News* (Summer 1962), 9.

D19a   Speech upon being made an Officer of the Legion of Honor (New Orleans, October 26, 1951).
Princeton University Library Chronicle, XVIII (Spring 1957), Pl. I.
Facsimile of speech manuscript, in French.

D20a   Delta Council Address (Cleveland, Mississippi, May 15, 1952).
An Address Delivered by William Faulkner.
Pamphlet in green wrappers, 8 pp., printing the address delivered by Faulkner at the Seventeenth Annual Meeting of the Delta Council on the campus of the Delta State Teachers College.

D20b   "The Rights of Man."
A reprint of the Delta Council speech appears in *The Delta Review: The Magazine of Memphis and the Mid-South,* II (July-August 1965), 40, 42.

D21a   Review of Ernest Hemingway's *The Old Man and the Sea.*
Shenandoah, III (Autumn 1952), 55.

D22a   "Sherwood Anderson: An Appreciation."

Atlantic Monthly, CXCI (June 1953), 27-29.

D22b   "Sherwood Anderson: An Appreciation."
The Achievement of Sherwood Anderson, ed. Ray Lewis White.
(Chapel Hill: University of North Carolina, 1966), 194-199.

D23a   Commencement Address: Pine Manor Junior College
(Wellesley, Massachusetts, June 8, 1953).
Press release, 11 sheets, printed on one side only.

D23b   "Before the Final Signature."
Time, LXI (June 22, 1953), 43.
Excerpt from the Pine Manor Commencement Address.

D23c   Commencement Address, Pine Manor Junior College.
"Faith or Fear."
Atlantic Monthly, CXCII (August 1953), 53-55.

D24a   For "A Note on *A Fable,*" written 1953 or 1954, see *Mississippi Quarterly,* XXVI (Summer 1973), 416-417. (1973.2)

D25a   "Mississippi."
Holiday, XV (April 1954), 33-47.

D25b   "Mississipi."
Les Temps Modernes, No. 103 (June 1954), 2115-2141. Trans.
Michel Zéraffa.

D25c   "Mississippi."
Encounter, III (October 1954), 3-16.

D25d   "Mississippi."
Ten Years of Holiday, intro. Clifton Fadiman (New York:
Simon and Schuster, 1956), 368-389.

D25e   "Mississippi."
American Panorama East of the Mississippi, A Holiday Magazine
Book (Garden City: Doubleday, 1961), 443-465.

D25f   "William Faulkner's Mississippi."
Country Beautiful, II (October 1962), 38-45. The revised version

At Sao Paulo, Brazil, 1954 (L15).

that forms the introduction to *Big Woods*.

D25g   "Mississippi."
               The Beautiful Country, ed. Arnold Ehrlich (New York:
               Viking, 1970), 36-38. A small portion of the *Holiday* version.

D26a   "A Guest's Impression of New England."
         New England Journeys Number 2, Ford Times Special Edition, 1954,
         6-8. Paintings by Paul Sample.

D26b   "A Guest's Impression of New England."
               The Ford Times *Guide to Travel in U. S. A.*, ed. C. H. Dykeman.
               (New York: Golden Press, 1962), 68-69.

D27a   Graham Greene. *Loser Takes All.*
         (London: Heinemann, 1955). On the rear of the jacket, among a
         group of excerpts from favorable reviews of Greene's *The End of the*
         Affair, is a brief quote by Faulkner.

D28a   "An Innocent at Rinkside."
         Sports Illustrated, II (January 24, 1955), 15.

D29a   National Book Award Address.
         (New York City, January 25, 1955).
         New York Times Book Review (February 6, 1955), 2, 24.

D29b   "Konstnären och samhället."
               All världens Berättare, XI (April 1955), 73.
               Trans. Mårten Edlund.

D30a   Address at the Universities of Montana and Oregon (April 1955).
         Transcription by Harry Runyan from recording made at the University
         of Montana, April 18, 1955.

D31a   "Kentucky: May: Saturday."
         Sports Illustrated, II (May 16, 1955), 22-24, 26.

D31b   "Kentucky: May: Saturday."
               Essays Today (New York: Harcourt Brace, 1956), 41-45.

Faulkner Digs Into Culture To Define Writers' Character

By WILLIAM FAULKNER
(Distributed by International News Service)

In a discussion in Tokyo, a statement of mine was misconstrued, if not misquoted. This was to the effect that I believed that America had no culture, that we were all savages, without intellect or spiritual tradition.

I did not say this because I don't believe it to be so.

As I see it, no peoples have a mutual culture save those who happened to believe primarily in the same things, like the peoples who believe in freedom, or the peoples who believe in serfdom.

I believe that all racial and ethnic groups have their own individual cultures.

The Japanese culture, for instance, is a culture of the intellect, just as the French culture is a culture of rationality and the British culture one of insularity. That is, each one makes its culture its national character.

Generosity With Success

Thus our American culture is not just success, but generosity with success—a culture of successful generosity.

We desire and we work to be successful in order to be generous with the fruits of that success. We get as much spiritual pleasure out of giving as we do out of gaining. All of these cultures are important, and in a way, they are interdependent.

A proof of this to me is that fact that we met in Japan, 10,000 miles from America, discussing in the English language American literature — that is, detached and compared our two separate cultures which produce our national literature.

Compared with the Japanese we are clumsy and awkward and even bad-mannered. Yet out of this clumsiness and awkwardness has come that power which produced the American writers whom the Japanese considered worthy of being discussed.

Out of our clumsiness and awkwardness there came that force which produced writers important enough to have a share in the seminar of intellects, the hosts to which were the people who have made a culture of the intellect.

I think it is our American culture of success and generosity which enabled our American writers to offer the Japanese something this last month.

I think that like our culture of material success, our writers are interested not merely in the success but in the generosity. We are as much interested in having what we have to offer acceptable to the writers of other nations as we are in being successful writers in our own country.

Universal Thinking

I think we are much more interested in universal writing than we are in being American writers.

I think that our American culture causes our writers to think of themselves only secondarily as American writers, that we think of ourselves first as men and women dealing in the universal quality which is literature.

I believe we are not really trying to produce American literature nor even to add to is prestige. I believe we are trying to increase the prestige of a universal literature. I believe that when we seem awkward, and provincial, it is because we are provincial.

It is because our culture of the intellect is so new that we have carried with us into the art of literature a certain naivete which we are too young in the craft as yet to have rid ourselves of.

A proof of this American naivete is that there is no jealously based on gender and very little even on material success among American writers.

No American assumes it the man's prerogative to have more talent or to be more important in literature than a woman writer.

We have been, as a nation, a lucky people.

We have escaped so much of the trouble and grief that other peoples have had to suffer and we are aware of this, and a part of our culture of success and generosity is a wish to share this good fortune with less fortunate people, if we can, through the qualities of the spirit as well as of the pocketbook; that the American writer is quite proud of his position in universal literature without being jealous of any other nation.

Hard To Conceive

I think that most other literary people can't quite conceive that the American can be a writer without being a man of ideas.

The European writer, if he is a writer, is per se a member of all other correlative intellectual processes. The American writer can be a writer and not be a part of the universality of ideas at all. What serves him for an idea is not a rational process at all, but an emotional concept of and belief in the universal truth of man's heart, and its record in literature.

It is this that we are proudest to participate in and share.

Nobel prize-winning author William Faulkner has just ended a three-week stay in Japan where he was the State Department's star contribution to a seminar on American literature. The Mississippi novelist records in his own words some of the differences and similarities between America and Japan and their writers, their ways or thinking, and the civilizations from which they sprang.

From Japan, August, 1955 (D34).

D31c   "Kentucky: May: Saturday."
The Spectacle of Sport, ed. Norton Wood. (Englewood Cliffs, N. J.: Prentice-Hall, 1957), 51-53.

D32a   "On Privacy. The American Dream: What Happened to It."
Harper's Magazine, CCXI (July 1955), 33-38.

D33a   *To the Youth of Japan.*
Tokyo: United States Information Service, August 1955.
A bilingual pamphlet printing Faulkner's message in Japanese and English.

D33b   "To the Youth of Japan."
Bei Kakidayori. A Monthly Review of American Books, No. 30 (September 1955), 28-32. English and Japanese texts.

D34a   "Faulkner Digs into Culture to Define Writers' Character." International News Service press release as printed in Memphis *Commercial Appeal,* Sunday, August 28, 1955.

D35a   Press dispatch for United Press on the Emmett Till case. New York *Herald Tribune* (September 9, 1955), 36. (Facsimile copy.)

D36a   "Impressions of Japan."
Memphis *Commercial Appeal,* in two parts: September 25, 1955, Section V, p. 14; October 2, 1955, Section V, p. 10. (Facsimile copies.)

D37a   Address at the meeting of the Southern Historical Association (Memphis, November 10, 1955).
"Equal Right to Opportunity Emphasized in Faulkner Text." Memphis *Commercial Appeal* (November 11, 1955), 8. (Facsimile copy.)

D37b   Address at the meeting of the Southern Historical Association.
"American Segregation and the World Crisis."
Three Views of the Segregation Decisions (Atlanta: Southern Regional Council, 1956). Pamphlet in gray wrappers, 29 pp., including Faulkner's address together with those of Benjamin E. Mays and Cecil Sims. Foreword by (and this copy signed by) Bell

I. Wiley.
The version of Faulkner's speech here is three paragraphs longer than that in the *Commercial Appeal.*

D37c   *Three Views of the Segregation Decisions.*
Another copy; "Second Printing, October 1956."
Wrappers are off-white.

D38a   "A Letter to the North."
Life, XL (March 5, 1956), 51-52.
An essay rather than a letter.

D38b   "A Letter to the North."
Reader's Digest, LXVIII (May 1956), 75-78.
Condensed (of course).

D39a   "On Fear: The South in Labor."
Harper's Magazine, CCXII (June 1956), 29-34.

D39b   "On Fear—The South in Labor."
Gentlemen, Scholars and Scoundrels, ed. Horace Knowles
(New York: Harper, 1959), 157-167.

D40a   *The Southern Reposure.*
Vol. 1, No. 1 (Summer, 1956).
The only issue printed of this satirical jab at segregation. Faulkner is said to have composed the headline:
EASTLAND ELECTED BY NAACP
AS OUTSTANDING MAN OF YEAR

D41a   "If I Were a Negro."
Ebony, XI (September 1956), 70-73.

D41b   "If I Were a Negro."
White on Black, ed. Era Bell Thompson and Herbert Nipson
(Chicago: Johnson Publishing, 1963), 69-75.

D42a   Aims of the People to People Program.
Faulkner's humorous approach to this program, expressed in 1956, is printed on p. 239 of *Requiem for a Nun: On Stage and Off,* by

EASTLAND ELECTED BY NAACP
AS OUTSTANDING MAN OF YEAR

★ ★ ★   ★ ★ ★   ★ ★ ★

The Southern Reposure

"Know Ye The Truth And Be Ye Then Free" JOHN 3:16

Volumn 1, Number One | Member: Confederate Press Association | Summer, 1956

News In Brief At A Glance

S.E.M. Rally Huge Success

Crawdad, Miss. (CPA) — A splendid attendance was reported for the first session in this year's Segregation Emphasis Month. A large crowd gathered to hear guest speaker Elsie Dinsmore discuss the topic "The Botch Made by the Scotch."

This was followed by a two-hour period of quite in which those present medi-hated and contemplated earnestly the many-faceted inferiority of the Scotch-Irish race.

After this fruitful interlude of hate, Dr. Praetorius P. Prudhomme closed by pronouncing the malediction.

AT & T To Segregate Party Lines

Port Olympic, Miss. (CPA) — Beginning immediately, say informers, the American Telegone and Telepath Company will have complete segregation on all party lines.

A spokesman described the new system as "simple and effective." He said, "The new system will be simple and effective."

He continued, "It will work thus: Any Scotch-Irishman who happens to get on already conversing lines must hang up immediately. As soon as enforcement is efficent, segregation will be completed by requiring any person who gets on line over which the same person is being discussed to refrain from listening. We think this will help to preserve the Southern Way of Life, and we want to do everything possible to help progress," he said.

Dr. Kershee Advised "It Would Be Tactless Of You To Come!"

Corn Pone, Miss. (CPA) — Dr. Boswell J. Kershee, D. D., pastor of the Second Baptist Church of Spring Falls Nebraska, and noted writer of inspirational books, was told Monday that his proposed address to the congregation of the Eighth Baptist Church here would have to be cancelled. The decision was reached, after due consideration, by a committee of prominent laymen. "Because of Dr. Kershee's background, we think it would prove to be tactless and bothersome of him to come," said Elmer P. Frisbey, spokesman for the committee.

The action was taken after it was disclosed that Dr. Kershee had recently contributed $30 to the Salvation Army and $50 to the March of Dimes. When questioned, Dr. Kershee did not deny this charge. "Yes, I have to both organizations given," he admitted. "I passed a Salvation Army lady ringing her bell on the street corner just before Christmastime and she looked so pitiful that I made a contribution. I do not regret my action."

Dr. Kershee was to have spoken on "Medieval Ascetism: its Kinship with Symbolist Existentialism in the 20th Century." Mr. Frisbey said that a replacement has not yet been found.

Terror Strikes Lelli White, Miss.

Lelli White, Miss. (CPA) — Reports coming in slowly from Mount Lelli White, Mississippi, place the number of injuries as high as fifteen in a recent uprising of rural Scotch-Irish against this small community's efforts to keep the rural element in its place.

The controversy arose three weeks ago when the Mount Lelli White village council placed restrictions on ancient and barbaric dancing and playing at crude wind instruments in the village square. The villagers protested the frequent gathering of the rural folk, resulting in the council's action.

It was agreed that the action should be taken after investigation proved that the Scotch-Irish did not pay taxes to support the city square, and, therefore, had no right to impose on the villagers' cultural benefits.

The injuries were caused by the pelting of eggs, corks, and mud balls by the villagers when the Scotch-Irish sneaked into town Saturday evening and began these wierd practices perculiar to their debased culture. Efforts have begun on the part of the village's more prominent citizens to organize and use economic coersion to prevent any more uprising by the rural elements.

Reverend Doctor I. E. Cokeman, leader of the group, said in an interview with our W. C. C. reporter, "This Scotch-Irish menace must be coped with before it engulfs us. It is time that the American people realize that separation in all respects is necessary for preservation of our civilization. Unless we stand united we shall fall as the pagan and loose moralled Nordic race has."

(Continued On Page 3)

Letters To The Editor

Dear Sirs:

For a long time I have suspected that my little son Ignatz was being influenced by insidious propaganda. But imagine my horror when I realized the full extent of his mental pollution. Today I found, securely hidden under his mattress, a copy of Emerson's Essays, God alone knows what strange ideas are seething now in my child's head. The reading of Emerson can only lead to questioning, thinking, and ultimately — yes, though I shudder to say it — to an open mind. Mothers, I implore you—sooner kill your own flesh and blood than see it come to this. If your child is hiding books by Emerson, Paine, Whitman, or Walt Kelly in his dresser drawers destroy them as the un-American trash that they are.

Respectfully,
Mrs. Wiener Wald, Jr.

Gentlemen:

I watched with dismay last Sunday's TV presentation of the opera Carmen. As you know, the lead roles were sung by two Scotch-Irish singers, Dennis Knight and McCormick Reeper. "Mercy!" I said to myself. "Did Bizet write it that way?" Now, I don't mind hearing the Scotch-Irish sing their own native spirituals like "Mother Tralee" or "Flow Gently, Sweet After," or even their own "folk operas" like Brigadoon; but I do mind their singing our music. Until this situation is remedied, I am withdrawing my membership molto

(Continued on Page 3)

Johnny Fred Dudley To Head New C.C.C.

Blue Blood, Miss. (CPA)—One of Mississippi's outstanding young lay leaders, Johnny Fred Dudley, III, has been elected to head the recently organized Campus Conservative Club, it was announced here today.

Officers and Board Members of the new club approved a Constitution, according to the news release. The Club will meet on alternate Black Mondays, Mr. Dudley said, with provisions for special sessions, if required. Dues, according to club officers, will be two bales of cotton annually, and membership is subject to the personal approval of Mr. Dudley, or anyone of his two or three close associates.

Club membership is limited to persons attending any one of the colleges in the state of Mississippi. Membership is not limited to either sex, but an applicant must be able to prove by birth certificate that they are white, Protestant, and native born.

"They have asked me why we are forming the club," Said Mr. Dudley. "Well, I'll tell you. There has been too much progress in this state. The Scotch-Irish are getting the upper hand. We don't like this filthy jazz music which is ruining our nervous systems, disintegrating our morals, and leading to juvenile delinquency and flagrant communism. It is a down right sin, and we want it stopped. The same goes for any

(Continued On Page 2)

Publisher's Introduction

It was late Spring that my son, Ernest Chris, returned to our plantation, "The Southern Manner," and brought the worst, certainly the most disturbing, news of my entire life.

As it was, I was stretched out on my hammock in the front yard, relaxing with a cool mint julip before dinner. Ernest Chris had returned from a college near Jackson, Mississippi, which he had attended during the year. I attended the same college; so did my father and so did his father.

Never have I been so upset by any news as by that brought home by my son, Ernest Chris.

He had been a member of the U.S.D.S. (United Sons and Daughters for Segregation) at our college. My son informed me, and I confirmed it, to be sure, that the Scotch-Irish among us were a real threat, indeed, a terrible menace to our way of life.

Here are some facts which I have confirmed about the Scotch-Irish in Mississippi today.

SMELL: The average Scottrish smells like smoke. This is most unpleasant, and is caused by drinking a concoction known as "Uisgebeatha". This drinking causes bad breath, naturally. It is only natural that if the Scotch Irish wanted to act civilized, as you and I, he would flavor his drink with mint. No, my friend, mint and smoke do not mix!

HABITS: The average Scotch Irish is a repulsive and obnoxious creature who is apt, if the notion strikes him, to pull a highland fling on the main street of any one of our towns in Mississippi. They are a group who, except for the women, carry long bladed knives to church with them. This, I assure you, is a heathen practice. In addition, they have come to expect to be served oatmeal in our finest restaurants simply because they have the required fifteen cents. Anyone with good breeding knows that oatmeal is horse food! And to top off the whole business, they eat pop corn in the movie houses. Which, of course, is not very couth, and, beside, it's damned annoying.

SPEECH: We Southerners have tried for years to keep the "R" sound out of our language, and have tried to teach the same basic good taste to the Scottrish among us. But, lo and behold, they insist on pronouncing the "R" and what's more, they do it with a roll. They are, no matter how hard we try, still barbaric.

MORALS: You should know the low morals of the Scottrish among us! Why, indeed, they breed like turtles! Their divorce rate is outrageous! They even like the smell that is their own, therefore they don't take baths every day as you and I do. To put it mildly, the Scotrish is a trifle lax in writing checks around the first of each month. They cannot and will not accept business responsibility, no matter how hard we try. You know this to be trus as well as I. In addition to their poor breeding, they are vulgar to an unbearable point. How many times have you heard one exclaim "Hoot Man," or Begorrrrah!" How disgusting!

In view of all the above information, I have taken the only means of which I know to bring certain news and views to you, I have undertaken the publication of this little paper, "THE SOUTHERN REPOSURE."

I have asked myself, as surely you must have, "Do I want my young daughter to marry a windbag, highland flinging, kilt wearing creature whose ancestry is questionable?"

Like yor answer, mine is the same: NO!

Knowing, of course, that the best thing that could be done would be to send them back to the bogs from which they came, I offer it to you for speculation. If that fails, then, we must stick together in an all out effort to make it clear to the Scotrish that we will theat them kind, but they MUST stay in their place.

In short, this paper proposes to maintain Segregation of the Scotch Irish, no matter what the cost! ·

It is a known fact that smoke and mint don't mix.

So, why try it at our expense?

Sincerely,
Nathan Bedford Cooclose

The Editor Makes—
Three Points To The Pointless

Physic Anglophilic disintegration (known in the medieval medical world as advanced auto-hypnotic melancholia) may be achieved in three easy stages. These are interposition, mullification, and secession. People with high blood pressure, if the stream hasn't been contaminated, have been known to skip the first or second step but this is frowned upon in best states rights circles. Sweet reason and gentle persuasion are most effective, although kicking in a guy's teeth or garrotting stimulate the disintegrating processes. Excessive brutality is never to be condoned except in the most stubborn cases and even then only after economic presure has been exhausted. Keep in mind at all times that the sole ultimate objective is the sacred cause of total mental intransigency.

Interposition is for the novice who has never indulged in sheeted night riding nor danced around the firey cross. Its childlike simplicity appeals to those who have hitherto

(Continued On Page 3)

ΑΜΕΡΙΚΑΝΙΚΗ ΥΠΗΡΕΣΙΑ ΠΛΗΡΟΦΟΡΙΩΝ
ΓΡΑΦΕΙΟΝ ΤΥΠΟΥ ΕΝ ΕΛΛΑΔΙ ΔΙΑ ΤΗΝ ΚΥΒΕΡΝΗΣΙΝ ΤΩΝ ΗΝΩΜΕΝΩΝ ΠΟΛΙΤΕΙΩΝ

**ΜΕΓΑΡΟΝ ΜΕΤΟΧΙΚΟΥ
ΤΑΜΕΙΟΥ 2ος ΟΡΟΦΟΣ
Οδος Βενιζελου 9Δ - ΑΘΗΝΑΙ
ΤΗΛΕΦΩΝΑ : 30-761 - ΕΣΩΤΕΡ. 769 - 668**

ΑΝΑΚΟΙΝΩΣΙΣ ΠΡΟΣ ΤΟΝ ΤΥΠΟΝ

Πέμπτη, 28η Μαρτίου 1957
PR-57-111

<u>ΣΗΜΕΙΩΣΙΣ ΠΡΟΣ ΤΟΥΣ κ.κ.ΣΥΝΤΑΚΤΑΣ:</u>
Παράκλησις ὅπως ἡ παροῦσα ἀνακοίνωσις μή δημοσιευθῇ πρός τῆς 6.30 μ.
τῆς Πέμπτης, 28ης Μαρτίου.

ΚΕΙΜΕΝΟΝ ΟΜΙΛΙΑΣ ΤΟΥ ΟΥΙΛΛΙΑΜ ΦΩΚΝΕΡ
ΕΠΙ ΤΗ ΑΠΟΔΟΧΗ ΤΟΥ ΑΠΟΝΟΜΗΘΕΝΤΟΣ ΑΥΤΩ
ΑΡΓΥΡΟΥ ΜΕΤΑΛΛΙΟΥ ΤΗΣ ΑΚΑΔΗΜΙΑΣ ΑΘΗΝΩΝ

ΑΘΗΝΑΙ--Παρατίθεται κατωτέρω τό κείμενον ὁμιλίας τοῦ κ. Οὐΐλλιαμ
Φῶκνερ, ἐπί τῆ ἀποδοχῆ τοῦ ἀπονεμηθέντος εἰς αὐτόν Ἀργυροῦ Μεταλ-
λίου τῆς Ἀκαδημίας Ἀθηνῶν, ἐκφωνηθείσης σήμερον, τήν 6.30 μ.μ.

o o o

Κύριε Πρόεδρε, Κύριοι Ἀκαδημαϊκοί, Κυρίαι καί Κύριοι:

Ἀποδέχομαι τό μετάλλιο αὐτό ὄχι μόνο σάν Ἀμερικανός, οὔτε μόνο
σάν λογοτέχνης, ἀλλά σάν ἔνας ποῦ ἡ Ἀκαδημία Ἀθηνῶν διάλεξε σάν
ἐκπρόσωπο τῆς ἀρχῆς ὅτι ὁ ἄνθρωπος θά παραμείνη ἐλεύθερος.

Τό ἀνθρώπινο πνεῦμα δέν ὑπακούει στούς φυσικούς νόμους. Ὅταν ὁ
ἥλιος τοῦ Περικλέους ἔρριξε τήν σκιά τοῦ πολιτισμένου ἀνθρώπου σ'ὁ-
κληρη τήν Γῆ, ἡ σκιά αὐτή ἀκολούθησε τήν καμπύλη τροχιά της, ὡς
ὅτου ἔπεσε πάνω στήν Ἀμερική. Ἔτσι, ὅταν κάποιος σάν κι'ἐμένα
ἔρχεται στήν Ἑλλάδα, μεταφέρει τήν σκιά αὐτή πίσω στήν πηγή τοῦ
φωτός ἀπό τήν ὁποία προῆλθε. Ὅταν ἕνας Ἀμερικανός ἔρχεται στήν
χώρα αὐτή, γυρίζει πίσω σέ κάτι ποῦ τοῦ εἶναι γνώριμο, σάν νά γυρίζη
σπίτι του. Γυρίζει στήν κοιτίδα τοῦ πολιτισμένου ἀνθρώπου. Εἶμαι
περήφανος ποῦ ὁ Ἑλληνικός λαός μέ θεώρησε ἄξιο γιά νά μοῦ ἀπονείμη
τό μετάλλιο αὐτό. Θά εἶναι καθῆκον μου νά ἐπιστρέψω στήν χώρα μου
καί νά πῶ στούς συμπατριῶτες μου ὅτι οἱ ἰδιότητες τῆς Ἑλληνικῆς
φυλῆς (ἡ ἀντοχή, τό θάρρος, τό αἴσθημα τῆς ἀνεξαρτησίας καί ἡ περη-
φάνεια) εἶναι πολύ πολύτιμες γιά νά χαθοῦν. Καθῆκον ὅλων τῶν ἀνθρώπ
εἶναι νά φροντίσουν νά μή χαθοῦν ἀπό τήν Γῆ.

o o o

Silver Medal Address in Greek (D43).

UNITED STATES INFORMATION SERVICE

PRESS OFFICE IN GREECE FOR THE UNITED STATES GOVERNMENT

METOCHIKON TAMEION BUILDING, SECOND FLOOR
9⁰ VENIZELOS STREET, ATHENS
TELEPHONE: 30-761, EXT. 769 or 668

PRESS RELEASE

Wednesday, March 28, 1957
PR-57-211

TEXT OF WILLIAM FAULKNER'S SPEECH OF ACCEPTANCE
OF THE ATHENS ACADEMY SILVER MEDAL

ATHENS — Following is the text of William Faulkner's speech of acceptance of the Athens Academy Silver Medal, delivered today, at 6.30 p.m.

o   o   o

Mr. President, Gentlemen of the Academy, Ladies and Gentlemen:

I accept this medal not alone as an American nor as a writer but as one chosen by the Greek Academy to represent the principle that man shall be free.

The human spirit does not obey physical laws. When the sun of Pericles cast the shadow of civilized man around the earth, that shadow curved until it touched America. So when someone like me comes to Greece he is walking the shadow back to the source of the light which cast the shadow. When the American comes to this country he has come back to something that was familiar. He has come home. He has come back to the cradle of civilized man. I am proud that the Greek people have considered me worthy to receive this medal. It will be my duty to return to my country and tell my people that the qualities in the Greek race — toughness, bravery, independence and pride — are too valuable to lose. It is the duty of all men to see that they do not vanish from the earth.

# # #

Silver Medal Address in English (D43).

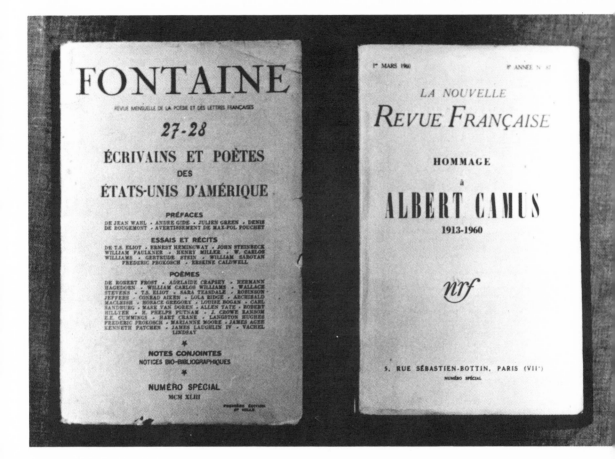

French language appearances preceding
English (B68a and D48a).

Barbara Izard and Clara Hieronymus. (1970.9)

D43a   *Acceptance Address, Silver Medal of the Athens Academy* (Athens,
Greece, March 28, 1957).
United States Information Service press release; two sheets, each printed
on one side only. One sheet is printed entirely in Greek, the other in
English.

D44a   "Presentation to John Dos Passos of The Gold Medal for Fiction" (New
York, May 22, 1957.)
*Proceedings of the American Academy of Arts and Letters and the
National Institute of Arts and Letters,* Second Series, No. 8 (1958),
192.
    An address of which Faulkner actually delivered only the last line.

D45a   "A Word to Virginians." (Charlottesville, Febraury 20, 1958.)
University of Virginia Magazine, II (Spring 1958), 11-14. Address
to the Raven, Jefferson, and ODK Societies of the University.
This issue also contains the second interview, "William Faulkner on
Dialect," 32-37. (For the first interview see G29a.)

D46a   *Address by William Faulkner at the Closing Plenary Session of the
Seventh National Conference of the U. S. National Commission for
UNESCO, in Denver, Friday, October 2, 1959.*
Press release, 3 sheets, printed on one side only.

D46b   UNESCO Address
"From Yoknapatawpha to UNESCO, the Dream."
Saturday Review, XLII (November 14, 1959), 21.

D47a   "Notice."
Advertisement posting Faulkner's land, Oxford *Eagle:*
    October 15, 1959, Sec. 2, p. 5.
    October 22, 1959, Sec. 2, p. 7.
    October 29, 1959, Sec. 3, p. 3.

D48a   "L'ame qui s'interroge."
La Nouvelle Revue Francaise, No. 87 (March 1960), 537-538.

Faulkner on Camus in a special memorial issue.

D48b   "Albert Camus."
             Transatlantic Review, No. 6 (Spring 1961), 5.
             First English language appearance of Faulkner's tribute.

D48c   "L'ame qui s'interroge."
             Hommage a Albert Camus, ed. Maurice Blanchot.
             (Paris: Gallimard, 1967), 143-144.

D49a "A Message from the Publisher."
      Life, XLVIII (May 16, 1960), 146-147.
      Four lines paraphrased from "On Privacy" spread across the pages in
      large red letters. Ironic, because that essay was prompted by Faulkner's
      reaction to the Robert Coughlan piece that had appeared in *Life.*

D50a Estate administrator notice.
      Form "Administrator's Notice to Creditors of Maude Butler Falkner"
      over the signature of "William C. Falkner" as Administrator.
      Oxford *Eagle,* October 20, 27; November 3, 1960.
         Faulkner's mother had died October 16.

D51a Acceptance Address, Gold Medal for Fiction of the National Institute
      of Arts and Letters (New York City, May 24, 1962).
      Press release, two sheets, printed on one side only.

D51b   Acceptance Address, Gold Medal for Fiction.
             Proceedings of the American Academy of Arts and Letters and the
             National Institute of Arts and Letters, Second Series, No. 13
             (1963), 226-227.
                Also includes the Presentation Address by Eudora Welty, pp.
             225-226. This copy signed by Miss Welty.

William Faulkner: Essays, Speeches and Public Letters.
Ed. James B. Meriwether. (A39a).
Reprints most of the essays and speeches listed above as well as many
of the letters in the category of "Published Correspondence."

SECTION E: PUBLISHED CORRESPONDENCE

A major source of published letters and excerpts is Joseph Blotner's *Faulkner: A Biography*, (1974.3).

The authoritative texts of Faulkner's "public letters" are found in *William Faulkner: Essays, Speeches and Public Letters*, edited by James B. Meriwether, (A39a).

Individual appearances include the following:

E1a February 1926.
   To Anita Loos, quoted in her, "A Girl Can't Go on Laughing All the Time," in *New York, N. Y.* (New York: American Heritage, 1968), 60.

E2a Summer 1927.
   To Fanny Butcher, Book Editor, Chicago *Daily Tribune,* (July 16, 1927), 12. (Photostatic copy.)

E3a Spring, 1930.
   To the Editor, *Forum,* LXXXIII (April 1930), p. lvi.

E4a April 14, 1932.
   To Maurice Edgar Coindreau, reproduced in *Princeton University Library Chronicle,* XVIII (Spring 1957), Plate II.

E5a June 27, 1933.
   To Ben Wasson, Faulkner's literary agent. *A Keepsake for the occasion of a lecture,* Gleeson Library Associates of the University of San Francisco, January 21, 1968. The lecture on Faulkner was given by Linton R. Massey.

E6a February 26, 1937.
   To Maurice Edgar Coindreau, reproduced in *Princeton University Library Chronicle,* XVIII (Spring 1957), Plate II.

E7a June 4, 1937.
   To Maurice Edgar Coindreau, *Shenandoah,* XVI (Winter 1965), 29. Also quotes E4a and E6a. (See 1965.l)

E8a 1938.
To the President of the League of American Writers, *Writers Take Sides: Letters about the War in Spain from 418 American Authors,* (New York: The League of American Writers, 1938), 23.

E9a July 6, 1941.
To Warren Beck, distinguished critic. In "Faulkner: A Preface and a Letter," *Yale Review,* LII (Autumn 1962), 157-160. Though excerpted, the quotations are substantial.

E10a July 1941.
To the Editor, Memphis *Commercial Appeal* (July 12, 1941), 4. (Facsimile copy.)

E11a July 1942.
To Whit Burnett, editor, *This Is My Best.* (New York: Dial Press, 1942), 522. Also reprint of "That Evening Sun Go Down."

E12a May 1944 to March 1957.
Twenty-three letters to Malcom Cowley; texts included in *The Faulkner-Cowley File.* (1966.14)

E13a Summer 1945.
To Richard Wright, author of *Black Boy.*
Richard Wright, by Constance Webb. (New York: Putnam's, 1968), 208-209. Two paragraphs of a three paragraph letter are printed.

E14a March 1947.
To the Editor, Oxford *Eagle* (March 13, 1947), 5.

E15a December 31, 1948.
To the American Academy of Arts and Letters.
In *The Faulkner-Cowley File,* 139. (1966.14)

E16a March 1950.
To the Editor, Memphis *Commercial Appeal* (March 26, 1950),

Section IV, 4.

E17a   April 1950.
To the Editor, Memphis *Commercial Appeal* (April 9, 1950),
Section IV, 4. (Facsimile copy.)

E18a   April 1, 1950.
To Mark Van Doren; in *The Faulkner-Cowley File,* 140. (1966.14)

E19a   June 12, 1950
To the Secretary of the American Academy of Arts and Letters,
*Proceedings of the American Academy of Arts and Letters and the
National Institute of Arts and Letters,* Second Series, No. 1 (1951),
19.
      Also includes "William Faulkner and the Nobel Award," by
Francis Hackett of the Institute, 68-80.

E19b   June 12, 1950.
The preceding material in the bound volume, *American Academy,
National Institute, Proceedings, Second Series, Numbers 1-5,
1951-1955.*

E20a   September 8, 1950.
To the Editor, Oxford *Eagle* (September 14, 1950), 13.
Also a second, proof copy.

E21a   November 1950.
To the Editor, *Time,* LVI (November 13, 1950), 6.

E22a   Autumn 1953 to ?
Four letters to Phillip E. Mullen, former associate editor of the Oxford
Eagle, printed in the Osceola (Arkansas) *Times* (December 22, 1966),
Sec. III, pp. 2, 3, 4.
      The entire section (except advertisements) is devoted to Mullen's
recollections of Faulkner. It also includes the texts of the Nobel Address,
the University High School Commencement Address, and the inscription Faulkner devised for Oxford's World War II monument.

E23a   1953?
        To Richard Walser, *The Enigma of Thomas Wolfe* (Cambridge: Harvard University Press, 1953), vii. Edited by Mr. Walser.

E23b   *The Enigma of Thomas Wolfe.*
            The Asheville Edition, limited to 301 copies signed by the editor. Number 269.

E24a   1954.
        To the publisher of Mac Hyman's *No Time for Sergeants.* Quoted by Harvey Breit in the *New York Times Book Review* (November 7, 1954).

E25a   December 22, 1954.
        To the Editor, *New York Times* (December 26, 1954), Section IV, 6.

E26a   For the texts of unpublished letters written 1955 through 1957, see *Mississippi Quarterly*, XXVI (Summer 1973), 375-386. (1973.2)

E27a   February 10, 1955.
        To the Editor, Memphis *Commercial Appeal* (February 20, 1955), Section V, 3.

E28a   March 1955.
        To the Editor, Memphis *Commercial Appeal* (March 20, 1955), Section V, 3.

E29a   March 18, 1955.
        To the Editor, *New York Times* (March 25, 1955), 22. (Facsimile copy.)

E30a   March 1955.
        To the Editor, Memphis *Commercial Appeal* (April 3, 1955), Section V, 3.

E31a   April 1955.
        To the Editor, Memphis *Commercial Appeal* (April 10, 1955), Section V, 3.

Paris, 1955.
U. S. I. S. photo.

E32a April 1955.
To the Editor, Memphis *Commercial Appeal* (April 17, 1955), Section V, 3.

E33a September 10, 1955.
To Arnoldo Mondadori, Faulkner's publisher in Italy. *Il Cinquantennio Editoriale di Arnoldo Mondadori: 1907-1957* (Verona: Mondadori, November 1957). Faulkner's letter is printed in Italian.

E34a March 8, 1956.
To David Kirk, University of Alabama student. Published in the student weekly *Crimson-White* (June 9, 1963), pp. 1, 3.

E35a March 1956.
To the Editor, *Life,* XL (March 26, 1956), 19.

E36a April 1956.
To the Editor, *The Reporter,* XIV (April 19, 1956), 7.

E37a April 1956.
To the Editor, *Time*, LXVII (April 23, 1956), 12.

E38a Winter of 1956-1957.
To Norman Mailer; published in *Advertisements for Myself* (New York: Putnam's, 1959), 333.

E39a December 1956.
To the Editor, *Time*, LXVIII (December 10, 1956), pp. 6, 9.

E40a December 11, 1956.
To the Editor, *New York Times* (December 16, 1956), Section IV, 8. (Facsimile copy.)

E41a February 1957.
To the Editor, *Time*, LXIX (February 11, 1957), 8.

E42a   September 1957.
        To the Editor, Memphis *Commercial Appeal* (September 15, 1957),
        Section V, 3. (Facsimile copy.)

E43a   October 7, 1957.
        To the Editor, *New York Times* (October 13, 1957).
        (Facsimile copy.)

E44a   February 24, 1960.
        To Paul E. Pollard, at one time Faulkner's butler. Published in *New
        York Times* (August 3, 1967), 15.

E45a   August 24, 1960.
        To the Editor, *New York Times* (August 28, 1960), Section IV, 10.

E46a   February 10 and June 25, 1962.
        To Major General William C. Westmoreland, then Superintendent of
        the United States Military Academy at West Point, New York.
        Faulkner at West Point (G37), Appendix.

SECTION F: UNPUBLISHED CORRESPONDENCE

F1 August 8, 1931.
Typed letter, signed "Faulkner," to Paul Romaine. Agrees to reprint arrangements that eventually produced *Salmagundi*. With hand addressed envelope to Casanova (booksellers), Milwaukee.

F2 October 12, 1931.
Telegram to Casanova (booksellers, Paul Romaine) excluding two short stories from *Salmagundi*.

F3 November 6, 1931.
Telegram to Anthony J. Buttitta limiting material to be published in *Contempo*.

F4 November 30, 1931.
Holograph note, signed "Bill," to Anthony Buttitta. Sorry they missed each other in New York, will send material for *Contempo* soon. With hand addressed envelope.

F5 No date (December 1931?)
Holograph letter to Harrison Smith concerning assembling verse for a new book *(A Green Bough)*. Signed "Bill."

F6 December 26, 1931.
Holograph letter to "Tony" (Buttitta) concerning latter's visit to Oxford in January. Signed "Bill."

F7 January 12, 1932.
Typed letter, signed "Bill Faulkner," to "Tony" (Buttitta). Concerning verse to appear in *Contempo*. With hand written envelope.

F8 January 27, 1932.
Typed letter, signed "Bill," to "Tony" (Buttitta). On literary matters concerning *Contempo*. With hand addressed envelope.

F9 March 4, 1932.
Typed note with holograph additions to "Tony" (Buttitta). Requests return of story and verse manuscripts. With hand addressed envelope.

Signed "Bill Faulkner."

F10   March 16, 1932.
Typed letter to Paul Romaine, signed "W Faulkner." Concerning auto-
graphing a few copies of *Salmagundi;* mentions Hemingway. With hand
addressed envelope.

F11   June 2, 1932.
Holograph note on Metro-Goldwyn-Mayer stationery. "Dear Romaine,"
signed "Faulkner." Acknowledges receipt of copy of book *(Salmagundi)*. With hand addressed envelope.

F12   May 1933.
Typed letter, signed "Bill," to Tod Browning. Acknowledges being
released by M-G-M story department.

F13   May (?) 1937.
Typed letter to a family member on a matter of family concern.

F14   December 28, 1937.
Typed letter to a friend concerning friend's recent visit to Oxford.

F15   1948 (?)
Typed letter to a friend concerning re-rigging Faulkner's sailboat.

F16   Spring 1949.
Typed letter to a friend concerning a Sunday aboard a houseboat;
makes humorous reference to the filming of *Intruder in the Dust.*
Signed "Bill."

F17   February 14, 1951.
Penciled note on back of restaurant menu to William Spratling introducing California artist.

F18   Early 1954.
Holograph letter to French friends concerning Faulkner's European

Dear Mr Romaine---

Thank you for the check. Excuse my not ~~fighting~~ writing sooner, but I have been sick. Certainly I'll sign a few for you. I hate to be stingy, but the damned autograph is like cotton down here: the more you make, the less it is worth, the less you get for it. And I have got to live on either it or cotton, and I cant make anything farming. Ler it be a mighty few, and I'll do better for you later on in something else. I will appreciate my complimentary copies.

The word from Hemingway is splendid. This is the second time he has said something about me that I wish I had thought to say first.

This is an out-of-way town and hard to reach, but I'll be glad to see you if you should straggle off into these wilds. I dont move much, but you had better give me some warning when you make the New Orleans trip.

Excuse the tardiness of this reply.

Yours sincerely,

W Fuller

Oxford, Miss.
something March. Wednesday, anyway.

To Paul Romaine concerning *Salmagundi*
(F10).

travel arrangements; signed "William Faulkner."

F19   June 25, 1956.
Telegram to California artist acknowledging receipt of painting.

SECTION G: INTERVIEW MATERIAL

G1a   "William Faulkner, 'Literary White Hope' from Mississippi, Likens Himself in City to a 'Houn' Dawg Under a Wagon'," *New York World-Telegram* (November 4, 1931). Interview by Evelyn Seeley.

G2a   "Slavery Better for the Negro Says Faulkner." *New York Herald Tribune* (November 14, 1931).

G3a   Marshall J. Smith. "Faulkner of Mississippi." *The Bookman*, LXXIV (December 1931), 411-417.

G3b   "Faulkner of Mississippi." Another copy. The photograph of Faulkner on p. 412 has been cut out. An inscription by Paul Romaine indicates this copy is the source of the photograph reproduced as the frontispiece in *Salmagundi*.

G4a   "Faulkner in Hollywood." *New York Sun* (September 3, 1932). By Laurence Stallings.

G5a   "Best Novel Still Unwritten, Falkner Admits at Oxford." Memphis *Commercial Appeal* (November 18, 1937).

G6a   "The Squire of Oxford." *New York Post* (October 17, 1939). By Michael Mok.

G7a   "An Interview with William Faulkner." *Western Review*, XV (Summer 1951), 300-304. A transcription of the April 16, 1947 session at the University of Mississippi; by Lavon Rascoe.

G7b   Account of 1947 University of Mississippi class sessions. Prepared by R. M. Allen and released in 1954 on six mimeographed legal size leaves printed on one side.

G8a   "Writer." *New York Times Book Review* (November 7, 1948). By Ralph Thompson.

G9a   "Author Faulkner Quietly Visits Gotham to 'Eat, Drink, Talk'," Memphis *Commercial Appeal* (February 19, 1950). By Rhea Talley.

G10a   "Gentle and Beloved Faulkner Places Human Problems First." Memphis *Commercial Appeal* (December 10, 1950). An interview conducted before Faulkner left for Stockholm.

G11a   "Conversation with William Faulkner." *Modern Fiction Studies*, V (Winter 1959-1960), 361-364. By Loic Bouvard, tr. Henry Dan Piper. At the Princeton Inn, November 30, 1952.

G12a   "An Interview with Faulkner." *Faulkner Studies*, III (Summer-Autumn 1954), 33-37. By A. M. Dominicis. In Rome, Italy, early in 1954.

G13a   "William Faulkner and Senator Mundt Attend A. Burks Summers' Big Party." *Washington Evening Star* (June 14, 1954). By Betty Beale.

G14a   "Unpublished Faulkner: Reply to Nathanael West Questionnaire." *American Book Collector*, XVII (September 1966), 27. Notes in response to a questionnaire sent to Faulkner in July 1954.

G15a   "Faulkner Speaking." *Time*, LXIV (August 23, 1954), 76. Comments made at the International Congress of Writers, São Paulo, Brazil.

G16a   "A Faulkner Fable." *Newsweek*, XLIV (August 30, 1954), 7. Report of an interview that never quite developed.

G17a   "A Walk with Faulkner." *New York Times Book Review* (January 30, 1955), pp. 4, 12. By Harvey Breit.

G17b   "William Faulkner."

The Writer Observed, comp. Harvey Breit. (Cleveland: World, 1956), 281-284.

G18a   "Happiest When He Had Nothing, Faulkner Says."
Associated Press Clipping (May 12, 1955). By Hal Boyle.

G19a   "An Interview with William Faulkner—September, 1955."
Accent, XVI (Summer 1956), 167-177. By Cynthia Grenier.

G19b   "L'art du roman: Dialogue de William Faulkner avec Cynthia Grenier." *La table ronde*, No. 109 (January 1957), 36-46.

G20a   *Faulkner at Nagano*. Ed. Robert A. Jelliffe.
(Tokyo: Kenkyusha, [July 15] 1956).
Text of interview sessions during the three weeks in August 1955 when Faulkner was in Japan. Also: "Message Given at Nagano," "Impressions of Japan," "To the Youth of Japan," and the by now inevitable Nobel Address.

G20b   "Faulkner In Japan."
Esquire, L (December 1958). Interview material on pp. 139, 141, 142. "Impressions of Japan," p. 140.

G21a   *faulkner on truth and freedom*
(Manila: Philippine Writers' Association, 1955). A pamphlet of excerpts from tape recordings made during Faulkner's Philippine visit.

G22a   "Faulkner Says Delinquents are Emotional Orphans."
Chicago Sun-Times (September 12, 1955), 13. United Press interview of September 11 carried in several papers.

G23a   Madeleine Chapsal. "A Lion in the Garden."
Reporter, XIII (November 3, 1955), 40. Cocktail party in the garden of Gallimard, Faulkner's Paris publisher.

G24a   "The Art of Fiction XII: William Faulkner."
Paris Review, No. 12 (Spring 1956), 28-52. Interview by Jean Stein early in 1956. Also contains reproduction of first manuscript page of

As I Lay Dying, 32-33.

G24b   "The Art of Fiction XII: William Faulkner."
Page proofs of the published interview including an introduction
composed by Faulkner that was deleted from the interview as
finally published in *Paris Review*.

G24c   "Faulkner Interviewed."
Quest, II (August-September 1956), 13-20. An abridgment of the
Jean Stein interview; published in Bombay.

G24d   "William Faulkner."
Writers at Work, ed. Malcolm Cowley (New York: Viking, 1958),
119-141.

G24e   *Writers at Work.*
Another copy, inscribed, "For Van Wyck, this record of how
writers write, and the editor's homage. Malcolm Cowley April
1958."

G24f   *Writers at Work.*
(New York: Viking, 1959). Compass Books C52 (paperback).

G24g   "The Art of Fiction XII: William Faulkner."
Reprint of the *Paris Review* (New York: Johnson Reprint,
1964). Lacks advertisements of the original.

G25a   "A Talk with William Faulkner."
Reporter, XIV (March 22, 1956), 18-20. An interview conducted by
Russell Warren Howe in New York on February 21, 1956.

G26a   "Segregation Issue Extremists Make Moderates Path Thorny."
Memphis *Commercial Appeal* (March 19, 1956). By Al Kuettner.

G27a   "William Faulkner Lambastes Press."
Washington Evening Star (June 12, 1957). By Betty Beale.

G28a   "Faulkner in the University: A Classroom Conference."
Ed. Frederick L. Gwynn and Joseph L. Blotner. *College English*, XIX
(October 1957), 1-6. A preview of the 1959 book.

G29a   "William Faulkner on Dialect."
University of Virginia Magazine, II (Winter 1958), 7-13. A radio interview at the University of Virginia. (For the second interview on this
topic see D45a pp. 32-37. These two interviews constitute Session
Fifteen in *Faulkner in the University*).

G30a   "Faulkner Says Parents and Educators are Endangering American Edu-
cation."
Oxford *Eagle* (March 13, 1958). Report of an interview session at
Princeton University.

G31a   *The Daily Princetonian* (March 19, 1958).
Two interview sessions at Princeton University; text of one on pp. 1
and 3, the other on p. 2.

G32a   *Faulkner in the University*. Edited by Frederick L. Gwynn and Joseph
L. Blotner. (Charlottesville: University of Virginia Press, 1959). The
subtitle indicates the contents: *Class Conferences at the University of
Virginia 1957-1958*. Thirty-six sessions.

G32b   *Gespräche mit Faulkner.*
(Zurich: Fretz & Wasmuth, 1961). Trans. Helmut Hilzheimer.
Introduction Erich Franzen. Wrappers.

G32c   *Gespräche mit Faulkner.*
(Stuttgart: Goverts, 1961). Text of the Hilzheimer translation.
Wrappers.

G32d   *Faulkner á l'Université.*
(Paris: Gallimard, 1964). Trans. René Hilleret. Intro. J. Gresset.
Wrappers. Number 28 of a limitation of 49 copies.

G32e   *Faulkner á l'Université.*
Another copy; wrappers. Regular first French edition, unnumbered.

G32f   *Faulkner in the University.*
(New York: Vintage Books, "First Vintage Edition, February
1965"). Vintage V-269. Includes corrections from the first printing.

G33a   "Joe Hyams Away from Hollywood."
New York *Herald Tribune*, April 28 and 29, 1959. Two part account
of a most difficult interview.

G34a   Phillipe Berard. "William Faulkner's Final Interview."
Rogue, VIII (February 1963), 69-70, 83. Primarily an account of a
Charlottesville encounter in the spring of 1961.

G35a   "Visit to Two-Finger Typist."
Life, LI (July 14, 1961), pp. 11, 12. Interview at Charlottesville by
Elliot Chaze.

G36a   "William Faulkner: An Interview."
Cate Review (June 1962), 3-6, 18-19. Interview conducted by Simon
Claxton at Oxford, Mississippi, March 23, 1962.

G37a   *Faulkner at West Point*. Edited by Joseph L. Fant and Robert Ashley.
(New York: Random House, [April 20] 1964). Transcript of a reading and conferences during Faulkner's visit to the United States Military Academy, April 19 and 20, 1962.

G37b   *Faulkner at West Point*.
(New York: Vintage Books, "Vintage Books Edition, February
1969"). Vintage V-485.

G37c   *Faulkner op West Point*.
(Utrecht: Bruna & Zoon, n. d.). Series: Witte Beertjes, No.
837. Trans. O. Falk. Wrappers.

G38a   *Lion in the Garden: Interviews with William Faulkner 1926-1962*.
Edited by James B. Meriwether and Michael Millgate. (New York:
Random House, [May 28] 1968). Transcripts of nearly three dozen
interviews; reprints many of the interviews listed above.

SECTION H: MOVIE WORK BY FAULKNER

Poster for the second Bogart-Bacall-
Hawks-Faulkner film collaboration (H4a).

H1a   Metro-Goldwyn-Mayer contract.
Copy of Faulkner's first film contract, April 15, 1932.

H2a   "Bride of the Bayou."
Lengthy typescript fragment of the screenplay on which Faulkner
was working when he was fired by M-G-M in May 1933.

H3a   *To Have and Have Not.*
Full sheet poster, 41x27 inches, 1944 release. Screenplay by Jules
Furthman and William Faulkner. Released January 20, 1945.

H3b   *To Have and Have Not.*
Four still photographs, 8 x 10 inches; one original 1945 release,
one 1952 re-release, two 1956 re-release.

H4a   *The Big Sleep.*
Full sheet poster, 40 x 26 inches, 1946 release. Screenplay by William
Faulkner, Leigh Brackett and Jules Furthman. Released August 31,
1946. Signed by Howard Hawks.

H4b   *The Big Sleep.*
Half-sheet poster issued at the time of the 1956 re-release.

H4c   *The Big Sleep.*
Four stills, 8 x 10 inches, published for the 1956 re-release.

H5a   *Land of the Pharaohs.*
Dialogue transcript.
Screenplay by William Faulkner, Harry Kurnitz and Harold Jack
Bloom. Released July 2, 1955.

H5b   *Land of the Pharaohs.*
Half-sheet poster, 22 x 28 inches, 1955.

H6a   George R. Sidney. "Faulkner in Hollywood: A Study of His Career As
a Scenarist. University of New Mexico Ph. D. dissertation, 1959.
Includes long quotations from Faulkner film treatments and screen-
plays.

H7a   *The New York Times Guide to Movies on TV*. Ed. Howard Thompson. Chicago: Quadrangle, 1970.

Includes capsule reviews of *The Big Sleep* and *Land of the Pharaohs*, on which Faulkner worked, and *The Long, Hot Summer, Sanctuary*, and *The Sound and the Fury*, adapted from Faulkner material.

SECTION I: RECORDINGS BY FAULKNER

I1a   *Faulkner Reads from His Works.*
Long playing record, Caedmon 1035, recorded in New York, September 30, 1954.

Contains the Nobel Prize Acceptance Speech and selections from *As I Lay Dying*, *A Fable*, and the "Old Man" portion of *The Wild Palms*.

I2a   Recording of an address made April 18, 1955, at the University of Montana, Missoula.
See also D30a.

I3a   *William Faulkner Reads from His Works.*
Long playing record, M-G-M E3617 ARC, recorded in 1957.

Contains two excerpts from *Light in August* and two excerpts from *The Sound and the Fury*.

I3b   *William Faulkner.*
Long playing record, Listening Library AA 3336.
Essentially a reissue of the 1957 M-G-M record with the same content. Issued 1971.

SECTION J: ADAPTATIONS OF FAULKNER

J1a   **The Unvanquished.**
Film script intended for production by Metro-Goldwyn-Mayer. Screenplay by Sidney Howard, September 1938. Never produced.

J2a   **Light in August.**
Thomas B. Hess. *Willem de Kooning.*
(New York: Braziller, 1959.)
Plate 68 is a reproduction of a de Kooning painting, *Light in August*, ca. 1946.

J3a   **Intruder in the Dust.**
Dialogue cutting continuity for the Metro-Goldwyn-Mayer film. Screenplay by Ben Maddow. Released February 3, 1950. (Continuity dated Sept. 21, 1949.)

J3b   **Intruder in the Dust.**
Half-sheet poster, 22x28 inches.

J4a   **Smoke** and **Barn Burning.**
Two plays adapted from Faulkner stories by Gore Vidal in *Visit to a Small Planet and Other Television Plays* (Boston: Little, Brown, 1957). *Smoke* on 217-233. *Barn Burning* on 235-252.

J5a   **The Long, Hot Summer.**
Film script ("First Draft Continuity"), July 15, 1957. Screenplay by Irving Ravetch and Harriet Frank, Jr. Produced by Twentieth Century-Fox. Released March 1958. (Adapted from material in *The Hamlet.*)

J5b   **The Long, Hot Summer.**
Quarter-sheet poster for the film.

J5c   **"The Long Hot Summer."**
Sheet music for movie theme, lyric by Sammy Cahn, music by Alex North. With 45 rpm record, Roulette R-4045, sung by Jimmie Rodgers.

J6a   **The Sound and the Fury.**
Full sheet poster, 40x26 inches, for the Twentieth Century-Fox film. Released March 1959. Screenplay by Irving Ravetch and Harriet Frank, Jr.

J6b   **The Sound and the Fury.**
          Vertical lobby card, 36 x 14 inches.

J7a   **As I Lay Dying.**
          Publicity photograph, 10 x 8, and program for Valerie Bettis ballet pro-
          duction, Goodman Theatre, Chicago, April 10, 1961. Actually a re-
          vival of an adaptation done by Miss Bettis as early as 1949.

J8a   **Tomorrow.**
          Still, 7 x 9, from CBS Television Network Playhouse 90 adaptation.
          Published for rebroadcast of July 18, 1961. Adaptation by Horton
          Foote.

J8b   **Old Man** and **Tomorrow.**
          Two plays adapted from Faulkner stories by Horton Foote in
          Three Plays (New York: Harcourt, Brace, 1962), *Old Man* on
          1-47, *Tomorrow* on 51-93. A Harvest Book paperback, HB 45.

J8c   **Tomorrow.**
          (New York: Dramatists Play Service, 1963).
          The Horton Foote play adaptation in a separate printed appear-
          ance for amateur acting groups.

J9a   **Sanctuary.**
          Twenty-eight publicity stills, 8 x 10 inches, from the 1961 production.
          (Twentieth Century-Fox, screenplay by James Poe.)

J9b   **Sanctuary.**
          Full sheet poster, 40 x 26 inches.

J9c   **Sanctuary.**
          Vertical lobby card, 36 x 14 inches.

J9d   **Sanctuary.**
          Exhibitor's Campaign Manual.

J10a   **The Long Hot Summer.**
          Six stills, 9 x 7 inches, from the ABC Television Network continuing
          series, season of 1965-66.

J11a **The Reivers.**
Film script of the Arthur Kramer-Irving Ravetch Production. Screen-play by Irving Ravetch and Harriet Frank, Jr., September 1, 1967.

J11b **The Reivers.**
Press book for the 1967 film.

J11c **The Reivers.**
Original sound track recording from the film adaptation; music-al selections only. Columbia Record OS 3510.

J12a **As I Lay Dying.**
Program for Chamber Theatre Production of an adaptation by Robert S. Breen. Produced by the School of Speech, Northwestern University, Evanston, Illinois, February 13 and 14, 1970.

J13a **A Rose for Emily.**
American Ballet Theatre announcement including mention of Agnes De Mille's adaptation. This ballet was done by North Carolina School of the Arts in October 1970 and by American Ballet Theatre in New York in December 1970. The announcement is of the latter production to be given in Chicago, March 1971.

SECTION K: THE FA(U)LKNER FAMILY

K1a   Col. William C. Falkner. *The White Rose of Memphis.*
(New York: Coley Taylor, 1953). Reprint of a novel by William Faulkner's great-grandfather, the original edition having appeared in 1881. Introduction for the 1953 printing by Robert Cantwell.

K2a   Maud Butler Falkner. Oil paintings by William Faulkner's mother, after William M. Harnett's *Emblems of Peace.* 10 x 8 inches.

K3a   (William and Estelle Faulkner.)
Cover of *Time* for January 23, 1939, with letter. The picture of William Faulkner on the cover sheet has been inscribed by Faulkner to Dan Brennan. It was then mailed to Brennan with a charming holograph letter (also present) written by Mrs. (Estelle) Faulkner.

K4a   *Exhibition of Paintings by Estelle Oldham Faulkner.*
Catalogue of an exhibit of paintings shown at the Alderman Library of the University of Virginia, October 12-31, 1964. The artist is Mrs. William Faulkner.

K5a   Jill Faulkner. Two part account of events surrounding awarding of Nobel Prize in Stockholm from the perspective of Faulkner's daughter. Oxford *Eagle*, December 28, 1950 and January 4, 1951, each on pp. 1 and 7.

K6a   John Faulkner. *Men Working.*
(New York: Harcourt, Brace, 1941). Marked "first edition" on copyright page. Advance copy in wrappers of the first novel by one of William Faulkner's brothers.

K6b   *Men Working.*
Another copy. Regular hardbound "first edition," 1941.

K6c   *Men Working.*
New York: Bantam paperback, [May] 1952.

K7a   John Faulkner. *Dollar Cotton.*
(New York: Harcourt, Brace, 1942). Marked "first edition" on copyright page.

K8a   John Faulkner. *Chooky.*
(New York: Norton, 1950). Advance copy in wrappers, marked
"First Edition" on copyright page.

K8b   *Chooky.*
Another copy, hardbound, no indication of edition on copyright page. On title page John Faulkner has inscribed this copy
to a friend he had known in New Orleans.

K9a   John Faulkner. *The Sin Shouter of Cabin Road.*
(New York: Fawcett, [January] 1955). Gold Medal paperback, 455.

K9b   *The Sin Shouter of Cabin Road.*
Another copy, "Third Printing, December 1960." Gold Medal
paperback, S1070.

K10a   John Faulkner. *Ain't Gonna Rain No More.*
(Greenwich, Conn.: Fawcett, [October] 1959). Gold Medal paperback, 927.

K11a   John Faulkner. *Uncle Good's Week-End Party.*
(Greenwich, Conn.: Fawcett, [August] 1960). Gold Medal paperback,
1031.

K12a   John Faulkner. "How Much Hate There is Now!"
Saturday Evening Post, CCXXXV (November 10, 1962), 24-25. Comment on aftermath of James Meredith's enrollment at the University
of Mississippi.

K13a   John Faulkner. *My Brother Bill: An Affectionate Reminiscence.*
(New York: Trident Press, 1963).

K14a   Murry C. Falkner. "The Day the Balloon Came to Town."
American Heritage, XVII (December 1965), 46-49. A prepublication
excerpt from the book of family reminiscences. By 1965 Murry Falkner was the only surviving brother.

K14b   Murry C. Falkner. "The Falkners of Oxford: The Enchanted Years."

Southern Review, III New Series (April 1967), 357-386. Another excerpt from Murry Falkner's book.

K14c Murry C. Falkner. *The Falkners of Mississippi.*
(Baton Rouge: L. S. U. Press, 1967). Inscribed by the author.

K15a Malcolm A. Franklin. "Pappy's Colored Family" and "Days and Nights in the Big Woods."
Mississippi Magazine, XII (Winter 1972), 7-8. Two reminiscences by Faulkner's stepson.
     Also: Ellis Byers, "Pappy's Honeymoon," 5-6.

SECTION L: GRAPHIC MATERIAL

L1   Two 10 x 8 photographs of William Faulkner: as a child with his brothers and as a young man with his friends. Reproduced from family photographs owned by Murry C. Falkner.

L2   Two 10 x 8 photographs, Faulkner in R.A.F. uniforms, 1918.

L3   Portrait photograph of Faulkner in Paris, 10 x 8, 1925. (William C. Odiorne.)

L4   Printed caricature by Arthur Hawkins, Jr., 6 x 4. Published as a Cape & Smith publicity piece in late 1930.

L5   Portrait photograph, 12 x 10, 1931. (J. R. Cofield.)

L6   Two 4 x 6 photographs, Chapel Hill, autumn 1931. (Anthony Buttitta.)

L7   "Mr. Faulkner is Visited by the Muse."
       The Bookman, LXXV (November 1932), 697. A caricature by A. E. Fisher.

L8   "William Faulkner." Photograph by Cofield Studio.
       The Bookman, LXXV (December 1932), 778.

L9   Sepia publicity photograph, 5 x 7, Faulkner beside his Waco aircraft, c. 1933.

L10   Photostat of caricature by D. C. Parrot, 7 x 5. Ca. 1936.

L11   Publicity photograph, 7 x 5, ca. 1938. (Random House.)

L12   Six 5 x 7 photographs taken at Rowanoak, July, 1940. (Dan Brennan.)

L13   Seven 7 x 9 photographs, Nobel Ceremony in Stockholm, December 10, 1950. (Swedish agency: Reportagebild.)

L14   Portrait photograph, 14 x 12, ca. 1954. (Sabine Weiss.)

L15   Photograph, 7 x 9, Faulkner at a snake farm, São Paulo, Brazil, August 12, 1954. (U. S. I. S.)

L16   Three 10 x 8 photographs, Faulkner at the National Book Award ceremony, January 25, 1955. (*Life* magazine.)

L17   Two 10 x 8 portrait photographs, Faulkner at the American Embassy in Paris, September, 1955. (U. S. I. S.)

L18   Photograph of Faulkner against background of Modern Library volumes, 9 x 7, ca. 1957. (Phyllis Cerf.)

L19   Faulkner at his niece's wedding, November 9, 1958. 10 x 8 photograph. (Cofield Studios.)

L20   Portrait photograph, wallet size, 1960. Made at Cofield's studio. Inscribed by Faulkner on the reverse and mailed to a California friend. With mailing envelope.

L21   Photograph of Faulkner outside his stable door, 13 x 9, March, 1962. (Martin Dain.)

L22   Portrait photograph, 10 x 8, March 20, 1962. (Jack Cofield.)

L23   Photographs by Ed Meek. "Spring Workout."
Mississippi Magazine, Spring 1962, cover, 12-13.

L24   *L'Atlantique,* Sunday, October 23, 1966. Daily newspaper of the French Line, the cover bearing a May 1962 Ralph Thompson portrait photograph of Faulkner.

L25   Photograph with Eudora Welty, 8 x 10, New York City, May 24, 1962. (United Press International.)

L26   Two Associated Press wirephotos of William Faulkner's funeral, July 7, 1962.

L27   Two Oxford *Eagle* photographs, 8 x 10, of the Faulkner funeral.

L28   Reissue of Phyllis Cerf photograph (L18) as a Random House memorial/promotional display easel, 24 x 18. Distributed in August, 1962. (In a white box superimposed on the right side of the picture is a list of Faulkner titles in print with current prices.)

L29   David E. Scherman and Rosemarie Redlich. "William Faulkner."
Literary America (New York: Dodd, Mead, 1952), 148-151. Primarily local-color photographs.

L30   Martin J. Dain. *Faulkner's County* (New York: Random House, 1964). Photographs of Lafayette County, Mississippi illuminated with fragments of Faulkner's prose to connote the atmosphere of Faulkner's Yoknapatawpha County.

L31   Two photographs, 10 x 14, Oxford Courthouse by day and by night. (Martin Dain.)

L32   Group of twenty-four 8 x 10 color photographs. Subjects include the interior and exterior of Faulkner's home (Rowanoak), scenes in Oxford and University, and the surrounding countryside of Lafayette County. Published in 1973. (Historical Graphics.)

L33   Original Edward Shenton wash drawing, 12 x 11. One of the illustrations for the *Saturday Evening Post* appearance of "The Bear," May 9, 1942 (B64a).

L34   Original Edward Shenton ink drawing for *Big Woods* (A33a), p. 143, 10 x 8. Portrays an Indian with a plow observed by the spirit of a noble ancestor. Blotner, in *Faulkner: A Biography* (1974.3), p. 1528, relates Faulkner's suggestions for this drawing.

L35   Original Edward Shenton ink drawing for *Big Woods*, p. 165. A deer caught in a flood.

L36   *Conversation*, by John McCrady. Original drawing, 12 x 16. McCrady lived much of his life in Oxford, Mississippi. The local color themes of his paintings, drawings and prints sometimes paralleled those of Faulkner's prose.

SECONDARY MATERIAL:

BACKGROUND AND CRITICAL

1860

Eug. W. Hilgard. *Report on the Geology and Agriculture of the State of Mississippi.* Jackson: Barksdale, 1860. On pp. 114, 297, and 307 are references to the stream in south Lafayette County as the Yockeney-Patafa.

1862

Preliminary Report on The Eighth Census, 1860. Washington: Government Printing Office, 1862. On pp. 10, 11 is an article on "negro slavery among the Indian tribes." On pp. 267, 268 a chart shows Lafayette County, Mississippi to have had a population in 1860 of 8,996 free and 7,129 slaves. For the entire state the figures are 354,674 free and 436,631 slaves.

1918

Major William A. Bishop. "Tales of the British Air Service." *National Geographic Magazine,* XXXIII (January, 1918), 27-37. Picture of the Sopwith Camel, p. 31. Background of Faulkner's R. A. F. service.

1924

University of Mississippi Post Office brick. Brick from the post office where Faulkner was postmaster, 1921-1924. The building was razed in 1965. (With letter from University faculty member authenticating source.)

1925

Sherwood Anderson. "A Meeting South." *The Dial,* LXXVIII (April 1925), 269-279. Fictionalized account of Anderson's first meeting with Faulkner.

1926

Sherwood Anderson. "A Meeting South." *Sherwood Anderson's Notebook.* New York: Boni & Liveright, 1926, 103-121. Book publication of the 1925 short story.
> Number 158 of a limitation of 225 copies, signed by Anderson.

1927

1 Publisher's announcement of publication of *Mosquitoes. Boni & Liveright: An Announcement of Publications for the Spring of 1927,* p. 9.

Review of *Mosquitoes:*
2 E. H. W., *NR,* July 20, p. 236.

1928

"FALKNER, William (surname originally Faulkner)." *Who's Who in America: Volume 15 1928-1929.* Chicago: Marquis, 1928, p. 741. A nine line entry.

1929

1 Publisher's announcement of publication of *The Sound and the Fury. Jonathan Cape & Harrison Smith: Fall List 1929,* p. 26.

Reviews of *The Sound and the Fury:*

2 Basil Davenport, *SRL* (Dec. 28), 601-602.

3 Clifton P. Fadiman, *Nation,* Jan. 15 (1930), 74-75.

4 Evelyn Scott. *On William Faulkner's* The Sound and the Fury. New York: Cape and Smith, 1929. Promotional pamphlet in an edition of 1000 copies.

1930

1 Publisher's announcement of publication of *As I Lay Dying. Jonathan Cape & Harrison Smith: Autumn Publications—1930,* p. 5.

2 Sherwood Anderson. "They Come Bearing Gifts." *American Mercury,* XXI (October 1930), 129-137.

Review of *As I Lay Dying:*
3 Clifton P. Fadiman, *Nation,* Nov. 5, 500-501.

1   James Burnham. "Trying to Say." *The Symposium,* II (January 1931), 51-59. "If every American novelist were to bring out a book tomorrow and I could have only one I should take William Faulkner's...it would have the best chance of being not dull."

2   Publisher's announcement of publication of *Sanctuary. Jonathan Cape & Harrison Smith: Spring Publications—1931,* pp. 3-4.

Reviews of *Sanctuary:*
3   Harry Hansen, *NYW,* Feb. 10, p. 13.
4   Edwin Seaver, *NYS,* Feb. 13, p. 31.
5   Anon., *Time,* Feb. 16, pp. 55-56.
6   George Britt, *NYTel,* Feb. 17.
7   Henry Seidel Canby, *SRL,* Mar. 21, pp. 673-674.
8   Philip E. Wheelwright, *Symposium,* Apr., pp. 422-423.
9   Clifton Fadiman, *Nation,* Apr. 15, pp. 422-423
10   Alexander Woollcott, *McCalls,* July.
11   Clifton Cuthbert, *Contempo,* Aug. 21, pp. 1-2.

English reviews of the Chatto & Windus edition:
12   Gerald Gould, *Observer,* Sept. 20, p. 6.
13   Anon., *TLS,* Sept. 24, p. 732.
14   Rebecca West, *Daily Telegraph,* Oct. 2, p. 18.

15   Weekly sales sheets for the publishing house of Jonathan Cape and Harrison Smith covering the period from February 11 to April 8, 1931.

16   William Harlan Hale. "The Future of the Novel." *The Harkness Hoot,* I (April-May 1931), 94-103.

17   Merle Johnson. "American First Editions: William Faulkner." *Publisher's Weekly,* CXX (August 15, 1931), 615.

18   Phil Stone. Letter to collector, August 27, 1931. Reviews publication history of *The Marble Faun;* disparages literary value while emphasizing monetary value to the collector. Offers copies at $25 or, if autographed, $75.

19   Granville Hicks. "The Past and Future of William Faulkner." *The Bookman,* LXXIV (September 1931), 17-24.

Reviews of *These 13:*
20   Lewis Gannett, *NYHT,* Sept. 22.
21   Laurence Stallings, *NYS,* Sept. 23, p. 29.
22   Anon., *NYTBR,* Sept. 27, p. 7.
23   Lionel Trilling, *Nation,* Nov. 4, pp. 491-492.

24   Robert Penn Warren, *Virginia Quarterly Review*, Jan. (1932), 160.

25   "William Faulkner's *Sanctuary...*" *Publisher's Weekly*, CXX (October 3, 1931), 1622.

26   Catalogue of the New School for Social Research, Inc., for Fall 1931, p. 30. As part of a lecture series on Modern Letters, to be given by Gorham B. Munson, the October 30 presentation is announced as "A new star in American fiction: Faulkner."

27   Donald Davidson. "Southern Literature—1931." *Creative Reading,* VI (December 1, 1931), 1229-1234.

28   "William Faulkner." *Living Authors: A Book of Biographies,* ed. Dilly Tante (Stanley J. Kunitz). New York: H. W. Wilson, 1931, 121-122. An early appearance of the usual biographical inaccuracies.

29   Junius Junior (pseud.). *Pseudo-Realists.* New York: Outsider Press, 1931. Pamphlet contrasting *Sanctuary* with Ben Hecht's *Jew in Love.*

30   *Checklists of Twentieth Century Authors: First Series.* Milwaukee: Casanova Booksellers, 1931. Pamphlet. On pp. 7-9 is a checklist of Faulkner material; on the inside front cover is an advertisement for *Salmagundi,* "in preparation."

31   Biographical clippings. Scrap book containing approximately 300 biographical clippings, 1931 to 1962, from newspapers and periodicals published in several American cities.

1932

1   Alan Reynolds Thompson. "The Cult of Cruelty." *The Bookman,* LXXIV (January-February 1932), 477-487.

2   John Riddell. "Popeye the Pooh." *Vanity Fair,* XXXVIII (March, 1932), 49, 66. First publication of this parody by Corey Ford.

3   Publisher's premature announcement of publication of *Light in August. Harrison Smith, Inc.: Spring Announcements 1932,* pp. 10-11. Announced for May, actually issued in October by the same publisher with a somewhat different corporate identity.

4   *First Editions of Twentieth Century Authors.* Catalogues of Casanova Booksellers of Milwaukee, No. 1 (Fall 1931) and No. 2 (Fall 1932). The latter contains brief excerpts of letters Faulkner wrote Paul Romaine during the period when Casanova was preparing *Salmagundi* for

publication.

5 Publisher's announcement of publication of *Light in August. Harrison Smith and Robert Haas, Inc.: Fall Announcements 1932,* pp. 4-5. Rescheduled to October.

Reviews of *Light in August:*
6 Lewis Gannett, *NYHT,* Oct. 6.
7 James T. Farrell, *NYS,* Oct. 7, p. 29.
8 Margaret Cheney Dawson, *NYHTBR,* Oct. 9, p. 3.
9 Dorothy Van Doren, *Nation,* Oct. 26, p. 405.
10 Geoffrey Stone, *Bookman,* Nov., pp. 736-738.
11 Parker Tyler, *New Act,* Jan. (1933), pp. 36-39.

12 Joseph Warren Beach. *The Twentieth Century Novel: Studies in Technique.* New York: Century, 1932. Several references to Faulkner.

13 Ernest Hemingway. *Death in the Afternoon.* New York: Scribner's, 1932. Reference to Faulkner with some sarcasm, p. 173.

14 John Riddell (Corey Ford). "Popeye the Pooh." *In the Worst Possible Taste.* New York: Scribner's, 1932, 84-89. Between pp. 88 and 89 is a delightful caricature by Miguel Covarrubias.

1933

1 *Vanity Fair,* XL (March, 1933). Photograph of George Raft (p. 25), scheduled to portray Popeye in movie version of *Sanctuary.* (He did not.)
Photograph of Joan Crawford (p. 36), "will appear as an English ambulance driver in *Today We Live,* from the bitter pen of Mr. William Faulkner."

2 Matthew Josephson. "The Younger Generation: Its Younger Novelists." *Virginia Quarterly Review,* IX (April 1933), pp. 243-261. References to Faulkner and *As I Lay Dying.*

3 Maurice Edgar Coindreau. *"Light in August,* par William Faulkner." *La Nouvelle Revue Francaise,* No. 239 (August 1933), 302-305. In French.

4 Typed letter, signed "A. B. Toklas," August 28, 1933. Answering a query from a Gertrude Stein enthusiast, Miss Toklas notes that Gertrude Stein did not write about Faulkner (presumably in *The Autobiography of Alice B. Toklas)* "because she has never met him."

5   *Random House Publications for Fall and Winter 1933-1934.* Announces publication "in early winter" of a limited edition of *The Sound and the Fury* printed in three colors. The edition was never published.

6   Morris U. Schappes. "Faulkner as Poet." *Poetry,* XLIII (October 1933), 48-52. Review of *A Green Bough.*

7   Andre Malraux. "Preface a *Sanctuaire* de W. Faulkner." *La Nouvelle Revue Francaise,* No. 242 (November 1933), pp. 744-747.

1934

Reviews of *Doctor Martino and Other Stories:*
1   Fred T. Marsh, *NYHT,* Apr. 15, p. 7.
2   Harry Hansen, *NYTel,* Apr. 16.
3   Fanny Butcher, *ChiDT,* Apr. 21, p. 17.
4   Philip Blair Rice, *Nation,* Apr. 25, p. 478.

5   Wyndham Lewis. "William Faulkner: The Moralist with the Corn-Cob." *Men Without Art.* London: Cassell, 1934, 42-64.

6   Robert Linn. "Robinson Jeffers and William Faulkner." *The* American Spectator *Yearbook.* New York: Frederick A. Stokes, 1934, 304-307.

7   Aubrey Starke. "An American Comedy: An Introduction to a Bibliography of William Faulkner." *Colophon,* Part 19 (1934).

1935

1   W. J. V. Hofmann. "Contemporary Portraits: William Faulkner." *Literary America,* II (March 1935), 193-195. Also a caricature by Herbert Fouts on p. 192.

Reviews of *Pylon:*
2   Harry Hansen, *NYW-T,* Mar. 24, p. 17.
3   Lewis Gannett, *NYHT,* Mar. 25, p. 13.
4   C. Jane-Mansfield, *NYS,* Mar. 27, p. 24.
5   Sterling North, *ChiDN,* Mar. 27, p. 15.
6   Clifton Fadiman, *NYr,* Mar. 30, p. 74.
7   Ben Ray Redman, *SRL,* Mar. 30, pp. 577, 581.
8   William Troy, *Nation,* Apr. 3, p. 393.
9   Malcolm Cowley, *NR,* Apr. 10, p. 254.

10   "Tenth Anniversary Number." *Virginia Quarterly Review,* XI (April

1935). References in "Modern with the Southern Accent," by John Crowe Ransom, 184-200; and "The Horrible South," by Gerald W. Johnson, 201-217.

11   Harlan Hatcher. *Creating the Modern American Novel.* New York: Farrar & Rinehart, 1935. References throughout, especially pp. 234-243.

1936

Reviews of *Absalom, Absalom!:*
1   Harry Hansen, *NYW-T,* Oct. 26, p. 19.
2   P. M. Jack, *NYS,* Oct. 30, p. 30.
3   Bernard DeVoto, *SRL,* Oct. 31, pp. 3-4, 14.
4   Dorothea Lawrance Mann, *Boston Evening Transcript,* Oct. 31, p. 6.
5   William Troy, *Nation,* Oct. 31, pp. 524-525.
6   Anon., *Newsweek,* Oct. 31, p. 26.
7   Harold Strauss, *NYTBR,* Nov. 1, p. 7.
8   Anon., *Time,* Nov. 2, p. 67.
9   Malcolm Cowley, *NR,* Nov. 4, p. 22.

10   Timothy Fuller. "The Story of Jack and Jill." *Saturday Review of Literature,* XV (December 19, 1936), 10. Parody of the nursery rhyme in Faulknerian context.

11   Henry Seidel Canby. *Seven Years' Harvest: Notes on Contemporary Literature.* New York: Farrar & Rinehart, 1936. References throughout.

1937

1   Asa Don Dickinson. *The Best Books of the Decade: 1926-1935.* New York: H. W. Wilson, 1937. The Faulkner choice (p. 61) is *Sanctuary.*

2   Virginia Faulkner. "Appomattox! Appomattox! or a Merry Christmas to William Faulkner." *Town & Country,* Christmas, 1937. Parody by an unrelated Faulkner.

1938

Reviews of *The Unvanquished:*
1   Lewis Gannett, *NYHT.*
2   Harry Hansen, *NYW-T,* Feb. 15, p. 19.
3   Clifton Fadiman, *NYr,* Feb. 19, pp. 60-61.
4   Louis Kronenberger, *Nation,* Feb. 19, pp. 212, 214.
5   Anon., *Time,* Feb. 21, p. 79.
6   Jack Lockhart, Memphis *Commercial Appeal,* Feb. 27, Sec. IV, p. 9.
7   Kay Boyle, *NR,* Mar. 9, pp. 136-137.

8   Anthony Buttitta. "William Faulkner: That Writin' Man of Oxford." *Saturday Review of Literature,* XVIII (May 21, 1938), 6-8.

9   *Mississippi: A Guide to the Magnolia State.* Compiled and Written by the Federal Writers' Project of the Works Progress Administration. New York: Viking Press, 1938. Part of the American Guide Series. Scattered references to Faulkner and the Falkner family.

10   *New Orleans City Guide.* Written and compiled by the Federal Writers' Project of the Works Progress Administration for the City of New Orleans. Boston: Houghton Mifflin, 1938, 117.

1939

Reviews of *The Wild Palms:*
1   Lewis Gannett, *NYHT.*
2   Burton Rascoe, *Newsweek,* Jan. 16.
3   Harry Hansen, *NYW-T,* Jan. 19, p. 19.
4   Clifton Fadiman, *NYr,* Jan. 21, pp. 60, 62.
5   Ben Ray Redman, *SRL,* Jan. 21, p. 5.
6   Jennie B. Gardner, Memphis *Commercial Appeal,* Jan. 22, Sec. IV, p. 9.
7   Peter Monro Jack, *NYTBR,* Jan. 22, p. 2.
8   Malcolm Cowley, *NR,* Jan. 25, p. 349.
9   Eleanor Fitzhugh, Jackson (Miss.) *News,* Feb. 6, p. 5.

10   *Time,* January 23, 1939. Cover story on Faulkner, taking off from the publication of *The Wild Palms.* This article was prepared by *Time* Associate Editor Robert Cantwell.

11   Announcement of William Faulkner's membership in the National Institute of Arts and Letters. *National Institute News Bulletin,* V (1939), p. 11.

12   George Marion O'Donnell. "Faulkner's Mythology." *Kenyon Review,* I (Summer 1939), pp. 285-299.

13   Conrad Aiken. "William Faulkner: The Novel as Form." *Atlantic Monthly,* CLXIV (November 1939), pp. 650-654.

1940

1   Leaf from Manuscript Auction Catalogue. Pp. 15-16 from a catalogue of manuscripts auctioned under the auspices of the League of American Writers and the Booksellers Guild of America for the aid of literary exiles, January 14, 1940. Reproduces the first page of the manuscript of *Absalom, Absalom!*

Reviews of *The Hamlet:*
2   Harry Hansen, *NYW-T,* Apr. 3, p. 27.
3   Clifton Fadiman, *NYr,* Apr. 6, p. 73.
4   Harold Strauss, *NYTBR,* Apr. 7, p. 2.
5   Louis Kronenberger, *Nation,* Apr. 13, pp. 481-482.
6   Malcolm Cowley, *NR,* Apr. 15, p. 510.
7   Anon., *Cue,* May.

8   Sherwood Anderson. "William Faulkner." *We Moderns: 1920-1940.* New York: Gotham Book Mart, (1940?), p. 29. Inscribed by Francis Steloff.

1941

1   Robert Penn Warren. "The Snopes World." *Kenyon Review,* III (Spring 1941), 253-257. Of importance beyond being a review of *The Hamlet.* This copy inscribed on the cover by Mr. Warren.

2   Joseph Warren Beach. *American Fiction: 1920-1940.* New York: Macmillan, 1941. References throughout, particularly pp. 123-169.

1942

1   Warren Beck. "A Note on Faulkner's Style." *Rocky Mountain Review,* VI (Spring-Summer, 1942), 5-6, 14.

Reviews of *Go Down, Moses and Other Stories:*
2   Lewis Gannett, *NYHT.*
3   John Temple Graves, II, *SRL,* May 2, p. 16.
4   James Robert Peery, Memphis *Commercial Appeal,* May 10, Sec. IV, p. 10.

5   Anon., *Time,* May 11, p. 95.
6   Milton Rugoff, *NYHTBR,* May 17, p. 2.
7   Malcolm Cowley, *NR,* June 29, p. 900.

8   Alfred Kazin. "Faulkner: The Rhetoric and the Agony." *Virginia Quarterly Review,* XVIII (Summer 1942), 389-402.

9   Phil Stone. "William Faulkner and His Neighbors." *Saturday Review of Literature,* XXV (September 19, 1942), 12.

10   Robert W. Daniel. *A Catalogue of the Writings of William Faulkner.* New Haven: Yale University Library, 1942. Issued as a pamphlet at the time of a Faulkner exhibition in the Yale University Library.

11   Maxwell Geismar. "William Faulkner: The Negro and the Female." *Writers in Crisis: The American Novel Between Two Wars.* Boston: Houghton Mifflin, 1942, 143-183.

12   Sven Møller Kristensen. "William Faulkner." *Amerikansk Litteratur 1920-1940.* Copenhagen: Atheneum, 1942, 59-73.

1944

Malcolm Cowley. "William Faulkner's Human Comedy." New York *Times Book Review,* October 29, 1944, p. 4.

1945

1   Malcolm Cowley. "William Faulkner Revisited." *Saturday Review of Literature,* XXVIII (April 14, 1945), 13-16.

2   Malcolm Cowley. "William Faulkner's Legend of the South." *Sewanee Review,* LIII (Summer 1945), 343-361.

3   Nelly Vacher-Zananiri. "William Faulkner, romancier saturnin." *Voix d'Amerique.* Cairo: Schindler, 1945, pp. 29-31. Wrappers.

1946

Reviews of *The Portable Faulkner:*
1   Caroline Gordon, *NYTBR,* May 5, pp. 1, 45.
2   Edmund Wilson, *NYr,* July 27, p. 65.

3   A. M. I. Fiskin, Chicago *Sun Book Week,* Feb. 9 (1947), 19.

4   Robert Penn Warren. "Cowley's Faulkner." *New Republic,* CXV (August 12 and 26, 1946), 176-180 and 234-237. Ostensibly a review of *The Portable Faulkner;* actually an important essay on Faulkner's career.

5   Jean-Paul Sartre. "American Novelists in French Eyes." *Atlantic Monthly,* CLXXVIII (August 1946), 114-118.

6   James T. Jackson. "Delta Cycle: A Study of William Faulkner." *Chimera,* V (Autumn 1946), 3-14.

7   George Snell. "The Fury of William Faulkner." *Western Review,* XI (Autumn 1946), 29-40.

8   Jean Pouillon. "William Faulkner, un témoin (à propos de *Pylone)."* *Les Temps Modernes,* No. 13 (October 1946), 172-178.

9   Pierre Brodin. "William Faulkner." *Les écrivains Américains de l'entre-deux-guerres.* Paris: Horizons de France, 1946, 147-170. Wrappers.

10   Norman Nicholson. "William Faulkner." *The New Spirit,* ed. E. W. Martin. London: Dobson 1946, 32-41.

11   Anne-Marie Soulac. "William Faulkner." *Romanciers Américains Contemporains,* pref. Etienne Gilson. Paris: Librairie Didier, 1946, 239-249. Wrappers.

1947

1   Hubert D. Saal. "Faulkner: Chronicler and Prophet." *Yale Literary Magazine,* CXV (December 1947), 8-15.

2   George Snell. "The Fury of William Faulkner." *The Shapers of American Fiction: 1798-1947.* New York: Dutton, 1947, 87-104.

3   Malcolm Cowley. "William Faulkner's Legend of the South." *A Southern Vanguard,* ed. Allen Tate. New York: Prentice-Hall, 1947, 13-27.

1948

1   Roark Bradford. "The Private World of William Faulkner." *'48,* II (May 1948), 83-94. With photographs by Bradley Smith.

2   Typed letter, signed, from Ben Wasson to a New York acquaintance, 18 June 1948, on the stationery of the Levee Press. Mentions with much pride the publication of a Faulkner novella "in the autumn." (*Notes on a Horsethief* was published by the Levee Press late in 1950.)

3   Caroline Gordon. "Notes on Faulkner and Flaubert." *Hudson Review,* I (Summer 1948), 222-231.

4   *Kenyon Review,* X (Autumn 1948). Contains: Richard Chase, "The Stone and the Crucifixion: Faulkner's *Light in August,"* 539-551. Lawrence Edward Bowling, "Faulkner: Technique of *The Sound and the Fury,"* 552-556.

5   John Arthos. "Ritual and Humor in the Writing of William Faulkner." *Accent,* IX (Autumn 1948), 17-30.

     Reviews of *Intruder in the Dust:*

6   Maxwell Geismar, *SRL,* Sept. 25, pp. 8-9.

7   Harvey Breit, *NYTBR,* Sept. 26, p. 4.

8   Paul Flowers, Memphis *Commercial Appeal,* Sept. 26, Sec. IV, p. 16.

9   Horace Gregory, *NYHTBR,*Sept. 26, p. 3.

10   Carter Brooke Jones, Washington *Sunday Star,* Sept. 26, p. 3-C.

11   Orville Prescott, *NYT,* Sept. 27, p. 21.

12   Anon., *Time,* Oct. 4, pp. 108, 110, 112.

13   Malcolm Cowley, *NR,* Oct. 18, pp. 21-22.

14   Paolo Milano, *Nation,* Oct. 30, pp. 496-497.

15   Eudora Welty, *Hudson Review,* Winter (1949), pp. 596-598.

16   Robert Bunker, *New Mexico Quarterly Review,* Spring (1949), 108-115.

17   Elizabeth Hardwick. "Faulkner and the South Today." *Partisan Review,* XV (October 1948), 1130-1135.

1949

1   Truman Capote. "Faulkner Dances." *Theatre Arts,* XXXIII (April 1949), 49. Review of Valerie Bettis ballet adaptation of *As I Lay Dying.*

2   *William Faulkner's Legend of the South by Malcolm Cowley.* Leaflet for a lecture sponsored by the Schools of English, University of Virginia, May 6, 1949.

3   W. M. Frohock. "William Faulkner: The Private versus the Public Vision." *Southwest Review,* XXXIV (Summer 1949), 281-294.

4   *Perspective,* II (Summer 1949). Faulkner issue, containing:
Ruel E. Foster, "Dream as Symbolic Act in Faulkner," 179-194.
Sumner C. Powell, "William Faulkner Celebrates Easter, 1928," 195-218.
Russell Roth, "The Brennan Papers: Faulkner in Manuscript," 219-224.
Phyllis Hirshleifer, "As Whirlwinds in the South: *Light in August,*" 225-238.
Ray B. West, Jr., "Atmosphere and Theme in Faulkner's 'A Rose for Emily'," 239-245.
Russell Roth, "William Faulkner: The Pattern of Pilgrimage," 246-254.

Reviews of *Knight's Gambit:*
5   Howard Mumford Jones, *SRL,* Nov. 5, p. 17.
6   Nelson Algren, *NYTBR,* Nov. 6, p. 4.
7   Irving Howe, *Nation,* Nov. 12, pp. 473-474.
8   Warren Beck, *ChiSTMB,* Nov. 13, p. 3.
9   Anon., *Newsweek,* Nov. 14, pp. 92-93.
10   Anon., *Time,* Nov. 21, p. 118.
11   Paul Flowers, Memphis *Commercial Appeal,* Dec. 4, Sec. IV, p. 12.
12   Edmund Wilson, *NYr,* Dec. 24, pp. 57, 59.

13   Eudora Welty. *Short Stories.* New York: Harcourt Brace, 1949, 39-47.
Commentary on "The Bear."

1950

1   William Poster. "Films." *Nation,*CLXX (January 14, 1950), 45. Review of the filmed *Intruder in the Dust.*

2   Barbara Giles. "The South of William Faulkner." *Masses & Mainstream,* III (February 1950), 26-40.

Reviews of *Collected Stories of William Faulkner:*
3   Horace Gregory, *NYHTBR,* Aug. 20, pp. 1, 2.
4   Harry Sylvester, *NYTBR,* Aug. 20, p. 1.
5   William Peden, *SRL,* Aug. 26, p. 12.
6   Carter Brooke Jones, Washington *Sunday Star,* Aug. 27, p. 3-C.
7   Anon., *Time,* Aug. 28, p. 79.
8   Paul Engle, *ChiSTMB,* Sept. 10, p. 3.
9   Granville Hicks, *New Leader,* Nov. 20, pp. 20-22.

10   *Perspective,* III (Autumn 1950). Second Faulkner issue, containing:
Olga Westland, *"As I Lay Dying,"* 179-191.
Edgar W. Whan, *"Absalom, Absalom!* as Gothic Myth," 192-201.
John L. Longley, Jr. and Robert Daniel, "Faulkner's Critics: A Select-

ive Bibliography," 202-208.
Harry M. Campbell, "Structural Devices in the Works of Faulkner," 209-226.
Tommy Hudson, "William Faulkner: Mystic and Traditionalist," 227-235.

11   Leslie A. Fiedler. "William Faulkner: An American Dickens." *Commentary,* X (October 1950), 384-387.

12   V. J. Jerome. *The Negro in Hollywood Films.* New York: Masses & Mainstream, (December 1950). An analysis of the film version of *Intruder in the Dust* by the chairman of the Communist Party's National Cultural Commission. Pamphlet.

13   Jean Simon. "William Faulkner." *Le Roman Américain au XXe Siècle.* Paris: Boivin, 1950, 119-131. Wrappers.

14   Edmund Wilson. "William Faulkner's Reply to the Civil-Rights Program." *Classic and Commercials.* New York: Farrar, Straus, 1950, 460-470.

1951

1   "William Faulkner." *Current Biography,* XII (January 1951), 22-25. Biographical sketch prompted by the awarding of the Nobel Prize.

2   Harvey Breit. "A Sense of Faulkner." *Partisan Review,* XVIII (January-February 1951), 88-94. Also contains a review by Isaac Rosenfeld of *Collected Stories,* 106-109.

Review of *Notes on a Horsethief:*
3   Carvel Collins, *NYHTBR,* Feb. 25, p. 8.

4   Robert Penn Warren. *William Faulkner and His South.* Text of lecture at the first Peters Rushton Seminar at the University of Virginia, March 13, 1951; mimeographed, 15 pp. Signed by Warren on first page.

5   Frank Sullivan. "A Distinguished Commuter." *Saturday Review of Literature,* XXXIV (June 9, 1951), 4. An incident from the early Thirties.

6   Cleanth Brooks. *"Absalom, Absalom!:* The Definition of Innocence." *Sewanee Review,* LIX (Autumn 1951), 543-558.

7   R. W. B. Lewis. "The Hero in the New World: William Faulkner's 'The Bear'." *Kenyon Review,* XIII (Autumn 1951), 641-660.

Reviews of *Requiem for a Nun* (novel):

8   Anthony West, *NYr*, Sept. 22, pp. 98, 101-102.

9   Anon., *Time*, Sept. 24, p. 114.

10   Irving Howe, *Nation*, Sept. 29, pp. 263-264.

11   Malcolm Cowley, *NYHTBR*, Sept. 30, pp. 1, 14.

12   Robert Penn Warren, *NYTBR*, Sept. 30, pp. 1, 31.

13   Paul Engle, *ChiSTMB*, Oct. 7, p. 6.

14   Granville Hicks, *New Leader*, Oct. 22, pp. 21-23.

15   Clifton Fadiman, *Holiday*, Nov., pp. 6, 8-9, 11.

16   Richard Match, *NR*, Nov. 5, pp. 19-20.

17   Robert Cantwell, *Freeman*, Feb. 11 (1952), 317-318.

18   Harvey Breit. "William Faulkner." *Atlantic Monthly*, CLXXXVIII (October 1951), 53-56.

19   Richard McLaughlin. "Requiem for Temple Drake." *Theatre Arts*, XXXV (October 1951), 50, 77.

20   *Harvard Advocate*, CXXXV (November 1951). William Faulkner Issue.
Contains:
William Faulkner, "Never Be Afraid," 7.
Alfred Kazin, "Faulkner's Vision of Human Integrity," 8, 9, 28-33.
Cleanth Brooks, "Notes on Faulkner's *Light in August*," 10, 11, 27.
Leonard Doran, "Form and the Story Teller," 12, 38-41.
Conrad Aiken, "William Faulkner: The Novel as Form," 13, 24-26.
Jerome Gavin, *"Light in August:* The Act of Involvement," 14, 15, 34-37.
Carvel Collins, "A Note on *Sanctuary*," 16.
John Crowe Ransom, "William Faulkner: An Impression," 17.
Archibald Macleish, "Faulkner and the Responsibility of the Artist," 18, 43.
Albert Guerard, *"Requiem for a Nun:* An Examination," 19, 41, 42.
Pierre Emmanuel, "Faulkner and the Sense of Sin," 20.
Also, brief letters by Albert Camus and Thomas Mann, 21.

21   Harry Modean Campbell and Ruel E. Foster. *William Faulkner: A Critical Appraisal.* Norman: University of Oklahoma Press, 1951.
Published after the Nobel Prize was awarded, this is the first of many, many books devoted entirely to the study of Faulkner.

22   Richard Chase. "The Stone and the Crucifixion: Faulkner's *Light in August.*" *The Kenyon Critics,* ed. John Crowe Ransom. Cleveland: World, 1951, pp. 115-126.

23   Frederick J. Hoffman and Olga W. Vickery, eds. *William Faulkner: Two Decades of Criticism.* East Lansing: Michigan State College Press, 1951. Contains:

Frederick J. Hoffman, "William Faulkner: An Introduction," 1-31.
A. Wigfall Green, "William Faulkner at Home," 33-48.
George Marion O'Donnell, "Faulkner's Mythology," 49-62.
Malcolm Cowley, "Introduction to *The Portable Faulkner,*" 63-82.
Robert Penn Warren, "William Faulkner," 82-101.
John Arthos, "Ritual and Humor in the Writing of William Faulkner," 101-118.
Rabi, "Faulkner and the Exiled Generation," 118-139.
Conrad Aiken, "William Faulkner: The Novel as Form," 139-147.
Warren Beck, "William Faulkner's Style," 147-164.
Lawrence E. Bowling, "The Technique of *The Sound and the Fury,*" 165-179.
Jean-Paul Sartre, "Time in Faulkner: *The Sound and the Fury,*" 180-188.
Olga W. Vickery, *"As I Lay Dying,"* 189-205.
Richard Chase, "The Stone and the Crucifixion: Faulkner's *Light in August,*" 205-217.
William R. Poirier, "'Strange Gods' in Jefferson Mississippi: Analysis of *Absalom, Absalom!,*" 217-243.
Elizabeth Hardwick, "Faulkner and the South Today," 244-250.
Andrew Lytle, "Regeneration for the Man," 251-259.
Ray B. West, Jr., "Atmosphere and Theme in Faulkner's 'A Rose for Emily'," 259-267.

24   Heinrich Straumann. "William Faulkner." *American Literature in the Twentieth Century*. London: Hutchinson House, 1951, pp. 86-89.

1952

Faulkner Studies, I. Four numbers for 1952. Contents include...
1   No. 1 (Spring):
       A General Introduction.
2   No. 2 (Summer):
       Cecil B. Williams, "William Faulkner and the Nobel Prize Awards," 17-19.
       John R. Marvin, *"Pylon:* The Definition of Sacrifice," 20-23.
3   No. 3 (Fall):
       William Van O'Connor, "A Short View of Faulkner's *Sanctuary,*" 33-39.
       H. Richard Archer, "Collecting Faulkner Today," 42-43.
       A. M. I. Fiskin. "Harvard Advocates...," 44-46.
4   No. 4 (Winter 1952):
       Walton Litz, "Genealogy as Symbol in *Go Down, Moses,*" 49-53.

Evans B. Harrington, "Technical Aspects of William Faulkner's 'That Evening Sun'," 54-59.
Each number also includes comments and reviews.

5   Maurice-Edgar Coindreau. "Preface aux *Palmiers sauvages.*" *Les Temps Modernes,* No. 75 (January 1952), 1187-1196.

6   Wright Morris. "The Violent Land: Some Observations on the Faulkner Country." *Magazine of Art,* XLV (March 1952), 99-103.

7   Russell Roth. "The Centaur and the Pear Tree." *Western Review,* XVI (Spring 1952), 199-205.

8   William Van O'Connor. "Protestantism in Yoknapatawpha County." *Hopkins Review,* V (Spring 1952), 26-42.

9   Harry M. Campbell. "Mr. Roth's Centaur and Faulkner's Symbolism." *Western Review,* XVI (Summer 1952), 320-321.

10   Edith Hamilton. "Faulkner: Sorcerer or Slave?" *Saturday Review,* XXXV (July 12, 1952), 8-10, 39-41.

11   Irving Howe. *William Faulkner: A Critical Study.* New York: Random House, 1952.

12   Ward L. Miner. *The World of William Faulkner.* Durham, N.C.: Duke University Press (Printed in France, 1952).

13   Robert Cantwell. "The Faulkners: Recollections of a Gifted Family." *New World Writing: Second Mentor Selection.* New York: New American Library, November 1952, pp. 300-315. A paperback.

14   Malcolm Cowley. "William Faulkner's Legend of the South." *Essays in Modern Literary Criticism,* ed. Ray B. West, Jr. New York: Rinehart, 1952, 513-526.

15   Wyndham Lewis. *The Writer and the Absolute.* London: Methuen, 1952. Scattered references.

16   Maurice Nadeau. *Littérature présente.* Paris: Corrêa, 1952. Scattered references.

17   Orville Prescott. *In My Opinion: An Inquiry into the Contemporary Novel.* Indianapolis: Bobbs-Merrill, 1952, 84-91.

18   Donald Robinson. "William Faulkner." *The 100 Most Important People in the World Today.* Boston: Little, Brown, 1952, 368-371.

19   Ray B. West, Jr. "Hemingway and Faulkner." *The Short Story in America.* Chicago: Regnery, 1952, 85-106.

20   *The Short Story in America.* Another copy, Gateway paperback edition.

1953

Faulkner Studies, II. Four numbers for 1953. Contents include
1   No. 1 (Spring):
        Olga W. Vickery, "Gavin Stevens: From Rhetoric to Dialectic," 1-4.
        Peter Lisca, "Some New Light on Faulkner's *Sanctuary,*" 5-9.
        Theodore Hornberger, "Faulkner's Reputation in Brazil," 9-10.
        Bradley T. Perry, "Faulkner Critics: A Bibliography Breakdown," 11-13.
2   No. 2 (Summer):
        Henry Nash Smith, "William Faulkner and Reality," 17-19.
        Douglas M. Thomas, "Memory-Narrative in *Absalom, Absalom!,*" 19-22.
        Carvel Collins, "Nathanael West's *The Day of the Locust* and *Sanctuary,*" 23-24.
        Bradley T. Perry, "Faulkner's Critics: A Bibliography Breakdown," 30-32.
3   No. 3 (Autumn):
        Leonard H. Frey, "Irony and Point of View in 'That Evening Sun'," 33-40.
        Marjorie Ryan, "The Shakespearean Symbolism in *The Sound and the Fury,*" 40-44.
4   No. 4 (Winter):
        Albert Gerard, "Justice in Yoknapatawpha County: Some Symbolic Motifs in Faulkner's Later Writing," 49-57.
        Carvel Collins, "A Note on the Conclusion of 'The Bear'," 58-60.
        Bradley T. Perry, "Faulkner Critics: A Bibliography Breakdown," 60-64.
        The numbers also include comments and reviews.

5   *Accent,* XIII (Winter 1953). Includes:
William Van O'Connor, "The Wilderness Theme in Faulkner's 'The Bear'," 12-20.
W. R. Moses, "Where History Crosses Myth: Another Reading of 'The Bear'," 21-33.

6   *Yale French Studies,* No. 10 (1953). Contains (in English):
Maurice Edgar Coindreau, "William Faulkner in France," 85-91.
Andre Malraux, "A Preface for Faulkner's *Sanctuary,*" 92-94.

Jean-Paul Sartre, "William Faulkner's *Sartoris,*" 95-99;
The Malraux and Sartre had originally appeared in French, in 1933 and 1938, respectively.

7 "Doom." *New Yorker,* XXIX (February 28, 1953), 18-20.

8 Robert Coughlan. "The Private World of William Faulkner." *Life,* XXXV (September 28, 1953), 118-136.
"The Man Behind the Faulkner Myth." *Life,* XXXV (October 5, 1953), 55-68.

9 Francisco Yndurian. *La obra de William Faulkner.* Madrid: Ateneo, 1953.

10 *Letters of Sherwood Anderson,* ed. Howard Mumford Jones and Walter B. Rideout. Boston: Little, Brown, 1953. Letters mentioning Faulkner are on pp. 145, 146, 154, 155, 252, 310, 314, 339, 393; a letter to Faulkner on p. 162.

11 Van Wyck Brooks. *The Writer in America.* New York: Dutton, 1953. References throughout.

12 Louis D. Rubin, Jr. and Robert D. Jacobs, eds. *Southern Renascence: The Literature of the Modern South.* Baltimore: Johns Hopkins Press, 1953. References throughout, particularly:
William Van O'Connor, "Protestantism in Yoknapatawpha County," 153-169.
Robert D. Jacobs, "Faulkner's Tragedy of Isolation," 170-191.
Irene C. Edmonds, "Faulkner and the Black Shadow," 192-206.

1954

Faulkner Studies, III. Four numbers in three for 1954. Contents include

1 No. 1 (Spring):
Robert H. Elias, "Gavin Stevens: Intruder?," 1-4.
Ruel E. Foster, "A Further Note on the Conclusion of 'The Bear'," 4-5.
Peter Lisca, *"The Hamlet:* Genesis and Revisions," 5-13.

2 Nos. 2 and 3 (Summer-Autumn):
John C. Sherwood, "The Traditional Element in Faulkner," 17-23.
Harry Runyan, "Faulkner's Poetry," 23-29.
Kenneth B. Sawyer, "Hero in *As I Lay Dying,*" 30-33.
A. M. Dominicis, "An Interview with Faulkner," 33-37.

3 No. 4 (Winter):
   William Faulkner, "Jealousy," 46-50, and "Episode," 51-53.
   William B. Bache, "Moral Awareness in 'Dry September'," 53-57.
 All numbers also include notes, comments, and reviews.

4 Melvin Backman. "Sickness and Primitivism: A Dominant Pattern in William Faulkner's Work." *Accent,* XIV (Winter 1954), 61-73.

5 Michel Carrouges. "Faulkner le voyant." *Monde Nouveau Paru,* No. 75 (January 1954), 74-79. Review of *Absalon! Absalon!*

Review of *Mirrors of Chartres Street:*
6   Carvel Collins, *NYTBR,* Feb. 7, p. 4.

Reviews of *The Faulkner Reader:*
7   Charles Poore, *NYT,* Apr. 1, p. 29.
8   Irving Howe, *NYTBR,* Apr. 4, pp. 1, 22.
9   Paul Engle, *ChiSTMB,* Apr. 18, p. 4.

10 Jack Goellner. "A Closer Look at *As I Lay Dying." Perspective,* VII (Spring 1954), 42-54.

11 William Styron. "The Art of Fiction V." *Paris Review,* II (Spring 1954), 42-57. Interview mentioning Faulkner.

12 *Random House: New Titles July-December 1954.* Announces publication of *A Fable* on August 2, p. 2.

Reviews of *A Fable:*
13   Maxwell Geismar, *SR,* July 31, pp. 11-12.
14   Carvel Collins, *NYTBR,* Aug. 1, pp. 1, 13.
15   Robert Coughlan, *ChiSunS-T,* Aug. 1, Sec. II, p. 4.
16   Malcolm Cowley, *NYHTBR,* Aug. 1, pp. 1, 8.
17   Paul Engle, *ChiSTMB,* Aug. 1, p. 3.
18   Max Herzberg, Newark *Sunday News,* Aug. 1, Sec. III, p. 2.
19   Anon., *Newsweek,* Aug. 2, pp. 48-52.
20   Anon., *Time,* Aug. 2, p. 76.
21   Lewis Gannett, *NYHT,* Aug. 2, p. 13.
22   Sterling North, *NYW-T&S,* Aug. 2, p. 2.
23   Orville Prescott, *NYT,* Aug. 2, p. 15.
24   Van Allen Bradley, *ChiDN,* Aug. 4, p. 16.
25   Carlos Baker, *Nation,* Aug. 7, pp. 115-118.
26   Leslie A. Fiedler, *NR,* Aug. 23, pp. 18-19.
27   Charles J. Rolo, *Atlantic,* Sept., pp. 79-80.
28   Irving Howe, *Reporter,* Sept. 14, pp. 43-45.
29   V. S. Pritchett, *Partisan Review,* Sept.-Oct., pp. 557-561.
30   Frances Neel Cheney, *Virginia Quarterly Review,* Autumn, pp. 623-626.

31   Thomas H. Carter, *Western Review,* Winter (1955), 147-158.

32   *Times Literary Supplement,* September 17, 1954. Special Number: "American Writing Today, Its Independence and Vigour." References throughout.

33   Arthur L. Scott. "The Myriad Perspectives of *Absalom, Absalom!" American Quarterly,* VI (Fall 1954), 210-220.

34   Norman Holmes Pearson. "Faulkner's Three 'Evening Suns'." *Yale University Library Gazette,* XXIX (October 1954), 61-70. Reproduces a manuscript page on p. 62 and quotes an unpublished reminiscence on pp. 69-70.

35   Carvel Collins. "The Interior Monologues of *The Sound and the Fury."* M. I. T. Publications in the Humanities, No. 6, 1954. An offprint from *English Institute Essays 1952,* New York: Columbia, 1954, pp. 29-56.

36   Robert Coughlan. *The Private World of William Faulkner.* New York: Harper, 1954. An expansion of the *Life* articles.

37   William Van O'Connor. *The Tangled Fire of William Faulkner.* Minneapolis: University of Minnesota Press, 1954.

38   Marcel Ayme. "What French Readers Find in William Faulkner's Fiction." *Highlights of Modern Literature.* New York: New American Library (March 1954), pp. 103-106. Mentor paperback.

39   Robert Coughlan. "The Private World of William Faulkner." *Prize Articles 1954,* ed. Llewellyn Miller. New York: Ballantine Books (1954), 121-156. Text of the two *Life* articles.

40   Malcolm Cowley. *The Literary Situation.* New York: Viking, 1954. References throughout.

41   Marcus Cunliffe. *The Literature of the United States.* London: Penguin, 1954. Scattered references.

42   "FALKNER, William." *Who's Who in America: Volume 28 1954-1955.* Chicago: Marquis, 1954, p. 833. Entry prepared from material supplied by Faulkner.

1955

1   Andrew Nelson Lytle. "The Son of Man: He Will Prevail." *Sewanee Review,* LXIII (Winter 1955), 114-137. Lengthy review of *A Fable.*

2   Bertram Rota. "The George Lazarus Library." *The Book Collector,* IV (Winter 1955), 279-284. Facing p. 279 is a reproduction of the first page of the manuscript of *Absalom, Absalom!*

3   Delmore Schwartz. "William Faulkner's *A Fable." Perspectives U. S. A.,* No. 10 (Winter 1955), 126-136.

4   Viola Hopkins. "William Faulkner's *The Hamlet:* A Study in Meaning and Form." *Accent,* XV (Spring 1955), 125-144.

5   *William Faulkner: Biography and Criticism, 1951-1954.* University of Oregon Library Humanities Division, April 29, 1955. Eleven mimeographed leaves printed on one side only.

6   Peter Swiggart. "Time in Faulkner's Novels." *Modern Fiction Studies,* I (May 1955), 25-29.

7   Arthur Knight. "Faulkner in Pharaoh-Land." *Saturday Review,* XXX-VIII (June 25, 1955), p. 24. Commentary on Faulkner's work in *Land of the Pharaohs.*

8   Ursula Brumm. "Wilderness and Civilization: A Note on William Faulkner." *Partisan Review,* XXII (Summer 1955), 340-350.

9   Roma King, Jr. "The Janus Symbol in *As I Lay Dying." University of Kansas City Review,* XXI (Summer 1955), 287-290.

10   Arthur Mizener. "The Thin, Intelligent Face of American Fiction." *Kenyon Review,* XVII (Autumn 1955), 507-524.

11   J. Maclaren-Ross. "A Cable, By W*LL**M F**LKN*R." *Punch,* CCXXIX (October 5, 1955), 399-401. Parody of and on *A Fable.*

    Reviews of *Big Woods:*
12   Van Allen Bradley, *ChiDN.*
13   Harrison Smith, *SR,* Oct. 29, p. 16.

14   Nemi D'Agostino. "William Faulkner." *Studi Americani 1.* Rome: Storia e Letteratura, 1955, 257-308.

15   Clifton Fadiman. "Puzzlements: William Faulkner." *Party of One.* Cleveland: World, 1955, 98-125. Inscribed by Fadiman.

16   Ann Lyon Haight. *Banned Books.* Second edition, rev., New York: Bowker, 1955. Page 100 reports a 1948 warrantless raid in Philadelphia in which titles seized included *Mosquitoes, Sanctuary,* and *The Wild Palms.*

17   Alfred Kazin. "Faulkner in His Fury." *The Inmost Leaf: A Selection of Essays.* New York: Harcourt, Brace, 1955, 257-273.

18   Sven Møller Kristensen. *Lidt om Amerikansk Litteratur*. Copenhagen: Carit Anderson, n. d. (1955?), 25-27.

19   Thelma M. Smith and Ward Miner. "Faulkner." *Transatlantic Migration: The Contemporary American Novel in France*. Durham, N.C.: Duke University Press, 1955, 122-145, 227-235.

1956

1   James Hafley. "Faulkner's *Fable:* Dream and Transfiguration." *Accent,* XVI (Winter 1956), 3-14.

2   Barbara Giles. "Whose South? A Reply to William Faulkner." *Masses & Mainstream,* IX (May 1956), 38-43.

3   *Modern Fiction Studies,* II (Autumn 1956). William Faulkner Special Number. Contains:
Melvin Backman, "Faulkner's Sick Heroes: Bayard Sartoris and Quentin Compson," 95-108.
Robert Flynn, "The Dialectic of *Sanctuary,*" 109-113.
David L. Frazier, "Gothicism in *Sanctuary:* The Black Pall and the Crap Table," 114-124.
W. R. Moses, "The Unity of *The Wild Palms,*" 125-131.
Roma A. King, Jr., "Everyman's Warfare: A Study of Faulkner's *Fable,*" 132-138.
Karl E. Zink, "Faulkner's Garden: Woman and the Immemorial Earth," 139-149.
Maurice Beebe, "Criticism of William Faulkner: A Selected Checklist with an Index to Studies of Separate Works," 150-164.

4   H. Richard Archer. "The Writings of William Faulkner: A Challenge to the Bibliographer." *Papers of the Bibliographical Society of America,* L (Third Quarter, 1956), 229-242.

5   James Baldwin. "Faulkner and Desegregation." *Partisan Review,* XXIII (Fall 1956), 568-573.

6   John W. Aldridge. *In Search of Heresy.* New York: McGraw-Hill, 1956. References throughout.

7   *The Reader's Companion to World Literature,* gen. ed. Calvin S. Brown. New York: New American Library (September 1956), 162-163. Mentor paperback.

8   Frederick J. Hoffman. *The Modern Novel in America.* Chicago: Regnery (1956 edition), 168-180. Gateway paperback.

9   Linton Massey. "Notes on the Unrevised Galleys of Faulkner's *Sanctuary.*" *Studies in Bibliography,* VIII (1956), 195-208. Offprint.

10   Sean O'Faolain. "William Faulkner or More genius than talent." *The Vanishing Hero: Studies in Novelists of the Twenties.* London: Eyre & Spottiswoode, 1956, 99-134.

1957

1   Beekman W. Cottrell. "Christian Symbols in *Light in August.*" *Modern Fiction Studies,* II (Winter 1956-1957), 207-213.

2   William Van O'Connor. "Hawthorne and Faulkner: Some Common Ground." *Virginia Quarterly Review,* XXXIII (Winter 1957), 105-123.

3   Marcel Schneider. "Une nonne americaine." *Cahiers des saisons,* No. 9 (February-March 1957), 232-233. Review of the Faulkner play as presented in the Camus adaptation.

4   *Princeton University Library Chronicle,* XVIII (Spring 1957).
William Faulkner, "Sherwood Anderson," 89-94.
Hodding Carter, "Faulkner and His Folk," 95-107.
Maurice Edgar Coindreau, "On Translating Faulkner," 108-113.
Carvel Collins, "The Pairing of *The Sound and the Fury* and *As I Lay Dying,*" 114-123.
George P. Garrett, Jr., "An Examination of the Poetry of William Faulkner," 124-135.
James B. Meriwether, "William Faulkner: A Check List," 136-158.
    Published to coincide with the opening of an exhibition, "The Literary Career of William Faulkner," at the Princeton University Library. Eight plates illustrate a few of the items exhibited.

5   John L. Longley, Jr. "Joe Christmas: The Hero in the Modern World." *Virginia Quarterly Review,* XXXIII (Spring 1957), 233-249. The Emily Clark Balch First Prize Essay for 1957.

6   *The Virginia Spectator.* "Writer-in-Residence Issue," CXVIII (April 1957). Student speculations on Faulkner.

Reviews of *The Town:*
7   James B. Meriwether, *SR,* Apr. 27, pp. 12-13.
8   Van Allen Bradley, *ChiDN,* May 1, p. 16.
9   Richard Ellmann, *ChiSunS-T,* May 5, Sec. III, p. 1.
10   Paul Engle, *ChiSTMB,* May 5, p. 4.
11   Alfred Kazin, *NYTBR,* May 5, pp. 1, 24.
12   Milton Rugoff, *NYHTBR,* May 5, p. 1.

13   Anon., *Newsweek,* May 6, pp. 116-117.
14   Anon., *Time,* May 6, p. 110.
15   Granville Hicks, *New Leader,* May 13, pp. 6-8.
16   Donald Malcolm, *NR,* May 27, pp. 20-21.
17   Norman Podhoretz, *NYr,* June 1, pp. 101-104.
18   Jacob Korg, *Nation,* June 8, pp. 503-504.

19   *The Literary Career of William Faulkner.* Souvenir leaflet from the
      Faulkner exhibit mounted at the Princeton University Library, May 10
      through August 30, 1957.

20   "Configuration critique de William Faulkner: I." *Revue des lettres
      modernes,* IV, Nos. 27-29 (June 1957). Published in France; contains:
      Melvin Backman, "Bayard Sartoris et Quentin Compson, héros malades
      de William Faulkner," 7-31.
      Robert Flynn, "La dialectique de *Sanctuary,"* 32-40.
      W. R. Moses, *"Les Palmiers Sauvages:* Structure et unité du Roman."
      41-54.
      Donald Torchiana, *"Pylone* et la structure du monde moderne," 55-85.
      David L. Frazier, "L'utilisation du 'gothique' dans *Sanctuary,"* 86-104.
      Beekman Cottrell, "Le symbolisme chrétien dans *Lumiere d'aout,"*
      105-118.
      Roma A. King, Jr., "Etude sur *Une Fable:* 'Everyman' et la guerre,"
      119-130.
      Karl E. Zink, "La femme et la terre immémoriale," 131-153.
      Maurice Beebe, "Critique Faulknérienne de langue Anglaise," 154-177.
      Stanley D. Woodworth, "La critique Faulknérienne en France: Essai
      de synthèse," 178-190.
      Stanley D. Woodworth, "Sélection bibliographique d'ouvrages ou
      d'articles sur 'William Faulkner en France' (1931-1952)," 191-196.

21   Andrew Lytle. *"The Town:* Helen's Last Stand." *Sewanee Review,*
      LXV (Summer 1957), 475-484.

22   Steven Marcus. "Snopes Revisited." *Partisan Review,* XXIV (Summer
      1957), 432-441. Review of *The Town.*

23   T. Y. Greet. "The Theme and Structure of Faulkner's *The Hamlet."*
      PMLA, LXXII (September 1957), 775-790.

24   Alfred Kazin. "The Stillness of *Light in August." Partisan Review,*
      XXIV (Fall 1957), pp. 519-538.

25   F. C. Riedel. "Faulkner as Stylist." *South Atlantic Quarterly,* LVI
      (Autumn 1957), 462-479.

26   Louis D. Rubin, Jr. "Snopeslore: Or, Faulkner Clears the Deck." *West-
      ern Review,* XXII (Autumn 1957), 73-76. Review of *The Town.*

27 Frederick J. Hoffman and Olga W. Vickery, eds. *Venti anni di critica.*
Parma: Guanda, 1957.
The Italian edition of *Two Decades of Criticism* deletes the John Arthos
essay from the original American edition and adds:
Emilio Cecchi, "Note su William Faulkner," 102-115.
Elio Vittorini, "Faulkner come Picasso?," 162-164.
Philip Blair Rice, "La Crocifissione di Faulkner: *A Fable,* 264-274.

28 Irving Malin. *William Faulkner: An Interpretation.* Stanford: Stanford
University Press, 1957.

29 Mary Cooper Robb. *William Faulkner: An Estimate of his Contribution
to the American Novel.* Pittsburgh: University of Pittsburgh Press, 1957.

30 *American Writing Today: Its Independence and Vigor,* ed. Allan Angoff.
New York: New York University Press, 1957. References throughout.

31 Donald Davidson. *Still Rebels, Still Yankees.* Baton Rouge: Louisiana
State University Press, 1957. References from p. 162 to p. 173.

32 Martha Mayes. "Faulkner Juvenalia." *New Campus Writing No. 2,*
ed. Nolan Miller. New York: Putnam's, 1957 , 135-144.
Quotes some of Faulkner's University of Mississippi material, all of
which was eventually republished in this country (1962) in *William
Faulkner: Early Prose and Poetry.*

33 W. S. Merwin. "William Faulkner." *Nobel Prize Winners,* ed. L. J.
Ludovici. London: Arco, 1957, 43-60.

34 Wright Morris. "The Function of Rage: William Faulkner." *The
Territory Ahead.* New York: Harcourt, Brace, 1957, 171-184.

35 Jean-Paul Sartre. *Literary Essays.* New York: Philosophical Library,
1957. Includes:
"William Faulkner's *Sartoris,*" 73-78.
"On *The Sound and the Fury:* Time in the Work of Faulkner," 79-87.

36 Robert E. Spiller. *The Cycle of American Literature.* New York: New
American Library, (January 1957), 219-226. Mentor paperback MD 188.

37 Hyatt H. Waggoner. "William Faulkner's Passion Week of the Heart."
The Tragic Vision and the Christian Faith, ed. Nathan A. Scott, Jr.
New York: Association Press, 1957, 306-323.

November 9, 1958 (L19).
Courtesy J. R. Cofield.

1958

1   Donald T. Torchiana. " Faulkner's *Pylon* and the Structure of Modernity." *Modern Fiction Studies,* III (Winter 1957-1958), 291-308.

2   Olga Vickery. "Faulkner's *Mosquitoes.* " *University of Kansas City Review,* XXIV (March 1958), 219-224.

3   Hyatt H. Waggoner. "William Faulkner: The Definition of Man." *Books at Brown,* XVIII (March 1958), 116-122.

4   Review of *New Orleans Sketches:* Alfred Kazin, *NYTBR,* Mar. 2, 4-5.

5   Olga W. Vickery. "The Making of a Myth: *Sartoris.* " *Western Review,* XXII (Spring 1958), 209-219.

6   George Monteiro. "Bankruptcy in Time: A Reading of William Faulkner's *Pylon.* " *Twentieth Century Literature,* IV (April-July 1958), 9-20.

7   Richard J. Stonesifer. "Faulkner's *The Hamlet* in the Classroom." *College English,* XX (November 1958), 71-77.

8   Masao Takahashi. *World of Faulkner.* Tokyo: Kenkyusha, 1958. In Japanese.

9   Maxwell Geismar. "William Faulkner: Before and After the Nobel Prize." *American Moderns: From Rebellion to Conformity.* New York: Hill and Wang, 1958, 91-106.

10   *Letters of Ellen Glasgow,* ed. Blair Rouse. New York: Harcourt, Brace, 1958. Scattered references.

11   Alfred Kazin. "The Stillness of *Light in August.* " *Twelve Original Essays on Great American Novels,* ed. Charles Shapiro. Detroit: Wayne State University Press, 1958, 257-283.

12   Randall Stewart. *American Literature and Christian Doctrine.* Baton Rouge: Louisiana State, 1958. References throughout.

13   Robert Penn Warren. "William Faulkner." *Selected Essays.* New York: Random House, 1958, 59-79.

1959

1   James B. Meriwether. "William Faulkner." *Shenandoah,* X (Winter 1959), 18-24. Published as part of a symposium: Modern Novelists and Contemporary American Society.

2   Walter F. Taylor, Jr. "Let My People Go: The White Man's Heritage in *Go Down, Moses.*" *South Atlantic Quarterly,* LVIII (Winter 1959), 20-32.

Reviews of the New York production of *Requiem for a Nun:*

3   Brooks Atkinson, *NYT,* Jan. 31, p. 13.

4   John Chapman, New York *Daily News,* Jan. 31, p. 21.

5   Robert Coleman, New York *Mirror,* Jan. 31, p. 27.

6   Walter Kerr, *NYHT,* Jan. 31, p. 7.

7   Richard Watts, New York *Post,* Jan. 31, p. 14.

8   Kenneth Tynan, *NYr,* Feb. 7, pp. 83-84.

9   Anon., *Time,* Feb. 9, p. 70.

10   Henry Hewes, *SR,* Feb. 14, p. 32.

11   Julia McGrew. "Faulkner and the Icelanders." *Scandinavian Studies,* XXXI (February 1959), 1-14.

12   Jerry Wald. "Faulkner and Hollywood." *Films in Review,* X (March 1959), 129-133.

13   "Configuration critique de William Faulkner: II." *Revue des lettres modernes,* V, Nos. 40-42 (March 1959).

Second part of this French study; contains:

Robert Penn Warren, "Introduction a William Faulkner," 205-230.

Roger Asselineau, "William Faulkner, moraliste puritain," 231-249.

Cyrille Arnavon, "*Absalon, Absalon!* et l'histoire," 250-270.

Warren Beck, "Faulkner et le sud," 271-291.

Maurice Le Breton, "Le théme de la vie et de la mort dans *As I Lay Dying,*" 292-308.

Melvin Backman, *"Tandis que j'agonise,"* 309-330.

Melvin J. Friedman, "Le monologue intérieur dans *As I Lay Dying,*" 331-344.

Stanley D. Woodworth, "Problèmes de traduction," 345-364.

Warren Beck, "Le style de William Faulkner," 365-384.

14   *Random House: New Titles July-December 1959.* Announces publication of *The Mansion* in October, p. 5.

15   William J. Handy. *"As I Lay Dying:* Faulkner's Inner Reporter." *Kenyon Review,* XXI (Summer 1959), 437-451.

16   Cecil D. Eby. "Faulkner and the Southwestern Humorists." *Shenandoah,* XI (Autumn 1959), 13-21.

17   Charles A. Raines. "Faulkner and Human Freedom." *Forum,* III (Fall 1959), 50-53.

18   *William Faulkner: Man Working 1919-1959.* Souvenir program from the Faulkner exhibit mounted at the Alderman Library of the University of Virginia, October 1 to December 23, 1959.

Reproduces page one from the typescript of *The Mansion.*

19   *William Faulkner: An Exhibition of Manuscripts.* Austin, University of Texas, October 15, 1959. Catalogue of a showing of rare Faulkner material at the Research Center of the University. Inscribed by James B. Meriwether.

20   *Times Literary Supplement,* November 6, 1959.
Special Number: "The American Imagination, Its Strength & Scope." Scattered references.

Reviews of *The Mansion:*
21   Anon., *Time,* Nov. 2, p. 90.
22   Waldon Porterfield, Milwaukee *Journal,* Nov. 8, Part V, p. 4.
23   Van Allen Bradley, *ChiDN,* Nov. 11, p. 8.
24   Orville Prescott, *NYT,* Nov. 13, p. 27.
25   Maurice Dolbier, *NYHT,* Nov. 14, p. 6.
26   Fanny Butcher, *ChiSTMB,* Nov. 15, p. 3.
27   Malcolm Cowley, *NYTBR,* Nov. 15, pp. 1, 18.
28   Harding Lemay, *NYHTBR,* Nov. 15, pp. 1, 14.
29   Hoke Norris, *ChiSunS-T,* Nov. 15, Sec. III, p. 1.
30   Gouverneur Paulding, *Reporter,* Nov. 26, pp. 41-44.
31   Anthony West, *NYr,* Dec. 5, pp. 236-243.

32   William Van O'Connor. *William Faulkner.* Minneapolis: University of Minnesota Press, 1959. No. 3 in the series: *Pamphlets on American Writers.*

33   Olga W. Vickery. *The Novels of William Faulkner.* Baton Rouge: Louisiana State University Press, 1959.

34   Hyatt H. Waggoner. *William Faulkner: From Jefferson to the World.* Lexington: University of Kentucky Press, 1959.

35   Stanley D. Woodworth. *William Faulkner en France (1931-1952).* Paris: Minard *Lettres Modernes,* 1959.

36   C. E. Zavaleta. *William Faulkner, novelista tragico.* Lima: Universidad Nacional Mayor de San Marcos, 1959.

37   Angela Giannitrapani. "Wistaria: le immagini in Faulkner." *Studi Americani 5.* Rome: Storia e Letteratura, 1959, 243-280.

38   Edith Hamilton. "Faulkner: Sorcerer or Slave?" *The* Saturday Review *Gallery,* ed. Jerome Beatty, Jr. New York: Simon and Schuster, 1959, 419-429.

39   R. W. B. Lewis. "William Faulkner: The Hero in the New World." *The Picaresque Saint.* Philadelphia: Lippincott, 1959, 179-219.

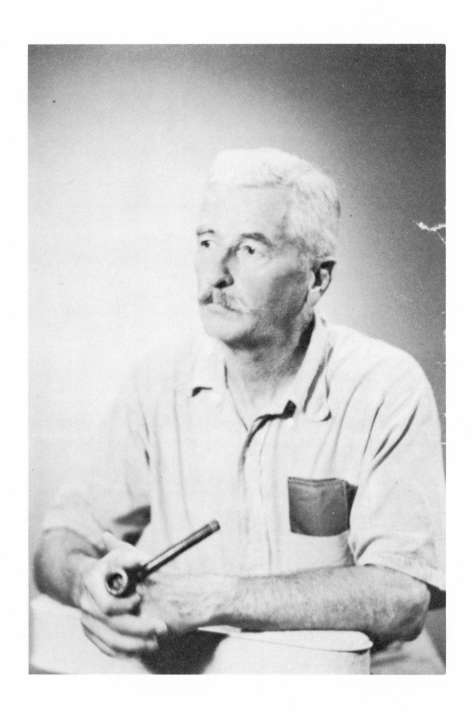

1960 (L20).
Courtesy J. R. Cofield.

40   William R. Mueller. "The Theme of Suffering: William Faulkner's *The Sound and the Fury." The Prophetic Voice in Modern Fiction.* New York: Association Press, 1959, 110-135.

41   Allen Tate. *Collected Essays.* Denver: Swallow, 1959. Scattered references.

42   Charlottesville, Virginia, City Map. (c. 1959) At this time Faulkner was a part-time resident.

1960

1   *Modern Fiction Studies,* V (Winter 1959-1960).
Includes:
Floyd C. Watkins and Thomas Daniel Young, "Revisions of Style in Faulkner's *The Hamlet,*" 327-336.
Donald Tritschler, "The Unity of Faulkner's Shaping Vision," 337-343.
Loic Bouvard, "Conversation with William Faulkner," 361-364.

2   Thomas H. Carter. Joint review of *The Mansion* and *The Novels of William Faulkner* by Olga W. Vickery. *Shenandoah,* XI (Winter 1960), 64-69.

3   Herbert A. Perluck. " 'The Heart's Driving Complexity': An Unromantic Reading of Faulkner's 'The Bear'." *Accent,* XX (Winter 1960), 23-46.

4   Ray B. West, Jr. "Faulkner's *Light in August:* A View of Tragedy." *Wisconsin Studies in Contemporary Literature,* I (Winter 1960), 5-12.

5   J. Robert Barth. "Faulkner and the Snopes Trilogy." *America,* CII (February 27, 1960), 638-640.

6   *Arizona Quarterly,* XVI (Spring 1960).
Includes:
Barbara M. Cross, *"The Sound and the Fury:* The Pattern of Sacrifice," 5-16.
J. L. Roberts, "The Individual and the Family: Faulkner's *As I Lay Dying,"* 26-38.
Allen Guttmann, "Collisions and Confrontations," 46-52.
Charles A. Allen, "William Faulkner: Comedy and the Purpose of Humor," 59-69.
Elmo Howell, "Faulkner's Jumblies: The Nonsense World of *As I Lay Dying,"* 70-78.

7   Warren Beck. "Faulkner in *The Mansion.*" *Virginia Quarterly Review,* XXXVI (Spring 1960), 272-292.

8   James B. Meriwether. "The Literary Career of William Faulkner: Catalogue of an Exhibition." *Princeton University Library Chronicle,* XXI (Spring 1960), 111-164.
    Included are twenty-one plates showing some of the more important pieces in the 1957 Princeton University Library exhibition.

9   Arthur Slobodin. "Faulkner's *Absalom, Absalom!*" *Amherst Review,* II (Spring 1960), 1-6.

10 Maurice Edgar Coindreau. "On Translating Faulkner." *Princeton Alumni Weekly,* LX (April 29, 1960), 3-4.

11 Elizabeth M. Kerr. "Snopes." *Wisconsin Studies in Contemporary Literature,* I (Spring-Summer 1960), 66-84.

12 Catherine Drinker Bowen. "Harold Ober, Literary Agent." *Atlantic Monthly,* CCVI (July 1960), 35-40.

13 Carvel Collins. "Miss Quentin's Paternity Again." Texas *Studies in Literature and Language,* II (Autumn 1960), 253-260. Offprint.

14 Frederick J. Hoffman and Olga W. Vickery, eds. *William Faulkner: Three Decades of Criticism.* East Lansing: Michigan State University Press, 1960.
    Contains:
    Frederick J. Hoffman, "William Faulkner: An Introduction," 1-50.
    Robert Cantwell, "The Faulkners: Recollections of a Gifted Family," 51-66.
    Jean Stein, "William Faulkner: An Interview," 67-82.
    George Marion O'Donnell, "Faulkner's Mythology," 82-93.
    Malcolm Cowley, "Introduction to *The Portable Faulkner,*" 94-109.
    Robert Penn Warren, "William Faulkner," 109-124.
    Ursula Brumm, "Wilderness and Civilization: A Note on William Faulkner," 125-134.
    Conrad Aiken, "William Faulkner: The Novel as Form," 135-142.
    Warren Beck, "William Faulkner's Style," 142-156.
    Jean-Jacques Mayoux, "The Creation of the Real in Faulkner," 156-173.
    Walter J. Slatoff, "The Edge of Order: The Pattern of Faulkner's Rhetoric," 173-198.
    Florence Leaver, "Faulkner: The Word as Principle and Power," 199-209.
    Lawrance Thompson, "Mirror Analogues in *The Sound and the Fury,*" 211-225.

Jean-Paul Sartre, "Time in Faulkner: *The Sound and the Fury*," 225-232.
Olga W. Vickery, "The Dimensions of Consciousness: *As I Lay Dying*," 232-247.
Alfred Kazin, "The Stillness of *Light in August*," 247-265.
John L. Longley, Jr., "Joe Christmas: The Hero in the Modern World," 265-278.
Ilse Dusoir Lind, "The Design and Meaning of *Absalom, Absalom!*," 278-304.
Joseph J. Moldenhauer, "Unity of Theme and Structure in *The Wild Palms*," 305-322.
William Van O'Connor, "The Wilderness Theme in Faulkner's 'The Bear'," 322-330.
T. Y. Greet, "The Theme and Structure of Faulkner's *The Hamlet*," 330-347.
William Faulkner, "The Stockholm Address," 347-348.
Heinrich Straumann, "An American Interpretation of Existence: Faulkner's *A Fable*," 349-372.
Philip Blair Rice, "Faulkner's Crucifixion," 373-381.
Steven Marcus, "Snopes Revisited," 382-391.

15   Walter J. Slatoff. *Quest for Failure: A Study of William Faulkner*. Ithaca: Cornell University Press, 1960.

16   Masao Takahashi. *William Faulkner*. Tokyo: Kenkyusha, 1960. In Japanese.

17   Carlos Baker. "William Faulkner: The Doomed and the Damned." *The Young Rebel in American Literature*, ed. Carl Bode. New York: Praeger, 1960, 145-169. Paperback PPS-26.

18   F. W. Dillistone. "The Friend Lays Down His Life." *The Novelist and the Passion Story*. London: Collins, 1960, 92-118. Discussion of *A Fable*.

19   Leslie A. Fiedler. *Love and Death in the American Novel*. New York: Criterion, 1960. References throughout.

20   Leon Howard. *Literature and the American Tradition*. Garden City: Doubleday, 1960, 318-323.

21   J. B. Priestley. *Literature and Western Man*. London: Heinemann, 1960. Scattered references.

22   Willard Thorp. "Southern Renaissance." *American Writing in the Twentieth Century*. Cambridge, Mass.: Harvard University Press, 1960, 263-274.

1   *Studies in Faulkner* (Carnegie Series in English No. 6), Pittsburgh: Carnegie Institute of Technology, 1961.
Contains:
Ann L. Hayes, "The World of *The Hamlet,"* 3-16.
Beekman W. Cottrell, "Faulkner's Cosmic *Fable:* The Extraordinary Family of Man," 17-27.
John A. Hart, "That Not Impossible He: Faulkner's Third-Person Narrator," 29-41.
Neal Woodruff, Jr., " 'The Bear' and Faulkner's Moral Vision," 43-67.
Ralph A. Ciancio, "Faulkner's Existentialist Affinities," 69-91.

2   W. T. Jewkes. "Counterpoint in Faulkner's *The Wild Palms." Wisconsin Studies in Contemporary Literature,* II (Winter 1961), 39-53.

3   Brian Way. "William Faulkner." *Critical Quarterly,* III (Spring 1961), 42-53. An English study in which *The Wild Palms* is designated "probably Faulkner's finest novel."

4   *Mississippi Quarterly,* XIV (Summer 1961).
Contains:
Harry M. Campbell, "William Faulkner: A New Look," 115-116.
Arlin Turner, "William Faulkner, Southern Novelist," 117-130.
Richard P. Adams, "Faulkner and the Myth of the South," 131-137.
Robert N. Burrows, "Institutional Christianity as Reflected in the Works of William Faulkner," 138-147.
Joe C. Shaw, "Sociological Aspects of Faulkner's Writing," 148-152.
Robert M. Slabey, "Faulkner's 'Waste Land' Vision in *Absalom, Absalom!,"* 153-161.
Also includes reviews of books dealing with Faulkner.

5   Joseph Gold. "Delusion and Redemption in Faulkner's *A Fable." Modern Fiction Studies,* VII (Summer 1961), 145-156.

6   Jere R. Hoar. "William Faulkner of Oxford, Mississippi." *Writer's Digest,* XLII (July 1961), 15-16, 77-78.

7   James B. Meriwether. "Some Notes on the Text of Faulkner's *Sanctuary." Papers of the Bibliographical Society of America,* LV (Third Quarter, 1961), 192-206. Offprint.

8   Melvin Backman. "The Wilderness and the Negro in Faulkner's 'The Bear'." *PMLA,* LXXVI (December 1961), 595-600.

9   Warren Beck. *Man in Motion: Faulkner's Trilogy.* Madison: University of Wisconsin Press, 1961. Issued without a jacket.

10   John B. Cullen in collaboration with Floyd C. Watkins. *Old Times in the Faulkner Country.* Chapel Hill: University of North Carolina Press, 1961.

11   Hiroshi Hayakawa. *Faulkner Studies: The Problem of Techniques and Styles.* Tokyo: Kenkyusha, 1961. In Japanese.

12   Frederick J. Hoffman. *William Faulkner.* New York: Twayne, 1961. No. 1 in Twayne's United States Authors Series.

13   James B. Meriwether. *The Literary Career of William Faulkner.* Princeton, N.J.: Princeton University Library, 1961. Thirty-three plates reproduce exhibits at the 1957 Princeton University Library Faulkner exhibition, including several manuscript pages.

14   Michael Millgate. *William Faulkner.* Edinburgh: Oliver and Boyd, 1961. No. 6 in the paperback Writers and Critics series. Inscribed by the author.

15   Edwin T. Bowden. *The Dungeon of the Heart.* New York: Macmillan, 1961, 124-138. Primarily on *Light in August.*

16   Donna Gerstenberger and George Hendrick. *The American Novel 1789-1959: A Checklist of Twentieth-Century Criticism.* Denver: Swallow, 1961, 71-89.

17   William Van O'Connor. "William Faulkner." *Tres escritores Norteamericanos.* Madrid: Gredos, 1961, 51-93. Trans. Angela Figuera. Wrappers. Contains Spanish translations of the University of Minnesota pamphlets on Hemingway, Faulkner, Frost.

18   Danforth Ross. *The American Short Story.* Minneapolis: University of Minnesota Press, 1961, 36-37. No. 14 in the series: *Pamphlets on American Writers.*

19   Kenneth Tynan. *Curtains.* New York: Atheneum, 1961, 276-278, 299-301. Reviews of English and American productions of *Requiem for a Nun.*

20   Stanley M. Vogel and Ella M. Murphy. "William Faulkner." *An Outline of American Literature,* Volume II. Boston: Student Outlines, 1961, 268-281.

21   *Studi Americani 7.* Rome: Storia e Letteratura, 1961.
Includes:
Glauco Cambon, "Stile e percezione del numinoso in un racconto di Faulkner," 147-162.
Mario Materassi, "Faulkner e la presentazione del personaggio," 163-193.

- -

THE WHITE HOUSE

STATEMENT BY THE PRESIDENT

It can be said with assurance of few men, in any area of human activity that their work will long endure. William Faulkner was one of those men. Since Henry James no writer has left behind such a vast and enduring monument to the strength of American literature. His death came in Oxford, Mississippi, in the heart of the setting for that turbulent world of light and shadow which was the towering creation of his mind and art. From this world he sought to illuminate the restless searching of all men. And his insight spoke to the hearts of all who listened.

A Mississippian by birth, an American by virtue of those forces and loyalties which guided his work, a guiding citizen of our civilization by virtue of his art, William Faulkner now rests, the search done, his place secure among the great creators of this age.

# # # #

President Kennedy's tribute (1962.18).

22 Joan Williams. *The Morning and the Evening.* New York: Atheneum, 1961. First novel by Faulkner's close friend.

1962

1 *Wisconsin Studies in Contemporary Literature,* III (Winter 1962).
Includes:
Elizabeth M. Kerr, *"As I Lay Dying* as Ironic Quest," 5-19.
Joseph Gold, "The 'Normality' of Snopesism: Universal Themes in
Faulkner's *The Hamlet,"* 25-34.

2 M. E. Bradford. "Faulkner's 'Tall Men'." *South Atlantic Quarterly,*
LXI (Winter 1962), 29-39.

3 Program, The American Academy of Arts and Letters and The
National Institute of Arts and Letters Ceremonial, May 24, 1962.
William Faulkner was awarded the Gold Medal for Fiction.

4 *Book-of-the-Month Club News,* June 1962. Essay by Clifton Fadiman
on choosing *The Reivers* as the July selection.

Reviews of *The Reivers:*
5   George Plimpton, *NYHT Books,* May 27, p. 3.
6   Anon., *McCalls,* June, pp. 12, 14.
7   Van Allen Bradley, *ChiDN,* June 2, p. 20.
8   Granville Hicks, *SR,* June 2, p. 27.
9   Irving Howe, *NYTBR,* June 3, pp. 1, 24-25.
10   R. A. Jelliffe, *ChiSTMB,* June 3, pp. 1-2.
11   Hoke Norris, *ChiSunS-T,* June 3, Sec. III, pp. 1, 3.
12   Anon., *Newsweek,* June 4, p. 100.
13   Anon., *Time,* June 4, p. 92.
14   Hilary Corke, *NR,* July 16, pp. 20-22.

15 Alwyn Berland. *"Light in August:* The Calvinism of William Faulkner."
Modern Fiction Studies, VIII (Summer 1962), pp. 159-170.

16 Allene Talmey. "William Faulkner at West Point." *Vogue,* CXL (July
1962), 70-73, 114, 116.

17 Faulkner's death.
Scrapbook containing newspaper and magazine clippings on Faulkner's
death, July 6, 1962, primarily from Oxford, Charlottesville, Memphis,
New Orleans, New York, and Chicago.

18 July 6, 1962. President John F. Kennedy's press release of tribute at
the time of Faulkner's death. Released by the Office of the White
House Press Secretary.

19   July 7, 1962. Broadside announcing memorial business closings in Oxford for a fifteen minute period on the afternoon of Faulkner's burial.

20   *Life,* LIII (July 20, 1962). Coverage of Faulkner's death includes: Editorial, "Faulkner's Legacy: 'Honor, Pity, Pride'," p. 4. William Styron, "As He Lay Dead, a Bitter Grief," 39-42.

21   *Saturday Review,* XLV (July 28, 1962). "A Special Section." Includes: Hamilton Basso, "William Faulkner: Man and Writer," 11-14. Lenore Marshall, "The Power of Words," 16, 17. Ruth Brown, "The Falkners of Mississippi," 17. Also includes photographs, caricatures, and reprints of material by and about Faulkner.

22   Sidney Finkelstein. "William Faulkner." *Mainstream,* XV (August 1962), 3-6.

23   Harold B. Meyers. "Faulkner." *USA*1,* I (August 1962), 49-53. Color portrait photograph by Vytas Valaitis, 48.

24   Richard Gilman. "Faulkner's Yes and No." *Commonweal,* LXXVI (August 10, 1962), 449-450.

25   W. J. Weatherby. "The Private Genius of William Faulkner." *The Novel Today,* program of the International Writers' Conference, Edinburgh International Festival 1962. (August 20-24).

26   Anne Taillefer. "As Faulkner Lies Dead." *The Catholic Worker,* XXIX (September, 1962), 2, 8.

27   *Emporia State Research Studies,* XI (September 1962). Contains: Robert L. Dorsch, "An Interpretation of the Central Themes in the Work of William Faulkner," 5-42. Dorothy D. Greer, "Dilsey and Lucas: Faulkner's Use of the Negro as a Gauge of Moral Character," 43-61.

28   *Mississippi Library News,* XXVI (September 1962). C. Hugh Holman, "William Faulkner Wrote of the Heart in Conflict with Itself," 99. Paul Flowers, "William Faulkner—Paradoxes or Contrasts?" 100-103.

29   Gay Wilson Allen. "With Faulkner in Japan." *American Scholar,* XXXI (Autumn 1962), 566-571.

30   James B. Meriwether. "Notes on the Textual History of *The Sound and the Fury." Papers of the Bibliographical Society of America,* LVI (Third Quarter, 1962), 285-316. Offprint.

31   John Pilkington, Jr. "William Faulkner and the University." *Ole Miss Alumni Review,* XV (October 1962), 2-5.

32   *William Faulkner: Henry Goverts Verlag.* Memorial (and promotional) pamphlet prepared after Faulkner's death by his German publisher, 24 pp.

33   Calvin S. Brown. "Faulkner's Geography and Topography." *PMLA,* LXXVII (December 1962), 652-659.

34   Martin Christadler. *Natur und Geschichte im Werk von William Faulkner.* Heidelberg: Carl Winter, 1962. (Jahrbuch für Amerikastudien, No. 8.)

35   Irving Howe. *William Faulkner: A Critical Study.* Second edition, revised and expanded. New York: Vintage (February 1962). Vintage paperback V-213.

36   Charles H. Nilon. *Faulkner and the Negro.* Boulder: University of Colorado Press, September 1962. University of Colorado Studies, Series in Language and Literature, No. 8. Paperback.

37   Irene Lynn Sleeth. *William Faulkner: A Bibliography of Criticism.* Denver: Swallow, 1962. Swallow Pamphlet Number 13.

38   Peter Swiggart. *The Art of Faulkner's Novels.* Austin: University of Texas Press, 1962.

39   Peter Bogdanovich. *the cinema of howard hawks.* New York: Film Library of the Museum of Modern Art, 1962, 13, 15, 23, 25, 33.

40   Deming Brown. *Soviet Attitudes Toward American Literature.* Princeton, N.J.: Princeton University Press, 1962. References throughout.

41   Leon Edel. "How to Read *The Sound and the Fury." Varieties of Literary Experience.* New York: New York University Press, 1962, 241-257.

42   Granville Hicks, ed. *The Living Novel: A Symposium.* New York: Collier, 1962. A paperback. Articles by ten writers with scattered references to Faulkner.

43   Isaac Rosenfeld. "Faulkner's Two Styles." *An Age of Enormity.* Cleveland: World, 1962, 268-272.

44   Colin Wilson. "William Faulkner." *The Strength to Dream.* London: Gollancz, 1962, 49-51, other scattered references.

45   James Woodress. *Dissertations in American Literature, 1891-1955,*

with Supplement, 1956-1961. Durham, N.C.: Duke University Press, 1962. Listings of dissertations on Faulkner on pp. 17-18 and 90-91, with other scattered references.

1963

1 "William Faulkner—A Moral Vision, by John James Stanfield." Adult evening school course announcement in the Chicago *Central YMCA Schools Bulletin,* Winter Term 1963, p. 10.

2 Charles R. Anderson. "William Faulkner." *Johns Hopkins Magazine,* XIV (February 1963), 17, 18, 24-27. Portrait drawing by Leonard Baskin, p. 16.

3 Aurelio Pego. "Lo que se desconocía de William Faulkner." *Horizontes,* VI (February 15—April 15, 1963), 6-7. Published in Mexico City.

4 Walter B. Rideout and James B. Meriwether. "On the Collaboration of Faulkner and Anderson." *American Literature,* XXXV (March 1963), 85-87.

5 Cleanth Brooks. "History, Tragedy, and the Imagination in *Absalom, Absalom!" Yale Review,* LII (Spring 1963), 340-351.

6 Richard Ellmann. "Faulkner as 'The Count'." *Dimension: Daily Northwestern* Supplement, May 27, 1963, 3, 4.

7 William J. Sowder. "Faulkner and Existentialism: A Note on the Generalissimo." *Wisconsin Studies in Contemporary Literature,* IV (Spring-Summer 1963), 163-171.

8 James B. Meriwether. "The Text of Faulkner's Books: An Introduction and Some Notes." *Modern Fiction Studies,* IX (Summer 1963), 159-170. Offprint.

9 Daniel Weiss. "William Faulkner and the Runaway Slave." *Northwest Review,* VI (Summer 1963), 71-79.

10 Robert N. Linscott. "Faulkner Without Fanfare." *Esquire,* LX (July 1963), 36, 38.

11 Hughes Rudd. "The Death of William Faulkner." *Saturday Evening Post,* CCXXXVI (July 13-20, 1963), 32-34, 37.

12 Nancy Hale. "Col. Sartoris and Mr. Snopes." *Vogue,* CXLII (August 1, 1963), 112, 113, 135, 136, 138, 139.

13   Martin J. Dain. "Faulkner Country." *Life,* LV (August 2, 1963), 46B-53. A photographic essay.

14   Richard Hughes. "Faulkner and Bennett." *Encounter,* XXI (September 1963), 59-61.

15   Joseph Blotner. "William Faulkner's Name Was in the Books He Loved Best." New York *Times Book Review,* December 8, 1963, 4-5, 45.

16   Bradford Daniel. "Faulkner on Race." *Ramparts,* II (Christmas 1963), 43-49. Quotes extensively from Faulkner letters and speeches.

17   Cleanth Brooks. *William Faulkner: The Yoknapatawpha Country.* New Haven: Yale, 1963.

18   Margaret Patricia Ford and Suzanne Kincaid. *Who's Who in Faulkner.* Baton Rouge: L. S. U., 1963.

19   Robert W. Kirk and Marvin Klotz. *Faulkner's People: A Complete Guide and Index to the Characters in the Fiction of William Faulkner.* Berkeley: University of California Press, 1963.

20   John Lewis Longley, Jr. *The Tragic Mask: A Study of Faulkner's Heroes.* Chapel Hill: University of North Carolina Press, 1963.

21   Monique Nathan. *Faulkner par lui-même.* Paris: Editions du Seuil, 1963. Paperback.

22   James L. Roberts. The Sound and the Fury *Notes.* Lincoln, Nebr.: Cliff's Notes, 1963.

23   Lawrance Thompson. *William Faulkner: An Introduction and Interpretation.* New York: Barnes and Noble, 1963.

24   *William Faulkner: An Introduction and Interpretation.* Another copy, Barnes and Noble paperback AC 10.

25   Brooks Atkinson. *Tuesdays and Fridays.* New York: Random House, 1963, 244-246, 260-262.

26   Cleanth Brooks. *The Hidden God: Studies in Hemingway, Faulkner, Yeats, Eliot, and Warren.* New Haven: Yale, 1963, 22-43 with other scattered references.

27   Hodding Carter. "Faulkner and His Folk." *First Person Rural.* Garden City: Doubleday, 1963, 71-85. A reprint of the piece from the Spring 1957 issue of the *Princeton University Library Chronicle.*

28   Chester E. Eisinger. *Fiction of the Forties.* Chicago: University of Chicago, 1963. References throughout, particularly pp. 178-186.

29 Martin Green. "Faulkner: the Triumph of Rhetoric." *Re-appraisals: Some Commonsense Readings in American Literature.* London: Hugh Evelyn, 1963, 167-195.

30 Robert F. Griffin. "Ethical Point of View in *The Sound and the Fury.*" *Essays in Modern American Literature,* ed. Richard E. Langford. DeLand, Florida: Stetson University Press, 1963. Issued without a jacket.

31 D. E. S. Maxwell. *American Fiction: The Intellectual Background.* London: Routledge and Kegan Paul, 1963, 275-278.

32 Boris Randolph. William Faulkner Crossword Puzzle. *50 American Authors* (Educational Crossword Puzzle Series: Volume I). New York: Pocket Books, (August 1963), 161-164.

33 Louis D. Rubin, Jr. *The Faraway Country: Writers of the Modern South.* Seattle: University of Washington Press, 1963. References throughout, especially pp. 43-71.

34 Maurice Sands and Paul A. Doyle. "William Faulkner." *An Outline of the Modern American Novel,* Revised ed. Boston: Student Outlines, 1963, 82-99.

1964

1 Donald M. Kartiganer. "The Role of Myth in *Absalom, Absalom!*" *Modern Fiction Studies,* IX (Winter 1963-1964), 357-369.

2 Esther M. Swift. "The Author—William Faulkner." *The Booklover's Answer No. 10,* (March-April 1964), 24-27, 30. Includes a checklist of incredible inaccuracy.

3 "The Curse and the Hope." *Time,* LXXXIV (July 17, 1964), 44-48. Cover story on Faulkner and the South.

4 *Mississippi Quarterly,* XVII (Summer 1964). Special issue: William Faulkner. Contains:
Gordon Price-Stephens, "Faulkner and the Royal Air Force," 123-128.
Mary Jane Dickerson, *"As I Lay Dying* and *The Waste Land*—Some Relationships," 129-135.
James B. Meriwether, "Early Notices of Faulkner by Phil Stone and Louis Cochran," 136-164.
Also: Reviews of books dealing with Faulkner.

5 Esperanza Aguilar. *Yoknapatawpha, propiedad de William Faulkner.*

Santiago: University of Chile, 1964.

6 *William Faulkner's Library—A Catalogue,* comp. Joseph Blotner. Charlottesville: University Press of Virginia, 1964. Issued in tissue wrapper.

7 Assis Brasil. *Faulkner e a técnica do romance.* Rio de Janeiro: Editôra Leitura, 1964.

8 Carvel Collins. *William Faulkner,* The Sound and the Fury. *Voice of America Forum Lectures: American Novel Series, 19.* c. 1964. Pamphlet.

9 Vartkis Kinoian. The Sound and the Fury *and Other Novels by Faulkner.* New York: Monarch Press, 1964. Study Guide 613.

10 James L. Roberts. Absalom, Absalom! *Notes.* Lincoln, Nebr.: Cliff's Notes, 1964.

11 James L. Roberts. As I Lay Dying *Notes.* Lincoln, Nebr.: Cliff's Notes, 1964.

12 James L. Roberts. Light in August *Notes.* Lincoln, Nebr.: Cliff's Notes, 1964.

13 Carol Z. Rothkopf, Series Consultant. *A Critical Commentary:* The Sound and the Fury. New York: American R. D. M., 1964. Study Master 448.

14 Harry Runyan. *A Faulkner Glossary.* New York: Citadel Press, 1964. Inscribed by Runyan.

15 Dorothy Tuck. *Crowell's Handbook of Faulkner.* New York: Crowell, 1964. Introduction by Lewis Leary.

16 *Bear, Man, and God: Seven Approaches to William Faulkner's "The Bear,"* ed. Francis Lee Utley, Lynn Z. Bloom, and Arthur F. Kinney. New York: Random House, 1964. Large paperback. Includes complete texts of two versions of "The Bear," the Nobel Prize Speech, and "Delta Autumn." Also includes material from several sources relating to "The Bear." A critical work rather than an anthology.

17 Olga W. Vickery. *The Novels of William Faulkner: A Critical Interpretation.* Baton Rouge: L. S. U., 1964. Revised edition of the 1959 title.

18 Edmond L. Volpe. *A Reader's Guide to William Faulkner.* New York: Farrar, Straus, 1964.

19 Walter Allen. *Tradition and Dream: The English and American Novel from the Twenties to Our Time.* London: Phoenix House, 1964, pp. 112-124.

20 Richard Armour. "William Faulkner." *American Lit Relit.* New York: McGraw Hill, 1964, pp. 154-158.

21 *Opinions and Perspectives from* The New York Times Book Review, ed. Francis Brown. Boston: Houghton Mifflin, 1964. Includes:
Irving Howe, "A Talent of Wild Abundance," 194-198.
Joseph Blotner, "The Books He Loved Best," 198-204.

22 Bradford Daniel. "William Faulkner and the Southern Quest for Freedom." *Black, White and Gray,* ed. Bradford Daniel. New York: Sheed and Ward, 1964, 291-308. Expanded from the 1963 *Ramparts* article.

23 Harriet Doar. "Interview with William Styron." *Red Clay Reader,* ed. Charleen Whisnat. Charlotte, N. C.: Southern Review, 1964, 26-30. Scattered references to Faulkner.

24 Leslie A. Fiedler. *Waiting for the End.* New York: Stein and Day, 1964. References throughout.

25 John Edward Hardy. "William Faulkner: The Legend Behind the Legend." *Man in the Modern Novel.* Seattle: University of Washington, 1964, 137-158. Washington paperback WP-13.

26 Arthur Mizener. *The Sense of Life in the Modern Novel.* Boston: Houghton Mifflin, 1964. References throughout; pp. 161-181 are adapted from the essay that appeared in the Autumn 1955 issue of *Kenyon Review.*

27 Geoffrey Moore. *American Literature and the American Imagination.* Hull, England: University of Hull, 1964. A pamphlet with references on 15-16.

28 Louis D. Rubin, Jr. "Notes on a Rear-Guard Action." *The Idea of the South: Pursuit of a Central Theme,* ed. Frank E. Vandiver. Chicago: University of Chicago Press, 1964, 27-41.

29 James W. Silver. *Mississippi: The Closed Society.* New York: Harcourt, Brace, and World, 1964. On p. xii appears the three paragraph addition Faulkner made, December 1, 1955, to the speech he had given before the Southern Historical Association on November 10, 1955. Other references to Faulkner appear.

30 *Reality and Myth: Essays in American Literature,* ed. William E. Walker and Robert L. Welker. Nashville: Vanderbilt University Press, 1964. Includes:
Robert L. Welker, *"Liebestod* with a Southern Accent," 179-211.
Frances Bowen Durrett, "The New Orleans *Double Dealer,"* 212-236.
O. B. Emerson, "Prophet Next Door," 237-274.
William E. Walker, *"The Unvanquished*—The Restoration of Tradition,"

275-297.

31 *Studi Americani 9.* Rome: Storia e Letteratura, 1964. Includes:
Mario Materassi, "Le immagini in *Soldiers' Pay*," 353-370.
Hans Bungert, "William Faulkner on *Moby-Dick:* An Early Letter,"
371-376.

1965

1 Maurice Edgar Coindreau. "The Faulkner I Knew." *Shenandoah,* XVI
(Winter 1965), 27-35. Includes texts of three Faulkner letters. (See
E4a, 6a, 7a.)

2 Louis Kronenberger. "Gambler in Publishing: Horace Liveright." *Atlantic Monthly,* CCXV (January 1965), 94-104.

3 H. Edward Richardson. "Oxford, Mississippi." *Books and Bookmen,*
X (February 1965), 39-40, 48, 33.

4 M. E. Bradford. "Escaping Westward: Faulkner's 'Golden Land'." *Georgia Review,* XIX (Spring 1965), 72-76.

5 Victor Strandberg. "Faulkner's Poor Parson and the Technique of In-
version." *Sewanee Review,* LXXIII (Spring 1965), 181-190.

6 *Mid-South Magazine:* Memphis *Commercial Appeal,* Sunday, April 4,
1965. Includes:
Thomas E. Michael, "Yoknapatawpha County Today," 6-7, 16-17.
William Boozer, "The Last Eight Are Hard to Find," 8, 31.

7 The William Faulkner Room: West Point. Invitation to the dedication
of the William Faulkner Room at the Library of the United States Military Academy at West Point, New York. With dedication program:
"20 April 1965—1315 hours."

8 *A Tribute to William Faulkner.* Program Leaflet, Southern Literary
Festival, 1965. University of Mississippi, April 22-24, 1965. Announced
speakers: Malcolm Cowley, Martin Dain, Ruth Ford, Robert Penn Warren, Eudora Welty.

9 The Oxford *Eagle,* April 22, 1965. William Faulkner Souvenir Edition.
Coincides with the Southern Literary Festival; reprints several pieces
by and about Faulkner that had appeared in earlier issues of the *Eagle.*

10 *Arizona Quarterly,* XXI (Summer 1965). Includes:
Glenn O. Carey, "William Faulkner as a Critic of Society," 101-108.
James F. Farnham, "Faulkner's Unsung Hero: Gavin Stevens," 115-

132.

H. Edward Richardson, "The Ways That Faulkner Walked: A Pilgrimage," 133-145.

Louise Dauner, "Quentin and the Walking Shadow: The Dilemma of Nature and Culture," 159-171.

11 *Mississippi Quarterly,* XVIII (Summer 1965). Special Issue. Entire contents:

Gordon Price-Stephens, "The British Reception of William Faulkner 1929-1962," 119-200.

12 *Modern Fiction Studies,* XI (Summer 1965). Includes:

Lawrence Bowling, "Faulkner: The Theme of Pride in *The Sound and the Fury,*" 129-139.

Charles Mitchell, "The Wounded Will of Faulkner's Barn Burner," 185-189.

13 Robert Penn Warren. "Faulkner: The South and the Negro." *Southern Review,* I New Series (Summer 1965), 501-529.

14 *The Delta Review: The Magazine of Memphis & the Mid-South,* II (July-August 1965). Faulkner issue, reporting on the April Southern Literary Festival. Includes:

Jane Sanderson, "A Kind of Greatness," 15, 17.

Robert Allen Carpenter, "Faulkner 'Discovered'," 27-29.

J. Giorgini, "Faulkner and Camus," 31, 74-79.

Lelia Clark Wynn, "A Bookman's Faulkner," 33, 35, 57.

Edwin Howard, "The Faithful Smith," 34-35, and "Foote-note on Faulkner," 37, 80.

Lucy Somerville Howorth, "The Bill Faulkner I Knew," 38-39, 73.

Jack Ryan, "The Lady of the Dakota," 44-45, 71-72.

Leon Z. Koury, "The Spark and the Flame," 46-47.

Kenneth R. Tolliver, "Truth and the Poet," 48, 67-69.

Also William Faulkner, "The Rights of Man," 40, 42. (The 1952 Delta Council speech.)

15 Program of the Philadelphia Orchestra concerts of September 23, 24, 25, 1965. Includes the World Premiere of David Diamond's "Elegies for Flute, English Horn and Strings." The first Elegy was written in memory of William Faulkner, the second in memory of e. e. cummings.

16 Eudora Welty. "Must the Novelist Crusade?" *Atlantic Monthly,* CCXVI (October 1965), 104-108.

17 Emily Whitehurst Stone. "How a Writer Finds His Material," *Harper's Magazine,* CCXXXI (November 1965), 157-161.

18 Oxford, Mississippi Telephone Directory, December, 1965. Three

years after his death a telephone is still registered to William Falkner.

19 *Faulkner's Mississippi: Land into Legend.* 16 mm sound film, narrated by Joseph Cotten, thirty-two minute running time. Educational Film Production of the University of Mississippi, 1965.

20 Thomas Goethals. As I Lay Dying: *A Critical Commentary.* New York: American R. D. M., 1965. Study Master 403.

21 Thomas Goethals. Light in August: *A Critical Commentary.* New York: American R. D. M., 1965. Study Master 404.

22 John W. Hunt. *William Faulkner: Art in Theological Tension.* Syracuse: Syracuse University Press, 1965.

23 Leslie A. Juhasz. *William Faulkner's* Light in August. New York: Monarch Press, 1965. Study Guide 666-8.

24 Michael Millgate. *The Achievement of William Faulkner.* London: Constable, 1965. Inscibed by Millgate in Chicago, July 1965.
This original issue of Millgate's important study was withdrawn by the publisher when it was discovered that the published book was mutilated by misprints that had not appeared in proof. Only a few copies of the 1965 issue survive and are in brown dust jacket. A corrected edition (in green jacket) was issued in 1966.

25 Charles H. Nilon. *Faulkner and the Negro.* New York: Citadel, 1965. A commercial paperback edition of the University of Colorado study of September 1962.

26 Elizabeth G. Phillips. *William Faulkner's* Absalom, Absalom! New York: Monarch Press, 1965. Study Guide 664-3.

27 George K. Smart. *Religious Elements in Faulkner's Early Novels: A Selective Concordance.* Coral Gables: University of Miami Press, 1965.

28 James W. Webb and A. Wigfall Green, eds. *William Faulkner of Oxford.* Baton Rouge: L. S. U. Press, 1965. Reminiscences by Faulkner's neighbors. Two whimsical "documents" devised by Faulkner concerning the ship *Minmagary* appear reproduced on 232-234.

29 *William Faulkner of Oxford.* Another copy; Louisiana Paperback L-43.

30 Kenneth Allsop. "The Farmer Who Scribbled a Bit on the Side." *Scan.* London: Hodder and Stoughton, 1965, pp. 54-58.

31 Douglas Grant. "The Last of William Faulkner." *Purpose and Place: Essays on American Writers.* London: Macmillan, 1965, 183-188.

32 J. Maclaren-Ross. *Memoirs of the Forties.* London: Alan Ross, 1965, p. 10.

33   Lewis P. Simpson. "Isaac McCaslin and Temple Drake: The Fall of New World Man." *Nine Essays in Modern Literature,* ed. Donald E. Stanford. Baton Rouge: L. S. U., 1965, 88-106.

1966

1   *Georgia Review,* XX (Winter 1966). Includes:
Calvin S. Brown, "Faulkner's Manhunts: Fact into Fiction," 388-395.
M. E. Bradford, "Faulkner, James Baldwin, and the South," 431-443.
M. Thomas Inge, ed., "Donald Davidson on Faulkner: An Early Recognition," 454-462.

2   Michael Millgate. "William Faulkner, Cadet." *University of Toronto Quarterly,* XXXV (January 1966), 117-132.

3   Kenneth Allsop. "Small, Sad and Silver." *Books and Bookmen,* XI (February 1966), 10-11, 63-64.

4   Thomas N. Walters. "On Teaching William Faulkner's 'Was'." *English Journal,* LV (February 1966), 182-188.

5   Rosemary Franklin. "Animal Magnetism in *As I Lay Dying.*" *American Quarterly,* XVIII (Spring 1966), 24-34.

6   Malcolm Cowley. "The Solitude of William Faulkner." *Atlantic,* CCXVII (June 1966), 97-98, 101-106, 108-115. A prepublication extract from *The Faulkner-Cowley File.*

7   Pyotr Palievsky. "Hemingway and Faulkner: A Russian View." *Soviet Life,* June 1966, 58-59.

8   *Mississippi Quarterly,* XIX (Summer 1966). Special Issue: William Faulkner. Contains:
Maurice Coindreau, "Preface to *The Sound and the Fury,*" 107-115. Tr. George M. Reeves.
Thomas L. McHaney, "Faulkner Borrows from the Mississippi Guide," 116-120.
Joyce M. Warren, "Faulkner's *Portrait of the Artist,*" 121-131.
Mary Jane Dickerson, "Some Sources of Faulkner's Myth in *As I Lay Dying,*" 132-142.
Michel Gresset, "Psychological Aspects of Evil in *The Sound and the Fury,*" 143-153.
Also: A brief review by James B. Colvert of *Essays, Speeches, and Public Letters,* 154-155.

9   Joseph Blotner. "William Faulkner, Roving Ambassador." *International*

Educational and Cultural Exchange, Summer 1966, 1-22.

10   Patrick G. Hogan, Jr., Dale A. Myers, John E. Turner. "Muste's 'Failure of Love' in Faulkner's *Go Down, Moses.*" *Modern Fiction Studies,* XII (Summer 1966), 267-270.

11   Richard Pearce. "Faulkner's One Ring Circus." *Wisconsin Studies in Contemporary Literature,* VII (Autumn 1966), 270-283.

12   Warren B. Benson. "Faulkner for the High School: 'Turnabout'." *English Journal,* LV (October 1966), 867-869, 874.

13   Melvin Backman. *Faulkner: The Major Years.* Bloomington: Indiana University Press, 1966.

14   Malcolm Cowley. *The Faulkner-Cowley File.* New York: Viking, 1966. Includes texts of several Faulkner letters and two speeches.

15   *The Faulkner-Cowley File.* Another copy. London: Chatto & Windus, 1966.

16   Joseph Gold. *William Faulkner: A Study in Humanism, from Metaphor to Discourse.* Norman: University of Oklahoma, 1966.

17   Edward M. Holmes. *Faulkner's Twice-Told Tales.* The Hague: Mouton, 1966.

18   Michael Millgate. *The Achievement of William Faulkner.* London: Constable, 1966. The corrected "first" edition.

19   *The Achievement of William Faulkner.* Another copy. New York: Random House, 1966. In dust jacket indicating "5/66"; together with a jacket for the originally intended American issue of "4/65."

20   Harry Runyan. *A Faulkner Glossary.* New York: Citadel, 1966. First paperback issue of the title; published hardbound in 1964.

21   Harry Runyan. Absalom, Absalom!: *A Critical Commentary.* New York: American R. D. M., 1966. Study Master 406.

22   *Faulkner: A Collection of Critical Essays,* ed. Robert Penn Warren. Englewood Cliffs, N. J.: Prentice-Hall, 1966. Includes the first appearance of an introduction by Warren, "Faulkner: Past and Present," as well as reprints of over twenty essays by American and European critics.

23   *Faulkner: A Collection of Critical Essays.* Another copy; Spectrum paperback S-TC-65, 1966.

24   John W. Aldridge. *Time to Murder and Create: The Contemporary Novel in Crisis.* New York: David McKay, 1966. References throughout.

25 Arnold Chapman. *The Spanish American Reception of United States Fiction.* Berkeley and Los Angeles: University of California Press, 1966, 127-150, 216-220. Volume 77 of University of California Publications in Modern Philology; wrappers.

26 Warren French. *The Social Novel at the End of an Era.* Carbondale: Southern Illinois University, 1966. References throughout.

27 C. Hugh Holman. "William Faulkner: The Anguished Dream of Time." *Three Modes of Modern Southern Fiction.* Athens, (Ga.): University of Georgia Press, 1966, 27-47; other references.

28 Irving Howe. "Faulkner and the Negroes." *Images of the Negro in American Literature,* ed. Seymour L. Gross and John Edward Hardy. Chicago: University of Chicago Press, 1966, 204-220.

29 Richard D. Lehan. *F. Scott Fitzgerald and the Craft of Fiction.* Carbondale, Ill.: S. I. U. Press, 1966, 45-48.

30 Andrew Lytle. *The Hero with the Private Parts.* Baton Rouge: L. S. U. Press, 1966, 103-147. Reprints reviews of *A Fable, Intruder in the Dust, The Town.*

31 D. Z. Phillips. *The Concept of Prayer.* New York: Schocken, 1966, 64-66, 132-134.

32 Katherine M. Rogers. *The Troublesome Helpmate: A History of Misogyny in Literature.* Seattle: University of Washington Press, 1966, 252-257.

33 Dan Brennan. *Cathy's Way.* New York: Tower, 1966. On the back cover of this paperback is a photograph of the author with Faulkner taken years earlier during one of Brennan's two visits to Faulkner's Oxford home.

1967

1 Addison C. Bross. *"Soldiers' Pay* and the Art of Aubrey Beardsley." *American Quarterly,* XIX (Spring 1967), 3-23.

2 *Modern Fiction Studies,* XIII (Spring 1967). William Faulkner Number; contains:
David M. Miller, "Faulkner's Women," 3-17.
Eric Larsen, "The Barrier of Language: The Irony of Language in Faulkner," 19-31.
Catherine B. Baum, "'The Beautiful One': Caddy Compson as Heroine of *The Sound and the Fury,"* 33-44.

John V. Hagopian, "Nihilism in Faulkner's *The Sound and the Fury.*" 45-55.

R. W. Franklin, "Narrative Management in *As I Lay Dying,*" 57-65.

Frank Baldanza, "The Structure of *Light in August,*" 67-78.

Floyd C. Watkins, "What Happens in *Absalom, Absalom!?,*" 79-87.

John Feaster, "Faulkner's *Old Man:* A Psychoanalytic Approach," 89-93.

Elizabeth M. Kerr, *"The Reivers:* The Golden Book of Yoknapatawpha County," 95-113.

Maurice Beebe, "Criticism of William Faulkner: A Selected Checklist," 115-161.

3   Jay Robert Nash. "One of Faulkner's People." *Chicago Omnibus and FM Guide,* IV (May 1967), 54-57.

4   *Mississippi Quarterly,* XX (Summer 1967). Special Issue: William Faulkner. Contains:

Nancy Dew Taylor, "The Dramatic Productions of *Requiem for a Nun,*" 123-134.

James M. Mellard, "The Biblical Rhythm of *Go Down, Moses,*" 135-147.

Carolyn H. Reeves, *"The Wild Palms:* Faulkner's Chaotic Cosmos," 148-157.

M. E. Bradford, "On the Importance of Discovering God: Faulkner and Hemingway's *The Old Man and the Sea,*" 158-162.

Matthew Bruccoli, "A Source for *Sartoris?,*" 163.

Bruce Harkness, "Faulkner and Scott," 164.

James B. Meriwether, "A Source in Balzac for *The Unvanquished,*" 165-166.

Wilmuth S. Rutledge, "How Colonel Falkner Built His Railroad," 166-170.

Also: Reviews of books dealing with Faulkner.

5   Hilda Nauman. "How Faulkner Went His Way and I Went Mine." *Esquire,* LXVIII (December, 1967), 173-175.

6   Kenneth E. Richardson. *Force and Faith in the Novels of William Faulkner.* The Hague: Mouton, 1967.

7   Joseph Blotner. "Faulkner in Hollywood." *Man and the Movies,* ed. W. R. Robinson. Baton Rouge: L. S. U. Press, 1967, 261-303.

8   *Fifty Works of English Literature We Could Do Without,* selected by Brigid Brophy, Michael Levey, Charles Osborne. London: Rapp & Carroll, 1967, pp. 145-146. The Faulkner selection is *The Sound and the Fury,* though anathema is pronounced on his entire output.

9   Stanley Cooperman. *World War I and the American Novel.* Baltimore:

Johns Hopkins, 1967, pp. 159-162; other scattered references.

10 Malcolm Cowley. *Think Back on Us...A Contemporary Chronicle of the 1930's.* Carbondale: Southern Illinois University Press, 1967. Reprints Cowley's reviews of *Pylon,* pp. 268-271, and *The Hamlet,* pp. 358-360.

11 Corey Ford. *The Time of Laughter.* Boston: Little, Brown, 1967. Scattered references including a reprint of the Covarrubias caricature of Faulkner.

12 *Essays on American Literature in Honor of Jay B. Hubbell,* ed. Clarence Gohdes. Durham: Duke University Press, 1967. Scattered references.

13 James Guetti. *"Absalom, Absalom!:* The Failure of Imagination." *The Limits of Metaphor: A Study of Melville, Conrad, and Faulkner.* Ithaca: Cornell, 1967, pp. 69-108; other references throughout.

14 Frederick J. Hoffman. *The Art of Southern Fiction: A Study of Some Modern Novelists.* Carbondale, Ill.: S.I.U. Press, 1967. References throughout.

15 Frederick J. Hoffman. *The Imagination's New Beginning: Theology and Modern Literature.* Notre Dame, Ind.: University of Notre Dame Press, 1967, 92-102.

16 Thomas Merton. " 'Baptism in the Forest': Wisdom and Initiation in William Faulkner." *Mansions of the Spirit: Essays in Religion and Literature,* ed. George A. Panichas. New York: Hawthorn Books, 1967, 19-44.

17 James E. Miller, Jr. "William Faulkner: Descent into the Vortex." *Quests Surd and Absurd: Essays in American Literature.* Chicago: U. of Chicago Press, 1967, 41-65.

18 Arthur Mizener. *"The Sound and the Fury." Twelve Great American Novels.* New York: New American Library, 1967, 142-159.

19 Louis D. Rubin, Jr. *The Curious Death of the Novel: Essays in American Literature.* Baton Rouge: L.S.U. Press, 1967. References throughout.

20 William Spratling. *File on Spratling.* Boston: Little, Brown, 1967, 21-34.

21 Dan Brennan. *Winged Victory.* New York: Tower, 1967. This paperback novel is dedicated to several people including "Estelle and Bill." Candace Compson appears briefly in the action of the story.

1968

1   Duncan Aswell. "The Puzzling Design of *Absalom, Absalom!" Kenyon Review,* XXX (Issue 1, 1968), 67-84.

2   Michael Millgate. "Faulkner in Toronto: A Further Note." *University of Toronto Quarterly,* XXXVII (January 1968), 197-202.

3   *Mississippi Quarterly,* XXI (Summer 1968). Faulkner issue. Includes:
Michel Gresset, "Weekend, Lost and Revisited," 173-178.
M. E. Bradford, "Faulkner's 'Elly': An Exposé," 179-187.
Phyllis Franklin, "Sarty Snopes and 'Barn Burning'," 189-193.
Charles C. Clark, " 'Mistral': A Study in Human Tempering," 195-204.
Elmo Howell, "Faulkner's Country Church: A Note on 'Shingles for the Lord'," 205-210.
Duncan Aswell, "The Recollection and the Blood: Jason's Role in *The Sound and the Fury,"* 211-218.

4   Edgar Simmons. "Faulkner." *Yale Review,* LVII (Summer 1968), 586-587. For a pleasant change, a poem.

5   Allen Tate. "Faulkner's *Sanctuary* and the Southern Myth." *Virginia Quarterly Review,* XLIV (Summer 1968), 418-427.

6   "Portrait of a Man Reading." William Styron interviewed on his reading habits by Charles Monaghan. Chicago *Tribune Book World,* October 27, 1968, p. 8. Cites influence of Faulkner.

7   Richard P. Adams. *Faulkner: Myth and Motion.* Princeton: Princeton University Press, 1968.

8   Walter Brylowski. *Faulkner's Olympian Laugh: Myth in the Novels.* Detroit: Wayne State University Press, 1968.

9   *Twentieth Century Interpretations of* The Sound and the Fury, ed. Michael H. Cowan. Englewood Cliffs, N. J.: Prentice-Hall, 1968. Includes reprints of several commentaries by Faulkner and others, as well as an original introduction by the editor.

10   *Twentieth Century Interpretations of* The Sound and the Fury. Another copy. Spectrum Book paperback S-809.

11   Malcolm Cowley. *The Faulkner-Cowley File.* Reprint. Viking Compass paperback edition C219, 1968.

12   Linton R. Massey. *"Man Working" 1919-1962 William Faulkner: A Catalogue of the William Faulkner Collections at the University of Virginia.* Charlottesville: Bibliographical Society of the University of Virginia, 1968.

13 Mario Materassi. *I romanzi di Faulkner.* Rome: Storia e Letteratura, 1968. Wrappers.

14 Heinrich Straumann. *William Faulkner.* Frankfurt am Main: Athenäum Verlag, 1968. German text.

15 James Gray Watson. *The Snopes Dilemma: Faulkner's Trilogy.* Coral Gables, Florida: University of Miami Press, 1968.

16 Jean Weisberger. *Faulkner et Dostoïevski, Confluences et influences.* Brussels: University of Brussels, 1968. Wrappers, rebound in boards.

17 Kay Boyle and Robert McAlmon. *Being Geniuses Together.* Garden City: Doubleday, 1968. Scattered references.

18 Albert Camus. *Lyrical and Critical Essays,* tr. Ellen Conroy Kennedy. New York: Alfred A. Knopf, 1968. Commentaries on Faulkner pp. 311-320.

19 Carvel Collins. "On William Faulkner." *Talks with Authors,* ed. Charles F. Madden. Carbondale: Southern Illinois University Press, 1968, 40-55. Transcription of a telephone interview rather than a formal essay.

20 Marc Connelly. *Voices Offstage: A Book of Memoirs.* New York: Holt, Rinehart & Winston, 1968. Pp. 215-216 and a photograph.

21 Leslie A. Fiedler. *The Return of the Vanishing American.* New York: Stein and Day, 1968, scattered references.

22 Frederick J. Hoffman. "William Faulkner." *American Winners of the Nobel Literary Prize,* ed. Warren G. French and Walter E. Kidd. Norman: University of Oklahoma Press, 1968, 138-157.

23 Bruce Kellner. *Carl Van Vechten and the Irreverent Decades.* Norman: University of Oklahoma Press, 1968. Brief references and a Van Vechten portrait photograph of Faulkner.

24 Archibald MacLeish. "Faulkner at Stockholm." *A Continuing Journey.* Boston: Houghton Mifflin, 1968, 163-137.

25 Robert Phelps and Peter Deane. *The Literary Life: A Scrapbook Almanac.* New York: Farrar, Straus and Giroux, 1968. References throughout.

26 Randall Stewart. *Regionalism and Beyond.* Nashville: Vanderbilt University Press, 1968, references throughout.

27 Allen Tate. "A Southern Mode of the Imagination." *Essays of Four Decades.* Chicago: Swallow Press, 1968, 577-592.

28 Willis Wager. *American Literature: A World View.* New York: N. Y. U.

Press, 1968, 235-238.

1969

1   Anthony West. "Remembering William Faulkner." *Gourmet,* XXIX (January 1969), 22, 23, 74, 75.

2   Erskine Caldwell. Typed letter, signed, October 27, 1969. In response to a letter asking about Faulkner, Caldwell notes that each of them had played in their own respective leagues.

3   William J. Clark. "Faulkner's *Light in August.*" *The Explicator,* XXV-III (November 1969), Item 19.

4   Sorin Alexandrescu. *William Faulkner.* Bucharest: Literatura Universala, 1969. In Rumanian.

5   Walter K. Everett. *Faulkner's Art and Characters.* Woodbury, New York: Barron's Educational Series, 1969. Limp board covers.

6   Elizabeth M. Kerr. *Yoknapatawpha: Faulkner's "Little Postage Stamp of Native Soil."* New York: Fordham University Press, 1969.

7   *Twentieth Century Interpretations of* Light in August, ed. David L. Minter. Englewood Cliffs, N. J.: Prentice-Hall, 1969. Includes reprints of commentaries by several critics as well as an original introduction by the editor. Spectrum Book paperback S-856.

8   H. Edward Richardson. *William Faulkner: The Journey to Self-Discovery.* Columbia, Mo.: University of Missouri Press, 1969.

9   *Apollo Handbook of Faulkner.* Another copy of Dorothy Tuck's *Handbook* issued as Apollo Editions paperback, A-224, in 1969.

10   Elizabeth Anderson and Gerald R. Kelly. *Miss Elizabeth: A Memoir.* Boston: Little, Brown, 1969, 39-43, 84, 85, 99-102.

11   Carlos Baker. *Ernest Hemingway: A Life Story.* New York: Scribners, 1969. Several references to Hemingway's attitudes toward Faulkner.

12   Nelson Manfred Blake. "The Decay of Yoknapatawpha County." *Novelists' America: Fiction as History, 1910-1940.* Syracuse: Syracuse University Press, 1969, 75-109.

13   *Southern Fiction Today: Renascence and Beyond,* ed. George Core. Athens: University of Georgia Press, 1969. Includes general essays by Walter Sullivan, C. Hugh Holman, and Louis D. Rubin, Jr. Scattered references to Faulkner throughout.

14 Bernard Dekle. "William Faulkner: 'Man Will Endure Because He Has a Soul'." *Profiles of Modern American Authors.* Rutland, Vermont and Tokyo: Charles E. Tuttle, 1969, 108-112. A paperback printed in Japan.

15 James K. Feibleman. *The Way of a Man: An Autobiography.* New York: Horizon Press, 1969, 268-277.

16 Lillian Hellman. *An Unfinished Woman—A Memoir.* Boston: Little, Brown, 1969, 177-179.

17 Daniel Hoffman. "William Faulkner: 'The Bear'." *Landmarks of American Writing,* ed. Hennig Cohen. New York: Basic Books, 1969, 341-352. Scattered references in other essays.

18 James B. Meriwether. "William Faulkner." *Fifteen Modern American Authors,* ed. Jackson R. Bryer. Durham: Duke University Press, 1969, 175-210. A survey of research and criticism.

19 Martha O'Nan. "William Faulkner's Benjy: Hysteria." *The Role of Mind in Hugo, Faulkner, Beckett and Grass.* New York: Philosophical Library, 1969, 13-22.

20 Edward Stone. "William Faulkner." *A Certain Morbidness: A View of American Literature.* Carbondale: Southern Illinois University, 1969, 85-120.

1970

1 William Rossky. "The Pattern of Nightmare in *Sanctuary;* or, Miss Reba's Dogs " *Modern Fiction Studies,* XV (Winter 1969-1970), 503-515.

2 *Mississippi Quarterly,* XXIII (Summer 1970). Faulkner Issue.
Contains:
Mary Montgomery Dunlap, "William Faulkner's 'Knight's Gambit' and Gavin Stevens," 223-239.
Raleigh W. Smith, Jr., "Faulkner's 'Victory': The Plain People of Clydebank," 241-249.
Carl Ficken, "The Christ Story in *A Fable*," 251-264.
Francois L. Pitavy, "The Landscape in *Light in August*," 265-272.
Gorman Beauchamp, "*The Unvanquished:* Faulkner's *Oresteia*," 273-277.
Rosemary Stephens, "Ike's Gun and Too Many Novembers," 279-287.
Margaret Yonce, "Faulkner's 'Atthis' and 'Attis': Some Sources of Myth," 289-298.
M. Gidley, "One Continuous Force: Notes on Faulkner's Extra-Literary Reading," 299-314.

Thomas L. McHaney, "A Deer Hunt in the Faulkner Country," 315-320.

James E. Kibler, Jr., "A Possible Source in Ariosto for Drusilla," 321-322.

Also: Reviews of books on Faulkner including:

Noel Polk, "The Critics and Faulkner's 'Little Postage Stamp of Native Soil'," 323-335.

3   *informations et documents,* Faulkner issue "Au pays de Faulkner,"
1 August, 1970. Contains articles by Claude Jannoud and Marc Saporta, an interview, and a reprint of "L'apres-midi d'une vache."

4   Father John Barry. "Glenmary in Faulkner Land." *Glenmary's Challenge,* XXXIII (Autumn 1970), 2-7. (A quarterly devoted to the Roman Catholic mission movement in rural America.)

5   "The Postmaster." *New Yorker,* XLVI (November 21, 1970), 50. Full text of the letter sent September 2, 1924 by Postoffice Inspector Mark Webster to errant Postmaster William C. Faulkner of the University, Mississippi post office.

6   Joan St. C. Crane. "Rare or Seldom-Seen Dust Jackets of American First Editions: III." *The Serif: Quarterly of the Kent State University Libraries,* VII (December 1970), 64-66.

7   *William Faulkner.* Paris: Armand Colin, 1970. In the series: U2. Contains a lengthy study of *As I Lay Dying* by André Bleikasten, a similar study of *Light in August* by Francois Pitavy, and an introduction by Michel Gresset.

8   *William Faulkner: "A Rose for Emily,"* ed. M. Thomas Inge. Columbus, Ohio: Charles E. Merrill, 1970. Includes the text of the story, an original introduction by the editor, and essays and essay fragments in reprint.

9   Barbara Izard and Clara Hieronymus. *Requiem for a Nun: On Stage and Off.* Nashville: Aurora, 1970. Includes a quotation of Faulkner's humorous notions for the 1956 People to People program, 239.

10   Martin Jarrett-Kerr. *William Faulkner: A Critical Essay.* Grand Rapids, Mich.: William B. Eerdmans, 1970. A pamphlet in the series, Contemporary Writers in Christian Perspective.

11   *The Merrill Studies in* The Sound and the Fury, comp. James B. Meriwether. Columbus, Ohio: Charles E. Merrill, 1970. Contains:
James B. Meriwether, "The Textual History of *The Sound and the Fury,*" 1-32.
Walter Brylowski, From "The Dark Vision: Myth in *The Sound and*

the Fury," 33-58.
Carvel Collins, "The Interior Monologues of *The Sound and the Fury*," 59-79.
Carvel Collins, "Miss Quentin's Paternity Again," 80-88.
Eileen Gregory, "Caddy Compson's World," 89-101.
John V. Hagopian, "Nihilism in Faulkner's *The Sound and the Fury,*" 102-113.
Michel Gresset, "Psychological Aspects of Evil in *The Sound and the Fury*," 114-124.
Michael Millgate, "The Problem of Point of View," 125-139.
Richard Gunter, "Style and Language in *The Sound and the Fury*," 140-156.

12   William Van O'Connor. "William Faulkner." *Quatre visages du roman Americaine.* Strasbourg and Paris: Nouveaux Horizons, 1970, 121-171. Tr. Denise Van Moppes. French translation of O'Connor's 1959 pamphlet text.

13   Richard P. Adams. "Focus on William Faulkner's 'The Bear': Moses and the Wilderness." *American Dreams, American Nightmares,* ed. David Madden. Carbondale: Southern Illinois University, 1970, 129-135.

14   Allen Cabaniss. *Liturgy and Literature: Selected Essays.* University, Alabama: University of Alabama Press, 1970. Brief references.

15   F. Garvin Davenport, Jr. "William Faulkner." *The Myth of Southern History: Historical Consciousness in Twentieth-Century Southern Literature.* Nashville: Vanderbilt University Press, 1970, 82-130.

16   Will and Ariel Durant. "William Faulkner." *Interpretations of Life: A Survey of Contemporary Literature.* New York: Simon and Schuster, 1970, 11-27.

17   Walker Gilmer. *Horace Liveright: Publisher of the Twenties.* New York: David Lewis, 1970, 125-127.

18   Jay Martin. *Nathanael West: The Art of His Life.* New York: Farrar, Straus and Giroux, 1970. Scattered references.

19   Theodore Solotaroff. *The Red Hot Vacuum.* New York: Atheneum, 1970. Scattered references to Faulkner's influence on the succeeding generation of writers.

1   Joan St. C. Crane. "Rare or Seldom-Seen Dust Jackets of American First Editions: IV." *The Serif: Quarterly of the Kent State University Libraries,* VIII (March 1971), 21-23.

2   *Mississippi Quarterly*, XXIV (Summer 1971). Faulkner Issue. Contains:
Thomas L. McHaney, "*Sanctuary* and Frazer's Slain Kings," 223-245.
Noel Polk, "Alec Holston's Lock and the Founding of Jefferson," 247-269.
Stephen E. Meats, "Who Killed Joanna Burden?," 271-277.
Gayle Edward Wilson, " '*Being Pulled Two Ways*': The Nature of Sarty's Choice in 'Barn Burning'," 279-288.
Frank Cantrell, "Faulkner's 'A Courtship'," 289-295.
Beverley E. Smith, "A Note on Faulkner's 'Greenbury Hotel'," 297-298.
Also two reviews including:
Noel Polk, "The Staging of *Requiem for a Nun*," 299-314.

3   *The Newberry Library Bulletin,* VI (July 1971). Special Sherwood Anderson Number. Includes "The Achievement of Sherwood Anderson: An Anniversary Exhibition," by Richard Colles Johnson, 268-287. Item 78 in the 1969 exhibition was a Faulkner letter to Anderson.

4   James B. Meriwether. "Two Unknown Faulkner Short Stories." *RANAM*, No. IV (1971). 23-30. Offprint.

5   Maurice Edgar Coindreau. *The Time of William Faulkner: A French View of Modern American Fiction,* ed. George McMillan Reeves. Columbia: University of South Carolina Press, 1971. On pp.25-110 appear English translations of eleven Coindreau essays on Faulkner, the originals having appeared between 1931 and 1963.

6   *Twentieth Century Interpretations of* Absalom, Absalom!, ed. Arnold Goldman. Englewood Cliffs, N. J.: Prentice-Hall, 1971. Includes an introduction by the editor and reprint material by Richard Poirier, John Paterson, Michael Millgate, Melvin Backman, James Guetti, Thomas E. Connolly and Cleanth Brooks.

7   *Twentieth Century Interpretations of* Absalom, Absalom! Another copy. Spectrum Book paperback S-879, 1971.

8   *Studies in* Light in August, comp. M. Thomas Inge. Columbus, Ohio: Charles E. Merrill, 1971. Contains a brief introduction by the compiler and reprint material from a variety of sources including critical essays by Richard Chase, Darrel Abel, C. Hugh Holman, Robert M. Slabey, John M. Kimmey, John L. Longley, Jr. and B. R. McElderry, Jr.

9   Gerald Langford. *Faulkner's Revision of* Absalom, Absalom! *A Collation of the Manuscript and the Published Book.* Austin: University of Texas Press, 1971.

10 James B. Meriwether. *The Literary Career of William Faulkner.* "Authorized reissue" of this important 1961 study. Columbia, S. C.: University of South Carolina Press, 1971.

11 Eric Mottram. *William Faulkner.* London: Routledge & Kegan Paul, 1971. In the Profiles in Literature Series.

12 Charles D. Peavy. *Go Slow Now: Faulkner and the Race Question.* Eugene, Oregon: University of Oregon, 1971.

13 Joachim Seyppel. *William Faulkner.* New York: Frederick Ungar, 1971. In the series: Modern Literature Monographs.

14 Light in August *and the Critical Spectrum*, ed. John B. Vickery and Olga W. Vickery. Belmont, California: Wadsworth, 1971. Reprint material from a number of sources.

15 Morris Beja. "William Faulkner: A Flash, a Glare." *Epiphany in the Modern Novel.* Seattle: University of Washington Press, 1971, 182-210.

16 Cleanth Brooks. *A Shaping Joy: Studies in the Writer's Craft.* New York: Harcourt Brace Jovanovich, 1971. References throughout, particularly 230-269.

17 Allen Churchill. *The Literary Decade.* Englewood Cliffs, New Jersey: Prentice-Hall, 1971. Scattered references.

18 *Cyril Connolly's One Hundred Modern Books from England, France and America 1880-1950.* Austin: The Humanities Research Center, 1971. Catalog of an exhibition at the University of Texas at Austin, March-December 1971. The Faulkner choice (item 69) is *Sanctuary*.

19 William J. Handy. "Faulkner's *As I Lay Dying*." *Modern Fiction: A Formalist Approach.* Carbondale: Southern Illinois University, 1971, 75-93.

20 Forrest L. Ingram. "William Faulkner: *The Unvanquished*." *Representative Short Story Cycles of the Twentieth Century.* The Hague: Mouton, 1971, 106-142.

21 Lewis A. Lawson. "William Faulkner." *The Politics of Twentieth-Century Novelists*, ed. George A. Panichas. New York: Hawthorn Books, 1971, 278-295. Also brief references in other essays in the volume.

22 James B. Meriwether. "The Short Fiction of William Faulkner: A Bibliography." *Proof: The Yearbook of American Bibliographical and Textual Studies Volume I, 1971*, ed. Joseph Katz. Columbia: University of South Carolina Press, 1971, 293-329.

23 Mark Schorer. "William Faulkner." *Atlantic Brief Lives: A Bibliographical Companion to the Arts,* ed. Louis Kronenberger. Boston: Little, Brown, 1971, 268-269, with an anonymous biographical sketch on 267.

24 Floyd C. Watkins. *The Flesh and the Word: Eliot, Hemingway, Faulkner.* Nashville, Vanderbilt, 1971, 169-273.

25 Joan Williams. *The Wintering.* New York: Harcourt Brace Jovanovich, 1971. "The love story of a young woman and a famous older man, by the author of *The Morning and the Evening*." A novel.

1972

1 Thomas L. McHaney. "Anderson, Hemingway, and Faulkner's *The Wild Palms*." *PMLA*, LXXXVII (May 1972), 465-474. Offprint.

2 *Mississippi Quarterly*, XXV (Summer 1972). Faulkner issue. Contains:
Thomas L. McHaney, "The Falkners and the Origin of Yoknapatawpha County: Some Corrections," 249-264.
Cleanth Brooks, "The Tradition of Romantic Love and *The Wild Palms*," 265-287.
Elisabeth S. Muhlenfeld, "Shadows with Substance and Ghosts Exhumed: The Women in *Absalom, Absalom!*," 289-304.
Noel Polk, "Faulkner's 'The Jail' and the Meaning of Cecilia Farmer," 305-325.
Albert J. Devlin, "*The Reivers:* Readings in Social Psychology," 327-337.
Robert W. Funk, "Satire and Existentialism in Faulkner's 'Red Leaves'," 339-348.
Michael Millgate, "Faulkner and Lanier: A Note on the Name Jason," 349-350.
Giliane Morell, "The Last Scene of *Sanctuary*," 351-355.
Beth B. Haury, "The Influence of Robinson Jeffers' 'Tamar' on *Absalom, Absalom!*," 356-358.
Also five reviews including:
Noel Polk, "The Manuscript of *Absalom, Absalom!*," 359-367.

3 *Modern Fiction Studies,* XVIII (Summer 1972). Includes:
David M. Monaghan, "The Single Narrator of *As I Lay Dying,*" 213-220.
Joseph Brogunier, "A Housman Source in *The Sound and the Fury,*" 220-225.

4 Eudora Welty. "The Art of Fiction XLVII." *Paris Review,* XIV (Fall 1972), 72-97. Interview with references to Faulkner.

5 *Southern Review,* VIII New Series (October 1972). Includes:
William Faulkner, "An Introduction for *The Sound and the Fury,*" ed. James B. Meriwether, 705-710.
Lewis M. Dabney, " 'Was': Faulkner's Classic Comedy of the Frontier," 736-748.
Panthea Reid Broughton, "*Requiem for a Nun:* No Part in Rationality," 749-762.
Andrew H. Pfeiffer, "Eye of the Storm: The Observers' Image of the Man Who Was Faulkner," 763-773.
Jim Faulkner, "Auntee Owned Two," 836-844.

6 Thomas B. Newsom. "Faulkner Work Found in Closet." *Pictures* (St. Louis *Post-Dispatch*), Sunday, December 10, 1972, 50, 54, 57, 59.

7 J. Robert Barth, S. J., ed. *Religious Perspectives in Faulkner's Fiction: Yoknapatawpha and Beyond.* Notre Dame, (Ind.): University of Notre Dame Press, 1972. Contains:
J. Robert Barth, S. J. "Religion and Literature: The Critical Context," 1-8.
J. Robert Barth, S. J., "Faulkner and the Calvinist Tradition," 11-31.
Harold J. Douglas and Robert Daniel, "Faulkner's Southern Puritanism," 37-51.
Cleanth Brooks, "Faulkner's Vision of Good and Evil," 57-75.
John W. Hunt, "The Theological Complexity of Faulkner's Fiction," 81-87.
Amos N. Wilder, "Vestigial Moralities in *The Sound and the Fury,*" 91-102.
Philip C. Rule, S. J., "The Old Testament Vision in *As I Lay Dying,*" 107-116.
Hyatt H. Waggoner, "*Light in August:* Outrage and Compassion," 121-137.
John W. Hunt, "The Theological Center of *Absalom, Absalom!,*" 141-169.
Herbert A. Perluck, " 'The Bear': An Unromantic Reading," 173-198.
Roma A. King, Jr., "*A Fable:* Everyman's Warfare," 203-210.
Additionally, the editor has supplied a commentary on each essay and an epilogue.

8   John Bassett. *William Faulkner: An Annotated Checklist of Criticism.* New York: David Lewis, 1972.

9   George C. Bedell. *Kierkegaard and Faulkner: Modalities of Existence.* Baton Rouge: L. S. U. Press, 1972.

10   James Early. *The Making of* Go Down, Moses. Dallas: S.M.U. Press, 1972.

11   Gerald Langford. *Faulkner's Revision of* Sanctuary. *A Collation of the Unrevised Galleys and the Published Book.* Austin: University of Texas Press, 1972.

12   Sally R. Page. *Faulkner's Women: Characterization and Meaning.* Deland, Florida: Everett/Edwards, 1972.

13   John W. Aldridge. *The Devil in the Fire.* New York: Harper's Magazine Press, 1972, 145-152 with other references throughout.

14   William Barrett. "Backward Toward the Earth." *Time of Need: Forms of Imagination in the Twentieth Century.* New York: Harper & Row, 1972, 96-129.

15   Van Allen Bradley. *The Book Collector's Handbook of Values.* New York: Putnam's, 1972. The entries for Faulkner first editions are on 161-163.

16   Fanny Butcher. *Many Lives—One Love.* New York: Harper & Row, 1972, 332-336.

17   Carl Ficken. "The Opening Scene of William Faulkner's *Light in August.*" *Proof: The Yearbook of American Bibliographical and Textual Studies Volume 2, 1972,* ed. Joseph Katz. Columbia: University of South Carolina Press, 1972, 175-184.

18   *Authors on Film*, ed. Harry M. Geduld. Bloomington: Indiana University Press, 1972. Excerpts from the *Paris Review* interview touching on Faulkner's Hollywood experiences, 198-199 and 203-205.

19   C. Hugh Holman. *The Roots of Southern Writing: Essays on the Literature of the American South.* Athens: University of Georgia Press, 1972. References throughout, particularly 149-176.

20   Jay B. Hubbell. *Who Are the Major American Writers?* Durham: Duke University Press, 1972. Extensive references throughout.

21   Stephen Longstreet. *We All Went to Paris.* New York: Macmillan, 1972. Faulkner quote on 446-448.

22   Reynolds Price. "*Pylon*—The Posture of Worship." *Things Themselves.* New York: Atheneum, 1972, 91-108. Also, on 109-113, an essay on

Cleanth Brooks' *William Faulkner: The Yoknapatawpha Country.*

23   *Soviet Criticism of American Literature in the Sixties,* ed. Carl R. Proffer. Ann Arbor: Ardis, 1972. Includes:
P. V. Palievsky, "Faulkner's Road to Realism," 150-168, English translation by the editor. Mikhail Landor, "Faulkner in the Soviet Union," 173-180, original English language text.

24   Budd Schulberg. *The Four Seasons of Success.* Garden City: Doubleday, 1972. Scattered references.

25   Walter Sullivan. "Allen Tate, Flem Snopes, and the Last Years of William Faulkner." *Death by Melancholy: Essays on Modern Southern Fiction.* Baton Rouge: L. S. U. Press, 1972, 3-21 with other references throughout.

1973

1   Robert Vare. "Oxford, Miss., Which Faulkner Transcended, Is As He Left It." New York *Times* Travel Section, Sunday, January 14, 1973, 3, 11.

2   *Mississippi Quarterly,* XXVI (Summer 1973). "Special Issue: William Faulkner." Issue editor, James B. Meriwether. Foreword by the editor. Includes Faulkner prose in first publication:
"And Now What's to Do," 399-402.
"Nympholepsy," 403-409.
"An Introduction to *The Sound and the Fury*," 410-415.
"A Note on *A Fable*," 416-417.
Other previously unpublished Faulkner material is included among the critical essays:
Noel Polk, "William Faulkner's *Marionettes*," 247-280.
Thomas L. McHaney, "The Elmer Papers: Faulkner's Comic Portraits of the Artist," 281-311.
Beatrice Lang, "An Unpublished Faulkner Short Story: 'The Big Shot'," 312-324.
Frank Cantrell, "An Unpublished Faulkner Short Story: 'Snow'," 325-330.
Keen Butterworth, "A Census of Manuscripts and Typescripts of William Faulkner's Poetry," 333-359.
Eileen Gregory, "Faulkner's Typescripts of *The Town*," 361-386.
Michael Millgate, "Faulkner on the Literature of the First World War," 387-393.
Noel Polk, " 'Hong Li' and *Royal Street*: The New Orleans Sketches

in Manuscript," 394-395.
Concludes with reviews of nine books about Faulkner.

3   André Bleikasten. *Faulkner's* As I Lay Dying. Bloomington: Indiana University Press, 1973. Revised and enlarged from the original French text published in Paris, 1970. Translated, with the author's collaboration, by Roger Little.

4   *Faulkner's* As I Lay Dying. Another copy. Midland Book paperback MB-159, 1973.

5   Edwin R. Hunter. *William Faulkner: Narrative Practice and Prose Style.* Washington, D. C.: Windhover, 1973.

6   Lewis Leary. *William Faulkner of Yoknapatawpha County.* New York: Crowell, 1973.

7   Francois Pitavy. *Faulkner's* Light in August. Bloomington: Indiana University Press, 1973. Revised and enlarged from the original French text published in Paris, 1970. Translated, with the author's collaboration, by Gillian E. Cook.

8   *Faulkner's* Light in August. Another copy. Midland Book paperback MB-166, 1973.

9   Joseph W. Reed, Jr. *Faulkner's Narrative.* New Haven: Yale, 1973.

10 *William Faulkner,* ed. Dean Morgan Schmitter. New York: McGraw-Hill, 1973. Paperback. Contains an original introduction by the editor and reprint material from a number of sources.

11 Linda Welshimer Wagner, ed. *William Faulkner: Four Decades of Criticism.* (East Lansing:) Michigan State University Press, 1973. Contains:
Linda W. Wagner, "Introduction," 1-6.
Richard P. Adams, "The Apprenticeship of William Faulkner," 7-44.
George Garrett, "The Poetry of William Faulkner," 44-54.
Mick Gidley, "One Continuous Force: Notes on Faulkner's Extra-Literary Reading," 55-68.
Otis Wheeler, "Some Uses of Folk Humor by Faulkner," 68-82.
George Marion O'Donnell, "Faulkner's Mythology," 83-93.
Robert Penn Warren, "William Faulkner," 94-109.
Lawrence Bowling, "William Faulkner, The Importance of Love," 109-117.
Cleanth Brooks, "William Faulkner, Vision of Good and Evil," 117-133.
Conrad Aiken, "William Faulkner: The Novel as Form," 134-140.
Warren Beck, "William Faulkner's Style," 141-154.

Walter J. Slatoff, "The Edge of Order: The Pattern of Faulkner's Rhetoric," 155-179.
Michael Millgate, "William Faulkner: The Problem of Point of View," 179-191.
Ray B. West, Jr., "Atmosphere and Theme in Faulkner's 'A Rose for Emily'," 192-198.
Lawrance Thompson, "Mirror Analogues in *The Sound and the Fury*," 199-212.
Floyd C. Watkins, "The Word and the Deed in Faulkner's First Great Novels," 213-230.
Elizabeth Kerr, "*As I Lay Dying* as Ironic Quest," 230-243.
Phyllis Hirshleifer, "Whirlwinds in the South: An Analysis of *Light in August*," 244-257.
Carl Benson, "Thematic Design in *Light in August*," 258-272.
Ilse Dusoir Lind, "The Design and Meaning of *Absalom, Absalom!*," 272-297.
Gorman Beauchamp, "Faulkner's *Oresteia*," 298-302.
Thomas Y. Greet, "The Theme and Structure of Faulkner's *The Hamlet*," 302-318.
Joseph Gold, "The 'Normality' of Snopesism: Universal Themes in Faulkner's *The Hamlet*," 318-327.
Stanley Tick, "The Unity of *Go Down, Moses*," 327-334.
Heinrich Straumann, "An American Interpretation of Existence: Faulkner's *A Fable*," 335-357.
William Rossky, "*The Reivers:* Faulkner's *Tempest*," 358-369.

12   Malcolm Cowley. "Faulkner: The Yoknapatawpha Story." *A Second Flowering: Works and Days of the Lost Generation.* New York: Viking, 1973, 130-155. One more reprint of Cowley's 1945 essay, with a few supplementary remarks.

13   Alfred Kazin. *Bright Book of Life: American Novelists and Storytellers from Hemingway to Mailer.* Boston: Little, Brown, 1973, 23-37. Other references throughout.

14   James B. Meriwether. "Faulkner's Correspondence With *Scribner's Magazine.*" *Proof: The Yearbook of American Bibliographical and Textual Studies Volume 3, 1973,* ed. Joseph Katz. Columbia: University of South Carolina Press, 1973, 253-282.

15   Michael Millgate. "Faulkner." *American Literary Scholarship: An Annual/1971*, ed. J. Albert Robbins. Durham: Duke, 1973, 104-119.

16   Lucio P. Ruotolo. "Isaac McCaslin." *Six Existential Heroes: The Politics of Faith.* Cambridge: Harvard, 1973, 57-78.

17   Lola L. Szladits. *New in the Berg Collection, 1970-1972.* New York:

New York Public Library, 1973. On page 43 is a list of Faulkner manuscript acquisitions including the typescript of *Soldiers' Pay*.

18 *The Harvard Lampoon Centennial Celebration 1876-1973*. Boston: Little, Brown, 1973. Faulkner parodies on 23 and 121.

1974

1 Michael Putney. "Yoknapatawpha's Mr. Bill." *The National Observer*, February 16, 1974, 22.

2 Roy Reed. "Faulkner's Mississippi Revisited: Some Change but Much the Same." New York *Times*, February 22, 1974, 35, 38.

3 Joseph Blotner. *Faulkner: A Biography*. New York: Random House, 1974.

4 Lewis M. Dabney. *The Indians of Yoknapatawpha: A Study in Literature and History*. Baton Rouge: L. S. U. Press, 1974.

5 Tony Buttitta. *After the Good Gay Times, Asheville—Summer of '35: A Season with F. Scott Fitzgerald*. New York: Viking, 1974, 57-63.

6 James B. Meriwether. "William Faulkner." *Sixteen Modern American Authors*, ed. Jackson R. Bryer. Durham, N. C.: Duke, 1974, 223-275. Updates material in a similar volume published in 1969.

7 One of William Faulkner's pipes; acquired in 1974. With a letter from a family member authenticating its source.

APPENDIX: POETRY PUBLICATION

APPENDIX

POETRY PUBLICATION

Title	*Double Dealer* appearance	*Contempo* appearance	*A Green Bough* number
Portrait	June 1922		
Dying Gladiator	Jan–Feb 1925		
The Faun	April 1925		
The Lilacs	June 1925		I
Visions in Spring		Feb 1, 1932	
Spring		Feb 1, 1932	XXXVI
April		Feb 1, 1932	

Next six poems appear in *Anthology of the Younger Poets* (Cl2a):

Title	*Double Dealer* appearance	*Contempo* appearance	*A Green Bough* number
I Will Not Weep for Youth		Feb 1, 1932	
My Epitaph		Feb 1, 1932	XLIV
To a Virgin		Feb 1, 1932	XXXIX
Winter Is Gone		Feb 1, 1932	
Knew I Love Once		Feb 1, 1932	XXXIII
Twilight		Feb 1, 1932	X

Title		*New Republic* appearance	*A Green Bough* number
A Child Looks from His Window		May 25, 1932	
The Flowers That Died		June 25, 1933	
The Race's Splendor	Apr 12, 1933		XXXVII
Gray the Day	Apr 12, 1933		XXX
Night Piece	Apr 12, 1933		VII
Over the World's Rim	Apr 12, 1933		XXVIII
The Ship of Night	Apr 19, 1933		XXXIV
Man Comes, Man Goes	May 3, 1933		VI

Next seven poems appear in *Mississippi Verse* (Al4c):

Title	*Double Dealer* appearance	*Contempo* appearance	*A Green Bough* number
Mirror of Youth			XVI
The Courtesan Is Dead			XXXV
Green Is the Water			XIX
If There Be Grief (My Epitaph)		Feb 1, 1932	XLIV
Here He Stands			XX
Boy and Eagle			XVIII
Mother and Child (The Ship of Night)	Apr 19, 1933		XXXIV

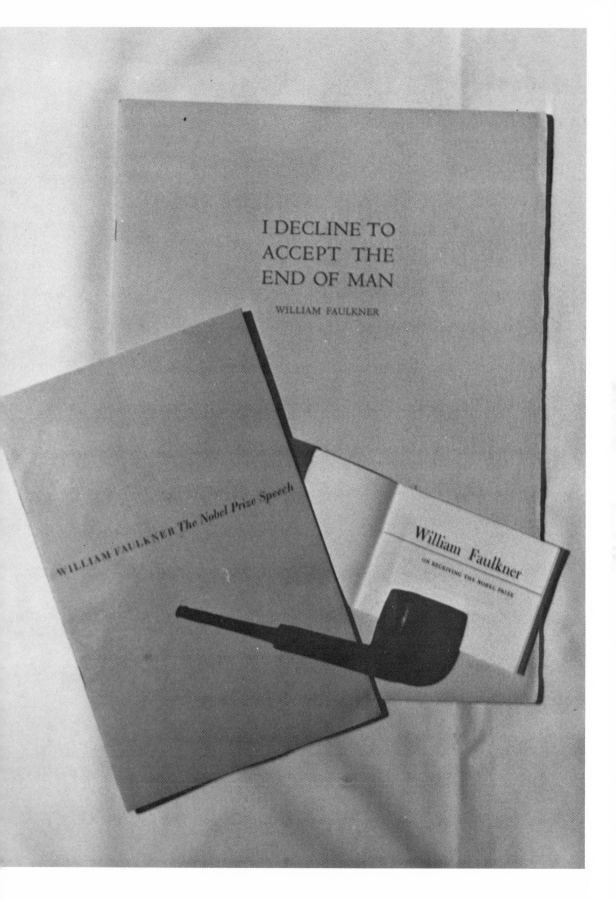

Nobel Laureate (D16p, D16g, D16k and 1974.7).

INDEX OF FAULKNER WORKS

Generally the letter coded entries denote appearances of Faulkner works, the dated entries refer to books and articles of criticism. See also the Index of Names.

x, B33

Pine Manor Junior College Commencement Address, D23

"A Point of Law," B56

"A Poplar," A38

The Portable Faulkner, A23; 1946.1-4, 1951.23, 1957.27, 1960.14

"Portrait," A11, 38b-h, C2, App.

Pylon, A16, 30l, n; 1935.2-9, 1946.8, 1952.2, 1957.20, 1958.1, 6, 1967.10, 1972.22

"Race at Morning," A26i, 30o, 33, B73

"The Race's Splendor," C19, App.

"Raid," A18, B42

"Red Leaves," A9, 23, 26a-c, e, g-i, l, o r-s, u, z, 30o B4; 1972.2

The Reivers, A37; 1962.4-14, 1967.2, 1972.2, 1973.11; J11 (film and recording)

Requiem for a Nun (novel), A23e-h, 28, 30a-c, i-k, q; 1951.8-17, 19-20, 1971.2, 1972.2, 5

Requiem for a Nun (play), A35; 1959.3-10, 1961.19, 1967.4, 1970.9, 1971.2

"Retreat," A18 (except m), B40

Review of *The Old Man and the Sea,* D21

"Riposte in Tertio," A18

"The Rosary," A29, 32a-c, e-f, h, k, m-o, q, u-w

"A Rose for Emily," A9, 22, 23, 26a-c, e g, i-j, m, o-p, t-u, y-z, 30a-c, g, i-k, m, B1; 1949.4, 1951.23, 1957.27, 1970.8, 1973.11; J13 (ballet)

A Rose for Emily and Other Stories, A22

Salmagundi, A11, F1-2, 10-11; 1931.30, 1932.4

Sanctuary, A8, 23, 30q; 1931.2-14, 25, 29, 1933.1, 7, 1937.1, 1951.20, 1952.3, 1953.1, 6, 1955.16, 1956.3 (2), 9, 1957.20 (2), 1961.7, 1968. 5. 1970.1, 1971.2, 18, 1972.2, 11; J9 (film)

"Sapphics," A38

Sartoris, A5, 30k, D7; 1953.6, 1957.35, 1958.5. 1967.4 (See also *Flags in the Dust,* A41)

Selected Short Stories of William Faulkner, A26i

"Sepulture South: Gaslight," B72, 1971.4

"Shall Not Perish," A26a-d, g, j, p, w-y, B69

"Sherwood Anderson" (1925), A32, D5; 1957.4

"Sherwood Anderson: An Appreciation" (1953), A30f, D22

Sherwood Anderson and Other Famous Creoles, A3

"Shingles for the Lord," A26a-d, g, w-x, 30a-c, f, i-j, B66; 1968.3

"The Ship of Night," C23, App.

The Sin Shouter of Cabin Road (John Faulkner), K9

"Skirmish at Sartoris," A18 (except m), B43

"Smoke," A15, 25 (except l), B26; J4 (play)

Soldiers' Pay, A2; 1964.31, 1967.1, 1973.17

The Sound and the Fury, A6, 23, 30a-c, k; 1929.1-4, 1933.5, 1948.4, 1949.4, 1951.23 (2), 1953.3, 1954.35, 1957.4, 27 (2), 35, 1959.40, 1960.6, 13, 14 (2), 1962.30, 41, 1963.22, 30, 1964.8-9, 13, 1965.12, 1966.8 (2), 1967.2 (2), 8, 18, 1968.3, 9-10, 19, 1970.11, 1972.3, 5, 7, 1973.2, 11; J6 (film)

Snopes trilogy, A20i, 34i, 36g; 1960.5, 11, 1961.9, 1968.15

Southern Historical Association Address, D37; 1964.29

INDEX OF NAMES

Bengtsson, Gun and Nils A., A16ee
Benson, Carl, 1973.11
Benson, Warren B., 1966.12
Berard, Phillipe, G34a
Berland, Alwyn, 1962.15
Bernardez, Aurora, A9l
Bettis, Valerie, J7a, 1949.1
Bianciardi, Luciano, A36o
Bishop, Maj. William A., 1918
Bizzarri, Edoardo, A21n, 23h, 30o
Blake, Nelson Manfred, 1969.12
Blanchot, Maurice, D48c
Blaustein, Albert P., B60c
Bleikasten, Andre, 1970.7. 1973.3-4
Bloom, Harold Jack, H5a
Bloom, Lynn Z., 1964.16
Blotner, Joseph L., A30g, D7a, G28a,
    32a, L34, 1963.15, 1964.6, 21, 1966.9,
    1967.7, 1974.3
Bode, Carl, 1960.17
Bogdanovich, Peter, 1962. 39
Bogoslovskaya, M., A26r
Bohmer, Gunter, A20p
Boisen, Mogens, A24m
Bolognese, Don, A40c
Boozer, William, 1965.6
Borges, Jorge Luis, A19r
Bosquet, Alain, B73e
du Bouchet, Andre, A25g
Bouvard, Loic, G11a, 1960.1
Bowden, Edwin T., 1961.15
Bowen, Catherine Drinker, 1960.12
Bowling, Lawrence Edward, 1948.4.
    1951.23, 1957.27, 1965.12, 1973.11.
Boyle, Hal, G18a
Boyle, Kay, 1938.7, 1968.17
Brackett, Leigh, H4a
Bradford, M. E., 1962.2, 1965.4, 1966.1,
    1967.4, 1968.3
Bradford, Roark, 1948.1

Bradley, Van Allen, 1954.24, 1955.12,
    1957.8, 1959.23, 1962.7, 1972.15
Braem, Helmut M., A6x-z, 19x-z, aa,
    20n-p, 26q
Braithwaite, William Stanley, C5b-c
Branner, H. C., A35n
Brasil, Assis, 1964.7
Bréant, J. and L., A34t-v, 39c
Breen, Robert S., J12a
Brehm, George, B35a
Breit, Harvey, A17e-f, E24a, G17a-b,
    1948.7, 1951.2, 18.
Brennan, Dan, A21a, K3a, L12, 1949.4,
    1966.33, 1967.21
Brickell, Herschel, A28d, B57b-c, 63b,
    71b
Britt, George, 1931.6
Brodin, Pierre, 1946.9
Brogunier, Joseph, 1972.3
Brooks, Cleanth, A13i, 1951.6, 20, 1963.5,
    17, 26, 1971.6-7, 16, 1972.2, 7, 22,
    1973.11
Brooks, Van Wyck, G24e, 1953.11
Brophy, Brigid, 1967.8
Bross, Addison C., 1967.1
Broughton, Panthea Reid, 1972.5
Brown, Calvin S., 1956.7, 1962.33, 1966.1
Brown, Deming, 1962.40
Brown, Francis, 1964.21
Brown, Leighton B., B1h
Brown, Ruth, 1962.21
Browning, Tod, F12
Bruccoli, Matthew, 1967.4
Brumm, Ursula, 1955.8, 1960.14
Brusar, Branko, 134q
Brussel-Smith, Bernard, B64e
Bryer, Jackson R., 1969.18, 1974.6
Brylowski, Walter, 1968.8. 1970.11
Bungert, Hans, 1964.31
Bunker, Robert, 1948.16

Burck, Jacob, A8j
Burnett, David, B75b
Burnett, Hallie, B67b
Burnett, Whit, B6h, 30b, 63d, 67b, E11a
Burnham, James, 1931.1
Burrell, Angus, B1e
Burrows, Robert N., 1961.4
Butcher, Fanny, E2a, 1934.3, 1959.26,
   1972.16
Butterworth, Keen, 1973.2
Buttitta, Anthony J., F3-4, 6-9, L6,
   1938.8, 1974.5
Byers, Ellis, K15a

Caballero, Agustín, A30l
Cabaniss, Allen, 1970.14
Cahn, Sammy, J5c
Caldwell, Erskine, 1969.2
Calvert, Elizabeth, A27a
Calvo, Lino Novás, A8dd, ii
Cambon, Glauco, A17o, 30p, 1961.21
Campbell, Allan, A29b
Campbell, Harry Modean, 1950.10,
   1951.21, 1952.9, 1961.4
Camus, Albert, A28q, 35h-l, o, q, D48,
   1951.20, 1957.3, 1968.18
Canby, Henry Seidel, B5c, 1931.7,
   1936.11
Cantrell, Frank, 1971.2, 1973.2
Cantwell, Robert, A5e-f, h, p, K1a, 1939.10,
   1951.17, 1952.13, 1960.14
Capote, Truman, 1949.1
Carbó, P., A30l
Carey, Glenn O., 1965.10
Carpenter, Margaret Haley, C5c
Carpenter, Robert Allen, 1965.14
Carrouges, Michel, 1954.5
Carter, Hodding, 1957.4, 1963.27
Carter, Thomas H., 1954.31, 1960.2

Cartier-Bresson, Henri, A30a-c
Cartmell, Van H., B1g
Carvalho, H. Santos, A6cc
Cassill, R. V., A19m
Cecchi, Emilio, 1957.27
Cerf, Bennett, B1e
Cerf, Phyllis, A37d, L18, 28
Chapman, Arnold, 1966.25
Chapman, John, 1959.4
Chapsal, Madeleine, G23a
Charteris, Leslie, A32j
Chase, Richard, 1948.4, 1951.22-23,
   1957.27, 1971.8
Chaze, Elliott, G35a
Cheney, Frances Neel, 1954.30
Christadler, Martin, 1962.34
Churchill, Allen, 1971.17
Ciancio, Ralph A., 1961.1
Clark, Charles C., 1968.3
Clark, William J., 1969.3
Claxton, Simon, G36a
Cochran, Louis, 1964.4
Cofield, J. R., L5, 8, 19-20
Cofield, Jack, L22
Cohen, Hennig, 1969.17
Coindreau, Maurice Edgar, A6s-v, 7n-r,
   9i, 13r-t, 19u-v, 28q, 30k, 37r-t,
   40f-h, B1c, 5b, 29b, 68a-b, E4, 6-7,
   1933.3, 1952.5, 1953.6, 1957.4,
   1960.10, 1965.1, 1966.8, 1971.5
Coleman, Robert, 1959.5
Collins, Carvel, A18g, 32d-f, k, m-o, q,
   s, u-w, 38a-f, 1951.3, 20, 1953.2, 4,
   1954.6, 14, 35, 1957.4, 1960.13,
   1964.8, 1968.19, 1970.11
Collins, Jimmy, D11a
Colvert, James B., 1966.8
Commins, Saxe, A22
Conklin, Groff, C24b
Connelly, Marc, 1968.20

Connolly, Cyril, 1971.18
Connolly, Thomas E., 1971.6-7
Cook, Gillian E., 1973.7
Cook, Howard, B53a
Cooperman, Stanley, 1967.9
Cordoba, Jeronimo, A4q
Core, George, 1969.13
Corke, Hilary, 1962.14
Costain, Thomas B., B25d
Cotten, Joseph, 1965.19
Cottrell, Beekman W., 1957.1, 20, 1961.1
Coughlan, Robert, D49a, 1953.8, 1954.15,
  36, 39
Courtin, A7p-q
Covarrubias, Miguel, 1932.14, 1967.11
Cowan, Michael H., 1968.9-10
Cowley, Malcolm, A13l, 23a-h, B16b,
  E12a, G24d-f, 1935.9, 1935.9, 1939.8,
  1940.6, 1942.7, 1944, 1945.1-2,
  1947.3, 1948.13, 1949.2, 1951.11, 23,
  1952.14, 1954.16, 40, 1957.27, 1959.27,
  1960.14, 1965.8, 1966.6, 14-15,
  1967.10, 1968.11, 1973.12
Crane, Joan St. C., 1970.6, 1971.1
Crawford, Joan, 1933.1
Crosby, Caresse and Harry, A8x
Cross, Barbara M., 1960.6
Crowther, Bosley, A24d
Cullen, John B., 1961.10
cummings, e. e., 1965.15
Cunliffe, Marcus, 1954.41
Curti, Merle, B10f
Cuthbert, Clifton, 1931.11

Daney, Lewis M., 1972.5, 1974.4
D'Agostino, Nemi, 1955.14
Dain, Martin J., L21, 30-31, 1963.13,
  1965.8
Daniel, Bradford, 1963.16, 1964.22

Daniel, Robert W., A2a, 3, 4b, 5a, 6b, 7e,
  1942.10, 1950.10, 1972.7
Dannay, Frederic ("Ellery Queen"), B70b
Dāriūsh, Parvīz, A18w
Dashiell, Alfred, B5c, 9b
Dauner, Louise, 1965.10
Dauphine, Augusto, A23h
Davenport, Basil, 1929.2
Davenport, F. Garvin, Jr., 1970.15
Davidson, Donald, 1931.27, 1957.31
Davis, Floyd, B55a, 60a, 66a
Dawson, Margaret Cheney, 1932.8
Day, Douglas, A41
Dean, Leonard F., B64d, D16f
Deane, Peter, 1968.25
De Angelis, Giulio, A4r, 7y
Dekle, Bernard, 1969.14
de Kooning, Willem, J2a
Delgove, Henri, A5k, 8y, 30k
De Mille, Agnes, J13a
Demopoulos, Mary, A29a
Déri, György, A13jj
Devlin, Albert J., 1972.2
DeVoto, Bernard, 1936.3
Diamond, David, 1965.15
Dickerson, Mary Jane, 1964.4, 1966.8
Dickinson, Asa Don, 1937.1
Dickmann, Max, A7t
Dillistone, F. W., 1960.18
Doar, Harriet, 1964.23
Dolbier, Maurice, 1959.25
Dominicis, A. M., G12a, 1954.2
Doran, Leonard, 1951.20
Dorsch, Robert L, 1962.27
Douglas, Harold J., 1972.7
Doyle, Paul A., 1963.34
Dubramet, Jean, A4n-p
Duncan, Robert David, A3d-f
Dunlap, Mary Montgomery, 1970.2
Durant, Ariel and Will, 1970.16

Durrett, Frances Bowen, 1964.30
Dutra, Lia Corrêa, B1j-k
Dykeman, C. H., D26b

Early, James, 1972.10
Eby, Cecil D., 1959.16
Edel, Leon, 1962.41
Edinga, Hans, A21y
Edlund, Mårten, A8nn, 28k, B6p, 60b, D29b
Edmonds, Irene C., 1953.12
Ehrlich, Arnold, D25g
Eijde, Brita, A32r
Eisinger, Chester E., 1963.28
Elias, Robert H., 1954.1
Ellmann, Richard, 1957.9, 1963.6
Emerson, O. B., 1964.30
Emmanuel, Pierre, 1951.20
Engle, Paul, B73d, 74b, 1950.8, 1951.13, 1954.9, 17, 1957.10
Everett, Walter K., 1969.5

Fadiman, Clifton, D25d, 1929.3, 1930.3, 1931.9, 1935.6, 1938.3, 1939.4, 1940.3, 1951.15, 1955.15, 1962.4
Falk, O., G37c
Falkner, Maud Butler, D50a, K2a
Falkner, Murry C., K14, L1
Falkner, Col. William C., K1a
Fant, Joseph L., G37a
Farnham, James F., 1965.10
Farrell, James T., 1932.7
Fass, John S., A10b
Faulkner, Estelle, K3-4, 1967.21
Faulkner, Jill, K5
Faulkner, Jim, 1972.5
Faulkner, John, A24e, K6-13
Faulkner, Virginia, 1937.2
Feaster, John, 1967.2

Feibleman, James K., 1969.15
Fein, Franz, A13u-y
Fenton, Charles A., B63g
Fernandez-Yañez, Julio, A16ff
Ferrari, Maria Stella, A5m
Ferreira, Armando, A13ll
Ficken, Carl, 1970.2, 1972.17
Fidler, William Perry, B6g
Fiedler, Leslie A., 1950.11, 1954.26, 1960.19, 1964.24, 1968.21
Figueiredo, Guilherme, A35o
Figuera, Angela, 1961.17
Finklestein, Sidney, 1962.22
Fisher, A. E., L7
Fiskin, A. M. I., 1946.3, 1952.3
Fitzhugh, Eleanor, 1939.9
Flesch, Richard K., A4t
Flowers, Paul, 1948.8, 1949.11, 1962.28
Flynn, Robert, 1956.3, 1957.20
Foley, Martha, B30b, 64b, 75b
Folsom, James K., B10f
Fonzi, Bruno, A19w
Foote, Horton, J8
Ford, Corey, 1932.2, 14, 1967.11
Ford, Margaret Particia, 1963.18
Ford, Ruth, A35a, m, p, 1965.8
de Forona, Ana-María, A21w, 30l
Foster, Ruel E., 1949.4, 1951.21, 1954.1
Fouts, Herbert, 1935.1
Frank, Harriet, Jr., J5-6, 11
Franklin, Malcolm A., K15a
Franklin, Phyllis, 1968.3
Franklin, R. W., 1967.2
Franklin, Rosemary, 1966.5
Franzen, Erich, A18t-v, 26l, B39b, G32b-c
Frazier, David L., 1956.3, 1957.20
French, Warren G., 1966.26, 1968.22
Frey, Leonard H., 1953.3
Friedman, Melvin J., 1959.13
Fritz-Crone, Pelle, A34n
Frohock, W. M., 1959.3

Fuller, Timothy, 1936.10
Funk, Robert W., 1972.2
Furthman, Jules, H3-4
Fussell, Paul, B64g

Gallo, Guarany, B44b
Gannett, Lewis, 1931.20, 1932.6, 1935.3, 1938.1, 1939.1, 1942.2, 1954.21
Gardner, Jennie B., 1939.6
Garrett, George P., Jr., 1957.4, 1973.11
Gaucher, Maxime, A2l-n
Gavin, Jerome, 1951.20
Geduld, Harry M., 1972.18
Geismar, Maxwell, 1942.11, 1948.6, 1954.13, 1958.9
Gerard, Albert, 1953.4
Gerstenberger, Donna, 1961.16
Giannitrapani, Angela, 1959.37
Gibson, William M., A30f
Gidley, Mick, 1970.2, 1973.11
Gigli, Lorenzo, A16w-y
Giles, Barbara, 1950.2, 1956.2
Gilman, Richard, 1962.24
Gilmer, Walker, 1970.17
Gilson, Etienne, 1946.11
Giorgini, J., 1965.14
Girard, Raymond, A37r-t
Giusti, George, B75a
Glaser, Milton, A37d
Goellner, Jack, 1954.10
Goethals, Thomas, 1965.20-21
Gohdes, Clarence, 1967.12
Gold, Joseph, 1961.5, 1962.1, 1966.16, 1973.11
Goldman, Arnold, 1971.6-7
Gordon, Caroline, B9c, 1946.1, 1948.3
Gotoh, Shoji, A16dd
Gould, Gerald, 1931.12
Goyert, Georg, A16u-v

Grant, Douglas, 1965.31
Graves, John Temple, II, 1942.3
Grayson, Charles, B1g, 25c
Green, A. Wigfall, 1951.23, 1957.27, 1965.28-29
Green, Martin, 1963.29
Greene, Graham, D27a
Greenwood, Sydney, A24j
Greer, Dorothy D., 1962.27
Greet, Thomas Y., 1957.23, 1960.14, 1973.11
Gregory, Eileen, 1970.11, 1973.2
Gregory, Horace, 1948.9, 1950.3
Grenier, Cynthia, G19a-b
Gresset, J., G32d-e
Gresset, Michel, B72b, 1966.8, 1968.3, 1970.7, 11
Griffin, Robert F., 1963.30
Gross, Seymour L, 1966.28
Gross, Theodore, B58c-d
Gruger, F. R., B39a, 40a, 42a, 51a, 52a, 62a
Grün, Herbert, A19dd
Guerard, Albert J., D16q
Guetti, James, 1967.13, 1971.6
Gunter, Richard, 1970.11
Gurza, Francisco, A2o, 5n
Guttmann, Allen, 1960.6
Gwynn, Frederick L, G28, 32

Hackett, Francis, E19a
Hafley, James, 1956.1
Hagopian, John V., 1967.2, 1970.11
Haight, Anne Lyon, 1955.16
Haislund, Niels, A19q
Hale, Nancy, 1963.12
Hale, William Harlan, 1931.16
Halman, Talât, A25j-k
Hamalian, Leo, A19j, B6o

Hāmid, Ādil, A25n
Hamilton, Edith, 1952.10, 1959.38
Hammar, Birgitta, B73c
Hammett, Dashiell, B1b
Handy, William J., 1959.15, 1971.19
Hanley, James, D9a
Hansen, Hagmund, A2v
Hansen, Harry, B34b, 47b, 54b, d, 55c,
    1931.3, 1934.2, 1935.2, 1936.1,
    1938.2, 1939.3, 1940.2
Hansen, Kurt Heinrich, A31k-l, B33b
Hardwick, Elizabeth, 1948.17, 1951.23,
    1957.27
Hardy, John Edward, 1964.25, 1966.28
Harkness, Bruce, 1967.4
Harnett, William M., K2a
Harrington, Evans B., 1952.4
Hart, Dick, A34l
Hart, Henry, C17a
Hart, John A., 1961.1
Hatcher, Harlan, 1935.11
Haury, Beth B., 1972.2
Hawkins, Arthur, Jr., A5a, 9a, 13a, 15a,
    L4
Hawks, Howard, H4a, 1962.39
Hayakawa, Hiroshi, A34w, 1961.11
Hayashi, Nobuyuki, A9m
Hayes, Ann L., 1961.1
Hecht, Ben, 1931.29
Heckman, Albert, C17a
Heins, John P., C17a
Hellman, Lillian, 1969.16
Helmrich-Hardt, Donata, D16s
Hemingway, Ernest, A11a-c, F10, 1932.13
Hendrick, George, 1961.16
Hendricks, Walter, B5d
Hennecke, Hans, A14g-h, B28b
Henning, Albin, B3a, 25a, 28a
Herlitschka, Herberth E., A8oo-pp
Hernandez, Ramon, A34r

Herzberg, Max, 1954.18
Hess, Albert, A7z, aa-bb
Hess, Thomas B., J2a
Hewes, Henry, 1959.10
Hicks, Granville, 1931.19, 1950.9, 1951.14,
    1957.15, 1962.8, 42
Hieronymus, Clara, D42a, 1970.9
Hilgard, Eug. W., 1860
Hilleret, René, A20q, 36l-m, G32d-f
Hilty, Hans Rudolf, A14i
Hilzheimer, Helmut, G32b-c
Hirshleifer, Phyllis, 1949.4, 1973.11
Hoar, Jere R., 1961.6
Hoel, Sigurd, A8mm, 13q
Hoffman, Daniel, 1969.17
Hoffman, Frederick J., 1951.23, 1956.8,
    1957.27, 1960.14, 1961.12, 1967.14-15,
    1968.22
Hofman, W. J. V., 1935.1
Hogan, Patrick G., Jr., 1966.10
Hogarth, Paul, A28f
Holman, C. Hugh, 1962.28, 1966.27, 1969.13,
    1971.8, 1972.19
Holmes, Edward M., 1966.17
Hopkins, Viola, 1955.4
Hornberger, Theodore, 1953.1
Howard, Edwin, 1965.14
Howard, Leon, 1960.20
Howard, Sidney, J1a
Howe, George, B61a
Howe, Irving, 1949.7, 1951.1 0, 1952.11,
    1954.8, 28, 1962.9, 35, 1964.21, 1966.28
Howe, Russell Warren, G25a
Howell, Elmo, 1960.6, 1968.3
Howes, Barbara, A32l
Howorth, Lucy Somerville, 1965.14
del Hoyo, Arturo, A7w, 30l
Hubbell, Jay B., 1967.12, 1972.20
Hudson, Tommy, 1950.10
Hughes, Richard, A2i, 6p, 1963.14

Hunt, John W., 1965.22, 1972.7
Hunter, Edwin R., 1973.5
Hunter, Jim, B61c
Hyams, Joe, G33a
Hyman, Mac, E24a

Inge, M. Thomas, 1966.1, 1970.8, 1971.8
Ingram, Forrest L., 1971.20
Inoue, Kenzi, A19t
Izard, Barbara, D42a, 1970.9

Jabra, Jabra I., A6dd
Jack, Peter Monro, 1936.2, 1939.7
Jackson, James T., 1946.6
Jacobs, Robert D., 1953.12
James, Alice, A14c
Jane-Mansfield, C., 1935.4
Jannoud, Claude, 1970.3
Janzon, Åke, B13b
Jarrett-Kerr, Martin, 1970.10
Jedde, Georg, A25i
Jedraszko, Sabina, A24l
Jelliffe, Robert A., G20a, 1962.10
Jerome, V. J., 1950.12
Jewkes, W. T., 1961.2
Johnson, Gerald W., 1935.10
Johnson, Merle, A13a, 1931.17
Johnson, Richard Colles, 1971.3
Jonason, Olov, B64h
Jones, Carter Brooke, 1948.10, 1950.6
Jones, Howard Mumford, 1949.5, 1953.10
Jonsson, Thorsten, A18p
Jørgensen, Gunnar Juel, A7v
Josephson, Matthew, 1933.2
Joyce, James, A4d
Juhasz, Leslie A., 1965.23
Junius Junior (pseud.), 1931.29

Kahn, Harry, A24s-u
Kahn, Joan, B5f
Kaila, Kai, A6ff, 13mm, 20v, 26z, 37x
Kaiser, Elisabeth, A6x-z, 19x-z, aa, 20n-p
Karasu, Bilge, A26n, B61b
Karl, Anita, A32k, 41a
Kartiganer, Donald M., 1964.1
Kashkin, I., A26r
Kato, Shozo, A24q
Katz, Joseph, 1971.22, 1972.17, 1973.14
Kauffer, E. McKnight, A8k, 24b, 25b, 28b
Kawatsu, Takashi, Blh
Kazantzés, Bas. L., A25m
Kazin, Alfred, 1942.8, 1951. 20, 1955.17,
     1957.11, 24, 1958.4, 11, 1960.14,
     1973.13
Kearns, Francis E., B4d
Kellner, Bruce, 1968.23
Kelly, Gerald R., 1969.10
Kelvin, Norman, B58c-d
Kennedy, Ellen Conroy, 1968.18
Kennedy, John F., 1962.18
Kerr, Elizabeth M., 1960.11, 1962.1, 1967.2,
     1969.6, 1973.11
Kerr, Walter, 1959.6
van Keulen, Johan, A8kk-ll
Kholmskaya, O., A26r
Kibler, James E., Jr., 1970.2
Kidd, Walter E., 1968.22
Kielty, Bernardine, B10e
Kierszys, Zofia, A2w, 8ss, 16gg, 17p, 21aa,
     25p, 26g, u, 33b
Kimmey, John M., 1971.8
Kincaid, Suzanne, 1963.18
King, Roma A., Jr., 1955.9, 1956.3, 1957.20,
     1972.7
Kinney, Arthur F., 1964.16
Kinoian, Vartkis, 1964.9
Kirk, David, E34a

Kirk, Robert W., 1963.19
Kissin, Eva H., B5g
Klotz, Marvin, 1963.19
Knight, Arthur, 1955.7
Knopf, Alfred, A6j
Knowles, Horace, D39b
Kocourek, Vítězslav, A26p
Koerner, W. H. D., B4a
Kollwitz, Käthe, A6b
Korg, Jacob, 1957.18
Koury, Leon Z., 1965.14
Krähenbühl, Olívia, A31m
Kramer, Arthur, J11a-c
Krešić, Stjepan, A6aa
Kreymorg, Alfred, B7a
Kristensen, Sven Møller, A8ee, 13ff, 19q,
    B6m, 1942.12, 1955.18
Kronenberger, Louis, A35b, 1938.4, 1940.5,
    1965.2, 1971.23
Kuettner, Al, G26a
Kunitz, Stanley J. ("Dilly Tante"), 1931.28
Kurnitz, Harry, H5

Lamb, Lynton, A25e, 31g
Landi, Attilio, A15g
Landor, Mikhail, 1972.23
Langford, Gerald, 1971.9, 1972.11
Langford, Richard E., 1963.30
Larbaud, Valery, A7n
Larsen, Eric, 1967.2
Lawson, Lewis A., 1971.21
Leary, Lewis, 1964.15, 1969.9, 1973.6
Leaver, Florence, 1960.14
Le Breton, Maurice, 1959.13
Lecuona, Pedro, A13dd
Lehan, Richard D., 1966.29
Lehtonen, Paavo, A26z
Leiria, Mario Henrique, A6cc
Lemay, Harding, 1959.28
Levey, Michael, 1967.8

Levinson, Riki, A31a
Lewicki, James, A37b
Lewis, R. W. B., 1951.7, 1959.39
Lewis, Wyndham, 1934.5, 1952. 15
Lind, Ilse Dusoir, 1960.14, 1973.11
Lindegren, Erik, A13ee, B13b
Linn, Robert, 1934.6
Linscott, Robert N., 1963.10
Linturi, Jouko, A26z
Lisca, Peter, 1953.1, 1954.1
Little, Roger, 1973.3-4
Litz, Walton, 1952.4
Livenzev, Arianna, A32t
Liveright, Horace, A2c, 1965.2, 1970.17
Lo Bue, Francesco, A9k
Lockhart, Jack, 1938.6
Longley, John Lewis, Jr., 1950.10, 1957.5,
    1960.14, 1963.20, 1971.8
Longstreet, Stephen, 1972.21
Loos, Anita, E1a
Louis-Rousselet, G., A16z, aa
Lozano, Jose Blaya, A9j
Luboff, Louis, B49a
Ludovici, L. J., 1957.33
Lustig and Barrows, A13d
Lytle, Andrew, B71d, 1951.23, 1955.1,
    1957.21, 27, 1966.30

Macauley, Robie, A2g
Maclaren-Ross, J., 1955.11, 1965.32
MacLeish, Archibald, 1951.20, 1968.24
Madden, Charles F., 1968.19
Madden, David, 1970.13
Maddow, Ben, J3a-b
Madsen, Gerhard, B59c
Magalaner, Marvin, B58d
Mailer, Norman, E38a
Malcolm, Donald, 1957.16
Maldini, Magda De Cristofaro, A30o
Malin, Irving, 1957.28

Malraux, Andre, A8y-z, aa-bb, 1933.7, 1953.6
Manfredi, Domingo, A4s
Mann, Dorothea Lawrance, 1936.4
Mann, Thomas, C17a, 1951.20
Marcus, Steven, 1957.22, 1960.14
Margarido, Alfredo, A7dd
Margherito, Rudy, B44b
Marichalar, Antonio, A8dd, ii
Marković, Božidar, A25l
Marmont, Alberto, A18o, 23h, 30p
Marsh, Fred T., 1934.1
Marshall, Lenore, 1962.21
Martin, E. W., 1946.10
Martin, Hansford, B73d
Martin, Jay, 1970.18
Marvin, John R., 1952.2
Massey, Linton R., E5a, 1956.9, 1968.12
Match, Richard, 1951.16
Materassi, Mario, 1961.21, 1964.31, 1968.13
Matson, Alex, A7u
Maurer, A16b
Maxwell, D. E. S., 1963.31
Mayberry, George, A13m
Mayes, Martha, 1957.32
Mayoux, Jean-Jacques, 1960.14
Mays, Benjamin E., D37b-c
Mazía, Floreal, A6w
McAlmon, Robert, 1968.17
McCrady, John, L36
McElderry, B. R., Jr., 1971.8
McGrew, Julia, 1959.11
McHaney, Thomas L., 1966.8, 1970.2, 1971.2, 1972.1, 1973.2
McLaughlin, Richard, 1951.19
Meats, Stephen E., 1971.2
Meek, Ed, L23
Mellard, James M., 1967.4
Meredith, James, K12a
Merino, Santos, A20s

Meriwether, James B., A2i, 5i, 6p, 7l, 8u, 9h, 13n, 15c, 16p, 17j, 18j, 19n, 20j, 21l, 24j, 25e, 26c-d, 28f, 30i, 31g, 34l, 39a-c, D10a-b, 13a, G38a, 1957.4, 7, 1959.1, 19, 1960.8, 1961.7, 13, 1962.30, 1963.4, 8, 1964.4, 1967.4, 1969.18, 1970.11, 1971.4, 10, 22, 1972.5, 1973.2, 14, 1974.6
Merton, Thomas, 1967.16
Merwin, W. S., 1957.33
Meyers, Harold B., 1962.23
Michael, Thomas E., 1965.6
Mihajlović, Milica, A8rr
Mihelić, Mira, A13hh
Milano, Paolo, 1948.14
Millay, Edna St. Vincent, A38a
Miller, David M., 1967.2
Miller, James E., Jr., 1967.17
Miller, Llewellyn, 1954.39
Miller, Nolan, 1957.32
Millgate, Michael, G38a, 1961.14, 1965.24, 1966.2, 18-19, 1968.2, 1970.11, 1971.6-7, 1972.2, 1973.2, 11, 15
Miner, Ward L., 1952.12, 1955.19
Minter, David L., 1969.7
Mitchell, Charles, 1965.12
Mize, Clell, A29a
Mizener, Arthur, 1955.10, 1964.26, 1967.18
Mjöberg, Jöran, A7s
Mohrt, Michel, A30k
Mok, Michel, G6a
Moldenhauer, Joseph J., 1960.14
Monaghan, Charles, 1968.6
Monaghan, David M., 1972.3
Mondadori, Arnoldo, E33a
Monicelli, Giorgio, A15g, 30o-q, 34s, 37m
Monteiro, George, 1958.6
Moore, Clement, C17a
Moore, Geoffrey, 1964.27
Moore, Nicholas, B11b

Morell, Giliane, 1972.2
Moreno de Sáenz, Lucrecia, A25f
Morris, Wright, 1952.6, 1957.34
Moses, W. R., 1953.5, 1956.3, 1957.20
Mottram, Eric, 1971.11
Mueller, William R., 1959.40
Muhlenfeld, Elisabeth S., 1972.2
Mullen, Phillip E., E22a
Mumford, Lewis, B7a
Munson, Gorham B., 1931.26
Murphy, Ella M., 1961.20
Myers, Dale A., 1966.10

Nadeau, Maurice, 1952.16
Napoletano, J., A30l
do Nascimento, Cabral, B64i
Nash, Jay Robert, 1967.3
Nathan, Monique, 1963.21
Nauman, Hilda, 1967.5
Nejgebauer, Aleksandar, A21u
Nelson, Beatriz Florencia, A17m
Newsom, Thomas B., 1972.6
Nicholson, Norman, 1946.10
Niederstenbruch, Alex, B64f
Nielsen, Kay, D16o
Nilon, Charles H., 1962.36, 1965.25
Nipson, Herbert, D41b
Nishikawa, Masami, A30n
Nishiwaki, Junzaburo, A30m
Nishizaki, Ichiro, A2s
Noel, Jacques, A30k
Norlén, Håkan, A18p
Norris, Hoke, 1959.29, 1962.11
North, Alex, J5c
North, Sterling, 1935.5, 1954.22
Novak, Michael, A31e

Oberfirst, Robert, A32g

O'Brien, Edward, B6b, e-f, 26b-c, 31b, 41b,
    45b, 50b, 55b, 59b
Ocampo, Victoria, A35k
O'Connor, William Van, A29a, 1952.3, 8,
    1953.5, 12, 1954.37, 1957.2, 1959.32,
    1960.14, 1961.17, 1970.12
O'Donnell, George Marion, 1939.12, 1951.23,
    1957.27, 1960.14, 1973.11
O'Faolain, Sean, 1956.10
Ohashi, Kenzaburo, A21bb
Ohashi, Kenzo, A16cc
Ohashi, Kichinosuke, A17r, 26m
Okubo, Yasuo, A19s, 25h
O'Nan, Martha, 1969.19
Onoe, Masaji, A6gg
Ormala, Marketta, A26z
de Ortiz, Raquel W., A20k
Osborne, Charles, 1967.8

Page, Sally R., 1972.12
Palievsky, Pyotr V., 1966.7, 1972.23
Palla, Victor, A26k
Panichas, George A., 1967.16, 1971.21
Park, Sung Hoon, A19bb
Parrot, D. C., L10
Paterson, John, 1971.6
Paulding, Gouverneur, 1959.30
Pavese, Cesare, A23h
Pearce, Richard, 1966.11
Pearson, Norman Holmes, 1954.34
Peavy, Charles D., 1971.12
Peden, William, B63i, 1950.5
de Pedrolo, Manuel, A13kk
Peery, James Robert, 1942.4
Pego, Aurelio, 1963.3
Percy, W. A. A38a
Perluck, Herbert A., 1960.3, 1972.7
Perry, Bradley T., 1953.1-2, 4
Pfeiffer, Andrew H., 1972.5

Robinson, W. R., 1967.7
Robredo, Agustin Caballero, A7w
Rodgers, Jimmie, J5c
Rodman, Seldon, A6o
Rogers, Katherine M., 1966.32
Rolo, Charles J., 1954.27
Romaine, Paul, A11, F1-2, 10-11, G3b, 1932.4
Rosenfeld, Isaac, 1951.2, 1962.43
Rosenfeld, Paul, B7a
Ross, Danforth, 1961.18
Rossky, William 1970.1, 1973.11
Rota, Bertram, 1955.2
Roth, Russell, 1949.4, 1952.7
Rothkopf, Carol Z., 1964.13
Rouse, Blair, 1958.10
Rovere, Richard H., A13e-f
Rubin, Louis D., Jr., 1953.12, 1957.26, 1963.33, 1964.28, 1967.19, 1969.13
Rubio, Jose Lopez, A35l
Rudd, Hughes, 1963.11
Rugoff, Milton, 1942.6, 1957.12
Rule, Philip C., S. J., 1972.7
Runnquist, Åke, B13b
Runyan, Harry, D30a, 1954.2, 1964.14, 1966.20-21
Ruotolo, Lucio P., 1973.16
Rutledge, Wilmuth S., 1967.4
Ryan, Jack 1965.14
Ryan, Marjorie, 1953.3

Saal, Hubert D., 1947.1
Sakata, Katsuzo, A28s
Salmaggi, Cesare, A32s
Salter, A20a
Sampaio, Jorge, A20t
Sample, Paul, D26a
Sanders, Walter, A24e
Sanderson, Jane, 1965.14

Sands, Maurice, 1963.34
Santesson, Hans, A32j
Saporta, Marc, 1970.3
Sartre, Jean-Paul, 1946.5, 1951.23, 1953.6 1957.27, 35, 1960.14
Sawyer, Kenneth B., 1954.2
Scagnetti, Aldo, A8ff
Schappes, Morris U., 1933.6
Scherman, David E., L29
Schmidt, Arno, A32u-w
Schmitter, Dean Morgan, 1973.10
Schnack, Elisabeth, A21q, 25o, 26h, q, y, 33c, 34o-p, 36j-k, 37p-q, B53c
Schneider, Marcel, 1957.3
Schnorr, Robert, A28n-p, 35c, e-g
Scholes, Robert, A30h
Schorer, Mark, B57d, 1971.23
Schulberg, Budd, 1972.24
Schulman, L. M., B54e
Schünemann, Peter, A7z, aa-bb
Schwartz, Delmore, 1955.3
Schwarz, Josef, A18x, 26p
Scott, Arthur L., 1954.33
Scott, Evelyn, 1929.4
Scott, Nathan A., Jr., 1957.37
Scott, Zachary, A35m, p
Seaver, Edwin, 1931.4
Seeley, Evelyn, G1a
de Sena, Jorge, A19ff, B4c
Seyppel, Joachim, 1971.13
Shalavar, Bahman, A6bb
Shapiro, Charles, 1958.11
Shaw, Joe C., 1961.4
Shenton, Edward, A18a, j, l, n, 33a, B38a, 43a, 48a, 50a, 64a, L33-35
Shepherd, J. Clinton, B24a
Sherwood, John C., 1954.2
Sidney, George R., H6a
Silveira, Breno, A37l
Silver, James W., 1964.29

Simmons, Edgar, 1968.4
Simon, Jean, 1950.13
Simpson, Lewis P., 1965.33
Sims, Cecil, D37b-c
Singleton, Ralph H., B6q
Škvorecký, Josef, A7cc
Slabey, Robert M. 1961.4, 1971.8
Slatoff, Walter J., 1960.14-15, 1973.11
Sleeth, Irene Lynn, 1962.37
Slobodin, Arthur, 1960.9
Słomczyński, Maciej, A13ii
Smart, George K., 1965.27
Smith, Beverley E., 1971.2
Smith, Bradley, 1948.1
Smith, Gregory Jay, A32l
Smith, Harrison, D16e, F5, 1955.13
Smith, Henry Nash, A12a, 1953.2
Smith, Ligia Junqueira, A8jj
Smith, Margarita G., B74c
Smith, Marshall J., G3
Smith, Raleigh W., Jr. 1970.2
Smith, Thelma M. 1955.19
Snell, George, 1946.7, 1947.2
Solotaroff, Theodore, 1970.19
Soulac, Anne-Marie, 1946.11
de Sousa, Antonio, A24x-y
de Sousa Rebelo, Luis, A6cc, 19gg, 28r
Sowder, William J., 1963.7
Spiller, Robert E., 1957.36
Spivak, Lawrence E., B6j
Spratling, William, A3, F17, 1967.20
Stallings, Laurence, G4a, 1931.21
Stanfield, John James, 1963.1
Stanford, Donald E. 1965.33
Starke, Aubrey, 1934.7
Starrett, Vincent, B70b
Stein, Gertrude, 1933.4
Stein, Jean, A30f, G24, 1960.14
Steloff, Frances, 1940.8
Stephens, Rosemary, 1970.2

Sterian, Margareta, A26o
Stewart, Randall, 1958.12, 1968.26
Stone, Edward, 1969.20
Stone, Emily Whitehurst, 1965.17
Stone, Geoffrey, 1932.10
Stone, Phil, A1, 34a, l, 1931.18, 1942.9, 1964.4
Stonesifer, Richard J., 1958.7
Storm, Ole, A21x
Storoni, Filiberto, A5l
Strandberg, Victor, 1965.5
Straumann, Heinrich, 1951.24, 1960.14, 1968.14, 1973.11
Strauss, Harold, 1936.7, 1940.4
Stresau, Hermann, A5r, 17l, 21p, r-t, 26q, 33c
Strøm, Leo, A8mm
Styron, William, 1954.11, 1962.20, 1968.6
Sükösd, Mihály, A13jj
Sullivan, Frank, 1951.5
Sullivan, Walter, 1969.13, 1972.25
Summers, A. Burks, G13a
Suyama, Shizuo, A13nn
Suzuki, Kenzo, A24r
Swift, Esther M., 1964.2
Swiggart, Peter, 1955.6, 1962.38
Sulvester, Harry, 1950.4
Szíjgyártó, László, A37w
Szladits, Lola L., 1973.17

Taillefer, Anne, 1962.26
Takahashi, Masao, A26j, m, 36q, 1958.8, 1960.16
Takigawa, Motoo, A15h
Takiguchi, Naotaro, A26j
Talley, Rhea, G9a
Talmey, Allene, 1962.16
Tamer, Ülkü, A26s
Tasso, Bruno, A34s

Warburton, Th., A5o, 24n
Ward, Lynd, A14a-b, C17a
Warren, Joyce W., 1966.8
Warren, Robert Penn, B6d, 1931.24,
     1941.1, 1946.4, 1951.4, 12, 23,
     1957.27, 1958.13, 1959.13, 1960.14,
     1965.8, 13, 1966.22-23, 1973.11
Wasson, Ben, E5a, 1948.2
Watkins, Ann, A8t
Watkins, Floyd C., 1960.1, 1961.10,
     1967.2, 1971.24, 1973.11
Watson, James Gray, 1968.15
Watts, Jean, B74a
Watts, Richard, 1959.7
Way, Brian, 1961.3
Weatherby, W. J., 1962.25
Webb, Constance, E13a
Webb, James W., 1965.28-29
Webster, Mark, 1970.5
Weisgerber, Jean, 1968.16
Weiss, Daniel, 1963.9
Weiss, Sabine, L14
Welker, Robert L., 1964.30
Wells, Oliver, C12
Welty, Eudora, D51b, L25, 1948.15,
     1949.13, 1965.8, 16, 1972.4
Werner, Vilém, A13z
Wertham, Frederic, A13l
West, Anthony, 1951.8, 1959.31, 1969.1
West, Nathanael, G14a
West, Ray B., Jr., 1949.4, 1951.23,
     1952.14, 19-20, 1957.27, 1960.4,
     1973.11
West, Rebecca, 1931.14
Westland, Olga, 1950.10 (See also Olga
     W. Vickery)
Westmoreland, Gen. William C., E46a
Whan, Edgar W., 1950.10
Wheeler, Otis, 1973.11
Wheelwright, Philip E., 1931.8

Whisnant, Charleen, 1964.23
White, Ray Lewis, D22b
Whittemore, Reed, B68c
Wilder, Amos N., 1972.7
Wiley, Bell I., D37b-c
Williams, Blanche Colton, B3b-c, 25b
Williams, Cecil B., 1952.2
Williams, Joan, 1961.22, 1971.25
Wilson, Colin, 1962.44
Wilson, Edmund, 1946.2, 1949.12,
     1950.14
Wilson, Gayle Edward, 1971.2
Wojciechowska, Kalina, A5q, 19cc
Wood, Norton, D31c
Woodcock, John, A17k, 36h, 37k
Woodress, James, 1962.45
Woodruff, Neal, Jr., 1961.1
Woods, Miriam, A33a
Woodworth, Stanley D., 1957.20, 1959.13,
     35
Woollcott, Alexander, 1931.10
Wright, Richard, E13a
Wynn, Lelia Clark, 1965.14

Xavier, Berenice, A13gg

Yañez, Julio Fernández, A30l
Yndurain, Francisco, 1953.9
Yonce, Margaret, 1970.2
Young, Thomas Daniel, 1960.1

Zakrzewski, Jan, A26g, u, 33b, B6n
Zalamea, Jorge, A28i-j
Zamattio, Paola Ojetti, A8gg-hh
Zavaleta, C. E., 1959.36
Zéraffa, Michel, D25b
Zink, Karl E., 1956.3, 1957.20
Zycieńska, Ewa, A17p, 18z, 24z, 26g, u

INTERNATIONAL ECONOMIC LAW SERIES
General Editor: John H. Jackson

REGIONAL TRADE AGREEMENTS AND THE WTO LEGAL SYSTEM

Regional Trade Agreements and the WTO Legal System

Edited by

LORAND BARTELS

and

FEDERICO ORTINO

OXFORD

UNIVERSITY PRESS

OXFORD
UNIVERSITY PRESS

Great Clarendon Street, Oxford OX2 6DP

Oxford University Press is a department of the University of Oxford.
It furthers the University's objective of excellence in research, scholarship,
and education by publishing worldwide in

Oxford New York

Auckland Cape Town Dar es Salaam Hong Kong Karachi
Kuala Lumpur Madrid Melbourne Mexico City Nairobi
New Delhi Shanghai Taipei Toronto

With offices in

Argentina Austria Brazil Chile Czech Republic France Greece
Guatemala Hungary Italy Japan Poland Portugal Singapore
South Korea Switzerland Thailand Turkey Ukraine Vietnam

Oxford is a registered trade mark of Oxford University Press
in the UK and in certain other countries

Published in the United States
by Oxford University Press Inc., New York

British Library Cataloguing in Publication Data
Data available

Library of Congress Cataloging in Publication Data

Regional trade agreements and the WTO legal system / edited by Lorand Bartels and
Federico Ortino.
  p. cm
Includes bibliographical references and index.
ISBN-13: 978-0-19-920699-5 (hardback : alk. paper)
ISBN-13: 978-0-19-920700-8 (pbk. : alk. paper) 1. World Trade Organization—
Rules and practice. 2. Foreign trade regulation. 3. Trade blocs. 4. Regionalism.
5. Tariff—Law and legislation. I. Bartels, Lorand. II. Ortino, Federico.
  K4610.RR 2006
  382′.92—dc22   2006032601

Typeset in Sabon by
RefineCatch Limited, Bungay, Suffolk
Printed in Great Britain
on acid-free paper by
Biddles Ltd., King's Lynn, Norfolk

ISBN 0-19-920699-6 (Hbk.)   978-0-19-920699-5 (Hbk.)
ISBN 0-19-920700-3 (Pbk.)   978-0-19-920700-8 (Pbk.)

1 3 5 7 9 10 8 6 4 2

General Editor's Preface

JOHN H. JACKSON[*]

One of the most perplexing and complex problems relating to the world trading system today, is the proliferation of a wide variety of so-called 'regional trade agreements (RTAs)'. These agreements vary greatly in composition and structure, from numerous bilateral 'Free Trade Agreements (FTAs)' to certain small regional or mini-lateral agreements such as NAFTA (North American Free Trade Agreement) or CAFTA (Central American Free Trade Agreement), and in some cases involving nations which are not even in the same region. These agreements have a wide variety of provisions, and often vary greatly even when involving one same partner. This volume, which is part of the Oxford University Press series of books on subjects of the extraordinarily broad landscape of international economic law, contains an excellent analysis of the various characteristics and problems of regional trade agreements.

This volume, edited by Lorand Bartels and Federico Ortino, is a very welcome contribution to the legal knowledge about international economic policy and the structure and configuration of the world trading system. The great proliferation of a wide variety of agreements poses considerable concern to the multilateral trade system, as most often represented by the WTO. On the other hand, many of these agreements can perform useful functions in a world that is often hobbled by difficult 'constitutional' problems of making timely decisions so as to keep abreast of rapid paced economic developments frequently described as 'globalization'.

Among other recent examples of commentary about the proliferation or 'spaghetti bowl' of RTAs is the annual WTO report for the year 2003, which includes an analytical section describing the multiplying development of regional trade agreements, in expressing some serious reservations about the policy implications of them, while recognizing some of the advantages. More recently, these issues were explored by the 'Sutherland' Consultative Board, which in its January 2005 report devoted an important chapter to the dangers to the multilateral system that can occur from the 'erosion of non-discrimination', attributed to the great growth in the number of FTAs and RTAs.

[*] *University Professor of Law*, Georgetown University Law Center (GULC), Washington, DC; *Director*, Institute of International Economic Law, GULC; *General Editor*, International Economic Law Series, Oxford University Press; *Editor in Chief, Journal of International Economic Law*, Oxford University Press.

Clearly there are some advantages for the RTAs, partly because, with a limited number of members, decisions often can be made more easily, more efficiently, and in a more timely way. Furthermore, these agreements often explore and experiment with subjects that have proven virtually impossible to develop in the broader multilateral framework of about 150 member countries or more.

On the other hand, many concerns are important. To some degree, RTAs can develop protectionist measures which discriminate against certain parts of the world trade and in any event create additional transaction costs because of the need of customs officials to analyse the 'origin' of goods (in a world where national origin becomes less and less meaningful for goods or services.) The rules of origin often themselves are manipulated in such a way to provide protectionist effects. In addition there are some subjects which do not well lend themselves to smaller grouping of states. For example, subsidies, particularly those on agriculture, cannot be effectively contained by agreements between small groups of countries, since the world market is what will drive many of the problems regarding subsidies and the market will restrict ways to diminish the distorting allocation effects of subsidies.

This book takes these various issues up in considerable detail and with very able perspective, in five parts which span very effectively these policy conundrums. Part I, entitled 'Framework Issues', sets the stage with an economic and political analysis of regional trade agreements and a discussion of 'constitutional functions' of the WTO and its relationship to regional trade agreements. Part II is entitled 'WTO Regulation of Regional Trade Agreements', and in this Part a series of some of the legal issues of regional trade agreements is explored. For example, the text explores whether these agreements and their rules of origin truly comply with the mandatory disciplines embodied in the norms expressed in Article XXIV of the GATT text incorporated in the WTO. Part III, which is entitled 'WTO-Plus Issues in Regional Trade Agreements', is a series of seven chapters and presents an awesomely extensive analysis of a number of different characteristics found in regional trade agreements, which in some cases push the frontiers of trade policy and ably provide answers in situations where the multilateral trade system has not been proven very effective. Subjects taken up include: services liberalization, foreign investment, intellectual property, competition law, harmonization ideas, constitutional reforms including possible interaction with human rights norms, and environmental issues of various sorts.

Part IV discusses 'Dispute Settlement in Regional Trade Agreements' and includes the perplexing problems of how these dispute settlement systems interact with each other. Finally, Part V, 'Interfaces Between the WTO and Regional Trade Agreements', begins to look more systemically at questions of overlap and jurisdiction between the WTO and RTAs and the question of applicability of WTO law in RTAs.

This book will certainly become a standard source of analyses which will influence future scholarship, and will be a necessary component of the thinking of policy makers, academics, and all professionals who have to grapple in-depth with the problems of world trade and globalization.

Acknowledgements

The contributions in this book are for the most part the proceedings of a conference of the same title held in Edinburgh in May 2005. We would like to express our deep gratitude to the International Law Association (British Branch), the British Academy, the University of Edinburgh, and Oxford University Press, for their generous support of the conference and of this publication. We would also like to thank the participants in the conference for their contributions, both formal and informal, which have enriched this publication. And we are grateful to Humberto Zúñiga Schroder for first class editorial assistance, and to John Louth and Gwen Booth at OUP for their helpfulness and efficiency with the production process of this book.

Contents

Table of Cases

A. GATT AND WTO DISPUTE SETTLEMENT REPORTS

(1) WTO Appellate Body Reports

Tables of Treaties and
International Instruments

A. WTO AGREEMENTS

GATT/WTO Decisions and Declarations

B. MULTILATERAL REGIONAL TRADE AGREEMENTS

Andean Community (Bolivia, Colombia, Peru, Ecuador, and Venezuela)

CAFTA–DR (United States, Costa Rica, El Salvador, Guatemala, Honduras, Nicaragua, and Dominican Republic)

Caribbean Community (Antigua and Barbuda, Bahamas, Barbados, Belize, Dominica, Grenada, Guyana, Haiti, Jamaica, Montserrat, Saint Kitts and Nevis, Saint Lucia, Saint Vincent and the Grenadines, Suriname, and Trinidad and Tobago)

C. BILATERAL REGIONAL TRADE AGREEMENTS

D. GENERAL

List of Abbreviations

ACP	African, Caribbean and Pacific
AJIL	American Journal of International Law
Alb L J Sci & Tech	Albany Law Journal of Science & Technology
ALCA	Área de Libre Comercio de las Américas (Free Trade Area of the Americas)
Am Rev Int Arb	American Review of International Arbitration
Am U Int L Rev	American University International Law Review
APEC	Asia-Pacific Economic Cooperation
Appl Econ Lett	Applied Economics Letters
Ariz J Int & Comp L	Arizona Journal of International and Comparative Law
ASEAN	Association of Southeast Asian Nations
ASEAN Econ Bull	ASEAN Economic Bulletin
Asian Econ J	Asian Economic Journal
ASIL Proc	American Society of International Law Proceedings
Asper Rev Int Bus & Trade L	Asper Review of International Business and Trade Law
Aust YIL	Australian Yearbook of International Law
BISD	Basic Instruments and Selected Documents (GATT Series)
BIT	Bilateral Investment Treaty
Brook J Int L	Brooklyn Journal of International Law
BYIL	British Yearbook of International Law
BYU L Rev	Brigham Young University Law Review
CACM	Central American Common Market
CAFTA-DR	Central American Free Trade Agreement
Cal W Int L J	California Western International Law Journal
Caricom	Caribbean Community
CCAEC	Canada–Chile Agreement on Environmental Cooperation
CCLCA	Canada–Chile Labour Cooperation Agreement
CCRLCA	Canada–Costa Rica Labour Cooperation Agreement
CEC	Commission for Environmental Cooperation
CEPA	Mainland and Hong Kong Closer Economic Partnership Agreement
CMLR	Common Market Law Review
Colo J Int Envtl L & Policy	Colorado Journal of International Environmental Law and Policy
Colum J Eur L	Columbia Journal of European Law

Comesa	Common Market for Eastern and Southern Africa
Cornell Int L J	Cornell International Law Journal
CRTA	WTO Committee on Regional Trade Agreements
CU	Customs Union
CUP	Cambridge University Press
CUSFTA	Canada–US Free Trade Agreement
DSB	Dispute Settlement Body
DSM	Dispute Settlement Mechanism
DSU	WTO Dispute Settlement Understanding
EBL Rev	European Business Law Review
EC	European Community or EC Treaty (after Article number)
ECHR	European Convention on Human Rights
ECJ	European Court of Justice
ECOWAS	Economic Community of West African States
ECR	European Court Reports
ECT	Energy Charter Treaty
ECtHR	European Court of Human Rights
EEA	European Economic Area
EFA Rev	European Foreign Affairs Review
EFTA	European Free Trade Association
EJIL	European Journal of International Law
EL Rev	European Law Review
ELJ	European Law Journal
EPA	Economic Partnership Agreement
EPL	European Public Law
ERPL	European Review of Private Law
EU	European Union or Treaty on European Union (after Article number)
Euratom	European Atomic Energy Community
Euromed	Euro-Mediterranean
Far East Econ Rev	Far Eastern Economic Review
Ford Int LJ	Fordham International Law Journal
FTA	Free Trade Agreement or Free Trade Area
FTAA	Free Trade Area of the Americas
GATS	General Agreement on Trade in Services
GATT	General Agreement on Tariffs and Trade
GCC	Gulf Cooperation Council
Geo Int Env L Rev	Georgetown International Environmental Law Review
Geo Wash Int L Rev	George Washington International Law Review
GSP	Generalized System of Preferences
GTAP	Global Trade Analysis Project
GYIL	German Yearbook of International Law

Harv Int L J	Harvard International Law Journal
Harv J L & Pub Policy	Harvard Journal of Law and Public Policy
HTS	Harmonized Tariff System
ICJ	International Court of Justice
ICJ Rep	International Court of Justice Reports
ICLQ	International and Comparative Law Quarterly
ICSID	International Centre for Settlement of Investment Disputes
ILC	International Law Commission
ILM	International Legal Materials
ILO	International Labour Organization
Ind J Glob Leg Stud	Indiana Journal of Global Legal Studies
Int Org	International Organisation
IOLR	International Organizations Law Review
IPE	International Political Economy
IPR	Intellectual Property Rights
ITL Rev	International Trade Law Review
ITO	International Trade Organization
J Asian Econ	Journal of Asian Economics
J Copyright Soc USA	Journal of the Copyright Society of the USA
J Econ Integration	Journal of Economic Integration
J Econ Lit	Journal of Economic Literature
J Econ Perspect	Journal of Economic Perspectives
J Int Trade Econ Devel	Journal of International Trade and Economic Development
J Pol Econ	Journal of Political Economy
JEPP	Journal of European Public Policy
JIEL	Journal of International Economic Law
JWIP	Journal of World Intellectual Property
JWT	Journal of World Trade
Law & Bus Rev Am	Law and Business Review of the Americas
LCP	Law and Contemporary Problems
LDC	Least Developed Country
Leiden J Int L	Leiden Journal of International Law
LIEI	Legal Issues of Economic Integration
LMO	Living Modified Organism
Loy LAL Rev	Loyola of Los Angeles Law Review
Marq Intell Prop L Rev	Marquette Intellectual Property Law Review
MEA	Multilateral Environmental Agreement
Mercosur	Mercado Común del Sur (Southern Common Market)
MFN	Most Favoured Nation
Mich J Int L	Michigan Journal of International Law

Minn J Global Trade	Minnesota Journal of Global Trade
MJIEL	Manchester Journal of International Economic Law
MLR	Modern Law Review
N Amer J Econ Finance	North American Journal of Economics and Finance
N C J Int L & Com Reg	North Carolina Journal of International Law and Commercial Regulation
NAAEC	North American Agreement on Environmental Cooperation
NAALC	North American Agreement on Labor Cooperation
NAFTA	North American Free Trade Agreement
NAO	National Administrative Office
Neth Int L Rev	Netherlands International Law Review
New Eng L Rev	New England Law Review
Nord J Int L	Nordic Journal of International Law
NTB	Non-Tariff Barrier
Nw J Int L & Bus	Northwestern Journal of International Law & Business
NYIL	Netherlands Yearbook of International Law
NYU J Int L & Pol	New York University Journal of International Law & Politics
OECD	Organisation for Economic Cooperation and Development
OJ	Official Journal of the European Union (formerly European Communities)
ONLR	Ohio Northern University Law Review
OPEC	Organization of the Petroleum Exporting Countries
ORC	Other Regulations of Commerce
ORRC	Other Restrictive Regulations of Commerce
OUP	Oxford University Press
Pac Rev	The Pacific Review
PCA	Partnership and Cooperation Agreement
Polish YIL	Polish Yearbook of International Law
RTA	Regional Trade Agreement
SAA	Stabilization and Association Agreement
SADC	Southern African Development Community
SPS	Sanitary and Phytosanitary (measures)
SYIL	Singapore Yearbook of International Law
TBT	Technical Barriers to Trade
TCE	Treaty Establishing a Constitution for Europe
TDCA	EC–South Africa Trade and Development Cooperation Agreement
TMB	WTO Textiles Monitoring Body
Tul L Rev	Tulane Law Review

TWQ	Third World Quarterly
U Chi L Rev	University of Chicago Law Review
U Ott Law & Tech J	University of Ottawa Law and Technology Journal
U Pa J Int Econ L	University of Pennsylvania Journal of International Economic Law
UN	United Nations
UNCED	United Nations Conference on Environment and Development
UNCITRAL	United Nations Commission for International Trade Law
UNCLOS	United Nations Convention on the Law of the Sea
UNCTAD	United Nations Conference on Trade and Development
UNDP	United Nations Development Programme
UNEP	United Nations Environment Programme
UNESCO	United Nations Educational, Scientific and Cultural Organization
UNTS	United Nations Treaty Series
US	United States of America or United States Supreme Court Reports
Vanderbilt J Transnatl L	Vanderbilt Journal of Transnational Law
VCLT	Vienna Convention on the Law of the Treaties
VER	Voluntary Export Restraint
Whittier L Rev	Whittier Law Review
WHO	World Health Organization
WTO	World Trade Organization
WTR	World Trade Review
Yale J Int L	Yale Journal of International Law

List of Contributors

Naomi Julia Barnes, Centre for Energy, Petroleum, and Mineral Law and Policy, University of Dundee

Lorand Bartels, Lecturer in International Economic Law, University of Edinburgh

Marie-Claire Cordonier Segger, Fellow, Lauterpacht Centre for International Law, University of Cambridge; Director, Centre for International Sustainable Development Law, Montreal

Thomas Cottier, Professor for European and International Economic Law; Managing Director, World Trade Institute, University of Berne

Chad Damro, Lecturer in Politics, University of Edinburgh

William J. Davey, Guy Raymond Jones Chair at the University of Illinois College of Law; former Director of the Legal Affairs Division, World Trade Organization

Gareth Davies, Lecturer in European Law, University of Groningen

Viet D. Do, PhD candidate, Department of Economics, McGill University

Piet Eeckhout, Professor of European Law and Director, Centre of European Law, King's College London; Associate Academic Member, Matrix Chambers

Marina Foltea, Research Fellow, World Trade Institute, University of Berne

Ignacio Garcia Bercero, Director, Bilateral Trade Relations I, DG Trade, European Commission

Melaku Geboye Desta, Senior Lecturer in International Economic Law, Centre for Energy, Petroleum, and Mineral Law and Policy, University of Dundee

Angela T. Gobbi Estrella, Counsel, Ministry of Finance, Brazilian Government

Gary N. Horlick, Partner, WilmerHale LLP, Washington DC

Locknie Hsu, Associate Professor, Faculty of Law, National University of Singapore

Markus Krajewski, Junior Professor, University of Potsdam

Kyung Kwak, Counsel, Legal Department, International Monetary Fund

Yan Luo, Teaching and Research Assistant and PhD Candidate, Centre for Commercial Law Studies, Queen Mary, University of London

Gabrielle Marceau, Counsellor, Office of the Director-General, World Trade Organization; Associate Professor, Faculty of Law, University of Geneva

James H. Mathis, Associate Professor, Department of International Law, University of Amsterdam, NL

Bryan Mercurio, Senior Lecturer, Faculty of Law, University of New South Wales

Armand de Mestral, Jean Monnet Professor of Law, McGill University

Federico Ortino, Fellow in International Economic Law and Director of the Investment Treaty Forum, British Institute of International and Comparative Law

Ernst-Ulrich Petersmann, Professor of International and European Law, European University Institute and Joint Chair at the Robert Schuman Center for Advanced Studies, European University Institute; Chairman of the International Trade Law Committee of the International Law Association and former legal advisor at the GATT and WTO

José Antonio Rivas, Director of Foreign Direct Investment, Ministry of Trade of Colombia; former counsel, International Centre for Settlement of Investment Disputes; Professor of Public International Law, Los Andes University, Bogotá

Audley Sheppard, Partner, Clifford Chance LLP, London

Isabelle Van Damme, PhD Candidate, University of Cambridge, Gonville & Caius College

William Watson, Associate Professor and Chair, Department of Economics, McGill University

Andreas R. Ziegler, Professor of Law, University of Lausanne, Visiting Professor at the Universities of New South Wales, Bocconi and at the Swiss Federal Institute of Technology; former Head of the International and European Economic Law Section of the Swiss Secretariat of Economic Affairs, Berne

Introduction

LORAND BARTELS AND FEDERICO ORTINO

It has become something of a commonplace, when introducing the subject matter covered in this book, to remark upon the steady proliferation of regional trade agreements. And yet it is difficult to imagine any other description that so well captures this phenomenon. In 1963, Kenneth Dam, in one of the first legal commentaries on regional trade agreements, spoke of proliferation when referring to a grand total of two bilateral agreements, the European project in its various forms, and a regional agreement in Latin America.[1] In retrospect, that appears rather to have been the golden age of multilateral trade: forty years later, over 300 regional trade agreements have been notified to the WTO and its predecessor, of which a full two-thirds have been notified within the past decade.[2] Among WTO Members regional trade agreements are practically universal,[3] economically significant,[4] and, as one observes in agreements such as the United States–Jordan and Korea–Chile free trade agreements, no longer even geographically 'regional'.[5] As the 21st century gets underway, trade on a most favoured nation basis risks becoming a rarity,

---

[1] K. Dam, 'Regional Economic Arrangements and the GATT, the Legacy of a Misconception' (1963) 30 U Chi L Rev, 615, at 615.

[2] By 31 March 2006, 346 agreements had been notified, of which 195 are currently in force: personal communication with WTO. For published earlier figures, *see* the Report of the WTO Committee on Regional Trade Agreements, WTO Doc. WT/REG/15, 3 November 2005, para. 4, www.wto.org/english/tratop_e/region_e/eif_e.xls (visited 30 May 2006) and, with discussion, J.A. Crawford and R.V. Fiorentino, 'The Changing Landscape of Regional Trade Agreements', WTO Discussion Paper No 8 (2005).

[3] Crawford and Fiorentino, *ibid.*, n 4.

[4] Regional trade agreements represent over 90 per cent of the trade of some WTO Members: *ibid*.

[5] In this sense the term 'regional trade agreement' is clearly a misnomer, but to be consistent with WTO practice, this book adopts this term. *See* the WTO Decision to establish a Committee on Regional Trade Agreements, which (at n 1) defines the agreements within its mandate to include 'all bilateral, regional, and plurilateral trade agreements of a preferential nature': WTO Doc. WT/L/127, 7 February 1996.

rather than the norm on which the world's trading system is supposedly founded.[6]

Whether this is a positive development raises difficult political, economic, and legal questions. In their favour, regional trade agreements provide countries with an opportunity for broader and deeper integration than is otherwise possible, with all attendant political and economic benefits. Who, then or now, would fault the Working Party on the European Economic Community for not taking a harder line on the EEC Treaty? More prosaically, regional trade agreements can serve as a laboratory for multilateral liberalization, as well as legal initiatives, such as in the realm of dispute settlement. Sometimes they also provide a forum for consenting parties to link trade with issues that are more controversial at the multilateral level, such as human rights, the environment, and cultural industries.

But of course regional trade agreements are also politically and economically risky. They are proving to be the basis for new political alliances in Asia, Latin America, and the Middle East to an extent that must evoke the warnings of the founders of the multilateral trading system six decades ago; and despite some successes, their economic credentials are often shaky. The authors of the 2004 Sutherland Report on the Future of the WTO expressed themselves to be 'deeply concerned' by the current spread of regional trade agreements, 'unconvinced' by their economic justification, and 'especially concerned that the preferential treatment is becoming merely a reward for governments pursuing non-trade related objectives.' They issued this warning: 'Governments need to show restraint or risk more damage to the multilateral trading system'.[7]

It is in this context that this book seeks to investigate both the specific features of these agreements and their regulation at the multilateral level. It is divided into five parts. Part I sets out the framework—economic, political, and constitutional—of regional trade agreements as they exist in the multilateral trading system, while Part II analyses the precise WTO rules under which regional trade agreements operate: an area singled out by a former Chairman of the Appellate Body as 'potentially explosive'.[8] Parts III and IV look at the way in which regional trade agreements have gone beyond the WTO, on both economic and social issues, as well as in their dispute settlement mechanisms. Finally, Part V looks at the way in which the two levels of trade liberalization interface with each other from the perspectives of the EU (the only regional trade agreement simultaneously a WTO Member) and international law.

Within this general structure, the contributions in this book deal with some

---

[6] If one includes its Generalized System of Preferences for developing countries, the EU trades on a most-favoured nation basis only with the US, Canada, Japan, Australia, New Zealand, Hong Kong, and Korea.

[7] P. Sutherland *et al. The Future of the WTO: Addressing Institutional Challenges in the New Millennium* (Geneva: WTO, 2004), at 79.

[8] C.-D. Ehlermann, 'Tensions between the Dispute Settlement Process and the Diplomatic and Treaty-making Activities of the WTO' (2002) 1 WTR, 301, at 303.

of the thorniest of legal questions provoked by the phenomenon of regional trade agreements: What political and economic explanations are there for regional trade agreements? What does it take for a regional trade agreement to comply with Article XXIV of GATT, that provision distinguished by both dubious origins[9] and (at least until *Turkey—Textiles*)[10] a tradition of non-application.[11] How is one to assess the legality of certain of the special features of regional trade agreements, such as their rules of origin and trade remedies provisions? To what extent has the regulatory action on such matters as services, investment, intellectual property, and competition moved to the regional level? And—an important question if it has—what are the impacts of regional and multilateral trade law on each other?

We hope that the essays in this volume will provide a basis for fruitful discussions on a topic of undoubted importance not only to professionals in the area of international trade, but in the wider community as well.

---

[9] Some of the background to Art. XXIV has recently been uncovered in K. Chase, 'Multilateralism Compromised: the Mysterious Origins of GATT Article XXIV' (2006) 5 WTR, 1; *see also* J.H. Mathis, *Regional Trade Agreements in the GATT/WTO: Article XXIV and the Internal Trade Requirement* (The Hague: T.M.C. Asser, 2002), especially Chs 1–2.

[10] WTO Appellate Body Report, *Turkey—Textiles*, WT/DS34/AB/R, adopted 19 November 1999.

[11] Of the hundreds of agreements notified so far to the GATT and WTO, only one (between the Czech and Slovak republics) was ever positively approved by its examining Working Party, and none definitively rejected.

PART I

Framework Issues

1

Economic Analysis of Regional Trade Agreements

VIET D. DO AND WILLIAM WATSON *

I. INTRODUCTION

The recent proliferation of regional trading arrangements (RTAs) poses a number of interesting and difficult questions for economists. The two most obvious are why it is happening and whether it is 'welfare-improving'—that is, a good thing or not in terms of its effects, via trade and investment, on people's lives. In this chapter we summarize recent economic work on these questions in hopes of deciding whether the discipline is yet able to offer reasonably conclusive answers to these questions. After a brief review of some stylized facts, we reverse what may seem a more natural order and begin with the normative question ('Is it good?'), which in theory at least may ultimately help us to answer the positive question ('Why is it happening?'). Governments do not always do what is welfare-improving, and they sometimes do what is clearly welfare-reducing, but if RTAs were in general a good thing, it might not be necessary to look much further in deciding why they are happening.

II. STYLIZED FACTS

Several very useful examinations of the rapid growth of preferential trade agreements have recently been published by agencies with the wherewithal for a comprehensive approach.[1] As a result of these investigations, several stylized facts have emerged.

* The authors would like to thank the Canadian Social Sciences and Humanities Research Council for its financial support for the research project on 'Regional Trade Agreements and the Multilateral Trading System'.

[1] *See* in particular *Global Economic Prospects 2005: Trade, Regionalism and Development* (Washington: World Bank, 2005), Regional Integration Agreements (Paris: OECD, 2001), available at www.oecd.org/dataoecd/39/37/1923431.pdf (visited 10 April 2006) and J.A. Crawford and R.V. Fiorentino, 'The Changing Landscape of Regional Trade Agreements', WTO Discussion Paper No 8 (2005).

Rapid growth. There has indeed been a very rapid proliferation of RTAs. As of this writing, the latest annual report of the WTO Committee on Regional Trade Agreements counts a total of 334 agreements and accessions to existing agreements as having been notified to the WTO. Of these, 183 were currently in force. The Committee was in the process of reviewing 141 agreements, many of which would already have come into effect.[2] Since the WTO's advent in 1995 it has received an average of 11 notifications per year, almost one per month.[3]

Periodic deaths. Regional agreements are not immortal. They do occasionally lapse, especially when countries that formerly had bilateral RTAs with one another enter into a plurilateral RTA. For instance, on 1 May 2004 fully 65 RTAs became defunct as 10 new members joined the European Union.[4] It is therefore important not to judge the scale of the phenomenon simply by counting the number of agreements entered into in the past.

Free trade areas mainly. The bulk of regional agreements are free trade areas (FTAs) rather than customs unions or other types of agreements. This appears to be true both on average and at the margin: Of 131 notified agreements in force in February 2005, 109 were intended to be FTAs, while only 11 were or had the goal of becoming customs unions. And of the RTAs not yet in force, not one was a customs union or intended customs union.[5] FTAs presumably are easier to negotiate than customs unions. No agreement on common external tariffs is required, though rules of origin must usually be established. The numbers cited probably should be weighted. The EU is clearly a very important customs union with aspirations to becoming even more important. But the majority of agreements are for FTAs and are likely to remain so. Economists customarily think of FTAs and customs unions as falling along a continuum that extends from autarky to economic union and sometimes seems to assume, following the postwar European model, that there is a natural tendency to move along that continuum over time. In fact, countries evidently feel themselves under no such obligation. FTAs may be final destinations.[6]

Most agreements are bilateral. More than 75 per cent of all RTAs that had been notified to the WTO and were in force in February 2005 were bilateral agreements, as well as almost 90 per cent of agreements then under negotiation.[7] That there is only one partner presumably makes bilateral agreements easier to negotiate than plurilateral agreements. Though small countries may

---

[2] WTO Report of the Committee on Regional Trade Agreements to the General Council, WTO Doc. WT/REG/15, 3 November 2005, at 1.

[3] Crawford and Fiorentino, above at n 1, at 3.   [4] *Ibid.*, at 8, fn 21.

[5] *Ibid.*, at 3. The 11 agreements not accounted for were 'partial scope' agreements.

[6] Repeated suggestions by business groups that NAFTA become a customs union have so far not had effect.

[7] Crawford and Fiorentino, above at n 1, at 4.

sometimes prefer safety in numbers bilateral FTAs are, on balance, the path of least resistance.

The WTO is implicated. Most tracking of agreements shows a sharp increase in the 1990s. Indeed, the trendline of RTAs seems to climb a cliff in the mid-1990s.[8] This may be partly illusory—as a result of WTO membership more countries were subject to more stringent reporting standards—and partly coincidental: the break-up of the Soviet Union probably had little to do with the WTO but gave rise to a substantial number of trade agreements among what had rather suddenly become independent countries. On the other hand, there may be a more substantive WTO link, in at least two ways: first, the continuing tariff reductions negotiated in the Uruguay Round will have helped lower the economic costs of preferential trading arrangements. Second, the perceived negotiating logjam coming out of the Uruguay Round may have persuaded many countries to seek alternative means of liberalization.

Agreements are not always implemented. Or are implemented more slowly than planned. As a result, 'many RTAs have more life on paper than in reality'.[9] Is non-implementation good or bad? If the rapidly growing number of agreements is a concern, concern may need to be downgraded, while if such agreements are thought to be a spur to multilateral liberalization, the spur may in fact be duller than supposed. Why would countries negotiate deals they end up not carrying through on? Implementation is an habitual difficulty in public policy; moreover, free trade agreements may be diplomatically useful even if they have minimal real consequences. During the Cold War friendly countries negotiated defence agreements with one another. In the age of globalization it seems only polite to negotiate free trade agreements.[10]

RTAs may not distort trade unduly. We return to this subject in greater detail below but despite the rapid growth of such agreements a declining share of world trade may be taking place on a preferential basis. One estimate of the total amount of world trade covered by such agreements is roughly 40 per cent.[11] But if account is taken of goods that face an MFN tariff of zero, so that a RTA provides no preference, the total falls to 21 per cent. And if trade where the MFN rate is less than three per cent is eliminated, the total falls to just 15 per cent. This may actually be a lower share than in the mid-1990s. There are more RTAs now but they may be less consequential.

---

[8] *See* World Bank, above at n 1, Fig 1, at xii.   [9] *Ibid.*, at xiv.

[10] Though as economists we are fully aware of the shortcomings of preferential agreements when compared with multilateral agreements, one of us recently found himself asking the ambassador of a G7 country why Canada and his country had not yet negotiated a free trade agreement, as if this were the default among allies. His response was that as we had taken different approaches during a recent world political crisis his country felt more comfortable pursuing an agreement with another developed country that had taken a position closer to its own.

[11] *Ibid.*, at 27. On the other hand, at 40 it is argued that one-third of world trade takes place among RTA members. The difference appears to be from non-reciprocal preferences such as the Generalized System of Preferences.

RTAs are not evenly distributed geographically. As of this writing, only one
WTO Member, Mongolia, was not party to an RTA.[12] But the agreements are
not uniformly distributed around the world. The EU has many bilateral
agreements, as does the United States. There are also concentrations of agreements in Southeast Asia and Africa. The image of a spaghetti bowl has been
the dominant metaphor in discussion of RTAs since Jagdish Bhagwati first
introduced it. But boiled spaghetti produces a tangle of largely random con-
nections of relatively uniform consistency. The reality of RTAs is a certain
lumpiness, with the spaghetti tangled in or around four or five discernible
clumps—meatballs, perhaps, or maybe it is time to think of a different pasta
entirely.[13]

RTAs exist for many different reasons. The EU, the granddaddy of RTAs,
came into being largely as a non-aggression device. Many of the RTAs Europe
itself has since negotiated have helped new countries prepare for membership,
while others have recognized longstanding historical and/or colonial ties.
Many agreements entered into by the countries of the former Soviet Union
were meant to facilitate the transition to market economics and were therefore
profoundly liberalizing. Others no doubt were illiberal. In the 1980s Canada
sought a free trade agreement with the US as insurance against contingent
protection and relative economic decline. Mexico sought such a deal to buy
international credibility for internal reforms. Canada then sought a tripartite
deal largely for defensive reasons. It would be surprising if deals with such
disparate motivations all had similar effects.[14]

III. IS THE PROLIFERATION OF RTAS A GOOD THING?

If RTAs are largely free trade agreements and if free trade is good, are RTAs
therefore not good almost by definition? Non-economists are likely to think
'Yes'. Economists worry about the theory of the second best.

A. Second best

At the end of trade economists' rainbow is full free trade, a world in which
consumers and firms can exchange goods and services as easily across international boundaries as within countries. It would not be a pure *laisser-faire*
world: governments would still intervene to try to correct market failures. But

---

[12] Crawford and Fiorentino, above at n 1, at 1, fn 4.

[13] The World Bank, above at n 1, introduces rigatoni to the analysis in Fig. 2.2, at 39. It may be
true, as the National Pasta Association claims, that 'Rigatoni's ridges and holes are perfect with
any sauce, from cream or cheese to the chunkiest meat sauces' but it is not clear why ridges make it
an apt metaphor for RTAs: *See* www.ilovepasta.org/shapes.html (visited 10 April 2006).

[14] Other things equal, those whose motivations were primarily economic presumably should
show higher economic payback than those whose motivations were political or geo-strategic.

addressing such failures generally would not require discriminating against foreign sellers of goods and services.[15] As a result, the laws of comparative advantage would cause such goods and services to be provided by whomever could provide them most cheaply.

The world as it exists is clearly some distance from the end of the rainbow. Tariffs have declined substantially since 1947, non-tariff barriers may well have increased, and there is some considerable way to go before all foreign suppliers will be treated in a non-discriminatory way. Non-economists probably assume that, in the progress from a world of substantial remaining trade barriers to a perfectly non-discriminating world, having more FTAs helps. If comprehensive free trade is better than partial free trade, then any movement in that direction presumably is good. If not all countries wish to engage in reasonably complete free trade, well, better that those who want to do. Unfortunately, common sense runs up against the economic 'theory of the second best'. In general, a more-liberalized world that is not yet fully liberalized may *not* produce greater welfare than one that is less liberalized.

If the idea that what seems to be progress toward a goal may actually be retrograde seems peculiar, think of a river's ability to provide transportation. If the river is completely frozen, trucks can be driven across it. If it is completely ice-free, vessels can navigate freely. But in the intermediate range, when it is filled with ice floes, transportation may be impossible. Welfare is higher at the extremes than in the stage between them. 'Second best' is not always a concern, however. For other purposes, irrigation or quenching thirst, for example, the river's transition from frozen to breaking up to completely open may involve continuously greater convenience. In general, partial change may or may not constitute an improvement. Whether any given change does so is therefore an empirical question. Unfortunately, that does not mean it is easy to answer.

The best-known complications arising from PTAs are 'trade creation' and 'trade diversion,' terms introduced to the literature by Jacob Viner in 1950.[16] An example may help. Until the 1980s Canada had a protected wine industry in the Niagara Peninsula south of Lake Ontario. The wine, expensive but not of high quality, was competitive domestically only because of tariff and non-tariff barriers. As a result of the Canada–US Free Trade Agreement of 1989, which liberalized the wine trade, the Canadian industry lost market share to California vintners.[17] This is an example of welfare-improving trade creation: Canadian wine prices fell; consumers were able to purchase more; Canadian vintners ceased producing goods that could be produced more cheaply in

---

[15] Even though, given the imperatives of democratic politics and the fact that foreigners do not vote, that will always be a temptation.

[16] J. Viner, *The Customs Union Issue* (New York: Carnegie Endowment for International Peace, 1950).

[17] *See* M. Hart, 'Great Wine, Better Cheese: How Canada can Escape the Trap of Agricultural Supply Management', in *Backgrounder 90* (Toronto: C.D. Howe Institute, April 2005).

California; this freed up resources for use elsewhere (in fact, many stayed in the wine industry and converted to specialty wines, including ice wines, where they have enjoyed some success); the Canadian government lost tariff revenue; but consumers gained by virtue of lower prices on imports. In sum, domestic producers and the domestic Treasury were hurt by trade liberalization but Canadian consumers enjoyed offsetting benefits. Net gains resulted from consumers' ability to drink more and better wine and from producers' migration out of the production of grades of wine in which Canada was not competitive.

On the other hand, the Canada–US FTA also caused trade diversion in wine. Tariffs on non-US suppliers remained in place. Where before Canadian consumers had paid the same tax on imports of California and, say, French wine, they now only paid tariffs on French wine. The introduction of preferential arrangements with the US therefore led to the substitution of some California wine production for some French wine production. Canadian trade was diverted from France to California. If on a level playing-field (or serving table) Canadians would have preferred French wine, this switch was welfare-reducing. In sum, the world moved from a situation, compared to the ideal, of too much Canadian wine to one of too much California wine. Whether on balance the increase in welfare from the trade creation outweighed the reduction in welfare from the trade diversion is an open question, one that must be asked many times over per trade agreement since such deals typically cover many hundreds if not thousands of goods.

At least one overall empirical guideline is available, however. Other things equal, the lower the level of multilateral tariffs, the less distorting will be the preference granted by a zero-tariff preference. Exemption from a 30 per cent tariff will be more valuable and create a greater distortion in trade flows than exemption from a five per cent tariff—which is why many countries that currently benefit from preferences drag their heels on further liberalization. But because multilateral tariffs have continued to decline the growth of preferential agreements may be less damaging than it would have been earlier. Economists typically examine the effects of trade deals by using two techniques: eyeballing trade data and building models, whether relatively simple 'gravity models' of overall trade flows or much more detailed 'computable general-equilibrium' models of specific trade deals.

1. Trends in trade data

The simplest measure of the degree of integration within a free trade region is the trend in the share of imports from regional partners in the total imports of a region. In fact, 'intra- trade' in major RTAs shows a substantial increase over the last 20 years. For example, the share of intra-NAFTA imports rose from less than 35 per cent of the three member countries' total imports in the late 1980s to almost 50 per cent in 1999. Over the same period, the volume of trade among Mercosur Members doubled from 10 to 20 per cent. In Africa, intra-trade is not as common but from the 1980s to 2000 the share of internal trade in the Economic Community of West African States (ECOWAS) and the Southern African Development Community (SADC) grew approximately fourfold, from 2.5 to 11 per cent.[18] This suggests at least the possibility of substantial trade diversion. On the other hand, in many cases intra-regional trade shares were growing strongly even before the agreements were effective, so the RTA may not be at fault, while in others there have been declines in intra-regional trade. And, in general, rising intra-trade has not crowded out trade with non-members. With the exception of Mercosur, all regions that have experienced an increasing share of intra-regional trade in total trade have also seen the ratio of their extra-regional trade to GDP increase.[19] The Association of Southeast Asian Nations (ASEAN) provides an interesting example. From the establishment of the ASEAN Free Trade Area (AFTA) in 1992 through 2000, within-area trade increased from 30 per cent to almost 45 per cent of total trade while external trade increased from seven to 14 per cent of regional GDP. In fact, the successful expansion of trade among the members of a regional trade agreement tends to be associated both with increasing extra-regional imports as a share of GDP and with the growth of world trade.[20] As Crawford and Laird concluded in 2001, 'the overall numbers do not point to clear evidence of diversion away from imports from nonmembers of RTAs'.[21]

The obvious difficulty with drawing inferences from simple trade flows is that causality is hard to untangle. Would intra-regional trade have increased even without a free-trade deal? What was its trend before the deal was made? What was happening to extra-regional trade? What are the principal influences on trade and did any of them change in ways that would either mask or exaggerate the effect of the RTA on trade flows? In short, were other things equal when the deal was introduced? Answering such questions is the purpose of economic models.

2. Economic models[22]

Two general types of economic model are used to analyse the welfare impacts of RTAs: *ex-ante* 'computable general-equilibrium' simulation studies and *ex-post* econometric analyses using the 'gravity model'. The *ex-ante* studies try to model the participating countries' economies explicitly and typically attempt to estimate the impact of RTAs at both the aggregate and sectoral levels. Because the effects of many non-tariff barriers are hard to quantify, the characterization of RTAs is often relatively simple (though the calculations rapidly become complex!), with most studies focusing on tariff removal. The

---

[18] *See* World Bank, above at n 1, at 58–9.   [19] *Ibid.*, at 59.   [20] *Ibid.*, at 60.
[21] J. Crawford and S. Laird, 'Regional Trade Agreements and the WTO' (2001) 12 N Amer J Econ Finance 193.
[22] For a comprehensive review of economic models used in assessing impacts of regional trade agreements *see* A. Panagariya, 'Preferential Trade Liberalization: The Traditional Theory and New Developments' (2000) 38 J Econ Lit 287 and J.E. Anderson and E. van Wincoop, 'Trade Costs' (2004) 42 J Econ Lit 691.

simulation exercises attempt to answer the question: 'What would be the impact of the preferential removal of tariffs against a limited set of trade partners, given the assumed model structure?'.

Ex-post econometric studies use gravity models to try to assess the actual impact of policy changes on trade flows between countries. They are 'gravity models' because they assume that, just as the gravitational attraction between planets is directly proportional to their mass and inversely proportional to their distance from each other, trade between nations is very likely directly proportional to their GDPs and inversely proportional to their distance from one another. As economists, we are unable to say whether just two variables adequately explain gravitational attraction. But the determinants of trade between countries are clearly more complicated. Thus gravity models generally also control for other potential influences on trade flows, such as common borders, past colonial relations, common languages, other measures of cultural proximity, and, key here, the presence of any form of preferential economic arrangements. If, when trade is 'regressed' against a collection of such variables, the presence of a trade deal has a statistically significant effect, the presumption is that the deal has in fact altered trade flows.

What do the models say? We briefly summarize some results by region.

The North American Free Trade Agreement (NAFTA) came into effect in 1994. Leading up to it, several studies examined its likely effects.[23] Although quantitative economic analysis of the potential effects of NAFTA was carried out in different ways and at various levels of aggregation, ranging from industry and sectoral studies to a number of studies using single and multi-country computable general-equilibrium models, there was a remarkable degree of consensus across studies that the effects of NAFTA would be net trade-creating and would benefit all three member countries, with the largest relative gains for Mexico. On the other hand, a number of *ex-post* studies on NAFTA conclude that, despite larger gross trade flows, implementation of the agreement may not have led to a substantial increase in trade.[24] One reason is that the member countries had already achieved substantial trade liberalization before 1994. In particular, the US and Canada had concluded their own free trade agreement in 1989, while the US had previously granted Mexico important trade preferences under the Generalized System of Preferences

---

[23] Surveys of the empirical work of this type include: US Department of Labour, *A Review of the Likely Economic Impact of NAFTA on the US* (Washington DC, 1992), US International Trade Commission, *Economy-Wide Modeling of the Economic Implications of a FTA with Mexico and a NAFTA with Canada and Mexico* (Washington DC, 1992), J.F. Francois and C.R. Shiells, *Modeling Trade Policy: Applied General Equilibrium Assessments of North American Trade* (Cambridge: CUP, 1994) and N. Lustig, B.P. Bosworth and R.Z. Lawrence, *North American Free Trade: Assessing the Impact* (Washington, DC: Brookings Institution, 1992).

[24] *See*, for example, M.E. Burfisher, S. Robinson and K. Thierfelder, 'The Impact of NAFTA on the United States' (2001) 15 J Econ Perspect 125.

(GSP).[25] A recent study disputes this conclusion, however.[26] Using a modified version of the gravity model, Tang finds that, after controlling for GDP, per capita income, distance, and exchange rate volatility, coefficients measuring the effects of NAFTA on bilateral trade flows change from negative in 1989–1992 to positive in 1993–2000. As previous studies focused primarily on the early and mid-1990s, it may be that the full effects of NAFTA are only now being felt.

A number of recent studies examine whether the implementation of the ASEAN Free Trade Area (AFTA) has contributed to any increase in trade among member countries. Although early results suggested little or no effect[27] a more recent study by Thornton and Goglio concludes that AFTA did facilitate trade, especially during the late 1990s.[28] Employing a modified version of the gravity model, Tang also found that the implementation of AFTA has contributed to the gradual but significant growth of trade among the member countries. The coefficient reflecting the effect of AFTA implementation on the region's intra-trade increased strongly from 1.284 in 1989–1992 to 1.826 in 1997–2000. It is interesting to note that the East Asian financial crisis apparently did not result in any appreciable decline in trade among ASEAN countries. Such trade may be expected to continue to grow as more of the AFTA provisions become effective.

A detailed simulation of the Southern Common Market (Mercosur), founded in 1991 by Brazil, Argentina, Uruguay, and Paraguay, indicated that it would raise member countries' welfare by stimulating their investment, production, and consumption.[29] Although external trade opportunities were to increase, intra-regional trade was to grow much faster than the total trade of Member Countries. Moreover, lowering Mercosur's common external tariff would allow Member Countries to benefit substantially more from their trade agreement and would also, not surprisingly, benefit third countries. *Ex-post* studies are divided, however. Soloago and Winters conclude that Latin American countries do trade with each other disproportionately but when gravity variables are taken into account the formation of Latin American RTAs, including Mercosur, does not seem to have been accompanied by a larger than expected increase in intra-bloc trade.[30] In a 2001 paper, Cernat

---

[25] *See also* I. Soloaga and A. Winters, 'Regionalism in the Nineties: What Effect on Trade' (2001) 12 N Amer J Econ Finance 1.

[26] *See* D. Tang, 'Effects of the Regional Trading Arrangements on Trade: Evidence from the NAFTA, ANZCER and ASEAN Countries, 1989–2000' (2005) 14 J Int Trade Econ Devel 241.

[27] *See* J.A. Frankel and S.J. Wei, 'Regionalization of World Trade and Currencies: Economics and Politics', in J.A. Frankel (ed), *The Regionalization in the World Economy* (Chicago: U Chicago Press, 1998), S.C. Sharma and S.Y. Chua, 'ASEAN: Economic Integration and Intra-regional Trade' (2000) 7 Appl Econ Lett 165 and Soloaga and Winters, above at n 25.

[28] *See* J. Thornton and A. Goglio, 'Regional Bias and Intra-regional Trade in Southeast Asia' (2002) 9 Appl Econ Lett 205.

[29] *See* Diao and Somwaru (2000).

[30] *See* Soloaga and Winters, above at n 25. Similar results were confirmed by Frankel and Wei, above at n 27.

concludes that 'South–South' RTAs are not in general more trade-diverting than other RTAs.[31] He does find, however, that trade among Mercosur Member Countries more than doubled between 1994 and 1998, while extra-regional imports fell by more than a third, which suggests an overall trade-diverting effect. Carrillo and Li's gravity-model analysis of bilateral trade flows found that Mercosur's effect on intra-industrial trade was relatively small compared to the effect of other important variables.[32] Moreover, it has only affected a subset of product classifications. Indeed, after controlling for size and distance effects, the only remaining positive effect is in one capital-intensive sub-category. In sum, the consensus seems to favour a positive, but small impact of Mercosur on intra-regional trade.

A recent 'meta-analysis' by the World Bank looked at the impact of 19 different RTAs as illuminated by 17 separate research studies that had all used gravity-model techniques. The average impact on total trade was negative while the average impact on intra-regional trade was positive, which suggests a net trade-diverting effect. On the other hand, 'For both parameters there is a high degree of variance about the mean values'.[33] For example, although the average effect on overall trade was negative, the effect was actually positive in 44 per cent of cases where results were statistically significant. Similarly, although the average effect on intra-regional trade was positive, in 18 per cent of statistically significant cases it was negative.[34] Results were not entirely random, however. 'In general, members of regional agreements that have been relatively open to imports have shown higher propensities to export to the global market than would otherwise be expected'.[35]

What of the future? What distorting effects could continued proliferation of RTAs have? The World Bank recently used the GTAP (Global Trade Analysis Project) of global trade to estimate the effects of several different possible scenarios for the global trading system over the next 10 years.[36] Compared to continuing multilateral liberalization, which produces a 0.8 per cent gain in world income, a scenario in which every country negotiates a bilateral free trade deal with the Quad countries (the US, the EU, Canada, and Japan) increases world income by only 0.3 per cent, while such a scenario in which the large developing countries (such as Brazil, China, and India) do not participate raises it by only 0.1 per cent. Moreover, although all regions share in the gains from multilateral liberalization, the gains from universal RTAs are mainly enjoyed by developed countries.

What is particularly intriguing is that according to the simulation results

[31] L. Cernat, 'Assessing Regional Trade Arrangements: Are South–South RTAs More Trade Diverting?', UNCTAD Doc. UNCTAD/ITCD/TAB/17 (2001).

[32] C. Carrillo-Tudela and C.A. Li. 'Trade Blocks and the Gravity Model: Evidence from Latin American Countries' (2004) 19 J Econ Integration 667.

[33] World Bank, above at n 1, in Box 3.2 at 62. The 19 studies examined provided a total of 254 estimates of the overall effect and 362 estimates of the internal effect.

[34] Authors' calculation based on *ibid.*   [35] *Ibid.*, at 62.   [36] *Ibid.*, at 126–32.

any developing country that could on its own negotiate a free-trade deal with the Quad would typically benefit—with gains varying from –0.1 per cent to 2.6 per cent of real income[37]—though only on the unrealistic assumption that it would be the only country to negotiate such an agreement. The proliferation of RTAs presumably has already shown that any such 'first-mover advantage' is fleeting. The World Bank authors conclude that multilateral liberalization is best. Few trade economists would disagree. On the other hand, the multilateral deal examined involves elimination of all 'merchandise trade distortions . . . domestic distortions in agriculture . . . [and] import quotas in the textile and clothing sectors'.[38] In view of the disappointing results of the Hong Kong ministerial in December 2005, this seems ambitious. A less ambitious deal presumably would give rise to smaller gains, which would reduce the opportunity costs of creeping bilateralism. On the other hand, bilateralism generally imposes costs compared to the status quo baseline, albeit not terribly large ones.[39] Whether recognition of the apparently perverse model results of widespread bilateralism—gains for rich countries, losses for poor—will persuade countries to re-double their Doha efforts time may tell.

In sum, although results are mixed, the proliferation of RTAs does not yet seem to have created a world trading system dominated by trade diversion. In most agreements intra-regional trade does seem to have grown. On the other hand, it was often growing before preferential agreements were struck. And extra-regional trade has also grown, albeit possibly not as much as it would have without the proliferation of preferential deals.

B. Transactions costs

Imagine a world in which every country had a bilateral free trade agreement with every other country. Though all tariffs would be zero, trade might yet be very difficult. Would-be multinational traders would have to familiarize themselves with many different sets of trading rules, including rules of origin. Such a world would be a boon to trade lawyers but seems likely to discourage trade by raising transactions costs. How much more convenient it would be if all countries had the same rules! Or, rather, to take a more scientific view, how much more convenient would it be if all countries had the same rules?

In estimating the transactions costs of the new regionalism it is important to be explicit on the point of comparison. If costs are compared to transactions costs as they would be in an end-of-the-rainbow world in which all tariffs were zero and non-tariff barriers had been eliminated, then it is true that in a multiple-RTA world costs might well be substantially higher. On the other hand, even in a perfectly liberalized world there would be national differences

---

[37] *Ibid.*, Table 6.2, at 129.   [38] *Ibid.*, at 128.
[39] On average, –0.1 per cent, with a maximum of –1.0 per cent to non-SACU sub-Saharan Africa: *ibid.*, Tables 6.1 and 6.2, at 128 and 129.

in habit, regulation, commercial practice and so on with which exporters would have to familiarize themselves. The French presumably would continue to speak French and the Germans German for some time to come. And, despite Brussels' best efforts, in many respects they might well continue to regulate their economies in idiosyncratic ways. Such differences impose fixed costs on exporters that are part of the reason why small firms tend not to export.

In fact the end-of-the-rainbow world is not the point of departure. MFN tariffs are not generally zero. Exporters must familiarize themselves with a wide range of tariffs and non-tariff barriers as-is. The cost of doing business across borders is already substantial.[40] Would transactions costs in an RTA-riddled world be that much higher than in a world in which each nation-state established its own tariffs and ran a full set of non-tariff barriers? It may depend on the type and number of RTAs. Some RTAs—the EU, for instance—bring several countries together under common trading rules and behind a common tariff wall. Trade within such RTAs may well involve *fewer* transactions costs than it used to. Indeed, reducing transactions costs so as to make trade easier within Europe has been a primary goal of the EU. Moreover, in most cases RTAs accept WTO rules as their foundational law. Would-be traders into them will find themselves in familiar legal territory. If the WTO's 149 Members divided themselves up into 10 or 15 RTAs within each of which WTO rules held sway and tariffs were zero, multinational traders might well find this a more congenial arrangement than a world of 150 nation-states heading only slowly toward common rules and zero tariffs under the auspices of the WTO.

An obvious qualification to this optimistic reverie is that as things stand there are many more than 10 or 15 RTAs. Countries now commonly belong to several deals that are, by virtue of that fact, overlapping.[41] The existence of such overlap can be an important strategic consideration. Canada lobbied to join the proposed Mexico–US Free Trade Area and turn it into NAFTA precisely in order to avoid a situation in which the US had a free-trade deal with each of its immediate neighbours and thereby became the hub in a 'hub-and-spoke' arrangement. What is the effect of such overlap on transactions costs for traders? Where the Canadian tariff schedule once included only two or three columns—for MFN, General, and GSP countries—it now includes 11 different tariff rates, including the MFN rate.[42] Still, although the proliferation of tariff rates clearly creates complications for academic economists wishing to know what 'the tariff' is on any particular good, the

---

[40] The cost of a Barbie doll that retails for $US10 in the US is just $US1 (quoted in Anderson and Van Wincoop, above at n 22, at 3).

[41] As of 2005, the average country belonged to 5 preferential arrangements (*ibid.*, Table 2.1, at 30).

[42] Headed, respectively, US Tariff, Mexico Tariff, Mexico–US Tariff, Chile Tariff, Costa Rica Tariff, Canada–Israel Agreement Tariff, General Preferential Tariff, Least Developed Country Tariff, Commonwealth Caribbean Countries Tariff, Australia Tariff, and New Zealand Tariff: *See* www.cbsa-asfc.gc.ca/general/publications/tariff2005/2005act-e.pdf (visited 10 April 2006), 8.

difficulty facing would-be exporters into the Canadian market may not be that great. There is still just one tariff per exporting country and with the customs schedule available on the Internet it is very easy to discover. Granted, the likelihood that a given exporter will face a different tariff than competitors from other countries is now greater than when MFN trade was more dominant. But in deciding how effective competitors will be, the tariff rate is probably the easiest part of the calculation. Production costs in other countries and transportation costs to Canada are much harder to gauge. The same is true for multinational enterprises trying to decide from which country to export to Canada. There are more tariffs to choose from, yes, but the hard part of the calculation is the cost of producing the good and getting it to Canada.

Different tariff rates are not the only complication, of course. Free Trade Areas generally also involve rules of origin, which can be very complicated indeed, even if they, too, will often be available on the web. Complying with the significant paper burden involved in such rules can impose substantial costs on businesses. Even so, in most cases the option is available to avoid the rules by paying the MFN tariff. In the late 1990s many firms trading between Canada and the US chose that option.[43] Thus the damage done by the spaghetti-bowl effect may be limited. If MFN tariffs are not raised as part of any deal and if the default of paying the MFN tariff remains, then businesses may decide to suffer increases in transactions costs only if there is an offsetting commercial gain from doing so.[44]

Unfortunately, any conclusion on this question must be agnostic. The most comprehensive recent survey of trade costs by economists is by Anderson and Van Wincoop. A reader is impressed mainly by their account of the difficulty of making estimates. There are very serious gaps in data: 'Direct measures of trade costs are remarkably sparse and inaccurate ... The seemingly simple question "how high are policy barriers to trade?" cannot usually be answered with accuracy for most goods in most countries at most dates ... The grossly incomplete and inaccurate information on policy barriers available to researchers is a scandal and a puzzle ...'.[45] Even if full information were available, the scale of the problem would be daunting. Counting countries, types of barriers and numbers of 'tariff lines' of products, 'tariffs and NTB's comprise some 10^5 lines, with large variation across the lines'.[46] Moreover,

---

[43] NAFTA take-up rates were as low as 55 per cent in some industries, although since US MFN rates were zero on a third of industries the incentive to trade under NAFTA procedures was muted. *See* D. Goldfarb, 'The Road to a Canada–US Customs Union: Step-by-Step or in a Single Bound?' (Toronto: C.D. Howe Institute Commentary, 2003), 10. She argues that from the Canadian side the cost of NAFTA rules of origin is unlikely to be less than 0.5 per cent of the value of Canadian exports.

[44] There is also the more general qualification that, as noted above, many RTAs apparently are never fully implemented. The paperwork problem may therefore look worse than it is in fact.

[45] Anderson and Van Wincoop, above at n 22, at 2, 5, and 2 fn 1.

[46] *Ibid.*, at 8.

'measuring the restrictiveness of each type of nontariff barrier requires an economic model'.[47]

Despite these difficulties, the World Bank has recently undertaken a very useful investigation of the costs of moving a typical 20-foot product container across borders.[48] A detailed questionnaire administered in 140 countries has produced data on the time and cost required for such things as 'trade document processing, approvals needed for import or export transactions, customs clearance, technical clearances, inland transport, terminal handling, and container security measures'.[49] The raw data suggest there are substantial differences across countries: 'For landlocked Zambia, for example, costs of trade-related transactions . . . amount to $4,616, compared with $969 in Côte d'Ivoire . . .' while 'Customs clearance times range from about 1 day for Hong Kong (China) and the Netherlands and 2 days for Ireland and Mauritius to 21 days for the Syrian Arab Republic and 25 days for Uzbekistan'.[50] In general, 'Institutional issues such as customs inspection and clearance, technical clearance, and document processing are among the most important factors in the cost and time of shipments, more important even than the physical condition of roads or rail'.[51]

Using the new data set, Hausman, Lee, and Subramanian have constructed a summary 'logistics index' that helps explain trade flows in an otherwise standard gravity model. What would be very interesting for present purposes but has not yet been done is a study of how customs costs vary with the number of RTAs a country belongs to. If there is such a correlation, is it causal? Do the extra RTA memberships increase costs or are memberships and costs jointly determined in a process in which some other factor is key? Unfortunately, at the moment the literature has produced many more questions than answers. We evidently are some distance from being able to generalize about how much greater transaction costs may be in a spaghetti-bowl world than they are in a not-perfectly-liberalized WTO world.

IV.   WHY ARE THERE SO MANY RTAS?

Economists' training teaches them to try to make testable hypotheses. Explaining a unique historical phenomenon such as the relatively sudden proliferation of RTAs in the 1980s and 1990s is not easy. The problem is not a paucity of possible explanations; the literature abounds with explanation. The problem is finding ways to decide among them. Anderson and Van Wincoop conclude their survey of trade costs thus: 'There is undoubtedly a rich relationship

---

[47] *Ibid.*

[48] *See* W. Hausman, H.L. Lee and U. Subramanian, 'Global Logistics Indicators, Supply Chain Metrics, and Bilateral Trade Patterns', World Bank Policy Research Working Paper 3773 (World Bank, 2005).

[49] *Ibid.*, at 6.   [50] *Ibid.*, at 10.   [51] *Ibid.*

between domestic and international trade costs, market structure and political economy'.[52] Unfortunately, rich relationships are notoriously difficult to parse.

They go on: 'Some trade costs provide benefits, and it is likely that the pursuit of benefits partly explains the costs'.[53] We have no suggestions in that regard but in brief concluding comments offer one or two observations that rely on our knowledge of the Canadian case and which may or may not generalize to the multilateral context. First, although there are probably many reasons why Canada sought, negotiated, and entered the Canada–US Free Trade Agreement (CUSFTA), including reasons having to do with particularities of the politics of the 1980s, a primary goal anticipated economic efficiency gains from access to the larger US market.[54] Canada sought the deal in the 1980s rather than the 1940s or 1950s because by then multilateral trade liberalization had reduced tariffs to a low enough level that although the gains from free trade were smaller so were the costs of adjustment.[55] By contrast, Canada entered the North American Free Trade Agreement largely for defensive reasons: it did not wish to become a spoke in a hub-and-spoke system centred on the US. Its current serial negotiation of free trade areas is also largely a defensive reaction to the US's decision to negotiate such deals. (Of the nine bilateral deals Canada has negotiated since 1991, six are with countries that also have agreements with the US.) It certainly is true that having secured preferential access to what is by far its largest trading partner, Canada's enthusiasm for multilateral negotiations seems to have dimmed. Influential commentators can be found who argue that further multilateral liberalization, though desirable, is not urgent.[56] That probably was not true in the 1950s and 1960s, when liberalization with the US was often secured through the GATT.[57]

The lack of enthusiasm for the WTO negotiations is not wholly a result of preferential arrangements with the US, however. Nor does it on its own explain the delays in the Doha Round. Problems in the WTO may be as much a cause as a consequence of regionalization. Although slow-moving negotiations do sometimes produce surprising and impressive results—witness the end of the Uruguay Round and the unexpected emergence of the WTO itself—

---

[52] Anderson and Van Wincooop, above at n 22, at 77.   [53] *Ibid.*

[54] *See* M. Hart, *A Trading Nation: Canadian Trade Policy from Colonialism to Globalization* (Vancouver: UBC Press, 2002) and G.B. Doern and B.W. Tomlin, *Faith & Fear: The Free Trade Story* (Toronto: Stoddart, 1991).

[55] Trefler argues that such gains were realized and that they amounted to a roughly six per cent increase in productivity in the Canadian manufacturing sector.

[56] *See* M. Hart and B. Dymond, 'The WTO Plays Hong Kong: So Little Accomplished by So Many', *Policy Options Politiques* (February 2006). As they put it (at 11 and 12) 'the simple fact is that Canada's most basic economic interests are now inextricably bound up with those of the United States and can no longer be addressed multilaterally in the WTO . . . [T]he days are long past when the results of multilateral negotiations had a significant impact on the Canadian economy'.

[57] And it may not be a sound position now: multilateral negotiations do continue, if slowly. By contrast the NAFTA/CUSFTA is not regularly revisited.

they are also a spur to freelancing. Quite apart from the growth of RTAs, there are perfectly understandable reasons why the WTO may no longer be the principal locus of liberalization. An organization with 80 Contracting Parties in 1986 had 149 Members at the end of 2005. Moreover, these members are very disparate; those with established preferences come with a built-in resistance to liberalization; and their growing numbers have encouraged more assertive participation on their part. It is hardly surprising that an increasingly inclusive institution is an increasingly unwieldy institution. But then neither should it be surprising that the momentum for multilateral free trade should have stalled. Pushing back the extensive margin so dramatically may have calcified the intensive margin.

We close with a conundrum. Reviews of the growth of RTAs customarily conclude with recommendations for how further proliferation might be discouraged. Sometimes what is recommended is merely transparency. In other cases, there are suggestions for mechanisms that would allow for the rewriting or perhaps even over-ruling of RTAs. But if member-nations could summon the will to restrict RTAs in any meaningful way, would they not also have the political will to provide the multilateral liberalization that would make such action unnecessary?

2

The Political Economy of Regional Trade Agreements

CHAD DAMRO *

I. INTRODUCTION

Regional trade agreements (RTAs) have proliferated widely since the creation of the World Trade Organization (WTO) in 1995.[1] Today, more than 40 percent of world trade is conducted within these regional trade arrangements.[2] The launch of the WTO alone did not cause governments to pursue RTAs. Rather, government decisions to enter into RTAs are the result of many international and domestic factors, including political imperatives and economic incentives.

The proliferation of RTAs and the interaction of these various factors have drawn considerable attention from political science scholars who investigate the International Political Economy (IPE).[3] IPE scholars explore both the political causes of international economic phenomena and the economic causes of international political phenomena. These scholars tend to ask questions about the political and economic factors that drive governments to enter into RTAs.[4]

* The author would like to thank Sophie Thomas for research assistance on this project. The author would also like to thank, for useful comments, Valentin Zahrnt and the participants of the International Law Association (British Branch) Annual Conference, Edinburgh University, Edinburgh, 27–28 May 2005.

[1] While this chapter employs the label 'RTA', many arguments below also apply to preferential trade agreements, which are often not regionally-specific.

[2] J. Ravenhill, *Global Political Economy* (Oxford: OUP, 2005), 117.

[3] For a useful and broad description of the subfield of political science known as IPE, *see* P.J. Katzenstein, R.O. Keohane, and S.D. Krasner, 'International Organization and the Study of World Politics' (1998) 52 Int Org 645, at 645–46. For discussions of differing perspectives in IPE, *see also* R. Gilpin, *Global Political Economy: Understanding the International Economic Order* (Princeton, NJ: PUP, 2001) and J.A. Frieden and D.A. Lake, *International Political Economy: Perspectives on Global Power and Wealth*, 4th ed. (London: Routledge, 2000).

[4] For recent examples of the growing political science literature on regionalism, *see* M. Smith, 'Regions and Regionalism', in B. White, R. Little, and M. Smith (eds), *Issues in World Politics*, 3rd ed. (Houndmills Basingstoke: Palgrave, 2005), 58–77, F. Söderbaum and T.M. Shaw, *Theories of New Regionalism* (Houndmills, Basingstoke: Palgrave, 2003), S. Breslin et al. (eds), *New*

At the same time, they argue about the contradictory and/or complementary nature of RTAs and multilateral trade liberalization via the WTO. The resulting IPE literature has identified a number of political factors that could lead governments to pursue RTA-driven regionalism over WTO-driven multilateralism.

RTAs have been seen as both building blocks and stumbling blocks to multilateral liberalization.[5] As building blocks, RTAs facilitate the further liberalization of trade through fora such as the WTO; they establish incentives that lead governments to oppose protectionism generally at both the regional and multilateral levels. As stumbling blocks, RTAs divert trade and clash with the economic goals of multilateral liberalization.[6] Governments may, thus, pursue regional liberalization at the expense of multilateral liberalization. RTAs may also be seen as politically-oriented stumbling blocks. This chapter reviews the political factors identified by the IPE literature that lead governments to pursue RTAs and argues that such motivations may encourage the negotiation of RTAs that become political stumbling blocks to multilateral liberalization.

The chapter accepts the possibility that RTAs can complement multilateral liberalization and the argument that they can function as a 'backbone' for a liberalizing international trade system.[7] Notwithstanding these arguments, the chapter suggests that many governments enter into RTAs for important political rather than economic reasons. If states do negotiate, sign and implement RTAs for political reasons, then these regional arrangements may become—albeit, likely unintentionally—political stumbling blocks that obstruct WTO multilateralism in the long term.

It is worth noting at the outset that this chapter does not attempt to provide a definitive conclusion on the comparative influence of political and economic factors in the signing of RTAs. Rather, the chapter highlights the political

---

Regionalisms in the Global Political Economy (London: Routledge, 2002), B. Hettne, A. Inotai, and O. Sunkel (eds), *Comparing Regionalism: Implications for Global Development* (Houndmills, Basingstoke: Palgrave, 2001), M. Schulz, F. Söderbaum, and J. Öjendal (eds), *Regionalization in a Globalizing World: A Comparative Perspective on Forms, Actors and Processes* (London: Zed Books, 2001), W. Mattli, *The Logic of Regional Integration* (Cambridge: CUP, 1999), K.P. Thomas and M.A. Tetreault (eds), *Racing to Regionalize, International Political Economy Yearbook*, Volume 11 (Boulder, CO: Lynne Reinner, 1999), A. Moravcsik, *The Choice for Europe: Social Purpose and State Power from Messina to Maastricht* (Ithaca, NY: Cornell University Press, 1998), and L. Fawcett and A. Hurrell, *Regionalism in World Politics: Regional Organization and International Orders* (Oxford: OUP, 1995). For a useful discussion of theoretical accounts of regional integration from political science and economics, *see* Gilpin, *Ibid.*

[5] For early works on this debate, *see* J. Bhagwati, *The World Trading System at Risk* (Princeton, NJ: PUP, 1991) and R. Lawrence, 'Emerging Regional Arrangements: Building Blocks or Stumbling Blocks?', in R. O'Brien (ed), *Finance and the International Economy, The AMEX Bank Review Prize Essays* (Oxford: OUP, 1991).

[6] For an argument on the ways in which regionalization can enhance the effectiveness of WTO negotiations, *see* V. Zahrnt, 'How Regionalization can be a Pillar of a More Effective World Trade Organization' (2005) 39 JWT 671.

[7] The author is grateful to Thomas Cottier for pointing out this possible complementary relationship between RTAs and the WTO.

motivations that may reflect a potential preference for regional over multilateral trade liberalization. If this is the case, serious discussions about RTAs and the WTO system must consider innovative ways to adjust legal provisions and economic incentives that will overcome these pro-regional political preferences. Without doing so, an ever increasing amount of world trade will be conducted through RTAs that act as political stumbling blocks to multilateral liberalization.

The chapter proceeds in the following manner. First, the chapter discusses the current state of RTAs and the WTO. This discussion supports the notion that governments should view RTAs as building blocks to multilateral liberalization. Second, the chapter discusses the development of IPE scholarship on RTAs and addresses the transition to 'new regionalism' in the literature. Third, the chapter introduces the IPE arguments on why governments decide to enter into RTAs. This section emphasizes the general political motivations that often inspire governments to pursue RTAs. The penultimate section discusses the potential implications of these political motivations for WTO multilateralism and suggests that these RTAs may become political blocks to multilateral liberalization. The chapter concludes with a summary of the preceding discussion and elaborates the importance of considering political factors when discussing RTAs and the WTO.

II. RTAS AS THE BUILDING BLOCKS OF MULTILATERALISM

This section outlines the current state of RTAs and the WTO.[8] The empirical record shows a significant increase in regional trade agreements, especially since the creation of the WTO in 1995. These trends tend to support the contention that RTAs function as building blocks for multilateral liberalization. However, as will be discussed below, the growth of RTAs may also create political stumbling blocks to multilateral liberalization in the long term.

Along with the creation of the WTO in 1995, and its corresponding legal developments in multilateral trade liberalization and dispute settlement, regional trade agreements remain a very important feature of the international trading system. Indeed, almost all of the Members of the WTO rely on RTAs as essential instruments through which they manage their trade relations. Reflecting the appeal and importance of regional trade, the trend toward RTAs has increased rapidly during the 1990s and continues today (see Figure 1).

Regional liberalization has clearly increased alongside multilateral liberalization, especially since the founding of the WTO in 1995. This empirical record suggests that governments might pursue regionalism as building blocks for multilateral liberalization.

---

[8] For an excellent accounting of RTAs, *see* J.A. Crawford and R.V. Fiorentino, 'The Changing Landscape of Regional Trade Agreements', WTO Discussion Paper No 8 (2005).

Number of RTAs

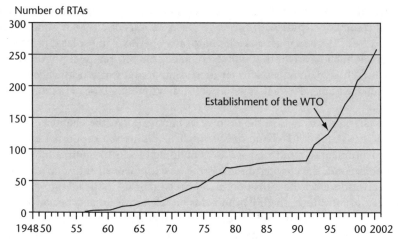

Figure 1. Evolution of Regional Trade Agreements, 1948–2002
Source: WTO Secretariat[9]

Many and diverse governments have negotiated, signed and implemented RTAs. According to the WTO, by 31 March 2006, 346 agreements had been notified, of which 195 are currently in force.[10] In general, each of these governments pursued their respective RTA for very specific reasons that supported and/or promoted their particular interests. This diversity of governments and interests creates a complex situation in which a number of factors and actors have come into play. What exactly were the factors that led governments to pursue these RTAs? The next section discusses the development of the IPE literature that began to formulate answers to this question.

III. FROM 'OLD' TO 'NEW' REGIONALISM

In the IPE literature, the scholarly study of regionalism has been divided into two different camps: old regionalism and new regionalism. These two camps are considered distinct for both empirical and analytical reasons.

The origins of the 'old regionalism' date to the mid-20th century. Although some scholars argue that the protectionist trend of the 1930s represented a first wave of regionalism, most agree that the old regionalism began with a wave of changes that followed World War II. During the 1950s–60s government efforts at regionalism were increased 'as an important strategy for achieving security, peace, development and welfare, particularly but by no means only in Europe'.[11] While political scientists spent considerable energy investigating the causes and logics of this regional integration in the post-WWII

---

[9] WTO Secretariat, Evolution of Regional Trade Agreements, available at www.wto.org/english/ tratop_e/region_e/regfac_e.htm (visited 29 January 2006).

[10] *See* Introduction, at n 2.   [11] *See* Schulz, Söderbaum, and Öjendal, above at n 4, at 3.

era,[12] 'the interest and enthusiasm for regional integration died out in the late 1960s and early 1970s because the grandiose projects actually had limited impact or simply never materialized'.[13]

The 'new regionalism' filled this empirical and academic vacuum. Developments in the 1980s pushed political science out of the malaise associated with the old regionalism and ushered in the study of new regionalism in IPE.[14] While given an appealing and modern label, the 'new regionalism' is simply a reflection of a new wave of regional integration. Political science scholars employ this label to identify the obvious proliferation of RTAs that began in or continued through the 1980s–90s. Commenting further about the study of regionalism, Higgott argues that, 'at a scholarly level, the study of comparative regionalism has been back in fashion for some time now—especially in the USA, where studies of NAFTA and the EU, and NAFTA and Asia–Pacific co-operation have emerged'.[15]

In addition to the simple temporal distinction between the old and new regionalism, Schulz *et al.* argue that the rise of the new regionalism is associated with or caused by a number of often inter-related changes in the international system:

(1) the move from bipolarity towards a multipolar or perhaps tripolar structure, centred around the EU, NAFTA, and the Asia–Pacific, with a new division of power and new division of labour;

(2) the relative decline of American hegemony in combination with a more permissive attitude on the part of the United States towards regionalism;

(3) the restructuring of the nation-state and the growth of interdependence, transnationalization and globalization;

(4) recurrent fears over the stability of the multilateral trading order, hand in hand with the growing importance of non-tariff barriers (NTBs) to trade; and

(5) the changed attitudes towards (neo-liberal) economic development and political systems in the developing countries as well as in the post-communist countries.[16]

Not only the causes, but the content of agreements associated with the new regionalism has also changed. Regional agreements signed during the old

---

[12] *See* E. Haas, *The Uniting of Europe: Political, Social, and Economic Forces, 1950–1957* (Stanford: Stanford University Press, 1958), J.S. Nye, *Peace in Parts: Integration and Conflict in Regional Organization* (Boston: Little, Brown & Co., 1971) and B. Russett, *International Regions and the International System* (Chicago: Rand-McNally, 1967).

[13] Schulz, Söderbaum, and Öjendal, above at n 4, at 3.

[14] For a further discussion of the 'newness' of new regionalism, *see* Söderbaum, above at n 4, at 3–6.

[15] R. Higgott, 'The International Political Economy of Regionalism', in W.D. Coleman and G.R.D. Underhill (eds), *Regionalism and Global Economic Integration: Europe, Asia and the Americas* (London: Routledge, 1998), 42.

[16] Schulz, Söderbaum, and Öjendal, above at n 4, at 4.

regionalism may have been 'imposed, directly or indirectly, from outside and above, in accordance with the bipolar structure of the Cold War and mainly in the interests of the superpowers'.[17] In stark contrast, the agreements signed during the new regionalism tend to represent 'more spontaneous' processes that have emerged from within the regions themselves and represent a 'heterogeneous, comprehensive, multidimensional phenomenon, which involves state, market and society actors and covers economic, cultural, political, security and environmental aspects'.[18]

Table 1 lists a number of the regional developments that are often cited as

Table 1. Two Waves of Regionalism

FIRST WAVE: 1950s–60s

Europe and Soviet Bloc
NATO (1949–)
Western European Union (1955–)
Warsaw Treaty Organization (1955–1991)
Council of Europe (1948–)
European Coal and Steel Community (1952–)
Euratom (1958–)
European Economic Community (1958–)
COMECON (1948–1991)

Africa
Organization of African Unity (1964–2002)

Latin America
Organization of American States (1948–)
Central American Common Market (1961–)
Andean Community (1969–)
Caricom (1973–)
LAFTA (1969–1980)

Middle East
Arab League (1947–)

West and East Asia
CENTO (1950s)
SEATO (1954–1975)
ASEAN (1967–)

SECOND WAVE: 1980s–90s

Europe
Conference on Security and Cooperation in Europe (1975–)
EEC–European Union (1992–)
Commonwealth of Independent States (1991–)

Latin America
Mercosur (1991–)
Free Trade Area of the Americas (1994–)
North American Free Trade Agreement (1993–)

---

[17] *Ibid.*

[18] *Ibid. See also* M. Bøås, M. Marchand, and T. Shaw, 'The Political Economy of New Regionalisms' (1999) 20 TWQ, 897 and J. De Melo and A. Panagariya (eds), *New Dimensions in Regional Integration* (Cambridge: CUP, 1993).

Asia and Asia-Pacific	*Africa*
Asia–Pacific Economic Cooperation (1989–)	Economic Community of West African States (1975–)
ASEAN Regional Forum (1994–)	Southern African Development Community (1992–)
Middle East	Common Market for Eastern and
Gulf Cooperation Council (1981–)	Southern Africa (1994–)

Source: Table adapted from Karns and Mingst (2004, 152).[19]

indicators of the waves of old and new regionalisms. These examples demonstrate that certain regional agreements, especially those established during the 1970s, do not always fall clearly within one of the two waves identified above (e.g., Caricom, CSCE). It should also be noted that some of the regional partnerships identified in Table 1 are not exclusively trade-related.

The transition from old to new regionalism within the IPE literature has been slow, empirical and important. The scholarly attention now being dedicated to the study of new regionalism has launched a rich discussion within political science that has identified a number of motivations for states to pursue RTAs. The next section reviews those various political motivations.

IV. IPE THEORY AND RTAS

Proponents of the new regionalism have dedicated themselves to identifying the reasons why states enter into regional arrangements. This section reviews the common IPE arguments for why governments might prefer to pursue liberalization through RTAs instead of through the WTO. Seven different political motivations are drawn from the IPE literature. These motivations are presented in abstract terms and supported with empirical evidence selected from various examples of regional trade agreements.

This section expands upon Ravenhill's authoritative classification of political motivations for RTAs.[20] Each of these political motivations depicts reasons why governments may enter into collaborative agreements, in particular RTAs. As such, the preference to pursue RTAs may be classified under the following themes:

(1) Marginalization syndrome
(2) Security via economic means

---

[19] M.P. Karns and K.A. Mingst, *International Organizations* (Boulder, CO: Lynne Rienner, 2004).
[20] Ravenhill, above at n 2.

(3) 'New security' needs
(4) Increase negotiating leverage
(5) Lock-in domestic reforms
(6) Accommodate domestic constituents
(7) Practical ease

A. Regionalism and the Marginalization Syndrome[21]

This motivation for regionalism identifies a 'marginalization syndrome' as the political reason why states enter into regional trade agreements. According to this motivation, states will enter into RTAs because they fear being left out, or marginalized, from important international economic and political developments. This marginalization syndrome encourages policy-makers to join negotiations and ultimately sign onto regional agreements that they might otherwise have ignored or avoided.

Typically countries that are politically weak, geographically isolated, and/or economically dependent are the most likely to succumb to this syndrome. These countries are already concerned with their vulnerable position in the international system and will view new regional agreements as potentially making them even more vulnerable unless they participate. As a result, the syndrome can create a fear-inspired, band-wagoning mentality in vulnerable governments that do not want to be left behind.

This political motivation can be found as a driving force in RTAs where regional competition is often intense and the fear of being left behind is perceived to be very real. However, it should be acknowledged that the marginalization syndrome can also motivate states to pursue multilateral trade liberalization with equal vigor. There should be no reason that this syndrome would manifest itself exclusively in a regional setting. Indeed, a vulnerable state might feel the syndrome just as strongly (or even more strongly) if it is presented with a scenario in which multilateral liberalization is occurring without its participation.

B. Security via Economic Means

According to this motivation, governments will enter into RTAs as a way to enhance economic cooperation, which will, in turn, create confidence within their region. This need for confidence may be in the greatest demand in regions that have had or are currently suffering from security problems. Thus regions suffering from security problems (very broadly defined) are likely to engage in RTAs. The impulse for confidence building can come from a desire for military security that is driven by developments both internal and external to the members of the RTA.

---

[21] For this insight, the author is grateful to the participants of the International Law Association (British Branch) Annual Conference, Edinburgh University, Edinburgh, 27–28 May 2005.

In regions that have histories of conflict and lack traditions of intergovern-mental partnership, the pursuit of economic cooperation can be a first step toward building security confidence. The EU has received considerable schol-arly attention as a case of regionalism and provides empirical evidence of governments pursuing an RTA in order to attain security via economic means. Many see the origins of the EU as a conscious decision to build confidence among its members and help to ensure their security. The motivation for the original six members to create the European Coal and Steel Community lay in the fundamental need to build confidence that Germany would not threaten their security in the future. By integrating their coal and steel industries, the logic followed that an attack by member A on member B would be the equivalent of member A attacking its own war-making capacity. Continued economic and atomic integration took this logic further by contributing to European economic recovery and restoring security confidence among the EU's members. The original political motivation has achieved its objective as today's EU has enlarged to include twenty-five members and military aggression among them seems inconceivable.

Scholars note similar motivations for the creation of ASEAN.[22] While the circumstances in Southeast Asia were quite different from those found in Europe, the founders of ASEAN strove to create a sense of regional identity as a means to promote conflict prevention and cooperative security.[23] ASEAN was established in 1967 'to promote economic cooperation in an attempt to build confidence and avoid conflict in a region that was the site of armed struggles in the Cold War era'.[24] Internal and external security threats pushed ASEAN's founding members to pursue regional cooperation. Internally, 'Indonesia and Malaysia, had engaged in armed conflict in the period 1963–66 as the Indonesian government of President Sukarno attempted to destabilize the newly independent Malaysia'.[25] To address similar internal security threats, ASEAN established as its core principle the non-intervention in the internal affairs of its members. Externally, the founding members were motiv-ated by other factors: 'threats from China, the heightened U.S. presence during the Vietnam War, and later from Vietnam's invasion of Cambodia played a

---

[22] A. Acharya, *Constructing a Security Community in Southeast Asia: ASEAN and the Problem of Regional Order* (New York: Routledge, 2001), A. Acharya, 'Ideas, Identity, and Institution-building: From the "ASEAN Way" to the "Asia–Pacific Way"?' (1997) 10 Pac Rev 319, and A. Acharya and E. Goh (eds), *Reassessing Security Cooperation in the Asia–Pacific* (Cambridge, MA: MIT Press, 2005).

[23] For further discussions of Asia–Pacific regionalism, *see* C.M. Dent, 'Networking the Region? The Emergence and Impact of Asia–Pacific Bilateral Free Trade Agreement Projects' (2003) 16 Pac Rev 1, M. Hund, 'ASEAN Plus Three: Towards a New Age of Pan-East Asian Regionalism? A Skeptic's Appraisal' (2003) 16 Pac Rev 383, D.K. Emmerson, 'What Do the Blind See? Reap-proaching Regionalism in Southeast Asia' (2005) 18 Pac Rev 1, B.D. Jorgensen, 'South Asia: An Anxious Journey towards Regionalization?', in Schulz, Söderbaum, and Öjendal, above at n 4, at 125–46, and R. Stubbs, 'Asia–Pacific Regionalism versus Globalization', in Coleman and Underhill, above at n 15.

[24] Ravenhill, above at n 2, at 122.   [25] *Ibid.*

major role in the formation and evolution of ASEAN'.[26] ASEAN was also designed to strengthen members against the external threat of 'Chinese-supported communist insurgencies'.[27]

Similar security motivations are found in the creation of other regional arrangements that promote trade liberalization. The Southern African Development Community (SADC, formerly Southern African Development Coordination Conference) was originally established in 1980 in an attempt to reduce the economic dependence of its members on South Africa during the apartheid era.[28] Because South Africa was seen as a destabilizing force in the region, the SADC partners pursued an RTA as a means to reduce their dependence on South Africa and, essentially, increase their security via economic means.

In Latin America, the political agenda of Mercosur seems to be focused on increasing security confidence, especially between Brazil and Argentina. Devlin and Ffrench-Davis argue:

> Today's integration in Latin America is often driven by powerful political objectives. This is most clearly manifest in MERCOSUR (including associates Chile and Bolivia), where countries with a history of conflictive relations are using economic integration to draw themselves more closely together into a common purpose of peace and prosperity. A similar phenomenon can be found with the reactivation of integration in other sub-regions such as the Andean Community and Central America.[29]

Finally, the Middle East also provides evidence of this political motivation for regional integration. The Gulf Cooperation Council (GCC), which covers various aspects of economic cooperation (e.g., finance, trade, customs, tourism, foreign investment), was established in 1981, in response to several new regional threats 'including the Iranian Revolution of 1979, the Soviet invasion of Afghanistan, and the war between Iran and Iraq'.[30] As a result, the members of the GCC, like so many other regions, are pursuing an RTA as an economic means to increase their security.

C. Regionalism and 'New Security' Needs

States may enter into regional trade liberalization agreements in order to address security threats that are not traditional military threats. This so-called 'new security agenda' is concerned with emerging causes of instability and

---

[26] *See* Karns and Mingst, above at n 19, at 149.   [27] *Ibid.*, at 192.   [28] *Ibid.*, at 205.

[29] R. Devlin and R. Ffrench-Davis, 'Towards an Evaluation of Regional Integration in Latin America in the 1990s', Inter-American Development Bank Integration and Regional Program Department, Working Paper No 2 (Buenos Aires: INTAL ITD, 1998), 13. For more on the political agenda of Mercosur, *see* M. Hirst, 'Mercosur's Complex Political Agenda', in R. Roett (ed), *Mercosur: Regional Integration, World Markets* (Boulder, CO: Lynne Rienner, 1999), 35–48.

[30] Karns and Mingst, above at n 19, at 208. For an argument that regional cooperation in the Middle East has been based on confidence building via macroregional and subregional cooperation schemes, *see* M. Laanatza, H. Lindholm Schulz, and M. Schulz, 'Regionalization in the Middle East?', in Schulz, Söderbaum, and Öjendal, above at n 4, at 42–60.

threats to security, such as environmental damage, illegal migration, organized crime, drug smuggling and international terrorism.[31] The 'newness' of these security threats is not necessarily an indication that they have recently started to occur, but rather an acknowledgment that academics are only now considering them significant causes of instability in the same sense as traditional military conflict.

This political motivation has recently been evident in the behaviour of developed states negotiating with their less developed regional partners. Regional economic cooperation agreements can address these new security threats either directly or indirectly. For example, the North American Free Trade Agreement included environmental provisions that would directly bolster Mexico's standards. Proponents also hope that RTAs will meet new security needs indirectly by 'promoting economic development and thereby ameliorating the conditions that were perceived as fostering the security threats. Concerns about new security threats played a part in European enthusiasm for new agreements with Mediterranean states, and in US interest in a free trade agreement with Mexico and its extension to other Western Hemisphere countries'.

The Free Trade Area of the Americas (FTAA) also provides considerable evidence of the new security concerns that propel RTAs. The FTAA originated with the Miami Summit of 1994, which agreed a Declaration of Principles and Plan of Action for various initiatives in twenty-three policy areas that included strengthening democracy, promoting human rights and cultural values, combating corruption, combating illegal drugs and related crimes, eliminating the threat of national and international terrorism, strengthening the role of women in society, sustainable energy use, and developing partnerships for biodiversity and pollution prevention.

This political motivation is not found exclusively in the behaviour of developed states in their relations with developing states. For example, Caricom reflects the strong concern of new security threats among Caribbean states. As Knight and Persaud argue, post-Cold War changes have posed 'a direct threat to the very survival of [Caricom states], whose fragile economies make them highly susceptible to any alterations in the status quo'.[32] Knight and Persaud argue that Caricom is changing to address the threats of drugs (including production, consumption and abuse, trafficking, and money laundering), migration, environmental changes (including hurricanes, pollution, oil spills, and foreign overfishing) and overpopulation pressures.[33] Without regional cooperation to counter these new security threats, the Caricom states face economic disaster brought on by declining tourism trade, a major revenue

---

[31] K. Krause and M. Williams, 'Broadening the Agenda of Security Studies: Politics and Methods' (1996) 40 Mershon Int Stud Rev, Supplement 2, 229–54.

[32] W.A. Knight and R.B. Persaud, 'Subsidiarity, Regional Governance, and Caribbean Security' (2001) 43 Latin Amer Politics Society, 29, at 39–40.

[33] *Ibid.*, at 40–1.

source for these states. The resulting instability would be a considerable threat to regional security.

Similar evidence can also be found in Africa where SADC's economic cooperation was originally designed to improve regional transportation networks and eliminate trade barriers. Now its 14 members promote an agenda that includes initiatives on refugees and environmental conservation.[34] One might also look to the recent enlargement of the EU to find evidence of this motivation pressuring new members to address various new security threats before entering the Union.

D. Regionalism to Increase Negotiating Leverage

States can also be motivated to enter into RTAs as a way to increase their bargaining power in international negotiations. This bargaining power can be used to increase leverage in negotiations with firms, other states and international organizations. The ability of an RTA to increase negotiating leverage lies in the ability of its members to speak with one voice.

RTAs can increase members' leverage when negotiating with transnational corporations (TNCs) and foreign investors. Many regional economic arrangements established by developing states in the 1950s–70s were designed to increase their bargaining power with TNCs.[35] According to Ravenhill, 'one approach, as in the Andean Pact ... was to adopt a system of region-wide industrial licensing. The intention was to prevent TNCs from gaining concessions by playing off governments of the region against one another, and to use the carrot of access to a larger regional market to extract concessions from potential investors'.[36]

Developing countries also found regional economic agreements as useful ways in which to leverage more aid from donor states and international organizations. The European Union, for example, is known to encourage regional economic integration as part of its development assistance to the African, Caribbean and Pacific (ACP) and other countries. Therefore, developing countries that promote regional cooperation increase their chances of receiving aid from the EU.

Developing states are also able to increase their negotiating leverage in international organizations by pooling their diplomatic resources with other members of a regional economic agreement. Sharing similar interests in areas affected by the RTA, these states often cooperate quite naturally and effectively *vis-à-vis* third parties. Ravenhill notes a study by the World Bank[37] that identifies the potential leverage gains that can follow from regional integration:

by pooling their diplomatic resources in a regional arrangement, less developed

---

[34] Karns and Mingst, above at n 19, at 205.   [35] Ravenhill, above at n 2, at 122.
[36] *Ibid.*   [37] World Bank, *Trade Blocs* (Oxford: OUP, 2000), 20.

countries are sometimes able to achieve greater prominence in international relations and to negotiate agreements that would not be available if they had acted individually, and to ensure election of their representatives to key positions in international organizations. The best example of successful pursuit of this strategy, the Bank suggests, is CARICOM, the Caribbean Community and Common Market.[38]

Some states face such significant obstacles due to regional characteristics that they find economic integration provides the only means through which their voice can be heard. Again, Caricom is the exemplar. Knight and Persaud identify Caricom's fundamental problem in this regard: 'Composed of a number of small, weak, and dependent states, the region does not possess a strong voice at the global level. This voice becomes even weaker when the Caribbean states do not pursue the same goals, or when they do not have a coordinated foreign policy'.[39]

In Asia, regionalization also shows evidence of increasing the negotiating leverage of regional partners. As Higgott argues,

It is now apparent that there is a growing desire on the part of a wide range of policy actors in the Asia–Pacific and East Asia to establish a greater sense of regional cohesion. This cohesion will permit the given region (APEC, the [East Asian Economic Caucus] or ASEAN depending on the level) to have an impact on the conduct of interstate relations within the region and between the region on the other international actors in a range of issues areas.[40]

It should also be noted that economic regionalization is not used exclusively by developing countries as a means to increase their negotiating leverage. Developed countries have also undertaken such measures for the same reason. Ravenhill notes some examples:

The Japanese Ministry of Economy, Trade and Industry, for instance, in advocating participation in discriminatory regional arrangements, pointed to the possibility that they could increase Japan's leverage within the WTO . . . The foundation (in 1989) of APEC was linked to perceptions that it could help to pressure the European Union into trade concessions during GATT's Uruguay Round of trade negotiations . . . And some authors have suggested that the negotiation of the Treaty of Rome, which established the European Economic Community in 1957, was at least in part motivated by European countries' desires to increase their leverage against the United States in the upcoming GATT talks.[41]

Developing and developed countries, therefore, have been motivated to enter into RTAs as a way to increase their leverage in negotiations with firms, other states, international organizations and other RTAs.

---

[38] Ravenhill, above at n 2, at 122–23.   [39] Knight and Persaud, above at n 32, at 42.
[40] *See* Higgott, above at n 15, at 53.   [41] Ravenhill, above at n 2, at 123.

E. Regionalism to Lock-In Domestic Reforms

Governments may also enter into RTAs as a means to lock-in liberalizing trade reforms. As Frankel argues, 'RTAs may lock-in and mobilize regional solidarity. When governments begin to adopt liberalization-trading agendas, their decisions can be "locked in" through RTAs so as to make it more difficult for future governments to reverse the pro-liberalization trading agenda'.[42]

Ravenhill develops this motivation further by elaborating the concepts of compliance and credibility that drive governments to use RTAs to lock-in reforms:

Countries' compliance with their commitments is likely to be more closely scrutinized within a regional grouping: the numbers of partners to be monitored is smaller than within the WTO with its close to 150 members, and any breaking of commitments is more likely to have a direct impact on regional partners and lead to swift retaliation. Some regional arrangements provide for regional institutions to monitor the implementation of agreements. Moreover, repeated interactions with a small number of partners within regional arrangements may make governments more concerned about their reputations (their credibility as collaborators) than they would be within more diffuse multilateral forums . . .[43]

Mexico's approach to NAFTA is often cited as a clear example of a government pursuing an RTA in order to lock-in domestic trade reforms. Since the mid-20th century, in order to avoid economic dependence on the US, Mexico pursued its development under a protectionist system of import-substituting industrialization. In the late 1980s, the Mexican government began an economic reform programme and 'Mexican Presidents Miguel de la Madrid and Carlos Salinas reversed a half-century of Mexican protectionism and imposed sweeping, unilateral liberalization measures'.[44] The proposed NAFTA fit nicely with this new programme of liberalization and reduced the likelihood that the reforms of the 1980s would be reversed. As Milner argues 'NAFTA provided a means to lock in the trade liberalization strategy that had been undertaken unilaterally. By joining a FTA, Mexico could not unilaterally change its policies and return to protectionism, at least not without incurring substantial costs . . . This increased the credibility of its policy moves and hence their effectiveness'.[45] Frankel seems to agree when he argues about Mexico's motivation for NAFTA: 'a good argument for NAFTA was that it locked in the reforms in a manner that would be difficult to reverse'.[46]

While Mexico may provide the best evidence of this motivation, developed countries may also pursue RTAs for similar reasons. Likewise, economies in

[42] J.A. Frankel, *Regional Trading Blocs in the World Economic System* (Washington, DC: Institute for International Economics, 1997), 216–17.

[43] Ravenhill, above at n 2, at 123.　　　[44] *See* Frankel, above at n 42, at 216.

[45] H. Milner, 'Regional Economic Co-operation, Global Markets and Domestics Politics: A Comparisons of NAFTA and the Maastricht Treaty', in Coleman and Underhill, above at n 15, at 28–9. *See also* F. Calvijo, 'Discussion', in De Melo and Panagariya, above at n 18, at 386.

[46] Frankel, above at n 42, at 216.

transition may also view RTAs as a way of locking-in reforms and establishing credibility with foreign investors.

F. Regionalism to Accommodate Domestic Constituents

The next motivation does not necessarily privilege regional trade liberalization over multilateral trade liberalization. Rather, the motivation for RTAs in this case is that they allow politicians to satisfy domestic constituents when compared to the policy alternative of unilateral liberalization. As such, politicians pursue regionalism (and multilateralism) to increase their chances of being re-elected.

Unilateral trade liberalization is politically difficult 'because domestic groups believe that the government is giving something away (tariff protection) and not receiving anything in return from other countries'.[47] The pursuit of an RTA, however, can be sold more easily by politicians to their constituents because of the reciprocal nature of the agreement. An RTA guarantees compensatory tariff reductions and ensures that 'economic activity and investment are more balanced' than they would be under unilateral liberalization.[48]

Milner provides evidence of the political motivation to pursue RTAs in order to accommodate domestic constituents.[49] NAFTA offered economic and political benefits and became a politically charged issue during elections in the US and Canada. According to Milner,

The administration was counting on it as 'a vote-winner for President Bush' (*New York Times*, 12 August 1992: 1). The prospect of increased growth, competitiveness and jobs motivated political leaders. Domestic politics also shaped the Canadian government's attitudes: 'Like President Bush, Mr Mulroney is expected to use positive features of the trade agreement in his own bid for reelection' (*New York Times*, 13 August 1992: 4).[50]

The domestic demand for reciprocity may lead governments to pursue RTAs for narrow domestic political gain. They will pursue RTAs based on their own political horizons—i.e., when is the next election? These domestic political calculations are not consistently tied to the potential long-term benefits of the liberal, multilateral trading system. Politicians enter into RTAs because they can argue that RTAs will—through a variety of developments that privilege constituent interests—increase their own constituents' economic growth and job creation, which will, in turn, increase their chances of being re-elected. And if the deliverables of RTAs are more easily communicated to domestic constituents than the deliverables of multilateral agreements, then it is possible

---

[47] Ravenhill, above at n 2, at 123.   [48] *See* Devlin and Ffrench-Davis, above at n 29, at 14.

[49] Constituents need not only be individual voters. Karns and Mingst argue that South American governments' promotion of the Mercosur initiative depended on a domestic political coalition of supporters that included strong export-oriented manufacturing industries. In sum, these strong constituents—export-oriented manufacturers—won out over local South American companies that would be harmed by increased trade competition: Karns and Mingst, above at n 19, at 150.

[50] *See* Milner, above at n 45, at 30.

that RTAs could be more important for re-election than multilateral agreements. Under such circumstances, politicians would likely prefer regional liberalization via RTAs over multilateral liberalization via the WTO. However, this chapter will assume that the deliverables of both regional and multilateral liberalization are equally easy to communicate.

G. Practical Ease of Regionalism v. Multilateralism

Simple practical matters can also lead governments to prefer RTAs over multilateral trade liberalization. Governments have limited resources and, thus, must take care when deciding where to direct those resources. Often following delicate internal political deliberations, they will decide to dedicate resources to negotiations that are more likely to reach a result than those that hold out the prospect of deadlock or minimal returns.

This political motivation suggests that states prefer RTAs because they are simply easier to negotiate than multilateral liberalization through the WTO. As Frankel argues, 'Within the context of multilateral negotiations, it can be slow and awkward to negotiate separately with over 100 small countries'.[51]

In addition, deadlock and minimal returns are features often associated with negotiations among large numbers of states. As the number of states increases, the diversity of interests also increases. As the diversity of interests increases, the complexity of negotiations also increases. As the complexity of negotiations increases, the likelihood of reaching an agreement decreases.[52] Under such circumstances, states may prefer to decrease the number of their negotiating partners and pursue an RTA. In addition, 'the larger the number of members, the more difficult it is to monitor behaviour and to enforce sanctions in the event of non-compliance . . . A regional agreement with a limited number of partners accordingly might be easier to negotiate and implement than one at the global level'.[53]

Of course, this logic does not always play out in reality; we do have evidence of agreements being reached among very large numbers of states. Nevertheless, the logic is compelling and states with limited resources will often make decisions based on their perception of a negotiation setting. Thus, states' perceptions can become more important than reality, and '. . . there is little doubt that many believe that regional agreements are easier to negotiate than those at the global level, given the numbers and diversity of WTO membership. The failure of the WTO ministerial meetings in Seattle in 1999 and in Cancun in 2003 reinforced these beliefs'.[54]

Frankel also identifies arguments in which states would first opt to pursue

---

[51] Frankel, above at n 42, at 218.
[52] For additional elaboration on this argument, *see* Zahrnt, above at n 6.
[53] Ravenhill, above at n 2, at 123.
[54] *Ibid.*, at 123–24. For a similar assessment, *see* Devlin and Ffrench-Davis, above at n 29, at 14.

regional integration as a way to increase efficiency before negotiating multi-laterally through the WTO:

Some authors have argued that the costs of negotiations rise with the number of coun-tries involved so that it is easier for a smaller group of countries to negotiate a customs union first. With a common external trade policy, they can then enter multilateral negotiations as a group . . . This is thought to increase the efficiency of the negotiations and to make a satisfactory worldwide agreement more likely. The European Union is certainly the most important example of this . . . negotiations among a small number of regional neighbors may allow more efficient treatment of new issues than do global negotiations.[55]

Thus, the ease—or at least perception of ease—provides significant motivation for states to pursue RTAs over multilateral liberalization through the WTO. This same logic may support preferences for regionalization as a means to homogenize interests, streamline participants and increase the efficiency of multilateral WTO negotiations.

V. RTAS AS POLITICAL STUMBLING BLOCKS TO WTO MULTILATERALISM

The chapter suggests that many states enter into RTAs for important political, rather than exclusively economic, considerations. In short, states are using economic means for political ends. It is important to reiterate at this point that this chapter does not argue that governments pursue RTAs for *exclusively* political reasons. Rather, governments pursue RTAs for important political reasons, which, at least indirectly, may often include the promised economic benefits of RTAs. Some of these economic benefits include larger markets, job growth, and increased foreign investment. While it is often difficult to delineate completely and clearly the interaction between political and eco-nomic motivations, this chapter merely argues that politicians frequently make decisions to pursue RTAs for political reasons.

Such political considerations could reflect a potential preference for regional over multilateral trade liberalization. As such, these political motivations might lead to the creation of RTAs that operate as political stumbling blocks to multilateral liberalization. An RTA designed to achieve political goals may overlook or even obstruct important economic objectives of multilateral trade liberalization. Likewise, the establishment of RTAs for political purposes does not necessarily result in sound economic implementation, which can also hinder multilateral liberalization.

So let us see whether the preponderance of these incentives drive states toward regionalism via RTAs or multilateralism via the WTO. How many of the seven motivations identified in the preceding section reflect a potential

---

[55] Frankel, above at n 42, at 218.

preference for regional over multilateral liberalization? Of the seven motivations, Table 2 shows that all but two—marginalization syndrome and domestic constituents—result in a preference for regional liberalization through RTAs over multilateralism through the WTO.

The marginalization syndrome can affect states negotiating both regional and multilateral liberalization. There is no clear reason that this syndrome would be more likely to manifest itself in a regional setting. Indeed, it seems likely that a vulnerable state would feel the pressure to participate in regional liberalization as strongly as in multilateral liberalization. It is possible that pressure and competition might manifest itself more immediately in a regional setting, but this chapter accepts that, overall, the marginalization syndrome affects equally states' preference for regional and multilateral liberalization.

The motivation of security via economic means leads to a clear preference for regionalism over WTO multilateralism. States are not known typically to engage in multilateral liberalization via the WTO in order to reap direct gains in traditional military security. Rather, by integrating economically with geographical neighbours, states are much more likely to reap the benefits of political cooperation and confidence building that increases security.

At first look, the motivation for economic cooperation as a means to address threats from the 'new security agenda' suggests that states may prefer RTAs and WTO liberalization equally. However, opposition to include such items—e.g., environmental measures linked to trade—in the Doha Round suggests such new security items have hit a dead end in the WTO. Thus, the best option for states motivated by this preference is to pursue RTAs as the

Table 2. Political Incentives and Preferences

		Preference	
		Pro-RTA	Pro-WTO
	Marginalization Syndrome	X	X
	Security via Economic Means	X	
Political Incentives	New Security Needs	X	
	Negotiating Leverage	X	
	Locking-In	X	
	Domestic Constituents	X	X
	Practical Ease	X	

only mechanism through which they can include provisions to address new security threats.

States that pursue regionalism to increase negotiating leverage are likely to prefer regional liberalization over multilateral liberalization through the WTO. Regional partnerships enhance bargaining power for developing countries when they negotiate in international forums with one voice. It increases their leverage *vis-à-vis* external actors, including firms, other states and international organizations. Both developing and developed countries can pool their diplomatic resources regionally as a way to increase their international prominence and leverage in multilateral trade negotiations.

The motivation for locking-in reforms leads to a preference for regionalism over multilateralism via the WTO. Compliance and credibility increase in RTAs because trade reforms are locked-in tighter when they are committed to regionally than when they are committed to multilaterally. This is not to claim that states cannot lock-in reforms by engaging in multilateral liberalization. Indeed, they can. But they prefer locking-in such reforms regionally for the greater certainty that follows from regional compliance and credibility.

States seeking to satisfy domestic political constituencies equally prefer RTAs and multilateral liberalization via the WTO as long as the deliverables of both regional and multilateral liberalization are equally easy to communicate to constituents. RTAs and multilateral liberalization allow politicians to satisfy domestic constituents when compared to the policy alternative of unilateral liberalization. In so far as liberalization satisfies important domestic constituents, politicians/states will prefer equally that liberalization proceeds regionally and multilaterally because both increase equally their chances of being re-elected.

The final motivation, practical ease of negotiation and implementation, leads states to prefer regionalism over multilateralism through the WTO. In general, the smaller the number of states, the fewer the interests involved and the simpler the negotiations for liberalization. While this calculation does not always follow in reality, the logic applies generally and certainly influences states' perceptions of negotiations. Despite reality, if states perceive RTAs as easier to negotiate and implement, than they are likely to prefer them over pursuing multilateral liberalization through the WTO.

VI. CONCLUSIONS

This chapter has reviewed some of the most important political reasons identified by the IPE literature for why governments may pursue RTAs. The chapter does not claim that RTAs are pursued exclusively for political reasons. Rather, it elaborates a common IPE argument that foreign economic policymaking is often determined by political motivations.

In the IPE literature, scholarly inquiry has followed empirical developments.

As a result, the so-called old regionalism has given rise to the new regionalism. The proponents of the new regionalism have dedicated themselves to identifying the reasons why states enter into regional arrangements. The resulting literature on comparative regionalism has generated a growing political science interest in the political economy of RTAs.

The chapter identified seven different political motivations for why states would enter into RTAs. Evidence of such motivations can be found in various regions among both developing and developed states. Five of the seven motivations result in state preferences that favour the pursuit of regional trade liberalization agreements over multilateral trade liberalization through the WTO. This finding may help to explain the current global slow down in multilateralism and continued increases in regionalism.

So do these preferences suggest that RTAs could serve as building or stumbling blocks for multilateral liberalization? A more systematic analysis of the causes of all RTAs would be useful for answering the question. However, the empirical evidence above does seem to suggest that RTAs are often based on political motivations. If states pursue RTAs for such non-economic reasons, then they may become significant political stumbling blocks to multilateral liberalization through the WTO. There is no reason to assume that RTAs that were originally pursued for political reasons and continue to develop for political reasons will necessarily complement and/or promote multilateral liberalization. Rather, the political objectives of RTAs could override or undermine the economic goals of multilateral liberalization.

These political factors could also result in a slow down of multilateral liberalization as governments shift attention and resources toward the negotiation of regional agreements. Because governments have limited resources, they may face the difficult choice of prioritizing different avenues of liberalization. The motivations identified above suggest that governments will prioritize regional liberalization via RTAs over multilateral liberalization through the WTO. Such regionalization for political reasons could also create vested regional interests that would resist future efforts at multilateral liberalization.

This chapter posits potential political preferences for regional over multilateral trade liberalization. Following this preference, politicians may increasingly seek regional over multilateral liberalization. If this is the case, serious discussions about RTAs and the WTO system must consider innovative ways to adjust legal provisions and economic incentives that will overcome these pro-regional political preferences. Without doing so, the preferences that drive regional liberalization may, indeed, result in RTAs becoming political stumbling blocks to multilateral liberalization.

3

Constitutional Functions of the WTO and Regional Trade Agreements

THOMAS COTTIER AND MARINA FOLTEA[1]

I. INTRODUCTION

Under general public international law, States are essentially free to enter any agreement of any kind and content. Equality of States entails the power to choose partners, and to discriminate against others. There are hardly any limitations in customary law on engaging in preferential or discriminatory treatment, beyond the principles and rules enshrined in the Charter of the United Nations. There is no general obligation to treat all States alike. Neither equal treatment nor most favoured nation (MFN) status are considered to be principles of general public international law. Norms relating to *jus cogens* hardly affect trade relations, except for the prohibition of slavery in its different forms, and of policies supporting racial segregation. The principle of *pacta tertiis nec nocent nec prosunt* (a treaty must neither benefit nor impair a third party) is of equally limited effect. Short of specific treaty provisions, it certainly does not limit the conclusion of preferential and discriminatory trade agreements, having the distorting effects of trade diversion.

The principles and rules pertaining to regional integration and preferential trade agreements of the World Trade Organization (WTO), which bind its Members (currently 148), are therefore of paramount importance in light of the increasing number and complexity of preferential agreements witnessed in the regions discussed in this study. They shape the conditions, requirements and limitations for such agreements on the basis of the General Agreement

---

[1] The chapter builds upon, and expands a working paper by T. Cottier, 'The Legal Framework for FTAs & CUs in WTO Law', in M. Godel and J. Gage (eds) *Multilateralism and Bilateralism after Cancun: Challenges and Opportunities of Regionalism* (Berne: Seco Publikation Welthandel No 2, 2004).

on Tariffs and Trade (GATT) 1994 and the General Agreement on Trade in Services (GATS). The WTO principles and rules pertain to treaty law; from a functional point of view, they assume the role of overriding, constitutional disciplines which structure the shape and contents of preferential agreements— all with a view to supporting trade creation, as building blocks to trade regulation and liberalization, while at the same time avoiding unnecessary trade distortions and diversions. The question arises of whether these WTO disciplines provide sufficient guidance and force to bring about the desired effects. The purpose of this chapter is to briefly assess the guiding principles, discuss efforts at reform, and seek to prepare for additional suggestions with a view to establishing a proper balance between the needs of multilateralism and of preferential and regional trade regulation and market access.[2] We first give a brief description of the economic and political reasons behind RTAs, followed by a description of the rules as applied in practice and in WTO jurisprudence, and how these rules embed the constitutional functions. We then attempt to clarify the unsettled WTO–RTA relationship in the treaty law framework. We assess the shortcomings and suggested proposals for reform submitted within the framework of the Doha Development Agenda. Finally, we explore some enforcement issues and submit further reform proposals with a view to stimulating further conceptual discussions.

II. ECONOMIC AND POLITICAL REASONS FOR RTAS

Throughout history, trade agreements have been concluded for a multitude of different reasons. They have formed part of peace agreements settling market access rights. The GATT, jointly with the Bretton Woods Institutions of the IMF and World Bank, formed part of the World War II settlement. Trade agreements were designed, most prominently in the case of the European Economic Community, to bring about lasting peace among Member States seeking deeper integration, starting with trade liberalization. Both multilateral and bilateral agreements share such traits. But it would seem that non-economic motivations are more prominent in the case of RTAs. Joining the WTO, and becoming a Member, is for most countries primarily induced by economic interests and advantages: Members benefit from MFN, market access rights and equal conditions of competition, backed by a strong system

---

[2] The term 'RTAs' should be used only if some geographical proximity or contiguity between the parties to the agreement exists, such as for example in the case of the European Union (EU), the North American Free Trade Agreement (NAFTA), the European Free Trade Association (EFTA), or the Southern Common Market (Mercosur). Since such agreements today are increasingly of a transcontinental nature, these authors are of the view that the term preferential trade agreements (PTAs) is more adequate in this context. However, for reasons of consistency with other contributions in this book we will further use the term 'RTA' without making distinctions between the two categories.

of dispute settlement. With regional agreements, trade liberalization is equally an economic end in itself. But often it is also a means to a political end.[3]

Economic rationales for concluding preferential agreements include the search for larger markets and for deeper integration, in particular among neighbouring countries. RTAs may become necessary for defensive reasons and as means to lock out competition from third countries. They often are motivated by the wish to improve conditions for foreign direct investment as they create larger markets. In particular, modern RTAs increasingly entail provisions on intellectual property rights, extending protection beyond the minimal standards of the agreement on Trade-Related Aspects of Intellectual Property Rights (TRIPS Agreement).[4] Finally, they may be induced to replace dependence upon unilateral General System of Preferences (GSP) programmes.

Political rationales for concluding RTAs are equally numerous. Preferential rights may honour closer trade relations, and back up closer political ties and political loyalty to larger partners. Preferential agreement may serve the prime purpose of enhancing negotiating powers. The example of the EFTA was a case in point. The main purpose of forming it was to increase bargaining power in relation to the EEC at the time, leading successfully to the 1972 EFTA–EC Free Trade Agreements. Preferential agreements may further serve the purpose of securing domestic reform and preventing backsliding. The constitutional function of taming and locking-in domestic protectionist forces is a common feature both of WTO and preferential agreements.

A report by the WTO Secretariat succinctly explains the various motivations which may lead to the conclusion of RTAs:[5]

22. The formation of RTAs is driven by a variety of factors which include economic, political and security considerations. As noted in the 2003 World Trade Report,[6] the conclusion of RTAs may be driven by the search for access to larger markets, which might be easier to engineer at the regional or bilateral level, particularly in the absence of a willingness among WTO Members to liberalize further on a multilateral basis. In this sense the setback of negotiations at Cancun apparently precipitated the forging of more regional partnerships; some countries argue that their participation in RTAs provides a competitive spur to liberalization at the multilateral level by promoting trade liberalization on multiple fronts, while others may increasingly be drawn into RTAs for

---

[3] *See* C. Damro, 'The Political Economy of Regional Trade Agreements', in this volume, at XXX.

[4] While legally consistent with the TRIPS Agreement, the policy of industrialized countries to seek higher standards of intellectual property protection in developing countries by means of RTAs risks undermining the flexibilities granted, and the balance achieved within the TRIPS Agreement between proprietary rights and information in the public domain: *see* F. Abbott, 'The WTO Medicines Decision: World Pharmaceutical Trade and the Protection of Public Health' (2005) 99 AJIL 317, at 349–54; *ibid.*, 'Toward a New Era of Objective Assessment in the Field of TRIPS and Variable Geometry for the Preservation of Multilateralism' (2005) 8 JIEL 77, at 88–97.

[5] WTO Secretariat, Regional Trade Agreements Section, Trade Policies Review Division, 'The Changing Landscape of RTAs' (paper prepared for a Seminar on Regional Trade Agreements and the WTO), 14 November 2003, paras 22–4.

[6] *World Trade Report* (Geneva: WTO, 2003).

defensive reasons, as a means of maintaining market access opportunities in the absence of MFN-driven liberalization.

23. RTAs can also be used by some countries as a vehicle for promoting deeper integration of their economies than is presently available through the WTO, particularly for issues which are not fully dealt with multilaterally, such as investment, competition, trade in services, environment and labour standards. Particularly as regards trade in services, preferential access may confer long term advantages in a market and may enable a supplier to steal an irreversible march on the competition. Discriminatory liberalization might also be attractive for countries which seek to reap gains from trade in product areas where they cannot compete internationally. Smaller countries particularly would see RTAs as a defensive necessity, while even larger economies may turn to RTAs to avoid being left out in the cold. Membership in RTAs can provide a means of securing foreign direct investment, particularly for a country with low labour costs which has preferential access to a larger, more developed market. The case of Mexico's FDI inflows in the wake of its membership in the NAFTA is a case in point. Developing countries, in particular, might be willing to forego the benefits conferred by GSP programmes and instead commit themselves to signing reciprocal RTAs with developed countries in order to secure access to their markets; such a strategy is usually deemed to have strong signalling effects and act as a pull for foreign investment. Thus, RTAs may perform a sort of dual locking function, locking out competition and locking in investment.

24. Political considerations are also reported to be key to the decision to foster regional trading arrangements. Governments seek to consolidate peace and increase regional security with their RTA partners, or to increase their bargaining power in multilateral negotiations by securing commitment first on a regional basis, or as a means to demonstrate good governance and to prevent backsliding on political and economic reforms. They may also be used by larger countries to forge new geopolitical alliances and cement diplomatic ties, thus ensuring or rewarding political support by providing increased discriminatory access to a larger market. Increasingly, the choice of RTA partners appears to be based on political and security concerns, thus potentially undermining or diluting the economic rationale which might be used in support of participation in RTAs.

The multitude of motivations for preferential agreements indicates that such agreements respond to economic and political needs. They inherently form part of the overall global system of international trade regulation. Efforts to avoid or reduce them may be well-founded from the point of view of limiting the erosion of non-discrimination (MFN).[7] The great numbers of preferential agreements as much as different motivations, however, indicate that they are likely to be here to stay. The multilateral trading system is thus composed both of the multilateral rules of the WTO and of preferential agreements, both bilateral and plurilateral.[8] Together they form the global system. The essential

---

[7] *See*, in particular, P. Sutherland et al., *The Future of the WTO: Addressing Institutional Challenges in the New Millennium* (Geneva: WTO, 2004), 19–27.

[8] On this point *see also* W.J. Davey, 'Dispute Settlement in the WTO and RTAS: A Comment', in this volume, at XXX, stating that: 'RTAs provide significant economic benefits, a conclusion that is not at all clear; they are singularly ill-suited to fulfill the full range of functions performed by the WTO'.

task thus consists of defining the relationship of its components and defining a framework of co-existence and corresponding conditions for preferential agreements within the global system.

III. CONSTITUTIONAL FUNCTIONS OF WTO LAW: PERTINENT RULES

Members of the WTO negotiating and concluding RTAs are obliged to comply with a number of principles and rules of the multilateral system. Since preferential agreements by definition restrict the application of MFN, WTO rules only exceptionally allow for sectoral bilateral or multilateral treaties. WTO law thus provides the framework within which Members may conclude preferential agreements between themselves and with third countries. In the field of goods, the main exceptions to MFN are set forth in Article XXIV GATT 1994 and the Understanding on the Interpretation of Article XXIV of the General Agreement on Tariffs and Trade 1994. In the field of services, a largely parallel provision is contained in Article V GATS and Article V bis GATS for Labour Market Integration Agreements. These provisions relate to the creation of separate customs territories (customs unions or 'CU'), free trade areas ('FTAs'), including interim agreements, and to economic integration agreements. The principles and rules are well-known and may be summarized briefly. They seek to balance multilateralism and the needs of RTAs by setting out a number of conditions which bilateral or multilateral preferential agreements are required to meet.[9]

Preferential arrangements are only lawful and possible under the definitions of FTAs or CUs. While the former establish free trade among members (such as EFTA or NAFTA), the latter, in addition, adopt a common external tariff and trade policy (such as EU). WTO law does not allow for preferential and non-reciprocal preferences under Part IV of GATT. Except for recourse to the general and temporary exceptions of waivers under Article IX:3 WTO Agreement, no provision was made to cover non-reciprocal agreements between industrialized and developing members.

A. Basic Requirements

Preferential agreements essentially need to meet three basic criteria.

1. *Substantial Trade Coverage*

First, a regional agreement (FTA or CU) needs to cover *substantially all the trade* in goods originating within members of the RTA (Article XXIV:8

---

[9] The following draws from T. Cottier, 'The Challenge of Regionalization and Preferential Relations in World Trade Law and Policy' (1996) 2 EFA Rev, 149, at 158–60. *See also* M. Krajewski, 'Services Liberalization in Regional Trade Agreements: Lessons for GATS "Unfinished Business"?', in this volume, at 175.

GATT). Similarly, a RTA on services is required to provide substantial sectoral coverage (Article V:1(a) GATS). In other words, policies of pick-and-choose among different products and sectors, or *à la carte*, are not consistent with WTO rules. The approach has to be comprehensive. This may, at first sight, seem illogical and disproportionate: limited liberalization is excluded and discriminations are lawful only when extensive areas of trade are covered. It may even lead to greater distortions and sectoral agreements. Yet, the requirement serves the purpose of preventing selectivity and limitations to goods or services of particular interest. It also serves to limit the number of RTAs, as comprehensive agreements are more difficult to negotiate than sector specific deals. The 'substantially all trade' and 'substantial sectoral coverage' requirements, if properly enforced, thus retard a gradual erosion of MFN trade and thus of the multilateral trading system.

In the area of goods, there is still controversy as to whether comprehensiveness amounts to a qualitative or a quantitative approach, or a combination of the two. Most RTAs, in particular those in Europe (including Switzerland), exclude preferential trade in agricultural goods or address it only in part. Parties to such agreements argue that entire goods sectors can be excluded from preferential agreements provided that the agreement covers the lion's share of total trade. An agreement covering only trade in industrial goods would fulfil that requirement, as up to 20 per cent of trade might be excluded. There is no agreement on this point, and it cannot be said that the exclusion of agriculture qualifies as subsequent treaty practice or even customary law due to persistent objection by agro-exporting countries.[10] Moreover, WTO jurisprudence points to a combined, quantitative and qualitative definition. In defining 'substantially all the trade' in the context of a CU, the Panel and the Appellate Body in *Turkey—Textiles* held that the ordinary meaning of the term 'substantially' in the context of Article XXIV:8(a) appears to contain both qualitative and quantitative elements for CUs.[11] The matter has not yet been adjudicated in relation to FTAs. Yet, it seems fair to say that essentially the same criteria apply and that in the authors' view it is no longer possible to generally exclude trade in agriculture from meeting the criteria of Article XXIV GATT in future FTAs.[12]

In the field of services, substantial sectoral coverage is explicitly defined

---

[10] *See* Negotiating Group on Rules, Compendium of Issues Related to Regional Trade Agreements, Background Note by the Secretariat, WTO Doc. TN/RL/W/8/Rev.1, 1 August 2002, at 18.

[11] WTO Appellate Body Report, *Turkey—Textiles*, WT/DS34/AB/R, adopted 19 November 1999, para 49. *See also* M. Oesch, 'Commentary on Turkey—Restrictions on Imports of Textiles and Clothing Products', *International Trade Law Reports*, Vol 5 (London: Cameron May, 2001), at 628–33.

[12] *See* T. Cottier and M. Panizzon, 'Die sektoriellen Abkommen und das Recht der WTO: Grundlagen und Spannungsfelder', in D. Felder and C. Kaddous (eds), *Accords Bilatéraux Suisse–UE (commentaires); Bilaterale Abkommen Schweiz–EU (Erste Analysen)* (Basel: Helbing & Lichtenhahn, 2001), 44–75.

both in quantitative and qualitative terms in the footnote to Article V GATS.[13] This further supports the findings above relating to goods if an overall coherent approach is being sought.

2. Abolition of Internal Trade Restrictions

Second, RTAs need to remove all tariffs and quantitative restrictions within a reasonable length of time.[14] Transitional arrangements may extend for up to ten years, and in exceptional cases (e.g. agriculture), may last even longer. The same is true in services. The elimination of discrimination and the granting of national treatment are required to take place either at the date of entry into force of the agreement or within a reasonable time frame. It is possible that the basic framework of ten years applied to goods will provide guidance in services as well.

3. Avoiding Additional Barriers for Third Countries

Third, RTAs must not result in more severe barriers to trade for third Member States of the WTO. Liberalization must not be achieved at the expense of others. In GATT, market access rights for third parties vary slightly depending on whether the RTA formed is a CU or a FTA. In the former, trade restrictions shall not be *on the whole* more severe than the general incidence of the duties and regulations prior to forming the CU. In the case of FTAs, such restrictions must not be higher in any instance.[15]

4. Minimum Requirements on Preferential Rules of Origin

Finally, it should be noted that the Agreement on Rules of Origin is of particular importance.[16] While this agreement primarily set the agenda for future (and largely failed) negotiations in this field with a view to applying equal rules in all areas (tariffs, tariff quotas, countervailing duties in dumping and subsidization, safeguards, QRs), there are nevertheless several principles and provisions which apply immediately upon ratification and can potentially be used for a challenge before a dispute settlement panel. Article 2 offers a number of

---

[13] 'This condition is understood in terms of number of sectors, volume of trade affected and modes of supply. In order to meet this condition, agreements should not provide for the a priori exclusion of any mode of supply'.

[14] A comprehensive account of this aspect is presented in A.T. Gobbi Estrella and G.N. Horlick, 'Mandatory Abolition of Antidumping, Countervailing Duties and Safeguards in Customs Unions and Free Trade Areas constituted between WTO Members', in this volume, at 109.

[15] Although generally not contemplated for RTAs because one (or more) developed country (countries) is involved, a third method of creating a preferential arrangement can use the Enabling Clause. A prohibition on raising barriers for third countries is also at the centre of such agreements. In addition, and without a counterpart in Art. XXIV GATT, such agreements must not impede the MFN reduction or elimination of tariff and non-tariff barriers. In services, a parallel provision states that the agreement shall not raise, with respect to any third Member, the overall level of barriers to trade in services with the respective sectors or sub-sectors.

[16] For further implications of rules of origin in RTAs *see* J. Rivas, 'Do Rules of Origin in Free Trade Agreements Comply with Article XXIV GATT?', in this volume, at 149.

detailed criteria against which preferential rules of origin can be assessed. They are of importance in arguments against arbitrary and discretionary determination by national customs authorities.

B. Additional Preferences

Preferential relations may be further justified by waivers granted under Article IX:3 of the WTO Agreement. Additionally, developing countries may benefit from preferences granted under the Enabling Clause (Decision on Differential and More Favourable Treatment, Reciprocity and Fuller Participation of Developing Countries), resulting from the 1979 Tokyo Round multilateral negotiations.[17]

Apart from this, the law of the WTO allows for permanent deviations from MFN only under certain specific conditions. Some of these conditions can be found in specific exceptions to the principle of MFN in Article 4 of the TRIPS Agreement.

Similarly, both the TBT Agreement and the SPS Agreement allow for bilateral mutual recognition agreements and even encourage Members to enter such preferential arrangements under Article 6.3 TBT and Article 4.2 SPS.[18] Members are entitled to enter into bilateral agreements recognizing diplomas and professional qualifications relating to the provision of services under Article VII GATS, provided that third Members are given a right to negotiate equal terms of access if they are able to show equal quality of their own diplomas and qualifications (conditional MFN). The Agreement on Safeguards allows that in exceptional cases measures may be limited to certain Members under Article 5.2(b) if it is established, and subject to additional conditions, that 'imports from certain Members have increased in disproportionate percentage in relation to the total increase of imports of the product concerned'. With this exception, measures under WTO law are strictly subject to MFN and deviations need to be based upon the specific exceptions provided for. For example, bilaterally negotiated tariff concessions including preferences in the field of inspections of sanitary and phytosanitary measures, were held to be applicable to all interested Members, notwithstanding the lack of reciprocal commitments made.[19] Similarly, MFN obligations arguably cannot be reduced, conditioned, or eliminated in services schedules under GATS, except where there are limited geographical boundary areas and temporary limitations scheduled under Annex II of the GATS Agreement. Given the long bilateral

---

[17] Differential and more favourable treatment reciprocity and fuller participation of developing countries, Decision of 28 November 1979, GATT Doc. L/4903.

[18] For a detailed discussion of TBT and SPS and regional integration *see* J.P. Trachtman, 'Towards Open Recognition? Standardization and Regional Integration under Article XXIV of GATT' (2003) 6 JIEL 459.

[19] *See* GATT Panel Report, *EEC—Imports of Beef*, adopted 10 March 1981, BISD 28S/92, 97. For an account on the EC approach to mutual recognition *see also* L. Bartels, 'The Legality of the EC Mutual Recognition Clause under WTO Law' (2005) 8 JIEL 691.

tradition of reciprocal relations in services, GATS allows for temporary selective privileges. Besides an exception for geographical boundary areas, exceptions had to be inserted under the provisions of Annex II into a particular MFN schedule. Importantly, they are of limited duration. They should be eliminated after ten years, i.e. by 2006. They are subject to review and further negotiations, and therefore cannot claim to be of a permanent nature upon which future bilateral relations in selectively liberalizing services can be built.

IV. COMPLIANCE: THE PROBLEM OF CONTRACTUAL FRAGMENTATION

A. The General Relationship of WTO and RTAs

WTO law as it stands, and despite refined criteria and enhanced transparency, will not effectively prevent or deter the proliferation of preferential agreements around the world which are not in compliance with the conditions set out in Article XXIV GATT 1994 and Article V GATS. This situation is rooted in the very structure of international law to which a hierarchy of treaties is still alien, or, at least, not well developed or generally recognized. All treaties, whether multilateral or bilateral, whether approved by Parliament or even the people, or mere executive agreements, are basically of a similar standing in international law. This is essentially because consent of nations provides the basis of all international law. No general hierarchy of sources exists in international law. Constitutional structures defining the relationships of different sources and layers of norms do not generally exist in international law. Except for the United Nations Charter under its Article 103, none of them per se prevails over another unless this is provided for by explicit treaty language either in a dominating or a submissive treaty.

The relationship of WTO law and RTAs therefore primarily depends on the specific language of the treaties. Answers need to be sought and developed primarily within WTO law. The definition of an appropriate relationship is supported by recourse to the relevant provisions of general treaty law. Such provisions inform treaty interpretation and apply in the absence of specific WTO rules addressing the relationship with RTAs. They should be taken into account to the extent that they form part of customary international law, in conformity with the rules of interpretation set forth in Article 3.2 of the Understanding on Rules and Procedures Governing the Settlement of Disputes (DSU).[20]

---

[20] Art. 3.2 of the WTO Dispute Settlement Understanding provides that this dispute system shall function within the WTO to clarify the existing provisions in accordance with the customary rules of interpretation of public international law. The question of applying other VCLT Articles to WTO provisions has not been settled. If limited to the portion of the VCLT only designated for interpretation, and only to determine the meaning of a WTO Agreement provision, then this narrow view would suggest that only Part III of the VCLT (Arts 26–38, entitled 'Observance,

The relation of RTAs to the WTO Agreements has rarely been examined according to the categories of hierarchy or amendments that govern the relation of subsequent treaties according to Articles 30 and 41 of the Vienna Convention on the Law of Treaties.[21] Articles XXIV GATT and Article V GATS, which regulate the conclusion of RTAs, are usually labelled and dealt with as 'exceptions' to the general obligations in these agreements. The same is true for agreements concluded under Paragraph 2(c) of the so-called Enabling Clause.[22] This specific perspective boils down to the question of the relation between the WTO Agreements and FTAs as well as CUs under WTO law.[23]

Addressing the relationship between WTO Agreements and FTAs has so far had little practical relevance within the WTO system. In the cases discussed above, the dispute settlement system had to deal with national implementation measures based on multilateral agreements and not with the relation of the agreements themselves.[24] While the panels and the Appellate Body examined whether a RTA fulfilled the requirements of Article XXIV:4 and XXIV:8 GATT,[25] they did not examine the relationship between the GATT and the RTA. Rather it was concluded that the national measure adopted upon the

---

application and interpretation of treaties') would be applicable. However, other authors advocate the application of public international law to treaties and necessarily to the relation of treaties to each other. The WTO Appellate Body has itself taken the view that Art. 3 DSU accommodates not only principles of international law relating to interpretation, but to principles of international law generally. *See* J.H. Mathis, *Regional Trade Agreements in the GATT/WTO: Article XXIV and the Internal Trade Requirement* (The Hague: T.M.C. Asser Press, 2002), 272. *See also* R. Bernhardt, 'Article 103', in B. Simma (ed), *The Charter of the United Nations: A Commentary*, Volume 2 (Oxford: OUP, 2002), 1294.

[21] For an exception *see* Mathis, *ibid.*, at 265–85. Even in the extensive work of J. Pauwelyn, *Conflict of Norms in Public International Law: How the WTO Law Relates to other Rules of International Law* (Cambridge: CUP, 2003), preferential agreements gained little attention, at 302–03.

[22] Differential and more favorable treatment reciprocity and fuller participation of developing countries, Decision of 28 November 1979, GATT Doc. L/4903. *See* WTO Appellate Body Report, *EC—Tariff Preferences*, WT/DS246/AB/R, adopted 20 April, 2004, paras 175–76.

[23] Para. 2(c) of the Enabling Clause speaks of 'regional or global arrangements entered into amongst less-developed contracting parties'.

[24] In the WTO Panel Report, *US—Line Pipe*, WT/DS202/R, adopted 8 March 2002, as modified by the Appellate Body Report, WT/DS202/AB/R, the Panel examined whether US safeguards which were discriminatory were justified as an exception based on a FTA (Art. XXIV GATT). The Appellate Body did not subsequently consider the matter as it found a violation of the Safeguards Agreements on other grounds. In the WTO Panel Report, *Turkey—Textiles*, adopted 19 November 1999, WT/DS34/R, as modified by the Appellate Body Report, WT/DS34/AB/R, both the Panel and the Appellate Body examined the imposition of quantitative restrictions by Turkey on imports from India based on a FTA with the EC.

[25] According to the Appellate Body in *Turkey—Textiles* (above at n 11) two conditions must be fulfilled for a national measure to be justified under Art. XXIV GATT: 'First, the party claiming the benefit of this defense must demonstrate that the measure at issue is introduced upon the formation of a customs union that fully meets the requirements of sub-paragraphs 8(a) and 5(a) of Article XXIV. And, second, that party must demonstrate that the formation of that customs union would be prevented if it were not allowed to introduce the measure at issue.' (para. 58).

formation of the RTA violated WTO obligations while not being justified under the Article XXIV exception.[26] Accordingly, the panel and Appellate Body did not require the Contracting Parties to terminate the RTA or correct its problematic provisions, but merely to bring the national measure based on the RTA into conformity with obligations under the WTO Agreement.

B. The Impact of the Vienna Convention on the Law of Treaties (VCLT)

1. *Articles XXIV GATT and V GATS and the Application of Successive Treaties Relating to the Same Subject Matter*

WTO law does not elaborate on norms regulating the potential conflict and tension of rules within and outside the multilateral system.[27] In particular, Articles XXIV GATT and Article V GATS contain no explicit rule which would apply in the event of a conflict between WTO obligations and the obligations stemming from a RTA. Therefore, general rules of international law on treaty conflict apply.[28] Here, the relationship of treaties is essentially defined in terms of freedom to contract, temporal sequencing (*lex posterior derogat legi priori*) and respect of third party rights (*pacta tertiis nec nocent nec prosunt*).[29] The basic rules are contained in the Vienna Convention on the Law of Treaties (VCLT).[30] It is considered to partly express customary international law.

According to Article 26 VCLT, Parties are subject to the principle of *pacta sunt servanda*. They are under an obligation to honour a binding treaty in good faith. This obligation essentially excludes them from entering into successive agreements incompatible with obligations entered into at an earlier stage; if they do so, the rights and obligations under the earlier treaty remain unimpaired and cannot be derogated. However, while the application of *pacta sunt servanda* is generally accepted, its actual effect in a case of conflicting treaties is not universally agreed upon.[31]

Article 30 VCLT addresses the issue of subsequent treaties and sets out the following rules for treaties having the same subject matter: a treaty may explicitly prescribe that it is subject to an earlier or later treaty or that it should

---

[26] *Ibid.*, at para. 63.   [27] *See* Pauwelyn, above at n 21, at 343–45.

[28] *See* K. Kwak and G. Marceau, 'Overlaps of Jurisdiction between the World Trade Organization and Regional Trade Agreements', in this volume, at 465, who express some doubts about the usefulness of these rules when it comes to conflicts between rules on dispute settlement established in RTAs and those within WTO.

[29] This article examines the VCLT relevant provisions with the view to establishing a hierarchy of the WTO rules over RTAs. For a different approach *see* I. Van Damme, 'What Role Is There for Regional International Law in the Interpretation of the WTO Agreements', in this volume, at XXX, examining VCLT with the view to clarifying the extent to which the WTO should defer to RTA in the interpretation process.

[30] Vienna Convention on the Law of Treaties, 1155 UNTS 331 (in force 27 January 1980).

[31] Some scholars interpret *pacta sunt servanda* as not favouring the earlier treaty but rather making each treaty enforceable, even though they may pose potentially incompatible obligations. Others, however, claim that *pacta sunt servanda* favours the earlier treaty. *See* C.J. Borgen, 'Resolving Treaty Conflicts' (2005) 37 Geo Wash Int L Rev, 573, at 588.

not be considered incompatible with its provision. In this case, the other treaty will prevail in accordance with Article 30(2) VCLT. Treaties concluded later in time prevail if they are concluded among the same Parties, even if the latter treaty does not include all the parties of the former.[32] The provisions of the previous treaty apply only to the extent that they are compatible with the later treaty, in accordance with Article 30(3). This rule does not apply in relation to third parties which are not parties to the new treaty, in accordance with Article 30(4)(b) VCLT.

Importantly, these provisions apply only to the extent that the subject matter of the successive treaties is identical and addressed on a comparable level in terms of normative density. Treaties addressing the subject matter in a more detailed and specialized manner are therefore not subject to the rules of Article 30. While the Vienna Convention does not express the principle of *lex specialis*, it applies as a general principle of law and by way of limiting the rules of Article 30 to treaties pertaining to the same subject matter.

Applied to WTO law, the rules produce complex constellations. A RTA concluded prior to the establishment of the WTO in 1995 (or successive treaty amendments) would need to give way to WTO rules, except when they can be considered of a more specialized nature. RTAs concluded after the advent of WTO rules would, in return, prevail under the later-in-time rule among the Parties concerned. Given the sequence of trade rounds and period package deals, the later-in-time rule may often produce unintended results. It is obvious that treating WTO rules and RTAs on an equal footing does not produce satisfactory, but rather confusing constellations in defining the applicable law in a particular case. The matter should be clarified in WTO law itself. The effort at grand-fathering pre-existing agreements is one attempt to create legal security. It may be neither sufficient, nor adequate, as it would exclude the application of more advanced WTO rules in the field. Moreover, the principle of *lex specialis derogat legi generali* (possibly derogating from *lex posteriori*)[33] may lead to similarly inadequate results as more detailed rules may alternatively either be found in WTO law or in RTAs. In conclusion, neither the temporal nor the more specialized rule approach to defining the proper relationship of WTO law and RTAs seems very suitable.

2. *Articles XXIV GATT and V GATS as Rules for Treaty Amendment*

Article 30 VCLT does not address the question of the legality of the conclusion of successive treaties. Also it does not regulate the consequences that stem from state responsibility in a case where a state violates its international obligations because the conclusion of the successive treaty was prohibited. Treaty amendment by way of successive treaties is particularly problematic when

---

[32] *See Oscar Chinn (UK v Belgium)* [1934] PCIJ Rep, Series A/B, No. 63, at 80.

[33] For a discussion of the relationship of the two principles *see* Pauwelyn, above at n 21, at 405 ss.

multilateral treaties, such as those of the WTO, are modified *inter se*[34] by an agreement by only a limited number of its parties.[35]

Article 30 VCLT is thus complemented with Articles 40 and 41 on amendments and modification of multilateral treaties.[36] In the context of RTAs, Article 41, which regulates the modification of multilateral agreements through subsequent agreements between only some of the parties to the treaty, is of special relevance in the context of WTO law and RTAs. It sheds light on the WTO–RTA legal relationship to the extent that the RTAs are regarded as 'modifications' to the WTO treaty.[37] In support of this proposition, it has been recognized that ' "*inter se*" modifications, in the wide sense, may also take the form of outside treaties whose very conclusion changes the legal relationship as between certain WTO Members.'[38] Apart from this, GATT Article XXIV:5 confirms that:

... the provisions of this Agreement shall not prevent, as between the territories of Contracting Parties, the formation of a customs union or of a free-trade area ... provided that ...

Article 41 VCLT provides for two alternative situations in which such modifications are permissible. Paragraph 1(a) applies to modifications where such a possibility is provided for by the multilateral treaty itself. Paragraph 1(b) governs the modification where the multilateral treaty does not 'prohibit' subsequent modifications. In this case, modifications are allowed only if the modification does not affect the rights and obligations of other parties and are not contrary to the object and purpose of the multilateral treaty. Either one or the other of the two paragraphs apply.

Consequently, one needs to establish which of the two possibilities provided in Article 41 VCLT governs *inter se* modifications that take the form of RTAs. Opinions are divided on this issue.[39] In our view it is Article 41(1)(a) that applies since RTAs represent an explicit authorization to modify the multilateral agreement. Article XXIV:5 GATT explicitly regulates 'the formation of a customs union', 'a free-trade area' or 'an interim agreement necessary

---

[34] The term *inter se* was employed by the International Law Commission as referring to '... an agreement entered into by some only of the parties to a multilateral treaty and intended to modify it between themselves alone': ILC, Report of the International Law Commission on the Work of the Second Part of its 17th Session, (1996) UN Doc. A/6309/Rev.1.

[35] Mathis noted that an *inter se* agreement was understood by the drafters of the Vienna Convention to be more likely to disrupt the object and purpose of a multilateral treaty than a treaty amendment that required the participation of all parties. *See* Mathis, above at n 20, at 274.

[36] According to Art. 30(5) VCLT paragraph 4 is without prejudice to Art. 41 VCLT.

[37] Here it is important to distinguish between 'modifications' and 'amendments'. Only for the latter, is the consent of all WTO Members required pursuant to Art. X of the WTO Agreement. Unlike amendments, such modifications would not affect WTO Members that did not agree to them.

[38] Pauwelyn, above at n 21, at 316.

[39] E.g. Mathis is of the view that it is Art. 41(1)(a) that applies, whereas Pauwelyn views RTAs as Art. XXIV modifications covered by Art. 41(1)(b). *See* Mathis and Pauwelyn, above at n 20 and 21 respectively.

for the formation of a customs union or a free-trade area'. Furthermore, paragraph 4 of the same provision, which informs paragraph 5, explicitly recognizes the freedom of Contracting Parties to develop closer integration between the economies of the parties 'through voluntary agreements'.[40] Article V GATS regulates the conclusion of an 'agreement liberalizing trade in services between or among the parties to such an agreement'. Both Article XXIV GATT and Article V GATS thus explicitly authorize the conclusion of international agreements in the form of CUs and FTAs, to the exclusion of other types of RTAs. In the authors' view, this is not without implications for the rights of third parties, that is, for non-parties to the RTA. Thus, Article 41(a) leaves the control of the legality of the *inter se* modification entirely with the granting treaty, *in casu* with WTO rules, in particular Article XXIV GATT and Article V GATS. This being established, Article 41(b) no longer has any bearing on the right to modify the WTO treaty. If paragraph (b) were to apply, that is if the WTO treaty had been silent on the possibility of its *inter se* modification—the control of the legality would have rested solely with the two-pronged test established therewith.[41] This is not the case.

3. The Primacy of WTO Law

Article 41 VCLT is of paramount importance in defining the relationship between WTO rules and RTAs. While these agreements are generally of similar standing under Article 30 VCLT, Article 41 VCLT establishes that WTO rules pertaining to the formation of FTAs and CUs are inherently of a higher ranking.[42] RTAs are compatible with Article 41 VCLT only to the extent that they are in compliance with the conditions and criteria set forth by WTO law. Whether or not WTO treaty relations among Members are lawfully modified by a preferential agreement essentially depends upon the compatibility with WTO rules of Articles XXIV GATT, and V GATS.

It is important to stress the supremacy of WTO law in this context. It differs from general international law. We recall again that international treaties, whatever their form, normally find themselves on the same level of hierarchy and their relationship is defined mainly by recourse to temporal criteria under

---

[40] Again Para. 2(c) of the Enabling Clause regulates 'regional or global arrangements'; *see* above n 23.

[41] In this context, an interesting open question is whether the terms of Art. XXIV GATT (which is a permissive modification under Art. 41 VCLT) accommodate to a larger or lesser extent concerns with the rights of third parties than the terms of Art. 41(1)(b) VCLT. Put differently, if GATT and GATS had been silent on the possibility to modify it *inter se* (in the form of RTAs) would Art. 41(1)(b) VCLT have offered more space for the interest of third parties? Since Art. XXIV has been criticized by economists for not reflecting a concrete mechanism for preventing trade diversion, it could be argued that Art. XXIV GATT and Art. V GATS provide for more extensive restrictions of third party rights than would be admissible under the terms of Art. 41(1)(b) VCLT.

[42] Similarly, Pauwelyn concludes that, when an *inter se* agreement is recognized as illegal under Article 41 VCLT, a normative conflict arises which should be resolved in favour of WTO law. The WTO treaty not only prevails, it leads to the illegality of the *inter se* agreement to the extent of the conflict. *See* Pauwelyn, above at n 21, at 321.

Article 30 VCLT. The same is generally true of other sources of international law, in particular customary law. However, under the WTO as a multilateral treaty defining terms and conditions for the deviation of non-discriminatory rights and obligations, a constitutional and hierarchical relationship between WTO rules and RTAs emerges under Article 41 VCLT. RTAs are subject to the conditions of WTO law, in the same way as legislation, in a domestic context, is subject to the requirements of constitutional law. In the case of conflict and non-compliance with WTO law, RTAs need to cede. They are not on the same footing.

According to the *inter se* Notification Requirement in Article 41(2) VCLT, the parties to the *inter se* shall notify the other parties of their *intention* to conclude the agreement and of the modification to the treaty for which it provides. The requirement is qualified by an exception applying to cases where agreements fall under paragraph 1(a) and do provide otherwise. Since we assert that RTAs are agreements covered by this provision, the current RTAs notification procedure—providing, if at all, merely for an ex-post notification requirement—cannot be challenged for being inconsistent with the VCLT. However, considering that the *inter se* agreements are likely to disrupt the object and purpose of a multilateral treaty—a widespread practice today— Article 41(2) VCLT supports the reform of notification procedures under WTO law towards comprehensive ex-ante modification, i.e. notification and examination should take place prior to the entry into force of an RTA. This would also be more consistent with the hierarchical relationship discussed above and supportive of bringing about WTO consistency of such agreements in the first place in accordance with the constitutional functions ascribed to the multilateral system. It goes without saying that ex-ante examination will also allow widening of the debate on FTAs domestically, and would eventually take into account concerns voiced in the process of examining compatibility, including those expressed by civil society organizations. The institutional reform of the WTO with a view to securing more adequate compliance of RTAs with WTO provision is further discussed in the subsection addressing conceptual reform proposals.

C. Legal Implications

The rules on treaty conflict and amendment have to be distinguished from the consequences resulting from state responsibility. A legal analysis has to distinguish between the legality of the conclusion of an international agreement and its applicability. We consider only the consequences of a violation of WTO obligations by way of concluding a RTA as between WTO Members, not as between WTO Members and third countries.

What are the consequences of a violation of Articles XXIV GATT or V GATS by the terms of a concluded RTA that is already in force? Under customary international law, a violation of obligations triggers state responsibility and the obligation to undertake any steps necessary to remedy the violation.[43] Within the WTO, a special regime operates. In our view, the general principles of state responsibility under international law do not apply.[44] WTO Members can request the establishment of a panel, which will examine whether benefits for WTO Members have been nullified or impaired. If a panel finds that a national measure which is based on a legal obligation in an RTA violates WTO law and is not justified by the RTA exception in either Article XXIV GATT or Article V GATS, it will recommend that the WTO Member should bring its measure into conformity with its WTO obligations. Provided that the measure is one based on a RTA, the WTO Member would either have to withdraw the measure or grant MFN treatment to all WTO Members. Alternatively, it may offer compensation to the third party affected, without changing the operation of the preferential agreement, all with a view to re-establishing the balance of mutual commitments. If the WTO Member fails to offer compensation, or the complaining party refuses compensation as unsuitable, it will ultimately have to face the suspension of concessions as provided for in Article 22 DSU. No financial compensation can be obtained either for past or for future damages. Obligations under the WTO hence remain unimpaired and subsequent treaties cannot be invoked to reduce the rights in particular of third Members affected by an agreement inconsistent with obligations under WTO law. We submit that this is supported by Article 34 VCLT, stating that a treaty cannot establish rights and obligations for third states without their consent. Members of WTO generally consented to RTAs, both in the form of CUs and FTAs, under the specific terms of WTO law, in particular Article XXIV GATT, Article V GATS and the Enabling Clause. Accordingly, they also consented to modifications under Article 41(1)(a) VCLT. Consent, however, cannot be presumed in the case of RTAs inconsistent with these terms, and additional obligations, or impairments of rights and benefits cannot be lawfully created vis-à-vis third parties.

The rules of the WTO, however, do not go beyond the protection of third States and therefore leave the freedom to enter into or conclude contracts among parties unrestrained. In the end all they risk is suspension of concessions by third parties. WTO Members will take this risk into account when concluding RTAs which are not fully consistent with the conditions of WTO law. Remedies intended to achieve compliance thus remain weak. It is here where the multilateral system has its main flaws. The question arises as to how it could be reinforced in a meaningful way.

---

[43] *See* A. Verdross and B. Simma, *Universelles Völkerrecht: Theorie und Praxis*, 3rd ed. (Berlin: Duncker & Humblot, 1984), 508; *see also* the ILC's Draft Articles on the Law of Treaties with Commentaries, text adopted in the 18th Session (1966), UN Doc. A/CN.4/SER.A/1966, at 217.

[44] But *see* D. Palmeter and P.C. Mavroidis, 'The WTO Legal System: Sources of Law' (1998) 92 AJIL 398.

V. IMPROVING COMPLIANCE AND ENFORCEMENT OF WTO LAW RELATING TO PREFERENTIAL AGREEMENTS

A. The Advent of Judicial Review

The rules protecting MFN in WTO law are fairly strict, although there is room for clarification and improvement. The concept of substantially all the trade, and thus the treatment of trade in agricultural goods, will certainly be among the most contentious issues. Moreover, negotiations and liberalization in the service sectors (including financial services and telecommunications) will test whether the comprehensive and unfettered MFN principle can be maintained in the long run. However, maintaining and enforcing the rules on RTAs amounts to a major challenge for reasons already discussed. It is a fact that most of the preferential agreements fail to comply fully with the conditions and criteria set out by the WTO. WTO Members, in reality, enjoy considerable leeway, as mechanisms to enforce substantive conditions and bring about compliance in the interests of the overall global system have remained weak, reflecting a predominance of sovereign treaty-making powers. Yet, the advent of judicial review with the conclusion of the Uruguay Round has brought about an important first step in the process of establishing the primacy of WTO law.

Up to the Uruguay Round, the enforceability of Article XXIV GATT 1947 was weak, if not non-existent. The examination of compatibility was completely left to a committee and to the consensus requirement, with the effect that parties failed to agree on whether the preferential agreements were consistent with GATT law. Ad hoc panels were not entitled to deal with the issue, except as a preliminary matter. Thus, the second Banana Panel (not adopted) had to assess as a preliminary matter whether or not the Lomé Agreement and its preferential schemes were basically and generally covered by Article XXIV GATT in order to assess preferential quotas under Article XIII GATT.[45]

The 1995 Understanding on Article XXIV brought about an important change and established original jurisdiction under Article XXII and XXIII GATT. Article 12 explicitly states that the provisions of Article XXIV are subject to dispute settlement and may be invoked by Members. In *Turkey—Textiles*, the Panel and the Appellate Body affirmed, albeit to different degrees, the justiciability of Article XXIV GATT and explicitly acknowledged the competence of panels to judicially review the legality of measures relating to RTAs.[46]

This case entailed examining additional quantitative restrictions imposed by Turkey upon concluding a CU with the EU. In aligning with EC trade restrictions, Turkey affected the market access rights, in textiles, of third parties, in

---

[45] WTO Panel Report, *EC—Bananas III (Article 21.5—EC)*, WT/DS27/RW/EEC (not adopted).
[46] WTO Panel Report, *Turkey—Textiles*, above at n 24, and WTO Appellate Body Report, *Turkey—Textiles*, above at n 11.

particular India. The panel and the Appellate Body examined the compatibility of these restrictions with the WTO obligations of Turkey. They both interpreted and applied Article XXIV. While the panel excluded the possibility that Article XXIV could justify exemptions to Article XI GATT 1994 (QRs), the Appellate Body, in principle, did not rule this out. Instead it adopted a necessity test: restrictions *vis-à-vis* third parties can be justified if two conditions are met: first, it must be shown that the measure was introduced upon forming the CU which fully meets the criteria of Article XXIV:8(a) and 5(a). Second, it must be demonstrated that the formation of the CU depends on the introduction of the measure.[47] In this case, the panel had simply assumed that the first condition of meeting the requirements of a CU had been met. It further held that panels 'arguably' do not have jurisdiction to assess the overall compatibility of the CU with WTO law, since this was primarily a matter for the political bodies, i.e. the Committee on Regional Trade Agreements (CRTA), to examine. Since this issue was not under appeal, the Appellate Body refrained from ruling on this point. However, it referred, *obiter dictum*, to its jurisprudence examining balance of payments measures even upon examination by a committee.[48] Moreover, jurisdiction to examine the matter is entailed in the first test established above. It is thus fair to conclude that WTO law currently allows panels and the Appellate Body to examine the conformity of RTAs with WTO law.[49] In addition to the *Turkey—Textiles* dispute, three other WTO disputes have cited the Regional Trade Articles XXIV GATT and V GATS, affirming jurisdiction to examine the compatibility of measures with these provisions.[50]

While judicial review of preferential agreements improves the effectiveness of Article XXIV and Article V GATS in assessing the compatibility of such agreements and of measures taken based upon them against third Members, it is important to note that the novel jurisdiction and submission of RTAs to WTO dispute settlement procedures also mark the emergence of a complex legal relationship—previously dormant—between WTO law and the ever increasing number of these agreements. While the panel in *Turkey—Textiles* held that 'the right of Members to form a customs union is to be exercised in such a way as to ensure that the WTO rights and obligations of third country Members (and of constituent Members) are respected, consistent with

---

[47] WTO Appellate Body Report, *Turkey—Textiles, ibid.*, at para. 59.

[48] *Ibid.*, para. 60.   [49] *See* above n 11.

[50] WTO Panel Report, *US—Line Pipe*, above at n 24 and WTO Appellate Body Report, *US—Line Pipe*, WT/DS202/AB/R, adopted 8 March 2002; WTO Panel Report, *Canada—Autos*, WT/DS139/R, WT/DS142/R, adopted 19 June 2000, as modified by the Appellate Body Report, WT/DS139/AB/R, WT/DS142/AB/R and WTO Appellate Body Report, *Canada—Autos*, WT/DS139/AB/R, WT/DS142/AB/R, adopted 19 June 2000; WTO Panel Report, *Argentina—Footwear (EC)*, WT/DS121/R, adopted 12 January 2000, as modified by the Appellate Body Report, WT/DS121/AB/R and WTO Appellate Body Report, *Argentina—Footwear (EC)*, WT/DS121/AB/R, adopted 12 January 2000.

the primacy of the WTO, as reiterated in the Singapore Declaration',[51] these WTO-inconsistent agreements are not per se invalid and void.

The hierarchy established between the WTO and RTA under Article 41 VCLT does not per se invalidate an inconsistent agreement. Lack of coherence of an agreement with the disciplines of WTO law merely allows affected third Members to claim nullification and impairment of benefits under WTO law. They may claim the abolition of measures inconsistent with MFN treatment and thus equal preferential market access. Such claims may eventually lead to the revision of the agreement among the parties to it, or even its abolition, if preferences cannot be extended under MFN in implementing an adopted decision of the Dispute Settlement Body. In cases such as *Turkey—Textiles*— which do not affect the validity of the RTA—implementation may be achieved by removing measures against third Members or replacing them with ones commensurate with the principle of proportionality. As a practical matter, however, the existence and operation of the Agreement itself are likely to continue despite inconsistencies and the effect of WTO law remains limited to compensation or the imposition of retaliatory measures, i.e. withdrawal of concessions. Under current rules, WTO law does not affect the relationship of the Parties *inter se* to a RTA, even if it is inconsistent with the criteria of Articles XXIV GATT and V GATS and thus Article 41 VCLT. Apart from protecting third party interests, WTO law does not provide effective disciplines in enforcing the balance struck between trade creation and trade diversion in regionalism and bilateralism. We shall return to these systemic issues when reviewing current efforts at reform below.

B. Current Efforts at Reform

While the Uruguay Round brought about jurisdiction of dispute settlement panels and the Appellate Body in relation to RTAs, current efforts mainly focus on improving the political process of assessing and examining RTAs. Under the WTO Agreement, the Committee on Regional Trade Agreements (CRTA) is mandated to monitor RTAs under GATT 1994. Members are obliged to notify such agreements to the Committee which is supposed to examine the compatibility of the treaty (i.e. the RTA) with WTO law. Since the Committee is a political body which operates under the consensus rule, the difficulties encountered under GATT 1947 persist. As substantial differences exist as to the interpretation in particular of the concept of substantially all the trade, as much as substantial sectoral coverage of services in GATS, the likelihood of consensus remains slim. Indeed, since 1995, it has not been possible to reach agreement in a single case. Moreover, Members often refrain from notifying agreements to the WTO, thus avoiding examination and discussion.[52]

---

[51] WTO Panel Report, *Turkey—Textiles*, above at n 24, at para. 9.183/4.
[52] *See* the listing of agreements relating to Eastern Europe in Godel and Gage, above at n 1.

There is a lack of transparency. These findings may reflect the newly confirmed jurisdiction of panels and the Appellate Body. Members are wary of fully exposing their agreements and having them examined because of the potential for dispute.[53]

Members interested in improving disciplines on preferential agreements have therefore tabled a number of proposals. Beginning with preparations for the Ministerial Conference in Seattle in 1999, these proposals have addressed a number of issues, mainly pertaining to improving transparency and the interpretation of the concept of substantially all the trade. Paragraph 29 of the Ministerial Declaration of Doha adopted the following negotiations mandate:

29. We also agree to negotiations aimed at clarifying and improving disciplines and procedures under the existing WTO provisions applying to regional trade agreements. The negotiations shall take into account the developmental aspects of regional trade agreements.

On 1 February 2002, the Trade Negotiations Committee created a Negotiating Group on Rules ('the Group'). In March 2002 Ambassador Tim Groser of New Zealand was appointed as Chairman of the Group. The Group is responsible for several aspects of applying rules which include anti-dumping, subsidies, and the rules to be applied to RTAs. Most submissions to the Group revolve around the first two items. The following assessment and the table in Appendix 1 summarize proposals relating to RTAs made up to the end of 2003:

The Chairman in his report TN/RL/6 (2 July 2003) reported:

The Group has substantively progressed in its work. The issue-identification phase has been practically completed, with issues being broadly structured as primarily 'procedural' and 'systemic'. Procedural questions, and in particular 'RTAs transparency', were identified as issues for initial consideration and have been tackled since last October, mostly in an informal mode. Systemic issues have been addressed only in formal meetings until now.

After two slow months, discussions in the Group regained momentum at the 11 June meeting, when three formal submissions were tabled. These submissions both built upon the progress achieved in informal discussions on 'RTAs transparency' and revived the debate on important systemic issues.

Progress achieved on 'RTAs transparency' suggests that the Group is heading to a common understanding on the elements to be included in an early package improving inter alia the procedures relating to the timing and content of RTAs notification, and a revived, more transparent and efficient RTA review process. It is difficult at this stage to know whether such a procedural package could be ready before the Cancún Ministerial, but it remains a possible achievement.

A number of systemic issues are now on the table for priority discussion: RTAs and development; RTAs coverage (in particular the definition of 'substantially all trade' in GATT Article XXIV:8); other (restrictive) regulations of commerce (in particular matters

---

[53] *See also* Compendium of Issues Relating to Regional Trade Agreements, above at n 10.

related to preferential rules of origin and safeguards); and the primacy of the multi-lateral trading system and possible RTA negative effects on third parties. The Group has also considered the question of 'grandfathering' of existing RTAs and retroactive application of any new rules, but it has been generally held that no useful outcome could be achieved on that issue until the negotiations had progressed significantly.

On development, the Group has before it certain RTA-related S & D proposals, referred to it by the Chairman of the General Council on 20 May 2003. The Group held a preliminary discussion of these proposals at its formal meeting of 11 June, and has scheduled a meeting on 21–23 July to further advance its consideration of these proposals.

The Group remains committed to achieving significant results in both the disciplines and procedures related to RTAs. It plans to accelerate work on the clarification and improvement of RTA disciplines under the existing WTO provisions in the post-Cancún period.

Specific proposals by the various delegations with respect to RTAs are included in Appendix 1. The proposals essentially reflect a long-standing list of issues of a procedural and substantive nature. These include: transparency (and its preventive effect), the relationship of the RTAs and dispute settlement, and the need to define *substantially all the trade* or *substantial sectoral coverage* and long-standing problems relating to *rules of origin*. Additional issues have emerged in relation to regional integration, safeguards, GSP, and SPS measures.[54]

India, for example, is mainly concerned that GSP provisions within RTAs may dilute the provisions of the Enabling Clause. India argues that this would be contrary to the spirit of the WTO framework and of the Doha Ministerial Declaration. According to India, the Enabling Clause is vital to the economic development of poorer nations and allows developing countries the policy space they need to adjust to greater competition in domestic and international markets.[55] The recent flood of RTAs threatens to divert trade away from India and other developing nations towards RTA signatories, which are sometimes developed countries, *despite* the benefits accruing to India and others under the Enabling Clause.

A recent case brought before the Dispute Settlement body at the WTO, *EC—Tariff Preferences*,[56] explored the issue of granting particular trade preferences, through RTAs, to developing countries that paid appropriate attention to labour rights, the environment and drug-trafficking. India argued that this was contrary to the MFN principle and to the Enabling Clause. It asked the panel to recommend that the EC withdraw these trade incentives. The panel found in India's favour with regard to the breach of Article I:1

---

[54] For a comprehensive listing of issues *see ibid.*

[55] WTO, Discussion Paper on Regional Trading Arrangements—Communication from India, WTO Doc. TN/RL/W/114, 6 June 2003.

[56] WTO Panel Report, *EC—Tariff Preferences*, WT/DS246/R, adopted 20 April 2004, as modified by the Appellate Body Report, WT/DS/246/AB/R.

GATT. The Appellate Body essentially upheld the decision and ruled that the Enabling Clause does not exclude conditionalities, but that such conditions need to be applied in a consistent and coherent manner, avoiding discrimination between different countries.[57]

While the clarifications sought in the current proposals are likely to improve legal security, they will not eliminate the fundamental weakness of the system in controlling and containing the proliferation of trade agreements, which are not fully compatible with WTO disciplines. We note that the problem of primacy of the multilateral trading system has been raised, but that discussions and proposals so far have not substantially addressed the more fundamental underlying structural issues regarding the legal relationship of WTO and RTAs. It is to these systemic issues we turn in concluding this paper.

VI. ASSESSING FUNDAMENTAL INTERESTS

In the absence of conflict rules within the WTO, it was found that the Vienna Convention on the Law of Treaties affirms the hierarchical relations of WTO rules and RTAs, but limits enforcement and implementation to preserve third party rights. The question therefore arises of whether the relationship of WTO law and regional or preferential agreements should not be further clarified and strengthened in WTO treaty law—beyond proposals currently tabled.

From a point of view of bilateral or regional commercial and political interests, such an effort would hardly be supported by the current state of affairs and the predominant views held by governments. Members using RTAs still seek to obtain as much leeway as they can. As long as third Members are not voicing objections, many Members of the WTO and their business communities will welcome the possibility of piecemeal and cherry-picking liberalization. From a systemic and long-term point of view, however, it is doubtful whether the current system with its emphasis on flexibility is sustainable and of long-term economic interest.

First, it is intellectually inconsistent to establish conditions and criteria for preferential agreements in WTO, and yet refrain from seeking to enforce them among members while leaving incentives to comply with and respect WTO weak rules. Second, the proliferation of preferential agreements around the world, many of them arguably not fully compatible with the disciplines of WTO law, may have the overall result of major trade diversion and distortions, which undermines the very goals of the multilateral system. Flexibility may no longer reflect the interests of businesses as they increasingly find themselves on the receiving end of discrimination on third markets. The growth of preferential trade in the three main regions of the globe, in particular in Asia,

---

[57] WTO Appellate Body Report, *EC—Tariff Preferences*, above at n 22, at para. 173.

may induce a rethink of the conventional policies dominant so far.[58] While preferential agreements and maximizing leeway were for many decades mainly of interest to Western Europe in building the European Theatre beyond the European Union, recourse to preferential agreements as a global feature of international trade regulation now provides the basis for rethinking the regime and for reinforcing disciplines. As Asian, African, American, and European countries alike pursue preferential policies, all members are mutually interested not only in the possibility, but also the containment of preferences in order to optimize market access. The sovereign interest in operating unfettered preferential relations is increasingly matched by the concern to avoid disadvantages imposed on third parties and to bring about an overall balanced global system. As regionalism develops, the main function of the WTO will consist in linking and bridging the trading blocs in the Americas, Europe, Russia, Asia, and Africa. The task of keeping markets open and of playing by the global rules will be of enhanced importance not only for world trade, but also for world peace. It is submitted that there is a shared interest in providing for a system of much more effective checks and balances. This could provide a basis for reform which goes beyond the modest proposals tabled during the Doha Agenda. Additional efforts to explore options for reforming WTO law should be made.

VII. CONCEPTUAL REFORM PROPOSALS

A. Distinguishing Preferential and Regional Integration

The current rules of Article XXIV GATT and Article V GATS fail to address the problem of trade diversion. Article XXIV GATT was drafted before Viner pioneered economic research and the doctrine of trade creation and trade diversion in the 1950s.[59] It would seem that the concept of substantially all the trade or of substantial sectoral coverage is able to bring about comprehensive agreements and thus to contain the proliferation of distorting piecemeal deals. It is unclear, however, to what extent comprehensive agreements also enhance diversions. In this context, further examination is needed of the extent to which different rules should be developed for regional integration, properly

---

[58] For an assessment of recent developments *see* L. Paez, 'Americas Regionalism', J. Gogo, 'East Asia & Oceanic Regionalism' and E. Evtimov, 'East European Regionalism', in Godel and Gage, above at n 1, at 51–107. *See also* J.A. Crawford and R.V. Fiorentino, 'The Changing Landscape of Regional Trade Agreements', WTO Discussion Paper No 8 (2005). For a historic account and earlier developments, *see* WTO Secretariat, *Regionalism and the World Trading System* (Geneva: WTO, 1995).

[59] *See* Mathis, above at n 20, at 103 citing J. Viner, *The Customs Union Issue*, (New York: Carnegie Endowment for International Peace, 1950) and J. McMillan, 'Does Regional Integration Foster Open Trade', in K. Anderson and R. Blackhurst (eds) *Regional Integration and the Global Trading System* (London: Harvester Wheatsheaf, 1993).

speaking, and preferential agreements.[60] Krugman suggested that trading blocs in close geographical proximity are unlikely to result in significant trade distortion.[61] Transcontinental agreements, on the other hand, rarely attain the same levels of integration but are limited to granting preferential concessions to partners that fall short of deeper integration. Moreover, they often need to respond to the needs of development cooperation and should be able to use non-reciprocal components. Indeed, from the point of view of the global system, reciprocal agreements should perhaps be limited to regional integration, requiring some geographical contiguity of trading partners. They should be reserved for proper and coherent trading blocs. Transcontinental relations should be essentially left to MFN, and thus to the rules of the WTO. Such a perception would be supported by the view that trading relations among the major partners and trading blocs should be left to WTO as the backbone of the global system. Additional and special rules should instead be designed to address the problems of developing countries, allowing, *inter alia*, for non-reciprocal relations in support of sustainable trade development under Part IV of GATT and the GATS. Different needs should be reflected in different rules. In conclusion, while we consider regional and deeper integration to be beneficial, there are doubts that reciprocal, transcontinental agreements produce the same benefits. Rather they undermine the global system. The point should be further examined and the results should be used in refining the substantive rules of WTO which, at this stage, do not distinguish between regional and preferential agreements, properly speaking. Beyond improving the substantive criteria for RTAs in Articles XXIV GATT (including the Understanding) and V GATS, a number of further suggestions may be made for different long-term systemic options.

---

[60] McMillan, *ibid.*, suggests that for Art. XXIV to become more workable its requirements must be phrased not in terms of height of tariffs but in terms of trade volumes, that is by looking at the trade consequences of the restrictions rather than trying to measure their effect on domestic prices. Accordingly, 'a proposed RIA, in order to get GATT imprimatur, would have to promise not to introduce policies that result in external trade volumes being lowered. And, if after some years the RIA is seen to have reduced its imports from the rest of the world, it would be required to adjust its trade restrictions so as to reverse this fall in imports . . .'. However, 'a possible disadvantage of focusing on trade volumes instead of tariff levels is that, in principle, tariff levels can be observed in advance, whereas trade volumes can be measured only after the RIA has been in existence for a few years. Yet, the implications of a new trading arrangement for trade volumes can, however, be predicted using an economic model'. He similarly suggests improvements in the adjudication of the compatibility of RTAs by allowing GATT panels to hear expert testimony about the predicted or observed effects of the agreement on trade volumes. For a summary of the economics of Art. XXIV GATT, *see* M. Foltea, 'The Legal Effects of Regional Trade Agreements under The GATT/WTO' (LLM Dissertation, World Trade Institute, Berne), also at www.wti.org, (visited 10 August 2005). *See also* R.H. Snape, 'History and Economics of GATT's Article XXIV', in Anderson and Blackhurst, *ibid.*, at 273–87.

[61] P. Krugman, 'The Move Towards Free Trade Zones', in *Policy Implications of Trade and Currency Zones* (Proceedings of a Symposium sponsored by the Federal Reserve Bank of Kansas, 1991). *See also* J. Gilbert, R. Scollay and B. Bora, 'Assessing Regional Trade Arrangements in the Asia-Pacific', Policy Issues in International Trade and Commodity Study Series No 15 (UNCTAD, 2001), at 16.

B. Strengthening the Legal Hierarchy of Norms

It may be argued that the complex interrelationship of WTO rules and RTAs should be developed through the case law over time. The triangular relationship between Articles XXIV GATT, V GATS, conflict rules, and the hierarchy of norms may thus be further clarified. This avenue, however, faces important limitations. First, panels and the Appellate Body are not entitled to apply the VCLT per se, but only customary international law.[62] Although Article 41 seems to express principles of customary international law, this may be contested in litigation. Second, existing rights and obligations bind panels and the Appellate Body. The case law would not offer the possibility for strengthening legal remedies and thus the proliferation of RTAs inconsistent with the WTO framework. It would essentially be limited to the protection of third party rights.

It would therefore seem important to further clarify the relationship of WTO law and RTAs in WTO negotiations and amend the agreements accordingly, while taking into account the relevant rules of the Vienna Convention. We reiterate that nothing in general international law and the VCLT would prevent the WTO Members from reinforcing the principle of primacy of WTO law. This would offer the possibility of clarifying the triangle of WTO rules, conflict rules, hierarchy of norms and the legal consequences of breach of obligations.

Considering that the VCLT does not offer comprehensive solutions for establishing the proper relationship between treaties,[63] a future reform could translate more clearly in adopting what lawyers today may call an explicit constitutional approach of regulating preferential agreements by and through the disciplines of WTO law. International law per se allows for considerable strengthening of the disciplines in treaty law. Nothing prevents States from agreeing on more rigorous obligations. Members could agree to an explicit commitment to refrain from entering a preferential agreement that fell short of compliance with WTO disciplines. As a matter of WTO law, agreements incompatible with WTO law could explicitly be defined to be not valid[64] and enforceable, both among the parties to an agreement and—as today—in

---

[62] *See* above n 20.

[63] The application of VCLT rules to solve conflicts of norms mostly leads to ending up with two treaties that are applicable among their respective parties, creating a need for renegotiation. Therefore, the modern style for solving these conflicts is political in nature, and based on power at the negotiation table—hoary legal principles hold little sway in the hard bargaining. *See* Borgen, above at n 31, at 24. Also, VLCT rules provide no real solution to the underlying conflict. Rather, the VCLT rules merely put the problem back into the arena of diplomatic negotiation. *See* A. Schulz, 'The Relationship Between the Judgments Project and Other International Instruments', available at hcch.e-vision.nl/upload/wop/genaff_pd19e.pdf (visited 10 August 2005).

[64] The VCLT does not provide for invalidity of an *inter se* agreement that is incompatible with the multilateral treaty. These norms are recognized illegal and would therefore trigger state responsibility. *See* Schulz, *ibid.*, at 12. It would therefore be necessary to bring about such effects by WTO treaty law.

relation to impaired third Members of the WTO. From the point of view of legal security, Members may be reluctant to adopt such an approach and to render inconsistent agreements null and void *ab initio*. Another, and less intrusive, option would consist in treating RTAs inconsistent with the disciplines of Articles XXIV and Article V GATS as unlawful, triggering state responsibility.[65] Unlike nullity, inconsistent agreements would not be invalid ex ante, but deploy obligations to remedy the constellation and to re-establish lawfulness *ex nunc*, i.e. upon assessing the agreement by a binding decision in dispute settlement.

It should be made clear that WTO rules relating to the formation of RTAs (free trade agreements, CU, economic integration, and perhaps also a future framework for non-reciprocal development agreements) trump regional agreements inconsistent with these rules, in a manner similar to Article 103 of the UN Charter, referred to in Article 30(1) VCLT. By so doing, a hierarchy of trade rules would be established, building upon Article 41 VCLT, to the effect that the multilateral system would prevail over preferential agreements that are not compatible with WTO law. Legal consequences, as discussed above, would need to be settled. They could range from rendering such agreements void *ab initio*, as part of the doctrine holds under Article 103 UN Charter, even for *inter se* relations.[66] Realistically, they could also be defined to be invalid and non-applicable *ex nunc* and thus bring relations back to the former MFN levels of the multilateral system. Such legal effects would provide important incentives to keep the shape of RTAs within legally permissible parameters.

Another, less ambitious option would be an obligation to insert mandatory provisions into RTAs, subjecting them to the rules of WTO law, in line with Article 30(3) VCLT. This obligation could be assumed by inserting corresponding provisions into preferential agreements themselves and render this a condition for lawfulness and approval of the agreement by the WTO. The EFTA Convention is an example in point.[67] Such reference to corresponding provisions could also establish jurisdiction of domestic courts to examine the compatibility of a RTA with WTO rules when assessing domestic foreign policy

[65] Invalidity as a sanction is explained on the grounds of lack of competence, contracting power or other related to the consent given to be bound by the norm in question, such as error, fraud, corruption, or coercion. Illegality, by contrast, is when the norm has been created; however, it is or becomes illegal because it constitutes conduct that is defined as wrongful under another norm. State responsibility is incurred only for the illegality.

[66] On the effects of Art. 103 UN Charter *see* Bernhardt, above at n 20, at 1295–299. RTAs between WTO Members and third parties would however remain valid.

[67] *See* the EFTA Preamble, which states: '. . . Building on their respective rights and obligations under the Agreement establishing the World Trade Organization and other multilateral and bilateral instruments of co-operation . . .'. *See* Annex to the Agreement Amending the Convention Establishing EFTA, Consolidated version of 4 January 1960, signed 21 June 2001, available at secretariat.efta.int (visited 10 August 2005).

measures based upon preferential agreements.[68] Up to now, domestic courts have not assumed such jurisdiction, as direct effect of WTO is largely rejected and treaty-making powers are generally restricted to the executive and legislative branches of government.[69] Nevertheless, avenues for exploring a proper role of domestic courts in the present context should be further examined. They may result in non-application of preferential treaty provisions found inconsistent with constitutional norms of the WTO, eventually inducing renegotiations and adjustments in treaty-making. From a point of view of dispute prevention, such jurisdiction would offer greater incentive to take seriously the disciplines of WTO law in treaty negotiations. This way, preferential trade would be shaped and limited to true regionalism, compliant with WTO disciplines. The role of WTO law would be strengthened, providing the essential linkages between the larger trading blocs and partners.

C. Procedural Reforms

In addition to defining the hierarchy of norms and jurisdictional issues, a number of procedural devices could be contemplated to prevent inconsistencies of RTAs with WTO rules.

1. *Notification and Ex Ante Examination*

It is generally recognized that the GATT process for reviewing RIAs is inadequate.[70] Therefore, efforts should be made to bring about a coherent system of notification of all RTAs to the WTO, whether they are concluded under Article XXIV GATT, Article V GATS or the Enabling Clause. These procedures should be unified. Proposals to this effect have been tabled.[71]

Under Article 41(2) VCLT, it was seen that Parties are obliged to notify their *intention* to conclude an agreement modifying their multilateral obligations. It could thus be contemplated that formal drafts of RTAs might be submitted to the WTO membership to allow for discussion. Examination and approval of RTAs could be required to take place prior to their entry into force, provided the examination occurs within a defined time frame. Existing procedures for examination of draft technical regulations under the umbrella of Article 2.9 of the TBT Agreement have proven the usefulness of such a device and assist in

---

[68] For a discussion on role of the judge in this context *see* T. Cottier and P.C. Mavroidis (eds), *The Role of the Judge in International Trade Regulation: Experiences and Lessons for the WTO* (Ann Arbor, Mich: U. Michigan Press, 2003).

[69] For a discussion of direct effect of WTO law *see* T. Cottier and M. Oesch, *International Trade Regulation, Law and Policy in the WTO, The European Union and Switzerland: Cases, Materials and Comments* (London: Cameron May, 2005), 209–27.

[70] *See* F. Abbott, *Law and Policy of Regional Integration: The NAFTA and Western Hemispheric Integration in the World Trade Organization System* (Dordrecht, London: Martinus Nijhoff, 1995), 40–2. For some proposals on improving the PTAs review procedure *see also* F. Roessler, 'The Relationship between Regional Integration Agreements and the Multilateral Trade Order', in Anderson and Blackhurst, above at n 59, at 320–34.

[71] *See* Appendix 1.

preventing unnecessary distortions and disputes. A similar model could be developed for formal draft RTAs.

2. *Review of RTAs by an Independent Expert Committee*

Second, an expert advisory committee, rather than the political body of the CRTA could examine and monitor RTAs. It is widely recognized that the main problem with the enforcement of Article XXIV GATT stems from the weak procedures within the CRTA, in particular due to its consensus rule. The problem, however, goes deeper. It has also been characterized as an Article XXIV paradox.[72] It stems from the fact that CRTA Members are bound to object to the formation of an RTA when it discriminates against only a portion of their external trade, but to support it when discrimination is against substantially all of their trade, thus conforming with the disciplines of Article XXIV GATT. The same is true of the conditions of substantial sectoral coverage in Article V GATS. We thus face a conflict of interest of individual Members between systemic interests and commercial interests affected as a third party by a RTA. Moreover, RTAs may be supported for political reasons or as policies of mutual support and reciprocity. For such reasons, it would be beneficial to allocate the task of reviewing RTAs to independent experts rather than Members of the WTO.

The independent permanent expert Committee could be given three main functions. First, it would provide assistance to members forming an RTA, advising on WTO legal requirements for creating a valid RTA. This assistance would be of great importance for developing countries as they are increasingly engaging in regionalism but frequently lack adequate expertise on WTO law. Second, the Committee would assess the degree of compliance of the envisaged RTA with the requirements of Article XXIV GATT or Article V GATS and issue a report on its findings. The report would be brought to the attention of WTO Members. However it would not represent an approval or disapproval of the RTA, nor would it be binding on dispute settlement panels. Nonetheless, considering the highly technical nature of the assessment exercise, panels would rely heavily on the findings of the Committee for their rulings on RTA compliance with WTO law. Thirdly, the Expert Committee would undertake an economic analysis of the trade creation and diversion effects which the RTA might induce for third Members. Because, at the stage of formation of a RTA, trade diversion and creation can be only estimated, this exercise would have to be carried out periodically for main agreements, in a manner comparable to the Trade Policy Review Mechanism. Similarly, dispute settlement panels would take such data into account in assessing the legal compatibility of the agreement with WTO rules. The Committee Report would contain specific recommendations for the RTA's members with a view to bringing their agreement into compliance with WTO law. The compatibility

---

[72] *See* above n 20, at 84.

assessment, however, would be left solely with the judiciary.[73] In this way power could be shifted from a political to a more impartial mechanism, hence, avoiding the political paradox discussed above.

Alternatively, in the case that political review of RTAs remains with the CRTA and improvements in decision-making beyond consensus can be found, the relationship between dispute settlement and the political functions of the body should be identified. It was suggested that positive decisions as to compatibility of a RTA could create the legal effect of presuming WTO-compatibility of the agreement.[74] Panels and the Appellate Body would only examine the conformity of a RTA if the claimant makes a prima facie case for the incompatibility of the agreement. Otherwise, the examination in dispute settlement would be limited to the 'necessity of an individual measure' implementing the RTA. Specific rules to this effect could contribute to a proper balance of power between the political and judicial branch of the WTO.

3. Monitoring Functions of the WTO Secretariat

Third, the functions of the WTO Secretariat in monitoring RTAs should be strengthened. Currently, it neither has the right to raise contentious issues in the CRTA, nor to challenge agreements inconsistent with WTO rules. The Director-General could therefore be given the right to challenge the compatibility of negotiated RTAs and to initiate dispute settlement. This function and right could be developed, complementing the work of the CRTA or a newly created expert committee. The Secretariat would thus play an active role in maintaining the balance between multilateralism and regionalism. Similarly to the Commission of the EC, the Secretariat would assume the role of a watchdog of the systemic common interest represented in the multilateral trading system affected by the proliferation of RTAs. Overall, the WTO as an international organization can play a stronger role in securing coherence between the different components—multilateral and bilateral—of the global trading system. Assigning these functions to the Director-General and the Secretariat adds to the proposals which reflect a constitutional approach, transcending the tradition of a purely 'member-driven' organization.

4. Strengthening Remedies

Finally, it will be important to consider RTAs in reforming remedies. The current limitation to remedies *pro futuro* (compensation, withdrawal of concessions) does not offer incentives to comply with the disciplines for RTAs under WTO law. In particular, WTO law does not imply an obligation to withdraw an agreement, or provisions therefore, which are found incompatible with WTO rules, despite primacy of the latter established under Article 41

---

[73] Currently, it is unclear as to how bound the CRTA is in exercising its authority in this consensual process, particularly, whether its 'decisions' or recommendations are also subject to 'appeal' in the DSU.

[74] Cottier, above at n 1, at 117–18.

VCLT. The thorny question arises of how remedies could be strengthened in a meaningful manner, seeking a proper balance between multilateral disciplines and treaty-making powers of WTO Members. Reform seeking to introduce nullity of inconsistent agreements would imply far-reaching retroactive remedies and obligations to compensate. Effects *ex nunc* ascribed to unlawfulness, however, would limit remedies to future effects, commensurate with existing WTO law. Given the difficulties of defining trade diversion and quantifying it, appropriate compensation would be difficult to assess. Likewise, attempts to define financial compensation would be extremely difficult not only as regards quantification, but also as a general remedy aimed at an international agreement held to be inconsistent with WTO law. The general obligation to comply with findings of dispute settlement decisions and to bring about compatibility leaves members with the option of either extending MFN treatment or suspending the operation of the inconsistent preference. WTO law could specify these remedies in terms of treaty language.

VIII. DECISION-MAKING AT WTO AND THE PROLIFERATION OF RTAS

International law thus offers a variety of options for bringing about enhanced disciplines in relation to RTAs and for promoting the constitutional functions of the WTO.[75] Whether or not Members are willing to engage in redefining rights and obligations depends upon their interests and their assessments of the pro and cons of a constitutional approach. It is evident that any progress will be difficult to achieve under the present consensus-based decision-making procedures as long as individual Members choose to protect treaty-making powers, taking into account potential distorting effects. Likewise, consensus renders the operation of procedural devices equally difficult. The problem has already been raised in relation to the CRTA above. Difficulties, however, are rooted more deeply. The cyclical proliferation of RTAs in relation to the multilateral trade negotiations shows that WTO Members revert to preferential or regional agreements to the extent that policy goals cannot be sufficiently and promptly achieved in WTO negotiations based upon MFN and formal equality of States.[76] These difficulties are, of course, partly the result of differences in substance. The containment of preferential agreements therefore will largely depend upon making progress, in particular in relation to trade in agriculture, the main stumbling block of the Doha Development Agenda.

---

[75] For a detailed discussion on constitutional functions of international economic law *see* E.-U. Petersmann, *Constitutional Functions and Constitutional Problems of International Economic Law*, Vol 3 (Fribourg, Switzerland: University Press, 1991). *See also* generally T. Cottier and M. Hertig, 'The Prospects of 21st Century Constitutionalism' in A. von Bogdandy and R. Wolfrum (2003) 7 Max Planck Yearbook of United Nations Law, 261.

[76] *See* above n 4.

Redefining the balance of rights and obligations by means of RTA in the field of legal standard setting, however, also reveals deeper structural problems. The problem of expanding the protection of intellectual property rights in RTAs begs the question of the extent to which the WTO Agreements need to define binding maximum standards, which must not be bypassed in preferential agreements, with a view to sustaining an appropriate balance between competition, trade and monopoly rights. From this perspective, the TRIPS Agreement should also serve as a maximum, and not merely and mainly as a minimum standard.[77] This raises entirely new issues of multilateralism, as such effects cannot be based upon traditional treaty law unless a prohibition on transgressing WTO standards in preferential agreements is explicitly inscribed in the agreement, or certain standards would be considered to be part of *jus cogens*. The triangle of multilateralism, preferential agreements, and competition thus raises new issues in defining the relationship of different agreements which need to be addressed in future negotiations and scholarly discussions.

Finally, difficulties in making progress within the WTO system and the proliferation of RTAs also relates to decision-making in WTO; i.e. the consensus rule per se and the lack of majority voting in WTO practice. The erosion of MFN, the proliferation of RTAs, and the consensus rule are closely intertwined. The problem of preferential trade and WTO compatibility is inherently linked to the broader issue of decision-making in the WTO. To the extent that the proliferation of RTAs is linked to the arcane and protracted process of decision-making based upon consensus, effective reform, and the achievement of a coherent relationship between WTO rules and preferential agreements will depend upon a broader reform of decision-making in the WTO. Effective containment of RTAs, which are inconsistent with WTO law, and the advancement of multilateral trade based upon MFN will thus depend on progress in general decision-making at the WTO.

Goals of limiting preferential trade to fully compatible CUs, FTAs, and RTAs thus cannot be disassociated from the structure of decision-making processes at the WTO. The best means of prevention of excessive regionalism lies in a workable and progressive multilateral system which is in a position to secure market access rights of a global reach. Under current decision-making procedures, containment of an excessive proliferation of RTAs depends on consensus and thus mutually agreed progress in multilateral negotiations. This is increasingly difficult to achieve. The system has reached its limits under the consensus rule. The reform of decision-making, in particular the review of consensus policies, is therefore key to preserving the multilateral system, to establishing a proper balance between global and regional integration, and to

---

[77] *See* T. Cottier, 'The Agreement on Trade-Related Aspects of Intellectual Property Rights', in P.F.J. Macroy, A.E. Appleton and M.G. Plummer (eds) *The World Trade Organization: Legal, Economic and Political Analysis* (New York: Springer, 2005), 1041, 1061–1063; *also* in T. Cottier, *Trade and Intellectual Property Protection in WTO Law: Collected Essays* (London: Cameron May, 2005), 117, 144–47.

limiting an escalation towards a multitude of distorting and trade-diverting preferential agreements around the globe.

This chapter will not explore the proposals for changing the voting system within the WTO and its implications on RTAs. We do note though that there is a growing awareness that the purely consensus-based system is no longer suitable to serve the goals of the multilateral system. As the Organization states:

> ... The WTO will likely suffer from slow and cumbersome policy-making and management—an organization with more than 120 member countries cannot be run by a 'committee of the whole'. Mass management simply does not lend itself to operational efficiency or serious policy discussion.
>
> Both the IMF and the World Bank have an executive board to direct the executive officers of the organization, with permanent participation by the major industrial countries and weighted voting. The WTO will require a comparable structure to operate efficiently. . . . [But] the political orientation of smaller . . . members remain strongly opposed. (WTO, 2003 p 103)

We agree that all of this raises fundamental questions. At this stage, we merely seek to encourage in-depth research and discussion of the structural shortcomings of the present system of decision-making. Effort should be made to seek a new system of carefully balanced weighted voting in the WTO. The Advisory Board of the Director General made some preliminary proposals. The group submitted that the problem of consensus deserves serious study. Members seeking to block consensus would be required to justify this step by recourse to vital national interests.[78] This is an important, albeit hardly sufficient step. It is submitted that solutions based upon carefully weighted voting rights should be discussed and could be achieved. This would provide a proper balance of voting rights and powers, commensurate with shares of world trade, openness of markets and population.[79] The fears of medium-sized and smaller WTO Members that they would lose influence and impact need to be replaced by the conviction that it is these countries who will benefit most from a global system which is able to discipline and contain preferential regionalism and bring about linkages between all the trading blocs around the world.

---

[78] *See* above n 7, at 65.
[79] *See* T. Cottier and S. Takenoshita, 'The Balance of Power in WTO Decision-Making: Towards Weighted Voting in Legislative Response' (2003) 2 *Aussenwirtschaft* (Swiss Review of International Economic Relations) 171.

APPENDIX I

DELEGATE SUBMISSIONS TO THE NEGOTIATING GROUP ON RULES REFERRING TO RTAS [80]

Document	Title of Document	Submitted by	Content Summary
TN/RL/W/2	Negotiations On Regional Trade Agreements: Key Issues For Consideration	Australia	Largely listed the procedural and systemic issues for consideration.
TN/RL/W/14	Submission On Regional Trade Agreements	European Communities	Points out that the CRTA has yet to complete a single evaluation of a RTA. EC believes RTAs can contribute to stability and development particularly for 'deep integration'. Reconfirmed flexibilities for SDT. Beyond that the submission largely once more lists clarification and procedural issues.
TN/RL/W/15	Submission On Regional Trade Agreements	Australia	'Substantially all trade' should require a defined percentage of all the six-digit tariffs listed in the HS ensuring sufficient flexibility to set aside product areas but the percentage should be sufficiently high to prevent carving out of a major sector.
TN/RL/W/16	Submission On Regional Trade Agreements	Chile	Addressing the Chair's request for submissions on procedural matters—when, where and what to notify.

[80] Summarized by J. Gage from WTO website.

Appendix 1—*continued*

Document	Title of Document	Submitted by	Content Summary
TN/RL/W/32	Submission On Regional Trade Agreements	Turkey	Proposed simplification of examination for CRTA and use of grandfathering. All RTAs (be it GATT XXIV, Enabling Clause, or GATS V) should be notified to the CRTA. Turkey favours a quantitative approach to the assessment of substantially all trade. Suggested a single set of Rules of Origin and general harmonization of regulations. Also emphasized SDT.
TN/RL/W/114	Discussion Paper On Regional Trading Arrangements	India	'Substantially all trade' should have a threshold limit of 6th level of HS tariff lines and identify trade flows at various stages of implementation. Argued the Enabling Clause and SDT should not be altered and against the notification to the CRTA for those agreements under that clause. Argued for a two-step notification before ratification. Concerned particularly about Rules of Origin for textiles. Argued harmonization of SPS/TBT standards cannot be per se a pre-condition for an RTA. Argued for consistency of anti-dumping, countervail between the RTA and WTO rules. Argued against grandfathering.
TN/RL/W/116	Submission On Regional Trade Agreements	Korea	Wants clarification on 'other [restrictive] regulations of commerce' particularly as it might impact third parties. Questions why Rules of Origin are more stringent than those applied on an MFN basis and whether to permit 'diagonal cumulation schemes'. Questions use of SPS/TBT practices against third parties. Safeguard and anti-dumping dual system should be considered not consistent.
TN/RL/W/117	Submission On Regional Trade Agreements	Australia; Chile; Hong Kong; China; Korea; and New Zealand	Addressing the Chair's request for submissions on procedural matters—when, where and what to notify.

PART II

WTO Regulation of Regional Trade Agreements

4

Regional Trade Agreements and Domestic Regulation: What Reach for 'Other Restrictive Regulations of Commerce'?

JAMES H. MATHIS *

INTRODUCTION

The GATT provisions for customs unions and free trade areas have a close legal relationship to the general most favoured nation obligation (Article I GATT). The relative ease or difficulty of forming a regional trade agreement between subsets of WTO Members defines how broadly MFN will be applied in practice. The exception acts to define the scope of the rule. This therefore renders Article XXIV a part of the core architecture of the GATT Agreement. The GATT 1947 Preamble recognized this by reciting as an objective 'the elimination of discriminatory treatment in international commerce'.

Article XXIV accomplishes this function by firstly defining which types of preferential entities members may entertain: customs unions, free trade areas, and interim agreements leading to either. Secondly it provides procedural and application requirements for them. In this sense Article XXIV appears to create a sort of self-standing regime. However, its character is inherently exceptional, especially when invoked by a regional member as a defence to a violation of MFN, or to some other GATT Article.

Substantively, there are 'internal' and 'external' requirements for a regional formation. Both aspects are captured in Article XXIV:4's 'purposive' expression. Here the desirability of increasing trade by voluntary agreements between regional members is recognized, and that 'the purpose of a customs

* The author wishes to thank Roland Fey and Kamala Dawar for their editorial assistance, and the conference participants and editors for their most helpful comments.

union or a free trade area should be to facilitate trade between the constituent territories' (the internal requirements of paragraph 8) and 'not to raise barriers to the trade of other Contracting Parties with such territories' (the external requirements of paragraph 5).

This chapter's focus is on one of Article XXIV's internal provisions: the requirement for regional members to eliminate 'other restrictive regulations of commerce' (ORRC). Section I will consider the definitional possibilities for this term as it may apply to the domestic regulations of RTA members. The section will look at the textual context, the drafting record, and the limited WTO Panel and Appellate Body treatment, in turn. It concludes that ORRC has a limited reach for domestic regulations. It is argued that the duty to eliminate other restrictive regulations of commerce only extends to domestic laws of an RTA member that are according less favourable treatment to the products of another regional member, in the sense of national treatment. With this narrow construction established, Section II considers the implications for regional members of an obligation for them to actively plan and schedule the elimination of their discriminatory ORRC. A second question of 'more favourable treatment' accorded among RTA members by acts of preferential recognition or harmonization is also considered. With a narrow scope for ORRC, the duty to eliminate does not appear to extend to acts of deeper integration. The scope of Article XXIV's exception does not intervene in the balance already struck in Annex 1A agreements for most-favoured nation between the general GATT Articles and the more specific and modifying TBT/SPS Agreement provisions.

The final Section III considers the role of restrictive measures that could be introduced between regional members for failing to fulfil an RTA regulatory benchmark. While the regulatory conditions established, for labour or human rights for examples, can all fall within the scope of domestic regulation, the relation to ORRC for these activities focuses rather on the legal form of any resulting trade-restrictive measure. Some restrictions entertained for violating a regulatory condition clearly fall within ORRC, such as an importation prohibition for example. These provisions, if contained in an RTA, should fall within the examination and qualification criterion under Article XXIV GATT. However, ORRC would not apply where the resulting restrictions remained within the scope of internal measures and were applied between the RTA members in a non-discriminatory manner. In these cases RTAs can set higher regulatory standards for their respective trade. These stricter regulations may at the same time impact the regional members underlying WTO most-favoured nation rights. The implications of this possibility are considered in the conclusion.

I. ARTICLE XXIV AND 'OTHER RESTRICTIVE REGULATIONS OF COMMERCE'

A. Paragraph 8, immediate context

Even a cursory reading of Article XXIV:8 will show that it is not possible to isolate the ORRC term from its immediate surroundings. Thus for a free trade area,

(*b*) A free-trade area shall be understood to mean a group of two or more customs territories in which the duties and other restrictive regulations of commerce (except, where necessary, those permitted under Articles XI, XII, XIII, XIV, XV and XX) are eliminated on substantially all the trade between the constituent territories in products originating in such territories.[1]

'Elimination' refers both to duties and ORRC, which could inform the meaning of the ORRC term. 'Elimination' is also conditioned in respect to 'substantially all the trade' (SAT), which might inform which types of ORRCs can be permitted within that parameter. In addition, the listing of Articles is provided for restrictions that need not be eliminated, and this also informs the meaning of ORRC since trade measures taken according to those Articles appear to constitute ORRC.

Paragraph 8 was not treated in the Uruguay Round Understanding on Article XXIV, except for the following single and not insignificant preamble expression. This states that the contribution of regional agreements to the expansion of world trade,

. . . is increased if the elimination between the constituent territories of duties and *other restrictive regulations of commerce* extends to all trade, and diminished if any major sector of trade is excluded;[2]

To the extent that this expression informs ORRC, it appears to push the interpretation toward greater levels of regional internal trade coverage rather than lesser.

B. Article XXIV and the broader context

The source of long-standing disagreement on the meaning and scope of the ORRC term is understandable if one considers the broader commercial and economic policy environment for the interpretation of Article XXIV. Since a preference granted between regional members will always raise a *relative* barrier to the trade of non-members, there is a clear tension presented by the Article's internal and external requirements. There is nothing inherently more

---

[1] Art. XXIV:8 (b) GATT.

[2] Understanding on the Interpretation of Article XXIV of the GATT 1994, preamble, third recitation, italics added.

trade-creating in a completed custom union than a lesser regional preferential exchange. Viner also famously noted the economic irrationality of demanding a 100 per cent preference, 'which suddenly turns to a maximum evil at 99 per cent . . .'.[3] To the extent to which the internal requirements suggest a very high degree of preference exchange, they are also not necessarily economically rational. This tension was recognized to favour a looser internal trade requirement by early calls for the functional re-interpretation of the Article in order to minimize an RTA's trade diverting potential.[4]

However, the issues raised by paragraph 8 requirements in their complex relationship to MFN are not all economic. Preferential trade discrimination raised political tensions among states during the interwar years. The failure to attain a generalized MFN clause for international trade in the settlement of World War I weighed upon the American post-World War II planners and eventually motivated the Suggested Charter for an International Trade Organization.[5] Sixty years later, MFN remains 'the core principle' of the WTO as a general obligation in each substantive annexed agreement. At the same time, recurrent eras of regional proliferation facilitated by a nearly systemic non-adherence to internal formation requirements has also raised serious problems for the WTO system. Not the least of which is, how much global trade can be rendered preferential before the value of a WTO membership is relegated to a secondary status?

No consistent practice or consensus has emerged for ORRC terminology in the GATT working groups, or later in the Committee on Regional Trade Agreements (CRTA) reviews of submitted free trade area and customs union plans. Regional members have tended to support their lack of internal trade coverage by emphasizing the absence of provable negative external effects. In reverse image, non-members have also challenged proposed regional arrangements for their lack of adherence to internal trade requirements. What has been nearly consistent in the review practice over time is a mixing and muddling of the internal and external requirements by the delegations on record in the review process.

---

[3] Viner posed a single qualification to support stronger internal requirements. A completed customs union (containing an across-the-board removal of duties) would be preferable, '. . . since the removal is non-selective by its very nature, the beneficial preferences are established along with the injurious ones, the trade-creating ones along with the trade-diverting ones. Preferential arrangements, on the other hand, usually are selective, and in practice probable that the preferences selected will be predominantly of the trade-diverting or injurious kind': J. Viner, *The Customs Union Issue* (New York: Carnegie Endowment for International Peace, 1950), 44, 51.

[4] The earliest complete critique being K. Dam, 'Regional Economic Arrangements and the GATT, the Legacy of a Misconception' (1963) 30 U Chi L Rev, 615, at 633. For a contemporary economic argument supporting a trade diversion criteria, *see* J. McMillan, 'Does Regional Integration Foster Open Trade', in K. Anderson and R. Blackhurst (eds), *Regional Integration and the Global Trading System* (London: Harvester Wheatsheaf, 1993), 292–310.

[5] Generally, R. Gardner, *Sterling–Dollar Diplomacy in Current Perspective* (New York: Columbia University Press, 1980). Generalized MFN and the status of future preferential systems were highlighted issues in the negotiations for the Atlantic Charter Declaration in 1941.

C. The role of internal requirements in qualifying formations

This author takes a 'sequential' or two-step view of the Article whereby commitments for internal requirements should be isolated and examined prior to considerations addressing the external effects of a regional formation.[6] This view is based upon the *definitional* lead generated by the terms of paragraph 8. This describes what, at the outset, constitutes a customs union or a free trade area that may be able to derive the Article XXIV exception ('. . . a customs union / free trade area *shall be understood to mean* . . .'). Following the assessment of the plan and schedule regarding these internal requirements of paragraph 8 (does the plan indicate that a free trade area or customs union is being formed?), *then* the external implications of potential new barriers to trade would be considered according to paragraph 5's external requirements. The lead sentence in paragraph 5 links the internal and external requirements by granting the 'exception' for FTAs and CUs (not for other preference systems) upon the additional condition of meeting the external requirements, the so-called *proviso*.[7]

A functional review regime might not consider either potential external welfare effects or external GATT Article violations for a proposed plan and schedule that does not appear to constitute a free trade area or a customs union in the first place. Since internal requirements have historically been either hedged or ignored by RTA proponents, the emphasis has inevitably tended to shift to controlling the external damage that might be caused by a given RTA, since the agreement itself cannot be 'blocked' in the review process for a failure to meet the internal requirements. The Appellate Body's well known two-part test for ruling whether an RTA member's GATT inconsistent external measures may be excepted by Article XXIV appears to re-confirm this relationship between internal and external formation requirements. Firstly,

. . . that the measure at issue is introduced upon the formation of a customs union that *fully meets the requirements of sub-paragraph 8*(a) *and 5*(a) of Article XXIV. Second, the party must demonstrate that the formation of that customs union would be prevented if it were not allowed to introduce the measure at issue.[8]

The second part of the test raises the need to examine whether an inconsistent measure is actually 'necessary' for the completion of a qualified formation. For an MFN challenge based on a non-accorded preference, it is reasonable to suggest that an RTA enactment eliminating a duty or other restrictive regulation of commerce would be found as 'necessary' to complete the regional formation. It appears evident that the first test cannot be passed without a

---

[6] J.H. Mathis, *Regional Trade Agreements in the GATT/WTO: Article XXIV and the Internal Trade Requirement* (The Hague: T.M.C. Asser, 2002), 231 *et seq.*

[7] Art. XXIV:5 head paragraph, '. . . nothing in the Agreement shall prevent the formation of a customs union or free-trade (or interim agreement) provided that . . .'.

[8] WTO Appellate Body Report, *Turkey—Textiles*, WT/DS34/AB/R, adopted 19 November 1999, para. 58.

commitment to this elimination being made evident, by the regional members, in a plan and schedule. Except for whatever flexibility is introduced for *substantially* all trade, (the remainder of trade between 'substantial' and 'all'), RTA enactments that fall within the scope of ORRC should be understood to fall within the exception. Likewise, measures that are not within the scope of ORRC should not likely be considered as 'necessary' for the establishment of a qualified Article XXIV formation. Although this point may not have been explicitly ruled by the Appellate Body in the test formulated above where the factual context was the introduction of new externally restrictive measures, at least one Panel has drawn this conclusion.[9]

There are well-recognized institutional difficulties with the WTO review process for RTAs. But, an absence of agreement on the substantive terms to be applied for internal trade requirements has meaningfully blocked progress for qualifying agreements. Some would suggest that the long-standing differences of opinion on the Article's paragraph 8 terms are so firmly entrenched in the WTO as to suggest a crippling ambiguity. Interpretation modes applied by the WTO Appellate Body may rather find that that the terms in their ordinary meaning are not as opaque as many members have long alleged. Whether true or not, the preparatory drafting and conference records relating to the ORRC term are considered now, not only for what they appear to clarify, but also for what they fail to address.

D. ITO preparatory conference record

The ORRC term was contributed by the US as a part of the original customs union paragraph within the Suggested Charter for the ITO prepared for the London preparatory conference (1946). Unlike many other GATT provisions, the term was not used in prior reciprocal US trade agreement practice. These agreements provided that reciprocal MFN rights accorded would be extended to newly formed customs unions of the other Contracting Party, and that preferences exchanged within customs unions would therefore be an exception to that Contracting Party's MFN obligations. This is similar to the operation of Article XXIV to the extent that the Article equates customs union formation with customs territories, which are also entities accorded the legal status of Contracting Parties in the GATT.[10] However, the earlier US bilateral agreements were also not in the practice of defining the requisite elements of what might constitute a customs union. The notion of providing some definitional contours for 'customs union' appears to have surfaced with this

---

[9] 'If the alleged violation of GATT 1994 forms part of the elimination of "duties and other restrictive regulations of commerce", there can be no question of whether it is necessary for the elimination of "duties and other restrictive regulations of commerce" ': WTO Panel Report, *US—Line Pipe*, WT/DS202/R, adopted 8 March 2002, as modified by the Appellate Body Report, WT/DS202/AB/R, para. 7.148, and note 137.

[10] Art. XXIV GATT, paras 1 and 2.

original paragraph for the Suggested Charter, numbered as Article 33 and as presented by the US in London as follows:

4. . . .A union of customs territories for customs purposes shall be understood to mean the substitution of a single customs territory for two or more customs territories, so that all tariffs and other restrictive regulations of commerce as between the territories of members of the union are substantially eliminated and the same tariffs and other regulations of commerce are applied by each of the members of the union to the trade of territories not included in the union.[11]

On this text the Preparatory Committee report indicated only that, 'they were in agreement that the provisions of the Charter regarding trade barriers should apply to each of the customs territories . . . that an appropriate exception . . . should be made . . . for advantages incident to the formation of a customs union . . . and that suitable definitions of customs territories and customs unions should be included in Chapter V'.[12]

The 'ORRC' term remained intact through the New York drafting session and the Geneva preparatory conference (GATT sessions, 1947). For those conference and committee documents available for examination, there is little recorded discussion of delegates ever seeking a clarification, or volunteering one, regarding the meaning of ORRC, or actually discussing the terminology used in the paragraph in any significant respect.

E. Havana Conference amendments

The existing Article XXIV GATT text comes from the Havana sessions where a significant re-working and expansion of the customs union Article was made. This occurred as a result of a referral to a specially formed joint subcommittee of both the Development and the Commercial Policy Committees to resolve the relationship between the MFN Article, the customs union Article, and the Charter's Development Chapter provisions. Article 15 of this Chapter permitted 'regional' preferences, but only subject to ITO membership vote and waiver. The general conference record is clear on a hostile developing-country response to the new generalized MFN clause that permitted 'standstill' provisions for existing preferential systems, but then requiring that all future preferential systems other than the customs unions would be subject to a voting

---

[11] Art. 33, Territorial Application of Chapter IV—Customs Unions—Frontier Traffic, Suggested Charter for an International Trade Organization of the UN, Department of State Publication, (September, 1946), WTO Library document. Note that from the outset the expression for internal trade referred to 'restrictive' (ORRC) while the expression for external trade (ORC) did not.

[12] The Preparatory Committee noted changes to this text including the introduction of the word 'formation', '. . . thus permitting measures which in fact represent a transitional stage towards a new customs union', and expressly providing for organizational control (by approval) for agreements that did not meet the conditions of the Chapter. *See* Report of the First Session of the Preparatory Committee of the UN Conference on Trade and Employment (the London Report), 11. The later Draft Charter re-numbered the Article as 38. These were the only subjects raised on this Conference relating to the Article.

waiver according to Article 15.[13] The task of reformulating the compromise was delegated to a working group of the joint sub-committee that held 29 meetings and presented the regional exception Article text as we now know it. The minutes and recorded comments (if there were any) are not available as part of the Conference record nor any of its indexes.[14] The revised text was conveyed in a joint-subcommittee report, which indicated the changes that were made but did not elaborate on the rationale for them.[15] These passed through the balance of the Conference without further proposals for amendments or any other apparent record of delegation comment or discussion.

The introduction of the free trade area exception was the notable outcome from this exercise. It is possible that other changes in the Article were made as part of the adjustments to accommodate the dual entities now being placed under the Article's exception.[16] The alterations made in Havana that could have a bearing on the meaning or the scope of the ORRC term include:

– the inclusion of the free trade area exception definition which also uses the ORRC term and also recites an identical requirement for the elimination of duties and ORRC
– the inclusion of a listing of Articles (XI-XV and XX)
– the change in placement of the term 'substantially' to its present position (substantially-all trade), from the earlier expression of 'substantially eliminated'.

F. ORRC viewed from the elements of customs union formation

If one considers that the terminology for 'elimination' is identical for both a customs union and the newly established free trade area, what elements constitute an ORRC might not have been so unclear from the view of the drafters. Particularly those drawn from what members would have commonly understood to be the requisites of a customs union. Members forming a single customs territory by way of a customs union would substitute their individual

---

[13] The referral charged the subcommittee to consider the Development Article and the MFN standstill paragraphs and the customs union Article '. . . with a view to finding a solution of the question of new preferential arrangements'. Havana document citations and discussion in Mathis, above at n 6, at 41.

[14] Some drafting sub-committees and working groups preserved their notes and others did not. Chase reviewed a collection of US diplomatic cablegrams and concluded that the US and Canada had decided to establish a free trade area and that the US was active in facilitating the introduction of a new exception, but not anxious to receive any attribution for 'loosening' the MFN obligation: K. Chase, 'Multilateralism Compromised: The Mysterious Origins of GATT Article XXIV' (2006) 5 WTR, 1.

[15] UN Doc. E/CONF.2/C.3/78, April 1948.

[16] Another view by Hudec and Southwick is that some changes (the shift of the word 'substantial') likely reflected the inclusion of the new Articles listing: R. Hudec and J. Southwick, 'Regionalism and WTO Rules', in M. Rodriguez Mendoza, P. Low and B. Kotschwar (eds), *Trade Rules in the Making: Challenges in Regional and Multilateral Negotiations* (Washington DC; OAS: Brookings, 1999).

and distinct external commercial policies in favour of a single external commercial policy. The subject matter of those policies would include the states' protectionist trade measures: tariff duties and importation restrictions 'other than duties and charges' (quantitative restrictions, Article XI GATT), and contingency trade defence measures such as anti-dumping and safeguard actions.

As is the case for any single national customs territory, one would also expect that these same policies would be eliminated from application within the territory. In a completed customs union, the elimination of commercial policies between the members would also be required. And this is what the paragraph appears to suggest. If this captures the general concept, then ORRC would refer to those trade measures other than tariff duties that would be necessary to 'eliminate' in order to give effect to a normally functioning customs territory operating in the form of a customs union, and probably not more.[17]

Where a new free trade area exception was created that did not require a common external commercial policy, the deal made for the new entity was that regional FTA members would still be required to eliminate the internal trade barriers akin to those of a single customs territory. This is a demanding requirement that each party to an FTA would maintain a separate commercial policy regime *vis-à-vis* its own external trade, but there is no context in the Article to suggest that the identical wording regarding the elimination of ORRCs in the customs union form was intended to be 'lesser', or different in any respect for the free trade area. While opening the provisions for a new regional exception, this identical obligation to eliminate duties and ORRC would also serve to preserve the organization's stronger oversight role for all other preference systems being sought to be established according to the Article 15 waiver requirement. The demarcation between Article 15 systems and the new free trade area exception is found in the more stringent internal requirements adopted for Article XXIV.

The extent of the elimination required for a customs union or free trade area would contemplate allowing some small portion of trade not to be eliminated within the 'substantially all the trade' (the SAT) requirement. Without detracting at all from the SAT requirement, regional members would also be required to apply to each other any restrictions taken in the form of the listed Articles (XI–XV and XX), each of which is provided by the GATT as exceptional for all Contracting Parties to address priority legitimate objectives that are not of an inherently protectionist nature. Not incidentally, all of the listed Articles employ MFN application to some degree or another when exercised at all.[18]

---

[17] A number of other policies can distort internal trade, subsidies for one example, but they are not trade measures and are not likely to be ORRCs. Many single national customs territories do not eliminate distorting policies affecting internal trade.

[18] This point is central to Hudec and Southwick's argument, that there is a distinction between what *must* be imposed between regional members if imposed at all, as compared to what *may* be

While the expression 'substantially all the trade' is said to raise aspects of both quantity and quality, the ORRC term refers to what 'types' of restrictive measures other than duties would be incorporated into a plan and schedule for eventual elimination. There is a relationship between ORRC and SAT where the type of measure permitted (because of its restrictive character, actual or potential) might undermine the SAT requirement if and when it would be applied by one regional member onto the trade of another. This link between the types of restrictions permitted by RTA members (as conditions subsequent to formation) and the SAT parameter has not been well illuminated in the review practice, although it has been raised as a subject on occassion in reference to potentially trade restrictive intra-regional safeguard clauses. This aspect becomes somewhat more central to consider in the domestic regulation area if RTA members use trade restrictions to enforce regulatory conditions.[19]

G. Panel and Appellate Body treatment

The Appellate Body has not had reason to consider the ORRC term directly for its definition or scope. The *Turkey—Textiles* Panel was presented with a challenge on the requirements for an external regime of a customs union according to Article XXIV:8(a)(ii).[20] The Appellate Body confirmed that whether the arrangement met the requirements of paragraphs 8(a) and 5(a) was not before it.[21] The word 'substantially' did receive treatment. However, this was for its position in sub-paragraph (ii). For sub-paragraph 8(a)(i), the Appellate Body noted that these terms 'provide that members of a customs union may maintain, where necessary, in their internal trade, certain restrictive regulations of commerce that are otherwise permitted under Articles XI through XV and under Article XX GATT 1994'.[22] This was indicative of offering members some flexibility, 'Yet we caution that the degree of "flexibility" that sub-paragraph 8(a)(i) allows is limited by the requirement that "duties and other restrictive regulations of commerce" be "eliminated with respect to substantially all" internal trade'.[23] These expressions may go more to the limits of 'substantial' than to the meaning of ORRC.

Two WTO cases have considered intra-regional safeguards where an RTA member excused another partner from the application of a safeguard. In both cases the regional members failed to match the investigation of origin sources with the application. The *Argentina—Footwear (EC)* Panel explicitly ruled that

---

eliminated between them. The 'must' requirement includes the Articles' listing, those exceptions that require an MFN application. Arts VI (anti-dumping) and XXI (security exception) do not present an MFN character. Categorizing safeguards (Art. XIX) was also problematic for their construction: *see* Hudec and Southwick, above at n 16.

[19] This subject is taken up in the final section of the chapter.
[20] WTO Panel Report, *Turkey—Textiles*, WT/DS34/R, adopted 19 November 1999, as modified by the WTO Appellate Body Report, WT/DS34/AB/R, paras 9.135–9.148.
[21] WTO Appellate Body Report, *Turkey—Textiles*, above at n 8, at para. 60.
[22] *Ibid.*, at para. 48.   [23] *Ibid.*, at para. 48.

safeguards could be entertained between the regional members as, 'In our view, that paragraph does not necessarily prohibit the imposition of safeguard measures between the constituent territories'.[24] In *US—Line Pipe*, the Appellate Body (again) explicitly refused to rule on whether regional members could be excluded from a safeguard application and noted the two circumstances whereby the issue would be properly raised.[25] Matsushita *et al.* concluded from the Panels that, 'On every occasion, the WTO adjudicating bodies held that parties to a PTA may impose safeguards against other parties to the PTA'.[26] Lockhart and Mitchell take the view that safeguards must certainly be ORRCs.[27] If one also accepts the 'may or must' construction of Hudec and Southwick, then safeguards, when applied to other WTO Members, are not *required* to be applied to other regional members since Article XIX is not a listed Article in paragraph 8.[28] However, when regional members do apply a safeguard to each other's trade, it may only be maintainable to that 'insubstantial' portion of the trade that need not be freed from duties and ORRC, according to the SAT requirement.[29]

This may be a proper characterization, but it raises questions between 'form' and 'application' that are puzzling. In an RTA agreement severe intraregional safeguard provisions can be agreed upon by the parties. By reducing injury thresholds and exempting WTO Safeguard Agreement notification and other control provisions, the mere existence of such a clause in an RTA suggests the potential to eliminate a significant amount of regional trade. At a later stage, during or after implementation, the use of such a clause by the parties means that an RTA could be 'qualified' one day, but then 'disqualified' the next day as its cumulated elimination of duties and other ORRCs meets the SAT test and then does not. The RTA parties assume their own risk for dispute settlement if their agreement does not respect the SAT requirement at the moment they might need to invoke the Article XXIV defence.

One poses the consideration of whether the *form* of the safeguard provision should at the outset be examined for its potential to suspend regional free

---

[24] WTO Panel Report, *Argentina—Footwear (EC)*, WT/DS121/R, adopted 12 January 2000, as modified by the Appellate Body Report WT/DS121/AB/R, para. 8.97. The Panel's treatment of Art. XXIV in the case was rejected by the Appellate Body (*see* WT/DS121/AB/R, para. 110).

[25] WTO Appellate Body Report, *US—Line Pipe*, WT/DS202/AB/R, adopted 8 March 2002, para. 198: 'We need not, and so do not, rule on the question whether Article XXIV of the GATT 1994 permits exempting imports originating in a partner of a free-trade area from a measure in departure from Article 2.2 of the Agreement on Safeguards'.

[26] M. Matsushita, T.J. Schoenbaum and P.C. Mavroidis, *The World Trade Organization: Law, Practice, and Policy* (Oxford: OUP, 2003), 363. It might be more correct to say that in each case the regional members were not permitted to excuse each other from the application, as they failed in each case to properly exclude each other's trade from the investigated sources. Whether they were 'allowed to apply' safeguards to regional trade was not the issue directed on point in the cases.

[27] N.J.S. Lockhart and A.D. Mitchell, 'Regional Trade Agreements under GATT 1994: An Exception and its Limits', in A.D. Mitchell (ed), *Challenges and Prospects for the WTO* (London: Cameron May, 2005), 237–38.

[28] Hudec and Southwick, above at n 16.   [29] Lockhart and Mitchell, above at n 27.

trade beyond paragraph 8's SAT requirements. Is there any systemic interest to document from the outset that the provisions adopted in an RTA demonstrate (or fail to demonstrate) a commitment to meet the coverage requirements over the interim period? A concluding review report could take note of the more draconian ORRC being reserved by the regional members. This could also note that the reviewers were unable to determine that a submitted plan and schedule could meet the SAT requirements of paragraph 8 over the interim period, since the parties had chosen to reserve certain rights to re-impose trade restrictions. This would at least make a record to inform a future dispute panel of structural defects in an RTA agreement, and additionally put regional members on notice that future dispute settlement claims may be more difficult to defend on Article XXIV.

A direct consideration of the definition for ORRC could occur in the post *Turkey—Textiles* environment where a WTO complainant would attack a denial of MFN to a regional party's eliminated trade or regulatory barrier that was not immediately and unconditionally extended to the complainant. This would call on paragraph 8 requirements to determine whether the liberalizing regional measure qualified as an ORRC that would then be required to be eliminated. A less direct but equally effective attack would be where the offending measure is a new or raised barrier in the meaning of paragraph 5 requirements, but where the complainant challenges the RTA member's Article XXIV defence on the underlying definitional requirements of paragraph 8. This is similar to the fact pattern set in *Turkey—Textiles*, but now with consideration of the Appellate Body's two-part test. The underlying qualification of the RTA is at issue if the Article XXIV defence is raised. This could call forth all the provisions (at least facially) of the trade agreement, and presumably the status of their implementation (to SAT).

The issue of whether certain types of provisions could be *facially* ruled incompatible with paragraph 8 should not be dismissed. This was the approach taken by both of the GATT (unadopted) *EC—Banana* Panels. They ruled that Article XXIV could not be successfully invoked as a defence if the absence of a reciprocal obligation to eliminate duties was expressly stated on the face of the RTA.[30]

The term 'other regulations of commerce' (ORC) did receive treatment in the *Turkey—Textiles* Panel. In relation to paragraph 5 barriers, ORC includes anything 'trade related' whether or not the subject matter falls within the WTO Agreements.[31] In addition to the obvious textual difference that has

---

[30] GATT Panel Reports *EEC (Member States)—Bananas I*, 3 June 1993, unadopted, DS32/R; and *EEC—Bananas II*, 11 February 1994, unadopted, DS38/R. The reciprocity requirement for para. 8 was found in the Panels' interpretation of the requirement to eliminate duties 'as between' the regional members.

[31] '. . . any regulation having an impact on trade . . .'. Although the Panel's indicative listing did not include a reference to rules of origin. WTO Panel Report, *Turkey—Textiles*, above at n 20, at para. 9.120.

been in place between ORC and ORRC since the original submitted draft version of the paragraph, there is good reason on the Panel's definition alone to conclude that ORC are not the same as ORRC. If the Panel's paragraph 5 ORC definition were to be applicable for ORRC, then the obligation to eliminate them would include any and all regulatory measures having an intra-regional 'impact on trade'. This would constitute a WTO commandment for regional members to form what might be considered as completed internal market regimes with characteristics of deep recognition to eliminate differing (but non-protectionist) regulatory barriers. Even single-territory federalized systems (such as the US) do not attempt to harmonize all state regulations affecting trade. The EU has a legal basis for elimination similar to what is expressed by the ORC definition (if applied to ORRC for intra-regional trade) where internal regulations 'hindering' trade are ruled 'measures of equivalent effect' to a quantitative restriction. But, it is difficult to conceive that this degree of harmonization would be established as an 'elimination' requirement for WTO Members establishing even a customs union, let alone a free trade area without institutional features.

H. Interpretation limited to internal discriminatory measures

Raising the Panel's ORC definition for possible application to ORRC sets the probable demarcation line for the term as it is applied to the field of domestic regulation. It is with an emphasis on the word 'restrictive', and this is *the* difference between the two expressions. While both refer to 'commerce', which can inclusively consider regulatory aspects as well as trade measures,[32] 'restrictiveness' equates well for border measures, duties and importation/exportation restrictions (other than duties). It is also for domestic regulations (fiscal or non-fiscal) that accord less favourable treatment to like imported products of the regional members.[33]

If the term ORRC extends at all to regulatory matters, then discrimination must be the core of the requirement. If the requirement is 'lesser' than national treatment, then there would be a free avenue for regional members to substitute new internal discriminatory measures for those duties eliminated by a plan and schedule. Since these new internal and discriminatory measures would only be levied upon the regional member, neither a national treatment nor an MFN violation would occur with respect to any third party rights. If the ORRC requirement is broader than that of national treatment, then the

---

[32] Otherwise the requirement would simply recite that regional members eliminate duties and quantitative restrictions within the meaning of Art. XI.

[33] Confirming, J.P. Trachtman, 'Toward Open Recognition? Standardization and Regional Integration under Article XXIV of GATT' (2003) 6 JIEL, 459, at 486. With the addition that he includes 'possibly unnecessary' measures as well. Trachtman considers that affirming national treatment for regional members may be superfluous if GATT parties have an obligation to provide it anyway. As between regional members, the question of whether they can lawfully suspend their respective national treatment obligations *inter se*, is considered in the final section of this chapter.

problems suggested above of mandating the elimination of non discriminatory but 'trade hindering' regulations arise. While certainly not conclusive, there is no other context in the original GATT 1947 provisions where economic integration at such a level was expressed as even an aspirational endeavour for the Contracting Parties.

One tangential but telling contemporaneous reference for the original text is offered to support an interpretation for ORRC that is limited to the field of internal discriminatory measures in addition to protectionist border measures. The 1949 US Tariff Commission Report on the Havana Charter, prepared for the House of Representatives Ways and Means Committee, referred to the objectives of the whole of the Havana Charter commercial policy chapter:

> The primary objective . . . is that, in the long run, governmental measures to *restrict* foreign trade shall be confined to non-discriminatory tariffs, and that the use of other *restrictive* measures, such as quantitative restrictions and *discriminatory internal taxes or discriminatory internal regulations*, shall be eliminated.[34]

This paragraph equates the core GATT obligations to eliminate protectionism by the prohibition on quotas (Article XI GATT) and the positive obligation of providing national treatment (Article III GATT) with the concept of 'restrictiveness'. While the quotation notes the longer term objectives for all members, it is fair to suggest that the same objectives, and not more, were being raised for regional members who sought to proceed at a faster pace toward the same ultimate ends by the use of Article XXIV arrangements.

Considered in the next section is how this limited ORRC scope, as enunciated above for internal discrimination, relates to domestic regulatory activities that have become a part of the modern RTA landscape.

II. ORRC AND DOMESTIC REGULATION

The treatment of regulatory regimes in RTAs has become the norm for regional endeavours and, with the exception of European internal integration, marks this generation of regionalism as distinct from the previous waves. For the US and the EU, although their external relations approaches to regulatory issues are clearly evolving, they also reflect the distinct emphases and commercial priorities of each party. The US agreements set stronger standards for enforcement of intellectual property rights and in some cases more fully delineate rights for investment and investors. The EU agreements pursue more detailed harmonization requirements for domestic competition laws, including distortionary state aids. With some other differences, both pay attention to domestic technical barriers to trade for products and food standards, and in

---

[34] US Tariff Commission, *Report on the Havana Charter for an International Trade Organization, for the Committee on Ways and Means, House of Representatives* (May 1949), WTO Library document, at 18, italics added.

varying degree raise some *possible* conditions (or exceptions) for labour or human rights or for the environment. Generally, the agreements are becoming more nuanced in tailoring to individual country situations and more comprehensive both in WTO rule-referencing, as well as treating regulatory aspects not otherwise covered in WTO annexed agreements. Some of the newer agreements could be said to reflect a sort of 'post-Doha' character that is indicative of the regulatory priorities that each major player might prefer to see incorporated in the multilateral trading system if only WTO Members were more amenable to extending the multilateral trading system into these regulatory domains.[35]

This is the environment within which the ORRC term, as it applies to domestic regulation, finds its current context. RTAs can certainly (in theory) bypass a recalcitrant WTO process for those fewer members willing to engage the process of enacting regulatory frameworks, or adopting regulatory conditions in exchange for the perceived benefits of preferential market access.[36]

Three areas of examination regarding the scope of the ORRC term to domestic regulatory matters are discussed below. The first considers what is required of regional members to eliminate as ORRCs in order to qualify a customs union or free trade area according to Article XXIV:8 (sub-section A). This informs a second consideration that defines third-party rights in respect of regional members' elimination of internal regulatory barriers (sub-section B). Section III will consider the treatment of new restrictive internal or importation measures that may result from a non-fulfilment of regulatory conditions imposed between members to an RTA.

A. What must be eliminated?

It has been suggested here that discriminatory (protectionist) regulatory matters are the only internal aspects that fall within the scope of ORRC and thus require an active removal by the regional members. The GATT law point of reference for the scope of eliminating internally discriminatory measures is that of Articles III:2 and III:4. The range of application for these two paragraphs is broad and encompasses not only other Annex 1A considerations, but also aspects of the other covered agreements. This is where measures drawn relating to services or intellectual property restrictions may somehow also *affect* the sale or distribution of a like imported product on the internal market of a regional member. Moreover, the two paragraphs cover discriminatory

---

[35] This refers to the Doha Round treatment for the so-called Singapore Issues. For both competition policy and investment, there are both elements of market access considerations and domestic regulatory treatment.

[36] Except that not all WTO Members are invited to formulate these more proactive exchanges. On assessing the use of regulatory provisions in North–South RTAs, *see Global Economic Prospects 2005: Trade, Regionalism and Development* (Washington: World Bank, 2005). The report relates the regulatory aspects of North–South RTAs to issues of economic development.

domestic regulations that are not treated at all by any WTO regimes. Non-covered regulations that could affect the internal sale of products can be drawn from taxation laws, competition laws, investment requirements, unfair trading laws, consumer protection laws, and so on.[37]

This implies that an examination of a regional member's ORRC to be eliminated may also require an active disclosure of 'non-WTO' regulations that provide less favourable treatment upon the internal sale of a regional member's like products. Although these would also constitute national treatment violations to all WTO Members as well, the context here is upon the affirmative obligation to place them in a plan if they exist and then to eliminate them according to a schedule. To the extent that this might likewise notify and then trigger national treatment claims from third members (assuming that this discrimination might be sought to be maintained as to them), this would seem to go part and parcel with the requirement to eliminate discriminatory measures between regional members.

B. What remains actionable?

The Article III GATT point of reference for defining the scope of ORRC also sets a demarcation line between what is an exceptional derogation of MFN to the other WTO Members and what is not. What must be eliminated as an ORRC is viewed here as falling within the exception. What need not be eliminated remains arguably subject to other WTO Members' rights to receive most favoured nation treatment.

1. Pre-existing violations

A question that arises is whether the elimination of a pre-existing, internally discriminatory regulation grants any exceptional right for the regional member to retain that same unlawful regulation as to third parties. The MFN obligation stated in Article I GATT extends to matters covered within paragraphs 2 and 4 of Article III GATT. Where one regional member eliminates a pre-existing discriminatory regulatory measure in favour of the other partner, how does this action (upon formation) trigger an MFN violation to third parties?

There are two inconsistencies to consider here. The first is the previous and underlying inconsistency of the pre-existing measure with the national treatment obligation with respect to all WTO Members. The second is generated by the implementation of the regional formation, which is a new MFN violation caused by eliminating the first inconsistency with respect to the regional members but not all others. The short answer is that the new violation may fall

---

[37] On national treatment application to competition laws: J.H. Mathis, 'WTO Core Principles and Prohibition: Obligations Relating to Private Practices, National Competition Laws, and Implications for a Competition Policy Framework', UNCTAD Doc. UNCTAD/DITC/CLP/2003/2 (2003).

within the Article XXIV exception but that the underlying inconsistency (the underlying national treatment violation) does not.

The test enunciated by the Appellate Body in its *Turkey—Textiles* report appears to address this problem. It refers to the validation of an otherwise 'inconsistent' measure, as they relate to other WTO Members, and where the regional agreement itself meets the conditions of paragraphs 8 and 5 and 'the formation of that customs union would be prevented if it were not allowed to introduce the measure at issue'. For this it appears that the inconsistent measure must be 'introduced upon the formation' of the RTA.[38] If so, this would disqualify pre-existing violations from falling within the exception and these would remain a violation to all members irrespective of the elimination to another regional partner.

2. *The introduction of a national treatment violation*

It might have been the commonly accepted wisdom prior to the *Turkey— Textiles* Appellate Body report that a violation of national treatment could not fall within the Article XXIV exception. This is because it was available only to excuse violations of most favoured nation. Although national treatment was not at issue in that case, the Appellate Body's ruling on the paragraph 5 exception leaves little doubt that violations of other provisions of the GATT, at least in theory, can fall within the exception.[39]

It is difficult to isolate an example for a new national treatment violation enacted as an aspect of a regional formation that would not also encompass a violation of most favoured nation. One can hypothetically take up such an example where the claimant simply chooses to pursue the national treatment claim, irrespective of the MFN elements that might also exist. One possible example might be drawn from the case of *EC—Trademarks and Geographical Indications*. The Panel here ruled that conditioning internal treatment upon a requirement of another member to adopt equivalent domestic laws and then positively accord reciprocity to the first member constitutes a violation of Article III GATT.[40] In this case, the EC did not apply an Article XXIV defence.[41]

Considering the limited scope for ORRC adopted above, where there is a new denial of national treatment as a result of an RTA formation, this new domestic measure must also then fall within the scope of an ORRC in order to

---

[38] WTO Appellate Body Report, *Turkey—Textiles*, above at n 8, at paras 58 and 46 respectively.

[39] *Ibid.*, at para. 43 *et seq*, ruling on the text '. . . the provisions of this agreement shall not prevent . . .'.

[40] WTO Panel Report, *EC—Trademarks and Geographical Indications (Australia)*, WT/DS290/ R, adopted 20 April 2005, at paras 7.255–7.276. at 7.262: 'The Panel notes that the European Communities concedes that the conditions of equivalence and reciprocity in Article 12(1) of the Regulation, if applied to WTO Members, are inconsistent with Article III:4 of GATT 1994'.

[41] Another historical example concerned a draft version of the EC second banking directive that proposed granting internal market recognition to non EC members if non-members accorded equivalent and reciprocal treatment to EC banks. *See* M. Dakolias, 'The Second Bank Directive: The Issue of Reciprocity' (1991) 2 LIEI 69.

fall within the possibility of an exception. If the domestic treatment imposed is not acting to eliminate an internally discriminatory measure (as between the regional members) and if there is no pre-existing internally discriminatory measure to eliminate prior to the formation, it does not seem possible that a new national treatment violation can be brought under the scope of the Article XXIV exception. Further, it seems difficult to conceive of any case where a new violation of national treatment to a WTO Member undertaken as an aspect of a regional formation would qualify as 'eliminating' an ORRC, if this term is viewed as being limited to eliminating pre-existing intra-regional discriminatory measures. It appears here that the Appellate Body has opened a theoretical possibility but perhaps not a practical possibility.

3. ORRC for harmonization and recognition

The general most favoured nation obligation of Article I GATT applies to the subject matter contained in paragraph 4 of Article III GATT. This establishes MFN treatment for internal domestic regulations, as a general right. It becomes applicable in activities where the domestic authority waives the application of its own product or service regulations and 'recognizes' a foreign authority's testing or certification process as equivalent to its own. Where one foreign product or service receives this positive treatment, but another foreign source does not, then the issue is the denial of most favoured nation.[42] National treatment is not at issue where the domestic regime for qualifying products or services remains in place for domestic products and is applied in the same measure to the second foreign source. This application is non-discriminatory for this second foreign source, but there is a difference in treatment between the two foreign sources. This raises a MFN issue and likewise, the question of whether the ORRC scope is broad enough to include this activity in order to bring discriminatory recognition within the regional exception. If the ORRC definition is taken narrowly to refer only to the requirement to eliminate discriminatory actions in the sense of national treatment denial, then the answer appears to be negative. The violation of recognizing one foreign source, but not another, does not fall within the action of eliminating a discriminatory domestic measure in favour of a regional partner. Article XXIV does not grant an exception for discriminatory recognition.[43]

Both the SPS and TBT Agreements state their own MFN provisions, but also go on to provide for some modifications of MFN mainly in the field of permissive and selective recognition, for example, the recognition of conformity assessment (testing results) in the TBT Agreement. These provisions are *lex*

---

[42] J.H. Mathis, 'Mutual Recognition Agreements: Transatlantic Parties and the Limits to Non-tariff Barrier Regionalism in the WTO' (1998) 32 JWT 5, at 14.

[43] Bartels appears to concur with the result, taking the view that the regional exception would not apply because the recognition undertaken is not 'necessary' as according to the Turkey—Textiles Appellate Body test: L. Bartels, 'The Legality of the EC Mutual Recognition Clause under WTO Law' (2005) 8 JIEL 691, at 713. The treatment here is perhaps emphasizing that the recognition is not 'necessary' where the 'barrier' being eliminated is not an ORRC in the first place.

specialis to the application of Article I GATT as described above,[44] but elements of MFN participation are preserved in various provisions of these agreements as well. The question of whether Article XXIV can affect these third party rights by incorporating recognition activities into an RTA plan would seem to call for the same answer concluded above.[45] The modified and conditional MFN regimes falling within TBT and SPS would remain in effect for all WTO Members irrespective of the existence of a RTA.

Without further clarification of the hierarchy between GATT–1994 and the other relevant Annex 1A agreements, it would seem that the Article XXIV:8 requirements as drafted would compel a result that those Annex 1A provisions will remain externally effective between regional members and other WTO Members. This may not be a very satisfactory result in those cases where regional members wish to close their regional recognition schemes to eliminate participation for other WTO Members, or to condition their participation by exacting equivalency and reciprocity. However, any broader scope granted for ORRC to include the elimination of trade cumbersome regulations by the use of recognition activities would also necessarily establish those same activities as ORRC elimination *obligations* for regional members. Perhaps a handful of WTO Members might accept this degree of regulatory integration as an Article XXIV requirement but most would not.

This is an 'either/or' situation. Either the ORRC term is broad enough to consider measures undertaken by regional members beyond those for the purpose of eliminating discriminatory regulations between them, or it is not. If it is broad enough to consider recognition as a type of activity falling within the exception to other GATT and Annex 1A obligations, then these activities should also be construed as mandatory requirements for paragraph 8 formations.

There is a parallel presented between Articles VII and V GATS. More advanced forms of integration to recognize the qualifications and certificates of foreign service providers are contained in Article VII GATS. This is also a general provision in the GATS and while modifying 'unconditional' MFN, it contains a strong MFN character to guarantee the possibility of participation in recognition agreements by other WTO Members. Article V GATS,

---

[44] This relationship between general GATT Articles and the Annex 1A Agreements is provided by the Annex 1A footnote to the WTO Agreement. For these measures, the TBT Agreement imposes obligations on members that seem to be different from, and additional to, the obligations imposed on members under the GATT 1994. WTO Appellate Body Report, *EC—Asbestos*, WT/DS135/AB/R, adopted 5 April 2001, at para. 80.

[45] One difference between the two is that the Art. XXIV exception in paragraph 5 only refers to 'this agreement', i.e. to GATT 1947, and arguably now only to GATT 1994, and not to the other Annex 1A agreements. Trachtman relies on the principle of effectiveness to argue that TBT and SPS are also part of the single undertaking and, 'should be treated in the same way as the provisions of the GATT, although Article XXIV:5 fails to refer specifically to them': Trachtman, above at n 33, at 473. If Art. XXIV is not applicable to SPS or TBT provisions, then there is no regional exception available to excuse any derogations from whatever rights are accorded for other WTO Members within those annexed agreements.

the regional exception, does not reference to this form of integration at all, and does not provide for any stated obligation for regional members to positively eliminate regulatory hindrances other than by respecting national treatment as within the meaning of Article XVII GATS.[46] The same reasoning applies as above. Since Article V does not require parties to engage in recognition of service provider diplomas or certificates, this area of regulatory liberalization does not fall within the scope of the Article V GATS exception at all.[47] The GATS construction of what must be eliminated is comparable to the Article XXIV interpretation suggested above, where ORRC is interpreted to only apply to internally discriminatory measures. The only apparent way of broadening these regional exceptions to include discriminatory recognition would be to establish an expansive interpretation of non-discrimination, within the meaning of national treatment.[48]

III. INTERNALLY RESTRICTIVE REGIONAL REQUIREMENTS

The question of introducing trade restrictive measures by agreement among subsets of WTO Members in the context of RTAs, raises an old GATT-law conundrum while also venturing into modern regulatory regionalism. If the requirement to eliminate ORRC is additionally understood to prevent the introduction of new restrictive border measures, then how are we to treat agreements between two WTO Members that incorporate regulatory norms or conditions that could result in terminating free trade commitments?

For the purpose of raising examples, regulatory measures that could in theory restrict intra-regional trade might include RTA provisions that:

– establish a stronger precautionary principle (SPS modification) for food safety;
– impose a higher regional standard than an international product standard;

---

[46] The only alternative reading supporting discriminatory recognition within a GATS V arrangement would say that the Article's stated requirements are minimum requirements. Once these are met then 'this agreement shall not prevent . . . an agreement liberalising trade in services': Art. V GATS.

[47] To the extent that GATS V notifications are incorporating recognition that falls within the meaning of GATS VII, then it is up to the members affected to bring their Panel cases accordingly. For example, WTO Doc. WT/TN/RL/M/15, 15 June 2004, para 22, '. . . within CTS discussions, a number of Members had indicated that RAs were not notified to the WTO because they were part of an economic integration agreement notified under GATS Article V'. Query whether any *ex ante* participation rights accorded by GATS VII could be secured if the recognition agreements are not notified to the CTS?

[48] This is not inconceivable, but rather at the limits of what 'de facto' analysis can really bear in respect to otherwise non-discriminatory domestic regulations. To the extent that national treatment is so broadened, then it would also call into question why the GATS would have a separate Article VII as a general provision to accommodate and regulate recognition. Recognition would then be an obligation undertaken by every specific commitment for national treatment (as a result of a market access commitment, Art. XVI GATS) except where parties conditioned their national treatment obligation to not include an obligation to accord recognition.

- condition market access commitments upon investment access or treatment;
- provide for trade measures in the absence of competition law enforcement;
- set a level of IP regulatory enforcement in addition to existing TRIPS provisions;
- condition sector free trade commitments upon prescribed labour rules;
- condition the entire agreement upon democracy or human rights indicators.

The common elements from the above may be identified as follows: 1) the subject area is internal and regulatory in nature, 2) a regulatory norm or level of internal treatment is established, 3) this norm either incorporates a non-WTO obligation or in some manner supplements or modifies an existing WTO provision, and 4) that some linkage may be made to the free-trade commitments, to the proper functioning of the agreement, or to the conditions established by the parties for concluding the agreement.[49]

These examples are arguably all 'GATT (or WTO) plus' in that higher levels of regulatory performance are 'locked in' (a NAFTA era term), and as suggested by some economists, deeper levels of integration can be accomplished within the laboratory of regulatory focused RTAs. The 'plus' effects upon economic development by increased trade and investment have also been cited by some as complementary to multilateralism.[50] There are voices on the other side of the issue. The Sutherland Report refers to the 'injection' of particular 'non-trade' objectives into trade agreements and expresses concern that such requirements become 'templates' for new demands in the WTO, which then will enter through the 'side door'.[51] A WTO Secretariat paper adopted a more technical flavour, referring to RTAs that have a broader scope to include policy areas not regulated multilaterally. 'This is likely to give rise to regulatory confusion, distortion of regional markets, severe implementation problems . . . and to greatly complicate future efforts to develop a consistent set of multilateral rules and procedures governing countries' trade-related policies'.[52]

A. Is typology possible?

The 'WTO plus' label for regulatory integration in an RTA is not very helpful for setting a description of the applicable legal regimes. Domestic regulatory norms are difficult enough to characterize since there are many ways to slice

---

[49] This renders the exercise hypothetical as no agreements are being cited or examined to establish the conditionality necessary to trigger an ORRC or SAT issue. It is acknowledged that in the absence of some trade conditionality there would be no issue for Art. XXIV provisions.

[50] For complementing multilateral trade, *see*, for example, W. Ethier, 'Regionalism in a Multilateral World' (1998) 106 J Pol Econ 1214. The Global Economic Prospects 2005 Report seems more tentative on whether some regulatory areas are so positive for economic development considerations.

[51] P. Sutherland et al., *The Future of the WTO: Addressing Institutional Challenges in the New Millennium* (Geneva: WTO, 2004), 83, para 87.

[52] WTO Secretariat, *Seminar on Regional Trade Agreements: Regional Trade Integration under Transformation* (WTO Trade Policies Review Division, 2003).

the regulatory cake. The 'WTO plus' concept can refer to supplementing an existing WTO regime (or provision) or to incorporating areas not covered by WTO Agreements at all. Either way, as with the term 'deep integration', it is less illuminating when it fails to delineate the potential for trade restrictiveness that could occur as a result of the new regulatory regional norm. For one example, WTO Members have a right provided by Article 2.4 TBT to rely upon international product standards for their traded goods. If regional members establish a set of product standards that are 'more strict' (higher) than the applicable international standard, this action could certainly be claimed to be 'WTO plus' since 'higher' standards are established. However, the result upon trade between the regional members could be more restrictive as a result and in this particular example, less favourable to the trade of a regional member than to other WTO Members who have a continuing WTO right to rely on the international standard.

Although the resulting 'restrictiveness' of a regulatory norm moves closer to the legal test to be applied for ORRC, it is also not an entirely clear basis for categorizing measures. As noted above, a more trade restrictive regulation may eliminate non-conforming regional trade, but it can also go on to raise a new level of market confidence so that the remaining regional trade is increased and a higher value-added trade results overall. For example, the incorporation of a labour standard as a condition to a free trade agreement can easily be characterized as a potentially trade restrictive measure, if the regional members agreed that importation barriers could result as a failure of that regulatory norm. At the same time, consumers' appetite for purchasing 'non-conforming' traded products may be so low within a regional member's market so as to prefer no free trade agreement in the absence of the regional labour standard. In this context, one cannot really say whether the imposed regulatory standard is more or less trade restrictive in the abstract.

This is one of the risks presented by applying conditionality in preferential trade agreements where new regulatory baselines are configured by regional parties. Detached as they may be from general MFN treatment, they lose an anchoring point of reference to determine whether these members are engaging in trade liberalization for Article XXIV internal requirements, or rather establishing for internal trade discrimination intended to trigger sector exclusions from their free trade commitments. No easy model emerges to assist in characterizing regulatory conditions, at least not in the legal sense in relating internal regulatory conditions to the ORRC requirements of paragraph 8.

B. Test based upon the resulting measure

The approach here is not to examine the validity of the regulatory objective, but to focus on the resulting trade measure undertaken if and when a regulatory norm is unfulfilled by a regional party. In other words, asking what type of measure, if any, will be applied in the event of non-compliance. More specifically, is this resulting measure an ORRC with qualification implications for the RTA? Where there is no linkage (no conditionality that can affect the trade whatsoever) then for Article XXIV purposes there would not seem to be any legal issue raised at all. An ORRC question is also avoided where the outcome is 'internal' in its mechanism and applied on non-discriminatory basis, within the meaning of national treatment. We have already examined why a non-discriminatory application of an internal regulation is not an ORRC. The outcome of a breached regulatory norm would be an imposition of a new ORRC if it was internal but discriminatorily applied between regional members, or was taken in the form of a restriction upon importation within the meaning of Article XI GATT.

This summation is only a starting point to determining how regulatory conditions (not regulatory objectives) may be treated within the Article XXIV qualification requirements. It is an attempt to characterize them according to their GATT law application, primarily between Article III GATT types of measures and Article XI GATT types of measures.

Before discussing these aspects, there are other short caveats that are raised on the subject of intra-regional regulatory restrictiveness. One is the point made in section I concerning the form of a provision where this may allow the 'introduction' of new restrictions after implementation of the formation. The Article XXIV text refers to elimination of ORRCs and this could be limited (certainly in the context of a submitted plan and schedule) to those measures only in existence at the time of notification or implementation. On the other hand, any value of a requirement to eliminate existing ORRCs in the first place is certainly undermined if members can re-introduce them all later via conditionality requirements.

Assume, for sake of example, that a regional partner's export trade to the other consists 90 per cent in the textile sector. A regulatory condition based on labour's right to organize in that sector becomes unfulfilled. The other partner imposes a prohibition upon the importation of textiles as a result. The balance of the trade (10 per cent) will continue to exchange at a zero-tariff rate. Irrespective of whether the regulatory objective is deemed valid or consensual between the regional members, if RTAs can make use of conditions 'subsequent' that link to trade restrictions, then there has to be a risk that RTAs will be designed to eliminate sensitive sectors under the guise of regulatory objectives. If there is no *ex post* control over RTAs in the review mechanism, then only the potential for third-party dispute settlement would seem to pose a remedy for affected WTO Members.

Another consideration is raised if the measure does not terminate the trade but rather returns it to a conventional (MFN) level, as in re-imposing the duty that would otherwise apply between the WTO Members. As with the safeguards example, a few RTAs do actually make reference to the underlying conventional rate as a remedy of first choice. This appears to be a far more enlightened approach from a WTO systemic view since the regional regime is preserving an underlying WTO right between the regional members. However, this may not totally vindicate the measure from 'disqualifying' the RTA according to paragraph 8 requirements. Where the result of the failed norm (or the safeguard if you choose) is a tariff duty, the obligation still remains to eliminate duties in respect of substantially all the trade. Some re-imposition is permitted but SAT still controls.[53]

Both of the examples above are identical to the results possible with the use of a regional safeguard clause, which is not servicing a regulatory objective but functions as a contingent trade measure employable according to an injury or threat of injury to domestic producers. This indicates that the subject matter of the regulatory endeavour being entertained, while perhaps very important economically, politically or socially, is quite irrelevant for the qualification requirements of a RTA. A measure imposed between regional members is either a duty or an ORRC, or it is not.

A third possibility is also noted where an entire agreement is conditioned upon certain behaviours of the regional members. This may not pose any issues for ORRC since an agreement completely terminated does not affect the WTO rights of the regional members or any of the other WTO Members. Regional members can terminate their trade agreements at will and according to their own agreed terms, and Article XXIV does not have anything to say about that.

C. Resulting importation restrictions

Since some resulting restrictions might constitute barriers upon importation, we first examine the application of Article XI GATT generally regarding *inter se* restrictive agreements, and then within the sphere of ORRC.

1. *General* inter se *restrictions in GATT law*

Pauwelyn offers the view that the GATT is a collective of bilateral relationships whereby *inter se* arrangements between subsets of members are only proscribed for 'liberalizing' activities, since these are the ones that directly affect third party rights by denying MFN. As such,

The WTO treaty is silent on inter se agreements that limit trade between some WTO Members only, for example, in order to protect cultural diversity, human rights or ethical standards in a way not permitted under normal WTO exceptions such as GATT Art. XX . . . WTO Members could agree that in the event either one breaches certain human rights or labour standards, the other can impose an import restriction to certain goods originating in the first state (and this is the case even if such restriction is otherwise inconsistent with WTO rules).[54]

---

[53] It might well be that this type of resulting measure if installed for all safeguards and regulatory conditions would be far easier to monitor *ex post* for the amount of trade covered by the elimination requirements.

[54] J. Pauwelyn, 'A Typology of Multilateral Treaty Obligations. Are WTO Obligations Bilateral or Collective in Nature?' (2003) 14 EJIL 907, at 947–48.

The same author goes on to qualify this right of restrictive *inter se* in those cases where such a restrictive agreement is outright prohibited by the WTO law. The example Pauwelyn offers is that of a voluntary export restraint (VER) agreement which is expressly contrary to Article 11 of the Safeguards Agreement. This is in contrast with those modifications that simply 'contradict' WTO rules.[55]

It would seem that many *inter se* restrictions might fall within the scope of what Article XI GATT prohibits: importation and exportation restrictions made effective other than by duties, taxes or other charges. This is also a general and quite unconditionally stated prohibition. However, unlike Article 11 SGA, it does not address the legality of *inter se* agreements among subsets of parties seeking to impose the restriction.[56] The question of whether a voluntary *inter se* restriction might fall somehow within the Article XI general prohibition has been a part of the GATT law dynamic since the earliest years,[57] but probably most pronounced in the intensive bilateral voluntary restraint era of the 1960s and 1970s.[58]

If we take Pauwelyn's characterization as a correct summation of treaty law with respect to *inter se* among WTO Members generally, then we could conclude that bilateral agreements to adopt quantitative restrictions (for cultural diversity, human rights or ethical standards) would be WTO lawful, except for those undertaken as voluntary export restraints within the meaning of Article 11 SGA or where otherwise prohibited in the Annex 1A agreements. Although this begs the question of why the objective of the measure, or the absence of any objective, should have any bearing on the legality of a bilateral restriction, it nevertheless raises the proper characterization to determine if

---

[55] J. Pauwelyn, 'How to Win a World Trade Organization Dispute Based on Non-World Trade Organization Law?' (2003) 37 JWT 997, fn 23, at 1004. An example of 'contradicting' given is the waiver of appeal rights under Art. 17 DSU as a part of a settlement, or an agreement permitting restrictions other than those listed according to Art. XX GATT. The former agreement (the VER) is 'illegal' since Art. 41(1)(b) VCLT does not permit a modification if 'prohibited' by the WTO treaty. The latter examples contradict (conflict) but are legal and then the question is, which rule prevails?

[56] Art. XIII GATT does expressly state an MFN obligation, but we pass for the purpose of this argument on whether that obligation might also control the members' right of *inter se* arrangements.

[57] The US Tariff Commission's opinion for Congress on the Havana Charter in respect of necessary changes to US trade laws, was that *bilateral* (but non-reciprocal) and *voluntary* quota agreements in the trade agreements' programme would have to be terminated by the US upon entry of the ITO, or the parties would have to apply for an ITO waiver. The example given was the Philippines Agreement (1946), where quotas were maintained against that country not otherwise generally applied: US Tariff Commission (1949).

[58] There has never been consensus in GATT law practice that restrictive *inter se* for quantitative restrictions was lawful, and many considered the practice at least voidable by action of the Contracting Parties. The commonly located expression was to note that no third party would ever likely bother with a complaint. For one characterization, *see* R. Hudec, *The GATT Legal System and World Trade Diplomacy* (Salem: Butterworth, 1990), 232, for his opinion on the 'GATT legality' of US endeavours to enlist and subscribe special arrangements for sensitive sectors among GATT party subsets.

this same open field for *inter se* is available for regional members, and in the same manner.

2. *Importation measures as ORRC*

Is it then possible that regional parties also have a free right of *inter se* for introducing new restrictions upon their bilateral trade resulting from a failure to comply with regulatory norms that they have chosen to set into their RTAs? The resulting restrictions could obviously include those that fall within the meaning of Article XI GATT. On Pauwelyn's analysis, there could be an argument for consistency where what is generally permissible in respect of Article XI GATT as free *inter se* between WTO Members should also be permissible as between regional members.

However, this result might also contradict a clear Article XXIV obligation for regional members to eliminate ORRC, as this term certainly includes importation restrictions in the form of quotas within its meaning.[59] The paragraph 8 text refers specifically to Article XI-XV measures as types of ORRCs ('. . . except where necessary *those* . . .'). Neither the right to conclude *inter se* agreements suggested above, nor the Article XI prohibition is in any way 'value sensitive' in permitting restrictions for some regulatory purposes but not for others. Thus, from a 'rules perspective', any restrictions of an Article XI character adopted or imposed by regional members would appear to be permissible only insofar as they cumulatively (with other ORRCs) eliminate only that insubstantial part of the trade that is not substantially all the trade (SAT). The SAT criterion is nullified if regional members can introduce importation restrictions on the same criteria that Pauwelyn finds controlling *inter se* generally in the GATT Agreement.

This view is not inconsistent with Pauwelyn's. Like Article 11 SGA, paragraph 8 of Article XXIV is also stating an obligation for members (seeking a regional exception) to avoid certain types of measures, essentially 'prohibiting' regional trade restrictions. Arguably the obligation to eliminate ORRC with respect to SAT is in the same legal position (illegal rather than contradicting) as is the prohibition on voluntary export restraint arrangements.

One difficult category of regulatory conditions that might result in importation restrictions within the meaning of ORRC are those that are drawn upon production-process methods (PPM), also including labour conditions. GATT law has only tentatively considered that these measures are not placed upon 'products as such,' and has characterized them on one (unreported panel) occasion as falling within the scope of Article XI GATT.[60] While Article III

---

[59] Subject to the author's continuing caveat that the obligation to eliminate also contemplates an obligation to not re-introduce or introduce anew.

[60] The unadopted but BISD reported GATT era, *US—Tuna Dolphin I* Panel treated a product distinction based on harvesting techniques as measures not being applied to 'products as such' within the meaning of either Art. III or the Note Ad Art. III. The measure therefore fell within Art. XI GATT: WTO Panel Report, *US—Tuna Dolphin I*, DS21/R, 3 September 1991, unadopted, BISD 39S/155, paras 5.11 and 5.18.

GATT Appellate Body reports (*Japan—Alcoholic Beverages II, EC—Asbestos*) have developed some concepts of like-product analysis that appear to allow some internal distinctions on the basis of production process methods (consumer taste and habits, for example), there also remains strong WTO Member sentiment on both sides of this characterization issue. For the purposes of ORRC, if these measures are importation restrictions and not internal regulatory enactments, then this entire arena of conditionality becomes 'off limits' for RTA members where ORRC includes a duty to eliminate quantitative restrictions.

While this discussion is not intended at all to resolve PPM characterization issues in GATT law, what is raised for interest is the possibility that regional members might choose to agree upon a stated interpretation of PPM characterization for the purpose of their regulatory undertakings. This could entail a declaratory statement indicating that all regulatory conditions imposed in their agreement shall be deemed to be internal regulatory measures and not falling within the province of Article XI GATT importation restrictions. While this would be a controversial provision, it would also be explicit in denoting the possible GATT rights being foregone by parties entering a RTA. This raises the question of whether the qualification of the agreement according to ORRC would have to yield to this modification. A tentative response is that ORRC is adjudged by objective criterion established by WTO law and the parties do not have a free right of *inter se* to modify it.

D. Inter se regulatory restrictions

Many restrictive measures enacted will not present an Article XI problem and will remain internal in the sense of Article III, together with Note Ad Article III.[61] This is the case for the types of control measures relating to 'marketability' such as those applied for product and food standards, at least for those that are descriptive of product characteristics, including labelling and additives. When the resulting restrictive measures are internal within the scope of Article III:4, then they also do not fall within ORRC when they are equally (non-discriminatorily) applied and an equivalent competitive opportunity is preserved between the regional members' like products. While less trade may result, the internal and non-discriminatory nature of the regulatory measures renders them outside of the ORRC category as defined in this discussion. Within the requirement of non-discrimination in the treatment accorded to the regional members, it appears that for measures that are wholly

---

[61] Note Ad Art. III says, 'Any internal tax or other internal charge, or any law, regulation or requirement of the kind referred to in paragraph 1 which applies to an imported product and to the like domestic product and is collected or enforced in the case of the imported product at the time or point of importation, is nevertheless to be regarded as an internal tax or other internal charge, or a law, regulation or requirement of the kind referred to in paragraph 1, and is accordingly subject to the provisions of Article III'.

internal, regional members are free to set their higher (or more strict) standards even where lower levels of trade would result. In this case, the measures are permissible according to the rules of the game for ORRC defined here, since they are not ORRC.

However, there is a resulting change of position between regional members and WTO Members when the RTA adopts a higher regulatory standard that was not applied to other WTO Members. The example noted was the inclusion of product technical requirement in an RTA set at a level 'higher than' an applicable international product standard. This would be a bilateral modification of a TBT Agreement provision (Article 2.4 TBT) and a suspension of the MFN rights accorded to WTO Members both in the TBT Agreement (Article 2.1 TBT), as well as Article I GATT MFN, as this applies to matters falling within paragraph 4 of Article III GATT.

This type of modification is not controlled by Article XXIV terms when the restriction does not fall either within the definition of duties or of ORRC. The question raised is whether there is any WTO legal basis to draw upon as a source for the protection of these underlying WTO rights. One reference is located in the preamble of the Uruguay Round Understanding on Article XXIV. That is, the objectives are best met when no major sector is excluded and that elimination of ORRC occurs for all of the trade. However here, ORRC does not appear to apply.

E. Restrictive regional conditions in VCLT analysis

An additional framework for analysis is provided by the Vienna Convention on the Law of Treaties (VCLT), specifically Article 41 governing modifications of multilateral treaties. This author has taken the view that Article XXIV functions in the GATT regime as a modification provision setting out the terms and conditions for allowable preferential deviations among WTO Members.[62] Others may differ on this point, and some have asserted a general position that rights and obligations among regional members are freely able to be varied between them as long as third-party rights are not affected.[63] This directly invokes the sentiment of Article 41(1)(b) VCLT, which is applicable in those cases where a multilateral agreement does not prohibit modifications. However, if one is going to invoke the VCLT modification Article as having a possible bearing on RTAs formed between subsets of WTO Members, then the first paragraph of Article 41(1)(a) VCLT should also be considered for its potential application. This subparagraph applies in the *alternative* case where 'the possibility of such a modification is provided for by the treaty'. In this case, the multilateral treaty terms themselves control the members'

---

[62] Mathis, above at n 6, at 265–85.

[63] For example, an EC submission to the Committee on RTAs stated that regional members may freely vary their rights and obligations as between them in the absence of any injury to third parties. WTO Doc. WT/REG/M/14, 24 November 1997, para. 13.

rights to modify, and the more open expression of modification contained in Article 41(1)(b) does not apply.

For Article XXIV GATT, only free trade area agreements and customs unions can be established for the purpose expressed by paragraph 4, governed by the definitional provisions of paragraph 8, and then subject to the institutional notification and control provisions of paragraphs 7, 10, and 12, and finally according to the implementation rules of paragraphs 5 and 6. This regime is established to provide a means for modifying the MFN rights that would otherwise be generally accorded to all WTO Members, and to do so in a manner that will derive a recognized (defensible) exception from the other GATT obligations. In this regime there are requirements stated for internal liberalization by regional members seeking to come under the Article XXIV exception. While the purpose of these provisions is to clearly insure that regional members do not raise new barriers to the trade of non-members, it is also the purpose of the regime to insure that regional members undertake meaningful trade liberalization in a RTA. Thus, the VCLT question for Article XXIV as a modification provision within the GATT is whether this Article is intended to be the exclusive means for regulating reciprocal preferential systems among subsets of members. If it is not so intended, then one asks why the Article regime was drafted and included in the GATT Agreement at all. If it is so intended, then Article 41(1)(a) VCLT is the only relevant VCLT reference for WTO Member preferential modifications.

Drawing Article 41(1)(a) VCLT into the analysis reinforces the application of Article XXIV GATT and establishes a basis for arguing that there is a hierarchy (as contrasted with Article 41(1)(b) VCLT) for the definitional and implementation components expressed within the Article's provisions. From our narrow interpretation of ORRC, this hierarchy controls later modifications for intra-regional importation barriers and for internally discriminatory measures. It does not however include the field of non-discriminatory regulatory restrictions even though a suspension of a regional member's underlying rights to receive most favoured nation treatment may result. As it stands, the determination of these modifications remain within the province of the regional members themselves.

Depending upon one's view of the advisability of including such regulatory restrictions in RTAs, there is either no need for additional action, or there is a need for clarification and/or further understanding regarding the role of regulatory regimes in RTAs. A point for consideration is whether there should be an express understanding by all the WTO Members affirming the underlying WTO rights of members to a RTA. This could take the form of an additional preamble expression within an Understanding stating that the benefits of regional integration are best realized and rendered most complementary to the multilateral trading system when the WTO rights of all members, including regional members, are sought to be preserved.

IV. CONCLUSION

The issue of trade restrictiveness within RTAs is not new, but it has moved from the realm of residual and contingent border measures to the regulatory area (as it has within the broader WTO context). The members have pledged to clarify the terms of Article XXIV in the Doha Round. There has been evident progress in the discussions to date, notably in promoting transparency in RTAs and also in proposals to define by agreement the elements of the SAT requirement. ORRC is also on the list for consideration, but further down the sequence, and it is possible that ORRC may not receive clarification prior to a final outcome. This may not be for worse. There is a certain hazard in opening this term in the current environment of regional proliferation. There is also the possibility that if the members can evolve some criterion for 'substantially-all trade', that some of the issues raised above for ORRC could dissolve in actual practice. More likely, there will remain a need to clarify the manner by which regional members do or do not continue to receive the benefit of their WTO rights in an RTA. Where many agreements are now concluded between developed and developing members and include regulatory commitments, this need for clarification is not on the wane. Thus far there are few citable examples in RTAs of trade restrictions being effected as a result of regulatory non-compliance. In this sense some of the questions raised in this chapter are, for now, theoretical. However, the RTA world is dynamic and where there may be evolution to stronger institutional and dispute settlement mechanisms within RTAs, then trade restrictive outcomes could be expected to follow.

5

Mandatory Abolition of Anti-dumping, Countervailing Duties and Safeguards in Customs Unions and Free Trade Areas Constituted between WTO Members: Revisiting a Long-standing Discussion in Light of the Appellate Body's Turkey—Textiles Ruling

ANGELA T. GOBBI ESTRELLA AND
GARY N. HORLICK[*]

I. INTRODUCTION

Article XXIV of the General Agreement on Tariffs and Trade (GATT) establishes an exception to GATT obligations (particularly to the obligation to provide all the parties to the Agreement with Most Favoured Nation treatment—MFN)[1] for customs unions and free trade areas (FTAs) constituted between Members of the World Trade Organization—WTO.[2] The availability

---

[*] The views expressed here are those of the authors in their personal capacity and not necessarily those of the entities with which they are affiliated.

[1] The MFN obligation (that is, providing all the Parties to the GATT with the same trade preferences) is set forth in Art. I of the GATT, and is a cornerstone of the multilateral trading system.

[2] Art. XXIV:5 GATT states: '[T]he provisions of this Agreement shall not prevent, as between the territories of the Contracting Parties, the formation of a customs union or of a free-trade area or the adoption of an interim agreement necessary for the formation of a customs union or of a free-trade area;'

of this exception is *conditioned* to the meeting of certain requirements set forth in paragraphs 5 to 9 of Article XXIV regarding the level of trade liberalization that shall be maintained in the external trade of the parties to these arrangements, and accomplished in the internal trade between them.[3]

The level of internal trade liberalization required in a regional trade agreement (RTA)[4] for it to qualify as a customs union or a FTA is set forth in Article XXIV:8(a)(i) and (b) of the GATT, and is virtually the same for both types of trade arrangements.[5] Subparagraph 8(a)(i) defines a customs union as the substitution of a single customs territory for two or more customs territories so that:

duties and other restrictive regulations of commerce (except, where necessary, those permitted under Articles XI, XII, XIII, XIV, XV and XX) are eliminated with respect to substantially all the trade between the constituent territories of the union or at least with respect to substantially all the trade in products originating in such territories . . .

Subparagraph (b) defines a FTA as a group of two or more customs territories in which

the duties and other restrictive regulations of commerce (except, where necessary, those permitted under Articles XI, XII, XIII, XIV, XV and XX) are eliminated with respect to substantially all the trade between the constituent territories in products originating in such territories.

Thus, for a RTA to benefit from the exception authorized in Article XXIV of the GATT its level of internal trade liberalization must be such that duties and other restrictive regulations of commerce are eliminated with respect to substantially all the trade (SAT) between the parties to these arrangements. The trade restrictions permitted under Articles XI, XII, XIII, XIV, XV and XX of the GATT are expressly listed as excepted from this rule. The listing does not mention 'trade remedies': Article VI which regulates the imposition of anti-dumping and countervailing duties, or Article XIX of the GATT, which governs application of safeguards.

---

[3] Right after the sentence establishing that the provisions of the GATT shall not prevent the formation of a customs union or a FTA (*see* the text quoted, *ibid.*), a second phrase in Art. XXIV:5 adds '*Provided* that:' From there on are set forth the requirements that a preferential trade arrangement between WTO Members must meet to be allowed to benefit from the exception established in Art. XXIV GATT. *See* J.H. Jackson, *The World Trade and the Law of the GATT: A Legal Analysis of the General Agreement on Tariffs and Trade* (Indianapolis: Bobbs-Merrill, 1969), 575–76, 581–85.

[4] The term 'Regional Trade Agreement—RTA' has been used to identify preferential trade arrangements in general, particularly those allegedly qualifying as customs unions or FTAs. *See* WTO, Trade Topics, Regional Trade Agreements: Scope of RTAs, available at www.wto.org/ english/tratop_e/region_e/scope_rta_e.htm (visited 10 April 2006).

[5] Art. XXIV:8 GATT establishes the definition of customs union and FTA, that is, what kind of regional trade agreement (RTA) *qualifies* as a custom union or as a FTA for the purposes of the Agreement. In both cases, the definition encompasses the level of trade liberalization that shall be accomplished in the RTA internal trade, and, in the case of customs unions, also the level of harmonization that shall be accomplished in the duties and regulations applied by its members in the trade with third parties.

The absence of Articles VI and XIX of the GATT in the exceptions list in Article XXIV:8 has raised the question of whether this provision mandates or allows abolition of trade remedies within customs unions and FTAs since early reviews of RTAs under the GATT.[6] No consensus has ever been reached on the subject,[7] nor a definite clarification provided specifically on the matter by the multilateral trading system dispute settlement mechanism.[8] Nonetheless, a

[6] *See* WTO Negotiating Group on Rules, Compendium of Issues Related to Regional Trade Agreements—Background Note by the Secretariat, WTO Doc. TN/RL/W/8/Rev.1, 1 August 2002, at paras 73–5. Discussions often centred on safeguards, although the same issue applies to anti-dumping and countervailing duties. *See* R. Hudec and J.D. Southwick, 'Regionalism and WTO Rules', in M. Rodríguez Mendoza, P. Low, and B. Kotschwar (eds), *Trade Rules in the Making: Challenges in Regional and Multilateral Negotiations* (Washington, DC; OAS: Brookings, 1999), 47, 67–71.

> The issue of how to deal with safeguards in a RTA arose in several working party reviews of RTAs before the Uruguay Round. Members of the working parties objected to RTAs in which the members exempted each other from the application of safeguards. Parties to RTAs have defended exemption of their RTA partners from safeguards on the grounds that Article XIX is not in the list of exceptions to the 'substantially all trade' rule, and therefore the 'substantially all trade' rule permits or indeed requires RTA members to exclude each other from the application of safeguards restrictions.
>
> . . .
>
> As with the absence of Article XIX, the absence of Article VI from the list of exceptions to the 'substantially all trade' rule could be read to suggest that members of an RTA may not apply Article VI measures to each other. (Citations omitted).

[7] *See* WTO Panel Report, *Argentina—Footwear (EC)*, WT/DS121/R, adopted 12 January 2000, as modified by the Appellate Body Report, WT/DS121/AB/R, para. 8.96, where the Panel notes that:

> Practice of the Contracting Parties to the GATT of 1947 and of WTO Members is inconclusive on the issue of imposition or maintenance of safeguard measures between the constituent territories of a customs union [or] of a free-trade area. It is a matter of fact that many agreements establishing free-trade areas or customs unions allow for the possibility to impose safeguard measures on intra-regional trade, while few regional integration agreements explicitly prohibit the imposition of intra-regional safeguard measures once the formation of such an integration area is completed.

See also WTO Negotiating Group on Rules, Compendium of Issues Related to Regional Trade Agreements—Background Note by the Secretariat (Revision), *ibid.*

[8] No ruling on the matter of application of trade remedies within customs unions and FTAs has ever been issued under the GATT, and the two only WTO Panel rulings on the issue were reversed and declared as having no legal effect by the Appellate Body. *See* WTO Negotiating Group on Rules, Compendium of Issues Related to Regional Trade Agreements—Background Note by the Secretariat (Revision), *ibid.*, at paras 76–7. Contrast M. Matsushita, T.J. Schoenbaum, and P.C. Mavroidis, *The World Trade Organization: Law, Practice and Policy* (Oxford: OUP, 2003), 362–63 who state that the WTO Appellate Body rulings in the discriminatory safeguard cases 'answer[ed] the question of whether the items figuring in the parenthesis of GATT Article XXIV:8 form an exhaustive list'. (The discriminatory safeguard cases are a series of disputes brought to the WTO dispute settlement system where a WTO Member that was party to a RTA applied a safeguard measure, and excluded imports originating in their RTA partners from the scope of the safeguard. The discriminatory safeguard cases brought so far to the WTO dispute settlement system are: *Argentina—Footwear (EC)*, *ibid.*, *US—Wheat Gluten*, WT/DS166, adopted 19 January 2001, *US—Lamb*, WT/DS177 and DS/178, adopted 16 May 2001, *US—Line Pipe*, WT/DS202, adopted 8 March 2002 and *US—Steel Safeguards*, WT/DS248, adopted 10 December 2003). According to Matsushita, Schoenbaum and Mavroidis '[o]n every occasion [in the discriminatory safeguard cases], the WTO adjudicating bodies held that parties to a PTA may impose safeguards against other parties to the PTA.' *See ibid.*, at 363. This assertion overstates the

couple of statements on Article XXIV:8 of the GATT in the WTO Appellate Body's *Turkey—Textiles* ruling,[9] which have passed mostly unnoticed so far, shed bright new light on the issue of application of trade remedies in customs unions and FTAs.[10]

In *Turkey—Textiles* the Appellate Body made its first (and only, as of the date this chapter is being written) excursion into the controversial interpretative issues involving the provisions governing customs unions and FTAs in Article XXIV of GATT, setting out of a framework for assessing the availability of a defence based on Article XXIV of the GATT.[11] Within that ruling it also made noteworthy remarks which provide meaningful guidance on whether Article XXIV:8 shall be interpreted as mandating or allowing elimination of trade remedies in RTAs.

First, the Appellate Body resolved in *Turkey—Textiles* the long lasting debate on the optional or mandatory nature of the list of exceptions in Article XXIV:8. This controversy centered on whether the exceptions listing provides for an *option* for parties to a RTA to maintain restrictions in their internal trade in certain fields, or rather establishes an *obligation* for those parties to maintain MFN treatment in the referred fields (i.e. maintaining the applicability of the

---

discriminatory safeguard rulings. The Appellate Body decisions in those cases merely interpreted and applied the provisions in the Agreement on Safeguards, whose Art. 2.2 expressly states that 'Safeguard measures shall be *applied* to *a product being imported irrespective of its source.*' (Italics added). It was on the basis of this express commandment on MFN application of safeguards that the Appellate Body held that the measures at stake in the discriminatory safeguard cases *had to* (rather than might) be applied to products from all sources, including those imported from the defendants' RTA partners. *See* e.g. WTO Appellate Body Report, *Argentina—Footwear (EC)*, WT/DS121/AB/R, adopted 12 January 2000, para. 112, where the Appellate Body stated: 'Argentina was ... *required under Article 2.2* to apply [safeguard] measures to imports from all sources, including from other Mercosur member States.' (italics added). The issue of Art. XXIV of the GATT (which could arguably provide a *defense* to justify a violation of Art. 2.2 SGA) was never addressed by the Appellate Body in the discriminatory safeguard cases. The Appellate Body has repeatedly refused to examine such matter on the grounds that it would only be relevant where a requirement of parallelism between the scope of the injury determination and the scope of application of the safeguard had been met (which the Appellate Body did not find to occur in any of the discriminatory safeguard cases). *See* WTO Appellate Body Report, *Argentina—Footwear (EC)*, paras 111–13, WTO Appellate Body Report, *US—Wheat Gluten*, paras 93–9, WTO Appellate Body Report, *US—Line Pipe*, paras 178–99, and WTO Appellate Body Report, *US— Steel Safeguards*, paras 433–74. For a further discussion on the relationship between parallelism and the discriminatory safeguard cases, *see* J. Pauwelyn, 'The Puzzle of WTO Safeguards and Regional Trade Agreements' (2004) 7 JIEL 109, at 119–24.

[9] WTO Appellate Body Report, *Turkey—Textiles*, WT/DS34/AB/R, adopted 19 November 1999.

[10] The regional arrangement at stake in *Turkey—Textiles* was an alleged customs union between Turkey and the European Community (EC); hence, the Appellate Body ruled there on sub-paragraph 8(a)(i) of Art. XXIV of the GATT, which sets forth the definitional requirements for a customs union, and did not address sub-paragraph 8(b), which establishes the definitional requirement for a FTA. Still, given that the wording of both provisions is virtually the same as regards the internal trade requirement, this chapter assumes that the guidance provided in the Appellate Body's *Turkey—Textiles* ruling informs the interpretation of Art. XXIV:8 with regard to both customs unions and FTAs.

[11] *See* WTO Appellate Body Report, *Turkey—Textiles*, above at n 9, at paras 58–9. *See also* WTO Analytical Index, available at www.wto.org/english/res_e/booksp_e/analytic_index_e/gatt1994_09_e.htm#articleXXIVD (visited 10 April 2006), para. 595.

trade restrictive measures in the listing also in the intra-RTA trade).[12] The Appellate Body did not discuss the issue in detail, but endorsed the first interpretation in its ruling, where it stated: 'We note . . . that the terms of subparagraph 8(a)(i) provide that members of a customs union *may* maintain, where necessary, in their internal trade, certain restrictive regulations of commerce that are otherwise permitted under Articles XI through XV and under Article XX of the GATT 1994'.[13]

Second, the above statement on the exceptions list referred to the trade restrictions that may be maintained in a customs union's internal trade as '*certain* restrictive regulations of commerce *that are otherwise permitted under Articles XI through XV and under Article XX*'.[14] This highlighting that it is permissible to maintain *certain* restrictions within a customs union, and the closed identification of such permissible restrictions with those governed by the provisions named in the exceptions list further suggests an exhaustive reading of the listing.[15]

Third, the Appellate Body identified both the permission to maintain the restrictions in the exceptions list, and the possibility to liberalize less than all the trade, and *thus* concluded that 'some flexibility' is afforded by the terms of Article XXIV:8 to the constituent members of a customs union when liberalizing their internal trade.[16] This reasoning suggests that the Appellate Body understands the leeway left to RTA parties when liberalizing their internal trade to subsume in what can be encompassed within the boundaries of one of those two identified mechanisms of flexibility. Moreover, the Appellate Body expressly *cautioned* that the degree of flexibility *allowed* by Article XXIV:8 is *limited* by the requirement that 'duties and other restrictive regulations of commerce' be 'eliminated with respect to substantially all' internal trade.[17] This warning further suggests that the Appellate Body would regard trade liberalization either falling short from *elimination* of duties and other restrictive regulations of commerce or encompassing a part of the RTA trade corres-

---

[12] *See* Hudec and Southwick, above at n 6, at 64.

[13] *See* WTO Appellate Body Report, *Turkey—Textiles*, above at n 9, at para. 48.   [14] *Ibid.*

[15] This point has been made recently by Lockhart and Mitchell. *See* N.J.S. Lockhart and A.D. Mitchell, 'Regional Trade Agreements under GATT 1994: An Exception and its Limits', in A.D. Mitchell, *Challenges and Prospects for the WTO* (London: Cameron May, 2005), 217, 239.

[16] *See* WTO Appellate Body Report, *Turkey—Textiles*, above at n 9, at para. 48 (italics added):

It is clear . . . that 'substantially all the trade' is not the same as 'all' the trade, and also that 'substantially all the trade' is something considerably more than merely 'some' of the trade. We note also that the terms of subparagraph 8(a)(i) provide that members of a customs union may maintain, where necessary, in their internal trade, certain restrictive regulations of commerce that are otherwise permitted under Articles XI through XV and under Article XX of the GATT 1994. *Thus*, we agree . . . that the terms of subparagraph 8(a)(i) offer 'some flexibility' to the constituent members of a customs union when liberalizing their internal trade in accordance with this sub-paragraph.

[17] *See* WTO Appellate Body Report, *Turkey—Textiles, ibid.*: 'Yet we caution that the degree of "flexibility" that the sub-paragraph 8(a)(i) allows is limited by the requirement that "duties and other restrictive regulations of commerce" be "eliminated with respect to substantially all" internal trade'.

ponding to less than 'substantially all' the trade as not meeting the internal trade requirement set forth in Article XXIV:8(a)(i) and (b).

The above statements lead to a construction of Article XXIV:8 of the GATT as *mandating* abolition of trade remedies as to the part of the trade within RTAs counting towards the fulfillment of the SAT threshold, and strongly indicate this to be the only way the text of that provision as currently written can be interpreted consistently with the Vienna Convention on the Law of the Treaties (VCLT).[18] The reasoning underlying this conclusion is developed in the following sections of this chapter, which revisit the controversies on the meaning of the relevant wording in Article XXIV:8 of the GATT in light of the *Turkey—Textiles* statements and applying the VCLT rules on treaty interpretation.

II. RELEVANT WORDING IN ARTICLE XXIV:8 INTERPRETED PURSUANT THE VCLT AND IN LIGHT OF THE APPELLATE BODY STATEMENTS IN *TURKEY—TEXTILES*

In the following sections, this chapter revisits the discussions on the meaning of relevant wording in Article XXIV:8 of the GATT in light of the Appellate Body statements in *Turkey—Textiles*. We first analyse the meaning of the expression 'duties and other restrictive regulations of commerce' and discuss whether it encompasses trade remedies—an issue not comprehended within the Appellate Body *Turkey—Textiles* ruling, but key to proceeding any further on a discussion on applicability of trade remedies in RTAs on the basis of Article XXIV:8 of the GATT. The authors argue that trade remedies are not comprehended within the meaning of 'duties' in Article XXIV:8, taking into account the text of the French and Spanish versions of the GATT, which indicate that the term 'duties' in this provision refers to customs duties only. Nonetheless, the authors conclude that trade remedies are encompassed within the meaning of 'other restrictive regulations of commerce' in Article XXIV:8. This conclusion relies on the wording on 'other restrictive regulations of commerce' informed by the wording on 'other regulations of commerce' in Article XXIV of the GATT and in the Understanding on Application of Article XXIV of the GATT, as well as on an analysis of the scope of the provisions in the exceptions list in Article XXIV:8.

The second section identifies the three distinct interpretations that have

---

[18] *See* Art. 31(1) Vienna Convention on the Law of Treaties, in force 27 January 1980, 1155 UNTS 331, which has been deemed to incorporate the customary rules of interpretation of public international law referred to in Art. 3.2 of the Dispute Settlement Understanding. See WTO Appellate Body Report, *Japan—Alcoholic Beverages II*, WT/DS8/AB/R, WT/DS/10/R, WT/DS/11/AB/R, adopted 1 November 1996, p. 10. *See also* WTO Appellate Body Report, *US—Gasoline*, WT/DS2/AB/R, adopted 20 May 1996, p. 23: '[o]ne of the corollaries of the general rule of interpretation in the *Vienna Convention* is that interpretation must give *meaning* and *effect* to *all* the *terms* of the treaty' (italics added).

been defended for the meaning of the rule on elimination of duties and other restrictive regulations of commerce (ORRC) and the list of exceptions to this rule, and their implications for the issue of abolition of trade remedies in customs unions and FTAs. The assumptions underlying each of these interpretations are discussed in light of the text of Article XXIV:8 and the Appellate Body's discarding of the 'must' interpretation of the exceptions list in *Turkey— Textiles*. The authors argue that only a 'must' interpretation of the listing would provide support for constructing Article XXIV:8 as *permitting* nonapplication of trade remedies within customs unions and FTAs without leaving the whole exceptions list meaningless. Hence the authors conclude that the Appellate Body's discarding of the 'must' interpretation in *Turkey— Textiles* confirms that the rule on elimination of duties and ORRC has to be interpreted as *mandating* abolition of trade remedies in customs unions and FTAs.

The third section further discusses the meaning of the phrase 'duties and other restrictive regulations of commerce . . . are eliminated with respect to substantially all the trade' in Article XXIV:8 of the GATT in light of the Appellate Body's finding that this provision expresses a requirement that limits the flexibility afforded to the parties to customs unions when liberalizing their internal trade. The authors argue that the *obligation* to '*eliminate*' duties and other restrictive regulations of commerce must be understood as requiring parties to customs unions and FTAs to *abolish* these trade restrictions on the part of their trade counting towards the fulfillment of the 'substantially all the trade' threshold. That is, the mere establishment of partial trade preferences, i.e. reduced duties or less restrictive regulations of commerce, or the simple nonapplication of duties and other restrictive regulations of commerce that are still in the books cannot be encompassed within the meaning of duties and restrictive regulations of commerce that 'are eliminated' in Article XXIV:8 of the GATT. In other words, the phrase 'duties and other restrictive regulations of commerce are eliminated with respect to SAT' means that *no duty and no other restrictive regulation of commerce can be applicable* in a part of the intra-RTA trade corresponding to substantially all the trade between the RTA parties. The authors find support for this understanding taking into account the ordinary meaning of the verb 'eliminate', and contrasting the wording used in Article XXIV:8(a)(i) and (b) of the GATT with that used in Article XXIV:8(a)(ii) of the GATT, as well as that used in Article V of the GATS.

The fourth section analyses the discussion on the exhaustive or illustrative character of the exceptions listing in Article XXIV:8 of the GATT, i.e. whether the Parties to RTAs aiming at qualifying as customs unions or FTAs would be allowed to maintain trade restrictions in their internal trade beyond those mentioned in the listing. The authors argue that the list of exceptions in Article XXIV:8 of the GATT must be understood as being exhaustive. We argue that a reading of the listing as merely illustrative does not find support in the text of Article XXIV:8 of the GATT, and would also leave the whole listing meaningless for allowing RTA parties to maintain whatever *sort* of trade restrictions they wish in their internal trade. We further argue that this interpretation is confirmed by the Appellate Body's statement on the exceptions' list in *Turkey—Textiles*. We then examine the drafting history of Article XXIV:8 of the GATT and discuss the argument that interpreting the exceptions listed in this provision as being exhaustive leads to a manifestly absurd result.[19] This argument is based on Article XXI of the GATT, which provides for an exception for security reasons that is the most broadly worded exception in the Agreement but is not included in the listing.[20] The authors review the drafting history of Article XXIV:8 of the GATT, which shows that there is a reasonable explanation for the non-inclusion of Article XXI in the exceptions listing, whereas there is no other reason, but a deliberate exclusion, for the provisions governing anti-dumping, countervailing duties and safeguards having been left out of the listing. Therefore, the authors conclude that the drafting history of Article XXIV:8 of the GATT confirms the interpretation that the exceptions listing is exhaustive. Accordingly, the authors also conclude that Article XXIV:8, interpreted in accordance with the ordinary meaning to be attributed to its terms, in light of GATT's object and purpose, mandates the *abolition* of trade remedies in 'substantially all the trade'[21] between the parties to customs unions and FTAs constituted between WTO Members.

The fifth section seeks to determine whether the interpretation that Article XXIV:8 mandates the *abolition* of anti-dumping, countervailing duties, and safeguards in substantially all the trade within customs unions and FTAs constituted between WTO Members is consistent with the context of GATT 1994, and the practice under the GATT and the WTO.[22] The authors argue that there are no decisions of the Contracting Parties on the matter of application of trade remedies in RTAs within the meaning of Article 1(b)(iv) of GATT 1994,[23] neither a consistent practice followed by the GATT Contracting Parties on Article XXIV:8 with regard to application of trade remedies in RTAs within the meaning of Article XVI:1 of the Agreement Establishing the World Trade Organization (WTO Agreement).[24] Yet, the authors recognize

[19] *See* Arts 31 and 32(b) VCLT.

[20] *See* Report of the Sub-group of the Committee on the European Economic Community (EEC), GATT Doc. L/778, adopted 29 November 1957, BISD 6S/70, 94, at para. 26, where the argument that the absence of Art. XXI in the exceptions list in Art. XXIV:8 demonstrates that the listing cannot be interpreted as being exhaustive was raised for the first time, within the examination of the consistency with Art. XXIV of the EEC Treaty provisions for the association of overseas territories.

[21] That is, the part of the intra-customs unions or intra-FTAs trade counting towards the fulfillment of the 'substantially all the trade' threshold.

[22] *See* Arts 31(1), (2), and (3)(b) VCLT.

[23] Art. 1(b)(iv) GATT 1994 states that decisions of the Contracting Parties to GATT 1947 make part of GATT 1994 ('The General Agreement on Tariffs and Trade 1994 ("GATT 1994") shall consist of . . . other decisions of the Contracting Parties to GATT 1947 . . .').

[24] Art. XVI:1 of the WTO Agreement provides that 'the WTO shall be guided by the decisions, procedures and customary practices followed by the Contracting Parties to GATT 1947 and the bodies established in the framework of GATT 1947'.

adopted Working Party reports on customs unions and FTAs as *decisions* of the Contracting Parties within the meaning of Article XVI:1 of the WTO Agreement, and, as such, an important part of GATT (and WTO) *acquis* that shall be taken into account to interpret Article XXIV:8 with regard to application of trade remedies in RTAs.[25] Nonetheless, the authors note that there is only one Working Party report where a RTA between GATT Parties was declared to be fully compatible with Article XXIV of the GATT,[26] and that report did not discuss or even note the issue of application of trade remedies to intra-RTA imports.[27] Therefore, the authors conclude that that Working Party report does not provide relevant guidance on the interpretation of Article XXIV:8 with regard to application of trade remedies in RTAs.

A. Meaning of 'Duties and Other Restrictive Regulations of Commerce'

The examination of the controversies on the meaning of the wording in Article XXIV:8 that is relevant for the issue of application of trade remedies in RTAs begins with the discussion of whether the expression 'duties and other restrictive regulations of commerce' in Article XXIV:8(a)(i) and (b) of the GATT (which describes the *types* of trade restrictions to be eliminated within a customs union or FTA)[28] encompasses anti-dumping, countervailing duties, and safeguards. The absence of Articles VI and XIX in the exceptions list in Article XXIV:8 has given rise to the general question of whether trade remedies should be considered as 'other restrictive regulations of commerce'— hence subject to the elimination rule—or not.[29] An answer in the negative would explain the absence of Articles VI and XIX in the exceptions listing on the basis that trade remedies are not comprehended within the trade restrictions whose elimination is required in Article XXIV:8. That is, if trade remedies are not encompassed within the meaning of 'duties and other restrictive regulations of commerce' their elimination in RTAs is neither required, nor allowed. This chapter argues though that trade remedies, while not falling within the meaning of 'duties', are within the meaning of 'other restrictive regulations of commerce' (ORRC) in Article XXIV:8(a)(i) and (b).

An argument that the term 'duties' in Article XXIV:8 encompasses trade

---

[25] *See* WTO Appellate Body Report, *Japan—Alcoholic Beverages II*, above at n 18, at 15.

[26] *See* WTO Committee on Regional Trade Agreements, Synopsis of 'Systemic' Issues Related to Regional Trade Agreements—Note by the Secretariat, WTO Doc. WT/REG/W/37, 2 March 2000, at para. 21. The RTA at stake in that case was an agreement notified as a customs union constituted between the Czech Republic and the Slovak Republic. *See* Working Party Report on the Agreement Establishing the Czech Republic-Slovak Republic Customs Union, L/7501, adopted 4 October 1994.

[27] *See* Working Party Report, *ibid.*, at 26.

[28] *See* J.H. Mathis, 'Regional Trade Agreements and Domestic Regulation, What Reach for "Other Restrictive Regulations of Commerce"?', in this volume, at 79. *See also* Lockhart and Mitchell, above at n 15, at 236.

[29] *See* WTO Negotiating Group on Rules, Compendium of Issues Related to Regional Trade Agreements—Background Note by the Secretariat (Revision), above at n 6, at para. 74.

remedies would be allowed based on the English version of the GATT, but does not find support in the French and Spanish versions of the Agreement. Anti-dumping and countervailing duties are described as 'duties' in Article VI of the GATT, as well as in the Agreement on Implementation of Article VI of the GATT 1994 (Antidumping Agreement) and in the Agreement on Subsidies and Countervailing Measures, and safeguard measures can be applied under the form of duties.[30] Therefore, it would be arguable that anti-dumping *duties* and countervailing *duties* are species comprehended within the broader genus 'duties' mentioned in Article XXIV:8. Yet, the French and the Spanish versions of Article XXIV:8 of the GATT use the terms 'droits de douane' and 'derechos de aduana', that is 'customs duties', as the equivalent to the term 'duties' used in the English version of the provision. The terms 'droits *de douane*' and 'derechos *de aduana*' obviously have a more specific meaning within which the terms 'droits anti-dumping' or 'derechos anti-dumping', and 'droits compensateurs' or 'derechos compensatorios' cannot be so easily encompassed.[31] Accordingly, given that all the versions of the Agreement are equally valid and have to be interpreted consistently, there is not support for the argument that 'duties' in the English version of Article XXIV:8 comprehends trade remedies. In contrast, the argument that trade remedies are within the meaning of 'other restrictive regulations of commerce' finds support in the text of Article XXIV:8(a)(i) and (b) of the GATT informed by the wording on 'other regulations of commerce' in paragraphs 5(a), (b) and 8(a)(ii) and by the Understanding on the Interpretation of Article XXIV of the GATT (Understanding on Article XXIV).

The wording on 'other regulations of commerce' (ORC) in paragraphs 5(a), (b) and 8(a)(ii) of Article XXIV coincides with that on 'other restrictive regulations of commerce' in paragraphs 8(a)(i) and (b), with the striking difference of the term 'restrictive', which qualifies the expression used in reference to the RTAs internal trade liberalization requirement. The coincident wording indicates that the measures referred to in Article XXIV:8(a)(i) and (b) are a subset of the regulations of commerce referred to in paragraphs 5(a), (b) and 8(a)(ii), distinguished by its restrictive nature, thus the meaning of ORC informs the meaning of ORRC. Hence the definition of ORC established in *Turkey—Textiles* (set out by the Panel and not rebutted by the Appellate Body) is relevant for defining ORRC. Referring to Article XXIV:5(a), the Panel stated there that

---

[30] *See* Lockhart and Mitchell, above at n 15, at 237–38.

[31] The difference in the terms used in the English version ('duties') and the French version ('droits de douane'—customs duties) of Art. XXIV:8 GATT was brought to light within a discussion on whether the requirement to eliminate 'duties' in Art. XXVI:8(a)(i) encompassed certain 'revenue duties' allegedly having a fiscal and non-discriminatory purpose (rather than a protective one), which members of certain RTAs constituted between the EC and third parties applied on imports from parties to the RTA. *See* GATT Doc. L/3665, adopted 29 May 1972, BISD 19S/90, 94, at para. 14. Of course, no conclusion was reached on the point. *See ibid.*

the ordinary meaning of the terms 'other regulations of commerce' could be understood to include *any regulation having an impact on trade* (such as measures in the fields covered by the WTO rules, e.g., sanitary and phytosanitary, customs valuation, anti-dumping, technical barriers to trade; as well as any other trade-related domestic regulation, e.g., environmental standards, export credit schemes).[32]

The *Turkey—Textiles* definition of ORC suggests the meaning of ORRC to encompass 'any regulation of commerce having a *restrictive* impact on trade'. That would comprehend either border measures, i.e. measures applied upon importation restricting the cross-border movement of goods, as marketplace regulations applied to imported products which adversely affect them as compared with domestic products in the sense of Article III of the GATT.[33] However, the definition of ORC set out by the *Turkey—Textiles* Panel seems to be excessively broad in scope in contrast with the text of Article XXIV:5(a) informed by the text of paragraphs 5(b) and 8(a)(ii), as well in the Understanding on Article XXIV, and the same is arguable with regard to ORRC and the text of Article XXIV:8(a)(i) and (b).

The chapeau of paragraph 8(a) uses the word 'customs', and paragraphs 5(a), (b) and 8(a)(ii) refer to regulations of commerce imposed (or applied) to 'the trade' (as opposed to 'the products' as in Article III of the GATT) of (or with) third parties. These terms suggests that the drafters intended the meaning of ORC to be of narrower scope, covering border measures only.[34] The requirement in the Understanding on Article XXIV that evaluation of ORC under Article XXIV:5(a) be made on the basis of 'import statistics' for goods originating in third countries (with no reference to statistics on exports to third countries)[35] further indicates that ORC refers to border measures on imports only.[36] As to ORRC, the text of Article XXIV:8(a)(i) and (b) also refers to elimination of duties and ORRC with respect to 'the trade' between the RTA parties, and the Understanding on Article XXIV refers to '*elimination between the constituent territories* of duties and other restrictive regulations of commerce'.[37] This equally suggests that the scope of ORRC in Article XXIV:8(a)(i) and (b) is limited to regulations that restrict the cross-border movement of goods between the RTA parties.[38] Moreover, a definition of

---

[32] *See* WTO Panel Report, *Turkey—Textiles*, WT/DS34/R, adopted 19 November 1999, as modified by the Appellate Body Report, WT/DS34/AB/R, para. 9.120 (italics added).

[33] *See* Lockhart and Mitchell, above at n 15, at 236–37, who, though not taking into account the *Turkey—Textiles* Panel ruling also state that ORRC are likely to include both border restrictions and marketplace regulations adversely affecting imported goods within the meaning of the national treatment obligation.

[34] *Ibid.*, at 246.

[35] *See* Understanding on the Interpretation of Article XXIV of the GATT 1994, para. 2.

[36] *See* Lockhart and Mitchell, above at n 15, at 245.

[37] *See* Understanding on the Interpretation of Article XXIV of the GATT 1994, preamble, fourth paragraph (italics added).

[38] *See* Lockhart and Mitchell, above at n 15, at 236–37, though the authors later conclude that 'ORRC are also likely to include marketplace regulations that adversely affect imported goods as compared with domestic goods'.

ORRC confined to restrictive border measures applicable on imports may be further confirmed by reference to the trade restrictions regulated in the provisions enumerated in the exceptions list in Article XXIV:8(a)(i) and (b) of the GATT.

All the provisions referred to in the exceptions list in Article XXIV:8(a)(i) and (b) of the GATT regulate measures that, by definition, *are* ORRC that were exempted from the rule on elimination of duties and ORRC. Therefore, the meaning of ORRC in Article XXIV:8 can be inferred through an analysis of the listed provisions, that is, Articles XI, XII, XIII, XIV, XV and XX of the GATT.

In brief, the scope of the listed provisions is as follows:

[Article] XI　　prohibits quotas and other restrictions on imports and exports other than duties and charges, except for certain import and export restrictions in the agricultural sector, such as those to support domestic supply management regimes.

[Article] XII　　Permits import restrictions in the event of balance of payments emergencies.

[Article] XIII　Requires that in those areas where quotas are allowed (for instance, agriculture) quotas be applied on a non-discriminatory basis.

[Article] XIV　Allows deviations from the non-discriminatory application of quotas under Article XIII if necessary for balance of payment reasons.

[Article] XV　Allows deviations from GATT rules to comply with commitments to the International Monetary Fund.

[Article] XX　Allows qualified deviation from GATT rules for measures to protect health, safety, the environment, [and other public policy purposes].[39]

The above descriptions show that Articles XI, XII, XIII, XIV and XV of the GATT basically regulate quantitative restrictions applicable at the border. Article XX, in contrast, has a much broader scope, which covers any kind of measures, applicable either at the border or internally, having any sort of restrictive effects on imports or adverse effects on imported products.[40] Notwithstanding, the presence of the broadly scoped Article XX in the exception's listing in Article XXIV:8(a)(i) and (b) does not necessarily imply that any kind of regulation having a restrictive effect on imports or an adverse effect on imported products would be encompassed within the meaning of

---

[39] *See* Hudec and Southwick, above at n 6, at 63.

[40] Once the requisites established in one of its paragraphs and in its chapeau are met, Art. XX of the GATT may justify either restrictions on the cross-border movement of goods such as measures prohibiting the importation of certain goods to pursue environmental or health purposes, as marketplace regulations providing less favourable treatment to imported products within the meaning of Art. III GATT.

ORRC. An interpretation more consistent with the wording in the other provisions in Article XXIV, and in the Understanding on Article XXIV would be that the presence of Article XX in the exceptions listing means that border restrictions justifiable under it are exempted from the rule on elimination of duties and ORRC, while marketplace restrictions are outside the scope of that rule. Still, the presence of Article XX in the exceptions list is instructive on the meaning of ORRC for indicating that this expression is not limited to quantitative restrictions as an examination of Articles XI to XV alone could suggest, but encompasses any sort of restriction on imports. This is significant to clarify that trade remedies (which are normally applied through increased duties rather than through quantitative restrictions)[41] are also encompassed within the meaning of ORRC. Trade remedies are, by definition, *border measures* taking the form of increased duties or quantitative restrictions, whose very purpose is *restricting imports* of certain products. For this reason, they are undoubtedly encompassed within the meaning of 'other restrictive regulations of commerce' in Article XXIV:8(a) and (b), irrespective of whether this expression is constructed broadly on the basis of the definition of ORC set out by the *Turkey—Textiles* Panel, or narrowly on the basis of the wording in Article XXIV and in the Understanding on Article XXIV.[42]

B. Interpretations proposed for the Rule on Elimination of Duties and Other Restrictive Regulations of Commerce and the List of Exceptions to this Rule—The 'May versus Must' Debate

The discussions between WTO Members on the meaning of the rule on elimination of duties and other restrictive regulations of commerce (ORRC) and the list of exceptions to this rule in Article XXIV:8(a)(i) and (b) of the GATT have centered in three distinct constructions of this provision, which lead to different conclusions on the issue of application of trade remedies in RTAs.[43]

---

[41] Anti-dumping and countervailing duties are applied through increased duties. *See* Arts VI:2 and 3 of the GATT, Art. 9 of the Antidumping Agreement, and Art. 19 of the Agreement on Subsidies and Countervailing Measures. Safeguard measures may be applied either through increased duties or through quantitative restrictions. *See* Art. 5.1 SGA.

[42] An interesting discussion (outside the scope of this chapter though) refers to whether a narrower definition of ORRC subsumed in border protectionist measures would permit an avenue for RTA parties to replace external restrictive measures for internal discriminatory measures such as discriminatory taxes levied upon RTA parties only, hence subverting the internal trade liberalization. *See* Mathis, above at n 28, at 10–1. The correlate problem is that a broader definition of ORC, on the other hand, 'would require customs unions members to externally harmonize all of the regulatory measures that can possibly affect trade, [which would be] far in excess of what a customs union could reasonably be understood to require'. *See* J.H. Mathis, *Regional Trade Agreements in the GATT/WTO: Article XXIV and the Internal Trade Requirement* (The Hague: T.M.C. Asser, 2002), 252.

[43] There is some additional variation on the opinions defended by WTO Members on the issue of application of trade remedies in customs unions and FTAs. *See* Committee on Regional Trade Agreements, Synopsis of 'Systemic' Issues Related to Regional Trade Agreements—Note by the Secretariat, above at n 26, at paras 56–8. See also Negotiating Group on Rules, Compendium of

All those constructions build on the 'may vs. must' debate on the nature of the list of exceptions to the rule on elimination of duties and ORRC in Article XXIV:8 of the GATT and make certain assumptions on the meaning of the relevant wording in that provision.

The debate on the mandatory or optional nature of the list of exceptions to the rule on elimination of duties and other restrictive regulations of commerce in Article XXIV:8 of the GATT focuses on how the phrase 'where necessary' in this provision shall be read.[44] The 'may' interpretation reads that phrase as providing that a party to a customs union or FTA is *allowed* to apply the restrictions listed to imports from its RTA partners, *when that party deems it necessary.*[45] The 'must' interpretation reads the same phrase as permitting a party to a customs union or FTA to apply the restrictions in the listing to the trade of its partners in the arrangement *whenever that is necessary pursuant the terms and principles of the listed provisions themselves.*[46] Since most listed provisions set forth criteria prescribing that the measures they regulate shall apply in a MFN basis, the 'must' interpretation implies that the measures

Issues Related to Regional Trade Agreements—Background Note by the Secretariat (Revision), above at n 6, paras 73–5. This chapter focuses in the three referred interpretations because they seek support for their arguments on a construction of the meaning of the relevant wording in Art. XXIV:8 GATT alone. Notwithstanding, it is worth mentioning that an argument has been made that Art. XXIV GATT shall not be construed as either mandating nor allowing non-application of trade remedies within customs unions and FTAs. This argument does not rely on an assumption on the nature of the exceptions list, but rather on the view that 'the invocation of Article XXIV d[oes] not mean that other Articles of the General Agreement should cease to apply'. *See* the Reports of the Working Parties concerning the agreements between the EC and Austria, Iceland, Portugal, Sweden, and Switzerland and Liechtenstein, respectively, BISD 20S/156, 169, 181, 194, 207 (and also in GATT Doc. L/6379, p. 36), and GATT Doc. L/7219, all adopted 19 October 1973. This argument will not be further discussed within this chapter, but the authors note their understanding that the broadly worded phrasing in the chapeau of para. 5 of Art. XXIV ('[n]othing in this agreement shall prevent the formation of a customs union or a free-trade area') makes clear that neither Art. XIX nor any other provision in the GATT is *a priori* excluded from the scope of the regional trade exception. See WTO Appellate Body Report, *Turkey—Textiles*, above at n 9, at para 45, where the Appellate Body stated: '[T]he chapeau makes it clear that Article XXIV may, under certain conditions, justify the adoption of a measure which is inconsistent with certain other GATT provisions, and may be invoked as a possible "defense" to a finding of inconsistency'. The authors argue furthermore that Art. XXIV of the GATT is not overruled by the prohibition on discriminatory safeguards set forth in Art. 2.2 of the SGA because there is no conflict between these rules within the meaning of the General Interpretative Note to Annex 1A of the WTO Agreement. Art. 1.1 SGA clarifies that the safeguards provided for in the Agreement and those in Art. XIX GATT are one and the same thing. *See* WTO Panel Report, *US—Line Pipe*, WT/ DS202/R, adopted 8 March 2002, as modified by the Appellate Body Report, WT/DS202/AB/R, para 7.150. *See also* WTO Appellate Body Report, *US—Lamb*, WT/DS177/AB/R, WT/DS178/AB/ R, adopted 16 May 2001, at para. 69, where the Appellate Body reconciled the reference to 'unforeseen developments' in Art. XIX with the absence of this expression in the SGA. For this reason, the exception in Art. XXIV, which covers the safeguards regulated in Art. XIX GATT, also encompasses the safeguards disciplined in the SGA. *See* WTO Appellate Body Report, *Turkey— Textiles*, above at n 9, at para. 45, note 13, where the Appellate Body ruled that Art. XXIV of the GATT may be invoked as a defence to a claim of inconsistency with the Agreement on Textiles and Clothing because Art. XXIV is incorporated in the ATC by Art. 2.4 of the ATC, which provides that '[n]o new restrictions . . . shall be introduced *except under* . . . the provisions of this Agreement *or relevant GATT 1994 provisions*'.

[44] *See* Hudec and Southwick, above at n 6, at 64.   [45] *Ibid.*   [46] *Ibid.*

regulated by the provisions in the listing *must* remain applicable in the intra-customs union or intra-FTA trade and *must* be imposed on RTA parties whenever imposed on third parties.[47]

One construction of Article XXIV:8 of the GATT builds on the interpretation that the exceptions listing refers to measures that *must* be applied on MFN basis to infer that other trade restrictions (those not listed, such as trade remedies) *may* (but do not have to) be applied to intra-customs union or intra-FTA imports. A second construction builds on the interpretation that the exceptions listing refers to trade restrictions that *may* be maintained in the intra-customs union and intra-FTA trade to infer that trade restrictions not listed (such as trade remedies) *must* be abolished within RTAs. A third view also builds on the interpretation that the exceptions listing refers to trade restrictions that *may* be maintained in the intra-RTA trade, but infers that non-listed restrictions (such as trade remedies) *may* be applied within the RTA to the extent that their application does not undermine the meeting of the 'substantially all the trade' requirement. This section discusses these constructions and the implications of the Appellate Body's *Turkey—Textiles* ruling endorsing a 'may' interpretation for the meaning of the exceptions listing in Article XXIV of the GATT for the issue of application of trade remedies within customs unions and FTAs.

1. Must *Apply Excepted Provisions to RTA Partners*—May *Eliminate Trade Remedies*

In several discussions reported under the GATT, RTA parties have relied on the '*must*' interpretation of the exceptions listing to argue that Article XXIV of the GATT *allowed* them to apply discriminatory safeguards (i.e. to exclude intra-customs union or intra-FTA imports from the scope of the safeguard). For instance, the Working Party Reports on the agreements between the European Communities (EC) and Austria, Iceland, Portugal, Sweden, and Switzerland and Liechtenstein all record a same statement by the representative of the EC, arguing that the omission of Article XIX among the provisions mentioned in Article XXIV:8(b) of the GATT implies that the EC is '*free to exempt*' its FTA partners from possible restrictions imposed under Article XIX.[48] Similar statements may be found in the records of various GATT Contracting Party meetings, such as the one made by the representative of Austria at the October 1991 GATT Council meeting, with respect to a safeguard which excluded imports originating in Austria's RTA partners in the European Free Trade Association (EFTA) from the scope of the measure.[49]

---

[47] *Ibid.*

[48] *See*, respectively, GATT Docs. L/3900, L/3902, L/3901, L/3899 and L/3898, all adopted 19 October 1973, and GATT Docs. 20S/145, 158, 171, 183 and 196. *See also* GATT Doc. 24S/73 (same views expressed in GATT Doc. L/3901 repeated in 1977 Report).

[49] *See* GATT Doc. C/M/252, p. 12–5 and GATT Doc. L/6899/Add.7/Suppl.1 (notification of import quota for cement of origin other than from EC or EFTA-Member State).

The representative of Austria argued there that 'since Article XIX was not mentioned in the list in Article XXIV:8(b), measures taken thereunder *might* be not applied to other members of a free-trade area'.[50]

Non-RTA parties are also reported to have relied on the 'must' interpretation of the exceptions listing to challenge the discriminatory application of measures regulated by the provisions *in the listing*. During the examination of the Free Trade Agreement between Canada and the United States a member of the Working Party argued that

> if a party to a free-trade agreement invoked *Article XX* to justify an export licensing scheme for short supply or conservation purposes, it *should apply* such measure in a *non-discriminatory manner* . . . *Article XXIV:8(b) did not allow* parties to a free-trade agreement *to exempt* other parties from the measures taken *under the exceptions provided in that article*.[51]

Also, within the examination of the European Free Trade Association (EFTA) and the Association between EFTA and Finland—Accession of Iceland certain members of the Working Party expressed the view that 'Article XXIV did not affect the obligations of Contracting Parties to apply *quota restrictions* in a *non-discriminatory manner*'.[52]

The argument could be made that the 'must—may' construction of the exceptions list and the elimination rule in Article XXIV:8 of the GATT finds support in an analysis of the nature of the measures regulated by the provisions in the listing.[53] The exceptions list refers to trade restrictions that are imposed to address global or external conditions (which are caused by imports from any source), and tend to apply across a range of products rather than as to particular products.[54] For this reason those measures, when applied, arguably *must* be imposed also to intra-RTA imports, either to be effective or to avoid undue harm to non-RTA parties.[55] On the other hand, all other types of trade restrictions (the ones not listed) *may* hypothetically be applied to address intra-RTA trade problems alone, therefore one can infer that these measures are always permitted between RTA parties.[56]

An arguable flaw in the above reasoning is that safeguards would also fall within the rubric of trade restrictions that are imposed to address conditions caused by imports from any source, and should therefore be imposed on MFN basis to avoid that non-RTA parties end up bearing a disproportionate burden of the effect of the measure.[57] A more precise distinction between safeguards and the measures regulated by the listed provisions may be drawn on the basis

---

[50] *Ibid.*, (italics added).

[51] *See* 1991 Report of the Working Party on Free Trade Agreement between Canada and the United States, GATT Doc. L/6927, adopted 12 November 1991, BISD 38S/47, 61, para. 45 (italics added).

[52] *See* Report of the Working Party on the Accession of Iceland to EFTA and FINEFTA, GATT Doc. L/3441, 18 September 1970, BISD 18S/174, 177, at para. 10 (italics added).

[53] *See* Mathis, above at n 42, at 245–46.   [54] *Ibid.*   [55] *Ibid.*   [56] *Ibid.*

[57] *Ibid. See also* Hudec and Southwick, above at n 6, at 68.

of a broader framework which the last share, but within which safeguards do not fall. All provisions in the listing regulate measures that are enacted to address *public policy concerns*.[58] Safeguards, on the other hand, (as well as tariff duties, anti-dumping, countervailing duties, quantitative restrictions) are enacted to address *commercial policy purposes*, providing a *domestic protection benefit* to domestic producers.[59] It would be arguable that public policy measures, by their own nature, are simply not encompassed within the purposes of 'substituting customs territories' or 'liberalizing trade'. Therefore, whenever a party to a RTA would have recourse to those measures, it would be *required* to do so in compliance with the MFN rule, i.e. applying the restrictions necessary to meet its public policy purposes also to its RTA partners. Yet, a distinction between measures addressing commercial policy purposes and measures addressing public policy purposes better supports the argument that safeguards (and the other trade remedies) *must* be eliminated in customs unions and FTAs, while the provisions in the listing *may* remain applicable, than the other way around.

Measures enacted to address public policy purposes arguably remain within the sovereign domain that parties to customs unions or FTAs would be less likely to give up to fulfill the requirement of 'substitution of a single customs territory for two or more customs territories' or liberalization of the trade between 'a group of two or more customs territories'.[60] As a matter of logic, it would then be up to the parties to these arrangements to decide the grade of sovereign domain they would be willing to refrain from exercising. For this reason, the exceptions listing can be more reasonably construed as indicating areas where parties to customs unions and FTAs are *allowed* to maintain restrictions in the trade between them, than areas where they would be *required* to maintain MFN treatment. That being said, the authors stress that the most striking flaw they see in the 'must—may' interpretation of Article XXIV:8 of the GATT does not reside on the nature of safeguard measures, but rather in the reading that interpretation makes of the rule on elimination of duties and ORRC.

To conclude that Article XXIV:8 of the GATT *permits* (rather than *mandates*) non-application of trade remedies within RTAs, the 'must—may' construction assumes that the rule on elimination of duties and ORRC with respect to SAT requires that trade restrictions not be *applied* (rather than applicable) to a portion of the intra-RTA trade correspondent to the SAT threshold.[61] This assumption (which is shared by the 'may—may' interpretation, as noted in

---

[58] *See* Mathis, *ibid.*, at 246–47. [59] *Ibid.* [60] *Ibid.*, at 245–47.

[61] *Ibid.*, at 68–69 and 238. This assumption (that the rule on elimination of duties and ORRC in Art. XXIV:8 only requires that trade restrictions not be *applied* to an amount of the trade significant enough to *jeopardize* the meeting of the threshold that a part of the intra-RTA trade equivalent to SAT between them is not *affected* by trade restrictions) seems to underlie the following reply of the EC to an argument by Argentina that application of safeguards was prohibited within customs unions or FTAs:

sub-section 'B.3' below), is inconsistent with an interpretation of the text of Article XXIV:8 of the GATT as currently written pursuant to the VCLT. As it is further discussed in section 'C' infra, to assume that the rule on elimination of duties and ORRC in Article XXIV:8(a)(i) and (b) merely requires *non application* of trade restrictions in a portion of the intra-RTA equal to SAT between them, the 'must—may' (and also the 'may—may') interpretation *reads into* the provision words that are *not* there, and *reads out* of the provision the words that *are* there.

In brief, the 'must—may' (as well as the 'may—may') interpretation reads the relevant wording in Article XXIV:8(a)(i) and (b) as if they provided that a customs union/FTA shall be understood to mean an area where 'duties and other restrictive regulations of commerce . . . are ~~eliminated~~ [*not applied*] with respect to substantially all the trade'. Yet, the text in Article XXIV:8(a)(i) and (b) of the GATT reads 'are eliminated', rather than 'are not applied'. For this reason, the authors argue that the 'must—may' interpretation of the exceptions list and the rule on elimination of duties and ORRC is not allowed under the VCLT, and cannot support a construction of Article XXIV:8 of the GATT as *permitting* application of trade remedies within customs unions or FTAs.[62]

2. May *Apply Excepted Provisions to RTA Partners*—Must *Eliminate Trade Remedies*

The 'may—must' construction for the exceptions list and the rule on elimination of duties and ORRC in Article XXIV:8 of the GATT was raised for the first time within the debates before the sub-group of the GATT Committee on the European Economic Community (EEC), which examined the consistency of the EEC Treaty provisions for the association of overseas territories with Article XXIV of the GATT. Members of the sub-group relied on the 'may' interpretation of the exceptions list to argue that the leeway Article XXIV:8 of the GATT left to RTA parties in what regards the restrictions applicable in their internal trade is limited. They asserted there that:

paragraph 8(b) [of Article XXIV of the GATT], in derogation of the rule regarding the elimination of internal obstacles, made provision for certain restrictive trade regulations authorized under certain Articles of the General Agreement; the list of these did

---

The European Communities contends that Article XXIV:8 of GATT does not prohibit the maintenance of the possibility to impose safeguard measures within customs unions or free-trade areas, either during the transitional period leading to their formation, or after their completion. The European Communities argues that safeguard measures are an exceptional emergency instrument of a temporary nature and *are limited to a specific product*, and that safeguard measures *do not as such affect the establishment and the nature of a customs union or a free-trade area*. Article XXIV of GATT *permits* the members of a customs union or free-trade area to *decide* whether, when applying a safeguard measure pursuant to Article XIX of GATT 1994 and the Agreement on Safeguards, to exempt other members of the customs union or free-trade area from the measure.

See WTO Panel Report, *Argentina—Footwear (EC)*, above at n 7, at para. 8.94 (italics added).

[62] The full reasoning underlying this conclusion is developed in sub-section 'C' below.

not, however, include Article XVIII, concerning governmental assistance to economic development. The application of the customs duties and of the restrictions instituted under Article XVIII did not therefore *benefit* from the exception for which provision was made in Article XXIV. The latter did not make provision for *allowing* one constituent territory of a FTA, in order to protect its industry, to levy import duties on imports from another constituent territory.[63]

In other words, according to this view a RTA party is *not allowed* to apply duties on the basis of Article XVIII of the GATT to the trade of other constituent parties because this provision is not included among those for which the exceptions listing *allows* a derogation from the rule that RTA parties shall eliminate internal obstacles to the trade between them. The same reasoning would apply to all trade restrictions regulated by provisions not included in the listing, such as anti-dumping, countervailing duties and safeguards, regulated, respectively, in Articles VI and XIX of the GATT.[64]

As it is evident from the above quotation, the 'may—must' interpretation relies, in the first place, on the assumption that the list of provisions excepted from the rule on elimination of duties and other restrictive regulations of commerce in Article XXIV:8 of the GATT is exhaustive, and that restrictions applied in the intra-RTA trade on the basis of the listing do not count against the meeting of the substantially all trade coverage requirement.[65] It draws furthermore, on the understanding that the rule on elimination of duties and other restrictive regulations of commerce covers the application of trade restrictions as a possibility, rather than only as a fact.[66] That is, areas and products where trade restrictive measures remain applicable count against meeting the 'substantially all the trade' threshold, even where those measures are not currently in place.[67] This particular aspect was underscored in a very enlightening way by a Participant of the Meeting of the WTO Negotiating Group on Rules held on March 7, 2005.[68] That Participant is reported to have made the following remarks after having stated that a submission on definition for SAT that had been presented by another Participant only proposed a partial definition for SAT, given that it did not deal with other directly or indirectly related issues:

[T]he concept of 'other restrictive regulations of commerce' (ORRCs) and its exemption list were directly linked to SAT . . . [hence] the proponent [should] clarify whether ORRCs applied under Articles VI and XIX of the GATT 1994—i.e. anti-dumping, countervailing duties and safeguards—should also be addressed as part of the SAT

---

[63] *See* GATT Working Party Report, above at n 20, at 94, para. 16 (italics added).

[64] As already discussed in sub-section 'A' supra, the authors purport that anti-dumping, countervailing duties, and safeguards fall within the meaning of ORRC in Art. XXIV:8 GATT.

[65] *See* Mathis, above at n 42, at 238. *See also* Lockhart and Mitchell, above at n 15, at 241–42.

[66] Lockhart and Mitchell present a very clarifying explanation on this assumption. *See* Lockhart and Mitchell, *ibid.*, at 238.

[67] *Ibid.*

[68] *See* Negotiating Group on Rules, Summary Report of the Meeting held on 7 March 2005, Note by the Secretariat, WTO Doc. TN/RL/M/24, 23 March 2005.

clarification. The balance that existed in Article XXIV:8 should be maintained; there-fore, a clarification of SAT should also encompass the extent to which such trade remedy measures could be applied in an RTA. *He noted his delegation's interpretation according to which trade remedy measures could not be applied to trade covered by free trade agreements or customs unions.*[69]

The 'may—must' interpretation of the exceptions list and the rule on elimin-ation of trade restrictions in Article XXIV:8 of the GATT was also invoked in the context of dispute settlement. In *Argentina—Footwear (EC)*, Argentina argued that it could not impose safeguard measures against imports from its RTA partners in the Southern Common Market (Mercosur) (an alleged cus-toms union) because Article XXIV of the GATT 'prohibit[ed] it from doing so'.[70] Argentina emphasized there that

Article XIX of GATT is not listed in Article XXIV:8(a)(i) or (b) of GATT among the exceptions from the requirement to abolish all the duties and other restrictive regula-tions of commerce on substantially all trade between the constituent territories of a customs union or a free-trade area. Therefore, it [was], in Argentina's view, *incompat-ible with the purpose of Article XXIV:8 of GATT* to impose safeguard measures within the Mercosur customs union.[71]

The Panel rejected Argentina's argument that Article XXIV:8 prevented it from applying safeguard measures to its RTA partners' imports.[72] Though having earlier noted that '[p]ractice of the Contracting Parties to the GATT of 1947 and of WTO Members is inconclusive on the issue of the imposition or maintenance of safeguard measures between the constituent territories of a customs union or of a free-trade area',[73] the Panel ended up endorsing the 'must—may' construction of Article XXIV:8.[74] The Panel also offered an

---

[69] *Ibid.*, para. 14 (italics added).
[70] *See* WTO Panel Report, *Argentina—Footwear (EC)*, above at n 7, at para. 8.93.
[71] *Ibid.*, (italics added).   [72] *Ibid.*, para. 8.101.   [73] *Ibid.*, para. 8.96.
[74] *Ibid.*, para. 8.97, where the Panel states:

Although the list of exceptions in Article XXIV:8 of GATT clearly does not include Article XIX, in our view, that paragraph itself does not necessarily prohibit the imposition of safeguard measures between the constituent territories of a customs union or free-trade area during their formation or after their completion. A frequently advanced justification for the maintenance or introduction of safeguards clauses within regional integration areas is the argument that the obligation of Article XXIV:8 to eliminate all duties and other restrictions of commerce applies only to '*substantially all*' but not necessarily to '*all*' trade between the constituent territories. It could be argued that for all practical purposes the application of safeguard measures to particu-lar categories of like or directly competitive products is unlikely to affect a trade volume that could put the liberalisation of 'substantially all trade' between the constituent territories of a customs union into question. But the persuasiveness of this argument depends mainly on the extent to which safeguard measures are actually imposed. Thus we do not exclude the possibility that extensive use of safeguard measures within regional integration areas for prolonged periods could run counter to the requirement to liberalise 'substantially all trade' within a regional integration area. In our view, the express omission of Article XIX of GATT from the lists of exceptions in Article XXIV:8 of GATT read in combination with the requirement to eliminate all duties or other restrictions of commerce on 'substantially all trade' within a customs union, leaves both options open, i.e. abolition of the possibility to impose safeguard measure between the Member States of a customs union as well as the maintenance thereof.

'alternative' understanding that in case imposition of safeguards within customs unions were to be deemed prohibited, the mechanism available for a customs union to implement that requirement would be the replacement of the application of safeguards by the customs union parties for the application of safeguards by the customs union as a single unit.[75] These findings of the *Argentina—Footwear (EC)* Panel on Article XXIV were later reversed by the Appellate Body on the basis that Argentina 'did not argue before the Panel that Article XXIV of the GATT 1994 provided it with a defence to a finding of violation of a provision of GATT 1994, hence [an] analysis of Article XXIV of the GATT 1994 was not relevant in th[e] case'.[76]

Interestingly, in a later dispute under the Mercosur dispute settlement system, Argentina relied on the *Argentina—Footwear (EC)* Panel decision to reply to the argument made by Brazil that a safeguard Argentina had imposed on textile imports from Brazil was illegitimate because 'imposition of safeguard measures has no place in a customs union'.[77] Argentina made reference to the *Argentina—Footwear (EC)* Panel decision to argue that the application

---

[75] *See* WTO Panel Report, *Argentina—Footwear (EC), ibid.,* at paras 8.99 and 8.102. In this 'alternative' finding the Panel applied Footnote 1 to the SGA, which is located right after the word 'Member' in Art. 2.1 of the Agreement. Art. 2.1 provides:

A Member[1] may apply a safeguard measure to a product only if that Member has determined, pursuant to the provisions set out below, that such product is being imported into its territory in such increased quantities, absolute or relative to domestic production, and under such conditions as to cause or threaten to cause serious injury to the domestic industry that produces like or directly competitive products.

Footnote 1 states:

A customs union may apply a safeguard measure as a single unit or on behalf of a member State. When a customs union applies a safeguard measure as a single unit, all the requirements for the determination of serious injury or threat thereof under this Agreement shall be based on the conditions existing in the customs union as a whole. When a safeguard measure is applied on behalf of a member State, all the requirements for the determination of serious injury or threat thereof shall be based on the conditions existing in that member State and the measure shall be limited to that member State. Nothing in this Agreement prejudges the interpretation of the relationship between Article XIX and paragraph 8 of Article XXIV of GATT 1994.

It is noteworthy, however, that, by implying that *the means* by which customs union parties implement a prohibition on application of safeguards to their partners eventually established in Art. XXIV is the application of the measure by the customs union as a single unit, instead of by its Member States, the *Argentina—Footwear (EC)* Panel *prejudged the interpretation of the relationship between Art. XIX and paragraph 8 of Art. XXIV GATT 1994.* That is, it did precisely what is forbidden by the last sentence in the Footnote 1 of the SGA.

[76] *See* WTO Appellate Body Report, *Argentina—Footwear (EC),* above at n 8, at paras 109–10. The Appellate Body also reversed the Panel findings on Footnote 1 to the SGA. In this regard, the Appellate Body first expressly stated that '[t]he ordinary meaning of the first sentence of footnote 1 [to Art. 2.1 SGA] appears to us to be that the footnote only applies when a customs union applies a safeguard measure "as a single unit or on behalf of a member State" '. *See* WTO Appellate Body Report, *Argentina—Footwear (EC), ibid.,* at para. 106. Then the Appellate Body noted that the safeguard at stake in that case had been applied by Argentina, on its own behalf (rather by the Mercosur customs union on its own behalf or on Argentina's behalf), therefore the Footnote 1 did not apply to the measures challenged in that case. *See ibid.,* at para. 108.

[77] *See* Laudo del Tribunal Arbitral, *Argentina—Aplicación de Medidas de Salvaguardia sobre Productos Textiles (Res. 861/99) del Ministerio de Economia y Obras y Servicios Publicos (Laudo III—Productos Textiles—de Brasil a Argentina),* 3 March 2000, III, F, 3.

of safeguard measures within customs unions and FTAs was *allowed* by Article XXIV:8(a) and (b) of the GATT.[78] The *Productos Textiles* Mercosur Arbitration Tribunal noted that the *Argentina—Footwear (EC)* Appellate Body Report did not prejudge the matter, and that the Panel Report had stated that the practice of GATT Contracting Parties and WTO Members was not conclusive on the issue.[79] The Arbitration Tribunal then stated that there was no need to further discuss that matter, given that the issue at stake in the case was rather if Mercosur law allowed the application of safeguards such as the challenged measure.[80]

Noteworthy, in a later Mercosur Arbitration Tribunal brought by Brazil against Argentina, this time challenging anti-dumping duties imposed on imports of chicken, Brazil explicitly argued that:

legal scholars assert that antidumping measures are incompatible with RTAS, and pursuant Article XXIV:8(a)(i) of the GATT a customs union implies the elimination of duties and other restrictive regulations of commerce between its constituent territories. Antidumping measures in Article VI of the GATT are evidently trade restrictive and moreover are not mentioned within the exceptions to Article XXIV.[81]

The *Pollo* Mercosur Tribunal ruled directly on the issue of whether Article XXIV:8 of the GATT prohibits application of trade remedies within customs unions and FTAs.[82] The *Pollo* Mercosur Arbitration Tribunal stated that Article XXIV:8 of the GATT envisions the free movement of goods within a RTA, with no exception but those made explicitly in the text, and expressly stated that the measures regulated by Articles VI and Article XIX of the GATT are not permitted within RTAs because they are not explicitly provided for in the parenthetical language in Article XXIV:8.[83] Yet, this decision left unad-

---

[78] *Ibid.*   [79] *Ibid.*   [80] *Ibid.*

[81] *See* Laudo del Tribunal Arbitral, *Aplicación de Medidas Antidumping contra la exportación de pollos enteros, provenientes de Brasil, Resolución No 574/2000 del Ministerio de Economía de la República Argentina* (*Laudo IV—Pollos—de Brasil a Argentina*), 21 May 2001, I-C-1–15. In the original:

medidas antidumping según la doctrina son incompatibles con esquemas de integración regional y según el artículo XXIV.8 (a) (i) del GATT 1947 una unión aduanera implica la eliminación de los aranceles y de otras reglamentaciones restrictivas del comercio entre los territorios que la componen. Las medidas antidumping del artículo VI del GATT son evidentemente restrictivas del comercio y además no son mencionadas entre las excepciones al artículo XXIV. *See ibid.*

Argentina this time replied that anti-dumping measures were not ORRC within the meaning of Art. XXIV:8, but rather 'measures against unfair trade practices' ('Las medidas antidumping son acciones contra prácticas comerciales desleales y no constituyen "reglamentaciones comerciales restrictivas" '). *See ibid.*, I-C-2–64.

[82] *Ibid.*, at II-E-3–245.

[83] In the original:

[L]a libertad de circulación de bienes y la ausencia de restricciones es propio de la naturaleza de las áreas de libre comercio y las uniones aduaneras, como lo recoge la normativa de la OMC. El artículo XXIV del GATT 1994 dispone en su párrafo 8 (a i) y (b) que esos sistemas de integración se caracterizan por la eliminación de los derechos y de las regulaciones restrictivas del comercio. Mientras que el Entendimiento para la Interpretación del artículo XXIV dispone que las áreas de libre comercio y las uniones aduaneras, para ser compatibles con dicho artículo han

dressed the main gap in the 'may–must' construction of the exceptions list and the rule on elimination of duties and ORRC in Article XXIV of the GATT, which is the absence of Article XXI, the broadly worded exception for security reasons, in the supposedly exhaustive list of restrictions that could be maintained within a customs union or FTA.

The counter-argument that the absence of Article XXI of the GATT shows that the exceptions listing in Article XXIV:8 cannot be interpreted as being exhaustive was made by the EC at the debates before the sub-group of the *Committee on the European Economic Community* where the 'may–must' construction of Article XXIV:8 of the GATT had been raised for the first time.[84] The EC argued there that a conclusion that the exceptions list is *not* exhaustive follows *a contrario* from the fact that the broadest worded exception in the GATT, the one for security reasons provided for in Article XXI, which the Contracting Parties' right to avail themselves of could not be disputed, is *not* included in the listing.[85] This argument has remained a shadow which the proponents of the 'may–must' interpretation for the exceptions list and the rule on elimination of trade restrictions in Article XXIV:8 of the GATT in the field of trade remedies have had difficulties in overcoming. The Delegation of Australia, for instance, argued in a Communication to the WTO Committee on Regional Trade Agreements (CRTA) that:

A fully implemented customs union or free-trade area does not permit anything between free trade between the partners to the arrangement and MFN treatment for third countries. Taking again Article XIX as an example, a judgement would therefore have to be made whether, if there is no plan to eliminate safeguard action between the partners, the MFN rule would apply instead.[86]

The paper presented by the Australian Delegation adds that '[s]imilar observations could be made about Article VI and its application in a fully developed free-trade area or customs union'.[87] These statements are preceded by a brief discussion on the provisions referred to in the exceptions list in Article XXIV:8 of the GATT, and the absence of Article XIX.[88] The Australian paper seems however to be reluctant to explicitly endorse the 'may–must' construction due

---

de satisfacer, entre otras de sus disposiciones, el párrafo 8. Las excepciones admitidas por el artículo XXIV y que son señaladas expresamente—artículos XI, XII, XIII, XIV, XV y XX—no incluyen el artículo VI relativo al dumping. De conformidad con este criterio la experiencia comparada de procesos de integración muestra que en el comercio dentro del espacio integrado no se aplican los mecanismos antidumping sino regímenes de defensa de la competencia sometidos a una disciplina común y administrados por organismos comunes y no por autoridades nacionales.

See ibid., at II-E-3-245.

[84] *See* 'Report of the Sub-group of the Committee on the "European Economic Community" ', above at n 20.

[85] *Ibid.*, at BISD 6S/97, para. 26.

[86] *See* Communication from Australia, WTO Doc. WT/REG/W/18, 17 November 1997, at para. 22.

[87] *Ibid.*, para. 23.   [88] *Ibid.*, paras 15, and 17–9.

to the difficulty in providing a reasonable explanation for the absence of Article XXI of the GATT in the listing. The paper notes in this regard that:

Delegations have in the past pointed out that Article XXI is not listed. In their view, if resort to general exceptions is permitted, there could hardly be a reason why security exceptions should be out of bounds. But there has always been a recognition that this Article applies to matters quite different to those listed in Article XX, and that no WTO Member will give up its right to judge when its essential security interests are involved. It would therefore be more profitable to consider the relevance of the list in Article XXIV:8 to other GATT articles.[89]

Nonetheless, on the one hand, the text of Article XXIV:8 leaves no room for the list of exceptions to be interpreted as being merely illustrative, and, on the other hand, the provision's drafting history provides a reasonable explanation for Article XXI having been left out of the listing, hence overcoming the gap raised in this interpretation. The authors further discuss the exhaustive or illustrative character of the exception's listing in sub-sections 'B.3' and 'D' *infra*.

3. May *Apply Excepted Provisions to RTA Partners*—May *Eliminate Trade Remedies*

The 'may–may' interpretation of the rule on elimination of duties and other restrictive regulations of commerce and the list of exceptions to this rule was initially relied upon by parties to RTAs under examination to rebut non-parties' arguments that Article XXIV:8 of the GATT requires RTA parties to apply the measures regulated by the provisions in the listing on a MFN basis. In the examination of the Free Trade Agreement between Canada and the United States, one member of the Working Party argued that Article XXIV:8(b) of the GATT did not allow parties to a free trade agreement to exempt other parties from measures taken under the provisions enumerated in the exceptions list, in case certain export control measures which had been justified under Article XX of the GATT.[90] The member of the Working Party added that '[s]uch measures could not be considered "other restrictive regulations of commerce" in terms of Article XXIV:8(b)'.[91] The representative of Canada is reported to have replied that:

[U]nder Article XXIV:8(b) of the GATT, restrictions meeting the exceptions of Article XX *could be maintained* in a free-trade agreement. Export control measures were included in 'other restrictive regulations of commerce' in this article.... *Article XXIV:8(b) . . . did not preclude the parties* in a free-trade agreement *from undertaking elimination of restrictions* vis-à-vis the other party to the agreement.[92]

Also, in light of earlier statements by certain members of Working Parties on

---

[89] *See* Communication from Australia, above at n 86, at para. 16.
[90] *See* 1991 Report of the Working Party on Free-Trade Agreement between Canada and the United States, above at n 51.
[91] *Ibid.*   [92] *Ibid.*, (italics added).

RTAs that 'Article XXIV did not affect the obligations of Contracting Parties to apply quota restrictions in a non-discriminatory manner',[93] representatives of the EEC and Finland 'replied' in the discussions on the *EC Agreements with Finland* that:

Article XXIV:8(b), specifically *mentioning Article XIII*, was *permissive* in this respect and covered certain *possibilities* in relation to the *maintenance of outward restrictive regulations of commerce* in certain circumstances, *while eliminating those between the parties to the Agreement.*[94]

Furthermore, within the debate on the consistency of the EEC Treaty provisions for the association of overseas territories with Article XXIV of the GATT, the EC relied on the 'may–may' interpretation of the rule on elimination of duties and other restrictive regulations of commerce and the list of exceptions to this rule to argue that *Article XXIV:8* of the GATT *allows* RTA parties to *maintain restrictions* in the trade between them, *not limited to those referred to in the listing.*[95]

More recently, the 'may–may' construction of Article XXIV:8 has also been at stake within dispute settlement procedures, more notably in *US—Line Pipe*, which is one of the discriminatory safeguard cases.[96] In *US—Line Pipe* Korea challenged a safeguard measure imposed by the United States which excluded imports originating in the United States RTA partners in the North American Free Trade Agreement (NAFTA) (an alleged FTA) from the scope of the measure.[97] The United States invoked Article XXIV as a defence,[98] and argued that:

the *list of measures* that Article XXIV:8 specifically *authorizes* free-trade area parties *to maintain* against each other *does not* include *safeguard* measures applied under Article XIX, . . . *therefore . . . by implication, safeguard* measures *either may or must* be made *part of the general elimination of 'restrictive regulations of commerce'* under any free-trade area.[99]

The United Stated further sustained the following interpretation for the relevant wording in Article XXIV:8 of the GATT:

Article XXIV *allows* FTA parties to *decide* whether to exclude each other from safeguard measures all of the time, some of the time, or not at all. Under Article XXIV:8, an

[93] *See* Report of the Working Party on the Accession of Iceland to EFTA and FINEFTA, GATT Doc. L/3441, above at n 52.

[94] *See* Report of the Working Party on the EC Agreement with Finland, GATT Doc. L/4064, adopted 30 October 1974, BISD 21S/76, 80, at para. 16 (italics added).

[95] *See* Report of the Sub-group of the Committee on the 'European Economic Community', above at n 20. Noteworthy, the 'may–may' interpretation of the exceptions list in Art. XXIV:8 of the GATT defended by the EC before the Sub-group of the Committee on the 'European Economic Community is inconsistent with the 'must–may' interpretation of the same provision later defended by the same EC before the above referred Working Parties on the agreements between the EC and Austria, Iceland, Portugal, Sweden, and Switzerland and Liechtenstein. *See* above at n 43 and 48.

[96] *See* above at n 8.

[97] *See* WTO Panel Report, *US—Line Pipe*, above at n 43, at para. 7.136.

[98] *Ibid.*, at para. 7.137.   [99] *Ibid.*, at para. 7.132 (italics added).

FTA *must eliminate* restrictive regulations of commerce—like safeguard measures—*on substantially all trade* among the parties. Thus, the *package of trade liberalizing measures* that accompanies formation of an FTA *need not eliminate all duties and restrictive regulations of trade. If* FTA parties, while retaining some duties and restrictive regulations of commerce, *can still achieve the Article XXIV:8 threshold (covering 'substantially all trade'),* they *may retain those regulations.* If the elimination of other restrictive regulations covers substantially all trade, the parties *may* also eliminate safeguard measures.[100]

The *US—Line Pipe* Panel implicitly endorsed the 'may–may' construction of Article XXIV:8 that was argued by the United States. The Panel identified Article 802 of the NAFTA Agreement, which *restricts* the use, but *does not abolish* the possibility of application of Article XIX safeguards within the NAFTA,[101] as a mechanism which provides for the elimination of safeguard measures between NAFTA members in certain circumstances.[102] Then, the Panel found that the non-application of a safeguard measure to intra-NAFTA imports on the grounds of Article 802 of the NAFTA Agreement 'forms part of the elimination of "duties and other restrictive regulations of commerce" ' 'which is the very raison d'être of any free-trade area'.[103]

As seen above, the 'may–may' construction of Article XXIV:8 of the GATT draws on two assumptions to make the argument that the exceptions listing provides for the areas where RTA parties *may* apply restrictive measures to the intra-RTA trade, but the absence of a provision in the listing does not imply that the measures regulated by that provision cannot be applied within RTAs. One, shared with the 'must–may' interpretation as discussed in sub-section 'B.1' above, is that the rule on elimination of duties and ORRC in Article XXIV:8 requires only that trade restrictions *not be applied* in a portion of the intra-RTA equal to SAT. The other is that the exceptions list in Article XXIV:8 is not exhaustive. The authors disagree with both.

The assumption that the rule on elimination of duties and ORRC in Article XXIV:8 may be read as requiring the mere *non-application* of trade restrictions in a portion of the intra-RTA equal to SAT cannot prevail for the reasons already stated in sub-section 'B.1' above and addressed in more detail in sub-section 'D' below. The presumption of the non-exhaustive character of the exceptions list is inconsistent with an interpretation of the text of Article XXIV:8 of the GATT pursuant to the VCLT because it *reads into* that

---

[100] *Ibid.*, at para. 4.260 (italics added).

[101] Art. 802 NAFTA Agreement establishes that the NAFTA Parties retain their rights and obligations on safeguards under Art. XIX of the GATT, but shall exclude imports originating in the NAFTA partners from the scope of the measure unless: (a) imports from a Party considered individually, account for a substantial share of total imports; and (b) imports from a Party, considered individually, or, in exceptional circumstances, imports from NAFTA Parties considered collectively contribute importantly to the serious injury or threat thereof, caused by imports.

[102] *See* WTO Panel Report, *US—Line Pipe*, above at n 43, at para. 7.141, note 127.

[103] *ibid.*, at para. 7.148. In so doing, the Panel agreed with the argument raised by the US that 'safeguard measures either may or must be made part of the general elimination of "restrictive regulations of commerce" under any free-trade area'. *See ibid.*, at para. 7.132 (italics added).

provision words that are *not* there: 'except, where necessary [*measures such as*] those permitted under Articles XI, XII, XIII, XIV, XV and XX'. Furthermore, an assumption on a non-exhaustive nature of the exceptions' list within the context of the 'may–may' interpretation renders the whole listing meaningless. This is so because the 'may–may' interpretation asserts that all sorts of trade restrictions remain potentially applicable, and that the criterion to determine whether the application of a specific trade restriction is permissible or not is the *part of the intra-RTA trade* that is *affected* by the ensemble of the trade restrictions applied. The *type* of trade restriction applied is not relevant within this reasoning, given that what matters is the *effect* of the restriction on the trade between the RTA parties, therefore, an *illustrative* list of types of permitted trade restrictions would be fully unnecessary and redundant.[104]

4. Resolution of the 'May vs. Must' Dispute in Turkey—Textiles

In *Turkey—Textiles* the Appellate Body resolved the long lasting debate on the optional or mandatory nature of the list of exceptions in Article XXIV:8. When stating its framework for assessing the availability of a defence based on Article XXIV of the GATT, the Appellate Body ruled in *Turkey—Textiles* that:

Sub-paragraph 8(a)(i) of Article XXIV establishes the *standard* for the internal trade between constituent Members *in order to satisfy* the definition of a 'customs union'. It *requires* the constituent members of a customs union to eliminate 'duties and other restrictive regulations of commerce' with respect to 'substantially all the trade' between them.[105]

Furthermore, the Appellate Body noted, with regard to the exceptions list in the same provision, that:

the terms of subparagraph 8(a)(i) provide that members of a customs union *may maintain*, where necessary, in their internal trade, certain restrictive regulations of commerce that are otherwise permitted under Articles XI through XV and under Article XX of the GATT 1994.[106]

The above quotations leave no doubt that the Appellate Body endorsed the 'may' interpretation of the meaning of the exception's listing.

5. Conclusion

The discussions reported above show that Article XXIV:8 of the GATT can be construed as *permitting* rather than *mandating* non-application of trade remedies within customs unions and FTAs on the basis of the 'must–may' and the 'may–may' interpretations of the meaning of the listing and the rule on elimination of duties and ORRC. The 'may–must' interpretation, in contrast,

---

[104] An alternative approach that could arguably render a 'may–may' construction meaningful would be to assume that the exceptions list *is exhaustive* and informs the trade restrictions that *may* be applied within RTAs *without counting against the meeting of the SAT threshold*.
[105] *See* WTO Appellate Body Report, *Turkey—Textiles*, above at n 9, at para. 48 (italics added).
[106] *Ibid.*, (italics added).

leads to a construction of Article XXIV:8 as *mandating* non-application of trade remedies within customs unions and FTAs.

The Appellate Body's endorsement of the 'may' interpretation on the nature of the exception's list in Article XXIV:8 of the GATT discards the 'must–may' construction for the meaning of the listing and the rule on elimination of duties and ORRC. That suggests either the 'may–must' or the 'may–may' constructions to be the appropriate reading. Yet, the 'may–may' construction for both the meaning of the exceptions list and the rule on elimination of duties and ORRC is not permitted because it would leave the exceptions list meaningless as pointed out above. Hence, the Appellate Body's discarding of the 'must' interpretation in *Turkey—Textiles* suggests that the rule on elimination of duties and ORRC has to be interpreted as *mandating* abolition of trade remedies in RTAs.

C. Meaning of the Phrase 'Duties and Other Restrictive Regulations of Commerce . . . are eliminated with respect to Substantially All the Trade'

In *Turkey—Textiles* the Appellate Body made clear that Article XXIV:8 of the GATT sets forth the *standard* that must be met in the internal trade between the constituent members for a RTA to satisfy the definition of customs union or FTA under the GATT.[107] The Appellate Body noted that this standard requires RTA parties 'to eliminate "duties and other restrictive regulations of commerce" with respect to "substantially all the trade between them" '.[108] It also noted that the terms of Article XXIV:8 offer some flexibility to the constituent members of a customs union when liberalizing their internal trade, upon having identified such 'flexibility' in the possibilities of on the one hand, liberalizing 'less than all' the trade, and on the other hand, maintaining the restrictions in the exceptions list within the RTA.[109] Finally, the Appellate Body further *cautioned* that the degree of flexibility that Article XXIV:8 *allows* is *limited* by the requirement that 'duties and other restrictive regulations of commerce' be 'eliminated with respect to substantially all' internal trade.[110] In light of these findings, this chapter now turns to the examination of the interpretative controversies on the meaning of the phrase 'other restrictive regulations of commerce . . . are eliminated with respect to substantially all the trade' with a view at the issue of application of trade remedies in customs unions and FTAs constituted between WTO Members.

The phrase 'duties and other restrictive regulations of commerce are eliminated . . . with respect to substantially all the trade' has been the subject of several proposed interpretations, many of which arguably pick and choose within the terms in its wording to build mosaics leading to targeted conclusions,

---

[107] *See ibid.*, at para. 48. The statement in *Turkey—Textiles* referred only to customs unions, but applies to FTAs as well given that the wording on the internal trade requirement is virtually the same for both types of RTAs as already observed *supra* under note 10.
[108] *Ibid.* at para. 48.   [109] *Ibid.*   [110] *Ibid.*

with no regard to the text of Article XXIV:8 of the GATT. The authors, however, argue that pursuant to the rules of treaty interpretation prescribed in the VCLT, the only reading allowed for the phrase 'are eliminated. . . with respect to substantially all the trade' in Article XXIV:8 of the GATT is the one sustained by the 'may–must' construction of the exceptions list and the rule on elimination of duties and ORRC. That is, the authors assert that the phrase 'are eliminated . . . with respect to substantially all the trade' in Article XXIV:8 of the GATT establishes a *standard* for RTAs internal trade liberalization which is only met if the imposition of duties and ORRC,[111] in any degree, is *eliminated as a possibility* for a part of the internal trade corresponding to 'substantially all the trade'[112] between the RTA parties.[113]

To begin with, we focus in the ordinary meaning of the expression 'are eliminated'. The ordinary meaning of the verb 'to eliminate' is 'to expel', 'to exclude', 'to remove', 'to get rid of',[114] which is univocal with the meaning of the verbs 'éliminer' ('exclure', 'supprimer', 'faire disparaître en supprimant l'existence')[115] and 'eliminar' ('excluir')[116] used in the French[117] and in the Spanish[118] versions of Article XXIV:8 of the GATT. This confirms that for the internal trade requirement established in Article XXIV:8 of the GATT to be met, duties and ORRC must be *abolished*, and that the intra-RTA trade to which any type of duty or ORRC remains *applicable* cannot be counted towards the fulfillment of the SAT threshold even where no duty or ORRC is effectively imposed. Indeed, it is clear that an ORRC *expelled, excluded,*

---

[111] Except those referred to in the list of exceptions.

[112] This chapter does not discuss the extent of coverage required by the 'substantially all the trade' threshold, nor whether its fulfillment shall be assessed in quantitative or qualitative terms. What the authors want to emphasize here is that the trade counted towards the fulfillment of the 'substantially all' threshold must be that which is *a priori* freed from the possibility that trade restrictive measures of any sort apply between the constituent territories.

[113] The point made here is that, as it is further discussed below, trade restrictions that are *not currently applied*, but *remain applicable* do *not* fall within the meaning of restrictions that 'are eliminated' in Art. XXIV:8 GATT. Also, the ordinary meaning of the words 'are eliminated' in Art. XXIV:8 does *not* encompass less than full abolition of duties and ORRC (that is, merely reducing duties or adopting less restrictive regulations does not result in a situation where duties and restrictive regulations of commerce 'are eliminated').

[114] See *The Compact Edition of the Oxford English Dictionary* (Oxford: Clarendon, 1971), 845.

[115] See P. Robert, *Dictionnaire Alphabetique et Analogique de la Langue Francaise* (Paris: Soc du nouveau Littré, le Robert, 1973), 552.

[116] See Real Academia Española, *Diccionario de la Lengua Española* (Madrid: Real Academia Española, 1953), 512.

[117] The French version of Art. XXIV:8 GATT provides in the relevant part:

les droits de douane et les autres réglementations commerciales restrictives (à l'exception, dans la mesure où cela serait nécessaire, des restrictions autorisées aux termes des articles XI, XII, XIII, XIV, XV et XX) *sont éliminés* pour l'essentiel des échanges commerciaux entre les territoires constitutifs.

[118] The Spanish version of Art. XXIV:8 of the GATT provides in the relevant part:

los derechos de aduana y las demás reglamentaciones comerciales restrictivas (excepto, en la medida en que sea necesario, las restricciones autorizadas en virtud de los artículos XI, XII, XIII, XIV, XV y XX) *sean eliminados* con respecto a lo esencial de los intercambios comerciales entre los territorios constitutivos.

removed cannot remain applicable, and that if an ORRC is still applicable it cannot be said to be expelled, excluded, removed, or, ultimately, *eliminated* with respect to substantially all the trade between RTA parties. Accordingly, it becomes evident that the interpretation that elimination of ORRC may be assessed on the basis of a volume of trade threshold (where ORRC would be considered 'eliminated' where the volume of intra-RTA trade *not being affected* by restrictive measures meets the SAT level), as asserted by the 'must—may' and the 'may—may' constructions, is inconsistent with the text of Article XXIV:8 of the GATT. Article XXIV:8 reads 'duties and ORRC . . . are *eliminated*'. Its drafters used a verb, 'to eliminate', which has a meaning and, as already underscored in sub-section 'B.1' above, cannot be *read out*— that would leave Article XXIV:8 to be read as if it stated 'duties and ORRC are *not applied* with respect to SAT'—even though that might be a more pleasant reading for RTA parties.

Second, the authors call attention to the precise wording adopted in Article XXIV:8(a)(ii) and (b) of the GATT. The relevant provision in Article XXIV:8 reads 'duties and other restrictive regulations of commerce . . . are eliminated with respect to substantially all the trade'. The authors note that some legal scholars have referred to the rule on elimination of duties and ORRC in Article XXIV:8 as requiring that 'duties and ORRC be *substantially elimin-ated*',[119] as if this wording were interchangeable with the wording 'duties and ORRC *are eliminated with respect to substantially all the trade*' effectively inscribed in Article XXIV:8 of the GATT.[120] Yet, the wording is different, since in the text in Article XXIV:8 of the GATT the term 'substantially' qualifies 'all the trade', whereas in the other wording the term 'substantially' qualifies 'eliminated'. These differences in wording must be ascribed some meaning pursuant to the VCLT, and this is even more relevant in this case because the phrase *'all tariffs and other restrictive regulations of members* as between the territories of the members are *substantially eliminated'*, was the *original phrasing of the internal trade requirement*, and was *replaced* by the current phrasing in Article XXIV:8 of the GATT.[121] The authors affirm that the differ-ences between the precise wording adopted in Article XXIV:8(a)(ii) and (b) of the GATT and the previous phrasing of the RTA exception have a bearing in further confirming that Article XXIV:8 requires abolition of duties and ORRC in customs unions and FTAs. The *Turkey—Textiles* discussion on the meaning of 'substantially the same regulations of commerce' in Article XXIV:8(a)(ii) is instructive on the point.

In *Turkey—Textiles* the Appellate Body discussed the meaning of the

---

[119] *See* e.g. Jackson, above at n 3, at 582–83: 'A customs union is defined in Article XXIV, paragraph 8(a), to have the two characteristics listed in the original United States proposal: (a) trade restrictions between union members are *"substantially eliminated"* . . .' (italics added).

[120] Emphasis and italics added.

[121] *See* Art. 33, Suggested Charter for an International Trade Organization of the United Nations, Department of State, September 1946.

requirement in Article XXIV:8(a)(ii) of the GATT that customs union members adopt 'substantially the same regulations of commerce' by customs union members.[122] There, the Appellate Body ruled that customs union members may be deemed to adopt 'substantially the same' regulations of commerce (i.e. most regulations of commerce would be the same), even when *some* regulations are different (in case, if some countries had quotas for textiles and others had not).[123] The above reasoning, however, is not extendable to the interpretation of the meaning of the requirement on *elimination* of duties and ORRC. The phrasing in Article XXIV:8(a)(i) and (b) of the GATT does not permit the interpretation that RTA parties would be allowed to *eliminate* 'less than all' duties and ORRC applicable to the part of the intra-RTA trade covered by the RTA trade liberalization programme and meant to account for meeting the SAT requirement. Article XXIV:8(a)(ii) of the GATT allows the interpretation made by the Appellate Body in *Turkey—Textiles* because it reads '*substantially the same duties and ORC are applied*'. This wording is different from the one used in Article XXIV:8 subparagraphs (a)(i) and (b) of the GATT, which state 'duties and ORRC . . . are eliminated with respect to in *substantially all the trade*'.[124]

The Appellate Body noted in *Turkey—Textiles* that the term 'substantially' in Article XXIV:8(a)(ii) of the GATT qualifies the expression '*the same regulations of commerce*'.[125] Hence, there was a textual basis for the Appellate Body's finding that *some* of the *regulations of commerce* applied by customs union members could be different, though *most regulations of commerce* shall be the same (i.e. *substantially the same regulations of commerce* are applied).[126] In contrast, as also noted by the Appellate Body in *Turkey—Textiles*, in Article XXIV:8 GATT subparagraphs (a)(i) and (b), the term 'substantially' qualifies the expression '*all the trade*',[127] not the verb 'eliminate' (and by a deliberate change in wording by the drafters). Accordingly, with regard to the internal trade requirement it is in the amount of trade to be liberalized that, as noted by the Appellate Body in *Turkey—Textiles*, resides the 'flexibility' offered by the terms of Article XXIV:8 of the GATT, not in the rule on elimination of duties and ORRC.[128] Therefore, there is no textual basis to affirm that the phrasing of GATT XXIV:8 sub-paragraphs (a)(i) and (b) allows for grades in the elimination of duties and ORRC. Again, the provision does *not* read 'duties and other restrictive regulations of commerce are *substantially eliminated*', but rather 'duties and other restrictive regulations of commerce . . . *are eliminated* with respect to substantially all the trade'. The

---

[122] WTO Appellate Body Report, *Turkey—Textiles*, above at n 9, at paras 48–63.
[123] *Ibid.*
[124] *Compare* also the wording of the RTA exception for trade in services in Art. V:1(b) of the General Agreement on Trade in Services, which states the internal trade liberalization in the following terms: 'provides for the absence or elimination of *substantially all discrimination* . . . among the parties, *in the sectors covered* . . .'
[125] *See* WTO Appellate Body Report, *Turkey—Textiles*, above at n 9, at para. 50.
[126] *Ibid.*, at para. 62.   [127] *Ibid.*, at para. 48.   [128] *Ibid.*

only interpretation consistent with this reading is that Article XXIV:8 of the GATT requires the *complete* elimination of the possibility that duties and ORRC apply to the part of the RTA trade covered by the RTA trade liberalization programme.[129]

Third, the authors take note of an additional element which further supports their conclusion on the inconsistency of constructing the rule on elimination of duties and ORRC in Article XXIV:8 of the GATT as providing for an assessment of its fulfillment on the basis of how much trade is being affected by duties and ORRC at any given moment in time. If the assessment of the portion of trade *affected* by duties and ORRC were to be the criterion for determining whether the requirement on elimination of duties and ORRC had been met, then the meeting of the Article XXIV:8 internal trade requirement would vary according to the number and type of ORRC imposed within the RTA at any given moment. By implication, the RTA compliance with Article XXIV:8 would be also variable, hence uncertain.[130]

Finally, the authors recall the Appellate Body's statements on the rule on elimination of duties and ORRC, which confirm that this rule requires the *complete* elimination of the possibility that ORRC apply to the *part* of the RTA trade that is meant to be the SAT threshold. In *Turkey—Textiles* the Appellate Body implicitly recognized that the possibility to liberalize less than 'all' the trade, together with the possibility to maintain the trade restrictions in the exceptions list in the RTA subsume all the flexibility that Article XXIV:8 of the GATT affords RTA parties in what regards the internal trade requirement.[131] The remarks on the 'substantially all the trade' threshold further highlight that this parameter provides for a leeway to RTA parties solely with regard to the *part of the trade* to be liberalized (which is defined as 'not the same as "all" the trade', but also 'something considerably more than merely "some" of the trade').[132] These remarks are followed by the warning that the degree of flexibility *allowed* by Article XXIV:8 'is *limited* by the requirement that "duties and other restrictive regulations of commerce" be "eliminated

---

[129] Needless to say, the requirement of complete elimination of duties and ORRC applicable in the part of the intra-RTA trade covered by the trade liberalization regime cannot be fulfilled by applying *reduced* duties or ORRC, or by merely *limiting* the possibility that ORRC apply in the intra-RTA trade as, for instance, in the NAFTA safeguards regime. *See* above at n 101. In essence, where a NAFTA partner undertakes a safeguard action on a global basis (in accordance with Art. XIX GATT), each NAFTA partner must be excluded from the action unless its exports account for a substantial share of total imports of the good and contribute importantly to the serious injury or threat thereof. See NAFTA, Ch. 8, Art. 802, at 8–3. The Agreement provides that a NAFTA country *normally* will not be considered as being accountable for a substantial share of total imports, unless it falls among the top five suppliers of the good. *See* L.A. Glick, *Understanding the North American Free Trade Agreement* (Deventer; Boston: Kluwer, 1993), 75.

[130] *See* Lockhart and Mitchell, above at n 15, at 238–39.   [131] *See* above at n 16.

[132] *See* WTO Appellate Body Report, *Turkey—Textiles*, above at n 9, at para. 48. This becomes even more evident in the Spanish and French versions of the report, which read: ' "lo esencial de los intercambios comerciales" significa algo bastante más amplio que tan sólo *parte* de los intercambios comerciales' and ' "l'essentiel des échanges commerciaux" est quelque chose de beaucoup plus important que simplement une *certaine partie* des échanges." '

with respect to substantially all" internal trade'.[133] This underscores that in the *part* of the trade meant to be deemed 'liberalized' duties and ORRC must be *eliminated*, that is *expelled, excluded, removed, gotten rid of*. It follows that no trade restrictions can remain applicable for any part of the intra-RTA trade which is intended to comprise part of the SAT threshold.

D. Exhaustive or Illustrative Character of the Exceptions Listing

As already noted in sub-section 'B' above, the discussion on the exhaustive or illustrative character of the exceptions listing in Article XXIV:8 of the GATT was part of the debates on the 'must—may', 'may—must' or 'may—may' constructions of the exceptions list and the rule on elimination of duties and ORRC. This discussion gains particular relevance in light of the Appellate Body's endorsement of the interpretation that the exceptions list indicates the areas where RTA parties *may* deviate from the general rule prescribing elimination of duties and ORRC, and of its implied recognition that the listing and the possibility to liberalize less than all the trade subsume all the flexibility Article XXI:8 of the GATT affords RTA parties as regards the internal trade requirement. An illustrative listing would allow RTA parties to maintain other trade restrictions in their internal trade beyond those regulated by the provisions in the listing, whereas an exhaustive listing would imply that restrictions regulated by provisions not listed, such is the case of anti-dumping, countervailing duties, and safeguards, must be abolished in customs unions and RTAs.

The authors already argued in sub-section 'B.3' *supra* that the list of exceptions in Article XXIV:8 of the GATT must be understood as being exhaustive. A reading of the listing as merely illustrative does not find support in the text of Article XXIV:8 of the GATT for *reading into* that provision words that are not there ('except, where necessary [measures such as] those permitted under Articles XI, XII, XIII, XIV, XV and XX'). This reading would furthermore leave meaningless the listing[134] and the rule on elimination of duties

---

[133] *See* WTO Appellate Body Report, *Turkey—Textiles, ibid.*, at para. 48; and above n 17.

[134] *See* Mathis, above at n 42, at 61: 'Indeed, [i]f the listing of GATT Article restrictions provided in [Art. XXIV:8 GATT] would be understood to be non-exhaustive, then they also must be considered to be essentially redundant'. Mathis also notes that the exhaustive character of the exceptions list is further confirmed by its legislative history. First, the provision originally encompassed only customs unions (CU), where there is 'the substitution of a single custom territory for two or more customs territories', so that 'substantially the same regulations of commerce are [to be] applied by all members'. *See ibid.* In such a case, the application of safeguards was probably viewed as more likely to be made by the CU (at least after the transitional period), and no longer by the individual territories composing it, hence, the issue of intra-RTA safeguards would not arise. *See ibid.* The FTA exception was included later, and after hard debates regarding preferential trade arrangements, whose trade-distortional effects the most favoured nation (MFN) obligation was aimed at eliminating. The fact that FTAs internal trade requirements mirror those of CUs, suggests that a high standard was established for FTAs to condition the MFN-regional exception only to those arrangements effectively aiming at and leading to a degree of internal trade liberalization as

and ORRC for allowing RTA parties to maintain whatever *sort* of trade restrictions they wish in their internal trade. The authors further noted their understanding that this interpretation is confirmed by the Appellate Body's statement on the exceptions' list in *Turkey—Textiles*, where it referred to the trade restrictions that may be maintained in a customs union internal trade as '*certain* restrictive regulations of commerce *that are otherwise permitted under Articles XI through XV and under Article XX*'.[135] As stated above, the Appellate Body's endorsement of the exhaustive character of the listing is suggested by the highlighting it made that *certain* restrictions may be maintained within a customs union, expressly referring to the provisions in the listing.[136]

In light of the above, it seems more relevant at this point to discuss the argument that interpreting the exceptions listing in Article XXIV:8 of the GATT as being exhaustive leads to a result that is 'manifestly absurd or unreasonable' because GATT's broadest worded exception, Article XXI on measures for security reasons, is not included in the listing either.[137] At a first sight, it seems difficult to explain, based on textual interpretation only, the absence of a reference to Article XXI of the GATT, which is the broadest and more deferential exception, while narrower and less deferential exceptions (XI, XII, XIII, XIV, and even XX) are referred to in the exceptions list in Article XXIV of the GATT. Yet, the singular wording in the chapeau of Article XXI of the GATT ('Nothing in this Agreement *shall be construed* . . .'; italics added) allows the argument to be made that Article XXI does not have to be mentioned in the exceptions list in Article XXIV:8 to remain applicable within RTAs. Given its peculiar reading, Article XXI of the GATT informs the meaning of every other provision in the Agreement, pervasively limiting all commitments undertaken under the Agreement, including the RTA parties' commitment to liberalize their internal trade to benefit from the Article XXIV exception.

---

high as those of CUs. *See ibid.* It is worth recalling that restricting the leeway for RTAs was the prevalent aim then, especially on the part of the United States, which was not part of such arrangements and viewed itself as harmed by them. *See ibid.*

[135] *See* WTO Appellate Body Report, *Turkey—Textiles*, above at n 9, at para. 48. *See also* the introduction to section II of this chapter.

[136] *See also* on this matter Lockhart and Mitchell, above at n 15, at 239.

[137] Art. XXI GATT states:

Nothing in this Agreement shall be construed

    (*a*) to require any contracting party to furnish any information the disclosure of which it considers contrary to its essential security interests; or

    (*b*) to prevent any contracting party from taking any action which it considers necessary for the protection of its essential security interests
        (i) relating to fissionable materials or the materials from which they are derived;
        (ii) relating to the traffic in arms, ammunition and implements of war and to such traffic in other goods and materials as is carried on directly or indirectly for the purpose of supplying a military establishment;
        (iii) taken in time of war or other emergency in international relations; or

    (*c*) to prevent any contracting party from taking any action in pursuance of its obligations under the United Nations Charter for the maintenance of international peace and security.

The VCLT provides that the interpreter may have recourse to legislative history for assistance in the clarification of the meaning of a provision when its textual interpretation 'leaves the meaning ambiguous or obscure or' leads to a result that is 'manifestly absurd or unreasonable'.[138] Then, reviewing the drafting history of Article XXIV:8 of the GATT, the authors conclude that there is a reasonable explanation for the non-inclusion of Article XXI in the exceptions listing, which confirms the interpretation that the drafters understood that mentioning Article XXI in the listing was not necessary.

The drafting history of Article XXIV:8 of the GATT shows that the non-inclusion of Article XXI in the exceptions list in Article XXIV:8 of the GATT comes from the original structure of the International Trade Organization (ITO) Charter, which went through changes when GATT had to replace the non-created ITO. The original structure of the ITO Charter contained separately titled chapters, among them Chapter IV, dedicated to Commercial Policy, and Chapter IX, containing ITO general provisions, which applied to *all* the provisions contained in the other chapters.[139] The provision corresponding to the current Article XXIV was part of the original Chapter IV of the ITO Charter, dedicated to Commercial Policy (as were the general exceptions now under Article XX of the GATT, which were listed as 'General Exceptions to Chapter IV').[140] The provision corresponding to current Article XXI of the GATT, on the other hand, was located under Chapter IX of the ITO Charter, and titled there as 'General Exceptions'.[141] Its preamble, which read: 'Nothing in this *Charter* shall be construed . . .'[142] made clear that the security exception provision applied to the whole ITO agreement. Therefore, it was not necessary and would have been redundant to have a specific reference to the security exception again in the provision that later became Article XXIV.[143] In contrast, it was necessary to make reference to the other restrictions permitted, which were inserted in the commercial policy chapter, under the title 'General Exceptions to Chapter IV' together with the provision that later became Article XXIV of the GATT.[144] This explains why when the corresponding provisions of the ITO Charter became Article XXIV of the GATT the security exception was omitted, maintaining the ITO Charter pattern. The drafters arguably understood that using the same wording ('Nothing in this *Agreement* shall be construed') was enough to make clear that the security exception applies to all provisions in the GATT, even though this may not stand out as evidently as it did in the ITO Charter structure with its separate chapters on Commercial Policy and General Exceptions.[145]

The above shows that the absence of Article XXI of the GATT from the

---

[138] *See* Art. 32(a) and (b) VCLT.   [139] *See* Mathis, above at n 42, at 62–3.
[140] *Ibid.*   [141] *Ibid.*   [142] *Ibid.*   [143] *Ibid.*   [144] *Ibid.*
[145] The GATT drafting history also raised another possible explanation for the absence of Art. XXI in the exceptions list in Art. XXIV:8. Mathis suggests that when the corresponding provisions of the ITO Charter became Art. XXIV GATT, the security exception was probably inadvertently omitted in spite of the absence of a General Exceptions chapter in the GATT. *See* Mathis, above at n 42, at 62–3.

exceptions list in Article XXIV of the GATT does have a reasonable explanation, and confirms the textual interpretation that the exceptions list in sub-paragraphs 8(a)(i) and (b) of Article XXIV is exhaustive. In contrast with the case of Article XXIV, the absence of a reference to Articles XIX (safeguards) and to Article VI (anti-dumping and countervailing duties) in the exceptions list cannot be explained by the texts of these provisions or through negotiating history. Unlike the former version of Article XXI, the earlier versions of Articles XIX and VI were part of the same Chapter IV dedicated to Commercial Policy, together with the former version of Article XXIV of the GATT. Therefore, as regards Articles XIX and VI of the GATT, one must conclude that they were *purposely* left out of the listing because the drafters did not want these trade restrictions to remain permissible in customs unions and FTAs. Therefore, this aspect of the drafting history of Article XXIV:8 of the GATT also supports the conclusion that abolition of trade remedies is mandatory in customs unions and FTAs constituted between WTO Members.

E. Practice on Customs Union and FTAs under the GATT and the WTO

Pursuant to Article 31(1), (2), and (3)(b) of the VCLT, the textual interpretation that Article XXIV:8 mandates the *abolition* of anti-dumping, countervailing duties, and safeguards in substantially all the trade within customs unions and FTAs constituted between WTO Members has to be informed by the context of GATT 1994, and the practice under the GATT and the WTO. The context of GATT 1994 comprehends the provisions in Article XXIV, in the GATT 1947, and in the Understanding on Article XXIV, which have already been taken into account in the discussions raised in the previous sections, and may also encompass decisions of the Contracting Parties on the matter of application of trade remedies in RTAs within the meaning of Article 1(b)(iv) of GATT 1994. Practice under the GATT and the WTO may cover any practice followed by the GATT Contracting Parties on Article XXIV:8 with regard to application of trade remedies in RTAs which falls within the meaning of Article XVI:1 of the WTO Agreement, as well as equivalent practice by WTO Members. The authors also take into account adopted Working Party reports on customs unions and FTAs, which are arguably decisions of the Contracting Parties within the meaning of Article XVI:1 of the WTO Agreement.

The context of GATT 1994 that is relevant for the discussion within this chapter does not go beyond the provisions in Article XXIV, in the GATT 1947, and in the Understanding on Article XXIV, already taken into account in the discussions raised in the previous sections. There are no decisions of the Contracting Parties within the meaning of Article 1(b)(iv) of GATT 1994 on the matter of application of trade remedies in RTAs. A decision of the Contracting Parties within the meaning of Article 1(b)(iv) of GATT 1994 is as 'a formal legal text which represent[s] a legally binding determination in respect of the rights and/or obligations generally applicable to all Contracting Parties to GATT 1947'.[146] In the case of RTA matters, however, none of the decisions adopted by GATT Contracting Parties on RTAs contains an express interpretation of Article XXIV:8 with regard to application of trade remedies within RTAs. On the contrary, there has been unwillingness by GATT Contracting Parties (and later WTO Members) to adopt decisions in respect of the rights and/or obligations generally applicable when the matter regards RTAs.[147]

There is also no practice followed by the GATT Contracting Parties on Article XXIV:8 with regard to application of trade remedies in RTAs within the meaning of Article XVI:1 of the WTO Agreement. The enduring controversies between WTO Members on the same interpretative issues since the early examinations under the GATT to date[148] provide striking evidence of the absence of any subsequent practice in the application of Article XXIV:8 which establishes the agreement of the parties regarding its interpretation within the meaning of Article 31(3)(b) of the VCLT.[149]

Adopted GATT Working Party reports on customs unions and FTAs are arguably decisions of the Contracting Parties within the meaning of Article XVI:1 of the WTO Agreement because these reports were adopted by a jointly decision of the Contracting Parties.[150] These adopted Working Party Reports shall therefore be taken into account in this analysis as an important part of GATT (and WTO) *acquis* whenever they provide relevant guidance on the

---

[146] *See* WTO Panel Report, *US—FSC*, WT/DS108/R, adopted 20 March 2000, as modified by the Appellate Body Report, WT/DS108/AB/R, para. 7.63.

[147] *See* e.g. Committee on Regional Trade Agreements, Background Note by the Secretariat, Systemic Issues Related to Other Regulations of Commerce, WTO Doc. WT/REG/W/17, 31 October 1997, at 3, which reports a draft decision on Art. XXIV GATT which circulated among Uruguay Round negotiators on September 24, 1990, proposing to address the relationship between Arts XIX and XXIV so as to clarify that a safeguard imposed by a member of a customs union or FTA *needed* not be applied to other members of the customs union or FTA. The report informs that the wording in that decision was rejected because 'the language . . . was found too permissive by delegations which held the view that Article XIX actions should not be applied to other members of the customs union and that the absence of any reference to Article XIX in paragraph 8 [of Article XXIV] supported this view'. *ibid.*

[148] *Compare* WTO Committee on Regional Trade Agreements, Synopsis of 'Systemic' Issues Related to Regional Trade Agreements—Note by the Secretariat, above at n 26, at paras 56–8, WTO Negotiating Group on Rules, Compendium of Issues Related to Regional Trade Agreements—Background Note by the Secretariat (Revision), above at n 6, at paras 73–5, and Report of the Sub-Group of the Committee on the 'European Economic Community', above at n 63, BISD 6S/70, 94, at para. 16 and BISD 6S/97, para. 26.

[149] The interpretative controversies show the absence of a '*concordant, common* and *consistent*' sequence of acts or pronouncements establishing a discernable pattern implying the agreement of WTO Members regarding the interpretation of Art. XXIV:8 GATT. *See* WTO Appellate Body Report, *Japan—Alcoholic Beverages II*, above at n 18, at 12 (italics added).

[150] *See* WTO Appellate Body Report, *EC—Poultry*, WT/DS69/AB/R, adopted 23 July 1998, at para. 40, where the Appellate Body clarified that the 'decisions, procedures and customary practices' referred to in Art. XVI:1 WTO Agreement 'include only those taken or followed by the Contracting Parties to the GATT 1947 acting *jointly*'.

issue of application of trade remedies within RTAs.[151] It is the authors' view that none of the Working Party Reports on RTAs adopted by the Contracting Parties has provided relevant guidance on the issue of application of trade remedies within customs unions or FTAs constituted between GATT Parties/ WTO Members.

The authors analysed the few Working Party Reports where the members of the Working Party have made a statement approving the RTAs under examination.[152] Most these arrangements involved non-Parties to the GATT, therefore their approval could only take place under Article XXIV:10 of the GATT (which allows for deviation from Article XXIV requirements),[153] even though reference to this provision was not expressly made in all the cases. That was the case of the Caribbean Free Trade Area (Carifta) and its later formation, the Caribbean Community and Common Market (Caricom). The Carifta Working Party Report stated that '[t]he Working Party agreed that the Agreement provided for the establishing of a free-trade area within the meaning of Article XXIV:8(b)'. The Caricom Working Party report stated that '[t]he Working Party generally agreed that the Caribbean Common Market constituted an interim agreement leading to the establishment of a customs union'. Yet, as both arrangements involved non-Parties to the GATT, they could not *qualify* as a FTA or a customs union under Article XXIV:8, which regulates customs unions and FTAs 'as between the territories of *contracting parties*'.[154] The only approved agreements involving GATT Parties alone were the South Africa–Southern Rhodesia Customs Union Agreement and the Czech Republic–Slovak Republic Customs Union. The South Africa–Southern Rhodesia Customs Union Agreement was 'granted the right to "claim the benefits of . . . Article XXIV" ', but was only provisionally accepted, and never

---

[151] *See* WTO Appellate Body Report, *Japan—Alcoholic Beverages II*, above at n 18, at 15, where the Appellate Body stated: 'Adopted GATT Panel reports are an important part of the GATT acquis. They are often considered by subsequent panels. They create legitimate expectations among WTO Members, and, therefore, should be taken into account where they are relevant to any dispute'.

[152] These are the Reports of the Working Parties that examined the Caribbean Community and Common Market (Caricom), GATT Doc. L/4470, 2 February 1977, BISD 24S/68, para. 13, Caribbean Free Trade Agreement, GATT Doc. L/3584, 29 September 1971, BISD 18S/129, para. 13, Czech Republic–Slovak Republic Customs Union, GATT Doc. L/7501, 15 July 1994, paras 13–18, El Salvador–Nicaragua Free Trade Area, Decision of 25 October 1951, BISD II/30, United Kingdom–Ireland Free Trade Area Agreement, GATT Doc. L/2633, 5 April 1966, BISD 14S/122 and Conclusions at BISD 14S/23, Participation of Nicaragua in the Central American Free Trade Area, GATT Doc. L/891, 25 October 1958, BISD 5S/29, and South Africa–Southern Rhodesia Customs Union Agreement, BISD II/176.

[153] Art. XXIV:10 allows the approval of 'proposals that do not *fully comply* with the requirements of paragraphs 5 to 9 inclusive, provided that such proposals lead to the formation of a customs union or a free-trade area *in the sense of this Article*' (italics added). There is certainly a distinction between a proposal leading to the establishment of a customs union or FTA 'in the sense' of Art. XXIV and an agreement that meets the requirements in Art. XXIV:8. The use of the expression *'fully meets'* in *Turkey—Textiles* suggests that the Appellate Body noted this difference. *See* WTO Appellate Body Report, *Turkey—Textiles*, above at n 9, at para. 48.

[154] *See* Art. XXIV:5 GATT (italics added).

fully recognized.[155] The Czech Republic–Slovak Republic Customs Union is recognized as the only Working Party report where a RTA between GATT Parties was declared to be fully compatible with Article XXIV of the GATT,[156] yet the report does not discuss or even note the issue of application of trade remedies to intra-RTA imports.[157]

The members of the Working Party report on the Agreement Establishing the Czech Republic–Slovak Republic Customs Union did not raise any questions, nor made any comments on the issue of application of trade remedies within the Czech Republic–Slovak Republic Customs Union.[158] The absence of any note on the matter looks odd, since the issue is admittedly highly controversial, and the agreement arguably provides for the replacement of countervailing duties for state aids regulation (Article 19) and elimination of Article XIX safeguards within the customs unions (Article 22).[159] Furthermore, the agreement is unclear on whether a party to the agreement may apply antidumping duties to imports of goods originating in the customs unions, or is allowed to impose anti-dumping duties only to the trade of third parties with the other party to the customs unions (Article 13), and shall apply competition regulation to intra-customs union goods (Article 18).[160] In light of the foresaid, the authors conclude that the adopted Working Party report on the Agreement Establishing the Czech Republic–Slovak Republic Customs Union does not provide relevant guidance on the interpretation of Article XXIV:8 with regard to application of trade remedies in RTAs, which could create legitimate expectations in the WTO Parties.

III. CONCLUSION

This chapter concludes that *abolition* of the *possibility* of applying anti-dumping, countervailing duties, and safeguards in the part of the intra-RTA trade counting towards the fulfillment of the 'substantially all the trade' threshold is mandatory for a RTA between WTO Members to qualify as a customs unions or a FTA under Article XXIV:8 of the GATT interpreted pursuant the VCLT. Accordingly, the authors also conclude that RTAs between WTO Members that were notified as customs unions or FTAs but generally allow

---

[155] *See* Jackson, above at n 3, at 589–90.

[156] *See* WTO Committee on Regional Trade Agreements, Synopsis of 'Systemic' Issues Related to Regional Trade Agreements—Note by the Secretariat, above at n 26, at para. 21. *See also* Working Party Report on the Agreement Establishing the Czech Republic–Slovak Republic Customs Union, above at n 26.

[157] *See* Working Party Report on the Agreement Establishing the Czech Republic–Slovak Republic Customs Union, *ibid*.

[158] *Ibid*.

[159] *See* GATT, Agreement establishing the Customs Union between the Czech Republic and the Slovak Republic, Joint Communication by the Government of the Czech Republic and the Government of the Slovak Republic, GATT Doc. L/7212, 30 April 1993.

[160] *Ibid*.

internal application of trade remedies are illegitimate departures of MFN that lack justification on the basis of Article XXIV of the GATT. The authors purport that this interpretation is further confirmed by the Appellate Body's statements on Article XXIV of the GATT in *Turkey—Textiles*, and bears no inconsistency with the context of the GATT 1994 and its practice.

6

Do Rules of Origin in Free Trade Agreements Comply with Article XXIV GATT?

JOSÉ ANTONIO RIVAS[*]

INTRODUCTION

The multilateral trading system under the World Trade Organization ('WTO') purports to achieve trade liberalization guided by the non-discrimination principle.[1] Simply stated, global trade should be conducted without discriminating between domestic and foreign products nor amongst foreign products. That is, commerce ought to conform to the most favoured nation treatment ('MFN') and national treatment obligations.[2]

The same multilateral trading system allows members of a regional trade agreement ('RTA') to distinguish between *RTA* countries and *non-RTA* countries.[3] Article XXIV exempts members from complying with the MFN principle when they trade with fellow members of a RTA, and allows them to extend and receive exclusive privileges consisting of duty-free and lower tariff

[*] The author is grateful for the rigorous comments of Professors Don Wallace, Christopher Parlin, Manuel Vazquez, and Lorand Bartels. I also would like to thank Mrs Rebecca Rivas-Rogers for her comments and editorial assistance. Of course the errors in this chapter remain my own.

[1] Preamble, GATT 1994.

[2] Arts I and III GATT. The promotion of free trade according to the principles of non-discrimination, most favoured nation and national treatment, is based on the assumption that free trade is desirable given the comparative advantage that nations have by producing either capital-intensive or labour-intensive goods. For a set of arguments assessing the benefits of free trade, *see* P. Krugman, *Strategic Trade Policy and the New International Economics* (Cambridge, Mass.; London: MIT Press, 1986).

[3] Regional Trade Agreements ('RTAs') include Free Trade Areas ('FTAs') as well as Customs Unions ('CUs'). *See* Art. XXIV:8 GATT.

treatment from each other. RTA countries keep these privileges exclusive and prevent trade *deflection*[4] through the use of rules of origin.[5]

Without FTA rules of origin the benefits of the FTA would not be exclusive to its members. Instead, non-FTA countries would also enjoy such benefits. With FTA rules of origin, products made in non-FTA countries which have entered an FTA country and have been re-exported to a second FTA country, can be distinguished from those products whose components are imported into the same FTA country, transformed there and then exported to the second FTA country. In the context of NAFTA, without the NAFTA rules of origin trade deflection could occur as non-NAFTA country imports that enter Mexico but are not transformed there, could be re-exported to the US and enjoy the NAFTA tariff, instead of being charged the higher MFN tariff.

Rules of origin are used to determine whether or not a good is of FTA origin and should therefore receive FTA preferential treatment. For instance, rules of origin can define the minimum percentage of the value of a good that must be added within the FTA, or certain manufacturing processes that must take place within the FTA, in order for a good to be classified as of FTA origin. If a good does not satisfy the FTA rule of origin, then the MFN and not the FTA tariff would be applied.

In determining which goods are of FTA origin the FTA rules of origin should remain *neutral*, i.e. they should simply identify the products qualifying for

---

[4] Trade deflection occurs when a product of a non-FTA member is introduced into the market of a particular FTA member but initially goes through the doorway of a second FTA member, because the latter charges lower tariffs on non-FTA products than the former. For instance US industries opposed the idea of allowing Mexico to become the doorway through which Japanese imports would enter the US market as NAFTA products. This opposition makes sense for FTA members since they do not wish to extend FTA lower tariffs to countries that were not invited to the specific FTA 'club', and which did not grant lower tariffs or duty free treatment to the FTA members. *See* M. Schiff, 'Will the Real "Natural Trading Partner" Please Stand Up?', World Bank Policy Research Working Paper 2161 World Bank, 1999), at 16, available at www.worldbank.org/html/dec/Publications/Workpapers/wps2000series/wps2161/wps2161.pdf (visited 7 September 2005). *See* J.M. Cooper (comment), 'NAFTA's Rules of Origin and Its Effects on the North American Automotive Industry' (1994) 14 Nw J Int L & Bus 442, at 452, D.A. Gantz, 'Implementing the NAFTA *Rules of Origin:* Are the Parties Helping or Hurting Free Trade?' (1995) 12 Ariz J Int & Comp L, 367, at 367, 377, D. Palmeter, *The WTO as a Legal System, Essays on International Trade Law and Policy* (London: Cameron May, 2003), at 148–49 and E. Vermulst, 'Rules of Origin as Commercial Policy Instruments?', in J. Bourgeois, E. Vermulst, and P. Waer (eds), *Rules Of Origin in International Trade: A Comparative Study* (Ann Arbor: U Michigan Press, 1993), 457. *See also* WTO Appellate Body Report, *Turkey—Textiles*, WT/DS34/AB/R, adopted 19 November 1999, paras 61–2. It is important to note that the economics literature refers to *deflection* and *diversion* as different phenomena while the Appellate Body in *Turkey—Textiles* makes no difference between the two concepts. What the Appellate Body refers to as *trade diversion* in its *Turkey—Textiles* report, is referred to in the economics literature as *trade deflection*. In this paper the view is that *deflection* and *diversion* are different concepts. *See* J. Bhagwati and A.O. Krueger, *The Dangerous Drift to Preferential Trade Agreements* (Washington DC: AEI Press, 1995), 24. Trade diversion occurs when non-FTA members are more efficient suppliers of intermediate goods or components than FTA countries and nonetheless, FTA countries shift their demand for those goods from FTA countries because the classification of the final good will have FTA preferential treatment if the components are originated within the FTA.

[5] *See* Art. 1 and Annex II, para. 2 of the Agreement on Rules of Origin.

FTA preferential tariff coverage. If the rules of origin are *overly restrictive* they would extend, in addition to the preferential tariffs, further protection to the goods from FTA countries.

The rules of origin of the US–Canada FTA ('CUSFTA') and NAFTA for ketchup demonstrate the effect that *overly restrictive* rules of origin can have. Under the applicable CUSFTA rule of origin, ketchup made in the US or Canada from tomato paste imported from third countries (e.g. Chile) was considered of CUSFTA origin and therefore enjoyed the CUSFTA preferential tariff. After NAFTA rules of origin replaced those of CUSFTA, only ketchup made from tomato paste from a NAFTA country could receive the NAFTA preferential tariff. As a result, after the creation of NAFTA Chile ceased being the leading exporter of tomato paste to the US and was overtaken by Mexico.[6]

This comparison between the CUSFTA and NAFTA rules of origin applicable to ketchup illustrates how FTA rules of origin can give further preferences and protection to goods from FTA countries beyond the MFN and FTA tariff differential. In addition to identifying those products that qualify for NAFTA tariffs, in practice, certain NAFTA rules of origin have directly discriminated against products of third countries by being more restrictive than the previously applicable CUSFTA rules of origin.

In textiles and apparel the NAFTA rules of origin replacing those of CUSFTA also increased barriers to imports from third countries into the FTA countries. Textiles and apparel were considered to be of CUSFTA origin when the yarn or fibre was transformed into apparel or textile within the CUSFTA region. This means that in order to qualify for the CUSFTA preferential tariff, the yarn or the fibre could be outsourced, i.e. imported from outside the CUSFTA region, and then transformed within the region.[7] In contrast, under NAFTA, only fibres, but no longer yarns can be outsourced.[8]

Certain FTA rules of origin, such as NAFTA's replacing those of CUSFTA for tomato paste or textiles and apparel, raise the question as to whether they are abusively crafted and applied. Clearly, not all FTA rules of origin are *neutral*, in fact, certain FTA rules of origin can negatively affect imports from third countries.

Although the Agreement on Rules of Origin and the Common Declaration with regard to Preferential Rules of Origin (the 'Declaration')[9] do not prohibit FTA rules of origin from being more restrictive for imports from third countries than the previously applicable rules of origin, this paper contends that Article XXIV, and in particular Paragraph 5(b) and its Chapeau[10] read in light

---

[6] *See* Annex 401, NAFTA, available at www.nafta-sec-alena.org (visited 7 September 2005). *See also* Palmeter, above at n 4, at 142–43.

[7] *See* M. Robert, *Negotiating NAFTA, Explaining the Outcome in Culture, Textiles, Autos and Pharmaceuticals* (Toronto: U Toronto Press, 2000), 100–01.

[8] *Ibid.*   [9] *See* Arts 1, 3(c) and Annex II of the Agreement on Rules of Origin.

[10] For the sake of brevity this chapter only refers to the external trade requirement with respect to FTAs, i.e. Art. XXIV:5(b) and its Chapeau, and does not include an analysis of the internal trade requirement of Art. XXIV:8. *See* Art. XXIV:8 GATT. For an extensive analysis of those conditions

of Paragraph 4,[11] govern such rules of origin. The interpretation of Article XXIV could clarify the limits to regulations, such as rules of origin, that countries craft and apply when creating an FTA.

Section I of this chapter argues that FTA rules of origin qualify as *other regulations of commerce* ('ORCs') in accordance with Article XXIV:5, and therefore FTA rules of origin should satisfy the conditions for ORCs set forth in Article XXIV. Section II explains why Article XXIV is a difficult case of interpretation requiring a strict interpretation. Section III interprets the requirements for new regulations of commerce under Article XXIV:5(b) and its Chapeau, and proposes that they should not be *overly restrictive*, i.e. i) ORCs should not be more restrictive after the creation of the FTA than they previously were; and ii) greater restrictiveness of ORCs may only be justified if without such ORCs the FTA's creation or integrity would have been prevented. Section IV, by reference to a classification of the *rules of origin of NAFTA* in terms of restrictiveness, distinguishes between rules of origin that are *overly restrictive* and *neutral* rules of origin which do not add an extra and unlawful layer of protection to the already permitted tariff differentials between the MFN tariffs and the FTA tariffs.

I. FTA RULES OF ORIGIN AS OTHER REGULATIONS OF COMMERCE AND THE APPLICABLE DISCIPLINES

Paragraph 2 of the Declaration defines preferential rules of origin as 'those laws, *regulations* and administrative determinations of general application applied by any member to determine whether goods qualify for preferential treatment under contractual or autonomous trade regimes leading to the granting of tariff preferences (. . .).'[12] The crucial characteristic of preferential rules of origin, including FTA rules of origin, is that they determine whether a product originates in a territory of a State to which a preference applies.[13]

Under the definitions of rules of origin (whether non-preferential, preferential or FTA rules of origin) in the WTO Agreement on Rules of Origin and the Declaration, and in commentaries on the subject,[14] they have been considered part of the more general categories of trade related laws, *regulations*, or administrative regulations. It can be difficult to find an authoritative source of law contradicting the description of rules of origin as *regulations*. Although

---

that RTA countries have to meet *vis-à-vis* RTA partners, *see* J.H. Mathis, *Regional Trade Agreements in The GATT/WTO: Article XXIV and The Internal Trade Requirement* (The Hague, T.M.C. Asser, 2002), 259–83.

[11] *See* Art. XXIV:4 GATT.   [12] *See* Annex II, para. 2 of the Agreement on Rules of Origin.
[13] *See* above at n 4.
[14] *See* W. Goode, *Dictionary of Trade Policy Terms*, 2nd ed. (Cambridge: CUP, 1998), 237 and N. Komuro, 'International Harmonization of Rules of Origin', in P. Ruttley et al., *The WTO and International Trade Regulation* (London: Cameron May, 1998), 86. *See also* Vermulst, above at n 4, at 457.

this observation may appear self-evident, it is pertinent due to a discussion on the nature of rules of origin, which itself may be for more political and strategic motives than for technical reasons.

The Compendium of Issues Related to Regional Trade Agreements of the Negotiating Group on Rules recognizes this discussion as follows:

RTA provisions on rules of origin have raised a number of issues. On the question of whether RTA rules of origin constitute an 'other regulations of commerce' (ORCs) under Article XXIV:5, distinct interpretations subsist:

• RTA origin rules constitute an ORC.
• RTA origin rules do not constitute an ORC, given that by definition they do not affect trade with third parties.
• A case-by-case examination of the preferential rules of origin in RTAs is needed. That examination would clearly indicate whether these rules had restrictive effects on the trade vis-à-vis third parties.[15]

In opposition to the view that FTA rules of origin do not constitute ORCs because they do not affect third parties, it has long been contended and demonstrated in various trade and economic studies that FTA rules of origin may divert trade.[16]

Beyond the views of GATT Working Parties in favor of rules of origin being ORCs[17] and of the Negotiating Group on Rules with regard to RTAs, there is an authoritative source of international law that holds the answer to this issue: Article XXIV:5 interpreted in conjunction with the Declaration.[18]

While interviewing trade economists for this chapter, the fact that Article XXIV does not mention 'rules of origin' was perceived as an impediment to considering that it covers *rules of origin*. Such a conclusion is flawed in that it

---

[15] Negotiating Group on Rules, Compendium of Issues Related to Regional Trade Agreements, Background Note by the Secretariat, WTO Doc. TN/RL/W/8/Rev.1, 1 August 2002, at para. 78.

[16] *See* E.W. James and M. Umemoto, 'NAFTA Trade with East Asia: Rules of Origin and Market Access in Textiles, Apparel Footwear and Electrical Machinery' (2000) 17 ASEAN Econ Bull, 293, H. Shibata, 'The Theory of Economic Unions: A Comparative Analysis of Customs Unions, Free Trade Areas and Tax Unions', in C.S. Shoup (ed), *Fiscal Harmonization In Common Markets*, Volume 1: Theory (New York: Columbia UP, 1967), E. Vermulst and P. Waer, 'European Community Rules of Origin as Commercial Policy Instruments?' (1990) 24 JWT 55 and E.W. James, 'APEC Preferential Rules of Origin: Stumbling Blocks for Liberalization of Trade?' (1997) 31 JWT 113, at 113–14. *See also* I. Forrester, 'The End of Innocence', in Bourgeois, Vermulst, and Waer, above at n 4, at 395.

[17] GATT Working Party Report on the Free-Trade Agreement between Canada and the US ('CUSFTA'), GATT Doc. L/6927, 12 November 1991, BISD 38S/47, 60, at 13, para. 37. For instance concerning the US–Canada FTA the representative of Canada stated: '[T]he question of whether rules of origin were one of other regulations of commerce" in terms of Article XXIV:5(b) had not led to a solution in previous working parties on free trade agreements. Rules of origin for the FTA would operate so as not to have adverse effects on the trade of third parties'. Similarly, one member of the Working Party reviewing the US–Canada FTA has also stated that: '[B]arriers to the trade of other contracting parties with free-trade areas should not be raised and that any new regulations of commerce shall not be more restrictive than those existing prior to the formation of free trade areas. The compatibility of the rules of origin in the FTA with GATT should be examined in the light of these criteria'.

[18] *See* Annex II of the Agreement on Rules of Origin.

disregards the rest of the treaty. On the contrary, interpreting the meaning of a treaty requires acknowledging the whole treaty and its context.

It is worth noting that the Panel in *Turkey—Textiles* stated that 'the ordinary meaning of the terms *other regulations of commerce* could be understood to include *any regulation having an impact on trade*'.[19] This statement further confirms that there is no unreasonableness, absurdity or contradiction in considering that preferential and FTA rules of origin are ORCs. This observation becomes even more obvious from the definitions of non preferential[20] and preferential[21] rules of origin, both of which stress that they are *regulations*.

Common sense leads to the same conclusion. If rules of origin were not ORCs, what would such measures be under WTO law? *Special* other regulations of commerce? *Other* other regulations of commerce? Rejecting that FTA rules of origin are ORCs therefore lacks a solid legal basis and amounts to an unreasonable and absurd conclusion under WTO law.

The conclusion that FTA rules of origin constitute ORCs is important as it implies that they are governed by the disciplines set out in Article XXIV. This conclusion is significant as the Declaration does not specifically prevent FTA members from imposing more restrictive *FTA rules of origin* than those rules of origin existing prior to the creation of the FTA.[22] In other words, the restrictiveness of FTA rules of origin is only limited by the disciplines set out in Article XXIV which prescribe that upon the formation of an FTA its ORCs should not be more restrictive than before.[23] Given that Article XXIV contains the applicable disciplines to ORCs, such as FTA rules of origin, we now turn to the interpretation of Article XXIV.

II. ARTICLE XXIV: A DIFFICULT CASE OF INTERPRETATION

Due to a number of factors Article XXIV is a difficult case of interpretation. First, the purposes of RTAs and the multilateral trade system of the WTO are *not synchronized*, creating a frictional relationship between multilateralism and regionalism. WTO Members directly seek *global trade liberalization*,[24] while the RTA partners directly seek *regional free trade* with the idea of liberalizing world trade as a secondary future goal. This friction becomes more evident as RTAs contain purposive language towards *global liberalization*, but

---

[19] WTO Panel Report, *Turkey—Textiles*, WT/DS34/R, adopted 19 November 1999, paras 9.105 and 9.120.

[20] *See* Art. 1 of the Agreement on Rules of Origin.

[21] *See* Annex II of the Agreement on Rules of Origin.

[22] *Ibid.*, Arts 1 and 3(c) and Annex II. It is worth noting that the disciplines of Art. 3(c) of the Agreement on Rules of Origin prescribing that rules of origin not be more stringent for imports than for domestic products, in accordance with Art. 1, are not applicable to *FTA rules of origin*.

[23] Art. XXIV:5(b) GATT.   [24] Preamble of the WTO Agreement.

not operative language in that direction, e.g. they lack transition schedules to gradually extend RTA preferences to third countries.

Second, applying an *exception* is in itself difficult because in order to prevent abuse of the exception, its application should not contradict the *aims* that the *principle* and its *exception* share.[25] In addition to the conditions that are often present in an exception, e.g. paragraphs 5 and 8 of Article XXIV, the consistency of an exception with the aims it shares with its respective principle is what distinguishes the exception from a mere violation of the principle. At the same time, attaining such consistency renders the application of an exception more complex than the application of a positive obligation. In this instance, Article XXIV, while an *exception* to the MFN principle,[26] should be applied taking into account the *aims* it shares with the MFN principle, i.e. mainly by contributing towards world trade liberalization. This could be achieved, for instance, by enhancing regional free trade without increasing trade barriers or imposing overly restrictive *regulations of commerce* on non-RTA members.

Third, various terms of Article XXIV have a *non-conclusive* character. For instance, the concept that may be comprised in '*other regulations of commerce*' is not defined by Article XXIV; and neither is the criterion to determine whether, after the creation of an FTA, new ORCs are more restrictive than those prior to the formation of the FTA.

Last and perhaps most importantly, political elements are involved in the interpretation of Article XXIV, as virtually all WTO Members are party to RTAs, or planning negotiations to become members thereto. These members may perceive the advantages of being party of RTAs loosely controlled under the WTO framework, i.e. creating regional import substitution zones before competing against the rest of the world. This contributes to a lack of consensus for the adoption of reports on RTAs and minimizes the incentives to strictly interpret, and comply with Article XXIV—since 1995, of the RTAs notified to the WTO Committee on Regional Trade Agreements ('CRTA'), none has been the subject of a report finalized by the CRTA and adopted by consensus.[27]

Article XXIV is a difficult case of interpretation requiring a strict application of the customary rules of interpretation,[28] i.e. the ordinary meaning of the words, the context, the object and purpose, the negotiating history, etc. In this

---

[25] H.L.A. Hart, *The Concept of Law*, 2nd ed. (Oxford: Clarendon, 1994), 260.

[26] *See* WTO Panel Report, *EC—Tariff Preferences*, WT/DS246/R, adopted 20 April 2004, as modified by the Appellate Body Report, paras 7.37 and 7.40. The Panel refers to paras 5 and 8 of Art. XXIV as exception provisions. *See also* WTO Appellate Body Report, *Turkey—Textiles*, above at n 4, paras 43, 58. Art. XXIV is an exception in the sense that it 'may justify a measure which is inconsistent with certain other GATT provisions'.

[27] *See* Statistics, available at the WTO website www.wto.org/english/tratop_e/region_e/summary_e.xls (last visited 7 September 2005).

[28] *See* Vienna Convention on the Law of Treaties, in force 27 January 1980, 1155 UNTS 331, Arts 31 and 32.

regard, the reliance on the object and purpose of a provision would only be to confirm the common meaning of its words;[29] or to clarify, with the use of examples, whether an interpretation conforms with the conditions of a provision examined in light of its object and purpose, e.g. *US—Shrimp.*[30] However, the reliance on a purposive provision should not go as far as directing the interpretative exercise by applying it as an operative provision to the facts of a case[31] because such application could lead to adding or diminishing the rights or obligations covered under the WTO Agreements.[32]

III. INTERPRETATION OF ARTICLE XXIV: 5 (B) — THE EXTERNAL TRADE REQUIREMENT FOR FTAS

Given that the Appellate Body has recognized that the provisions of Article XXIV should be read in light of Article XXIV:4,[33] the analysis of Article XXIV:5(b) is preceded by an examination of Article XXIV:4.

---

[29] *See* WTO Appellate Body Report, *Argentina—Footwear (EC)*, WT/DS121/AB/R, adopted 12 January 2000, paras 94, 146–47. *See* WTO Appellate Body Report, *Korea—Dairy*, WT/DS98/AB/R, adopted 12 January 2000, paras 87 and 90. *See also* WTO Appellate Body Report, *Brazil—Desiccated Coconut*, WT/DS22/AB/R, adopted 20 March 1997, at 18.

[30] *See* WTO Appellate Body Report, *US—Shrimp*, WT/DS58/AB/R, adopted 6 November 1998, paras 16, 155, 156, 169, 172 and 174–76. In concluding that the US ban of shrimp imports, as applied, had a *'plainly discriminatory and unjustifiable effect'* contrary to the Chapeau of Art. XX, the Appellate Body provided examples of how the defeat of the conditions of the Chapeau read in light of the object and purpose of Art. XX could have been avoided, i.e. instead of banning their imports, the US could have negotiated with the complainants as it did with other nations for the protection of sea turtles. *See also* WTO Appellate Body Report, *US—Gasoline*, WT/DS2/AB/R, adopted 20 May 1996, at 7, 14, 17 and 28.

[31] *See Military and Paramilitary Activities in and against Nicaragua Case (Nicaragua v United States of America)* (Merits) [1986] ICJ Rep 94, paras 275–76. Contrary to the interpretative practice of the WTO Appellate Body, the ICJ has given a predominant role and a binding character to the object and purpose of treaties. In *Nicaragua v United States of America*, the ICJ concluded that the US attacks on oil installations and ports, and its general trade embargo constituted 'a violation of the obligation not to defeat the object and purpose of the treaty'; i.e. 'they undermined the whole spirit of a bilateral agreement directed at sponsoring friendship and commerce between the two States party'. *See* Art. XXIII:1 GATT. It is worth noting that in accordance with Art. XXIII:1 GATT a WTO Member may bring a complaint alleging that the attainment of an objective of a WTO Agreement is being impeded as a result of any measure whether or not it conflicts with the WTO Agreements. Under the practice of the ICJ, e.g. *Nicaragua v United States of America*, contradicting the object and purpose of a treaty has constituted a basis to conclude that the treaty at issue has been breached. By contrast, undermining the object and purpose of WTO Agreements has not been interpreted by the Appellate Body as sufficient ground to conclude that an obligation of a WTO Agreement has been violated.

[32] *See* Annex 1A of the WTO Agreement and Arts 3.2 and 19.2 of the DSU. WTO Appellate Body Report, *India—Patents (US)*, WT/DS50/AB/R, adopted 16 January 1998, paras 46–8, where the Appellate Body rejected the view of the Panel that the legitimate expectations of members always had to be taken into account in interpreting the TRIPS Agreement, is a case that reflects how the Appellate Body favours a textual interpretation. In that case the Appellate Body emphasized as a principle of interpretation that it 'must not add to or diminish rights and obligations provided in the *WTO Agreement*'. *See also* WTO Appellate Body Report, *Chile—Alcoholic Beverages*, WT/DS110/AB/R, adopted 12 January 2000, para. 79.

[33] *See* WTO Appellate Body Report, *Turkey—Textiles*, above at n 4, at paras 57, 61–6.

A. Interpreting Article XXIV in Light of the Purpose set forth in Article XXIV:4

Article XXIV:4 reads as follows:

The contracting parties recognize the desirability of increasing freedom of trade by the development, through voluntary agreements, of closer integration between the economies of the countries parties to such agreements. They also recognize that the *purpose of a customs union* or of a *free-trade area* should be to *facilitate trade between the constituent territories and not to raise barriers to the trade of other contracting parties with such territories.* (emphasis added)

In *Turkey—Textiles*, Turkey, a party to a customs union with the EC (the Association between Turkey and the European Communities), relied on Article XXIV in its attempt to justify the introduction of quotas on nineteen categories of Indian textile and clothing products.[34]

In this case, Article XXIV:4 was interpreted incorrectly by the Panel when it was applied to the measures under review in order to test whether they are justified under Article XXIV. The Panel concluded:

[T]he conditional right to form a regional trade agreement has to be understood and interpreted within the parameters set out in paragraph 4.[35]

By stating that Article XXIV:4 *determines the parameters* for Article XXIV, the Panel suggested that Paragraph 4 contains operative language and thus could be a legal basis to test the measures under review. Similarly, for Marceau and Reiman[36] it seems clear that paragraph 4 'proscribes RTAs from "rais[ing] barriers to trade with third countries."' [37]

The Appellate Body disagreed with the view of the Panel and differentiated between those paragraphs which contain operative language, such as Paragraph 5 and its Chapeau, and Paragraph 4 which only has purposive language.[38] However, it explained that the Chapeau of Paragraph 5 must be interpreted in light of the purpose set forth in Paragraph 4.[39]

When the Appellate Body decided on the legality of the quota restrictions issued by Turkey, it tested their consistency by relying on the Chapeau of Paragraph 5, which concerns the question of whether the absence of the measures at issue would have prevented the existence of the RTA.

The Chapeau of Paragraph 5 reads as follows:

Accordingly, *the provisions of this Agreement shall not prevent,* as between the territories of contracting parties, *the formation of a customs union or of a free-trade area* or

---

[34] *Ibid.*, paras 17, 18, 20, 41 and 42.
[35] *See* WTO Panel Report, *Turkey—Textiles*, above at n 19, at para. 9.105.
[36] G. Marceau and C. Reiman, 'When and How Is an RTA Compatible with the WTO?' (2001) 28 LIEI 297.
[37] *Ibid.*, at 319.
[38] *See* WTO Appellate Body Report, *Turkey—Textiles*, above at n 4, at paras 57, 61–6.
[39] *Ibid.*

the adoption of an interim agreement necessary for the formation of a customs union or of a free-trade area (. . .).[40]

The Appellate Body found that Turkey's quantitative restrictions were not justified under Article XXIV because Turkey had 'not demonstrated that the formation of a customs union between Turkey and the European Communities would be prevented if it were not allowed to adopt [the] quantitative restrictions'.[41] The measures in question were not *necessary*[42] for the formation of the Association between Turkey and the EC as Turkey could have adopted alternative measures such as:

Rules of origin for textile and clothing products that would allow the European Communities to distinguish between those textile and clothing products originating in Turkey, which would enjoy free access to the European Communities under the terms of the customs union, [and those originating in third countries.][43] (emphasis added).

By concluding that Turkey could have adopted alternative measures to preserve the integrity of the RTA, the Appellate Body strictly complied with the operative provision (i.e. the Chapeau of Paragraph 5). The implication is that Turkey neither took into account the 'purpose' of RTAs 'not to raise barriers to trade',[44] nor made any effort to avoid 'creating adverse effects on the trade of [non-RTA countries]'.[45] Therefore, the Appellate Body implicitly followed the purpose of RTAs contained in Paragraph 4 and effectively interpreted the Chapeau of Paragraph 5 in *light of the purpose* of RTAs set out in Paragraph 4.

B. Strict Requirements for New Measures upon the Formation of an FTA under the Article XXIV Defence.

In *Turkey—Textiles* the Appellate Body stated:

Article XXIV may justify a measure which is inconsistent with certain other GATT provisions.[46]

---

[40] *See* Art. XXIV:5 GATT.

[41] WTO Appellate Body Report, *Turkey—Textiles*, above at n 4, at para. 63.

[42] *Ibid.* For the sake of clarity, it is important to note that the term 'necessary' contained in the Chapeau refers to 'the adoption of an interim agreement' that would be required for 'the formation of an RTA' (an FTA or a CU). The requirement that the measures created upon the formation of an RTA be necessary for the creation and existence of the RTA does not come directly from the language of the Chapeau. In *Turkey—Textiles* the Appellate Body concluded that Turkey could not rely on the Art. XXIV defence because 'Turkey ha[d] not demonstrated that the formation of a customs union between Turkey and the European Communities would be prevented if it were not allowed to adopt these quantitative restrictions'. It is from this conclusion of the Appellate Body that the measures at issue are required to be *necessary* for the creation or existence of the RTA.

[43] *Ibid.*, para. 62.   [44] Art. XXIV:4 GATT.

[45] Preamble, Understanding on the Interpretation of Article XXIV of the GATT 1994.

[46] *Ibid.*, para. 58. *See also* WTO Appellate Body Report, *US—Line Pipe*, WT/DS202/AB/R, adopted 8 March 2002, para. 199 and J. Pauwelyn, 'The Puzzle of WTO Safeguards and Regional Trade Agreements' (2004) 7 JIEL 109. *See also* WTO Appellate Body Report, *Argentina—Footwear (EC)*, above at n 29, at para. 114.

Article XXIV therefore may justify the introduction of measures that violate other WTO provisions. The RTA country imposing such a measure has the burden of invoking the *Article XXIV defence* and meeting its two part test.

1. The Two Part Test of Article XXIV

In *Turkey—Textiles*, for the first time, the Panel and the Appellate Body extensively analysed and interpreted the requirements of Article XXIV: 4, 5, and 8. The Appellate Body analysed the issue of whether new measures can be successfully justified by the *Article XXIV defence*, and it established a comprehensible criterion to determine whether new restrictive measures are necessary to create the RTA.[47]

The relevant issue in *Turkey—Textiles* was whether the exception provided by Article XXIV regarding the right of a member to lower tariffs and trade barriers exclusively to countries belonging to the same RTA (and not to non-RTA countries) also includes a right to impose quotas on imports from non-RTA countries (i.e. Turkey's right to impose quotas on Indian Textile).[48]

The Appellate Body concluded that the quotas introduced by Turkey were inconsistent with Articles XI and XIII GATT, and with Article 2.4 of the Agreement on Textiles and Clothing.[49] The Appellate Body also found that the quotas were not allowed under Article XXIV[50] and laid out a two part test for analysing whether the restrictions imposed on imports from non-RTA countries can successfully rely on *the Article XXIV defence*. It explained that:

In a case involving the formation of a customs union [or a free trade area], this 'defence' is available only when two conditions are fulfilled. First, the party claiming the benefit of this defence must demonstrate that the measure at issue is introduced upon the formation of a customs union that fully meets the requirements of sub-paragraphs 8(a) and 5(a) of Article XXIV, [or the requirements of sub-paragraphs 8(b) and 5(b) of Article XXIV in the case of a free trade area]. And, second, that party must demonstrate that the formation of that customs union [or the free trade area] would be prevented if it were not allowed to introduce the measure at issue. Again, both these conditions must be met to have the benefit of the defence under Article XXIV.[51]

In accordance with the two part test, this chapter applies the operative provisions, Article XXIV:5(b) and the Chapeau, to a particular case read under the Article XXIV defence: *US—Line Pipe*.

The Chapeau and Article XXIV:5(b) read as follows:

Accordingly, the provisions of this Agreement shall not prevent, as between the territories of contracting parties, the formation of (. . .) a free-trade area; Provided that:
(. . .)

---

[47] *See* WTO Appellate Body Report, *Turkey—Textiles*, above at n 4, at paras 17, 18, 20, and 22.
[48] *Ibid.*, paras 17, 18, 20, 41 and 42.   [49] *See* Arts XI and XIII GATT and Art. 2.4 ATC.
[50] *See* WTO Appellate Body Report, *Turkey—Textiles*, above at n 4, at paras 17, 18, 20, 41 and 42.
[51] *Ibid.*, para. 58.

(b) with respect to a free-trade area, (. . .) the duties and other regulations of commerce maintained in each of the constituent territories and applicable at the formation of such free-trade area (. . .) to the trade of contracting parties not included in such area (. . .) *shall not be higher or more restrictive than the corresponding duties and other regulations of commerce existing in the same constituent territories prior to the formation of the free-trade area,* (emphasis added).

A. REQUIREMENTS OF ARTICLE XXIV:5(B): THE LEVEL OF
RESTRICTIVENESS OF THE DUTIES AND OTHER REGULATIONS OF
COMMERCE APPLICABLE BY THE FTA MEMBERS IN THEIR RESPECTIVE
TERRITORIES PRIOR TO THE FTA

i. An incorrect interpretation of article XXIV:5(b): The Reading of the Panel in US—Line Pipe

On February 11, 2000, after an investigation conducted by its International Trade Commission (the 'ITC'), the US imposed a safeguard measure on imports of circular welded carbon quality line pipe (the *'line pipe safeguard'*). The *line pipe safeguard*, which was applicable only to non-NAFTA countries, entered into effect on March 1, 2000.[52]

Korea contended that the US could not successfully rely on the *Article XXIV defence* to apply the *line pipe safeguard*, which arguably breached Articles I, XIII and XIX GATT, and the Agreement on Safeguards. The issue was whether *the Article XXIV defence* justified the application of *the line pipe safeguard* solely to non-NAFTA countries.

In *US—Line Pipe* the Panel had an opportunity to interpret the external trade requirement for an FTA, i.e. the conditions that in accordance with Article XXIV an FTA member has to meet concerning third countries. However, instead of conducting a detailed analysis of Article XXIV:5(b), the Panel found that NAFTA was a *prima facie* case of conformity with this provision,[53] and the exclusion of imports from Canada and Mexico from the scope of *the line pipe safeguard* was justified under Article XXIV.[54] The Panel stated:

Concerning Article XXIV:5(b) (. . .) while the *United States ha[d] placed on the record extensive evidence supporting its right to rely on Article XXIV as a defense,* Korea has not disputed any of this evidence, either in terms of its accuracy or its sufficiency.[55] (emphasis added)

The Panel did not explain why or how the extensive evidence submitted by the US proved that NAFTA was consistent with Article XXIV:5(b). It simply found that *the line pipe safeguard* constituted an *elimination of duties and*

---

[52] *See* WTO Panel Report, *US—Line Pipe*, WT/DS202/R, adopted 8 March 2002, as modified by the Appellate Body Report, WT/DS202/AB/R, paras 2.1–2.5 and 7.310. The *line pipe safeguard* would allow the first 9,000 short tons of imports from each country, with annual reductions in the rate of duty in the second and third years. A 19 per cent rate of duty would be imposed to imports above 9,000 short tons during the first year. This percentage would decrease to 11 per cent in the third year.

[53] *Ibid.*, paras 7.144–145.   [54] *Ibid.*, para. 7.146 and 7.163.   [55] *Ibid.*, para. 7.145.

other restrictive regulations of commerce among NAFTA countries,[56] and reasoned that such elimination occurred upon the formation of NAFTA when:

[I]mports from Canada and Mexico were excluded from the line pipe measure on the basis of Article 802 of NAFTA.[57]

For the Panel the *line pipe safeguard* and Article 802 were equivalent. It stated:

Since the line pipe measure introduces a tariff quota, we consider that the line pipe measure constitutes a 'dut[y] [or] other restrictive regulation [ ] of commerce' within the meaning of Article XXIV:8(b). *As the exclusion of imports from Canada and Mexico therefore forms part of the elimination of 'duties and other restrictive regulations of commerce' between NAFTA members, it is in principle authorized by Article XXIV:5* (. . .)[58] (emphasis added)

However, the Appellate Body declared that the Panel finding that Article XXIV justified *the line pipe safeguard* had no legal effect. The Appellate Body considered that in order to adjudicate the *US—Line Pipe* matter it was unnecessary to analyse the Article XXIV defence because the US did not meet the 'parallelism' requirement.[59] According to this requirement the imports included in the serious injury investigations (under Articles 2.1 and 4.2 of the Agreement on Safeguards)[60] should correspond to the imports included in the application of the measure.[61] The rationale behind this requirement is that safeguard measures should be applied to those imports that caused the serious injury, and to the extent that they caused such an injury.

The Appellate Body noted that while the ITC performed an investigation including line pipe imports both from NAFTA and non-NAFTA countries, the

---

[56] *Ibid.*, para. 7.144.   [57] *Ibid.*, fn 128.   [58] *Ibid.*, para. 7.141.

[59] *See* WTO Appellate Body Report, *US—Line Pipe*, above at n 46, at paras 181, 199. *See also* Pauwelyn, above at n 46. Pauwelyn criticizes the Appellate Body's requirement of parallelism and offers members of RTAs a range of options of WTO safeguards from which to choose.

[60] Art. 2.1 of the Agreement on Safeguards reads:

A Member may apply a safeguard measure to a product only if that Member has determined (. . .) that such product is being imported into its territory in such increased quantities (. . .) as to cause or threaten to cause serious injury to the domestic industry that produces like or directly competitive products.

Art. 4.2 reads:

(a) In the investigation to determine whether increased imports have caused or are threatening to cause serious injury to a domestic industry (. . .) the competent authorities shall evaluate *all relevant factors* of an objective and quantifiable nature having a bearing on the situation of that industry (. . .) (emphasis added).

(b) The determination referred to in subparagraph (a) shall not be made unless this investigation demonstrates (. . .) the existence of the causal link between increased imports of the product concerned and serious injury or threat thereof. When factors other than increased imports are causing injury to the domestic industry at the same time, such injury shall not be attributed to increased imports.

Accordingly, all factors having a bearing on the situation of the affected industry shall be evaluated in the serious injury investigation. Therefore the factors under investigation shall include all increases of imports of the product concerned, notwithstanding their place of origin.

[61] *See* WTO Appellate Body Report, *US—Line Pipe*, above at n 46, at para. 181.

US only applied the *line pipe safeguard* to non-NAFTA countries. Thus, such application was done:

[W]ithout providing a reasoned and adequate explanation that establishes explicitly that imports from non-NAFTA sources by themselves satisfied the conditions for the application of a safeguard measure.[62]

In addition to not reviewing the *line pipe safeguard* under the parallelism requirement, the interpretation of the Panel is in error because it mixed-up Article 802 and the *line pipe safeguard*. Article 802, effective since 1995, proscribed the application of safeguards among NAFTA countries.[63] By contrast, the *line pipe safeguard*, effective since March 1, 2000,[64] consisted of tariff quotas applied to non-NAFTA countries.[65]

Distinguishing between these two measures leads then to a complete analysis of the *line pipe safeguard*, and to the application of the two part test to the facts of *US—Line Pipe*.

ii. An Appropriate Interpretation of Article XXIV:5(b) in US—Line Pipe

The first part of the test is to determine whether safeguard measures fall within the meaning of the terms '*duties or other regulations of commerce*'. Safeguard measures, as considered by the Panel,[66] qualify as *other regulations of commerce*.

The next issue in the examination of the *line pipe safeguard* is whether 'the existing' ORCs in the constituent territories (Mexico, Canada, and the US) prior to NAFTA's entry into force, became 'higher or more restrictive' than those 'applicable' once NAFTA was formed.

Under Article 802, once NAFTA entered into force the possibility of applying safeguards to imports from NAFTA countries was limited, but remained with respect to third countries. Since the potential for introducing safeguard measures on imports from countries such as Korea (i.e. third countries once NAFTA was formed) existed before and after NAFTA, *other regulations of commerce* did not become more restrictive after NAFTA's creation. Therefore, the existence of Article 802 was consistent with Article XXIV:5(b) and the actual measure applied, i.e. *the line pipe safeguard*, was in principle justified. However, the examination of *the line pipe safeguard* continues under the Chapeau.

---

[62] *Ibid.*, para. 197.   [63] *See* Art. 802 NAFTA.

[64] *See* Pauwelyn, above at n 46. Pauwelyn describes Art. 802 as the provision that reserves the right of NAFTA Members to take safeguards under GATT Art. XXIV. Considering this description, it can also be inferred, as argued in this paper, that Art. 802 and the actual safeguards are different in nature.

[65] *See* WTO Panel Report, *US—Line Pipe*, above at n 52, at paras 7.127–7.134. In their arguments the parties did not rely on the difference between Art. 802 exempting the NAFTA Members from the application of safeguards, and the actual *line pipe safeguard* applied by the US to third countries. While the US argued that it was entitled to apply the *line pipe safeguard* only to third countries in accordance with the Chapeau, Korea argued that it had not been demonstrated that NAFTA was in compliance with Art. XXIV:8, i.e. that NAFTA was a FTA.

[66] *Ibid.*, para. 7.148.

B. THE CHAPEAU OF ARTICLE XXIV:5 APPLIED TO US—LINE PIPE

The second part of the test refers to the Chapeau which requires the FTA country imposing the trade restriction to demonstrate that the restrictions were *indispensable or necessary* for the creation of the free trade area.[67]

In *Turkey—Textiles* the Appellate Body read the phrase 'shall not prevent' of the Chapeau in the sense that the 'provisions of the GATT Agreement *shall not make impossible* the formation of a customs union [or an FTA]'.[68] The Appellate Body reasoned:

(. . .) *Article XXIV can justify the adoption of a measure which is inconsistent with certain other GATT provisions* only if the measure is introduced upon the formation of a customs union [or and FTA], and *only to the extent that the formation of the customs union [or an FTA] would be prevented if the introduction of the measure were not allowed.*[69] (emphasis added).

Similarly, in applying the Chapeau to *US—Line Pipe* the question would be whether *the line pipe safeguard* of March 1, 2000, indeed a new measure, was necessary for the formation and coherence of NAFTA as an FTA. If a safeguard was to be applied to non-NAFTA Members, in order to maintain the coherence of NAFTA by fulfilling the Article 802 undertaking of eliminating *other restrictive regulations of commerce* such as safeguards, such measure should not cover NAFTA Members. In this regard, the *line pipe safeguard* was argued to be instrumental to maintain the coherence of NAFTA.[70]

Although NAFTA would not have disappeared if the safeguard had covered Mexico and Canada, with such coverage NAFTA would not be an FTA without safeguards amongst its members. It can thus be argued that the application of a safeguard among NAFTA Members could directly affect the condition set out under Article XXIV:8(b) of eliminating other restrictive regulations of commerce on substantially all trade between the FTA countries. Maintaining the existence of the FTA[71] in accordance with the liberalization agreed by its members is the standard favoured by this paper because a lower standard, i.e. guaranteeing a mere formal existence of the FTA, would run contrary to the condition of eliminating trade barriers on substantially all regional trade.[72]

So far the analysis in this section would lead to a similar conclusion to the Panel's finding. Yet, the question of whether the *line pipe safeguard* was

---

[67] *See* WTO Appellate Body Report, *Turkey—Textiles*, above at n 4, at para. 63.
[68] *Ibid.*, para. 45.   [69] *Ibid.*, para. 46.
[70] *See* WTO Panel Report, *US—Line Pipe*, above at n 52, at para. 7.132.
[71] *See* WTO Appellate Body Report, *Turkey—Textiles*, above at n 4, at para. 46. In limiting the application of measures inconsistent with WTO Agreements, the formation of the FTA should not be prevented. Maintaining the existence of an FTA should also be guaranteed as the formation of a short-lived FTA would make no sense.
[72] *See* Art. XXIV:8(b) GATT.

necessary can only be completely addressed by solving the issue of whether *an alternative and less restrictive measure* could have been applied.[73]

Clearly, no measures other than safeguards could have been applied because the specific *other restrictive regulations of commerce* that NAFTA Members chose to eliminate, i.e. safeguards, could only be *NAFTA exclusive* if they could still be applied to non-NAFTA Members.

However, in this particular case, the specific characteristics of, and the manner in which the *line pipe safeguard* was applied (i.e. they were applied only to non-NAFTA countries though the serious injury investigation giving rise to the safeguards did not distinguish between the rise in imports from NAFTA and non-NAFTA countries as different causes of serious injury) leads to the conclusion that the application of the specific *line pipe safeguard* was not necessary. In other words, a different sort of safeguard could have been imposed: A safeguard different from the *line pipe safeguard* in that it could have been applied to imports from non-NAFTA countries to the extent that such imports would have caused, by themselves, a serious injury to the US industry, i.e. a safeguard in compliance with the parallelism requirement.

IV. ANALYSIS OF NAFTA RULES OF ORIGIN, OTHER REGULATIONS OF COMMERCE, UNDER THE ARTICLE XXIV REQUIREMENTS

This chapter contends that FTA rules of origin (e.g. NAFTA's) are indeed ORCs and therefore should be analysed under the requirements of Article XXIV:5(b) and the Chapeau. They should be subject to an analysis parallel to the review of the tariff quotas by the Appellate Body in *Turkey—Textiles*; and to the review proposed above of the line pipe safeguard of *US—Line Pipe* (*see* table on facing page).

Under this methodology, as ORCs, FTA rules of origin would have to meet the two part test: i) they should not become more restrictive than the respective *regulations* existing before the formation of the FTA; and ii) as new restrictive measures, they would only be permitted if without them the formation or coherence of the FTA would have been 'prevented'.

A. FTA Rules of Origin should not be more restrictive than the respective *Regulations* existing prior to the Formation of the FTA

FTA rules of origin are necessary to identify the goods that qualify for the preferential tariffs. This qualification is a means to prevent extending the

---

[73] *See* WTO Appellate Body Report, *Turkey—Textiles*, above at n 4, at para. 62. A similar analysis was used by the Appellate Body in *Turkey—Textiles* when it explained that rules of origin instead of quotas could have been used in order to maintain the preferences of the RTA members.

Table 1.

ORCs:	Turkey—Textiles Tariff Quotas	US—Line Pipe Line Pipe Safeguard
i. Test under Article XXIV:5(b): Have ORCs *vis-à-vis* third countries become more restrictive?	Yes. The new tariff quotas were imposed on third countries.	No. Although the application of the line pipe safeguard was a new restrictive measure, the possibility of applying it to third countries existed even before NAFTA.
ii. Test under the Chapeau: Would not applying the new restrictive regulations otherwise have prevented the creation or coherence of the FTA?	No, there were less restrictive alternative measures that could have been applied: Rules of origin.	No, there were less restrictive alternative measures that could have been applied: Safeguards complying with the parallelism requirement.

FTA's preferences to goods which originate outside the territory covered by the FTA,[74] i.e. to avoid trade deflection.[75]

As set out by the GATT Working Party reviewing the Spain–EFTA Agreement, 'the purpose of the rules was to prevent deflection of trade and not to limit the scope of free trade nor create obstacles to third country exports,'[76] e.g. not to cause trade diversion.[77]

While FTA rules of origin ensure, as necessary, the privileges of FTA partners, they should still be *neutral*.[78] That is, the preferential treatment

---

[74] *See* E.I. Kingston, 'The Economics of Rules of Origin', in Bourgeois, Vermulst, and Waer, above at n 4, at 14. FTA rules of origin appear to be fundamental to maintain the privileges of FTA countries as seen in the case of motor vehicles under the US–Canada FTA. In that case while the local value content demanded by the US industry of products of non-FTA origin was 70–80 per cent, the value content under such FTA was 50 per cent. This means that a motor vehicle product with Canadian components would be considered of US origin by having 50 per cent US value content, while if instead it had Korean components it would only be considered of US origin by having 70–80 per cent US value content. *See also* GATT Working Party Report on CUSFTA, above at n 17, at paras 35 and 40.

[75] *See* above at n 4 on trade deflection. *See also* P. Brenton, 'Rules of Origin in Free Trade Agreements' (2003) Trade Note 4 (World Bank, 2000).

[76] *See* GATT Working Party Report on the Spain–EFTA Countries Agreement, GATT Doc. L/5045, 24 October 1980, at 9, para. 28.

[77] *See* Bhagwati *et al.*, above at n 4.

[78] *See also* J. Matthies, 'EC Rules of Origin from an Official's Point of View', in Bourgeois, Vermulst, and Waer, above at n 4, at 419. Matthies contends that rules of origin should not be used

amongst FTA members *vis-à-vis* non-FTA countries would be provided by the tariff differential between the MFN and NAFTA tariffs,[79] but not by the FTA rules of origin. In other words, under the concept of *neutrality* FTA preferences would not be further increased by highly restrictive rules of origin of particular industries, e.g. NAFTA rules of origin in textiles and apparel.[80]

The *neutrality* of FTA rules of origin, and hence their consistency with Article XXIV, runs parallel to the idea of minimizing the adverse effects on non-FTA parties.[81] In this regard a Working Party member stated that:

Rules of origin in the context of the [U.S-Canada] FTA had to be operated in such a manner as not to cause adverse effects on the trade of third parties, as provided in Article XXIV.[82]

Commentators have opposed the analysis of FTA rules of origin under the framework of Article XXIV by relying both on the lack of a WTO agreement on preferential rules of origin, as well as on the difficulty of comparing the FTA rules of origin once created, to previous existing regulations of the same nature. For instance, Mathis appears to oppose such a review on the grounds that there are no FTA rules of origin preceding the creation of the FTA.[83] He also argues that there is a 'stretch engaged' in reviewing FTA rules of origin under Article XXIV because the term *rules of origin* is not mentioned therein.[84]

---

as instruments of commercial policy nor to create restrictive distorting or disruptive effects on international trade. They should not be manipulated according to the requirements of certain sectors. *See also* Kingston, above at n 74.

[79] The tariff differential equals the MFN tariff minus the NAFTA tariff (i.e. tariff differential = MFN tariff – NAFTA tariff).

[80] Administratively, the trade effects of an FTA can be traced to the regulations accompanying the formation of the FTA. By means of econometric regressions the change in the flow of imports from third countries can be attributed to tariff differentials while others to, among other factors, rules of origin. From the effects attributed to rules of origin, a determination can be made on whether they are overly restrictive or neutral. This determination is two-fold. The first element of this determination relies on whether the new rule of origin applicable to a specific industry is more restrictive than the previously applicable rule of origin. The comparison between pre-FTA and post-FTA trade flows of a particular industry into the FTA territory would be accompanied by an assessment of whether the modification of the rules of origin in that particular industry caused trade diversion. The second element concerning whether the rules of origin are overly restrictive is whether their greater restrictiveness with respect to previous rules of origin was necessary for the integrity of the FTA. In this regard, what makes the FTA rules of origin of a particular industry overly restrictive, as opposed to neutral, are their effects compared to those of rules of origin of the universe of industries of the same FTA.

[81] *See* M.E. Burfisher et al., *Regionalism: Old and New, Theory and Practice* (International Food Policy Research Institute, February 2004), available at www.ifpri.org/divs/mtid/dp/mtidp65.htm (visited 7 September 2005), at Annex: Analytical Tools in the Viner-Meade Framework. It is important to note that upon the formation of an FTA, trade diversion is likely to exist due to a series of factors (inelastic export supply of the fellow FTA members, tariff differentials, FTA rules of origin). Hence, rather than eliminating trade diversion overall, *neutral rules of origin* would minimize trade diversion.

[82] GATT Working Party Report on CUSFTA, above at n 17, at 2.

[83] *See* Mathis, above at n 10, at 253.   [84] *Ibid.*, at 254.

In response to arguments that complete discretion is sanctioned under WTO law to craft FTA rules of origin, is it worth noting that the limits to the freedom of creating an FTA and the regulations that go with it are set forth by Article XXIV.

In this connection, comparing newly created FTA rules of origin to regulations of the same nature is not only possible but necessary. Otherwise, adopting any *restrictive* rule of origin under the label of a rule of origin of an FTA would be open authorization for protectionism.

The shift of the US and Canada from their preferential *CUSFTA rules of origin* to the *NAFTA rules of origin* with regard to textiles and apparel, as explained above, illustrates how *FTA rules of origin* can raise barriers to imports from third countries.[85] While under CUSFTA the yarn or the fibre could be outsourced, under NAFTA only fibres, but not longer yarn, could be outsourced.[86]

Remarks by a Canadian official during the NAFTA negotiations further confirm that the yarn-forward rule was more restrictive than the existing CUSFTA rule. The official stated that 'under the yarn forward proposal, 90 per cent of US and Mexican apparel production will qualify for trade preferences, while less than 50 per cent of Canadian production, which relies heavily on imported yarn will qualify'.[87] Similarly, the former president of Canadian Apparel Manufacturers Institute noted that 'much of the fabric sold by Canadian textile firms is comprised of imported yarn or is merely converted and finished in Canada, meaning that garments made of those fabrics would not meet the NAFTA rules of origin'.[88] Clearly the more restrictive NAFTA rules of origin on textiles and apparel directly affected yarn imports from non-NAFTA countries into Canada for further transformation and exportation into the US.

This example shows that FTA rules of origin can indeed be more restrictive than their respective prior ORCs. The next question is whether there are less restrictive alternative measures.

B. Classification of NAFTA Rules of Origin in Terms of Restrictiveness

Given that FTA rules of origin by definition enable the FTA countries to maintain their FTA tariff preferences solely amongst themselves, measures different from rules of origin would not be an alternative. However, the

---

[85] *See* above para. 8.   [86] *See* Robert, above at n 7, at 100–01.   [87] *Ibid.*

[88] *Ibid.* It is worth noting that though the NAFTA yarn-forward rule was more restrictive than CUSFTA's rules of origin, in order to protect the Canadian textiles and apparel industry special tariff rate quotas were adopted under the NAFTA. These tariff quotas kept permitting the Canadian industry to import limited quantities of yarn from non-NAFTA countries and to transform them under NAFTA's preferential coverage. These special provisions protect the Canadian industry but not necessarily the volume of yarn imported from third countries that used to be transformed and exported into the US under the CUSFTA.

comparison can be made between FTA rules of origin with different degrees of restrictiveness.

To this effect, an attempt has been made to classify the *NAFTA rules of origin* in terms of restrictiveness in 'NAFTA Rules of Origin Criteria Applied to the Harmonized Tariff System Classification of Goods'.[89] There, three groups of general rules of origin criteria were identified: the change in classification ('CC') criterion, the regional value content ('RVC') criterion and the processing operations ('PO') criterion.

Under the CC criterion NAFTA rules of origin may demand a change from a chapter, heading, subheading or tariff, to a different chapter, heading, subheading or tariff item of the Harmonized Tariff System ('HTS') Classification, e.g. the product manufactured in one or more of the NAFTA countries has a different classification from its *non-NAFTA originated* components or parts. For instance, *surgical stockings with graduated compression for orthopedic treatment* (under item number 61159330) have to be made from goods classified under a different chapter (e.g. from *special woven fabrics* classified under chapter 58 of the HTS Classification, which is different from chapter 61). However, the change in classification may also be from one specific category to another specific category, but within the same broad classification e.g. the NAFTA rule of origin requires the good to shift from a heading to another heading but within the same chapter. For instance *Solid or cushion tires of rubber* (under item number 40129010) have to be made from goods classified under a different heading, although they can be made from goods classified under the same chapter (e.g. *Natural rubber latex, whether or not prevulcanized*, are classified under item number 40011000, which belongs to chapter 40 and to a different heading from heading 4012, i.e. heading 4001).

According to the RVC criterion a good is considered of NAFTA origin depending on the percentage (%) of the good's value that has been added within the NAFTA area.

In turn, under the PO criterion specific processing operations (e.g. cutting, knitting to shape, sewing and assembling) are required in the manufacturing of certain goods (e.g. textiles and apparel) for them to be considered of NAFTA origin.

Within each of these groups (i.e. CC, RVC and PO criteria) a classification in terms of restrictiveness was made.[90] Such classification was made by groups

---

[89] *See* the table 'NAFTA Rules of Origin Criteria Applied to the Harmonized Tariff System Classification of Goods', Annex 1, in J.A. Rivas, *How Regional Trade Agreements and their Rules of Origin Comply with GATT Article XXIV* (Doctoral Dissertation on file with the author, March, 2005). The table was created based on Annexes 401 and 300b of NAFTA. *See also* Annexes 401 and 300b of NAFTA. The dissertation and its table present an in-depth study on the classification of NAFTA rules of origin in term of restrictiveness.

[90] *Ibid.* Concerning CC, three degrees of restrictiveness were identified: Low CC ('L_{cc}') for goods that have to change from a subheading to a different subheading but within the same heading and chapter; Medium CC ('M_{cc}') for goods that have to change from a heading to a different heading but within the same chapter; and High CC ('H_{cc}') for goods that have to change from a chapter to another chapter. The CC classification was made under the assumption that when a good has to go

of combinations of rules of origin criteria, because most of the imports under the *NAFTA rules of origin* have to comply with a combination of rules of origin criteria (e.g. CC from chapter to chapter and over 65 per cent of RVC).

After classifying, item by item, the groups of combinations of NAFTA rules of origin criteria,[91] econometric regressions were used to test whether a specific combination of *NAFTA rules of origin* has been more restrictive[92] on imports from the countries of the Americas into the US, than other combinations of rules of origin.[93] The conclusion to this question was that the *rules of origin* combination classified as High under the CC and PO criteria (i.e., H_{po} H_{cc}: the combination requiring processing operations and a change from chapter to chapter which covers various textile and apparel goods such as cotton yarn, anoraks, trousers, breeches, gloves, etc)[94] could be said to be more restrictive than the other combinations of *rules of origin*. This because the H_{po} H_{cc} combination of rules of origin applied to NAFTA goods of certain industries (e.g. textile and apparel) have a greater power to influence these industries' imports from the Americas into the US, than the other combinations of rules of origin exert on the imports of their respective industries. In other words, the effect of the H_{po} H_{cc} combination of rules of origin on the diversion of trade in the textile and apparel is more significant than the effect of other combinations of rules of origin on the diversion of trade in their respective industries.

Given that there are *neutral* rules of origin that permit maintaining the NAFTA tariff benefits amongst NAFTA countries, such *neutral* rules of origin (e.g. the rules of origin applicable to facsimile machines; teleprinters and part thereof; synthetic detergents; polishes and creams for footwear, wood,

through a change of classification from a general category (e.g. chapter) to another general category, such rule of origin is more restrictive than that requiring a change between specific categories but within the same general category. Concerning RVC, three degrees of restrictiveness were identified: Low RVC ('L_{rvc}') for goods that are required to have at least a 50 per cent of RVC; Medium RVC ('M_{rvc}') for goods that are required to have at least a 70 per cent of RVC; and High RVC ('H_{rvc}') for goods that are required to have a minimum number of specific NAFTA components (e.g. TV tubes made in NAFTA for TVs to be of NAFTA origin). Concerning PO, two degrees of restrictiveness were identified: Low PO ('L_{po}') for goods not governed by the PO criterion; and High PO ('H_{po}') for goods for which processing operations need to occur within NAFTA.

[91] *Ibid.* The combinations of the NAFTA rules of origin criteria included the following groups: 1) H_{po} H_{cc}; 2) H_{po} L_{cc} M_{rvc}; 3) H_{po} M_{cc} L_{rvc}; 4) L_{po} H_{cc} L_{rvc}; 5) L_{po} L_{cc} H_{rvc}; 6) L_{po} M_{cc} M_{rvc}; and L_{po} L_{cc} M_{rvc}.

[92] *Ibid.*; see also above at n 80, on *neutrality* and *overly restrictiveness*. The test used compared the effects of FTA rules of origin of particular industries on their respective trade flows, with those effects of FTA rules of origin of the universe of industries of the same FTA.

[93] *See* Rivas, above at n 89, for details of the regressions used to test the classification of NAFTA rules of origin.

[94] *Ibid.* The combination H_{po} H_{cc} includes goods such as single cotton yarn, less than 85 per cent cotton by weight, of combed fibers (under number 52062200); Men's or boys' anoraks, windbreakers and similar articles, not knitted (62019215); men's or boys' trousers and breeches, of wool, not containing elastic (62034118); women's or girls' anoraks, windbreakers and similar articles imported as pants of ski-suits (62112054); gloves, mittens and mitts, for sports use, including ski and snowmobile (62160046).

furniture, glass and metal; glues; penicillin, fireworks; and chemical preparations for photographic use)[95] constitute alternative measures to the highly restrictive NAFTA rules of origin.

V. CONCLUSION

This chapter has relied, for the review of FTA rules of origin, on a parallel analysis to the review of the tariff quotas by the Appellate Body in *Turkey— Textiles*; and to the review proposed above of the line pipe safeguard of *US— Line Pipe*. This analysis (*see* table below) has been followed to present an alternative for the clarification of Article XXIV[96] and the creation of greater discipline of FTAs by submitting that *overly restrictive* FTA rules of origin (i.e. FTA rules of origin being both i. more restrictive than the *rules of origin* existing prior to the formation of the FTA, and ii. more restrictive than necessary for the formation and integrity of the FTA) are inconsistent with WTO law.

Table 2.

ORCs:	Case of NAFTA rules of origin
	NAFTA rules of origin for the Textiles and Apparel Industry
i. Test under Article XXIV:5(b): Have ORCs *vis-à-vis* third countries become more restrictive?	Yes. Although by definition NAFTA rules of origin are only applicable to goods from NAFTA countries, the very definition of NAFTA goods may now prevent imports and components of third countries from receiving a treatment as favourable as the one applicable before NAFTA.
ii. Test under the Chapeau: Would not applying the new restrictive regulations otherwise have prevented the creation or coherence of the FTA?	No, there were less restrictive alternative measures that could have been applied: Neutral FTA rules of origin of the sort applied to other industries.

[95] *Ibid.* The examples of *neutral rules* of origin refer to those products classified under the groups of combinations of the NAFTA rules of origin criteria $L_{po}\, L_{cc}\, M_{rvc}$ and $L_{po}\, L_{cc}\, H_{rvc}$.

[96] Doha Ministerial Declaration, WT/MIN(01)DEC/1, adopted 14 November 2001, para. 29. It reads as follows: 'We also agree to negotiations aimed at clarifying and improving under the existing WTO provisions applying to regional trade agreements'. The central provision of WTO law on RTAs is Article XXIV. Clarification and improvement of this provision is most likely to involve its interpretation.

This proposal on Article XXIV with respect to FTA rules of origin does not call for new agreements or understandings to the already considerable amount of WTO provisions. It simply calls for strictly interpreting Article XXIV and reducing the layer of protectionism created by unscrutinized FTA rules of origin.

PART III

WTO-plus Issues in Regional Trade Agreements

7

Services Liberalization in Regional Trade Agreements: Lessons for GATS 'Unfinished Business'?

MARKUS KRAJEWSKI *

I. INTRODUCTION

The relationship between the WTO legal system and regional trade agreements (RTAs) is a complex one as the contributions to this volume aptly demonstrate. The complexity is growing with the proliferation of RTAs, in particular of bi- or trilateral free trade agreements among non-neighbouring countries.[1] Many RTAs increasingly include chapters or protocols on trade in services rendering the relationship between regional and multilateral trade rules even more complicated. While trade in goods aspects of that relationship are classic issues of trade law, the services dimension is relatively novel, because services entered the trade agenda as late as the mid-1980s. Regional and multilateral rules on services trade liberalization co-exist only since the entry into force of the WTO's General Agreement on Trade in Services (GATS) in 1995.

Comparisons between regional and multilateral liberalization of services trade focussed so far predominantly on issues such as the scope of the agreements, the way they cover services ('negative' versus 'positive' list approaches)[2]

* I would like to thank Maika Engelke for valuable research assistance and the participants of the ILA British Branch 2005 Spring Conference for a stimulating debate. Federico Ortino and Elisabeth Türk provided extremely helpful suggestions on an earlier draft of this contribution. I would also like to gratefully acknowledge the useful comments of two anonymous reviewers of OUP. All errors remain mine.

[1] For a comprehensive account of this development, see J.A. Crawford and R.V. Fiorentino, 'The Changing Landscape of Regional Trade Agreements', WTO Discussion Paper No 8 (2005).

[2] A negative list approach refers to agreements, according to which market access and national treatment apply generally, but members of the agreement may exempt certain sectors or measures from these obligations by including them on a 'negative list'. A positive list approach refers to an agreement, according to which market access and national treatment only apply to sectors, which are positively included in a list, and only subject to the conditions contained in such a list. Many RTAs follow negative list approaches, while GATS follows a positive list approach.

and on the substantive obligations of market access and national treatment.[3] Often these studies aimed at deriving lessons for the multilateral trading system. This paper will pursue a similar objective, but it will focus on elements of services agreements, which have not yet received much attention in the literature: domestic regulation, government procurement, subsidies, and emergency safeguard measures. These four issues are subject to negotiations in the context of the current GATS negotiations and involve a number of contentious questions. The paper will analyse these four issues through the lens of selected RTAs enabling the paper to suggest whether and which lessons can be learned from RTAs. The practical relevance of this exercise is underlined by a recent request of the Members of the WTO's Working Party on Domestic Regulation to the WTO Secretariat to compile a list of provisions relating to domestic regulation in RTAs. The Secretariat produced a 190-page long overview of such provisions which shows the importance of studying regional agreements as examples in the context of the ongoing negotiations.[4]

The chapter is organized as follows: section II will briefly sketch the main aspects of the general relationship between regional and multilateral services trade liberalization as shaped by Article V GATS, which addresses this relationship from the perspective of WTO law. Even though this provision does not have a direct impact on the comparative study at the core of this chapter, the general relationship between RTAs covering services and the GATS forms the background of any comparative analysis between regional and multilateral rules on trade in services. Section III will then give a short overview of the 'unfinished business of GATS', i.e. negotiations on disciplines on domestic regulation (Article VI:4 GATS), government procurement (Article XIII GATS), subsidies (Article XV GATS), and emergency safeguard measures (Article X GATS). Readers familiar with these negotiations may wish to proceed immediately to section IV, which is the core of the chapter. After introducing the RTAs selected for comparison, the treatment of each of the four issues (domestic regulation, government procurement, subsidies, and emergency safeguard measures) in the different RTAs will be analysed. Based on the findings of this analysis, the final section of the chapter will suggest some lessons for the negotiations in the GATS context.

---

[3] *See* e.g. R.H. Snape and M. Boswort, 'Advancing Services Negotiations', in J.J. Schott (ed), *The World Trading System: Challenges Ahead* (Washington, D.C.: Institute for International Economics, 1996), 185–203 and S.M. Stephenson, 'Regional versus Multilateral Liberalisation of Services' (2002) 1 WTR 187.

[4] Working Party on Domestic Regulation, Overview of Regulatory Provisions in Services Economic Integration Agreements, Informal Note by the Secretariat, JOB(05)175, 14 September 2005.

II. REGIONAL AND GLOBAL SERVICES TRADE LIBERALIZATION: THE FRAMEWORK OF ARTICLE V GATS

The relationship between regional and multilateral integration is characterized by conflicting interests and objectives.[5] On the one side, regional integration can serve as a 'building block' for further integration and therefore provide incentives for multilateral trade liberalization. On the other side, regional trade agreements can turn into trading blocs making liberalization beyond the regional level more difficult ('stumbling block').[6] WTO rules on the compatibility of regional trade agreements with the principles of the multilateral trading system recognize these two conflicting perspectives and try to reconcile them.

In GATS, the general rule is contained in Article V, entitled 'Economic integration'.[7] The most important substantive rules are paragraphs 1 and 4 of Article V GATS. According to Article V:1(a) GATS, members may form an agreement liberalizing trade in services provided that the agreement has substantial sectoral coverage. Footnote 1 of the GATS specifies that '[t]his condition is understood in terms of number of sectors, volume of trade affected and modes of supply. In order to meet this condition, agreements should not provide for the a priori exclusion of any mode of supply'.

Furthermore, a RTA must provide 'for the absence or elimination of substantially all discrimination, in the sense of Article XVII, between or among the parties' (Article V:1(b) GATS). This can be achieved through the elimination of existing and/or prohibition of new discriminatory measures. Measures permitted under Articles XI, XII, XIV and XIVbis GATS do not fall under that requirement. Since Article XVII GATS contains the national treatment obligation, it would seem that Article V:1(b) GATS only requires non-discrimination on a national treatment level. However, the Panel in *Canada—Autos* extended this requirement to most-favoured-nation treatment among the parties of a RTA.[8]

Paragraph 4 of Article V GATS holds that any RTA in the services area shall be designed to facilitate trade between the parties and shall not raise the overall level of barriers to trade in services within the respective sectors or subsectors compared to the level applicable prior to such an agreement.

The other paragraphs of Article V GATS contain, *inter alia,* special rules for

---

[5] *See* generally B. Hoekman and M.M. Kostecki, *The Political Economy of the World Trading System,* 2nd ed. (Oxford: OUP, 2001), 346–68.

[6] B. Hoekman and P. Sauvé, 'Regional and Multilateral Liberalisation of Service Markets: Complements or Substitutes?' (1994) 32 JCMS 283, at 313 ff and C. Damro, 'The Political Economy of Regional Trade Agreements', in this volume, at 23.

[7] For a discussion of this provision *see* S.M. Stephenson, 'GATS and Regional Integration', in P. Sauvé and R.M. Stern (eds), *GATS 2000—New Directions in Services Trade Liberalisation* (Washington, DC: Brookings, 2000), 509–29.

[8] WTO Panel Report, *Canada—Autos,* WT/DS139/R, WT/DS142/R, adopted 19 June 2000, as modified by the WTO Appellate Body Report, WT/DS139/AB/R, WT/DS142/AB/R, paras 10.269–10.272.

developing countries and provide for the notification of a RTA covering services to the Council for Trade in Services, which can establish a working group examining the consistency of a RTA with Article V GATS.[9] As of November 2005, 31 RTAs and two accessions to services agreements have been notified under Article V GATS.[10] However, no report on the consistency of a regional agreement with Article V GATS has been adopted so far.[11]

Comparing Article V GATS with Article XXIV:4–8 GATT, the corresponding provision on RTAs in GATT, one notes that GATS does not distinguish between customs unions and free trade agreements, because this distinction has no relevance regarding trade in services. A free trade area and a customs union differ with regard to the establishment of a common external tariff. Since services are typically not subject to tariffs, a distinction based on tariffs would not make much sense for trade in services. Instead, Article V uses the term 'Economic integration'. According to paragraph 2 of Article V, '[i]n evaluating whether the conditions under paragraph 1(b) are met, consideration may be given to the relationship of the agreement to a wider process of economic integration or trade liberalization among the countries concerned'. This shows that services trade liberalization usually happens at a higher level of regional integration than the liberalization of trade in goods: Not all customs unions or free trade agreements also provide for the liberalization of trade in services, but services trade liberalization at the regional level takes place in an integration context which also involves trade in goods.

Despite this difference and the more complex nature of services trade liberalization, the GATS rules on RTAs are modelled after the GATT rules and require similar conditions:[12] The agreement must have substantial sectoral coverage according to Article V:1(a) GATS (compare to 'substantially all the trade' in Article XXIV:8 GATT) and the agreement shall not raise the overall level of barriers to trade according to Article V:4 GATS (compare to the prohibition of higher trade barriers in a customs union or free trade area in Article XXIV:5 GATT).

III. 'UNFINISHED BUSINESS' IN GATS

Five provisions of GATS mandate further negotiations concerning trade in services. One of them, Article XIX GATS, calls for successive rounds of

---

[9] For example, the Working Group on NAFTA or on the Enlargement of the European Community in 1995. *See* Council for Trade in Services, Report of the Meeting held on 30 May 1995, WTO Doc. S/C/M/3, 26 June 1995.

[10] *See* Notifications of RTAs in force to the WTO as of 22 November 2005, available at www.wto.org/english/tratop_e/region_e/summary_e.xls (visited 13 February 2006).

[11] *Ibid.*

[12] For a comprehensive discussion of Arts XXIV GATT and V GATS *see* T. Cottier and M. Foltea, 'Constitutional Functions of the WTO and Preferential Trade Agreements', in this volume, at 43.

negotiations directed at the reduction or elimination of measures with adverse effects on trade as a means for providing effective market access. The first round of such negotiations began—as mandated by Article XIX—five years after the entry into force of the GATS, i.e. in 2000 ('GATS 2000 negotiations'). These negotiations have now become part of the overall Doha Development Agenda.[13]

The other four provisions contain negotiating mandates relating to aspects on which the negotiators of the Uruguay Round could not reach consensus at the end of that round. They are part of the 'built-in agenda' otherwise referred to as the 'unfinished business' of GATS.[14] These provisions are Article VI:4 GATS providing for negotiations on disciplines on domestic regulation, Article X:1 GATS calling for negotiations on emergency safeguard measures, Article XIII:2 GATS mandating negotiations on government procurement, and Article XV:1 GATS concerning negotiations on subsidies.

A. Disciplines on domestic regulation

Article VI:4 GATS entitles the Council for Trade in Services to establish— through subsidiary bodies—disciplines on domestic regulation 'with a view to ensuring that measures relating to qualification requirements and procedures, technical standards and licensing requirements do not constitute unnecessary barriers to trade in services'. Article VI:4 GATS further holds that these disciplines shall aim to ensure that such regulations are, *inter alia,* '(a) based on objective and transparent criteria, such as competence and the ability to supply the service; (b) not more burdensome than necessary to ensure the quality of the service; (c) in the case of licensing procedures, not in themselves a restriction on the supply of the service'.

From 1995 to 1998 the negotiations mandated by Article VI:4 GATS took place in the Working Party on Professional Services (WPPS). Work in the WPPS focussed on sectoral disciplines for regulation of accountancy services. The WPPS drafted a set of such disciplines (Accountancy Disciplines), which was adopted by the Council for Trade in Services in December 1998.[15] These disciplines have, however, not yet been formally integrated into the GATS framework, but their integration is anticipated for the end of the current round of GATS negotiations.[16] In the meantime, members 'shall, to the fullest extent consistent with their existing legislation, not take measures which would be inconsistent with these disciplines'.[17]

---

[13] Doha Ministerial Declaration, WT/MIN(01)/DEC/1, adopted 14 November 2001, para. 15.

[14] P. Sauvé and R.M. Stern, 'New Directions in Services Trade Liberalisation: An Overview', in Sauvé and Stern, above at n 7, at 9.

[15] Council for Trade in Services, Disciplines on Domestic Regulation in the Accountancy Sector, WTO Doc. S/L/64, 14 December 1998.

[16] Council for Trade in Services, Decision on Disciplines Relating to the Accountancy Sector, WTO Doc. S/L/63, 14 December 1998.

[17] *Ibid.*

In 1999, the WPPS was replaced with the Working Party on Domestic Regulation (WPDR), which received a broader mandate and aimed at disciplines for all sectors. These negotiations have not yet been concluded and include a number of contentious issues.[18] Among others, the scope and application of such disciplines is not yet clear: should they apply to all sectors or only to committed sectors? The elements of a necessity test are another subject of the negotiations: should it only refer to the quality of the service as a legitimate regulatory objective as in Article VI:4(b) GATS or should a larger range of national policy goals be considered legitimate as in the Accountancy Disciplines? Another topic in the debates concerns the role of international standards: should members be obliged to follow them or should international standards only be taken into account as suggested in Article VI:5(b) GATS? Finally, members have discussed the proper role of recognition of equivalence: should members be obliged to recognize qualifications obtained abroad or should they only be encouraged to do so as mentioned in Article VII GATS?

In light of the many unresolved questions, the future scope and content of disciplines on domestic regulation is difficult to predict. However, a couple of core elements are emerging from the negotiations in the WPDR. In particular, since the Accountancy Disciplines have served as a raw-model and reference point in these negotiations it is possible that general disciplines will be developed along the lines of the Accountancy Disciplines. General disciplines on domestic regulation will hence most likely specify the conditions of the necessity test of Article VI:4(b) GATS and include references to international standards and to recognition of equivalence. It is therefore of special interest how the RTAs studied subsequently address these issues.

B. GATS rules

The other three pending negotiations are commonly referred to as 'GATS rules' and take place in the Working Group on GATS Rules (WPGR).[19] In all three areas, the negotiations have not produced any substantive outcome and are still at an early stage despite many years of negotiations.[20] WTO Members differ substantially on a number of fundamental issues concerning these negotiations, which is why there has been so little progress.

Article X:1 GATS calls for 'multilateral negotiations on the question of emergency safeguard measures based on the principle of non-discrimination'.

---

[18] *See* M. Djordjevic, 'Domestic Regulation and Free Trade in Services—A Balancing Act' (2002) 29 LIEI, 305 and M. Krajewski, *National Regulation and Liberalization of Trade in Services* (London and The Hague: Kluwer, 2003), 134–51.

[19] For a discussion of these negotiations *see* P. Sauvé, 'Completing the GATS Framework: Addressing Uruguay Round Leftovers' (2002) 57 Aussenwirtschaft (Swiss Review of International Economic Relations), 301.

[20] For the most recent summary of the negotiations *see* Working Party on GATS Rules, Annual Report of the Working Party on GATS Rules to the Council for Trade in Services, WTO Doc. S/WPGR/15, 22 September 2005.

Despite a clear deadline in Article X:1 GATS ('The results of such negotiations shall enter into effect on a date not later than three years from the date of entry into force of the WTO Agreement'), the Council for Trade in Services has prolonged the deadline several times, most recently until the end of the current round of negotiations.[21] Elements discussed in the negotiations on emergency safeguard measures included the justification of safeguards, applicable measures, duration, compensation and surveillance. Some members also questioned the desirability and feasibility of rules on safeguards in the context of trade in services.

According to Article XIII GATS, the core disciplines of most favoured nation treatment (Article II GATS), market access (Article XVI GATS) and national treatment (Article XVII GATS) shall not apply to measures regulating government procurement.[22] Article XIII:2 GATS mandates 'negotiations on government procurement in services'. Aspects of government procurement discussed in the WPGR concern the application of the most favoured nation principle, the relationship of rules under Article XIII GATS to the plurilateral Agreement on Government Procurement, and the possibility of distinguishing between procurement of goods and services.

Unlike government procurement, subsidies are not exempt from the GATS disciplines. Yet, there are no rules on the permissibility of subsidies in services sectors and on possible countervailing measures. According to Article XV:1 GATS, members recognize that subsidies may have distortive effects on trade in services. They therefore agreed to 'enter into negotiations with a view to developing the necessary multilateral disciplines to avoid such trade-distortive effects', which shall also address the appropriateness of countervailing procedures (Article XV:1 GATS). So far, members of the WPGR are still in the process of exchanging information on subsidies and discussing a working definition of subsidies.

Given the early stage of the debates on GATS rules in the WTO, it will be interesting to see whether RTAs address these issues in general and which concepts they utilize when addressing them. For example, it could be asked whether RTAs contain specific disciplines for subsidies and government procurement regarding services or whether they do not distinguish between goods and services in this respect. Concerning emergency safeguard measures, the existence of provisions on such measures in RTAs could show that emergency safeguard measures are feasible in the services context.

---

[21] Council for Trade in Services, Fifth Decision on Negotiations on Emergency Safeguard Measures, WTO Doc. S/L/159, 15 March 2004.

[22] It should be recalled that the Plurilateral Agreement on Government Procurement applies to services pursuant to Annex 4 of each Party's Appendix I, *see* Arts I:1 and I:2 GPA.

IV. TREATMENT OF 'UNFINISHED BUSINESS' IN SELECTED REGIONAL TRADE AGREEMENTS

In light of the generally low level of progress concerning the four areas of GATS negotiations studying how these aspects have been treated in other agreements on trade in services could provide useful lessons for the GATS context. The following section of the chapter will therefore analyse the treatment of domestic regulation, government procurement, subsidies, and emergency safeguard measures in selected regional trade agreements.[23]

A. Regional trade agreements selected for comparison

The selection of RTAs for the purpose of the study was based on the availability of the texts of the agreements in English and through the Internet, and on the desire to use a sample of different types of agreements (free trade agreements/customs unions) and different 'generations' (before and after entry into force of GATS). Furthermore, I deliberately, but admittedly somewhat arbitrarily, excluded bilateral agreements between non-neighbouring countries. As a result, the following legal instruments were selected for comparison:

- North American Free Trade Agreement (NAFTA), signed on 17 December 1992, entered into force 1 January 1994;
- ASEAN Framework Agreement on Services (AFAS), signed on 15 December 1995, not yet in force;[24]
- Protocol of Montevideo on Trade in Services in the Southern Common Market (Mercosur), signed on 15 December 1997, entered into force on 7 December 2005;[25]
- General Framework of Principles and Rules and for Liberalizing the Trade in Services in the Andean Community, Decision of the Andean Commission of 11 June 1998;[26]
- Revised Treaty of Chaguaramas Establishing the Caribbean Community including the Caricom Single Market and Economy, signed on 5 July 2001, not yet in force, but applied on the basis of the Protocol on the Provisional

---

[23] For a similar approach regarding provisions on competition law *see* M.G. Desta and N.J. Barnes, 'Competition Law in Regional Trade Agreements', in this volume, at 239.

[24] As of January 2006 only the ratification by Malaysia was missing. Information taken from www.aseansec.org/Ratification.pdf (visited 13 February 2006).

[25] Decision 13/97 of the Council of the Common Market, 15 December 1997, Boletín Oficial del Mercosur, No 4 (1998). The Protocol entered into force for Argentina, Brazil and Uruguay, while Paraguay has not yet ratified the Protocol as of December 2005.

[26] Decision 439 of the Commission of the Andean Community, 11 June 1998, Gaceta Oficial del Acuerdo de Cartagena, Año XIV Número 347, 17 June 1998, at 34. This Decision is based on Article 79 of the Andean Subregional Integration Agreement (Cartagena Agreement), codified version of 25 June 2003. The Decision is part of Andean Community Law according to Article 25(2) of the Cartagena Agreement.

Application of the Revised Treaty of Chaguaramas of 5 February 2002;[27] and

• Dominican Republic, Central America, and United States Free Trade Agreement (CAFTA-DR), signed on 5 August 2004, not yet in force.[28]

Table 1 shows an overview of the respective provisions of the GATS and the selected regional trade agreements and instruments for each of the four areas studied. A first look already indicates that the treatment of these issues differs significantly in the various agreements and instruments. Some of them go further than existing (or even potential) GATS rules, while others are less far reaching. The following sections of this paper will analyse these provisions in greater detail.

A word of caution is necessary before the detailed analysis of the texts of these agreements and instruments. Three of them are in force (NAFTA, the Montevideo Protocol, and the Andean Community General Framework), one is applied provisionally (the Revised Treaty of Chaguaramas) and two (CAFTA-DR and AFAS) await entry into force. Thus, in a strict legal sense, these two instruments can only be considered emerging international law. Furthermore, the actual functioning and application of the rules in some of these agreements may less depend on their exact legal status and more on the political willingness and administrative capacities to enforce them. It may, in fact, be the case that some of the rules discussed below have little to do with the practical realities of the respective RTAs.

A comprehensive analysis of these RTAs would therefore have to take the political, economic and social reality into account. However, such an in-depth study is not only beyond the scope of this contribution. It is also not necessarily required in order to achieve the main objective of this contribution, i.e. to compare the approaches taken by different RTAs to the four sets of issues, which are still subject to negotiations in the WTO, and to suggest some lessons for GATS in this respect.

[27] As of January 2006, the Revised Treaty was signed and ratified by 12 of the 15 Caricom Members. The Bahamas, Haiti, and Montserrat (the latter awaiting entrustment from the UK) still need to sign and ratify. *See* 'Establishment of the Caricom Single Market and Economy. Summary of Status of Key Elements', 10 August 2005, available at www.sice.oas.org/TPD/CAR/MatxAug10_2005.pdf (visited 13 February 2006) and 'Single Market will transform the region', News Release of the Caricom Secretariat, 24 January 2006, available at www.caricom.org/jsp/pressreleases/pres17_06.jsp (visited 13 February 2006).

[28] As of October 2005, El Salvador, Guatemala, Honduras, Nicaragua, and the US had ratified the treaty. Information taken from www.sice.oas.org/TRADEE.ASP (visited 13 February 2006).

Table 1. Synopsis of Key Provisions in the Areas of Comparison

	Domestic Regulation	Government Procurement	Subsidies	Emergency Safeguard Measures
GATS (1994)	Art. VI:4 (Accountancy Disciplines concluded; negotiations on further disciplines pending)	Art. XIII:2 (negotiations pending)	Art. XV:1 (negotiations pending)	Art. X:1 (negotiations pending)
NAFTA (1992)	Art. 904(4) (necessity test for standards) Art. 1210 (disciplines for licensing and certification)	Chapter Ten (full procurement regime)	no special provision	no special provision
ASEAN (AFAS, 1995)[29]	no provision	no special provision	no special provision	no special provision, but Art. 14 ASEAN Investment Area Framework Agreement (safeguard provision for investments)
Mercosur (Montevideo Protocol, 1997)	Art. X (discipline similar to Art. VI:4 GATS, but binding)	Art. XV (negotiations required) Protocol on Public Procurement (2004), not yet in force	Art. XVI (negotiations required)	no special provision

[29] AFAS contains a general reference to GATS (Art. XIV:1 AFAS).

Andean Community (General Framework, 1998)[30]	no special provision except Art. 13 (recognition of licenses, etc., in accordance with Commission decision)	Art. 4 (only requirement of national treatment)	Art. 18 (application in a non-competitive manner)	no special provision
CARICOM (Revised Treaty of Chaguaramas, 2001)	no special provision, but Arts 36, 37 (general prohibition of restrictions on services) and Art. 67 (mandate to harmonize standards)	Art. 239 (b) (mandate to establish protocol on government procurement)	Art. 96–115 (full subsidies regime) Art. 69 (mandate to harmonize investment incentives)	Art. 47 (safeguard provision for establishment, services, capital, and movement of persons)
CAFTA-DR (2004)	Art. 11(8) (discipline equivalent to VI:GATS, but binding)	Chapter 9 (full procurement regime)	no special provision	no special provision

[30] The General Framework contains a general reference to GATS (Art. 26 General Framework).

B. Domestic regulation

1. NAFTA

Of the RTAs chosen for comparison, NAFTA provides the most detailed regime for domestic regulation. However, NAFTA does not contain a provision on disciplines on domestic regulation specifically relating to trade in services. Instead, the NAFTA chapter on standards-related measures (Chapter Nine) applies to measures directly or indirectly affecting trade in goods or services trade (Article 901(1) NAFTA). Article 904 NAFTA establishes basic rights and obligations concerning such standards-related measures. Paragraph 4 of that provision contains a necessity test:

No Party may prepare, adopt, maintain or apply any standards-related measure with a view to or with the effect of creating an unnecessary obstacle to trade between the Parties. An unnecessary obstacle to trade shall not be deemed to be created where:
(a) the demonstrable purpose of the measure is to achieve a legitimate objective; and
(b) the measure does not operate to exclude goods of another Party that meet that legitimate objective.

Even though Article 904(4) NAFTA is comparable to Article VI:4 GATS, the standard of the necessity test applied in the two provisions differs: whereas the necessity test of Article VI:4 GATS only refers to the quality of the service, Article 904(4) NAFTA refers to (any) legitimate objective. Thus, Article 904(4) NAFTA is less strict on domestic regulation.

An interesting element can be found in Article 904(4)(b) NAFTA. According to this provision, a standard does not create unnecessary obstacles to trade if it does not exclude goods from another country which meet the objective of that standard. Article 904(4)(b) hence alludes to the principle of mutual recognition.[31] However, the provision applies only to goods and not to services even though the reason for this exclusion is not entirely clear.[32]

A stronger and clearer obligation regarding mutual recognition which also extends to services can be found in Article 906(4) NAFTA. This provision obliges members to treat foreign regulations as equivalent to domestic ones if the foreign regulation adequately fulfils the domestic policy objectives.

A further obligation addressing an issue which is also discussed in the GATS

[31] This view is shared by the NAFTA Panel in the Trucking case. The Panel stated that Art. 904(4) 'should be considered in conjunction with Article 906.4, which contains a requirement that where an exporting country maintains a technical regulation, and the exporting country, in cooperation with the importing Party, demonstrates to the satisfaction of the importing Party that its technical regulation adequately fulfils the importing Party's legitimate objectives, the importing Party must treat such a technical regulation as equivalent'. NAFTA Panel Report, *Cross Border Trucking Services and Investment*, adopted 6 February 2001 [2001] NAFTA 1, para. 272, fn 309, available at www.worldtradelaw.net (visited 13 February 2006).

[32] It is possible that this is a drafting mistake. Art. 904(4) NAFTA is based on Art. 603 of the CUSFTA of 1989, which is seen as the predecessor of NAFTA. Art. 603 CUSFTA only applied to goods, because all provisions on technical standards of CUSFTA (Chapter Six) applied to goods only. The drafters of NAFTA may have copied the wording of Art. 603 CUSFTA without amending it to suit the scope of Chapter Nine NAFTA.

domestic regulation context is Article 905 NAFTA. This provision requires the use of relevant international standards as a basis for standards-related measures. Articles 905 and Article 906(4) NAFTA hence supplement the basic rule of Article 904(4) NAFTA and show the relevance of the use of international standards and recognition of equivalence in the context of domestic regulation, which has also been recognized by the negotiations in the WTO.[33]

NAFTA's Chapter Twelve concerning trade in services contains only one provision specifically addressing domestic regulation: Article 1210. Its paragraph 1 reads:

With a view to ensuring that any measure adopted or maintained by a Party relating to the licensing or certification of nationals of another Party does not constitute an unnecessary barrier to trade, each Party shall endeavor to ensure that any such measure:
(a) is based on objective and transparent criteria, such as competence and the ability to provide a service;
(b) is not more burdensome than necessary to ensure the quality of a service; and
(c) does not constitute a disguised restriction on the cross-border provision of a service.

The substantive standard of this provision resembles the standard of Article VI:4 GATS. In particular, letters (a) and (b) are almost identical to the respective parts of Article VI:4 GATS. However, unlike Article VI:4 GATS, which covers qualification requirements and procedures, technical standards and licensing requirements, the scope of Article 1210(1) NAFTA is limited to licensing and certification of natural persons. Furthermore, unlike the disciplines envisioned by Article VI:4 GATS, Article 1210(1) NAFTA only contains a best effort approach ('each Party shall endeavor').

To briefly summarize: NAFTA Chapter Nine applies to (goods and) services standards, whereas Article 1210 applies to licensing and certifications of natural persons. Even though both provisions contain a necessity test, their scope and level of legal obligation is more limited than the scope of potential disciplines according to Article VI:4 GATS.

The NAFTA Telecommunications Chapter (Chapter Thirteen) also contains a provision on domestic regulation. Article 1304(1) NAFTA requires each Party to ensure that its standards-related measures relating to the attachment of equipment to the public telecommunications transport networks are adopted or maintained only to the extent necessary to achieve five specific policy objectives. These include the prevention of damage to or interference with public telecommunications transport services, the prevention of billing equipment malfunction and users' safety, and access to public telecommunications networks or services. This provision thus establishes a specific necessity test with a closed list of legitimate objectives. Unlike Article 1210(1) NAFTA, Article 1304(1) NAFTA contains a strict legal obligation ('each Party shall ensure').

---

[33] *See* above Section III.A.

Finally, NAFTA Chapter 11 on investment must also be mentioned in this context, because NAFTA excludes investment from the definition of trade in services (Article 1213(2) NAFTA) and devotes a special chapter to investment. It can be argued that the obligation to treat investments fair and equitable according to Article 1105(1) NAFTA performs similar functions as disciplines on domestic regulation according to Article VI:4 GATS.[34] Even though the standard of 'fair and equitable treatment' under international investment law is not precisely defined,[35] it seems to include minimum principles of objectiveness, transparency and due process.[36] However, it does not generally require a measure to be no more burdensome than necessary.

2. *Mercosur and CAFTA-DR*

The Montevideo Protocol on Trade in Services and the CAFTA-DR Agreement contain provisions on domestic regulation for trade in services, which are of striking similarity to Article VI:4 GATS. Article X:4 (National Regulation) of the Montevideo Protocol holds:

In order to assure that measures relative to technical norms, requirements and procedures for qualification certificates and requirements in terms of licensing do not constitute unnecessary impediments to trade in services, Member States shall see to it that these requirements and procedures, among other things:
i.   are based on objective and transparent criteria, such as the competence and capacity for providing the service;
ii. are not unnecessarily onerous for assuring quality of service, and
iii. in the case of procedures in regard to licenses, do not constitute in themselves restrictions on the provision of services.

Article 11(8)(2) (Domestic regulation) of CAFTA-DR reads as follows:

With a view to ensuring that measures relating to qualification requirements and procedures, technical standards, and licensing requirements do not constitute unnecessary barriers to trade in services, each Party shall endeavor to ensure, as appropriate for individual sectors, that any such measures that it adopts or maintains are:
(a) based on objective and transparent criteria, such as competence and the ability to supply the service;
(b) not more burdensome than necessary to ensure the quality of the service; and
(c) in the case of licensing procedures, not in themselves a restriction on the supply of the service.

Article X:4 of the Montevideo Protocol and Article 11(8)(2) CAFTA-DR contain almost the same wording as Article VI:4 GATS with the notable exception that the standards stipulated in these provisions are directly applicable and do not require any further negotiations. They therefore seem similar to an early Uruguay Round proposal for Article VI GATS, which also contained directly

---

[34] I am thankful to Federico Ortino for bringing this to my attention.
[35] P. Muchlinski, *Multilateral Enterprises and the Law* (Oxford: Blackwell, 1995), 625.
[36] A.F. Lowenfeld, *International Economic Law* (Oxford: OUP, 2002), 475.

applicable rules for domestic regulation.[37] However, the level of obligation in the CAFTA-DR and Mercosur provisions is not entirely clear. While Article 11(8)(2) CAFTA-DR only contains a best endeavour approach, Article X:4 of the Montevideo Protocol seems to be stronger. The Spanish original 'los Estados Partes asegurarán' is translated to 'Member States shall see to it' in the English version, but could also be translated to 'Member States ensure'. Nevertheless, the wording seems to fall short of a binding obligation. The ambiguous notion is reinforced by the peculiar use of 'among other things': It is unclear which other things Member States should ensure apart from those mentioned in Article X:4 of the Montevideo Protocol.

Article 11(8) CAFTA-DR contains an additional, interesting element not found in the other RTAs studied. Its paragraph 3 requires an amendment of Article 11(8) CAFTA-DR in order to take into account the results of negotiations under Article VI:4 GATS once GATS disciplines on domestic regulation enter into effect. The amendment shall bring the results of the GATS negotiations into effect under the CAFTA-DR Agreement. Furthermore, CAFTA-DR parties will coordinate on the GATS negotiations as appropriate.

3. Andean Community and ASEAN

Neither the General Framework of the Andean Community nor the ASEAN Framework Agreement on Services (AFAS) has special provisions on domestic regulation.

The only provision which touches upon a subject also discussed in the GATS negotiations on domestic regulation is Article 13 of the Andean Community General Framework. This Article requires the recognition of licences, certifications, professional degrees, and accreditations granted by another member in accordance with criteria established by a Decision of the Andean Community Commission.[38] Recognition of equivalence is also discussed in the GATS context of disciplines on domestic regulation, because it could contribute to the reduction of trade-distortive effects of domestic regulations.

Interestingly, the Andean Community General Framework and the AFAS contain references to the GATS in general. Article 26 of Andean Community General Framework states:

In order to ensure the consistency and clarity of the General Framework established by this Decision, the ideas, definitions and interpretive elements contained in the General Agreement on Trade in Services (GATS) shall be applied to said General Framework, whenever pertinent.

Article XIV:1 AFAS holds:

[37] J. Wouters and D. Coppens, 'Domestic Regulation Within the Framework of GATS', in K. Byttebier and K. Van den Borght (eds), *Issues of International Legal Trade Policy and Implementation: Challenges for the World Trade Organization* (London: Cameron May, 2006), forthcoming.

[38] As far as it could be ascertained, the Andean Commission has not yet taken such a decision.

The terms and definitions and other provisions of the GATS shall be referred to and applied to matters arising under this Framework Agreement for which no specific provision has been made under it.

At least one commentator seems to suggest that the reference in Article XIV:1 AFAS includes Article VI:4 GATS and incorporates that provision into the AFAS.[39] A similar argument could be made about Article 26 of the Andean Community General Framework.

It is not clear whether the wording of Article XIV:1 AFAS ('terms and definitions and other provisions') and Article 26 of the Andean Community General Framework ('ideas, definitions and interpretative elements') can be read as a direct incorporation of all provisions of GATS or whether they only refer to general principles and terms. Even if one assumes that the references to GATS incorporate all provisions covering aspects for which the respective agreements do not contain a specific rule, the scope of such a reference to Article VI:4 GATS is unclear. In light of the contentiousness of the issues involved, it does not seem plausible that the drafters of AFAS and the Andean Community General Framework meant to incorporate the standard of Article VI:4 GATS as a binding standard. However, it is also unlikely that the drafters intended to incorporate the negotiating mandate of Article VI:4 GATS without specifying the institutional framework of such negotiations on disciplines on domestic regulation. Because of the ambiguities involved in such a reference, it can be assumed that the drafters had explicitly stated it had they intended such a reference. It is therefore more plausible to interpret the relevant provisions of AFAS and the Andean Community General Framework as references to the broader concepts and definitions of GATS, but not as specific disciplines or negotiating mandates.

4. Caricom

Chapter III of the Revised Treaty of Chaguaramas, which covers establishment, services, capital, and the movement of persons, does not contain a provision similar to Article VI:4 GATS. Article 36 of the Treaty generally prohibits the introduction of new restrictions on the provision of services and Article 37 calls for the establishment of a programme to abolish existing discriminatory restrictions on the provision of services. Because of their focus on (discriminatory) restrictions, these provisions seem to serve similar functions as the market access and national treatment provisions of GATS, with the exception that the latter only apply on the basis of specific commitments.

Article 67 of the Revised Treaty of Chaguaramas also needs to be mentioned in this context even though it is not restricted to services. The provision addresses standards and technical regulations and contains a legislative

---

[39] S.M. Stephenson, 'A Comparison of Existing Services Trade Arrangements within APEC', in C. Findlay and T. Warren (eds), *Impediments to Trade in Services, Measurement and Policy Implications* (London: Routledge, 2000), 287, 309.

mandate for the Caricom Council for Trade and Economic Development to develop a standardization programme aimed at trade facilitation, enhanced efficiency in the production and delivery of services, improved quality, and consumer and environmental protection. The programme shall, *inter alia*, include harmonization of standards and technical regulations, transparency in their development, and recognition of conformity assessment procedures through mutual recognition agreements. Such a standardization programme could fulfil similar objectives as GATS disciplines on domestic regulation. It would, however, achieve those objectives through harmonization of regulations. Arguably, the mandate of Article VI:4 GATS does not include regulatory harmonization, because—unlike Article 67 of the Revised Treaty of Chaguaramas —it does not state any direct and positive regulatory objectives. The members of the Working Party of Domestic Regulation seem to share that view and have not made any proposals concerning harmonization.

5. Summary

A mixed picture emerges when summarizing the survey of provisions on domestic regulation in RTAs. Some legal instruments, such as AFAS, the Andean Community General Framework and the Revised Treaty of Chaguaramas do not contain specific references to domestic regulation. The effects of these agreements will likely be more lenient on domestic regulation than future disciplines on domestic regulation developed under the mandate of Article VI:4 GATS. The provisions of NAFTA are also narrower than the potential scope of future GATS disciplines. Two legal instruments, CAFTA-DR and the Montevideo Protocol, contain a provision with a standard similar to the standard of Article VI:4 GATS. It could be argued that these agreements go beyond the scope of GATS, because they contain directly applicable disciplines and do not call for negotiations. However, the exact level of their obligation is not clear. In any event, no RTA studied in this contribution went beyond the possible scope of future GATS disciplines on domestic regulation.

C. Government procurement

1. NAFTA and CAFTA-DR

Two agreements studied, NAFTA and CAFTA-DR, contain a comprehensive legal regime on government procurement covering goods and services (NAFTA Chapter Ten and CAFTA-DR Chapter Nine). Both agreements provide for general non-discrimination treatment and include detailed regulations on tendering and bid challenging procedures. NAFTA rules on government procurement apply to services in accordance with Annex 1001.1b–2 NAFTA and construction services in accordance with Annex 1001.1b–3 NAFTA which contain a common classification system and schedules of each of the three NAFTA parties excluding certain sectors and subsectors from the application of the rules on government procurement. CAFTA-DR government procurement rules apply to services in general without extensive sectoral exclusions.

2. Mercosur

The provision of the Montevideo Protocol on Trade in Services on government procurement relating to services is again almost identical to the respective provision in GATS (Article XIII GATS). Article XV (Public Contracting) of the Montevideo Protocol states:

(1) Articles III, IV, and V[40] shall not be applicable to the laws, rules, and regulations that govern government contracting of services directed at official functions, nor to commercial re-sale or to its utilization in the provision of services for commercial sale.

(2) Maintaining the terms established in Paragraph 1, and recognizing that such laws, rules, and regulations may have distorting effects on trade in services, the Member States agree to establish common guidelines that in terms of government purchases in general shall be established in the MERCOSUR.

In December 2004, members of Mercosur agreed on a Protocol on Public Contracts covering goods and services (Protocolo de Contrataciones Públicas del Mercosur).[41] The protocol, however, contains different approaches towards goods and services. Whereas goods are covered subject to Annex II of the Protocol, which contains a negative list, services are covered subject to a positive list contained in Annexes III and IV. Consequently, the rules on government procurement only apply to services sectors, which have been included specifically in the lists of the different members compiled in Annexes III and IV. The classification of these annexes follows the GATS classification (so-called 'W/120' classification).[42] The Protocol establishes a full-fledged regime concerning public procurement. It contains non-discrimination provisions (Articles 3 and 4 of the Protocol) and detailed rules on contract awarding and challenging procedures.

3. Andean Community, Caricom and ASEAN

The General Framework of the Andean Community contains a general provision addressing government procurement. Its Article 4 states:

(. . .) The procurement of services by government agencies or public institutions of Member Countries shall be subject to the principle of national treatment among

---

[40] Art. III of the Montevideo Protocol provides for most favoured nation treatment, Art. IV for market access and Art. V for national treatment (Explanation added by the author).

[41] Decision 27/04 of the Council of the Common Market, 9 December 2004. As of December 2005, no Mercosur Member had ratified this protocol. Information taken from www.mre.gov.py/dependencias/tratados/mercosur/registro%20mercosur/mercosurprincipal.htm (visited 13 February 2006).

[42] GATT Secretariat, Services Sectoral Classification List, Note by the Secretariat, MTN.GTS/W/120, 10 July 1991.

Member Countries, pursuant to a Decision to be adopted no later than January 1st, 2002. In the event that the Decision in question fails to be adopted by that date, the Member Countries shall grant national treatment immediately. (. . .)

Apparently, a decision extending national treatment to public procurement was never taken. Hence, national treatment applies to procurement now by the virtue of Article 4 of the Andean Community General Framework. The General Framework does not contain any further obligations, in particular concerning awarding procedures.

The Revised Treaty of Chaguaramas does not contain rules on government procurement, but Article 239 (b) of that treaty calls upon Caricom Members to undertake to elaborate a Protocol relating, *inter alia*, to government procurement. Caricom Members have taken upon themselves to develop a regional government procurement policy in their work programme for 2004 and 2005.[43] This could then be incorporated into a protocol on the basis of Article 239 (b).

The only agreement not addressing government procurement at all is AFAS. Apparently, government procurement is also not considered part of the general ASEAN economic integration programme.[44] One could point again to Article XIV:1 AFAS, which incorporates terms and definitions and other provisions of GATS into AFAS. However, as argued above, such a general reference clause would not be sufficient to also incorporate the negotiating mandate of Article XIII:2 GATS.

4. Summary

A summary of the survey of provisions on government procurement in the RTAs studied reveals a picture, which is even more mixed than the picture concerning domestic regulation: three RTAs (NAFTA, CAFTA-DR, and Mercosur) have comprehensive legal frameworks for government procurement. They contain non-discrimination obligations and detailed tendering procedures. They do not, however, provide for market access, which is a contentious issue in the GATS context. Two of these agreements (NAFTA and CAFTA-DR) adopt negative list approaches concerning their application to services, and one (Mercosur) adopts a positive list approach.

Other RTAs are less ambitious regarding government procurement: one instrument, the General Framework of the Andean Community, requires national treatment for government procurement. One agreement, the Revised Treaty of Chaguaramas, refers to government procurement as a potential future policy objective. Finally, one RTA, the AFAS, is silent on government procurement altogether. There is thus no common approach to government

---

[43] Caricom, Programme 15: Legal and Institutional Development, Thrust of the Programme for 2004 and 2005, available at www.caricom.org/jsp/archives/work%20programme/prog15_04.htm (visited 13 February 2006).

[44] ASEAN Secretariat, *Annual Report 2004–2005*, available at www.aseansec.org/AR05/TOC.pdf (visited 13 February 2006).

procurement relating to trade in services in the RTAs studied. However, one conclusion can be drawn from this survey: If the RTAs address government procurement, they usually cover goods and services. Put differently, no RTA contains rules on government procurement only covering goods or only covering services. This observation is important for the lessons to be drawn from RTAs for GATS in the last section of this contribution.

D. Subsidies

1. *Caricom and Andean Community*

Compared to the other RTAs studied, the most comprehensive treatment of subsidies can be found in the Revised Treaty of Chaguaramas. Chapter Five on trade policy of this treaty devotes an entire part (Part Three) with no less then 21 provisions (Articles 96–115) to subsidies applying to goods and services. Article 96 defines a subsidy as 'a financial contribution by a Government or any public body' such as direct transfer of funds, government revenue that is not collected, and government provision of services other than general infrastructure. Article 97 (Types of Subsidies) categorizes subsidies into three groups: prohibited subsidies; subsidies which cause injury to a domestic industry, result in nullification or impairment of benefits, or seriously prejudice interests of a Member State; and subsides which cause serious adverse effects to a domestic industry of any Member State which would be difficult to repair. Article 98 entitles members to take actions against subsidized products, and Article 99 proscribes the granting or maintenance of export subsidies and local content subsidies. Additional provisions of this chapter concern investigations, consultations and the withdrawal of subsidies.

Also of relevance is Article 69 of the Revised Treaty of Chaguaramas, which requires Caricom Members to 'harmonise national incentives to investments in the industrial, agricultural and services sectors'. The Council for Finance and Planning is entrusted with formulating respective proposals, which shall accord 'support for industries considered to be of strategic interest to the Community' and may, *inter alia*, provide for non-discrimination in the granting of incentives among Community nationals.

Article 18 of Andean Community General Framework contains a general obligation to apply subsidies to services in a competitively neutral way and requires the adoption of further rules on this subject.

Member Countries shall ensure that such promotional measures as they may apply to service activities do not distort competition within the subregional market and shall adopt Community rules regarding incentives for the trade in services.

In 1999, the Andean Commission enacted special rules to prevent and correct distortive effects of subsidies (Normas para prevenir o corregir las distorsiones en la competencia generadas por prácticas de subvenciones en importaciones de productos originarios de Países Miembros de la Comunidad Andina).[45] These rules apply to subsidies in general and do not distinguish between goods and services subsidies. The rules contain detailed provisions on the definition of a subsidy in general, of actionable and of specific subsidies, and on the calculation of the benefit element of a subsidy. The rules also specify the determination of a damage caused by a subsidy and possible remedies, including preliminary measures.

2. Mercosur

Article XVI of the Montevideo Protocol resembles—like Articles X and XV of that Protocol—the respective GATS provision (Article XV GATS):

(1) The Member States recognize that in certain circumstances subsidies may have distorting effects on trade in services. The Member States agree that common guidelines shall be applied that in the matter of subsidies in general shall be established in MERCOSUR.

(2) The mechanism stated in Paragraph 2 of Article XV of GATS shall be applied.

As far as it could be ascertained, the common guidelines on subsidies mandated by Paragraph 1 of Article XVI of the Montevideo Protocol have not yet been agreed upon. Paragraph 2 of Article XVI refers to Article XV:2 GATS, according to which a member that considers itself to be adversely affected by a subsidy may request consultations from the subsidizing member. Such a request shall be considered sympathetically.

3. NAFTA, CAFTA-DR and ASEAN

NAFTA, CAFTA-DR, and AFAS do not contain special rules addressed at subsidies to services. Article 1201(2)(d) NAFTA specifically excludes subsidies from the coverage of the services chapter. NAFTA Chapter Nineteen provides for the review of antidumping and countervailing duty matters based on domestic laws and does not contain substantive obligations. Importantly, the provisions apply only with respect to goods and not to services according to Article 1901 NAFTA. According to Article 8(8)(2) CAFTA-DR, nothing in the agreement shall be construed 'as imposing rights and obligations on the Parties with respect to antidumping or countervailing duty measures'. Article 8(8)(3) CAFTA-DR maintains each Party's 'rights and obligations under the WTO Agreement with regard to the application of antidumping and countervailing duties'. AFAS or other ASEAN agreements do not address subsidies or countervailing measures at all.

4. Summary

When assessing the treatment of subsidies in the RTAs surveyed, one can—once again—observe a variety of different approaches to the subject. Two

---

[45] Decision 457 of the Commission of the Andean Community, 4 May 1999, Gaceta Oficial del Acuerdo de Cartagena, Año XV Número 436, 7 May 1999, at 20.

RTAs studied, Caricom and the Andean Community, have a detailed regime addressing the legality of subsidies and possible remedies. Both agreements address subsidies for goods and services and do not contain special rules for services subsidies. One RTA, the Montevideo Protocol, follows the example of GATS, i.e. recognizing the importance of the subject and calling for negotiations on the subject. One agreement (NAFTA) restricts its already limited legal regime concerning subsidies and countervailing measures to goods and two agreements do not contain rules on subsidies at all.

E. Emergency safeguard measures

1. Caricom

The treatment of the last issue—emergency safeguard measures—in the selected RTAs is less complex than the aspects discussed above. While some of the legal instruments studied contain provisions on balance-of-payment safeguard measures (Article 2104 NAFTA, Articles 20 and 21 of the General Framework of the Andean Community, Article 43 of the Revised Treaty of Chaguaramas), only Article 47 (Restrictions to Resolve Difficulties or Hardships Arising from the Exercise of Rights) of the Revised Treaty of Chaguaramas addresses emergency safeguard measures for services.[46] Paragraph 1 of that provision reads:

Where the exercise of rights granted under this Chapter[47] creates serious difficulties in any sector of the economy of a Member State or occasions economic hardships in a region of the Community, a Member State adversely affected thereby may, subject to the provisions of this Article, apply such restrictions on the exercise of the rights as it considers appropriate in order to resolve the difficulties or alleviate the hardships.

According to Paragraph 5 of Article 47, restrictions applied by a Member State pursuant to paragraph 1 shall be confined to those necessary to resolve the difficulties in the affected sectors and to alleviate economic hardships in a particular region. Article 47(6) requires the minimization of damage to the commercial or economic interests of other Member States. According to Article 47(7), restrictions shall not be discriminatory and shall be progressively relaxed as relevant conditions improve and maintained only to the extent that the conditions mentioned in paragraph 1 continue to justify their application.

Article 47(2) contains procedures for the notification of emergency measures. Article 47(3) requires the Member State applying an emergency measure to submit a programme through which it intends to resolve its difficulties or

---

[46] A very similar provision is contained in Art. 38(a) of the 1997 Protocol II Amending the Treaty establishing the Caribbean Community on Establishment, Services and Capital (Protocol of Montego Bay).

[47] Chapter Three covers establishment, services, capital, and movement of persons (explanation by the author).

hardships to the Council for Trade and Economic Development or the Council for Finance and Planning. The competent organs will assess the programme and determine whether the measures shall be continued and if so, for how long, and whether additional conditions should be applied.

2. ASEAN

An interesting aspect can be found in the ASEAN context: While AFAS does not mention emergency safeguard measures, the 1998 Framework Agreement on the ASEAN Investment Area (AIA)[48] contains a provision on this matter. Its Article 14 (Emergency Safeguard Measures) provides:

(1) If, as a result of the implementation of the liberalisation programme under this Agreement, a Member State suffers or is threatened with any serious injury and threat, the Member State may take emergency safeguard measures to the extent and for such period as may be necessary to prevent or to remedy such injury. The measures taken shall be provisional and without discrimination.

(2) Where emergency safeguard measures are taken pursuant to this Article, notice of such measure shall be given to the AIA Council within 14 days from the date such measures are taken.

(3) The AIA Council shall determine the definition of serious injury and threat of serious injury and the procedures of instituting emergency safeguards measures pursuant to this Article.

When comparing Article 47 of the Revised Treaty of Chaguaramas with Article 14 of the AIA Framework Agreement, the similarities between both provisions become apparent: The measures which a member may take as emergency safeguard measures are not specified further. However, they must be applied on a non-discriminatory basis. Their application is limited to the extent and for the time they are deemed necessary. Measures must be notified and the preconditions and the modalities of application are subject to institutional controls by competent organs.

3. NAFTA, CAFTA-DR, Mercosur, and Andean Community

The other agreements studied in this survey do not address safeguards concerning trade in services: Article 801(1) NAFTA allows the suspension of the further reduction or the increase of duties if imports 'constitute a substantial cause of serious injury, or threat thereof, to a domestic industry producing a like or directly competitive good'. However, this right only applied to goods and ceded after the 10 year transition period. An almost identical provision exists in Article 8(1) CAFTA-DR, which also addresses only safeguards in reaction to the importation of goods and which also restricts the right to impose safeguard measure to a 10 year transition period. The Treaty of Asunción Establishing a Common Market (Mercosur-Treaty) of 1991 also provided for

---

[48] Text available at www.aseansec.org/6466.htm (visited 13 February 2006).

temporary safeguard measures in its Annex IV.[49] The right to apply such safeguards subsided on 31 December 1994. The Andean Community General Framework does not contain emergency safeguard provisions.

4. Summary

The preceding analysis shows that only one of the agreements studied, the Caricom treaty, contains a provision on emergency safeguard measures which also applies to services. In the ASEAN context, the AIA Framework Agreement allows safeguard measures concerning investment. This shows that some countries forming a RTA thought that the possibility to use safeguard measures was necessary and found ways to implement such provisions. GATS negotiators can therefore study these examples. However, there is no common approach towards emergency safeguard measures in the RTAs studied, which could be used as a raw-model in the GATS negotiations.

V. CONCLUSION: LESSONS FOR GATS

The above analysis of domestic regulation, government procurement, subsidies, and emergency safeguard measures in selected RTAs covering trade in services shows a mixed picture: some agreements and legal instruments go further than GATS with regard to the four issues studied and some are less far-reaching: for example, on the one hand, some agreements contain directly applicable disciplines on domestic regulation or detailed rules on government procurement relating to services. On the other hand, some agreements do not even mention these issues, or mandate negotiations on these subjects like GATS. It should also be noted, however, that there is no uniform trend. For example, while NAFTA and CAFTA-DR contain a full procurement regime, they have no special rules on subsidies. Similarly, Caricom and Andean Community have regimes of subsidies, but they have no specific rules on domestic regulation.

In light of this observation and the mixed results emerging from the comparative study of the treatment of the aspects of GATS' 'unfinished business' in RTAs, are there any lessons to be drawn from RTAs, which might be of value in the GATS context? It is suggested that the following considerations extracted from the comparative study could be considered by GATS negotiators and policy makers:

Concerning disciplines on domestic regulation, the mixed results indicate that disciplining domestic regulation is a complex and difficult subject even within RTAs. It also reflects different legal and regional approaches to this idea. This suggests that caution, rather than too much ambition, might be the

---

[49] Treaty Establishing a Common Market between the Argentine Republic, the Federal Republic of Brazil, the Republic of Paraguay and the Eastern Republic of Uruguay, signed 26 March 1991, in force 29 November 1991.

appropriate route to take in the GATS context. Furthermore, it should be noted that those RTAs which address the subject provide for similar standards to those suggested in Article VI:4 GATS. However, none of the RTAs contained detailed prescriptions for specific regulatory measures or limited the choice of instruments. As a consequence, broader and general disciplines might react better to the ambiguity of the subject than disciplines which are overly strict and reduce national regulatory autonomy to a greater degree than necessary to achieve the purpose of such disciplines. In particular, it might be sufficient to install a general necessity test following the example of Articles 904(4) and 1210(1) NAFTA, Article X:4 of the Montevideo Protocol, and Article 11(8)(2) CAFTA-DR. However, in light of the contentiousness of the issue, the list of legitimate objectives should not be restricted to the quality of the service, but should include all legitimate policy objectives as in the case of Article 904(4) NAFTA. The use of international standards and of mutual recognition could be encouraged, but not made binding in the strict sense. Even though recognition is not an untypical feature of regional integration, the RTAs studied in this survey remain reluctant to the use of mutual recognition concerning services.

With regard to government procurement, it is notable that some RTAs contain a full-fledged regime on the regulation of government procurement (CAFTA-DR, NAFTA, and Mercosur), while others are completely silent on the subject (ASEAN). A similar picture can be found in relation to subsidies. Therefore, it is difficult to suggest any specific lessons that could be learned from the RTAs experience with regard to the GATS negotiations. However, one aspect is noteworthy: almost all provisions and regulations concerning government procurement and subsidies treat services and goods in the same way: In other words, if a RTA contains a full regime on government procurement or subsidies, it extends to goods and services. For the GATS context, this raises some highly challenging questions. It can be asked whether special rules on services procurement or services subsidies are desirable or achievable in light of the experience of RTAs. In particular concerning government procurement, it is difficult to explain why there are multilateral negotiations on services procurement, while there is no multilateral agreement or negotiations leading to such an agreement concerning goods. In this light, it might be useful to critically re-assess the feasibility of the negotiations on services procurement in the WTO context.

Finally, concerning emergency safeguard measures, the rules on safeguard measures contained in Article 47 of the Revised Treaty of Chaguaramas and Article 14 of the ASEAN Investment Agreement are worth studying as examples in the current GATS negotiations. These provisions show that it is possible to integrate emergency safeguard measures in a services context. Both provisions suggest that institutional procedures to assess the validity and legality of safeguard measures may be important. Yet, there is no uniform approach to emergency safeguards in the RTAs studied in this contribution.

In general, RTAs and their treatment of domestic regulation, government procurement, subsidies, and emergency safeguard measures provide interesting examples and may be useful models to study in the context of the negotiations on the unfinished business of GATS. However, anyone who expects clear-cut lessons and ready-made propositions which can be adapted in the GATS context, should be warned: there is no one-size-fits-all solution in this context.

8

International Agreements Covering Foreign Investment in Services: Patterns and Linkages

FEDERICO ORTINO AND AUDLEY SHEPPARD [*]

I. INTRODUCTION

With the growth of the service industry in the last 30 years, it is not surprising that the number of international agreements purporting to liberalize and promote trade and investment in the service sector has increased dramatically.[1] In particular, the multilateral trade disciplines embodied in the General Agreement on Trade in Services (GATS) expressly apply to both international trade and foreign investment in services. Article I:2(c) of GATS defines trade in services *inter alia* as both the supply of a service from the territory of one member into the territory of any other member (i.e., 'cross-border supply') and the supply of a service by a service supplier of one member through commercial presence in the territory of any other member (so called 'commercial presence').

More than 2300 bilateral investment treaties (BITs) are aimed at promoting and protecting all kinds of foreign investment, including investment in the service sector. There exist several hundred regional integration agreements, including free trade agreements (FTAs) with specific chapters covering investment in services and/or trade in services (e.g. NAFTA, ASEAN Framework

---

[*] We are extremely grateful for comments and discussions with Lorand Bartels, Lothar Ehring, and Gaetan Verhoosel. We are also grateful to Dora Costa for her research assistance. All errors remain ours alone.

[1] For purposes of understanding the global legal framework dealing with the international supply of services (including both cross-border trade and foreign direct investment), one cannot but include, next to FTAs and CUs, BITs. Contrary to Art. XXIV GATT, Art. V GATS (providing for the 'regional economic integration' exception) does not limit its scope exclusively to FTAs and CUs but applies more generally to any 'agreement liberalizing trade in services'. Thus, for purposes of this chapter, we will consider BITs, FTAs, and CUs as the relevant regional economic integration (or trade) agreements. *See* UNCTAD, The REIO Exception in MFN Treatment Clauses (2004).

Agreement) and customs unions (CUs) which also include provisions relating to services. The result of this almost frenetic treaty-making activity is a complex and multilayered network of international rules regulating the transnational movement of services and service providers.[2]

This chapter considers the issue of coordination, or lack of coordination, between the many international agreements covering investment in services. In particular, it focuses on the question of whether bilateral and regional economic integration agreements are consistent with the multilateral disciplines embodied in the GATS. The chapter briefly introduces the legal disciplines in international agreements dealing with investment in services, highlighting the, at times stark, differences in the levels of liberalization and protection of investment flows in services among the complex network of such agreements (section II). The chapter then focuses on the linkages between bilateral and regional economic integration agreements, on the one hand, and the multi-lateral disciplines within the WTO, on the other. First, we posit that BITs and FTAs, by providing more favourable treatment to certain categories of investors, violate the Most Favoured Nation (MFN) obligation enshrined in Article II GATS (section III). Secondly, we also posit that such violation cannot be justified on the basis of the 'Economic Integration' exception of Article V GATS (section IV).

II. INTERNATIONAL DISCIPLINES REGULATING FOREIGN INVESTMENT IN SERVICES

The disciplines contained in international agreements dealing with foreign investment in the services field differ quite substantially. This is evidenced even by a brief overview of the three main features of such disciplines: (a) investment liberalization provisions; (b) investment protection provisions; and (c) dispute settlement provisions.

A. Investment liberalization provisions

In line with the traditional approach to trade liberalization (developed in the field of trade in goods),[3] liberalization provisions covering trade/investment in services under the GATS (a) require the elimination of an exhaustive list of

---

[2] While simultaneity of production and consumption is an essential attribute of services, there exist several ways in which services may be provided between countries: (a) from the territory of one Member into the territory of any other Member (cross-border supply); (b) in the territory of one Member to the service consumer of any other Member (consumption abroad); (c) by a service supplier of one Member, through commercial presence in the territory of any other Member (commercial presence); (d) by a service supplier of one Member, through presence of natural persons of a Member in the territory of any other Member (presence of natural persons). (Art. I:2 GATS).

[3] Although the focus of trade liberalization has at least historically been on reducing border measures (or market access restrictions), provisions dealing with internal measures have come under the overarching liberalization agenda.

specific 'market access' restrictions (Article XVI)[4] and (b) subject all other measures affecting trade in services to the National Treatment principle (Article XVII).

Accordingly, the investment liberalization effects of Articles XVI and XVII GATS are potentially quite broad. First of all, most of the market access restrictions listed in (and prohibited by) Article XVI:2 focus on freeing up investment flows. Secondly, the national treatment obligation covers potentially any governmental measure 'affecting' *inter alia* investment in services, thus including measures that restrict investment entry or admission to the host state (even if not included under the exhaustive list of market access restrictions in Article XVI).[5]

In the investment field, on the other hand, the traditional emphasis of international rule-making has been on the provision of disciplines addressing post-entry concerns of foreign investors.[6] International disciplines have thus focused on protecting foreign investors after entry in the host state, usually through establishing some basic treatment guarantees.[7] Only recently have international investment agreements included provisions aimed at liberalizing investment flows through the reduction of entry barriers (liberalization *stricto sensu*). This has occurred principally by extending national treatment guarantees beyond the post-entry phase to cover also entry or admission restrictions.[8] While a broad national treatment obligation does not recognize *per se* a right of establishment to foreign investors (as that contained in Article 43 of the EC Treaty, for example), it has the potential of recognizing a *de facto* right of entry, as long as a service sector is open to domestic operators.[9]

B. Investment protection provisions

Investment protection disciplines encompass basic treatment guarantees against discriminatory, unfair and expropriatory conduct by host states *vis-à-vis* foreign investments or investors (once they have been admitted in the

---

[4] The market access restrictions listed in Art. XVI:2 GATS include *inter alia*: limitations on the number of service suppliers; limitations on the total value of service transactions or assets; limitations on the total number of service operations; measures which restrict or require specific types of legal entity or joint venture; and limitations on the participation of foreign capital.

[5] WTO Appellate Body Report, *EC—Bananas III*, WT/DS27/AB/R, adopted 25 September 1997, para. 220. However, the liberalization effects of Arts XVI and XVII GATS are greatly curtailed (at least for the time being) since GATS subjects these two provisions to Members' specific commitments.

[6] UNCTAD, World Investment Report 2004—The Shift towards Services (2004), at 224. *See* M. Sornarajah, *The International Law on Foreign Investment* (Cambridge: CUP, 2004), 97 ff.

[7] These agreements contain mere hortatory language aimed at promoting foreign investment as in Art. 2 of the 1999 BIT between UK and Lebanon.

[8] *See* for example Art. 1102 of NAFTA, Art. 3 of the 2004 Canada Model BIT and Art. 2 of the 2002 BIT between Korea and Japan.

[9] Nevertheless, even BITs and FTAs that include investment liberalization provisions usually provide for the possibility of Contracting Parties to complement such provisions with a number of limitations and reservations.

territory of the host state). In particular, these disciplines include the national treatment and MFN treatment obligations (prohibiting discrimination on the basis of the nationality of the investment or investor), fair and equitable treatment, and full protection and security obligations, the obligation to compensate foreign investors for expropriation (under certain circumstances), transparency requirements, transfer of funds obligations, and the requirement to observe any general or specific obligation entered into with the foreign investor (the so called 'umbrella clause').[10]

International agreements that take an investment-based approach (providing for a single, uniform discipline for all investment sectors, whether in goods or services) will usually contain all the standard investment protection provisions mentioned in the previous paragraph.[11] On the other hand, international agreements that take the service-based approach (where investment in services is covered by the disciplines regulating more broadly trade in services) tend to be less far-reaching in terms of investment protection guarantees, focusing only on non-discrimination obligations (such as national and MFN treatment), transparency requirements, and certain disciplines on domestic regulation requiring host states to conform to 'necessity' and/or 'least-restrictive measure' tests. The GATS and certain FTAs, such as the 2003 EFTA–Chile FTA,[12] follow this approach.

The point that should be made here is perhaps an obvious one: the protections offered to foreign investors in the service sector (even more so than in the goods sector) differ, sometimes dramatically, from agreement to agreement. More importantly, even BITs or FTAs that are signed by the same country differ depending on the contracting party or parties with whom those agreements are signed, as well as the time in which these agreements are drafted.[13] Differences may also stem from more subtle differences in the wording of investment protection provisions as well as in the manner in which they are interpreted by arbitral panels.[14]

---

[10] *See* generally Sornarajah, above at n 6 and P. Muchlinski, *Multinational Enterprises and the Law* (Oxford: Blackwell Publishers, 1999).

[11] Most (if not all) BITs and certain FTAs (such as NAFTA or the 2000 New Zealand–Singapore FTA) follow this approach. *See* the 1996 Canada–Chile FTA which contains a chapter on Investment (covering also investment in services) and a chapter on cross-border trade in services.

[12] The 2003 EFTA–Chile FTA contains a chapter on Trade in Services (covering also investment in services) which includes only GATS-type protection provisions. *See* Arts 22–42.

[13] The 2001 China–Jordan BIT grants foreign investments *inter alia* full protection and security and fair and equitable treatment (Art. 3), national and MFN treatment (Art. 4) and expropriation guarantees (Art. 5). On the other hand, the older, but still in effect, 1988 China–New Zealand BIT grants foreign investments *inter alia* fair and equitable treatment (Art. 3, para. 2), MFN treatment (Art. 4) and expropriation guarantees (Art. 6) but it does not include full protection and security or national treatment.

[14] *Compare*, for example, the FET obligations in the 1999 BIT between Australia and India and in the 2005 FTA between Australia and the US.

C. Dispute settlement provisions

International agreements concerning investment generally contain mechanisms by which disputes arising between states (State–State) and/or between a foreign investor and a host state (investor–State) may be resolved. State–State dispute settlement mechanisms usually provide that any dispute between states concerning the interpretation or application of the treaty (which cannot be resolved through negotiations or consultations) shall at the request of either party be submitted to an arbitral tribunal. Investor–State dispute settlement mechanisms generally grant foreign investors the option of submitting a dispute arising between the investor and the host country to international arbitration.

Several differences may be noted with regard to dispute settlement provisions. Agreements taking the investment-based approach, such as BITs and most recent FTAs, usually contain mechanisms for both State–State and investor–State dispute settlement (e.g. NAFTA Chapter Twenty, Section B and Chapter Eleven, Section B). On the other hand, agreements that follow the services-based approach, such as the GATS and certain FTAs (such as the 2003 Chile–EFTA FTA), only provide for State–State dispute settlement.

Furthermore, as highlighted in a recent UNCTAD study,[15] several differences exist in both State–State and investor–State dispute settlement mechanisms concerning: (a) the scope of the subject matter that can be referred to dispute settlement; (b) the rules governing the procedural aspects of arbitration proceedings; (c) the relationship between international arbitration and recourse to domestic tribunals; (d) the applicable rules for the settlement of disputes; and (e) the effect and enforcement of arbitral awards.

III. COMPATIBILITY OF BITS AND FTAS WITH THE MFN OBLIGATION IN GATS?

The argument advanced in this section is that potentially a large number (if not all) BITs and many FTAs violate the general MFN provision of the GATS (Article II) by failing to accord immediately and unconditionally to service suppliers of any other member treatment no less favourable than that accorded to like service suppliers of any other country.[16]

We consider the following hypothetical example: Country A, a WTO Member, by signing a BIT or an FTA with Country B (whether a WTO Member or not) may be found to violate the MFN principle of Article II GATS *vis-à-vis* WTO Member C if Country A provides, through the BIT or FTA more

---

[15] UNCTAD, Key Terms and Concepts in IIAs: A Glossary (2005), at 43 ff.

[16] For an examination of the linkages (in the opposite direction) between WTO law and BITs, *see* G. Verhoosel, 'The Use of Investor–State Arbitration under Bilateral Investment Treaties to Seek Relief for Breaches of WTO Law' (2003) 6 JIEL 493.

favourable treatment to the investors of Country B compared to the treatment it affords to like investors (or service suppliers) of WTO Member C (as well as any other WTO Members).

This argument is premised on two (undisputable) assumptions. First, no country maintains equivalent BITs or FTAs with all its partners; on the contrary, as evidenced in section II above, the liberalization and protection commitments offered by BITs and FTAs differ extensively from agreement to agreement, even among those agreements concluded by the same country. Secondly, and in any event, no WTO Member maintains BITs or FTAs with all other WTO Members.

The MFN provision in GATS sets out three conditions to its application. In other words, in order to determine the consistency of a member's conduct with the MFN obligation in Article II GATS, a dispute settlement panel will need to address: (a) whether the measure at issue is a 'measure covered' by the GATS; (b) whether the services or service suppliers concerned are 'like' services or service suppliers; and (c) whether the member accords 'less favourable treatment' to the services or service suppliers of another member.

A. Measure covered

A measure is covered by the GATS if it is a 'measure by a Member' and is 'affecting trade in services'.

The GATS takes a broad definition of what may be a measure by a Member. Article I:3 states that measures by Members will include 'any measure taken by central, regional or local governments and authorities, as well as non-governmental bodies in the exercise of powers delegated [by those governments and authorities]'. Moreover, Article XXVIII (a) defines 'measure' as 'any measure by a Member, whether in the form of a law, regulation, rule, procedure, decision, administrative action, or any other form'.

BITs and FTAs are formally international agreements, which at a minimum need to be ratified to become binding in the international plane (usually through an act of the Government which may be accompanied by consent of Parliament) and some will subsequently be incorporated into the domestic legal system either directly or through *ad hoc* legislation. The question may be raised whether the mere signature or ratification of these agreements are deemed to be 'measures' for purposes of Article II GATS. The definition of a 'measure' in Article XXVIII (a) is quite broad—including any measure by a Member whatever its form—and is thus apparently broad enough to include even measures of a pure international nature. This broad reading is in line with the objective of the MFN provision, which is to guarantee the equality of opportunities between service and service providers of different countries.[17]

---

[17] P. van den Bossche, *The Law and Policy of the World Trade Organization—Text, Cases and Materials* (Cambridge: CUP, 2005), 319.

Whether the measure potentially upsetting this equality is of an international or national nature should not make a difference for purposes of determining the scope of the MFN provision in Article II GATS. Accordingly, not only laws, regulations, administrative actions applying, or taken pursuant to, a BIT or FTA, but also the mere signature or ratification of such a treaty or agreement, should be considered as measures by a member for purposes of Article II GATS.[18]

Similarly broad is the definition of a 'measure affecting trade in services'. As noted above, 'trade in services' is defined as including any of the four modes of supply listed in Article I:2 of GATS. Mode 3, commonly referred to as 'commercial presence', clearly covers foreign investment with regard to services ('the supply of a service by a service supplier of one Member, through commercial presence in the territory of any other Member'). Article XXVIII of GATS defines 'commercial presence' as 'any type of business or professional establishment, including through (a) the constitution, acquisition or maintenance of a juridical person, or (b) the creation or maintenance of a branch or a representative office, within the territory of a Member for purpose of supplying a service'.

Secondly, WTO jurisprudence has interpreted broadly the term 'affecting'. A measure affects trade in service (including service FDI) when the measure 'modifies the conditions of competition in supply of a service'.[19] In its Report on *EC—Bananas III*, the Appellate Body noted that the use of the term 'affecting' indicates that the GATS has 'a broad scope of application' wider in scope than such terms as 'regulating' or 'governing'.[20] Furthermore, in order to determine whether a measure 'affects' trade in services, there is no need to determine actual effects, rather it is enough to demonstrate a potential effect on trade. Albeit within the context of determining the meaning of 'affecting'

---

[18] The recent WTO Appellate Body Report in *Mexico—Soft Drinks* interpreted the terms 'laws and regulations' in Art. XX(d) GATT as referring only 'to rules that form part of the domestic legal system of a WTO Member'. This general statement should not, however, modify our conclusion for two reasons. First, the term 'measure' in Art. II GATS is broader than the terms 'laws and regulations' in Art. XX(d) (or in Arts I and III GATT). Second, the central issue raised before the Appellate Body in *Mexico—Soft Drinks* was limited to whether the terms 'to secure compliance with laws or regulations' in Art. XX(d) of the GATT encompass WTO-inconsistent measures applied by a WTO Member to secure compliance with *another* WTO Member's obligations under an international agreement. The Appellate Body concluded that 'laws and regulations' in Art. XX(d) included 'obligations of *another* WTO Member under an international agreement'. WTO Appellate Body Report, *Mexico—Soft Drinks*, WT/DS308/AB/R, adopted 24 March 2006, paras 68–9.

[19] *See* WTO Panel Report, *EC—Bananas III (US)*, WT/DS27/R/USA, adopted 25 September 1997, as modified by the Appellate Body Report, WT/DS27/AB/R, at para. 7.281 and GATT Panel Report, *Italy—Agricultural Machinery*, adopted 23 October 1958, BISD 7S/60.

[20] WTO Appellate Body Report, *EC—Bananas III*, above at n 5, at para. 220. *See* W. Zdouc, 'WTO Dispute Settlement Practice Relating to the General Agreement on Trade in Services' in F. Ortino and E.-U. Petersmann (eds), *WTO Dispute Settlement System: 1995–2003* (London: Kluwer, 2004), Ch 21 and A. Mattoo, 'MFN and the GATS', in T. Cottier et al. (eds), *Regulatory Barriers and the Principle of Non-Discrimination in World Trade Law* (Ann Arbor: U Michigan Press, 2000), 53.

in Article III:4 GATT, in *Canada—Autos*, the Panel held that a measure can be considered to be a measure affecting the internal sale of imported products even if it is *not* 'shown to have an impact under current circumstances on decisions of private firms' to buy imported products.[21] Accordingly, in determining the coverage of the MFN provision in the GATS, it is sufficient to show that a governmental measure has the potential to affect (i.e. to have an effect on) trade in service (including investment in services).

As mentioned in section II above, BITs and FTAs provide for a variety of investment liberalization and protection provisions which are aimed at promoting foreign investment including investment in the service sectors. In order for such investment provisions to be considered 'measures affecting trade in services' within the meaning of Article I:1 GATS, it is not required that they have an 'actual' effect on investment in services or that this effect be a 'positive' one (i.e. that they encourage foreign investment). It is simply sufficient that investment provisions in international agreements have the potential to modify the conditions of competition between investments or investors in services from any WTO Member.

B. Like services or service suppliers

The second element of the three-tier test of consistency concerning the MFN obligation of Article II GATS deals with the relationship between the service suppliers (including service investors)[22] at issue. The non-discrimination obligation embodied in the MFN clause only applies between 'like' service investors. Accordingly, it is necessary to answer the following question: Are service investors of non-BIT/FTA origin (i.e. not covered by a BIT or FTA) *like* service investors of BIT/FTA origin (i.e. covered by a BIT or FTA)? In the example that we have given above (i.e. WTO Member A has concluded a BIT or FTA with Country B but not with WTO Member C), the relevant legal question here is the following: Are service investors (e.g. banks or engineering companies) from Country B *like* service investors from WTO Member C?

The GATS does not contain a definition of the term 'like' service providers. The issue of likeness under Article II GATS has only been addressed twice in GATS/WTO jurisprudence, albeit very briefly. In *EC—Bananas III* and *Canada—Autos*, a relevant statement by both Panels was that 'to the extent that entities provide like services, they are like service suppliers'.[23] Looking at the extensive jurisprudence on the issue of the likeness of products under

---

[21] WTO Panel Report, *Canada—Autos*, WT/DS139/R, WT/DS142/R, adopted 19 June 2000, as modified by the Appellate Body Report, WT/DS139/AB/R, WT/DS142/AB/R, paras 10.80 and 10.84. *See* GATT Panel Report, *Italy—Agricultural Machinery*, above at n 19, at para. 12.

[22] Art. XXVIII(g) defines a 'service supplier' as 'any person who supplies a service', including natural and legal persons as well as service suppliers providing their services through forms of commercial presence, such as a branch or a representative office (*see* footnote 12).

[23] WTO Panel Report, *EC—Bananas III*, above at n 19, at para. 7.322 and WTO Panel Report, *Canada—Autos*, above at n 21, at para. 10.248.

GATT,[24] it may be said that the likeness test in the GATS should be based *inter alia* on the following factors: (a) service's end-uses in a given market; (b) consumer habits and preferences regarding the service or the service supplier; (c) characteristics of the service or the service supplier; and (d) classification and description of the service in the United Nations Central Product Classification (UN CPC) system.[25]

However, the issue of likeness does not raise problems when the governmental measure under review is a measure that expressly differentiates between (service) investors and investments *on the basis of the nationality* of the investor (i.e. it is a formally discriminatory measure). Since a formally discriminatory measure presupposes by definition that the regulated service investors and investments are, for purposes of that same measure, identical (that is, identical except for their different nationality), an examination of the service investors' relationship is not (or at least should not be) a relevant issue in the case at issue.[26]

In our hypothetical example, it is the BIT or FTA itself that uses nationality as the discriminating criterion: it is only nationals of WTO Member A and Country B that can avail themselves of the investment protections of the BIT or FTA between countries A and B. Accordingly, any investors from WTO Member C (whether e.g. a financial service provider or an engineering firm) will be potentially 'like' investors from Country B that are covered by the investment protections provided for in the BIT or FTA between countries A and B.

C. 'Less favourable treatment'

The third and final element of the MFN test under Article II GATS focuses on the obligation to accord to services and service providers of Members no less favourable treatment than the treatment they accord to like services and service providers of any other country.[27]

Looking at WTO jurisprudence, the Appellate Body in *EC—Bananas III* took the view that 'treatment no less favourable' in Article II:1 GATS should be taken to include both *de jure* and *de facto* discrimination.[28]

Further insights may be had from WTO jurisprudence interpreting the term 'less favourable treatment' in the field of trade in goods. From the early GATT practice, the phrase 'no less favourable' has been described as an expression of

---

[24] WTO Appellate Body Report, *EC—Asbestos*, WT/DS135/AB/R, adopted 5 April 2001, at para. 101.

[25] A. Mattoo, 'National Treatment in the GATS—Corner Stone or Pandora's Box' (1997) 31 JWT 107, at 128, Zdouc, above at n 20 and van den Bossche, above at n 17, at 323–24.

[26] F. Ortino, *Basic Legal Instruments for the Liberalisation of Trade: A Comparative Analysis of EC and WTO Law* (Oxford, Hart 2004), 124 ff.

[27] The MFN obligation in GATS thus extends also to the treatment afforded to services and service providers of a non WTO Member ('of any other country').

[28] WTO Appellate Body Report, *EC—Bananas III*, above at n 5, at paras 231–34.

the underlying principle of *effective* equality of treatment between imported products, under the most favoured national standard. Accordingly, a measure affords less favourable treatment if it *adversely* modifies the conditions of competition between imports from two different countries. As mentioned above, in order to establish whether the 'no less favourable standard' has been met, panels need to determine whether the particular measure at issue has the *potential* to lead to the application to imported products of treatment less favourable, and not whether it had actually done so. Both non-discrimination norms in WTO law are there to protect *expectations* on the competitive relationship between products.[29]

Affording service providers (or investors) from Country B, for example, an *additional* dispute settlement option (in the form of international arbitration), which is not available (or as favourable as that afforded) to service providers from WTO Member C may represent a breach of the MFN obligation as it may upset the equality of competitive opportunities between providers of Country B and WTO Member C.[30] Similar arguments may be raised with regard to the investment protection and liberalization provisions in BITs and FTAs, whereby investors from Country B would enjoy *higher* market access or post-entry guarantees (due to the BIT or FTA) compared to those accorded to investors from WTO Member C.

IV. AVAILABILITY OF THE 'ECONOMIC INTEGRATION' EXCEPTION OF ARTICLE V GATS?

Using the above hypothetical example, this section posits that Country A may not be able to resist a claim of a GATS MFN violation by having recourse to the 'Economic Integration' exception provided for by Article V GATS since BITs lack 'substantial sectoral coverage' and FTAs do not always provide for the 'elimination of substantially all discrimination' in the sense of Article XVII GATS, as required, respectively, by subparagraphs (a) and (b) of Article V:1 GATS.

Aside from the exemptions to MFN that Article II:2 GATS allows WTO Members to maintain (for a limited period of time, and if listed in their

---

[29] *See* GATT Panel Report, *Italy—Agricultural Machinery*, above at n 19, at paras 11–2 and GATT Panel Report, *US—Section 337*, adopted 7 November 1989, BISD 36S/345, at paras 5.10–5.13.

[30] Although it dealt *in casu* with the National Treatment obligation in Art. III GATT, the GATT Panel Report in *US—Section 337* found that the United States provided 'less favourable treatment' to imports *vis-à-vis* domestic products in light of the fact that Section 337 of the Tariff Act of 1930 allowed holders of US intellectual property rights to obtain *expedited relief* from the International Trade Commission against imports which infringe upon these rights, while patents infringement by domestic products were subject to *normal domestic judicial proceedings*.

Schedules of Commitments),[31] Article V GATS on 'Economic Integration' provides for the only permitted departure from MFN treatment under the GATS. Modeled on Article XXIV GATT, Article V GATS provides for an exception to the MFN obligation in order to permit WTO Members to be party to or enter into an agreement liberalizing trade in services between or among the parties to such an agreement. Article V GATS, however, sets out the necessary requirements for such an economic integration exception to come into operation. It requires that the economic integration agreement:

(a) has substantial sectoral coverage,[32] and
(b) provides for the absence or elimination of substantially all discrimination, in the sense of Article XVII, between or among the parties, in the sectors covered under subparagraph (a), through:
    (i) elimination of existing discriminatory measures, and/or
    (ii) prohibition of new or more discriminatory measures, either at entry into force of that agreement or on the basis of a reasonable time frame, except for measures permitted under Articles XI, XII, XIV and XIV *bis*.

A. 'Substantial sectoral coverage'

With regard to the 'substantial sectoral coverage' requirement, footnote 1 to Article V specifies that 'this condition is understood in terms of numbers of sectors, volume of trade affected and modes of supply. In order to meet this condition, agreements should not provide for the *a priori* exclusion of any mode of supply'.

Both the meaning of Article V GATS in this regard and the concept of how substantial sectoral coverage should be measured are not very clear.[33] It would appear that the 'substantial sectoral coverage' requirement is there to prevent members from using the Article V exception for economic agreements that are limited to one specific mode of supply, such as cross-border services (mode 1) or foreign direct investment (mode 3). As noted by the WTO Secretariat, the requirement in Article V:1(a) 'is designed to prevent the conclusion of regional agreements with limited coverage, for example covering one or few sectors, or exchanging preferential treatment in limited domains such as foreign direct investment'.[34]

The three relevant factors mentioned in footnote 1 (numbers of sectors,

[31] These exemptions could be taken only at the time the negotiations were concluded. Most of them are subject to a ten-year expiration period since the entry in to force of the GATS (i.e. they should have expired in January 2005).

[32] *See* below sub-section A on 'substantial sectoral coverage'.

[33] S.M. Stephenson, 'GATS and Regional Integration', in P. Sauvé and R. Stern (eds), *GATS 2000: New Directions in Services Trade Liberalization* (Washington DC: Brookings, 2000), 514–15.

[34] *See* WTO Secretariat document, available at www.wto.org/english/thewto_e/whatis_e/eol/e/ wto06/wto6_17.htm (visited 10 April 2006).

volume of trade affected and modes of supply) seem to apply cumulatively. In other words, the failure to cover a high number of service sectors or the exclusion of one or more modes of supply would mean that the international agreement lacks substantial sectoral coverage for purposes of Article V:1(a). Accordingly, while determining the sectoral coverage of an economic integration agreement is generally a very difficult exercise,[35] it may not be so in the case of a BIT because of its evident lack of 'substantial sectoral coverage'. It should be emphasized in this regard that BITs generally limit their scope of application expressly to investors and investment of one party in the territory of the other party.[36] In other words, in GATS terminology, BITs cover principally 'commercial presence'. Thus, having regard to the 'modes of supply' factor, a BIT that only covers investment in services (i.e. commercial presence) but not cross-border trade in services (or consumption abroad) may not be said to have substantial sectoral coverage.

This conclusion is supported also by the additional requirement in footnote 1 to Article V specifying that the relevant agreement should not provide for the *a priori exclusion* of any mode of supply. Even if one were to interpret footnote 1 as requiring an *express* exclusion of any mode of supply, it appears that the provision in a BIT that limits the scope of application *ratione materiae* to foreign investment (in service) would be enough to fail the requirement of 'substantial sectoral coverage' in Article V:1(a) GATS.

A related issue is whether, for purposes of the 'substantial sectoral coverage' test, a BIT (covering investment in services) may be analysed in conjunction with an FTA (covering the cross-border trade in services, consumption abroad and presence of natural persons) which has been concluded between the same parties. If the combined effect of the two international agreements is to *substantially* cover service sectors, volume of trade affected and modes of supply, it may be argued that these two agreements would meet the requirement of Article V:1(a), even if taken individually they would fail such test. This conclusion is reinforced by the provision in Article V:2 GATS which states that 'In evaluating whether the conditions under paragraph 1(b) are met, consideration may be given to the relationship of the agreement to a wider process of economic integration or trade liberalization among the countries concerned'.

---

[35] Stephenson, above at n 33, at 515. The author in particular notes the difficulty of measurement of the volume of trade in services because of the severe limitations on the availability of accurate data on services trade and the aggregate nature of the categories reported in statistical publications.

[36] Art. 2 on 'Scope and Coverage' of the 2004 US Model BIT provides that the treaty 'applies to measures adopted or maintained by a Party relating to: (a) investors of the other Party; (b) covered investments; and (c) with respect to Arts 8, 12, and 13, all investments in the territory of the Party'. The US Model BIT defines 'investor of a Party' and 'covered investment' as follows: *investor of a Party* means a Party or state enterprise thereof, or a national or an enterprise of a Party, that attempts to make, is making, or has made an investment in the territory of the other Party; *covered investment* means, with respect to a Party, an investment in its territory of an investor of the other Party in existence as of the date of entry into force of this Treaty or established, acquired, or expanded thereafter.

B. 'Elimination of substantially all discrimination'

Even if the BIT or FTA in question is found to meet the 'substantial sectoral coverage' test, the international agreement would still need to comply with the non-discrimination requirement of Article V:1(b).

For purposes of determining the availability of the MFN exception of Article V GATS, the agreement in question needs to provide for the absence or elimination of substantially all discrimination, in the sense of Article XVII GATS, between or among the parties in the sectors covered by the agreement (except as permitted *inter alia* by general public policy exceptions and balance of payments safeguards). Albeit that GATS Article V:1(b) requirement is not as strict as the parallel requirement of Article XXIV:8 GATT,[37] it is nevertheless quite broad given the scope of application of the National Treatment provision in Article XVII GATS. As noted above, the National Treatment provision in GATS covers potentially any governmental measures 'affecting' *inter alia* investment in services, including both measures that restrict investment entry or admission to the host state (pre-establishing phase) and measures that apply to the post-establishment phase of foreign investment.

This broad interpretation has been followed in *Canada—Autos*, where the Panel considered that, with respect to an import duty exemption available to only a limited number of firms, Canada could not claim an exemption from its MFN obligation under Article II by invoking Article V:1 GATS. The Panel noted that the Canadian measures at issue did not grant more favourable treatment to all services and service suppliers of members of NAFTA (i.e. only a small number of manufacturers/wholesalers of the United States and of Mexico enjoyed more favourable treatment).[38]

Although some recent BITs and FTAs provide for broad national treatment obligations with regard to investment (including both pre and post-establishment investment measures), the majority of BITs and a number of FTAs still tend to limit the scope of their national treatment obligations to post-establishment, only. Focusing on this point, these latter agreements may fail the broad non-discrimination requirement of Article V:1(b) GATS.[39]

However, Article V:1(b) does not require the elimination of all discrimination, but only the elimination of *substantially* all discrimination. As noted by the Appellate Body in *Turkey—Textiles* with regard to the similar provision in Article XXIV:8 GATT, 'substantially all' is not the same as 'all', and is something considerably more than merely 'some'.[40] Furthermore, while recognizing

---

[37] *See* J.H. Mathis, 'Regional Trade Agreements and Domestic Regulation: What Reach for "Other Restrictive Regulations of Commerce" ', in this volume, at 79.

[38] WTO Panel Report, *Canada—Autos*, above at n 21, at para. 10.271.

[39] A more complex issue is whether the national treatment provisions in BITs and FTAs (even if applicable to both pre and post-establishment) need to be formulated or (at least) interpreted as provided for in Art. XVII GATS.

[40] WTO Appellate Body Report, *Turkey—Textiles*, WT/DS34/AB/R, adopted 19 November 1999, at para. 48.

that the terms of Article XXIV:8(a) offer 'some flexibility' to the constituent members of a RTA when liberalizing their internal trade (as members may maintain in their internal trade certain restrictive regulations of commerce permitted under Articles XI through XV and under Article XX GATT), the Appellate Body cautioned that the degree of 'flexibility' is limited by the requirement that 'duties and other restrictive regulations of commerce' be eliminated with respect to 'substantially all' internal trade.[41]

It is difficult to determine whether a BIT or FTA limiting its national treatment obligation only to post-establishment measures will satisfy the 'elimination of substantially all discrimination' requirement of Article V:1(b) GATS. This determination cannot but involve a case-by-case analysis, where particular attention will have to be paid to any exclusion or exemption of the scope of application of the national treatment obligation provided for in the BIT or FTA (for example, through exclusions included in an annex to the agreement or through conditions imposed on a Member's positive list of commitments). Furthermore, with regard to FTAs, determining whether the agreement provides for the elimination of substantially all discrimination will necessarily imply an analysis of all modes of supply (and not just the 'commercial presence' mode of supply). In other words, it may be that by maintaining certain discriminatory measures to the pre-establishment phase, an FTA will nevertheless meet the requirement of Article V:2(b) GATS if overall the agreement eliminates all discrimination in relation with the other three modes of supply ('cross border', consumption abroad', 'presence of natural persons').

V. BRIEF CONCLUSION

As the process of integration of the global market place continues, efforts to steer such process at the international level through treaty-making (whether of a bilateral, regional or multilateral nature) should at a minimum seek to achieve a certain level of coordination, and in particular consistency with such fundamental instruments as GATS. The current legal framework relating to liberalization of the international provision of services does not appear to achieve that objective. It may be inevitable that inconsistencies will occur between so many bilateral and regional international agreements, which are negotiated by different people in different countries with different policy aims, but government trade officials, academics and international organizations need to consider carefully how better to coordinate BITs and FTAs with obligations under GATS, if the whole system is not to tie itself in knots.

---

[41] *Ibid.* In the context of Art. XXIV:8(a)(ii), the Appellate Body agreed with the Panel that the ordinary meaning of the term 'substantially' appears to provide for both qualitative and quantitative components: *ibid.*, at para. 49 citing the WTO Panel Report, *Turkey—Textiles*, WT/DS34/R, adopted 19 November 1999, as modified by the Appellate Body Report, WT/DS/34/AB/R, at para. 9.148.

9

TRIPS-Plus Provisions in FTAs: Recent Trends

BRYAN MERCURIO

I. INTRODUCTION

While many believed the introduction of minimum standards and greater enforcement for intellectual property rights (IPRs) through the Agreement on Trade-Related Aspects of Intellectual Property (TRIPS) sufficiently placated the major industrialized nations' demands for strong IPRs, it now appears that this agreement only served as another step in the pursuit of stronger IPRs. In fact, having failed to achieve all they sought in the TRIPS negotiations, the US and other developed nations almost immediately began negotiating for the inclusion of more protectable subject matter, broader and more extensive coverage, increased harmonization, stronger enforcement mechanisms, and a weakening of 'flexibilities' and 'special and differential treatment' granted to developing and least developed countries in the TRIPS.

Having unsuccessfully attempted to strengthen IPRs in TRIPS in the years following its implementation, and following the spectacular failure of the Seattle Ministerial in 1999, these nations shifted the focus of their efforts from the multilateral forum to bilateral and regional Free Trade Agreements (FTAs). Thus, while many developing countries were still struggling to implement their obligations under TRIPS, developed countries were already raising the level of IPRs through FTAs. In this regard, the US is the clear leader in promoting higher standards of intellectual property (IP) protection than required in TRIPS (so called TRIPS-Plus provisions).[1]

---

[1] For its part, the EC has not attempted to negotiate TRIPS-Plus provisions. However, the EC already has an extensive network of FTAs and preferential arrangements and is currently negotiating FTAs for geo-political reasons. In addition, Member Countries have extensive BITs which include IP-related activities in the definition of investment and TRIPS-Plus provisions, particularly encompassing geographical indications, may appear in future EC FTAs. Moreover, newly acceded EU countries had to meet TRIPS-Plus standards and the EC has used internal trade mechanisms recently against both Turkey and South Korea. *See* R. Mayne, 'Regionalism, Bilateralism, and "TRIP Plus" Agreements: The Threat to Developing Countries' (2005) UNDP Human Development Report Office Occasional Paper, 10–2.

This chapter does not attempt to provide a comprehensive analysis of the history of IPRs in the international trading system. Nor does it attempt to analyse all present negotiations involving TRIPS-Plus provisions. Instead, it seeks to make two more limited points: first, that TRIPS should never have been viewed as the final statement on international IPRs, but rather as merely a stage (albeit an important one) in a larger cycle alternating between bilateral, regional, and multilateral forums; and second, that the world has moved beyond the multilateral phase and into a bilateral phase; a phase which is seeing the negotiation increased IPRs and placing increased obligations on signatories.

This chapter focuses on patents as one particular form of intellectual property to demonstrate that a rotating cycle between bilateralism, regionalism and multilateralism not only exists but also strengthens IPRs and obligations of nations. This is not to underemphasize the importance and potential consequences of TRIPS-Plus provisions in other areas of IP, such as plant varieties protection, breeders' protection, copyright, trademark, technological protection measures, and geographical protections and enforcement mechanisms.[2] These are all important areas being re-negotiated bilaterally with the introduction of every TRIPS-Plus provision.

II. THE NEGOTIATING CYCLE: BILATERALISM, REGIONALISM AND MULTILATERALISM

While the US may be using bilateralism to undermine the substantive and strategic gains, protections and flexibilities of developing countries by weakening or even overriding TRIPS, such a view fails to fully grasp the broader, more historical context of IPRs. When one broadens the scope of review, it becomes clear that TRIPS is not the definitive agreement on IPRs that some thought or hoped it would be but instead represents one part of a larger cycle in which developed countries engage in bilateralism, regionalism, and multilateralism to advance their interests and secure concessions from other nations, particularly developing nations.[3]

In fact, the cycle of bilateralism, regionalism, and multilateralism is evidenced from the beginning of IPRs. Early IPRs (and other trade-related

[2] Even though these provisions correspond to US law, they fail to contain many safeguards built into US law. *See* P. Yu, 'Intellectual Property at a Crossroads: The Use of the Past in Intellectual Property Jurisprudence: Currents and Crosscurrents in the International Intellectual Property Regime' (2004) 38 Loy LAL Rev, 323, at 395–96 and R. Okediji, 'TRIPS Dispute Settlement and the Sources of (International) Copyright Law' (2001) 49 J Copyright Soc USA, 585.

[3] This perspective is substantiated by the long history of international IP policymaking impacting upon 'trade interests'. For instance, early English patents were revocable if they were not exploited or communicated to workers so as to ensure enhanced domestic production and export capacities. A similar experience can be found in Italy and France: R. Okediji, 'Back to Bilateralism? Pendulum Swings in International Intellectual Property Protection' (2003) 1 U Ott Law & Tech J 125, at 131–32.

interests) were granted nationally and applied in a discriminatory manner in an effort to develop domestic manufacturing and export facilities. Realizing the inefficiencies of the system, the principles of MFN and NT became features of early bilateral commercial and Friendship, Commerce and Navigation (FCN) agreements, to which IPRs were included. By the mid-1800s, however, trading nations had created a complex web of agreements in which MFN and NT applied bilaterally. When the 'spaghetti bowl' agreements became unmanageable, practitioners and government realized the rights needed to be formally adopted in an international framework.[4] Such efforts built upon the bilateralism by filling gaps and providing coherence to IPRs. This process culminated in the Paris Convention for the Protection of Industrial Property (1883) (patents, trademarks, and industrial designs) and the Berne Convention for the Protection of Literary and Artistic Works (1886) (copyright).[5] The World Intellectual Property Organization (WIPO) was subsequently created to oversee and administer these and other IP-related treaties.

Many years later, and following the failure of the GATT 1947 to encompass all topics traditionally covered by FCN treaties, nations shifted to bilateralism and negotiated Bilateral Investment Treaties (BITs) to protect a range of private rights, including IPRs. Increasingly, the BITs negotiated in the 1970s and early 1980s represented a return to bilateralism in IPRs by providing more detailed provisions relating to IP.

At the same time, multilateralism was further developing through WIPO and its various treaties. Developed countries, however viewed WIPO as a developing country dominated institution incapable of adequately protecting IPRs. It was therefore an unacceptable forum to developed countries and the proliferation of BITs continued.[6] However, as a result of government policies and recession in the late 1970s and early 1980s, developing countries allowed their multilateral advantage to erode and developed countries orchestrated a shift away from multilateralism.[7] This forum shift occurred mainly as a result of the failure of the BITs to effectively protect IPRs (in fact, counterfeiting and other transgressions flourished) coupled with the realization on the part of the US that counterfeit goods were annually costing the nation between

---

[4] This phrase, christened by economist Jagdish Bhagwati in the context of goods, has become part of the vernacular to describe 'a chaotic crisscrossing of preferences, with a plethora of different trade barriers applying to products depending on which countries they originate from'. *See* J. Bhagwati, 'Reshaping the WTO' (2005) 168 Far East Econ Rev 25. Its usage is equally applicable to IPRs pre-Berne and Paris.

[5] *See* Berne Convention for the Protection of Literary and Artistic Works (Paris Act), 1161 UNTS 30, revised 24 Jul 1971 and Paris Convention for the Protection of Industrial Property, 20 March 1883, 13 UST 2, 828 UNTS 107, as last revised at the Stockholm Revision Conference 14 July 1967, 21 UST 1538, 828 UNTS 303.

[6] *See* J. Braithwaite and P. Drahos, *Global Business Regulation* (Cambridge: CUP, 2000).

[7] *See* H. El-Said and M. El-Said, 'TRIPS, Bilateralism & Implications for Developing Countries: Jordan's Drug Sector' (2005) 2 MJIEL 59. For detailed analysis, *see* S. Sell, *Power and Ideas* (New York: SUNY Press, 1998).

US$43–61 billion.[8] As the US now had a comparative advantage in IP (while at the same time losing its comparative advantage in other areas, namely manufacturing), IPRs became an international policy priority for the US. It was not until this shift in international policy norms that strong protection and exploitation of IPRs internationally was meaningfully linked to international trade.[9] Thereafter, the US strengthened the link between IPRs and international trade regulation and took several steps to fortify its dominance in the area, including by naming transgressor countries and designating a 'priority watch' list in the annual *USTR National Trade Estimates Report*, applying pressure through bilateral negotiations and by filing cases and obtaining favourable decisions or concessions on the basis of unfair acts under Section 301–310 of the US Trade Act of 1974 (even though the actions of the foreign company/country violated no international law).[10] At the same time, the US completed the shift away from the perceived ineffectiveness of multilateralism through WIPO by negotiating for IPRs into the North American Free Trade Agreement (NAFTA) and by linking IPRs to its Generalized System of Preferences (GSP) programme granting preferential access to the US market.[11] Importantly, these measures were only taken after failing to obtain an agreement on trade in counterfeit goods in the Tokyo Round (1979) and in the face of strong developing country resistance to the addition of IPRs in the Uruguay Round. Thus, by the mid-1980s, bilateralism through BITs (approximately 500 BITs existed at the time of the finalization of the Uruguay Round) coupled with aggressive unilateralism dominated the international scene.

The forum soon shifted back to multilateralism, however, as the US, with the assistance of developed nations (notably the EC, Switzerland, and Japan), managed to eventually get IP on the negotiating table in the Uruguay Round and successfully negotiated for a more uniform system not only providing more protection, but also an adequate remedy in the form of a binding

---

[8] *See* F. Abbott, 'Commentary: The International Intellectual Property Order Enters the 21st Century' (1996) 29 Vanderbilt J Transnatl L 471, at 473.

[9] Despite the efforts of WIPO, intellectual property regimes differed widely in a number of important areas and only minimally protected through the agreements administered by WIPO: B. Mercurio, 'TRIPS, Patents and Access to Life-Saving Drugs in the Developing World' (2004) 8 Marq Intell Prop L Rev 211, at 215–16.

[10] *See* generally A. Sykes, 'Constructive Unilateral Threats in International Commercial Relations: The Limited Case for Section 301' (1993) 23 Law & Policy Int Bus 263, at 318–19; *see also* K. Maskus, 'Implications of Regional and Multilateral Agreements for Intellectual Property Rights' (1997) 20 World Economy 681, at 681–82. The US also passed the *Bayh-Dole Act* to assist the commercialization of federally funded research, ratified the Berne Convention, and established a specialized patent Court as part of its shift in policy priorities. *See* Okediji, above at n 3, at 135.

[11] *See* Title V of the Trade and Tariff Act of 1984 (so called GSP Renewal Act) (conditioning GSP on, *inter alia*, protection of IPRs in order to maintain their preferential trading status). *See also* the reauthorization of the Act in 1996, which now requires the President to 'take into account the extent to which such country is providing adequate and effective protection of intellectual property rights'. For more on the US's use of GSP to influence IPRs, *see* International Intellectual Property Alliance, available at www.iipa.com/gsp.html (visited 10 April 2006).

and enforceable dispute settlement mechanism.[12] The resulting agreement—TRIPS—is comprehensive in coverage and includes several sectors of IPRs (such as copyright and related rights; trademarks; geographical indications; industrial designs; patents; layout-designs of integrated circuits; and protection of undisclosed information). Like other covered agreements of the WTO, the basis of TRIPS is MFN and NT; however, TRIPS also establishes minimum levels of protection that each member must provide and grant to other nations.[13] Importantly, members may apply higher levels of protection if they so desire, so long as the principles of MFN and NT are respected.[14]

While the criticisms of TRIPS from a development perspective are well known, developed countries also failed to achieve all their goals in the Uruguay Round and, perhaps due to constant lobbying of IP holders, increasingly argue the multilateral standards are insufficient to protect their interests. Thus, as noted above, the US and other developed nations sought to negotiate higher levels of WTO IP protection in the late 1990s. Developing countries organized to resist these efforts, which not only contributed to the collapse of the Seattle Ministerial, but later the confirmation of the flexibilities built into TRIPS via the Doha Declaration on TRIPS and Public Health[15] and a prolonged Doha Round (including the failure of the Cancun Ministerial in 2003). As a result of the strong and unwavering resistance, the US has again shifted its negotiating focus and sought to use bilateralism/regionalism to increase IPRs by requiring FTA partners to implement TRIPS-Plus provisions in the following form:

(a) inclusion of new areas of IPRs; or
(b) implementation of more extensive levels or standards of IP protection than is required by TRIPS; or
(c) elimination of an option or flexibility available under TRIPS.

On the one hand, the strategy of consolidating gains and then almost immediately moving to another forum to seek additional gains does make sense from a nationalistic policy perspective for a number of reasons. First, multilateral gains are always, to some extent, small and resemble the least common

[12] Eventually, with the threat of continued unilateral action and decreased trade aid, developing countries agreed to the inclusion of IPRs in the Uruguay Round in exchange for concessions in other areas, notably agriculture and textiles. Developing countries also succeeded in negotiating several flexibilities into TRIPS, the most notable being deferred implementation provisions.

[13] In formulating minimum standards, TRIPS incorporates the substantive obligations of WIPO, the Paris Convention, the Berne Convention, and certain provisions of the Treaty on Intellectual Property in Respect of Integrated Circuits and the Rome Convention. In addition, TRIPS also sets standards in areas which were either not addressed in or, according to members, were not sufficiently covered in the WIPO Agreements.

[14] It is imperative to understand at the outset that such a regulatory, harmonized approach to this issue is unlike the approaches of the other covered agreements of the WTO.

[15] The Doha Declaration affirms the right of each WTO Member to make use of the provisions of the TRIPS Agreement providing flexibility for the protection of public health and promoting access to medicines.

denominator that can be achieved when a large number of varied opinions and interests attempt to achieve consensus. This is especially the case at the WTO, where every member, no matter the size or economic clout, essentially can use the consensus decision-making process to veto the entire process. In such a situation, the interests of a nation or lobbyist (such as the pharmaceutical industry) will never fully be placated through multilateralism. Thus, when the US is unable to gain concessions through multilateral negotiations due to, among other reasons, consensus-decision making, it simply shifts the parameters and sidesteps multilateral impediments (and the 'won't do' countries) through bilateral/regional agreements with those 'can do' countries willing to make concessions in order to secure a potentially lucrative agreement with, to many, the most important market in the world.[16]

In addition, and intertwined to the above, is the fact that multilateral agreements also contain special and differential treatment and other opt-out clauses, resulting not only in unfulfilled negotiating goals but also scope for bilateral movement. As a result, members find it advantageous to shift the forum. As one commentator stated of recent bilateralism:

> From the United States' standpoint, the switch to bilateralism has at least two benefits. By changing the forum and reducing the number of negotiating parties, the United States can provide side payments that it would not be able to offer in a multilateral forum, given the diversity of interests the United States has vis-à-vis the contracting states. By switching to bilateralism, the United States can also prevent less developed countries from reopening the TRIPS negotiations with a better bargaining position.[17]

Quite obviously, the TRIPS-Plus provisions and resulting standards are designed to best protect US domestic interests. While some commentators may disagree with this approach, it is in fact no different to any negotiation: the US is putting forth its position and the negotiation partner can choose to accept the demand, conditionally accept it in exchange for a US concession or outright reject the demand.[18] It is also clear that the TRIPS-Plus provisions appearing in US FTAs (or, in other words 'internationalizing') are identical to aspects of its domestic law. This is not hidden, and in fact can be seen in the US law providing the President with the power to conclude trade agreements ('Trade Promotion Authority' or so called 'fast track'), which states the promotion of an IP regime that 'reflect(s) a standard of protection similar to that found in United States law' is a US negotiating objective. This negotiating

---

[16] R. Zoellick, 'America will not wait for the won't-do Countries', Financial Times (London), 22 September 2003, 23. It should be noted that the US and others are also still negotiated BITs which incorporate IP-related activities. In fact, there are now over 2,200 BITs. *See* 'Making Investment Work for Development' (2004), available at www.unctad.org (visited 10 April 2006). For more on recent BITs, *see* D. Vivas-Eugui, 'Regional and Bilateral Agreements and a TRIPS plus world: the case of the FTAA' TRIPS Issues Paper No 1 (2003), available at www.qiap.ca/documents/FTAASupptableA42.pdf (visited 10 April 2006), 7–9.

[17] Yu, above at n 2, at 395.

[18] The issue of power in bilateral negotiations will be addressed later in this chapter and has been addressed in other chapters of this book.

strategy can be seen in the similarities between recent US FTAs (such as, for instance, the US–Singapore and US–Australia FTAs).

The negotiation of similar, or in fact identical, standards is again not unexpected. As with any other system of standards, it is always more manageable if more than one country operates a similar system. In addition to administrative reasons for negotiating identical standards, developed countries are also meeting their own economic needs and persuading others to fit in with their cultural and philosophical traditions. In this regard, countries agreeing to such heightened standards must fully recognize they not only are agreeing to amend their IP laws, in most cases without full discussion and input of the IP community and, perhaps more importantly, any economic analysis as to the overall costs of the changes, but that they may be agreeing to standards that are far removed from their own the economic and social needs.[19]

On the other hand, and unlike in the 1960s and 1970s when increased standards (such as investment and IP protection) were cast in terms of assisting development (i.e. encouraging investment),[20] the current bilateralism unashamedly seeks to fragment developing country coalitions while at the same time taking advantage of unequal bargaining power in bilateral negotiations. It is apparent that such a strategy encompasses 'dividing' developing country coalitions and negotiating with those nations willing to compromise.[21] It must be noted, however, that many developing countries do not hesitate to trade off IPRs in exchange for market access.[22] In the vast majority of cases, such a trade off is not included nefariously by the larger trading nation but instead a conscious choice of the developing nation.[23] This is why, despite protests from mainly Western NGOs purporting to represent the interests of the developing world, developing countries continue to negotiate FTAs.[24] The reason for this

---

[19] P. Drahos, 'Expanding Intellectual Property's Empire: the Role of FTAs' (2003), available at www.grain.org (visited 10 April 2006). French President Jacques Chirac called the US strategy 'tantamount to blackmail' *See* Mayne, above at n 1, at 5.

[20] *See* Okediji, above at n 3, at 141.

[21] It seems clear that the US is employing a strategy of dividing and conquering by excluding leading G-20 members from FTA negotiates and conditioning GSP access to increased IP protection. *See* P. Drahos, B. Faunce, T. Goddard and D. Henry, 'The FTA and the PBS' (2004) Submission to the Senate Select Committee on the US–Australian Free Trade Agreement.

[22] On whether the gains eventuate, *see* C. Freund, 'Reciprocity in Free Trade Agreements' World Bank Policy Research Paper 3061 (World Bank, 2003).

[23] Canadian academic Michael Geist stated, in the context of copyright: 'Developing countries such as the Dominican Republic view the inclusion of stronger copyright protections as a costless choice. For those countries, the harm that may result from excessive copyright controls pales in comparison to more fundamental development concerns and they are therefore willing to surrender copyright policy decisions in return for tangible benefits in other trade areas': M. Geist, 'Why We Must Stand on Guard Over Copyright', Toronto Star (Toronto), 20 October 2003, D3. *See also* F. Abbott, 'The Cycle of Action and Reaction: Latest Developments and Trends in IP and Health' (2004) ICTSD-UNCTAD Dialogue on Ensuring Policy Options for Affordable Access to Essential Medicines, available at www.iprsonline.org/unctadictsd/bellagio/docs/Abbott_Bellagio3rev1.pdf (visited 10 April 2006).

[24] For instance, Mexico has FTAs with over 42 countries, many of which were negotiated subsequent to NAFTA.

is that bilateral agreements offer developing countries real gains instead of the mainly pyrrhic or symbolic victories of multilateralism (where the resulting gains may not flow to every country and must be divided among all competitors).[25] It must be also noted that the practice of negotiating TRIPS-Plus provisions is not limited to FTAs with developing countries. For instance, the US–Australia FTA imposes a strict IP regime, modelled on the US–Chile and US–Singapore FTAs, requiring Australia to amend several laws.[26]

All of the above illustrates how the US is supporting its overall trade agenda by strategically rebalancing the landscape and creating new norms for IPRs through multiple FTAs with both developed and developing countries.[27] Peter Drahos refers to this as the 'global ratchet' for IPRs.[28] According to Drahos, the 'ratchet' is dependent upon three factors. First, the standard setting agenda must be shifted from a forum where difficulty is being encountered to a more amenable forum. In IP, as with others aspects of international trade, this process has repeated several times. For instance, as explained above, in the early 1980s industrialized countries objected to the increasing domination of WIPO by developing countries and responded by including IPRs in BITs (and later FTAs) and pushing for IPRs to be included in the Uruguay Round. However, since the US does not have enough support to strengthen IPRs multilaterally, it has again shifted the forum to back to bilateralism in order to promote its agenda.

Second, there must be a coordination of bilateral and multilateral IP strategies. For instance, this could see the US negotiate BITs/FTAs requiring other parties to comply with certain multilateral IP standards. Such policies expedite compliance with TRIPS while at the same time force certain developing countries to relinquish their rights granted by the TRIPS (i.e. longer implementation periods). To illustrate, Nicaragua agreed to forego its implementation period and immediately comply with its TRIPS obligations in exchange for preferential access to the US market and increased prospects of foreign direct investment.[29]

---

[25] *See*, e.g. M. Leaffer, 'Protecting United States Intellectual Property Abroad: Toward a New Multilateralism' (1991) 76 Iowa L Rev 273, at 295 and M. Baucus, 'A New Trade Strategy: The Case for Bilateral Agreements' (1989) 22 Cornell Int L J 1.

[26] The US–Australia FTA was controversial as it impacted upon Australia's Pharmaceutical Benefits Scheme (PBS) for providing access to affordable medications. For more information, *see* B. Mercurio, 'The Impact of the AUSFTA on the Provision of Health Services in Australia' (2005) 26 Whittier L Rev, 1051 and P. Drahos et al., 'Pharmaceuticals, Intellectual Property and Free Trade: The Case of the US–Australia Free Trade Agreement' (2004) 22 Prometheus, 243.

[27] *See* R. Zoellick, 'Globalization, Trade and Economic Security', Remarks at the National Press Club, 1 October 2002 (on file with author) and 'Advisory Group Reports on U.S.-Bahrain FTA' (2004), available at www.ustr.gov/Trade_Agreements/Bilateral/Bahrain_FTA/Reports/Section_Index.html (visited 10 April 2006).

[28] Peter Drahos has coined the practice of viewing TRIPS as purely a minimum standard which can be superseded as the 'global regulatory ratchet for intellectual property': Drahos, above at n 19, at 7.

[29] R. Rajkumar, 'The Central American Free Trade Agreement: An End Run Around The Doha Declaration on TRIPS and Public Health' (2005) 15 Alb L J Sci & Tech 433, at 450. The agreement was signed less than a year after Nicaragua was added to the USTR Special 301 list.

Finally, in order for the ratchet to take hold there must be a re-setting of minimum standards through multilateral entrenchment. In this regard, it is important to note that many of the US FTAs explicitly commit the parties to the agreement to provide adequate and effective protection of IPRs in accordance with 'the highest international standards'.[30] The setting of minimum standards in each agreement is important because the minimum standards clauses can ratchet up the lowest level of protection with each subsequent bilateral or multilateral agreement. While such standards are not clearly defined, nor is the term mentioned in TRIPS, it has long been thought that such notations refer not to the standards existing at the time of negotiation but to any standards which subsequently emerge as a matter of international practice.[31] In this regard, each bilateral agreement negotiated by the US not only further supports their framework of increased protection but also adds to it upon the completion of subsequent agreements.[32]

Closely related is the fact that the MFN clause in TRIPS further assists the US in the process of recalculating and resetting international standards. The reason for this is that Article 4 of TRIPS states that any member which grants 'any advantage, favour, privilege or immunity' to the nationals of *any* other country (whether that country be a Member of the WTO/TRIPS or not) must accord the same treatment to the nationals of other Members of TRIPS. The clause operates in a relatively unqualified way because, unlike Article XXIV of the GATT, which may serve to exempt FTAs from the operation of MFN, TRIPS does not contain a similar provision; thus, the principle of MFN applies to FTAs. To illustrate, if the US and a developing country member negotiate an FTA, MFN will force the developing nation to make the same IP concessions it accepted in the FTA available to all nations.[33] This provision clearly serves to 'ratchet up' international IP. Therefore, those nations negotiating for TRIPS-Plus provisions are at the same time utilizing the MFN principle to harmonize the protection of IP rights, resulting in more far reaching implications than FTA provisions dealing with, for instance, goods.[34] Therefore, if enough FTAs are negotiated containing TRIPS-plus provisions, these provisions will essentially become the new minimum standard from which any future WTO trade round will proceed.

---

[30] *See*, e.g. US FTAs with Jordan (Art. 4(1)), Morocco (Art. 15(1)(1)), Bahrain (Art. 14(1)(1)), Singapore (Art. 16(1)(1)), Australia (Art. 17(1)(1)), and Chile (Art. 17(1)(1)).

[31] P. Drahos, 'Bilateralism in Intellectual Property' (2001) 4 JWIP 6, at 13 (noting the framework established under the EU–Mexico FTA makes clear that the meaning of 'highest standard' is 'not confined to standards prevailing at the time of the FTA, but may well include other subsequent standards that emerge, especially if the failure to adhere to those standards gives rise to difficulties in the protection of intellectual property').

[32] The 'highest international standard' phrase also appears in numerous EC agreements (including with Palestine, Mexico, Tunisia, and South Africa). The EC claims, however, that it no longer negotiates such language into its agreements. *See* Mayne, above at n 1, at 10–2.

[33] Subject to the qualifications in Art. 4 TRIPS.

[34] At least one commentator has asserted that developing countries may not fully appreciate this point of difference with the GATT. Mayne, above at n 1, at 1.

III. TRIPS-PLUS PROVISIONS

As the US is the main driver of the global IP ratchet, this section examines certain TRIPS-Plus provisions negotiated by the US to illustrate how the US is raising minimum standards by progressively building upon the level of IP protection through the development of FTA models or prototypes.[35] Further, this section focuses only on a few provisions that potentially have serious implications in the area of patents relating to medicines. It must be noted that attempting to evaluate the social and economic implications of the TRIPS-Plus provisions in the FTAs is difficult. It requires not only an understanding of the changes in laws and regulations but also involves complex economic forecasting.[36] This chapter does not attempt such an analysis, but does point out where changes may impact upon the ability of a nation to promote public health as well as rebutting the US claim that its 'side letters' adequately protect the flexibilities built into TRIPS and public health.[37]

A. TRIPS-PLUS Provisions

1. Linking 'market approval' to the patent status of a drug

Several US FTAs introduce provisions which prevent national drug regulatory authorities from registering a generic version of a drug that is under patent in the country without the consent of the patent holder. Identical language in several agreements states:

> If a party permits a third person to use the subject matter of a subsisting patent to generate information necessary to support an application for marketing approval of a pharmaceutical . . . that Party shall provide that any product produced under such authority shall not be made, used, or sold in the territory of that Party other than for purposes related to generating information to meet requirements for approval to market the product once the patent expires, and if the Party permits exportation, the product shall only be exported outside the territory of that party for purposes of marketing approval requirements of that Party.[38]

This provision represents a significant shift from traditional operating standards, where the market approval of a drug, that is the regulatory approval

---

[35] The Acting Director of the US Patent and Trademark Office stated: '. . . [I]n order to lower the transaction costs of bilateralism, the US has developed models or prototypes of the kind of bilateral trading it wishes to have with other countries. Once a model treaty is ratified by the Senate, US trade negotiators know that if they stick to its terms in other negotiations there is a good chance the treaties flowing from these negotiations will also be approved . . .'. J. Dudas, Testimony to the United States Senate Subcommittee on Oversight of Government Management, 20 April 2004.

[36] C. Fink and P. Reichenmiller, 'Tightening TRIPS: The Intellectual Property Provisions of Recent US Free Trade Agreements' (2005) The World Bank Group Trade Note, 7 February 2005.

[37] For more on this issue, *see* S.F. Musungu and C. Oh, 'The Use of Flexibilities in TRIPS by Developing Countries: Can they Promote Access to Medicine' (2005), available at www.who.int/intellectualproperty/studies/TRIPS_flexibilities/en/ (visited 10 April 2006), 55.

[38] *See* Arts 19(5)(3) of CAFTA-DR; 17(9)(4) of US–Chile; 15(9)(6) of US–Morocco; 16(7)(5) of US–Singapore; and 14(8)(5) of US–Bahrain.

granted to a product which proves its safety and efficacy, has not been linked to a drug's patent status. Thus, the patent status of a drug has never had bearing on whether a drug is of sufficient quality, safety and efficacy to be marketed in a particular nation or region. The reason for the separation of patent status and regulatory approval is simple—the authorities granting patents and those granting regulatory and marketing approval offer very different areas of expertise and competency. Simply stated, authorities which assess and grant patents (commonly called patent offices) decide whether the drug at issue is innovative and novel and otherwise meet the criteria for a patent in that country whereas national drug regulatory authorities, on the other hand, simply assess whether the drug at issue is of sufficient quality, safety, and efficacy to be marketed as a potential medical treatment. Thus, national drug regulatory authorities have traditionally not been concerned with the patent status of a drug they are assessing. Therefore, potential infringement of a patented drug by the applicant generic manufacturer has never had a bearing on the decision of a national drug regulatory authority.

As a result, if a patent holder believes a generic manufacturer is infringing its patent, it traditionally has the responsibility to enforce its rights. In practice, this entails the patent holder bringing suit against the alleged infringer in an effort to prevent further sales of the infringing product and recover damages. This process can be lengthy and costly, but ensures the validity of a patent before enforcing the rights asserted by the plaintiff. In addition, IPRs have always been recognized as 'private rights' (TRIPS explicitly supports this position) and it seems logical that the owner of private rights should be responsible for their enforcement. The newly delegated role of the regulatory authority as an 'enforcer' of a private right is therefore a significant benefit to the rights holder.

TRIPS does not specifically address the rights of generic manufacturers to make use of a patented drug prior to its expiration for the purpose of obtaining marketing approval of their generic product. However, Article 30 authorizes limited exceptions to patent rights for such things as research, prior user rights, and pre-expiration testing. The provision has been used to advance science and technology by allowing researchers to use patented inventions to gain a better understanding of the technology. In addition, the provision is also used to allow manufacturers of generic drugs to apply for marketing approval without the patent owner's permission and before the expiration of the patent. The Panel in *Canada—Pharmaceutical Patents* held this practice is preserved by Article 30.[39] Moreover, state practices both prior and subsequent to TRIPS is consistent with the understanding that the research exception is permitted by Article 30.

Not only will these provisions delay access to generic drugs, importantly,

---

[39] *See* WTO Panel Report, *Canada—Pharmaceutical Patents*, WT/DS114/R, adopted 7 April 2000, at para 4.15 (also holding that manufacturing and stockpiling drugs prior to the exhaustion of patent protection is not a 'limited exception' under Article 30).

the linkage between market approval to patent status could also be detrimental to countries taking advantage of the TRIPS recognized flexibility of a compulsory licence.[40] More specifically, it is unclear whether a compulsory licence may be issued to provide entry of generic drugs where the law does not allow registration prior to the expiration of the patent. This potential impediment results from the fact that a manufacturer granted authority to produce under compulsory licence still must be registered by the national drug regulatory authority. Thus, if the regulatory authority is prohibited from registering generics until the patent expires, the compulsory licence will be prevented from coming to fruition.

2. *Data exclusivity periods*

As discussed above, before marketing or distributing a drug the manufacture must apply for regulatory/marketing approval with a national drug regulatory authority to ensure that the drug is safe, effective, and of sufficient quality. The regulatory authority does not undertake clinical trials or otherwise test the drugs; instead, it relies on the clinical trials and other data conducted and submitted by the applicant. When a later applicant (a generic manufacturer) seeks registration of the same drug, it need not re-conduct the same clinical trials but only must submit and prove that the drug it seeks to distribute is of the same quality and therapeutically equivalent to the previously approved drug. This process facilitates the introduction of generic drugs to the market and, without having to conduct clinical trials, generic manufactures save a significant amount of resources and can introduce their drug on the market at a reduced rate.

TRIPS does not explicitly require members to provide any period of data exclusivity to an original applicant. While the interpretation of TRIPS on this point is contentious, the wording of Article 39.3 merely states the need to protect 'undisclosed test or other data' from 'unfair commercial use' and 'disclosure', provided that the data required 'considerable effort' to generate, that it is undisclosed and that the product involves a 'new chemical entity'. TRIPS does not dictate how protection should occur or the limits of such protection. On the contrary, the text indicates that it is up to the individual member to determine what constitutes 'unfair'.[41] In addition, the provision does not define what is meant by a 'new chemical entity'.[42]

Recent US FTAs, however, seek to bring its FTA partners into line with

---

[40] It is well established that the introduction of generic drugs results in lower prices. *See*, e.g. Treasury Board of Canada, 'Patented Medicines Price Review Board, Prices of the Top Selling Multiple Source Medicines in Canada' (June 2003).

[41] Indeed, during TRIPS negotiations, negotiators rejected the option to include stronger 'data exclusivity' provisions, as originally proposed by the US.

[42] The US–Jordan FTA first provided a definition for 'new chemical entity' by stipulating that 'new chemical entity' includes 'protection for new uses for old chemical entities for a period of three years'. *See* Art. 4(22).

American domestic law[43] by preventing the later applicant and the national authority from relying on the clinical studies and data provided by the original applicant when seeking to register the generic version of the drug for a given period of time following the first registration (US FTAs generally seek a five-year period of exclusivity).[44] Thus, a generic manufacturer wishing to market and distribute a generic whilst the period of data exclusivity is in force must conduct its own clinical trials and other data and submit its findings to the national authority. This approach raises a number of practical concerns, not least of which is that conducting tests and generating clinical data is extremely expensive (sometimes costing into the tens of millions of dollars).[45] From a public health perspective, this requirement is difficult to justify and the generic industry will find it difficult to implement such onerous requirements.[46] Even if generic manufacturers were able to generate this data, the cost of the resulting drugs produced would rise considerably as well as delay the generics introduction into the marketplace. Moreover, such duplication of testing is arguably unethical, as it simply is repetition in testing and clinical trials where the safety and efficacy of a product has already been determined.[47]

Even more, the US has sought to include provisions in certain FTAs which apply a period of data exclusivity from the approval date of another country even if the manufacturer has not sought to register the drug in that particular country; thus, the generic manufacture would still be prohibited from relying on the data for a certain time period with the end result being that the country does not have access to that particular drug until the expiration of the data exclusivity period.

Several US FTAs also effectively prohibit generic manufacturers from using evidence of registration of the originator drug in another country to prove the safety and efficacy of their version. The only condition that can be imposed on the originator is to require marketing approval be sought within five years of registering the product in a country other than a member of that particular FTA.[48] This TRIPS-Plus provision is difficult to justify as, depending on how the originator times entry into the market, the effect of the provision could result in ten years of test data protection. For example, a pharmaceutical company could register the original drug in one of the FTA-member countries but wait five years before submitting the market approval application in

---

[43] *See* J. Watal, *Intellectual Property Rights in the WTO and Developing Countries* (New Delhi: OUP, 2001), 200.

[44] *See* Arts 17(10)(1) of US–Chile; 15(10)(1) of US–Morocco; 14(9)(1)(a) of US–Bahrain; 16(8)(1) of US–Singapore; and 17(10)(1) of US–Australia FTA.

[45] R. Weissman, 'Dying for Drugs: How CAFTA Will Undermine Access to Essential Medicines' (2004), available at www.health-now.org/site/article.php?articleId=75&menuId=13 (visited 10 April 2006).

[46] Musungu and Oh, above at n 37, at 66.   [47] Rajkumar, above at n 29, at 465.

[48] These provisions are found in FTAs between the US and CAFTA-DR (Art. 15(10)(1)(b)), Singapore (Art. 16(8)(2)), Morocco (Art. 15(10)(2)), Bahrain (Art. 14(9)(1)(b)), and Australia (Art. 17(10)(1)(b)). The provisions do not appear in US FTAs with Chile or Jordan.

another FTA-member country. It would then be entitled to a further five years of exclusivity from that date.

In addition, certain FTAs eliminate the Article 39.3 requirement in TRIPS which protects data only in cases where the pharmaceutical in question utilizes 'new chemical entities' and where the generation of data involves considerable effort.[49] The provision requires data protection with respect to any new product (with 'new product' being loosely defined as 'one that does not contain a chemical entity that has previously been approved by the Party').[50] The effect of this provision is to allow a first registrant of a new pharmaceutical product to obtain protection even in the case of old and well known products and such protection may be sought irrespective of whether any effort was spent in the generating the data.[51]

Finally, as noted above, US FTAs link test data protection to the patent term, generic manufacturers may not obtain marketing approval at any time during the patent period, even when a compulsory license is issued, and even in preparation to enter the market upon patent expiry, both of which are allowed under TRIPS.[52] Thus, and without question, a period of data exclusivity increases the final cost of the marketed product as well as possibly delays its entry onto the market.[53] Data exclusivity can also act as a *de facto* patent, ensuring a minimum period of monopoly for pharmaceutical companies, preventing competition, and in some instances, it may even prohibit a generic manufacturer from seeking registration in a country. Furthermore, a period of exclusivity relying upon the registration in another country potentially deprives a country of the drug for the entirety of that period.

It is also important to note that the period data exclusivity negotiated in FTAs is independent from the patent process and applies regardless of whether the drug is patented in the country. Thus, the effect of a period of data exclusivity where a patent does not exist serves to maintain an artificial barrier to entry into the marketplace and higher prices to consumers.

As with the linkage of market approval to patent status, a period of data exclusivity could be detrimental to countries taking advantage of a compulsory licence. Again, a manufacturer granted authority to produce a generic drug under compulsory licence still must be registered by the national drug regulatory authority and if the generic manufacturer cannot rely on existing data to gain regulatory approval it cannot respond to the compulsory licence

---

[49] *See* CAFTA-DR (Art. 15(10)(1)(c)), Morocco (Art. 15(10)(1)), and Bahrain (Art. 14(9)(1)(c)). There are no similar provisions in US–Chile; US–Jordan or US–Singapore.

[50] This extends the provision found in US–Jordan FTA which restrictively defined 'new chemical entity'.

[51] *See* F. Abbott, 'The Doha Declaration on the TRIPS Agreement and Public Health and the Contradictory Trend in Bilateral and Regional Trade Agreements' (2004) QUNO Occasional Paper 14, at 8.

[52] These rules are embodied in the FTAs with CAFTA-DR (Art. 15(10)(3)), Singapore (Art. 16(8)(4)), Morocco (Art. 15(10)(4)), and Bahrain (Arts. 14(9)(4)). *Contra*, US FTAs with Jordan and Chile.

[53] It also must be queried whether duplicating tests is the best allocation of resources.

and supply the needed drug. Thus, where a medicine is protected by patent, data exclusivity effectively could render the compulsory licence meaningless if it cannot make effective use of the licence without repeating time-consuming and costly tests to obtain marketing approval of its drug.[54] Therefore, exclusivity provisions can effectively prevent the use of compulsory licensing during the patent term as well as extend the life of the patent.[55]

The US counters by contending that, 'if circumstances ever rise in which a drug is produced under a compulsory licence and it is necessary to approve that drug to protect public health or effectively utilize the TRIPS/health solution, the data provision provisions in the FTA would not stand in the way . . .'.[56] Leaving aside for the moment the legal affect of such statements (addressed later in the chapter), the meaning from a US standpoint is if the compulsory licence fits within the US view of 'necessary' than it would not allow the FTA to stand in the way of the licence. Such a stance removes the ability to protect public health from the signatory country and gives it to the US.

3. Patent term extensions

TRIPS requires members to grant patent protection for a period of at least 20 years from the date of filing of an application for a patent. However, as medical products require lengthy testing periods and regulatory approval, pharmaceutical companies wishing to apply for patent protection must do so at a very early stage of basic research, many years before filing an application for regulatory approval. In total, the patent and regulatory approval process often lasts between eight and twelve years, meaning a company which has gained a patent for a drug will have its monopoly period significantly shortened.

TRIPS does not obligate members to 'compensate' patent holders for 'unreasonable' delays in approving a patent or registering the product by extending the patent term.[57] However, in order to rebalance the effects of the time delay, provisions in certain US FTAs 'compensate' the pharmaceutical companies for any 'unreasonable' delay caused by the national drug regulatory authority in examining an application for registration or from a patent office in assessing the application for a patent by extending the patent term in the same amount of time as the 'unreasonable' delay (often stated as a period extending beyond five years from the date of the filing or three years after a request for an extension).[58] For example, Article 15(9)(6) of the CAFTA-DR states:

---

[54] Some FTAs limit the use of compulsory licensing to emergency situations. In such circumstances, due to time constraints, it will be impossible to conduct the necessary tests and obtain registration of the drug.

[55] Rajkumar, above at n 29, at 461.

[56] *See*, e.g. Executive Office of the President, Office of the USTR, 'Letter to Congressman Levin concerning US Morocco FTA', 19 July 2004.

[57] In fact, countries rejected such proposals when originally negotiating the TRIPS Agreement.

[58] The provisions negotiated by the US reflect domestic American law and have their origins in the US Drug Price Competition and Patent Term Restoration Act of 1984 (Hatch–Waxman Act).

Each party, at the request of the patent owner, shall adjust the term of a patent to compensate for unreasonable delays that occur in granting the patent. For the purposes of this paragraph, an unreasonable delay shall at least include a delay in the issuance of the patent of more than five years from the date of filing of the application in the Party, or three years after a request for examination of the application has been made, whichever is later.[59]

Similarly, Article 15(10)(2) of the CAFTA-DR relating to delays in market approval continues:

With respect to any pharmaceutical product that is subject to a patent, each Party shall make available a restoration of the patent term to compensate the patent owner for unreasonable curtailment of the effective patent term as a result of the marketing approval process.[60]

Proposals for the Andean FTA provide yet another avenue for extending the patent term by requiring signatory countries that have granted a patent on the basis of the patent being granted in another country to grant an extension if the term is extended in the granting country relied upon.

It should be noted that it is common international practice to grant extensions for delays caused by registration and examination, especially in developed countries. However, there is concern for developing countries from a public health perspective over what is considered 'reasonable'. Given the resource constraints on national drug regulation authorities and patent offices in developing countries, an arguably 'reasonable' delay could possibly exceed six years. But would the US view this delay as reasonable? The extra years added to a patent may not have serious implications in developed nations or even industrialized developing countries, but may have serious consequences for public health in poorer developing countries due to the fact that the provisions extend the time period drug companies are free from generic competition, thereby delaying significant reductions in price which follow the introduction of generic competition. Such delays could prevent large portions of the population from accessing needed drugs and further deepen the public health crises currently engulfing much of the developing world. Therefore, while it seems reasonable to extend patents when 'unreasonable' delay prevents the patent holder from exploiting their invention, and while it is easy to imagine abuse from patent offices and regulatory authorities, the undefined nature over what is considered 'unreasonable' is troublesome, especially given the complex

---

[59] *See also* Art. 17(9) of US–Chile FTA. Other US FTAs have similar provisions, the only variation being the number of years considered 'unreasonable'. For example, FTAs with Singapore (Art. 16(7)(7)), Morocco (Art. 15(9)(7)), Bahrain (Art. 14(8)(6)), and Australia (Art. 17(9)(8)) refer to four and two years respectively. In the Singapore FTA, a further provision regarding a five-year extension of the patent term when a patent is granted based on the examination conducted in another country awards an extension when at the same time it has been awarded in the other country (Art. 16(7)(8)).

[60] *See* US–Chile (Art. 17(10)(2)(a)); US–Singapore (Art. 18(8)(4)(a)); US–Australia (Art. 17(10)(4)); US–Morocco (Art. 15(10)(3)). In each case what is regarded as 'unreasonable' is not specified. Note the US–Jordan FTA does not contain a similar provision.

applications coupled with resource constraints on patent offices and national authorities.

4. *Limits on compulsory licences*

Compulsory licensing is a TRIPS-recognized public health safeguard allowing a government to temporarily override a patent and authorize the production of generic versions of a patented product.[61] Since the implementation of TRIPS, the US has sought to restrict the flexibility through FTAs, despite the 2001 Doha Declaration, which affirmed countries' right to use compulsory licensing and to determine the circumstances warranting this action.[62]

The restrictions placed on compulsory licensing through FTAs exist at two levels. First, FTAs indirectly restrict compulsory licensing as a result of the data exclusivity provisions discussed above. Second, direct restrictions limit the grounds on which compulsory licences can be issued. For instance, and unlike TRIPS, these provisions are drawn in the negative and confine the use of compulsory licences to specified cases (such as remedying an anti-competitive practice, public non-commercial contexts, national emergencies and other cases of extreme urgency, and the failure to meet working requirements).[63] Moreover, the US–Singapore FTA restricts the use of compulsory licensing even further by raising the level of compensation required ('reasonable and entire' rather than the TRIPS language of 'adequate') and expressly restricting the transfer of 'know how' (a term not found in TRIPS).[64] The restriction of 'know how' is important because 'know how' licensing agreements frequently accompany a licensing arrangement and enable the licensee to make efficient use of the patent. Without access to 'know how', the commercial value of access to a patent is often worth much less to a licensee.

It should be noted that the above agreements are not necessarily indicative of the US forcefully imposing restrictions on compulsory licensing. In fact, Australia and Singapore willingly restricted the use of compulsory licences to cases of emergency or other circumstances of extreme urgency. The draft text of the FTAA, however, is similar to the US–Singapore FTA despite the vastly different circumstances of the countries involved.[65] Thus, a similarly restrictive

---

[61] For more on compulsory licensing, *see* C. Correa, '*Intellectual Property Rights and the Use of Compulsory Licences: Options for Developing Countries*' (1999) South Centre Working Paper, available at www.southcentre.org/publications/complicence/toc.htm (visited 10 April 2006).

[62] The US unsuccessfully negotiated for such provisions in the TRIPS negotiations. *See* Watal, above at n 43, at 320.

[63] Such provisions appear in US FTAs with Jordan (Art. 4(20)), Singapore, (Art. 16(7)(6)), and Australia (Art. 17(9)(7)).

[64] A similar term exists in the US–Australia FTA (Art. 17(9)(7)(b)(iii)).

[65] There are two versions of Art. 6.1 concerning compulsory licensing. The less restrictive uses TRIPS Art. 31 as a guide. The more restrictive include the following limits: (1) public, non-commercial use or in cases of national emergency; (2) governmental purchases produced under license; (3) prohibition of exports of goods produced under a compulsory licence; (4) requires 'reasonable and entire' compensation.

approach potentially has far more significant public health implications.[66] For instance, the inability to import ingredients or pharmaceutical products in situations other than those stated in the FTA could greatly undermine the accessibility of generic medicines and other key public health strategies in Latin America.[67]

Furthermore, the expiration of transitional implementation periods in 2005 (when all Members to the WTO—except least developed countries—were obligated to provide patents for pharmaceutical products and processes) increased the negative implications of stricter compulsory licensing laws for developing countries. This is due to the fact that, post-2005, any production of patented drugs by generic manufacturers relies entirely upon voluntary or compulsory licences. While the 'Implementation Agreement' reached by the WTO General Council on 30 August 2003 allows a compulsory licence to be issued allowing a country to produce generic drugs for export in a public health crisis, many in the international community believe that meeting the requirements of the Implementation Agreement will make it hard to exploit the waiver. This change will greatly affect the ability to supply affordable generic medicines in both the public and private sectors of the developing countries who are FTA partners with the US.

5. Limits on parallel importing

Parallel importing occurs when the patent holder sells a product to a buyer who exports the product to a second buyer in another country.[68] Such practice arises when the price of the imported product, taking into account transportation and tariffs, remains lower than the price of the same product legally made or imported into the country. Quite obviously, parallel importation undercuts the ability of a patent holder to engage in price discrimination across national boundaries and can severely reduce profit levels of international companies. Importantly, the Doha Declaration confirmed the existing right available in TRIPS that each WTO Member may establish its own regime of exhaustion of IPRs.[69] Parallel importing is therefore not in and of itself a violation of TRIPS.

---

[66] Interestingly, by adopting TRIPS-Plus compulsory licensing provisions in their patent law, several countries negotiating the FTAA may be adopting more restrictive laws than required in US domestic law. Drahos, above at n 19, at 11. Compulsory licensing is not part of US patent law, but provisions on compulsory licensing are found in other parts of US law such as the Clean Air Act and the Atomic Energy Act and are a key remedy in the context of antitrust litigation. Therefore, countries that adopt a restrictive approach to compulsory licensing as part of their patent law and do not compensate by having licensing access provisions in other parts of their law are offering patent owners stronger rights than exist in US domestic law. *Ibid.*

[67] For strategies to calculate the effect of these provisions, *see* Musungu and Oh, above at n 37, at 65.

[68] For more information, *see* 'Health Care and Intellectual Property: Parallel Imports', available at www.cptech.org/ip/fsd/health-pi.html (visited 10 April 2006).

[69] *See* Doha Ministerial Declaration, WT/MIN(01)/DEC/1, adopted 14 November 2001, at para. 5(d).

International price discrimination (i.e. tiered pricing) benefits developing countries and other countries with elastic demand for the product. It also allows companies to charge a high price in countries able and willing to meet the higher price (most often developed nations) in order to recoup the costs of offering a lower price to those markets unable or unwilling to meet the higher price. Manufacturers often engage in price discrimination between national boundaries, as the elasticity of demand differs widely between markets; thus, when there is a low elasticity of demand in one country (low rate of exit) and a high elasticity of demand in another (high rate of exit), manufacturers will price products accordingly.

Traditionally, IPRs are 'exhausted' once a product is sold once (placed on a market anywhere in the world); in other words, the initial sale ends the IP holders' rights and control over what can be done with that product. Therefore, nothing prevents the importing nation that acquired the pharmaceuticals at reduced prices from exporting the drugs back to the original market or any other market for profit. Attempts at curbing parallel imports, even under the context of a compulsory licence, are fraught with uncertainty.[70] In such a circumstance, the US has sought to impose strict standards on other nations via FTAs providing for the restriction and/or prohibition on parallel importation. For example, US FTAs with Morocco (Article 15(9)(4)) and Australia (Article 17(9)(4)) prohibit parallel importation; however, both agreements provide the prohibition may be limited to cases where the patent owner has placed restrictions by contract or other means. Notwithstanding this footnote, the provision may effectively prohibit parallel importation and essentially allow patent holders, through contract law, to segment markets and maintain price discrimination. Furthermore, the US–Singapore FTA (Article 16(7)(2)) also restricts parallel importation by allowing patent holders to block parallel importation into either country when the same is done in violation of a distribution agreement anywhere in the world.

It must be noted that countries such as Australia and Singapore advocate restricting or prohibiting parallel importation and as such, already prohibited such action. The agreements, however, remove the flexibility of a future government to amend the law and ease restrictions. In addition, while there may be a case for these countries prohibiting parallel importation, it is harder to justify such action from a public health perspective in developing countries.

Interestingly, a number of US FTAs with developing countries, including Chile, Jordan, and CAFTA-DR, are silent on the exhaustion of patent rights; thus, these countries have retained the flexibility granted by TRIPS. On the

---

[70] Of course, such conduct on the part of developing countries would be against the spirit of the Doha Declaration and prevent the goal of facilitating access to medicines from being reached. Therefore, supplying pharmaceuticals to developing countries at reduced prices must be conditioned on the fact that the drugs will be used to ease their health crisis, not simply re-exported to a market willing to pay a higher price for the drugs. Para 4. of the 30 August Agreement attempts to resolve the uncertainty. For criticism, *see* Mercurio, above at n 9, at 244–45.

other hand, the draft text of the FTAA only partially allows for the retention of the TRIPS flexibility, allowing each country to determine its own rules on parallel importation but then obliging them to set up regional exhaustion under their domestic laws within five years. In effect, this would allow parallel importation within the FTAA zone, while keeping the world market segmented. Scepticism already exists that the US will pressure members to set up national exhaustion, thus preventing the use of parallel importation.[71]

B. Side Letters on Public Health

The above demonstrates that the newly granted IPRs pose a threat to the public health and welfare by removing the flexibilities granted in TRIPS and mandating a more restrictive system of healthcare.[72] The US, however, has responded by claiming side letters in the FTAs contain a waiver for public health purposes. For instance, the US–CAFTA–DR side letter states that the obligations set forth in the FTA 'do not affect the ability of either Party to take necessary measures to protect public health by promoting access to medicines for all, in particular concerning such cases as HIV/AIDS, tuberculosis, malaria and other epidemics, as well as circumstances of extreme urgency or national emergency', and that the FTA 'does not prevent the effective utilization of the TRIPS/health solution'. While the USTR asserts that the side letter will have interpretative value and that 'the United States has no intention of using dispute settlement to challenge any country's actions that are in accordance with that solution', such statements cannot to be relied upon as side letters are not part of the actual text and therefore will likely carry little legal weight in a dispute settlement proceeding. In any event, the side letter itself lends itself to interpretative difficulties, as some disagreement still exists as to what is a 'TRIPS/health solution'. Thus, the US could still use pressure partners to submit to its understanding or initiate dispute settlement proceedings for clarification of the understanding.

For instance, and importantly, the side letter states that the FTA does not affect 'necessary' measures to protect public health. Such a term is not used in the Doha Declaration and could be used to restrictively limit many health alternatives. Such vague language is part of an unfortunate trend in many negotiating areas, where FTA texts are increasingly dependent upon the interpretation of complex and often poorly drafted side letters of understanding.

---

[71] *See*, e.g. OXFAM Briefing Note, *Undermining Access to Medicines: Comparison of five US FTAs* (2004), available at www.oxfamamerica.org/newsandpublications/publications/briefing_papers/pdfs/fta_comparison.pdf (visited 10 April 2006).

[72] In addition, the net gains analysis presumes that earnings in agriculture or other sectors due to increased market access translate into ability to afford higher priced medicine; this presumption is questionable. Musungu and Oh, above at n 37, at 55. For other concerns, *see* Abbott, above at n 51 and UK Commission on Intellectual Property Rights, 'Integrating Intellectual Property Rights and Development Policy' (2002), available at www.iprcommission.org/graphic/documents/final_report.htm (visited 10 April 2006).

The World Bank's annual report recognized potential difficulties with the side letters:

Notwithstanding the potential flexibilities provided by these side letters, they raise several questions. How widely will the parties to the three agreements define the 'protection of public health'- or, what definitions would an arbitration panel use? Uncertainty, in this respect may become itself a barrier to making use of the flexibilities and may open the door for restrictive interpretations by vested interest. Also, several of the other U.S FTAs do not contain comparable side letters, raising questions about conflicts between intellectual property obligations and public health objectives in at least some of the affected countries.[73]

IV. CONCLUSION

International intellectual property policy making consists of a never-ending cycle of multilateral standard-setting which lead to increased standards via bilateralism/regionalism followed by consolidation in the form of more multilateralism. The US has recently re-invigorated a process of recalculating the IP standards bilaterally in parallel to the multilateral system. The US, in particular, consistently and strategically embraces bilateralism to further a range of foreign policy objectives. Such a pattern can be discerned from its FCN, BITs, and pre- and post- TRIPS behaviour. Such a pattern of bilateralism reflects the Americans' deep-seated inclination of isolationism.[74]

The recent cycle of forum shifting began in the 1970s–1980s with a 'wave' of bilaterals followed by the multilateral standard-setting and then another 'wave' of bilaterals and more multilateral standard setting.[75] Of course, each wave of bilaterals builds and extends existing standards until the multilateral forum accepts and incorporates the standards into its agreements. It is obvious that we are currently in a bilateral phase, with the US and almost all trading countries having recently entered into, or about to enter into several FTAs. If history is to once again repeat itself, a push for higher multilateral standards may be in the near future.[76] However, consensus decision making in the multilateral forum is complex and with FTAA negotiations stalled (in large part due to a controversial draft text on IPRs and other divisive issues),[77] the shift back to multilateralism may not occur for some time.

It is also clear that the purported crowning achievement of TRIPS was greatly exaggerated and/or badly misread. Again, bilateralism is the US default

---

[73] World Bank, 'Global Economic Prospects 2005: Trade Regionalism and Development' (2004), available at www.worldbank.org (visited 10 April 2006), at 110.

[74] *See* Okediji, above at n 3, at 142–43.

[75] Drahos, above at n 31, at 10. *See also* L. Helfer, 'Regime Shifting: The TRIPS Agreement and the New Dynamics of International Intellectual Property Lawmaking' (2004) 29 Yale J Int L 1.

[76] *See* Drahos, above at n 19, at 8.

[77] On the restiveness of the FTAA on intellectual property, *see* EFF Action Alert, www.eff.org (visited 10 April 2006) and Vivas-Eugui, above at n 16.

negotiating strategy and history coupled with recent events suggest it will remain as such for the foreseeable future.[78] This is not to suggest that multilateralism is unimportant or past its use by date. Far from it, as multilateralism is an important part of the cycle of standards modification; multilateralism harmonizes the law and thus contributes to the ratchet up of standards. Thus, once countries negotiate enough bilateral/regional agreements with similar provisions, it becomes easier to manipulate multilateralism. In this regard, bilateralism naturally leads to multilateralism by creating common negotiating positions as well as through a 'laboratory effect' of trialling at the bilateral/regional level.[79] This process played itself out in the Berne Convention, repeated to some extend in TRIPS and will likely repeat again in the future to consolidate the TRIPS-Plus provisions.[80]

This chapter has demonstrated, however, that this cycle is currently reducing the flexibilities of TRIPS and possibly negatively impacting the public health choices of US FTA partners. The question of how to correct for the current cycle of bilateralism is beyond the scope of this chapter, but the question of how to forestall US advancement of TRIPS-Plus provisions must be addressed. Leaving aside the argument that IP should be set by careful public policy balancing the interests of the rights holder with that of the public, developing and developed countries (such as Australia in terms of the PBS) must resist being coerced into granting IPRs to the detriment of the welfare of its people. Developing countries in particular have a long history of ignoring public health and instead prioritizing military and other spending. These governments must commit to improving the health and welfare of their nations by, *inter alia*, allocating more funds to health, stemming corruption, improving infrastructure, and encouraging doctors to train and remain in the country. Such factors require significant monetary resources (partly in the form of increased and more targeted aid), but these nations *can* simply make the decision to refrain from placing the promise of economic benefits over the welfare of their populations.[81]

In this regard, Brazil has taken the lead and opposed the FTAA in part over IPRs, arguing that if the US refuses to confront the agricultural subsidies bilaterally/regionally, IPRs should likewise be discussed in the WTO. While there are obvious flaws with the analogy, it does represent one country refusing to accommodate US interests in the name of perceived economic gain in other areas. In addition, and more significantly, Brazil has also lowered the

---

[78] *See*, e.g. the comments of Bill Thomas, outgoing chair of the House Ways and Means Committee, that the Doha Round was condemned to failure and that the US should focus on FTAs. 'No Breakthroughs in Rio; US Lawmaker Urges Bush Admn to Switch Focus to Bilateral FTAs' 10(12) Bridges Weekly Trade News Digest, 5 April 2006.

[79] S. Cho, 'A Bridge Too Far: The Fall of the Fifth WTO Ministerial Conference in Cancun and the Future of Trade Constitution' (2004) 7 JIEL 219, at 238.

[80] One must also not forget that this process plays itself out under the stick of a Section 301 action and/or other unilateral action.

[81] *See* Musungu and Oh, above at n 37.

cost of several antiretroviral drugs by threatening to issue a compulsory licence if the manufacturer does not lower the price. In every instance, the manufacturer has capitulated. Moreover, in *US—Cotton Yarn*, Brazil threatened to cross-retaliate in the area of IP if the US did not come into compliance with the DSB. Interestingly, the US and Brazil reached temporary agreement on compliance shortly thereafter.[82]

Such approaches, however useful, will not work for every developing country. For most, strength in numbers through strong coalitions working multilaterally is the strongest option to reverse the TRIPS-Plus trend and protect the flexibilities written into TRIPS. Equally, developing countries must insist upon some development friendly provisions in FTAs, including the recognition of the Doha Declaration at the minimum.[83] Another (albeit less likely to be successful) option for developing countries is to negotiate more FTAs among themselves which recognize strong pro-development rights. In essence, this approach would create a new negotiating template. Thus instead of allowing developed countries to set the agenda and then reacting to the template presented by the developed nation, a developing country could set its own agenda and negotiating priorities.[84] Whether developing countries are willing, or even able, to contemplate an alternative system of IPRs remains to be seen.

---

[82] Ecuador similarly used this strategy in *EC—Bananas*. See *EC—Bananas III (Ecuador) (Article 22.6—EC)*, WT/DS27/ARB/ECU, 24 March 2000. For analysis, *see* J. McCall Smith, 'Compliance Bargaining in the WTO: Ecuador and the Bananas Dispute': Document prepared for UNCTAD Conference on Developing Countries and the Trade Negotiation Process, 6–7 November 2003, Geneva.

[83] It is discouraging that such language was rejected by the US in, at least, the Andean negotiations. *See* Mayne, above at n 1, at 14.

[84] For more possibilities, *see* Abbott, above at n 23.

10

Competition Law in Regional Trade Agreements: An Overview

MELAKU GEBOYE DESTA AND NAOMI JULIA BARNES

I. COMPETITION LAW: GENERAL REMARKS

Competition law[1] is a key element of virtually all advanced national legal systems based on free market principles. Competition law is concerned with the structure and behaviour of enterprises on the market. It aims to create a market in which producers and traders compete freely on the quality of products and services they offer and the prices they charge rather than through the improper exercise of market power, whether acquired unilaterally or in concert with others. More broadly, competition policy is designed to address 'industry structures and practices that give excessive market power to sellers—power to raise prices above, or reduce quantities below, the levels that would prevail in competitive markets'.[2]

The competition laws of almost all countries target and discourage or even prohibit two forms of practices by business enterprises—concerted practices such as price-fixing and market-segmentation cartels (hereafter anti-competitive agreements) and abuse of dominant position such as monopolies (hereafter disciplines on dominant market position).[3] For example, Section 1 of the Sherman Antitrust Act of 1890 in the United States (US) provides, in part: 'Every contract, combination in the form of trust or otherwise, or conspiracy, in restraint of trade or commerce among the several States, or with

---

[1] The term 'competition law' is generally used here in the narrow sense and does not include such governmental or governmentally-backed practices as subsidies covered by the WTO rule book. In the few cases where we refer to such government-related practices, we intend only to make a point relevant to our narrower subject rather than address such practices for their own sake.

[2] See D.K. Tarullo, 'Norms and Institutions in Global Competition Policy' (2000) 94 AJIL 478, at 483.

[3] See, e.g. Arts 81 and 82 of the EC Treaty together with the 1989 Merger Regulation (Council Regulation (EEC) No 4064/89 of 21 December 1989 on the Control of Concentrations between Undertakings [1989] OJ L395/1).

foreign nations, is declared to be illegal'.[4] Likewise, Section 2 of the same Act on monopolies provides as follows: 'Every person who shall monopolize, or attempt to monopolize, or combine or conspire with any other person or persons, to monopolize any part of the trade or commerce among the several States, or with foreign nations, shall be deemed guilty of a felony . . .'.[5] Sanctions for violation of competition law range from administrative behavioural or structural orders to, in some cases such as the US and since 2002 the UK,[6] criminal penalties against officers acting on behalf of those operators.

Competition laws are generally triggered only by voluntary business conduct and not by actions compelled by the state. When a state compels specific business behaviour, companies may have the defence of 'government compulsion', which is normally available in cases where private anti-competitive conduct is compelled by a government. In a US case, a group of crude oil suppliers participated in a concerted boycott designed to deny an oil refining company (Interamerican Refining Corporation) crude oil from Venezuela. In the antitrust proceeding that followed, the defendants argued that they could not supply the required grade and type of oil to the refiner because the Venezuelan government had forbidden sales which, directly or indirectly, reached Interamerican. The US district court for the District of Delaware held that 'the undisputed facts demonstrate[d] that defendants were compelled by regulatory authorities in Venezuela to boycott plaintiff . . . [and] that such compulsion is a complete defence to an action under the antitrust laws based on that boycott'.[7]

National competition laws can also specifically address the status of state enterprises. In Mexico, for example, the Federal Economic Competition

---

[4] The full text of this Act is available at www.usdoj.gov/atr/foia/divisionmanual/ch2.htm#a (visited 4 April 2006). For detailed guidelines on the application of US antitrust law, see the Antitrust Enforcement Guidelines for International Operations, issued by the US Department of Justice and the Federal Trade Commission, April 1995, available at www.usdoj.gov/atr/public/guidelines/internat.htm (visited 4 April 2006).

[5] *Ibid. See also* Section 7 of the Clayton Act of 1914 on Mergers and Acquisitions.

[6] *See* Art. 188 of the UK Enterprise Act of 2002 (UK).

[7] *Interamerican Ref. Corp. v Texaco Maracaibo, Inc.*, 307 F. Supp. 1291, 1296 (D. Del 1970). It is notable however that national law requirements would not serve as a defence in a WTO-type of situation where members undertake to eliminate anti-competitive conduct. In *Mexico—Telecoms* Mexico argued that acts by its telecommunications enterprise, Telmex, could not be anti-competitive practices since they were required by national law. The Panel rejected Mexico's argument and rightly observed:

> International commitments made under the GATS 'for the purpose of preventing suppliers . . . from engaging in or continuing anti-competitive practices' are . . . designed to limit the regulatory powers of WTO Members. . . . In accordance with the principle established in Article 27 VCLT, a requirement imposed by a Member under its internal law on a major supplier cannot unilaterally erode its international commitments made in its schedule to other WTO Members to prevent major suppliers from 'continuing anti-competitive practices'. The pro-competitive obligations in Section 1 of the Reference Paper do not reserve any such unilateral right of WTO Members to maintain anti-competitive measures.

See WTO Panel Report, *Mexico—Telecoms*, WT/DS204/R, adopted 1 June 2004, at para. 7.244 (footnotes omitted).

Law provides that state enterprises are subject to the prohibition against monopolies and monopolistic activities unless the enterprise is engaged in strategic activities protected by the Constitution.[8] In the US, state enterprises are relatively uncommon, but those in existence generally enjoy sovereign immunity against antitrust lawsuits.[9]

In the regional setting, competition-based provisions have allowed challenges to state enterprises and their market power and market behaviour. In an arbitration brought under the North American Free Trade Agreement (NAFTA), a private corporation has claimed that the Canada Post Corporation, a Canadian state enterprise, has engaged in anti-competitive conduct and that Canada's failure to redress such conduct is a breach of NAFTA's provisions governing monopolies and state enterprises.[10] The arbitration is ongoing and has not been finally resolved. In the European system, the German postal monopoly Deutsche Post was ordered by the European Community to divest itself of its parcel delivery enterprise due to cross-subsidization issues contrary to the EC Treaty's state aid provision.[11]

Finally, competition laws do not generally apply to inter-governmental anti-competitive practices such as the various international commodity agreements made up of producing and consuming countries aimed at regulating prices and supplies through production quotas,[12] or those established only by producing countries such as the Organization of Petroleum Exporting Countries (OPEC).[13] Such practices could however be captured by the rules of the WTO

---

[8] Ley Federal de Competencia Económica [L.F.C.E.] (Federal Economic Competition Law), Chapter 1, Articles 3 and 4, Diario Oficial de la Federación [DO], 22 December 1992, available at www.apeccp.org.tw/doc/Mexico/Competition/mxcom1.html (visited 4 April 2006).

[9] *United States Postal Service v Flamingo Indust. (USA), Ltd.*, (2004) 540 US 736, at 746 (holding that the Postal Service was not subject to suit under the Sherman Act despite the fact that it was an independent establishment of the Federal Government), *Webster County Coal Corp. v Tennessee Valley Authority*, (1970) 476 F Supp, 529, at 532 (holding that the Tennessee Valley Authority as an instrumentality of the Federal Government was not subject to suit under US antitrust laws).

[10] *United Parcel Service of America, Inc. v Government of Canada*, Award on Jurisdiction, 22 November 2002, at para. 10, available at www.dfait-maeci.gc.ca/tna-nac/parcel-en.asp (visited 4 April 2006).

[11] D.E.M. Sappington and J.G. Sidak, 'Competition Law for State-Owned Enterprises' (2003) 71 ALJ 479, at 481–82, D.D. Sokol, 'Express Delivery and the Postal Sector in the Context of Public Sector Anti-Competitive Practices' (2003) 23 Nw J Int L & Bus 353, at 358 and Art. 87 EC Treaty.

[12] *See*, e.g. the International Coffee Agreements, particularly the earlier ones, which 'allowed for the suspension of quotas if prices were high and their reintroduction if prices became too low'. *See* dev.ico.org/history.asp#ica2 (visited 4 April 2006).

[13] Although this view is widely shared among international lawyers and competition specialists, two judicial actions were brought against OPEC based on US antitrust law. In both cases, however, the courts dismissed the cases on grounds of the 'act of state' doctrine and service of process. For more on this, *see* M.G. Desta, 'OPEC, the WTO, Regionalism, and Unilateralism' (2003) 37 JWT 523. *See also* M. Rezzouk, 'The Organization of Petroleum Exporting Countries, Competition and the World Trade Organization: Might a WTO Agreement on Competition Constitute a Threat to OPEC?', UNCTAD Doc. UNCTAD/DITC/CLP/2003/11 (2004), observing that the behaviour of governments is outside 'the conventional range of national competition law', at 2. Tarullo, above at n 2, at 483 also notes that 'competition law generally applies only to private conduct'.

system, due to the direct governmental act involved, unless justified by any of its exceptions.[14]

II. COMPETITION LAW AND REGIONAL TRADE AGREEMENTS

A. The Backdrop of Trade Liberalization

Although national competition law had its historical origins independently of international trade, the current discussions about regional and international competition law and policy are taking place in the backdrop of broader international trade liberalization through bilateral, regional, plurilateral, and multilateral means. With the proliferation of RTAs aimed at closer economic integration through the dismantling of barriers against the free movement of goods and services, and in many cases also of capital and persons, the need for competition law at the regional level has become ever more apparent, and regional competition laws and policies are increasingly commonplace. According to UNCTAD, over 100 of the around 300 bilateral and regional RTAs in force or under negotiation today include competition-policy related provisions.[15]

The reasons behind this development are fairly well-known. Firstly, although multilateral and regional trade liberalization have succeeded in the reduction/elimination of most governmental barriers to trade, the lack of similar arrangements to deal with 'private trade barriers'[16] to international trade has created doubts about the effectiveness of the multilateral trading system. Competition law is thus perceived as a necessary anti-circumvention supplement to regional trade agreements designed to protect the fruits of trade liberalization from being undermined by private sector barriers.[17]

Secondly and related to the first, closer integration between markets means that the likelihood of private measures in one country causing adverse effects on another country's interests is much higher. More specifically, the creation of RTAs, if not supplemented by appropriate arrangements about enforcement of competition law, has the potential to exacerbate this problem since RTAs by definition make it easier for companies to cause damage in partner countries.[18]

---

[14] *See* Desta, *ibid.*

[15] *See* L. Puri, 'Executive Summary', in P. Brusick *et al.* (eds), 'Competition Provisions in Regional Trade Agreements: How to Assure Development Gains', UNCTAD Doc. UNCTAD/DITC/CLP/2005/1 (2005), ix.

[16] Private trade barriers here refer to 'arrangements by domestic producers such as boycotts or refusals-to-deal that exclude imported products from their market'. *See* R. Hudec, 'A WTO Perspective on Private Anti-Competitive Behavior in World Markets' (1999) 34 New Eng L Rev 79.

[17] It is in fact difficult to find any RTA competition provision that does not mention as its primary objective the protection of the achievements of the RTA from being undermined by private anti-competitive behaviour.

[18] P. Holmes *et al.*, 'Trade and Competition in RTAs: A Missed Opportunity?', in Brusick *et al.*, above at n 15, at 71.

In the absence of inter-state cooperation or harmonization on competition issues, the standard reaction in such circumstances by any government would be to apply its competition law to practices that took place outside its territorial jurisdiction, as is often the case with US antitrust law, thereby causing serious international frictions.[19] Regional competition law is thus as much an instrument of minimizing trade distortions as of building confidence and amicable international relations at the regional level. Indeed, the recent growth in the number of countries with competition laws in many parts of the developing world is directly linked to the unprecedented growth in the number of regional trade agreements with competition provisions over the past decade or so.[20]

At the global level as well, the WTO system already contains bits and pieces of competition provisions, such as Article 9 of the WTO Agreement on Trade-Related Investment Measures, Articles 8, 31, and 40 of the Agreement on Trade-Related Aspects of Intellectual Property Rights, Articles VIII and IX of the GATS, and the 1996 Reference Paper on Telecommunication Services.[21] Moreover, intense effort has been taking place on this topic particularly since the 1996 Singapore Ministerial Conference with the object of introducing a generic competition agreement that would apply to every sector in the same way as the WTO Agreements on subsidies and countervailing measures or on anti-dumping measures. This effort has not been successful yet,[22] and the competition policy instruments in existence today at the international level are limited to the soft-law provisions of the 1976 OECD Guidelines for Multinational Enterprises (revised in 2000)[23] and the 1980 United Nations Set of Principles and Rules on Restrictive Business Practices.[24]

---

[19] On the extraterritoriality aspects of competition law, *see* A.T. Guzman, 'Is International Antitrust Possible?' (1998) 73 NYUL Rev 1501.

[20] For relevant information, *see* V. Silva, 'Cooperation on Commodity Policy in Latin America in Latin American and Caribbean Bilateral Trade Agreements' (UN Economic Commission for Latin America and the Caribbean (ECLAC), Santiago: 2004), 7. Silva reported that '. . . in 1990, only five nations in this region had competition laws. At present, 12 of the 33 countries of the region possess such laws, while eight—not including Caribbean nations—are at the drafting stage and a greater number have sectoral and constitutional laws or other relevant provisions'. This is not accidental; it reflected the rapid growth in the number of RTAs worldwide since the 1990s. According to a recent WTO paper, 196 RTAs were notified to the WTO between 1 January 1995 and February 2005, while the total number of RTAs over the 47 years lifetime of the GATT stood at just 124. *See* J.A. Crawford and R.V. Fiorentino, 'The Changing Landscape of Regional Trade Agreements', WTO Discussion Paper No 8 (2005), 3.

[21] For practical experience in the application of these competition rules under the WTO, *see* the WTO Panel Report *Mexico—Telecoms*, above at n 7. For an in-depth analysis of these rules, *see* K. Kennedy, *Competition Law and the World Trade Organisation: The Limits of Multilateralism* (London: Sweet & Maxwell, 2001), Ch 3.

[22] Following the Cancun WTO Ministerial setback in September 2003, which was largely attributed to agriculture and the Singapore issues (one of which is competition), the effort to create a WTO competition agreement has been suspended.

[23] *See OECD Guidelines for Multinational Enterprises Revision 2000*, available at www.oecd.org/dataoecd/56/36/1922428.pdf (visited 4 April 2006).

[24] See the UN Set of Principles and Rules on Competition, UNCTAD Doc. TD/RBP/CONF/10/Rev.2 (2000), available at www.unctad.org/en/docs/tdrbpconf10r2.en.pdf (visited 4 April 2006).

B. A Survey of Competition Law in RTAs

Almost every modern RTA devotes a chapter or so to competition law issues.[25] Although significant divergence exists in the form and substantive content of the competition law obligations created by different RTAs,[26] the relative goals and ambitions of competition provisions fall loosely within three major categories. First, there are some RTAs with competition provisions that seek only cooperation on competition issues between signatory states. An extreme example of this cooperative category is the New Zealand–Singapore bilateral trade agreement which is limited to broad and non-binding language and omits any express obligation to adopt or enforce competition measures.[27] The New Zealand–Singapore Agreement states:

> The Parties recognise the strategic importance of creating and maintaining open and competitive markets which maximise total welfare. The Parties *shall endeavour to implement* the APEC Principles to Enhance Competition and Regulatory Reform with a view to protecting the competitive process rather than competitors and ensuring that the design of regulation recognises options that minimise distortions to competition.[28]

The APEC Principles to Enhance Competition and Regulatory Reform referred to here are the non-binding principles of competition issued in 1999 by the Asia–Pacific Economic Cooperation group that are intended to encourage and promote competition throughout the Member States.[29] To promote competition and the attendant benefits, the Principles endorse non-discrimination, comprehensiveness of competition policies, transparency, accountability, and implementation.[30] The Principles simply state, *inter alia*, that Member States will make efforts to adopt appropriate measures and address anti-competitive behaviour. The language of both the New Zealand–Singapore Agreement and the Principles to which it refers provides an example of the least restrictive type of trade-related competition provisions.

A second and more ambitious category of RTA competition provisions require enactment of national competition laws, and in some cases, see harmonization of the substantive provisions of those laws. For example, Chapter 15 of the NAFTA[31] requires each signatory government to 'adopt or maintain

---

[25] For a useful and recent survey on this, *see* OECD, *Competition Provisions in Regional Trade Agreements*, OECD Doc. COM/DAF/TD(2005)3/FINAL. Surprisingly, the Central American-Dominican Republic–US Free Trade Agreement (CAFTA-DR) does not contain a generalized competition provision and only specifically addresses the issue in relation to the privatization and liberalization of Costa Rica's telecommunications industry. *See* CAFTA-DR, signed 5 August 2004, not yet in force, available at www.ustr.gov/Trade_Agreements/Bilateral/CAFTA/CAFTA-DR_Final_Texts/Section_Index.html (visited 4 April 2006).

[26] *See* Holmes, above at n 18, at 107.   [27] *See* OECD, above at n 25, at 9.

[28] New Zealand–Singapore Closer Economic Partnership, signed 14 November 2000, in force 1 January 2001, Part II, Art. 3 (emphasis added).

[29] APEC Principles to Enhance Competition and Regulatory Reform, adopted 13 September 1999, available at www.apec.org/apec/leaders__declarations/1999/attachment_-_apec.html (visited 4 April 2006).

[30] *Ibid.*   [31] Ch. 15 NAFTA.

measures to proscribe anti-competitive business conduct and take appropriate action with respect thereto ...'.[32] While Canada and the US already had long-established competition law systems, Mexico adopted a competition law in 1992 and created the Federal Competition Commission to enforce it in 1993.[33]

On the most advanced end of the spectrum fall such region-wide common competition regimes as the EC and a few South–South regional agreements which not only impose common substantive obligations directly on the private operators in member countries but also create a supranational authority with power to enforce the law throughout the Community. RTAs with this level of harmonization are however rather limited in number. For the most part, existing RTAs fall somewhere between loose, non-binding aspirations and complete harmonization of laws and enforcement within the trade area.

A closer look at the text of different RTAs today reveals some interesting distinctions and similarities based to some extent on the parties to the RTAs. A common distinction has been drawn between RTAs based on either the US and Canada model or RTAs based on the EC model.[34] In this respect, an OECD study has found it appropriate to distinguish between two 'families' of RTAs—the EC-style agreements which tend to contain specific substantive provisions, and the US-style agreements which tend to focus on coordination and cooperation provisions.[35] These distinctions, however, are not bright-line rules; there are variations among each category. RTAs have also been categorized by virtue of the development status of the parties, such as North–North RTAs, North–South RTAs, and South–South RTAs.[36] The discussion below attempts to outline generally the similarities and differences of these commonly utilized categories by analysing a sampling of various RTAs from each category.

RTAs with a US or Canadian influence have been classically characterized as geared toward a cooperative approach in developing and enforcing national competition laws, regardless of the specific content of the competition laws of either party.[37] These cooperative RTAs tend to require the enactment of competition laws, if none exist, and enforcement of those laws. However, the content of such laws is not specified beyond a general reference to anti-competitive conduct. In addition, these agreements generally contain provisions for cooperation by competition authorities regarding enforcement, notification, exchange of information and consultation and can also include a positive comity commitment to consider requests from the other party to

[32] Art. 1501 NAFTA.
[33] Competition Law and Policy in Mexico: An OECD Peer Review, Paris 2004, available at www.oecd.org/dataoecd/57/9/31430869.pdf (visited 4 April 2006).
[34] *See* OECD, above at n 25, at 14 and Holmes *et al.*, above at n 18, at 72.
[35] OECD, *ibid.*, at 14.
[36] L. Cernat, 'Eager to Ink, but Ready to Act? RTA Proliferation and International Cooperation on Competition Policy', in Brusick *et al.*, above at n 15, at 11–2.
[37] OECD, above at n 25, at 16.

enforce national competition provisions. US and Canada-style agreements also address specifically the issues of monopolies and state enterprises and usually require that these entities act in accordance with the trade agreement.

On the other end of the spectrum of the US–Canada/EC distinction are the EC-oriented RTAs that tend to require closer, if not complete harmonization of essential competition provisions, namely anti-competitive agreements and abuse of dominant market position.[38] These agreements tend not to emphasize extensive cooperation and coordination. EC-oriented agreements also tend to exclude agriculture from the competition provisions of the trade agreement.[39] However, there are exceptions to these broad characterizations and indeed the agreements between the EC and developing countries outlined below provide examples of such exceptions.

The inclusion of competition provisions in North–South RTAs is often a result of demands from the developed countries parties to such agreements.[40] The potential benefit to developed countries of this policy transfer is to create and protect a competitive market for exports.[41] But also, such provisions may protect developing countries from international cartels that can do substantial damage to developing economies. Competition provisions in RTAs that prohibit anti-competitive agreements and provide for notification and positive comity can assist developing countries in constraining the effect of such cartels.[42]

Finally, with regard to South–South RTAs, a general tendency toward close integration is evident. In the examples discussed below the level of integration is intense; three of the four RTAs discussed here involve customs unions and there is one common market. In each case, the parties have created some form of supranational regulation and enforcement, thereby showing integration similar to that of the EC. There is also an effort to require development of national competition regimes that can assist the supranational organizations and coordinate investigations and enforcement actions. It is obvious that this level of integration imposes heavy administrative burdens on the Member States and thus far, the implementation of such ambitious integration within South-South RTAs has been mixed.[43]

This section will provide a brief survey of the competition provisions of several bilateral and regional trade agreements with a view to demonstrating how the general features just mentioned are reflected in treaty provisions. To that end, we start with a brief outline of EC competition law both as an example of a system of competition law in a North–North RTA as well as laying the ground for subsequent discussion on the influence of this system on other RTAs. Likewise, the key features of the US–Australia FTA will also be outlined so as to demonstrate the features of US-oriented North–North RTAs as well as lay the background for the subsequent discussion on the influence of

---

[38] *Ibid.*, at 14.   [39] *See* Cernat, above at n 36, at 29–30.   [40] *Ibid.*, at 23.
[41] *Ibid.*, at 17–8.   [42] *Ibid.*, at 12.   [43] *Ibid.*, at 22.

the US/Canada systems on other RTAs. This will then be followed by a brief look at four South–South RTAs and five North–South RTAs involving both the EC and the US.

C. Competition Provisions in North–North RTAs

1. EC Competition Law

Given the depth and complexity of EC competition law, it is impossible to provide any detailed description of the system here. The following brief introduction is intended mainly to outline the general principles contained in the Treaty of Rome and key secondary legislation.

The EC boasts the most advanced and near-uniform system of regional competition law with a powerful Competition Directorate-General that has the competence to enforce its rules directly on private enterprises throughout the Community.[44] Indeed, 'the competition sector is the only one in which the commission is entrusted with the application of community rules to individual undertakings'.[45]

The basic substantive rules of EC competition law are contained in Articles 81 and 82 of the Treaty Establishing the European Community (EC Treaty) on anti-competitive agreements and abuse of dominant market position, respectively.[46] Article 81(1) prohibits 'all agreements between undertakings, decisions by associations of undertakings and concerted practices which may affect trade between Member States and which have as their object or effect the prevention, restriction or distortion of competition within the common market'. This general principle is supplemented by a list of specific practices such as price fixing, supply restriction, and market sharing agreements which 'shall be automatically void'. Article 81(3) provides a list of conditions under which anti-competitive agreements otherwise falling under paragraph 1 would be exempted, which will be discussed in the next section.

Article 82 of the EC Treaty also provides that '[a]ny abuse by one or more undertakings of a dominant position within the common market or in a substantial part of it shall be prohibited as incompatible with the common market in so far as it may affect trade between Member States'. Once again, this general principle is also supplemented by a list of specific practices which may qualify as such an abuse of a dominant position. These practices include the imposition of unfair purchase or selling prices or other unfair trading conditions, and limitation of production, markets or technical development to the prejudice of consumers.

Article 86 of the EC Treaty then singles out public undertakings and

---

[44] F. Jenny and P.M. Horna, 'Modernization of the European System of Competition Law Enforcement: Lessons for other Regional Groupings', in Brusick *et al.*, above at n 15, at 287–331.

[45] *See* C.-D. Ehlermann, 'The Modernization of EC Antitrust Policy: A Legal and Cultural Revolution' (2000) 37 CMLR, 537, at 537–40.

[46] Arts. 81 and 82 EC Treaty.

undertakings to which Member States grant special or exclusive rights and declares that they, too, are subject in principle to the rules of competition law contained in the Treaty. However, paragraph 2 goes further and provides:

Undertakings entrusted with the operation of services of general economic interest or having the character of a revenue-producing monopoly *shall be subject to the rules contained in this Treaty, in particular to the rules on competition, in so far as the application of such rules does not obstruct the performance, in law or in fact, of the particular tasks assigned to them.* The development of trade must not be affected to such an extent as would be contrary to the interests of the Community. (Emphasis added).

The power to issue regulations and directives necessary for the enforcement of EC competition law was initially given to the European Council. The Council also had the power 'to define, if need be, in the various branches of the economy, the scope of the provisions of Articles 81 and 82'.[47] We shall see later on how the Council exercised its power under this provision in adapting the scope of competition law to the various branches of the economy. EC competition law may be enforced by the competition authorities and national courts of the Member States as well as the European Courts at the initiation of any interested party, private as well as public.[48]

The EC's specificity regarding prohibited conduct in Articles 81 and 82 of the EC Treaty are generally carried forward into most EC-oriented RTAs. The level of specificity can take the form of explicit references to the EC Treaty or merely the inclusion of similar language.[49] This is the harmonization process that has been associated with EC-oriented RTAs. However, that is not always the case, as will be seen below in the discussion of North–South RTAs to which the EC is a party.

2. Competition Law and Policy in the US–Australia FTA

The US–Australia FTA mostly follows the classical US RTA model in that it requires the maintenance of measures prohibiting anti-competitive conduct and a competition authority to enforce such provisions.[50] As is characteristic in US RTAs, the FTA contains cooperation and coordination provisions. The US–Australia Agreement also specifically refers to previous cooperation agreements on antitrust matters and renews the commitment to further cooperate on the enforcement of their national competition laws and to facilitate such cooperation through a joint working group.[51]

---

[47] Art. 83(2)(c) EC Treaty.

[48] *See,* e.g. Art. 6 of Council Regulation (EC) No 1/2003 of 16 December 2002 on the implementation of the rules on competition laid down in Articles 81 and 82 of the Treaty [2003] OJ L1/1.

[49] *See* Cernat, above at n 36, at 24.

[50] Art. 14(2)(1) of the US–Australia Free Trade Agreement, signed 18 May 2004, in force 1 January 2005 available at www.ustr.gov/Trade_Agreements/Bilateral/Australia_FTA/Section_Index.html (visited 4 April 2006).

[51] *Ibid.,* Arts 14(2)(3) and 14(2)(4).

In addition, and as is mostly the case in US RTAs, the US–Australia FTA specifically addresses monopolies and state enterprises. Designating monopolies is not prohibited, but any designated monopoly must comply with the terms of the FTA, must act solely with commercial considerations in the sale of any goods or services, provide non-discriminatory treatment to covered investments under the FTA and not use its monopoly position to engage in anti-competitive practices in a non-monopolized market within its territory.[52] Similarly, all state enterprises must refrain from creating obstacles to trade and investment and must comply with the terms of the FTA as well as provide non-discriminatory treatment in the sale of goods or services.[53]

Provisions peculiar to the US–Australia FTA include cooperation on cross-border consumer protection issues.[54] Both parties agreed to cooperate and coordinate on such issues and to recognize existing agreements addressing such matters. Also specific to the US–Australia Agreement is a provision addressing recognition and enforcement of monetary judgments issued by their respective competition and securities authorities.[55]

Finally, as is generally the case in US RTAs, the US–Australia FTA does not allow for the dispute resolution provisions to be invoked for any matter arising under the obligation to maintain competition laws, the ability to designate monopolies, consumer protection provisions, or the obligation to cooperate or consult.[56]

D. Competition Provisions in South–South RTAs

1. The Caribbean Community (Caricom)

As early as 1973, the Chaguaramas Treaty establishing Caricom[57] provided a set of principles governing restrictive business practices. In language that clearly bears the influence of the EC system described above, Article 30 of the Annex to the Chaguaramas Treaty declares a category of private sector practices which would nullify the benefits expected from the agreement to liberalize intra-regional trade to be incompatible with the terms of the Treaty. These practices include the following: (a) agreements between enterprises, decisions by associations of enterprises and concerted practices between enterprises which have as their object or result the prevention, restriction or distortion of competition within the Common Market; and, (b) actions that take unfair advantage of a dominant position, within the Common Market or a substantial part of it. Furthermore, Article 30(4) also committed Member States to introduce 'as soon as practicable' uniform legislation for the control of restrictive business practices.

The sketchy provisions of Article 30 were later amended and replaced by a

---

[52] *Ibid.*, Art. 14(3) [53] *Ibid.*, Art. 14(4) [54] *Ibid.*, Art. 14(6) [55] *Ibid.*, Art. 14(7)
[56] *Ibid.*, Art. 14(11)
[57] Treaty establishing the Caribbean Community (Caricom), signed 4 July 1973, in force 1 August 1973 (1973) 12 ILM, 1033.

new and more detailed protocol in 2000.[58] Protocol VIII amending the Caricom treaty provides that the Community will 'establish appropriate norms and institutional arrangements to prohibit and penalize anti-competitive business conduct' and 'establish and maintain information systems to enable enterprises and consumers to be kept informed about the operation of markets within the CSME [Caricom Single Market and Economy]'.[59]

Protocol VIII establishes a regional competition commission invested with powers necessary for the enforcement of the rules, including powers to secure the attendance of any person before it to give evidence, order termination of anti-competitive conduct and impose fines and/or order payment of compensation to affected parties.[60] The protocol also imposes on Member States the obligation to take all necessary legislative measures to ensure compliance with the rules of competition, impose penalties for anti-competitive business conduct and establish national competition authorities to that end.[61] The national competition authorities are required to cooperate with the Community Competition Commission.

At the substantive level, the protocol prohibits anti-competitive business conduct, which is defined to mean the following:

(a) agreements between enterprises, decisions by associations of enterprises, and concerted practices by enterprises which have as their object or effect the prevention, restriction or distortion of competition within the Community; (b) actions by which an enterprise abuses its dominant position within the Community; or (c) any other like conduct by enterprises whose object or effect is to frustrate the benefits expected from the establishment of the CSME.[62]

This broad definition is further supplemented by a long illustrative list of specific practices, such as price fixing, supply restriction, and unauthorized denial of access to networks or essential infrastructure.

In summary, Caricom's competition provisions provide for common RTA-wide competition rules with a supranational enforcement mechanism. The provisions further require all Member States to enact appropriate competition legislation and establish competition authorities to enforce such legislation against prohibited conduct. This level of integration is also characteristic of the other regional RTAs discussed below.

2. *The Southern Common Market (Mercosur)*

The Mercosur customs union was formed in 1991 by the Treaty of Asunción between Argentina, Brazil, Paraguay, and Uruguay. The Treaty provides that 'States Parties shall co-ordinate their respective domestic policies with a view to

---

[58] Protocol Amending the Treaty Establishing the Caribbean Community, Protocol VIII: Competition Policy, Consumer Protection, Dumping and Subsidies, signed 14 March 2000, Art. 30(b), available at www.caricom.org/jsp/secretariat/legal_instruments/protocolviii.jsp?menu=secretariat (visited 4 April 2006) (hereinafter Protocol VIII).
[59] *Ibid.*, Art. 30(b).   [60] *Ibid.*, Art. 30(f).   [61] *Ibid.*, Art. 30(b).
[62] *Ibid.*, Art. 30(i)(1).

drafting common rules for trade competition'.[63] In 1996 the Mercosur parties agreed to the Mercosur Protocol for the Defence of Competition to provide for specific RTA-wide competition rules.[64] The Protocol applies to 'natural and legal persons under public and private law, and other entities whose purpose is to influence or to bring influence to bear upon competition in the framework of the Mercosur and consequently to influence trade between the States Parties'.[65] Thus, the conduct captured by the Protocol is conduct that has an effect within the Mercosur market, not individual national markets or markets outside Mercosur.[66] The prohibited conduct includes concerted acts or agreements that 'distort competition or access to the market or which constitute an abuse of a dominant position'.[67] Such acts include price fixing, reduction of output and input, predatory practices, and market manipulation.[68] State monopolies are included unless application of the terms of the Protocol would prevent 'the regular exercise of their legal attributions'.[69]

Each Mercosur signatory must enact common rules that prohibit anti-competitive conduct, specifically, acts 'which may limit or in any way cause prejudice to free trade, or result in the domination of the relevant regional market of goods and services, including [acts] which result in economic concentration, with a view to preventing their possible anti-competitive effects in the framework of the Mercosur'.[70]

With respect to investigation and enforcement, the signatories to the Protocol agreed to establish an intergovernmental Committee for the Defence of Competition, which has the power to promulgate procedural rules for the application of the Protocol, subject to referral to the Trade Commission.[71] Interested parties may initiate individual proceedings with the national competition authorities and investigations of the matter will be conducted by those authorities.[72] The competition authorities of the other States parties must cooperate with the investigation. If the proceeding implicates effects on the Mercosur market, the competition authority must refer its final decision to the Committee for the Defence of Competition which has the authority to determine whether the Protocol has been violated and order cessation of the

---

[63] Treaty of Asunción, signed 26 March 1991, in force 29 November 1991, Art. 4.

[64] *See* Mercosur Protocol for the Defence of Competition, signed 17 December 1996, in force 8 September 2000, text in Portuguese available at www.sice.oas.org/Trade/MRCSRS/Decisions/AN1896p.asp (visited 4 April 2006).

[65] *Ibid.*, Art. 2.

[66] J. Tavares de Araujo and L. Tineo, 'Harmonization of Competition Policies among Mercosur Countries' (1998) 24 Brook J Int L 441, at 455.

[67] Art. 4 of the Mercosur Protocol for the Defence of Competition.   [68] *Ibid.*, Art. 6.

[69] *Ibid.*, Art. 2.   [70] *Ibid.*, Art. 7.

[71] *Ibid.*, Art. 9. The Trade Commission is a body formed to assist the Common Market Group (the Mercosur legislative body) and to 'monitor the application of the common trade policy instruments agreed by the States Parties in connection with the operation of the customs union'. Art. 16 of the Protocol of Ouro Preto, signed 17 December 1994.

[72] Tavares de Araujo and Tineo, above at n 66, at 455 and Art. 15 of the Mercosur Protocol for the Defence of Competition.

conduct at issue.[73] If a party subject to an order of cessation fails to comply, the Committee can impose fines or take other action.[74] Fines will be enforced by the competition authority of the jurisdiction where the violating party is domiciled. Any decision of the Committee must be referred to the Trade Commission which has the authority to make a ruling by issuing a Directive.[75] If consensus in the Trade Commission is not reached, the matter will be referred to the Common Market Group, the executive organ of the common market,[76] which has the authority to issue a decision by resolution.[77] If the Common Market Group does not reach consensus with respect to the matter, the complaining party may seek redress under the dispute resolution provisions of the Brasilia Protocol.[78] Sanctions for anti-competitive conduct include fines, exclusion from public procurement processes in any of the States Parties and exclusion from contracts with public financial institutions.[79]

Each national competition authority must adopt mechanisms for technical coordination and must cooperate with the other Mercosur authorities. Disputes regarding the application or the interpretation of the Protocol can be brought by any State party before the Trade Commission or be settled through the dispute settlement provisions of the Brasilia Protocol.[80]

In summary, the Mercosur competition provisions provide substantive rules which govern anti-competitive conduct having an effect on the Mercosur market, specifically conduct comprising concerted practices or abuse of dominant market position. The competition provisions create an intergovernmental Committee for the Defence of Competition that has the power to promulgate rules regarding the competition Protocol and to review all cases that have an effect on the Mercosur market. The Committee can also order cessation of conduct and impose fines, but enforcement of such action is left to the national competition authorities. All Member States are required to enact common competition rules and national competition authorities are vested with the power to investigate and sanction anti-competitive conduct. If the conduct at issue has an effect on the Mercosur market, national competition authorities are required to refer the issue to the Committee for review.

---

[73] Art. 13 of the Mercosur Protocol for the Defence of Competition.

[74] Tavares de Araujo and Tineo, above at n 66, at 455 and Art. 13 of the Mercosur Protocol for the Defence of Competition.

[75] Art. 15 of the Mercosur Protocol for the Defence of Competition.

[76] *See* Art. 13 of the Treaty of Asunción.   [77] *Ibid.*, Art. 21.

[78] *Ibid.* The Brasilia Protocol, signed 26 March 1991, provides for dispute resolution between States Parties to the Treaty of Asunción and between private parties and a State Party. A private party can submit its claim to the National Section of the Common Market Group. The Section can attempt to decide the dispute or refer it to the Common Market Group. If the complaint is referred to the Common Market Group, it will refer the case to a group of experts. The experts will then submit a report to the Common Market Group. If the report supports the complaining party's case against the State Party, any other State Party 'can then demand that corrective measures be adopted or that the disputed measure be annulled'. If the request for corrective measures is not granted, the requesting State Party can invoke the binding ad hoc arbitration provisions of the Brasilia Protocol.

[79] *See* Art. 28 of the Treaty of Asunción.   [80] *Ibid.*, Art. 31.

3. Andean Community

In 1969 the Andean Community was formed between Bolivia, Colombia, Ecuador, Peru, and Venezuela.[81] The treaty requires the Commission of the Andean Community, the entity responsible for formulating and carrying out trade integration policy, to 'adopt the essential provisions to guard against or correct practices that may distort competition within the subregion, such as dumping, improper price manipulations, manoeuvres to upset the normal supply of raw materials, and others with a like effect'.[82] The Commission of the Andean Community and of the Andean Council of Foreign Ministers issued Decision 608 on competition on 25 March 2005.[83] The purpose of Decision 608 is to promote market efficiency and consumer welfare by addressing anti-competitive conduct that produces effects within the Community. Like the Mercosur competition provisions, Decision 608 aims not to regulate purely national anti-competitive conduct, but to capture conduct having an effect within the Community, whether that conduct originates within or outside the Community. This attempt to constrain conduct arising outside the Community, but having an effect within the Community is an added dimension beyond that of Mercosur.[84] The Decision applies to any 'economic agent' which includes any public or private, natural or legal person.[85]

Chapter X of the Treaty of Cartagena governing the Andean Community states only that the Commission of the Andean Community shall adopt measures to prevent practices that distort competition within the Community. It does not explicitly require Member States to enact harmonized competition legislation. Decision 608 on Competition merely suggests that national competition laws must be based on principles of non-discrimination, transparency and due process.

The proscribed conduct under Decision 608 includes concerted practices, such as price fixing, restriction of supply or demand, and bid rigging, as well as abuse of dominant market position.[86] The General Secretariat may investigate any incidence of prohibited conduct on its own initiative or at the request of a national competition authority or any other interested party, whether governmental or otherwise.[87] A request for investigation must be accompanied by a thorough description of the conduct and its duration.[88] If an investigation is opened, the General Secretariat will notify all interested parties, including the

---

[81] Agreement on Andean Subregional Integration (Cartagena Agreement), signed 26 May 1969, in force 16 October 1969 (1969) 8 ILM, 910.

[82] Chapter X of the Cartagena Agreement.

[83] Normas para la Protección y Promoción de la Libre Competencia en la Comunidad Andina ('Rules for the Protection and Promotion of Free Competition in the Andean Community'), Decision 608, signed 29 March 2005, available in Spanish at www.sice.oas.org/trade/JUNAC/junaind.asp (visited 4 April 2006). The authors are relying upon an unofficial translation of Decision 608 for this chapter and would like to express their thanks to Brendan Oviedo for his help in translating relevant material on the Andean Community.

[84] *Ibid.*, Art. 5.   [85] *Ibid.*, Art. 1.   [86] *Ibid.*, Arts. 7 and 8.   [87] *Ibid.*, Arts. 10.

[88] *Ibid.*, Arts. 11.

national competition authority of any interested Member State. The General Secretariat will then instruct the appropriate competition authority to investigate the matter in accordance with an agreed investigation plan.[89] Both the General Secretariat and the national competition authority have the power to request documents, and conduct inspections and interviews.[90] The General Secretariat also has the power to order a public hearing at the request of any interested party. If the investigation reveals the presence of prohibited anticompetitive conduct, the General Secretariat may order the cessation of such conduct and impose sanctions based on an evaluation of factors such as the gravity of the conduct, cooperation with the investigation, the damage to competition and the duration of the conduct. A fine can be imposed up to a maximum of 10 per cent of the gross income of the responsible party.[91]

In summary, the Andean Community has established a supranational authority with power to enforce the common competition law throughout the region. The authority has the power to oversee the national competition authorities' investigations and possesses its own investigative and enforcement powers.

4. Common Market for Eastern and Southern Africa (Comesa)

Comesa became a free trade area in 2000 and plans to become a customs union by 2008.[92] The treaty establishing Comesa provides that the 'Member States agree to prohibit any agreement between undertakings or concerted practice which has as its objective or effect the prevention, restriction or distortion of competition within the Common Market'.[93] The Comesa Council of Ministers, the entity responsible for ensuring the 'proper functioning and development of the Common Market in accordance with the provisions of this [Comesa] Treaty', adopted competition regulations in 2004 which echo this proscription and which expand this prohibition to also specifically include abuse of dominant market position.[94] Prohibited conduct specifically includes price fixing, bid rigging, customer or market allocation, and sales or production quotas.[95] The regulations also address mergers and consumer protection and safety.[96] The Council of Ministers adopted the competition regulations under powers vested in it by Article 55 of the Comesa Treaty. Article 5 of the competition regulations imposes on Member States an obligation to 'take all appropriate measures, whether general or particular, to ensure fulfilment of the

---

[89] *Ibid.*, Art. 15.   [90] *Ibid.*, Art. 16.   [91] *Ibid.*, Art. 34.

[92] G.K. Lipimile and E. Gachuiri, 'Allocation of Competences between National and Regional Competition Authorities: The Case of COMESA', in Brusick et al., above at n 15, at 381.

[93] Treaty Establishing the Common Market for Eastern and Southern Africa, signed 5 November 1993 (1994) 33 ILM, 1067.

[94] *See* Lipimile and Gachuiri, above at n 92, at 365 and Arts 9, 16, and 17 of the Comesa Competition Regulations, adopted 17 December 2004, available at www.comesa.int/trade/issues/policy/ (visited 4 April 2006).

[95] *See* Art. 19 Comesa Competition Regulations.   [96] *Ibid.*, Arts 23–38.

obligations arising out of these Regulations or resulting from action taken by the Commission under these Regulations'.

The Comesa competition regulation establishes a Competition Commission with extensive powers and functions. The commission is required to, *inter alia*, assist Member States in the promotion of national competition laws and institutions with the objective of harmonizing national competition laws with the Comesa competition regulations. The goal of such harmonization is the uniform application and interpretation of competition law and policy within the common market. The Commission also has the power and obligation to, among other things: (1) monitor anticompetitive conduct and mediate disputes between Member States; (2) assist Member States to harmonize national competition laws with the regulations; (3) cooperate with national competition authorities; (4) facilitate the exchange of expertise and information; and, (5) enter into arrangements that assist in monitoring conduct occurring outside Comesa that has an effect within it.[97] The Commission has broad investigative powers in cases in which anti-competitive conduct within Member States has the effect of restricting competition in the common market that include the power to compel testimony and the submission of evidence.[98] If the Commission determines that any particular conduct has an adverse impact on competition, it has the power to: (1) order the termination or nullification of any agreement; (2) order any party to cease the anti-competitive conduct and to take measures to overcome the abuse of a dominant market position or any other anti-competitive conduct; (3) order payment of compensation; or, (4) impose fines.[99] The Commission can also grant authorizations to engage in anti-competitive conduct if the public benefits outweigh the detrimental effects of such conduct.[100]

Any person may file a request for an investigation with the Commission and the Commission will consult with all interested parties to determine whether the Commission has jurisdiction and whether the investigation is justified.[101] The Commission may also initiate an investigation on its own.[102] If an investigation is opened, the Commission has six months to notify the concerned party, allow that party to present a defence and conclude the investigation.[103]

In summary, the Comesa competition scheme requires Member States to prohibit anti-competitive conduct and creates a supranational competition authority that possesses broad investigative and enforcement powers.

5. *Summary*

The South–South RTAs discussed above have many similarities and fewer differences. All of the RTAs proscribe anti-competitive conduct, particularly concerted practices. With the exception of Comesa, they also expressly include

---

[97] *Ibid.*, Art. 7.   [98] *Ibid.*, Arts 7 and 8   [99] *Ibid.*   [100] *Ibid.*, Art. 20.
[101] *Ibid.*, Art. 21.   [102] *Ibid.*, Art. 22.   [103] *Ibid.*, Art. 21.

abuse of dominant market position. All four RTAs establish some form of supranational competition authority or commission. In the case of Comesa, the Andean Community, and Caricom, the supranational authorities have extensive investigative and enforcement powers. In the case of Mercosur, the authority has broad supervisory powers, but national competition authorities have the ultimate power to enforce sanctions. Member States are usually required to prohibit anti-competitive conduct through the adoption of national legislation and, in the case of Caricom and Mercosur for instance, that legislation must be uniform among Member States.

E. Competition Provisions in North–South RTAs

1. Trade Agreements with the United States

Bilateral trade agreements with the US tend to contain provisions that require the signatory governments to enact competition laws, if none exist, or to amend existing competition laws to prohibit anti-competitive conduct. Specifically, US bilateral agreements generally require each party to adopt or maintain competition laws or measures that 'proscribe anti-competitive business conduct'.[104] The US–Singapore Free Trade Agreement required Singapore to enact competition laws by September 2005 and also to make such laws applicable to government enterprises.[105] In 2004, Singapore enacted such competition legislation.[106] The provisions of the Competition Act 2004 governing concerted practices and abuse of dominant market position were to take effect on 1 January 2006.[107] The provisions governing mergers and acquisitions will take effect at least 12 months later.[108] Singapore's enactment of competition legislation demonstrates the effectiveness of the transfer of competition policy from developed to developing countries by means of trade agreements.

US bilateral trade agreements often require the formation of competition authorities with the power to enforce competition laws[109] and tend to focus on cooperation and coordination between the signatory states in furthering the development of competition law and policy as well as requiring cooperation

---

[104] US–Singapore Free Trade Agreement, signed 6 May 2003, in force 1 January 2004, available at www.ustr.gov/Trade_Agreements/Bilateral/Singapore_FTA/Section_Index.html (visited 4 April 2006), Article 12(2)(1); *see also* Art. 14(2)(1) US–Australia FTA and Art. 16(1) US–Chile Free Trade Agreement, signed 6 June 2003, in force 1 January 2004, available at www.ustr.gov/Trade_Agreements/Bilateral/Chile_FTA/Section_Index.html (visited 4 April 2006).

[105] US–Singapore FTA, fn 12–1.

[106] Singapore Competition Act 2004, available at statutes.agc.gov.sg/ (visited 4 April 2006).

[107] Singapore Competition Commission, Background of the Competition Act 2004, available at www.ccs.gov.sg/Legislation/CompetitionAct/index.html (visited 4 April 2006).

[108] *Ibid.*

[109] Art. 12(2)(2) US–Singapore FTA, Art. 14(2)(2) US–Australia FTA, and Art. 16(1)(2) US–Chile FTA.

and coordination between competition authorities with respect to enforcement of competition laws.[110]

US trade agreements do not prohibit the designation of privately-owned monopolies, but such monopolies may not act contrary to the terms of the agreements. Monopolies must act solely with commercial considerations, provide non-discriminatory treatment to investments covered by the trade agreement and must not use their monopoly position to engage in anti-competitive conduct.[111]

US trade agreements also specifically address state enterprises. The US–Chile Agreement, for example, does not prohibit state enterprises, but generally requires that state enterprises act in conformance with the terms of the trade agreement, even when exercising regulatory, administrative or other governmental authority.[112] A state enterprise must also ensure non-discriminatory treatment in the sale of its goods or services.[113]

The terms of the US–Singapore Trade Agreement are more comprehensive with respect to state enterprises. Like the US–Chile Agreement, the Singapore Agreement also requires that a state enterprise act in accordance with the terms of the agreement in the exercise of any governmental authority and accord non-discriminatory treatment in the sale of its goods or services.[114] But, with respect to Singapore, the trade agreement specifically requires that state enterprises refrain from entering into agreements to restrain competition or engage in exclusionary practices and that Singapore refrain from influencing or directing the decisions of its government enterprises.[115] However, Singapore may exercise any voting rights it has as long as such exercise conforms to the terms of the trade agreement. Of particular interest in this respect is the provision requiring Singapore to 'continue reducing, with the goal of substantially eliminating, its aggregate ownership and other interests that confer effective influence in entities organized under the laws of Singapore, taking into account, in the timing of individual divestments, the state of relevant capital markets'.[116] Singapore has an obligation to annually report its ownership interests in all state enterprises.[117]

The US bilateral trade agreements do not allow the dispute resolution provisions to be invoked for certain provisions related to competition. For example, the US–Chile Agreement states that parties may not invoke the

---

[110] Arts 12(4) and 12(6) US–Singapore FTA and Art. 16(2) US–Chile FTA. As mentioned above, Art. 14(6) of the US–Australia FTA (which is not a North–South agreement despite physical geography) in particular, also requires coordination on issues of consumer protection laws.

[111] Art. 12(3)(1)(c) US–Singapore FTA, Art. 14(3)(1) US–Australia FTA, and Art. 16(3) US–Chile FTA.

[112] Art. 16(4) US–Chile FTA.

[113] Art. 16(4) US–Chile FTA. In the US–Australia FTA, the US agreed not to exclude sub-federal state enterprises from its anti-trust laws. Australia also agreed to ensure that all levels of government accord non-discriminatory treatment to state and non-state enterprises: Art. 14(4)(2)–(3) US–Australia FTA.

[114] Art. 12(3)(2) US–Singapore FTA.   [115] *Ibid.*   [116] *Ibid.*, Art. 12(3)(2)(f).

[117] *Ibid.*, Art. 12(3)(2)(g).

dispute settlement provisions for violations of the agreement to maintain competition laws and competition authorities, the agreement to cooperate or the agreement to consult. The US–Singapore Agreement contains similar provisions.

2. Trade Agreements with the EC

As discussed above, the EC generally follows the standard practice of including competition provisions in agreements it signs with developing countries, but those provisions generally specify the conduct that is prohibited, namely concerted practices and abuse of dominant market position. This is in contrast to the US model which often only states that each party will generally prohibit 'anti-competitive business conduct'. The EC–South Africa Trade and Development Cooperation Agreement (TDCA),[118] the Euro-Mediterranean Association Agreement between the EC and Algeria (EC–Algeria),[119] and the EC–Mexico Free Trade Agreement[120] show that the EC has effectively made competition policy an essential aspect of preferential trade agreements. The TDCA and the EC–Algeria Agreement follow the classical EC format in that they specify the prohibited conduct. Article 35 of the TDCA and Article 41 of the EU-Algeria Agreement identify concerted practices and abuse of dominant market position as being prohibited conduct.[121] The EC–Mexico Agreement, on the other hand, simply states that the parties undertake to 'eliminate anti-competitive activities by applying the appropriate legislation'.[122] Also specific to the EC–Mexico Agreement is the EC's agreement to give particular attention to 'agreements between companies, decisions to form an association between companies and concerted practices between companies' and to prevent the abuse of dominant market position.[123] Mexico specifically agreed to give particular attention to 'absolute or relative monopolistic practices and mergers'.[124] In addition, the EC–Algeria Agreement provides that within five years of executing the agreement, Algeria must adjust state monopolies to ensure no discrimination in the sale of any goods and must take measures to ensure that state enterprises with special or exclusive rights do not distort trade between the parties.[125]

The provisions of the EC trade agreements require that the parties to the agreements apply existing competition laws, or enact new competition laws if none exist, to implement the terms of the trade agreement. In this respect, the TDCA specifically provides that 'if, at the entry into force of this Agreement,

---

[118] Art. 35 of the EC–South Africa Trade, Development and Cooperation Agreement [1999] OJ L311/3

[119] Art. 41 and Annex 5 of the EC–Algeria Euro-Mediterranean Association Agreement, signed 12 April 2002 (in process of ratification) COM (2002) 157 Final.

[120] Art. 1 of the EC–Mexico Free Trade Agreement, Decision No 2/2000 of 23 March 2000 [2000] OJ L157/10.

[121] Art. 35 EC–South Africa Agreement and Art. 41 EC–Algeria AA.

[122] Art. 1 EC–Mexico FTA.	[123] *Ibid.*	[124] *Ibid.*

[125] Arts 42 and 43 EC–Algeria AA.

either Party has not yet adopted the necessary laws and regulations for the implementation of Article 35, in their jurisdictions it shall do so within a period of three years'.[126]

In all three cases, the enforcement of the competition commitments is left to the respective competition authorities of the EC and the partner countries but the agreements also provide for administrative cooperation and coordination, provisions that are not normally comprehensive in EC RTAs.[127] The TDCA's cooperation provisions are the least detailed of the three EC RTAs discussed here. The TDCA provides for consultation regarding any action that affects the interests of the other party as well as the exchange of information and technical assistance consisting of the exchange of experts, seminars, and training activities.[128] Unlike the EC–Algeria or EC–Mexico Agreements, however, the TDCA provides for a positive comity obligation under which the Parties agree that 'whenever the Commission or the South African Competition Authority has reason to believe that anti-competitive practices, defined under Article 35, are taking place within the territory of the other authority and are substantially affecting important interests of the Parties, it may request the other Party's competition authority to take appropriate remedial action in terms of that authority's rules governing competition'.[129] The TDCA also specifically prohibits state aid that favours 'certain firms or the production of certain goods' and that results in distorting or threatening competition and is not supported by a specific public policy objective.[130]

Cooperation provisions are more detailed in EC–Mexico and EC–Algeria Agreements, especially with respect to exchange of information and notification of enforcement activities and coordination thereon, consultations when a party's important interests are affected, as well as technical assistance in terms of exchange of experts, seminars, joint studies, and training.[131]

In contrast to the agreements discussed above, and in apparent recognition of the weaker position of the African, Caribbean, and Pacific Group of countries (the ACP), the competition provisions of the Cotonou Agreement[132] are largely limited to a restatement of general principles and future aspirations. Article 45 of the Cotonou Agreement simply declares the crucial importance of a sound and effective competition policy and commits the ACP countries:

to implement national or regional rules and policies including the control and *under certain conditions* the prohibition of agreements between undertakings, decisions by associations of undertakings and concerted practices between undertakings which have as their object or effect the prevention, restriction or distortion of competition. The Parties further agree to prohibit the abuse by one or more undertakings of a dominant

---

[126] *See* Art. 36 EC–South Africa Agreement.   [127] *See* Holmes, above at n 18, at 72.
[128] Arts 38–40 EC–South Africa Agreement.   [129] *Ibid.*, Art. 38.   [130] *Ibid.*, Art. 41.
[131] Arts 3–6 and 9 EC–Mexico FTA; and Annex 5, Arts 6–7 EC–Algeria AA.
[132] ACP–EU Cotonou Partnership Agreement, signed 23 June 2000, in force 1 April 2003 [2000] OJ L317/3.

position in the common market of the Community or in the territory of ACP States. (Emphasis added).

This is then followed by a statement of cooperation including technical assistance in the drafting of an appropriate legal framework and its administrative enforcement. It is notable at this juncture that this softly-softly approach is likely to change as competition policy is being pursued more vigorously by the EC in the context of the ongoing negotiations for the establishment of Economic Partnership Agreements with ACP sub-regions.[133]

III. EXEMPTIONS FROM COMPETITION LAW[134]

It is noteworthy that not every cartel-like activity or every monopoly situation is prohibited whether at the national or regional levels. Indeed, the US RTAs specifically recognize that designated monopolies are not prohibited. And, although the economic principles of productive and allocative efficiency underlying competition law would be undermined by most anti-competitive activities,[135] the laws of many countries and regions provide for a host of grounds for exemptions from the application of their respective competition rules. Exemptions from competition law do not necessarily imply the total exclusion of competition law provisions from a particular sector but tend to broadly cover modifications or adaptations of general competition law with a view to making it more lenient and accommodative of private behaviour in a particular sector or activity. Some of these exemptions are motivated by considerations of the strategic significance of particular industries in an economy (e.g. agriculture and the energy sector in general); some others are dictated by the nature of the industry—such as the so-called natural monopolies in the network-bound industries (e.g. electricity and natural gas); and still others by the mercantilistic urge to promote exports (e.g. the exemption of export cartels in the US, EC, and many other developed legal systems).[136]

Reflecting the structural considerations at the core of competition law, exemptions from the ban on anti-competitive agreements are mostly available only to small players in the market. Special competition law regimes are

---

[133] *See*, e.g. K. Falkenberg, 'EPAs and DDA—Parallelism or Crossroads?' (2004) 3(4) *Trade Negotiations Insights* 1, arguing that trade alone is not sufficient for development and that the Economic Partnership Agreements should cover competition since 'enterprises in developing countries can stitch up markets at least as successfully as in developed countries' which 'plays against new entrants into the markets and hence against economic growth and employment,' at 3.

[134] For more on exemptions, *see* M.G. Desta, 'Exemptions from Competition Law in Regional Trade Agreements—A Study Based on Experiences in the Agriculture and Energy Sectors', in Brusick *et al.*, above at n 15, at 443–72.

[135] *See also* R.D. Anderson and P. Holmes, 'Competition Policy and the Future of the Multilateral Trading System' (2002) 5 JIEL 531.

[136] *See* P. Victor, 'Export Cartels: An Idea Whose Time has Passed' (1992) 60 ALJ 571, at 577, stating that all major trading partners of the US have some form of antitrust immunity for export cartels, an approach which is like 'each country trying to benefit at everyone's expense'.

thus often created to apply to farmers, fisheries and the like owing to the small and fragmented nature of the individual actors in those industries;[137] the strategic significance of food production also plays an important role. Such exemptions are usually available in many legal systems to what are called small and medium-size enterprises (SMEs) in all sectors. SMEs often benefit from exemptions from competition law rules prohibiting concerted practices either expressly[138] or through the minimum anti-competitive threshold requirements set by the competition laws of many countries.[139] According to the OECD, the reasons for this include the structural concern that SMEs 'have no chance of survival in competition with large firms if the latter use economies of scale'.[140] Several governments attempt to offset those structural disadvantages of the SMEs by, *inter alia*, allowing them to enter into co-operative agreements amongst themselves.[141]

Exemptions from competition law applying to dominant market position are often indirect and limited to the big national utilities and natural monopolies.[142] Furthermore, recent developments in many countries show that the scope and significance of those exemptions are becoming increasingly limited. A good example here would be the application of EC competition rules to the network-bound segments of the energy industry, which has been traditionally limited. Although undergoing change over the past decade or so,[143] such networks are what are often called natural monopolies generally immune from competition law requirements. The EC experience on the relationship between its network-bound energy industry and its common competition policy could be a useful example here.

---

[137] L. Altman and R. Callmann, *Callmann on Unfair Competition, Trademarks and Monopolies*, 4th ed. (Eagan, Minnesota: Thomson West, 2005), para. 4.4 (recognizing that under US antitrust law, some exemptions from competition are based on 'concern for the economic weakness of isolated groups, such as farmers').

[138] Examples include the EU, the US, and Japan. For more on this, *see*: General Cartel Bans: Criteria for Exemption for Small and Medium-Sized Enterprises, OECD Doc. OCDE/GD(97)53, available at www.oecd.org/dataoecd/34/54/1920345.pdf (visited 4 April 2006).

[139] Examples include Canada and Norway, *ibid.* [140] *Ibid.*, at 8.

[141] For example, German competition law allows inter-company cooperation agreements that are primarily directed to the promotion of efficiency including 'production, research and development, financing, administration, advertising, purchasing and distribution', but not agreements designed to eliminate competition such as price-fixing or market sharing, *ibid.*, at 11. In the effort to minimize the structural disadvantage of SMEs, in 1990 Germany extended the exemption from the ban on concerted practices to joint purchasing by SME on certain conditions: 'if the participating companies are not compelled to purchase, if competition on the relevant market is not substantially impaired and if the agreement serves to promote the competitiveness of SME', *ibid.*, at 12.

[142] Note however that exemptions from disciplines on dominant market position are not necessarily limited to the big players. Section 24 of Japan's Anti-Monopoly Act, for example, provides an exemption for SMEs from the anti-monopoly law by allowing them to form co-operative unions so that 'small-scale enterprises that find it difficult to effectively compete with large-scale enterprises become part of an effective unit of competition in the market, and thereby actively contribute to the maintenance and promotion of the fair and free competition order as set out in the Anti-Monopoly Act'. *See* OECD, above at n 138, at 35.

[143] *See* P. Cameron, *Competition in Energy Markets: Law and Regulation in the European Union* (Oxford: OUP, 2002), 7–9.

Unlike in some national legal systems,[144] there is no explicit exemption for energy from EC competition law; the claim about the limited application of EC competition to the sector is arrived at only indirectly. Firstly, the EC Treaty provides for an exemption for 'undertakings entrusted with the operation of services of general economic interest'. According to Article 86(2) of the EC Treaty, '[u]ndertakings entrusted with the operation of services of general economic interest or having the character of a revenue-producing monopoly shall be subject to the rules contained in this Treaty, in particular to the rules on competition, in so far as the application of such rules does not obstruct the performance, in law or in fact, of the particular tasks assigned to them'. The energy industry squarely fits into this description due to the general economic interest of the energy industry and its tendency toward monopoly. Although the EC Commission later introduced several pro-competition initiatives for the energy sector, both in the form of legislative proposals and judicial actions, several competing interests conspired to keep the network-bound energy sector largely shielded from the EC rules of competition law for long.[145] A lack of political will from Member States and the cautious approach of the ECJ in the interpretation of the EC Treaty, and particularly Article 86(2) played a major part in this. At the national level, many EC member countries reconciled the competing demands of competition law on the one hand and the natural monopoly status of the network-bound sectors with their public service requirements on the other through establishment of independent regulators as 'a surrogate for competition'.[146] This anti-competitive role of networks is gradually being addressed especially in the EC gas and electricity sectors, through network unbundling and particularly regulated and non-discriminatory third-party access to networks.[147] However, it remains that energy is still one of the least-developed common policies at the EC level.[148]

---

[144] For example, although Mexico's constitution prohibits monopolies and monopolistic practices, it exempts from this prohibition specific sectors in what it calls 'strategic areas' including petroleum, hydrocarbons, petrochemicals, radioactive mining, and electricity. *See* OECD, above at n 33, at 15.

[145] For more on how this provision was used to exempt the network-bound energy industry, *see* Cameron, above at n 143, at Ch 5.

[146] *Ibid.*, at 23.

[147] Non-discriminatory access to upstream production (generation in the case of electricity; imports or national production in the case of gas), non-discriminatory access to transmission and distribution networks, and non-discriminatory access to consumers are essential conditions for competitive entry to occur in the energy industry. For more on this, *see* OXERA, The Relative Extent of Energy Market Competition in the EU and G7: Report by on Behalf of the UK Department of Trade and Industry, September 2003, available at www.dti.gov.uk/energy/gas_and_electricity/competitiveness_structure/oxera_report.pdf (visited 4 April 2006), 8–9. *See also* Cameron, above at n 143, at 4, 23–8 and T. Waelde and A. Gunst, 'International Energy Trade and Access to Networks: the Case of Electricity', in J. Bielecki and M.G. Desta (eds), *Electricity Trade in Europe: Review of Economic and Regulatory Challenges* (The Hague: Kluwer, 2004), 179–212.

[148] By contrast, the Treaty of Rome devoted a whole section to agriculture (Title II of the EC Treaty, Arts 32–39) and the Common Agricultural Policy (CAP) is perhaps 'the most highly developed' of all the common policies of the EC. *See* J. Steiner and L. Woods, *Textbook on EC Law*, 7th ed. (London: Blackstone, 2000), 208.

In sum, competition law, whether regional or national, does not apply equally to every economic sector or operator; it is rather carefully adapted to suit the realities of different sectors of the economy in the form of exemptions or modifications. Indeed, the type of competition law applying to different sectors and operators is largely determined by the structure of particular industries and their role in the overall economy.

IV. CONCLUSION

This chapter has shown that competition law has its origins in national regimes designed to regulate private business conduct that is perceived to distort the proper functioning of a free market economy. This concept has become a common element of bilateral and regional trade agreements because private business conduct, if left unregulated, can distort and defeat the intended effects of trade agreements. Despite the fact that competition provisions have become a common element of trade agreements, they are by no means consistent in their scope or terms. As we have seen, competition provisions can vary from mere statements of aspiration to harmonized national laws and supranational institutions with broad powers. We have seen that similarities can be drawn based on the parties to RTAs or their source of inspiration, such as the US-and-Canada-based agreements or the EC-based ones, but significant differences can also exist within these categories. For instance, while the EC-based RTAs are generally associated with minimal cooperation and coordination provisions, the EC–Mexico and the EC–Algeria Agreements are very detailed on these matters. In addition, we have seen that the development level of the trading partners does not necessarily translate to different forms of competition provisions other than the broad categories of US- and EC-style RTAs. An interesting parallel can be drawn, however, between the comprehensive regional agreements of the EC on the one hand and the South–South RTAs discussed in this chapter on the other. These RTAs all contemplate common competition policies and rules and supranational authorities with the power to enforce those provisions on a region-wide basis. Finally, despite the consistent presence of competition provisions in some form or another in many RTAs, there are often important exemptions from competition regimes.

11

Is Mutual Recognition an Alternative to Harmonization? Lessons on Trade and Tolerance of Diversity from the EU

GARETH DAVIES

I. INTRODUCTION

This chapter draws on European experience with mutual recognition of standards for goods and services, and asks what conclusions can be drawn for other RTAs and the WTO. Its main conclusion is that mutual recognition, while apparently offering an attractive alternative to harmonized rules, has a self-destructive quality which gives it a short life. It is effective at enabling trade, but also rapidly creates the conditions in which domestic lobbies push for harmonized rules. These rules extend far beyond standards, into social and environmental legislation. Mutual recognition is thus the first domino in a row at the end of which lies broad international governance.

The chapter proceeds in three sections. The following discusses the nature of the dichotomy between mutual recognition and harmonization in an abstract way. After that the EU experience with this tension is related. This is followed by an analysis of that experience, and then an attempt to extract lessons applicable outside the EU.

II. THE VIRTUES OF MUTUAL RECOGNITION

Any system of free trade runs very quickly into the problem of different standards for goods and services. These differences prevent products made according to the rules of one state from being sold in others. The most obvious apparent solution is harmonization of the standards to a common rule, yet this often turns out to be politically difficult. The many parties with an interest in the nature of the rule simply cannot, or will not, agree.

At this point it is convenient to distinguish between the different kinds of rules that may be at stake. Some will concern matters such as health and safety that should, perhaps, in an ideal world, be susceptible to an objective, thus non-national, analysis. Levels of chemicals, resistance to fire, are subjects that are culturally specific insofar as nations find different levels of risk acceptable, but where one can at least imagine a neutral and objective process of discussion. Science is international, and one may have hope that such rules could be too.

However, other rules are more broadly culturally specific. Standards that protect consumer expectation, such as advertising and description rules, or requirements for durability or reliability, will inevitably vary enormously from state to state. Particularly where services are involved, complicated services such as financial, medical, personal, or advisory ones especially, rules to protect transparency and comprehensibility and fairness will have great global diversity. These standards may be harder to harmonize because, while everyone may agree that some rule is necessary, there is no objective way of agreeing what that rule should be; there is no unique best way of regulating such matters. It is often the fact of a rule, to which consumers adapt their expectations, that does the protecting, rather than the unique content of the rule itself. Discussion over which form is best for a harmonized rule could continue forever for the simple reason that there may well be no right answer.[1]

These culturally specific standards are not always a great problem. It will often be no great difficulty to make for export. If France wants one kind of packet and the USA another then Chinese factories will simply put their products in different packets for each market. However, in a mature trading system this becomes undesirable. To obtain the full gains from regional, or global, trade integration, producers want to be able to make a single product for both their home and export markets and sell this without the bother or cost of additional product adjustments. Benefits of scale, including in marketing, argue against such a fragmented production process, and certainly as wealth differences between countries become less, and trade becomes more a balanced exchange, and less a huge flow of goods from certain states, making for export represents a significant efficiency loss.

Thus it is only a matter of time before attention turns to mutual recognition as a possible way of achieving trade while sidestepping the political and bureaucratic nightmare of harmonization.[2] This allows states to maintain their own product rules, which they may apply to producers based within their

---

[1] *See* K. Nicolaïdis and M. Egan, 'Regional Policy Externality and Market Governance: Why Recognise Foreign Standards?' (2001) 8 JEPP 454.

[2] For accounts of the movement towards mutual recognition in different contexts *see* J. Clarke, 'Mutual Recognition Agreements' (1996) 2 ITL Rev 31 and S.M. Stephenson, 'Mutual Recognition and its Role in Trade Facilitation' (1999) 33 JWT 141.

jurisdiction, on condition that they accept products made according to the rules of other states onto their markets. Mutual recognition is a system which requires that each producer be regulated by a single authority only, and that this be the authority where the production facility is located. It can be used for specific products, or between specific states, or with certain exceptions, or, most magnificently of all, as a general principle of trading law. However, the character of the rule that it entails is the same however broad or narrow its context of application.

Economists tend to love mutual recognition. As well as its low implementation costs it permits regulatory competition between states, which may use the quality or attractiveness of their product legislation as a means of attracting investment.[3] It also results in a diverse marketplace, where products made according to a range of standards are available. This increases consumer choice, and at least according to some views of the consumer may also therefore increase consumer satisfaction. After all, the choice of buying domestic goods made according to the familiar domestic standards remains.

Political scientists often also get quite excited about mutual recognition. For one thing it avoids the centralization which harmonization entails. As with other monopolies, a monopoly of regulation is not seen as necessarily good for quality, and a centralized regulator also becomes a target for regulatory capture by business lobbies.[4] A diversity of regulators, as well as keeping the world more interesting, increases the chance of diverse interests being represented, at least somewhere, and also allows for experiment and innovation.[5] National regulators are also closer to the public, which gives decentralization of standards more democratic legitimacy, and may increase the chance that rules will be responsive to public desires and needs.[6]

Even lawyers are becoming less sceptical of mutual recognition.[7] While certainty, precision and uniformity, high legal values, might tend to lead to harmonization as a preferred choice, the sheer power and elegance of a mutual recognition solution cannot fail to make an impact on even the most codified legal mind. It is, perhaps, more deserving of the name 'harmonization' than harmonization is. A common rule ends the disharmony by what may be

---

[3] *See*, e.g. P. Griffin, 'The Delaware Effect: Keeping the Tiger in its Cage. The European Experience of Mutual Recognition in Financial Services' (2001) 7 Colum J Eur L 337. For an overview of the arguments and citations of numerous works: A. Ogus, 'Competition between National Legal Systems: A Contribution of Economic Analysis to Comparative Law' (1999) 48 ICLQ 405 and J.M. Sun and J. Pelkmans, 'Regulatory Competition in the Single Market' (1995) 33 JCMS 67.

[4] *See*, e.g. D. Charny, 'Competition among Jurisdictions in Formulating Corporate Law Rules: An American Perspective on the "Race to the Bottom" in the European Communities' (1991) 32 Harv Int L J 423.

[5] *Ibid.*

[6] *See* K. Nicolaïdis and G. Schaffer, 'Transnational Mutual Recognition Regimes: Governance without Global Government' (2005) 68 LCP, 263 (also available at www.ssrn.com under the title 'Managed Mutual Recognition Regimes: Governance without Global Government') (visited 4 April 2006).

[7] They have tended to be more critical of the resulting regulatory competition. *See* N. Reich, 'Competition between Legal Orders: A New Paradigm of EC Law?' (1992) 29 CMLR 459.

compared to force—the elimination of the capacity to disagree. But is that harmony? Harmony entails more than one tone. Mutual recognition, by contrast, provides a mechanism for differences to continue without conflict. Truly it seems a method for our age.[8]

III. THE EUROPEAN EXPERIENCE

The EU has been wrestling with the choice between mutual recognition and harmonization for several decades now, and while mutual recognition has done well in the legal battles it is too early to call either the legal or the political war. Nevertheless, the rise and rise of mutual recognition has been sufficient to note some of its effects and impact.

After early and unsuccessful attempts to achieve free trade through harmonization, which failed because of the political and administrative difficulties of producing harmonized rules quickly or broadly enough to respond to the pace of product development and the needs of the market, it was the Court of Justice which indicated a new direction for the EU (or EEC as it then was) in its famous judgment in *Cassis de Dijon*.[9] In this it famously announced that products made according to the standards of one Member State could in principle be sold in any other Member State. There were exceptions—mutual recognition does not of course have to be absolute, indeed never is—but recognition was the general rule and from then on the starting point.[10]

The reaction of the European Commission was both rational and admirable. They indicated that wherever the *Cassis* principle applied successfully there was clearly no need for harmonization of standards; there was no obstruction to inter-state trade any more. As a result they would concentrate new harmonization legislation on areas where mutual recognition did not or could not successfully apply. They envisaged a future in which many fewer harmonized standards would be necessary.[11]

Mutual recognition has certainly been a huge success. At the time when the Court delivered its judgment in *Cassis* harmonization in the European Community had more or less come to a stop, and the failure to agree common

---

[8] *See* G. Davies, *Nationality Discrimination in the European Internal Market* (The Hague, London: Kluwer, 2003).

[9] Case 120/78 *Cassis de Dijon* [1979] ECR 649.

[10] S. Weatherill and P. Beaumont, *EU Law*, 3rd ed. (London: Penguin, 1999), 568–69. Mutual recognition was rapidly extended beyond goods to services and qualifications, and is now a generally applicable principle. *See*, e.g. Case 272/80 *Criminal Proceedings against Frans-Nederlandse Maatschappij voor Biologische Producten* [1981] ECR 3277 and Case C–76/90 *Säger and Dennemeyer* [1991] ECR I–4221.

[11] Commission White Paper, *Completing the Single Market* COM (85) 310, para 65 and Commission Communication 3 October 1980 [1980] OJ C256/2, analysed in L. Gormley, 'Cassis de Dijon and the Communication from the Commission' (1981) 6 EL Rev 454.

standards was proving a serious obstacle to trade.[12] *Cassis* broke through this barrier, and its principle, applied by courts and incorporated into legislation, has been the basis of a dramatic increase in cross-border trade, and is the conceptual cornerstone of the current internal market. Since it is now widely accepted that a policy of total harmonization, such as was once pursued, is politically undesirable and practically impossible, it is probably no exaggeration to say that the EU owes its trade integration largely to mutual recognition.[13]

However, the introduction of non-conforming foreign products onto domestic markets was experienced by various domestic lobbies as highly threatening. Consumer groups often saw it as undermining standards.[14] They questioned the value, for the consumer, of a standard that is not applied to all goods on a market, and regarded mutual recognition as leading to a lowering of marketplace quality.[15] Producers simply objected to the competition. Mutual recognition made imports easier. Moreover, since it does not require goods to be made for export, exporters can use standard domestic stock to penetrate foreign markets, which encourages a more adventurous or speculative approach. Without the need for specialized production facilities the costs of foreign ambitions are lower, and so more producers are inclined to have a go.[16] Domestic markets became much more competitive.[17]

Both of these groups—consumer organizations and producers—may well have objected to *ex ante* harmonization of standards. National product rules are often prized by consumer groups as protecting and entrenching age-old philosophies of quality and certainty, and there is commonly a—quite understandable—instinct against amending them in the direction of foreign equivalents, perish the thought of entirely replacing them.[18] Producers will often have found the existing national standards, in a pre-mutual recognition age, to be comfortably protective.[19] They prevented foreign competition, unless the competitors were prepared to make especially for that market, which entailed risk and cost. Even if they did so, the generally domestic character of markets without mutual recognition or harmonization preserves consumer prejudices, making it even harder for the foreigner to gain entry.

[12] *See* K.J. Alter and S. Meunier-Aitshalia, 'Judicial Politics in the European Community: European Integration and the Pathbreaking Cassis de Dijon Decision' (1994) 26 Comp Pol Stud 535.

[13] Weatherill and Beaumont, above at n 10, at 594–98 and Alter and Meunier-Aitshalia, *ibid*.

[14] Alter and Meunier-Aitshalia, *ibid*.

[15] H.-C. Von Heydebrand u.d. Lasa, 'Free Movement of Foodstuffs, Consumer Protection and Food Standards in the European Community: Has the Court of Justice got it Wrong?' (1991) 16 EL Rev 391.

[16] This economic argument is one of the major justifications for mutual recognition in the context of goods in the EU. *See* Weatherill and Beaumont, above at n 10, at 608–09; Joined Cases C–267 and 268/91 *Keck and Mithouard* [1993] ECR I–6097 and Joined Cases C–401 and 402/92 *Tankstation* [1994] ECR I–2199.

[17] *See* S.K. Schmidt, 'The Impact of Mutual Recognition—Inbuilt Limits and Domestic Responses to the Single Market' (2002) 9 JEPP 935.

[18] Von Heydebrand, above at n 15.   [19] Davies, above at n 8, at 65–6.

Under pressure to concede some kind of import possibilities the groups may well have decided that mutual recognition presented less of a threat than harmonization. It seems to leave the national rule, the fundamental market regulatory structure, intact. The possibility of a few odd foreign products at the margins may seem less dramatic than a total overhaul of the product rules. Both parties may be sceptical of how many of these products, with their strange labels and ingredients, there will ever be. At least they have the comfort that their trusted domestic products will continue to be made according to trusted domestic standards, maintaining the cosy relationship between domestic consumer and producer.

In the EU mutual recognition was perhaps more successful than anticipated.[20] It may be that risks never experienced are difficult to calculate, and it is psychologically inevitable that domestic lobbies will *ex ante* see mutual recognition as more palatable than harmonization. There is some discussion of why this may be below. However, if and when mutual recognition succeeds in enabling significant international trade the political dynamic changes, and this is the critical factor in the analysis of how mutual recognition works. Before its application it is seen as a preferable choice. After it comes into effect producers and consumers find that their interests have changed and harmonization has become more desirable.

This balance of interests changes for two reasons. From the point of view of the consumer, once a diversity of standards on the marketplace becomes the norm it starts to look as if there is therefore no standard.[21] The national rule may remain in force for domestic producers, but as a guarantee of product composition it is largely lost. Harmonization then looks more attractive. Any guarantee is better than no guarantee. Mutual recognition has rendered the initially preferred option, of a national guarantee, impossible, and harmonization is the logical second choice. Of course, some consumers may be happy with reading labels or contracts and taking their chances with foreign products,[22] but for the consumer accustomed to a regulated quality marketplace, a flight to harmonization will be a rational reaction to mutual recognition in full bloom.

Producers will make a similar transition in agenda. They will note that the foreign standards may have lower associated production costs, giving their new competitors a market advantage. Harmonization would remove this. Thus, under threat from new competitors harmonization will become a weapon to protect them from 'unfair' competition, where previously they saw

---

[20] The tendency of EU commentators is to emphasize the limits of the principle; e.g. C. Barnard, *The Substantive Law of the EU: The Four Freedoms* (Oxford: OUP, 2004), 508. However, if the comparison is made not with what might be, but with what was, or with what is elsewhere, then the extent of the power and effect of *Cassis* becomes apparent.

[21] Von Heydebrand, above at n 15 and S. Weatherill, 'Recent Case Law Concerning the Free Movement of Goods: Mapping the Frontiers of Market Deregulation' (1999) 36 CMLR 51.

[22] Weatherill, *ibid.*

it as a threat to domestic dominance.[23] Once again, this transition occurs once mutual recognition succeeds in creating a significant amount of trade.

It may be that the initial harmonization is voluntary; states align their national laws as a result of regulatory competition and domestic lobby pressure.[24] Those with high standards wish to avoid disadvantaging domestic industry, while those with low standards wish to avoid exemption clauses being used against them. In this latter case mutual recognition, by raising the possibility of acceptance of domestic standard goods abroad, provokes the state to adjusting those domestic standards to achieve this acceptance. However, voluntary alignment remains an unstable position.[25] The potential for a race to the bottom remains, and for renewed regulatory competition. Thus it does not fully meet the arguments for centralized regulation. On the other hand, since the differences between national laws have been reduced, it does make such regulation much easier to achieve.[26]

Mutual recognition therefore works in two steps. Firstly, it enables trade. Secondly, by doing this, it creates a situation in which harmonization is politically necessary and possible. Mutual recognition is in practice not so much an alternative to harmonization as a methodology to prepare the ground for it; it is the ante-chamber to harmonization.

This process is visible in the EU. In fact, despite the Commission's optimism product harmonization has continued apace since *Cassis*.[27] Indeed, the different national rules on alcohol levels which that case concerned, and which the Court said could be addressed by mutual recognition, have nevertheless since been harmonized.[28] Rather than each case of successful mutual recognition defining an area where no harmonization is necessary, each case of successful mutual recognition tends rather to define an area where domestic lobbies will shortly begin arguing the need for common rules—which will gradually lead to harmonization. Mutual recognition has functioned almost as an educative, discursive tool. It translates market making into concrete examples which involve diverse groups in the integration process. Their instinct seems to be overwhelmingly hostile to the live-and-let-live diversity approach of mutual

---

[23] *See* R. Van der Laan and A. Nentjes, 'Competitive Distortions in EU Environmental Legislation: Inefficiency versus Inequity' (2001) 11 Eur J Law Econ 131.

[24] Sun and Pelkmans, above at n 3, at 67.

[25] A comparison may be made with voluntary convergence based on soft law coordination, which is also increasingly seen as leading to harmonization rather than being a long-term alternative to it. *See* S. Velluti, 'The European Employment Strategy and Enlargement', in T. Tridimas and P. Nebbia (eds), *European Law for the Twenty-First Century—Rethinking the New Legal Order*, Volume 1 (Oxford: Hart, 2004), D. Trubek and L. Trubek, 'Hard and Soft Law in the Construction of Social Europe: The Role of the Open Method of Co-ordination' (2005) 11 ELJ 343 and D. Trubek, P. Cottrell, and M. Nance, ' "Soft law", "Hard Law", and European Integration: Toward a Theory of Hybridity', available at eucenter.wisc.edu/OMC/Papers/EUC/trubeketal.pdf (visited 4 April 2006).

[26] Clarke also notes that the cooperation between governments necessary to operate a successful mutual recognition scheme promotes subsequent harmonization. *See* Clarke, above at n 2.

[27] *See* Nicolaïdis and Egan, above at n 1.

[28] Council Regulation 1576/89 [1989] OJ L160/1.

recognition, and overwhelmingly in favour of certainty and uniformity. Mutual recognition is essentially a philosophy of multiculturalism in products,[29] and the disjunction between an academic or intellectual attraction to this, and a popular aversion, is equally apparent.

Moreover, as well as the continued growth of product standards, mutual recognition has served as the launching pad for a wider range of harmonized rules. As product regulation is equalized other differences between national laws become relatively more important. Partly the removal of standard-based reasons to lobby against foreign products leads producers to look for other arguments, and partly, as any cost differences resulting from different standards are harmonized away, the cost differences resulting from other laws become relatively more important.

Hence in the EU the character of harmonization has changed with the years. Product harmonization continues, but as a relatively technical and uncontroversial activity. The centre of EU market-building is now harmonization to remove distortions of competition.[30] These are rules not directly related to product composition, but which do have an effect on cost of production.[31]

Initial attention was on industry-specific distortions, such as environmental or safety rules of particular importance to certain manufacturing processes, and harmonization in these areas is now the rule. However, matters have gone much further. As each distortion is removed, others become relatively more important, and ever more attention was paid to more general aspects of regulation which nevertheless impacted on competitive advantages.[32] Thus broader environmental and planning rules, and labour law—varying from anti-discrimination rules and maternity leave to health and safety in the workplace—have been the subject of considerable harmonization.[33] Recently enforcement of the law has been a focus of interest—equal rules only make a level-playing field if there is also enforcement on equivalent terms. Provisions of national procedural and contract law, and taxation, are also never far from discussion. While often of great impact on the operating economics of companies, they are also extremely politically sensitive and difficult to harmonize. It takes a high level of integration before countries feel themselves forced to negotiate over such matters. Whether that point is entirely reached is a matter of controversy, but such issues are no longer strange to the Commission's agenda.[34]

---

[29] *See* Nicolaïdis and Schaffer, above at n 6, at 83.

[30] *See* S. Weatherill, 'Why Object to the Harmonisation of Private Law?' (2004) 5 ERPL 633, K. Mortelmans, 'The Relationship between the Treaty Rules and Community Measures for the Establishment and Functioning of the Internal Market—Towards a Concordance Rule' (2002) 39 CMLR, 1303, at 1308–309 and P.J.G. Kapteyn and P. Verloren van Themaat, *Introduction to the Law of the European Communities*, 3rd ed. (London: Kluwer, 1998), 774–83.

[31] Case C–376/98 *Germany v Parliament and Council* [2000] ECR I–8419.   [32] *Ibid.*

[33] *See*, e.g. Kapteyn and Verloren van Themaat, above at n 30.

[34] *See* K. Mortelmans, 'The Common Market, the Internal Market and the Single Market: What's in a Market?' (1998) 35 CMLR 101.

IV. THE TWO DRIVERS: DISHONESTY AND UNPREDICTABILITY

The starting point for this harmonization chain-reaction is a fundamental dishonesty at the heart of mutual recognition. The justification usually given for it is usually that different standards are functionally equivalent, at least to an acceptable degree.[35] They are different but equal. The rationale for accepting foreign standards is that in all important aspects they achieve pretty much the same ends as domestic ones, just in different ways.

This is controversial, since at least in some ways it is often possible to clearly rank standards in a hierarchy of protection. Not everything different is just as good. However, where differences are great enough it is possible to allow exceptions to the general principle, as does EU law. Mutual recognition is an ingredient that does not have to be used to excess.[36]

Nevertheless, this does not solve a more fundamental problem. Functional equivalence is considered, as its name suggests, from the perspective of the user, not the producer. Yet even where two standards can be considered equivalent in functional terms they may well not be equivalent in terms of costs of production. This fact is precisely what leads, or may lead, to regulatory competition. States seek out the rules which achieve the desired level of protection with the least burden on the producer. However, not all states are equally good or fast at competing; this depends on their domestic political processes.

Hence even where mutual recognition is entirely justifiable from the user's perspective it will continue to create pressures for harmonization from the production side. The producer's voice is ignored in the logic of the principle, and this creates an inherent, and in a way creative, tension.

The second important factor in the process that this paper describes is the apparent inability of parties to predict the impact of mutual recognition. Its surprising power relies on it being seen as less threatening than harmonization initially, with that balance reversing as the full impact of its application becomes clear. Why do parties not anticipate this?

In the EU it was because mutual recognition was introduced by the Court of Justice rather than as a result of negotiation by states. Any need for a consensus of involved parties was bypassed. This does render the EU story unique. However, there are reasons to believe that even negotiated mutual recognition may be agreed upon without a full appreciation of the consequences.

For one thing, mutual recognition is a system which magnifies its own importance. By achieving trade it reduces wealth differences which in turn increases the importance of regulatory diversity. The cost advantage of

---

[35] J.H.H. Weiler, 'The Constitution of the Common Market Place: Text and Context in the Evolution of the Free Movement of Goods', in P. Craig and G. de Búrca (eds), *The Evolution of EU Law* (Oxford: OUP, 1999).

[36] Nicolaïdis and Schaffer say that the fundamental mutual recognition question is whether systems are compatible enough for it to work. *See* Nicolaïdis and Schaffer, above at n 6, at 35.

Chinese goods does not largely derive from less burdensome local production rules. One day it might do. Trade will help bring about this day. As well as this, the fact that harmonization of one aspect of regulation increases the importance of others creates a chain reaction of surprising length, as described above. It takes a great deal of vision to see where that path will lead before one has gone down it.

Partly that is because the specific product story may diverge from the general pattern. Mutual recognition does not cause imports of all products to increase significantly, nor trade between all states. It is hard to predict how product markets will change, where a regulatory difference will hugely affect trade and where it will seem to be unimportant. In this post-planning age trade is inherently unpredictable, and *ex ante* review of the effects of mutual recognition on a product market is probably as difficult and as unreliable as *ex ante* constitutional review of legislation. One can never imagine all the ways that things may develop. This is particularly so given that whereas rules may remain static for some time products often do not. Mutual recognition allows producers to adapt their product and relocate to exploit regulatory advantage dynamically.[37] The consequences will therefore not be easily calculated in advance.

More procedurally, consumers and producers may be less involved in negotiation of mutual recognition agreements than they would be in the creation of new harmonized standards. Not only is the technical need for their participation less, but since the national systems are being left largely in place their inclination to be involved may be less too. Indeed, the classical argument for mutual recognition is that it preserves national autonomy to a greater extent, with associated economic and democratic advantages.[38] The premise of this argument is clearly that mutual recognition is a less intrusive and threatening policy than harmonization. Domestic lobbies can be forgiven for accepting this consensus.

Yet in product areas where regulatory competition is of importance its economic effect may be much greater or dramatic than that of harmonization. Harmonization may even result in less trade, by reducing regulatory incentives. Mutual recognition can be by far the broader and deeper integratory approach.

Finally, mutual recognition agreements usually have conditions—general interest clauses that provide for exemptions to the principle. These provide comfort to states and seem to reinforce the myth of equivalence. However, once trade begins the issue of policing comes to the fore—who interprets the exemptions? It may be an international body, or national courts, or arbitrators, but it is unlikely to be governments, since no trading party would accept such a system. These interpreters are operating in a trade environment, and will inevitably take a more or less strict approach to derogation. The outcome

---

[37] *See* similarly Sun and Pelkmans, above at n 3. [38] Nicolaïdis and Schaffer, above at n 6.

of the debate before them is also influenced by the fact that relying on a derogation puts the state on the defensive. They are at a rhetorical and often legal disadvantage before they even begin. Thus exemption clauses promise more than they tend to deliver.[39]

For all these reasons mutual recognition is seductive. The scholarship and outward appearance suggest that for states it is the safe option, and sometimes perhaps it will be. However, it starts a dynamic process of exploitation of regulatory difference that is too multi-polar and chaotic to be predicted, and as trade brings countries closer in wealth and economic ties it will often turn out to have created a situation in which avoidance of harmonization is no longer tenable.

V. IS THERE A LESSON?

The EU embraces this story. It has the legal tools available for a wide range of harmonization measures, and in fact this step-by-step integration of Member States fits its agenda precisely.[40] It is commonly argued that from its inception it made a conscious choice not to integrate everything at once, but to begin with free trade and use this to draw states into closer social and political ties.[41] Mutual recognition and its effects could have been created to implement the post-war European master plan.

However, this suggests that for other regional trade agreements, that may be less politically ambitious, mutual recognition is a dangerous toy. It sucks states in to a place where they may not want to be. Once the economic integration is advanced it is difficult to avoid harmonization, even involving social and political matters, yet the economic integration is difficult to undo.[42] A humane mousetrap is created, in which states can only go forward. On the other hand, it would be too narrow to say that therefore mutual recognition should be avoided. Without it, it is difficult to achieve economic integration, with the many benefits that this brings.

The first question that other RTAs, or the WTO, should ask is how far the story above is specifically European. Could it really play out in the same way in other contexts?[43] Certainly an argument could be made that a passion for

---

[39] *See* P. Craig and G. de Búrca, *EU Law*, 3rd ed. (Oxford: OUP 2003), 638–39 and Barnard, above at n 20, at 107.

[40] Nicolaïdis and Egan (above at n 1), describe the importance of such institutional factors in the implementation of mutual recognition.

[41] *See* Craig and de Búrca, above at n 39, at 5–7.

[42] Nicolaïdis and Schaffer, above at n 6, at 51.

[43] The Australia–New Zealand mutual recognition system is discussed in the Government of Australia Productivity Commission Research Report, *Evaluation of the Mutual Recognition Schemes* (Canberra, 2003), available at www.pc.gov.au/study/mra/finalreport/mra.pdf (visited 4 April 2006) and Q. Hay, 'Trans-Tasman Mutual Recognition: A New Dimension in Australia–New Zealand Legal Relations' (1997) 3 ITL Rev 6. Hay notes that there is pressure resulting for voluntary harmonization of national measures.

precise regulation of matters that are not life-and-death, but primarily to do with expectation and satisfaction, is a particularly European characteristic, as is a tendency to squabble and an instinctive desire for uniformity. A case could be made that particularly European traits have driven both the failure to harmonize initially and the violence of the reaction against regulatory competition.

Yet the alternative is probably more convincing. One could equally say that if Europe, with its cultural similarity, cannot agree on harmonized rules, and cannot find the trust and tolerance to operate a stable mutual recognition rule, then what region can? Moreover, the behaviour of the European actors can be understood in terms of rational self-interest, and the pressures they have experienced as a result of mutual recognition are not essentially context-specific.

If there is a specifically European element it seems less likely to be culture than circumstances, which may have meant that regulatory competition was and remains particularly impactful there. A number of factors determine the impact of regulatory competition. The primary one is probably relative wealth. Where there are great differences these swamp regulatory costs. Also important are the characteristics of the products—services and consumer goods may be areas where standards are central to the market structure. Finally, other regulatory or cost differences, such as transport and tax and planning regulation will affect the impact of a given standard or rule.

In Europe, countries of similar wealth engage in complex trade of which a large part is consumer goods and services. Comparative advantage is sometimes very slight, and there is great potential for a given rule to have significant impact. By contrast, WTO attention is focused to a greater extent on maximizing the benefits of trade between countries of significantly different wealth and circumstances, not to say resources or structure. This kind of trade is such that mutual recognition may be efficient without being destructive. It is simple law, and the inequalities it creates may be of marginal importance, while practical matters may be made easier.

The challenge for the WTO, and for other RTAs, is one of prediction. How fast will countries become economically similar, and at what point will regulatory competition become an issue? Precisely a system where it is not of great importance is one where mutual recognition can be most seductive, yet this can in the long term maximize its impact—it becomes established and entrenched so that parties become accustomed to it, and will only realize its threat to their interest after that becomes concrete.

Perhaps therefore the WTO and other RTAs should ask a second question; given that the effects of mutual recognition cannot fully be foreseen, and that there is a real risk of an EU-style suck-in in the medium or longer-term, do they or their Member States have the capacity to cope with that politically difficult situation? As the referendum in France on the EU constitution showed, unmanaged regulatory competition is politically destabilizing. Therefore any trade system that creates trade before it creates harmonization has to face the possibility that in the future it will have to create frameworks for rules far beyond mere trade itself, but extending to the circumstances surrounding production.[44] That is so sensitive that it requires both political will and maturity. A failure of states to engage on this level will either lead to enormous political backlash as countries are laid waste by competition, or unilateral imposition of trade barriers, and a potential unravelling of the trade system, with all the economic consequences that entails.[45] In short, however much trade may make everyone richer in the long term, while that point is being reached it creates winners and losers, and to think that the effects of this can be managed by a purely economic international legal framework seems, on the basis of the EU experience, naive.

VI. A THIRD WAY

Mutual recognition represents economic integration without social or political integration; trade without other common laws. It is ultimately rooted in ideas of tolerance and diversity, and its attraction is obvious and powerful. Yet it does not seem to be a stable long-term policy. The idea that states can retain autonomy while being open to each other is a myth. Nor is it even, on closer examination, such an attractive myth. A criticism of multi-culturalism is that it can easily topple into neglect and lack of interest, and 'different but side-by-side' can become 'side-by-side but far away'. Such isolation of parties who in fact need each other is dangerous. Mutual understanding and trust suffer, and the risk is that when conflicts arise the basis for dealing with them rationally is not in place, and they can escalate.

Whether it be human rights, the environment, labour conditions, or taxation, countries that trade with each other have an important interest in each other's rules, and while total harmonization may not be either realistic or desirable, mutual recognition is simply a form of avoidance of the problem, with all the risks that that brings: the problem will return later, in a more pressing form.

In practice this means that trade bodies who do not wish to look back on

---

[44] Nicolaïdis and Schaffer note that mutual recognition of production regulation is implicit in trade. Until recently this was a non-issue. By contrast, mutual recognition of the standards of the traded goods and services was unusual. The current trend is to reverse this position; mutual recognition of product standards, or of policing of those standards, is increasing, whereas extra-territorial conditions are increasingly being imposed on the circumstances surrounding production, i.e. import is made conditional upon human rights or environmental principles being respected at source. If this harmonization pressure results partly from increasing trade, as seems likely, and mutual recognition is partly responsible for that increase, as also seems likely, then their description fits the thesis of this paper. *See* Nicolaïdis and Schaffer, above at n 6.

[45] *See* R. Dehousse, 'Completing the Internal Market: Institutional Constraints and Challenges', in R. Bieber et al. (eds), *1992: One European Market?: A Critical Analysis of the Commission's Internal Market Strategy* (Baden-Baden: Nomos 1998), 336.

their articles of free trade as extended political suicide notes, but who are not in a realistic position to engage in widespread harmonization, must look for a third way. To some extent the EU offers a tentative example here. Partly this is through techniques of harmonization—framework harmonization which allows some national diversity, and minimum harmonization which limits the impact of regulatory competition are both ways in which it has attempted to react to the conflict under discussion here.[46] However, in recent years assessment of both techniques has tended to conclude that their success is at best limited.[47] They bring a large part, sometimes just as much, of the bureaucratic and political costs of complete harmonization, to reduce, but not remove, the problem. Yet is in the nature of cost competition that if differences are made smaller everywhere then smaller differences will become more important. The sense of threat from regulatory competition does not seem to have been in any way diminished by these partial protection measures. On the contrary, such measures can be seen as enacting partial mutual recognition and regulatory competition, and as such they have worked in the same way as *Cassis*—trade is increased, and so is consequent panic about differences.

A different approach which has attracted hope and attention recently, although it is too early to draw conclusions, is the open method of coordination.[48] This is a form of semi-formalized discussion and peer review. In certain areas of policy Member States retain autonomy but agree on certain general goals and meet regularly to discuss their achievements and learn from each other. Whether this process achieves much, and certainly whether it can ever be a communicative channel to rival the many other ways in which governments and policy-makers learn from each other, is open to question.[49] However, it can also be understood as partially reflecting a desire to finesse the brutal choice between centralized rule making and regulatory war. Perhaps there can be convergence that avoids the worst effects of regulatory competition on a voluntary and gradual basis, without conceding regulatory power to a third party, even one owned by the states. Moreover, maybe the process can be begun before the economic pressure reaches its peak. The politicians can perhaps anticipate the economic needs, avoiding the situation where they are merely reacting to regulatory competition-driven crisis—the situation of Germany and France today—and thus giving them greater opportunity to reflect, plan, and be prepared. Such fora for discussion may, insofar as they are

[46] *See* M. Dougan, 'Minimum Harmonization and the Internal Market' (2000) 37 CMLR 853 and B. Kurcz, 'Harmonisation by Means of Directives—Never Ending Story?' (2001) 12 EBL Rev 287.

[47] *Ibid.*, P. Rott, 'Minimum Harmonization for the Completion of the Internal Market? The Example of Consumer Sales Law' (2003) 40 CMLR 1107, P.J. Slot, 'Harmonisation' (1996) 21 EL Rev 378 and A. McGee and S. Weatherill, 'The Evolution of the Single Market—Harmonisation or Liberalisation?' (1990) 53 MLR 578.

[48] D. Ashiagbor, 'Soft Harmonisation: The Open Method of Co-ordination in the European Employment Strategy' (2004) 10 EPL 305.

[49] J. Mosher and D. Trubek, 'EU Social Policy and the European Employment Strategy' (2003) 41 JCMS 63.

understood as reflecting a desire for such a convergence process, or at least consideration of it, have an impact beyond the conversations within their walls. They may influence and restructure broader debates.

Talk is not cheap. There are political obstacles to putting broader harmonization of rules on the agenda, even if the aim is no more than to create a forum to discuss the feasibility of voluntary convergence. However, the obstacles may not be insurmountable, and the price of introducing fora of these types into the WTO and other RTAs may be repaid manyfold if states are better prepared for regulatory competition crises when they come.[50]

VII. CONCLUSION

Whether or not voluntary coordination offers a true alternative, the dichotomy between mutual recognition and harmonization is false anyway. The more real choice is between pre-trade harmonization or post-trade harmonization (or no trade).

The first is difficult to agree, slow, and likely to be inefficient. Great energy may be invested in standards that do not in fact lead to great trade, for other reasons, such as changing economic circumstances or consumer tastes. On the other hand, it does give Member States control, and makes the progress towards free trade a managed one.

Post-trade harmonization, following mutual recognition-led trade, is not only a much more effective way of creating a free trade environment, but it ensures that harmonization is led by need. Harmonization efforts will be focussed on areas and products where mutual recognition has caused significant trade. Products that are not exchanged to any great extent can perhaps be left to trickle over the border in their non-harmonized state. Of course, if the very fact of differences in regulation is a major motor behind the trade then harmonization will reduce the trade flows created by mutual recognition. In some products and markets this may be the case, but in the majority the differences between regulatory environments and standards are probably enough to distress producers without themselves generating a significant market that would not otherwise exist. On the other hand, once the choice is made for post-trade harmonization, Member States begin a journey to an unknown destination. Even the EU, with its commitment to integration is finding the public reaction within Member States to trade-led harmonization difficult to manage.

The most plausible conclusion is therefore this: if there is going to be trade, there will be far-reaching harmonization and the only real question is how fast. Structures such as the WTO, which propose pure trade agreements, will

---

[50] *See* A.T. Guzman, 'Global Governance and the WTO' (2004) 45 Harv Int L J 303 on the need to address non-trade issues within the WTO framework, and J.O. McGinnis and M.L. Movsesian, 'Against Global Governance in the WTO' (2004) 45 Harv Int L J 353, replying to his arguments.

either be ineffective or unstable. The EU, with its highly accelerated history, is therefore both an example and a warning of where other trade agreements are likely to be heading towards.

The risk that trade systems face is that a failure to accept this leads to future instability. The upside is perhaps that, if the risk is faced, trade may provide a means to address other issues of international concern. Discussing non-trade issues as such may provoke arguments about national autonomy. Linking them to trade may provide a way round this. Certainly it has in the EU.

There are of course risks in this too. The danger is that non-trade issues are looked at in a narrowly economic way. Nevertheless, one may speculate from the European experience that the greatest impact of the WTO in the long term may be in entwining nations messily with each other, and so paving the way for global governance.

12

The WTO and Regional Trade Agreements as Competing Fora for Constitutional Reforms: Trade and Human Rights

ERNST-ULRICH PETERSMANN

STATE-CENTRED OR CONSTITUTIONAL APPROACHES TO WTO LAW: DOES IT MATTER?

The customary rules of international treaty interpretation (e.g. Article 5 VCLT) and the jurisprudence of international courts recognize that the 'contractual dimensions' of international agreements (e.g. the GATT and GATS schedules of reciprocal commitments) may require interpretative approaches (e.g. judicial protection of 'non-violation complaints' aimed at maintaining the reciprocal 'balance of concessions') that may not be warranted for interpreting the 'constitutional dimensions' of agreements constituting and limiting international organizations for the collective supply of global public goods. For instance, a 'contractual reading' of the WTO Dispute Settlement Understanding (DSU) may suggest that WTO Members intended to limit the adjudicative powers and applicable law in WTO dispute settlement proceedings to 'the covered agreements' (Articles 1, 7 DSU); a 'constitutional interpretation' of WTO law as part of the international legal system may argue, however, that the explicit recognition, in numerous WTO provisions, of 'basic principles underlying this multilateral trading system' (Preamble of the WTO) requires interpreting WTO rules in conformity with other principles of international law. The customary methods of treaty interpretation also recognize (e.g. in the Preamble of the VCLT) 'respect for, and observance of, human rights and fundamental freedoms for all' as a general principle of modern international law. This contribution examines the relevance of non-economic objectives (*Section I*), 'constitutional approaches' (*Section II*) and of the human rights

obligations of all WTO Members for regional trade agreements (RTAs) and
WTO law (*Section III*); it concludes (in *Section IV*) that WTO rules and RTAs
should be seen as competing *fora* not only for trade liberalization, but also for
constitutional reforms inside trading countries.

Most WTO Members justify the WTO's treatment of reciprocal trade liberalization—based on most favored nation treatment as a non-discriminatory
first-best policy and on RTAs as *second-best* policies—on grounds of economic
efficiency and non-discriminatory conditions of competition. This 'contractual
interpretation' does not explain the empirical fact that many RTAs—not only
in Europe, but also in the Americas, Africa, and Asia—progressively move
from trade and economic liberalization to *domestic policy coordination* and
foreign policy coordination (notably in customs unions like the EC). The
more than 60 RTAs concluded since the failure of the 2003 WTO Ministerial
Conference to advance the worldwide Doha Round negotiations confirm that
many WTO Members perceive bilateralism or regionalism as *policy alternatives* to lengthy WTO negotiations. The WTO and RTA provisions on dispute
settlement (e.g. forum choice in RTAs of the United States, exclusive dispute
settlement fora in European RTAs) further illustrate the importance of legal
policy objectives. To the extent RTAs are used for political and legal reasons
(e.g. for promoting peaceful cooperation and dispute settlement, rule of law,
high human rights standards in a limited region), WTO negotiations focusing
only on the *economic* dimensions of RTAs may fail.

I. NON-ECONOMIC JUSTIFICATIONS OF WTO RULES AND RTAS

The European Community progressively evolved from a customs union and
common market to an economic and monetary union which, since the 1977
Joint Declaration on Human Rights adopted by the Parliament, Council, and
Commission of the EC, increasingly emphasized the need for respect for human
rights and democratic governance by all EC institutions and EC Member
States.[1] Since the 1990s, it became official European Union (EU) policy to
include 'human rights clauses' in all new trade and cooperation agreements
with third countries.[2] Also in Africa and in the Americas, an increasing number of RTAs explicitly refer to human rights as an objective or fundamental
principle of economic integration, or implicitly limit membership to countries
committed to protection of human rights.[3] Such legal and economic linkages

---

[1] *See* A. Williams, *EU Human Rights Policies: A Study in Irony* (Oxford: OUP, 2004).
[2] *See* L. Bartels, *Human Rights Conditionality in the EU's International Agreements* (Oxford:
OUP, 2005).
[3] *See* the contributions by S.F. Musungu, 'International Trade and Human Rights in Africa: A
Comment on Conceptual Linkages' and by F.J. Garcia, 'Integrating Trade and Human Rights in
the Americas' to F. Abbott, C. Breining-Kaufmann, and T. Cottier (eds), *International Trade and
Human Rights* (Michigan, U Michigan Press, 2006), Chs 15 and 16.

between trade rules and human rights reflect both the longstanding economic insight that trade and economic welfare are only *instruments* for enabling and promoting individual freedom as the ultimate goal of economic life and the most efficient means of realizing general welfare,[4] and the idea that the rule of law and respect for human rights (such as freedom of information and expression, freedom of profession, property rights) are also legal preconditions for the proper functioning of markets and for the realization of many trade policy objectives (such as reduction of transaction costs, non-discriminatory conditions of competition, legal security, consumer welfare).[5]

In the Preamble to the WTO Agreement, all WTO Members commit themselves to 'the basic principles and . . . objectives underlying this multilateral trading system,' including the objective of 'sustainable development'. As every WTO Member has ratified one or more UN human rights conventions, the explicit WTO commitment to sustainable development should be interpreted in conformity with the universally recognized 'right to development' and the human rights obligations of WTO Members.[6] The 2004 WTO Appellate Body report on *EC—Tariff Preferences*, for example, prompted the EC to offer special incentives—in its 2005 EC system for generalized tariff preferences (GSP)—depending on whether less-developed countries (LDCs) 'ratify and effectively implement' International Labour Organization (ILO) and UN human rights conventions and whether tariff preferences can effectively address the development and trade needs of LDCs in their implementation of ILO labour standards and UN human rights conventions.[7] Similar human rights justifications of tariff preferences could also be made in the examination of the WTO consistency of RTAs. Both WTO rules (such as the 2001 Protocol on the accession of China) and many RTAs have proven to be 'transformation agreements' of crucial importance for peaceful cooperation in Europe, rule of law, independent courts, and protection of private rights in many other regions and countries (like China).

---

[4] On 'development as freedom' and substantive 'opportunity to achieve', *see* A. Sen, *Rationality and Freedom* (Cambridge, MA: HUP, 2002), Ch 17 on 'markets and freedoms' and E.-U. Petersmann (ed), *Developing Countries in the Doha Round*, (Florence: EUI, 2005), 3–18. *See also* F.A. Hayek, *The Constitution of Liberty* (Chicago, IL: U Chicago Press, 1960), 35: 'Economic considerations are merely those by which we reconcile and adjust our different purposes, none of which, in the last resort, are economic (except those of the miser or the man for whom making money has become an end in itself)'.

[5] These interrelationships are explained in various contributions to the books by Abbott, Breining-Kaufmann and Cottier, above at n 3 and T. Cottier, J. Pauwelyn and E. Bürgi (eds), *Human Rights and International Trade* (Oxford: OUP, 2005).

[6] *See* E.-U. Petersmann, 'Human Rights and the Law of the WTO' (2003) 37 JWT, 241; *ibid.*, 'Human Rights and International Trade Law—Defining and Connecting the Two Fields', in Cottier, Pauwelyn and Bürgi, *ibid.*, at 29–94.

[7] WTO Appellate Body Report, *EC—Tariff Preferences*, WT/DS246/AB/R, adopted 20 April 2004, paras 163–64). Council Regulation 980/2005 of 27 June 2005 on the EC's new GSP scheme for 2006–2015 [2005] OJ L169/1 was explicitly designed to reflect 'the integral nature of the concept of sustainable development' as defined by the Appellate Body, *see* J. Harrison, 'Incentives for Development: The EC's Generalized System of Preferences, India's WTO Challenge and Reform' (2005) 42 CMLR 1663.

The universal recognition of human rights, and the acceptance of 'human rights clauses' in an ever larger number of RTAs among WTO Members, are likely to increasingly influence the interpretation of WTO rules. The customary rules of international treaty interpretation require taking into account 'any relevant rules of international law applicable in the relations between the parties' (Article 31(3)(c) VCLT), including the universal human rights obligations of WTO Members. Yet, human rights also require respect for the legitimate diversity of human rights and democratic traditions at national and regional levels, which help to explain the diversity of 'constitutional approaches' and of the legal regulation of RTAs (Section II). Section III concludes by arguing that the legal relevance of human rights for the interpretation of WTO rules in WTO dispute settlement proceedings might differ depending on whether they are invoked (1) by the complainant or by the defendant, (2) for the protection of human rights at home or abroad, and (3) in support of discriminatory or non-discriminatory trade measures; notably, WTO rules and policies must distinguish between *national (unilateral)* and *internationally agreed* human rights standards, and should accord more deference to 'defensive' uses of human rights as a justification of import restrictions protecting domestic citizens *at home* than to 'offensive' uses of human rights as a justification of trade sanctions or trade preferences *vis-à-vis* third countries in order to promote human rights *abroad* in foreign countries with different constitutional traditions.

II. THE WTO AGREEMENT AS PART OF THE INTERNATIONAL LEGAL ORDER: STATE-CENTRED VS HUMAN RIGHTS APPROACHES AND CONSTITUTIONAL APPROACHES

The Westphalian system of international law evolved as a power-oriented system focusing on state sovereignty and 'order' rather than on justice and human rights.[8] WTO jurisprudence interprets WTO rules as parts of international law and may soon be confronted with legal claims that WTO obligations are to be construed and applied with due regard to the human rights obligations of WTO Members. As goods and services are produced and consumed by individuals, WTO dispute settlement panels have emphasized that 'one of the primary objects of the GATT/WTO . . . is to produce certain market conditions which would allow . . . individual activity to flourish' by protecting the international division of labour against discriminatory trade restrictions and other distortions.[9] WTO law differs from most other

---

[8] On the pursuit of order rather than 'justice' in international relations *see* R. Foot, J.L. Gaddis, and A. Hurrel (eds), *Order and Justice in International Relations* (Oxford: OUP, 2003) and J.L. Goldsmith and E.A. Posner, *The Limits of International Law* (Oxford: OUP, 2005).

[9] *See* WTO Panel Report, *US—Section 301 Trade Act*, WT/DS152/R, adopted 27 January 2000, para. 7.73 *et seq.*

international agreements by extending the legal protection of private freedoms across national frontiers. The WTO commitments (e.g. in TRIPS) for the protection of private rights, and the explicit guarantees—in the 2001 WTO Protocol on the accession of China—of private 'rights to trade' (including 'rights to import and export goods') and of individual access to judicial remedies in China[10] illustrate that many WTO rules pursue not only intergovernmental 'foreign policy functions' for the protection of rights and obligations among governments, but also 'domestic policy functions' for the protection of private freedom of trade, legal security, and property rights.[11]

A. 'Realist' Approaches to WTO Law and Human Rights

Most states and governments adopt a 'realist approach' to international relations and perceive international law as a system based on 'sovereign equality of states' and the pursuit of state interests. Intergovernmental organizations are viewed as mere frameworks for intergovernmental bargaining driven by national interests and by the relative power of governments. From such a 'realist perspective', the agenda of intergovernmental negotiations is legitimately shaped by national interests and bargaining power. Realists argue that human rights are deliberately not mentioned in WTO law; the disregard for human rights in many WTO Members should not be an impediment for welfare-increasing trade liberalization and trade regulation in the WTO. The restrictions of the trade opportunities of LDCs are explained by the lack of active participation of LDCs in past GATT and WTO negotiations, i.e. they are viewed as political rather than legal problems of the WTO. Most governments believe that—in order to facilitate the WTO's task of liberalizing international trade as a means for 'enhancing human welfare', 'reducing the prices of basic consumer goods', and promoting 'exposure of governments and their citizens to an international institutional framework dedicated to openness'[12]—protection of human rights and labour standards should be left to specialized agencies. However, such 'realist approaches' and opposition by WTO diplomats to explicit linkages of WTO rules with human rights have been increasingly challenged by human rights activists and UN human rights bodies which continue to call for a 'human rights approach to international trade'.

---

[10] *See* WTO Doc. WT/L/432, 23 November 2001, Part I, section 2 (D).

[11] On these diverse foreign policy functions, domestic policy functions and constitutional functions of certain GATT and WTO rules *see* E.-U. Petersmann, *Constitutional Functions and Constitutional Problems of International Economic Law* (Fribourg, Switzerland: University Press, 1991), Ch 7.

[12] These three objectives are emphasized in the recent 'Sutherland Report' on *The Future of the WTO: Addressing Institutional Challenges in the New Millennium* (Geneva: WTO, 2004), 10.

B. UN Proposals for a 'Human Rights Approach to Trade'

In a number of recent reports on the human rights dimensions of various WTO Agreements, the UN High Commissioner has called for a 'human rights approach to trade'.[13] These reports underline that, what are referred to—in numerous WTO provisions—as *rights* of WTO Members to regulate, may be *duties* to regulate under human rights law (e.g. so as to protect and fulfil human rights of access to water, food, essential medicines, basic health care, and education services at affordable prices). The UN reports neither propose inserting human rights provisions into WTO law nor specify what changes in WTO rules and institutions may be required to realize a 'human rights approach to trade'. However, in a consultant report, Robert Howse has claimed that mainstreaming the right into the WTO 'actually yields a very concrete agenda for transformation of practice and structure' and 'reorientation of the WTO project' including:

– determination of the negotiating agenda and gains from trade in terms of their contribution to the meeting of human needs as reflected in human rights;
– more open consultation and deliberation processes at domestic and WTO levels with civil society, parliamentarians and other non-governmental actors (NGOs) so as to take into account the rights and views of citizens (e.g. in the Trade Policy Review Mechanism of the WTO) and ensure 'direct citizen access to the process of international policy-making';
– inclusion of UN human rights institutions in the delivery of WTO technical assistance programs;
– sensitizing governments and civil society (which may submit *amicus curiae* briefs in WTO dispute settlement proceedings) about the possibilities for invoking human rights in WTO proceedings and in elaborating a more convincing ethos of the WTO community.[14]

The now regular inter-parliamentary meetings of representatives from national parliaments during WTO Ministerial Conferences, the annual public seminars organized by the WTO with WTO trade diplomats and NGOs on topical subjects of international trade law and policies, the increasing transparency of WTO publications (e.g. on the WTO website), and some of the negotiating proposals in the Doha Round negotiations (e.g. for opening

---

[13] UN Doc. E/CN.4/Sub.2/2002/9 of 25 June 2002, p 2. For a discussion of the various UN reports *see*: E.-U. Petersmann, 'The Human Rights Approach Advocated by the UN High Commissioner for Human Rights and by the ILO: Is It Relevant for WTO Law and Policy?' (2004) 7 JIEL 605.

[14] Mainstreaming the right to development into international trade law and policy at the WTO, UN Doc. E/CN.4/Sub.2/2004/17, 9 June 2004. For earlier such proposals, *see* Report of the 71st Conference of the ILA in Berlin 2004 (London 2004), at 543–47; Report of the 70th Conference of the ILA in New Delhi 2002 (London 2002), at 672–75 and Report of the 69th ILA Conference at London 2000 (London 2000), at 184–85.

meetings of WTO dispute settlement panels and the Appellate Body to the public) reflect the increasing awareness of WTO Members for the need to enhance the transparency, democratic legitimacy, and accountability of the WTO.[15] Yet WTO bodies refer to human rights only rarely (e.g. in the 2003 'waiver decision' for the Kimberley Protocol on the control of conflict diamonds), and have refrained from any official response to the UN initiatives for a human rights approach to trade. Likewise, UN human rights conventions nowhere address the importance of international trade rules for reducing poverty and for empowering individuals to satisfy their basic needs through a welfare-increasing, worldwide division of labour.

Also legal experts fail to agree on whether, and to what extent, the limited jurisdiction of WTO panels and Appellate Body includes the right to apply international as well as regional or national human rights law (e.g. as relevant legal context for interpreting WTO rules if they are invoked by national or regional authorities as legal justification for limiting and regulating imported goods and services or trade-related intellectual property rights at home). Just as national laws, RTAs, and worldwide treaties legitimately differ in their approaches to the regulation of economic freedom and human rights, so are the related practices of national, regional, and worldwide courts characterized by different judicial approaches and 'balancing principles' depending on the different legal and constitutional context of the respective systems and institutions.[16] International consensus on the relevance of human rights for WTO rules and policies is further impeded by the different constitutional and human rights approaches to economic and social regulation in the various regions of the world.[17]

Like the UN initiatives for a human rights approach to trade, the WTO must focus on the *international law perspective*, without prejudice to diverse national or regional perspectives on human rights and trade law which may legitimately vary among countries.[18] As governments protect human rights and apply WTO rules primarily in the context of *national* laws and institutions, WTO judges have to respect the broad margin of appreciation which

---

[15] *See* P. Lamy, 'Economic, Social and Cultural Rights in the context of the Development Activities of International Organizations', Geneva, 7 May 2001 (on file with this author).

[16] On these different levels of regulation and 'balancing principles' *see* E.-U. Petersmann, 'Constitutional Approaches to International Law: Interrelationships between National, International and Cosmopolitan Constitutional Rules', in J. Bröhmer et al (eds), *Internationale Gemeinschaft und Menschenrechte* (Berlin: Carl Heymanns Verlag, 2005), 207–22.

[17] On differences between UN and European constitutional and human rights traditions *see* Petersmann, above at n 6. On the 'federal rejection', but 'state protection' of economic and social rights in the US, *see* J.M. Woods and H. Lewis, *Human Rights and the Global Marketplace. Economic, Social and Cultural Dimensions* (Ardsley, NY: Transnational Publishers, 2004), Ch 10.C.

[18] These legitimate differences among national, regional and worldwide levels of human rights and of trade rules and policies were not adequately taken into account in the criticism by P. Alston, 'Resisting the Merger and Acquisition of Human Rights by Trade Law' (2002) 13 EJIL 815; *see* E.-U. Petersmann, 'Taking Human Dignity, Poverty and Empowerment of Individuals More Seriously: Rejoinder to Alston' (2002) 13 EJIL 845.

UN law and WTO law leave to governments for implementing their international legal obligations inside their respective constitutional systems in conformity with their often diverse democratic preferences, social needs, and legitimate traditions. UN and WTO bodies also have to respect the reality that regional human rights conventions and RTAs often go far beyond the worldwide minimum standards prescribed in UN human rights conventions and WTO law.

C. Constitutional Approaches to International Law: Lessons from Europe?

Most WTO Members have adopted constitutions that constitute and limit government powers, subject governments to constitutional restraints, and commit government policies to respect for human rights. The more governments cooperate internationally for the collective supply of 'international public goods', the more multilevel governance in international organizations is leading to multilevel legal restraints on national policy powers. Since the Constitution Establishing the ILO of 1919, many constituent agreements of international organizations such as the World Health Organization (WHO) and the UN Educational, Scientific and Cultural Organization (UNESCO) are named 'constitutions' in view of the fact that, e.g. they:

(1) constitute a new legal order with legal primacy over that of the Member States;
(2) create new legal subjects and hierarchically structured institutions with limited governance powers;
(3) provide for institutional checks and balances (e.g. among rule-making, administrative and dispute settlement bodies in the WTO);
(4) legally limit the rights of Member States (e.g. regarding withdrawal, amendment procedures, dispute settlement procedures);
(5) provide for the collective supply of 'public goods' that—as in the case of the above-mentioned treaty constitutions (of the ILO, WHO, and UNESCO)—are partly defined in terms of human rights (such as core labour rights, the human rights to health, and education); and often
(6) operate as 'living constitutions' whose functions—albeit limited in scope and membership—increasingly evolve in response to changing needs for international cooperation.

The worldwide 'treaty constitutions' differ fundamentally from national constitutions by their limited policy functions and much less effective constitutional restraints (e.g., on intergovernmental and national policy powers). State-centred international lawyers therefore prefer to speak of 'international institutional law'[19] or of an intergovernmental 'constitutionalism

---

[19] *See* N. Blokker and H.G. Schermers, *International Institutional Law*, 4th ed. (Boston, Mass: Martinus Nijhoff, 2003).

lite'.[20] From citizen-oriented economic and constitutional perspectives, however, international organizations have become no less necessary for the collective supply of public goods than national organizations. Human rights require designing national and international governance as an integrated, multilevel constitutional framework for the protection of citizen rights, democratic self-government and cooperation among free citizens across frontiers. *International constitutionalism* is a functionally limited, but necessary complement to *national constitutionalism* which, only together, can protect human rights and democratic self-government more effectively across frontiers in a globally integrating world. In Europe, multilevel trade governance and multilevel constitutionalism have become a reality that is no longer contested by governments, parliaments, courts, and citizens, notwithstanding the continuing differences of view on whether, and to what extent, EC citizens and EC Member States should be entitled to judicial protection by the EC courts against the frequent violations by EC institutions of their WTO obligations.[21]

None of the supporters of 'international constitutionalism' claims that international 'treaty constitutions' constituting and limiting international rule-making, executive, and judicial powers for the collective supply of international public goods are, or should become, constitutions in the same sense as national constitutions. In line with the diverse national constitutional traditions, constitutional approaches to multilevel governance differ inevitably. Some use the notion of a 'WTO constitution' in view of:

(1) the comprehensive rule-making, executive and (quasi-) judicial powers of WTO institutions;[22]
(2) the 'constitutionalization' of WTO law resulting from the jurisprudence of the WTO dispute settlement bodies;[23]

---

[20] *See* J. Klabbers, 'Constitutionalism Lite' (2004) 1 Int Org L Rev 31, at 45. On the general recognition of multilevel constitutionalism in Europe *see* C. Joerges and E.-U. Petersmann (eds), *Constitutionalism, Multilevel Trade Governance and Social Regulation* (Oxford: Hart, 2006).

[21] Notwithstanding the longstanding EC jurisprudence that GATT and WTO obligations form an 'integral part of the Community legal system' binding on all EC institutions and judicially enforceable *vis-à-vis* EC Member States, the Court consistently denies 'direct effects' of GATT and WTO rules as well as judicial protection of EC citizens and EC Member States against violations of WTO rules by EC institutions. Unsurprisingly, the EC legal services support this power-oriented, judicial self-restraint *vis-à-vis* the EC's violations of WTO law, *see* P.J. Kuijper and M. Bronckers 'WTO Law in the European Court of Justice' (2005) 42 CMLR 1313; Kuijper claims 'that it is rarely or never possible to speak of a sufficiently serious breach of WTO law' by the EC justifying intervention by the EC Court (at 1334), and welcomes that also 'the *Nakajima* doctrine has never really been applied . . . because this doctrine . . . (is) untenable on grounds of legal logic' (at 1340). The frequent disregard by the EC's 'guardians of law' *vis-à-vis* WTO law, and the lack of effective parliamentary and judicial control of the EC's trade policy powers, illustrate the 'constitutional deficits' of the EC's foreign trade law.

[22] *See* J.H. Jackson, *The World Trade Organisation: Constitution and Jurisprudence* (London: Royal Institute of International Affairs, 1998).

[23] *See* D.Z. Cass, 'The "Constitutionalization" of International Trade Law: Judicial Norm-Generation as the Engine of Constitutional Development in International Trade' (2001) 12 EJIL 39.

(3) the domestic 'constitutional functions' of WTO rules, for example, for protecting constitutional principles (like freedom, non-discrimination, rule of law, proportionality of government restrictions) and domestic democracy (for example, by limiting the power of protectionist interest groups) for the benefit of transnational cooperation among free citizens;[24]

(4) the international 'constitutional functions' of WTO rules, for example, for the promotion of 'international participatory democracy' (e.g. by holding governments internationally accountable for the 'external effects' of their national trade policies, by enabling countries to participate in the policy-making of other countries)[25] and of the enhancement of 'jurisdictional competition among nation states'[26] and 'the allocation of authority between constitutions';[27] or

(5) in view of the necessity of 'constitutional approaches' for a proper understanding of the law of comprehensive international organizations which use the term 'constitution', as well as constitutional methods and principles, for more than 80 years (see, e.g. the 'Constitutions' of the ILO, WHO, FAO, EU).[28]

All these constitutional approaches agree that the WTO should not be simply viewed in narrow *economic* terms (for example, as an institution promoting economic welfare through trade liberalization). WTO rules and policies also pursue *political* as well as *legal* objectives that are no less important than the economic benefits from liberal trade, as illustrated by the guarantees of private 'rights to import and export', of private access to independent courts and rule of law in the 2001 WTO Protocol on the accession of China. The introduction of rule of law in China and of a system of independent trade courts (supervised by a chamber of the Chinese Supreme Court specialized in WTO law) illustrates that the WTO Agreement is one of the most revolutionary 'transformation agreements' in the history of international law.

The progressive transformation of the intergovernmental EC Treaty rules into constitutional and judicial guarantees of individual rights was largely the result of the struggle of citizens and courts (including the EC Court and European Court of Human Rights) against welfare-reducing abuses of foreign

---

[24] *See* Petersmann, above at n 11 and J.O. McGinnis and M.L. Movsesian, 'The World Trade Constitution' (2000) 114 Harv L Rev 511. Gerhart contrasts the 'inward-looking, economic vision of the WTO' in helping Member Countries addressing internal political failures with the 'external, participatory vision of the WTO' helping WTO Members to address concerns raised by policy decisions in other countries: P.M. Gerhart, 'The Two Constitutional Visions of the World Trade Organisation' (2003) 24 U Pa J Int Econ L 1.

[25] *See*, for example, P.M. Gerhart, 'The WTO and Participatory Democracy: The Historical Evidence' (2004) 37 Vanderbilt J Transnatl L 897.

[26] *See* J.O. McGinnis, 'The WTO as a Structure of Liberty' (2004) 28 Harv J L & Pub Policy 81.

[27] J.P. Trachtman, 'Constitutions of the WTO', in 17 EJIL 2006 at 623–646.

[28] *See*, for example, E.-U. Petersmann, 'Multilevel Trade Governance Requires Multilevel Constitutionalism', in Joerges and Petersmann, above at n 20, at Ch 1 and N. Walker, 'The EU and the WTO: Constitutionalism in a New Key', in: G. de Búrca and J. Scott (eds), *The EU and the WTO: Legal and Constitutional Issues* (Oxford: Hart, 2001).

policy powers. In Europe, this struggle for individual freedom and democratic self-government across frontiers has led to the legal and judicial protection of ever more 'new' fundamental rights (as codified in the 2000 EU Charter of Fundamental Rights) and 'constitutional principles' of EU law (as codified in Part I of the 2004 Treaty Establishing a Constitution for Europe (TCE)).[29] Their underlying value premises of *normative individualism* and rule of international law (see Article I–2 TCE on the 'Union's values'), rather than foreign power politics, remain contested by many politicians and their legal advocates.[30] The universal recognition of human rights entails a 'dédoublement fonctionel' (G. Scelle) of states and international organizations for protecting human rights in national as well as in international law and requires construing international guarantees of freedom, rule of law and human rights not only as rights and obligations among states, but also as obligations of governments *vis-à-vis* their own citizens constituting corresponding individual rights to freedom and respect for international law subject to democratic legislation.

Citizen-oriented constitutional approaches also better explain why 'constitutional reforms' of international law (such as the tri-partite membership in the ILO, the compulsory dispute settlement system in the WTO, judicial interpretation of the EC Treaty's customs union rules as creating individual 'market freedoms' with legal primacy and 'direct effect') resulted so often from individual complaints and civil society pressures. Human rights and legal restraints on abuses of government powers have hardly ever become effective without struggles by self-interested citizens for additional constitutional safeguards. Multilevel constitutionalism, including the explicit linkage of trade law with human rights, has proven to be the most successful strategy for transforming Europe into a peaceful constitutional order[31] and also seems to offer the only realistic strategy for a legitimate international rule of law.

D. Constitutional Functions and Structures of WTO Law?

Prior to his appointment as WTO Director-General, Pascal Lamy famously criticized the decision-making processes of the WTO as 'medieval' and called for new forms of 'cosmopolitics' and 'cosmopolitan constituencies' in support of global public goods like a rules-based world trading system, emphasizing

---

[29] Treaty Establishing a Constitution for Europe, signed 29 October 2004, not in force [2004] OJ C310/1. *See also* A. von Bogdandy and J. Bast (eds), *Principles of European Constitutional Law* (Oxford: Hart, 2006).

[30] *See* the justification of the frequent EC violations of WTO law by members of the EC legal services such as Kuijper, above at n 21, who criticizes the rule-oriented 'Kupferberg jurisprudence' of the EC Court as politically 'naïve' (at 1320). Also Klabbers' 'constitutional approach would, as much as possible, avoid using the language of rights' (above at n 20, at 57).

[31] Even though the process of ratification of the TCE has been blocked by two negative *referenda* in France and the Netherlands, it appears realistic to assume that the basic constitutional principles codified in the TCE will continue to prevail in EU constitutional law.

the need to learn from the EU's governance experiences with international economic integration without a common state.[32] The negotiators of the WTO Agreement wisely refrained from enumerating all 'the basic principles and . . . objectives underlying th(e) multilateral trading system', to which the Preamble and many other provisions of the WTO Agreement refer. Even though primarily constituting rights and obligations among WTO Members, numerous WTO provisions acknowledge that—since trade takes place between private producers, traders and consumers—WTO law requires legal protection also of private 'rights to trade'.[33] WTO law expresses these 'constitutional functions' of certain WTO guarantees of freedom, non-discrimination, rule-of-law and social safeguards—not only in *intergovernmental* relations, but also inside countries for the protection of private rights against protectionist abuses of government powers—only in very imperfect ways, for instance in the TRIPS and Preshipment Inspection Agreements and in the WTO Protocol for the accession of China.

WTO law uses all three formal techniques characteristic of 'constitutionalism': (1) the distinction between 'constitutional choice' and 'post-constitutional choices' (e.g. more stringent WTO requirements for the entry into force and amendments of the WTO Agreement (Articles X, XIV) than for normal decision-making by consensus or majority-voting (Article IX WTO Agreement)); (2) recognition of a higher legal rank of constitutional rules over post-constitutional rules (e.g. the primacy of the WTO Agreement (Article XVI:3 and 4 and Articles IX, X)); and (3) the general and abstract nature of constitutional rules which should bind all without discrimination (e.g. Articles I, II, III, XI GATT; Articles II, XVI, and XVII GATS; Article 4 TRIPS Agreement).

Although only a functionally limited 'world trade constitution', WTO law also uses the various *substantive* principles that are characteristic of the historical evolution of constitutionalism such as: (4) the rule of law requirement (Article XVI WTO Agreement and Article 3 DSU); (5) respect for human dignity and human rights (the WTO is committed to 'sustainable development' (Preamble of the WTO Agreement) and to (quasi) judicial interpretation of WTO law in accordance with customary rules of interpretation (Article 3 DSU)); (6) separation of powers and other horizontal and vertical 'checks and balances' (Article IX WTO Agreement); and (7) 'social justice' as a precondition for maintaining the needed social consensus over time (e.g. aiming at 'raising standards of living, ensuring full employment', promoting 'sustainable development', and 'positive efforts designed to ensure that developing countries, and especially the least developed among them, secure a share in the growth of international trade commensurate with the needs of their economic development' (Preamble of the WTO Agreement)).

[32] *See*, e.g. P. Lamy, *La démocratie-monde. Pour une autre gouvernance globale* (Paris: Seuil, 2004).
[33] WTO Doc. WT/L/432, above at n 10 and related text.

This use of 'constitutional methods' (above 1–3) and 'constitutional principles' (above 4–7) supports the increasingly held view that WTO law can usefully be conceived as a multilevel 'constitutional framework' for limiting multilevel trade governance for the benefit of producers, traders, and consumers.[34] The constitutional approach views the WTO not only in narrow *economic* terms (e.g. as an institution promoting economic welfare through trade liberalization); WTO rules and policies also pursue *political* as well as *legal* objectives that are no less important than the economic benefits from liberal trade. National constitutions turn out to be only 'partial constitutions' which—in a globally interdependent world—cannot protect the basic needs and human rights of citizens effectively without international cooperation in international organizations that must remain, like national organizations, subject to multilevel constitutional restraints limiting abuses of government powers. However, even though constitutional approaches may be of crucial political importance for constituting and limiting effective multilevel governance, they must not detract WTO judges from their obligation to 'clarify the existing provisions of those agreements in accordance with customary rules of interpretation of public international law' (Article 3 DSU).

E. Political Opposition to Mainstreaming Human Rights into WTO Law

WTO diplomats and most WTO experts continue to oppose discussing human rights and 'constitutional approaches' in WTO bodies. WTO bodies have, therefore, not formally responded to the UN proposals for a 'human rights approach to international trade'. WTO jurisprudence likewise focuses on the state-centred, customary methods of international treaty interpretation and has never referred—in WTO panel and Appellate Body findings—to human rights law. There are many reasons why the political WTO bodies prefer to avoid spending their time on clarifying the controversial relevance of human rights for the interpretation and application of WTO rules and policies:

1. National vs. Multilevel Constitutionalism

The 'realist approach' and the 'constitutional approach to international law' share the constitutional premise that the reality of international power politics requires 'domestic constitutional scrutiny' of international rules. In constitutional democracies, international rules should be applied only to the extent that they respect and promote the human rights and democratic self-governance of domestic citizens. Constitutional traditions differ, however, so widely among WTO Members that proposals for 'constitutional reforms' of WTO rules and institutions (e.g. establishment of a parliamentary WTO

---

[34] *See* E.-U. Petersmann, 'Constitutionalism and WTO Law: From a State-Centered Approach towards a Human Rights Approach in International Economic Law', in D.L.M. Kennedy and J.D. Southwick (eds), *The Political Economy of International Trade Law* (Cambridge: CUP, 2002), 32–67; *see also* Petersmann, above at n 28.

body, public access to WTO meetings) have proven to be very controversial. Even among constitutional democracies, the US focus on *national constitutionalism* and *hegemonic, unilateralist foreign policy options*[35] differs fundamentally from the EU's commitment to *multilevel constitutionalism* and 'strict compliance with international law' (Article I–3 TCE).[36] Whereas the EU Parliament and Commission supported the regular inter-parliamentary meetings at WTO Ministerial Conferences since 1999, US Congressmen have hardly participated in such inter-parliamentary conferences outside the US and tend to oppose 'international constitutionalism' as a potential threat to democratic governance inside the US.[37]

2. *Fragmentation vs. Indivisibility of Human Rights*

More than 30 WTO Members have not ratified the UN Convention on Economic, Social and Cultural Human Rights. Also other UN human rights conventions have not been ratified by major trading countries like China (e.g. non-ratification of the UN Covenant on Civil and Political Rights) and the US (e.g. non-ratification of the UN Covenant on Economic, Social and Cultural Rights, of many ILO Conventions, the UN Convention establishing the International Criminal Court).[38]

Notwithstanding the almost universal recognition—in the 1993 Vienna Declaration of the UN World Conference on Human Rights—that 'all human rights are universal, indivisible and interdependent and interrelated', the reality of UN human rights law (e.g. in terms of membership in UN human rights conventions and UH human rights bodies) remains fragmented. Human rights in the US, for example, are characterized by the higher degree of legal and judicial protection of civil and political human rights compared with economic and social rights.[39] The comprehensive guarantees of individual 'market freedoms' and transnational 'freedom to conduct a business in accordance with Union law' (as codified in Articles I–4 and II–76 TCE of the EU Charter

---

[35] On the US penchant for power-oriented, unilateral foreign policies, notwithstanding US-leadership in promoting multilateral legal disciplines for other countries after World Wars I and II, *see* I. Daalder and J. Lindsay, *America Unbound: The Bush Revolution in Foreign Policy* (Washington DC; Brookings Institution, 2004). On the often skeptical US attitude *vis-à-vis* international law *see* J.F. Murphy, *The United States and the Rule of Law in International Affairs* (Cambridge: CUP, 2004).

[36] *See* E.-U. Petersmann, 'The 2004 Treaty Establishing a Constitution for Europe and Foreign Policies: A New Foreign Policy Paradigm?', in R. Iglesias *et al.* (eds), *Festschrift für Manfred Zuleeg* (Nomos: Baden-Baden 2005), 165–83. On the importance of the various forms of 'civil power' (like democratic governance and law), *see* J.S. Nye, *Soft Power: The Means to Success in World Politics* (New York: Public Affairs, 2003).

[37] On EU proposals for 'WTO cosmopolitics' (P. Lamy) and an advisory parliamentary assembly of the WTO, and US skepticism *vis-à-vis* 'international constitutionalism', *see* the contributions by E. Mann, D. Skaggs, J. Bacchus, G. Shaffer, and S. Charnovitz, in E.-U. Petersmann (ed), *Reforming the World Trading System: Legitimacy, Efficiency and Democratic Governance* (Oxford: OUP 2005).

[38] On double standards in US human rights policies and foreign policies *see* M. Ignatieff, *American Exceptionalism and Human Rights* (Princeton, Oxford: PUP, 2005).

[39] *See* Woods and Lewis, above at n 17.

of Fundamental Rights), their explicit foundation on 'the indivisible, universal values of human dignity, freedom, equality and solidarity',[40] and the EC jurisprudence on judicial protection of human rights in EC law have no equivalent in national and regional economic law outside Europe, such as the North American Free Trade Agreement (NAFTA) and the jurisprudence of NAFTA bodies.

III. NEED FOR CLARIFYING THE LEGAL IMPACT OF HUMAN RIGHTS ON WTO LAW AND JURISPRUDENCE

A. A WTO Declaration on 'The WTO and Human Rights'?

In their 1996 Singapore Ministerial Declaration, WTO Members renewed their commitment to the observance of internationally recognized core labour standards, affirmed their support for the ILO's work in promoting these standards, and rejected protectionist abuses of such standards. In a similar way, WTO Members could respond to the UN proposals for a 'human rights approach to trade' by a WTO Ministerial Declaration that could, for example:

(1) renew the commitment of WTO Members to respect, protect and promote universal human rights in all policy areas, both individually and through international cooperation, and to ensure the consistency of WTO rules and policies with universal human rights;

(2) affirm their support for the proposals by UN human rights bodies to clarify the impact of universal human rights on trade rules and policies, with due respect for the limited competences of the WTO, for the legitimate diversity of human rights traditions at national, regional and worldwide levels, and for the need to carry out the proposed 'human rights impact studies' by competent human rights bodies;

(3) acknowledge the need for harnessing the complementary functions of WTO rules and human rights for welfare-increasing cooperation among free citizens in international trade, in conformity with the worldwide recognition—in the 1993 Vienna Declaration of the UN World Conference on Human Rights—that 'democracy, development and respect for human rights and fundamental freedoms are interdependent and mutually reinforcing' (para. 8);

(4) recognize that the customary rules of international treaty interpretation may require WTO bodies to take into account human rights obligations of

---

[40] The quotation is from the Preamble of the EU Charter and is discussed by J. Kenner, 'Economic and Social Rights in the EU Legal Order: The Mirage of Indivisibility', in T. Hervey and J. Kenner (eds), *Economic and Social Rights under the EU Charter of Fundamental Rights* (Oxford: Hart, 2003), Ch 1.

WTO Members as relevant legal context for the interpretation of WTO rules;

(5) are convinced that the objectives, principles and exception clauses of WTO Agreements are flexible enough to enable each WTO Member to implement WTO rules in conformity with its obligations to promote and protect the human rights of its citizens;

(6) urge WTO dispute settlement bodies, if they are requested by WTO Members to take into account human rights as relevant legal context for the interpretation of WTO rules, to exercise judicial restraint and fully respect the margin of appreciation which every WTO Member may legitimately claim in designing its domestic human rights laws and policies in conformity with its international obligations and in response to the democratic preferences and social needs of its citizens.

From the perspective of human rights activists, such a Declaration might appear disappointing. Yet, just as human rights were only gradually introduced into EC law in order to limit (rather than enlarge) the discretion and regulatory powers of the EC, so should a WTO Declaration on trade policies and human rights proceed cautiously by beginning to clarify the 'limiting functions' of human rights for preventing abuses of trade governance powers, before addressing the more controversial 'empowering functions' of human rights in the field of trade law and policies. The experience of European integration suggests that the functional interrelationships between human rights and international economic law are bound to intensify over time in order to protect basic human needs more effectively in the international division of labour across frontiers. The proposed collective pledge by WTO Members to respect their existing, universal human rights obligations could—without creating new legal obligations or new WTO competencies, and without attempting to define the contested scope of universal human rights obligations and their impact on WTO rules—improve the limited 'input' and 'output-legitimacy' of WTO rules and WTO negotiations by acknowledging that the numerous 'public interest clauses' in WTO law are flexible enough to be interpreted in conformity with the human rights obligations of WTO Members and to take into account the social adjustment problems of international trade (e.g. for small subsistence farmers in poor countries, for vulnerable 'losers' in international competition, for sick people depending on access to foreign medicines at affordable prices).

However, political support for the adoption of a WTO Declaration on *WTO and Human Rights* appears very unlikely. The narrow trade policy mandate of WTO diplomats, and the lack of human rights expertise in the WTO make it unlikely that the political WTO bodies will attempt to clarify the impact of human rights on WTO rules and policies. WTO instruments (like the 2001 WTO Declaration on access to medicines) usually avoid explicit references to human rights and, in the rare exceptional cases (such as the reference to 'gross violations of human rights' in the 2003 WTO waiver for the 'Kimberley Protocol' limiting trade in 'conflict diamonds'),[41] do not clarify the legal relationships between WTO rules and human rights. While these instruments 'illustrate the flexibility of the WTO legal system in response to human rights arguments, they also show that political agreement on such Declarations and 'waivers' may be possible only as part of comprehensive 'package negotiations' (e.g. on the 2001 and 2005 WTO Ministerial Declarations on the Doha Development Round).

B. Human Rights Arguments and 'Balancing Principles' in WTO Dispute Settlement Proceedings

The more than 300 GATT and WTO dispute settlement reports since 1949[42] include neither references to human rights arguments by the parties to the dispute nor legal findings on the relevance of human rights for the interpretation of GATT and WTO rules. This surprising fact reflects the narrow conception of the applicable law and jurisdiction in GATT and WTO dispute settlement proceedings prevailing among GATT and WTO Members. Even after the establishment of a GATT Legal Office in 1983, it took years to persuade the diplomats and non-lawyers acting as GATT dispute settlement panelists that GATT Contracting Parties had to comply with all their international legal obligations in good faith, and that GATT panels could not consistently apply GATT rules and the incomplete GATT dispute settlement procedures without recourse to general international law rules (e.g. on treaty interpretation, burden of proof, international jurisdiction, representation before panels, abuse of rights, state responsibility).

The following sections explore four different contexts in which arguments based on national, regional or UN human rights law might be raised in WTO dispute settlement proceedings.

1. Applicable Law and Jurisdiction in WTO Panel Proceedings

In WTO dispute settlement practice, panels and the Appellate Body have explicitly rejected interpreting WTO rules 'in clinical isolation' from other fields of international law, and increasingly resort to MEAs, RTAs and general rules of international law in interpreting WTO rules.[43] There is broad agreement that the DSU requires the complainant to base its legal claims on the

---

[41] World Trade Organization, Waiver Concerning Kimberley Process Certification Scheme for Rough Diamonds, WTO Doc. WT/L/518, Decision of 15 May 2003.

[42] *See* the lists of working party, panel, appellate, and arbitration reports in the Annexes to E.-U. Petersmann (ed), *International Trade Law and the GATT/WTO Dispute Settlement System* (London, Boston: Kluwer, 1997), 587 ff, and F. Ortino and E.-U.Petersmann (eds), *The WTO Dispute Settlement System 1995–2003* (London, Boston: Kluwer, 1994), at 558 ff.

[43] *See* above at n 13 and J. Pauwelyn, *Conflict of Norms in Public International Law. How WTO Rules Relate to Other Rules of International Law* (Cambridge: CUP, 2003), e.g. at 244–72.

'covered WTO Agreements' (Articles 1, 7 DSU). Complaints based on human rights would be outside the limited jurisdiction of WTO dispute settlement panels. WTO lawyers disagree on whether the DSU implicitly authorizes WTO dispute settlement panels to apply non-WTO law as a defence against WTO complaints and to 'fill gaps' in WTO rules and dispute settlement procedures;[44] whether the DSU limits the mandate of WTO dispute settlement bodies to the application of the 'covered WTO Agreements';[45] and whether the recognition, in numerous WTO rules, of 'basic principles underlying this multilateral trading system' offers a source of WTO law that is sufficiently flexible for interpreting WTO rules in conformity with other multilateral obligations of WTO Members.[46] All these views recognize that many WTO rules explicitly refer to international treaties negotiated outside the WTO, and that the requirement to clarify WTO rules 'in accordance with customary rules of interpretation of public international law' (Article 3 of the DSU) implicitly calls for taking into account 'any relevant rules of international law applicable in the relations between the parties' (see Article 31(3)(c) VCLT). The controversy is thus essentially over the correct interpretation of the definition—in the DSU—of the jurisdiction of WTO dispute settlement panels, i.e. whether the DSU excludes direct application of non-WTO international law in WTO dispute settlement proceedings; or whether the DSU implicitly authorizes application of general principles of law and of non-WTO international law not only for interpreting WTO rules but also as directly applicable law (e.g. for 'filling gaps' in WTO law or justifying departures from WTO rules in the unlikely case of a conflict with international *ius cogens*).

So far, WTO dispute settlement panels and the Appellate Body have been reluctant to directly apply bilateral agreements[47] or legal defences directly based on general international law,[48] and have avoided dispute settlement findings on whether non-WTO international law is applicable directly, and whether non-WTO law can waive or amend WTO rules outside the formal WTO procedures for waivers and amendments (Articles IX and X of the WTO Agreement).[49] In most WTO disputes, interpreting the WTO Agreement as

---

[44] This is the view of e.g. Pauwelyn, *ibid.*, at 459–61.

[45] This is the view of, e.g. J.P. Trachtman, 'The Domain of WTO Dispute Resolution' (1999) 40 Harv Int L J 333, at 342; *see also* Trachtman's critical review of the above-mentioned book by Pauwelyn in (2004) 98 AJIL 855.

[46] This is the view of E.-U. Petersmann, 'Future Challenges for the WTO Dispute Settlement System', in Y. Taniguchi *et al.* (eds), *The WTO at Ten: Dispute Settlement, Multilateral Negotiations, Regional Integration* (Cambridge: CUP, 2006).

[47] *See* the Appellate Body's refusal to apply the bilateral oilseeds agreement in the *EC—Poultry* dispute, WT/DS69/AB/R, adopted 23 July 1998.

[48] *See* the Appellate Body's refusal to determine whether the precautionary principle was applicable as a rule of customary international law in the *EC—Hormones* case, WT/DS26/AB/R and WT/DS48/AB/R, adopted 13 February 1998.

[49] In the WTO Panel Report on *Korea—Procurement*, WT/DS163/R, adopted 19 June 2000, the Panel noted as *obiter dictum*: 'Customary international law applies generally to the economic relations between the WTO Members. Such international law applies to the extent that the WTO Agreements do not "contract out" from it. To put it another way, to the extent there is no conflict

implicitly authorizing panels to apply general international law rules to the extent necessary for accomplishing their dispute settlement functions (e.g. for determining a 'violation' of WTO obligations, providing 'security and predictability' in terms of Article 3 DSU) is likely to lead to the same legal findings as in the case of the more controversial, 'direct' application of general international law or the less controversial, 'indirect' application of non-WTO rules binding on the disputing parties based on a wide notion of treaty interpretation under Article 31(3) VCLT.[50] For example, as the Appellate Body has held that WTO panels must check their own jurisdiction at their own initiative,[51] interpreting the jurisdiction of WTO dispute settlement bodies might require taking into account agreements among the parties to the dispute limiting or excluding WTO jurisdiction (e.g. Article 292 EC on exclusive jurisdiction of the EC Court of Justice, Article 2005 NAFTA on exclusive jurisdiction of NAFTA panels). Arguably,

- the large number of 'public interest clauses' in WTO law (e.g. in Article 7 TRIPS Agreement on 'objectives', Article 8 TRIPS on 'principles') and
- of WTO 'exceptions' (e.g. in Article XX GATT, Article XIV GATS, Article 30 TRIPS);
- the broad mandate of panels, e.g. to 'make such findings as will assist the DSB in making the recommendations or in giving the rulings provided for in that/those agreement(s)' (Article 7 DSU);
- a broad reading of the customary international law rules of treaty interpretation (e.g. Article 31(3) VCLT) and on the admissibility of *inter se* agreements, and
- the judicial clarification of 'the principles underlying this multilateral trading system' (Preamble WTO Agreement) for the interpretation and 'balancing' of WTO rights and obligations

offer enough flexibility for WTO dispute settlement bodies to interpret WTO rules in conformity with the human rights obligations of the WTO Members concerned.

Human rights law and WTO jurisprudence suggest that, in examining the potential impact of human rights on the interpretation of WTO rules, three different kinds of trade regulations should be distinguished and might require

or inconsistency, or an expression in a covered WTO Agreement that implies differently, we are of the view that the customary rules of international law apply to the WTO treaties and to the process of treaty formation under the WTO' (para. 7.96). Yet, this finding does not specify whether WTO panels have jurisdiction to *directly* apply customary international law rules, or whether the WTO Agreement must be interpreted as implicitly authorizing panels to apply general international law rules to the extent necessary for accomplishing their dispute settlement functions.

[50] *See* J. Pauwelyn, 'How to Win a World Trade Organization Dispute Based on Non-World Trade Organization Law?' (2003) 37 JWT 997, at 1004.

[51] In *US—1916 Act* (WT/DS136AB/R and WT/DS162/AB/R adopted 26 September 2000), the Appellate Body referred to the 'widely accepted rule that an international tribunal is entitled to consider the issue of its own jurisdiction on its own initiative, and to satisfy itself that it has jurisdiction in any case that comes before it' (fn 30).

different 'balancing principles'. These are examined in the three following sections.

2. *International Trade Sanctions/Preferences for the Promotion of Human Rights Abroad*

In past GATT and WTO dispute settlement proceedings over international trade sanctions, the respondent countries often refrained from requesting establishment of a GATT panel (e.g. in the case of trade sanctions against Argentina and Cuba). In the few cases where a GATT working party (e.g. in the case of US trade sanctions against Czechoslovakia) or a GATT panel (e.g. in the case of trade sanctions against Nicaragua and South Africa) examined the trade embargoes, human rights arguments were neither raised nor addressed in the dispute settlement findings. If a WTO dispute settlement body has to examine the influence of human rights law on the interpretation of WTO rules in international relations among WTO Members, it has to respect their 'sovereign equality' (e.g. as regards ratification of international human rights conventions) and the 'margin of appreciation' of each WTO Member in designing its domestic human rights legislation and prioritizing scarce resources for the realization of human rights and social needs.

The respective scope of freedom of WTO Members might have been limited by international rules or UN resolutions 'that sanctions and negative conditionalities which directly or indirectly affect trade are not appropriate ways of promoting the integration of human rights in international economic policy and practice'.[52] As Article XXI GATT explicitly provides that 'nothing in this Agreement shall be construed ... (c) to prevent any contracting party from taking any action in pursuance of its obligations under the United Nations Charter for the maintenance of international peace and security', UN Security Council resolutions prescribing economic sanctions can justify departures from WTO rules (*see* Article 103 UN Charter). The legal relevance of other UN resolutions on the interpretation of WTO rules remains to be examined case-by-case.[53] Other questions to be clarified relate to the WTO-consistency of trade restrictions in response to alleged violations of human rights in international relations among WTO Members which have explicitly committed themselves to respect for human rights in their reciprocal trade relations (e.g. in the human rights clauses included in the Cotonou Agreement and in other trade agreements between the EC and less-developed WTO Members). Multilateral agreements on the collective promotion of human health (e.g. through the Framework Convention on Tobacco Control adopted by the

---

[52] UN Commission on Human Rights, Sub-Commission on Promotion and Protection of Human Rights, Resolution 1999/30 of 26 August 1999 on 'Trade Liberalization and its Impact on Human Rights', adopted by the UN Doc. E/CN.4/Sub.2/RES/1999/9.

[53] Myanmar, a WTO Member, refrained from invoking WTO dispute settlement procedures against the trade sanctions imposed by various WTO Members (e.g. under the Burmese Freedom and Democracy Act 2003 adopted by the US Congress).

World Health Organization in 2003) and of other human rights values (e.g. the 2003 Kimberley Process Certification Scheme) may likewise support recourse to human rights arguments as relevant context for interpreting WTO rules (such as Article XX(b) GATT on protection of human health).

In response to India's challenge of the discriminatory effects of certain preferences granted under the EC's generalized system of tariff preferences (GSP), the WTO Appellate Body clarified

- 'that the term "non-discriminatory" . . . does not prohibit developed-country Members from granting different tariffs to products originating in different GSP beneficiaries, provided that . . . identical treatment is available to all similarly-situated GSP beneficiaries that have the "development, financial and trade needs" to which the treatment in question is intended to respond'.[54]
- the existence of a 'development, financial (or) trade must be assessed according to an objective standard';[55] and
- 'the particular need at issue must, by its nature, be such that it can be effectively addressed through tariff preferences', without imposing 'unjustifiable burdens on other Members'.[56]

In June 2005, the EU adopted a new GSP system aimed at promoting 'sustainable development' by differentiating tariff preferences depending on whether LDCs have ratified and effectively implemented major UN human rights conventions, ILO conventions, UN environmental convention, UN conventions on drugs, and the UN convention against corruption.[57] This use of UN human rights law as 'objective standard' for differentiating trade preferences for less-developed countries may also influence the interpretation of the WTO-consistency of future RTAs and may entail future WTO disputes on whether preference-granting WTO Members have correctly interpreted and applied UN human rights standards as justifying trade discrimination among less-developed countries. As the jurisdiction of WTO panels is limited to examining legal claims under the covered WTO Agreements, WTO dispute settlement bodies should leave it to the WTO Members concerned to bear the burden of proving the existence of alleged violations of human rights (e.g. by invoking special dispute settlement procedures available under human rights conventions or under regional trade agreements).

3. International Trade Restrictions for the Protection of Human Rights Inside the Domestic Jurisdiction

The WTO disputes over the EC's import restrictions on hormone-fed beef,[58] asbestos,[59] and the US restrictions on gambling services[60] illustrate that WTO

---

[54] WTO Appellate Body Report, *EC—Tariff Preferences*, above at n 7, at paras 173, 190.
[55] *Ibid.*, paras 161–63.   [56] *Ibid.*, paras 164–67.   [57] *See* above at n 7.
[58] WTO Doc. WT/DS48/AB/R, above at n 48.
[59] WTO Appellate Body Report, *EC—Asbestos*, WT/DS135/AB/R, adopted 5 April 2001.
[60] WTO Appellate Body Report, *US—Gambling*, WT/DS285/AB/R, adopted 20 April 2005.

rules grant importing countries broad regulatory discretion regarding restrictions of imported goods with proven and potential health risks. As UN human rights conventions prescribe minimum standards that do not prevent WTO Members from accepting higher human rights standards in regional human rights conventions such as the ECHR and the EU Charter of Fundamental Rights (as well as in national human rights laws), the WTO-consistency of import restrictions designed to protect the human rights of domestic citizens (e.g. health protection measures pursuant to Article XX(b) GATT or Articles 30–31 TRIPS) may be legitimately influenced by arguments based on *regional* (as well as national) human rights law rather than on UN human rights conventions. Many human rights arguments in trade disputes before the European Court of Justice (ECJ) and the European Court of Human Rights (ECtHR) could be similarly raised in WTO dispute settlement proceedings.

In the *Omega* case, for instance, the ECJ held that a national restriction on the importation of foreign services was legally justified on the ground that it was necessary for protecting public policy by prohibiting a commercial activity affronting human dignity (laser games simulating acts of homicide).[61] The respondent referred to the constitutional protection of human dignity as a human right in Article 1 of the German Basic Law as well as in Article 1 of the EU Charter of Fundamental Rights. UN human rights conventions, by contrast, recognize respect for human dignity only as a legal principle and source of inalienable human rights, but not as a human right in itself.[62] If the same import restrictions on the supply of international services (laser games simulating acts of homicide) had been challenged in the WTO, the importing country (Germany) and the EC could have invoked the same human rights arguments in support of the legal justification of the import restrictions as being 'necessary to protect public morals' or 'to maintain public order' in terms of Article XIV(a) GATS. As these WTO concepts recognize that 'public morality' and 'public order' may legitimately vary from one community to the other,[63] WTO dispute settlement bodies would have to respect the legitimate 'margin of appreciation' of the national authorities concerned to define 'public morality' and 'public order' in conformity with the national constitutional guarantees (here, the guarantee of a human right to respect for human dignity in Article 1 of the German Basic Law). In terms of the customary methods of international treaty interpretation, WTO dispute settlement bodies might also have been justified taking into account the legal guarantee of respect for

---

[61] *See* Case C–36/02 *Omega Spielhallen- und Automatenaufstellungs-GmbH v Oberbürgermeisterin der Bundesstadt Bonn* [2004] ECR I–9609

[62] *See* K. Dicke, 'The Founding Function of Human Dignity in the Universal Declaration of Human Rights', in D. Kretzmer and E. Klein (eds), *The Concept of Human Dignity* (The Hague, London: Kluwer, 2002), 111–20.

[63] *See*, e.g. the footnote to Art. XIV(a) GATS which states: 'The public order exception may be invoked only where a genuine and sufficiently serious threat is posed to one of the fundamental interests of society'.

human dignity in Article 1 of the EU Charter of Fundamental Rights[64] as a 'relevant rule of international law applicable in the relations between the parties': Even though these terms in Article 31(3)(c) VCLT are often construed as referring to international law rules accepted by all parties to the treaty concerned (i.e. all WTO Members), they—arguably—also include lawful *inter se* agreements among some of the parties (like EC law adopted by the 25 EC Member States in conformity with Article XXIV GATT and Article V GATS).

In the *Schmidberger* case, the ECJ had to examine the extent of an EC Member State's obligation to ensure the free movement of goods and freedom of transit in situations where a demonstration permitted by the Austrian authorities on the most important Alpine transit route between Austria and Italy had the effect of blocking this motorway for nearly 30 hours.[65] If the private transport company—which claimed that the failure of the Austrian authorities to ban the demonstration amounted to a trade restriction inconsistent with the EC Treaty (Article 28)—had had the nationality of a third WTO Member State, an intergovernmental WTO dispute settlement proceeding on a similar legal complaint (i.e. inconsistency of the authorization of the political demonstration with the obligation under Article V GATT to protect freedom of transit) could have been admissible; this could have confronted the WTO dispute settlement bodies with the same methodological question of how to reconcile the trade obligations of the country concerned with its human rights obligations to protect the freedom of expression and freedom of assembly of the demonstrators, as guaranteed in the ECHR (Articles 10,11) and in the national constitution of the country concerned.

In its judgment of 12 June 2003, the ECJ confirmed its settled case law that the prohibition of trade restrictions in Article 28 EC also applies where a Member State abstains from adopting the measures required in order to deal with *private* obstacles to the free movement of goods which are not caused by the state.[66] Having recalled its longstanding jurisprudence that both the EC and EC Member States are required to respect fundamental rights, the Court examined how to reconcile the EC Treaty guarantees of free movement of goods with the protection of freedom of expression and freedom of assembly, as guaranteed in the ECHR (Articles 10, 11). The Court followed from the express wording of Articles 10 and 11 that

the exercise of those rights may be restricted, provided that the restrictions in fact correspond to objectives of general interest and do not, taking account of the aim of the restrictions, constitute disproportionate and unacceptable interference, impairing the very substance of the rights guaranteed [. . .]. In those circumstances, the interests involved must be weighed having regard to all the circumstances of the case in order to determine whether a fair balance was struck between those interests.[67]

---

[64] The text is published in [2000] OJ C364/1 and is also included into the 2004 Treaty establishing a Constitution for Europe (above at n 31).
[65] *See* Case C–112/00 *Schmidberger v Austria* [2003] CMLR 1043, at 1069.
[66] *Ibid.*, at 1086, para. 64.   [67] *Ibid.*, at 1089, paras 80–1.

The Court then emphasized and applied two 'balancing principles' which could prove important also for similar judicial review problems in other worldwide and regional *fora* (e.g. WTO and NAFTA panels). First, the competent national government authorities 'enjoy a wide margin of discretion in that regard. Nevertheless, it is necessary to determine whether the restrictions placed upon intra-Community trade are proportionate in the light of the legitimate objective pursued, namely, in the present case, the protection of fundamental rights'.[68] In this respect, the Court concluded that 'the national authorities were reasonably entitled . . . to consider that the legitimate aim of that demonstration could not be achieved in the present case by measures less restrictive of intra-Community trade'.[69]

Second, rather than examining the human rights concerned under the *rule of reason*-exception to Article 28 (or as a justification under Article 30 EC), the Court ruled that '(t)he fact that the authorities of a Member State did not ban a demonstration in circumstances such as those of the main case is not incompatible with Articles 30 and 34 of the EC Treaty (now, after amendment, Articles 28 EC and 29 EC), read together with Article 5 of the EC Treaty (now Article 10 EC)'.[70] This judicial method of deliberately avoiding to 'pigeonhole a justification based on the need to respect for human rights into one of the justificatory categories'[71] of the EC Treaty might be more difficult to follow by WTO dispute settlement bodies unless all parties to the dispute agree that the WTO panel has jurisdiction to apply human rights conventions directly as applicable law in the WTO dispute concerned.

4. Human-Rights-Related Non-Discriminatory Trade Regulation

The proposals for further harmonization of (non-discriminatory) domestic laws in the context of the WTO—for instance, by elaborating WTO rules on intellectual property rights, technical and health regulations, trade facilitation, competition and environmental rules, investments, and public services—may raise different human rights concerns. For example, future WTO rules on private rights (such as the private 'rights to trade' protected in the 2001 WTO Protocol on the accession of China), anti-competitive private practices, private access to financial assistance in the context of trade-facilitation, limitations on private intellectual property rights, and the administration of a WTO Register for private geographical indications may give rise to legal challenges whether such WTO rules are themselves consistent with human rights law.

The ECJ prefers to balance economic freedoms with other 'fundamental

---

[68] *Ibid.*, at 1089, para. 82.

[69] *Ibid.*, at 1091, para. 93. *See* Case C–71/02 *Herbert Karner Industrie-Auktionen* [2004] ECR I–3025.

[70] Above at n 65, at 1092.

[71] C. Brown, 'Case C–112/00, *Eugen Schmidberger, Internationale Transporte und Planzüge v Austria*. Judgment of 12 June 2003, Full Court' (2003) 40 CMLR 1499, at 1504.

rights' case-by-case without explicit recognition of human rights as hierarchically superior to 'fundamental economic rights'. Yet, the ECJ has noted that—in interpreting fundamental rights—the EC judicature 'must take into account' the case law of the European Court of Human Rights.[72] However, in ECJ proceedings, the burden of proving the 'necessity' and 'proportionality' of restrictions of the EC's market freedoms may fall on the government invoking the need to protect fundamental rights whether the restrictions are discriminatory or not.[73]

The European Court of Human Rights (ECtHR), by contrast, imposes a higher burden of proof on those who claim that economic freedoms should prevail over fundamental political rights; the Court tends to apply a 'strict interpretation' to the scope of exception clauses in the ECHR, but recognizes a 'margin of appreciation' of national authorities regarding the 'necessity' of non-discriminatory, domestic restrictions (e.g. economic regulation) balancing different human rights values.[74] For example, in *Hertel*, the ECtHR had to review the consistency of Swiss court judgments on 'unfair competition' and freedom of commercial speech with the guarantees of freedom of expression in Article 10 ECHR. The commercial court in the Canton of Berne had, on the basis of the 'principle that there is no hierarchy of fundamental rights', considered it necessary to weigh against the constitutional rights invoked by Dr. Hertel (such as freedom of expression and freedom to carry out scientific research) the right to freedom of trade and industry as guaranteed by the Swiss Constitution.[75] Based on the Swiss Unfair Competition Act, the court prohibited Dr. Hertel 'from stating that food prepared in microwave ovens is a danger to health and leads to changes in blood of those who consume it that indicate a pathological disorder and present a pattern that could be seen as the beginning of a carcinogenic process'. The Swiss Federal Court dismissed the appeal by Dr. Hertel, *inter alia* on the ground that the 'smooth operation of competition and economic freedom, freedom of expression, scientific freedom and freedom of the press must be guaranteed as well

---

[72] For a discussion of these cases *see* A. Rosas, 'The Legal Sources of EU Fundamental Rights: A Systemic Overview', in N. Colneric *et al.* (eds), *Une Communauté de Droit. Festschrift für G. C. R. Iglesias* (Berlin: Berliner Wissenschafts-Verlag, 2003).

[73] WTO dispute settlement bodies tend to apply stricter standards of judicial review to discriminatory trade restrictions under WTO exceptions clauses (e.g. Art. XX GATT) than to nondiscriminatory regulations based, for example, on the SPS Agreement. *See* V. Heiskanen, 'The Regulatory Philosophy of International Trade Law' (2004) 38 JWT 1, at 25–9, 33.

[74] On these two principles, and their inherent tensions, in the jurisprudence of the European Court of Human Rights *see*, e.g. D. Gomien, D. Harris and L. Zwaak, *Law and Practice of the European Convention on Human Rights and the European Social Charter* (Strasbourg: Council of Europe Publishing, 1996), 211–19.

[75] The quotations and facts are taken from the Judgment of the ECtHR of 25 August 1998, *Hertel v Switzerland* (59/1997/843/1049), published in Reports 1998–VI and discussed by T. Cottier and S. Khorana, 'Linkages between Freedom of Expression and Unfair Competition Rules in International Trade: The *Hertel* Case and Beyond', in Cottier, Pauwelyn, and Bürgi, above at n 5, at 245–71.

as possible, but at the same time limited so that the various constitutional objectives may be reconciled in practice'.

The ECtHR proceeded from the premise that exceptions to freedom of expression (Article 10) must be construed strictly, and that the margin of appreciation of the Swiss authorities in matters of commercial speech was reduced by the fact that the statements by Dr. Hertel had been part of 'a debate affecting the general interest, for example over public health'. The majority of the judges considered the Swiss court injunction as not 'necessary in a democratic society', and therefore a violation of Article 10. The three dissenting judges argued that the ECtHR should respect the considerable margin of appreciation of national authorities in unfair competition cases rather than 'substitute its own evaluation for that of the national courts, where those courts considered, on reasonable grounds, the restrictions to be necessary'. By way of implementing the ECtHR judgment, the Federal Court revised the previous court injunction and acknowledged the freedom of Dr. Hertel to make public statements on the dangerous effects of the use of microwave ovens; but the Federal Court subjected the freedom of expression of Dr. Hertel to the condition that such statements must also refer 'to current differences of opinion' so as to avoid unfair distortions of competition.[76]

The different 'balancing approaches' applied by the Swiss commercial court, as confirmed by the Swiss Federal Court, and by the ECtHR illustrate that—in Europe—views on the proper balancing of economic and non-economic 'fundamental freedoms' may differ considerably. These different views may be relevant before WTO dispute settlement bodies.

Article 2 of the TRIPS Agreement, for example, incorporates the unfair competition rules of the Paris Convention on the Protection of Industrial Property (Article 10 *bis*) into the TRIPS Agreement. WTO law also includes other prohibitions of 'anti-competitive practices', false or misleading information that can be enforced through national and WTO dispute settlement proceedings so as to limit market failures (such as information asymmetries) and protect the proper functioning of markets (e.g. in their role as information mechanisms and dialogues about values).[77] WTO dispute settlement bodies may, therefore, be asked to interpret national and international competition and intellectual property regulations in conformity with the human rights obligations of WTO Members. As freedom of information and expression, including freedom of speech and of the press, are of constitutional importance for the proper functioning of *economic* markets no less than of *political* markets (i.e. democracy), the European jurisprudence and 'balancing principles' on reconciling economic and non-economic 'fundamental freedoms' may

---

[76] Bundesgericht Entscheidungen, Volume 125 III 185. *See* Decision of the ECtHR of 17 January 2002, Application No 53440/99.

[77] *See*, e.g. the comprehensive competition rules included into the 1997 GATS Protocol on Telecommunications, which were applied in the WTO Panel Report on *Mexico—Telecoms*, WT/DS 204/R, adopted 1 June 2004.

inspire future WTO jurisprudence. Even though the WTO Agreement is drafted in terms of rights and obligations of WTO Members, numerous WTO rules recognize obligations to protect the private rights of market participants, such as private 'rights to trade', procedural rights, property rights, and judicial remedies.

C. An ILA Declaration on 'International Trade Law and Human Rights'?

A Declaration from an academic association of international law experts, such as the International Law Association (ILA), could go beyond the six political principles suggested for a WTO Declaration (above section III.A) and elaborate more precise legal rules for the methodology and judicial standards necessary for promoting the mutual consistency of human rights law and international trade law. At the 72nd biennial ILA Conference at Toronto (Canada) in June 2006, the ILA approved the proposal by its International Trade Law committee to elaborate a Draft ILA declaration on 'International Trade Law and Human Rights'. The discussions in the ILA could focus on the following questions regarding the legal interrelationships between WTO rules and policies and the human rights obligations of WTO Members:

(1) How could the ILA contribute best to clarifying the legal impact of the universal recognition of 'inalienable', 'indivisible' and interrelated human rights on the future interpretation (e.g. in WTO jurisprudence) and implementation of international trade rules (e.g. in WTO negotiations and domestic laws implementing WTO obligations)?

(2) As UN human rights law prescribes minimum standards that do not prevent WTO Members from committing themselves to additional human rights and 'fundamental freedoms' in national and regional laws (like the EU Charter of Fundamental Rights): Should worldwide UN and WTO bodies only focus on UN human rights law? Or does the examination of the consistency of trade measures with WTO rules require taking into account also national and regional human rights, e.g. if the WTO Member concerned justifies the trade measure concerned as being necessary for protecting national or regional human rights or 'fundamental rights' of domestic citizens inside the domestic jurisdiction? To what extent have the principles of the Universal Declaration of Human Rights (1948) evolved into general international obligations of all WTO Members?

(3) What does the limitation of the mandate of WTO dispute settlement bodies imply for the 'applicable law' and 'jurisdiction' in WTO dispute settlement proceedings? Can WTO dispute settlement bodies fulfill their dispute settlement function if their findings of 'violations' of WTO rules do not take into account non-WTO legal rules which may exclude the jurisdiction of WTO dispute settlement bodies (e.g. Articles 292 EC, 2005 NAFTA, 1(2) of the MERCOSUR Olivos Protocol of 2002

constituting exclusive jurisdiction for certain trade disputes), or may justify departures from WTO rules (e.g. in the case of international *ius cogens* and WTO-consistent *inter se* agreements among the disputing WTO Members)?

(4) Do the customary methods of international treaty interpretation (e.g. Article 31(3)(c) VCLT) permit WTO dispute settlement bodies to take into account only *universal* human rights obligations of all WTO Members, or also human rights obligations accepted by some WTO Members (e.g. in an *inter se* agreement permitted by Article XXIV GATT and Article V GATS and accepted by all parties to the WTO dispute concerned)? Do the customary methods of treaty interpretation permit recourse to the 'General Comments' adopted by UN human rights committees also as relevant context for interpreting WTO rules?

(5) Do the explicit objectives of WTO law (such as 'raising standards of living', 'ensuring full employment', 'sustainable development', 'protection of intellectual property rights in a manner conducive to social and economic welfare'), the legal 'principles underlying this multilateral trading system' (as referred to in the Preamble to the WTO Agreement and defined in 'public interest' clauses such as Article 8 of the TRIPS Agreement), the numerous 'general exceptions' from WTO rules (e.g. for protecting 'public morals', 'public order', human health, 'essential security interests'), and the 'balancing methods' applied in WTO jurisprudence offer adequate 'policy space' for interpreting and implementing WTO rules in conformity with the human rights obligations of WTO Members? Is the European practice of defining 'public morals' and 'public order' in conformity with human rights relevant for the future interpretation of these legal terms in WTO law?

(6) Are the 'balancing principles' applied in WTO jurisprudence (such as the 'necessity requirements' in Article XX GATT) consistent with those applied in the context of UN human rights conventions? Would a WTO Declaration acknowledging the legal relevance of universal human rights for the interpretation and progressive development of WTO law be politically and legally desirable (e.g. for clarifying the jurisdiction of WTO dispute settlement bodies)? Under what conditions can violations of human rights justify recourse to international trade sanctions? Do WTO Members have a larger 'margin of appreciation' in democratically designing their respective *domestic* human rights laws for the protection of their *domestic citizens* than for resorting to international sanctions in response to human rights violations by *foreign* governments?

(7) Is there empirical evidence for 'conflicts' between WTO rules and human rights that cannot be resolved by interpreting WTO rules in conformity with the human rights obligations of WTO Members? Does the universal recognition of respect for human dignity and for human liberty as sources of 'inalienable human rights' imply that the 'inalienable core' of human

rights must always prevail (as *ius cogens*) over other conflicting rules of international law?

(8) Should UN human rights law and practices offer more guidance for designing a world trading system aimed at promoting the social welfare of all citizens and protecting fundamental rights (such as freedom of profession, freedom of opinion) also in the economic area? What is the relevance of human rights for WTO rules in favour of less-developed countries and related WTO assistance (such as 'trade facilitation')?

Even if the ILA should fail to reach agreement on answers to these and other related questions regarding the interrelationships between human rights and trade rules, promoting a worldwide discussion—inside and beyond the ILA membership—on these legal questions could assist WTO bodies in their task of promoting synergies between international trade law and human rights.[78]

IV. CONCLUSION: RTAS AND WTO NEGOTIATIONS AS COMPETING FORA FOR TRADE LIBERALIZATION AND CONSTITUTIONAL REFORMS

As long as the WTO continues to be perceived as lacking democratic legitimacy and efficiency in its task of promoting social welfare and 'sustainable development' through liberal trade, the ever increasing recourse to RTA's offers a second-best policy and welcome pressure on those governments that block trade liberalization and democratic reforms inside their own countries and in the WTO. The failure of the DDR negotiations on stricter WTO disciplines for RTAs is also due to the fact that both WTO rules and RTAs are rightly perceived as instruments not only of trade liberalization, but also of legal and political reforms inside trading countries.

It seems to be only a matter of time until WTO dispute settlement bodies will be confronted with human rights arguments (e.g. for interpreting the WTO provisions on protection of 'public morals', 'public order', and 'public health'). As the political WTO bodies are unlikely to take up this challenge, this chapter has argued that the ILA and other civil society institutions should follow the invitation by WTO DG Pascal Lamy to participate in 'cosmopolitics' and 'cosmopolitan constituencies' in order to support WTO dispute settlement bodies in developing appropriate legal methodologies and judicial methods for interpreting WTO rules in conformity with the human rights obligations of WTO Members.[79] European law and the WTO legal and dispute settlement system offer the most successful attempts to-date to overcome

---

[78] *See* ILA's Resolution on 'The Rule of Law in International Trade', adopted at the ILA Conference in July 2000 at London, Report of the 69th Conference at London, 2000, at 18–25.

[79] *See* above at n 15 and 25 and P. Lamy, *Towards World Democracy* (London : Policy Network, 2005).

failures of 'constitutional nationalism', as well as of UN law, in the search for more effective, legitimate and democratic global trade governance.[80]

The jurisprudence of regional courts (like the ECJ and the ECtHR) offers important examples of 'balancing principles' for reconciling trade rules and human rights. It also seems to confirm that the objectives, principles and 'general exceptions' of trade law (including WTO law) are flexible enough to avoid conflicts between trade rules and human rights. Yet, as suggested by Advocate-General Jacobs in *Schmidberger*, in view of the diversity of national human rights traditions, it 'cannot be automatically ruled out that a Member State which invokes the necessity to protect a right recognized by national law as fundamental nevertheless pursues an objective which as a matter of Community law must be regarded as illegitimate'.[81] Similarly, human rights arguments may not justify all kinds of departures from WTO rules (e.g. trade sanctions in response to human rights violations by foreign governments if the trade sanctions increase the suffering of the foreign people concerned).

There is, so far, no empirical evidence for conflicts among human rights and WTO rules on the level of legal principles. Yet, such conflicts may arise in the implementation of WTO rules and may not be easily resolved by claims of legal hierarchy of human rights, or by recourse to traditional conflict avoidance rules (like *lex posterior* and *lex specialis*). Views on the legitimacy and WTO consistency of trade-related human rights measures are likely to be influenced by civil society discussions and public perceptions of how WTO Members should protect fundamental rights in the trade policy area. The history of human rights as well as of trade law (e.g. since the guarantees of freedom of trade in the Magna Carta of 1215) suggests that legal protection of individual freedoms may not become effective without civil society struggles in defense of private freedom against protectionist abuses of government powers. Protection of human liberty inevitably entails specialization, exchange, and markets as decentralized, citizen-driven information-, coordination- and sanctioning-mechanisms. Yet, European history also teaches that the social acceptability of international market competition depends on promoting 'social justice', as reflected in the explicit commitments of the EC Treaty Constitution to a 'social market economy' (Article I–3) and of the WTO's Doha Round negotiations to a 'Development Round'.

The moral legitimacy and democratic importance of 'cosmopolitics' and of 'cosmopolitan constituencies' (like the ILA) for clarifying the cosmopolitan 'human rights dimensions' of WTO law and policies can be appreciated best by recalling their Kantian origins. According to Kantian legal philosophy, the moral 'categorical imperative' of protecting human dignity and maximum equal freedoms of individuals through a 'universal law of freedom' requires

---

[80] *See* Petersmann, above at n 37.
[81] Opinion delivered on 11 July 2002 in Case C–112/00, above at n 65, at paras 96–8.

national and *international* as well as *cosmopolitan* constitutional rights limiting abuses of power inside states, in intergovernmental relations, as well as in cosmopolitan relations among individuals and foreign governments.[82] The needed 'public enlightenment' and antagonistic struggles for progressively realizing such interrelated constitutional rights require democratic discourse in a communicating public that may eventually turn into a cosmopolitan community of world-citizens.[83] Commitment to 'universalizable principles', rational public criticism and social antagonism (which Kant described as the 'unsocial sociability' of rational individuals) are the only reliable guides, even if they entail 'an uncomfortable condition of permanent revolution'.[84]

Since the entry into force of the WTO Agreement in 1995, the civil society claims for more transparency and 'deliberative democracy' in WTO decision-making processes have influenced WTO Members to accept an impressive number of legal and institutional reforms (such as participation of ever more NGOs in WTO Ministerial Conferences, annual WTO symposia with NGOs, public access to almost all WTO documents and—for the first time in 2005— to a WTO dispute settlement panel meeting, WTO decisions facilitating access to medicines and control of 'conflict diamonds', WTO jurisprudence accepting *amicus curiae* briefs). Civil society pressures have also been of crucial importance for democratic reforms of RTAs, notably in Europe. It seems to be no coincidence that many recent proposals for constitutional reforms of multi-level trade governance in the WTO—such as proposals for the creation of advisory WTO bodies with representatives from parliaments and civil society, transformation of the *ad hoc* WTO dispute settlement panels into a 'permanent Panel', WTO competition and investment rules, and more generous preferential treatment of less-developed WTO Members—have been initiated by the EU. The rights-based, cosmopolitan European constitutionalism differs fundamentally from the constitutional nationalism in most democracies outside Europe.[85] RTAs in Europe and in the Americas have elaborated policy

---

[82] For a discussion of Kant's constitutional and cosmopolitan legal theories, and for a criticism of the lack of constitutional theory in public international law doctrine, *see* E.-U. Petersmann, 'How to Constitutionalize International Law and Foreign Policy for the Benefit of Civil Society?' (1998) 20 Mich J Int L 1.

[83] *See* A.W. Wood, *Kant's Ethical Thought* (Cambridge: CUP, 1999), 298. On Kant's concept of 'Weltbürgerrecht' (cosmopolitan law) *see*, e.g. R. Brandt, 'Vom Weltbürgerrrecht', in O. Höffe (ed), *Zum Ewigen Frieden* (Berlin: Akademie, 1995), 133–48 and V. Gerhardt, *Immanuel Kant's Entwurf 'Zum Ewigen Frieden'* (Darmstadt: Wiss. Buchgesellschaft, 1995), at 102 ff. On democratic discourse theory, *see* J. Habermas, *Between Facts and Norms—Contributions to a Discourse Theory of Law and Democracy* (Cambridge, Mass.: MIT Press, 1996), 315–28.

[84] Wood, *ibid.*, at 333.

[85] For some Anglo-Saxon communitarian lawyers, even Europe cannot be properly described as 'constitutionalized' until it embodies a European polity and *demos* legitimizing its community (*see* J. Weiler, *The Constitution of Europe* (Cambridge: CUP, 1999)). Some Anglo-Saxon lawyers also challenge the cosmopolitan recognition of 'market freedoms' in European constitutional law on the ground that neither individual economic freedom nor other individual rights are 'a matter considered essential to constitutionalisation in the received tradition' of 'mature constitutional systems, for example in the United States, Canada and Australia' (D.Z. Cass, *The*

alternatives that could inspire future WTO reforms. Following the ECJ jurisprudence that fundamental rights are part of the common constitutional principles of EC law, respect for fundamental freedoms, for human rights and
democracy has become progressively recognized as an explicit objective of
internal EU policies (*see* Articles 6, 7 EU) as well as of the EU's external
development policy (Article 177 EC), cooperation agreements with developed
countries (Article 181(a) EC) and common foreign and security policy (Article
11 EU).[86]

It could be a logical consequence of the EU's human rights policy in the
trade policy area if—just as Article 5 of the EC's Lomé Convention and Article
9 of its Cotonou Agreement with more than 70 LDCs define their 'development' objectives in terms of respect for human rights—the EU would propose
a similar rights-based definition of the WTO objective of 'sustainable development' (WTO Preamble). Such an EU and WTO initiative should emphasize
Europe's experience that:

- respect for human rights is a democratic precondition of the legitimacy of
  international trade law and of its democratic support by citizens and
  parliaments;
- European courts have hardly ever identified conflicts between fundamental
  rights and liberal trade rules and, if so, have given preference to human
  rights (e.g. freedom of opinion, freedom of assembly, respect for human
  dignity, privacy and family life) rather than to liberal trade rules;
- almost all the complaints in European courts about alleged conflicts
  between trade rules and human rights could likewise arise in WTO dispute
  settlement proceedings;
- neither the several hundred past GATT and WTO dispute settlement proceedings nor the human rights analyses of WTO rules (e.g. by the UN) have
  identified conflicts among WTO law and human rights on the level of
  principles;
- WTO Members should not—once again—leave the clarification of the
  human rights dimensions of WTO law to WTO dispute settlement bodies
  without giving political guidance on how to reconcile WTO rules and
  human rights; and
- acknowledgment of the existing human rights obligations would be without
  prejudice to the diverse national and regional human rights traditions of
  WTO Members, the limited competences of the WTO, and to the different
  approaches of WTO Members to implementing WTO rules in domestic
  laws.

Constitutionalization of the WTO (Oxford: OUP, 2005), 168, 176, 191). For a criticism of 'constitutional nationalism' and of the book by Cass *see* my book review in CMLR 2006 at 890–892
and E.-U. Petersmann, 'Introduction and Summary', in Joerges and Petersmann, above at n 20.

[86] *See* above at n 1, 2, 5 and 40.

13

Sustainable Development in Regional Trade Agreements

MARIE-CLAIRE CORDONIER SEGGER *

I. INTRODUCTION

Sustainable development is recognized as an objective of global and regional trade law and policy. In *EC—Tariff Preferences*, the WTO Appellate Body affirmed that the Preamble of the 1994 WTO Agreement sets sustainable development as 'an objective of the WTO'.[1] An explicit commitment 'to promote sustainable development' is also found in the preambles of many regional trade agreements (RTAs) that have been negotiated over the past decade in the Americas. What does it mean to set sustainable development as an objective of a trade agreement, and how can treaty parties which have set this objective for their RTAs make it operational through innovative procedures and provisions? This chapter discusses these questions with reference to RTAs in the Americas.

A. Contours and legal foundations of sustainable development

A brief consideration of the ordinary meaning of sustainable development and how the concept has been addressed in international law (including WTO law

* The author thanks Kristin Price, CISDL Researcher at Cambridge University, for her exemplary contributions, Oana Dolea, CISDL Researcher at McGill University, for her excellent research, Dr. Markus Gehring, and the editors of this volume for their advice. She acknowledges Foreign Affairs Canada, the International Development Research Centre, the Social Sciences and Humanities Research Council of Canada (SSHRC), and the British Chevening Award, also colleagues in the SSHRC Research Group on Regional Integration Agreements and the database funded by the Dobson Fund, McGill University Faculty of Law, for their support in this continuing legal research. The chapter builds on legal research published in M.C. Cordonier Segger and M. Leichner Reynal (eds), *Beyond the Barricades: The Americas Trade and Sustainability Agenda* (Aldershot: Ashgate, 2005), and M. Gehring and M.C. Cordonier Segger (eds), *Sustainable Development in World Trade Law* (The Hague: Kluwer, 2005).

[1] WTO Appellate Body Report, *EC—Tariff Preferences*, WT/DS246/AB/R, adopted 20 April 2004, para. 94.

and policy) can shed light on how it might be implemented as the objective of an RTA.

Development can be defined as the process of expanding people's choices, enabling improvements in collective and individual quality of life, and in the exercise of full freedoms and rights.[2] These freedoms include the opportunities for individuals to utilize economic resources for the purposes of consumption, production or exchange.[3] Though development means more than mere economic growth, the expansion of economic opportunities is usually considered an important component of the development process.

The concept of *sustainable* development has gained great currency in recent years. While its underlying ideas may have governed ancient cultures and traditions for millennia,[4] the term itself likely originated in laws and policies governing forest industry management practices.[5] According to these rules, only as much of the forest should be harvested as could re-grow each year, in order to maintain the forest as a whole (the natural capital). As such, the sustainable development concept, from inception, did not involve preventing economic activity but rather a *re-directing* of such activity, in order to promote the potential for long-term, *sustained* yields from development activities. The most accepted definition today, from the 1987 Brundtland Report, describes sustainable development as '. . . development that meets the needs of the present without compromising the ability of future generations to meet their own needs'.[6] This definition is usefully vague enough to have meaning in many diverse contexts and cultures, but it seems to lack certain precision for an international legal rule. Indeed, scholarly debates continue as to whether sustainable development can be considered a principle of customary international law, and if so, what its normative effect would be.[7] This chapter does not seek to resolve these questions.[8] Rather, it starts from the recognition that the

---

[2] *See* A. Sen, *Development as Freedom* (Oxford: OUP, 1999), 35. *See also* the UN Development Programme, Human Development Reports, available at hdr.undp.org (visited 23 January 2006). *See also* UN Development Programme, *Making Global Trade Work for People* (London: Earthscan, 2003), xi.

[3] Sen, *ibid.*, at 39.

[4] As observed by H.E. Judge C.G. Weeramantry in his extraordinary Separate Opinion for the International Court of Justice, Advisory Opinion, *Danube Dam Case (Hungary v Slovakia)* (1997) 37 ILM 162.

[5] *See* H.C. von Carlowitz, *Sylvicultura Oeconomica* (Leipzig: Braun, 1713).

[6] World Commission on Environment and Development, *Our Common Future* (Oxford: OUP, 1987), 43.

[7] *See* V. Lowe, 'Sustainable Developments and Unsustainable Arguments', in A. Boyle and D. Freestone (eds), *International Law and Sustainable Development: Past Achievements and Future Challenges* (Oxford: OUP, 1999), 26.

[8] For further discussion, *see* M.C. Cordonier Segger and A. Khalfan, *Sustainable Development Law: Principles, Practices and Prospects* (Oxford: OUP, 2004), 45–50, 95–8. *See also* D. French, *International Law and Policy of Sustainable Development* (Manchester: Manchester UP, 2005), M.C. Cordonier Segger and Judge C.G. Weeramantry (eds), *Sustainable Justice: Reconciling Social, Economic and Environmental Law* (Leiden: Martinus Nijhoff, 2004) and Boyle and Freestone, *ibid.*

promotion of sustainable development is the explicit object and purpose of many binding treaties, including the WTO Agreement and a host of RTAs in the Americas. In the context of the decisions of trade dispute settlement bodies which have sought to interpret this objective, this chapter examines provisions used by parties to make it operational.

The 1992 United Nations Conference on Environment and Development (UNCED) in Rio de Janeiro,[9] which attracted over 140 heads of state, offers a starting point. In Agenda 21, States jointly called for '[t]he further development of international law on sustainable development, giving special attention to the delicate balance between environmental and developmental concerns'.[10] Similarly, in the 1997 *Danube Dam Case* the International Court of Justice noted that the 'need to reconcile economic development with protection of the environment is aptly expressed in the concept of sustainable development'.[11] In 2002, the Johannesburg Declaration on Sustainable Development, and the Johannesburg Plan of Implementation affirmed a collective commitment by countries to 'advance and strengthen the interdependent and mutually reinforcing pillars of sustainable development—economic development, social development and environmental protection—at the local, national, regional, and global levels,'[12] explicitly recognizing the third 'social' pillar of the concept. And in the 2005 *Iron Rhine* decision, arbitrators in the Permanent Court of Arbitration[13] recognized a duty to prevent or mitigate harm to the environment in international law, and suggested that in accordance with the notion of sustainable development, parties must take this duty into account when implementing economic development treaties.

B. Incremental Promotion of Sustainable Development in WTO Negotiations, Law and Policy

Building on the GATT 1947,[14] the Preamble of the 1994 WTO Agreement recognizes that WTO Members' 'relations in the field of trade and economic endeavour should be conducted with a view to . . . allowing for the optimal use of the world's resources in accordance with the objective of sustainable

---

[9] *See* Rio Declaration on Environment and Development, done at Rio de Janeiro, 14 June 1992, UN Doc. A/CONF.151/26/Rev.1 (Vol. I), 3–8; reprinted in (1992) 31 ILM 874 and Report of the UNCED ('Agenda 21'), done at Rio de Janeiro, 13 August 1992, UN Doc. A/Conf.151/26 (Vol. II).

[10] Agenda 21, *ibid.*, at Ch 39(1)(a).

[11] *Danube Dam Case*, above at n 4. *See also* Lowe, above at n 7, at 36 and Boyle and Freestone, above at n 7, at 16–8.

[12] 2002 Johannesburg Declaration, done at Johannesburg, 26 August to 4 September 2002, UN Doc. A/AC.257/32.

[13] The Permanent Court of Arbitration reaffirmed the imperative of balancing development and environmental protection in its Arbitral Award for the *Arbitration Regarding the Iron Rhine ('Ijzeren Rijn') Railway (Belgium v Netherlands)*, 24 May 2005, at paras 59, 114, available at www.pca-cpa.org (visited 23 January 2006).

[14] The Preamble of the GATT 1947 referred to '[. . .] developing the full use of the resources of the world [. . .]'.

development . . .'.[15] This was amplified by the 1996 Singapore Ministerial Declaration, which stated that '[f]ull implementation of the WTO Agreements will make an important contribution to achieving the objectives of sustainable development'.[16] Here, sustainable development objectives are clearly linked to the implementation of trade agreements, rather than simply the optimal use of natural resources. Further, the 1998 Geneva Ministerial Declaration states, at paragraph 4: 'We shall also continue to improve our efforts towards the objectives of sustained economic growth and sustainable development'.[17] As such, the WTO and Member States have formally recognized that sustainable development is not only related to natural resources, or an automatic result of the liberalization process, but is actually one of the objectives of the WTO itself. Indeed, during the 1998–1999 negotiations leading toward the Seattle Ministerial Conference, several Members sought to strengthen the WTO's sustainable development mandate, or to clarify its environmental focus.[18] Other Members resisted addressing 'non-trade' (social or environmental) issues in the WTO, and sought to underline the development aspect of the concept.[19] This debate led to the recognition, in the 2001 Doha Ministerial Declaration[20] launching the Doha Round of trade negotiations, at paragraph 6, that:

We strongly reaffirm our commitment to the objective of sustainable development, as stated in the Preamble to the Marrakesh Agreement. We are convinced that the aims of upholding and safeguarding an open and non-discriminatory multilateral trading system, and acting for the protection of the environment *and the promotion of sustainable development* can and must be mutually supportive . . . We encourage efforts to promote cooperation between the WTO and relevant international environmental *and developmental organizations*, especially in the lead-up to the World Summit on Sustainable Development to be held in Johannesburg, South Africa, in September 2002.[21] (emphasis added).

As such, members recognized sustainable development as an objective of the WTO, placing it into a strengthened context, and emphasized, in the explicit

[15] Preamble, WTO Agreement. *See* M. Gehring and M.C. Cordonier Segger (eds), *Sustainable Development in World Trade Law* (The Hague: Kluwer, 2005), at 1–24.

[16] Singapore Ministerial Declaration, WT/MIN(96)/DEC, adopted 13 December 1996.

[17] Geneva Ministerial Declaration, WT/MIN(98)/DEC, adopted 20 May 1998.

[18] *See*, e.g. Preparations for the 1999 Ministerial Conference—Trade and Sustainable Development, Communication from the US, WTO Doc. WT/GC/W/304, 6 August 1999, at 8; Preparations for the 1999 Ministerial Conference—Trade and Environment, Communication from Norway, WTO Doc. WT/GC/W/176, 30 April 1999 and Preparations for the 1999 Ministerial Conference—EC Approach to Trade and Environment in the New WTO Round, Communication from the EC, WTO Doc. WT/GC/W/194, 1 June 1999.

[19] *See*, e.g. Preparations for the 1999 Ministerial Conference—Trade, Environment and Sustainable Development, Communication from Cuba, WTO Doc. WT/GC/W/387, 15 November 1999. *See also* the statements from Kenya: WTO Doc. WT/GC/W/233; Bangladesh: WTO Doc. WT/GC/W/251; Pakistan: WTO Doc. WT/GC/W/126; Dominican Republic–Honduras–Pakistan: WTO Doc. WT/GC/W/255 and Cuba–Dominican Republic–Honduras–Pakistan: WTO Doc. WT/GC/W/163, as referenced in (1999) 3(46) Bridges Weekly Trade News Digest.

[20] *See* Doha Ministerial Declaration, WT/MIN(01)/DEC/1, adopted 4 November 2001.

[21] *Ibid.*, at para. 6.

reference to 'development' organizations, its social development element. Indeed, in paragraph 51, Members went further, stating that:

[t]he Committee on Trade and Development and the Committee on Trade and Environment shall, within their respective mandates, each act as a forum to identify and debate developmental and environmental aspects of the negotiations, in order to help achieve the objective of having sustainable development appropriately reflected.[22]

Questions remain as to whether these two Committees, even abetted by the myriad concurrent global processes, will be able to fulfill these tasks in the Doha Round. Decisions within the WTO dispute settlement system can also shed light on how trade law has evolved in recognizing and implementing this objective.

C. Sustainable Development in WTO Dispute Settlement

The WTO Appellate Body has been called upon to interpret the concept of sustainable development in trade law. Two cases, *US—Shrimp*[23], and *EC—Tariff Preferences*[24] are particularly relevant. In this chapter, a few brief comments must suffice.[25]

In *US—Shrimp*, the Panel concluded that 'the best way for the parties to this dispute to contribute effectively to the protection of sea turtles in a manner consistent with WTO objectives, including sustainable development, would be to reach cooperative agreements on integrated conservation strategies'.[26] On appeal, this finding was not overturned. The US stated that in the light of the preamble of the WTO Agreement, '[a]n environmental purpose is fundamental to the application of Article XX . . .'.[27] The Appellate Body Report considered the Preamble, but found that:

The preamble of the WTO Agreement—which informs not only the GATT 1994, but also the other covered agreements—explicitly acknowledges 'the objective of sustainable development.[28]

Footnote 107 in this finding deserves particular attention in understanding the concept from the WTO Appellate Body's perspective. The note explained that '[t]his concept has been generally accepted as *integrating economic and social*

---

[22] *Ibid.*, at para. 51.
[23] *See* WTO Panel Report, *US—Shrimp*, WT/DS58/R and Corr. 1, adopted 6 November 1998, as modified by the Appellate Body Report, WT/DS58/AB/R. *See also* WTO Appellate Body Report, *US—Shrimp*, WT/DS58/AB/R, adopted 6 November 1998.
[24] WTO Appellate Body Report, *EC—Tariff Preferences*, above at n 1.
[25] This section is based on a discussion that is further developed in Gehring and Cordonier Segger, above at n 15, at 129–87.
[26] WTO Panel Report, *US—Shrimp*, above at n 23, at para. 9.1.
[27] WTO Appellate Body Report, *US—Shrimp*, above at n 23, at para. 12.
[28] *Ibid.*, at para. 129.

development and environmental protection[29] (emphasis added). This is remarkable for two reasons. First, the WTO Appellate Body expresses itself on the nature of sustainable development, recognizing that it is an objective of the WTO Agreements, and that this objective informs interpretation of these Agreements. Second, the Appellate Body specifically emphasizes the need to integrate all three elements or 'pillars' of sustainable development, recognizing the important social dimension of the concept. This reasoning was adopted and applied in *US—Shrimp (Article 21.5—Malaysia)*,[30] when Malaysia argued that the measures taken by the United States did not comply with the recommendations and rulings of the DSB. In particular, the Panel at paragraph 5.54 stated that:

In that framework, assessing first the object and purpose of the WTO Agreement, we note that the WTO preamble refers to the notion of 'sustainable development'.[31] This means that in interpreting the terms of the chapeau, we must keep in mind that sustainable development is one of the objectives of the WTO Agreement.[32]

In defining this objective, the Panel at footnote 202 cites the Rio Declaration and the Agenda 21, which refer to the need to balance environmental protection with the social and economic development needs of developing countries, and to ensure that trade and environment policies are 'mutually supportive'. On appeal, this interpretation was not overturned by the WTO Appellate Body.[33]

In *EC—Tariff Preferences*,[34] the WTO Appellate Body, citing its report in *US—Shrimp*, noted that the objectives of the WTO could be fulfilled through 'General Exceptions', observing that 'the optimal use of the world's resources in accordance with the objective of sustainable development' could be achieved through application of the WTO exceptions, such as Article XX(g) GATT.

The reasoning of the WTO Appellate Body and Panel with regard to the 'explicit recognition by WTO Members of the objective of sustainable development in the preamble of the WTO Agreement'[35] in these cases, taken together with recent negotiations among Members, suggests that the sustainable development commitment in the Preamble has legal relevance. As such, it could also be used to interpret trade obligations also in regional trade

---

[29] *Ibid.*, at note 107 reads (in part): 'This concept has been generally accepted as integrating economic and social development and environmental protection . . .'

[30] WTO Panel Report, *US—Shrimp (Article 21.5—Malaysia)*, WT/DS58/RW, adopted 21 November 2001, as upheld by the Appellate Body Report, WT/DS58/AB/RW.

[31] *Ibid.*, at para. 5.54. Note 202 reads (in part): 'the concept is elaborated in detailed action plans in Agenda 21 so as to put in place development that is sustainable—i.e. that "meets the needs of the present generation without compromising the ability of future generations to meet their own needs" . . .'

[32] *Ibid.*   [33] *Ibid.*

[34] WTO Appellate Body Report, *EC—Tariff Preferences*, above at n 1.

[35] WTO Appellate Body Report, *US—Shrimp (Article 21.5—Malaysia)*, WT/DS58/AB/RW, adopted 21 November 2001, at para. 131.

agreements. The rest of this paper examines the negotiation processes and texts of RTAs that explicitly recognize sustainable development as an object-ive, and considers how these treaties can contribute to 'development that is sustainable',[36] by 'integrating economic and social development and environ-mental protection'.[37] Such procedures and provisions would encourage parties 'reach cooperative agreements on integrated ... strategies'.[38] With these thoughts in mind, this chapter now turns to its primary focus: a brief discus-sion of recent innovations in Americas RTAs that appear to respond to this sustainable development objective.

II. SUSTAINABLE DEVELOPMENT AND RTAS IN THE AMERICAS

In the Americas, a web of different bi-lateral, regional, and other economic cooperation agreements has entered into force in the last decade. Four regional (or 'sub-regional') integration arrangements include the Caricom,[39] the Andean Community,[40] the Mercosur,[41] and the Central American Com-mon Market.[42] These projects incorporate innovative institutional and other social and environmental cooperation mechanisms, and have potential to sup-port sustainable development.[43] A second model, similar to the 1994 North American Free Trade Agreement, is the 'straight' free trade agreement (FTA). The 1995 Bolivia–Mexico FTA,[44] the Canada–Chile FTA,[45] the Canada–Costa Rica FTA,[46] the Chile–US FTA[47] and the US–Peru FTA[48] are examples of such

[36] WTO Panel Report, *US—Shrimp (Article 21.5—Malaysia)*, above at n 30, at note 202.
[37] WTO Appellate Body Report, *US—Shrimp*, above at n 23, at note 107.
[38] WTO Panel Report, *US—Shrimp* above at n 23, at para. 9.1
[39] Caricom Free Trade Agreements, done at Costa Rica, 9 March 2004 and the Dominican Republic, 22 August 1998, available at www.caricom.org (visited 23 January 2006).
[40] Andean Subregional Integration Agreement, done at Cartagena, 25 June 2003, available at www.sice.oas.org/agreemts/Comand_e.asp (visited 23 January 2006).
[41] Treaty of Asuncion, signed 26 March 1991, in force 29 November 1991 (1991) 30 ILM 1044.
[42] General Treaty on Central American Economic Integration, signed 13 December 1960, in force 4 June 1961 (Guatemala, El Salvador and Nicaragua), 27 April 1962 (Honduras) and 23 September 1963 (Costa Rica), 455 UNTS 3
[43] For discussion, *see* M.C. Cordonier Segger *et al.*, *Trade Rules and Sustainability in the Americas* (Winnipeg: IISD, 1999), *Social Rules and Sustainability in the Americas* (Winnipeg: IISD/OAS, 2004) and *Ecological Rules and Sustainability in the Americas* (Winnipeg: IISD/UNEP, 2002). *See also* Cordonier Segger and Khalfan, above at n 8, at 281–93.
[44] Bolivia–Mexico Free Trade Agreement, signed 10 September 1994, in force 1 January 1995.
[45] Canada–Chile Free Trade Agreement, signed 5 December 1996, in force 5 July 1997.
[46] Canada–Costa Rica Free Trade Agreement, signed 23 April 2001, in force 1 November 2002.
[47] Chile–US Free Trade Agreement, signed 6 June 2003, in force 1 January 2004. Additionally, US Trade Representative, Press Release: The US–Chile Free Trade—An Early Record of Success, available at www.ustr.gov (visited 23 January 2006) and J. Sagar, 'The Labour and Environment Chapters of the United States–Chile Free Trade Agreement: An Improvement over the Weak Enforcement Provisions of the NAFTA Side Agreements on Labour and the Environment' (2004) 21 Ariz J Int & Comp L, 913.
[48] US Trade Representative, Press Release: US and Peru Conclude Free Trade Agreement, Negotiations with Colombia, Ecuador to Continue Early Next Year (07/12/2005), available at www.ustr.gov (visited 23 January 2006).

agreements. Thirty-four states have also embarked on hemispheric negotiations, which, if successful, will result in a Free Trade Agreement of the
Americas (FTAA).[49] Such regional trade agreements 'RTAs' are the focus of the
present chapter. Some contain parallel or 'side agreements' on environmental
cooperation and labour issues, while others, negotiated under the current US
trade promotion authority, actually incorporate social and environmental
chapters, and others contain only specific provisions on these issues throughout the text of the treaty.[50] Provisions from the NAFTA and these newer RTAs
in the Americas, including certain procedural innovations in the negotiations
for the FTAA, provide examples for the discussion in this chapter.

A. Procedural Innovations in the Negotiation of Americas RTAs

Sustainable development has an important procedural element. Prior to the
negotiation of an RTA, states may seek to promote openness, consultation,
assessment, capacity-building, and cooperation, in order to contribute to
sustainable development.

1. Impact assessments and reviews

One particularly important procedural step for sustainable development
involves impact assessment of new trade rules. Critics of trade agreements
have warned that the economic growth stimulated by a trade agreement may
have significant negative impacts on social and environmental sustainability.[51]
Partly in response to this pressure, States have begun to seek ways to identify,
then prevent or mitigate environmental and social impacts of new trade rules.
Through the use of national and regional environmental impact assessments,
potential impacts can be considered, taken into account and even avoided;
social or human rights impact assessments can also be conducted, running
parallel to environmental impact assessments.[52] Further, social and environmental impacts can be considered together in an assessment, using integrated
or 'sustainability impact assessments' that are usually applied to specific chapters of a trade agreement, sector by sector.[53] While not all sustainability impact

---

[49] M.C. Cordonier Segger and M. Leichner Reynal (eds), *Beyond the Barricades: The Americas
Trade and Sustainability Agenda* (Aldershot: Ashgate, 2005). *See also* M.C. Cordonier Segger,
'Sustainable Development in the Negotiation of the FTAA' (2004) 27 Ford ILJ 1118.

[50] Cordonier Segger and Khalfan, above at n 8, at 281–93.

[51] *See*, e.g. The Public Citizen, Global Trade Watch: Promoting Democracy by Challenging
Corporate Globalization, available at www.citizen.org/trade/nafta/ (visited 23 January 2006),
Stop CAFTA, available at www.stopcafta.org/ (visited 23 January 2006) and Anti-GATT, available
at www.gatt.org/ (visited 23 January 2006).

[52] UN Environment Programme, Reference Manual for the Integrated Assessment of Trade-
Related Policies, Geneva 2001. *See also* S. Walker, 'Human Rights Impact Assessments of Trade-
Related Policies', in Gehring and Cordonier Segger, above at n 15, at 217–56.

[53] C. Kirkpatrick and N. Lee, 'WTO New Round: Sustainability Impact Assessment Study
(Phase Two Report): Sustainability Impact Assessment', available at www.sia-trade.org/wto/
Phase2/EXSUMFINAL.htm (visited 23 January 2006).

assessments include a strong social dimension, it is becoming increasingly accepted to do so.[54] At present, several States have committed to perform regular impact assessments of global and regional trade negotiations.[55] Pilot studies have been conducted for the North American Symposium for the Assessment of Trade and Environment policies,[56] and for the United Nations Environment Programme.[57]

These commitments are reflected in the side agreements of several Americas RTAs. For example, the North American Agreement about Environmental Cooperation contains the obligation to assess environmental effects of the NAFTA. The Commission on Environmental Cooperation is, institutionally, separate from the NAFTA Commission. However, according to Article 10(6)(d) of the NAAEC, the Council of Ministers of the CEC is responsible for 'considering on an ongoing basis the environmental effects of the NAFTA' in cooperation with the NAFTA Commission.[58] While seeking broad public participation,[59] the CEC studied methodological approaches[60] and tested them in case studies,[61] leading the CEC Ministerial Council to adopt an Analytic Framework for Assessing the Environmental Effects of the North American Free Trade Agreement.[62] The Analytical Framework has since been applied in three case studies, examining Mexican corn, beef production in the US and in Canada, and the electricity market in all three countries.[63]

National reviews can also be conducted. For instance, the US carried out a Final Environmental Review of the US–Chile FTA.[64] It also found that trade in environmental goods is likely to increase and thus could yield positive effects.

[54] H. Blanco, 'Evaluación de la Sustentabilidad de los Acuerdos Comerciales y su Aplicación en el Contexto Latinoamericano y del ALCA', in H. Blanco, M. Araya and C. Murillo, *ALCA y Medio Ambiente: Ideas desde Latinoamerica* (Santiago de Chile: CIPMA / GETS / CINPE, 2003).

[55] For example, WTO Doc. WT/GC/W/304, above at n 18, and Preparations for the 1999 Ministerial Conference—Canadian Approach to Trade and Environment in the New WTO Round, Communication from Canada, WTO Doc. WT/GC/W/358, 12 October 1999.

[56] K.P. Gallagher and H. Blanco, 'Sustainability Assessments: Tools for Effective Trade Policy in the Hemisphere' (IRC Paper, 9 April 2003).

[57] Centro de Investigación y Planificación del Medio Ambiente (CIPMA), *Environmental Impacts of Trade Liberalization and Policies for the Sustainable Management of Natural Resources: A Case Study of Chile's Mining Sector* (Geneva: UNEP, 1999), available at www.unep.ch/etu/etp/acts/capbld/rdone/chile.htm (visited 23 January 2006).

[58] J. Barr, 'Final Analytical Framework to Assess the Environmental effects of NAFTA', in WWF and Fundación Futuro Latinoamericano, *The International Experts' Meeting on Sustainability Assessments of Trade Liberalisation—Quito, Ecuador 6–8 March 2000, Full Meeting Report* (Gland: WWF, 2000), 100.

[59] *Ibid.*, at iii.

[60] Commission for Environmental Cooperation, *Building a Framework for Assessing NAFTA Environmental Effects* (Montreal: CEC, 1996).

[61] *Ibid.*, Assessing Environmental Effects of the North American Free Trade Agreement (NAFTA)—An Analytic Framework (Phase II) and Issue Studies (Montreal: CEC 1999).

[62] *Ibid.*, *Analytic Framework for Assessing the Environmental Effects of the NAFTA* (Montreal: CEC, 1999), available at www.cec.org/files/pdf/ECONOMY/Frmwrk-e_EN.pdf (visited 23 January 2006).

[63] CEC, above at n 61, at 65.

[64] Final Environmental Review of the US–Chile FTA, June 2003, available at www.ustr.gov (visited 23 January 2006).

In another example, the US carried out an Interim Environmental Review of the US–Andean Free Trade Agreement (Peru, Ecuador and Colombia).[65] It found that degradation of mahogany forests, marine resources, and marine water quality might be exacerbated by the trade agreement, if environmental laws and standards were not implemented effectively.[66] In 2001, the Canadian Cabinet Decision on Environmental Assessment of Trade Negotiations[67] began to mandate examinations, *ex ante*, of environmental impacts for new trade agreements. As such, while there are no environmental assessments for either the Canada–Chile FTA or the Canada–Costa Rica FTA, an Initial Environmental Assessment was carried out for the Canada–Chile Government Procurement Chapter to be added to the Canada–Chile FTA.[68] The ministry concluded that there were no significant environmental impacts *in Canada*, and thus refrained from conducting a draft environmental assessment. Such studies provide one procedural mechanism to support the achievement of sustainable development through a trade agreement, as they can both identify and recommend areas for greater social or environmental cooperation between parties to an RTA, and also find ways to adjust the drafting of certain provisions in order to minimize their potential impacts on the environment. However neither the Canadian nor the US assessments consider social impacts at this point, and the Canadian studies only assess potential impacts within Canada.

2. *Other procedural innovations related to sustainable development*

Americas RTA negotiations have sought to promote sustainable development through other procedural innovations, as can be demonstrated using examples from ongoing negotiations for a Free Trade Area of the Americas (FTAA). First, in the interest of transparency, Trade Ministries can periodically release draft texts of trade negotiations, inviting public comment. For example, there have been consecutive releases of the FTAA draft text during the course of FTAA negotiations, and Ministers have established a Committee of Government Representatives for the Participation of Civil Society to consider comments received.[69] The need to promote openness in order to be consistent with sustainable development was part of the arguments used by States to secure this innovation.[70] Second, civil society organizations, in the context of sustainable

---

[65] Interim Environmental Review of the US–Andean FTA, February 2005, available at www.ustr.gov (visited 23 January 2006).

[66] *Ibid.*, at 10.

[67] Framework for Conducting Environmental Assessments of Trade Negotiations, available at www.dfait-maeci.gc.ca/tna-nac/EAF_Sep2000-en.asp (visited 23 January 2006).

[68] Initial Environmental Assessment of the Canada–Chile Government Procurement Chapter to be added to the Canada–Chile FTA, available at www.dfait-maeci.gc.ca/tna-nac/RB/report_chileen.asp (visited 23 January 2006).

[69] M. Rivas 'ALCA y Participación de la Sociedad Civil', in Blanco, Araya and Murillo, above at n 54 and M.C. Cordonier Segger and J. Cabrera, 'Public Participation in Americas Trade and Environment Regimes', in Cordonier Segger and Leichner Reynal, above at n 49.

[70] Hemisphere Ministers Agree To Release FTAA Texts, Set Deadlines, Inside US Trade, 9 April 2001.

development, are often capable of organizing themselves to provide construct-ive input into RTA negotiations. For instance, during the FTAA negotiations civil society organizations prepared an 'Americas Trade and Sustainable Development Forum' parallel to each meeting of the FTAA ministers.[71] Third, national trade authorities are increasingly consulting with national environment and development authorities on specific issues related to RTA negotiations. Such consultations can also be carried out through relevant intergovernmental organizations, which also provide training for such author-ities where this is needed to ensure meaningful input.[72] Finally, State and civil society officials, particularly from smaller economies, can also benefit from commitments for capacity-building in areas of concern in order to build their capacity to respond to requests for participation, requests for information regarding social and environmental measures that might be affected by trade disciplines, and other demands.[73] For instance, upon the request of the smaller economies in the FTAA negotiations, a Hemispheric Cooperation Programme has been established and has begun to support capacity building in trade issues, including civil society, environment, and development projects.[74]

B. Americas RTA Provisions Related to Sustainable Development

Procedural innovations, as well as other reasons, have led parties to set sus-tainable development as an objective of several RTAs in the Americas. Putting this commitment into practice may prove challenging. However, the objective is by no means impossible to achieve. As noted above, the WTO Appellate Body has found the sustainable development means 'development that is sus-tainable', and involves 'integrating social and economic development and environmental protection', developing 'cooperative agreements on integrated . . . strategies', and ensuring that trade, environment and development policies are 'mutually supportive'. Indeed, parties to RTAs have developed several types of innovative substantive provisions to deliver on this objective. A few of the most common provisions can be briefly surveyed.

---

[71] Ministerial Declaration of Miami, FTAA 8th Ministerial Meeting, done at Miami, adopted 20 November 2003, available at www.ftaa-alca.org/Ministerials/Miami/Miami_e.asp (visited 23 January 2006): 'We appreciate the recommendations made by the . . . Americas Trade and Sustainable Development Forum, organized with a broad representation of civil society, and with whom we met here in Miami, Florida . . .'

[72] *See* references to UNEP and UNDP collaboration in M. Pérez-Esteve 'Oportunidades para Reforzar los Beneficios resultantes de la Globalización en America Latina y el Caribe: Mejorami-ento de la Capacidad en materia de Comercio, Medio Ambiente y Desarrollo', in Blanco, Araya, and Murillo, above at n 54.

[73] Tripartite Committee of the FTAA—Consultative Group on Smaller Economies, Summary Matrix of Project Profiles, FTAA.Sme/Inf/105/Rev.3, adopted 14 July 2003.

[74] *See also* Draft FTAA, Annex III, available at www.ftaa-alca.org/FTAADraft03/Index_e.asp (visited 23 January 2006).

1. Sustainable Development Objectives Recognized in RTA Preambles

The Preamble of the 1994 North American Free Trade Agreement between the Government of Canada, the Government of the United Mexican States, and the Government of the United States of America (NAFTA) states that 'The Government of Canada, the Government of the United Mexican States and the Government of the United States of America, resolved to: ... promote sustainable development; ... have agreed as follows ...'.[75] Among other recently negotiated FTAs in the Americas, this commitment is also found in the preambles of the Canada–Chile FTA,[76] the Canada–Costa Rica FTA, the Chile–United States FTA, and the Peru–United States FTA. It is also found, in Spanish, in the Bolivia–Mexico FTA. These explicit joint resolutions set the promotion of sustainable development as a shared objective of these RTAs, among other priorities. How to render this objective operational? What kinds of provisions, in a regional or bi-lateral trade agreement, can be included to promote sustainable development?

The following discussion focuses on a few specific provisions and mechanisms. It considers whether and how such provisions might contribute to the promotion of 'development that is sustainable' by ensuring mutual supportiveness and integration between economic and social development and environmental protection.

2. Exceptions for Social Development and Environmental Measures

One of the ways to provide for mutual supportiveness between trade liberalization, social development, and environmental protection regimes is to ensure that one regime does not actually conflict with the other, or unduly constrain the adoption of legitimate measures to deliver on the commitments of the other. An 'exceptions' provision is commonly included in trade treaties modelled on the GATT Article XX, providing space for certain legitimate government measures which trade policies might otherwise inadvertently limit or constrain'.[77]

The Americas RTAs contain a modified version of this exception. For instance, the Peru–US FTA at Article 22.1(1) simply states that Article XX of the GATT 1994 and its interpretive notes are incorporated into and made part of the Agreement, *mutatis mutandis*. It also clarifies that the:

Parties understand that the measures referred to in Article XX(b) of the GATT 1994 *include environmental measures* necessary to protect human, animal, or plant life or health, and that Article XX(g) of the GATT 1994 applies to measures relating to the conservation of *living and non-living* exhaustible natural resources. (emphasis added).

As such, if an otherwise inconsistent measure can be shown (by the party claiming the exception) to fall under certain limited exceptions, and also to

---

[75] *See* Preamble, NAFTA.   [76] *See* Preamble, Canada–Chile FTA.
[77] Art. XX GATT 1994.

comply with a 'chapeau' which requires that it does not result in arbitrary or unjustifiable discrimination and does not constitute disguised protectionism, it will be permitted by the RTA. Against a background of continuing debates concerning these cases, the parties appear to set out these 'understandings' to clarify their own interpretation of the GATT exceptions. For instance, in *US— Shrimp*, it was contested as to whether living natural resources could fall within the scope of Article XX(g), though the Appellate Body eventually found that it did. These provisions clarify that the parties intend to give more policy space to their regulators, in the interest of environmental and natural source conservation measures. Such space may be helpful to ensure a 'mutual supportiveness', or at least to prevent one priority (trade) from almost always overriding the other, in spite of limited exceptions. However, unlike Article XX, which applies to the GATT and all other WTO Agreements, such exceptions apply only to certain enumerated provisions of the FTA. As such, health or environment regulators will not have access to exceptions to the excluded chapters, unless otherwise provided. Further, exceptions from trade disciplines for 'measures necessary to protect human . . . health' covers only one aspect of the 'social pillar' of sustainable development highlighted in the World Summit on Sustainable Development.[78] While the parties do not take the opportunity to extend general exceptions to measures taken to protect other important social priorities, such as education or water, in many of the RTAs surveyed, such social priorities are exempted through specific reservations in certain chapters.[79]

Specific exceptions may also be provided in certain chapters of the RTAs, responding to concerns that have been identified in global debates or impact assessments. For instance, in the WTO, concerns have been raised about the need for flexibility for regulators in the area of services.[80] And indeed, a set of specific exceptions is provided in the Canada–Chile FTA. Subject to a 'chapeau', this Agreement provides exceptions for 'measures necessary to secure compliance with laws or regulations that are not inconsistent with the provisions of this Agreement, *including those relating to health and safety and consumer protection*'.[81] In *Korea—Various Measures on Beef*, the Appellate Body suggested that similarly worded provisions might be interpreted through a two-step test: 'First, the measure must be one designed to "secure compliance" with laws or regulations that are not themselves inconsistent with some

---

[78] M.C. Cordonier Segger and M. Gehring, 'Precaution, Health and the World Trade Organization: Moving Toward Sustainable Development' (2003) 29 Queen's L J 133.

[79] Canada–Chile FTA contains reservations for services at Art. H–06; Canada–Costa Rica FTA provides reservations to services at Art. VIII:3.

[80] WTO Council for Trade in Services, Ministerial Decision on Trade in Services and the Environment, Decision on Trade in Services and the Environment, WTO Doc. S/C/M/1, 1 March 1995.

[81] *See* the Canada–Chile FTA, at Art. G–01.

provision of the GATT 1994. Second, the measure must be "necessary" to secure such compliance'.[82]

3. Parallel cooperation agreements on environmental and social matters

A second approach to ensure that an RTA contributes to sustainable development was pioneered with the NAFTA, and has continued to be developed in other RTAs of the Americas. This approach involves developing 'value-added' cooperative agreements during trade treaty negotiations, typically addressing labour and environment issues. Some RTAs contain 'chapters' which also refer to further cooperation strategies or agreements, while others are negotiated with parallel social or environmental 'side agreements'.[83]

With regards to social development and labour rights, the first side agreement was the North American Agreement on Labour Cooperation (NAALC), which commits to 'improve working conditions and living standards' in all parties, to 'protect, enhance and enforce basic workers' rights', through eleven core labour principles.[84] A Commission for Labour Cooperation (Ministerial Council and Secretariat, assisted by National Administrative Offices (NAOs) in each country) is established,[85] and the NAALC provides for a complaints process[86] also a compliance mechanism in the event that an arbitral panel finds a persistent pattern of failure by a country to effectively enforce its labour law.[87] If a country fails to correct the problem, the panel may impose a fine, with certain caps. A similar model is used by the 1997 Canada–Chile Labour Cooperation Agreement (CCLCA). Under the CCLCA, parties commit to maintain and improve labour standards, to effectively enforce their labour law and other guarantees,[88] and create a Commission for Labour Cooperation structured similar to the one in the NAALC.[89] The CCLCA has two main components: a Cooperative Work Program and a procedure for handling

---

[82] WTO Appellate Body Report, *Korea—Various Measures on Beef*, WT/DS161/AB/R, adopted 10 January 2001, at para 157.

[83] *See* Cordonier Segger *et al.*, *Ecological Rules and Sustainability in the Americas*, above at n 43. *See also* Cordonier Segger and Leichner Reynal, above at n 49 and A. Barcena *et al.*, *Financing for Sustainable Development in Latin America and the Caribbean: From Monterrey to Johannesburg* (Santiago: ECLAC and UNDP, 2002).

[84] Art. 1 NAFTA.

[85] *Ibid.*, at Arts 8–9, 12, 15, and 21. *See* NAALC Secretariat, available at www.naalc.org (visited 23 January 2006). *See* in particular: Commission for Labour Cooperation, Comparative Guide to Labour and Employment Laws in North America: Labour Relations Law in North America (Washington: NAALC, 2000).

[86] *See* K. Banks 'Civil Society and the North American Agreement on Labor Cooperation', in J. Kirton and V. Maclaren (eds), *Linking Trade, Environment and Social Cohesion: NAFTA Experiences, Global Challenges* (Aldershot: Ashgate, 2002).

[87] Arts 23–26, 27–29, 37–39 NAFTA. For a summary of disputes to date under the NAALC, *see* Human Rights Watch, available at www.hrw.org/reports/2001/nafta/nafta0401–05.htm (visited 23 January 2006).

[88] *See* Canada–Chile Agreement on Labour Cooperation, First Annual Report (July 1997–June 1998), available at www110.hrdc-drhc.gc.ca/doc/ialc-cidt/eng/e/backen.htm (visited 23 January 2006).

[89] *Ibid.*

issues of concern, in a way that is similar to the NAALC.[90] The Canada–Costa Rica Labour Cooperation Agreement (CCRLCA) has certain differences. Administratively, the CCRLCA is much simpler, and does not include provisions for national secretariats, evaluation committees of experts, or panel rosters, in order to be simpler to implement for a Party with less administrative capacity. In terms of scope and coverage, all three agreements cover eleven principles and rights. However, the CCRLCA obligations, in Annex 1, are directly related to the 1998 ILO Declaration on Fundamental Principles and Rights at Work, which came into effect after the Canada–Chile LCA and the NAALC. Further, the CCRLCA does not provide for monetary fines.[91]

The Chile–US FTA provides a slightly different model. It includes a Labour Chapter 18 which lays out a cooperative agenda to promote worker rights.[92] In the accord, parties agree that it is inappropriate to weaken or reduce domestic labour protections to encourage trade or investment, and it requires that parties shall effectively enforce their own domestic labour laws, and a cooperative mechanism is provided specifically to promote respect for the principles embodied in the 1998 ILO Declaration on Fundamental Principles and Rights at Work, and compliance with ILO Convention 182 on the Worst Forms of Child Labour. The labour chapter is subject to the dispute settlement provisions of the Chile–US FTA with high standards of openness and transparency, including open public hearings, public release of legal submissions by parties, a special roster of labour or environmental experts for disputes in these areas, and rights for interested third parties to submit views. The emphasis is put on the promotion of compliance through consultation, joint action plans and trade-enhancing remedies, but the enforcement mechanism also includes monetary penalties.[93]

Environmental agreements/chapters seek to facilitate cooperation on environmental protection objectives, including the strengthening of environmental laws and regulations. An early model is the North American Agreement on Environmental Cooperation (NAAEC) between Canada, Mexico, and the US, which has been well documented in academic literature.[94] NAAEC

---

[90] *See* Ministerial Council, Report on the Three-Year Review of the Canada–Chile Agreement on Labour Cooperation (December 2002), available at www.hrsdc.gc.ca/en/lp/spila/ialc/2003_2004/02canada_chili_agreement.shtml (visited 23 January 2006).

[91] Communication with Dale Whiteside, Deputy Director, Strategic Trade Policy, Department of Foreign Affairs and International Trade, Government of Canada, 26 June 2003, on file with authors.

[92] Art. 18 Chile–US FTA.

[93] Summary of Chile–US FTA, available at www.ustr.gov (visited 23 January 2006).

[94] North American Agreement for Environmental Cooperation ('NAAEC'), adopted 1 January 1994 (1993) 32 ILM 1482, available at www.cec.org (visited 23 January 2006). *See* M.C. Cordonier Segger 'Enhancing Social and Environmental Cooperation in the Americas', in Cordonier Segger and Leichner Reynal, above at n 49, at 183–222 and C. Deere and D. Esty (eds), *Greening the Americas: NAFTA's Lessons for Hemispheric Trade* (Cambridge, MA: MIT Press, 2002). *See also* A.L.C. de Mestral, 'The NAFTA Commission on Environmental Cooperation— Voice for the North American Environment?', in A. Kiss, D. Shelton, and K. Ishibashi (eds), *Economic Globalization and Compliance with International Environmental Agreements* (The Hague, London: Kluwer, 2003).

objectives are assigned to an institution, the Commission for Environmental Cooperation (CEC), which is served by a Secretariat and governed by the Tripartite Council of Environment Ministers that works to promote environmental cooperation among the parties.[95] If a persistent pattern of non-enforcement of environmental laws is identified, a factual report process also exists.[96] With guidance from its Joint Public Advisory Committee, the CEC has become a strong intergovernmental voice in North America for the environment.[97] Elements of the NAAEC, and certainly the CEC itself, demonstrate the usefulness of a credible institution as part of any regional regime that seeks to harmonize environment and trade objectives. Modeled on the NAAEC, the Canada–Chile Agreement on Environmental Cooperation (CCAEC) also provides a framework for bilateral cooperation on environmental issues.[98] The CCAEC provides a commission for environmental cooperation, the provision of environmental information and a joint public advisory council process.[99] It establishes national secretariats to implement its mandate and recognizes prior commitments under other environmental agreements. The annexes, which phase in the application of the Agreement to Chilean environmental law, led to a comprehensive and valuable revision of environmental law in Chile.[100] The Canada–Costa Rica Environmental Cooperation Agreement focuses more on environmental information exchange and capacity building in the area of environmental enforcement and monitoring,[101] with a stronger focus on access to environmental information and capacity building for environmental policy and law-makers.[102] Rather than an enforcement process, it includes provisions granting rights to request

[95] Specifically, the Council has a cooperative work plan based on priority areas, including: establishing limits for specific air and marine pollutants; environmental assessments of projects with trans-boundary implications; and reciprocal court access for damage or injury resulting from trans-boundary pollution.

[96] *See* G. Alanis Ortega, 'Public Participation within NAFTA's Environmental Agreement' and S. Wilson, 'Article 14–15 of the North American Agreement on Environmental Cooperation: Intent of the Founders', in Kirton and Maclaren above at n 86.

[97] Additional details on the North American Commission for Environment Cooperation are available at www.cec.org (visited 23 January 2006).

[98] A. Bowcott, Manager, Environment Canada, International Relations Canada, and Canada's Chief Negotiator for the Canada–Chile, Canada–Costa Rica, and Canada–Central America Environmental Side Agreements (Series of interviews January–April, 2003, notes on file with the author).

[99] W. Durbin, *A Comparison of the Environmental Provisions of the NAFTA, the Canada–Chile Trade Agreement and the Mexican–European Community Trade Agreement* (New Haven: Yale Centre for Environmental Law and Policy, 2000).

[100] Canada–Chile Agreement on Environmental Cooperation, signed 6 February 1997, in force 5 July 1997 (1997) 36 ILM 1196, Arts 2 and 10, Sections 1 and 2. Available at www.sice.oas.org/trade/chican_e/chcatoc.asp#environ (visited 23 January 2006).

[101] E. Gitli and C. Murillo, 'A Latin American Agenda for a Trade and Environment Link in the FTAA', in Deere and Esty, above at n 94.

[102] Canada–Costa Rica Agreement on Environmental Cooperation, signed 23 April 2001, in force 1 November 2002, available at www.sice.oas.org/Trade/cancr/English/enve.asp (visited 23 January 2006)

information from any party on the effective implementation of environmental law in its territory and the duty to respond publicly to this request.[103]

The Chile–US FTA provides, in Chapter 19 (Environment), for the establishment of an Environmental Affairs Council,[104] and a common, detailed work programme on specific topics.[105] As with the labour chapters, the Chile–US FTA and the Peru–US FTA both include provisions which permit access to the FTA dispute settlement mechanisms for non-enforcement of environmental laws, with penalties as monetary assessments rather than trade sanctions. Both refer to an Environmental Cooperation Agreement that will be negotiated at a later date between the parties.

In the FTAs which locate environmental considerations in 'chapters,' measures for capacity-building and cooperation on the implementation of environment regulations appear more concrete and detailed. However, both the 'chapter' and the 'side agreement' approaches provide for environmental cooperation and social development through institutional structures such as committees and ongoing cooperation agendas, and by encouraging public and civil society engagement in the process.

4. Specific operational provisions

Beyond the exceptions and the parallel side agreement/chapters, a more strategic approach is beginning to evolve which addresses instances where specific provisions related to the same subject-matter in the RTAs and other treaties related to sustainable development might overlap, constraining policy choices and affecting the potential for effective implementation of social and environmental commitments. For instance, the 2001 Cartagena Protocol on Biosafety,[106] and its 1992 United Nations Convention on Biological Diversity[107] (UN CBD) appear to contain provisions which could overlap with the provisions of several Americas RTAs.

First, the 2001 Cartagena Protocol to the 1992 UN CBD procedures on Advance Informed Agreement and Living Modified Organisms (LMOs) for Food, Feed and Processing require both risk assessment and risk management, and expressly permit parties to apply the precautionary principle in their reasoning.[108] Problems may arise from intersections between the right of parties under the Cartagena Protocol to use precaution in making decisions concerning LMOs, and WTO Sanitary and Phytosanitary measures (SPS) obligations only to maintain SPS measures that can be justified by scientific

---

[103] *Ibid.*, Art. 9.   [104] Art. 19(3) US–Chile FTA.

[105] H. Corbin, 'The Proposed United States–Chile Free Trade Agreement: Reconciling Free Trade and Environmental Protection' (2003) 14 Colo J Int Envt L & Policy 119.

[106] *See* the Cartagena Protocol on Biosafety to the Convention on Biodiversity, in force 11 September 2003 (2000) 39 ILM 1027.

[107] UN Convention on Biological Diversity, adopted 5 June 1992, in force 29 December 1993, 1760 UNTS 79, (1992) 31 ILM 818, at 15.

[108] Arts 15 and 16 Cartagena Protocol.

methods.[109] The WTO Appellate Body has recognized the challenge of applying the precautionary principle in the context of members' obligations in the SPS Agreement.[110] Under the WTO SPS Agreement, a party enacting a measure to restrict trade must bear a burden of proof to defend its measure by demonstrating that it is transparent, science-based, and strictly necessary for the protection of human, animal, and plant health. As such, WTO SPS obligations could be used to restrict measures aimed at controlling trade in LMOs, affecting both health and environmental priorities.

With regard to SPS, the WTO SPS Agreement and the NAFTA contain provisions similar to the Bolivia–Mexico FTA at Article 4(11) on Scientific Principles, which commit only to implement SPS measures based on science. The Chile–US FTA and the Peru–US FTA specifically re-confirm their WTO obligations. The RTAs then establish Standing Committees which might provide a cooperative forum for discussions to develop integrated strategies. Perhaps the most cooperative approach is adopted in the Canada–Chile FTA and the Canada–Costa Rica FTA, which establish cooperation mechanisms on SPS measures in the context of the environmental side agreements.[111] If it is not the intention of RTA parties that are also party to the Cartagena Protocol to permit their measures to be constrained, it could be useful to include provisions in the RTAs which offer clear guidance to States in the event of overlaps or conflicts between the two sets of rules, rather than simply re-confirming problematic obligations then providing forums for discussion (and further debate).

Second, the intellectual property rights (IPRs) provisions in the NAFTA, the Chile–US FTA and others may overlap with provisions of the 1992 UN CBD as well as human rights commitments to provide access to essential medicines.[112] Concerns have been raised as to how, under strict IPR disciplines, parties will have the policy space to fulfil their UN CBD commitments to ensure that local and indigenous communities have control over and can benefit from their biodiversity-related traditional knowledge and 'informal'

---

[109] *See*, e.g., H. Trudeau and C. Nègre, 'Precaution in Multilateral Environmental Agreements and Its Impact on the World Trading System', in Gehring and Cordonier Segger, above at n 15, at 593–630. *See also* C. Button, *The Power to Protect: Trade, Health and Uncertainty in the WTO* (Oxford: Hart, 2004).

[110] *See* WTO Appellate Body Report, *EC—Hormones*, WT/DS26/AB/R, WT/DS48/AB/R, adopted 13 February 1998, at para. 124.

[111] For instance, in order to apply the WTO SPS Agreement, Canada and Costa Rica, at Art. IX:5, inaugurated a Committee for consultation and cooperation purposes, which may consider: '. . . co-operation programs; . . . mutual recognition and equivalence agreements, and product control, inspection and approval procedures; . . . the identification and resolution of SPS-related problems; . . .' etc. *See* the Canada–Costa Rica Agreement on Environmental Cooperation.

[112] *See* M. Prabhu and K. Garforth, 'International Public Health and Trade Law', in Gehring and Cordonier Segger, above at n 15, at 549–73. *See also* K. Balasubramaniam, 'Access to Medicines and Public Policy Safeguards under TRIPS' and N.B. Zaveri, 'The TRIPS Agreement and Generic Production of HIV/AIDS Drugs', in C. Bellmann, G. Dutfield and R. Meléndez-Ortiz (eds), *Trading in Knowledge: Development Perspectives on TRIPS, Trade and Sustainability* (London: Earthscan, 2003), 135–42, 149–56.

innovations,[113] and how, in accordance with sovereignty over genetic resources recognized in the UN CBD, countries can decline to patent life-forms, and balance plant breeders' rights with others.[114]

Two innovative approaches are found in the context of the Peru–US FTA. At Article 16, this RTA contains relatively strict and detailed provisions to protect intellectual property rights, including a commitment that by 2008, both parties will be members of the 1991 International Convention for the Protection of New Varieties of Plants (UPOV Convention),[115] which has attracted critique due to its requirements on patenting of plant genetic resources.[116] These commitments may be balanced by a Draft Agreement, included in the Peru–US FTA package, titled Understanding regarding Biodiversity and Traditional Knowledge. The Understanding recognizes the importance of obtaining prior informed consent from appropriate authorities, equitably sharing the benefits arising from the use of traditional knowledge and genetic resources; and promoting quality patent examination to ensure the conditions of patentability are satisfied. It refers to the use of contracts that reflect mutually agreed terms between users and providers of traditional knowledge and genetic resources, and includes an operational commitment to share information through publicly accessible databases and an opportunity to cite, in writing, to the appropriate examining authority prior art that may have a bearing on patentability.[117] Under strong IPR regimes, genetic resources based on traditional knowledge ('prior art') could be patented without benefit sharing. In such situations, biodiversity-rich states can be unwilling to grant strong IPR protections, and may need trade measures to prevent such resources from being patented beyond their control. The Understanding commits to cooperation between the parties on such issues. It builds on experience of the Andean

---

[113] *See* CBD, above at 107, at 8(j) and 10. *See* R.J.L. Lettington, 'The Biodiversity Convention and TRIPS', in P. Konz et al. (eds), *Trade, Environment and Sustainable Development: Views from Sub-Saharan Africa and Latin America* (Geneva: ICTSD and UNU–IAS, 2000).

[114] CBD, *ibid.*, at 1. *See* D. Vivas Eugui, 'Requiring the Disclosure of the Origin of Genetic Resources and Traditional Knowledge: the Current Debate and Possible Legal Alternatives', G. Aguilar, 'Access to Genetic Resources and Protection of Traditional Knowledge in Indigenous Territories' and B. Dhar, 'The Convention on Biological Diversity and the TRIPs Agreement: Compatibility or Conflict?', in Bellmann, Dutfield and Meléndez-Ortiz, above at n 112, at 175–83, 196–208 and 77–88.

[115] There have been three versions of the UPOV Convention, two of which are of concern here: International Convention for the Protection of New Varieties of Plants, 2 December 1961, as revised on 23 October 1978, in force 8 November 1981, International Convention for the Protection of New Varieties of Plants, 2 December 1961, as revised on 23 October 1978 and 19 March 1991, in force 24 April 1998 and the International Convention for the Protection of New Varieties of Plants, done in Geneva, adopted at 2 December 1961, revised at 23 October 1978 and 19 March 1991.

[116] *See* M. Ruiz, 'The Andean Community regimes on access to Genetic Resources, Intellectual Property and Indigenous Peoples' Knowledge', in Bellmann, Dutfield, and Meléndez-Ortiz, above at n 112, at 238–45.

[117] Understanding Regarding Biodiversity and Traditional Knowledge, Draft, 6 January 2006, as part of the Peru–US Free Trade Agreement, not yet in force, available at www.ustr.gov/assets/Trade_Agreements/Bilateral/Peru_TPA/Final_Texts/asset_upload_file869_8728.pdf (visited 23 January 2006).

Community in Decision 391 on Common Access Regime for Genetic Resources,[118] which responds to Article 15 UN CBD, regulating access to genetic resources and the equitable distribution of benefits derived from their use, and recognizing the contributions of indigenous peoples' traditional knowledge.[119] Such regimes, also found in Central America, guarantee the direct participation of communities and local populations, and seek ways to equitably distribute benefits from genetic resources that are identified using traditional knowledge.[120] As such, this aspect of the RTA may accommodate the parties' desire to ensure benefits from traditional knowledge accrue to the originators. For Peru, this recognition could be helpful to meet their obligations in the UN CBD. Much will depend on how this DRAFT Understanding is implemented, and if substantive progress is made.

The Peru–US FTA package includes a second DRAFT Understanding which explicitly recognizes the need to ensure affordable access to essential medicines. In particular, in the DRAFT Understanding regarding Certain Public Health Measures included with Article 16 on IPRs in the FTA, the parties state: 'The obligations of Chapter Sixteen of the Agreement do not affect a Party's ability to take necessary measures to protect public health by promoting access to medicines for all, in particular concerning cases such as HIV/AIDS, tuberculosis, malaria and other epidemics as well as circumstances of extreme urgency or national emergency'. It also reaffirms the WTO 2003 Decision on TRIPS and Public Health[121] which addresses such measures, specifically clarifying that Chapter Sixteen is not intended to prevent effective use of this provision. These provisions appear to demonstrate not only that States are aware of potential overlaps between trade regimes and environmental and social (health) regimes, but that RTAs can incorporate provisions for cooperative strategies toward more integrated trade, social development and environmental decision-making. Since the UN CBD and the Cartagena Protocol share sustainable development objectives with the WTO and these RTAs, it is hoped such strategies will be further developed in the future.

It is clear from the analysis above that in certain areas, there is potential for the negotiation of integrated cooperative strategies and provisions to seek greater levels of 'mutual supportiveness' between the trade, social and environmental regimes. However, there is also potential for less supportive overlaps. Beyond the use of substantive provisions and specific exceptions to

---

[118] International Regime on Access and Benefit-Sharing: Proposals for an International Regime on Access and Benefit-sharing, adopted 7 January 2003, UN Doc. UNEP/CBD/MYPOW/6, at 6–7. Decision 391 of the Commission of the Andean Community, 2 July 1996, Gaceta Oficial del Acuerdo de Cartagena, Año XII, Número 213, 17 July 1996.

[119] CBD, above at n 107, at 15.

[120] *See* J.C. Medaglia, 'The Central American Regional Protocol on Access to Genetic and Biochemical Resources', in Bellmann, Dutfield and Meléndez-Ortiz, above at n 112.

[121] Implementation of Paragraph Six of the Doha Declaration on the TRIPS Agreement and Public Health, WTO Doc. WT/L/540, 2 September 2003 and the WTO General Council Chairman's Statement Accompanying the Decision JOB(03)/177. *See also* Minutes of the General Council, WTO Doc. WT/GC/M/82, 13 November 2003.

accommodate the specific areas of overlaps, a fourth approach has also been attempted with mixed success: to provide rules on the relationships between regimes themselves.

5. Rules on Relationships between Treaties

Disagreements about the appropriateness of using trade measures to achieve the goals of 'non-trade' regimes are possible and in some cases, well documented. Trade agreements might also simply limit policy space, constraining the use of economic instruments to achieve the goals of sustainable development treaties. For example, measures to support emissions reductions and the use of market-based instruments (carbon taxes) to implement the 1997 Kyoto Protocol to the 1992 UN Framework Convention on Climate Change might be constrained by commitments to reduce subsidies, or to avoid certain types of border adjustments and non-tariff barriers to trade; measures to develop a multi-lateral system of access and benefit sharing in the 2004 International Treaty on Plant Genetic Resources for Food and Agriculture (FAO Seed Treaty) might conceivably be limited by commitments to liberalize agriculture; regional measures to reduce air or water pollution might be found to infringe on the rights of investors, and be subject to compensation claims in closed arbitral processes; or other regional or national measures to meet human rights commitments regarding access to water, health care, or education might be blocked by the results of services liberalization processes. When trade, environment and social development regimes overlap, there is seldom a direct conflict of positive obligations, though some parties may see rights gained in one regime limited by commitments in the *lex posteriori*. However, trade rules may work formally or informally to constrain the use of social or environmental measures, affecting parties' ability to implement other important social or environmental commitments and frustrating the sustainable development objectives of all.

Where constraints are not intended by the parties, provisions can be included in RTAs which directly address potential overlaps and clarify which regime will have precedence. This approach precludes, in a limited way, measures taken under these accords from the purview of trade disciplines. This approach was taken by the NAFTA, and also appears in the Canada–Chile FTA at Articles A-03 and A-04, and the Canada–Costa Rica FTA at Articles I:3 and I:4. A useful example is provided by Articles 102 and 104 of the NAFTA. Chapter 1 sets forth the Agreement's basic objectives and rules of interpretation. Article 102 states the objectives of the NAFTA, and that agrees that it will be interpreted in accordance with the applicable rules of international law. Article 103 affirms existing rights and obligations under both bilateral and multilateral agreements, including the WTO Agreements, providing that the NAFTA prevails in the event of any inconsistency between it and such other international agreements, except as otherwise noted.[122] Then,

---

[122] Overview of the NAFTA Agreement, available at www.sice.oas.org/summary/nafta/nafta1.asp (visited 23 January 2006).

Article 104 reverses the general rule of Article 103 in regard to certain international environmental agreements. The 'listed MEAs' (Multilateral Environmental Agreement(s)) were already in force during the negotiation of the NAFTA in 1994, and each authorizes the use of trade measures to achieve its objectives. These measures include trade bans against products made with CFCs in non-parties to discourage 'free-riders', bans on trade in endangered species products to discourage their exploitation, and bans on the import/export of hazardous wastes, as well as other restrictions. If not for Article 104, these measures would be disallowed by the former provision. Further, to prevent parties from bringing trade cases related to these MEAs to other bodies, a choice of forum provision was added so that the party which relied on the MEA in their defence, could have the dispute adjudicated under a NAFTA panel. Under the NAFTA, Article 2005(3) states that if NAFTA Article 104 is being used as a defence, recourse exists only under the NAFTA. Without such a provision, the complaining party could simply pursue any claims at the WTO, which likely lacks the authority to apply a NAFTA 'precedence' provision.

Mutual supportiveness, and integration, implies an element of balance between overlapping provisions. A straightforward declaration that environmental treaties will have *precedence* in the event of conflicts may not actually provide for a *balanced* relationship between trade, environment, and social obligations. However, in this instance, the granting of precedence is balanced by certain conditions.[123] These conditions introduce this element of balance, and are important. While the non-application of NAFTA disciplines to these limited instances would not necessarily have a great impact on the NAFTA's effectiveness, non-application of the MEA trade measures could act as a significant and disproportionate constraint on the ability of parties to the MEAs to implement the treaty regimes. Two futher points can be highlighted, however. First, though they do provide for further accords to be 'placed under the protection' of this limited exemption from NAFTA rules disallowing trade measures of this sort, no such further accords have as yet been designated. It remains to be seen whether other sustainable development related treaties signed later than the NAFTA would be subjected to Article 103 provisions in the event of 'inconsistencies'. Second, the treaty is clear that these provisions contemplate only environmental agreements. However, if the social pillar of sustainable development is to be taken seriously, it might be equally important that the relationship between the RTA and social development accords, including human rights covenants and other instruments, be made equally clear.

The NAFTA approach is also found in the Canada–Chile FTA and the Canada–Costa Rica FTA. This can be compared with a second approach found in the environment chapter of the Peru–US TPA at Article 18(10) and the Chile–US FTA at Article 19(9). The Peru–US TPA commit to 'seek

---

[123] K. Gray, 'Accommodating MEAs in Trade Agreements' (Presentation given at the International Environmental Governance Conference, Paris, March 2004).

means to enhance the mutual supportiveness of multilateral environmental agreements to which they are all party and trade agreements to which they are all party . . .' It also commits to 'consult, as appropriate, with respect to negotiations on environmental issues of mutual interest'. And at paragraph 3, it states that 'Each Party recognizes the importance to it of the multilateral environmental agreements to which it is a party'.[124] This provision is located in a different context than Articles 103 and 104 of the NAFTA, and the comparable articles of the Canada–Chile FTA and the Canada–Costa Rica FTA. This provision does not commit to *precedence* in the event of conflict. Rather, it simply commits to seek means to enhance 'mutual supportiveness,' and that parties will consult, as appropriate, on 'issues of mutual interest'. It limits the commitment to MEAs to which the TPA parties are 'all parties,' and trade agreements to which they are all parties. The commitment to mutual supportiveness would not apply to measures taken under environmental agreements to which some parties are parties, but others are not. This problem is clearly acknowledged in the final provision that '[e]ach Party recognizes the importance to it' of the MEAs to which it is a party, but it is not resolved. Perhaps the least problematic approach can be found in the Chile–US FTA Environment Chapter at Article 19(9), which simply states: 'The Parties recognize the importance of multilateral environmental agreements, including the appropriate use of trade measures in such agreements to achieve specific environmental goals'.

With regards to social development, the Peru–US TPA provides an example of an innovative provision in the body of the text which indicates the relationship of the trade agreement to international social development (labour) treaties and bodies, at Article 17(1) (Statement of Shared Commitments). In particular, it commits that all parties 'shall strive to ensure that such labor principles and the internationally recognized labor rights . . . are recognized and protected by its law'. and that the parties 'reaffirm their full respect for their Constitutions and recognize the right of each Party to adopt or modify its labor laws and standards. Each Party shall strive to ensure that it provides for labor standards consistent with the internationally recognized labor rights . . .' This commitment is made operational at Article 17(5) (and following), on the Labor Cooperation and Capacity Building Mechanism, which also states that the mechanism 'shall operate in a manner that respects each Party's law and sovereignty'. The rights protected include: a) the right of association; b) the right to organize and bargain collectively; c) a prohibition on the use of any form of forced or compulsory labour; d) labour protections for children and minors, including a minimum age for the employment of children and the prohibition and elimination of the worst forms of child labour; and e) acceptable conditions of work with respect to minimum wages, hours of work, and occupational safety and health, but not a common minimum wage. The

---

[124] Peru–US Trade Promotion Agreement, signed 12 April 2006, not yet in force.

provision does not commit to precedence for all labour agreements, as such. The ILO enshrines over 190 Conventions, but the TPA only mentions ILA Convention No. 182 Concerning the Prohibition and Immediate Action for the Elimination of the Worst Forms of Child Labour.[125] Nor does it address other human rights, such as the right to health. It addresses only *common* commitments. Essentially, the provisions remain fairly limited, as do the similar provisions in the 2003 Chile–United States FTA.[126] They only extend to social agreements to which all parties are already parties, which suggests that in other cases, the trade rules might 'trump' labour standards. However, on contentious social issues, such provisions may hold some potential to become tools for 'reconciliation' of the trade treaty norms with other social norms.[127]

It can be seen that several models for innovative provisions have been recently included in Americas RTAs in the interest of sustainable development and related environmental and social development objectives. It is not yet clear which strategies or instruments will have the most success in helping to integrate social and economic development and environmental protection. It is likely that no one single type of provisions has an answer to this problem. Rather, many different provisions and instruments are being developed and tested in the regional context. These provisions alone will not necessarily ensure that sustainable development objectives are given more weight by the parties in complying with their obligations, and by dispute settlement bodies in interpreting FTAs, as compared to the other relevant objectives of FTAs (promotion and protection of foreign investment, for example). However, they appear likely to contribute to the achievement of a greater degree of balance in the agreements, which is a first step.

III. CONCLUSIONS: RTA PROVISIONS RELATED TO SUSTAINABLE DEVELOPMENT

The explicit recognition of the objective of sustainable development in the preamble to a trade agreement has relevance in trade law, and can be used to interpret trade measures, shedding light, in particular, on the meaning of exceptions and other aspects of a trade agreement.[128] However, there is no stand-alone strategy to ensure that a trade agreement will be able to promote sustainable development. Rather, many mechanisms are possible. Several

---

[125] ILO Convention No 182 concerning the Prohibition and Immediate Action for the Elimination of the Worst Forms of Child Labour, adopted 17 June 1999, in force 10 November 2000 (1999) 38 ILM 1207, Arts 7(1) and 8.

[126] Art. 19(3) Chile–US FTA.

[127] Additional Protocol to the American Convention on Human Rights in the Area of Economic, Social and Cultural Rights (Protocol of San Salvador), in force 16 November 1999, OAS Treaty Series No 69, at 67.

[128] Gehring and Cordonier Segger, above at n 15, at 1–24 and 129–86.

are currently being tested in the Americas. These RTAs appear to have been influenced by recent WTO debates on sustainable development, including negotiations and dispute settlement decisions, as parties learn from and are interactionally shaped by their participation in the WTO and other international trade regimes.

At a time when many States are only just establishing new social and environmental laws and policies, new trade rules could be used to limit or constrain the use of measures to implement another internationally agreed social or environmental regime. In this situation, an RTA with a sustainable development objective would be seen to constrain implementation of other regimes that share this sustainable development objective. Unsustainable development ensues when economic objectives trump all others, or growth takes place at the expense of a country's social or natural capital, limiting the ability of future generations to meet their needs. Various processes and provisions can, at the minimum, identify and reduce these instances by providing exceptions or other forms of 'windows' in the text of the RTA where overlaps are likely. Parties have also included certain specific provisions in the Americas RTAs, which may help trade, environment and social development issues to be addressed cooperatively in an 'integrated' manner. These provisions could benefit from further legal analysis and from informed debate as to their implications.

How to investigate and compare these preventive provisions, cooperative mechanisms and procedural innovations, in future legal research in this area? This chapter suggests the use of a typology, which may also provide a source of ideas for States seeking to deliver on a commitment to sustainable development in the context of an RTA.

First, certain procedural innovations can be undertaken by the parties during trade negotiations. These may also assist parties (and others) in identifying useful innovations for the agreement:

(1) *ex ante* (or ongoing) environment, development, human rights, or sustainability impact assessments and reviews of trade liberalization policies and draft treaties;
(2) consultations between economic, environment and development authorities;
(3) mechanisms to ensure transparency, including in negotiations;
(4) mechanisms to strengthen public participation in trade negotiations and dispute settlement;
(5) capacity-building and financing mechanisms for social and environmental cooperation related to negotiation and implementation of RTA regimes.

In addition, certain substantive provisions can be included in the text of the FTAs. In addition to the preambular commitments to promote sustainable development, which have been highlighted above, the Americas FTAs include, for instance:

(1) Provisions which create 'windows' or exemptions from trade rules, where trade obligations might otherwise constrain regulators and policy-makers, mitigating their effects, such as:

    a. general exceptions related to the conservation of natural resources, and the use of measures, including environmental measures, necessary to protect human, animal, or plant life or health;

    b. general interpretive statements to guide potential areas where trade rules could otherwise constrain the use of measures agreed in other international (or regional) agreements;

    c. specific exceptions in sections of the RTA where it is clear that trade rules on, for example, sanitary and phytosanitary standards, technical barriers to trade, intellectual property rights, public procurement, services, or investment, might constrain the use of environmental and social measures;

    d. explicit reservations by the parties of socially or environmentally sensitive sectors (such as nature reserves and parks reserved from investment provisions, or health and education sectors from services disciplines).

(2) Provisions which develop 'value-added' but parallel (non-integrated) social and environmental cooperation strategies, such as:

    a. parallel agreements (or chapters) for cooperation on environmental and social matters;

    b. the development of institutions for social and environmental cooperation;

    c. common work programmes on specific environmental or social projects, particularly when accompanied by reliable capacity-building, technology transfer and financing commitments;

    d. factual report/complaints mechanisms to provide recourse when environmental or social rules are violated.

(3) Constructive 'sustainable development' oriented trade rule enhancement initiatives, where a positive 'triple-win' might be achieved within the trade agreement, which might include:

    a. sanitary and phytosanitary provisions which promote cooperation to improve levels of protection;

    b. technical barriers to trade provisions to improve certification processes and promote mutual recognition;

    c. intellectual property rights provisions which support biodiversity protection, the recognition of traditional knowledge or public access to essential medicines;

    d. liberalization of environmental services; or

    e. the promotion and protection of investments which deliver on international environmental and social priorities (e.g. investments under the Clean Development Mechanism of the Kyoto Protocol).

Such procedural steps, and innovations in the provisions of the trade agreements themselves, carried out in support of sustainable development objectives, suggest that 'those negotiating treaties, . . . or environmental controls, at the national or the international level, are likely to approach that task within the context of sustainable development. The concept colours the whole approach to this area of international law'.[129] In conclusion, though regional trade may have unsustainable impacts, regional trade rules might also promote development that is sustainable. Through innovative procedures and provisions that can integrate economic and social development and environmental protection in a balanced, mutually supportive way, RTAs could still limit recourse to trade-related measures not based on international consensus while demonstrating respect for environmental protection and social development as goals of national and international policy. Depending on the policies pursued and the detailed legal rules negotiated, and the way that these are implemented in practice, such regional innovations may have the potential to provide and test cooperative, integrated strategies toward a shared sustainable development objective.

---

[129] V. Lowe, 'The Politics of Law-Making: Are the Method and Character of Norm Creation Changing?', in M Byers (ed), *The Role of Law in International Politics: Essays in International Relations and International Law* (Oxford: OUP, 2000), 216.

PART IV
Dispute Settlement in Regional Trade Agreements

14

Dispute Settlement in the WTO and RTAs: A Comment

WILLIAM J. DAVEY

The debate has long raged over the comparative economic benefits of preferential trade liberalization pursuant to regional trade agreements (RTAs) and multilateral liberalization under the World Trade Organization (WTO) and whether RTAs are a long term threat to the WTO.[1] In my view, any such threat is mitigated by the fact that, even if RTAs provide significant economic benefits, a conclusion that is not at all clear,[2] they are singularly ill-suited to fulfill

---

[1] For a more detailed discussion of this issue, *see* W.J. Davey, 'Regional Trade Agreements and the WTO: General Observations and NAFTA Lessons for Asia', a paper presented at the International Symposium on Development of International Economic Law from an Asian Perspective (13th annual meeting of the Japanese Association of International Economic Law), Nagoya, Japan, 1 November 2003 (publication forthcoming by the JAIEL), also available as Illinois Public Law Research Paper No 05–18, available at ssrn.com/abstract=863846 (visited 3 April 2006).

[2] As explained in Davey, *ibid.*, it is difficult to assess the economic effects of RTAs, as one is always forced to speculate on what would have happened without the RTA in question and that can never be known with any certainty. A 2001 OECD report reviewed the economics literature on the effects of RTAs on trade and investment flows: *Regional Integration: Observed Trade and Other Economic Effects*, OECD Doc. TD/TC/WP(2001)19/FINAL (19 October 2001). In examining recent *ex post* studies, the report concludes that results are 'mixed'. Some studies showed significant increases in intra-bloc trade, but others did not. As to trade diversion, there was no indication found that it is a major problem, although some evidence indicated that it may exist to a limited degree. The review reports that *ex post* studies on the economic growth effects of RTAs suggest that they 'have had little impact on economic growth' (*ibid.*, at para. 3). The *ex ante* studies reviewed showed 'weak evidence of trade diversion, but that the recent wave of regionalism has been trade creating on a net basis and welfare improving for member countries and trading blocs as a whole' (*ibid.*, at para. 3). The *World Trade Report* (Geneva: WTO 2003), concluded that for the most part there is not strong evidence of trade creation in most RTAs, at 55–7. In respect of the more general issue of trade creation versus trade diversion, it notes a divergence of opinion amongst economists and studies of specific RTAs (*ibid.*, at 58–9). The conclusion to be drawn by a non-economist would seem to be straightforward: The overall economic impact of RTAs may not be all that great.

the full range of functions performed by the WTO.[3] Indeed, there are two WTO functions in particular—to serve as a negotiating forum and dispute settlement—that RTAs cannot duplicate or perform adequately for reasons that I would argue are inherent.[4]

First, they cannot supplant the WTO's role as a forum for trade negotiations because the existing regional agreements do not, and will likely never, include enough major trading nations to enable deals to be struck on key global issues involving a broad range of nations with disparate interests. Agricultural trade is the prime example. One of the major stumbling blocks to the negotiation of the long-proposed Free Trade Area of the Americas (FTAA) is that some participants in the negotiations want concessions on agricultural trade, which others are unwilling to give except in the context of global negotiations.[5] This inherent inability of RTAs to offer sufficient trade-offs between major trading countries and issues would seem to guarantee the primacy of the WTO negotiating process for a long time to come, notwithstanding its unwieldiness and dismal performance to date in the Doha Round negotiations.[6]

Second, RTAs cannot perform the dispute settlement function as effectively as the WTO. In this brief comment, I will focus on this issue. I would suggest that the apparent superiority of the WTO dispute settlement system is a significant reason why regional trade agreements do not ultimately threaten to supplant or even burden the operation of the WTO system. In the following paragraphs, I will outline the operation of the WTO's Dispute Settlement Understanding and evaluate the results it has produced in its first decade of operation. I will then compare these results with the limited information that is available on the operation of RTA dispute settlement systems. For the most part, the formal procedures of RTA dispute settlement do not appear to be much used at all, except in certain aspects in NAFTA and in Mercosur. I then consider reasons for this disparity in use and ultimately conclude that the

---

[3] Art. III of the WTO Agreement designates five functions for the WTO, i.e. (i) to provide for the administration of the WTO Agreements, (ii) to serve as a negotiating forum, (iii) dispute settlement, (iv) trade policy review, and (v) global economic coherence.

[4] RTAs also cannot duplicate the global economic coherence function, but to date that function has been somewhat ill-defined in any event.

[5] 'Mexican Efforts to Revive FTAA appear to have failed', Inside US Trade, 26 August 2005 ('One source close to the talks said he thought it was "fair to say" that the talks would essentially be on hold until after the WTO meeting in Hong Kong. This source said a positive outcome on the issue of domestic support in Hong Kong could have a positive impact on FTAA negotiations that might allow progress to be made. This refers to the position of Brazil and other members of Mercosur, who initially argued that the US should agree to reduce domestic subsidies as part of the FTAA negotiations, which is something the US has refused to do outside the WTO talks').

[6] RTAs may, in some instances, facilitate multilateral negotiations. The experience gained in RTA (or other plurilateral) negotiations on various issues may help resolve them at the multilateral level. Moreover, in customs unions that negotiate as one entity (i.e. the European Union), the need to agree on a common position may lead to a more moderate position for the group as a whole than would be followed by some individual members of the group—an important consideration for WTO negotiations where consensus is ultimately required. Of course, if the group follows the position of its less moderate members, WTO negotiations may become more difficult.

WTO dispute settlement system seems to be a more legitimate and effective mechanism than those used in RTAs.

I. WTO DISPUTE SETTLEMENT

The WTO dispute settlement system has been quite active since it came into existence at the beginning of 1995. In its first 10 years, there were 324 consultation requests, involving 229 distinct disputes.[7] The number of consultation requests has moderated over time. In the 1996–1998 period, it was running at about 40 requests a year. More recently, the rate has fallen to 20 to 30 a year. Even so, the system remains very active for an international, i.e. state-to-state, dispute settlement system. Interestingly, over time, developing countries have become more active in participating in the system, including using it to raise issues with other developing countries as well as to attack developed country measures.[8] Indeed, some of the more newsworthy cases in recent years were Brazil's challenges to US cotton subsidies and EU sugar subsidies, both of which succeeded.[9]

The extensive use of the WTO system is probably explained in large part because of several key features.[10] First, the system requires a period of consultations, such that invocation of the system does not commit a country to litigation.[11] This provides the possibility that matters may be raised and settled on a formal or informal basis, and, as noted below, this often happens. Second, the WTO system operates automatically, by which I mean that there are specified time periods for the various phases of dispute settlement and mechanisms to ensure that a complainant can push the matter forward to the next phase if it wishes to do so.[12] While WTO Members typically do not take maximum advantage of the various possibilities for moving cases forward,[13]

---

[7] For overall statistics and information on the operation of the WTO dispute settlement system, *see* the dispute settlement section of the WTO website (www.wto.org, visited 3 April 2006). For a more detailed analysis of the first ten years' operation of the system, *see* W.J. Davey, 'The WTO Dispute Settlement System: The First Ten Years' (2005) 8 JIEL 17.

[8] Davey, *ibid.*, at 24.

[9] WTO Appellate Body Report, *US—Upland Cotton*, WT/DS267/AB/R, adopted 21 March 2005, and WTO Appellate Body Report, *EC—Export Subsidies on Sugar*, WT/DS265/AB/R, WT/DS266/AB/R, WT/DS283/AB/R, adopted 19 May 2005. In the Sugar case, Brazil was a co-complainant with Australia and Thailand.

[10] For a general overview of the WTO dispute settlement system, *see* W.J. Davey, 'The WTO Dispute Settlement Mechanism', Illinois Public Law Research Paper No 03–08, available at ssrn.com/abstract=419943 (visited 3 April 2006).

[11] Art. 4 of the WTO Dispute Settlement Understanding (DSU).

[12] Arts 4.7, 6.1, 8.7, 12.9, 16.4, 17.5, 17.14, 21.3, 22.2, and 22.6 DSU (establishing time limits in respect of consultations, panel establishment, panel composition, panel proceedings, panel report adoption or appeal, appellate proceedings, appellate report adoption, establishment of reasonable period of time for implementation, and agreement on compensation or authorization of suspension of concessions).

[13] W.J. Davey, 'Implementation of the Results of WTO Trade Remedy Cases' (paper presented at International Conference on 'Trade Remedy System': An East Asian Perspective, Chung-Hua

the fact that these mechanisms exist mean that they can initiate cases with confidence that the cases will go forward if desired. This was a notable change from the GATT system, which initially permitted a country to block movement forward in a case at several different stages, most importantly by blocking adoption of the panel's report and thereby consigning it to a legal limbo.[14]

Third, the WTO system results in a very thorough vetting of the issues by neutral experts. This thoroughness occurs because of the approach followed by panels in considering cases and because of the existence of an appellate review option. At the panel stage, the parties have the possibility to agree on the identity of the three experts that will consider their case.[15] In practice, they are usually unable to agree on all three, with the result that the panel selection is completed by the WTO Director-General on request of one of the parties. The Director-General, as well as the parties, have an interest in ensuring that the best possible panellists are selected so as to avoid criticism and second-guessing later. As for the panel process,[16] the practice of holding two hearings, preceded by the filing of written submissions by the parties and followed by written questions from the panel, means that the issues in a case are thoroughly explored. The appellate process then provides an opportunity for a second look, which helps ensure that a panel has not lost its way in the morass of facts and arguments.[17] For the most part, the WTO Appellate Body, which consists of seven individuals appointed for four-year terms (once renewable), has not changed the basic results of many cases, but it has had a very significant impact on the reasoning used to reach results and on the general approach to interpretation of WTO Agreements in general. This very thorough and neutral process on an international plane gives a distinct aura of legitimacy to the results of WTO dispute settlement.

Fourth, the WTO system has detailed rules for monitoring the implementation of the decisions rendered by panels and the Appellate Body.[18] These include reporting requirements to help ascertain whether there has been implementation of the decisions and the possibility of negotiating compensation or suspending concessions if there has not been implementation within a reasonable period of time, which itself is either agreed or set by arbitration. This enforcement mechanism helps strengthen the overall credibility of the WTO system. It has to be conceded, however, that the rules for this last phase of dispute settlement were negotiated conceptually, as there had been no real experience in GATT with this phase of dispute settlement. As a consequence, this phase is probably the least satisfactory part of WTO dispute settlement,

---

Institution for Economic Research (Taiwan WTO Center), Taipei, August 29–30, 2005), at 7. Also available as Illinois Public Law Research Paper No 05–20, available at ssrn.com/abstract=863905 (visited 3 April 2006).

[14] On the operation of the GATT system and the problem of delays, *see* W.J. Davey, 'Dispute Settlement in GATT' (1987) 11 Ford ILJ 51.

[15] Art. 8 DSU.   [16] *Ibid.*, Art. 12 and App. 3.   [17] *Ibid.*, Art. 17.

[18] *Ibid.*, Arts 21 and 22.

although, as discussed next, the results of WTO dispute settlement to date suggests that overall it works fairly well.

What has resulted from the hundreds of consultation requests brought to the WTO? The aim of the WTO dispute settlement system is, of course, the resolution of trade-related disputes between WTO Members. In cases where a violation is found, removal of the inconsistent measure is the goal.[19] Otherwise, a mutually agreed solution is the preferred result.[20] In any case, prompt settlement is said to be essential.[21] In considering how the system has performed in meeting these goals, in a recent article I examined the 181 disputes that involved a consultation request made prior to July 1, 2002.[22] Of those 181 disputes, there were 107 disputes that either did not result in an adopted panel report or were not pending before an active panel as of the Summer of 2004 when the article was written. The remaining 74 cases involved disputes where panels had been established and had reported or were actively working. The results of the 181 disputes were as follows:

Results	Number	%
Panel, complainant lost	10	6
Panel, respondent lost and implemented	48	27
Panel, respondent lost, not implemented or disputed	10	6
Panel pending (or implementation period not expired)	6	3
Settled or dropped, after panel established	18	10
Settled, with notification to DSB	26	14
Settled, without notification	20	11
Dropped (for legal, political, commercial reasons)	24	13
Dropped (trade remedy measure not imposed/removed/expired)	15	8
Consultations pending	4	2

This overall record is impressive. With respect to the 74 cases where panel reports were issued or expected, six were pending cases. Of the remaining 68 disputes where reports had been adopted and implementation was due, the complainant had lost in 10 of them, such that no implementation was required. Of the 58 other disputes, there had been implementation in 48. That leaves 10 disputes where there had been no implementation or a disagreement

---

[19] *Ibid.*, Art. 3.7; *see also* Art. 3.5.   [20] *Ibid.*, Art. 3.7.   [21] *Ibid.*, Art. 3.3.

[22] The statistics presented here are reproduced from Davey, above at n 7. Dispute proceedings initiated by consultation requests made subsequent to June 2002 were not considered because so many of them were still pending. Additional detail on the settled or dropped cases can be found in W.J. Davey, 'Evaluating WTO Dispute Settlement: What Results have been Achieved Through Consultations and Implementation of Panel Reports?', paper presented at the conference 'WTO at 10: Dispute Settlement, Multilateral Negotiations, Regional Integration', Tokyo, Japan, 25–27 October 2005, also available as Illinois Public Law Research Paper No 05–19, available at ssrn. com/abstract=863865 (visited 3 April 2006).

between the parties over implementation as of mid-2004.[23] That suggests a successful implementation rate of 83 per cent. In fact, several of the ten have subsequently been resolved.[24] It should be mentioned, however, that there have been a number of cases, now resolved, where there were long-running disputes over implementation. Examples of such cases would include the *EC—Bananas III* (WT/DS27), *Australia—Salmon* (WT/DS18) and *Canada—Dairy* (WT/DS103 and DS/113) cases. Moreover, the record of successful implementation must also be tempered by the fact that in some cases, the complaining parties have accepted what they have claimed was less than full implementation. Nonetheless, for an international system of dispute settlement in which any case may be brought, this is an impressive record.[25]

Perhaps even more significant is the fact that the other 107 disputes—representing 59 per cent of the total cases—were mostly settled without panel proceedings. It appears that 35 per cent of the total cases, roughly one-third, were settled, and that in another 21 per cent, the matter was dropped because the challenged measure disappeared or the commercial interest changed. A few

---

[23] WTO Appellate Body Report, *EC—Hormones*, WT/DS26/AB/R, WT/DS48/AB/R, adopted 13 February 1998, WTO Appellate Body Report, *Brazil—Aircraft*, WT/DS46/AB/R, adopted 20 August 1999, WTO Appellate Body Report, *Canada—Aircraft*, WT/DS70/AB/R, adopted 20 August 1999, WTO Panel Report, *Canada—Aircraft Credits and Guarantees*, WT/DS222/R and Corr.1, adopted 19 February 2002, *Canada—Measures Affecting the Export of Civilian Aircraft* (request for consultations by Brazil), WT/DS71, WTO Appellate Body Report, *US—FSC*, WT/DS108/AB/R, adopted 20 March 2000, WTO Appellate Body Report, *US—1916 Act*, WT/DS136/AB/R, WT/DS162/AB/R, adopted 26 September 2000, WTO Panel Report, *US—Section 110(5) Copyright Act*, WT/DS160/R, adopted 27 July 2000 and WTO Appellate Body Report, *US—Offset Act (Byrd Amendment)*, WT/DS217/AB/R, WT/DS234/AB/R, adopted 27 January 2003 where compensatory or retaliatory measures were in place or authorized, or were being sought, as well as three cases where there appeared to be an ongoing dispute over whether recent action amounted to implementation. Likewise, WTO Appellate Body Report, *Chile—Price Band System*, WT/DS207/AB/R, adopted 23 October 2002; *Chile—Price Band System and Safeguard Measures relating to certain Agricultural Products*, (request for consultations by Guatemala), WT/DS220, WTO Appellate Body Report *US—Countervailing Measures on Certain EC Products*, WT/DS212/AB/R, adopted 8 January 2003 and WTO Appellate Body Report, *Japan—Apples*, WT/DS245/AB/R, adopted 10 December 2003.

[24] As of early 2006, the United States had repealed the 1916 Antidumping Act and the Byrd Amendment on a prospective basis, as of December 2004 and October 2007, respectively. The United States also implemented the FSC decision in late 2004, except for certain transitional provisions that the EC later successfully challenged. The prospective nature and timing of the repeals raise obvious issues of short-term WTO inconsistency, but the repeals do presage ultimate compliance. The EC claims to have implemented the *Hormones* decision and launched a challenge to the continuation of US and Canadian sanctions in 2004 (WT/DS320 and DS321). While a compliance panel found that there had not been complete implementation in the *Japan Apples*, Japan subsequently announced new rules that the US has accepted.

[25] T. Ginsburg and R.H. McAdams, 'Adjudicating in Anarchy: An Expressive Theory of International Dispute Resolution' (2004) 45 Wm & Mary L Rev 1229, at 1308–312 (finding a 68 per cent compliance rate, as defined by the authors, for a sample of cases before the International Court of Justice). The WTO success rate is comparable to the rate achieved by the GATT dispute settlement system through 1989. R. Hudec, *Enforcing International Trade Law: The Evolution of the GATT Legal System* (Salem NH: Butterworth 1993), Ch 11. It is probably true, however, that some difficult cases were never brought to the GATT system because of the right of the losing party to 'block' any adverse consequences of a decision against it (Davey, above at n 14). Moreover, the success rate of the GATT system declined considerably in the 1990s.

of these dropped cases undoubtedly involved valid legal claims that could have been pursued, but were not for one reason or another. This overall summary reinforces the positive record that the system has achieved.

One caveat to this record must be noted: while the dispute settlement system's record for dispute resolution is quite good, its performance in terms of promptness is not so impressive. In the first four years or so of the system's operation (through April 1999), the overall average time from panel establishment to report adoption was slightly more than 15 months, as opposed to the 12 months' goal in the DSU for appealed cases (9 months for non-appealed cases). Recent statistics compiled by Mexico suggest that the 15 to 16 month average remains true today, even though the rate of non-appealed cases has doubled.[26] To this time, must be added the reasonable times set for implementation, which have averaged around 9 months. In addition, some cases take much longer.

To summarize briefly: the WTO dispute settlement rules are comprehensive and provide a procedure that ensures that disputes can be settled bilaterally or, if necessary, adjudicated by neutral third parties in proceedings that are credible and that generally lead to enforceable results, albeit sometimes with considerable delay.

II. RTA DISPUTE SETTLEMENT

Compared to the WTO experience, the record of RTA dispute settlement is more difficult to assess. Generally, RTAs have dispute settlement systems. There are typically provisions for consultations to resolve differences and many RTAs have dispute settlement systems that resemble the GATT/WTO systems, i.e. disputes may be referred to a panel of experts that will issue a report on the merits of the dispute. The details vary from agreement to agreement, often as a function it would seem of the date of the agreement. In other words, parties often seem to adopt a state-of-the-art dispute settlement system when they initially negotiate an RTA or significantly revise it. This has promoted the spread of WTO-like dispute settlement systems.

On the question of usage, the picture is quite different from that of WTO dispute settlement: RTA dispute settlement seems to be used much less frequently than WTO dispute settlement. Indeed, it appears that a number of relatively complex dispute settlement mechanisms have never been used. An example would be that of ASEAN, which otherwise resembles the WTO system. The two systems that have seen some use are those of NAFTA and Mercosur.

---

[26] This figure is taken from a paper submitted by Mexico to the DSU negotiations. The paper was circulated as JOB(03)208, 10 November 2003; it has not been circulated as a TN/DS document. It did, however, receive coverage in the trade press. D. Pruzin, 'Mexican Study Cites Non-Compliance as Top Problem in WTO Dispute Settlement' (2003) 20 BNA Int Trade Rep, 1902.

A. NAFTA

The North America Free Trade Agreement (NAFTA), which includes Canada, Mexico, and the United States, has multiple dispute settlement mechanisms.[27] In addition to a general dispute settlement mechanism contained in Chapter 20, it includes in Chapter 19 a system for 'appealing' the results of antidumping and countervailing duty decisions by Canadian, Mexican, or US administrative authorities in Chapter 19, and a mechanism for resolving investor-state disputes in Chapter 11. Chapter 19 has been used extensively under NAFTA,[28] as it was under the Canada–US FTA,[29] effectively replacing appeals to the courts. Panels under Chapter 19 have been fairly intrusive in reviewing administrative decisions and frequently remand them. Chapter 11 has also been used rather extensively.[30] Although investors have been successful only in a few cases, the mere idea of a trade agreement providing such a remedy is very controversial.[31] However, since the Chapter 11 and 19 procedures are not state-to-state systems and have no true WTO analogue, I have not considered them in this paper.

The general dispute settlement system contained in NAFTA Chapter 20 resembles the WTO system. Indeed, it was negotiated at roughly the same time as the WTO system was put together. It provides in the first instance for consultations,[32] followed by referral of the dispute to a five-person panel if consultations fail to resolve the matter.[33] Chapter 20 generally imposes tighter deadlines than the WTO system[34] and provides for the establishment of a short roster of panellists from which panellists are normally to be drawn (by lot, if necessary).[35] If a panel finds a measure to be inconsistent with NAFTA, the complaining party may suspend concessions in the absence of an agreement on compensation.[36]

In contrast to the dispute settlement mechanisms established under Chapters

---

[27] *See* generally A.L.C. de Mestral, 'NAFTA Dispute Settlement: Creative Experiment or Confusion?', in this volume, at 359.

[28] According to the NAFTA secretariat website (www.nafta-sec-alena.org, visited 3 April 2006), there have been 18 decisions in cases challenging Canadian AD/CVD actions (none now active); 13 decisions in cases challenging Mexican actions (5 now active); and 55 decisions in cases challenging US actions (27 now active).

[29] According to the NAFTA secretariat website, *ibid.*, there were 16 decisions in cases challenging Canadian AD/CVD actions and 33 decisions in cases challenging US actions.

[30] The US State Department website (www.state.gov/s/l/c3741.htm, visited 3 April 2006) lists 11 Chapter 11 cases involving Mexico, 4 involving Canada and 12 involving the United States. There are additional matters where an intention to initiate a case has been filed.

[31] *See*, e.g. Public Citizen, 'NAFTA Chapter 11 Investor-State Cases', available at www.citizen.org/trade/nafta (visited 3 April 2006). It reports that as of February 2005, there had been two successful claims against Mexico (one for $15.6 million; one for $1.5 million) and two successful claims against Canada (one for $4.8 million; one for $450,000), plus a settlement where Canada paid $13 million.

[32] Art. 2006 NAFTA.   [33] *Ibid.*, Art. 2007.

[34] *Ibid.*, Arts. 2006, 2007, 2016, 2017, 2019 (relating to consultations, panel establishment, panel proceedings, and suspension of concessions).

[35] *Ibid.*, Arts 2009–2011.   [36] *Ibid.*, Arts 2018–2019.

11 and 19, the NAFTA general dispute settlement system under Chapter 20 has not been much used. According to information from the NAFTA dispute settlement website,[37] there have only been three cases since NAFTA entered into force in 1994 (two successful Mexican complaints: one about US trucking services restrictions and another about a broomcorn broom safeguard; and an unsuccessful US complaint about Canadian agricultural tariffs). This is a very low usage rate. It may be explained in part by the questionable effectiveness of the system. Mexico has had to wait considerable time for US implementation of the decisions in Mexico's favour.[38] It is striking, in fact, to consider that in the same period there have been many US–Mexican and US–Canadian disputes brought to the WTO system,[39] suggesting that the principal system for resolving these disputes is the WTO system, not the NAFTA system.

Several additional points about NAFTA should be noted. First, the NAFTA system was designed to be automatic in operation through the used of a pre-agreed roster of panellists. Unfortunately, after more than a decade, the roster has never been made public, apparently because it has yet to be agreed upon.[40] Second, the general dispute settlement system of the Canada–US Free Trade Agreement was also not much used—five cases during the FTA's seven years—and received only mixed reviews.[41]

In short, the general NAFTA dispute settlement system of Chapter 20 does

[37] See www.nafta-sec-alena.org/DefaultSite/index_e.aspx?ArticleID=5 (visited 3 April 2006).

[38] In the Broomcorn case, the safeguard at issue was imposed on 28 November 1996: 61 Federal Register 64431 (4 December 1996). The NAFTA panel found the safeguard to violate NAFTA rules in the case of Mexico on 28 January 1998. NAFTA Chapter 20 Panel Report, *US Safeguard Action Taken on Broomcorn Brooms from Mexico*, 30 January 1998, available at www.sice.oas.org/DISPUTE/nafdispe.asp (visited 3 April 2006). The safeguard was terminated on 3 December 1998, officially because the US industry failed to take adjustment measures as required by US law: 63 Federal Register 67761 (8 December 1998). No mention was made of the NAFTA panel report in the termination decision. In the Trucking case, the decision was issued on 6 February 2001. NAFTA Chapter 20 Arbitral Panel Report, *Cross-Border Trucking Services*, available at www.sice.oas.org/DISPUTE/nafdispe.asp (visited 3 April 2006). The report apparently remains unimplemented. 'Mexican Trucks Still Halted at Border as Sides Discuss Inspections', Inside US Trade, 12 November 2004.

[39] Canada has brought 13 consultation requests against the United States in the WTO (WT/DS144, DS167, DS180, DS194, DS221, DS234, DS236, DS247, DS257, DS264, DS277, DS310, DS311), while the US has brought 4 cases against Canada (WT/DS31, DS103, DS170, DS276). Mexico has brought 6 cases against the US (WT/DS49, DS234, DS280, DS281, DS282, DS325) and the US has initiated 6 cases against Mexico (WT/DS101, DS132, DS203, DS204, DS295, DS308). There have been no Canada–Mexico cases. Most of the cases concern US trade remedy measures, and, in the case of Canada, most of the cases are related to the Softwood Lumber dispute.

[40] This has meant that it is necessary for the parties to agree on panellists, which removes the intended automaticity from the system. This allows one party to block effectively panel formation. An apparent example of this is indicated on the USTR website, which lists one Mexican request for a panel under NAFTA Chapter 20, made in August 2000 in respect of US tariff rate quotas on sugar, as unresolved. USTR, Dispute Settlement Update (15 November 2005), 29, available at www.ustr.gov/Trade_Agreements/Monitoring_Enforcement/Section_Index.html (visited 3 April 2006).

[41] On the FTA's dispute settlement system, see W.J. Davey, *Pine & Swine: Canada–United States Trade Dispute Settlement: The FTA Experience and NAFTA Prospects* (Ottawa: Centre for Trade Policy and Law, 1996).

not seem to have enjoyed success comparable to that of the WTO dispute settlement system.

B. Mercosur

Mercosur was established in 1991. It is a customs union, consisting of Argentina, Brazil, Paraguay, and Uruguay. It has had a dispute settlement system since its inception, although the use of WTO-like panels was provided only as of 1993. More recently, the 2002 Olivos Protocol, which came into force in 2004, provides for a more WTO-like system with, *inter alia*, a permanent review tribunal to hear appeals from ad hoc panels.[42]

In the case of Mercosur,[43] its website indicates there have been ten arbitral decisions since 1999, although only two since 2002. All four of the Mercosur parties have invoked the system, with Argentina being the most frequent complainant in panel cases (three cases against Brazil and one against Uruguay), while Uruguay has brought three complaints leading to panels (one against Argentina and two against Brazil). Brazil has initiated two panel cases (both against Argentina) and Paraguay has started one (against Uruguay). As in the case of NAFTA, the Mercosur parties have made some (albeit rather limited) use of the WTO dispute settlement in their trade dealings as well. To be precise, there have been two WTO cases brought by Brazil against Argentina—one of which was related to a Mercosur dispute.[44]

The evaluations of the Mercosur system as a system—particularly with the innovations introduced by the Olivos Protocol—have been rather positive.[45] It is difficult to square that view, however, with the apparent reduced use of the system in recent years. Nonetheless, it would appear that the Mercosur system seems to be unusual in its status as a functioning and relatively effective RTA dispute settlement system. Perhaps its success can be explained by the fact that Mercosur is a customs union and that as an entity that has committed to much deeper integration than the typical RTA does, it both needs and can support a more effective dispute settlement system. The creation of a customs union, after all, arguably presupposes that the constituents parts will have common traditions and effective institutions in respect of dispute settlement.

---

[42] On the Mercosur system generally, *see* UNCTAD Course on Dispute Settlement: Regional Approaches: Mercosur (Volume 6.2, 2003), C. Leathley, 'The Mercosur Dispute Resolution System', The Royal Institute of International Affairs (Chatham House), Mercosur Study Group, 27 September 2002, E.J. Cardenas and G. Tempesta, 'Arbitral Awards under Mercosur's Dispute Settlement Mechanism' (2001) 4 JIEL 337, J. Lacarte and J. Granados (eds), *Solución de Controversias Comerciales Inter-Gubernamentales: Enfoques Multilaterales y Regionales* (Buenos Aires: BID-INTAL 2004). The latter volume discusses dispute settlement in Mercosur at pages 139–48, and in other Latin American trading systems at pages 133–38 and 159–86.

[43] *See* 200.40.51.219/msweb/principal/contenido.asp (visited 3 April 2006).

[44] WT/DS190 and DS241.   [45] *See* sources cited, above at n 42.

C. ASEAN

ASEAN was established in 1967. It is a free trade area and is currently comprised of Brunei Darussalam, Cambodia, Indonesia, Lao People's Republic, Malaysia, Myanmar, the Philippines, Singapore, Thailand, and Vietnam. Initially, the ASEAN agreements provided for relatively informal dispute settlement, but in 1996 a WTO-like system was adopted (with the possibility of appealing a panel decision to the ASEAN ministers).[46] Reportedly, this new more judicial-like system was adopted because of some dissatisfaction with the prior informal system, where disputes could be put on the agenda of officials' meetings for discussion, but were often resolved only after a very long time.[47] Whatever the reason for adopting it, however, the new system has yet to be used even though it has been in place for a considerable period of time. It may be that ASEAN countries are more comfortable with negotiating compromises to disputes, but they have occasionally used the WTO system,[48] even against each other.[49]

D. Other RTAs

RTAs typically provide for periodic meetings of the parties at a reasonably high political level. These meetings often contain agenda items involving trade disputes. It is clear that such meetings do succeed in resolving some disputes, although there seems to be no systematic study of their overall efficacy. The anecdotal evidence that is available suggests that disputes often languish on such agendas for a long period before finally be resolved or otherwise being disposed of.[50]

---

[46] *See* generally UNCTAD Course on Dispute Settlement: Regional Approaches: ASEAN (Volume 6.3, 2003).

[47] Statement of ASEAN Secretariat official, International Conference on 'Trade Remedy System': An East Asian Perspective, Chung-Hua Institution for Economic Research (Taiwan WTO Center), Taipei, 29–30 August 2005.

[48] Indonesia has initiated 3 consultation requests, 2 of which went to panels (WT/DS123, DS217, DS312); Malaysia pursued 1 panel case against the US (WT/DS58); the Philippines launched 4 cases, one of which it pursued in panel proceedings (WT/DS22, DS61, DS270, DS271); and Thailand started 11 cases against 6 different WTO Members (WT/DS17, DS35, DS47, DS58, DS181, DS205, DS217, DS242, DS283, DS286, DS324). In contrast, ASEAN members have not often been the target of WTO dispute settlement proceedings. There has been 1 dispute involving the Indonesian auto regime (WT/DS54, DS55, DS59, DS64); a challenge to Thai anti-dumping duties on H-Beams (WT/DS122) and several cases against the Philippines (WT/DS74, DS102, DS195, DS215).

[49] The only example was the first WTO case: *Singapore v Malaysia* (WT/DS1) in respect of certain Malaysian quotas on plastics.

[50] *See* I. Garcia Bercero, 'Dispute Settlement In European Union Free Trade Agreements: Lessons Learned?', in this volume, at 383.

E. Summary

In short, most dispute settlement provisions in RTAs do not seem to have been used, beyond those that simply provide for consultations. In the two RTAs where there has been some use of a general trade dispute settlement system, use has been rather limited and of questionable success, at least in the case of NAFTA.

III. THOUGHTS ON COMPARING DISPUTE SETTLEMENT IN THE WTO AND RTAS

The foregoing evidence suggests that, with the possible exception of Mercosur, dispute settlement in RTAs does not seem as successful as WTO dispute settlement.[51] That is certainly the case of NAFTA versus WTO dispute settlement. And it seems to be generally true. What explains this?

One possible reason is that the WTO dispute settlement system is a more sophisticated mechanism for resolving disputes, with superior rules. On paper, this does not seem to be true, however. Many RTAs have dispute settlement mechanisms that are quite similar to that of the WTO—ASEAN, Mercosur and NAFTA are examples, although NAFTA has no form of appellate review. Indeed, as noted above, there has seemed to be a tendency to model dispute settlement systems for new RTAs on the recently adopted systems. The apparent similarities between systems may be deceiving, however, when one examines how the system actually operate in practice. For example, the automaticity of the WTO system may not in fact be duplicated in RTAs.[52] More significantly, WTO panellists and Appellate Body members benefit from the assistance of trained experts provided by the WTO secretariat, while RTA dispute settlement typically relies much more heavily on the panellists themselves to do all of the work. One can argue about whether such staffs should be independent (as is the case with the WTO Appellate Body, whose staff exists solely to serve it) or not (the WTO Secretariat personnel working for panels have other responsibilities, including involvement in servicing negotiations). It is clear, however, that a dispute settlement system benefits from such support—especially in terms of educating panellists on standard procedures and precedents; in helping to ensure that the factual and legal arguments are adequately developed, in necessary through extensive questions; and in terms

---

[51] Of course, it is possible that parties to RTAs don't have trade disputes, but that seems improbable. It may be, however, that adjudicating the disputes that do arise is viewed as less acceptable amongst some nations. The countries of ASEAN might be an example of this, although they have used WTO dispute settlement (Indonesia, Malaysia, Singapore, and the Philippines have initiated cases), even amongst themselves (e.g. Malaysia Polyethylene (WT/DS1)).

[52] The example that immediately comes to mind is NAFTA where the system for automatically appointing panellists is not operational, and arguably would still depend on the cooperation of the respondent in any event.

of ensuring consistency in decisions across time. It is, of course, essential that the key decisions are in fact made by the panellists/Appellate Body members, but their decision-making process is helped if there is adequate staff support, since they may devote more of their time to the key issues. Thus, while the WTO dispute settlement system resembles those of some major RTAs on paper, it actually operates in a much more sophisticated and effective manner.

A second possible reason that trade dispute settlement seems to concentrated at the WTO could be that the WTO has a more effective enforcement system. However, this is not clearly the case. While it is true that the WTO procedures for surveillance and for suspension of concessions may be more developed than those in most RTA systems, the reality is that the sort of retaliatory actions that are the ultimate sanction under WTO rules are generally thought not to be effectively available to any countries except the most powerful—probably just the US and the EU.[53] Thus, differences in the formal enforceability of results would not seem to explain the difference, although as noted below, it appears that informal pressures to comply are much greater in the WTO system than in a bilateral situation arising under an RTA.

Third, and the most significant reason explaining the differences in results between dispute settlement in the WTO and under RTAs is that the WTO decisions are viewed as more legitimate—in part because the panels are typically from neutral states, in part because the decisions are subject to appellate review and in part because WTO dispute settlement is more adjudicative in nature and therefore less power-based than many RTA dispute settlement systems.

In terms of neutrality, it was certainly the case that the Canada–US FTA general dispute settlement suffered in part from suggestions, particularly in one case, that panellists were too nationalistic.[54] Similar concerns have occasionally arisen in Chapter 19 proceedings.[55] Thus, although by and large there may not be a problem with using nationals of the disputing parties to rule on disputes,[56] it takes only a very few cases where allegations of national bias are made for the legitimacy of a system to be substantially undermined. Thus far, nationality bias has not seemed to be a problem for the WTO.

The desirability of appellate review in enhancing legitimacy may be seen in the problems that NAFTA has had with Chapter 11 panel in investor-state disputes. Each panel is left on its own to interpret the key phrases of Chapter 11

[53] W.J. Davey, 'Implementation in WTO Dispute Settlement: An Introduction to the Problems and Possible Solutions', at 12–14, Illinois Public Law Research Paper No 05–16, available at ssrn.com/abstract=862786 (visited 3 April 2006).

[54] Davey, above at n 41, at 71–2 ('[I]n [one] case, some felt that the [panel] process was tainted by nationalism'.)

[55] *See* Davey, *ibid.*, at 232–44 (describing controversy over alleged conflicts of interest in one case).

[56] WTO Appellate Body members sit on cases involving their countries, but panellists typically do not. There has been only one panel proceeding where nationals of the two parties served on the panel: *US—Laws, Regulations and Methodology for Calculating Dumping Margins (Zeroing)* (WT/DS294).

and while there may be some adherence to prior rulings, the desirability of a tribunal that could ensure standard practice seems obvious. It also ensures a second, more detached look at a case after the initial sorting out of the facts and legal issues. The mere existence of an appeal right probably gives some comfort to a losing party, even if the appeal is unlikely to lead to a reversal of the result.

Finally, WTO dispute settlement is viewed as more legitimate because it is less power-based and more rule-based than RTA dispute settlement.[57] While RTAs may be concluded between trading partners of roughly equal size and power, they often include parties that vary to a great degree in relative size and power—NAFTA and, to a lesser degree, Mercosur—are prime examples, as are almost any RTA entered into by the United States or the European Union. While such RTAs may appear to have WTO-like rule-based dispute settlement, they often in fact exhibit aspects of power-based dispute settlement. For example, as noted above, Mexico has had difficulty in obtaining compliance from the United States in the two NAFTA Chapter 20 cases it brought and was apparently unable to proceed with a third;[58] Canada currently appears to be facing difficulties in obtaining US compliance with NAFTA Chapter 19 panel rulings in the long-running softwood lumber anti-dumping and countervailing duty cases.[59] While the same power disparities exist in the WTO, they are more effectively offset, even if they can never be eliminated, in a multilateral setting than in a bilateral one.

Thus, it would appear that the relative disuse of RTA dispute settlement (or less successful use thereof) than WTO dispute settlement may be explained by the fact that the WTO, as a multilateral system, offers a more legitimate result—a result that is more likely to be accepted by the parties and complied with than the results of RTA dispute settlement. Failure to comply with an RTA dispute settlement ruling is an irritant in bilateral relations; failure to comply with a WTO ruling is not only a bilateral irritant, but has multilateral consequences. Non compliance is raised at least monthly at the WTO and the defending party will be accused of cavalierly undermining an otherwise successful dispute settlement system. Countries may often want to avoid those consequences and accusations and thus be more likely to comply with a WTO ruling. Certainly the analysis of the results of WTO dispute settlement that is set out above support the view that compliance with WTO rulings is relatively good. Indeed, to the extent that the WTO system is perceived to be effective

---

[57] On the desirability of an adjudicative or rule-based approach to dispute settlement, as opposed to a power-based or negotiation approach, *see* Davey, above at n 14, at 65–81 and J.H. Jackson, 'Governmental Disputes in International Trade Relations: A Proposal in the Context of GATT' (1979) 13 JWT 1.

[58] *See* above at n 38 and 40.

[59] *See*, e.g. 'Canada's Prime Minister Calls Bush, Links Complaints on Softwood, NAFTA to Energy', BNA International Trade Daily (17 October 2005) (reporting that 'the prime minister stressed Canada's concerns that the refusal of the United States to respect a recent dispute panel ruling in the softwood case raises issues about the validity of free trade under [NAFTA]').

(and WTO Members have frequently lauded it as basically successful and only needing fine-tuning in DSU reform negotiations),[60] its further success is facilitated as there is more pressure on WTO Members not to be the one that fails to implement. Thus, its success starts to feed on itself and to have aspects of a self-fulfilling prophecy. It is not clear that RTA dispute settlement could produce comparable results. Certainly it seems that NAFTA has not.

I would not want to overstate this conclusion. It is largely based on a comparison of NAFTA and WTO dispute settlement as there are so few other examples of RTA dispute settlement. Nonetheless, I think that the analysis makes sense and is a major reason why the WTO is likely to survive and prosper in a world with an ever increasing number of RTAs.

---

[60] W.J. Davey, 'Reforming WTO Dispute Settlement', in D. Ahn and M. Matsushita (eds), *New Perspectives on the World Trading System: WTO and East Asia* (London: Cameron May 2004).

15

NAFTA Dispute Settlement: Creative Experiment or Confusion?

ARMAND DE MESTRAL *

I. INTRODUCTION

Regional trade agreements (RTAs) are generally said to offer a range of advantages and entail possible disadvantages for the parties. On the positive side of the ledger, it is asserted that an RTA can allow the parties to proceed towards closer economic integration at a faster pace than is possible under the World Trade Organization (WTO). It is also asserted that an RTA allows for greater flexibility of arrangements: the parties can experiment with new forms of integration and incidentally can adopt measures that may serve as models for future multilateral arrangements. Apart from allegedly weakening the multilateral trade system, it is said of RTAs that virtually all suffer from rigidity and an incapacity for organic change and development. This debate usually revolves around trade provisions such as rules of origin and the preferential exemption from safeguards or other multilateral rules but the same questions can be asked of the working of dispute settlement systems in RTAs. Several recent WTO dispute settlement proceedings have revealed conflicts between the requirements of WTO membership and the provisions or practice under certain RTAs.[1]

The purpose of this chapter is to provide an analysis of the working of the various dispute settlement systems which exist under the North American Free

* The author expresses his thanks to Mohammad Nsour, Ph.D. candidate, McGill University and to the Canadian Social Sciences and Humanities Research Council for its financial support for the research project on 'Regional Trade Agreements and the Multilateral Trading System'.

[1] *See*, e.g. WTO Panel Report, *Canada—Autos*, WT/DS139/AB/R, WT/DS142/AB/R, adopted 19 June 2000, WTO Appellate Body Report, *US—Wheat Gluten*, WT/DS166/AB/R, adopted 19 January 2001, WTO Panel Report, *Turkey—Textiles*, WT/DS34/R, adopted 19 November 1999, WTO Appellate Body Report, *Argentina—Footwear (EC)*, WT/DS121/AB/R, adopted 12 January 2000, WTO Appellate Body Report, *EC—Bananas III*, WT/DS27/AB/R, adopted 25 September 1997, *EEC—Bananas II*, 11 February 1994, unadopted, DS38/R, and *EC (Member States)— Bananas I*, 3 June 1993, unadopted, DS32/R.

Trade Agreement (NAFTA)[2] with a view to determining whether NAFTA displays the same alleged advantages and disadvantages in respect of dispute settlement. It will be shown that, far from being totally separate, there is a strong interrelationship between certain NAFTA procedures and the WTO Dispute Settlement Understanding (DSU). The many procedures existing under NAFTA, far from being self-contained, have the capacity to overlap and interweave in a manner that was not planned by the drafters of the treaty. While NAFTA itself has not shown much capacity to develop, it may be asked whether some incremental change is being fostered by various dispute settlement procedures in a manner comparable to the impact of the European Court of Justice on EU Law. Arguably these changes may affect both NAFTA and the WTO DSU. Finally, what judgment can be made of allowing several private rights of action? Is this the positive feature that is alleged or is it turning out to be a means of encouraging private parties to raise public issues better left to interstate litigation?

A. General Features of NAFTA

NAFTA was built upon the Canada–United States Free Trade Agreement (CUSFTA) which entered into force on January 1, 1989.[3] When Mexico proposed the negotiation of a bilateral RTA with the United States in 1990, the Government of Canada waited almost six months before calling for a trilateral negotiation in 1991, but then proceeded to defend the acquis of CUSFTA, including the dispute settlement provisions throughout the ensuing negotiations. The dispute settlement provisions which emerged, as described below, are either expanded versions of those of the CUSFTA or new forms of dispute settlement which did not appear in the CUSFTA, such as those respecting investments in Chapter 11 B. A further point concerning the drafting of NAFTA is that negotiations occurred during the latter stages of the Uruguay Round of Multilateral Trade Negotiations. Chapter 18 of CUSFTA and Chapter 20 of NAFTA, the residual chapters, were influenced by and may even have led the search for more binding and compulsory procedures evidenced by the GATT Mid-term Agreement[4] but, having entered into force on January 1, 1994, NAFTA did not adopt the more binding solution enshrined in the WTO Dispute Settlement Understanding.[5] Chapter 11 B on investment disputes may reflect the solution that might have been had the Uruguay Round successfully

---

[2] *See* NAFTA Implementation Act, S.C. 1993, c. 44. *See also* NAFTA Agreement, signed 17 December 1992, in force 1 January 1994, at Chs 11, 14, 18, 19 and 20.

[3] *See* Canada–US Free Trade Agreement Implementation Act, S.C. 1988, c. 65. *See also* Canada–US Free Trade Agreement (the CUSFTA Agreement), signed 2 January 1988, in force 1 January 1989.

[4] *See* GATT, Decisions Adopted at the Mid-Term Review of the Uruguay Round, 8 April 1989 (1989) 28 ILM 1023, 1033.

[5] Understanding on Rules and Procedures Governing the Settlement of Disputes ('DSU'), Annex 2 to the WTO Agreement.

pursued broader negotiations on investments. The ultimate result of comparison of the two agreements is that, while CUSFTA/NAFTA was at one point ahead of the GATT in the search for more binding and compulsory dispute settlement procedures, it ultimately maintained its lead on many issues but lost it on Chapter 20.

NAFTA provides strong evidence for the proposition that RTAs allow the parties to be more inventive and proceed more quickly than may be possible at the multilateral level. NAFTA enshrines no less than seven forms of dispute settlement. The different forms are as follows: (1) Chapter 20, the residual procedure based on the GATT panel model; (2) Chapter 14 on financial services disputes, which adopts the same approach as Chapter 20, but which provides for panels made up of financial experts; (3) Chapter 19 which provides a recourse to challenge domestic decisions imposing anti-dumping and countervailing duties (AD/CV) before a bi-national panel; (4) Chapter 11 B which deals with investment disputes under Chapter 11 A; (5) Article 2002 envisages recourse to the WTO procedures where they might lie under both agreements; (6) Article 2022 envisages the possibility of recourse to arbitration and other alternative means of dispute resolution between the Parties; and (7) the 'side agreements' on environmental and labour cooperation[6] provide both for a private party complaints procedure before the respective Commissions, designed more as a dispute avoidance rather than dispute settlement mechanisms, as well as a formal dispute settlement procedure which is available in limited circumstances to the three governments.

It must also be noted that, as well as providing a variety of specialized dispute settlement procedures, NAFTA and the side agreements provide not only for inter-state remedies but also create the possibility of private rights of action. The private rights of action take the form of investor-state actions under Chapter 11 B, as well as an appeal to a bi-national panel process to challenge domestic administrative decisions imposing AD/CV duties under Chapter 19, and the private rights of complaint leading to investigative procedures under the side agreements. A further point to be made is that Chapter 19 provides for a right of remand by the bi-national panel seized of an AD/CV appeal. This remand may involve a duty of the domestic administrative agency to return before the bi-national panel should its decision on the remand not satisfy the complainant private party.

The general picture which emerges from NAFTA and the side agreements is

---

[6] *See* Canada–Mexico–US North American Agreement on Labor Cooperation, signed 14 September 1993, in force 1 January 1994, 32 ILM 1499, at 5 (NAALC) (the NAALC adopted 11 internationally-recognized rights for workers including the freedom of association and the right to strike. NAALC defines two main avenues to enhance labour rights: first, demanding that domestic legislations conform to NAALC criteria; and second, by creating a dispute settlement mechanism. It should be noted that NAALC contains a body that is referred to as the Evaluation Committee of Experts (ECE). The ECE primarily intervenes upon a party's request if consultations did not succeed). *See also* Canada–Mexico–US North American Agreement on Environmental Cooperation, in force 1 January 1994 (1993) 32 ILM 1480 (NAAEC).

of an RTA which seeks to tailor dispute settlement procedures to a variety of quite different negotiated settlements. Rather than impose a single top down procedure, the negotiators of NAFTA grafted different solutions to a text which can legitimately be described as reflecting a range of 'bottom up' solutions. This reflects the reality of NAFTA where the onus of economic integration is very much upon the private sector, which has always been the driving force for integration. The three Parties to NAFTA in 1994 limited themselves essentially to removing obstacles to economic integration in a context where the integration of many enterprises had already achieved levels exceeding the integration of most countries of the European Community. NAFTA, as a free trade agreement, is essentially a complex, fairly rigid, and highly detailed agreement which does not provide for the kind of extensive common regulatory activity which has been characteristic of the EU. Canada and the United States already possessed two very closely entwined economies and sought to provide a framework in which private business could continue down the path of further intra-firm and sectoral specialization. Mexico accepted and contributed to this model, in part because there was little choice, but also because it embraced the same approach based on opening up sectors and markets on the basis of private initiative and private investment. The different dispute settlement procedures which emerged reflect this fact. These procedures also reflect the fact that NAFTA remains, despite its differences, much closer to the matrix of the WTO model than to that of a customs union such as the EU; there is virtually no hint of supranationality to be found in NAFTA.

One final point must be made by way of introduction: this is the complex and sometimes uneasy relationship of NAFTA to the law of the WTO. NAFTA is based on the principles of WTO law. There is a presumption of compatibility between the two and the deep structure of NAFTA is grounded in the multilateral system. This is certainly true of the substantive law of NAFTA, but curiously it is less true of the procedural law pertaining to dispute settlement. The two basic procedures, the WTO DSU and NAFTA Chapter 20 while similar, are in some ways more rivals than complementary, while the other procedures of NAFTA often depart considerably from the general matrix of WTO procedural law.

II. ASSESSMENT OF EACH PROCEDURE

A. Chapter 20

Like Chapter 18 of the CUSFTA before it, this is the residual procedure for NAFTA when no other procedure exists and when a State Party considers that a measure of another party is inconsistent with NAFTA or is causing nullification or impairment. The procedure is essentially a WTO-like panel process, composed of five panellists and subject to fixed and roughly similar deadlines. Very detailed rules exist for the constitution of a roster of panellists and their selection in individual cases. The roster was designed to be a college of experts, but in practice parties have not kept up the roster faithfully and have chosen panellists on and off the roster by bilateral negotiation. The whole Chapter 20 process is governed by the NAFTA Free Trade Commission composed of the three Ministers of International Trade. Under Article 2008, upon receiving a request to constitute a panel, the Commission is under a legal obligation to constitute it. However, in a three way relationship it seems that political choice and pressure have played a considerable role, particularly with respect to the speed with which the panel is actually constituted and the moment when it actually begins its work. The formal automaticity of Article 2008(2) has never been legally tested but the object was clearly to have an obligatory process. The Final Report of the panel is undoubtedly less binding than panel reports under the WTO DSU. Article 2017 states:

1. On receipt of the final report of a panel, the disputing Parties shall agree on the resolution of the dispute, which normally shall conform with the determinations and recommendations of the panel, and shall notify their Sections of the Secretariat of any agreed resolution of any dispute.
2. Wherever possible, the resolution shall be non-implementation or removal of a measure not conforming with this Agreement or causing nullification or impairment in the sense of Annex 2004 or, failing such a resolution, compensation.

However, the Article 2018(1) does strengthen the obligatory character of the panel report since it states that:

1. If in its final report a panel has determined that a measure is inconsistent with the obligations of this Agreement or causes nullification or impairment in the sense of Annex 2004 and the Party complained against has not reached agreement with any complaining Party on a mutually satisfactory resolution pursuant to Article 2018(1) within 30 days of receiving the final report, such complaining Party may suspend the application to the Party complained against of benefits of equivalent effect until such time as they have reached agreement on a resolution of the dispute.

On the basis of relatively little experience, it appears that these rules lead to a satisfactory solution only when an existing measure is upheld and no changes are required, as was the case in *Tariffs Applied by Canada to certain US-Origin Agricultural Products*.[7] But when positive action is required, as in the *Cross Border Trucking Services and Investment Case*,[8] the bilateral or tripartite political relationship has not always been conducive to rapid settlement on the basis of the Panel Report. The only relatively uncontroversial case lost by the United States was *US Safeguard Action Taken on Broomcorn Brooms from*

---

[7] *See Re Tariffs Applied by Canada to Certain US-Origin Agricultural Products (United States v Canada)* (1996) CDA-95–2008–01 (Ch 20 Panel).

[8] *See Re Matter of Cross-Border Trucking Services (Mexico v United States)* (2001) USA–MEX-98–2008–01 (Ch 20 Panel).

Mexico[9]. A Chapter 20 panel held that the US safeguard measures adopted by the International Trade Commission were not adequately grounded in law or fact.

Article 2005 contains several choice of forum rules. The Article accepts that matters arising under both the WTO and NAFTA may be decided under either procedure at the election of the complainant. The election is final and binding on both parties. However, under Article 2005(3) and (4), where the dispute relates to a multilateral environmental agreement covered by Article 104, the dispute can only be heard under NAFTA and where the dispute relates to matters arising under Chapter 7 B (SPS) and Chapter 9 (Standards) the respondent, not the complainant, is free to insist upon proceeding under NAFTA. Implicitly, this Article constitutes a challenge to the primacy of the DSU and since there is no *forum non conveniens* rule before the WTO, it does not seem possible that it could be raised there if violated by a party. None of these forum selection rules have been tested before a panel under either jurisdiction.

Two questions stand out with respect to Chapter 20; the first relates to the number of cases and the second relates to the choice of this chapter when the WTO DSU is also available. Experience under Chapter 18 would have suggested a relatively stable number of decisions under Chapter 20, but there have only been three Chapter 20 decisions in ten years under NAFTA, in contrast to the FTA Chapter 18, under which there were five in five years.[10] This may result from the fact that the WTO DSU provides both a more obligatory and a more binding process backed up by tighter enforcement procedures than was the case of FTA Chapter 18. Of the three Chapter 20 decisions, only *Broomcorn Brooms from Mexico* offered a choice of recourses before both fora. It is not known why Mexico chose to proceed under NAFTA. In the other two cases, the United States and Mexico had to proceed under NAFTA as their pleas were based entirely on specific NAFTA provisions which they could not plead before a WTO panel.

The disaffection from Chapter 20 was highlighted by the success of the United States when it chose to make a complaint against Canadian preferential measures against 'split run' periodicals. Had the United States made its complaint under NAFTA it would have been met by a Canadian defence based on Article 2106 permitting preferential measures in favour of cultural industries

---

[9] See *Re US Safeguard Action Taken on Broom Corn Brooms from Mexico (Mexico v United States)* (1998) USA-97-2008-01 (Ch 20 Panel).

[10] See, e.g. *Re Puerto Rico Regulations on the Import Distribution and Sale of UHT Mill from Quebec (Canada v United States)* (1993) USA-93-1807-01 (Ch 18 Panel), *Re Durum Wheat Sales (United States v Canada)* (1993) CDA-92-1807-01 (Ch 18 Panel), *Re Treatment of Non-Mortgage Interest under Article 304 (Canada v United States)* (1992) USA-92-1807-01 (Ch 18 Panel), *Re United States Regulations on Lobster (Canada v United States)* (1990) USA-89-1807-01 (Ch 18 Panel) and *Re West Coast Salmon and Herring from Canada (United States v Canada)* (1998) CDA-89-1807-01 (Ch 18 Panel).

between Canada and the United States.[11] Before the WTO panel, the United States successfully argued that the measures constituted a denial of national treatment and a quota.[12] Canada did not consider that it was entitled to raise a defence based on NAFTA before the WTO and was faced with the loss of the case and the necessity to reach a negotiated solution with the United States on a measure which was justified under NAFTA and which enjoyed widespread public support.[13]

The impression left by Chapter 20 at this time is of a chapter overtaken and weakened by comparison to the WTO DSU. The WTO process, adopted after both the FTA Chapter 18 and NAFTA Chapter 20 is clearly stronger in many respects, and more serious still is the fact that NAFTA law cannot be pleaded before the WTO. This is surely a most serious issue. Perhaps Canada was mistaken in not raising the NAFTA defence before the *Canada—Periodicals*

---

[11] Art. 2106 of the NAFTA is the equivalent to Art. 2005 in the CUSFTA. Art. 2005 was an exemption to the cultural industries from the liberalization agreed upon under the CUSFTA. Nevertheless, though Art. 2106 of the NAFTA applies between Canada and Mexico and between Canada and the United States, it is not applicable between Mexico and the United States. *See* Art. 2106 NAFTA; *see also* Art. 2005 CUFSTA.

[12] *See* WTO Panel Report, *Canada—Periodicals*, WT/DS31/R, adopted 30 July 1997. *See also* generally V. Ross, 'Canadian magazines duffer body blow', Globe & Mail, 18 January 1997, C2; C. Goar, 'U.S. threatens retaliation for magazine tax, Kantor blasts' dictionary Canadian move', Toronto Star, 16 December 1999; D. Crane, 'Big bucks at stake in local-content war', Toronto Star, 19 January 1999; B. McKenna, 'Canada on front line in cultural battle', Globe & Mail, 18 January 1999, BI; P. Morton, 'Kantor's attack on Canada is a warning to world', Financial Post, 12 March 1996, 7; J. Stoffman, 'U.S. magazines ignore Canadian threat', Toronto Star, 9 February 1999; B. McKenna, 'The View from Washington, Unlikely ally backs bid to shelter culture', Globe & Mail, 1 December 1998, B10; 'Right way and wrong way to foster Canadian culture', Financial Post, 17 September 1996, A14; A. Coyne, 'A second read on saga of split-runs', Toronto Star, 21 January 1997, D3; J. Stoffman, 'Delay expected in trade appeal', Toronto Star, 21 January 1997, D2; L. Eggerston, 'Magazine invasion looms, Up to 80 from U.S. poised to flood Canada', Toronto Star, 11 July 1998, A12; L. Eggerston, 'Trade body sinks magazine policy', Toronto Star, 1 July 1997, AI; E. Stewart, 'Ottawa out to skirt ruling on magazines', Toronto Star, 2 July 1997, 3; B. Dagliesh, 'Canadian publishers say WTO ruling is a "technical problem" ', Financial Post, 2 July 1997, 3; D. Saunders, 'Magazine publishers social on ruling', Globe and Mail, 1 July 1997, DI; P. Morton, 'U.S. eyes spuds in next trade fray with Canada: Fries and Fish on Menu: Barshefsky finds new irritants in two-way trade', National Post, 20 March 1998; B. Mckenna, 'Ottawa may seek WTO ruling on Bill C-55, Washington reacts coolly to magazine law review', Globe & Mail, 21 January 1999, BI; G. Fraser and B. Mckenna, 'Canada's bid to protect culture provokes warning from Washington', Globe & Mail, 12 January 1999, CI; H. Scoffield, 'The Magazine Deal, "Canada won, Copps insists" ', Globe & Mail, 27 May 1999, A3; P.C. Newman, 'Au revoir but not good-bye', MacLean's, 7 June 1999 and D. Crane, 'Magazine war shows U.S. wants to own us', Toronto Star, 29 May 1999.

[13] The Canada and the US agreed on three method plan the American publishers may follow in the Canadian market : first, American split-run magazine distributors shall have at least 18 per cent of the advertising targeting Canadian audience; second, if advertising was with 0 per cent Canadian content, foreign publishers may deduct 50 per cent of their advertising expenses, and 100 per cent when 80 per cent Canadian content exists; third, any new periodical established in Canada should have the majority of content is Canadian related, while existing periodicals at that time could not be acquired. Moreover, the agreement recognizes the right of Canada to subsidies up to $50 million dollars per annum the Canadian owned and controlled magazines. *See* 'Canada and the U.S. sign an agreement on periodicals', The Canadian Heritage, News Release/Communiqué, 26 May 1999, available at www.canadianheritage.gc.ca/newsroom/news_e.cfm?Action=Display&code=9NR031E (visited 10 April 2006).

panel? But there is a serious anomaly resulting from the fact that WTO law is central to the interpretation of an FTA, while the WTO dispute settlement procedure is blind to the fact of an increasing body of FTA law and practice around the world.

B. Chapter 14

This chapter dealing with Financial Services provides for the same procedure as Chapter 20, except that the members of the panel shall be selected from a roster of fifteen persons who 'have expertise in financial services law or practice . . .' The roster has never been made public and no dispute has yet occurred under this chapter.

C. Chapter 19

This chapter is probably the most innovative of the dispute settlement procedures to be found in NAFTA. The chapter deals with disputes arising under anti-dumping and countervailing duty (AD/CV) legislation. It first appeared in the CUSFTA, where it was negotiated as a last minute solution to a negotiating impasse, after the United States refused the accede to the Canadian proposal that AD/CV laws no longer be applied to trade between the two countries in the context of their future free trade agreement. The proposal to abolish or exclude the application of AD/CV laws to Canada–United States trade had been made early in the negotiations as a response to widespread concern in Canada that too many Canadian industries and jobs were subject to AD/CV proceedings in the United States; for this reason the Canadian Government had indicated that it was a matter of high priority to Canada and essential to the conclusion of an agreement. Faced with the refusal of the American negotiators to accept the principle of exclusion or alternatively of replacement of AD/CV laws with competition law, the Canadian delegation withdrew from the negotiations and only returned when it was agreed that a solution would be found. Negotiations on the future Chapter 19 were rushed through in a final month, thus permitting the entry into force of CUSFTA on January 1, 1988. After that date, sporadic efforts continued to be made by Canadian ministers to seek exemption from American AD/CV laws or to stimulate debate on the wisdom of replacing them with competition law, but when the trilateral NAFTA negotiations began, it was on the basis of the CUSFTA Chapter 19, which, with some amendments, became NAFTA Chapter 19. Thus, although it was an original solution to a difficult negotiating problem, NAFTA Chapter 19 was never the first choice of Canada or the United States, and Mexico had little to say in the matter at all. Given the relatively undeveloped nature of Mexican AD/CV law, Mexico was put to considerable trouble to ensure the existence of an appropriate legislative and administrative structure to ensure full implementation of Chapter 19.

Chapter 19 is a complex mix of private and international remedies. Each country is entitled to retain its AD/CV laws, which in fact are based on their common commitments as WTO Members to the Agreement on Subsidies and Countervailing Duties and the Agreement on the Implementation of Article VI of the GATT 1994. Both agreements set out requirements for the decision-making process to determine the existence of dumping and subsidies and the degree to which they have or will cause serious injury to the production of like goods by the domestic industry. In order to restrain protectionist impulses by domestic regulators, Chapter 19 provides that judicial review may, at the option of the foreign private party, be exercised by a bi-national panel composed of five experts who are authorized to hear and adjudicate upon complaints that the domestic administrative or quasi-judicial decision has not been adopted according to the domestic law of the state where the complaint has been heard. A bi-national panel must apply the standard of judicial review applicable to like cases according to local law; it may confirm a decision or reject it in whole or in part: in which case it shall remand the matter to the administrative authority for a further hearing and decision as directed. The decisions of a bi-national panel do not constitute *res judicata* in other proceedings in the domestic legal order, but have the force of law and are binding on the domestic regulatory authorities and the private parties involved. Article 1904 requires that the election of a bi-national tribunal is binding and precludes, any return to the domestic courts which would normally exercise judicial review.[14] In clearly defined circumstances, Article 1904(13) provides an Extraordinary Challenge Procedure (ECP) to challenge a bi-national panel decision. It is important to note that the ECP can only be invoked by a government and not by the private parties who here invoked the bi-national panel procedure of Article 1904(1) in the first place.

This procedure is by far the most widely used of the NAFTA dispute settlement processes. As of April 2005 there had been 71 cases completed before bi-national panels and two ECPs;[15] 30 cases were active before bi-national panels and one ECP was pending.[16] Under the CUSFTA, between 1988 and 1994 there had been 49 proceedings including 3 ECPs.[17] The purpose of recourse to a Chapter 19 bi-national panel is to ensure that the domestic law has been properly applied and has not been interpreted and applied in a manner designed to give protection to the domestic industry. Bi-national

---

[14] But not a complaint before the WTO DSB on related issues. *See*, e.g. *Certain Softwood Lumber Products from Canada (Canada v the United States)* (2003) USA–CDA-2002–1904–02 (Ch 19 bi-national Panel), *Certain Softwood Lumber Products from Canada (Canada v United States)* (2003) USA–CDA-2002–1904–03 (Ch 19 bi-national Panel) and *Certain Softwood Lumber Products from Canada (Canada v United States)* (2003) USA–CDA-2002–1904–07 (Ch 19 bi-national Panel).

[15] 19 in Canada; 41 in the United States and 11 in Mexico. NAFTA Decisions & Reports, available at www.nafta-sec-alena.org/DefaultSite/index_e.aspx (visited 10 April 2006).

[16] 27 in the United States; 3 in Mexico and none in Canada. The ECP involved a Softwood Lumber decision in the United States. *See ibid.*

[17] 19 in Canada and 30 in the United States. *See ibid.*

panels apply the standard of administrative law review applicable in the country where the litigation takes place; they do not apply an international standard derived from either NAFTA or the WTO. The standard of review for each country is specified in Annex 1911.[18] In all three jurisdictions, the central policy is to respect the choices made by the administrators and quasi-judicial agencies charged with making determinations and decisions under their respective laws and only to upset these decisions in limited circumstances where the decision maker has exceeded their authority or fundamental procedural principles of administrative law have been violated.

In the United States, the standard of review is a complex issue. It is probably the broadest standard of the three NAFTA countries and has been a constant source of concern for bi-national panels.[19] In Canada, the standard of review depends very much upon the existence of a privative clause or failing express statutory directives upon context.[20] In Mexico the standard of review is based on a complex appreciation of fact and law as set out in the requisite statute.[21]

---

[18] In Canada, the Federal Court Act R.S.C., c. F-7, s. 18.1(4) (1985); in the United States, the Tariff Act of 1930, 19 U.S.C. § 1516a(b)(1)(A) and (B) & § 751(b) (1994); in Mexico the Codigo Fiscal de la Federacion [Federal Fiscal Code], Art. 238.

[19] It has been described by one panel in the following manner:

Article 1904(3) of the NAFTA requires that this Panel apply the 'standard of review' and 'general legal principles' that a U.S. court would apply in its review of a Department determination. The standard of review that must be applied by the Panel is dictated by § 516A(b)(1)(B) of the Act, which requires the Panel to 'hold unlawful any determination, finding, or conclusion found . . . to be unsupported by substantial evidence on the record, or otherwise not in accordance with law. . .'. The question in an appellate review is whether the administrative record adequately supports the Department's determination, which must be adjudged only on the grounds and findings actually stated in its determination, not on the basis of post hoc argumentation of counsel. In carrying out its review of an agency determination, a reviewing court or binational panel must stay strictly within the confines of the administrative record already in existence. Panels may not engage in *de novo* review and, as a consequence, may not make new factual findings that would amend the agency record. Indeed, the statutory requirement that review be 'on the [administrative] record' means that the reviewing court or binational panel is limited to 'information presented to or obtained by [the Department] . . . during the course of the administrative proceeding . . .

See *Certain Durum Wheat and Hard Red Spring Wheat from Canada (United States v Canada)* (2005) USA–CDA-2003–1904–05 at p. 17 (Ch 19 Panel).

[20] See *Re Certain Iodinated Contrast Media Used for Radiographic Imaging, Originating in or Exported from the United States of America (Including the Commonwealth of Puerto Rico) (Canada v United States)* (2003) CDA–USA-2000–1904–01 (Ch 19 Panel). This decision described the standard of review as:

[it] identifies three possible standards of review: correctness, and two deferential standards: unreasonableness and patent unreasonableness. Which standard applies is determined on the basis of a 'pragmatic and functional analysis'. The principal components of that analysis are: the nature of the particular issue on which review is being sought, the expertise of the decision-maker, legislative indicia (if any), and the overall statutory purpose. The Supreme Court has also held that the critical factor in most instances will be expertise.

[21] See *Re Imports of High Fructose Corn Syrup, Originating from the United States of America (United States v Mexico)* (2001) Mex–USA-98–1904–01 (Ch 19 Panel). The standard was described in the following terms in this decision as follows:

274. (c) in the case of Mexico, the standard set out in Article 238 of the Codigo Fiscal de la Federacion, or any successor statutes, based solely on the administrative record.

In each NAFTA country, the standard of review is a complex matter which is driven by legislative fiat, fundamental principles of law, the exercise of judicial discretion, and the facts of each case. It is inevitably a moving target which evolves along with the whole corpus of administrative law applicable to judicial review. More than any other parts of NAFTA, the language of Article 1904, which determines the jurisdiction of bi-national panels, is applied directly by panels. Particular problems arise in Mexico where, unlike the United States and Canada, many parts of the NAFTA treaty can be applied directly by panels and courts.

Significant points of similarity and of difference exist between NAFTA and the law of the WTO on this matter. Under the WTO, the fundamental objective of requiring bi-national panels to apply and respect the national standard of review is also reflected in the policy of Article 17(6)(ii) of the WTO Agreement on Implementation of Article VI of the GATT 1994 (AD Agreement). This similarity of concerns inevitably invites comparison of the two systems. However, comparison reveals some major differences: while the WTO procedure can deal with particular decisions, it is only invoked by one state and against another; it is addressed to the legislative measures of states and can only call on the state to act in response to a determination that a decision has been taken in violation of the AD Agreement. NAFTA Chapter 19, on the other hand, is invoked by a private party and addresses the complaint of the private party. It focuses directly upon the administrator or quasi-judicial tribunal and the bi-national tribunal is empowered to remand the decision with instructions as to how the error may be remedied. During the period of the remand, the bi-national panel remains seised of the case and may rule upon the adequacy of the response and ultimately, in the event of a blatant refusal of the administrative body to respond appropriately, can decide the case. The

275. This standard of review comprises two parts. The first one is article 238 of the Federal Fiscal Code, which establishes:
276. An administrative determination shall be declared illegal when one of the following grounds is established:
277. I. Lack of jurisdiction of the official who issued, ordered, carried out the proceeding from which the said determination was derived.
278. II. Omission of the formal requirements provided by law, which affects an individual's defenses and goes beyond the result of the challenged determination, including the lack of legal grounding or reasoning, as the case may be.
279. III. Procedural errors which affect an individual's defenses and goes beyond the result of the challenged determination.
280. IV. If the facts, which underlie the determination, do not exist, are different or were erroneously weighed, or if (the determination) was issued in violation of applicable legal provisions or if the correct provisions were not applied.
281. V. When an administrative determination issued under discretionary powers does not correspond with the purposes for which the law confers those powers.
282. The Federal Fiscal Tribunal may declare sua sponte, because it is a matter of public order, the incompetence of the authority to render the challenged determination and the total absence of grounding or reasoning of this determination.
283. Likewise, based on the second part of the standard of review, the Panel shall apply the general principles of law.

Rules of Practice, issued under Chapter 19[22] provide relatively tight deadlines for the hearing of complaints before bi-national tribunals, although it must be noted that these deadlines are seldom met to the day.

All this would appear to suggest the superiority of the NAFTA system over that of the WTO. However the picture is not that clear. While many cases have been resolved as provided by Chapter 19 and the record of compliance is relatively good, several factors suggest the presence of important inadequacies. In a number of important cases, particularly those involving softwood lumber[23] and high fructose corn syrup,[24] Chapter 19 has revealed the potential for the multiplication of procedures, as the chapter allows for a challenge to every 'final' decision along the way. The result is that a well-financed litigant, such as a major industry lobby group, is able to multiply and draw out the process and thus wear out even the strongest opponent. The cost of even a short procedure is considerable and, particularly in the United States, can resemble complex anti-trust litigation. Furthermore, although bi-national panels are empowered to order return of AD and CV duties which have been levied in violation of domestic law, as a result of the Byrd Amendment legislation,[25] the return of duties has become problematic and has not yet been resolved. Thus it appears that some of the alleged advantages of Chapter 19 may not be as real as might be thought.

A further factor in this calculus is the relationship of Chapter 19 to the WTO DSU. Although the choice of forum rule of Chapter 19 appears to ensure the irrevocability of the choice *vis-à-vis* domestic courts, it now appears that there is nothing to stop a state, dissatisfied with a particular Chapter 19 decision, from taking some aspect of the dispute before the WTO. This has in fact happened in both the *Softwood Lumber* and the *High Fructose Corn Syrup* litigation.[26] The result has been to lengthen the process and complicate efforts to ensure compliance with the Chapter 19 decisions.

Decisions of bi-national panels are final and are not subject to appeals to national courts. However, the drafters of Chapter 19 thought it prudent to add a safety valve in the form of the Extraordinary Challenge Procedure. The ECP is triggered only by a government in the face of an extraordinary situation such as allegations of conflict of interest or violation of some fundamental procedural principle. It is heard before three retired judges rather than by trade experts. The true nature of this procedure became the object of debate

---

[22] *See NAFTA Rules of Procedures*, available at www.nafta-sec-alena.org/DefaultSite/index_e.aspx?DetailID=187 (visited 10 April 2006).

[23] *See Softwood Lumber*, above at n 14.

[24] *See High Fructose Corn Syrup*, above at n 21.

[25] Dumping and Subsidy Offset Act of 2000 (Byrd Amendment), Pub. L. No. 106–387, 114 Stat. 1549 (2000) (codified at 19 U.S.C. § 1675c (2000)). *See* WTO Appellate Body Report, *US—Offset Act (Byrd Amendment)*, WT/DS217/AB/R and WT/DS234/AB/R, adopted 27 January 2003.

[26] *See High Fructose Corn Syrup*, above at n 21, at paras 14–127. *See also Softwood Lumber*, above at n 14 (containing arguments on the applicability of WTO jurisprudence within NAFTA's scope).

and much comment at the time of the second round of *Softwood Lumber* litigation,[27] which occurred under the CUSFTA. After one decision where a panel was split along national lines, the United States Government called for an ECP alleging a finding of conflict of interest on the part of some Canadian panellists and serious errors of law. The ECP panel also split along national lines with the dissenting American judge arguing that there had been a conflict of interest and arguing also that the two Canadian judges had failed to comprehend American law governing the standard of review. In Judge Wilkey's view, the ECP resembled an appeal from a failure to correctly apply the appropriate standard of review while the majority judges, both Canadians, considered that they were exercising a form of judicial review available only in the most extraordinary circumstances. The debate continues as to the true nature of the ECP and it should be noted that the NAFTA Article 1094(13)(a)(iii) concerning the ECP adds 'failing to apply the appropriate standard of review', to the prior language of the CUSFTA. The ECP was invoked three times under the CUSFTA and has been invoked only twice under NAFTA.[28] In every decision rendered so far the decision of the bi-national panel has been maintained, thus leaving the suspicion that it is only invoked when governments, so far only that of the United States, may be pressed to go the extra mile in support of domestic interests.

D. Chapter 11

No chapter of NAFTA has attracted more public and scholarly comment than Chapter 11.B. Chapter 11.B is devoted to dispute settlement concerning the protection of investments.[29] While the issue of investments was covered by the CUSFTA, Chapter 16 of the CUSFTA has no particular provisions on dispute settlement. It appears that the need of a special form of investment dispute settlement did not arise between Canada and the United States. However, the memory of Mexican nationalizations of American oil interests in the 1920s was sufficiently strong in the United States and the desire to allay these fears was sufficiently strong in Mexico, that the United States and Mexico both came to see the advantage of having additional guarantees in the form of

---

[27] *See Re Certain Softwood Lumber Products from Canada* (1993) U.S.A.-92–1904–01 (Ch 19 Panel). *See also Re Certain Softwood Lumber Products from Canada* (1994) ECC-94–1904–01USA (Ch 19 Panel).

[28] An important ECP decision in the ongoing softwood lumber dispute was rendered on 10 August 2005. *See Re Certain Softwood Lumber Products from Canada (United States v Canada)* (2005) USA–CDA-2004–1904–01 USA (Ch 19 Panel).

[29] *See*, e.g. R.C. Jones, 'NAFTA Chapter 11: Investor-to-State Dispute Resolution: A Shield to Be Embraced or a Sword to Be Feared?' (2002) BYU L Rev, 527 at 529–31 (highlighting the evolution of investment treaties), D.A. Gantz, 'Potential Conflicts Between Investor Rights and Environmental Regulation under NAFTA's Chapter 11' (2001) 33 Geo Wash Int L Rev 651, at 719–20; D.A. Gantz, 'The Evolution of FTA Investment Provisions: From NAFTA to the United States—Chile Free Trade Agreement' (2004) 19 Am U Int L Rev 679 (identifying possible impacts of Chapter 11 on the US–Chile FTA).

special dispute settlement procedures as they negotiated NAFTA. The Government of Canada, made no objection to the insertion of Section B of Chapter 11. What was perhaps insufficiently clear at the time of negotiation was that, when a legal remedy is offered in two of the most litigious societies of the world, the remedy will inevitably be invoked. Both Canada and the United States, as well as Mexico, have been the object of a number of Chapter 11 claims. These claims have become controversial as they are seen by some public interest groups as giving foreign private interests a right of action not possessed by nationals. There is also suspicion of the process because the claims are made in an arbitral forum and not before a domestic court, and because the claims are seen as granting corporate interests a method of challenging widely supported domestic public policies concerning access to public services. One Canadian critic has suggested that NAFTA Chapter 11 has been used as a disguised means of bringing American constitutional protections of property and contract into Canadian law where they do not otherwise exist.[30] American critics have seen the *Loewen* litigation[31] as evidence of an attack upon the sanctity of the jury system in civil matters in the United States, while the *Mondev*[32] case has been seen as an attaint to the authority of the judiciary.[33]

Chapter 11 Section B provides that a foreign investor who alleges to have suffered financial loss from a government's failure to respect the guarantees given to foreign investors and foreign investments in Section A (MFN, NT, fair and equitable treatment and direct or indirect expropriation) has a right to invoke arbitration under the ICSID or UNCITRAL rules with a view to recovering damages. The establishment of the arbitral tribunal is assured as Section B functions very much like a bilateral investment treaty (BIT). This is

[30] D. Schneiderman, 'Investment Rules and the New Constitutionalism' (2000) 25 Law & Soc Inquiry, 757. *See also* H. Mann, 'Private Rights, Public Problems: A Guide to NAFTA's Controversial Chapter on Investment Rights' (2001), available at www.iisd.org/publications/publication.asp?pno=270 (visited 10 April 2006).

[31] *See* J. Atik, Repenser NAFTA Chapter 11: A Catalogue of Legitimacy Critiques' (2003) 3 Asper Rev Int Bus & Trade L 215, at 232. *See also The Loewen Group, Inc. v The United States of America* (2003) ARB(AF)/98/3 (International Centre for Settlement of Investment Disputes) (Arbitrators, Sir A. Mason, A.J. Mikva, Lord Mustel).

[32] Mondev is a Canadian real estate company. A Mondev subsidiary agreed with the City of Boston and the Boston Redevelopment Authority to build shopping malls in Boston. In 1990, the Mondev subsidiary brought a law suit against a bank which foreclosed on a shopping mall owned by the former. Though the lower court of Boston ruled in favour of Mondev's subsidiary, the Supreme Court of Massachusetts reversed the decision. Mondev then requested arbitration under Chapter 11 of the NAFTA to challenge the decision of the Supreme Court of Massachusetts. The NAFTA tribunal rejected the Mondev subsidiary's claim because, according to the tribunal, the American Court did not violate international law, and did not treat Mondev's subsidiary unfairly. *See Mondev Int'l Ltd. v United States* (2002), ARB(AF)/99/2 (International Centre for Settlement of Investment of Disputes) (Arbitrators, Sir N. Stephan, Professor J. Crawford, S.M. Schwebel).

[33] *See* A. Liptak, 'Review of U.S. Ruling by NAFTA Tribunals stirs Worries', The NY Times, 18 April 2005, p. 20, available at the web page of the New York Times, at www.nytimes.com (visited 10 April 2006) (the author cites M.H. Marshall, the Chief Justice of Massachusetts, when she declared her dissatisfaction with the possibility of an international tribunal reviewing a judgment of the Massachusetts' courts).

not surprising as Section B follows the pattern of the then current United States Model BIT,[34] which, largely as a result of concerns flowing from Chapter 11, has now been changed.[35] Panels of arbitrators are constituted by the complaining investor and the government in question and conducted according to the appropriate arbitral rules. Under Article 1131(2), governments are empowered to issue interpretations of the NAFTA text which are binding upon arbitral tribunals. This power has been exercised once, and initially give rise to considerable controversy.[36]

The first case to attract public attention in Canada involved a Canadian import prohibition of a chemical additive to gasoline adopted in lieu of an outright ban. When faced with a claim the Canadian Government did not contest and paid some $16 million damages.[37] Soon after, the cancellation of export permits of hazardous wastes from Canada led to a decision in the claimant's favour in the *S.D. Myers* case.[38] In Mexico a claim for damages from an indirect expropriation of a waste treatment facility was highly controversial and was challenged by the government of Mexico, with partial success, before the British Columbia courts, whose law was applicable to the arbitration.[39] In the United States two procedures have been launched challenging judicial decisions,[40] and a major environmental case somewhat similar to the *Ethyl* case continues has attracted great attention in California.[41] Despite the expression of much public concern, the United States has never

---

[34] *See* 1994 Model Bilateral Investment Treaty, 1997 BDIEL AD Lexis 6.

[35] *See* The Office of the Unites States Trade Representative, 2004 Model BIT, Treaty between the Government of the United States of America and the Government of [...] Concerning the Encouragement and Reciprocal Protection of Investment, available at www.ustr.gov/assets/ Trade_Sectors/Investment/Model_BIT/asset_upload_file847_6897.pdf (visited 10 April 2006).

[36] NAFTA Free Trade Commission, Notes of Interpretation of Certain Chapter 11 Provisions, available at www.dfait-maeci.gc.ca/tna-nac/NAFTA-Interpr-en.asp (visited 10 April 2006). *See Re Pope & Talbot, Inc. v Canada* (2002) 41 ILM 1347. *See also Re Methanex Corporation v United States of America, Second Opinion of Professor Sir Robert Jennings Q.C. (6 September, 2001)* (Arbitrators V.V. Veeder, W. Christopher, W. Rowley), available at www.naftalaw.org/ (visited 10 April 2006) (explaining the meaning of Article 1105(1)); *see also* Art. 1105 NAFTA. *See Methanex* tribunal at Part II, Ch H, at 11, and Part IV, Ch C., at 6 (where it reviewed various other decisions on the issue of Chapter 11 interpretation. Like *Mondev*, and the *Waste Management* decisions).

[37] *Re Ethyl Corp. and Government of Canada, Award on Jurisdiction* (1999) 38 ILM 708, (Ch 11 Arbitration).

[38] *See S.D. Myers, Inc. v Canada, Award* (2000) 2004 FC 38 (NAFTA Chapter 11 Arbitration Tribunal), available at decisions.fct-cf.gc.ca/fct/2004/2004fc38.html (visited 10 April 2006).

[39] *See Mexico v Metalclad Corp.* (2001), Case no. ABF(ARF)1/97/1 (International Centre for Settlement of Investment Disputes) (Arbitrators E. Lauterpacht, B. Civiletti, J.L. Siquieiros).

[40] *See The Loewen Group, Inc. v The United States of America*, above at n 31, *Mondev Int'l Ltd. v United States* (2002), above at n 32.

[41] *See Re Methanex Corporation v United States of America* (2005) at Part VI (Ch 11 Panel), available at www.iisd.org/investment/methanex.asp (visited 10 April 2006) (the tribunal rejected all Methanex' arguments on both jurisdiction pursuant to Art. 1101 of NAFTA and Art. 21 of the UNCITRAL Arbitration Rules, and on merits pursuant to Arts 1102, 1105, and 1110 of NAFTA and pursuant to Art. 21(4) of the UNCITRAL Arbitration Rules).

lost a case and Canada and Mexico have lost five. The total number of decisions and pending cases is now 42.[42]

While it was presumed that investment disputes would be a very separate category under NAFTA, this has not proven to be entirely the case. There now appears to be a possibility of overlapping between Chapters 19 and 11 as well as between Chapter 19 and the WTO/DSU. The protean *Softwood Lumber* litigation has now transformed itself into several investment claims.[43] A similar claim has been launched under Chapter 11 by American High Fructose Corn Syrup producers who have been disappointed by the results inter-governmental litigation under Chapter 19 and before the WTO DSU.[44]

Equally interesting is the potential impact of Chapter 11 on the conduct of litigation in other forums. Chapter 11 has been the object of considerable criticism from trades unions, environmental NGOs, and other groups concerned with the perceived negative impact of trade liberalization. Much of their criticism has focused upon the fact that arbitral proceedings are conducted at the behest of private parties by privately chosen arbitrators rather than publicly appointed judges. They also focus upon the fact that pleadings before arbitral tribunals have not been public and on the difficulties encountered by public interest groups in presenting *amicus curiae* briefs.[45] Similar criticism has been made of other international trade dispute procedures, particularly those under the WTO DSU.[46] Interestingly, more progress seems to have been made on these issues in the NAFTA context than in the WTO. This has happened both through the action of arbitral tribunals themselves as well as through governmental action. A major arbitral panel responded positively to a request by various public interest groups to make *amicus* submissions. In the *Methanex* case, the tribunal accepted the arguments that since they were dealing with both public and private issues, it was appropriate that they receive *amicus* briefs.[47] In doing so, the tribunal decided that the advantages of public debate outweighed any disadvantages of additional cost and additional complexity of the proceedings. This was followed by the decision of the parties before the *UPS* tribunal to make available a room where the public

[42] As of September 2005. *See* the 'NAFTA Claims' website (Disputes), available at www.naftaclaims.com/disputes.htm (visited 10 April 2006).

[43] *See, inter alia, Tembec Inc. et al. v United States of America*, available at www.state.gov/s/l/c11070.htm (visited 10 April 2006).

[44] *See Corn Products International v The United Mexican States*, available at naftaclaims.com/corn_products.htm (visited 10 April 2006).

[45] *See* Mann, above at n 30, at 41.

[46] *See* generally R. Howse and M.J. Trebilcock, 'The Fair Trade—Free Trade Debate: Trade, Labor and the Environment' (1996) 16 Int Rev L & Econ 61, R. Howse 'The Boundaries of the WTO: From Politics to Technocracy and Back Again: The Fate of the Multilateral Trading Regime' (2002) 96 AJIL 94, at 107 (highlighting examples to show the broad historical sweep of the WTO) and R. Howse and M.J. Trebilcock, *The Regulation of International Trade*, 2nd ed. (New York: Routledge, 1999), 57–8.

[47] *See Methanex* above at n 41, Decision of the Tribunal on Petitions from Third Parties to Intervene as Amici Curiae (15 January 2001), at para. 49.

could view the oral proceedings on a videoconference link.[48] In the Note of Interpretation of July 31, 2001, the three NAFTA governments stated that NAFTA did not preclude Chapter 11 arbitral proceedings announced by making all documents publicly accessible. Subsequently the Free Trade Commission on October 7, 2003 issued a statement on non-party participation and Canada announced the intention of holding all oral proceedings, in which it was involved in public.[49]

Chapter 11 has also had a considerable impact upon the substantive law applicable to United States and Canadian investment disputes and even upon ideas concerning the development of permanent investment dispute tribunals. The *obiter dicta* in the decision of the tribunal in the *Pope and Talbot*[50] case concerning the standard of fair and equitable treatment provided by NAFTA compared to the other BITs and the many claims in subsequent Chapter 11 cases based upon this view, caused concern among politicians and officials. Similarly there has been concern in all three countries that the concept of indirect expropriation might be expanded to cover a broader range of regulatory action than that allowed by customary international law or by United States law. As a result, the United States Congress has legislated to require that the United States Model BIT be changed to stipulate that the law governing indirect expropriation not exceed the standard set out in United States law.[51] Congress has also called on United States BITs negotiators to work towards the creation of permanent investment arbitration courts. As a result, provisions calling for further negotiations on the creation of some kind of appellate tribunal have been included in several draft BITs.[52] The debate in the United States, flowing from Chapter 11, concerning the utility of replacing *ad hoc* arbitral tribunals with permanent investment dispute courts has also had its impact upon the discussions in ICSID on a more extensive appeals

---

[48] *See* The US Department of State, *United Parcel Service of America, Inc. v Government of Canada* (NAFTA/UNCITRAL Arbitration Rules Proceeding), available at www.state.gov/s/l/c3749.htm (visited 10 April 2006). *See also United Parcel Service of America, Inc v Government of Canada* (NAFTA/UNCITRAL Arbitration Rules Proceeding), The World Bank, News Release (28 May 2001) (declaring that the proceedings will be open to public in a video conference room).

[49] International Trade Canada, above at n 36 and NAFTA Commission Joint Statement and Statement of Canada on Open Hearings in Chapter 11 Proceedings, available at www.dfait-maeci.gc.ca/tna-nac/NAFTA-Interpr-en.asp (visited 10 April 2006).

[50] *See Pope & Talbot*, above at n 36, at para. 44.

[51] *See* Bipartisan Trade Promotion Authority Act, 19 U.S.C. § 3802 (b)(3) (2005). *See also* 2004 Model BIT, above at n 35 at Annex B (limiting indirect expropriation and regulatory takings).

[52] *See* US–Central American Free Trade Agreement (1 June 2004), at Annex 10-F, available at www.ustr.gov/assets/Trade_Agreements/Bilateral/CAFTA/CAFTA-DR_Final_Texts/asset_upload_file328_4718.pdf (visited 10 April 2006) (stating that 'the FTC shall establish a Negotiating Group to develop an appellate body or similar mechanism to review awards rendered by tribunals under the Investment Chapter of the Agreement'), US–Chile Free Trade Agreement, in force 9 September 2003, at Ch 22. The Office of the US Trade Representative, Exchange of letters on the Possibility of Bilateral Appellate Mechanism (6 May 2003), available at www.ustr.gov/assets/Trade_Agreements/Bilateral/Singapore_FTA/Final_Texts/asset_upload_file159_4060.pdf (visited 10 April 2006).

mechanism[53] as well as in the context of negotiations for a Free Trade Agreement of the Americas.[54] It has also found its way into proposals for a revamped WTO TRIMs Agreement.[55] So far these proposals have not garnered much support in the wider international community.

A final important point of contact between NAFTA dispute settlement and the law governing the WTO DSU is the substantive law applicable. Virtually every chapter of NAFTA asserts the compatibility of the agreement with the law of the WTO.[56] In the same vein, NAFTA is replete with interpretative provisions requiring interpretations of words and concepts in a manner compatible with the law of the GATT 1947 and successor agreements, unless the contrary is required.[57] The impact of this requirement is most obvious with respect to Chapter 20, and these decisions, like the CUSFTA Chapter 18 decisions before them.[58] Equally interesting, although more complex, is the impact of WTO law on Chapter 11. The basic concepts of Chapter 11, MFN and NT are derived from WTO law and arbitral tribunals have not hesitated to draw upon this body of law when it is appropriate.[59] In this, Chapter 11 cases are no different from other investor state cases before the ICSID[60] or other major arbitral bodies.[61] However, controversy surrounds the interpretation of the NT and MFN standards as they apply to the situation of 'investors' and 'investments' rather than to goods and services. To what extent do standards developed in the GATT with respect to goods, and now extended to

[53] *See* ICSID, 'Possible Improvements of the Framework for ICSID Arbitration', October 2004.

[54] *See* D.A. Gantz, 'Government-to-Government Dispute Resolution under NAFTA's Chapter 20: A Commentary on the Process' (2000) 11 Am Rev Int Arb 481, at 527. *See also* Canada, Parliament, *Report of the Sub-Committee on International Trade Disputes and Investment and assigned it the responsibility of examining a Free Trade Area of the Americas (FTAA)* (1999) No 33, at Ch 16. *See also* E. Dannenmaier, 'Inter American Perspective: Trade Democracy, and the FTAA: Public Access to the Process of Constructing a Free Trade Area of the Americas' (2004) 27 Ford ILJ 1066, at 1084 (highlighting concerns about the dispute settlement mechanism in the FTAA).

[55] Doha Ministerial Declaration, WT/MIN(01)/DEC/1, adopted 14 November 2001 (holding in paras 20–22 that WTO working groups on trade and investment will take into account the agreed upon rules in the bilateral investment treaties and regional trade agreements).

[56] *See*, e.g. Arts 102, 103, 301, 409, and 315 NAFTA (stating that NAFTA ought to be interpreted according to the international law rules, in general, and WTO in particular).

[57] Art. 103 NAFTA.

[58] The cases that dealt with NT/MFN are numerous within the WTO. *See* WTO Panel Report, *EC—Commercial Vessels*, WT/DS301/R, adopted 20 June 2005 and GATT Panel Report, *Italy— Agricultural Machinery*, adopted 23 October 1958, BISD 7S/60, at para. 12. *See also UHT Mill*, above at n 10.

[59] *See Mondev*, above at n 32, at paras 81, 152–60; *ADF Group Inc. v the United States of America* (2003), Case No ARB(AF)/00/1 at paras 177–80, (International Centre for Settlement of Investment Disputes) (Arbitrators, F. Feleciano, A. de Mestral, C.B. Lamm).

[60] *See Plama Consortium Limited v Republic of Bulgaria* (2005), ICSID Case No. ARB/03/24 (Arbitrators: C. Salans, A. Jan van Dan Berg, V.V. Veeder); *Saini Construttori S.p.A and Italstrade S.p.A v the Hashemite Kingdom of Jordan* (2004) ICSID Case No. ARB/02/13 (Arbitrators G. Guillaume, B. Cremades, I. Sinclaire).

[61] *See*, e.g. *Ronald S. Lauder v the Czech Republic* (2003) (UNCITRAL ad hoc Tribunal, London) (Arbitrators L. Cutler, R. Briner, B. Klein). The tribunal found that the investor was discriminated against because of his national origin.

services, extend to the situation of investors and investments? The search for the appropriate comparator is arguably best made in the context of the facts of each case but it clearly raises complex issues which are far from being resolved.[62] Making this search all the more complex is the issue of the ambit of 'fair and equitable treatment' and the applicability of US regulatory takings case law in the definition of 'indirect expropriation' of Article 1110, referred to above. One major difference from the law of the WTO is that Chapter 11 excludes the application of GATT Article XX exceptions and relies on the affirmation of Article 1101(4) that 'nothing in the chapter shall prevent a Party from performing a public service'. There appear to be differences as well as similarities between the substantive law of Chapter 11 and the law of the WTO.

To conclude, Chapter 11 has shown a capacity to reach out to the other chapters governing NAFTA dispute settlement in a way probably quite unsuspected by the drafters. Aspects of cases not fully resolved under other Chapters of NAFTA or even by the WTO are coming up before Chapter 11 arbitral tribunals and these tribunals are called on to apply or adopt the principles of international trade law developed in other fora.

E. NAFTA Side Agreements

NAFTA entered into force with two 'side agreements', one dealing with environmental cooperation[63] and the other devoted to cooperation on the protection of labour standards.[64] In all probability these agreements made the adoption of NAFTA possible, as candidate Clinton had made his commitment to NAFTA conditional upon reaching further and more extensive agreement on the protection of environmental and labour standards. Since Canada and Mexico refused to reopen the already signed NAFTA with President Clinton, upon his election, it became necessary to negotiate separate and complementary agreements. Both agreements take the form of commitments of the three countries to maintain high labour and environmental standards. Each country retains the right to adopt its own laws and is subject to no common standards. However the three countries agree establish quasi-independent secretariats which answer to a Commission for Environmental Cooperation and a Commission for Labour Cooperation composed of the respective ministers of the three Parties. Both agreements provide for a fairly well circumscribed but nevertheless autonomous process of private complaint to the secretariats. In both cases the complaints from citizens or groups have to meet various procedural requirements and must allege that a state '. . . is failing to effectively enforce its own law . . .' with respect to the NAAEC[65] or '. . . there has been a persistent pattern of failure by that other Party to effectively enforce

---

[62] *See Methanex*, above at n 41, at Part II, Ch B at p. 2, and Part VI, Ch B at p. 2.
[63] *See* NAAEC above at n 6.   [64] *See* NAALC, above at n 6.   [65] *Ibid.*, at Art. 14(1).

such standards . . .' with respect to the NAALC.[66] The complaints are made on environmental issues to the Secretariat of the CEC and the Secretariat is empowered to prepare an independent report in appropriate circumstances. The procedure on labour standards is somewhat more complex, since the complaint must proceed through several stages, beginning with the most public: a 'Public Communication' from a private person or organisation to the National Administration Office of a Party, and then to an Expert Committee only at the request of a Party. In both cases the reports return to the full Commissions for further action. Formal dispute settlement between governments is possible under both side agreements but it has been made so complex that it is virtually unthinkable that it will ever be invoked by a government.

The environmental and labour proceedings are both more designed as fact finding and dispute avoidance than as dispute settlement proceedings. Neither gives a binding decision and this has led to considerable disappointment in the labour and environmental communities. However, many complex and interesting matters have been taken through these procedures, including a few matters that, in other forms and in other contexts, have also been the object of formal dispute settlement under other chapters of NAFTA.[67]

F. Recourse to the WTO

Article 2005(1) states the principle that disputes in respect of matters arising under both NAFTA and the GATT and successor agreements may be referred to either forum. As indicated above, all three governments have availed themselves of this right. The motives are varied. Sometimes, as with *Canada— Periodicals*,[68] the purpose is to avoid limits placed by NAFTA substantive rules; in other cases, it is to find a solution which has eluded parties to litigation under different NAFTA chapters and in other cases it must reflect a judgment that the WTO provides a more effective venue and range of enforcement remedies. The later is particularly the case in respect of disputes arising both under Chapter 20 and the WTO/DSU. Since the creation of both fora, the three NAFTA Parties have had recourse against each other 31 times,[69] three times under Chapter 20 and 28 times before the WTO DSU, thus putting in doubt the efficacy of Chapter 20. Some disputes have also used the WTO to review AD/CV decisions which might otherwise have been run under Chapter 19.[70] NAFTA has faced serious competition from the DSU, to the

[66] *Ibid.*, at Art. 27(1)

[67] Such as the right to cut timber, fisheries regulation, migrant farm labour, the production of pork and wheat etc.

[68] See *Canada—Periodicals*, above at n 12.

[69] The total of NAFTA members' disputes before the WTO tribunals is 28 disputes, and 3 before Chapter 20 Panels. *See* WTO, The Dispute Chronologically, available at www.wto.org/english/tratop_e/dispu_e/dispu_status_e.htm (visited 10 April 2006).

[70] *See*, e.g. WTO Doc. WT/DS281/1, *United States—Anti-Dumping Measures on Cement from Mexico (Complaint by Mexico)* (2003) (pending Panel Report).

point that it is necessary to ask whether, in the final analysis, despite the existence of specific NAFTA forum selection rules,[71] these choice of forum rules can resist recourse by another NAFTA Party to the DSB. It appears that any merely implicit choice of forum such as Article 1904(11), which does not explicitly rule out recourse to another procedure, cannot withstand recourse to the DSB. Equally powerless to lay claim to exclusivity is Article 1903 which provides for the creation of a bi-national panel to judge the compatibility of new domestic legislation with the requirements of the law of the GATT or successor agreements on AD/CV. This procedure has never been used. Canada joined other states in challenging the 'Byrd Amendment' legislation[72] before the DSB, rather than using its potential recourses under NAFTA.[73]

In the final analysis, one important lesson of the NAFTA–WTO/DSU relationship, is the power of the multilateral remedy. It alone can successfully lay claim to exclusivity in the face of competing claims, and the multilateral remedy appears to provide strength to a weaker party against more powerful partners that a regional agreement cannot provide. Beyond this, one must note the advantages of having a judgment on the merits backed by all the Members of the DSB and the correlative advantages of multilaterally ordered sanctions.

G. Recourse to Domestic Law

It is beyond the scope of this chapter to go far into the recourse to domestic legal remedies. Suffice it to say that in many areas they exist and are more powerful that the international remedies created by NAFTA. In most cases this recourse is always present and litigants will look first to their domestic remedies then only to NAFTA when all else is unavailing.[74] Under Chapter 11 the normal recourses in domestic law for the reform of arbitral proceedings are not precluded and have been used by both the governments of Mexico and Canada.[75] In some instances, such as Article 1904(1), the choice of the domestic remedy or NAFTA is explicit. Article 2020(1) contains a tantalizing option, but one which has never been used to date:

1. If an issue of interpretation or application of this Agreement arises in any domestic judicial or administrative proceeding of a Party that any Party considers would merit its intervention, or if a court or administrative body solicits the views of a

---

[71] *See*, e.g. Arts 2005(4), 103, and 104 NAFTA.   [72] *See* Byrd Amendment, above at n 25.

[73] For further discussion of forum selection issues *see* A.L.C. de Mestral, 'The North American Free Trade Agreement: A Comparative Analysis' (1998) 275 *Recueil des Cours* 223, J. Pauwelyn, *Conflict of Norms in Public International Law: How WTO law relates to other Rules of International Law* (Cambridge: CUP, 2003) and D.M. McRae, 'The Contribution of International Trade Law to the Development of International Law' (1996) 260 *Recueil des Cours* 99.

[74] A good example is the *Loewen* case where Mr. Loewen and his companies were precluded from using the normal diversity jurisdiction rules under US Federal Court Rules.

[75] *See Canada (Attorney General) v S.D. Myers Inc.* (2004) 3 FCR 368 and *United Mexican States v Metalclad Corp.* (2001) 89 BCLR (3d) 359.

Party, that Party shall notify the other Parties and its Section of the Secretariat. The Commission shall endeavor to agree on an appropriate response as expeditiously as possible.

Article 2022 provides for recourse to 'alternative dispute settlement' under domestic law concerning the resolution of international commercial disputes between private parties. Apart from the creation of an Advisory Committee on Private Commercial Disputes and a virtual dispute resolution centre, the Commercial Arbitration and Dispute Resolution Centre for the Americas (CAMCA),[76] this provision does not seem to have given rise to any procedural initiatives or legislative initiatives between the three NAFTA Parties.

It should be noted that Article 2021 explicitly prohibits any party giving '. . . a right of action under its domestic law against any other Party on the ground that a measure of the other Party is inconsistent with this Agreement'. This is a partial ban on the granting of direct effect to the rules of NAFTA. Nothing would seem to prevent a Party from granting direct effect against itself, but there appears to be no interest in such an option.[77] In April and August, 2005 the Government of Canada, together with several lumber producers, launched a challenge to the legality of the 'Byrd Amendment' in the United States Court of International Trade.[78] Another issue is that of the possibility of giving something akin to the direct effect of NAFTA in Mexico, given that treaties have the same status as legislation under the Mexican Constitution.[79] This issue has arisen in several Chapter 19 cases[80] but so far has not become a central issue in private litigation or NAFTA proceedings.

Finally, the possibility of constitutional challenges to the legality of various forms of NAFTA dispute settlement, particularly Chapters 11 and 19, can never be ruled out. Attempts have already been made in all three NAFTA countries, so far without success, but some challenges are currently pending.[81]

---

[76] *See* Commercial Arbitration and Mediation Centre for the Americas (CAMCA), available at: www.sice.oas.org/dispute/comarb_e.asp (visited 10 April 2006).

[77] *See* A.L.C. de Mestral, A. and J. Winter, 'Giving Direct Effect to NAFTA: Analysis of the Issues', in T.J. Courchene et al., *Thinking North America* (Institute for Research on Public Policy: Montreal, 2004), at 35–98.

[78] *See* Department of Foreign Affairs and International Trade, 'Canada takes action on Byrd Amendment' (Ottawa, 2005), available at webapps.dfait-maeci.gc.ca/MinPub/Publication.asp?Language=E&publication_id=382501 (visited 10 April 2006).

[79] *See* the Mexican Constitution. Art. 133 states that:
[A]ll the treaties . . . shall be the supreme law of the whole Union. The judges of each State shall conform to the [. . .] Constitution, the laws, and treaties, in spite of any contradictory provisions that may appear in the constitutions or laws of the States.

[80] *See*, e.g. *Re Urea from the United States of America (Mexico v the United States)* (2002) MEX-USA-00–1904–01 (Ch 19 Panel), *Re Polysternene and Impact Crystal from the United States of America (Mexico v the United States)* (1996) MEX-94–1904–03 (Ch 19 Panel) and *Re Cut-to-Length Plate Products from the Unites States of America (Mexico v the United States)* (1995) MEX-94–1904–02 (Ch 19 Panel).

[81] *See*, e.g. *Bhullar v United States*, 259 F. Supp. 2d 1332 (2003). *See also Metalclad*, above at n 75. *See also* I. Austen and C. Krauss, 'U.S. Gets Lift in Lumber Fight with Canada', New York Times, 31 August 2005, p. 6.

III. CONCLUSIONS

NAFTA dispute settlement procedures clearly demonstrate the capacity of an FTA to foster experimentation beyond the level possible in the multilateral system. Has this variety of recourses had a positive impact? Arguably it has, both within NAFTA and even outside the confines of the agreement. Private remedies have been created, new forms of action designed to restrict protectionist behaviour have been adopted. The cost may be high for the litigants but at least they have options not available under the WTO. Arguably the experience of NAFTA, particularly under Chapter 11 has been instructive for those arguing for the adoption of investment dispute settlement in the context of wider investment protection agreements. Both the advantages for private investors and the political pitfalls for their governments have become clearer and have even led to certain changes in policy respecting the conclusion of Bilateral Investment Agreements by the NAFTA governments. The side agreements have given a slight hint of what may be accomplished even by the most modest supranational bodies. More has been learned concerning the interrelationship between international trade law and domestic law.[82]

Have the NAFTA procedures promoted incremental change not otherwise directly possible? Again the answer should be modestly affirmative. Insofar as change is possible to an FTA independently of the NAFTA governments, it has come through dispute settlement when the inadequacies of the agreement have been highlighted by the results of a dispute settlement procedure.

In the final analysis, can an FTA prevail over the multilateral rules and thus undermine the global system? Here the experience of NAFTA may suggest that the multilateral trade system is more resilient than many have thought. Experience of the various NAFTA dispute settlement procedures seems to point squarely to the paramountcy of the multilateral order, which, for the defenders of the WTO, still mired in the Doha Round, may be a source of some modest satisfaction.

---

[82] *See* Pauwelyn, above at n 73, at 15–6 (highlighting the interaction between domestic factors and public international law and international trade law).

16

Dispute Settlement in European Union Free Trade Agreements: Lessons Learned?

IGNACIO GARCIA BERCERO *

I. INTRODUCTION

Within the framework of the WTO, the European Union (EU) has become a major proponent and user of a 'quasi-judicial' approach to the solution of trade disputes. Until recently, however, EU bilateral agreements relied, almost exclusively, on traditional diplomatic means for dispute resolution. A fundamental shift occurred with the conclusion of the free trade agreements with Mexico (2000) and Chile (2001), both of which incorporate a quasi-judicial model of trade adjudication, which is largely inspired by the WTO Dispute Settlement Understanding. Since then, the EU has sought to introduce similar dispute settlement procedures to all ongoing negotiations for free trade agreements.

This chapter explores the reasons for the increasing EU preference for a quasi-judicial model of adjudication as far as trade disputes is concerned. Section II makes a brief presentation of the current network of EU free trade agreements. Section III describes the traditional 'diplomatic' dispute settlement mechanism, which until recently characterized all EU free trade agreements. Section IV discusses the main characteristics of the quasi-judicial model of trade adjudication as reflected in the free trade agreements with Mexico and Chile. Section V examines how these two agreements have tried to address

* The author wishes to thank Edna Ramirez Robles for her contribution to this chapter, in particular for drafting Section I and preparing Table 1. In preparing this chapter, the author has benefited from discussions with Ms. Ramirez Robles, who is currently preparing a doctoral thesis on dispute settlement in the EU–Mexico FTA. I also wish to thank Lothar Ehring and Lorand Bartels for their detailed comments. The opinions expressed in this chapter are personal and do not necessarily represent the views of the European Commission.

the vexed question of the relationship between bilateral and WTO dispute settlement. Section VI draws some conclusions.

II. THE CURRENT NETWORK OF EUROPEAN UNION FREE TRADE AGREEMENTS

All the EU agreements which are discussed in this chapter have one feature in common: they are all free trade agreements (FTAs) within the meaning of Article XXIV GATT.[1] The only exception is the customs union agreement with Turkey. It should be noted, however, that recent agreements go well beyond the requirements of Article XXIV GATT, since they often include trade in services and/or envisage common disciplines in a number of regulatory areas (standards, procurement, competition policy, investment, etc.)[2]

Although different criteria can be used to classify EU FTAs, this chapter uses a classification based on the degree of 'proximity' between the EU and its FTA partners. On this basis, three types of FTAs can be considered:

(a) FTAs with countries that are part of the 'European space' and which are normally recognized as potential EU members. In such cases a classic FTA is often complemented with provisions by which the partner country undertakes to align its legislation with EU norms in a broad range of economic areas.

(b) FTAs with neighbouring countries. These often include a component of alignment with EU norms, although to a lesser extent than for countries that are candidates for EU membership. The EU has established *vis-à-vis* those countries a 'neighbourhood policy', under which neighbouring countries are expected to participate in the internal market. This often implies 'partial alignment' with EU norms.

(c) FTAs with non-neighbouring countries. These agreements include no reference to alignment with EU norms. However—and paradoxically—they are sometimes more comprehensive in their scope and subject to stronger enforcement mechanisms.

The agreements within the 'European space' are the European Economic Area (EEA), the Customs Union with Turkey, the Stabilization and Association Agreements (SAAs) with the Western Balkan countries, and the

---

[1] A free trade area is a group of two or more countries or economies that have eliminated tariffs and all or most non-tariff measures affecting trade among themselves: W. Goode, *Dictionary of Trade Policy Terms* (Cambridge: CUP, 2003), 146.

[2] Many contemporary FTAs include goods and services, and cover such issues as investment, government procurement, and competition. FTAs also contain provisions like mutual recognition of technical standards, intellectual property, etc.: S. Woolcock, 'A Framework for Assessing Regional Trade Agreements: WTO-plus', in G.P. Sampson and S. Woolcock (eds), *Regionalism, Multilateralism and Economic Integration, the Recent Experience* (Hong Kong: UN University, 2003), 18–31.

Europe Association Agreements with Romania and Bulgaria (until their accession to the EU). The FTAs concluded with neighbouring countries are the 'Euro-Mediterranean' Association Agreements with Egypt, Lebanon, Morocco, Algeria, Tunisia, Israel, the Palestine Authority, and Jordan. Neighbouring countries in Europe—such as Ukraine and Russia—have so far only concluded non-preferential Partnership and Cooperation Agreements (PCAs) but not FTAs. The countries in the last category are South Africa, Mexico, and Chile. Negotiations are ongoing with Mercosur, ACP countries, and the Gulf Cooperation Council (GCC), and are currently being considered with ASEAN, the Andean Community, and the Central American Common market.

A. Free trade agreements within the European space

The European Economic Area (EEA) is an agreement that has undergone many changes as regards its Contracting Parties. The EEA was signed in 1992 by the EC and the European Free Trade Association (EFTA).[3] At the time, the members of EFTA were Austria, Finland, Iceland, Liechtenstein, Norway, Sweden, and Switzerland (the latter, however, did not ratify the EEA Agreement). Today only Iceland, Liechtenstein, and Norway remain parties to the EEA.

Of the agreements concluded with countries within the European space, the EEA is *sui generis* in that it provides an alternative to rather than a preparation for EU membership. In order to participate in the internal EU market, the EEA requires almost full alignment with the EU *acquis*, also with respect to legislation adopted after the entry into force of the EEA. It is the only agreement which provides for judicial enforcement procedures, modelled on those of the European Court of Justice. Although the EEA has sometimes been presented as a possible model for the EU neighbourhood policy, so far no other EU FTA has adopted similar institutional provisions.

The Customs Union with Turkey came into force in 1995 within the framework of the Association Agreement between the European Economic Community (EEC) and Turkey, which was signed in Ankara in 1963.[4] The Ankara Agreement includes an article that regulates the settlement of disputes relating to the application or interpretation of the agreement. An innovative feature is that the article provides that, if the parties so agree, they can use other fora to settle disputes and notably the Court of Justice of the European Communities. These 'alternative' procedures have, however, never been used.

The Europe Agreements with Romania and Bulgaria are in force *until the*

---

[3] European Economic Area Agreement, signed 2 May 1992, in force 1 January 1994 [1994] OJ L1/3.

[4] *See* the EEC–Turkey Supplementary Protocol to the Association Agreement, signed 28 November 1977, in force 3 January 1978 [1977] OJ L361/1 and Decision 1/95 of the EC–Turkey Association Council [1995] OJ L96/142.

accession of these two countries to the EU. This will take place on 1 January 2007 unless a Council decision postpones it for a further year.[5]

The Stabilization and Association Agreements (SAAs) with the Balkans, have been signed with Bosnia and Herzegovina, Croatia, and the former Yugoslav Republic of Macedonia. Negotiations have been launched with Albania and Serbia and Montenegro.[6] The aims of these agreements include the fostering of respect for democratic principles, as well as the reinforcement of links between this region and the EU single market, and include a membership perspective. These agreements create a free trade area and provide for the alignment with the EU *acquis* in several areas such as in competition, state aid and intellectual property which will allow the economies of the region to integrate better with the EU.[7]

The Europe Agreements and the SAAs are all based on a 'diplomatic model' for the settlement of disputes. As further discussed below, the main features of such a model are consultations within the framework of a Joint Committee, including the possibility of having recourse to arbitration. However, the establishment of an arbitration panel requires consensus by the parties.

B. Association Agreements with neighbouring countries

The Euro-Mediterranean Partnership was launched in 1995 with the Barcelona Declaration, which establishes a framework of political, economic and social relations between the EU and the Southern Mediterranean Partners.[8] Those partners currently are Algeria, Egypt, Israel, Jordan, Lebanon, Morocco, the Palestine Authority, Syria, Tunisia, and Turkey.

One of the main objectives of the Barcelona Declaration is the establishment of a Euro-Mediterranean free trade area by 2010. The means of achieving this free trade area will be through association agreements concluded between the EU and the Mediterranean Partners as well as FTAs among the Mediterranean Partners themselves. The FTAs between EU and the Mediterranean Partners replaced the cooperation agreements signed in the 1970s.[9] So far the agreements

---

[5] Notice concerning the entry into force of the Treaty of Accession of Romania and Bulgaria [2005] OJ L157/10.

[6] Those agreements are part of the of the Stabilization and Association Process (SAP), which is the framework to support domestic reforms and is based on aid, trade preferences, dialogue, technical advice, and contractual relations

[7] *See* europa.eu.int/comm/external_relations/see/index.htm (visited 10 April 2006).

[8] On the Barcelona process, *see* A. Galal and B. Hoekman, *Regional Partners in Global Markets: Limits and Possibilities of the Euro-Med Agreements* (London: Centre for Economic Policy Research, 1997).

[9] *See* europa.eu.int/comm/external_relations/euromed/med_ass_agreements.htm (visited 10 April 2006).

with Tunisia,[10] Israel,[11] Morocco,[12] Jordan,[13] and Egypt[14] have been ratified and are in force. For Lebanon, the Palestinian Authority, and Algeria the trade provisions are in force through interim agreements. The Agreement with Syria has been initialled.

Euro-Mediterranean Agreements in force include similar dispute settlement provisions, which correspond essentially to a 'diplomatic model'. In general, the dispositions are included only in one article, i.e. Euro-Mediterranean Agreements with Tunisia (Articles 86 and 34 of the Protocol concerning the definition of originating products and methods of administrative cooperation), Israel (Articles 75 and 33 of the Protocol), Morocco (Articles 86 and 34 of the Protocol), Jordan (Articles 97 and 32 of the Protocol), and Egypt (Articles 82 and 33 of the Protocol).

C. FTAs with non-neighbouring countries

The FTAs with South Africa, Mexico, and Chile are the first signed with countries outside the European neighbourhood.

South Africa is a Contracting Party of the EU–African Caribbean Pacific (ACP) Cotonou Agreement, but is excluded from its trade and financial co-operation provisions. The Trade, Development and Cooperation Agreement (TDCA) between South Africa and the EU was signed in 1999 and the ratification process by the Member States is still ongoing.[15] However its trade provisions have been applied under an interim agreement since 2000. The settlement of disputes under this TDCA goes, in certain aspects, beyond the provisions of the Euro-Mediterranean Agreements or the agreements concluded with countries that are candidates to become EU members.

A provision (Article 104) encompasses a set of rules for arbitration. Consensus is required to establish the arbitration panel and compliance procedures are not specified. Nevertheless, for trade-related disputes there are certain innovations, i.e. time limits are established, as well as working procedures for arbitration, and a reasonable period of time to comply. The arbitrators are expected to report their findings within 6 months and implementation should take place within a 'reasonable period of time' not exceeding 15 months.

[10] EC–Tunisia Euro-Mediterranean Association Agreement, signed 17 July 1995, in force 1 March 1998 [1998] OJ L97/2.

[11] EC–Israel Euro-Mediterranean Association Agreement, signed 20 November 1995, in force 1 June 2000 [2000] OJ L147/3.

[12] EC–Morocco Euro-Mediterranean Association Agreement, signed 26 February 1996, in force 1 March 2000 [2000] OJ L70/2.

[13] EC–Jordan Euro-Mediterranean Association Agreement, signed 24 November 1997, in force 1 May 2002 [2002] OJ L129/3

[14] Agreement in the form of an exchange of letters concerning the provisional application of the trade and trade-related provisions of the EC–Egypt Euro-Mediterranean Association Agreement, signed 25 June 2001, in force 1 January 2004 [2003] OJ L345/115.

[15] Council Decision No 1999/753 (Provisional application of the EC–South Africa Agreement) [1999] OJ L311/1.

Issues relating to each Party's WTO rights and obligations can be referred to the FTA arbitration proceeding only if the parties agree.

The EU–Mexico contractual relationship was established in two agreements (the Global and the Interim) along with a Final Act signed in 1997.[16] The EU–Mexico FTA was established through two Decisions of the Joint Council, which entered into force in different years.[17] Decision 2/2000 established a free trade area in goods, and entered in to force on 1 July 2000,[18] while Decision 2/2001 established a free trade area in services and entered into force on 1 March 2001.[19]

The Global Agreement provides that the Joint Council shall decide on the establishment of a compatible dispute settlement procedure with the WTO.[20] The set of rules on dispute settlement include detailed norms and specific time frames. They encompass the different stages of the procedure (consultation plus arbitration), the appointment of arbitrators, the content of the panel reports (interim and final), and the procedures to implement the final report. They also include rules of procedure[21] and a code of conduct[22] for the arbitrators.

Negotiations for the EC–Chile Association Agreement began in 2000, and its trade provisions entered into force on an interim basis in February 2003 under the EC–Chile FTA.[23]

The settlement of disputes is regulated in depth in the consultations, arbitral, and compliance stage. It contains rules about the appointment of arbitrators, the arbitration panel ruling, as well as model rules of procedure[24] and a code of conduct.[25]

FTAs are currently being negotiated with Mercosur (Argentina, Brazil, Paraguay, and Uruguay) and the Gulf Cooperation Council (Saudi Arabia, Kuwait, Bahrain, Qatar, United Arab Emirates, and Oman). The FTAs being negotiated with Mercosur and the GCC have some common features. In both

---

[16] The first move towards the signature of these Agreements was in 1975 with a Cooperation Agreement between Mexico and the EEC which was substituted in 1991 with another Cooperation Agreement but of the *third generation* type. Later in 1995, in a Joint Declaration, both parties stated their interest in deepening the relationship. *See* E. Ramírez Robles, *Solución de Controversias en los Acuerdos Celebrados entre México y la Comunidad Europea* (Guadalajara: Universidad de Guadalajara, 2003), 85–104.

[17] On the EU–Mexico FTA, *see* J. Reiter, 'The EU–Mexico Free Trade Agreement: Assessing the EU approach to Regulatory Issues in Regionalism, Multilateralism and Economic Integration, the Recent Experience', in Sampson and Woolcock, above at n 2, at 66.

[18] Decision No 2/2000 of the EC-Mexico Joint Council of 23 March 2000 [2000] OJ L157/10 and annexes [2000] OJ L245/1. For the chronology *see* www.economia-bruselas.gob.mx/ls23al.php?s=501&p=4&l=2 (visited 10 April 2006).

[19] EU–Mexico Joint Council Decision No 2/2001 [2001] OJ L70/7.

[20] Art. 50 of the Global Agreement.

[21] Annex III with reference of Art. 43 of Decision No 2/2001.

[22] Appendix I of Decision No 2/2001.

[23] EC–Chile Association Agreement, in force 1 Mar 2005 [2002] OJ L352/3.

[24] Model Rules of Procedure for the Conduct of Arbitration Panels. Annex XV referred to in Art. 189(2).

[25] Code of Conduct for Members of Arbitration Panels, Annex XVI.

cases, the counterpart of the EU is a customs union concluded amongst developing countries. The objective is to negotiate 'comprehensive' FTAs which—as is already the case in the EU–Chile FTA—cover substantially all trade in goods and services, as well as common disciplines on a number of regulatory areas, such as investment, public procurement, intellectual property, competition policy, etc. Negotiations are well advanced on a dispute settlement mechanism which is, in many respects, similar to those included in the EU–Mexico and EU–Chile agreements.

Negotiations are also ongoing on regional Economic Partnership Agreements (EPAs). These agreements are being negotiated between the EU and regional groups established among African Caribbean Pacific (ACP) countries (6 regions with 79 countries).[26] The current ACP–EC Agreement was concluded for a twenty-year period in Cotonou. The mechanism for the settlement of disputes in the Cotonou Agreement is innovative, i.e. the option for a multi-party dispute is incorporated, arbitration is possible after consultations; where the second and/or third arbitrator is not designated, either party can ask the Secretary General of the Permanent Court of Arbitration to appoint one.[27] Negotiations of EPAs with the six regional groups have not yet started to consider future dispute settlement mechanisms.

III. THE TRADITIONAL 'DIPLOMATIC' DISPUTE SETTLEMENT MECHANISM IN EU FTAS

With the exception of the EEA, all pre-2000 EU FTAs are based on a traditional diplomatic approach to dispute settlement. Such an approach relies essentially on consultations and diplomatic negotiations as the key mechanism to solve disputes relating to the interpretation or implementation of the agreement. The option of having recourse to legal adjudication (arbitration) is normally available but requires agreement of the parties. The limited effectiveness of legal adjudication is balanced with the preservation of unilateral measures of self-help, through the inclusion of a non-execution clause, although these often have a high diplomatic cost and are only used as measures of last resort.

The Europe Agreements which were concluded with countries in Central and Eastern Europe after the regime-changes of 1989 are all based on such a diplomatic model, which had its origins in prior association agreements.[28] The absence in such cases of binding arbitration procedures for trade disputes is hardly surprising, since the Europe Agreements were negotiated for essentially

---

[26] *See* europa.eu.int/comm/development/body/cotonou/index_en.htm. (visited 10 April 2006).

[27] ACP–EU Cotonou Partnership Agreement, signed 23 June 2000, in force 1 April 2003 [2000] OJ L317/3, Art. 98.

[28] *See* J. Gomula, 'Dispute Settlement under Association Agreements with Central and Eastern European States' (1995) 22 Polish YIL 107.

political reasons and their main objective was to prepare countries for eventual EU membership. It is also likely that recourse to legal adjudication was considered as potentially disruptive of important bilateral relationships.[29] Once countries in Central and Eastern Europe entered into enlargement negotiations, most differences related to the extent to which the *acquis* was being properly implemented. Although not explicitly stated, it may be assumed that the leverage provided by the process of enlargement negotiations was considered a more effective instrument to achieve compliance than legal adjudication. Moreover, the frequent references in the Europe Agreements to the EU *acquis* raise complex legal issues as regards the extent to which a bilateral arbitration panel may apply EU law, thereby increasing the reluctance to have recourse to arbitration.

The Europe Agreements provided the model for the Stabilization and Association Agreements with countries in the Western Balkans, which respond to a similar political rationale. It is, perhaps, less clear why the Euro-Mediterranean Agreements include dispute settlement provisions which are almost identical to those in the agreements negotiated with countries that are candidates for EU accession. Since the political sensitivity of the bilateral relationship or the preference for asymmetrical leverage are less relevant in the absence of a membership perspective, it may be assumed that until the EU–Mexico FTA was concluded in the year 2000, there was a consistent EU preference for a non-judicial approach to bilateral dispute settlement. While some of the Euro-Mediterranean Agreements and the Stabilization and Association Agreements were concluded after 2000, the maintenance of the traditional diplomatic model was mainly due to institutional conservatism and the tendency to follow the same approach for all agreements concluded within a region. Indeed, as previously noted, the basic features of the diplomatic model of dispute resolution predate the Europe Agreements and, until recently, had been applied to all EU association agreements, including both their trade and non-trade related provisions.

This preference for non-judicial dispute settlement can therefore be best explained in historical terms. Prior to the entry into force of the WTO Agreements, there was very limited experience with legal adjudication as an instrument to solve commercial disputes. GATT panels were only established and adopted by consensus and disputes were often solved through complex negotiations, including the threat (or actual application) of retaliation. The first free trade agreement to include binding arbitration procedures was NAFTA, which was concluded in 1992, i.e. shortly before the conclusion of negotiations of the new WTO Dispute Settlement Understanding. It took some time

---

[29] The Trade Barriers Regulation (Council Regulation (EC) No 3286/94 [1994] OJ L349/71) excluded from the procedure for industry complaints the enforcement of bilateral agreements. The main reason was concern by some Member States that the TBR could result in difficult to solve disputes under the Europe Agreements. For a discussion of the TBR, *see* M. Bronckers and N. McNelis, 'The EU Trade Barriers Regulation Comes of Age' (2001) 35 JWT 427, at 434.

before countries became used to the new procedures under the WTO and sought to include similar provisions in bilateral agreements.

This historical explanation is further corroborated by the fact that the first EU agreement to include binding arbitration was the FTA with Mexico. The EU had taken some timid steps towards more effective arbitration procedures in the FTA with South Africa and in the Cotonou Agreement. It was, however, Mexico that took the initiative of requesting the establishment of detailed and binding arbitration procedures, which were largely based on NAFTA. Whereas the EU had a number of reservations with the NAFTA model, it accepted the basic rationale for moving towards a quasi-judicial dispute resolution in the trade field.

This shift of EU preferences can be best explained through a combination of three factors. First, as already noted, the EU had by this time become a major user of WTO dispute settlement and could therefore see the advantages of quasi-judicial procedures as a means of seeking neutral and less political resolution of disputes. Second, the EU–Mexico Agreement was the first FTA in which leadership within the Commission was allocated to DG Trade, which is institutionally more inclined towards procedures that ensure a rapid solution of commercial disputes. Finally, and most importantly, there was growing dissatisfaction within the EU with the effectiveness of the traditional diplomatic approach to dispute resolution.

In order to better understand the weaknesses of the traditional diplomatic model of dispute resolution, it is useful to refer briefly to the key elements of the dispute settlement clauses included in EU association agreements. These are as follows:

(a) Any of the parties may refer to the Association Council any dispute concerning the application or interpretation of the Association Agreement. The Council may, by consensus, adopt a binding decision to resolve the dispute. In practice this procedure is used to encourage consultations and diplomatic negotiations to reach a mutually acceptable solution. This diplomatic approach has often proved effective to solve a number of 'low profile' trade irritants. Indeed, consultations remain the preferred means to solve disputes under the quasi-judicial procedures followed in more recent agreements. However, in the absence of a credible arbitration option, there have been numerous examples of issues that figure year after year in the agendas of the Association Council without any effective resolution.[30] This is particularly so if influential producer interests are affected. In those circumstances, diplomatic negotiations may prove ineffective, whereas

---

[30] An example is provided by the dispute concerning the non-adoption by Turkey of the EU-acquis as regards the protection of data exclusivity for pharmaceuticals. This issue had been first raised in the Association Council in April 2002. However, a partial solution has only been found in 2005 following a complaint under the Trade Barriers Regulation. The TBR report recommended a negotiated solution, joint reference to the ECJ, or recourse to WTO dispute settlement.

the EU, in the absence of a major economic impact, may be reluctant to exercise political leverage or apply retaliatory measures.

(b) In the event that a dispute is not settled through a decision of the Association Council, any of the parties may have recourse to arbitration. Each of the parties appoints an arbitrator and the third arbitrator is appointed by the Association Council. The parties are required to take steps to implement the decision of the arbitrators. This procedure has three obvious weaknesses:

 (i) arbitration procedures can be blocked if one of the parties fails to appoint an arbitrator or opposes a consensus decision on the third arbitrator,[31]

 (ii) there are no deadlines or established procedures for the conduct of the arbitration, and

 (iii) there are no procedures for compliance with the arbitration ruling.

 In the light of this, it is not surprising that the arbitration procedure has hardly ever been used.

(c) Most agreements also include a non-execution clause, which allows a party to take 'appropriate measures' if it considers that the other party has failed to fulfil an obligation under the agreement. Normally the parties should first seek a solution within the framework of the Association Council, although in cases of urgency, measures may be taken immediately. In comparison with the retaliation options provided under WTO-type dispute settlement procedures, 'appropriate measures' have two distinguishing features:

 (i) recourse to dispute settlement procedures is not a precondition for the application of remedial action, and

 (ii) there are no clearly defined limits on the measures that may be adopted as a response to a failure by the other party to fulfil its obligations under the agreement.[32]

 It might have been thought that the high degree of self-help involved in the procedure leaves the EU—as the strongest party in the bilateral relationship—with substantial leverage to ensure asymmetrical compliance. In practice, however, this procedure has been used very sparingly

---

[31] A party that blocks arbitration proceedings can be said to be in breach of its obligations under the agreement, thereby triggering the right of the other party to resort to other remedies under international law, including invocation of the non-execution clause. In practice, however, the parties may be reluctant to have recourse to such 'exceptional' remedies and prefer to continue efforts to seek a diplomatic solution to a dispute. The absence of a pre-established procedure with clear time limits acts as a disincentive for having recourse to arbitration. For instance, in a case concerning the Ukraine, arbitration proceedings were not pursued because of a disagreement on how to share the costs of the arbitration.

[32] Non-execution clauses normally provide that the measures adopted must be those that 'least disturb the functioning of the agreement'. Some also include reference to the principle of 'proportionality' or to the need to ensure consistency with international law. For a discussion on the non-execution clause, *see* L. Bartels, *Human Rights Conditionality in the EU's International Agreements* (Oxford: OUP, 2005), 29, 131.

and most of the cases involved Russia, a partner with not insignificant bargaining power. A possible explanation is that decision making in the EU Council on the adoption of retaliatory measures is facilitated if such action is as the outcome of a quasi-judicial adjudication procedure.[33]

IV. TOWARDS A QUASI-JUDICIAL MODEL OF ADJUDICATION: THE EU–MEXICO (2000) AND EU–CHILE (2002) FTAS

As noted in the prior section, the introduction of quasi-judicial procedure for dispute settlement was the result of dissatisfaction with the effectiveness of the diplomatic model as an instrument to solve trade disputes, experience with WTO dispute settlement and the demands of EU's trading partners. Some of the more obvious weaknesses of the standard arbitration clauses in EU agreements were already corrected in the 1999 EU–South Africa Trade and Development Cooperation Agreement (TDCA) and in the 2000 Cotonou Agreement. However, a fully developed arbitration procedure has only been introduced, so far, in the FTAs concluded with Mexico and Chile. The EU–Mexico Agreement includes a Title on Dispute Settlement comprising seven articles, as well as a separate set of rules of procedure and a Code of Conduct for arbitrators. The EU–Chile Agreement has a Title on Dispute Settlement comprising nine articles, rules of procedure and a Code of Conduct. These innovations only relate, however, to the trade and trade-related parts of the agreements. No dispute settlement has been envisaged as regards the political or cooperation provisions of the agreements. It should be noted that the EU–South Africa TDCA was different in that the traditional dispute settlement model was retained for economic, development, financial or other areas of cooperation, while stricter time-limits were limited to disputes relating to trade or trade-related areas.

The main source of the arbitration procedures in the two agreements is WTO dispute settlement, which provides the basic structure of a procedure based on a consultation phase, arbitration panels, an obligation to comply within a 'reasonable period of time' and commensurate retaliation in case of lack of compliance (or agreement on temporary compensation). At the same time, the parties tried to improve on WTO dispute settlement, in particular, in order to have faster procedures. The parties—and, particularly, the EU and Chile—also experimented with some of the ideas being discussed in the WTO DSU negotiations. NAFTA was also an important source for the EU–Mexico Agreement, particularly as regards the Rules of Procedure and the Code of Conduct.

The arbitration procedures in the EU–Mexico and the EU–Chile agreements have many elements in common, but also important differences. For ease of reference, Table 1 summarizes the main differences between the two

---

[33] The Council adopted Regulations on retaliatory measures following WTO disputes with the US concerning steel safeguards, the Foreign Sales Cooperation, and the so-called Byrd Amendment.

Table 1. Main Differences in the Dispute Settlement Mechanism FTAs EC–Mexico and EU–Chile*

LEGAL PROVISIONS	EC/MEXICO OJ L157/26 of 30.06.2000	EC/CHILE FTA OJ L353 of 30.12.2002
Forum Exclusion	WTO and the procedures of the FTA, **are not mutually exclusive** but the proceedings can not be concurrent (Art. 47(4))	WTO and the procedures of the FTA (Art. 189(4)(c)) are mutually exclusive
Transparency	Not regulated	*Hearings*: Opportunity to the Parties to have **open hearings** (Rule 23) <u>*Amicus curiae*</u>: **submissions are allowed** but the arbitration panel shall not be obliged to address them, in its ruling (Rule 35 to 37)
Establishment of the panel (timeframes)	Within 45 days of the request for the establishment, the panel shall be constituted (Art. 44).	Within 3 days of the request for the establishment of the arbitration the panel shall by constituted (Art. 185).
Composition of the panel	Panel composed of 3 arbitrators. Each Party appoint one arbitrator. Each party proposes up to 3 arbitrators to serve as chair. If one of the parties fail to propose an arbitrator or if there is no agreement on the chair, they will be chosen by lot (Art. 44)	Panel composed of 3 arbitrators selected by lot, from a **roster** of 15 persons (5 EU, 5 Chile, 5 non-nationals). (Art. 185). Roster to be established by Association Committee no later than 6 months after entry into force of agreement.

Initial report	**Initial Report** will be issued within 3 or 5 months from the constitution of the panel. (Art. 45(1))	No initial report.
Timeframe for panel examination	Final Report shall be issued within 30 days form the presentation of the initial report (Art. 45(2)) (Initial + Final = 4 or 6 months)	Final report will be issued in **3 or 5 months** from the constitution of the panel. (Art. 187(1))
Implementation procedures	The Party concerned shall notify the measures adopted in order to implement the final report before the expiry of the reasonable period of time (**RPT**) previously determined (either by agreement of the parties or by arbitration, the ruling should be given within 15 days). (**Art. 46**)	The complained against party will notify the measures required to comply, a reasonable period of time (**RPT**) for doing so, and a concrete proposal for a **temporary compensation** until full implementation (Art. 188(3)). In case of disagreement of any of the 3 previous issues, there is the possibility to ask arbitration. If the party does not agree with the notification, could ask the original panel to make a ruling within 45 days (Art. 188(4))

* *Source:* Edna Ramirez Robles, 2006

agreements. What follows is a presentation of the key features of the new 'quasi-judicial' approach:

A. Shorter timeframes than under the WTO DSU

A potential advantage of bilateral dispute settlement is to secure speedier resolution of commercial disputes than is possible under the WTO DSU. This was an important consideration when negotiating the arbitration procedures under both agreements. The main source of procedural time-savings is the absence of an appellate review, which in any event would have been difficult and unusual to establish within the institutional framework of a bilateral agreement. There are, in addition, other time-saving provisions. The mandatory consultation period has been reduced from 60 days under the DSU to 45 days. The arbitration panel is to be established within no more than 45 days (Mexico) and within three days (Chile). The shorter timeframe in the EU–Chile Agreement is due to the differences in panel-establishment procedures, which are discussed below. As regards the timeframe for the issuance of a final report (since the date of establishment of a panel), this is four to six months (Mexico) and three to five months (Chile). The reason for this difference is the elimination in the EU–Chile Agreement of the DSU requirement to prepare an interim panel report. As a result of all these time-savings, under the EU–Chile Agreement, it should in principle be possible to obtain a definitive ruling on a dispute within less than seven months of a complaint being launched.[34]

B. Automatic procedure for the establishment of an arbitration panel

Under both agreements the need for consensus in the Association Council disappears, although the institutional solutions found to avoid blockages are different. Under the EU–Mexico Agreement, each of the parties is to appoint one arbitrator and propose up to three candidates as a Chair. If no agreement is reached on the Chair, or if a party fails to appoint its arbitrator, the remaining arbitrators are selected by lot. In negotiating these procedures, an important consideration for both the EU and Mexico was to avoid the procedural complexities of the panel composition procedure under NAFTA, which had often resulted in a failure by the parties to agree on a panel.[35]

The EU–Chile panel composition procedure is more innovative in that it departs from the DSU model, which relies on efforts by the parties to agree on ad-hoc panelists. Instead, the parties are to agree on a roster of fifteen

---

[34] A word of caution is, however, necessary since, under the WTO, Panels have often taken longer to finalize their work than the time periods stipulated in the DSU. This is despite the fact that panelists can rely on the support of the WTO secretariat. It can not be excluded, therefore, that bilateral panelists, which have very limited institutional support, may require more time to issue a ruling, particularly in complex disputes.

[35] On NAFTA dispute settlement, *see* A.L.C. de Mestral 'NAFTA Dispute Settlement: Creative Experiment or Confusion?', in this volume, at 359.

panelists—five from Chile, five from the EU and five non-nationals. All three arbitrators are then selected by lot within three days of the request for the establishment of the panel. Unlike in the case of NAFTA, the establishment of a roster is conceived as an alternative to the ad-hoc selection procedure. Despite this, it has proved easier than in NAFTA to agree on the roster, which has already been established.[36]

C. Detailed procedural rules for the arbitration

Whereas prior EU agreements only had one article to regulate all aspects of dispute settlement procedures, the FTAs with Mexico and Chile include detailed rules on arbitration procedures both in the main body of the agreement and in the annexes on rules of procedure and Code of Conduct. As already noted, the procedural rules are a combination of DSU and NAFTA rules. In one important aspect, however, the EU–Chile Agreement is more innovative than either the DSU or NAFTA (and, indeed, than the EU–Mexico Agreement). The EU–Chile Agreement explicitly provides that rulings should be made public and that, provided both parties agree, hearings may also be opened to the public. It also provides for the admissibility, under certain conditions, of *amicus curiae*. These transparency provisions are essentially identical to those proposed by the EU in the DSU negotiations. The agreement with Chile was the first bilateral FTA to provide for open hearings and admissibility of *amici*, although similar provisions have been included in agreements subsequently negotiated by the US.

D. Compliance proceedings

Both agreements have established detailed compliance proceedings inspired by Articles 21 and 22 of the DSU, although they go beyond the current rules of DSU in two respects: (a) the establishment of rules on sequencing—i.e. retaliation is only allowed if the original panel rules that the measures taken to comply with the initial ruling are still in breach of the FTA, and (b) a procedure to allow for the lifting of sanctions if compliance is achieved after concessions have been suspended. These provisions are very similar to rules supported by most WTO Members in ongoing DSU negotiations.[37]

The EU–Chile Agreement is again more innovative. In particular, it provides that, within thirty days of the ruling, the defending party must notify: (a) the specific measures it intends to take in order to comply, (b) a proposed

---

[36] The NAFTA roster is larger than in EU–Chile—30 individuals—and arbitrators are still selected by the parties rather than by lot. At the time of writing, it appears that NAFTA parties have not yet agreed on the roster.

[37] For a discussion of the DSU Negotiations, *see* I. Garcia Bercero and P. Garzotti, 'DSU Reform—Why have Negotiations to Improve WTO Dispute Settlement failed so far and what are the Underlying Issues' (2005) J World Invest & Trade, 847.

timeframe for compliance, and (c) a concrete proposal on temporary compensation until full implementation. If there is disagreement on any of these three issues, the matter may be referred to arbitration by the same panel that ruled in the original dispute. This procedure is more far-reaching than what has been proposed so far in the DSU negotiations. First, it requires the defending party to indicate, within a very short deadline, the specific measures it intends to take to comply with the ruling. Moreover, the arbitration panel is given jurisdiction to rule on a measure before it has been adopted. This represents a significant departure from DSU rules and practice, under which compliance proceedings normally only start at the end of the reasonable period of time and where there is no obligation to formally notify in advance the measures a party intends to take in order to comply. Second, an obligation is introduced to present an offer for temporary compensation during the time required to achieve compliance with bilateral obligations. The arbitration panel has jurisdiction to rule on whether the compensation offer presented is 'manifestly disproportionate'. The obligation to present a compensation offer is, however, non-enforceable since retaliation may only be applied in case there is lack of compliance at the end of the reasonable period of time.

Both agreements include rules on retaliation which are similar to those in the DSU. The original arbitration panel may be asked to rule on whether a proposed suspension of concessions is equivalent to the level of nullification and impairment. The arbitrator may also rule on whether the principles governing the selection of countermeasures have been followed. These principles require specific justification in case the suspension relates to a different title to that in which the arbitrators have found a breach and to the need to select measures that 'least disturbs the functioning of this agreement'.[38] It should be noted that parties are only authorized to 'suspend the application of benefits granted under this Part of the Agreement . . .'. This appears to exclude the suspension of benefits under the non-trade related part of the agreement.[39]

---

[38] Under the EU–Chile Agreement, the trade-related part includes separate titles on Free Movement of Goods, Trade in Services and Establishment, Government Procurement, Current payments and Capital movements, Intellectual Property Rights, and Competition (this last title is excluded from the application of Dispute Settlement).

[39] In principle, it would appear that retaliation could include measures which are in breach of obligations under the WTO Agreement. However, the application of such retaliatory measures would give rise to complex issues as regards the relationship between bilateral and WTO dispute settlement. An important question is whether a WTO Panel has jurisdiction to apply WTO law in relation to countermeasures that have been properly adopted under a bilateral dispute settlement procedure. This issue underlies the WTO dispute between US and Mexico on discriminatory taxes applied by Mexico on US sugar products as a retaliation against a US breach of NAFTA provisions, although in this case Mexico's retaliation was not based on the provisions of NAFTA but was rather a response to the obstruction by the US of NAFTA procedures. The Appellate Body, however, has ruled that it has no jurisdiction to adjudicate non-WTO disputes. (*See* WTO Appellate Body Report, *Mexico—Soft Drinks*, WT/DS308/AB/R, adopted 6 March 2006, para. 56). It should be noted that these findings were not strictly necessary to solve the dispute and could be regarded as *obiter*.

As a conclusion, it should be noted that both the EU–Mexico and the EU–Chile Agreements represent a radical departure from prior EU practice. In both cases the main purpose was to introduce an arbitration proceeding for trade disputes based on the WTO model, but with reduced timeframes. The EU–Chile FTA represents a more significant departure from the established WTO model, because of the willingness of the parties to experiment with a number of ideas being discussed in the DSU negotiations. Some of these innovations are close to the current consensus of the broader WTO membership—i.e. sequencing. Others may be more difficult to emulate at the multilateral level-procedures for *amicus curiae*, establishment of a roster of panelists, obligation to present a compensation offer. On one issue, however, the two agreements reached highly contrasting approaches. This is the vexing question of the relationship between bilateral and WTO dispute settlement. This issue is discussed in the next section.

V. AN UNRESOLVED ISSUE: ARTICULATION BETWEEN BILATERAL DISPUTE SETTLEMENT AND WTO PROCEEDINGS

The relationship between the dispute settlement proceedings of the WTO and of FTAs is a subject of great legal complexity. This article will not consider the extent to which there may be overlaps and conflicts of jurisdiction between the two legal orders or whether WTO dispute settlement proceedings may take into account provisions of regional trade agreements or the fact that the same measure may be (or have been) subject of bilateral dispute settlement proceedings under a regional trade agreement.[40] The focus of the present inquiry is limited to explaining how this relationship has been addressed in recent EU FTAs and to suggest that further reflection on the relationship between bilateral dispute settlement and the WTO is needed, since neither of the approaches followed in the agreements with Mexico and Chile are fully satisfactory.

The complexity of finding an 'ideal' solution to the relationship between WTO and bilateral dispute settlement procedures is due to the fact that the substantive law of free trade agreements is very largely influenced—and, indeed, dependent upon—WTO law. In order to illustrate this point, it is useful to consider some examples drawn from the substantive provisions of the EU–Chile FTA. On the basis of these examples, it appears possible to distinguish at least four possible 'types' of relationship between WTO law and the law of the FTA.

---

[40] *See* the contribution by K. Kwak and G. Marceau, 'Overlaps and Conflicts of Jurisdiction between the World Trade Organization and Regional Trade Agreements', in this volume, at 465.

A. Bilateral provisions which are largely independent from WTO obligations

Examples are the preferential schedules of market access commitments for goods and services, the provisions on the right of establishment or capital movements (areas not regulated by WTO rules), or the title on government procurement (since Chile is not a party to the WTO plurilateral Government Procurement Agreement). However, even in these areas, WTO law may exercise an influence since many of the underlying legal concepts are common in WTO and FTA law. It can not be excluded, therefore, that in interpreting the meaning of a market access concession or of a term in the government procurement title, a bilateral arbitration panel may wish to consider how similar issues have been addressed in WTO jurisprudence. Indeed, it may well be argued that, in order to enhance the predictability and coherence of international trade law, it would be highly desirable if bilateral panels were to consider relevant WTO rulings.

B. Areas where the FTA essentially confirms WTO obligations

The clearest example is Article 78 on Antidumping and Countervailing Measures. This article states that the parties retain the right to apply such measures in accordance with the relevant WTO provisions. Presumably, the reason for including such a provision in a bilateral agreement is simply to confirm that the right to apply such measures is not affected by the FTA. Regardless of whether the parties explicitly exclude the application of bilateral dispute settlement to such provisions or not, it could hardly be their intention that a bilateral panel adjudicates on the interpretation and application of the WTO Antidumping Agreement.[41] A more complex case is Article 92 on the Safeguard Clause. Article 92(1) essentially confirms the application of Article XIX GATT and the Safeguards Agreement. However, the article also provides for a number of obligations that are additional to those provided for in the WTO. While most of these obligations are procedural—and, thus, not easily subject to adjudication—at least one of the provisions is substantive and largely independent from WTO law. It can not be excluded therefore that a bilateral panel may be asked to adjudicate on the interpretation and application of Article 92(6) of the EU–Chile Agreement.[42]

---

[41] The EU–Mexico Agreement explicitly excludes the application of bilateral dispute settlement to antidumping and countervailing measures, whereas EU–Chile is silent on the matter. However, in both cases, the purpose of referring to the Antidumping Agreement is to confirm an exception from the obligation to eliminate duties in bilateral trade.

[42] Art. 92(6) obliges the parties to select safeguard measures which least disturb the achievement of the objectives of the agreement, which do not exceed what is necessary to remedy serious injury, and which preserve the level/margin of preference under the agreement.

C. Areas of overlap between WTO and bilateral obligations

In certain areas, parties to an FTA seek to establish rules that go beyond WTO obligations (so-called WTO-plus provisions). However, in doing so the negotiators are not drawing on a blank piece of paper since often the point of departure is a confirmation of existing WTO obligations. For instance, the EU–Chile Agreement seeks to develop disciplines on technical standards and regulations and on sanitary and phytosanitary measures which go beyond the provisions of the WTO, TBT, and SPS Agreements. (Arguably, however, many of the provisions included in the agreement are non-binding in nature). At the same time, the FTA confirms WTO obligations under the TBT and SPS Agreements and clarifies that a number of terms are used with the same meaning than they have under the WTO Agreements. In such cases, it is difficult to see how a bilateral panel could properly apply the provisions of the FTA without also referring to WTO law. To a certain extent, similar issues can arise as regards the EU–Chile provisions on trade facilitation, intellectual property and, possibly, customs valuation.

D. Areas where the FTA reproduces (without referring to) WTO provisions

A clear example is Article 77 of the EU–Chile Agreement on national treatment of internal taxes and regulations which simply reproduces Article III GATT. Similarly, the regulatory provisions on services are largely modelled on the equivalent provisions of the GATS. Even if no explicit reference is made to the WTO, it is difficult to envisage how a bilateral panel could interpret these provisions without making reference to relevant rulings of the WTO Dispute Settlement Body. NAFTA panels, for instance, have often referred to GATT and WTO law in their rulings.[43]

This complex relationship between WTO law and FTA law gives rise to two questions: (a) May bilateral arbitration panels apply WTO law which is reproduced or referred to in the provisions of the FTA or, at least, take into account WTO provisions for the interpretation of FTA law? and (b) Do the parties retain the freedom to use both bilateral and WTO dispute settlement or do they need to operate a choice of forum? Both issues were highly controversial in the negotiations with Mexico and Chile and could only be solved at the final stage of the negotiations. As will be seen the solutions found are not only different, but also not fully satisfactory.

1. Application of WTO Law by bilateral panels

As was already the case in the EU–South Africa FTA, the agreement with Mexico provides that 'Arbitration proceedings established under this title will

---

[43] For a theoretical framework on the extent to which WTO law may be applied by bilateral panels, including a discussion of NAFTA practice, *see* L. Hsu, 'Applicability of WTO law in Regional Trade Agreements: Identifying the Links', in this volume, at 525.

not consider issues relating to each party's rights and obligations under the Agreement establishing the World Trade Organization' (Article 47(3)). Moreover, the articles that have a closer connection to WTO rules—antidumping and countervailing measures, balance of payments restrictions, trade agreements with third parties, and intellectual property—are explicitly excluded from the application of bilateral dispute settlement.

The EU–Chile FTA only explicitly excludes from bilateral dispute settlement a non-WTO related area—i.e. competition. It includes, however, a provision that, if broadly interpreted, could result in bilateral panels having to decline jurisdiction whenever WTO law appears to be relevant for the resolution of a dispute. Article 189(4)(c) reads as follows: 'Unless the Parties otherwise agree, when a Party seeks redress of a violation of an obligation under this part of the agreement which is equivalent in substance to an obligation under the WTO, it shall have recourse to the relevant rules and procedures of the WTO . . .'.

What are the consequences of these two approaches for the jurisdiction of a bilateral panel to apply WTO law or to use WTO law as a tool for the interpretation of provisions in the bilateral agreement that are closely related to WTO law? First, it would appear that under both agreements a bilateral panel may not rule on bilateral provisions that go no further than a confirmation of existing WTO rules and obligations. In any event, in order to increase legal certainty, the EU–Mexico FTA explicitly excludes a number of provisions that appear to fall under this category. Second, the EU–Chile FTA appears to go much further in that it excludes—unless the parties agree—bilateral provisions that are equivalent in substance to WTO obligations, even if the FTA may not at all refer to WTO law. Thus, it would appear that, under such a clause, the responding party could object to the jurisdiction of a bilateral panel to rule, for instance, on a breach of national treatment on the grounds that the bilateral obligation is substantially equivalent to Article III of GATT. Third, it is submitted that bilateral panels should always be able to use WTO law as a tool to interpret FTA provisions. This appears to be, in any event, required under public international law and both EU–Mexico and EU–Chile indicate that arbitration panels shall interpret the provisions of the agreement in accordance with customary rules of public international law.[44] Finally, in so far as interpretation is not a sufficient tool to take WTO law into account, none of the approaches above provides a satisfactory solution to address areas in which there is a genuine overlap between WTO and bilateral obligations. In those cases, it may be impossible for a bilateral panel to apply a bilateral provision without at the same time considering issues relating to each party's rights and obligations under the WTO. Moreover, recourse to WTO dispute

[44] An unfortunate legal ambiguity has been created with the requirement that arbitration proceedings should not 'consider' issues relating to WTO rights and obligations. A strict reading of such provision could even imply a prohibition to use WTO law as a tool to interpret FTA provisions. It is submitted that such a 'clinical isolation' of FTA and WTO law would be highly undesirable.

settlement does not provide an alternative, since WTO panels may not enforce the WTO plus elements included in the FTA.

2. *Choice of Forum*

Under the NAFTA and subsequent US FTAs, there is a 'choice of forum' clause which essentially provides that: (a) the complaining party may select whether to refer a dispute to the WTO or bilateral dispute settlement, and (b) once a panel has been requested under either one of these fora, the forum selected shall be used to the exclusion of the others.

In the negotiations of the EU–Mexico FTA, Mexico took the position that there should be an equivalent 'choice of forum' clause to that included in NAFTA. The EU was strongly opposed to the NAFTA approach. It was argued that the consequence of a 'choice of forum' clause would be that, whenever both options were available, the complainant would have a clear preference to have recourse to WTO dispute settlement, since the DSU was well tested. Moreover, in the light of the evolutionary nature of WTO law and jurisprudence, there was a reluctance to any procedural solution which implied giving up future WTO rights. The compromise reached was a rule against concurrent proceedings. Thus, while there is no forum exclusivity, once a forum has been chosen, proceedings in a different forum may only be initiated after the first proceedings have ended. This is intended to limit the risk of procedural harassment by the complainant.

The compromise above was not acceptable to Chile. Thus the EU–Chile Agreement includes a rule on forum exclusivity. However, within 10 days of the establishment of a bilateral panel, a jurisdictional objection may be raised, on which a preliminary ruling must be made within 30 days. In practice, this means that the defendant would normally be able to avoid a bilateral proceeding if the claims by the complainant include a breach of bilateral provisions that are substantially equivalent to WTO obligations. As indicated above, the consequence is likely to be a much greater reluctance by the parties to have recourse to bilateral dispute settlement.

To sum up, it would appear that a simpler and more effective solution should be found to the relationship between bilateral and WTO dispute settlement. In this connection, the author would favour the following approach: (a) bilateral dispute settlement panels should be in a position to apply WTO law which is referred to in a bilateral FTA, unless the parties have explicitly excluded the applicability of bilateral dispute settlement to a particular provision.[45] Article 41(3) of the EU–Mexico FTA is not satisfactory since it can limit the scope to apply WTO-plus provisions, where such provision

---

[45] Some may argue that such an approach contradicts Art. 23.1 DSU, under which WTO Members may only seek a redress of a violation of WTO law through WTO dispute settlement proceedings. However, from the moment WTO law is incorporated into a bilateral agreement, it becomes part and parcel of the bilateral rights and obligations which may be enforced under bilateral dispute settlement.

can only be applied in conjunction with existing WTO obligations. Article 189(4)(c) of EU–Chile is, of course, even more limitative and could seriously impair the effectiveness of bilateral dispute settlement. b) A rule against concurrent proceedings is sufficient to prevent any risk of legal harassment. A rule on forum exclusion is, on the other hand, likely to be to the detriment of bilateral dispute settlement except for issues not covered by WTO disciplines, since complainants are likely to be reluctant to lose WTO remedies.

VI. CONCLUSIONS: LESSONS LEARNED?

The evolution towards a quasi-judicial model of adjudication in EU FTAs appears now irreversible. Ongoing negotiations of FTAs with Mercosur and the GCC include dispute settlement provisions which are similar to those included in the FTAs concluded with Mexico and Chile. The initialled EU–Syria FTA is the first Euro-Mediterranean Agreement which includes quasi-judicial dispute settlement procedures. Recently, the EU Council authorized the Commission to open negotiations with all Euro-Mediterranean countries with a view to introducing more effective dispute settlement procedures. Consideration of such an approach is also being discussed in ongoing negotiations for the conclusion of an SAA with Serbia and Montenegro. Indeed, quasi-judicial dispute settlement appears to be the norm in all recently concluded FTAs, not only of the EU, but of all major trading partners.

Despite the above, it is perhaps premature to conclude that lessons have been learned and that the EU has decided to move away from the traditional diplomatic approach of bilateral dispute resolution. After all, at the time of writing, there has not been a single case in which the dispute settlement provisions of the FTAs with Mexico and Chile have been invoked. This contrasts with the relatively frequent recourse by the EU to WTO dispute settlement. What explains this limited recourse to the new quasi-judicial dispute settlement procedures?

A first possible reason is that the trend towards quasi-judicial dispute settlement is still very recent and limited to a few trading partners, which are not frequent 'targets' of EU dispute settlement. In these circumstances, it is likely that the traditional diplomatic approach to dispute resolution is still preferred. The fact that the EU Trade Barriers Regulation does not allow industry complaints to enforce obligations under FTAs may also limit the potential for recourse to bilateral dispute settlement. It can be expected, however, that both the EU (and its trading partners) will over time overcome this initial reluctance to test the new quasi-judicial procedures. One or two successful examples may be all it takes for recourse to bilateral arbitration to become accepted as a 'normal' occurrence in bilateral trade relations. It may also be the case that the mere existence of quasi-judicial arbitration procedures acts as an incentive to solve more disputes at the consultation/diplomatic phase.

Another possible reason relates to the substantive normative content of EU FTAs. As indicated above, bilateral dispute settlement is not applicable to disputes concerning trade remedies measures (i.e. antidumping, countervailing duties, and safeguards). These are, however, a large majority of the cases that the EU (and other WTO Members) bring to WTO dispute settlement. Indeed, the only WTO case launched by the EU *vis-à-vis* Mexico concerns the application of countervailing duties on olive oil and the only WTO case launched by Chile against the EU concerned a safeguard measure on salmon. None of these cases could have been brought under the bilateral dispute settlement procedures in the FTAs. Bilateral dispute settlement would appear to be particularly appropriate in the case of WTO plus provisions in the FTAs. However, most of these relate to the schedules of market access concessions, which normally are faithfully implemented and are not a source of trade disputes. In case future FTAs were to include more ambitious WTO plus provisions in regulatory areas, it could be expected that more frequent recourse would be made to bilateral dispute settlement.

Finally, there is possibly a more structural reason. As Bill Davey has noted, WTO dispute settlement may be viewed as more legitimate and effective both in terms of the adjudication process and the pressure to comply with a ruling.[46] This is due to a combination of factors, including the existence of a well established WTO jurisprudence, the role of the Appellate Body in ensuring high legal standards and coherence of rulings, the support provided to panels by the WTO Secretariat, and the existence of multilateral surveillance for the implementation of rulings. As a result of these factors, it is likely that if a certain trade dispute can be addressed under either bilateral or WTO dispute settlement, there will still be a clear preference to have recourse to WTO procedures. So, in all likelihood while bilateral dispute settlement will become a more important part of EU toolbox, it will not eclipse the priority given to WTO dispute settlement.

---

[46] *See* W.J. Davey, 'Dispute Settlement in WTO and RTAs: A Comment', in this volume, at 343.

17

Dispute Settlement in Bilateral Trade Agreements: The EFTA Experience

ANDREAS R. ZIEGLER

I. THE EFTA CONVENTION

A. The Stockholm Convention of 1961

The EFTA Convention, governing the economic relationship between Norway, Iceland, Liechtenstein, and Switzerland, is a wonderful example to show the development of dispute settlement in international trade agreements over the last half-century.

The original EFTA Convention of 1961, the so-called Stockholm Convention,[1] in its Article 31, primarily relied on bilateral and possibly multilateral consultations within the main organ of the Convention. However, not unlike the GATT 1947, it provided for a possibility to arrange for an examining committee to make recommendations to the Council.

Article 31: General consultations and complaints procedure
1. If any Member State considers that any benefit conferred upon it by this Convention or any objective of the Association is being or may be frustrated and if no satisfactory settlement is reached between the Member States concerned, any of those Member States may refer the matter to the Council.
2. The Council shall promptly, by majority vote, make arrangements for examining the matter. Such arrangements may include a reference to an examining committee constituted in accordance with Article 33. Before taking action under paragraph 3 of this Article, the Council shall so refer the matter at the request of any Member State concerned. Member States shall furnish all information which they can make available and shall lend their assistance to establish the facts.
3. When considering the matter, the Council shall have regard to whether it has been

[1] Convention establishing the European Free Trade Association (EFTA), signed at Stockholm on 4 January 1960, in force 3 May 1960, SR 0.63.31.

established that an obligation under the Convention has not been fulfilled, and whether and to what extent any benefit conferred by the Convention or any objective of the Association is being or may be frustrated. In the light of this consideration and of the report of any examining committee which may have been appointed, the Council may, by majority vote, make to any Member State such recommendations as it considers appropriate.

4. If a Member State does not or is unable to comply with a recommendation made in accordance with paragraph 3 of this Article and the Council finds, by majority vote, that an obligation under this Convention has not been fulfilled, the Council may, by majority decision, authorise any Member State to suspend to the Member State which has not complied with the recommendation the application of such obligations under this Convention as the Council considers appropriate.

5. Any Member State may, at any time while the matter is under consideration, request the Council to authorise, as a matter of urgency, interim measures to safeguard its position. If it appears to the Council that the circumstances are sufficiently serious to justify interim action, and without prejudice to any action which it may subsequently take in accordance with the preceding paragraphs of this Article, the Council may, by majority decision, authorise a Member State to suspend its obligation under this Convention to such an extent and for such a period as the Council considers appropriate.

The EFTA solution of 1961 was thus very similar to the model enshrined in the GATT of 1947. While the EC had already a fully-fledged court in place for the settlement of disputes among its members, the EFTA relied on a very traditional GATT-oriented model not even including classical arbitration.

In view of the modesty of this system and its similarity to the GATT 1947, it seems not surprising that after the entry into force of the WTO's Dispute Settlement Understanding (DSU) the general need for an overhaul of the EFTA convention as it arose in the late 1990s was used for a modification of the EFTA dispute settlement mechanism.

B. The Vaduz Convention of 2001

The so-called Vaduz Convention[2] of 2001 led to a major revision of the original Stockholm Convention. This overhaul was primarily necessary in view of the fact that all EFTA partners had more ambitious relations with the European Community (EC) than those foreseen among the EFTA States themselves. For Norway, Iceland, and Liechtenstein these bilateral relations are based on the EEA Agreement[3] while Switzerland has concluded in 1999 a first series of bilateral agreements with the EC and its Member States. But the revision of the EFTA Convention was also justified by the fact that the EFTA

---

[2] Convention of 21 June 2001 to consolidate the Convention establishing the European Free Trade Association (EFTA) of 4 January 1960, in force 1 June 2002. An English version is available at secretariat.efta.int/Web/EFTAConvention/EFTAConventionTexts/EFTAConventionText (visited 10 April 2006).

[3] European Economic Area Agreement, signed 2 May 1992, in force 1 January 1994 [1994] OJ L1/3.

States had concluded an important number of bilateral free trade agreements with third States. Namely, the latter contained normally dispute settlement provisions inspired by the WTO while the EEE Agreement and the bilateral agreements between Switzerland and the EC contain surprisingly modest dispute settlement provisions.

The Agreement between the European Community and the three EFTA States—Norway, Iceland, and Liechtenstein—for the creation of the European Economic Area (EEA) of 1992 includes only purely diplomatic consultation procedure within the EEA Joint Committee.[4] This limitation applies equally to the bilateral agreements between Switzerland and the EC of 1999.[5] Although Switzerland had repeatedly requested the introduction of mandatory arbitration, the EC has always refused this—officially out of fear to cut inadmissibly the authority of the European Court of Justice.[6]

The new Vaduz Convention of 2001 provides with regard to dispute settlement for consultations (Article 47) and the possibility of classical inter-state arbitration (Article 48). However, a specific Annex T contains rules on implementation very much inspired by the WTO DSU:

Article 47 Consultations

1. The Member States shall at all times endeavour to agree on the interpretation and application of this Convention, and shall make every attempt through cooperation and consultations to arrive at a mutually satisfactory resolution of any matter that might affect its operation.

2. Any Member State may bring any matter, which concerns the interpretation or application of this Convention before the Council. The Council shall be provided with all information, which might be of use in making possible an in-depth examination of the situation, with a view to finding an acceptable solution. To this end, the Council shall examine all possibilities to maintain the good functioning of the Convention.

3. A meeting of the Council shall be held within 30 days from the receipt of the request for consultations.

Article 48 Arbitration

1. In case a Member State considers that a measure applied by another Member State violates the Convention and the matter has not been resolved within 45 days after consultations have been held pursuant to Article 47, such matter may be

---

[4] *See* Art. 111(1) and (2) EEA.

[5] *See* Bilateral Agreements between Switzerland and the EC of 1999 (with exception of the Agreement between the European Community and the Swiss Confederation on Air Transport, which intends a different procedure before the European Court of Justice). Only the Cooperation Agreement between the European Atomic Energy Community (Euratom) and the Swiss Confederation in the field of controlled thermonuclear fusion and plasma physics of the 14 September 1978 (SR 0.424.11) and the Agreement between the European Economic Community and the Swiss Confederation of 10 October 1989 pertaining to direct insurance other than life insurance (SR 0.961.1) contain exceptionally mandatory arbitration clauses.

[6] *See* in addition D. Felder, 'Appréciation juridique et politique du cadre institutionnel et des dispositions générales des accords sectoriels', in D. Felder and C. Kaddous (eds), *Accords bilatéraux Suisse-UE: Commentaires* (Basel: Helbling & Lichtenhahn, 2001), 117–48, 134 f.

referred to arbitration by one or more Member States parties to the dispute by means of a written notification addressed to the Member State complained against. A copy of this notification shall be communicated to all Member States so that each may determine whether it has a substantial interest in the matter. Where more than one Member State requests the submission to an arbitration tribunal of a dispute with the same Member State relating to the same question a single arbitration tribunal should be established to consider such disputes whenever feasible.

2. A Member State which is not a party to the dispute, on delivery of a written notice to the disputing Member States, shall be entitled to make written submissions to the arbitration tribunal, receive written submissions of the disputing Member States, attend all hearings and make oral submissions.

3. The award of the arbitration tribunal shall be final and binding upon the Member States parties to the dispute and shall be complied with promptly.

4. The establishment and functioning of the arbitration tribunal and the implementation of arbitral awards are governed by the rules set out in Annex T.

Annex T Arbitration (Art. 48)

Article 1: Establishment and functioning of the arbitral tribunal and the implementation of arbitral awards

1. The arbitral tribunal shall comprise three members.

2. In its written notification pursuant to Article 48 of this Convention, the Member State(s) referring the dispute to arbitration shall designate one member of the arbitral tribunal.

3. Within 15 days from the receipt of the notification referred to in paragraph 2, the Member State(s) to which it was addressed shall, in turn, designate one member.

4. Within 30 days from the receipt of the notification referred to in paragraph 2, the Member States concerned shall agree on the designation of a third member. The third member shall not be a national of the parties to the dispute, nor permanently reside in the territory of either Member State. The member thus appointed shall be the President of the arbitral tribunal.

5. If all three members have not been designated or appointed within 30 days from the receipt of the notification referred to in paragraph 2, the necessary designations shall be made, at request of either party to the dispute, by the President of the International Court of Justice applying the criteria of paragraphs 3 and 4. If the President is unable to act under this paragraph or is a national of a party to the dispute, the designations shall be effected by the next senior member of the Court who is neither unable to act nor a national of a Member State.

6. Unless otherwise agreed between the parties to the dispute, and subject to Article 48 of the Convention and this Annex, the Optional Rules for Arbitrating Disputes between Two States of the Permanent Court of Arbitration (PCA), effective 20 October 1992, shall apply.

7. The arbitral tribunal shall take its decisions by majority vote. Minority opinions shall not be disclosed.

8. A Member State which is not a party to the dispute, on delivery of a written notice to the disputing parties, shall be entitled to make written submissions to the arbitral tribunal, to receive written submissions of the disputing parties, attend all hearings and make oral submissions.

9. The arbitral award shall be rendered within six months of the date at which the

President of the arbitral tribunal was appointed. This period can be extended by a maximum of three additional months, if the parties to the dispute so agree.

10. The expenses of the arbitral tribunal, including the remuneration of its members, shall be borne by the parties to the dispute in equal shares. Fees and expenses payable to members of an arbitral tribunal established under these Articles will be subject to schedules established by the Council and in force at the time of the establishment of the arbitral tribunal.

Article 2 Implementation of the arbitral award

1. On receipt of the arbitral award, the parties to the dispute shall agree on the implementation of the arbitral award, which, unless they decide otherwise by common accord, shall conform with the determinations and recommendations of the arbitral tribunal. The parties to the dispute shall notify the other Member States of any agreed resolution of the dispute.

2. Wherever possible, the resolution shall be non-implementation or removal of a measure not conforming with this Convention or, failing such a resolution, compensation.

3. In case of disagreement as to the existence or consistency of a measure implementing the arbitral award with the recommendations of the arbitral tribunal, such dispute shall be decided by the same arbitral tribunal before compensation can be sought or suspension of benefits can be applied in accordance with Article 3 below.

4. The complaining Member State may not initiate arbitration under the preceding paragraph before a period of 12 months has expired following the rendering of the award pursuant to paragraph 3 of Article 48. The award of the tribunal referred to in the preceding paragraph shall normally be rendered within three months of the request for arbitration.

Article 3 Non-implementation—suspension of benefits

1. If the arbitral tribunal, in accordance with paragraph 3 of Article 48, has determined that a measure is inconsistent with the obligations of this Convention, and the Member State complained against has not reached agreement with any complaining Member State on a mutually satisfactory resolution within 30 days of receiving the arbitral award, or if no implementing measures have been taken, such complaining Member State or Member States may:
   (a) seek compensation through an agreement with the Member State complained against; or
   (b) suspend the application to the Member State complained against of benefits of equivalent effect until such time as the disputing Member States have reached agreement on a resolution of the dispute.

2. Upon written request of any party to the dispute delivered to the other Member State or Member States, the same arbitral tribunal shall be reconvened to determine whether the level of benefits suspended by a Member State pursuant to paragraph 1 is of equivalent effect.

3. The proceedings of the arbitral tribunal shall be conducted in accordance with paragraph 2 of Article 1 above. The arbitral tribunal shall present its determination within 60 days after the date of the request referred to in paragraph 2 or such other period as the parties to the dispute may agree.

The EFTA States, thus, continue to try to solve disputes primarily by bilateral consultations and negotiations (Article 47(1) Vaduz Convention). The possibility to discuss the matter in the Joint Committee remains, although this organ has no longer the authority to adopt resolutions by majority vote and is therefore reduced to a pure consent institution (Article 47(2) and (3) Vaduz Convention). Since a proper arbitration procedure has been introduced, the possibility for the Council to authorize retaliation by majority vote has been given up.

II. FREE TRADE AGREEMENTS BETWEEN THE EFTA STATES AND THIRD STATES

A. Overview

The developments with regard to dispute settlement in the EFTA Convention itself correspond clearly to the general trend regarding dispute settlement in bilateral trade agreements by both the EFTA States and the EC. In particular, the EC and the EFTA States have concluded—under different titles—a set of free trade agreements containing specific arbitration mechanisms.

B. First Generation Agreements

For a long time these agreements by the EFTA States were limited to Eastern Europe and the Mediterranean. Of these, many of the former have been terminated in view of the accession of many of these States to the European Union (EU) in 2004. Generally these association agreements contained relatively slim dispute settlement provisions. They provided basically for bilateral consultations and the involvement of a Joint Committee before applying retaliatory measures. This model stemmed originally from the free trade agreements negotiated between the EFTA States and the EC (at that time the European Economic Community was still the EEC) in the early 1970s.[7] A typical example is the dispute settlement provision of the Agreement between the EFTA States and Turkey:

Article 23: Procedure for the application of safeguard measures
1. Before initiating the procedure for the application of safeguard measures set out in this Article, the States Parties to this Agreement shall endeavour to solve any differences between themselves through direct consultations, and shall inform the other States Parties thereof.
2. In the cases specified in Articles 16 to 22 a State Party to this Agreement which is considering to resort to safeguard measures shall promptly notify the Joint Committee thereof. The Parties concerned shall provide the Joint Committee with all relevant information and give it the assistance required to examine the case.

---

[7] *See*, for example, EEC–Switzerland Agreement, signed 22 July 1972, in force 1 January 1973 [1972] OJ L300/189.

Consultations between them shall take place without delay in the Joint Committee with a view to finding a commonly acceptable solution.

3. If, within three months of the matter being referred to the Joint Committee, the State Party in question fails to put an end to the practice objected to or to the difficulties notified and in the absence of a decision by the Joint Committee in the matter, the concerned State Party may adopt the safeguard measures it considers necessary to remedy the situation.

C. First Generation Agreements including Arbitration

From 1997 onwards, however, the EFTA States tried to include arbitration provisions in their bilateral agreements in order to have some judicial mechanism for the settlement of disputes.[8] In some cases, this even led to the renegotiation of the agreements concerned in order to include an arbitration provision. For example, the Agreement with Bulgaria of 1993 was amended by Joint Committee Decision No. 8 of 16 December 1997 in order to include the following provision:

Article 26 bis: Arbitration procedure
1. Disputes between States Parties to this Agreement relating to the interpretation of rights and obligations of States Parties to this Agreement, which have not been settled through consultation or in the Joint Committee within six months, may be referred to arbitration by any State party to the dispute by means of a written notification addressed to the other State party to the dispute. A copy of this notification shall be communicated to all States Parties to this Agreement.
2. The constitution and functioning of the arbitral tribunal is governed by Annex XIV.
3. The arbitral tribunal shall settle the dispute in accordance with the provisions of this Agreement and applicable rules and principles of international law.
4. The award of the arbitral tribunal shall be final and binding upon the States parties to the dispute.

Annex XIV Constitution and Functioning of the Arbitral Tribunal
1. In its written notification made pursuant to Article 26 bis of the Agreement, the State referring the dispute to arbitration shall designate one member, who may be its national.
2. Within thirty days from the receipt of the notification referred to in paragraph 1,the State to which it was addressed shall, in turn, designate one member, who may be its national.
3. Within sixty days from the receipt of the notification referred to in paragraph 1, the two members already designated shall agree on the designation of a third member who shall be confirmed by the States parties to the dispute within 15 days. The third member shall not be a national of either State party to the dispute, nor permanently reside on the territory of either State. The member thus appointed shall be the President of the arbitral tribunal.
4. If all three members have not been designated or appointed within sixty days from

---

[8] *See*, for example, EFTA States–Macedonia Free Trade Agreement, signed 19 June 2000, in force 1 May 2002 (Article 31) or EFTA States–Jordan Free Trade Agreement, signed 21 June 2001, in force 1 September 2002 (Article 31). Texts available at www.efta.int (visited 10 April 2006).

the receipt of the notification referred to in paragraph 1, the necessary designations shall be made, at request of either State party to the dispute, by the President of the International Court of Justice. If the President is unable to act under this paragraph or is a national of a State party to the dispute, the designations shall devolve on the Vice-President of the Court. If the latter, in turn, is unable to act or is a national of a State party to the dispute, the designations shall be effected by the next senior member of the Court who is neither unable to act nor a national of a State Party.

5. The tribunal shall lay down its own rules of procedure and take its decisions by majority vote.

6. The arbitral award shall be rendered within six months of the date at which the President of the Tribunal was appointed. At the request of the tribunal the Joint Committee may grant an extension of this time period up to six additional months. In the event of a dispute over the meaning and scope of the award, any State party to the dispute can, within 60 days from the communication of the arbitral award, ask for clarification by the tribunal. The tribunal shall deliver its clarification within 60 days from the day the issue was brought before it.

7. The expenses of the Tribunal, including the remuneration of its members, shall be borne by the States parties to the dispute in equal shares.

D. The Introduction of More Substantive Competition Provisions and Dispute Settlement

A specific problem with regard to the development of bilateral dispute settlement mechanisms was encountered, when the scope of these bilateral agreements evolved. This became particularly obvious once rules on competition were included into the EFTA States' bilateral agreements. While this issue remains under discussion relating to the potential inclusion of competition provisions into the WTO Agreement, the EFTA States opted to exclude competition from the scope of their arbitration provisions in some later agreements, such as in Article 78 of the Free Trade Agreement between the EFTA States and the Republic of Chile of 26 June 2003[9] or in Article 9(1) of the Free Trade Agreement between the EFTA States and South Korea of 15 December 2005.[10]

E. Second-Generation Free Trade Agreements

On the whole, in Eastern Europe and the Mediterranean the EFTA Members have signed agreements with the same States as the EC. This holds also true for Latin America (Chile, Mexico). However, on other continents EFTA has only partly followed the EC's track record. While the attempted negotiations for an agreement with Canada have never been concluded, the EFTA States have for the first time concluded an Agreement with Singapore in a situation where the EC was not envisaging trade negotiations. On 15 December 2005 the EFTA States signed also a substantive agreement with South Korea. The EC has only

---

[9] *See* secretariat.efta.int/Web/ExternalRelations/PartnerCountries/Chile (visited 10 April 2006).

[10] *See* secretariat.efta.int/Web/News/korea_fta_initialed (visited 10 April 2006).

concluded a Framework Agreement on Trade and Cooperation with South Korea of 28 October 1996 (entered into force in 2001) which does not contain any substantive trade preferences.

The agreements signed between the EFTA States and States outside Europe and the Mediterranean regularly foresee consultation within a Joint Committee and mandatory arbitration in order to settle trade disputes. The texts, however, are not always identical as the preferences differ between various partner countries, which is often a result of their own involvement in specific treaty negotiations with other States. In South America, e.g. with regard to Chile and Mexico, the influence of NAFTA and the respective bilateral agreements by the NAFTA States can clearly be felt. Similar observations apply to the agreements concluded by the EC with both countries.[11]

A further example is the Free Trade Agreement between the EFTA States and Singapore signed on 26 June 2002 in Egilstadir (Iceland).[12] In this Agreement the influence of the arbitral rules developed between Singapore and New Zealand (which themselves are based on the rules of the Closer Economic Relationship Agreement between New Zealand and Australia) can be felt. This leads to an interesting fusion of the rules from agreements of the Pacific area[13] with European standards. All these agreements contain dispute settlement procedures based on the three elements: (a) bilateral consultations, (b) consultations in a joint organ—for the agreements by the EFTA States or the EC normally referred to as 'Joint Committee'—and (c) *ad hoc* arbitration.[14] However, a few potential problems have evolved over time which may lead to tensions in the future.

III. POTENTIAL PROBLEMS

A. Choice of Forum

Some, but not all of the agreements negotiated by the EFTA States provide for rules as to whether a trade dispute may be settled using the WTO DSU or the mechanism of the bilateral agreement.

In their agreement with Korea, the EFTA States have chosen to allow for either to be chosen, but to exclude the use of the other mechanism once this has be done. The same is true for the aforementioned agreement between the

---

[11] EC–Mexico Free Trade Agreement, Decision No 2/2000 of 23 March 2000 [2000] OJ L157/10. This Agreement was adopted as a Joint Committee decision. A separate decision deals with trade in services and establishment. *See also* EFTA States–Mexico Free Trade Agreement, signed 27 November 2000, in force 1 July 2001, available at www.efta.int (visited 10 April 2006).

[12] *See* Neue Zürcher Zeitung, No 84 of 12 April 2002, 19.

[13] *See* e.g. New Zealand-Singapore Closer Economic Partnership, signed 14 November 2000, in force 1 January 2001. This agreement is characterized by an extremely simplified dispute settlement without creation of special instruments like the Joint Committee known from the European agreements.

[14] *See*, for example, Chapter 9 of the EFTA–South Korea FTA.

EFTA States and Chile. Would this mean that the Dispute Settlement Body (DSB) of the WTO would have to refuse to establish a panel if the other party to a dispute invokes the rule of the bilateral agreement and the existence (or completion) of parallel proceedings under the FTA?

Chapter 9 Dispute Settlement (FTA EFTA–South Korea)
Article 9(1) Scope and Coverage

...

2. Disputes on the same matter arising under both this Agreement and the WTO Agreement may be settled in either forum at the discretion of the complaining Party. The forum thus selected shall be used to the exclusion of the other.
3. For purposes of this Article, dispute settlement proceedings under the WTO Agreement or this Agreement are deemed to be initiated upon a request for a panel by a Party.
4. Before a Party initiates dispute settlement proceedings under the WTO Agreement against another Party or Parties as regards a matter arising under both this Agreement and the WTO Agreement, it shall notify all the Parties of its intention.

In some agreements, such as the one between the EFTA States and Mexico there is a possibility to force the other party into the dispute settlement mechanism of the bilateral agreement. But can it be enforced, in cases where the other party to the dispute requests nevertheless the establishment of a panel under the WTO?

Article 77 (EFTA States–Mexico): Choice of forum

...

2. Before an EFTA State initiates a dispute settlement proceeding against Mexico or Mexico initiates a dispute settlement proceeding against any EFTA State in the WTO on grounds that are substantially equivalent to those available to the Party concerned under this Agreement, that Party shall notify the other Parties of its intention. If another Party wishes also to have recourse to dispute settlement procedures as a complainant under this Agreement regarding the same matter, it shall inform promptly the notifying Party and those Parties shall consult with a view to agreement on a single forum. If those Parties cannot agree, the dispute shall be settled under this Agreement.

B. Applicable Law

The applicable law is not always stated in the same way in EFTA's bilateral agreements. In some cases, any other rule of international law applicable between the Parties is included as part of the applicable law for the arbitration tribunal, while in other agreements only the 'rules of interpretation of public international law' are mentioned as applicable law besides the agreement as such.

Article 9.6: Procedures of the Arbitration Panel (EFTA–South Korea)[15]

...

[15] The Agreement with Chile contains a very similar wording.

5. The arbitration panel shall make its ruling based on the provisions of this Agreement, applied and interpreted in accordance with the rules of interpretation of public international law.

However in the Agreement between the EFTA States and Bulgaria of 1993 the following provision was included:

Article 26 bis Arbitration procedure

. . .

3. The arbitral tribunal shall settle the dispute in accordance with the provisions of this Agreement and applicable rules and principles of international law.

C. Incorporation of WTO Law

The EFTA third country agreements contain many direct or indirect references to WTO law, as most bilateral trade agreements do today. They either refer to WTO law and declare it to be part of the bilateral agreement (incorporation) or simply repeat the text of corresponding WTO provisions. It will be very interesting to see what happens if bilateral dispute settlement proceedings under theses bilateral agreements lead to the application of WTO law or the interpretation of identical provisions. While it is likely (but not absolutely certain) that bilateral arbitration tribunals may follow many of the previous Panel and Appellate Body Reports under the WTO, it is probably less clear whether the WTO Appellate Body would in any way accept to refer to existing awards resulting from arbitration under bilateral agreements with regard to identical provisions.

IV. CONCLUSION

This short overview is not intended to show all the WTO DSU elements contained in some of the more recent free trade agreements concluded by the EFTA States. Furthermore, it has only highlighted some of the interesting features and questions without even trying to discuss them in detail. However, the remarks with regard to the inclusion of new disciplines (such as competition) in trade agreements and its influence on dispute settlement may be of relevance if, in the (remote) future, competitions should be on the WTO agenda again. Similarly the issues arising from the similarities and differences between the dispute settlement mechanisms of the bilateral agreements discussed and the WTO, as well as their potential incompatibilities, may lead to interesting question before bilateral arbitration tribunals and/or the organs of the WTO dispute settlement mechanism in a not so distant future.

18

Dispute Settlement in the Proposed East Asia Free Trade Agreement: Lessons Learned from the ASEAN, the NAFTA, and the EU

YAN LUO *

I. INTRODUCTION

East Asia has a long history of being a geographic or cultural identity for many Asian countries. However, as a concept of a regional trade bloc, it is relatively new.[1] Historically, even if the Chinese culture, Confucianism, and Buddhism influenced all of East Asia considerably, there have been only minimal diplomatic interchanges between governments and only small-scale, unofficial trade in the area.[2] It has therefore long been argued that it is in the interest of East Asian economies to put their focus on maintaining an open global economy through the World Trade Organization (WTO), rather than favouring Regional Trade Agreements (RTAs), due to the dependence of extra-regional trade of most East Asian economies.[3]

Nevertheless, East Asia became a distinctive locus for regional integration recently. Many countries in East Asia have dramatically changed their attitudes towards regionalism and show increasing interest in creating regional

---

* The author wishes to thank Professor Marise Cremona, Professor Locknie Hsu, and Mr Simon Wu for their comments to early drafts and Professor Junji Nakagawa for the helpful discussion in the conference.

[1] T. Terada, 'Constructing an "East Asian" Concept and Growing Regional Identity: From EAEC to ASEAN+3' (2003) 16 Pac Rev 251, at 251.

[2] L. Byung-Woon, 'Building the Northeast Asian Community' (2004) 11 Ind J Glob Leg Stud 257, at 261.

[3] B. Desker, 'In Defence of FTAs: From Purity to Pragmatism in East Asia' (2004) 17 Pac Rev 3, at 4.

vehicles for economic cooperation.[4] Among all recent high-profile RTAs in East Asia, the blueprint of an East Asia Free Trade Agreement (East Asia FTA) is the most exciting one.[5] If materialized, it will be a big step forward for East Asia integration—a broad and deep RTA which is rule-governed, institutionalized, and WTO-consistent.

Behind the cheerful picture of the proposed East Asia FTA, an important point has to be bear in mind—the success of a RTA is very much contingent on the design of such agreement and its implementation.[6] Among the possible reasons leading to the failure of a RTA, the most significant one is the absence of a properly designed dispute settlement mechanism (DSM) to secure adequate implementation of commitments. In this sense, an 'appropriate' DSM will be one of the crucial prerequisites for the success of the proposed East Asia FTA. But what makes a DSM 'appropriate' to East Asia?

This chapter attempts to answer this question by analysing both the regionalism in East Asia and the experience of existing DSMs in other regions. In section II, the recent development of regionalism in East Asia will be examined, demonstrating the general trend of East Asian countries from 'single track'—mainly supporting multilateral trade liberalization through the WTO—to 'double track'—promoting free trade at both international and regional level. It will provide the political economy background of the proposed East Asia FTA. In section III, the focus turns to the rationale of the design of DSMs in RTAs, highlighting six legal factors, which differentiate the DSMs and should be taken into account in designing a new DSM. The DSMs in three typical RTAs—the Association of Southeast Asian Nations (ASEAN), the North American Free Trade Agreement (NAFTA), and the European Union (EU)—will be accessed, including their efficiency and their contributions to the respective integration processes. Section IV will provide several legal alternatives to the proposed East Asia FTA and access their merits. Finally, section V as a conclusion will contain a proposal for the proposed East Asia FTA.

---

[4] *Ibid.*, at 3. This shift in East Asia has been described as from a focus on multilateral trade liberalization through the WTO to a pragmatic approach favouring bilateral and regional FTAs while continuing to support the WTO system.

[5] Terada, above at n 1, at 274. On the other side, several impediments to the creation of an East Asia FTA have also been widely discussed. For instance, the ASEAN's fear to be possibly marginalized has been recognized as a major one. Moreover, the increased concerns from some non-member countries, in particular US, could also be an impediment.

[6] H. Shams, 'Regional Integration: Comparative Experience—Introduction' (2004) 10 Law & Bus Rev Am 457, at 458.

II. THE DEVELOPMENT OF REGIONALISM IN EAST ASIA

A. Regional Integration in East Asia

More and more countries in the world are now enjoying significant benefits from the regional integration process of their region.[7] Closer European integration and a number of regional initiatives from the US fundamentally transformed the global economic climate after 1980s.[8] Under this global trend of regionalism, East Asian countries have also been alerted to the potential benefit of promoting regionalism in economic diplomacy.[9] The ideas of an integrated East Asia started emerging in early 1990s.[10] Without a strong conceptual framework and not well-designed, the later development of East Asia integration was rather slow and painful. Nonetheless, the past decade has witnessed both the de facto economic integration and the changing perception of East Asian countries towards regionalism.

Economically, East Asian countries have realized that their economics were much more deeply interconnected than they might have imagined before. The trade volume between East Asian countries was doubled or even tripled in the last decade.[11] In 2003, total intra-regional trade volume hit US$918.02 billion, accounting for 54.5 per cent of the region's total exports.[12] Unfortunately, this interdependence and interconnection has not only been evidenced by the increase of the intra-regional trade, but also by the Asia Financial Crisis in 1997–1998. After about 30 years economic boosting, of which the extra-regional trade, rather than intra-regional trade, was believed as the main engine, the Asia Financial Crisis made East Asian countries painfully aware of their mutual dependence. The fact that the financial crisis in Thailand, which appeared to be isolated, soon spread to other East Asian countries, highlighted the negative aspect of interdependence.[13] In a way, this crisis shed light on the refreshed enthusiasm of regionalism in East Asia. After that, it is impossible to deny that the de facto economic integration has gone much deeper and the

[7] Terada, above at n 1, at 252.

[8] R.R. Elliott and K. Ikemoto, 'AFTA and the Asian Crisis: Help or Hindrance to ASEAN Intra-Regional Trade?' (2004) 18 Asian Econ J 1, at 2.

[9] Desker, above at n 3, at 9.

[10] Terada, above at n 1, at 251. The first comprehensive proposal for East Asia integration was East Asian Economic Caucus (EAEC), which was put forward by Prime Minister Mahatir of Malaysia in early 1990s.

[11] A. Carstens, 'Making Regional Economic Integration Work', Speech at the 20th Annual General Meeting and Conference of the Pakistan Society of Development Economists, Islamabad, Pakistan, 12 January 2005, available at www.imf.org/external/np/speeches/2005/011205.htm (visited 3 March 2006). The speaker stated that intra-regional trade is particularly large within Europe and Asia—in the European Union (EU), about 60 per cent of the countries' external trade remains within the region and in East Asia the share is about 50 per cent.

[12] 'China, Japan, ROK, ASEAN to Start FTA Feasibility Study soon', People's Daily, 24 January 2005, available at english.people.com.cn/200501/24/eng20050124_171679.html# (visited 3 March 2006).

[13] Terada, above at n 1, at 266.

institutionalization of cooperation mechanism is more or less a catch-up in responding to economic reality.

On the other side, the development of regionalism in East Asia has been boosted not only because the East Asian countries felt isolated when other regional institutions have successfully created or advanced their regional identities, but also because of their gradual, but fundamental, change of perception towards regionalism: from building a closed trade bloc to open regionalism.[14]

The history of East Asia integration in 1990s clearly reflects this changing perception. In the early 1990s, the first proposal for comprehensive East Asia integration, East Asian Economic Caucus (EAEC), from Prime Minister Mahatir of Malaysia, was sought to create a 'yellow Asian' entity and embraced a racist notion of Asianism.[15] Not surprisingly, this proposal, which was aiming to create a closed, discriminatory, and race-oriented bloc, gained very little support from Japan, China, and even other ASEAN countries and finally failed to be realized.[16] After that, for almost 10 years, no influential proposal for comprehensive integration emerged. Instead, East Asian countries actively engaged in WTO-consistent bilateral or plurilateral RTAs within or across the regime and gradually built up an open RTA network for regional integration.

The shifting attitudes of two leading economies in the past decade also illustrated the changing theme of regionalism in East Asia. In the early 1990s, Japan's lukewarm attitude towards the EAEC and East Asia integration can be explained by two main reasons: Japan's self-imposed international identity and its US-centred foreign policy.[17] The desire to avoid reminding Asian countries of the Pacific War and to eliminate the long-standing mistrust of its neighbours was the first important consideration behind Japan's hesitation towards East Asia integration.[18] The US's overwhelming position in Japan's security and economic policies also makes it rather difficult for Japan to take the lead in East Asia integration, which would exclude the participation of the US.[19] However, after the Asian Financial Crisis, along with the materialization and the gradual development of ASEAN + 3 meeting,[20] Japan started realizing its growing political interest in the region.[21] The motivation is relatively simple: Japan cannot afford to be 'left-out' in this process and lose its leading position in East Asia area, especially in front of a fast-growing China.

---

[14] For general discussion of open regionalism, *see* H.E.S. Nesadurai, *Globalization, Domestic Politics and Regionalism: The ASEAN Free Trade Area* (London: Routledge, 2003), 50.

[15] Terada, above at n 1, at 260.   [16] *Ibid.*   [17] *Ibid.*, at 258.

[18] For example, Byung-Woon, above at n 2, at 301 and also J. Wang, 'China's Regional Trade Agreements: The Law, Geopolitics, and Impact on the Multilateral Trading System' (2004) 8 SYIL 119, at 140.

[19] Terada, above at n 1, at 259.

[20] From 1997, ASEAN invited Japan, South Korea and China to their informal summit meeting, so-called ASEAN + 3. After several years' development, ASEAN + 3 became an important foundation for further integration. For more details, *see* Strengthening ASEAN + 3 Co-operation (Chairman's Statement of the 8th ASEAN + 3 Summit), available at www.aseansec.org/16847.htm (visited 3 March 2006).

[21] Terada, above at n 1, at 268.

To a certain extent, China's dynamic movements in initiating, negotiating, and signing RTAs within the region are one of the direct stimuli for the recent development of regionalism in East Asia. After its accession to the WTO, China showed the world not only its irrevocable and irreversible commitment to international trading system, but also its changing perception of both globalization and regionalism.[22] By being an active player in multilateral and regional forums, China made itself clear that it is no longer that isolated, dangerous 'dragon' which may threat its neighbours and the world.[23] Rather, it is playing the regionalism card in a constructive way, intending to share the benefits of each other's growing economics with its neighbours and promoting peace and common security in the region.[24] In the long run, China is also expecting that a closer regional tie with other East Asian countries can enhance its bargaining power and influence over rule making of multilateral fora, *inter alia*, the WTO.

In sum, regional integration in East Asia, unlike European integration, started without a strong conceptual framework and a strong leadership. Rather, it went through a pragmatic and slow process.[25] In the late 1990s, economic incentives, such as the surge of intra-regional trade and the regional resolution of Asian Financial Crisis, largely promoted the development of regionalism in East Asia. More ideologically, the changing perception of regionalism in East Asian countries, in particular Japan and China, confirm the belief that open regionalism, by following a WTO-consistent path, is in the interest of all East Asian states. The recent high profile of RTAs in the region best evidenced this changing perception.

B. Proliferation of RTAs: An overview

The past decade, in particular after the Asian Financial Crisis, witnessed not only the conceptual construction of an East Asia identity, but also, the institutionalization of East Asia regional cooperation. One aspect is the significant increase of RTAs in the region—East Asia is quickly becoming a locus of proliferating RTAs.[26] The oldest regional cooperation mechanism, ASEAN, by shifting its emphasis into greater economic cooperation, launched its relatively ambitious ASEAN Free Trade Area (AFTA) project in 1992.[27] Other economies, either intending to catch up the worldwide trend of regionalism, or disappointed by the slowdown in trade liberalization in the WTO, have also

---

[22] Q. Kong, 'China's WTO Accession and the ASEAN-China Free Trade Area—The Perspective of a Chinese Lawyer' (2004) 7 JIEL 839, at 842.

[23] Wang, above at n 18, at 140.   [24] *Ibid.*, at 141.

[25] J.L. Tongzon, *The Economics of Southeast Asia: Before and After the Crisis*, 2nd ed. (Cheltenham: Edward Elgar, 2002), 3.

[26] W. Choi, 'Regional Economic Integration in East Asia: Prospect and Jurisprudence' (2003) 6 JIEL 49, at 55.

[27] L. Tan, 'Will ASEAN Economic Integration Progress Beyond a Free Trade Area?' (2004) 53 ICLQ 935, at 935.

moved into high gear in engaging bilateral or plurilateral RTAs, within or across the region.

1. The ASEAN—Achievements and Limitations

On 8 August 1967 in Bangkok, the ASEAN was born with five founding members of Indonesia, Malaysia, the Philippines, Singapore, and Thailand.[28] The *raison d'etre* of ASEAN was a political one—to promote regional peace, security, and stability.[29] After more than 30 years' development, ASEAN formally encompassed all ten countries of Southeast Asia in 1999, becoming the first and the foremost formalized regional vehicle in East Asia.

Despite its long history, however, the development of ASEAN and its impact on both economic and socio-political integration can never compare to the EU and the NAFTA. Economic empirical studies indicate that ASEAN has had only a modest impact on trade liberalization in the East Asia, even after the launch of a rather ambitious AFTA project in 1992.[30] Due to its problematic implementation, it is unsafe to conclude that the AFTA has in fact increased intra-ASEAN trade and promoted regional growth.[31]

The major reason for the limited success of AFTA is, arguably, lack of proper institutional and legal framework.[32] The ASEAN has remained as a loose agreement for three decades. Instead of emulating the Western concept of 'rule-based' regionalism, the ASEAN countries chose to go in an 'ASEAN Way'—cooperation without supranational institutions for decision-making or enforcing community rules.[33] In absence of such kind of legal framework, the governments frequently abused and backtracked the trade liberalization commitments that have been made.[34]

The implementation of CEPT can be an illustrative example of this problem. Despite its achievements on tariff cuts,[35] the implementation of CEPT is, however, a mixed blessing rather than a clear victory. Since it is at a member's discretion to decide what products should be excluded from the tariff reduction, the implementation of CEPT was at times problematic as one or another

---

[28] Tongzon, above at n 25, at 3.

[29] Tan, above at n 27, at 935 and also M.T. Yeung, N. Perdikis, and W.A. Kerr, *Regional Trading Blocs in the Global Economy—The EU and ASEAN* (Cheltenham UK, Northampton, MA: Edward Elgar, 1999), 45.

[30] For general comments on AFTA: T.C. Fischer, 'A Commentary on Regional Institutions in the Pacific Rim: Do APEC and ASEAN Still Matter?' (2003) 13 Duke J Comp & Int L, 337, at 353; for the economic analysis of the effect of AFTA on intra- and extra- regional trade flow: Elliott and Ikemoto, above at n 8, at 16. The authors concluded that trade flows were not significantly affected in the years immediately following the signing of the AFTA agreement in 1993. However, they did find some evidence of a positive AFTA effect that, although limited at first, gradually increased.

[31] Nesadurai, above at n 14, at 51.   [32] *Ibid.*, at 58.   [33] Tan, above at n 27, at 949.

[34] *Ibid.*, at 941.

[35] *Ibid.*, at 940–41. As reported, in 2003, CEPT Package showed that 99.55 per cent of intra-ASEAN 6 trade were in the 0–5 per cent category and zero tariff rates are expected to be achieved by 2010 for the ASEAN 6 and 2015 for the other members with flexibility on some sensitive products until 2018.

government attempted to withhold participation in CEPT or backtracked on commitments already made for certain products.[36] This led to a number of disputes among members.[37] For instance, a dispute emerged between Malaysia and Thailand, when the former backtracked on its early commitment to reduce the tariff on its automotive sector. Malaysia's request was opposed by Thailand, which intimated that it would delay cuts on its palm-oil duties.[38]

The flexibility of CEPT or AFTA is not, in itself, a weakness. Rather, the absence of strong and effective DSM in ASEAN is more likely to contribute to the abuse or backtracking of the programs.[39] As argued, the preference in ASEAN for political rather than administrative or juridical arrangements for dispute settlement and problem resolution has actually placed a substantial burden on agendas in AFTA.[40] Although it is unfair to conclude that the 'ASEAN way' has done nothing good for the regional cooperation in East Asia, it is quite clear that the inability of ASEAN to have any legal controls over the economic cooperation is very dangerous to further integration.

2. *Other Bilateral and Plurilateral RTAs*

Reflecting the positive approach of key East Asian economies towards open regionalism, apart from ambitious AFTA programme among ASEAN countries, other economies have also taken their own initiatives to engage in bilateral or plurilateral RTAs, within or across the region, as demonstrated by Figure 1.[41] Even though at the moment, it is too early to draw a conclusion as to the real effect of most of those RTAs, or proposed RTAs, they are, as argued, forming a lattice network within the region, which may pave the way to a single trading bloc, an East Asia FTA.[42]

A. CHINA'S INITIATIVES TOWARDS FTAS[43]

Soon after the conclusion of China's negotiations for accession to the WTO, in November 2000, Chinese Premier Zhu Rongji proposed the establishment of a China–ASEAN FTA (ACFTA) at his meeting with ASEAN leaders.[44] After a careful feasibility study, China and ASEAN agreed to set up a Free Trade Area over a period of 10 years at the fifth China-ASEAN Summit.[45] On November 2002, the Framework Agreement for the ACFTA has been reached at the summit in Cambodia. This agreement, much more than a declaration of economic cooperation, officially commenced the process for the establishment of the ACFTA by prescribing guiding principles and laying down a general

---

[36] Nesadurai, above at n 14, at 50.

[37] *Ibid.* In the last few years, the disputes greatly increased in agriculture, automobiles, and petrochemicals sectors.

[38] Tan, above at n 27, at 941.   [39] Nesadurai, above at n 14, at 58.   [40] *Ibid.*

[41] *Ibid.*   [42] Desker, above at n 3, at 3.

[43] Many commentators have addressed to the details of China's movements on RTAs, their impacts and the motivations behind those initiatives. For example, Wang, above at n 18, Kong, above at n 22 and S. Chirathivat, 'ASEAN–China Free Trade Area: Background, Implications and Future Development' (2002) 13 J Asian Econ 671.

[44] Wang, *ibid.*, at 124.   [45] Kong, above at n 22, at 841.

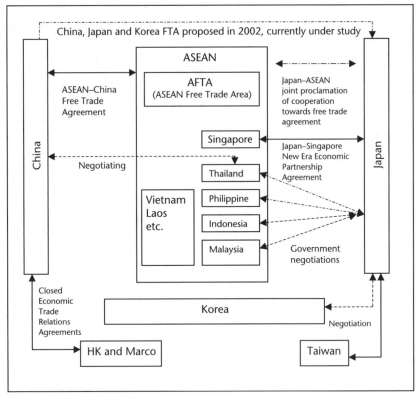

Figure 1. The Current State of East Asia's FTAs
Sources: adapted from EU–Japan Business Dialogue Round Table 2004, June 2004, Tokyo

pattern and a timetable for the ACFTA.[46] If successful, such ACFTA would involve 1.7 billon people, a GDP of about US$2 trillion and two-way trade valued at US$1.23 trillion—so far, the largest free trade area in the world.[47]

Meanwhile, China concluded its first official FTA with Hong Kong Special Administrative Region (Hong Kong SRA), a separate customs territory under WTO, in June 2003.[48] This FTA is formally entitled the Mainland and Hong Kong Closer Economic Partnership Agreement (CEPA). Three and a half months later, the Mainland concluded an identical agreement with Macao.[49] On 27th August 2004, the Mainland and Hong Kong SAR governments

---

[46] *Ibid.*, at 842.   [47] Desker, above at n 3, at 13.

[48] The official website of the China–HK CEPA is www.tid.gov.hk/english/cepa/index.html (visited 3 March 2006). Wang, above at n 18, at 122. For the legal status of CEPA: W. Wang, 'CEPA: A Lawful Free Trade Agreement under "One Country, Two Customs Territories?"' (2004) 10 Law & Bus Rev Am 647.

[49] The official website of the China–Macau CEPA is www.macau.gov.mo/cepa.phtml?lang=en (visited 3 March 2006).

signed Supplement to CEPA (CEPA II), in providing further liberalization and market access for good and services.[50]

As an adopted and materialized version of the early idea of a China Free Trade Area linking Greater China, the CEPA covers three broad areas—trade in goods, trade in services, and trade and investment facilitation.[51] In respect of trade in goods, as of 1 January 2005, China undertook to eliminate tariffs on total 1087 categories of HK products.[52] Non-tariff measures, except for safeguards, are precluded by CEPA.[53] In terms of trade in services, CEPA grants market access to the mainland to a total of 26 service sectors. In the prescribed 26 industries, HK service providers can enjoy preferential treatment ahead of China's WTO timetable.[54] In addition, CEPA also provided trade and investment facilitation through greater transparency, standardization and enhanced information change.

B JAPAN'S ENTHUSIASTIC ENGAGEMENT WITH REGIONALISM

As indicated in the previous section, Japan has been uncommitted to East Asia integration for quite a long time.[55] However, the changing climate, both inside and outside Japan, has prompted Japan to work out its new policy— enthusiastically supporting East Asia integration and showing its readiness to lead the creation of an East Asian community.[56]

The first fruit of Japan's paradigm shift is the Agreement between Singapore and Japan for a New-Age Economic Partnership (JSEAP). It is the first bilateral RTA Japan has ever negotiated. As a comprehensive RTA, it covers not only traditional trade issues which are staples of WTO negotiation, but also issues such as competition policy, supporting research and development in science and technology.[57] In the hope of Japan, this forward-looking FTA may anchor Japanese commitment to the region and provide a model of cooperation for further regionalism.[58]

Moreover, in responding to China's move of establishing the China–ASEAN FTA, Japan also signed a joint Declaration in 2002 that ASEAN and Japan would realize the Comprehensive Economic Partnership (AJCEP) within 10 years, including elements of an FTA.[59] By announcing this AJCEP proposal, Japan made its intention of maintaining a strategic balance in the region very clear.

Meanwhile, Japan has also worked with its northeast neighbour, the Republic of Korea (ROK), for a comprehensive bilateral FTA between these

---

[50] Supplement to CEPA, available at www.tid.gov.hk/english/cepa/cepa2.html (visited 3 March 2006).
[51] Wang, above at n 18, at 122 and Desker, above at n 3, at 14.
[52] Prior to CEPA II, a total of 374 categories were eligible for zero tariff. According to the Main Agreement of CEPA, Art. 5(3) and Arts 1 and 5 of Annex 1, 713 product categories were added in CEPA II: www.tid.gov.hk/english/cepa/files/CEPAII_summary.pdf (visited 3 March 2006).
[53] Arts 6, 7 and 8 of the Main Agreement of CEPA.   [54] Wang, above at n 18, at 123.
[55] Terada, above at n 1, at 273.   [56] Choi, above at n 26, at 52.
[57] Desker, above at n 3, at 11–2.   [58] Choi, above at n 26, at 53.
[59] Desker, above at n 3, at 12.

two most advanced economics in East Asia. In early 2004, Japan and ROK formally launched their negotiation in establishing a Japan–ROK FTA (JKFTA).[60] This ambitious FTA would, as proposed in a feasibility study released in 2001, aim at a comprehensive framework for economic integration encompassing market integration measures, such as investment promotion, trade facilitation, and harmonized trade and investment rules and standards, in addition to eliminating tariff and non-tariff barriers to trade.[61]

C SINGAPORE: HUB OF EAST ASIAN REGIONALISM?[62]

Strategically placed as a hub for the region, Singapore has been most active in promoting FTAs. Not including AFTA, it concluded, or is embarking on, FTAs with almost all strategic trading partners in the world.[63] To some extent, Singapore would prefer the accolade that it is playing a 'path-finder' role, an outreach partner of ASEAN eager to forge strategic and economic alliances with other regions and countries around the world.[64]

Among its FTAs, US–Singapore Free Trade Agreement (USSFTA), which came into force on 1 January 2004, is a landmark one.[65] Generally patterned after NAFTA, this agreement covers a considerable range of subjects including trade in goods, trade in services, investment, e-commerce, intellectual property rights, competition policy, and so on.[66] It is, as its proponents claimed, an FTA that covers substantially all trade and consistent with WTO obligations.[67]

C. Prospect of a Broad East Asia RTA

Given the dynamics of recent East Asia integration, it is not surprising that the prospect of a single trading bloc in East Asia has been widely discussed in both academic and diplomatic circles.[68] Most recently, with the experience of CAFTA-DR and ASEAN + 3 meetings, China took the first move by officially proposing an East Asia FTA, which will cover China, Japan, the Republic of Korea, and the 10-member ASEAN nations in 2003, and urging a feasibility study for this envisaged FTA.[69] It is fair to observe that this broad East Asia FTA is still at the conceptual stage. Nevertheless, with the surge of RTAs in East Asia, which, to a certain degree, has underpinned the eventual

---

[60] *Ibid.*, at 11.   [61] *Ibid.*

[62] For general comments on Singapore's recent movements on RTAs: C. Feng, 'Recent Developments in Singapore on International Law' (2004) 8 SYIL 207.

[63] So far, Singapore has concluded FTAs with New Zealand, the US, Japan, Canada, Mexico, India, Korea, EFTA, and Australia.

[64] Desker, above at n 3, at 19.

[65] Feng, above at n 62, at 210; for general comments on USSFTA: S.S. Lim, 'The US–Singapore Free Trade Agreement: Fostering Confidence and Commitment in Asia' (2004) 34 Cal W Int L J 301.

[66] Desker, above at n 3, at 18.   [67] *Ibid.*, at 19.

[68] For example, Choi, above at n 26, Desker, above at n 3, Tan, above at n 27, and Terada, above at n 1.

[69] People's Daily, above at n 12.

establishment of a single trading bloc, one can cautiously anticipate an East Asia FTA may emerge as the result of consolidation of the existing bilateral and regional FTAs.[70]

This proposed FTA might bring several key benefits to East Asian countries. First and foremost, the proposed East Asia FTA is expected to significantly boost intra-regional trade and investment. On the demand side, a broadened East Asian FTA will, on the basis of already vigorous trade and investment flow in the region, create a giant common market similar to EU and NAFTA.[71] As illustrated in Table 1, along with an expanded EU and an FTAA, three nearly equal giant markets will emerge.[72] On the supply side, elimination of internal barriers within the region is supposed to build efficient inner region production/distribution networks as a single unit.[73] Varying tariff rates on parts in each country are now burdensome and weakening the competitiveness of Asian products in the global market.[74] Thus, the creation of an East Asia FTA would, in theory, enhance the economic welfare of participating states and maintain the competitiveness of East Asian economics.[75]

The potential socio-political benefits of a broad East Asia FTA are also clear.

Table 1. Market Scales of East Asia FTA, EU and FTAA

Market Scale – Broad East Asia FTA, EU and FTAA (2003)

		East Asia	Expanded EU	FTAA
Population		2,005 million	480 million	810 million
Nominal GDP	2003	$7.4 trillion	$11.0 trillion	$13.4 trillion
	2013*	*$15.6 trillion*	*$19.9 trillion*	*$23.3 trillion*
Real GDP Growth Rate* (Annual average 2004–13)		3.7%	2.3%	3.3%
Imports	Actual	$1.7 trillion	$2.9 trillion	$1.8 trillion
	Global Share	22%	37%	23%

* Estimates by Marubeni Research Institute.

Source: IMF and US CENSUS.

[70] Terada, above at n 1, at 272.   [71] Byung-Woon, above at n 2, at 290.

[72] T. Tsuji, 'Towards an East Asia FTA', a presentation in EU–Japan Business Dialogue Round Table 2004, available at www.eujapan.com/roundtable/presentations_marubenicorporation_june04.pdf (visited 3 March 2006).

[73] *Ibid.* For instance, in the motor vehicle industry, a production network has been forming, within which the ASEAN countries or China produce different components such as gasoline engines, while Japan or Korea produce the advanced engine related parts.

[74] *Ibid.*   [75] Byung-Woon, above at n 2, at 262.

A more economically interdependent East Asia community would facilitate the resolution of existing mistrust and disputes among participating states.[76] Moreover, as the successful experience of the ASEAN countries in Uruguay Round suggested, speaking as a single voice may significantly increase the weight of East Asian countries in multilateral fora. In particular, Japan and China are anticipating that an East Asia trading bloc may enhance their bargaining powers in the future multilateral trade talks.[77]

Despite all potential benefits from the creation of an East Asia FTA, several serious concerns are also worth mentioning. First, it is argued, this East Asia FTA will be the most difficult to conclude as it mirrors the divisions within the WTO which have slowed down Doha Round negotiations.[78] For instance, Japan and South Korea are opposed to agriculture liberalization, the sector offering greatest gains for ASEAN countries such as Thailand and the Philippines. The divergence between East Asian countries implies their comparative advantages in different products, which in a way guarantees potential benefits of creating a common market. Nevertheless, it also indicates the difficulty of harmonization, which is an essential impediment of further integration.

More crucially, even if the agreement could be concluded, the process of realizing such an expanding FTA will be nothing if not painful. As the experience of AFTA indicated, there is always a tension between the 'Asian Way' to achieve economic cooperation—i.e. not through rules and regulations, but through discussion, consultation and consensus—and the treaty compliance.[79] The preference of diplomacy rather than litigation in settling disputes may leave the proposed RTA vulnerable and powerless in preventing abuse and backtracking. Hence, how to adopt a legalistic DSM is one of the key challenges for future regionalization in East Asia.

III. DISPUTE SETTLEMENT MECHANISMS (DSMS) IN RTAS

A. Legal Factors to Differentiate DSMs

In the last decade, as a reflection of the growing importance of the rule of law in regional integration, more and more regional DSMs are moving towards an adjudication regime, patterning the WTO and other advanced RTAs such as EU and NAFTA.[80] While it sometimes appears as if each new regional agreement is reinventing the wheel, some general rules can be detected in designing

---

[76] Kong, above at n 22, at 844.   [77] *Ibid.*, at 845.   [78] Desker, above at n 3, at 16.

[79] P.J. Davidson, 'The ASEAN Way and the Role of Law in ASEAN Economic Cooperation' (2004) 8 SYIL 165, at 165.

[80] M. Cremona, 'Regional Integration and the Rule of Law: Some Issues and Options', in R. Devlin and A. Estevadeordal (eds), *Bridges for Development—Policies and Institutions for Trade and Integration* (Washington DC: Inter-American Development Bank, 2003), 156.

a new DSM.[81] In particular, a combination of six legal factors—jurisdiction, institutional feature, binding effect and enforcement, standing of non-state actors, enforceability of awards at national court, and transparency of proceedings—may legally classify various types of DSM and provide alternatives to construct an effective DSM.[82]

In this combination, jurisdiction indicates the coverage of a particular DSM, i.e. whether it applies to the disputes relating to all agreements, such as the WTO DSM, or covers only disputes with a specific subject. The institutional feature of a DSM refers to the distinction between the permanent tribunals such as ECJ and the *ad hoc* arbitration tribunals, such as NAFTA Chapter 11 tribunal, or the combination of both, such as the WTO panels and Appellate Body. Binding effect of dispute settlement awards or reports considers whether decisions of dispute settlement tribunals are binding to the Member States, while enforcement, as the opposite side of the same coin, measures the effectiveness of DSM by focusing upon its mechanisms for treaty compliance. Both the direct access of non-state actors to the DSM and the enforceability of dispute settlement awards or reports at national court are important factors differentiating the impact of a DSM to domestic legal system of a Member State. Finally, transparency refers to the clarity of procedures and decisions, and the extent to which they are made public. The differences in each of the six factors and the combination of them may dictate the form and function of different DSMs.

The following sections will use these factors in analysing the DSMs in three typical RTAs—the ASEAN, the NAFTA, and the EU, as summarized at Table 2. It has to be borne in mind that the DSM has always evolved along with the development of regionalism in the respective regions. The focus here is, however, the current status of DSMs, rather than their evolutionary history.

B. The ASEAN DSM

Traditionally, ASEAN has followed the 'ASEAN way' in both decision-making and dispute settlement.[83] Embodied in Malay terms *musyawarah* (decision-making through discussion and consultation) and *mufakat* (unanimous decision that is arrived at), the ASEAN way reflects the reluctance of members to be too legalistic and the preference of political and diplomatic rather than judicial or quasi-judicial resolution of disputes.[84] Nevertheless, the 2004 Protocol on Enhanced Dispute Settlement Mechanism (the Protocol) indicates the ASEAN's movement towards a legalistic, rule-based institution.[85] In comparison with its predecessor, the Protocol considerably improved the

[81] A.K. Schneider, 'Getting Along: The Evolution of Dispute Resolution Regimes in International Trade Organizations' (1999) 20 Mich J Int L 697, at 700.

[82] *Ibid.*, at 703.   [83] Davidson, above at n 79, at 166.   [84] *Ibid.*, at 167–71.

[85] This Protocol was signed on 29 November 2004 and replaced the 1996 Protocol on DSM. The text is available at www.aseansec.org/16755.htm (visited 3 March 2006).

Table 2. Legal Factors of DSMs in the ASEAN, NAFTA and the EU

	Jurisdiction	Institutional Feature	Binding Effect and Enforcement	Standing of non-state actors	Enforceability at national court	Transparency
ASEAN DSM	Existing and future ASEAN Economic Agreements	Combined *ad hoc* penal and permanent Appellate Body	Yes, similar enforcement measures to the WTO DSM, with several improvements	No	No	No
NAFTA	Chapter 20	All NAFTA Chapters without special DSM	*Ad hoc* arbitration	Not binding, weak enforcement	No	No
	Chapter 19	Chapter 19 of NAFTA (AD/CVD Disputes)	Bi-national panel (*ad hoc*)	Binding and enforceable	Yes	Yes
	Chapter 11	Chapter 11 of NAFTA (Investor-state Disputes)	*Ad hoc* arbitration (Under ICSID and UNCITRAL)	Binding, but only monetary damage involved	Yes	Yes
EU	Direct Actions Against MS (Arts 226 and 227)	All EU Treaties and Secondary legislations	Permanent Court (ECJ and CFI)	Binding, after TEU, with monetary punishment	Yes, but only the Commission, not the private actors	No
	Preliminary Ruling (Art. 234)	All EU Treaties and community acts	Permanent Court (ECJ and national courts)	Binding	Yes	Yes

institutional framework of DSM, particularly by establishing an independent Appellate Body. On paper, this new DSM has moved away from a negotiation forum and is adjudicatory in nature.

This new Protocol, with 21 articles and two Annexes, provides detailed rules for the whole dispute settlement process—from consultation, panel proceeding, appeal, to implementation and compensation. Articles 1 and 2 set out the general framework of this DSM, i.e. the coverage of application and administration of the Protocol. Here, the Senior Economic Officials Meeting (SEOM) is introduced as an equivalent of the DSB in the WTO DSM.[86] Articles 3 and 4, identical to Articles 4 and 5 of DSU, provide the consultation, and good office, conciliation, or mediation procedures, with the same timetable as the DSU.[87]

Articles 5 to 11 of the Protocol concern the panel process, from the establishment of the panel to the function of the panel. The ASEAN panel, established by SEOM, has its own working procedures, as provided by Annex II of the Protocol. Notably, the ASEAN panels are under even tougher time pressure than the WTO panel, since they have to submit their findings and recommendations within 60 days of their establishment.[88]

The panel ruling is appellable to an independent Appellate Body established by the ASEAN Economic Ministers (AEM), which has a similar function to the WTO Appellate Body, according to Article 12.[89] This is one of the most significant improvements of the 2004 Protocol. This Appellate Body, composed of seven persons who are unaffiliated with any government, has the power to uphold, modify or reverse the legal interpretations adopted by the panel. Once issued, its report shall be adopted by the SEOM and 'unconditionally accepted by the parties', unless the SEOM decides by consensus not to adopt the report.[90] Moreover, the ASEAN panel or Appellate Body report may not only recommend that the member concerned should bring the measure into conformity, as the WTO panels and Appellate Body do, but also suggest 'ways in which the Member could implement the recommendations'.[91]

With respect to implementation, the Protocol imposes a fixed period—60 days—to comply with the report after the adoption of that report from panels or Appellate Body, unless the parties to the dispute agree on a longer period of time, as provided by Article 15(1).[92] In exceptional circumstances, if the actions required to comply with the panel or Appellate Body report are complex enough, the request for a long period of time shall not be unreasonably denied.[93] Most importantly, the issue of implementation may be raised at the SEOM by 'any' member at any time after their adoption and will remain on the SEOM's agenda until the issue is resolved.[94] Before finally resolved, the party concerned is obligated to provide the SEOM with a status report in

---

[86] Art. 2(1) of the Protocol.   [87] *Ibid.*, Art. 3(4).   [88] *Ibid.*, Art. 8(2).
[89] *Ibid.*, Art. 12(1).   [90] *Ibid.*, Arts 12(3), 6 and 13.   [91] *Ibid.*, Art. 14(1).
[92] *Ibid.*, Art. 15(1).   [93] *Ibid.*, Art. 15(2).   [94] *Ibid.*, Art. 15(6).

writing of its progress in the implementation at least 10 days prior to each such SEOM meeting.[95]

The Protocol also differentiates from the DSU in terms of compensation and the suspension of concessions, since it takes a broader interpretation of the 'sector', supplementary to the principle that the suspension of concessions should be in the same sector.[96] Article 16(3)(e) reads, 'for the purpose of this article, "sector" means: with respect to goods, all goods'. Accordingly, if the losing party fails to implement a panel or Appellate Body report concerning trade in goods, the retaliation may involve all sectors of trade in goods and the pressure for compliance is therefore increased.

Finally, Article 17 of the Protocol established an ASEAN DSM Fund to meet the expenses of the panels, the Appellate Body and any related administration costs.[97] This fund is a revolving fund, separate from ASEAN Secretariat's regular budget.[98]

Generally, the new ASEAN DSM is predominantly modelled on the WTO DSM. Most provisions in the Protocol can find their equivalents in the WTO DSU. However, at some points, the Protocol may be considered as an advanced version of the DSU, since it learned lessons from the current controversies of the WTO DSM and cured some of its drawbacks. For example, the new ASEAN panels and Appellate Body are entitled not only to draw the conclusion of consistency of the national measures in dispute, but also to make practical suggestions to the implementation. This might be an effective means to avoid future disagreements on the meaning of compliance in the panel or Appellate Body reports. The 60 days deadline also ensures the promptness of compliance, which is always controversial due to the ambiguous 'reasonable period of time' in Article 21.3 of the DSU. Moreover, the possibility of any member to raise the issue of implementation in the SEOM and the obligation of the losing party to report its implementation status to the SEOM significantly increases the pressure of compliance and, indeed, makes the process more focused on securing the community rules than on pure dispute resolution. It provides, in another sense, an example of the potential advantage of regional arrangements—although the insufficiencies suffered by the DSU have been widely discussed, the slow process of multilateral trade negotiation makes it impossible to improve them in a short period of time. But at the regional level, given the limited number of members, it is easier to reach consensus and improve the DSM.

As indicated in Table 2, the ASEAN DSM covers all ASEAN economic agreements, even the future ones. Institutionally, it is a combination of an *ad hoc* panel system and a permanent Appellate Body. The reports from this DSM are binding and there are strong enforcement mechanisms. In addition to the menu of enforcement options similar to the WTO, the Protocol also

---

[95] *Ibid.*, Art. 15(6).   [96] *Ibid.*, Art. 16(3)(a).   [97] *Ibid.*, Art. 17(2).
[98] *Ibid.*, Art. 17(1).

placed the issue of implementation on the agenda of every SEOM meeting until it has been resolved.[99] In this way, there will be public embarrassment for non-compliance, which could be a very powerful punishment for governments of ASEAN Members, given the cultural tradition of ASEAN countries.

Nevertheless, there is no standing for non-state actors and its reports are not enforceable at national court. With respect to transparency, the whole proceeding is confidential although, in limited circumstance, the non-confidential summary of the information contained in parties' written submissions could be disclosed to the public.[100]

C. The NAFTA DSMs

When the NAFTA became effective in 1994, it incorporated several specialized DSMs to deal with disputes relating to different subject matters.[101] In particular, there are three principle mechanisms, namely the general DSM in Chapter 20, the Anti-dumping and Countervailing Duty (AD/CVD) DSM in Chapter 19, and the investor-state dispute resolution in Chapter 11.[102] With different rules of procedures, these three mechanisms vary considerably as indicated in Table 2. However, they have something in common: they all serve as the main channels for resolving trade and investment conflicts in North America.[103] As argued, the overall record of litigation between NAFTA partners over the past 10 years indicates that 'agreed rules, not power politics, have determined outcomes (of disputes)'.[104]

The legal basis of dispute resolution relating to NAFTA's interpretation or application is the dispute settlement provisions of Chapter 20.[105] This general DSM, similar with DSMs contained in most FTAs and the WTO DSM, is characterized as 'a traditional state-to-state *ad hoc* arbitration system', with an intention to resolve dispute by agreement, if at all possible.[106] Before the issue of the panel report, the Chapter 20 DSM is almost identical to the WTO DSM. However, Chapter 20 proceedings produce only non-binding findings and recommendations.[107] Article 2018 of NAFTA provides that upon receipt

---

[99] *Ibid.*, Art. 15(6)   [100] *Ibid.*, Arts 8(5), 12(9), and 13(2).

[101] A. Ortiz Mena, 'Dispute Settlement under NAFTA', in E. Chambers and P. Smith (eds), *NAFTA in the New Millennium* (San Diego: Center for US–Mexican Studies, 2002), 426.

[102] F. Abbott, 'The Political Economy of NAFTA Chapter Eleven: Equality Before the Law and the Boundaries of North American Integration' (2000) 23 Hastings Int & Comp L Rev 303, at 304.

[103] Ortiz Mena, above at n 101, at 426.

[104] G.C. Vega and G.R. Winham, 'The Role of NAFTA Dispute Settlement in the Management of Canadian, Mexican and US Trade and Investment Relations' (2002) 28 ONLR, 651, at 705.

[105] NAFTA Secretariat, Overview of the Dispute Settlement Provisions of the NAFTA, available at www.nafta-sec-alena.org/DefaultSite/index_e.aspx?DetailID=8 (visited 3 March 2006). The full text of NAFTA is available at www.nafta-secalena.org/DefaultSite/index_e.aspx?DetailID=78 (visited 3 March 2006).

[106] *Ibid.* Also M. Sher, 'Chapter 20 Dispute Resolution under NAFTA: Fact or Fiction?' (2003) 35 Geo Wash Int L Rev 1001, at 1007.

[107] *Ibid.*, at 1008.

of the final report, the parties shall agree on a resolution, and such a resolution 'normally shall confirm with the determinations and recommendations of the panel', but the finding itself is not binding.[108] If within 30 days no agreement on resolution has been reached, sanctioned retaliation is retained as an option to ensure compliance, as provided by Article 2019 of NAFTA.

In practice, the Chapter 20 DSM has been called into action much less frequently than its Chapter 11 and Chapter 19 counterparts, partly due to the frequently systematic delays on panellist selection.[109] The long delays of the panel process have in most circumstance exacerbated political and economic tensions instead of easing them.[110] Some observers therefore concluded that the flexible nature of this process has become more of a liability than an asset.[111]

Apart from Chapter 20, NAFTA also includes Chapter 11 and Chapter 19 DSMs that allow the participation of private parties. Among them, as the busiest DSM in NAFTA, the Chapter 19 bi-national panel process is quite novel in the sense that it is directed to complaints alleging a failure to correctly apply national Anti-dumping and Countervailing Duty (AD/CVD) law.[112] Formally, it is an inter-state DSM, but in practice, the private party is the engine of this DSM.[113] Only when an industry asking for a review of an AD/CVD determination by national authorities files a request for panel Review, can the NAFTA Secretariat establish a bi-national panel accordingly.

Article 1904 is at the heart of what normally referred to as the Chapter 19 DSM, which establishes a mechanism to provide an independent bi-national panel as an alternative of a domestic court for the judicial review of final determination from investigation authorities.[114] The binational panels, established on an *ad hoc* basis, do not exactly make a third party arbitration. Rather, by applying the importing party's AD/CVD law, they can only uphold or remand an administrative authority's determination—the panel decision contains no relief by itself, partly because NAFTA Chapter 19 provides no substantive body of AD/CVD law.[115] Nevertheless, this has not affected the binding effect of the panel decisions. Only in the exceptional circumstance that a NAFTA government invokes the Extraordinary Challenge Committee (ECC) procedure, which addresses the issue where a party alleges there has been gross misconduct on the part of the panel, can the panel report be reviewed by a three-person, binational EEC.[116]

---

[108] Art. 2018 of NAFTA.   [109] Ortiz Mena, above at n 101, at 432.   [110] *Ibid.*

[111] *Ibid.*, at 430.

[112] *Ibid.*, at 427. In fact, the vast majority (about 88 per cent) of NAFTA disputes fall under Ch 19.

[113] G. Cavazos Villanueva and L.F. Martinez Serna, 'Private Parties in the NAFTA Dispute Settlement Mechanisms: The Mexican Experience' (2003) 77 Tul L Rev, 1017, at 1020.

[114] NAFTA Secretariat, above at n 105.

[115] Cavazos Villanueva and Martinez Serna, above at n 113, at 1020.

[116] NAFTA Secretariat, above at n 105.

This original DSM, as approved, provides legal certainty for the partici-pants.[117] Nevertheless, the difficulty in appointing panelists and doubt as to the competence of foreign panellists to interpret domestic law have been recog-nized as two major problems.[118] Interestingly, given the considerable overlaps between Chapter 19 and WTO AD/CVD rules, there is also 'forum shopping' between the Chapter 19 DSM and the WTO DSM. In the recent *Mexico—Corn Syrup* case,[119] the delay in the appointment of the panellists promoted the US to use a parallel forum approach, i.e. resort to the WTO DSM even before the NAFTA panel was actually established.[120]

Among the three principal DSMs in the NAFTA, the Chapter 11 investment DSM is by far the most profound one, but also most controversial one. Being cited as the 'single most significant legal development' in the NAFTA, this investor-state DSM is actually similar to the DSM of many bilateral investment treaties (BITs).[121] The basic logic of it is to allow NAFTA investors to bypass the local courts of a host government through access to binding arbitration under the World Bank's International Centre for the Settlement of Investment Disputes (ICSID) or the rules of United Nations Commission for International Trade Law (UNCITRAL).[122] Distinctively, the final award of the international arbitration tribunal is enforceable in domestic courts. This kind of enforce-ability in fact created an innovative form of 'judicial dialogue' between the international tribunal and domestic courts.[123]

But also because of the enforceability of all arbitration awards, including undesired ones, there are bitter criticisms of the Chapter 11 DSM.[124] Although foreign investors are largely satisfied by this mechanism, critics challenged the right of Chapter 11 international tribunals to scrutinize sensitive domestic legislation, *inter alia*, environmental and labour regulations.[125] As rightly concluded by Professor Abbott, the Chapter 11 DSM went as far as establish-ing a legal framework, which provides attractive financial guarantees to the investors, but did not build a framework strong enough to accommodate social policies.[126] Moreover, the proceedings have been accused of lacking

[117] Cavazos Villanueva and Martinez Serna, above at n 113, at 1022 and Ortiz Mena, above at n 101, at 431.
[118] Cavazos Villanueva and Martinez Serna, *ibid.*, at 1022.
[119] WTO Panel Report, *Mexico—Corn Syrup*, WT/DS1323shR and Corr. 1, adopted 24 February 2000.
[120] Cavazos Villanueva and Martinez Serna, above at n 113, at 1024.
[121] Vega and Winham, above at n 104, at 678 and Ortiz Mena, above at n 101, at 427.
[122] Ortiz Mena, *ibid.*, at 426 and Cavazos Villanueva and Martinez Serna, above at n 113, at 1027.
[123] R.B. Ahdieh, 'Between Dialogue and Decree: International Review of National Courts' (2004) 79 NYUL Rev 2029, at 2031.
[124] For example, Abbott, above at n 102, at 308 and A. Afilalo, 'Towards a Common Law of International Investment: How NAFTA Chapter 11 Panels Should Solve Their Legitimacy Crisis' (2004) 17 Geo Int Env L Rev 51, at 52.
[125] Afilalo, *ibid.*   [126] Abbott, above at n 102, at 309.

transparency, due to the secretive nature of the arbitration process and non-obligatory publication requirement.[127]

As summarized in Table 2, the three principal DSMs in the NAFTA have different legal characters, although institutionally all of them are *ad hoc* arbitration systems. The Chapter 20 DSM, similar to general DSMs in most FTAs, covers disputes from all other NAFTA chapters without specific DSMs and provides no standings for non-state actors. Chapter 20 panel reports are not binding and only relatively weak enforcement procedures are available. Chapter 20 panel reports are also not enforceable at national court and there is only limited transparency in Chapter 20 proceedings.

In the case of Chapter 11 and 19 DSMs, both of them grant standing to private parties. Their arbitration awards are binding and enforceable in domestic courts, although the awards concern not the change of domestic law, but only monetary compensation. Moreover, their non-transparency and unaccountability are the focus of criticisms.

D. The European Court System

In their journey towards the court of a constitutionalized EU, the European Court of Justice (ECJ) and its Court of First Instance (CFI) have gone very far from a simple DSM in a Customs Union.[128] Referred to as a 'supranational court', the ECJ is different from the DSMs discussed above in all legal factors indicated in Table 2.[129] In fact, if we factor in the novel character of Community legal order, none of the existing DSMs are comparable to it at all. Only when we identify some of the Court's key functions relating to the Customs Union aspects of the EU, is it then within the scope of this essay to analyse the Court in the context of regional integration.

If it is the underlying philology of NAFTA in designing its DSM that agreements with different subject matters should have different DSMs, the EU took the approach that a single institution framework, including a single court, should cover all agreements, from its early days.[130] Therefore, the ECJ is armed with treaties with an extremely wide jurisdiction.[131] Only when the Court serves as an 'international adjudication' body by hearing suits brought against a Member State (MS) for an alleged violation of the treaties or giving preliminary rulings upon the question of the interpretation of Community law, is it functioning more like a DSM in an RTA.[132]

---

[127] Ortiz Mena, above at n 101, at 435.

[128] L. Brown and T. Kennedy, *The Court of Justice of the European Communities*, 5th ed. (London: Sweet & Maxwell, 2000), 7. For the convenience of discussion, the ECJ and CFI will be referred as 'the Court'.

[129] Schneider, above at n 81, at 723–24.

[130] Brown and Kennedy, above at n 128, at 1. At the time that the EEC and the Euratom were established, the six founding Member States decided that there should be only a single Court to serve all three Communities.

[131] *Ibid.*, at 111.   [132] *Ibid.*

First and foremost, the Court provides a primary mechanism, direct actions against MSs, for monitoring and enforcing MS compliance with the treaties and with secondary legislations—a key function of DSMs in FTAs.[133] Articles 226 and 227 of the EC Treaty entitle either the Commission or the MS to bring 'direct action' to the Court in order to enforce the provisions of EC law *vis-à-vis* non-complying MSs.[134] While actions under Article 227 have been very rare, largely due to the reluctance of MSs to challenge each other directly before the Court, enforcement actions by the Commission under Article 226 have been increasingly frequent with the development of the Communities.[135] Here, the Commission, acting as a watchdog of the Community, brings the cases against MSs that break the Community rules.

Another particularly effective means by the Court to secure rights claimed under Community law is to give preliminary rulings under Article 234 of the EC Treaty, when requested by a national court.[136] Under Article 234, when a national court and tribunal faces a question of EC law, it can request a preliminary ruling from the Court regarding the interpretation of the treaty, or the validity or interpretation of the acts of the Community institutions.[137] From a functional perspective, the preliminary reference procedure plays a dual role: it provides an additional opportunity for both enforcement and judicial review of Community acts.[138] The preliminary references to Luxembourg have almost the same effect as certain direct actions in putting a particular MS in the dock for a Treaty infringement.[139] Through it, private parties play a critical role in developing Community law across a wide range of issues that may never have been covered by the enforcement action of the Commission or other MSs.[140]

Other jurisdictions of the Court, *inter alia*, judicial review of Community acts, although having equal importance, if not more, in the Community legal order, are outside the scope of this chapter. Most other existing FTAs have no institutional framework resembling the EU, and, therefore, their DSMs may not be required to serve as an inter-institution debate forum, as ECJ does.

To sum up, the ECJ, as a well-established institution with full jurisdiction for all EC treaties and Community acts, has two categories of jurisdiction relating to the alleged violation of the treaties and the interpretation of the Community law: direct actions against MSs under Articles 226 and 227, and the preliminary ruling procedure under Article 234. The first one, granting no standing to private parties, is normally initiated and motivated by the Commission, a non-state actor. The judgment is more than binding—it has

---

[133] M. Pollack, *The Engines of European Integration—Delegation, Agency and Agenda Setting in the EU* (Oxford: OUP, 2003), 161.

[134] *Ibid.* [135] *Ibid.*; *also*, Brown and Kennedy, above at n 128, at 115.

[136] Pollack, above at n 133, at 163. In the case of a national court as final instance, it has to refer the question concerning EC law to the ECJ.

[137] *Ibid.*, at 162. If a national court is acting as a court of final instance, it has to refer the questions concerning EC law to the ECJ.

[138] *Ibid.* [139] *Ibid.*, at 113. [140] Abbott, above at n 102, at 308.

supremacy over domestic law and has direct effect, i.e. a private party can rely on this judgment at national court. Before the TEU, there was no sanction for non-compliance, but after it, financial penalties could be imposed on the infringing MS. With respect to the preliminary ruling, private parties have standing since the litigation takes place at national courts. The preliminary reference from the ECJ has supremacy over domestic law and is enforceable through the national courts. Both the proceedings are transparent according to the procedures of the Court, although the pre-trial process in Article 226 actions is not public.

IV. ALTERNATIVE DSM TO THE PROPOSED EAST ASIA RTA

A. Political Economy of the Design of DSM—'Asian Way' vs. Legalization

In previous sections, the discussion of existing DSMs in three typical RTAs— ASEAN, NAFTA, and the EU—involved not only their nature of *ex ante* institutional designs, but also the record of *ex post* state behaviours. Indeed, during trade negotiations, governments stand, arguably, behind a veil of ignorance with regard to future implementation and disputes.[141] In advance of actual integration, it is difficult to predict what kind of DSM can guarantee greater compliance, if this is at all possible. Given this uncertainty, this section, on the purpose of setting the political economy background for the design of a DSM in the proposed East Asia RTA, will only highlight the factors that may count for significant variation in the general institutional design of the DSM.[142]

As international relations scholars have argued, when negotiating a trade pact and deciding how legalistic its DSM should be, governments always confront a trade-off between two mutually exclusive goals: policy discretion and treaty compliance.[143] On the one hand, political leaders are motivated to retain power over domestic policies.[144] Under a legalistic DSM, the power and discretion of national governments are threatened and *ex post* protection is under the risk of complaints from trading partners that could lead to rulings of violation, with attendant costs to their reputations and perhaps sanctions.[145] On the other hand, political leaders also care about compliance with the treaty. The very legalistic procedures that constrain the policy autonomy of governments also, as proved by the economic success of EU and NAFTA, improve the economic value of the treaty, yielding domestic political benefits.[146] In short, it is nothing but a balance—if the benefits from a legalistic DSM are sufficiently large they may offset the potential costs of policy constraints, making the legalistic DSM an attractive institutional option.[147]

---

[141] J. McCall Smith, 'The Politics of Dispute Settlement Design: Explaining Legalism in Regional Trade Pacts' (2000) 54 Int Org 137, at 138.
[142] *Ibid.*   [143] *Ibid.*, at 143–44.   [144] *Ibid.*, at 145.   [145] *Ibid.*   [146] *Ibid.*
[147] *Ibid.*, at 146.

Apart from the general cost of policy constraints, East Asian countries have to pay extra costs to adopt a more legalistic DSM because of their anti-litigation tradition.[148] Under this legal culture, litigation was mostly viewed negatively, which caused both sides to 'lose face'.[149] Bringing a lawsuit against the other party might even embarrass the winning party, because it ruins the harmony of the community.[150] The history of East Asia integration from the 1960s to the 1990s, therefore, offered an example of low legalization and possibly an explicit aversion to legalization, clearly in contrast to the institution and legal framework-building concentrated in the West Europe and North America.[151]

Over the past decade, however, East Asian countries have changed dramatically, starting to catch the global phenomenon of legalization and localizing it.[152] By endorsing the WTO DSM, East Asian countries implicitly accepted legalization as an emerging 'transnational norm'.[153] Statistically, the proportion of complaints brought by East Asian states has doubled as a share of total complaints when compared to the historical average under the GATT, though arguably they continue to underutilize the WTO DSM when compared with their importance in world trade.[154]

In addition to their willingness to resolve disputes in legalized forums outside the region, *inter alia* the WTO, East Asian countries, in particular the ASEAN governments, also showed their endorsement of legalization in regional integration.[155] The adoption of a DSM by ASEAN in 1996 backed up the argument that ASEAN is on its way from a consensus-based diplomatic forum to a more legalized institution.[156] When the ASEAN countries chose the WTO DSM as the model, which bore little resemblance to an ASEAN way of settling disputes, and improved its DSM most recently, they clearly indicated their strong desires to be active norm-takers to build congruence between legalization—the 'transnational norm', and the ASEAN way—the local beliefs and practices.[157] Although no conclusive empirical evidence is available yet to assess the utilization of the ASEAN DSM and it is too early to come to a conclusion as to its real impact on the future FTAs in East Asia, this movement, at least, makes the ASEAN governments' undertaking to create 'a more predictable and rules-based free trade area' very clear and will definitely

---

[148] S. Peng, 'The WTO Legalistic Approach and East Asia: From the Legal Culture Perspective' (2000) Asian-Pac L & Policy J 1, at 10–1.

[149] *Ibid.*, at 12.   [150] *Ibid.*

[151] M. Kahler, 'Legalization as Strategy: The Asia-Pacific Case' (2000) 54 Int Org 549, at 550.

[152] For definition of localization and norm diffusion: A. Acharya, 'How Ideas Spread: Whose Norms Matter? Norm Localization and Institutional Change in Asian Regionalism' (2004) 58 Int Org, 239, at 239.

[153] *Ibid.*, at 241.

[154] Kahler, above at n 151, at 563; for the general description of the profile of East Asian countries in the WTO DSM: N. Park, 'Overview on the State of WTO Dispute Settlement Involving the ASEAN+3', in M. Matsushita and D. Ahn (eds), *WTO and East Asia: New Perspectives* (London: Cameron May, 2004), 241.

[155] Kahler, above at n 151, at 565.   [156] *Ibid.*   [157] Acharya, above at n 152, at 241.

influence the attitudes of other East Asian countries in terms of the design of a DSM.

However, the problem still exists of how to incorporate this 'foreign norm' to the pre-existing and, to a large extent, stubborn, Asian tradition. East Asian countries are facing the challenge to be creative learners to 'restructure the norms to ensure a better fit with prior local norms', so that the localized norm may enhance, but not undermine, the performance of their institutions.[158]

B. Legal Alternatives to the Proposed East Asia RTA

Theoretically, there are several legal alternatives available for East Asian countries, namely modelling the WTO, the NAFTA, and the EU. An important assumption is that although it has been argued that 'good' global norms should prevail over the 'bad' local beliefs and practices, many local beliefs are themselves part of a legitimate normative order, which conditions the acceptance of global norms.[159] Therefore, East Asian states are expected to choose one that can best combine the long-term interest of moving towards legalization and the short-term political and social acceptance. The following section will access the merits of these three alternatives, in particular the feasibility of their utilization in the proposed East Asia FTA.

1. A New Mechanism on the Basis of the WTO DSM

The first alternative for the proposed East Asia FTA is to establish a new DSM resembling the WTO DSM with several improvements. There are two main reasons for this choice. First, the above discussion of political economy dynamics of East Asia regionalism shows that a DSM resembling the WTO DSM, which is less legalistic than the European Court system but still highly legalized, would best match the level of East Asia integration. Second, the WTO rules as a whole have been generally accepted by East Asian countries, as indicated in previous trade disputes, such as the Japan–China 'Welsh Onion War' in 2000. In settling that dispute, the parties concerned frequently referred to the WTO Agreements in the course of negotiation, although at that time China was still not a Member of the WTO.[160] Therefore, the choice of modelling the WTO DSM and making several improvements that address the special concerns of the East Asian countries, as the ASEAN did to its new DSM, will be more likely to be accepted by East Asian countries in negotiations and function well.

In building up a new DSM in East Asia, it would be very helpful to take lessons from two controversial issues in the ASEAN DSM. First is the reluctance of ASEAN states to use this DSM in promoting the treaty compliance. Although the first formalized ASEAN DSM has been established from 1996,

---

[158] *Ibid.*, at 240.   [159] *Ibid.*, at 239.
[160] J. Nakagawa, 'Lessons from the Japan–China "Welsh Onion War" ' (2002) 36 JWT 1019, at 1019.

during its eight year history (1996–2004), no ASEAN government has ever utilized this DSM in resolving their disputes under AFTA.[161] During this period, there were plenty of disputes between ASEAN Members over the implementation of AFTA, in particular CEPT, but none of those disputes have been brought to the 1996 DSM. It is therefore important to take the resistance of East Asian states to litigation-style dispute settlement into account when designing a new DSM for the proposed FTA.

One possible explanation for this is that in East Asia tradition, litigation is considered more as an expression of hostility than an effective way of settling disputes.[162] In light of this tradition, the EU's experience of introducing an independent watchdog to secure Community law is worth considering as it may effectively avoid the direct conflicts between MSs. Although a strong institution serving the full Commission-type function is very unlikely to appear in East Asia in the foreseeable future, to establish an independent body in charge of the surveillance might be a good alternative in that it may increase the public pressure for compliance whilst maintaining the good relationship between states.

Second, given the sensitivity of sovereignty in East Asian countries, the ASEAN DSM granted no standing to private parties to challenge treaty-inconsistent national laws and regulations. However, from the experience of NAFTA and EU, there will be obvious benefits of granting access to legal remedies to private parties in developing 'community law' and promoting regional integration in the long run.[163] Thus, as will be extensively discussed with the NAFTA's experience, the proposed East Asia FTA should also consider how and to what extent the regional DSM may be open to private parties, not only in the highly demanding investment regime, but also in other subject matters such as competition policy.

2. *The NAFTA Model DSM*

Of the three principal DSMs in the NAFTA, the Chapter 20 general DSM and the Chapter 19 AD/CVD DSM have less significance than the Chapter 11 investment DSM to East Asia integration. In terms of interstate dispute, as discussed above, a WTO DSM would be a better model for East Asian countries. Moreover, most East Asian countries are not frequent users of AD and CVD rules. Chapter 19 DSM is therefore less meaningful to them.

As the most dynamic DSM in the NAFTA, the Chapter 11 DSM, not only its achievements but also its recent legitimacy crisis, does provide an example to East Asian countries in designing their DSMs. Although the success of the Chapter 11 DSM might push East Asian states to provide better legal protection for foreign investors, it is still questionable whether the proposed East Asia FTA should follow the exact pattern of NAFTA Chapter 11, given the

---

[161] Kahler, above at n 151, at 566.   [162] Peng, above at n 148, at 12.
[163] Abbott, above at n 102, at 307.

greater reluctance of accepting rulings from international tribunals and the sensibility of sovereignty in East Asian states. The legitimacy crisis facing Chapter 11 also indicates the necessity to reform the *ad hoc* investor-state arbitration system, especially when the involvement of sensitive domestic regulation, such as environmental and health policy, is by and large inevitable.

One possible choice for the proposed East Asia FTA is to identify several sectors that the private parties may have direct access to and introduce different set of rules of procedure for different subject matters, as the NAFTA system does. NAFTA's approach to submit the disputes to *ad hoc* binational penal or arbitration tribunals in other international institutions might be acceptable. Nevertheless, eventually, a single regional institution, such as an independent Appellate Body, should stand as the tribunal of final instance and have the right to review legal merits of *ad hoc* arbitration awards. Under the same roof of regional institutions, stronger judicial authority and greater stability and consistency is expected, although different DSMs are involved in disputes with different subject matters.

3. The ECJ Model DSM

As noted above, the EU-type dispute resolution, based on strong institutions and a clear idea of supranationalism, is by and large beyond the acceptance of East Asian states and the level of East Asia integration. Again, only the indications from the evolution of EU's legal regime, but not the exact rules of the ECJ, are within the scope of this chapter.

Given the critical role played by the Commission in the Article 226 direct actions against MS, it is worth considering how far that the proposed FTA can, or should, go to strengthen the regional institutions in improving treaty compliance. To empower some regional institutions to play more important roles in dispute settlement is very likely to be beneficial to East Asia integration in the long term.

V. CONCLUSION

Given the recent dynamic development of regionalism in East Asia, it is important to review East Asia not only as a geographic or cultural identity, but also as a potential trade bloc under the WTO system. Together with economic integration, the changing attitudes of East Asian countries towards regionalism largely enhance the proliferation of RTAs in the region and the likelihood of a broad and deep East Asia FTA.

Among prerequisites of a successful RTA, the design of an appropriate DSM would be the toughest task, which continuously tests the wisdom of governments. In theory, a combination of six different legal factors, namely jurisdiction, institutional feature, binding effect and enforcement, standing of non-state actors, transparency, and enforceability at national court, can differentiate the DSMs and provide alternatives to a new DSM. Corresponding to the different stage of their regional integration respectively, the DSMs in three typical RTAs—the ASEAN, the NAFTA, and the EU—also provide valuable examples for the design of a new DSM in East Asia.

With the background that both the global trend of legalization and economic integration in East Asia may push the East Asian countries to adopt a more legalistic approach different from their previous practice, it is more important to make sure that legalization, as a transnational norm, has been appropriately localized to serve the East Asia integration constructively.

This chapter therefore proposes, first, a general DSM, which is modelled on the WTO and draws experience from the new ASEAN DSM, to resolve interstate trade disputes. There are two main reasons for this choice: the proper legalistic level of the WTO DSM and the general acceptance of WTO rules in East Asian states. Given the considerable resistance of East Asian states to litigation style dispute settlement, it is also advisable to introduce a stronger and more independent body in charge of treaty compliance in order to avoid direct conflicts between East Asian states. Hopefully, this institution can better secure the treaty and increase the pressure of compliance, although it may not have the full function of the EC Commission.

In addition to the general interstate DSM, which grants no standing to non-state actors, this chapter has also suggested opening several sectors of the proposed FTA to the private parties, i.e. granting them direct access to the DSM in selected subject matters with different rules of procedure. The most highly demanding regime is of course the investment regime, but private parties may also have the same need to access other sectors, such as competition. Based on the experience of the EU and NAFTA, it is rational to anticipate that separate rules of procedure, as supplements to the general DSM, may appropriately promote the compliance of the 'community rules'. However, to avoid the legitimacy crisis of NAFTA tribunals, it is important to keep different rules of procedure under the same legal framework, and a single regional institution, such as an independent appellate body, is placed to provide the judicial authority, stability, and consistency of the regional dispute settlement.

PART V

*Interfaces Between the WTO and
Regional Trade Agreements*

19

The EU and its Member States in the WTO—Issues of Responsibility

PIET EECKHOUT [*]

I. INTRODUCTION

The EU is no doubt the most accomplished system of regional integration currently extant. It is a unique transnational polity, with a legal system broadly federal in nature. Its policies have long surpassed the limited domain of trade. And yet it is always helpful to remember one's origins—in particular if they are modest. The EU started off with an economic treaty aimed at establishing a common market between six European countries. Still today, the EC Treaty provides in Article 23(1) that 'the Community shall be based upon a customs union'.[1] The EU is therefore an example of what the establishment of a customs union may lead to. It is not clear, though, whether it is in that sense a model, or simply a unique experiment unsuited for replication.

The unique character of the EU has many facets. One of those consists of its activities and position in international relations. The EC has international legal personality,[2] and makes an active use of that personality. It has concluded literally hundreds of international agreements, and acts in many international organizations. It has its own, in many ways fascinating, constitutional-type law which governs its international action. This aspect of its legal system continues to develop at great speed, and to throw up challenging questions, for example relating to external competence,[3] to the relationship between

* The author is grateful for the excellent research assistance by Ms Christina Eckes, funded by the Centre of European Law, and for the stimulating discussions with and suggestions by Lorand Bartels.

[1] The Treaty establishing a Constitution for Europe abandons this notion, but at present does not look like ever entering into force.

[2] On the question of the legal personality of the EU, as distinct from the EC, *see* P. Eeckhout, *External Relations of the European Union: Legal and Constitutional Foundations* (Oxford: OUP, 2004),154–60. Reference in this paper to the EU generally denotes the EU *as encompassing* the EC; reference may occasionally be made to the EC for the purpose of legal precision.

[3] *Opinion 1/03 (Lugano Convention)*, 7 February 2006, not yet reported.

international law and the EC's domestic law,[4] or to the Member States' position with respect to dispute settlement under a so-called mixed agreement.[5]

Much of the EU's international action is conducted within the framework of the WTO. The EC is the only customs union which is a founding member of the WTO in its own right.[6] The WTO Agreement is a mixed agreement, and thus the EU Member States are also founding members: the Court of Justice decided in *Opinion 1/94* that the Community and its Member States shared competence to conclude the agreement.[7] In the current daily practice of the WTO this mixed membership is hardly visible. The EU generally operates as a single actor, with the European Commission acting as negotiator and litigant, and with the Council of Ministers and the so-called 133 Committee[8] acting as political minders and ultimate decision-makers. Individual action by EU Member States is exceedingly rare.

Much has been said and written about this shared external competence in WTO matters, and about issues related to the effect of WTO law in EC and national law. However, much less attention has hitherto been paid to the international law dimension of shared membership. The most successful of the WTO's functions (listed in Article III WTO Agreement) is its dispute settlement system. The WTO is an intense litigation forum, where members' obligations are regularly enforced. It is in this sense quite unique in the international legal system. Considering the broad scope of WTO law, which encompasses large segments of international economic law, the importance of the WTO dispute settlement system is clearly beyond dispute.

How does the WTO dispute settlement system tackle the joint membership of the EC and its Member States? This is an important question, for a number of reasons. From a pragmatic perspective it is important for the EC, its Member States, and other WTO Members to know where responsibility for breaches of WTO law may lie: with the EC, with the individual Member States, or with both. From an internal constitutional perspective it is equally important for the EC and its Member States to know what are the international law consequences of joint membership of an international organization. And for the international legal system the case of EC membership of the WTO is a particularly significant manifestation of responsibility of an international organization, a topic currently considered by the International Law Commission (ILC).

This chapter does not aim to offer a definitive treatment of the international

---

[4] Case C-377/02 *Van Parys v BIRB* [2005] ECR I-1465.

[5] Case C-459/03 *Commission v Ireland (Mox Plant)*, Opinion of Maduro AG, 18 January 2006, not yet reported; a mixed agreement is an agreement to which both the EC and its Member States are Contracting Parties.

[6] *See* Art. XI of the WTO Agreement.

[7] *Opinion 1/94 (WTO Agreement)* [1994] ECR I-5267.

[8] This is the Committee of Member State representatives which prepares the Council's work under Art. 133 EC.

responsibility of the EC and its Member States for violations of WTO law. Much more modestly, its objective is to contribute to the debate and the reflection. The chapter is divided in two parts. The next section concentrates on the actual practice in WTO dispute settlement. As will be seen, that practice is rather straightforward and pragmatic. The paper then turns to underlying theoretical questions, for which the current debates in the ILC offer a nice angle. Though the practice may be straightforward, it will be seen that the theoretical questions are more complex.

II. PRACTICE

Before analysing the actual practice in WTO dispute settlement it is useful to set out some basic legal facts concerning the joint membership of the EC and its Member States. Article XI:1 WTO Agreement provides that 'the contracting parties to GATT 1947 . . . and the European Communities . . . shall become original Members of the WTO'.[9] Accordingly, the then EC Member States and the EC became full original WTO Members, each apparently bound by all obligations resulting from the WTO Agreement. In contrast with what often happens in the context of other international organizations or agreements there was no express limitation of the EC's membership, either through a list or declaration of competences,[10] or through an indication in the agreement itself as to which obligations the EC, respectively its Member States, entered into. This is a consequence of the sequence of events. The legal questions of EC and Member State competence were not resolved by the time the WTO Agreement was drafted and the Uruguay Round Final Act signed at Marrakesh in April 1994. Signature was followed by municipal approval procedures, which were all completed by the end of 1994 for the purpose of enabling the entry into force of the WTO Agreement by 1 January 1995. In those few months the European Commission requested and obtained *Opinion 1/94*, in which the Court of Justice analysed the division of competences between the EC and its Member States.[11] It is important to bear in mind that some WTO Members may in fact have signed *and approved* the WTO Agreement before the Court's Opinion was delivered (15 November 1994). This may be relevant to the question whether other WTO Members can be presumed to have had sufficient knowledge about the division of competences.

In *Opinion 1/94* the Court of Justice clarified the scope of EC and national competence, but only up to a point. The Court focused solely on the question whether the EC had *exclusive* competence to conclude the WTO Agreement, and therefore did not address the question of what parts of the WTO Agreement came within the EC's non-exclusive external competences.[12] The Court

---

[9] *See also* Art. XIV WTO Agreement.   [10] *See,* e.g. UNCLOS.
[11] *See* above at n 7.   [12] Para. 14.

distinguished between, on the one hand, Annex 1A of the WTO Agreement, Multilateral Agreements on Trade in Goods, and, on the other, Annexes 1B and 1C, respectively containing GATS and TRIPS. All the agreements pertaining to trade in goods were considered to come within the exclusive competence of the EC pursuant to Article 133 EC (the provision on the common commercial policy). GATS and TRIPS, by contrast, were held to come within the shared (or joint) competence of the EC and its Member States. For GATS the division of competences cut right through the agreement: the cross-border mode of providing services (Article I:2(a) GATS) came within the scope of Article 133 EC, whereas the other modes did not. In addition there may be exclusive competence for those parts of GATS which affect internal EC legislation (the so-called AETR principle).[13] That principle also applies to TRIPS, which was not considered to be covered by Article 133 EC, with the exception of its provisions on enforcement of IP rights at border crossing points.

However, the authority of *Opinion 1/94* is limited in two ways. First, as mentioned the Opinion considered the question of exclusive competence only. Second, such exclusive competence is evolutionary in character, again in two ways. Exclusive competence expands with the adoption of further internal EC legislation in areas covered by WTO law, due to the AETR principle. This is particularly relevant for TRIPS, in light of the increased activity of the EC in the intellectual property field. Exclusive competence has also expanded, so it seems, through the amendments to Article 133 EC which the Treaty of Nice introduced.[14] Article 133(5) EC extends the common commercial policy to 'agreements in the fields of trade in services and the commercial aspects of intellectual property', an apparent reference to GATS and TRIPS.[15]

The Court of Justice has made a couple of statements about international responsibility in the case of a mixed agreement where no declaration of competences was made and where the agreement contains no indication of which obligations were entered into by which party (Community or Member States). In *Parliament v Council*, regarding the Lomé IV Convention, Jacobs AG stated that under a mixed agreement the Community and the Member States are jointly liable unless the provisions of the agreement point to the opposite conclusion.[16] The Court appeared to confirm this. In *Hermès*, which concerned the WTO Agreement, the Court referred to the fact that the agreement was concluded by the Community and ratified by its Member States without any allocation between them of their respective obligations towards the other

---

[13] *See* Case 22/70 *Commission v Council* [1970] ECR 263.

[14] *See*, e.g. H.G. Krenzler and C. Pitschas, 'Progress or Stagnation? The Common Commercial Policy after Nice' (2001) 6 EFA Rev, 291 and C.W. Hermann, 'Common Commercial Policy after Nice: Sisyphus Would Have Done a Better Job' (2002) 39 CMLR, 7.

[15] It is not clear, though, whether competence under Art. 133(5) EC is exclusive or shared. *See* Eeckhout, above at n 2, at 51.

[16] Case C-316/91 *Parliament v Council* [1994] ECR I–625, para. 69.

Contracting Parties.[17] However, in *Commission v Ireland*, a case concerning the EEA Agreement, Mischo AG took a different view, by stating:[18]

It does not appear certain to me, however, that the simple fact that the respective obligations of the Community and the Member States to the other Contracting Parties have not been defined enables the latter to infer that the Community assumes responsibility for fulfilment of the whole of the agreement in question, including those provisions which do not fall within its competence. On the contrary, the very fact that the Community and its Member States had recourse to the formula of a mixed agreement announces to non-member countries that that agreement does not fall wholly within the competence of the Community and that, consequently, the Community is, *a priori*, only assuming responsibility for those parts falling within its competence.

As can thus be seen, there is no consensus within the ECJ on the issue of joint or separate liability.

But what is the practice at WTO level? The first point to note is that, apparently, none of the EC Member States have ever attempted to become an active litigant ('complainant') in WTO dispute settlement. We can leave aside whether this is purely for political or institutional reasons, or whether there are legal objections, resulting from EC law, which are considered to preclude this. Matters are different with respect to passive litigation, i.e. Member States being a defendant. Other WTO Members (the US in particular) have addressed complaints to individual Member States, but in all cases which have led to a panel the EC has effectively taken up the defence of the measures in question.[19]

In one of the earliest cases, *EC—Computer Equipment* (the so-called LAN case), the US took action against the EC, Ireland, and the UK. The EC expressed the view that the customs administrations of the Member States were acting as implementing authorities of EC law in a field of exclusive EC competence; that the actions of those authorities should be attributed to the EC itself; and emphasized its readiness to assume responsibility.[20] The US nevertheless requested that the panel clarify the responsibility of the respective defendants. The panel, however, did not directly reply to that request and simply stated that its examination would focus on whether customs authorities in the EC, including those located in Ireland and the UK, had or had not deviated from the obligations assumed under the EC Schedule.[21] In the end the

---

[17] Case C–53/96 *Hermès International v FHT* [1998] ECR I–3603, para. 24; *see also* the Opinion of Tesauro AG, paras 14 and 20 and Joined Cases C–300 and 392/98 *Parfums Christian Dior v Tuk Consultancy* [2000] ECR I–11307, para 33.

[18] Case C–13/00 *Commission v Ireland* [2002] ECR I–2943, para. 30 of the Opinion.

[19] A useful overview is supplied in the European Commission's comments and observations to the ILC for the purpose of its work on the responsibility of international organizations. *See* ILC, Responsibility of International Organizations—Comments and Observations received from International Organizations, 56th Session, UN Doc. A/CN.4/545, at 19–20 and 34–5.

[20] *Ibid.*, at 20.

[21] WTO Panel Report, *EC—Computer Equipment*, WT/DS62/R, WT/DS67/R and WT/DS68/R, adopted 22 June 1998, as modified by the Appellate Body Report, WT/DS62/AB/R, WT/DS67/AB/R and WT/DS68/AB/R, para. 8.16.

panel concluded that the EC had acted inconsistently with Article II:1 GATT 1994.[22]

The Commission also reported to the ILC that in the area of TRIPS, largely subject to Member State competence, some variation in the dispute settlement practice was noticeable. Requests for consultations were first addressed solely to the Member State concerned and the solution was reached between the claimant and that State, whereas in some subsequent similar cases the Community participated in the settlement negotiations. More recently, consultation as well as the establishment of a panel was requested against both the Member State concerned and the EC separately, while the settlement was negotiated among the claimant, the Member State concerned, and the EC.[23] However, whilst such settlements no doubt constitute practice under WTO law, they are not decisions by a panel or the Appellate Body, which are judicial-type bodies.

There are some further developments, subsequent to the Commission's submissions to the ILC. In *EC—Trademarks and Geographical Indications* the panel examined the consistency of an EC Regulation with various TRIPS provisions.[24] It noted that there were various executive authorities involved in the implementation of the Regulation, including representatives of EC Member States. The panel observed that the EC delegation had confirmed that the statements made by agents of the European Commission before the panel committed and engaged the EC. The EC delegation had also indicated that Community laws are generally not executed through authorities at EC level but rather through recourse to the authorities of its Member States which, in such a situation, acted as *de facto* organs of the EC for which the EC would be responsible under WTO law and international law in general. The panel accepted this explanation of what it called the EC's domestic constitutional arrangements, and accepted that the submissions were made on behalf of all the executive authorities of the EC.[25]

In the *Biotech* case, where at the time of writing no definitive panel report is as yet available, but where the findings of the interim report are on the internet, there are also a couple of interesting statements. The complainants challenged three types of measures: an EC moratorium on approvals of biotech measures; various product-specific measures affecting the approval of specific biotech products; and various EC Member State safeguard measures prohibiting the import and/or marketing of specific biotech products. As regards the last type of measures, the panel noted that the EC as a whole was the responding party in respect of those Member State measures. This was a

---

[22] *Ibid.*, para. 9.1.

[23] *See* UN Doc. A/CN.4/545, above at n 19, at 20 and 35, for further details.

[24] Council Regulation 2081/92 on the Protection of Geographical Indications and Designations of Origin for Agricultural Products and Foodstuffs, as amended [1992] OJ L208/1.

[25] WTO Panel Report, *EC—Trademarks and Geographical Indications (US)*, WT/DS174/R, adopted 20 April 2005, paras 7.97–7.98 and *passim*.

direct consequence of the fact that the complainants had directed their complaints against the EC, and not individual EC Member States. The panel further noted that the EC had never contested that, for the purposes of the dispute, the challenged Member State measures were attributable to it under international law (note the term 'attributable') and hence could be considered EC measures.[26] As the interim report stands, it is primarily these Member State measures which according to the panel violate WTO law.

Finally, the award of the arbitrator in *EC—Chicken Cuts* may be worth mentioning. The arbitration concerned the reasonable period for implementation under Article 21.3 of the DSU. The EC argued that it could not change the classification of chicken prior to obtaining a ruling from the World Customs Organization. The arbitrator observed that such envisaged action was *outside* the lawmaking procedures of the EC. He noted that disputes that give rise to WTO dispute settlement focus exclusively on 'measures taken' by a WTO Member, and that, accordingly, a measure that is the subject of a challenge in WTO dispute settlement must be 'attributable' to that member.[27] The arbitrator went on to say that implementation would ordinarily be achieved by means entirely within the implementing member's lawmaking procedures. Recourse to external processes would not ordinarily form part of the implementation of the recommendations and rulings of the DSB. Accordingly, the arbitrator continued, the mere assertion by a member of the need for recourse to such external decision-making processes was not entitled to the same deference as in the case of an implementation procedure that was entirely within that member's domestic legal system. The member concerned bore the burden of establishing that this external element of its proposed implementation was necessary for, and therefore indispensable to, that member's full and effective compliance with its obligations.[28]

The question to which these observations give rise is whether the approach is likely to be similar in a case where implementation requires action by an EC Member State. Would such action also be considered an external process, or would it be considered to be within the EC's lawmaking procedures? What if the EC were to argue that, insofar as a Member State measure is considered contrary to WTO law, the only means at its disposal consist of an enforcement action by the European Commission pursuant to Article 226 EC—which in any event may take around two years to be decided upon by the Court of Justice?

---

[26] *Ibid.*, paras 7.101 and 7.102.

[27] The arbitrator referred to para 121 of the WTO Appellate Body Report in *US—Gambling* (WT/DS285/AB/R, adopted 20 April 2005), which in turn makes a reference to para. 81 of the WTO Appellate Body Report, *US—Corrosion-Resistant Steel Sunset Review* (WT/DS244/AB/R, adopted 9 January 2004); in *US—Gambling* the AB stated that 'a "nexus" must exist between the responding Member and the "measure", such that the "measure"—whether an act or omission—must be "attributable" to that Member'.

[28] WTO award of the arbitrator, *EC—Chicken Cuts (Brazil and Thailand)*, WT/DS269/13 and WT/DS286/15 respectively, paras 51–2.

What conclusions can be drawn from this overview of WTO practice? The first conclusion is that the EC is eager to take up responsibility. This of course is counterintuitive. One would expect issues of responsibility to arise as a consequence of attempts to deny or evade such responsibility. Here the opposite appears to happen. The main reason for the EC's eagerness may well be the European Commission's quest for integration and for international confirmation and acceptance of the role of the EC as such. The Commission vigorously battled to have the Court of Justice say that the EC had sole competence in WTO matters. It failed to convince the Court, but it may well be achieving its goal in the daily practice of the WTO.

The second conclusion is that panels have hardly interfered. In the cases where the issue came up they accepted that the EC takes responsibility. It is noteworthy that there appears to be no ruling which establishes, in its conclusions, that an EC Member State has violated its WTO obligations. The panels accept the federal-type arguments by the EC. Their approach is characterized by pragmatism.

On this basis it is possible to develop some more theoretical reflections.

III. THEORY

As mixed agreements have been a permanent feature of the EC's external policies, there is plenty of academic literature on questions of responsibility connected to such agreements.[29] Much of this literature is abstract and general, however, essentially because for a long time there was hardly any relevant practice. It is only in the last ten years or so, with EC membership of the WTO and EC participation in other multilateral agreements, such as UNCLOS, that practice is developing. In addition, the theoretical debate has acquired more depth with the work of the ILC on responsibility of international organizations. This short contribution therefore does not aim to paint a complete portrait of the theoretical debate. It is considered more convenient to focus on a couple of major contributions, with contrasting positions: the reports of the Special Rapporteur to the ILC on international responsibility, Giorgio Gaja;[30] the reports of the ILC itself;[31] the European Commission's comments and observations to the ILC;[32] and an article by

---

[29] For a recent overview *see* M. Björklund, 'Responsibility in the EC for Mixed Agreements—Should Non-Member Parties Care?' (2001) 70 Nord J Int L 373.

[30] Respectively: ILC, First Report on Responsibility of International Organizations, 55th session, UN Doc. A/CN.4/532; Second Report, 56th session, UN Doc. A/CN.4/541; and Third Report, 57th session, UN Doc. A/CN.4/553.

[31] ILC Report on the Work of its 55th, 56th and 57th sessions, UN Docs. A/58/10, Ch IV; A/59/10, Ch V and A/60/10, Ch VI (years 2003, 2004, and 2005, respectively).

[32] Cited above, at n. 19.

Kuijper and Paasivirta, both EC Commission lawyers, reflecting and deepening those comments and observations.[33]

A. Apportionment of obligations?

The central provision in the draft articles on international responsibility of international organizations (hereafter 'draft articles') is Article 2, which provides in paragraph 2 that:

There is an internationally wrongful act of an international organization when conduct consisting of an action or omission:
(a) Is attributable to the international organization under international law; and
(b) Constitutes a breach of an international obligation of that international organization.

This provision identifies the two constituent elements: breach of an international obligation, and attributable conduct. As they currently stand the draft articles do not address the specific question of determining the respective obligations of an international organization and of its Member States under mixed agreements such as those concluded by the EC. As described above, the Court of Justice in *Parliament v Council* appeared to accept the position of Jacobs AG that the EC and its Member States are jointly liable for all obligations under a mixed agreement, unless the agreement says otherwise. The majority of academic literature adopts the same approach.[34] In the case of the WTO that would mean that there would be no need to distinguish between the various parts or provisions of WTO law, and that, where a breach of WTO law is established, the only question would be whether conduct is attributable to the EC and/or its Member States.

There is however minority academic opinion,[35] as well as the Opinion of Mischo AG in *Commission v Ireland*.[36] The Commission elaborated on this in the observations it submitted to the ILC. In the Commission's view the question of what it calls 'apportionment' of obligations between the international organization and its members needs to be distinguished from the question of attribution of conduct. The former question needs to be answered first, and it is 'entirely determined by the rules of the organization'.[37] Applied to the case

[33] P.J. Kuijper and E. Paasivirta, 'Further Exploring International Reponsibility: The European Community and the ILC's Project on Responsibility of International Organizations' (2004) 1 IOLR 111.
[34] *See* e.g. E. Stein, 'External Relations of the European Community; Structure and Process', in *Collected Courses of the Academy of European Law*, Volume I, Book 1, (Dordrecht: Nijhoff, 1991), 162, G. Gaja, 'The European Community's Rights and Obligations under Mixed Agreements', in D. O'Keeffe and H.G. Schermers (eds), *Mixed Agreements* (Deventer: Kluwer, 1983), 137, and C. Tomuschat, 'Liability for Mixed Agreements', in Keeffe and Schermers, *ibid.*, at 130.
[35] J. Groux and P. Manin, *The European Communities in the International Order* (Brussels: European Commission, 1985), 143.
[36] Cited above, at n 18.
[37] UN Doc. A/CN.4/545, above at n 19, at 13–4; *see* further Kuijper and Paasivirta, above at n 33, at 116–23.

of the WTO, this would mean that, prior to determining whether a measure challenged in dispute settlement can be attributed to the EC, one would need to establish whether the relevant obligation needs to be apportioned to the EC, or rather to its Member States.[38] In order to do so, one would need to examine the 'rules of the organization'.[39] Thus, EC law on external competence would need to be applied first. With respect to GATS and TRIPS in particular, the conclusion from that analysis might be that the relevant provision of WTO law does not come within EC competence—say a TRIPS provision on patents, where there is as yet very little EC law—and thus the EC has not assumed any particular obligation, and cannot be held responsible.

Neither the special rapporteur nor the ILC itself appear inclined to incorporate this approach in the draft articles, but that of course does not mean that it is incorrect. What could be the justification for the Commission's position? According to Mischo AG, the very fact that the agreement is concluded in mixed form announces to third countries that the agreement does not wholly fall within EC competence and the EC is only assuming responsibility for the parts within its competence.[40] Björklund advances further arguments in support of limits to joint liability in the case of mixed agreements.[41] He points out that an indiscriminate invocation of joint liability by other Contracting Parties appears inconsistent with the requirement of good faith in the performance of a mixed agreement. This would for example permit such parties to ask an EC Member State to act on a matter where they actually know that competence has been transferred to the EC, or to ask the EC to act *ultra vires*. He also draws attention to the rule in Article 46(2) of the Vienna Convention on the Law of Treaties between States and International Organizations or between International Organizations, according to which a breach of an organization's competence rules does not affect its consent to be bound by a treaty, 'unless that manifestation was manifest and concerned a rule of fundamental importance'. In Björklund's view, 'the idea of a rule of international law stipulating absolute joint liability for mixed agreements appears to conflict with the idea that acts which are manifestly *ultra vires* do not bind the organization'.[42]

There is of course some force to such arguments. But let us examine a little further what would be the consequences of either approach—apportionment, or no apportionment—in the framework of the WTO. If the Commission's position were followed, it would fall to WTO panels to establish the apportionment of obligations, in accordance with EC law. This is straightforward for the multilateral agreements on trade in goods, since they all come within the EC's exclusive competence under Article 133 EC. But it is much less so for

---

[38] In the Commission's view apportionment is the primary question, and attribution the secondary one, *ibid.*, at 14.

[39] For a definition *see* Art. 4(4) of the draft articles.   [40] Cited above, at n. 18.

[41] Björklund, at n 29, at 388–402.

[42] *Ibid.*, at 391. For criticism *see* L. Bartels, *Human Rights Conditionality in the EU's International Agreements* (Oxford: OUP, 2005), 153.

GATS and TRIPS, in particular where exclusive competence is based on the AETR principle.[43] Then there is the further question of the scope of the EC's non-exclusive external competences; is the existence of such a competence sufficient to apportion an obligation to the EC? It is hardly realistic to expect panels fully to engage with such difficult questions of EC law. Nor is it from a WTO perspective desirable to have panels confronted with complex issues of non-WTO law, since many cases are complex enough already, and further legal complication does not contribute to prompt settlement.[44] From an EU perspective such panel involvement is not desirable either, as the question of how to determine the scope of the EC's external competence is better left to the Court of Justice.[45]

There is, moreover, no textual basis in the WTO Agreements for an apportionment of obligations, and the arguments advanced by those who support such apportionment seem based on the idea that joint liability may not be appropriate in all cases. But does a lack of apportionment lead to a situation were there would be joint liability of the EC and its Member States in each and every case?[46] That is not a foregone conclusion. The draft articles require attribution of conduct. Imagine a case where an EC Member State is claimed to be in breach of certain TRIPS provisions on patent protection. As was mentioned, patent law is largely untouched by EC law. Let us therefore assume that the EC does not have external competence in this respect, and could therefore not have entered into the relevant WTO obligations. Perhaps, then, it would be impossible to attribute the relevant conduct to the EC? If there is no EC competence or EC law in the matter, it is hard to see what 'conduct consisting of an action or omission' (Article 3(2) draft articles) could be attributable to the EC. In other words, joint liability could be avoided through appropriate rules on attribution, and it would seem unnecessary to require apportionment of obligations first. There is a further advantage to such an approach. Imagine the EC acting *ultra vires*. It adopts a regulation or directive outside the sphere of its competences. If one would first need to apportion the relevant obligation in accordance with EC law on competence, the conclusion would need to be that the obligation could not be apportioned to the EC, and therefore no responsibility could be established. Surely this would be wrong. Whether or not the EC (or indeed a Member State) acts *ultra vires* is irrelevant from a WTO perspective; other WTO Members may expect the EC and its Member States to comply with their WTO obligations.

---

[43] For an illustration of the complexity of the AETR principle, *see Opinion 1/03*, above at n 3.

[44] *See* Art. 3.3 DSU.

[45] In *Opinion 1/91 (EEA Agreement)*, the Court objected to the fact that the envisaged EEA Court would be ruling on the respective competences of the EC and its Member States, *see* [1991] ECR I–6079, paras 31–5.

[46] On the distinction between joint responsibility and joint-and-several responsibility *see* Bartels, above at n 42, at 160–62.

B. Attribution of conduct

Chapter II of the draft articles addresses the issue of attribution of conduct. Article 4 contains the general rule, and refers to the conduct of an organ or agent of an international organization in the performance of functions of that organ or agent. Article 5 extends attribution to cases where an organ of a State, or an organ or agent of an international organization, is placed at the disposal of another organization: if the latter exercises effective control the conduct by such an organ or agent shall be considered an act of that organization. Article 6 provides that it does not matter whether the conduct of an organ or agent of an international organization exceeded the authority of that organ or agent or contravened instructions. Article 7, lastly, provides:

Conduct which is not attributable to an international organization under the preceding draft articles shall nevertheless be considered an act of that international organization under international law if and to the extent that the organization acknowledges and adopts the conduct in question as its own.

Those draft articles are of course written so as generally to cover responsibility of international organizations. It is not *prima facie* clear that they are particularly suited for the kind of mixed agreements which the EC concludes. As the European Commission rightly pointed out in its comments to the ILC, the EC case is special in the sense that its Member States so often act as implementing authorities of EC law. The Commission further referred to its observations in the LAN case,[47] where it took the view that the actions of these authories (*in casu* Member States' customs authorities) should be attributed to the EC itself and where it emphasized its readiness to assume responsibility for all measures within the particular field of tariff concessions.[48] Kuijper and Paasivirta take this point a little further. They are critical of the suggestion that, in cases where Member States' authorities implement EC law, such authorities are placed at the disposal of the EC (see Article 5 of the draft articles). They argue that this 'grates at the ears of the average Community lawyer, since it is inherent in the Community legal order, and in particular in the primacy of Community law, that Member States' legislative, administrative and judicial organs carry out and implement Community law'.[49] They submit that from a standpoint of pure Community law the idea that Member States' authorities act in the exercise of the authority of the EC is certainly the right one.

The problem should be further refined, though. The LAN case involved EC customs law, a segment of the common commercial policy extensively regulated through EC regulations, and indeed through international obligations assumed by the EC, where the role of the EC Member States is confined to implementing and applying EC law. Here the Member States act as agents of the EC. But even in the sphere of the common commercial policy, an area of

---

[47] Cited above, at n 21.   [48] UN Doc. A/CN.4/545, above at n 19, at 19–20.
[49] Kuijper and Paasivirta, above at n 33, at 127.

exclusive EC competence, there are other types of cases. The taxation of products, for example, is only partially harmonized by the EC (e.g. VAT and excise duties), and certain forms of taxation are not regulated by the EC at all (e.g. road taxes). It is generally accepted that, in the absence of EC harmonization, taxation is within the competence of the Member States. In an international trade context, however, such taxation is subject to the disciplines of Article III:2 GATT, a provision which comes within the exclusive competence of the EC. The Member States could not on their own have concluded GATT 1994, nor can they be regarded as agents of the EC or as exercising EC authority when adopting e.g. road taxes, and yet they are subject to Article III:2. *EC—Asbestos* offers another example. In that case French legislation banning asbestos was challenged under Article III:4 GATT and under the TBT Agreement. The EC took up the defence of the French legislation, and could well have been found responsible if a breach had been established (*quod non*).[50] And yet it was difficult to see how the French conduct could in any way be attributed to the EC, since France had adopted the relevant legislation for public-health reasons, and since there was no link whatsoever with EC legislation. In fact, if one considers, along with the Commission, that first one needs to *apportion* the relevant international obligation and only subsequently *attribute conduct*, the outcome appears wholly incongruous: the obligations (Article III:4 GATT and the TBT Agreement) need to be apportioned to the EC, and cannot be apportioned to France, whereas the conduct would seem attributable to France alone. No international responsibility therefore?

In his second report (2004) Gaja addressed some of these issues. He discussed EC mixed agreements, and referred to the ECJ's judgment in *Parliament v Council*, according to which the EC and its Member States were jointly liable under the Fourth Lomé Convention.[51] He took the view that in such cases attribution of conduct to the EC or a Member State was not relevant, and that even if it was ascertained that conduct was attributable only to one of those actors, they would all be jointly responsible.[52] He then looked at the case of an agreement concluded by the EC under the common commercial policy, where implementation is left to the Member State.[53] He referred to the Commission's observations which suggested that in such cases the conduct of a Member State should be attributed to the international organization because of its exclusive competence. The special rapporteur did not however approve of this approach. He considered that there was no need to devise special rules on attribution for this purpose. It could well be that an organization undertakes an obligation in circumstances in which compliance depends on the conduct of its Member States:[54]

[50] *EC—Asbestos*, WT/DS135.   [51] Cited above, at n 18, para 29.
[52] Cited above, at n 30, at 4–5.
[53] It may in fact be noted that issues of responsibility do not only arise for mixed agreements, but even more so for pure EC Agreements.
[54] Cited above, at n 30, at 6.

Should member States fail to conduct themselves in the expected manner, the obligation would be infringed and the organization would be responsible. However, attribution of conduct need not be implied. Although generally the organization's responsibility depends on attribution of conduct . . . this does not necessarily occur in all circumstances.

In its subsequent report (2004) the ILC took this up, without further clarifying: it simply stated that responsibility of an international organization may in certain cases arise also when conduct is not attributable to that international organization.[55]

Kuijper and Paasivirta then rightly pointed out that it remained somewhat mysterious how this approach could be squared with Article 2 of the draft articles, which generally requires both breach of an international obligation and attributable conduct.[56]

In his third report (2005) Gaja attempted to unveil the mystery. He indicated that there are two alternative ways of considering the implementation by States of treaties concluded by an international organization of which they are members. He proposed to focus on the content of the obligation breached rather than on attribution. The first alternative was that the organization may be under an obligation to take the necessary steps to ensure a certain conduct on the part of its Member States. The conduct of the Member States would not *per se* be wrongful under the treaty; it would only be the occasion for the organization to comply with its obligation or fail to do so. The second possible explanation was that the obligation for the international organization concerns the achievement of a certain result, irrespective of which entity takes the conduct that is necessary to that end. Thus the EC could be under an obligation to reach a result which may be attained by its Member States; under the rules of the organization the Member States may even be the only competent entities to do so. The special rapporteur did not consider it necessary to specify in the draft articles the possible existence of such types of obligation. He recognized that the breach of an obligation to achieve a certain result appears to imply an exception to the general principle of attribution of conduct expressed in Article 3 of the draft articles. That was not in his view a problem, since 'general principles are not stated as non-derogable rules'.[57] The ILC endorsed this approach in its 2005 report.[58]

These clarifications call for a couple of comments. It is not clear whether the two alternatives are really alternatives, or rather two different expressions of the same idea. Where the EC assumes a tariff obligation in the WTO it does appear to assume an obligation of result, which will require action both by itself and by its Member States. This obligation of result therefore includes an obligation to ensure that conduct by its Member States complies with the obligation. This is presupposed by the EC's commitment, and other

---

[55] Cited above, at n 31, at 101.   [56] Kuijper and Paasivirta, above at n 33, at 127.
[57] Cited above, at n 30, at 5–6.   [58] Cited above, at n 31, at 90.

Contracting Parties obviously base themselves on the assumption that the EC will be able to guarantee compliance. The second comment is that it may not be necessary to see this as an exception to the general principle of attribution of conduct. If the obligation is one of result, is there not simply an 'omission' (Article 3 of the draft articles speaks of 'an action or omission'), attributable to the EC, where it fails to prevent action by its Member States in breach of the relevant treaty obligation?

This approach to attribution of conduct would be consonant with the nature of the EC's external competence, for example in trade policy matters. It does not, however, resolve all issues. In particular, there does seem a need to look again at the question of apportionment of obligations. Take the patent law example. Assuming that the EC had no competence in this area when it concluded the WTO Agreement, the consequence is that it could not have assumed an obligation of result in this respect. For such cases, there is therefore still the question whether other WTO Members are supposed to be aware of the 'rules of the organization', and whether a panel could hold that a violation of TRIPS by a Member State is not attributable to the EC; or whether, by contrast, the EC is in any even jointly liable, since no apportionment of obligations took place at the time of the conclusion of the WTO Agreement and no declaration of competences was made.

IV. SOME CONCLUSIONS

Practice in the WTO appears to accept that the EC is responsible for violations, even by its Member States. The EC itself has suggested that Member State authorities act as agents of the EC, when implementing, e.g. EC customs law. It has also suggested that it acknowledges and adopts Member State conduct as its own. It is true that no hard cases, i.e. cases involving provisions of WTO law which are clearly not within the EC's competence, have been decided by a panel as yet. The practice does suggest that the EC is keen on accepting its responsibility.

There are two potential disadvantages to such an approach. First, it would seem that by accepting responsibility for measures by its Member States the EC exposes itself to suspension of concessions pursuant to Article 22 DSU extending to products originating from any Member State, and not just from the Member State whose legislation or action violates WTO law. Second, there is the question whether the EC can actually force a Member State to comply with WTO law in cases outwith the EC's external competences. In *Commission v Ireland* the Court of Justice ruled that, in the case of a mixed agreement, an enforcement action by the Commission under Article 226 EC is limited to the provisions of the agreement which are within EC competence.[59]

---

[59] Cited above, at n 18.

It is not clear therefore whether the EC has any internal legal mechanisms for acting upon its international responsibility in case a Member State violates a provision of WTO law which does not come within the EC's competences.

At a theoretical level it does not appear desirable to advocate a strict separation between apportionment of obligations and attribution of conduct. In fact mixed agreements (or indeed pure EC Agreements requiring implementation by Member States) can be brought within the scope of the draft articles as they currently stand, if one considers that the EC's obligations are in many cases obligations of result. Conduct can thus be attributed to the EC, either where the EC itself acts in breach of its obligations, or where it omits to prevent that a Member State so acts.

Applied to the WTO this approach would seem to cover most cases. The question nevertheless remains whether there is any room left for apportioning the relevant obligations. This would be in the sense of looking at EC law on external competence for determining those cases where the EC could not have entered into any obligation of result, because it lacks competence. One can see the arguments for accepting that other Contracting Parties ought to be aware of *manifest* cases of lack of competence. However, whether there are any such cases with respect to WTO law is doubtful, in particular since the re-writing of Article 133 EC at Nice. The conclusion would therefore seem to be that there is joint liability.

20

Overlaps and Conflicts of Jurisdiction between the World Trade Organization and Regional Trade Agreements

KYUNG KWAK AND GABRIELLE MARCEAU *

I. INTRODUCTION

The relationship between the dispute settlement mechanism of the World Trade Organization (WTO) and that of regional trade agreements (RTAs) demonstrates the difficulties surrounding the issues of overlaps/conflicts of jurisdiction and of hierarchy of norms in international law.[1] Jurisdiction is often defined in terms of either legislative or judicial jurisdiction—that is, the authority to legislate or to adjudicate on a matter. Jurisdiction may be analysed from horizontal points of view (the allocation of jurisdiction among states or among international organizations) and from a vertical point of view (the allocation of jurisdiction between states and international organizations).[2]

---

* The views expressed in this article are strictly personal to the authors and do not engage the WTO Secretariat or its members. We are grateful to John Kingery, Maria Pellini, Carmen Pont-Vieira and Yves Renouf for their useful comments on earlier drafts. Mistakes are only our own. The chapter is reprinted by and permission of the Publisher from The Canadian Yearbook of International Law Vol. 41 by Dan M. McRae © University of British Columbia Press, 2003. All rights reversed by the Publisher.

[1] On the issue of jurisdiction generally and the relationship between the jurisdiction of the WTO and that of other treaties and institutions, see J.P. Trachtman, 'Institutional Linkages: Transcending "Trade and . . ." ' (2002) 96 AJIL 77. On the issue of universal and criminal jurisdiction, see the recent judgment of the International Court of Justice and the separate opinions of Judge G. Guillaume, and Judges R. Higgins, P.H. Kooijmans, and T. Buergenthal in *Case Concerning the Arrest Warrant of 11 April 2000 (Democratic Republic of Congo v Belgium)*, Judgment [2002] [2002] ICJ Rep 1.

[2] This categorization is suggested by J.P. Trachtman who argues that the linkage problem between '[t]rade and . . . is a problem of allocation of jurisdiction; he suggests that there are three basic, and related, types of allocation of jurisdiction: (i) horizontal allocation of jurisdiction

This article addresses the issue of horizontal allocation of judicial jurisdiction between RTAs and the WTO, as expressed in the dispute settlement provisions of each treaty. The choice of a dispute settlement forum is often an expression of the importance that states give to the system of norms that may be enforced by the related dispute settlement mechanism. For instance, if the same states—which are parties to two treaties A and B that contain similar obligations—provide that priority or exclusivity is given to the dispute settlement mechanism of A over that of B, it may be that the states are expressing their choice to favour the enforcement of treaty A over treaty B.

In the case of RTAs, the situation is further complicated because the General Agreement on Tariffs and Trade (GATT) authorizes WTO Members to form RTAs. The WTO jurisprudence has made it clear that members have a 'right' to form preferential trade agreements. This right is however conditional. In the context of an RTA, Article XXIV may justify a measure that is inconsistent with certain other GATT provisions. However, in a case involving the formation of a customs union, this RTA 'defence' is available only when two conditions are fulfilled. First, the party claiming the benefit of this defence must demonstrate that the measure at issue is introduced upon the formation of a customs union that fully meets the requirements of sub-paragraphs 8(a) and 5(a) of Article XXIV. Second, this party must demonstrate that the formation of the customs union would be prevented if it were not allowed to introduce the measure at issue. Again, *both* of these conditions must be met to have the benefit of the defence under Article XXIV of GATT.[3]

Many RTAs include (substantive) rights and obligations that are parallel to those of the Marrakesh Agreement Establishing the World Trade Organization (WTO Agreement). Generally, these RTAs may provide for their own dispute settlement mechanism, which makes it possible for the states to resort to different but parallel dispute settlement mechanisms for parallel or even similar obligations. This situation is not unique as states are often bound by multiple treaties, and the dispute settlement systems of these treaties operate in a parallel manner.[4] At the same time, the WTO dispute settlement system claims to be compulsory and exclusive. Article 23 of the Understanding on Rules and Procedures Governing the Settlement of Disputes (DSU) mandates exclusive

among States, (ii) vertical allocation of jurisdiction between states and international organizations and (iii) horizontal allocation of jurisdiction among international organisation'. Trachtman, *ibid.*, at 79.

[3] WTO Appellate Body Report, *Turkey—Textiles*, WT/DS34/AB/R, para 58. Presently, Art. XXIV and WTO jurisprudence clearly establish that it is for the parties to the regional trade agreement (RTA) to prove that the concerned free trade area or customs union is compatible with Art. XXIV of GATT (and/or Art. IV of the GATS. This test has, however, been severely criticized for being unrealistic.

[4] The arbitral tribunal established under Annex VII of the UN Convention for the Law of the Sea stated that '[t]here is frequently a parallelism of treaties, both in their substantive content and in their provisions for settlement of disputes arising thereunder': *Southern Bluefin Tuna (Australia and New Zealand v Japan)*, Award on Jurisdiction and Admissibility of 4 August 2000 (2000) 39 ILM 1359, p. 91 (hereinafter *Southern Bluefin Tuna* case).

jurisdiction in favour of the DSU for WTO violations. By simply alleging that a measure affects or impairs its trade benefits, a WTO Member is entitled to trigger the quasi-automatic, rapid, and powerful WTO dispute settlement mechanism, excluding thereby the competence of any other mechanism to examine WTO law violations. The challenging member does not need to prove any specific economic or legal interest nor provide any evidence of the trade impact of the challenged measure in order to initiate the DSU mechanism.[5] The WTO will thus often 'attract' jurisdiction over disputes with (potential) trade effects even if such disputes could also be handled in fora other than that of the WTO.

II. OVERLAPS OF JURISDICTION BETWEEN RTAS AND THE WTO

Overlaps of jurisdiction in dispute settlement can be defined as situations where the same dispute or related aspects of the same dispute could be brought to two distinct institutions or two different dispute settlement systems. Under certain circumstances, this occurrence may lead to difficulties relating to 'forum-shopping,' whereby disputing entities would have a choice between two adjudicating bodies or between two different jurisdictions for the same facts. When the dispute settlement mechanisms of two agreements are triggered in parallel or in sequence, there are problems on two levels: first, the two tribunals may claim final jurisdiction (supremacy) over the matter and, second, they may reach different, or even opposite, results.[6]

Various types of overlaps of jurisdiction may occur. For the purpose of the present discussion, an overlap of jurisdiction occurs: (1) when two fora claim to have exclusive jurisdiction over the matter; (2) when one forum claims to have exclusive jurisdiction and the other one offers jurisdiction, on a permissive basis, for dealing with the same matter or a related one; or (3) when the dispute settlement mechanisms of two different fora are available (on a non-mandatory basis) to examine the same or similar matters. Conflicts are possible in any of these three situations. All of the RTAs examined in Table 1 in the

---

[5] The WTO jurisprudence has confirmed that any WTO Member that is a 'potential exporter' has the sufficient legal interest to initiate a WTO Panel process (WTO Appellate Body Report, *EC—Bananas III*, WT/DS27/AB/R, adopted 25 September 1997, at para. 136); and in WTO disputes, there is no need to prove any trade effect for a measure to be declared WTO inconsistent (Art. 3.8 DSU). This is to say, in the context of a dispute between two WTO Members, involving situations covered by both the RTA and the WTO Agreement, any member that considers that any of its WTO benefits have been nullified or impaired has an absolute right to trigger the WTO dispute settlement mechanism and request consultations and the establishment of a panel (WTO Appellate Body Report, *US—Wool Shirts and Blouses*, WT/DS33/AB/R and Corr. 1, adopted 23 May 1997, at para. 13). Arguably, a single WTO Member cannot even agree to take its WTO dispute in another forum.

[6] The issue of forum shopping is not new. In the old GATT days, parties to the Tokyo Round codes had the choice between the general GATT dispute settlement mechanism and that of the codes (Article 15 of the Agreement on Implementation of Article VI of the GATT).

annex of this chapter have dispute settlement mechanisms with jurisdiction that may potentially overlap with that of the WTO Agreement.

Table 1 examines different dispute settlement mechanisms of RTAs and attempts to describe systematically the dispute settlement mechanisms provided in the RTAs according to two different categories—the characteristics of the dispute settlement system and the region. Furthermore, the table identifies several important elements of RTA dispute settlement mechanisms, including: (1) the compulsory or non-compulsory nature of the RTA jurisdiction; (2) the reference to the WTO dispute settlement mechanism; (3) the exclusive or priority forum prescription clause; (4) the choice of forum clause; (5) the binding nature of dispute settlement conclusions; and (6) the remedy provided by the agreement, including the explicit right to take countermeasures in trade matters with or without the permission of RTA dispute settlement bodies.

III. EXAMPLES OF OVERLAPS OF JURISDICTION BETWEEN THE WTO AND RTAS' DISPUTE SETTLEMENT MECHANISMS

A. Canada–United States Free Trade Agreement / North American Free Trade Agreement (NAFTA) and the GATT/WTO Dispute Settlement Mechanisms

NAFTA provides that a forum can be chosen at the discretion of a complaining party and gives preference to the NAFTA forum when the action involves environmental, sanitary and phytosanitary (SPS) measures, or standards-related measures.[7] At the time of the conclusion of NAFTA, these provisions were more advanced than those of GATT. It further provides that, if the complaining party has already initiated GATT procedures on the matter, the complaining party shall withdraw from these proceedings and may initiate dispute settlement proceedings under NAFTA.[8]

However, in light of Article 23 of the DSU, which provides that a violation of the WTO Agreement can be addressed only according to the WTO DSU mechanisms, would the invocation of this NAFTA provision be sufficient to halt the WTO adjudicating body? How can Article 23 and the quasi-automatic process of the DSU be reconciled with the preference and, in some

[7] Art. 2005(3) NAFTA.

[8] Art. 2005(7) NAFTA, concludes that for purposes of Art. 2005, dispute settlement proceedings under the GATT are deemed to be initiated by a party's request for a panel, such as under Art. XXIII:2 of GATT 1947. Indeed, the explicit references to 'GATT' and to the 'General Agreement on Tariffs and Trade 1947' raise the question whether the same rules would continue to apply to the new DSU of the WTO. However, since the first paragraph of Art. 2005 refers to 'any successor agreement (GATT)' and the recent NAFTA panel described GATT as 'an evolving system of law' that includes the results of the Uruguay Round, the provisions of Art. 2005 of NAFTA would be applicable to the dispute settlement rules of the WTO. Arbitral Panel Established Pursuant to Article 2008 of the North American Free Trade Agreement, *In the Matter of Tariffs Applied by Canada to Certain US—Origin Agricultural Products*, Final Report (2 December 1996).

circumstances, the exclusive priority given to the NAFTA dispute settlement mechanism for obligations that are similar in NAFTA and in the WTO for the same facts? For instance, Article 301 of NAFTA explicitly refers to Article III of GATT. In a hypothetical case where a NAFTA state's domestic regulation violates Article III of GATT and Article 301 of NAFTA, the defending party may prefer to have the matter submitted to a NAFTA panel—it may have a valid defence under NAFTA—but the complaining party may prefer to have the matter addressed in the WTO. The situation may also be reversed if the defending party sees some procedural or political advantage in having its case debated in the WTO.[9]

In light of the quasi-automaticity of the mechanism, once a dispute is initiated under the DSU, it is unlikely that a WTO panel would give much consideration to the defendant's request to halt the procedures just because similar or related procedures are being pursued under a regional arrangement. To take the NAFTA/WTO example again, a WTO panel would not examine any allegation of a NAFTA violation, rather it would be asked to examine an alleged WTO violation, which would be similar to a NAFTA violation. Could it be said that the NAFTA and the WTO provisions are dealing with the same subject matter (which could be defined as the measure plus the type of obligation imposed by the law)? Strictly speaking, the matter is different, although the content of the obligations is similar. For instance, the Free Trade Agreement between the EU and Mexico[10] states that arbitration proceedings established under this agreement will not consider issues relating to parties' rights and obligations under the WTO Agreement. Would the insertion of this type of provision mitigate the problem of conflicts of jurisdiction or would it aggravate the situation?

If there is an allegation of WTO violation, it would be difficult for a WTO panel to refuse to hear a WTO Member complaining about a measure claimed to be inconsistent with the WTO Agreement on the ground that the complaining or defending member is alleged to have a more specific or more appropriate defence or remedy in another forum concerning the same legal facts. Before a WTO panel, should the NAFTA parties have explicitly waived their rights to initiate dispute settlement proceedings under the WTO, the situation would be the same. However, in such a case, in initiating a parallel WTO dispute, a NAFTA party may be found to be violating its obligation under NAFTA—that is, not to take a dispute outside of NAFTA. In these circumstances, the NAFTA party opposed to the parallel WTO panel (the 'opposing NAFTA party') could claim that the WTO panel initiated by the other NAFTA party is impairing some of its benefits under NAFTA. The opposing NAFTA party would arguably win this claim before the NAFTA panel. Theoretically, that opposing

---

[9] WTO Appellate Body Report, *Canada—Periodicals*, WT/DS31/AB/R, adopted 30 July 1997, is a good example of potential overlap. The US initiated its dispute against Canada under the DSU of the WTO rather than that of the NAFTA.

[10] Decision No 2/2000 of the EC-Mexico Joint Council of 23 March 2000 [2000] OJ L157/10 and annexes [2000] OJ L245/1, Art. 41.

NAFTA party would then be entitled to some retaliation—the value of which could probably correspond to (part of) the benefits that the other NAFTA party could gain in initiating its WTO panel.

In other words, even if it may not be practical or useful for a NAFTA party to duplicate in the WTO a dispute that should be handled in NAFTA, there does not seem to be any legal impediment against such a possibility, since, legally speaking, the NAFTA and WTO panels would be considering different 'matters' under different 'applicable law', providing for different remedies and offering a different implementation and retaliation mechanisms.

B. Other Free Trade Agreements with a 'Forum Election Clause' and an 'Exclusivity Forum Clause'

Some recent free trade agreements contain even further detailed and articulate provisions on the overlap with the WTO dispute settlement system. The Free Trade Agreement between the European Free Trade Association States and Singapore[11] explicitly provides that disputes on the same matter arising under both this agreement and the WTO Agreement, or under any agreement negotiated thereunder, to which the parties are party, may be settled in either forum at the discretion of the complaining party but that the forum thus selected shall be used to the exclusion of the other.[12]

The Free Trade Agreement between Canada and Costa Rica contains a general provision on the compulsory nature of the dispute settlement system provided for in the same agreement.[13] The agreement also provides that '[s]ubject to paragraph 2, Article VI:4 (Dispute Settlement in Emergency Action Matters), Article VII:1.5 (Antidumping Measures), Article IX:5.1.2 (Sanitary and Phytosanitary Measures) and Article XI:6.3 (Consultations), disputes regarding any matter arising under both this Agreement and the WTO Agreement, any agreement negotiated there under, or any successor agreement, may be settled in either forum at the discretion of the complaining Party'.[14] It also adds that once dispute settlement procedures have been initiated under Article XIII:8 or dispute settlement proceedings have been initiated under the WTO Agreement, the forum selected shall be used to the exclusion of the other unless a party makes a request pursuant to paragraph 2.[15]

These free trade agreements prohibit their members from initiating a second dispute on the same or related matters once the dispute settlement process of these free trade agreements or of the WTO has been initiated. It is doubtful whether this type of provision would suffice to allow a WTO panel to refuse to

---

[11] EFTA States–Singapore Free Trade Agreement, signed 26 June, 2002, in force 1 January 2003, available at www.efta.int (visited 10 April 2006).

[12] *Ibid.*, Art. 56(2).

[13] Canada–Costa Rica Free Trade Agreement, signed 23 April 2001, in force 1 November 2002, available at www.sice.oas.org/Trade/cancr/English/cancrin.asp (visited 10 April 2006), at Article XIII:6.

[14] *Ibid.*   [15] *Ibid.*

hear the matter in situations where the dispute settlement process of the free trade agreement has been triggered. It may be difficult at the early stage of a WTO panel to assess whether the matter is indeed exactly the same as the one raised in the free trade forum. The WTO panel may simply continue its investigation to find out whether the measure is inconsistent with the WTO provisions while assessing whether the obligations are the same under both treaties. However, the WTO Member party to the free trade agreement that initiates a WTO dispute process in parallel or subsequently to that of the free trade agreement could very well be in violation of that free trade agreement and lose, in application of the free trade agreement, all the benefits that it would/could otherwise have obtained from the WTO dispute settlement system.

C. Mercosur/WTO Dispute Settlement Mechanisms

The Southern Common Market (Mercosur)[16] provides that '[t]he controversies which arise between the State Parties regarding the interpretation, application or non-compliance of the dispositions contained in the Treaty of Asuncion, of the agreements celebrated within its framework, as well as any decisions of the Common Market Council and the resolutions of the Common Market Group, will be submitted to the procedure for resolution established in the present Protocol' and that 'the state parties declare that they recognize as obligatory, *ipso facto* and without need of a special agreement, the jurisdiction of the Arbitral Tribunal which in each case is established in order to hear and resolve all controversies which are referred to in the present Protocol'.[17] The Protocol of Olivos[18] now provides that the forum chosen by the complaining party should be the forum of the dispute and adds that once a forum has been selected it shall deal with the dispute at the exclusion of other fora.

In 2000, Argentina decided to impose safeguard quotas on entries of certain cotton products from Brazil, China, and Pakistan. Brazil asked an arbitral panel to rule on the trade dispute. The three arbitrators concluded that Argentina's safeguard measure was incompatible with the Mercosur Agreement. Argentina did not remove its quotas immediately, thus Brazil asked the WTO Textiles Monitoring Body (TMB) to review the legality of the Argentina quotas.[19] Although the WTO rules on textiles allow members to take some safeguard actions, the TMB concluded that Argentina's safeguard measures

[16] Mercosur was created by the 1991 Treaty of Asunción, signed 26 March 1991, in force 29 November 1991.

[17] Protocol of Brasilia for the Solution of Controversies, Council Decision MERCOSUR/CMD/DEC No 01/91, Arts 1 and 8, signed 17 December 1991, available at www.sice.oas.org/Trade/MRCSR/brasilia/pbrasilia_e.asp (visited 10 April 2006).

[18] Protocol of Olivos for the Settlement of Disputes in Mercosur, signed 18 February 2002, in force 10 February 2004 (2003) 42 ILM 2, at Art. 1.

[19] The legal issues in the WTO were slightly different from those before the Mercosur arbitrators and could have led to very complicated questions relating to the WTO compatibility of the Mercosur customs union and whether countries in a customs union can impose safeguard measures against imports from another member.

were incompatible with the WTO Agreement. Since Argentina continued to refuse to comply, Brazil was forced to take the dispute to the dispute settlement body (DSB) and could have requested the establishment of a panel. In the end, the parties settled amicably.

In 2002, Brazil initiated a WTO dispute complaint relating to the imposition of anti-dumping measures against the importation of poultry from Argentina.[20] Before the WTO panel, Argentina argued that Brazil had failed to act in good faith by first challenging Argentina's anti-dumping measure before a Mercosur ad hoc tribunal and then, having lost that case, initiating WTO dispute settlement proceedings against the same measure. Argentina raised a preliminary issue concerning the fact that, prior to bringing WTO dispute settlement proceedings against Argentina's anti-dumping measure, Brazil had challenged that measure before a Mercosur ad hoc arbitral tribunal.[21] According to Argentina, a member is not acting in good faith if it first has recourse to the mechanism of the integration process to settle its dispute with another WTO Member and, then, dissatisfied with the outcome, files the same complaint within a different framework, making matters worse by omitting any reference to the previous procedure and its outcome.[22] Argentina considered that 'Brazil's conduct in bringing the dispute successively before different fora, first Mercosur and then the WTO, constitutes a legal approach that is contrary to the principle of good faith which, in the case at issue, warrants invocation of the principle of estoppel'.[23] Argentina requested that, in light of the prior Mercosur proceedings, the panel refrain from ruling on the claims raised by Brazil in the present WTO dispute settlement proceedings. In the alternative, Argentina submitted that the panel should be bound by the ruling of the Mercosur tribunal. In the alternative, Argentina submitted that 'in view of the relevant rule of international law applicable in the relations between parties pursuant to Article 31(3)(c) of the Vienna Convention the Panel cannot disregard, in its consideration and substantiation of the present case brought by Brazil, the precedents set by the proceedings in the framework of Mercosur'.[24]

According to Brazil, the simple fact that it had brought a similar dispute to the Mercosur Tribunal did not represent that Brazil has consented not to bring the current dispute before the WTO, especially when the dispute before this Panel is based on a different legal basis than the dispute brought before the Mercosur Tribunal. Brazil asserted that the Mercosur Protocol of Olivos on Dispute Settlement, signed on 18 February 2002, cannot be raised here as an implicit or express consent by Brazil to refrain from bringing the present case to the WTO dispute settlement, again because the object of the earlier Mercosur proceedings was different from that of the present WTO proceedings.

---

[20] *See* WTO Panel Report, *Argentina—Poultry Antidumping Duties*, WT/DS241/R, adopted 19 May 2003.
[21] *Ibid.*, at para. 7.17. [22] *Ibid.*, at para. 7.19. [23] *Ibid.*, at para. 7.18.
[24] *Ibid.*

Furthermore, the Protocol of Olivos does not apply to disputes that have already been concluded under the Protocol of Brasilia.[25]

It is worthwhile to note the United States's argument as a third party. The United States submitted that the Mercosur dispute settlement rules are not within the Panel's terms of reference:

> Article 7.1 of the DSU makes quite clear that a Panel's role in a dispute is to make findings in light of the relevant provisions of the 'covered agreements' at issue. The Protocol of Brasilia is not a covered agreement, and Argentina has not claimed that Brazil's actions with respect to the Protocol breach any provision of a covered agreement. Rather, Argentina's claim appears to be that Brazil's actions could be considered to be inconsistent with the terms of the Protocol. A claim of a breach of the Protocol is not within this Panel's terms of reference, and there are no grounds for the Panel to consider this matter. Argentina may, however, be able to pursue that claim under the Mercosur dispute settlement system.[26]

The panel decided to limit itself to the arguments raised by Argentina— allegations of bad faith on the part of Brazil and the invocation of estoppels that would prohibit Brazil from challenging Argentina's actions before the WTO—and to reject them as inherently inconsistent. The panel concluded that 'two conditions must be satisfied before a Member may be found to have failed to act in good faith. First, the Member must have violated a substantive provision of the WTO agreements. Second, there must be something "more than mere violation". With regard to the first condition, Argentina has not alleged that Brazil violated any substantive provision of the WTO agreements in bringing the present case. Thus, even without examining the second condition, there is no basis for us to find that Brazil violated the principle of good faith in bringing the present proceedings before the WTO'.[27] The Panel then discussed the international law criteria for estoppel and concluded that there was nothing on the record to suggest that Argentina actively relied in good faith on any statement made by Brazil, either to the advantage of Brazil or to the disadvantage of Argentina. There was nothing on the record to suggest that Argentina would have acted any differently had Brazil not made the alleged statement that it would not bring the present WTO dispute settlement proceedings.

The panel also rejected Argentina's argument based on Article 3.2 of the DSU and Article 31(3)(c) of the Vienna Convention on the Law of Treaties.[28] The panel recalled that Article 3.2 of the DSU is concerned with international rules of treaty interpretation:

> Article 3.2 of the DSU is concerned with treaty *interpretation*. Article 31(3)(c) of the Vienna Convention is similarly concerned with treaty *interpretation*. However, the

---

[25] *Ibid.*, at para. 7.22.   [26] *Ibid.*, at para. 7.30.   [27] *Ibid.*, at para. 7.36.
[28] Vienna Convention on the Law of Treaties, signed 23 May 1969, in force 27 January 1980, 1155 UNTS 331.

Panel noted that Argentina has not sought to rely on any law providing that, in respect of relations between Argentina and Brazil, the WTO Agreements should be *interpreted* in a particular way. In particular, Argentina has not relied on any statement or finding in the Mercosur Tribunal ruling to suggest that we should interpret specific provisions of the WTO agreements in a particular way. Rather than concerning itself with the interpretation of the WTO agreements, Argentina actually argues that the earlier Mercosur Tribunal ruling requires us to *rule* in a particular way. In other words, Argentina would have us *apply* the relevant WTO provisions in a particular way, rather than *interpret* them in a particular way. However, there is no basis in Article 3.2 of the DSU, or any other provision, to suggest that we are bound to rule in a particular way, or apply the relevant WTO provisions in a particular way.[29]

This report was not appealed to the Appellate Body.[30] It is clear that WTO adjudicating bodies do not have the authority to enforce provisions of a RTA as such.[31] In a case such as this one, however, the WTO adjudicating bodies would seem to be assessing the concerned states' situation in light of their WTO obligations and not in light of their Mercosur obligations. Yet, contrary findings based on similar rules from the Mercosur and WTO institutions would have unfortunate consequences for the trust that the states are to place in their international institutions.

IV. HOW CAN STATES AND WTO PANELS DEAL WITH OVERLAPS OF JURISDICTION BETWEEN DISPUTE SETTLEMENT MECHANISMS OF RTAS AND THE WTO?

A. Solutions Suggested by International Law

Overlaps and conflicts of jurisdictions are now of relevance in international law generally because of the multiplication of international jurisdictions. In recent years, treaties and organs of jurisdiction have increased drastically in number. An obvious example is the multiplicity of treaties, organs, and jurisdictions that are involved in human rights issues.[32] The accepted practice seems to be that states may adhere to different but parallel dispute settlement mechanisms for parallel or even similar obligations. The arbitral tribunal of the International Centre for the Settlement of Investment Disputes/International Tribunal for the Law of the Sea in the recent *Southern Bluefin Tuna (New Zealand v Japan; Australia v Japan)* case stated:

---

[29] *See* WTO Panel Report, *Argentina—Poultry Antidumping Duties*, above at n 20, at para. 7.41.

[30] It is interesting to note that the new Protocol of Olivos on Dispute Settlement, above at n 18, now contains an exclusive forum clause: 'Once a dispute settlement procedure pursuant to the preceding paragraph has begun, none of the parties may request the use of the mechanisms established in the other fora, as defined by article 14 of this Protocol'. At the time of this dispute, it was not yet in force.

[31] Contracting Parties Decision, *US—Margin of Preferences*, 9 August 1949, BISD II/11.

[32] *See* E. Roucounas, 'Engagements parallèles et contradictoires' (1987) 206 *Recueil des Cours* 9, at 197.

But the Tribunal recognizes as well that there is a commonplace of international law and State practice for more than one treaty to bear upon a particular dispute. There is no reason why a given act of a State may not violate its obligations under more than one treaty. *There is frequently a parallelism of treaties, both in their substantive content and in their provisions for settlement of disputes arising thereunder* ... the conclusion of an implementing convention does not necessarily vacate the obligations imposed by the framework convention upon the parties to the implementing convention.[33]

A call for increased coherence was also made by a former president of the International Court of Justice (ICJ), Stephen Schwebel,[34] and again by Gilbert Guillaume,[35] against the dangers of forum shopping and the development of fragmented and contradictory international law. Roselyn Higgins believes, however, that there may not be any need for such an international structure, and coherence may be best ensured through awareness and exchanges between jurisdictions:

With the greatest respect to the past two Presidents of the International Court, I do not share their view that the model of Article 234 (the renumbered Article 177) of the Rome Treaty provides an answer. It is simply cumbersome and unrealistic to suppose that other tribunals would wish to refer points of general international law to the International Court of Justice. Indeed, the very reason for their establishment as separate judicial instances militates against a notion of intra-judicial reference.

The better way forward, in my view, is for us all to keep ourselves well informed. Thus the European Court of Justice will want to keep abreast of the case law of the international Court, particularly when it deals with treaty law or matters of customary international law; and the International Court will want to make sure it fully understands the circumstances in which these issues arise for its sister court in Luxembourg. Many ways of achieving this can be suggested; and events such as this lecture may perhaps be seen as counting among them.[36]

In the absence of provisions such as a choice of forum clause and an exclusive forum clause, it is possible that the dispute settlement forum of an RTA and that of the WTO may be seized, at the same time or sequentially, of very

---

[33] *Southern Bluefin Tuna* case, above at n 4, at 91 (emphasis added).

[34] '[I]n order to minimize such possibility as may occur of significant conflicting interpretations of international law, there might be virtue in enabling other international tribunals to request advisory opinions of the International Court of Justice on issues of international law that arise in cases before those tribunals that are of importance to the unity of international law ... There is room for the argument that even international tribunals that are not United Nations organs, such as the International Tribunal for the Law of the Sea, or the International Criminal Court when established, might, if they so decide, request the General Assembly—perhaps through the medium of a special committee established for the purpose—to request advisory opinions of the Court': S.M. Schwebel, President of the ICJ, Address to the Plenary Session of the General Assembly of the United Nations, 26 October 1999, available at www.icj-cij.org (visited 10 April 2006).

[35] *See*, for instance, the note by G. Guillaume, 'La Mondialisation et la Cour Internationale de Justice' (2000) 2 International Law Forum du Droit International, 242.

[36] R. Higgins, 'The ICJ, The ECJ, and the Integrity of International Law' (2003) 52 ICLQ 1, at 20.

similar matters, to the extent that obligations under the RTA and the WTO are similar and applicable. In the absence of any other specific treaty prescription, the rules and principles of treaty interpretation and of conflicts applicable to the substantive provisions of treaties would also be applicable to the issue of the overlap or conflict of their respective dispute settlement mechanisms. The issue is whether these rules of conflict *(lex posterior* and *lex specialis)* are such as to be able to invalidate the WTO dispute settlement process or nullify its access. It is doubtful.

As long as a treaty provides for a dispute settlement mechanism in its text, parties to the treaty may invoke that mechanism to settle a dispute concerning the interpretation or application of the treaty. In the absence of any clear prescription, such a cumulative application of various dispute settlement mechanisms under different treaties seems possible. In initiating a WTO dispute, the RTA member may, however, nullify the benefits of another RTA member and may be subject to RTA dispute settlement procedures and eventually retaliation in the RTA context. The WTO recognizes the legitimacy of RTAs (with conditions). It may be argued that RTAs' dispute settlement mechanisms are used to enforce the disciplines of RTAs (which themselves must be compatible with Article XXIV and with the WTO) and are therefore 'necessary' to allow members to enforce RTA rules (and the related countermeasures).

B. Treaty Clauses Addressing Dispute Settlement Mechanisms of Other Treaties

Article 23 of the DSU is a specific treaty clause[37] that seems to prevent other jurisdictions from adjudicating WTO law violations. However, Article 23 cannot prohibit tribunals established by other treaties from exercising jurisdiction over the claims arising from their treaty provisions that run parallel to, or overlap with, the WTO provisions. Hence, there is a need for WTO Members to further address the issue of overlapping WTO/RTA dispute settlement jurisdictions. Table 1 at the end of this chapter identifies a number of aspects relevant to RTA jurisdiction. A large number of RTAs provide for compulsory jurisdiction mandating the parties to refer their disputes to an institution established by the constituting treaty. Some RTAs provide for forum shopping or a forum choice clause, allowing for the settlement of disputes either in the RTA forum or in the GATT forum at the discretion of the complaining party. Other RTAs contain exclusive forum clauses, in addition to the choice of forum clause, providing that, once a matter has been brought before either forum, the procedure initiated shall be used to the exclusion of any other, as is the case with NAFTA and the free trade agreements between the United States

---

[37] Art. 30(2) VCLT.

and Singapore,[38] Japan and Singapore,[39] or Singapore and Australia.[40] The purpose of this rule was not to recognize the existence of *res judicata* as such (since the applicable law was strictly different—the law of the free trade agreement in one forum, GATT law in the other) but rather to introduce certainty and avoid multiple dispute settlement proceedings. In fact, NAFTA goes further than the Canada—United States Free Trade Agreement, which preceded NAFTA and, in the area of sanitary and phytosanitary measures (SPS) and environment and other standard disputes, obliges a NAFTA state to withdraw from a GATT dispute if the other NAFTA state prefers the NAFTA jurisdiction.[41] The Free Trade Agreement between Chile and Mexico[42] and the Free Trade Agreement between Canada and Chile[43] have similar provisions.[44]

There is no clear rule in regard to the relationship between the WTO jurisdiction and other jurisdictions. Article XXIV of GATT does not make any reference to the dispute settlement mechanisms of RTAs. In order to govern the legal relationships between RTAs' dispute settlement mechanisms and those of the WTO, a set of principles can be devised. If both processes were triggered at the same time, it is quite probable that the WTO panel process

---

[38] US–Singapore Free Trade Agreement, signed 6 May 2003, in force 1 January 2004, available at www.ustr.gov/Trade_Agreements/Bilateral/Singapore_FTA/Section_Index.html (visited 10 April 2006).

[39] Japan-Singapore New Age Economic Partnership Agreement, signed 13 January 2002, in force 30 November 2002, available at www.mofa.go.jp/region/asia-paci/singapore/jsepa.html (visited 10 April 2006).

[40] Singapore–Australia Free Trade Agreement, signed 17 February 2003, in force 28 July 2003. Art. 1801 of the Canada–US Free Trade Agreement, signed 2 January 1988, in force 1 January 1989, envisaged that disputes arising under both this agreement and GATT (including the Tokyo Round codes) could be settled in either forum at the discretion of the complaining party but that once a matter has been brought before either forum, the procedure initiated shall be used to the exclusion of any other.

[41] Art. 2005 of NAFTA, provides that after consultation 'the dispute normally shall be settled under this Agreement'. Paras 3 and 4 of Art. 2005 go further and prescribe the exclusive application of NAFTA to the detriment of GATT: when the responding party claims that its action is subject to Art. 104 of the Environmental and Conservation Agreements (inconsistency with certain environmental and conservation agreements), sanitary and phytosanitary measures, or standards-related measures adopted or maintained by a party to protect its human, animal or plant life or health, or its environment, and that raises factual or scientific issues on these aspects, 'the complaining Party may, in respect of that matter, thereafter have recourse to dispute settlement procedures solely under [NAFTA]'. According to para. 5 of Art. 2005, if the complaining party has already initiated GATT procedures on the matter, 'the complaining Party shall promptly withdraw from participation in those proceedings and may initiate dispute settlement procedures under Article 2007'. *See* the Agreement between the Government of Canada and the Government of the United States of America Concerning the Transboundary Movement of Hazardous Waste, signed 28 October 1986, in force 8 November 1986, TIAS 11099; and the Agreement between the United States of America and the United Mexican States on Cooperation for the Protection and Improvement of the Environment in the Border Area, signed 14 August 1983, in force 16 February 1984 (1983) 22 ILM 1025.

[42] Chile–Mexico Free Trade Agreement, signed 17 April 1998, in force 1 August 1999.

[43] Canada–Chile Free Trade Agreement, signed 5 December 1996, in force 5 July 1997.

[44] Art. N–05 of the Canada–Chile Free Trade Agreement and Article 18–03, para. 2 of Chile–Mexican States Free Trade Agreement.

would proceed much faster than the RTA process. What arguments may be raised before a WTO adjudication body with respect to the RTA dispute settlement mechanism? Are there rules of general international law that may be useful? Principles and rules that have been developed in private international commercial law for dealing with overlaps and conflicts of jurisdictions are also informative. It may be worthwhile to examine whether such rules could be used in situations of multiple jurisdictions of international law tribunals.

C. Abuse of Process, Abuse of Rights, and Good Faith

In public international law, a state, by initiating a second proceeding on the same matter, may be viewed as abusing its process or procedural rights. A tribunal could decline jurisdiction if it considers that the proceedings have been initiated to harass the defendant or that they were frivolous or groundless. It is not the multiple proceedings that are condemned 'but rather the inherently vexatious nature of the proceedings'.[45] Such a prohibition against 'abuses of rights' could be considered a general principle of law.[46] However, it is unlikely that any adjudicating body, including those of the WTO, would find the allegations that their constitutional treaty has been violated to be 'vexatious,' especially when, in all probability, the claims would be drafted to capture the specific competence of that tribunal.

One could possibly argue that a state may be bound by its implied commitment to respect a previous ruling and thus may have to refrain from resorting to another forum to challenge the previous ruling. However, at the same time, states may be bound by two different jurisdictions sequentially and this situation happens often in international law. One may also argue that the general obligation of states to enforce their treaty obligations in good faith obliges them to use the most appropriate forum to settle their disputes or to use them in any sequence. However, if states have negotiated the possibility of referring disputes to various fora, it has to be assumed that they intended to retain the possibility of using such fora freely, yet in good faith.

In addition, it may be argued that a WTO panel could consider consultations and the use of the RTA dispute settlement mechanism in an RTA context or the efforts to reach a mutually agreeable solution to the dispute as an evidence of the good faith of its member(s), which may be relevant for the determination of compliance with the WTO provisions. As shown in Table 1, RTAs generally provide for consultation mechanisms. Once consultations have been requested by a party, the other party usually has to respect such a

---

[45] Lowe affirms that the doctrine of abuse of process is 'well established, though occasions for its application are likely to be very rare': V. Lowe, 'Overlapping Jurisdictions in International Tribunals' (2000) 20 Aust YIL 1, at 13.

[46] Brownlie wrote that '[i]t is not unreasonable to read the principle of abuse of right as a general principle of law': *See* I. Brownlie, *Principles of Public International Law*, 5th ed. (Oxford: OUP, 1998), 447–48. *See also* WTO Appellate Body Report, *US—Shrimp*, WT/DS58/AB/R, adopted 6 November 1998, at para. 158.

request. Consultations normally take place in an RTA institution composed of representatives of participating member states.

D. Exhaustion of RTA Remedies

There does not seem to be any rule that demands the exhaustion of one dispute settlement mechanism prior to the initiation of another one. There is a principle in general international law that obliges states to ensure that local remedies have been exhausted before bringing a claim on behalf of a national to international dispute settlement mechanisms, but many would argue that this doctrine does not apply under WTO law.[47] In any case, the dispute settlement mechanism of a RTA does not provide for any 'local' remedy therefore it is difficult to consider that such a principle could be invoked to oblige a state to exhaust RTA remedies before going to the WTO.[48]

E. Reference to the ICJ

Another solution to address the proliferation of international jurisdictions is to adopt the suggestion of Judge Guillaume and empower the ICJ with some form of reference jurisdiction to be used by international tribunals, possibly through advisory opinion requests.[49] However, as he points out, it is unrealistic to expect states to empower the ICJ in this way or to expect international tribunals to surrender their judicial power. In addition, states or tribunals may not be able to agree on the type of questions to be referred to the ICJ.

V. PRINCIPLES OF PRIVATE INTERNATIONAL COMMERCIAL LAW DEALING WITH OVERLAPS AND CONFLICTS OF JURISDICTION

A. *Forum Conveniens* and *Forum Non Conveniens*[50]

The *forum conveniens* doctrine is defined as 'a court taking jurisdiction on the ground that the local forum is the appropriate forum (or an appropriate forum) for trial or that the forum abroad is inappropriate. It is said to be a

[47] *See*, for instance, E.-U Petersmann, 'Settlement of International Disputes through the GATT: The Case of Anti-Dumping Law', in E.-U Petersmann and G. Janicke, *Adjudication of International Trade Disputes in International and National Economic Law* (Fribourg: University Press, 1992), 126.

[48] On the issue of the exhaustion of local remedies in international law and its application in WTO law, *see* P.J. Kuijper, 'The Law of GATT as a Special Field of International Law' (1994) NYIL 227; *ibid.*, 'The New WTO Dispute Settlement System' (1995) 29 JWT, 49 and J.M. Rutsel Silvestre, 'World Trade Dispute Settlement and the Exhaustion of Local Remedies Rule' (1996) 30 JWT 107.

[49] He referred to the model found in Art. 177 of the EC Treaty (now Art. 234). *See* for instance Guillaume, above at n 35 at 242.

[50] On this issue, *see* T. Sawaki, 'Battle of Lawsuits—Lis Pendens in International Relations' (1979) 23 Japanese Ann Int L 17.

positive doctrine, unlike *forum non conveniens* which is a negative doctrine defined as a general discretionary power for a court to decline jurisdiction'.[51] However, the objective of both doctrines is the same—that is, to identify which forum is the most convenient one or which forum is not convenient. The criteria to determine which jurisdiction is to be preferred vary with each state. Most states rely on criteria such as connecting factors, expenses, the availability of witnesses, the law governing the relevant transactions, the place where the parties reside or carry on business, the interest of the parties, and the general interest of justice. In some states, courts use the *forum conveniens* doctrine as one of the discretionary criteria on which to base their jurisdiction. Other states explicitly refer to the doctrine and provide when and how such assessment must be performed by national courts and based on what criteria.

In the current state of international jurisdictional law, the doctrine of *forum non conveniens,* or of *forum conveniens*, absent an agreement among states, appears to be inapplicable to an overlap of jurisdictions in public international law tribunals. In domestic jurisdictions, the defendants have usually agreed to subject themselves to any such available jurisdiction, while it may not be the case with international jurisdictions. The location of evidence, witnesses, and lawyers is usually of minimal importance in international disputes. Although demands of efficiency in the administration of justice may indicate that a specific court should decline to exercise its jurisdiction, 'criteria developed in the context of a proper concern for the interest of private litigants make little sense in the context of inter-State proceedings'.[52]

Article 23 of the DSU reflects the clear intention of WTO Members to ensure that WTO adjudicating bodies can always exercise exclusive jurisdiction on any WTO-related claim. The WTO forum is always a 'convenient forum' for any WTO grievance. In fact, it seems to be the exclusive forum for WTO matters. In order to change this situation, members would have to negotiate amendments to Article 23 of the DSU and would risk reopening the debate on the prohibition of unilateral counter-measures, mandated by Article 23 of the DSU.

B. *Lis Alibi Pendens* and *Res Judicata*

The rule on *lis alibi pendens* (litispendence) provides that once a process has begun, no other parallel proceedings may be pursued. The object of the *lis alibi pendens* rule is to avoid a situation in which parallel proceedings, which involve the same parties and the same cause of action, simultaneously continue in two different states and with the possible consequence of irreconcilable judgments.[53] The *res judicata* doctrine provides that the final

---

[51] J.J. Fawcett, *Declining Jurisdiction in Private International Law* (Oxford: OUP, 1995), 5–6 and 10.

[52] Lowe, above at n 45, at 12.   [53] Fawcett, above at n 51, at 26.

judgment rendered by a court of competent jurisdiction on the merits is conclusive as to the rights of the parties and, as between them, constitutes an absolute bar to a subsequent action involving the same claim, demand, or cause of action.

It is generally difficult to speak of *res judicata* or *lis alibi pendens* between two dispute settlement mechanisms under two different treaties. The parties may be the same and the subject matter may be a related one but, legally speaking, in the WTO and RTAs, the applicable law would not be the same—certain specific defences may be available only in one treaty or time-limits, procedural rights, and remedies may differ. Therefore, it is difficult to speak of *lis pendens* or *res judicata* between two international law jurisdictions.[54] However, RTAs such as the Central American Common Market (CACM) and Mercosur refer to the effect of *res judicata*. The CACM, for instance, states that the arbitration award has the effect of *res judicata* for *all Contracting Parties* so far as it contains any ruling concerning the interpretation or application of the provisions of this treaty. Thus, once the interpretive ruling is rendered, all CACM parties are bound by it, even if they are not parties to the dispute. However several questions remain. Does it mean that the WTO panel's ruling, as long as it concerns the interpretation and application of the General Treaty on Central American Economic Integration between Guatemala, El Salvador, Honduras, and Nicaragua[55] (CACM) cannot be challenged (or risk to have it changed) in the WTO forum? How then can it be used? What if a WTO panel, in its assessment of the WTO compatibility of the RTA or one of its specific measure reads a provision of an RTA differently from the CACM formal interpretation? Should the CACM judgment not be considered as a fact—a legal fact—which the WTO panel will have to assess?

In the WTO context, Article 23 of the DSU provides that WTO grievances can only be debated within the parameters of the WTO institutions. It is difficult to see how WTO panels could decline jurisdiction for reasons of *res judicata, lis pendens*, or *forum non conveniens*.[56] This is not to say that the decisions and conclusions of those other RTA jurisdictions would be of no relevance to the WTO process. On the contrary, similar to any other court

---

[54] As Lowe points out, in most cases, the fact that a State has sought adjudication under one treaty cannot deprive it of the right to seek a declaration in respect of another treaty. *See* Lowe, above at n 45, at 14.

[55] General Treaty on Central American Economic Integration, done at Managua, adopted on 13 December 1960; Protocol of Tegucigalpa to the Charter of the Organization of Central American States, 13 December 1991; Protocol of Guatemala to the General Treaty on Central American Economic Integration, 29 October 1993; Convenio del Estatuto de la Corte Centroamericana de Justicia, 13 December 1992, available at www.sice.oas.org/cp_disp/English/dsm_II.asp (visited 10 April 2006).

[56] This is not to say that other jurisdictions do not have the capacity to read, take into account, and somehow interpret WTO provisions to the extent that it is necessary to interpret their own treaty.

decision on a similar matter, they will be examined as a judicial interpretation by another international tribunal of a similar provision.

VI. POSSIBILITY OF INVOKING ARTICLE 13 OF THE DSU TO OBTAIN (EXPERT) EVIDENCE FROM RTA PROCEEDINGS

Article 13 of the DSU allows any WTO panel to request from the parties, or from any source, any relevant information. Arguably, this information could include evidence from the proceedings in another forum. The WTO panel may want to require expert information from an RTA secretariat, or, with the agreement of the parties, it may also want to use the analysis or data collected during a RTA dispute process as expert data. However, how should a WTO panel treat submitted evidence that relates to a RTA proceeding? Panels are at all times bound by the provisions of Article 11 of the DSU, which mandates an 'objective' assessment of the facts and the law. If the panel respects due process, nothing would limit the right of a panel to inquire about members' actions in another forum dealing with similar claims.

VII. DISCUSSION ON OVERLAPPING DISPUTE SETTLEMENT MECHANISMS

In the absence of any treaty prescription, the state initiating the dispute will make its choice, taking into account the specific facts of the case, which include the expertise of adjudicators of each forum, the need for efficiency and specific remedies, and the procedural aspects of each forum. In addition, there are other factors of a more political nature that may affect the state's choice of forum, such as whether the state will seek a dispute settlement or a systemic declaration or what type, importance, or influence the forum will have, which will affect the state's choice of forum.

Is it conceptually possible that an RTA adjudicating body reach a conclusion contrary to that of the WTO adjudicating body on exactly the same factual allegation? The applicable law—that is, the treaty provision being interpreted and applied—would be different (on the one hand, RTA law and, on the other hand, WTO law), although it may happen that the said provisions of the two treaties are almost identical. Even if WTO Members are not faced with a formal conflict between two mutually exclusive jurisdictions, it may be that an RTA jurisdiction and the WTO jurisdiction adjudicate the same dispute or related aspects of the same dispute, and this situation in itself, can be problematic.

In the absence of the agreement of the parties to suspend the DSU mechanism, it is most doubtful whether a WTO adjudicating body would terminate its process solely on the ground that a related dispute or aspects of the same dispute are being examined or have been examined in another forum. Article 23 of the DSU and the quasi-automaticity of the DSU mechanism do not allow for such suspension of the DSU mechanism to happen. However, in initiating a WTO process, the RTA member may be in violation of the RTA and be subject to dispute settlement and possibly retaliation or other sanctions or countermeasures. It is thus argued that since dispute settlements are inherent to the application of Article XXIV, countermeasures are necessary instruments for effective RTAs and are therefore WTO compatible pursuant to Article XXIV.[57]

It is equally wrong to argue for an exclusive allocation in favour of the WTO forum for any 'trade' matter. Could one argue that Article 23 of the DSU goes as far as denying WTO Members the right to sign RTAs or other treaties with dispute settlement provisions where rights and obligations are parallel to those of the WTO? Such an argument is rather extreme since RTAs are explicitly permitted (with conditions attached) under Article XXIV of GATT and Article XIV of the General Agreement on Trade in Services, and such is the practice of states as well.

If an RTA contains an exclusive forum clause, nothing appears to prevent a WTO panel from proceeding to examine a claim of WTO violation even if, in doing so, one of the parties to the WTO dispute would be in violation of its RTA obligation. As mentioned earlier in this chapter, in such a case, the WTO Member that is also an RTA state, may, in initiating a parallel WTO dispute, be found to be violating its obligation under the RTA not to take a dispute outside the RTA and not to trigger a WTO claim regarding a related violation under the RTA. In these circumstances, the RTA state that is opposed to the parallel WTO panel could claim that the WTO panel initiated by the other RTA party is impairing some of its benefits under the RTA. The RTA state that is opposed to a WTO dispute would arguably win this claim before the RTA dispute settlement body. Theoretically, that RTA state would then be entitled to some retaliation, the value of which could probably correspond to (part of) the benefits that the other RTA party could gain in initiating its WTO panel. In other words, a distinction must be made between the fact that parallel dispute settlement proceedings can be triggered (and arguably cannot be stopped since there is as yet no international agreement on this issue) and the international responsibility of the concerned states that in doing so may be in violation of their treaty obligations.

A large number of difficult issues remain unresolved. Members may consider the possibility of providing for the suspension or the exhaustion of either the WTO or the RTA process in certain circumstances subject to identified criteria. Exchanges of information between RTAs and the WTO Secretariats can also be envisaged. Finally, the relationship between the rulings of RTAs and those of the

---

[57] The assumption is that the RTA otherwise respect the prescriptions of Art. XXIV. *See* the WTO Appellate Body Report, *Turkey—Textiles*, above at n 3, at para. 48.

WTO can also be negotiated. Since there is no 'international constitution' regulating the relationship between the dispute settlement procedures of regional and other multilateral agreements, nor any treaty provision on the matter in the WTO or elsewhere, the position taken by the parties to one of these agreements cannot be sufficient to prevent a different forum from adjudicating on a similar matter within its jurisdiction. Hence, the potential for tensions in their overlaps and the need to consider the issue is authentic. At the moment, there is no solution for this matter until a set of common rules is negotiated.

VIII. CONCLUSION

There could be overlaps or conflicts of judicial jurisdiction between the dispute settlement mechanism of the WTO and RTAs. The wording of Article 23 and the quasi-automaticity process of the DSU makes it evident that a WTO adjudicating body always has the authority and even the obligation to examine claims of violations of WTO obligations. WTO rights and obligations can be challenged only pursuant to the WTO dispute settlement procedures and only before a WTO adjudicating body (Article 23 of the DSU).[58] In addition, as stated earlier, in the context of a dispute between two WTO Members involving situations covered by both an RTA and the WTO Agreement, any WTO Member that considers that any of its WTO benefits have been nullified or impaired has the absolute right to trigger the WTO dispute settlement mechanism and to request the establishment of a panel.[59] Such a WTO Member cannot be asked, and arguably cannot even agree, to take its WTO dispute to another forum, even if that other forum appears to be more relevant or better equipped to deal with the sort of problems at issue. In so doing, the WTO Member may be in violation of an RTA, but this matter is not for the WTO adjudicating body (under the existing WTO provisions). However, this WTO Member may risk RTA retaliation that could be considered WTO compatible.

There appears to be no legal solution for a situation where two members are faced with two treaties that contain overlapping and potentially conflicting jurisdictions. Members remain obliged at all times to respect both treaties. However, this obligation on states may not suffice to stop a dispute settlement mechanism process triggered by a WTO Member contrary to its RTA obligations. Tensions may also arise from the availability of non-compulsory RTA dispute settlement mechanism with no binding effect even in the absence of strict *de jure* conflicts. It is not clear how members' benefits or their nullification in another forum could be taken by the WTO adjudicating bodies. For the time being, international law does not appear to offer any solution. It is

[58] Even an arbitration performed pursuant to Art. 25 of the DSU would be a WTO arbitration, hence, covered by the exclusivity provision of Art. 23 of the DSU.

[59] *See* note 5.

therefore for WTO Members to negotiate how they want to allocate jurisdiction between RTAs and the WTO and how the dispute settlement mechanisms of RTAs and that of the WTO will operate. In the meantime, the general principle of good faith and principles of interpretation call for the 'awareness' by jurisdictions and adjudicators of others' jurisdictions.

Table 1. Dispute Settlement Mechanisms of Regional Trade Agreements[1]

Section 1: Consultation, Good Offices, Conciliation, and Mediation

Dispute Settlement Provision	Jurisdiction	Reference to WTO Dispute Settlement (DS) Mechanism	Binding Effect of Decision	Remedy or Other Countermeasures	Potential for Overlap
Asia and the Pacific[2] Australia–New Zealand Closer Economic Relations Trade Agreement (ANZCERTA)[3]	Non-compulsory	WTO DS mechanism not mentioned	No binding effect	Unilateral safeguard measures	Low
• In addition to the provisions for consultations elsewhere in the agreement, ministers of the member states shall meet annually or otherwise as appropriate to review the operation of the agreement.					
• Consultations: The member states shall, at the request of either, promptly enter into consultations with a view to seeking an equitable and mutually satisfactory solution if the party that requested the consultation considers that an obligation under the agreement is not being fulfilled; a benefit conferred upon it by the agreement is being denied; the achievement of any objective of the agreement is frustrated; and a case of difficulty has arisen or may arise.					

	Non-compulsory	WTO DS mechanism not mentioned	Binding effect	Appropriate measures	Low
First Agreement on Trade Negotiations among Developing Member Countries of the Economic and Social Commission for Asia and the Pacific (Bangkok Agreement)[4] • Consultations: If a participating state should consider that another participating state is not duly complying with any given provision under this agreement, and that such non-compliance adversely affects its own trade relations with that participating state, the former may make formal representation to the latter, which shall give due consideration to the representation made to it. • Referral to the Standing Committee:[5] If no satisfactory adjustment is effected between the participating states concerned within 120 days following the date on which such representation was made, the matter may be referred to the Standing Committee, which may, by majority vote, make to any participating state such recommendation as it considers appropriate. • Decision of the Standing Committee: If the participating state concerned does not comply with the recommendation of the Standing Committee, the latter may, by majority decisions authorize any participating state to suspend in relation to the non-complying state, the application of such obligations under this agreement as the Standing Committee considers appropriate.				• The measures considered to be appropriate by the Standing Committee can be taken by the affected party. Unilateral suspension of concessions (safeguard measures) • Suspension of concessions is possible but should be notified to the other party, and the committee shall enter into consultations. • If the consultations fail, the party affected by such suspension shall have the right to withdraw equivalent concession(s)	

Continued overleaf

Table 1. *continued*

Dispute Settlement Provision	Jurisdiction	Reference to WTO Dispute Settlement (DS) Mechanism	Binding Effect of Decision	Remedy or Other Countermeasures	Potential for Overlap
Agreement on South Asian Association for Regional Cooperation (SAARC) Preferential Trading Arrangement (SAPTA)[6] • Consultations: Each contracting state shall accord sympathetic consideration to, and shall afford adequate opportunity for consultations regarding such representations as may be made by, another contracting state with respect to any matter affecting the operation of this agreement. • The Committee of Participants[7] may, at the request of a contracting state, consult with any contracting state in respect of any matter for which it has not been possible to find a satisfactory solution through such consultation. • Agreement between parties: Any dispute regarding the interpretation and application of the provisions of this agreement or any instrument adopted within its framework shall be amicably settled by agreement between the parties concerned. • Referral to committee: In the event of a failure to settle a dispute, it may be referred to the committee by a party to the dispute. The committee shall review the matter and make a recommendation thereon within 120 days from the date on which the dispute was submitted to it.	Non-compulsory	WTO DS mechanism not mentioned	No binding effect	Unilateral suspension of concessions (safeguard measures) • Same as Bangkok Agreement	Low

South Pacific Regional Trade and Economic Agreement (SPARTECA)[8] • Consultations: A party may at any time request consultations on any matter related to the implementation of the agreement. • Director: Any such request shall be submitted in writing to the director of the South Pacific Bureau for Economic Co-operation. On receipt of a request for consultations, the director shall inform the parties accordingly and arrange for consultations between interested parties.	Non-compulsory	WTO DS mechanism not mentioned	No binding effect	Unilateral variation or suspension of obligations (unilateral safeguard measures) • If, after consulting the other party, a mutually satisfactory solution is not available, then the party may vary or suspend its obligations.	Low
Melanesian Spearhead Group[9] • Consultation: Consultation shall take place between the parties, if a party is of the opinion that any benefits conferred on it by this agreement are not being achieved. • Institutional Framework.[10] The consultations shall take place through the institutional framework of the agreement.	Non-compulsory	WTO DS mechanism not mentioned	No binding effect	Unilateral suspension of obligations (safeguard measures): • Same as SPARTECA	Low
Europe and the Mediterranean Central European Free Trade Agreement (CEFTA)[11] • Exchange of information and consultation within the committee: For the purpose of the proper implementation of this agreement, the parties to it shall exchange information and, at the request of any party, shall hold consultations within a joint committee.	Non-compulsory	WTO DS mechanism not mentioned	No binding effect	Unilateral safeguard measures • If the party considers that the other party has failed to fulfil its obligations under the agreement, the party may take appropriate measures.	Low

Continued overleaf

Table 1. *continued*

Dispute Settlement Provision	Jurisdiction	Reference to WTO Dispute Settlement (DS) Mechanism	Binding Effect of Decision	Remedy or Other Countermeasures	Potential for Overlap
• Decision-making at the Joint Committee:[12] The Joint Committee is responsible for administration and implementation, keeps under review the possibility of removing further obstacles to trade between the parties. The committee shall/may make decisions in the cases provided for in the agreement and make recommendations on other matters.					
FTAs between European Free Trade Association (EFTA)[13] • Same as CEFTA	Same as CEFTA	Same as CEFTA	Same as CEFTA	Same as CEFTA	Low
FTAs between two states[14] • Same as CEFTA	Same as CEFTA	Same as CEFTA	Same as CEFTA	Same as CEFTA	Low
FTAs between European Community (EC) and other countries:[15] • Same as CEFTA	Same as CEFTA	Same as CEFTA	Same as CEFTA	Same as CEFTA	Low
Association agreements:[16] EC–Cyprus and EC–Malta • Exchange of information and consultation within Association Council:[17] For the purpose of the proper implementation of this agreement, the parties shall exchange information and, at the request of any party, hold consultations.	Non-compulsory	WTO DS mechanism not mentioned	No binding effect	Unilateral safeguard measures • In case of serious difficulties in the economic situation of either party, the party may take the necessary protective measures. Such measures shall be notified to the Association Council.	Low

• Decision-making at Association Council: The Association Council is responsible for administration and implementation, shall keep under review the possibility of removing further obstacles to trade between the parties. The council shall make decisions by common agreement in the cases provided for in the agreement. On other matters, the council may make recommendations.					
Cooperation Agreement between the EC and the former Yugoslav Republic of Macedonia (FYROM)[18] • Decision-making at the Cooperation Council:[19] Each party may refer to the cooperation council any dispute relating to the application or interpretation of the agreement. The council may settle the dispute by means of a binding decision.	Non-compulsory	WTO DS mechanism not mentioned	Binding effect.	Direct recourse to retaliation • If a party considers that the other party has failed to fulfil an obligation under the agreement, it may take appropriate measures. Unilateral safeguard measures	Low
Cooperation agreements:[20] EC–Jordan; EC–Lebanon; and EC–Syria • Referral to Cooperation Council:[21] The parties shall take any general or specific measures to fulfil their obligations under the agreement. If either party considers that the other party has failed to fulfil an obligation under the agreement, it may take appropriate measures. Before so doing, it shall supply the Cooperation Council with all relevant information for a thorough examination of the situation with a view to seeking a solution acceptable to the parties.	Non-compulsory	WTO DS mechanism not mentioned	Binding effect.	Direct recourse to retaliation Unilateral safeguard measures: • Same as the Cooperation Agreement between the EC–FYROM	Low

Continued overleaf

Table 1. *continued*

Dispute Settlement Provision	Jurisdiction	Reference to WTO Dispute Settlement (DS) Mechanism	Binding Effect of Decision	Remedy or Other Countermeasures	Potential for Overlap
Bilateral Agreement between Kyrgyz and Uzbekistan[22] • Negotiation or other means: Disputes between the parties regarding the interpretation or application of the provisions shall be settled by way of negotiations or by any other way acceptable for the parties.	Non-compulsory	WTO DS mechanism not mentioned	No binding effect		Low

America
Latin American Integration Association (ALADI)[23]
• Resolution 114:
   • Any member state may request that consultations be held with any member country or countries that, in their view, take measures that are inconsistent with the commitments undertaken by virtue of the provisions of the 1980 Treaty of Montevideo or of relevant resolutions of the association. The request shall also be forwarded to the Committee of Representatives.
   • Consultations: Consultations shall begin within five days after the request is processed and shall conclude ten working days after consultations begin. The member countries agree to respond diligently to requests for consultations and to carry them out without delay in order to reach a mutually satisfactory solution.
	Non-compulsory	WTO DS mechanism not mentioned	No binding effect		Low

- Referral to the Committee of Representatives:[24] Should no satisfactory solution be achieved between the parties directly involved in the dispute at the end of the consultation period, the member countries may submit the matter to the Committee of Representatives.
- The Committee shall propose to the countries directly involved in the dispute, 15 days after the matter was submitted to its consideration, the formulas deemed most appropriate for settling the dispute.
- Article 35 of 1980 Treaty of Montevideo:
- The Committee has the obligation to propose formulas for the resolution of matters raised by the member states, when the failure to observe some of the rules or principles of the present Treaty has been alleged.

Inter-regional Agreement on the Global System of Trade Preferences among Developing Countries (GSTP)[25]	Non-compulsory	WTO DS mechanism not mentioned	No binding effect.	Unilateral suspension of concessions	Low

- Consultations: Any dispute that may arise among the participants regarding the interpretation and application of the agreement or any instrument adopted within its framework shall be amicably settled by agreement between the parties through consultation.
- Recommendation of Committee:[26] In the event of a failure to settle a dispute through consultations, it may be referred to a committee by a party to the dispute. The committee shall review the matter and make a recommendation within 120 days from the date on which the dispute was submitted to it.

Unilateral suspension of concessions
- If a party considers that the value of concessions or any benefit from the agreement is being nullified or impaired, the party may consult the other party.
- If the consultations fail, the matter may be referred to the committee, which may make recommendations.
- If no satisfactory adjustment is made within ninety days after the recommendations, the party may suspend concessions.

Continued overleaf

Table 1. *continued*

Section 2: Arbitration[27]

Dispute Settlement Provision	Jurisdiction	Reference to GATT/ WTO DS Mechanism	Binding Effect of the Decision	Remedy[28]	Potential for Overlap
Asia and the Pacific Asean Free Trade Area (AFTA)[29] • Protocol on Dispute Settlement Mechanism:[30] • A member state involved in a dispute can resort to other fora at any stage before the Senior Economic Officials Meeting (SEOM)[31] has made a ruling on the panel report. • Consultations: Members shall accord adequate opportunity for consultations regarding any representation made by other members with respect to any matter affecting the implementation of the agreement. Any differences between the members concerning the interpretation or application of the agreement shall, as far as possible, be settled amicably between the parties. • Good offices, conciliation, or mediation: Member states that are parties to a dispute may at any time agree to good offices, conciliation, or mediation. They may begin at any time and be terminated at any time. Once procedures for good offices, conciliation, or mediation are terminated, a complaining party may then proceed to raise the matter to the SEOM.	Non-compulsory	WTO DS mechanism not mentioned	Binding effect • Arbitration: The party shall comply with the rulings of the arbitration tribunal within a reasonable time-period. If the party fails to do so, that party may consult with the complaining party. If no mutually satisfactory	Arbitration award • Decision by the AEM	High

Continued overleaf

- Referral to the SEOM: If the consultations fail to settle a dispute within sixty days after the date of receipt of the request for consultations, the matter shall be raised in the SEOM. The SEOM shall establish a panel or, where applicable, raise the matter to the special or additional rules and procedures for its consideration. However, if the SEOM considers it desirable to do so in a particular case, it may decide to deal with the dispute to achieve an amicable settlement without appointing a panel.
- Establishment of the panel: The SEOM shall establish a panel within thirty days after the date on which the dispute has been raised to it. The SEOM shall make the final determination of the size, composition, and terms of reference of the panel. The panel shall submit its findings to the SEOM.
- Decision by the SEOM: The SEOM shall consider the report of the panel in its deliberations and make a ruling on the dispute within thirty days from the submission of the report.
- Appeal: Parties to the dispute may appeal the ruling by the SEOM to the ASEAN Economic Ministers (AEM)[32] within thirty days of the ruling. The AEM shall make a decision based on a simple majority.

resolution is reached, the complaining party may request authorization for suspension of benefits from the AEM.

- Appeal with the AEM: The decision of the AEM on appeal shall be final and binding on all parties to the dispute.

Table 1. *continued*

Dispute Settlement Provision	Jurisdiction	Reference to GATT/WTO DS Mechanism	Binding Effect of the Decision	Remedy[28]	Potential for Overlap
Agreement between New Zealand and Singapore on a Closer Economic Relationship (ANZSCEP)[33] • Consultation: The parties shall consult each other concerning any matter that may affect the operation of the agreement. The parties shall try to reach a mutually satisfactory resolution of any matter through consultations. The parties may at any time agree to good offices, conciliation, or mediation. • Arbitral stage: If the consultations fail to settle a dispute within sixty days after the date of the receipt of the request for consultations, the complaining party may make a written request to the other party to appoint an arbitration tribunal. • Composition of the arbitral tribunal: The tribunal consists of three members. Each party shall appoint an arbitrator within thirty days of the receipt of the request, and the two arbitrators appointed shall designate by common agreement the third arbitrator, who shall chair the tribunal. If the chair has not been designated within one month from the appointment of second arbitration, the directorate-general of the WTO, at the request of either party, may select the chair.	Compulsory	WTO DS mechanism not mentioned However, the rules and procedures of dispute settlement under the agreement shall apply to the parties in dispute but without prejudice to the rights of the parties to dispute settlement procedures under other agreements to which they are parties.	Binding effect • The rulings of the arbitral tribunal shall be final and binding on the parties.	• The party shall comply with the rulings of the arbitration tribunal within a reasonable time period. • If the party fails to do so within the time limit, that party may consult with the complaining party. • If no mutually satisfactory resolution is reached, the complaining party may suspend the application of equivalent benefits.	Medium/High

Europe and the Mediterranean

Free trade area agreements:[34] EFTA–Morocco and EFTA–PLO

- Referral to the Joint Committee:[35] For the purpose of the proper implementation of this agreement, the parties to it shall exchange information and, at the request of any party, shall hold consultations within a joint committee.

- Decision-making at the Joint Committee: The Joint Committee is responsible for the administration and implementation, shall keep under review the possibility of further removing the obstacles to trade between the parties. The Joint Committee may make decisions in the cases provided for in the agreement. On other matters, the committee may make recommendations.

- Arbitral stage: Disputes relating to the interpretation of rights and obligations of the parties, which have not been settled through consultation or the committee within six months, may be referred to arbitration by any party to the dispute by means of a written notification.

- Composition of the Arbitral Tribunal: The complaining party will designate one panel member in its notification. Within a month from the receipt of the notification, the other party will designate one member. Within two months from the receipt of the notification, the two members already designated shall agree on the designation of a third member, who will become the president of the Arbitral Tribunal. The tribunal takes its decision by majority vote.

Non-compulsory	WTO DS mechanism not mentioned	Binding effect	Direct recourse to retaliation	Medium
		• The arbitration award is binding and final upon the parties.	• If a party considers that the other party has failed to fulfil an obligation under the agreement, it may take appropriate measures. Decision of arbitration panel • However, once the matter is referred to arbitration, the decision of the arbitration panel is binding.	

Continued overleaf

Table 1. *continued*

Dispute Settlement Provision	Jurisdiction	Reference to GATT/WTO DS Mechanism	Binding Effect of the Decision	Remedy[28]	Potential for Overlap
Free trade area agreements between EFTA and certain countries[36] • Referral to Joint Committee:[37] The parties shall make every attempt through cooperation and consultations to arrive at a mutually satisfactory resolution of disputes. At the request of a party, the consultations shall take place in the Joint Committee if any of the parties so request. • Arbitral stage: Disputes between the parties to this agreement, relating to the interpretation of rights and obligations under this agreement, which have not been settled through direct consultations or in the Joint Committee within ninety days from the date of the receipt of the request for consultations, may be referred to arbitration by any party to the dispute. • Composition of the Arbitral Tribunal: The complaining party will designate one panel member in its notification. Within a month from the receipt of the notification, the other party will designate one member. Within two months from the receipt of the notification, the two members already designated shall agree on the designation of a third member, who will become the president of the Arbitral Tribunal. The tribunal takes its decision by majority vote.	Non-compulsory	WTO DS mechanism not mentioned	Binding effect • The arbitration award is binding and final upon the parties.	Direct recourse to retaliation • Same as EFTA—Morocco/PLO Decision of arbitration panel: • Same as EFTA—Morocco/PLO	Medium

EFTA–Mexico[38]	Compulsory jurisdiction	Exclusive forum clause	Binding effect	Decision of arbitration panel	Medium
• Consultation: The parties shall at all times endeavour to agree on the interpretation and application of the agreement and shall make every attempt through cooperation and consultations to arrive at a mutually satisfactory resolution of any matter that might affect their operation. • Referral to Joint Committee:[39] Each party may request consultations within the Joint Committee with respect to any matter relating to the application or interpretation of the agreement. The Joint Committee shall convene within thirty days of delivery of the request and shall endeavour to resolve the dispute promptly by means of a decision. That decision shall specify the implementing measures to be taken by the party concerned and the period of time to do so. • Arbitral stage: In case a party considers that a measure applied by the other party violates the agreement and such matter has not been resolved within fifteen days after the Joint Committee has convened or forty-five days after the delivery of the request for a Joint Committee meeting, either party may request in writing the establishment of an arbitration panel. • Composition of arbitration panel: The panel consists of three members. Each party shall appoint an arbitrator, and the two arbitrators appointed shall designate by common agreement the third arbitrator, who shall chair the panel. If not all three members have been appointed within thirty days from receipt of notification, any party may request that the directorate-general of the WTO designates the member.		• Once the dispute settlement provisions of this agreement or the WTO Agreements have been initiated, the procedure initiated shall be used to the exclusion of any other. Forum election clause • Disputes regarding any matter arising under both this agreement and the WTO Agreement may be settled in either form at the discretion of the complaining party. Recourse to DS procedure by a third party	• The decision of the arbitration panel is final and binding	• The party shall comply with the rulings of the arbitration tribunal within a reasonable time period. • If the party fails to do so within the time limit, that party may consult with the complaining party. • If no mutually satisfactory resolution is reached, the complaining party may suspend the application of equivalent benefits.	

Continued overleaf

Table 1. *continued*

Dispute Settlement Provision	Jurisdiction	Reference to GATT/WTO DS Mechanism	Binding Effect of the Decision	Remedy[28]	Potential for Overlap
		• If a third party wishes to resort to DS procedures as a complainant under this agreement on the same matter, it must inform the notifying party. If these parties cannot agree on a single forum, the dispute normally shall be settled under this agreement			
Customs Union between the EC and Andorra[40] • Referral to Joint Committee:[41] Any disputes arising between the contracting parties over the interpretation of the agreement shall be put before the Joint Committee. • Arbitral stage: If the Joint Committee does not succeed in settling the dispute at its next meeting, each party may notify the other of the designation of an arbitrator; the other party shall then be	Compulsory	WTO DS mechanism not mentioned	Binding effect • The arbitration award is binding and final upon the parties.	Direct recourse to retaliation • Same as EFTA–Morocco/PLO Decision of arbitration panel: • Same as EFTA–Morocco/PLO	High

required to designate a second arbitrator within two months. The Joint Committee shall designate a third arbitrator. The arbitrator's decisions shall be taken by majority vote.

Customs Union between the EC and Turkey[42] • Consultation: In harmonizing the legislation, each party may consult each other within the Customs Union Joint Committee.[43] • Referral to Joint Committee: If a mutually acceptable solution is not found by the committee and if either party considers that discrepancies in the legislation may affect the free movement of goods, deflect trade, or create economic problems, it may refer the matter to the committee, which may make recommendations. If discrepancies cause or threaten to cause impairment of the free movement of goods or the deflection of trade, the party may take the necessary protection measures. • Arbitral stage: If the Association Council[44] fails to settle a dispute relating to the scope or duration of protection measures, either party may refer the dispute to arbitration. • Composition of arbitration panel: There shall be three arbitrators, two appointed by each party and a third appointed by common agreement. The panel shall take its decisions by majority.	Compulsory	WTO DS mechanism not mentioned	Binding effect • The arbitration award shall be binding on the parties.	Decision of arbitration panel	High
Europe Agreements[45] • Referral to Association Council:[46] Each of the two parties may refer to the Association Council any dispute relating to the application or interpretation of the agreement. The Association Council may settle the dispute by means of a	Compulsory	WTO DS mechanism not mentioned	Binding effect • The arbitration award is binding and final	Direct recourse to retaliation • If a party considers that the other party has failed to fulfil an obligation, it may take appropriate measures. Decision of arbitration panel	High

Continued overleaf

Table 1. *continued*

Dispute Settlement Provision	Jurisdiction	Reference to GATT/WTO DS Mechanism	Binding Effect of the Decision	Remedy[28]	Potential for Overlap
decision. Each party shall be bound to take the measures involved in carrying out the decision. • Arbitral stage: If it is impossible to settle the dispute by means of a decision, either party may notify the other of the appointment of an arbitrator; the other party must then appoint a second arbitrator within two months. The Association Council shall appoint a third arbitrator. The arbitrator's decisions shall be taken by majority vote.			upon the parties.		
Association agreements between the EC and certain countries:[47] • Same as Europe Agreements	Compulsory	WTO DS mechanism not mentioned	Same as Europe Agreements	Same as Europe Agreements	High
Cooperation Agreement between the EC and Algeria • Same as Europe Agreements	Compulsory	WTO DS mechanism not mentioned	Same as Europe Agreements	Same as Europe Agreements	High
Bilateral agreements[48] • Same as Europe Agreements	Compulsory	WTO DS mechanism not mentioned	Same as Europe Agreements	Same as Europe Agreements	High

	Compulsory	Exclusive forum clause	Binding effect	Decision of arbitration panel	High
EC–Mexico[49] • Consultation: The parties shall endeavour to agree on the interpretation and application of the agreement and shall make every attempt through cooperation and consultations to arrive at a mutually satisfactory resolution of any matter that might affect their operation. • Referral to Joint Committee:[50] Each party may request consultations within the Joint Committee with respect to any matter relating to the application or interpretation of the agreement. The Joint Committee shall convene within thirty days of delivery of the request and shall endeavour to resolve the dispute promptly by means of a decision, which should specify the implementing measure and the period for implementation. • Arbitral stage: In case a party considers that a measure applied by the other party violates the agreement and such matter has not been resolved within fifteen days after the Joint Committee has convened or forty-five days after the delivery of the request for a Joint Committee meeting, either party may request in writing the establishment of an arbitration panel. • Composition of an arbitration panel: The panel consists of three members. Each party shall appoint an arbitrator, and the two arbitrators appointed shall designate by common agreement the third arbitrator, who is the chair of the panel.	Compulsory	• Recourse to the dispute settlement provisions of the agreement shall be without prejudice to any action in the WTO framework. However, where a party has instituted a DS proceeding under this agreement or the WTO Agreement, it shall not institute a DS proceeding on the same matter under the other forum until the end of the first proceeding. Arbitration proceedings under the agreement will not consider parties' rights and obligations under the WTO Agreement.	• Each party shall be bound to take the measures involved in carrying out the final arbitration report.		High

Continued overleaf

Table 1. *continued*

Dispute Settlement Provision	Jurisdiction	Reference to GATT/WTO DS Mechanism	Binding Effect of the Decision	Remedy[28]	Potential for Overlap
Commonwealth of Independent States (CIS)[51] • Any disputes and disagreements between the members shall be settled in the following manner: conduct immediate consultations, through a special conciliatory procedure; in the Economic Court of the CIS; through other procedures provided by international law. • Transition to the subsequent procedure is possible by mutual consent of the disputing parties or by the order of one of them if agreement is not reached within six months from the day of the beginning of the procedure.	Non-compulsory	WTO DS mechanism not mentioned	Binding effect		Medium/High
America[52] Central American Common Market (CACM)[53] • General Treaty on Central American Economic Integration: • Agreement: The parties may settle disputes concerning interpretation or application of the agreement amicably through the Executive Council[54] or the Central American Economic Council.[55] • Arbitral stage: If agreement cannot be reached, they shall submit the matter to arbitration. For the purpose of constituting the arbitration tribunal, the secretary-general of the Organization of Central American States and	Compulsory	WTO DS mechanism not mentioned	Binding effect: • The award of the arbitration tribunal shall require the concuring votes of not less than three members and shall	Decision of arbitration panel	High

Continued overleaf

Provisions	Binding effect	Relationship with WTO	Nature	Remedies	Intensity
the government representatives in the organization shall select, by drawing lots, one arbitrator for each contracting party from a list containing the names of arbitrators proposed by each member state. • Protocol of Tegucigalpa: • Article 35: Any disagreement on the application or interpretation of the provisions contained in this protocol and any other convention, agreement, or protocol between the members (bilateral or multilateral) on Central American integration shall be put before the Central American Court of Justice. • Transitional provisions (Article 3) provides that, for the purposes of what is established in paragraph 2 of Article 35, until the Central American Court of Justice is established, disputes on the application or interpretation of the provisions in the protocol will be submitted to the Central American Judicial Council.	have the effect of *res judicata* for all the contracting parties so far as it contains any ruling concerning the interpretation or application of the provisions of this treaty.		Compulsory		Medium
US–Israel FTA[56] • Consultations: The parties shall make every attempt to arrive at a mutually agreeable resolution through consultations whenever: a disputes arises concerning the interpretation of the agreement; a party considers that the other party has failed to carry out its obligations under the agreement; or a party considers that measures taken by the other party severely distort the balance of trade benefits accorded by the agreement or substantially undermine fundamental objectives of the agreement.	No binding effect • The panel report is not binding but the Joint Committee will make a final decision taking into account the	WTO DS mechanism not mentioned. However, Exclusive forum clause • If the dispute settlement panel under the agreement or any other international dispute settlement mechanism is invoked with		Appropriate measures • After a dispute has been referred to a panel and the panel has presented its report, the affected party shall be entitled to take any appropriate measure.	

Table 1. *continued*

Dispute Settlement Provision	Jurisdiction	Reference to GATT/WTO DS Mechanism	Binding Effect of the Decision	Remedy[28]	Potential for Overlap
• Referral to Joint Committee:[57] If the parties fail to resolve a matter through consultations within sixty days, either party may refer the matter to the joint committee. • Arbitral stage: If a matter referred to the joint committee has not been resolved within three months, or within such other period as agreed upon, either party may refer the matter to a dispute settlement panel. The panel shall be composed of three members: each party will appoint one, and two appointees will choose a third.		respect to any matter, the mechanism shall have exclusive jurisdiction over that matter.	panel decision.		
Southern Common Market (Mercosur)[58] There are two tracks of dispute settlement mechanisms to which the parties can resort. Member states can either go straight to the Brasília Protocol, which is faster, or through the Ouro Preto Protocol, which is longer but provides for a technical committee phase and could allow more easily for mutually agreeable solutions. (1) Brasília Protocol—Chapter IV: • Direct negotiations: The state parties to any controversy will first attempt to resolve it through direct negotiations. They will inform the Common Market Group[59] regarding the actions undertaken during the negotiations and their results.	Compulsory: • The state parties declare that they recognize as obligatory, *ipso facto* and without need of a special agreement, the jurisdiction of the Arbitral Tribunal, which in each case is	WTO DS mechanism not mentioned	Binding effect: • The decisions of the tribunal cannot be appealed, and are binding on the parties to the controversies from the moment	Decision of arbitration panel	High

Continued overleaf

the respective notification is received and will be deemed by them to have the effect of *res judicata*.

established in order to hear and resolve all controversies that are referred to in the present protocol.

- Participation of the Common Market Group: if the direct negotiations do not resolve the matter, any of the parties can submit for consideration by the Common Market Group, which will evaluate the situation. At the conclusion of the procedure (not exceeding thirty days), the Common Market Group will formulate its recommendations to the parties.

- Arbitral stage: If direct negotiations and intervention by the Common Market Group fail, any of the state parties to the controversy can communicate to the Administrative Secretariat its intention to resort to the arbitral procedure. The tribunal shall issue its decision within sixty days, extendable for an additional thirty days, from the time its president is designated. The tribunal will take decision by majority vote.

- Composition of the Arbitral Tribunal: Each state party will designate one arbitrator from a pre-existing list of names deposited at the Administrative Secretariat. The third arbitrator will be designated upon common agreement and will reside over the arbitral tribunal. The arbitrators should be named within fifteen days from the date on which the intention of one of the parties to resort to arbitration was communicated to the other parties to the controversy.

Table 1. *continued*

Dispute Settlement Provision	Jurisdiction	Reference to GATT/ WTO DS Mechanism	Binding Effect of the Decision	Remedy[28]	Potential for Overlap
(2) Protocol of Ouro Preto—Article 21 + Annex: • Mercosul Trade Commission: The commission receives complaints originating from member states or from private parties. It must consider the complaint in the first subsequent meeting. If no solution is agreed upon, then a technical committee (intergovernmental) is established. There are thirty days to elaborate joint recommendation or individual conclusions. The commission evaluates joint recommendation or conclusions in its next meeting. • Submission of Complaint to Common Market Group: If there is no consensus, the complaint is submitted to the Common Market Group, which will have thirty days to consider the complaint. If a consensus is reached, a deadline is given to the member state to take measures. If there is no consensus or the member state does not implement measures, Chapter IV of the Brasilia Protocol—Ad Hoc Arbitral Tribunal is invoked. (3) Protocol of Olivos for the Solution of Controversies:					

- The new Protocol of Olivos Protocol was signed in Buenos Aires on 18 February 2002 and changes the mechanism in fundamental ways (Appellate Body, WTO clause, and so on) and will enter into force after ratification and will replace the Brasília Protocol.

		Exclusive forum clause	Binding effect:	Suspension of benefits	High
North American Free Trade Agreement (NAFTA)[60] • Cooperation: The parties shall at all times endeavour to agree on the interpretation and application of the agreement and shall make every attempt through cooperation and consultations to arrive at a mutually satisfactory resolution of any matter that might affect its operation. • Consultations: If the matter is not settled through cooperation, either party may request in writing consultations with the other party regarding the interpretation or application of the agreement, or wherever a party considers that an actual or proposed measure of the other party is, or would be, inconsistent with the obligations of this agreement or cause nullification or impairment. • Commission[61]—Good Offices, Conciliation and Mediation: If the parties fail to resolve a matter through consultations within the time limit (thirty days of delivery of a request for consultations, fifteen days of delivery of a request for consultations on matters of urgency, or any other period as they may agree), either party may request in writing a meeting of the commission.	Compulsory	• Once the dispute settlement provisions of this agreement or the WTO Agreement have been initiated, the procedure initiated shall be used to the exclusion of any other. Forum election clause • Disputes regarding any matter arising under both this agreement and the WTO Agreement may be settled in either form at the discretion of the complaining party:	• On receipt of the final report of a panel, the disputing parties shall agree on the resolution of the dispute, which normally shall conform with the determinations and recommendations of the panel, and shall notify their	• If the final panel report determined that a measure is inconsistent with the obligations of the agreement or causes nullification or impairment, and the respondent party has not agreed with the complaining party on a mutually satisfactory solution within thirty days of receiving the final report, the complaining party may suspend the application of benefits of equivalent effect until the measures complained against have been removed or a mutually satisfactory solution is reached.	

Continued overleaf

Table 1. *continued*

Dispute Settlement Provision	Jurisdiction	Reference to GATT/WTO DS Mechanism	Binding Effect of the Decision	Remedy[28]	Potential for Overlap
• Arbitral stage: If the matter has not been resolved, either party may request in writing the establishment of an arbitral panel within the time limit (thirty days after the commission has convened for the meeting, thirty days after the commission has convened with respect to the matter most referred to it, where proceedings have been consolidated, and such other period as the parties may agree). On delivery of the request, the commission shall establish an arbitral panel. The panel issues the initial report and the parties have the opportunity to submit their comment. The panel issues its final report. • Composition of arbitration panel: The panel shall comprise three members. Each party shall select one panellist and will agree on a third panellist, who shall serve as chair of the panel.		• An exception is made in respect to claims involving environmental, SPS, and technical standards matters, for which the responding party may demand that the matter be settled by a NAFTA panel. • Recourse to DS procedure by a third party: If a third party wishes to have recourse to NAFTA DS procedures on the same matter and if these parties cannot agree on a single forum, the dispute normally shall be settled under NAFTA agreement.	sections of the Secretariat of any agreed resolution of any dispute.		

Canada–Israel FTA[62] • Same as NAFTA	Compulsory	Exclusive forum clause Forum election clause • In the event of any inconsistency between this agreement and the WTO Agreement, this agreement shall prevail to the extent of the inconsistency, except as otherwise provided in the agreement.	Binding effect • Same as NAFTA.	Suspension of benefits: • Same as NAFTA, except, insert '30 days of receiving the final report if the measure was found to be inconsistent with the agreement or within 180 days if the measure was found to cause nullification or impairment' instead of '30 days of receiving final report.'	High
Canada–Chile FTA[63] • Same as NAFTA	Compulsory	Exclusive forum clause Forum election clause • If the party claims that its action s subject to Article A-4 (relation to environmental and conservation agreements) and request that the matter be considered under this agreement,	Binding effect • Same as NAFTA.	Suspension of benefits • Same as NAFTA	High

Continued overleaf

Table 1. *continued*

Dispute Settlement Provision	Jurisdiction	Reference to GATT/ WTO DS Mechanism	Binding Effect of the Decision	Remedy[28]	Potential for Overlap
		then the party has the sole recourse to dispute settlement under the agreement.			
Chile–Mexico FTA[64] • Same as NAFTA	Compulsory	Exclusive forum clause Forum election clause • If the responding party claims that its action is subject to Article 1–06 (relation to environmental and conservation agreements) and request that the matter be considered under this agreement, the complaining party may have recourse to dispute settlement procedures solely under this agreement.	Binding effect • Unless the Commission decides otherwise, the final report of the panel shall be published. The final report of the panel is binding on the parties.	Suspension of benefits • Same as NAFTA	High

		Exclusive forum clause / Forum election clause	Binding effect	Suspension of benefits	
Israel–Mexico FTA[65] • Same as NAFTA	Compulsory		• Same as NAFTA.		High
US–Jordan FTA[66] • Consultations: The parties shall make every attempt to arrive at a mutually agreeable resolution through consultations whenever: a disputes arises concerning the interpretation of the agreement; a party considers that the other party has failed to carry out its obligations under the agreement; or a party considers that measures taken by the other party severely distort the balance of trade benefits accorded by the agreement; or substantially undermine fundamental objectives of the agreement. • Referral to the Joint Committee:[67] If the parties fail to resolve a matter through consultations within sixty days, either party may refer the matter to the joint committee. • Arbitral stage: If a matter referred to the joint committee has not been resolved within three months, or within such other period as agreed upon, either party may refer the matter to a dispute settlement panel. The panel shall be composed of three members: each party will appoint one, and two appointees will choose a third.	Compulsory	WTO DS mechanism not mentioned. However, exclusive forum clause • If the panel under the agreement or any other international dispute settlement mechanism is invoked with respect to any matter, the mechanism shall have exclusive jurisdiction over that matter.	No binding effect • After the presentation of the panel report, the Joint Committee shall try to resolve the matter taking into account the report. • If the committee does not resolve the dispute within one month, the affected party is entitled to take appropriate measures.	Appropriate measures	Medium

Continued overleaf

Table 1. *continued*

Dispute Settlement Provision	Jurisdiction	Reference to GATT/ WTO DS Mechanism	Binding Effect of the Decision	Remedy[28]	Potential for Overlap
Inter-regional African Caribbean Pacific–EC Partnership Agreement • Referral to the Council: Any dispute arising from the interpretation or application of this agreement between one or more member states or the EC and one or more ACP states, shall be submitted to the Council of Ministers.[68] Between the meetings of the Council of Ministers, such disputes shall be submitted to the Committee of Ambassadors. • Arbitral stage: If the Council of Ministers does not succeed in settling the dispute, either party may request settlement of the dispute by arbitration. To this end, each party shall appoint an arbitrator within thirty days of the request for arbitration. In the event of failure to do so, either party may ask the secretary-general of the Permanent Court of Arbitration to appoint the second arbitrator. • The two arbitrators shall in turn appoint a third arbitrator within thirty days. In the event of failure to do so, either party may ask the secretary-general of the Permanent Court of Arbitration to appoint the third arbitrator. • The arbitrators' decisions shall be taken by majority vote within three months.	Non-compulsory	WTO DS mechanism not mentioned	Binding effect • Each party to the dispute shall be bound to take the measures necessary to carry out the decision of the arbitrators.		

Section 3: Standing Tribunal[69]

Dispute Settlement Provision	Jurisdiction	Binding Effect of the Decision	Potential for Overlap
Europe European Economic Area (EEA) Agreement[70] • Alleged infringement of European Economic Area (EEA) law by a state party • Informal stage • Pre 31-Letter sent to the concerned state by the Surveillance Authority • The EFTA state submits comments to the authority (within one to two months) • Letter of formal notice • The EFTA state submits comments to the authority (normally within two months) • Reasoned opinion by the authority • The EFTA state replies to the opinion (normally within two months) • Decision on referral to the EFTA Court Proceedings before the EFTA Court • The court is mainly competent to deal with infringement actions brought by the EFTA Surveillance Authority against an EFTA state with regard to the implementation, application, or interpretation of an EEA rule, for the settlement of disputes between two or more EFTA states, for appeals concerning decisions taken by the EFTA Surveillance Authority and for giving advisory opinions to courts in EFTA states on the interpretation of EEA rules.	Compulsory jurisdiction: • The EFTA Court has jurisdiction with regard to EFTA states that are parties to the EEA Agreement (at present Iceland, Liechtenstein, and Norway). Exclusive jurisdiction	Binding effect Direct effect	High

Continued overleaf

Table 1. *continued*

Dispute Settlement Provision	Jurisdiction	Binding Effect of the Decision	Potential for Overlap
Customs Union[71] • The community court will provide guarantees of uniform enforcement by the parties of this agreement and other agreements between the community members and decisions taken by community institutions. • The court shall also consider economic disputes arising between the parties on issues of implementation of decisions of the community institution and provisions of agreements effective between members, and provide explanations and opinions.	Compulsory jurisdiction Exclusive jurisdiction	Binding effect	High
America Andean Subregional Integration Agreement[72] (Cartagena Agreement) • Action of nullification: It is up to the court to nullify the decisions taken by the commission[73] and the resolutions issued by the Board that violate the rules comprising the legal system of the Cartagena Agreement. When the Board considers that a Member State has failed to fulfil the obligations from the Cartagena Agreement, it shall make its observations in writing, to which the member country must reply within two months. The Board shall issue a reasoned opinion. If in the Board's opinion the member country failed to fulfil the obligations mentioned above and continues to do so, the Board may request a verdict from the court. • Action of non-compliance: When a member country considers that another member country has failed to fulfil the obligations from the agreement, it may raise its claim with the Board, stating all of the background of the case, so that the Board can issue a reasoned opinion. If, in the Board's opinion, the member country failed to fulfil its obligations and continues to do so, the Board may request a verdict from the court. Should the Board not file the action within	Compulsory jurisdiction Exclusive Jurisdiction • Member countries shall not submit any controversy arising from the application of rules comprising the legal system of the Cartagena Agreement to any court, arbitration system, or proceeding other than those contemplated herein. • Member countries hereby agree to make use of the procedure established in Article 23 (action for non-compliance) of the Cartagena Agreement only for controversies arising between any one of them and another contracting party of the Montevideo Treaty that is not a member of the agreement.	Binding effect • If the court rules finds non-compliance, the member country at fault shall take the necessary steps to execute the judgment within three months after notification.	High

Binding effect   High

Compulsory jurisdiction
Exclusive jurisdiction

two months after the date of its judgment, the claiming country may appeal directly to the court. Should the Board fail to pronounce judgment within three months from the date the claim was submitted, or rule against the non-compliance, then the claiming country may appeal directly to the court.

• Prejudicial interpretation: It is up to the court to issue a pre-judicial interpretation of the rules comprising the legal system of the Cartagena Agreement, in order to ensure its uniform application in the territories of member countries.

Treaty Establishing the Caribbean Community (Caricom)[74]

• Modes of dispute settlement: Disputes shall be settled only by recourse to the following modes: good offices, mediation, consultation, conciliation, arbitration, and adjudication. If a dispute is not settled using one of the modes other than arbitration or adjudication, either party may have recourse to another mode.

• Expeditious settlement of disputes: When a dispute arises between member states, the parties shall proceed expeditiously to an exchange of views to agree on a mode of settlement and a mutually satisfactory implementation method.

• Notification of existence and settlement of dispute: Member states to a dispute shall notify the secretary-general of the existence and nature of the dispute and any mode of dispute settlement agreed upon or initiated. When a settlement is reached, the member states concerned shall notify the secretary-general of the settlement and the mode used in arriving at the settlement.

• Good offices, mediation, and consultations: Parties to a dispute may agree to employ the good offices of a third party or agree to settle the dispute by recourse to mediation.

Continued overleaf

Table 1. *continued*

Dispute Settlement Provision	Jurisdiction	Binding Effect of the Decision	Potential for Overlap
• Consultations: A member state shall enter into consultations upon the request of another member state where the requesting member state alleges that an action taken by the requested member state constitutes a breach of obligations arising from, or under, the provisions of the treaty.			
• Conciliation Commission: Where member states parties to a dispute have agreed to submit the dispute to conciliation, any such member state may institute proceedings by notification addressed to the other party or parties to the dispute. The complaining party chooses one conciliator from a list of conciliators and the other party does the same. Two conciliators will appoint a third conciliator from the list, who will be the chairman. The decision shall be made by majority vote.			
• Arbitration tribunal: A party to a dispute may, with the consent of the other party, refer the matter to an arbitration tribunal. Each of the parties will appoint one arbitrator from the list of arbitrators. The two arbitrators shall appoint a third arbitrator.			
• Judicial settlement: The court has compulsory and exclusive jurisdiction to hear disputes concerning the interpretation and application of the treaty. The court has exclusive jurisdiction on inter-state disputes, disputes between members and the Caricom, referrals from national courts of members, and persons. The court shall have exclusive jurisdiction to deliver advisory opinions concerning the interpretation and application of the treaty.			

	Compulsory jurisdiction	Binding effect	High
Africa Common Market for Eastern and Southern Africa (COMESA)[75] • The court has jurisdiction to hear the following: disputes between states, disputes between the state and the COMESA institutions, claims from members, the secretary general, legal and natural persons, claims against COMESA or its institutions by COMESA employees and third parties, and claims arising from arbitration clauses and special agreement.	Compulsory jurisdiction: • The court shall have jurisdiction to adjudicate upon all matters that may be referred to it pursuant to the treaty.	Binding effect	High
Economic Community of Central African States (CEEAC); Communauté et monétaire de l'Afrique Centrale (CEMAC)[76] • La Cour de Justice Communautaire comporte deux Chambres: Une Chambre Judiciaire et une Chambre des Comptes. • La Cour de Judiciaire de la Communauté est régie par une Convention spécifique.	Compulsory jurisdiction: • La Chambre Judiciaire de la Communauté connaît des litiges liés à la mise en oeuvre de la Convention régissant l' Union Économique de l'Afrique Centrale.	Binding effect	High
East African Community (EAC)[77] • The court can hear claims from members, the secretary general, persons, claims against the EAC or its institutions by EAC employees and third parties, and claims arising from the arbitration clause and special agreement.	Compulsory jurisdiction • The Court shall initially have jurisdiction over the interpretation and application of the treaty. • The court shall have such other original, appellate, human rights, and other jurisdictions as will be determined by the council at a suitable subsequent date. To this end, the partner states shall conclude a protocol to operationalize the extended jurisdiction.	Binding effect	High

Continued overleaf

Table 1. *continued*

Dispute Settlement Provision	Jurisdiction	Binding Effect of the Decision	Potential for Overlap
Traité de l'Union Economique et Monetaire Ouest Africaine (UEMOA) West African Economic Monetary Union (WAEMU)[78] • La Cour de Justice connaît, sur recours de la Commission ou de tout Etat member, des manquements des Etats membres aux obligations qui leur incombent en vertue du Traité de L'Union. • La Cour de Justice statue à titre préjudicionnel sur l'interpretation du Traité de l'Union sur la légalité et l'interpretation des status des organismes créés par un acte du Conseil. • La Cour de justice connaît des litiges relatifs à la réparation des dommages causés par les organes de l'Union, des litiges entre l'Union et ses agents, et des différends entre membres relatifs	Compulsory jurisdiction • La cour de Justice veille au respect du droit quant à l'interprétation et à l'application du Traité de L'Union au Traité de l'Union.	Binding effect	High

[1] Table 1 is based on the wording of the treaties, but the practices of states may differ. The table does not include regional trade agreements that have not been notified to the World Trade Organization (WTO).

[2] The Agreements in Table 1 only include the agreements that have been notified to the WTO.

[3] The Agreement entered into force on 1 January 1983.

[4] The Agreement is a preferential tariff arrangement that aims at promoting intra-regional trade through exchange of mutually agreed concessions by member countries. The Agreement entered into force on 17 June 1976. Current signatories are Bangladesh, China, India, Republic of Korea, Lao People's Democratic Republic, and Sri Lanka.

[5] A Standing Committee of the participating states members of the Economic and Social Commission for the Asia and the Pacific (ESCAP) Trade Negotiations Group consists of the representatives of the countries participating in the agreement.

[6] The Agreement entered into force on 7 December 1995. Current signatories are Bangladesh, Bhutan, India, Maldives, Nepal, Pakistan, and Sri Lanka.

[7] The Committee of Participants is composed of the contracting states.

[8] SPARTECA is a non-reciprocal trade agreement under which the two developed nations of the South Pacific Forum, Australia and New Zealand offer duty free and unrestricted or concessional access for virtually all products originating from the developing island member countries of the forum. SPARTECA was signed by most forum members at the forum's eleventh meeting in Kiribati on 14 July 1980. It came into effect for most Forum Island countries (FIC) on 1 January 1981. With the joining of new members to the forum, the current list of FIC signatories to SPARTECA includes the Cook Islands, the Federated States of Micronesia, Fiji, Kiribati, Marshall Islands, Nauru, Niue, Papua New Guinea, Solomon Islands, Tonga, Tuvalu, Vanuatu, and Western Samoa.

[9] The Agreement entered into force on 22 July 1993. The initial members were Papua New Guinea, Solomon Islands, and Vanuatu. Fiji became a formal member of the agreement on 14 April 1998.

[10] Under the Melanesian Spearhead Group Institutional framework, the Annual Summit of Heads of Governments of the Melanesian Spearhead Group provides policy directions with respect to the implementation of the agreement. Trade officials of the parties meet annually prior to the annual summit of heads of governments to jointly review trade matters among the parties. The annual summit of the heads of governments may decide from time to time to establish technical committees to oversee the implementation of specific fields of activity of this agreement.

[11] On 21 December 1992, the former Czechoslovakia, Hungary, and Poland signed the Central European Free Trade Agreement (CEFTA). On 1 March 1993, CEFTA entered into force. Slovenia, Romania, and Bulgaria joined afterwards.

[12] The Joint Committee is composed of the representatives of the parties, who act by common agreement.

[13] These agreements include the FTAs concerning: EFTA–Czech Republic; EFTA–Hungary; EFTA–Poland; EFTA–Romania; EFTA–Slovak Republic; and EFTA–Turkey. The FTA with the former Czech and Slovak Federative Republic (CSFR) entered into force on 1 July 1992. In the wake of the dissolution, two separate but identical FTAs with the Czech Republic and the Slovak Republic superseded the original one. The FTA with Hungary entered into force on 1 October 1993 and the FTA with Poland entered into force on 1 September 1994. FTAs entered into force on 1 May 1993 for Romania. The FTA with Turkey entered into force on 1 April 1992.

[14] Croatia–Hungary, Czech Republic–Estonia, Czech Republic–Latvia, Czech Republic–Turkey, Faroe Islands–Estonia, Faroe Islands–Iceland, Faroe Islands–Norway, Faroe Islands–Poland, Faroe Islands–Switzerland, Hungary–Estonia, Hungary–Latvia, Hungary–Lithuania, Hungary–Slovenia, Hungary–Turkey, Latvia–Estonia, Latvia–Slovak Republic, Latvia–Poland, Latvia–Slovenia, Romania–Turkey, Slovak Republic–Estonia, Slovenia–Croatia, Slovenia–Estonia, Slovenia–FYROM., Slovenia–Latvia, Slovenia–Lithuania, Turkey–Bulgaria, Turkey–Estonia, Turkey–Latvia, Turkey–Lithuania, Turkey–Slovak Republic and Ukraine–Estonia.

[15] These agreements concern: EC–Faroe Islands; EC–Iceland; EC–Norway; and EC–Switzerland. The agreements entered into force for Faroe Islands on 1 January 1997, for Iceland on 1 April 1973, for Norway on 1 July 1973, and for Switzerland on 1 January 1973.

[16] The EC–Cyprus Agreement entered into force on 1 June 1973 and the EC–Malta Agreement entered into force on 1 April 1971.

[17] The Association Council consists of the members of the Council and members of the Commission of the EC and of members of the government of the Republic of Cyprus/Malta.

[18] The EC–FYROM Agreement entered into force on 1 January 1998.

[19] The Cooperation Council is composed of representatives of the EC and its member states and of representatives from the FYROM.

[20] The EC–Jordan, EC–Lebanon, and EC–Syria agreements all entered into force on 1 July 1977.

[21] The Cooperation Council is composed of representatives of the EC and of its member states and of representatives of Jordan/Lebanon/Syria. The Cooperation Council acts by mutual agreement between the EC and Jordan/Lebanon/Syria.

[22] The Agreement entered into force on 20 March 1998.

[23] The Agreement entered into force on 18 March 1981. Argentina, Bolivia, Brazil, Chile, Colombia, Cuba, Ecuador, Mexico, Paraguay, Peru, Uruguay, and Venezuela are current signatories.

[24] The committee is the permanent organ of the association and is constituted by one permanent representative from each member state with the right to one vote. Each permanent representative has an alternate.

[25] The Agreement entered into force on 19 April 1989. Forty-four countries are GSTP participants. *See* www.g77.org/gstp/#members (visited 10 April 2006) for the full list.

[26] A Committee of Participants consists of the representatives of the governments of participants. The committee takes decisions by two-thirds majority on matters of substance and a simple majority on matters of procedure.

27 Arbitration is a more judicial and adversarial system, whereas consultations mechanism in a political and diplomatic system. The arbitration procedure is normally used after the consultation mechanism is exhausted.

28 In addition to the remedy provided by the arbitration panel, unilateral safeguard measures adopted by either party are generally available for the agreements in this section (*see* Section 2: Arbitration).

29 The Agreement entered into force on 31 August 1977. Brunei Darussalam, Cambodia, Republic of Indonesia, Malaysia, Myanmar, the Republic of the Philippines, the Republic of Singapore, the Kingdom of Thailand, and Vietnam are the current signatories.

30 The protocol has not been notified to the WTO.

31 The SEOM consists of senior economic officials of the contracting states.

32 The AEM consists of economic ministers of the contracting states.

33 The Agreement entered into force for 1 January 2001.

34 The EFTA–Morocco FTA entered into force on 1 December 1999. The interim EFTA–PLO FTA entered into force on 1 July 1999.

35 The Joint Committee consists of the representatives of the parties and acts by common agreement.

36 These agreements concern: EFTA–Bulgaria; EFTA–Croatia; EFTA–Estonia; EFTA–FYROM; EFTA–Israel; EFTA–Jordan; EFTA–Latvia; EFTA–Lithuania; and EFTA–Slovenia. The agreements entered into force for Bulgaria on 1 July 1993, for Croatia on 1 January 2002, for Estonia on 1 October 1997, for FYROM on 19 June 2000, for Israel on 1 January 1993, for Jordan on 21 June 2001, for Latvia on 1 June 1996, for Lithuania on 1 January 1997, and for Slovenia on 1 September 1998.

37 The Joint Committee consists of the representatives of the parties and acts by common agreement.

38 The EFTA–Mexico Agreement entered into force on 1 July 2001.

39 The Joint Committee consists of representatives of the parties and acts by consensus.

40 The Agreement entered into force on 1 July 1991.

41 The Joint Committee is composed of representatives of the EC and of representatives of the Principality of Andorra.

42 The Agreement entered into force on 31 December 1995.

43 The Joint Committee consists of the representatives of EC and Turkey. It acts by common agreement.

44 The Association Council consists of the members of the Council of the EC and members of the Commission of the EC and of representatives of the government of Turkey.

45 The Europe Agreements were concluded with respect to: EC–Bulgaria; EC–Czech Rep.; EC–Estonia; EC–Hungary; EC–Latvia; EC–Lithuania; EC–Poland; EC–Romania; EC–Slovak Rep.; and EC–Slovenia. The agreements entered into force for Bulgaria on 31 December 1993, for Czech Republic on 1 March 1992, for Estonia on 1 January 1995, for Hungary on 1 March 1992, for Latvia on 1 January 1995, for Lithuania on 1 January 1995, for Poland on 1 March 1992, for Romania on 1 May 1993, for Slovak Republic on 1 March 1992, and for Slovenia on 1 January 1997.

46 An Association Council consists of the members of the Council of the EC and of members of the Commission of the EC and of members of the governments of participating states.

47 These agreements concern: EC–Israel; EC–Morocco; EC–PLO; and EC–Tunisia. The agreements entered into force for Israel on 1 June 2000, for Morocco on 1 March 2000, for the PLO on 1 July 1997, and for Tunisia on 1 March 1998.

48 These agreements are: Czech Republic–Israel, Israel–Poland, Israel–Slovak Republic, Israel–Slovenia, Israel–Turkey, and Slovenia–Turkey.

49 The EC–Mexico Agreement entered into force on 1 July 2000.

50 The Joint Committee consists of the representatives of the parties and acts by common agreement.

[51] The Agreement entered into force on 30 December 1994. Azerbaijan Republic, Republic of Armenia, Republic of Belarus, Republic of Georgia, Republic of Kazakhstan, Kyrgyz Republic, Republic of Moldova, Russian Federation, Republic of Tajikistan, Republic of Uzbekistan, and Ukraine are the current signatories.

[52] The agreements in America, especially in North America, are organized in a chronological manner in order to show the evolution of RTA dispute settlement provisions. Dispute settlement mechanism in Latin American arrangements became more sophisticated with the addition of protocols.

[53] The Agreement entered into force for Guatemala, El Salvador, and Nicaragua on 4 June 1961, for Honduras on 27 April 1962, and for Costa Rica on 23 September 1963.

[54] The Executive Council consists of one titular official and one alternate appointed by each contracting party. Before ruling on a matter, the Executive Council shall determine unanimously whether the matter is to be decided by a concurrent vote of all its members or by a simple majority.

[55] The Central American Economic Council is composed of several ministers of economic affairs of several contracting states.

[56] The Agreement entered into force on 19 August 1985.

[57] The Joint Committee is composed of representatives of the parties and shall be headed by the United States trade representatives and Jordan's minister primarily responsible for international trade, or their designees. All the decisions by the Joint Committee are taken by consensus.

[58] The Treaty of Asuncion entered into force on 29 November 1991. The members are Argentina, Brazil, Paraguay, and Uruguay.

[59] The Common Market Group consists of four members and four alternates for each country, representing the following public bodies: Ministry of Foreign Affairs; Ministry of Economy or its equivalent (areas of industry, foreign trade and/or economic co-ordination); and the Central Bank.

[60] The NAFTA Agreement entered into force on 4 January 1994.

[61] The Free Trade Commission comprises representatives of both parties. The principal representative of each party shall be the cabinet level officer or minister primarily responsible for international trade, or a person designated by the cabinet level officer or minister. All the decisions of the commission is taken by consensus.

[62] The Agreement entered into force on 1 January 1997.

[63] The Agreement entered into force on 5 July 1997.

[64] The Agreement entered into force on 1 August 1999.

[65] The Agreement entered into force on 1 July 2000.

[66] The Agreement entered into force on 17 December 2001.

[67] The Joint Committee is composed of representatives of the parties and shall be headed by the United States trade representatives and Jordan's minister primarily responsible for international trade, or their designees. All the decisions by the Joint Committee are taken by consensus.

[68] The Council of Ministers comprises the members of the Council of the EC and members of the EC Commission, and a member of the government of each ACP state. The council takes its decisions by common agreement of the parties.

[69] Standing tribunal is the most sophisticated dispute settlement mechanism to adjudicate disputes within regional trade organizations. One of the most developed regional trade integration system, European Communities, is not included here because the European Communities and its member states are treated as one member of the WTO. For the agreements written in French, the original French text was used.

[70] The EEA entered into force on 1 January 1994. The EEA Agreement unites fifteen EU member states and three EFTA states (Norway, Iceland, and Liechtenstein) into a single market.

[71] The Agreement entered into force on 8 October 1997. The members are the Kyrgyz Republic, the Russian Federation, Belarus, and Kazakhstan.

[72] The Andean Subregional Integration Agreement entered into force on 25 May 1998. The Customs Union was established in February 1995. ON 10 March 1996, the countries signed the Act of Trujillo for the creation of an Andean Community. The members of Andean Community are Bolivia, Colombia, Ecuador, Peru, and Venezuela.

[73] The Commission of the Andean Community is comprised of a plenipotentiary representative from each one of the governments of the member countries.

[74] The Treaty Establishing the Caricom entered into force on 1 August 1973. Antigua and Barbuda, Bahamas, Barbados, Belize, Dominica, Grenada, Guyana, Haiti, Jamaica, Montserrat, Trinidad and Tobago, St. Kitts and Nevis, St. Lucia, St. Vincent and the Grenadines, and Suriname are CACM members.

[75] The COMESA treaty entered into force in December 1994. Angola, Burundi, Comoros, Democratic Republic of Congo, Djibouti, Egypt, Eritrea, Ethiopia, Kenya, Madagascar, Malawi, Mauritius, Namibia, Rwanda, Seychelles, Sudan, Swaziland, Tanzania, Uganda, Zambia and Zimbabwe are COMESA members.

[76] The CEMAC members are Cameroon, Central African Republic, Congo Republic, Equatorial Guinea, Gabon, and Chad.

[77] The EAC treaty was signed on 30 November 1999. Kenya, Uganda, and Tanzania are members.

[78] The Agreement entered into force on 1 August 1994. Benin, Burkina Faso, Côte d'Ivoire, Guinea Bissau, Mali, Niger, Senegal, and Togo are members.

21

Applicability of WTO Law in Regional Trade Agreements: Identifying the Links

LOCKNIE HSU *

I. INTRODUCTION

Of late, there has been much discussion about the numerous RTAs concluded and under negotiation. The polarized views regarding their popularity reflect two sides of the coin on the relationship between the WTO and RTAs: the speed (or lack thereof) of progress of the Doha Development Agenda negotiations for further liberalization, and the role of RTAs in the WTO universe of trade liberalization. Views range from the decrying of such proliferation as a detraction from the multilateral process, to its defence in the name of pragmatic response to slow progress in multilateral negotiations. However, like it or not, RTAs are here to stay, with new ones being announced with great frequency. While participants may change 'dance partners' with each new RTA, many provisions are becoming easily recognizable, as they resemble those in WTO Agreements.

It is hardly surprising that many RTA provisions mimic WTO provisions. Trade negotiators who negotiate many of these RTAs may also have been involved in the Uruguay Round of negotiations which gave birth to the WTO. Furthermore, when RTA negotiators seek language which both/all partners are comfortable with, WTO language often provides a convenient 'model' or yardstick which is acceptable, since the RTA partners are likely to be already bound by WTO Agreements.

At the same time, RTAs generally carry dispute settlement systems of their own. This concomitant spawning of dispute settlement systems in RTAs is not, as yet, attracting a great deal of in-depth analysis, as many of them are

* The writer wishes to thank Lorand Bartels for his helpful comments on an earlier draft.

dormant at the moment. This chapter examines the interface between WTO law (treaty and dispute settlement interpretations), and the large number of dispute settlement panels that can potentially burst into life under RTAs. Specifically, what role should WTO law play in decisions by such panels, in interpreting RTA provisions that either incorporate or resemble WTO language? What could be the theoretical underpinnings that could link them?

As a matter of practice, RTA panels will have to deal with WTO cases where disputants raise them in support of their legal arguments. In addition, WTO case law is now often cited by RTA panels themselves, often without an indication of the basis for doing so. Such a lack of theoretical explanation indicates a lacuna in current thinking and is unsatisfactory.

The following discussion suggests a theoretical framework for the interface of WTO law—particularly WTO case interpretations—with RTA dispute settlement panels. The starting point in interpreting RTAs would be to recognize that they are treaties, which would bring into play international principles of interpretation, such as those under the Vienna Convention on the Law of Treaties (VCLT). The application of Articles 31 and 32 VCLT, in particular, has already been clearly recognized in the interpretation of WTO Agreements.[1] Taking this approach, the precise role in RTA interpretation of WTO treaty language, and its interpretation in case law, would depend on the text and context of the RTA itself, and the extent to which the parties have expressed an intention to apply or refer to such case law. It is further argued that WTO case law could, in some aspects, be forming a body of specialized international rules within the wider universe of public international law, as a matter of custom. Where it is established that such case law does form such specialized international law rules, they could bind RTA parties unless they have opted out of these rules through the RTA provisions.

II. INTERPRETATION OF RTAS: THE VCLT AND THE PLACE FOR WTO CASE LAW

Should an RTA dispute settlement panel refer to and rely on WTO law, particularly case law, in interpreting the RTA's provisions, and if so, to what extent?

As a matter of practice, it is apparent that WTO cases will have some influence on such panels. One explanation is that of pressure to heed juris-

---

[1] *See,* for example, WTO Appellate Body Reports, *US—Gasoline,* WT/DS2/AB/R, adopted 20 May 1996 and *Japan—Alcoholic Beverages II,* WT/DS8/AB/R, WT/DS10/AB/R, WT/DS11/AB/R, adopted 1 November 1996.

prudence of other international tribunals.[2] Another is because WTO law is seen as providing legal context for other international agreements.[3]

Consistency has also been a factor cited by tribunals in considering prior decisions. International arbitration tribunals, such as those of ICSID, have made observations about the bearing that prior decisions of other ICSID tribunals may have on the dispute at hand. In one ICSID case, the arbitrator said that:

30. An identity of the basis of jurisdiction of these tribunals, even when it meets with very similar if not even identical facts at the origin of the disputes, does not suffice to apply systematically to the present case positions or solutions already adopted in these cases. Each tribunal remains sovereign and may retain, as it is confirmed by ICSID practice, a different solution for resolving the same problem; but decisions on jurisdiction dealing with the same or very similar issues may at least indicate some lines of reasoning of real interest; this Tribunal may consider them in order to compare its own position with those already adopted by its predecessors and, if it shares the views already expressed by one or more of these tribunals on a specific point of law, it is free to adopt the same solution.

31. One may even find situations in which, although seized on the basis of another BIT as combined with the pertinent provisions of the ICSID Convention, a tribunal has set a point of law which, in essence, is or will be met in other cases whatever the specificities of each dispute may be. Such precedents may also be rightly considered, at least as a matter of comparison and, if so considered by the Tribunal, of inspiration.

32. The same may be said for the interpretation given by a precedent decision or award to some relevant facts which are basically at the origin of two or several different disputes, keeping carefully in mind the actual specificities still featuring each case. If the present Tribunal concurs with the analysis and interpretation of these facts as they generated certain special consequences for the parties to this case as well as for those of another case, it may consider this earlier interpretation as relevant.

33. From a more general point of view, one can hardly deny that the institutional dimension of the control mechanisms provided for under the ICSID Convention might well be a factor, in the longer term, for contributing to the development of a common legal opinion or *jurisprudence constante*, to resolve some difficult legal

---

[2] For instance, in discussing the investor–State arbitration regime of the Energy Charter Treaty (ECT), Wälde asserts that despite there being no formal *stare decisis*, there is pressure to 'heed jurisprudence' of international; tribunals on identical or similar legal language; T.W. Wälde, 'Investment Arbitration under the Energy Charter Treaty: An Overview of Key Issues', in (2004) 1(2) Transnational Dispute Management, available at www.transnational-dispute-management. com/samples/freearticles/tv1–2-article224b.htm (visited 10 October 2005). For a more recent comment, see Pan American Energy LLC and BP Argentina Exploration Co v Argentina, ICSID Case No ARB/03/13, Decision on Preliminary Objections, 27 July 2006, para. 42.

[3] *See*, for instance, E.-U. Petersmann, 'Justice as Conflict Resolution: Proliferation, Fragmentation and Decentralization of Dispute Settlement in International Trade', European University Institute, Working Paper No 2004/10, available at www.iue.it/PUB/law04–10.pdf (visited 10 October 2005), 10–1. *See also* G. Verhoosel, 'The Use of Investor-State Arbitration under Bilateral Investment Treaties to Seek Relief for Breaches of WTO Law' (2003) 6 JIEL 493, at 503–06, where he argues that WTO law may provide an interpretative context for bilateral investment treaties (BITs) under Art. 31(3)(c) VCLT.

issues discussed in many cases, inasmuch as these issues share the same substantial features.[4]

In the present context, while an RTA tribunal has no institutional relationship with the WTO, the considerations expressed in the first paragraph quoted above are of relevance. An RTA tribunal may be find itself 'dealing with the same or very similar issues' as what a WTO Panel has dealt with (for example, because interpretation of text that is common to the RTA and a WTO Agreement).

Further, judging from actual practice of NAFTA tribunals (discussed later in this article), it is apparent that WTO law does have an impact on interpretation outside the WTO. At the very least, the relationship will be one of influence and persuasiveness where there is common treaty language.

If one refers to the list of sources of law for the International Court of Justice in its Statute, Article 38(1)(d) permits reference, as a 'subsidiary means' for determining the rules of law, to 'judicial decisions'. This can arguably include the decisions of international or multilateral organization tribunals such as WTO Panels or the Appellate Body. Hence, although there is formally no doctrine of *stare decisis* in international law, prior decisions are seen as useful and may be properly referred to by a tribunal.[5] There is thus at least this justification for NAFTA/RTA panels to refer to 'judicial decisions' of WTO, albeit not as a primary source of law. It will be seen from the NAFTA cases discussed below, however, that even this justification is either overlooked or not explicitly given in the NAFTA panel decisions even though they often refer to WTO reports.

Beyond such reference to WTO decisions as such 'subsidiary means', there is a case for arguing that WTO interpretations are a potential source of customary international law rules.

In addition, the current practice of the United States of using 'templates' with 'standard terms' for its free trade agreements or Trade and Investment Framework Agreements (TIFAs) may also be arguably contributing to evolution of customary international law insofar as certain provisions are concerned.[6]

---

[4] *AES Corporation v The Argentine Republic*, ICSID Case No ARB/02/17. Decision on Jurisdiction, 26 April 2005, available at www.worldbank.org (visited 10 October 2005).

[5] This is so even though such decisions are not primary sources of law, and do not necessarily form customary law. See R. Jennings and Sir A. Watts (eds), *Oppenheim's International Law*, 9th ed., Volume 1 (Harlow: Longman, 1992), para 13. *See also* the recent ICSID arbitration in *Sempra Energy International v The Argentine Republic*, ICSID Case No ARB/02/16, 11 May 2005, available at www.worldbank.org (visited 10 October 2005), at paras 147–48. Admittedly, WTO cases may be viewed differently from 'judicial decisions' of other tribunals, for a number of reasons. For instance, unlike other tribunals, WTO Panel and Appellate Body decisions must be adopted by the WTO Dispute Settlement Body. Also, they culminate in *recommendations*, rather than judgments or awards.

[6] The editors of *Oppenheim's International Law*, *ibid.*, state in para. 13, note 12, that '[a] general and constant practice of numerous bilateral treaties containing similar provisions may afford evidence of a rule of customary law in that sense . . .'. This is pertinent to the said US practice, especially where they replicate WTO language and their own language consistently.

In analysing the role of WTO cases in RTA dispute settlement, it is useful to set out the process of interpretation faced by an RTA tribunal.

Since an RTA is an international treaty, it is subject to the textual approach of interpretation of the VCLT. Article 31(1) states:

A treaty shall be interpreted in good faith in accordance with the ordinary meaning to be given to the terms of the treaty in their context and in the light of its object and purpose.

This provision has been repeatedly applied by WTO Panels and the Appellate Body in interpreting WTO provisions. The basis cited by them is Article 3.2 DSU, which provides:

The dispute settlement system of the WTO is a central element in providing security and predictability to the multilateral trading system. The Members recognize that it serves to preserve the rights and obligations of Members under the covered agreements, and to clarify the existing provisions of those agreements *in accordance with customary rules of interpretation of public international law*. Recommendations and rulings of the DSB cannot add to or diminish the rights and obligations provided in the covered agreements. (emphasis added).[7]

The following diagram indicates possible reactions by an RTA panel to WTO law. At the two extremes, a panel could either completely ignore or completely adopt WTO interpretations where there are WTO-like provisions in the RTA. However, applying the VCLT approach to interpreting the RTA, the panel is unlikely to take either of these extreme approaches. Rather, it will have to examine the text, context, and objective of the RTA to determine its interpretation, and the extent of the role of WTO jurisprudence thereunder. It is further argued here that certain aspects of WTO treaty language, coupled with its interpretation, may be shown to be evolving into customary international law, and may also need to be taken into account by an RTA panel as such.

Much of the current debate on lawmaking by the WTO dispute settlement branch has focused on the creation of 'WTO law' by that branch for its members, and whether such law has precedential value, or is of binding effect on the parties.[8] Another debate revolved around the role of WTO law in the

---

[7] Art. 33 VCLT has also been applied in WTO: *see* WTO Appellate Body Report, *Chile—Price Band System*, WT/DS207/AB/R, adopted 23 October 2002, para. 271 (in contrast with the WTO Appellate Body Report, *EC—Tariff Preferences*, WT/DS246/AB/R, adopted 20 April 2004, where the Appellate Body significantly did not raise Art. 33). Although the words emphasized refer specifically to customary rules of interpretation, the view has been expressed that the WTO Panels and the Appellate Body are not confined to applying only, say, Arts 31–33 VCLT. *See*, for instance, J. Pauwelyn, *Conflict of Norms in Public International Law: How WTO Law Relates to Other Rules of International Law* (Cambridge: CUP, 2003).

[8] *See* R.H. Steinberg, 'Judicial Lawmaking at the WTO: Discursive, Constitutional, and Political Constraints' (2004) 98 AJIL 247, at 254, in which he discusses the precedential value of Appellate Body decisions. On the binding effect of WTO dispute settlement decisions as regards compliance, *see* J. Jackson, *The World Trading System: Law and Policy of International Economic Relations* (Cambridge, Mass.; London: MIT Press, 1997), 25, and his response to J.H. Bello, 'The WTO Dispute Settlement Understanding: Less is More' (1996) 90 AJIL 416 in 'The WTO Dispute

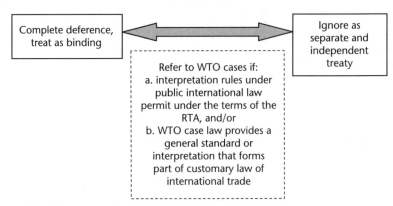

Figure 1. Possible responses by RTA tribunals to WTO case law

international law system, as to whether it forms part of or is separate from general international law. A majority of writers favour the view that WTO law is a part of the public international law system—as one writer has put it, '. . . WTO law is, therefore, not a "system" in and of itself but a "sub-system" of international law'.[9] Elsewhere, the debate has been about the 'constitutionalization' of WTO law the effect of WTO law in municipal systems or legal orders and whether, for instance, WTO law has direct effect in such systems.[10]

Settlement Understanding—Misunderstandings on the Nature of Legal Obligations' (1997) 91 AJIL 60. One article refers briefly to the reverse issues, i.e. how a WTO Panel should treat information and facts from an RTA: *see* K. Kwak and G. Marceau, 'Overlaps and Conflicts of Jurisdiction between the WTO and RTAs', in this volume, at 465. In the European context, *see* Case C–377/02 *Van Parys v BIRB* [2005] ECR I–1465.

[9] Pauwelyn, above at n 7, at 38. *See also* J. Jackson, 'Global Economics and International Economic Law' (1998) 1 JIEL, 1, at 9 and 19 and J. Charney, 'The Impact of the International Law System of the Growth of International Courts and Tribunals' (1999) 31 NYU J Int L & Pol 697. The Appellate Body has stated that Art. 3.2 DSU reflects 'a measure of recognition that the [GATT 1994] is not to be read in clinical isolation from public international law': WTO Appellate Body Report, *US—Gasoline*, above at n 1, at 17. For a view on the reasons why international law did not traditionally embrace international economic law, *see* D.M. McRae, 'The WTO in International Law: Tradition Continued or New Frontier?' (2000) 1 JIEL 27 and 'The Contribution of International Trade Law to the Development of International Law' (1996) 260 *Recueil des Cours* 99. Pauwelyn disagrees with McRae's view at pp. 29–35 of his book.

[10] *See*, for instance, S. Peers, 'Fundamental Right or Whim? WTO Law and the European Court of Justice', in G. de Búrca and J. Scott (eds), *The EU and the WTO—Legal and Constitutional Issues* (Oxford: Hart, 2001); and more recently, D. de Mey, 'The Effect of WTO Dispute Settlement Rulings in the EC Legal Order: Reviewing *Van Parys v Belgische Interventie- en Restitutiebureau* (C377/02)' (2005) 6 German L J 1025, available at www.germanlawjournal.com (visited 10 October 2005) and T. Cottier and K.N. Schefer, 'The Relationship between World Trade Organization Law, National and Regional Law' (1998) 1 JIEL 83. *Van Parys*, above at n 8, for instance, illustrates the resistance to using WTO law in interpreting EC obligations within the Community. Another aspect of the debate relates to the issue of competing jurisdiction of dispute settlement fora arising under different treaty regimes: *see*, for instance, Y. Shany, *The Competing Jurisdictions of International Courts and Tribunals* (Oxford: OUP, 2003). In the context of WTO and RTAs, Kwak and Marceau, above at n 8, at 465, conclude that there is 'no "international constitution" regulating the relationship between the dispute settlement procedures of regional and other multilateral agreements, nor any treaty provision on the matter, in the WTO or elsewhere . . .'.

It is argued here that since WTO treaty and interpretation (referred to here as WTO law) is part of the public international law system, it may contribute customary international law concepts, principles, and practices to that system, where they are shown to have become accepted as custom. While the actual outcome of the dispute will bind only the parties to the dispute, the legal principles and reasoning that emerge in the case can bind all trading nations if they are successfully shown to have come to be accepted as custom.[11] If WTO law is accepted as part of the public international law system, it can play a part in contributing to the formation of the law under that system. This can be achieved by proving that WTO law has set new norms by treaty, or by case interpretations springing from its dispute settlement system.

The sources of international law set out in Article 38(1)(a)–(d) of the Statute of the International Court of Justice are well-known. This has been argued to be a non-exhaustive list of sources, with new sources having arisen.[12]

A. Customary International Law Formation and Trade Law

Although the view may be taken that treaties do not necessarily start out being a source of international law (since they only create legal rights and obligations *inter se* for the treaty-makers),[13] it is arguable that WTO treaty provisions and their interpretations may *evolve* into 'international custom as evidence of a general practice which accepted as law' under Article 38(1)(b) of the Statute of the ICJ. As one eminent writer has pointed out, with regard to the evolution of treaty provisions into rules of general international law as *opinio juris*:

In each instance, whether such a metamorphosis has taken place or not is a question of fact to be established by concrete evidence, as in attempts to ascertain the existence of any rule of general international law.[14]

Further, Article 38 VCLT makes it clear that treaty language may become binding on parties not privy to the treaty, where its acceptance as customary international law is shown:

Nothing in articles 34 to 37 precludes a rule set forth in a treaty from becoming binding upon a third State as a customary rule of international law, recognized as such.

---

[11] The Appellate Body has indicated that adopted Panel reports bind only the disputing parties— *see*, for instance, WTO Appellate Body Report, *Japan—Alcoholic Beverages II*, above at n 1, at 14.

[12] Pauwelyn, above at n 7, at 99.

[13] For instance, Cheng and the editors of *Oppenheim* are of the view that treaties merely constitute a source of rights and obligations in international law. *See* B. Cheng, 'Custom: The Future of General State Practice in a Divided World', in R.St.J. Macdonald and D.M. Johnston (eds), *The Structure and Process of International Law: Essays in Legal Philosophy Doctrine and Theory* (Dordrecht: Lancaster: Nijhoff, 1986), at 526–28 and Jennings and Watts, above at n 5, at para 11. Cheng further agreed with the view that treaties may, however, 'metamorphosize' into custom: at 532–33.

[14] Cheng, *ibid.*, at 533.

This article argues that treaties in the WTO and specific legal interpretations of these treaties may evolve into customary international law, where such interpretations fulfil the twin requirements of consistent state practice and *opinio juris*.

A starting point is to argue that the requirement of *consistent state practice* by a large-enough number of states is satisfied by the near-universal consent of states—in the form of WTO membership—to the principles, practices, and interpretations of WTO Agreements. There is reference in the WTO Agreement itself to 'basic principles'.[15] Moreover, the WTO Members have agreed to 'be guided by the decisions, procedures and customary practices' of the Contracting Parties of GATT 1947.[16] This provision acknowledges that a series of decisions, procedures, and practices existed prior to formation of the WTO and these continue to 'guide' members. While it does not state that these 'bind' members in law, it goes toward showing state practices accepted by members. Hence, WTO Members arguably exhibit consistent state practice (which may form the subject matter of customary international law) through the continual observation of GATT decisions, procedures, and practices. Many of these have now been carried over into the WTO system.

A second aspect of WTO Members exhibiting consistent state practice is through the machinery of the WTO dispute settlement system and, in particular, its rulings and practices. Because WTO Members have bound themselves to the 'single undertaking' of the WTO Agreements—including the system under the Dispute Settlement Understanding (DSU)—they (in large part) observe the principles, commitments, and legal interpretations arising. The Dispute Settlement Body mechanism for adopting Panel and Appellate Body reports containing legal interpretations arguably represents a collective state practice of acceptance of such treaty interpretations.

Brownlie lists the following as material sources of state practice: 'diplomatic correspondence, policy statements, opinions of official legal advisors, official manuals on legal questions, . . . *international and national judicial decisions* . . . a pattern of treaties in the same form, the practice of international organs . . .'.[17] (emphasis added). Consistent and repeated interpretations by WTO Panels and the Appellate Body of trade agreement terms (and the repeated replication of identical terms in other agreements such as RTAs) can thus offer one form of evidence of state practice in accepting certain legal interpretations.

Secondly, in terms of *opinio juris*, it is necessary to prove that WTO Members have accepted as binding principles under customary international law, certain rules, interpretations, and practices.

In the *Libya—Malta Continental Shelf* dispute, the International Court of Justice identified elements for formation of customary international law:

---

[15] Preamble, WTO Agreement.   [16] Art. XVI:1 WTO Agreement.
[17] I. Brownlie, *Principles of Public International Law*, 6th ed. (Oxford: OUP, 2003), 6.

It is of course axiomatic that the material of customary international law is to be looked for primarily in the actual practice and *opinio juris* of States.[18]

In the same case, the Court acknowledged that multilateral treaties have an important role in recording, defining and developing customary international law. In the field of economic—relating to investment, specifically—law, this possibility has also been acknowledged by an ICSID arbitral tribunal, which had to decide whether there was customary international law prohibiting or regulating anti-competitive behaviour.[19]

It is also not an obstacle to formation of custom where it may not be possible to show a long practice.[20] This means that the fact that the WTO treaties and the DSU mechanism have existed for only ten years is not necessarily an obstacle to WTO jurisprudence contributing to customary international law. Indeed, as has been noted elsewhere, the possibility of 'instant' customary international law is not as bizarre as it may first seem.[21]

WTO Members have committed to the agreements of membership by way of treaty obligations, and therefore are bound by law under the treaties. This binding nature of the principles and commitments in the WTO Agreements is further enhanced by acceptance by members, *as a matter of law*, of rulings of the WTO Panels and Appellate Body which 'clarify' these principles and commitments.[22]

There are reasons for arguing that members consider themselves bound by such rulings as a matter of law. WTO case law represents the legal 'clarification' of WTO Agreements that 149 members accept, through subscribing to the WTO system and its DSU process. The adoption of Panel and Appellate Body reports by negative consensus in the DSB lends to the argument that members have been accepting the decisions (and their legal interpretations) so far. There are, of course, arguments about the democratic deficit in the WTO process, and that in reality, many countries face a 'take it or leave it' system,[23]

---

[18] *Case concerning the Continental Shelf (Libyan Arab Jamahiriya v Malta)* [1985] ICJ Rep 13, at 29, para. 27.

[19] NAFTA Chapter 11 Report, *United Parcel Service of America Inc v Government of Canada*, NAFTA Arbitration Award on Jurisdiction, 22 November 2002, available at www.state.gov/s/l/c3749.htm (visited 10 October 2005), at para. 84. On the facts of that case, the tribunal found that Canada had not established such a rule of customary international law.

[20] *See* Brownlie, above at n 17, at 7: '[p]rovided the consistency and generality of a practice are proved, no particular duration is required: the passage of time will of course be a part of the evidence if generality and consistency. A long (and, much less, an immemorial) practice is not necessary, and rules relating to airspace and the continental shelf have emerged from fairly quick maturing of practice. The International Court does not emphasize the time element as such in its practice'.

[21] *See* Cheng, above at n 13, at 536.

[22] Art. 3.2 DSU refers to this 'clarifying' role. Art. IX:2 of the WTO Agreement reserves the right to adopt 'authoritative interpretations' of the Agreements exclusively to the Ministerial Conference and the General Council.

[23] *See*, for instance, J.H.H. Weiler and I. Motoc, 'Taking Democracy Seriously: The Normative Challenges to the International Legal System', in S. Griller (ed), *International Economic Governance and Non-Economic Concerns* (Vienna: Springer, 2003), particularly at 66–7.

but these do not alter the fact that the WTO operates on the treaty-provided method of consensual decision-making, particularly with respect to its DSB decisions.

Secondly, a majority of members who receive rulings implement them. The actual practice of these states in accepting the rulings of the DSB satisfies the first condition for custom formation. As has been observed, while having a majority number of states take a certain view on a certain rule is not conclusive that an international tribunal will find *opinio generalis*,[24] it is one factor. The general adherence to the DSB procedures and compliance (in a majority of cases) with rulings and recommendations may be evidence of the fact that members consider themselves bound by the recommendations and legal interpretations.[25]

Moreover, there are indications that WTO treaty language and case law are accepted as binding by members, such as the following:

• The acceptance of WTO treaties and DSU rights and obligations (including case determinations) as a binding 'single undertaking';[26]
• Compulsory and exclusive jurisdiction under the DSB creates a centralized dispute settlement system for all WTO Members in respect of disputes arising from the agreements covered by the DSU. Members have thus expressed their intention and belief, in treaty form, of being bound by the judicial authority and interpretations of the Panels and Appellate Body in applying the WTO Agreements.[27]

Where there are any strong objections in the course of DSB debate, they could be taken into account under the persistent objector rule in the formation of customary international law.[28] Interpretations which are not so accepted would not form customary international law. For instance, the Appellate Body's treatment of *amicus curiae* briefs during *EC—Asbestos* attracted a

[24] *Ibid.*, at 541. *See also* S. Zamora, 'Is there Customary International Economic Law?' (1989) 22 GYIL, 9, for a general discussion of the hitherto weak relationship between customary international law and international economic law.

[25] For the breakdown of compliance with WTO dispute settlement rulings, *see* W.J. Davey, 'The WTO Dispute Settlement System: The First Ten Years' (2005) 8 JIEL 17, where he concludes that a majority of members do implement such rulings, even though there is a problem with timeliness of compliance.

[26] Art. II:2 of the WTO Agreement states that '[t]he agreements and associated legal instruments included in Annexes 1, 2 and 3 (hereinafter referred to as "Multilateral Trade Agreements") are integral parts of this Agreement, binding on all Members'.

[27] Arts 1.1 and 23.1 DSU.

[28] It should be noted, however, with respect to *a particular Member's measures*, some WTO Panels have expressed the view that silence on the part of a member does not necessarily mean agreement that the measures of the other member are in conformity with WTO obligations: the WTO Panel in *EC—Export Subsidies on Sugar (Australia)*, WT/DS265/R, adopted 19 May 2005, as modified by the Appellate Body WT/DS265/AB/R, observed in para. 7.211: '... silence or failure to challenge a measure by a Member does not create the presumption that said Member has agreed that the measure at stake is consistent with the *WTO Agreement*' (following the reasoning in the WTO Panel Report, *EC—Bananas III (Article 21.5—EC)*, WT/DS27/RW/EEC and Corr.1, 12 April 1999, at para. 4.13).

significant dissent from many members during a General Council meeting.[29] This demonstrates that members may choose to object to interpretations or applications of the WTO provisions where they do not accept them. In such a case, the interpretation of the relevant provisions of the DSU or practice adopted would arguably not satisfy the requirement of having been accepted by state practice as being binding *for the purpose of establishing customary international law*. Such dissent has, however, been absent in respect of the vast majority of adopted WTO reports, so their legal interpretations offer possible material for the establishment of customary international law.

In the above context, it is thus arguable that WTO treaty interpretations satisfy the requirement of *opinio juris*. Although there is a view that, for the formation of customary international law, it must be shown that WTO Members consider themselves bound by certain principles and practices *qua* customary international law, rather than *qua* treaty commitments alone, it is submitted that the WTO system, being *sui generis*, with its matrix of case interpretation and adoption mechanisms among more than 149 Members just explained, would sufficiently provide an exception to the requirement under this view.[30]

B. What WTO matters may constitute customary international law

If the above argument is accepted, it merely sets the stage for the proposition that WTO treaty provisions and case interpretations may contribute to the pool of public international law as a matter of custom.

The next—and more difficult—question is: *What* aspects of WTO law might be proven to have evolved into customary law? Clearly, not all matter that emanates from WTO Panels or the Appellate Body is, operationally, of such character as to form general rules of international law. Certain considerations may pertain only to the particular disputants or dispute, where they relate to the particular fact situation presented. The difficulty would lie in identifying what is so 'generalizable' and what is not, and proving that the former has gained acceptance as custom.[31] There are two possible categories in terms of WTO treaty provision and interpretation:

– interpretations of terms that are in common use in the WTO; and
– practices and steps derived from applying WTO provisions.

[29] *See* WTO Appellate Body, Communication of 8 November 2000, WTO Doc. WT/DS135/9 and General Council, Minutes of meeting held on 17 November 2000, WTO Doc. WT/GC/M/60, 22 November 2000.

[30] For this view, *see* M.E. Villinger, *Customary International Law and Treaties: A Manual on the Theory and Practice of the Interrelation of Sources*, 2nd ed. (The Hague, London: Kluwer, 1997), Ch 1, paras 31–3 and at 133, para. 199. The author acknowledges that conventions or treaties may codify customary international law, or promote progressive development of customary international law; *see* Ch 3 generally.

[31] *See* discussions on the concept of what is 'generalizable' by Cheng, above at n 13, at 530 and 535.

In respect of the first category, it would be necessary to prove that a particular term has been consistently interpreted within the WTO dispute settlement system so as to form a common principle, such as the need to interpret the notion of 'like products' flexibly according to the context.[32] Another area where the WTO has established interpretations is in relation to non-violation complaints under Article XXIII GATT. Several RTAs contain language that replicates the relevant portion of this GATT provision, and its consistent interpretation (albeit there have been few cases) by panels may offer evidence of custom in interpreting such a provision.[33]

In respect of the second category, it may include interpretation of provisions such as the General Exceptions.[34] It is not uncommon to see a replication in RTAs of the chapeau-plus-exceptions formulation under Article XX GATT. Other practices may include the interpretation of trade measures covered under RTAs as including 'as such' measures. WTO jurisprudence has provided several examples of such measures being subject to WTO disciplines, so that where the language of an RTA replicates WTO Agreement language, it could arguably cover such measures as a matter of custom.[35]

It would thus fall to a party seeking to rely on an aspect of WTO law as having metamorphosed into binding custom, to bring evidence of this, both in establishing state practice and *opinio juris* to this effect.[36] Such a party would have to bring evidence of some government statement, practice or judicial decision supporting the practice of applying WTO interpretations as customary international law, as well as proof that such practice is a result of an

---

[32] WTO jurisprudence has provided this and other general interpretative principles *vis-à-vis* the term 'like product', such as the need to take into its account and allow for flexibility, allowing it to 'stretch' like an 'accordion': *Japan—Alcoholic Beverages II*, above at n 1, cited by a NAFTA panel (below, at n 61). For a discussion of some 'general principles' and concepts that have emerged from WTO jurisprudence, *see* M. Hilf and G.J. Goettsche, 'The Relation of Economic and Non-Economic Principles in International Law' in Griller, above at n 23. Note that the most favoured nation (MFN) obligation has not been accepted as a customary law right, but is, rather a consensual treaty right: *see* Zamora, above at n 24, at 28–9. At the same time, the author points to the possibility that there can be customary rules of law 'concerning the *interpretation* of MFN clauses' (at 29, emphasis added). Further, it is noteworthy that in the area of investment law, it has been ruled that *lex specialis* is not precluded from forming the subject of customary international law: *see Sempra v Argentina*, above at n 5, at paras 156–57.

[33] For a discussion of non-violation complaint provisions in some recent RTAs, *see* L. Hsu, 'Non-Violation Complaints—World Trade Organization Issues and Recent Free Trade Agreements' (2005) 39 JWT 205.

[34] For instance, WTO jurisprudence has provided a two-tier process for interpreting Art. XX GATT: the first is the proof of applicability of one of the sub-paragraphs to the measure in question. If this is shown, one proceeds to the second step of examining consistency of the measure in question with the chapeau of Art. XX. *See* WTO Appellate Body Reports, *US—Gasoline*, above at n 1, *US—Shrimp*, WT/DS58/AB/R, adopted 6 November 1998 and *US—Gambling*, WT/DS285/AB/R, adopted 20 April 2005.

[35] In one NAFTA arbitration, the tribunal even 'borrowed' and applied the notion of the 'single undertaking' from the WTO in interpreting the NAFTA provisions: *see* NAFTA Chapter 11 Report, *SD Myers v Government of Canada*, Partial Award dated 13 November 2000, available at www.state.gov/s/l/c3746.htm (visited 10 October 205), paras 291–92.

[36] *See* above n 14.

acceptance of its binding nature as customary international law. This will not be easy as it has been recognized that the exercise of proving something has become a norm as part of customary law or general principles of law is a 'much more difficult task' as compared with identifying treaty norms, '. . . because the criteria for recognition of these norms are less clear'.[37] Moreover, a custom is 'a clear and continuous habit of doing certain actions which has grown up under the aegis of the conviction that these actions are, according to international law, obligatory or right'.[38]

C. Difficulties with the argument

It is recognized that there are some difficulties arising from the above argument.

First, one indication of such a continuous habit of doing certain actions would be state practice. In this respect, a party arguing that WTO law has evolved in some respect into custom might not be able to rely on WTO jurisprudence as an indication of 'subsequent practice' for the purposes of Article 32 VCLT. Further, some writers question if there is any WTO customary international law, while one leading writer is prepared to consider that '. . . custom [in the area of trade] could emerge *with reference to GATT/WTO law*'.[39] While it is advanced here that WTO case law may evolve into customary international law, it is not by any means clear that such an argument would be generally accepted.

Secondly, a question may arise as to 'whose custom' it is. Examples of proving *opinio juris* include the conclusion of bilateral and multilateral treaties, attitudes in international meetings and state representative statements.[40] While mere inclusion of a provision in a treaty, e.g. in a WTO Agreement or in an RTA, is not conclusive that the parties consider such provision reflective of a custom in international law, consistent use in a number of treaties may indicate use amounting to custom.[41] Given the use of 'templates' by certain countries for a number of RTA provisions with different partners, this

---

[37] Pauwelyn, above at n 7, at 91–3.

[38] Jennings and Watts, above at n 5, at 27. The writers distinguish a custom from an usage. The latter is 'a habit of doing certain actions which has grown up without there being the conviction that these actions are, according to international law, obligatory or right'.

[39] *See*, for instance, Pauwelyn, above at n 7 at 47–50, citing W. Benedek, *Die Rechtsordnung des GATT aus Völkerrechtliche Sicht* (Berlin, London: Springer, 1990), 123–31 and D. Palmeter and P.C. Mavroidis, 'The WTO Legal System: Sources of Law' (1998) 92 AJIL 398 and Zamora, above at n 24.

[40] Jennings and Watts, above at n 5, at 28. A tentative argument that there could be a customary international law in the area of *investment* through similarly-worded Bilateral Investment Treaties (BITs) was raised in J.W. Salacuse and N.P. Sullivan, 'Do BITs Really Work?: An Evaluation of Bilateral Investment Treaties and their Grand Bargain' (2005) 46 Harv Int L J 67.

[41] *See* Jennings and Watts, *ibid.*, at 28 note 15, and the last paragraph of n 6 above regarding consistent use of certain provisions in a number of bilateral treaties. However, Zamora noted that observance of rules out of treaty obligation 'do not establish that a State would feel legally compelled to observe the rule if the treaty were absent' and that certain rules arise as consensual treaty obligations and not customary international law. *See* Zamora, above at n 25, at 19.

interesting phenomenon may be argued by such countries to be proof that certain provisions are evolving into customary trade law. If successful, this argument could encourage a powerful state to proactively enter into numerous bilateral treaties on certain terms which it wishes to promote as being customary international trade law. From a developing country point of view, entering the treaty may be an economic and/or political necessity, so that a developing country treaty partner may have no real choice in accepting the provisions or 'custom' at all. The current slew of RTAs with a mishmash of WTO, NAFTA, and other 'template' language reflects certain state interests and the question is whether these can be shown to represent customary international law, accepted sufficiently generally by states. Custom does not have to be accepted by every state, as in some fields, 'it is the practice and attitude of states directly concerned in that field which may be of most importance'.[42] In this respect, while it could be argued that the practice and attitudes of WTO Members would be of relevance since they are the ones 'directly concerned' in the field of international trade law, the question would be whether all WTO Members' practice should be viewed, or only those involved in the 'field' of promoting RTAs.

Thirdly, as pointed out above, the precise content of an alleged custom will be a potential source of contention.[43] For instance, would the fact that a particular rule appears in 99 per cent of RTAs surveyed make that rule the subject of custom? Questions will arise in respect of proof and the extent of the 'metamorphosis'. Politically, it will also raise the question of whether economically less influential states should be bound by such provisions found in a slew of RTAs promoted by economically more influential states.

The argument may also be anticipated that under Article IX:2 of the WTO Agreement, only the Ministerial Conference and the General Council have exclusive authority to adopt interpretations of WTO Agreements, and that Article 3.2 of the DSU merely permits Panels and the Appellate Body to 'clarify' the rights and obligations. No doubt these provisions were negotiated to ensure that final authority on meaning of WTO Agreements lay with the

---

[42] Jennings and Watts, *ibid.*, at 29. In the analysis of another writer, it is *power* which is crucial in shaping customary international law, in that '[t]he more powerful the economy, the greater the presence of its government and nationals in international transactions. Trade, foreign investment, and technical know-how emanate disproportionately from the advanced economic powers; they carry with them, as a rule, the political views of their respective States, together with social attitudes bearing on international relations. Moreover, for these reasons the affluent States are objects of attention by others. Their views and positions are noticed and unusually respected. Their official legal opinions and digests of State practice are available along with international law treatises that influence professional opinion and practical outcomes': O. Schachter, 'New Custom: Power, *Opinio Juris* and Contrary Practice', in J. Makarczyk (ed), *Theory of International Law at the Threshold of the 21st Century—Essays in Honour of Krzysztof Skubiwzewski* (The Hague; Boston: Kluwer, 1996), 537. These words may be apt to describe what developed nations are propagating in terms of 'trade law' through their numerous 'template' agreements.

[43] For the content of a customary international law rule, it is possible to look beyond state practice, to 'multilateral conventions which 'may have an important role to play in recording and defining rules deriving from custom, or indeed in developing them': Jennings and Watts, above at n 5, at 29. The WTO Agreements would be such a source to refer to.

Ministerial Conference or all the members acting in the General Council. However, under Article 3.2 of the DSU, the 'clarifications' by Panels and the Appellate Body may involve the development of legal interpretations of WTO provisions. One way to read this harmoniously with Article IX:2 would be to say that the authoritative interpretations adopted under that article refer to interpretations *vis-à-vis* all members.[44] Therefore, where legal interpretations of certain provisions are consistently applied over and over in different individual cases, such interpretations may form the subject of customary international law *vis-à-vis* the provisions interpreted. Should an RTA replicate those provisions, there is room to argue that the WTO case law applies as customary international law in interpreting the RTA provisions.

Finally, particularly in areas of high contentiousness such as interpretation of WTO treaty rights and obligations *vis-à-vis* trade issues—particularly where they share an interface with policy areas where there exist controversial debates, such as environmental protection—there may be general disagreement about WTO Panels or the Appellate Body being the appropriate forum to 'create' customary trade law that becomes binding on all states. The DSU system was not, in short, formed with such far-reaching influence in mind, as it was established to allow the prompt settlement of inter-member disputes in accordance with their WTO treaty rights and obligations.

Apart from these arguments, other difficulties have been raised earlier by other writers concerning difficulties in applying customary international law to the area of international economic law. These include—at least pre-WTO— the view that there has been 'relatively little case law, either at the international or national level, concerning customary international law, economic or otherwise'.[45] Another obstacle appears to be the difficulty of applying customary law to 'shifting economic relations'.[46] One would now need to look afresh at both these premises, in light of the numerous legal pronouncements emanating from the WTO's dispute settlement system. This development may challenge both these arguments, given that the WTO law being developed could in effect be engaging in the process of shaping customary international trade law (even if it is not expressly stated to be so) while precisely dealing with economic relations between members. In addition, to some extent, the WTO Agreements have helped to stabilize these 'shifting economic relations' in many areas through its labyrinth of rules and their interpretations, so that the argument against applying customary law to the area may not be quite as persuasive today.[47]

---

[44] The WTO itself appears to be of this view: *see* www.wto.org/english/tratop_e/dispu_e/disp_settlement_cbt_e/c1s3p2_e.htm (visited 10 October 2005).

[45] Zamora, above at n 24, at 38–9.   [46] *Ibid.*, at 40–1.

[47] In fact, the aims of the DSU system include providing 'security and predictability to the multilateral trading system' and to 'preserve the rights and obligations of Members under the covered agreements . . .': *see* Art. 3.2 DSU. It is recognized, however, that many WTO provisions remain largely unlitigated—or arise in argument but whose analysis may be avoided by Panels— under the DSU system and to that extent, there is still debate in some areas.

D. Framework for Linking RTA Disputes and WTO Law

If it is accepted (and in a given case, proven) that certain aspects of WTO treaty language and interpretation can evolve into customary international law (as illustrated by Figure 2), how does this branch interact with RTA provisions that either incorporate or resemble WTO provisions? If one starts by examining an RTA as a treaty, its provisions should be subject to the interpretative principles under public international law. This includes Articles 31 and 32 VCLT—which have by now become regular components in interpretation of WTO treaty language as well. Thus, a Panel faced with an RTA provision would, under Article 31, examine the text of the RTA provision for its ordinary meaning, determined in the light of its context and object. WTO case law may enter the examination in the following ways:

- By express incorporation of WTO provisions and their interpretations by WTO Panels and the Appellate Body;[48]
- By express inclusion of language identical to WTO treaty language;
- By express inclusion of language evocative of WTO jurisprudence language;
- By implication, where application of Articles 31 and/or 32 VCLT leads to the need for examining WTO jurisprudence;
- By express inclusion of a provision to apply general international law—this would include WTO treaty and case interpretations which can be proven to have evolved into customary international law or general principles of law, or WTO cases as 'judicial decisions and teachings of the most highly qualified publicists', under Article 38(1)(b)–(d) of the Statute of the ICJ;[49]

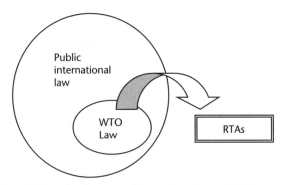

Figure 2. WTO law which evolves into general international law, and RTAs

---

[48] Art. 31(4) VCLT allows parties to give such special meaning to a treaty term: '4. A special meaning shall be given to a term if it is established that the parties so intended'.

[49] Art. 31 VCLT states: '3. There shall be taken into account, together with the context: (a) any subsequent agreement between the parties regarding the interpretation of the treaty or the application of its provisions; (b) any subsequent practice in the application of the treaty which establishes the agreement of the parties regarding its interpretation; (c) *any relevant rules of international law applicable in the relations between the parties*'. (emphasis added).

- Under Article 31(3)(c) VCLT—this could permit an RTA panel to refer to WTO treaty law or case interpretations that can be proven to have evolved into custom or general principles of law, or WTO cases as 'judicial decisions and teachings of the most highly qualified publicists', under Article 38(1)(b)–(d) of the Statute of the ICJ;
- Under Article 32 VCLT, where it is necessary under that Article to resort to the 'preparatory work of the treaty and the circumstances of its conclusion' under that article, and such preparatory work and circumstances point to application of WTO interpretation of the provision in question.

At the very least, WTO cases may form 'judicial decisions' to be used by an RTA panel as subsidiary source of international law under Article 38(1)(d) of the ICJ Statute.

It should be noted that the current discussion seeks to provide a basis for applying WTO case interpretations for interpreting identical language in RTAs (subject to the VCLT); it does not seek to argue that WTO case law should be used to fill gaps which arise in RTAs.[50]

These are shown in Table 1 below.

Under this framework of links, examination of an RTA's language begins with the principles of treaty interpretation. The RTA should be viewed, in accordance with Articles 31 and 32 VCLT, in the light of its text, context and objective. Where there is language in the RTA that is similar or identical to that WTO treaty language, an RTA panel would have to interpret the RTA language in accordance with these principles, and might therefore, in light of *that* RTA's text, context and objective, come to an interpretation that differs from what is in a particular WTO case. As has been observed elsewhere in the context of determining the question of competing jurisdiction under two treaty regimes:

> . . . [T]he application of international law rules on interpretation of treaties to identical or similar provisions of different treaties may not yield the same results, having regard to, *inter alia*, differences in the respective contexts, objects and purposes, subsequent practice of parties and *travaux préparatoires*.[51]

In other words, there should not be blind or slavish reference to WTO interpretations since the RTA is a separate treaty, equally subject to international law interpretation rules.

The RTA may, however, *through such interpretation*, be found to either expressly or impliedly refer the interpreters to WTO interpretations, either expressly or implicitly.

---

[50] The issue on using international law for gap-filling in WTO interpretation is taken up elsewhere, e.g. by J. Pauwelyn, 'The Role of Public International Law in the WTO: How Far Can We Go?' (2001) 95 AJIL 535 and L. Bartels, 'Applicable Law in WTO Dispute Settlement Proceedings' (2001) 35 JWT 499.

[51] *Mox Plant Case (Ireland v United Kingdom), Order on Provisional Measures*, 3 December 2001 (2002) 41 ILM 405 at 413.

Table 1. Links between RTA Interpretation and WTO Treaties and Case Interpretations

Link between RTA and WTO jurisprudence	RTA Panel Treatment of WTO jurisprudence	Examples
Express incorporation of WTO provision and interpretation in RTA	Generally interpret RTA in accordance with Arts 31 and 32 VCLT. Refer to and apply WTO interpretation in accordance with and to the extent of incorporation by RTA of WTO jurisprudence, by virtue of RTA parties' express treaty intention.	Art. 301 NAFTA
Express inclusion of language identical to those in WTO Agreements	Interpret RTA provisions/language in accordance with Arts 31 and 32 VCLT. Apply WTO jurisprudence if such interpretation of the RTA text calls for it; or b) it is established that WTO jurisprudence on the language in question has achieved the status of customary international law on such provisions/language.	NAFTA and numerous RTAs which use terms such as: 'like product' 'like circumstances' General Exceptions identical to Art. XX GATT or Art. XIV GATS
Express inclusion of language evocative of WTO jurisprudence language	Interpret RTA language in accordance with Arts 31 and 32 VCLT. Refer to WTO jurisprudence if such interpretation calls for it; or b) it is established that WTO jurisprudence on the language in question has achieved the status of customary international law on the language used.	Art. 701 US-Canada FTA: use of term 'reasonable expectations'
By implication	Where Arts 31 and 32 VCLT interpretation of the RTA requires an implication of party intention to apply WTO case law.	Dependent on text of RTA
By express inclusion of a provision to apply general international law	WTO treaty or case law which can be proven to have evolved into custom, general principles of law, or WTO case law which is shown to be relevant 'judicial decisions' (ICJ Statute Art. 38(1)(a)–(d) sources), may be applied under this provision.	Art. 101(2) NAFTA
By virtue of Art. 31(3)(c) VCLT	WTO treaty or case law which can be proven to have evolved into custom, general principles of law, or WTO case law which is shown to be relevant 'judicial decisions' (ICJ Statute Art. 38(1)(a)–(d) sources), may be applied under this provision.	–
By virtue of Art. 32 VCLT	Where supplementary means of interpretation are needed and they point to WTO case interpretations.	–

Apart from express or implicit intention gleaned from the RTA text, the above framework also provides for the possibility of proving WTO interpretation as having separately evolved—or to use Professor Bin Cheng's language, 'metamorphosized'—into customary international law *on a given term or provision*. Where this is proven, the RTA panel may take into account such custom even if there is no express incorporation of it by the RTA provisions, provided the RTA has not expressly provided *against* such adoption (ie, RTA partners have not 'contracted out' of any customary international law, including any established under WTO law).

While the treaty negotiators in the Uruguay Round may not have foreseen such far-reaching effects for the decisions of WTO Panels and Appellate Body, or the proliferation of RTAs using WTO language, it is necessary to address these links between the areas. The proposed framework would give some certainty to the international law system by providing RTA tribunals a structured means of judging whether and when to follow WTO case interpretations. At the same time, it would permit RTA negotiators wishing to adopt interpretations of their own, differing from WTO interpretations, to expressly state such intention in their treaties.

The next section examines the actual practice of some NAFTA panels, to discern the role that WTO case law plays in their decision-making. The practice shown in a selected number of Panel decisions under NAFTA Chapter 20, Chapter 11 and of ICSID is discussed. NAFTA panel decisions were chosen since NAFTA provisions have been replicated in many recent RTAs; furthermore, NAFTA panels have been so far the most active RTA panels.

III. NAFTA PRACTICE

A. NAFTA Chapter 20 Panels

There have so far been only three completed arbitral panel reviews under Chapter 20 of NAFTA. These deal with state-to-state disputes between the NAFTA parties. These are:

- *In the Matter of Cross-Border Trucking Services*
- *In the Matter of the US Safeguard Action taken on Broomcorn Brooms from Mexico*
- *Tariffs Applied by Canada to Certain US-origin Agricultural Products*

The first two cases mentioned above are discussed here in view of their panels' usage of GATT and WTO case interpretations.[52]

---

[52] The third case focused on the rights and obligations under the US–Canada FTA in connection with obligations created by the WTO Agreement on Agriculture, with little on the guidance offered by WTO case law.

In the *Broomcorn Broom* case,[53] the NAFTA panel was confronted with having to deal with WTO law at two levels: procedure and substance. At the procedural level, there were two issues. First, the panel was asked by the US to rule that it had no jurisdiction to adjudicate Mexico's claims based on obligations under Article XIX GATT and the WTO Agreement on Safeguards. Secondly, the panel was asked by the US to rule that Mexico's failure to raise an article during consultations (Article 803 and Annex 803(3)) was a failure to give timely notice of its claim under Articles 2012(3) and 2007(3) NAFTA, so that the claim under that article was not in the Panel's terms of reference.

On the jurisdictional point, the panel chose to confine its decision to the NAFTA provisions on safeguards, stating that:

Since the NAFTA and the WTO versions of the rule are substantively identical, application of the WTO version of the rule would have in no way changed the legal conclusion reached under NAFTA Annex 803.3(12). Accordingly, the Panel chose to rest its decision entirely on NAFTA Annex 803.3(12), without relying on the WTO Safeguards Code.

The panel seemed content to focus only on the bilateral safeguards provision in NAFTA, even though clearly, the agreement is a treaty which would have been governed in its interpretation by the VCLT. The VCLT has been applied numerous times by WTO Panels and the Appellate Body in interpreting WTO Agreements, ruling that Article 3.2 DSU provided the basis for this application of the VCLT. Though NAFTA Chapter 20 does not contain the same DSU language to apply 'customary rules of interpretation of public international law', NAFTA should be interpreted according to the VCLT since it is clearly a treaty. Secondly, Article 101(2) NAFTA in its objectives provision states:

2. The Parties shall interpret and apply the provisions of this Agreement *in the light of its objectives set out in paragraph 1 and in accordance with applicable rules of international law*. (emphasis added).[54]

A NAFTA panel should therefore interpret NAFTA provisions in accordance with Articles 31 and 32 of the VCLT. Article 31(1) therefore requires a panel to interpret NAFTA:

. . . in good faith in accordance with the ordinary meaning to be given to the terms of the treaty in their context and in the light of its object and purpose.

Two observations may be made of the Panel's ruling. The panel appears to have considered primarily the substantive similarity between the NAFTA bilateral safeguard provision (Article 801) and the 'WTO version of the rule' (above), in concluding that application of the WTO 'version' would not have

---

[53] NAFTA Chapter 20 Panel Report, *US Safeguard Action Taken on Broomcorn Brooms from Mexico*, 30 January 1998, available at www.sice.oas.org/DISPUTE/nafdispe.asp (visited 10 October 2005).

[54] The full text of the NAFTA is available at the NAFTA Secretariat website: www.nafta-sec-alena.org (visited 10 October 2005).

affected the legal conclusion under the NAFTA 'version'. No discussion of the ordinary meaning of the terms of Article 803 *in the context of NAFTA and in the light of the object and purpose of NAFTA* appears to have been undertaken by the panel to reach this conclusion. Secondly, in considering the substantive issue of the ITC's application of the terms 'domestic industry' and 'like or directly competitive', the NAFTA panel referred freely to decisions of WTO Panels and the Appellate Body.

What about the status of such WTO decisions *vis-à-vis* the NAFTA dispute? While there is no stated *stare decisis* relationship here,[55] in effect, the panel was applying standards and reasoning used in the WTO. Judging from the unquestioned reference by the panel to WTO standards and interpretations, it would appear to have considered itself very much guided by the WTO decisions, to the point of excluding discussion of NAFTA's own context and objectives.[56] Even if there is some kind of informal or *de facto* application of *stare decisis* being observed, a NAFTA panel is still obliged to consider the provisions under NAFTA in accordance with Articles 31 and 32 of the VCLT. A panel should not, and cannot, simply adopt the interpretations of a WTO Panel or the Appellate Body without considering NAFTA's own language, context and object and purpose. By contrast, under the agreement preceding the NAFTA, the US–Canada Free Trade Agreement, panels did refer to and apply Articles 31 and 32 of the VCLT in interpreting the provisions in question.[57]

At the substantive level, the panel had to determine whether the US application of bilateral safeguard action under Article 801 NAFTA was in proper, particularly whether the US had properly applied the provision 'domestic industry' in determining that increasing imports of broomcorn brooms had caused serious injury to the domestic industry. In dealing with this issue, the panel considered two aspects: whether the US had applied a 'like product' analysis and satisfied Article 801, and whether the US had applied the factor of 'like or directly competitive products' therein properly. In its discussion, the panel referred not only to WTO dispute settlement reports but also to a GATT panel report, for guidance.[58]

In summary, the *Broomcorn Brooms* Panel referred to WTO and GATT decisions for the following purposes:

[55] The panel stated that it 'noted' certain WTO cases: *see*, e.g. para. 66.

[56] The panel did make one brief reference to the overall objective of NAFTA as contained in its preamble, in considering whether the ITC had made a proper legal determination for the application of its bilateral safeguard action: *see* para. 71.

[57] *See*, for instance, *In the Matter of Canada's Compliance with Article 701.3 with respect to Durum Wheat Sales* (1993), available at www.nafta-sec-alena.org/DefaultSite/index_e.aspx?DetailID=380#USA–99–1904–03 (visited 10 October 2005), paras 14–20, 74–5, and 86. *See also In the Matter of Article 304 and the Definition of Direct Cost of Processing or Direct Cost of Assembling* (1992), available at www.nafta-sec-alena.org/DefaultSite/index_e.aspx?DetailID=10#usa9701 (visited 10 October 2005).

[58] Para. 69, referring to GATT Panel Report, *Korea—Resins*, ADP/92 and Corr.1, adopted 27 April 1993, BISD 40S/205.

- Determining the standard for the requirement of timely notice under Articles 2012(3) and 2007(3) NAFTA, by considering the equivalent standard under Article 6.2 DSU;[59]
- Interpretation of 'like product' in Article 801 NAFTA;[60]
- Gleaning the general principle from WTO jurisprudence that the definition of 'likeness' 'can vary from WTO provision to WTO provision according to the legal context in which it is being used', like an accordion being squeezed.[61]

In the Notes of the NAFTA, it is noteworthy that paragraph 16 states that for NAFTA Annex 300-B, sections 4 and 5, the terms 'serious damage' and 'increased quantities' are to be interpreted 'in the same manner' and 'in the light of its meaning' respectively with (the then) draft Agreement on Textiles and Clothing and Annex A of the Multifibre Agreement.[62] The parties clearly intended for interpretation of these phrases in NAFTA to be linked to their interpretation in the said WTO Agreements. Notably, the NAFTA parties did not single out 'domestic industry' or 'like products' for such linkage. It may be argued that the exclusion of express linkage to WTO interpretation for these other terms implies that they did not necessarily require NAFTA panels to apply WTO interpretations throughout. Secondly, paragraph 16 of the Notes distinguishes the interpretation of the said terms in sections 4 and 5 of Annex 300-B as compared with their interpretation under Article 801. Under Article 801 is understood to provide more narrowly and stringently for these two terms, respectively, than the interpretation in Annex 300-B which should follow WTO interpretation. This means that Article 801 is intended to have a different scope and breadth from the WTO standards. The Panel in *Broomcorn Brooms* ought to have examined the interpretation of the terms 'domestic industry' and 'like product' in the light of such (and any other) contextual information and the objectives of the NAFTA as a whole. The outcome may well have been the same but it would have been a more complete analysis based on the VCLT principles of interpretation.

---

[59] Para. 53, referring to WTO Panel Report, *Brazil—Desiccated Coconut*, WT/DS22/R, adopted 20 March 1997, as upheld by the Appellate Body Report WT/DS22/AB/R.

[60] The parties agreed on the factors to be used in determining 'likeness', as established by WTO: para. 64 of the Panel decision, and paras 36 and 38 of Mexico's and the US's arguments respectively. The Panel in this case also referred to WTO decisions on 'like product' in paras 66–7. *See also* n 7, above.

[61] Para. 66, citing the WTO Appellate Body's words in *Japan—Alcoholic Beverages II*, above at n 1, at 21.

[62] In NAFTA Ch 19, which deals with review of anti-dumping and countervailing measure actions, Art. 1911 on Definitions also contains a link to the GATT: '*goods of a Party* means domestic products as these are understood in the *General Agreement on Tariffs and Trade*'. (emphasis added). It should be noted that Ch 19 binational Panels have also referred to WTO interpretations of language similar to that in NAFTA and the Special Import Measures Act: *see*, for instance, Binational Panel Review, *In the Matter of Certain Refrigerators, Dishwashers and Dryers Originating in or Exported from the USA etc*, 16 January 2002, available at www.sice.oas.org/DISPUTE/nafdispe.asp (visited 10 October 2005), at 23–6.

In the more recent panel decision in *Cross-Border Trucking Services*, the Panel again did not refer to interpretative provisions of the VCLT. It referred to WTO cases for 'guidance'.[63] In this case, the panel had to interpret Articles 1202 and 1203 of the NAFTA; specifically, it had to interpret the phrase 'in like circumstances' therein. In doing so, it also referred to other agreements, such as the US–Canada Free Trade Agreement, which preceded the NAFTA.[64] The panel also referred to WTO jurisprudence in interpreting an exception in Article 2101, as the language in Article 2101:2 'closely tracks the GATT Article XX language',[65] and to 'long-established doctrine under the GATT and WTO'.[66]

The panels in these two cases did not discuss the theoretical basis for referring to WTO case law but appeared, rather, to accept doing so as a natural interpretative act in view of the common language involved.

1. NAFTA Chapter 11 Panels

By contrast, NAFTA Chapter 11 panels appear to have been more mindful of Article 102(2), which requires them to 'interpret and apply the provisions of [NAFTA] in the light of its objectives set out in paragraph 1 and in accordance with applicable rules of international law'.

Panels have read this to include principles under the VCLT. Hence, in the *Ethyl* award on jurisdiction, the panel applied Article 31 VCLT,[67] as did the Panels in *Methanex*[68], *Metalclad*[69] and *Firemen's Fund*.[70]

The Panel in *SD Myers v The Government of Canada* also considered the interpretative principles in Articles 31 and 32 VCLT as being applicable to NAFTA.[71] It proceeded to examine other international treaties which the disputants were party to. In respect of WTO case law, the panel considered it for the following purposes:

- As a yardstick for measuring the principles which the panel gleaned from various international treaties governing the level of environmental protection that the parties were privy to;[72]

---

[63] *See* paras 251 and 260–70.   [64] *Ibid.*, para. 249.

[65] *Ibid.*, para. 260.   [66] *Ibid.*, para. 289.

[67] *Ethyl Corporation v The Government of Canada*, Award on Jurisdiction, 24 June 1998, available at (1999) 38 International Legal Materials 708.

[68] First Partial Award, 7 August 2002, paras 97–102, available at www.state.gov/s/l/c5818.htm (visited 10 October 2005). *See* further discussion of the Final Award on page 549.

[69] *Metalclad Corporation v United Mexican States*, Award dated 30 August 2000, available at www.state.gov/s/l/c3752.htm (visited 10 October 2005), para 70.

[70] Case CIADI No ARB(AF)02/1, *Fireman's Fund Insurance Co v United Mexican States*, Decision on the Preliminary Question, available at www.economia-snci.gob.mx (visited 10 October 2005), para. 63.

[71] Available at www.dfait-maeci.gc.ca/tna-nac/SDM-en.asp (visited 10 October 2005).

[72] *Ibid.*, paras 220–21.

- As guidance in interpreting the phrase 'like circumstances' in the national treatment obligations under Article 1102(1) and (2) NAFTA;[73]
- As an example of a treaty which was a 'single undertaking' whose components were to be interpreted with a view to complementarity, to apply to NAFTA.[74]

Extensive discussion of WTO case law was undertaken by the Panel in *Pope & Talbot*, in which a US investor brought a claim against the Government of Canada.[75] The case law was raised by Canada, to support its argument of 'disproportionate disadvantage', in the context of national treatment under NAFTA.[76] Interestingly, however, with respect to a separate argument relating to interpretation of the phrase 'like circumstances', no reliance was placed on WTO or GATT interpretations of 'like', unlike in *SD Myers* above. The Panel in *Pope & Talbot* was mindful that NAFTA provisions should be interpreted in accordance with Articles 31 and 32 VCLT.[77] In the *ADF* case, the Panel referred to WTO case law for interpretative guidance in examining the object and purpose of the NAFTA provisions in question.[78] Again, the panel was mindful of the need to interpret these provisions in light of the VCLT.[79]

While the Tribunal in *ADF* was not convinced by the investor that the standard it was arguing for had evolved to form part of customary international law, it (and the Tribunal in *Mondev* which it quoted) acknowledged the possibility:

The Investor, for instance, has not shown that such a requirement has been brought into the corpus of present day customary international law by the many hundreds of bilateral investment treaties now extant. It may be that, in their current state, neither concordant state practice nor judicial or arbitral caselaw provides convincing substantiation (or, for that matter, refutation) of the Investor's position. It may also be observed in this connection that the Tribunal in *Mondev* did *not* reach the position of the Investor, while implying that the process of change is in motion:

Thirdly, the vast number of bilateral and regional investment treaties (more than 2000) almost uniformly provide for fair and equitable treatment of foreign investments, and largely provide for full security and protection of investments. Investment treaties run between North and South, and East and West, and between States in these spheres inter se. On a remarkably widespread basis, States have repeatedly obliged themselves to accord foreign investment such treatment. In the Tribunal's view, such a

---

[73] *Ibid.*, paras 243–46, referring to the overall legal context of the term 'like' in GATT case law. Apart from GATT cases interpreting the phrase 'like products', the panel also referred to other documents and rulings for the legal context for the NAFTA provisions in question: *see* paras 247–50.

[74] *Ibid.*, paras 291–93.

[75] Available at www.dfait-maeci.gc.ca/tna-nac/pope-en.asp (visited 10 October 2005).

[76] *Pope & Talbot Inc v The Government of Canada*, Award on the Merits Phase 2, 10 April 2001, available at www.dfait-maeci.gc.ca/tna-nac/pope-en.asp (visited 10 October 2005).

[77] *See* fn 68 of the award, as well as paras 115–18.

[78] Case No ARB(AF)/00/1, *ADF Group Inc v USA*, Award, 9 Jan 2003, available at www.state.gov/s/l/c3754.htm (visited 10 October 2005), fn 152 and para 147.

[79] *Ibid.*, para. 149.

body of concordant practice will necessarily have influenced the content of rules governing the treatment of foreign investment in current international law. *It would be surprising if this practice and the vast number of provisions it reflects were to be interpreted as meaning no more than the Neer Tribunal (in a very different context) meant in 1927'.* (emphasis added).[80]

The *ADF* tribunal also observed that recourse to customary international law 'must be disciplined by being based on State practice and judicial or arbitral case law or other sources of customary or general international law'.[81]

Finally, in the most recent decision of *Methanex Corporation v USA*,[82] the claimant, Methanex, sought to show that it was a producer 'in like circumstances' as US domestic ethanol producers under Article 1102, by arguing that Methanex produced the same good—or 'like products' under GATT terminology—as the US producers. Methanex then sought to rely on WTO jurisprudence to provide assistance in interpreting 'like goods'. However, the Tribunal declined to rely on WTO jurisprudence in this context since Chapter 11 did not contain what it called, 'the term of art in international trade law, "like products", which appears in and plays a critical role in the application of GATT Article III'.[83] The Tribunal thus seemed to acknowledge that certain words under WTO Agreements could be legal 'terms of art'. This lends some support to the argument that WTO terms which are 'terms of art', with their interpretations, could pass into the realm of customary international law. This argument would apply *a fortiori* in the interpretation of a BIT or FTA provision containing the precise words, 'like products' and the surrounding GATT language.[84]

IV. CONCLUSION

From the above discussion, it is argued that interpretation of the NAFTA and other RTAs should be subject to the principles in Articles 31 and 32 of the VCLT. In the case of NAFTA, Article 102(2) makes specific provision for the application of international law in interpreting its provisions. In other RTAs, where such an express provision may not be present, it is submitted that the international law principles of treaty interpretation encapsulated in the VCLT should still apply to the treaties. In both the NAFTA and other RTAs, WTO case law can have a place in treaty interpretation. Where under the analysis provided by Article 31 VCLT there is a need to refer to WTO cases, they should be referred to, to the extent that the treaty itself directs. The present

---

[80] *Ibid.*, para. 183.   [81] *Ibid.*, para. 184.

[82] Final Award of the Tribunal on Jurisdiction and Merits, 3 August 2005, available at www.state.gov/s/l/c5818.htm (visited 10 October 2005).

[83] Part IV, Ch B, paras 23–38, especially para. 29.

[84] Indeed, the Tribunal observed that the NAFTA Parties did use the term 'like products' and other WTO terms in other provisions of the agreement; *see* paras 30–5.

situation where some panels choose to refer to WTO interpretations without explanation of the basis for such reference is unsatisfactory. Where such reference is warranted, one may find that WTO case law can offer direction in procedural practice and substantive interpretation of treaty language; such direction is already being sought *de facto* by several panels at present, as seen from the examples discussed above.

Secondly, NAFTA and RTA panels are likely to seek guidance from WTO case law as a matter of practice in certain situations: where the NAFTA or RTA directly incorporates WTO provisions;[85] contains language similar to that in a WTO Agreement; where the NAFTA or RTA contains language evocative of WTO concepts developed in its jurisprudence; and where by implication the interpretation of the text requires reference to WTO case law.[86]

Further, where an aspect of WTO interpretation is shown to have reached

---

[85] For instance, Article 301 NAFTA on National Treatment states:

1. Each Party shall accord national treatment to the goods of another Party in accordance with Article III of the *General Agreement on Tariffs and Trade* (GATT), *including its interpretative notes, and to this end Article III of the GATT and its interpretative notes, or any equivalent provision of a successor agreement to which all Parties are party, are incorporated into and made part of this Agreement.* (emphasis added).

Interestingly, Art. 301 NAFTA dropped the sub-paragraph in Art. 501 of the US–Canada FTA, which states that '[f]or purposes of this Agreement, the provisions of this Chapter shall be applied in accordance with existing interpretations adopted by the Contracting Parties to the GATT.' This provision was considered in the Chapter 18 case, *Lobsters from Canada* (1990), available at www.nafta-sec-alena.org/app/DocRepository/1/Dispute/english/FTA_Chapter_18/USA/uc89010e. pdf (visited 10 October 2005).

Again, Art. 309 NAFTA on Import and Export Restrictions provides:

1. Except as otherwise provided in this Agreement, no Party may adopt or maintain any prohibition or restriction on the importation of any good of another Party or on the exportation or sale for export of any good destined for the territory of another Party, except *in accordance with Article XI of the GATT, including its interpretative notes, and to this end Article XI of the GATT and its interpretative notes, or any equivalent provision of a successor agreement to which all Parties are party, are incorporated into and made a part of this Agreement.* (emphasis added).

Finally, Art. 2101 NAFTA provides:

1. For purposes of:
(a) Part Two (Trade in Goods), except to the extent that a provision of that Part applies to services or investment, and
(b) Part Three (Technical Barriers to Trade), except to the extent that a provision of that Part applies to services, *GATT Article XX and its interpretative notes, or any equivalent provision of a successor agreement to which all Parties are party, are incorporated into and made part of this Agreement.* (emphasis added.)

Under the US–Canada FTA, a Ch 18 panel examined Art. XX(g) GATT (and its jurisprudence) as incorporated by Art. 1201 of the FTA: *see Canada's Landing Requirement for Pacific Coast Salmon and Herring* (1989); available at www.nafta-sec-alena.org/DefaultSite/index_e.aspx?DetailID=425#CDA–89–1807–01 (visited 10 October 2005).

[86] In a dispute under Ch 18 of the US-Canada FTA, a Panel interpreted the phrase '. . . any benefit reasonably expected to accrue . . .'. in Art. 2011 to incorporate the GATT-developed notion of reasonable expectations, even though no express reference was made in Art. 2011 to Art. XXIII GATT which gave rise to that notion; *see* Final Report of the Panel, *In the Matter of Puerto Rico Regulations on the Import, Distribution and Sale of UHT Milk from Quebec,* 3 June 1993, available at www.nafta-sec-alena.org/DefaultSite/index_e.aspx?DetailID=431#USA–93–1807–01 (visited 10 October 2005), at para. 5.56.

the status of custom, such interpretation may be applied by a panel where the RTA permits application of general international law to its interpretation. With the large number of RTAs in existence—and being negotiated—it can be expected that future RTA panels will frequently encounter the need to interpret common WTO-like terms, such as 'like products', 'like services', 'domestic industry', 'material injury', 'necessary', and general exceptions worded exactly like those in Article XX GATT and Article XIV GATS. NAFTA tribunals have already acknowledged the possibility of *investment treaty* language exhibited consistently in numerous BITs—disciplined by state practice and case law—may evolve into customary international law. A parallel evolution in the interpretation of trade *'terms of art'* should therefore also be possible. Should it be accepted that a particular term used in WTO is such a term of art, through state practice and case law, and it is replicated exactly in a RTA, a dispute settlement tribunal under the RTA would be able to apply WTO law on the interpretation of that term as customary international law.

In addition, WTO jurisprudence will be watched keenly by RTA panels in 'newer' areas, such as in the interpretation of GATS obligations and Schedules.[87] At the same time, the concomitant proliferation of RTA dispute settlement fora means that there will be a need to clarify the relationship between RTA interpretation and WTO interpretations of common terms.[88] Judging from NAFTA experience, dispute settlement panels currently either do not refer to the VCLT interpretative principles or refer to them without discussion of the role of WTO law *vis-à-vis* RTA interpretation under the VCLT. This leaves the role of WTO law in RTA interpretation, ambiguous. This chapter has thus proposed a framework of reference linking WTO law and RTAs, within the VCLT interpretative principles.

Having a clear theoretical framework within which RTA panels are to deal with WTO case interpretations would be beneficial for at least four reasons:

1. RTA dispute settlement would be more predictable. Panels would be guided as to when to refer to WTO case law. For states which have entered into RTAs with a 'template' based on WTO provisions that have been interpreted, they can be assured of consistency of interpretation by an RTA panel with WTO principles. For investor claimants in RTA investor-state disputes, this would be particularly important as investors can be

---

[87] The Appellate Body recently offered its first ruling on a dispute based purely on the GATS, in *US—Gambling*, above at n 34, where it had to interpret the Schedule of specific commitments of the US.

[88] For a discussion of the role of specialized dispute settlement fora in the international law system, *see* generally, Charney, above at n 9, also in 'Is International Law Threatened by Multiple International Tribunals?' (1998) 271 *Recueil des Cours* 101 and C. Romano, 'The Proliferation of International Judicial Bodies: The Pieces of the Puzzle' (1999) 31 NYU J Int L & Pol 709, particularly at 735–38.

better advised on the potential interpretation of provisions in the FTA being relied on.[89]

2. RTA dispute panels would, where the RTA permits, be able to draw upon the expertise of WTO dispute panels and the Appellate Body in the development of legal concepts and principles. In particular, since RTA provisions often contain terms identical to GATT language, the wealth of pre-WTO, GATT Panel interpretation can be drawn upon as well.

3. It would help to ameliorate the potential fragmentation of international trade law into pockets of interpretation for RTA provisions that mimic WTO provisions.

4. RTA partners wishing to have provisions interpreted otherwise than in accordance with WTO jurisprudence (where such jurisprudence might be applicable through one of the interpretative reasons in Table 1) continue to have a choice of expressly contracting away from such jurisprudence in their RTA, by setting out their own interpretative or definitional provisions.

---

[89] Given the slew of RTAs being negotiated and signed by the US and other countries, in time to come, their dispute panels' jurisprudence may also form a significant subject of study, in their relation to international law. The challenges to 'lesser states' which sign these agreements are discussed in Weiler and Motoc, above at n 23, especially at 65.

22

What Role is there for Regional International Law in the Interpretation of the WTO Agreements?

ISABELLE VAN DAMME [*]

I. INTRODUCTION

The interpretation of WTO law in the light of international law is a highly contested matter among scholars, practitioners, and diplomats, more often from a policy than a legal perspective. The emergence of diffuse and often conflicting regional trade agreements ('RTAs') has raised concerns for the future 'predictability and security' of the multilateral trading system. Regionalism is certainly a 'hot topic' these days, not only in Geneva, Brussels, or Washington DC, but in almost every capital. But the rhetoric on regionalism often takes for granted or simply ignores the validity and meaning of regionalism in terms of the sources of public international law.

This chapter seeks to identify 'regionalism' as a source of international law;[1] and how regional international law has and should be relied on by panels and the Appellate Body in the interpretation of WTO law and in the light of Article 31(3)(c) of the Vienna Convention on the Law of Treaties ('VCLT').[2] First, the chapter touches briefly on the treaty interpretation practice of WTO panels and the Appellate Body. Following this short overview, the chapter

[*] This chapter is part of a broader study on the relevance of international law for the interpretation of WTO law in the context of WTO dispute settlement. The author would like to thank the organizers of the Conference, in particular Lorand Bartels and Federico Ortino, and the participants for their feedback. The author also thanks Professor Joanne Scott and Professor James Crawford for their helpful comments.

[1] References to regionalism and 'regional' international law in this chapter include bilateral treaties.

[2] Done at Vienna, in force 27 January 1980, 1155 UNTS 331.

looks at the legal basis for the reliance on norms of other sub-systems of international law and general international law for treaty interpretation, i.e. Article 31(3)(c) VCLT. According to Article 31(3)(c) VCLT, the interpretation of a treaty shall take into account, along with the context of the treaty, 'any relevant rules of international law applicable in the relations between the parties'. This interpretation rule has so far been mostly overlooked in WTO dispute settlement probably because of its ambiguous and vague wording. This raises the question of how to resolve interpretation questions of an interpretation rule. One of the interpretation problems with Article 31(3)(c) VCLT is the definition of 'rules of international law'. Regionalism has various meanings in public international law, and several of these understandings will be explored. The chapter discusses the practice of WTO panels and the Appellate Body in considering regionalism as a source of international law and as a means to interpret the WTO covered agreements. The chapter concludes with a few preliminary conclusions on the relationship between regionalism and international law in the context of the interpretation of the WTO covered agreements. It is not a question of 'if' panels and the Appellate Body are looking at regional international law for interpretative purposes, but rather of 'when', 'how', and 'how much'. So far, the jurisprudence has offered unsatisfactory answers to those questions.

II. THE INTERPRETATION OF WTO LAW AND THE RELEVANCE OF INTERNATIONAL LAW: A CLOSER LOOK AT ARTICLE 31(3)(C) VCLT

WTO panels and the Appellate Body have established themselves as progressive and innovative front runners in treaty interpretation among the continuously expanding network of regional and international dispute settlement systems. They have consistently relied on the customary rules of international law on treaty interpretation, as partially codified in the VCLT, to support and confirm the legal analysis in their reports; and they have systemically explained the 'mechanics' of their reasoning under the VCLT.

Interpretation lies at the heart of the WTO dispute settlement system and this is reflected in the Dispute Settlement Understanding ('DSU'). Under Article 3.2 DSU, the WTO dispute settlement bodies must 'clarify the existing provisions of those agreements in accordance with customary rules of interpretation of public international law'.[3] Under this authority, panels and the Appellate Body have explored a wide range of customary rules and principles

---

[3] Art. 3.2 DSU: 'The dispute settlement understanding of the WTO is a central element in providing security and predictability to the multilateral trading system. The Members recognize that it serves to preserve the rights and obligations of Members under the covered agreements, and to clarify the existing provisions of those agreements in accordance with customary rules of interpretation of public international law. Recommendations and rulings of the DSB cannot add to or diminish the rights and obligations provided in the covered agreements'.

of treaty interpretation, beyond those embedded in Articles 31, 32, and 33 VCLT.

The Uruguay Round negotiators of the DSU understood 'customary rules of interpretation of public international law' as meaning Articles 31, 32, and 33 VCLT, and not necessarily other principles of treaty interpretation. Although the negotiators, most of them being not lawyers, were in general agreement on the precise scope of Article 3.2 DSU, they were somewhat ignorant of the interpretation problems arising from especially Articles 31 and 32 VCLT. There was no discussion, in the course of the Uruguay Round negotiations on the DSU, of the substance and scope of the treaty interpretation rules in the Vienna Convention. Article 31(3)(c) VCLT might be the most prominent example. With over 26,000 pages of treaty law, panels and the Appellate Body face a substantial responsibility in the interpretation of the WTO covered agreements.[4]

Some caution is appropriate when characterizing the interpretation 'methodology' of any dispute settlement system, including that of WTO panels and the Appellate Body. Interpretation is in essence an intangible reflection process of the adjudicator, which is submitted to the rule of law. Treaty interpretation is a reasoning process that is premised on the identity of the interpreter, the context of the interpretation, and the tools of interpretation at the disposal of the interpreter. The principles and rules of treaty interpretation are not mathematical formulas that predict the outcome of a legal sum. Instead, these principles and rules of interpretation structure the multiple dimensions of the interpretation process. The legitimacy and authority of the interpretation process is embedded in these principles and rules, but are nevertheless a function of the respect for the rule of law. Therefore, one should not generalize too much when it comes to describing methodologies. Especially in the context of WTO dispute settlement where, despite a strong precedent or persuasive value, DSB reports are only binding on the disputants one should be vigilant in making grand statements about interpretation doctrines by panels and the Appellate Body. The international (and national) judicial mandate encompasses a certain degree of discretion to include various values and interests that 'colour' the dispute before an international court or tribunal. When interpreted liberally, Article 31(3)(c) VCLT offers the adjudicator a broad palette of values and rights protected by various international norms, which he can then consider when deciding disputes brought before him.

---

[4] The power to adopt authoritative interpretations is reserved to the Ministerial Conference and the General Council and this requires a three-fourths majority (Art. IX:2 Marrakesh Agreement). In practice, WTO Members have been reluctant to adopt such authoritative interpretations. There are, however, examples of interpretative guidance by WTO Members. For example, WTO Members agreed in the Doha Ministerial Declaration that the TRIPS Agreement '. . . can and should be interpreted and implemented in a manner supportive of WTO Members' right to protect public health and, in particular, to promote access to medicines for all': WTO Doha Declaration on the TRIPS Agreement and Public Health, WTO Doc. WT/MIN(01)/Dec/2, adopted 14 November 2001, at para. 4.

Even with this qualification in mind, the Appellate Body's interpretation 'methodology' has been described as an emerging 'WTO ethos' in the interpretation of the covered agreements.[5] Appellate Body reports like *US—Shrimp* and *EC—Hormones* have been subject to public and academic scrutiny. This chapter does not aim to repeat, reformulate, or add to the rich and diverse commentaries on these cases. Rather, this chapter offers a forward-looking perspective on the potential ramifications of the use of Article 31(3)(c) VCLT for the interpretation of the WTO covered agreements.[6] According to Article 31(3)(c) VCLT, a treaty should be interpreted taking into account, along with the context of the treaty, 'any relevant rules of international law applicable in the relations between the parties'. The VCLT, therefore, appears to contemplate (relevant) regional sources of international law as means of treaty interpretation.

The interpretation practice of panels and the Appellate Body when it comes to considering other rules of international law, and especially RTAs, is ambivalent to say the least. After ten years of WTO dispute settlement, there is little or no mention of Article 31(3)(c) VCLT in the case law of panels and the Appellate Body, in shrill contrast to the elaborate, often theoretical, elucidation on the other provisions in the VCLT in DSB reports. This is not to proclaim that panels and the Appellate Body have not interpreted the WTO covered agreements in the light of the wider corpus of international law. The jurisprudence of the WTO shows that '[r]eference to other rules of international law in the course of interpreting a treaty is an everyday, often unconscious part of the interpretation process'.[7] In its very first report, the Appellate Body in *US—Gasoline* left no doubt over the fact that the WTO covered agreements should not be read 'in clinical isolation from public international law'.[8] The WTO dispute settlement system has been receptive to various sources of both general international law and other sub-systems of international law. For example, the Appellate Body recognized in *US—Shrimp* that it should seek 'additional interpretative guidance, as appropriate, from the general principles of international law'.[9] But the minimalist use of Article 31(3)(c) VCLT by panels and the Appellate Body is somewhat puzzling.[10] Generally, disputants, panels, and the Appellate Body have relied on other rules of international law as context, subsequent practice, and supplementary means of interpretation.

One possible explanation for the Appellate Body's practice of using inter-

---

[5] ILC, Study on the Function and Scope of the Lex Specialis Rule and the Question of 'Self-Contained Regimes': Preliminary Report by Mr. M. Koskenniemi, Chairman of the Study Group (7 May 2004), UN Doc. ILC(LVI)/SG/FIL/CRD.1, at para. 152.

[6] The WTO covered agreements include the agreements listed in Appendix 1 and 2 to the DSU (Art. 1 DSU).

[7] C. McLachlan, 'The Principle of Systemic Integration and Article 31(3)(c) of the Vienna Convention' (2005) 54 ICLQ 279, at 280.

[8] WTO Appellate Body Report, *US—Gasoline*, WT/DS2/AB/R, adopted 20 May 1996, at 16.

[9] WTO Appellate Body Report, *US—Shrimp*, WT/DS58/AB/R, adopted 6 November 1998, at para. 158.

[10] *See* section II.B of this chapter.

national law as the interpretative framework for the WTO covered agreements could be Article 31(1) VCLT.[11] Article 31(1) VCLT sets forth the primary rule of interpretation according to which 'a treaty shall be interpreted in good faith in accordance with the ordinary meaning to be given to the terms of the treaty in their context and in the light of its object and purpose'. A treaty should not only be interpreted in good faith (Article 31(1) VCLT), it must also be applied in good faith (Article 26 VCLT). The good faith obligation is also said to encapsulate a presumption that states negotiate treaties taking into account all relevant international law.[12] Therefore, the Appellate Body might feel compelled by Article 31(1) VCLT to consider international law in the interpretation of the WTO covered agreements, rather than by Article 31(3)(c) VCLT. The good faith interpretation offers the interpreter more discretion in the choice of rules of international law to which he or she may want to refer. Discussions and choices about the meaning of the inter-temporal element and the 'parties' in Article 31(3)(c) VCLT are only some of the questions that can be avoided by relying on Article 31(1) VCLT. Nevertheless, Article 31(3)(c) VCLT should be read as a further elaboration and application of the obligation to interpret a treaty in good faith. Although panels and the Appellate Body have relied on a kaleidoscope of sources of non-WTO law for the interpretation of the covered agreements, they should not avoid Article 31(3)(c) VCLT to justify their recourse to rules of international law.[13] Other international courts and tribunals have also generally declined to give explicit recognition to Article 31(3)(c) VCLT. The predominant reason for the hesitance to apply this coherence-enforcing interpretation rule, was eloquently expressed by Judge Weeramantry when he wrote that Article 31(3)(c) VCLT, '. . . scarcely covers [this] aspect with the degree of clarity requisite to so important a mater'.[14]

While drafting the VCLT, the negotiators assumed that international law should, or rather 'shall' as the text of Article 31(3)(c) VCLT reads, be considered as an authentic means of interpretation, not as a supplementary means

[11] By 'interpretative framework' we mean the entire spectrum of norms of international law and other elements of treaty interpretation that qualify under the customary rules and principles of treaty interpretation.

[12] G. Marceau, 'Conflict of Norms and Conflicts of Jurisdictions—The Relationship between the WTO Agreement and MEAs and other Treaties' (2001) 35 JWT 1081, at 1089 and 1107.

[13] Panel and Appellate Body reports in which Art. 31(3)(c) VCLT was mentioned, but only rarely applied, include: Appellate Body Report, *US—Shrimp*, above at n 9, at para. 158, fn 157; Panel Report, *US—Gambling*, WT/DS285/R, adopted 20 April 2005, as modified by the Appellate Body Report, WT/DS285/AB/R, at para 18, fn 44; Decision by the Arbitrators, *Brazil—Aircraft (Article 22.6—Brazil)*, WT/DS46/ARB, 28 August 2000, at fn 48; Panel Report, *Chile—Price Band System*, WT/DS207/R, adopted 23 October 2002, as modified by the Appellate Body Report, WT/DS207/AB/R, at para. 7.85; Panel Report, *Argentina—Poultry Antidumping Duties*, WT/DS241/R, adopted 19 May 2003, at para 7.41; Appellate Body Report, *EC—Chicken Cuts*, WT/DS269/AB/R, WT/DS286/AB/R, adopted 27 September 2005, at para. 199, fn 384.

[14] *Danube Dam Case (Hungary v Slovakia)*, Judgment 5 February 1997, Separate Opinion Judge Weeramantry [1997] ICJ Rep 88, at 114.

under Article 32 VCLT.[15] The case law of various international courts and tribunals, including that of WTO panels and the Appellate Body, is not entirely respectful of the preparatory work of the VCLT. Only in a handful of cases have international courts and tribunals relied on Article 31(3)(c) VCLT.[16] Several reasons for this hesitance can be identified: uncertainty about the evolving general structure and sources of international law; the so-called 'organic' nature of interpretation; concerns of state consent and sovereignty; and especially the ambiguity of the wording of Article 31(3)(c) VCLT. The 'organic' nature of treaty interpretation implies that the process of treaty interpretation is inherently context-dependent, fact-specific, and on a case-by-case basis. The process of interpretation is a subjective exercise in which many factors play a role, including the legal background of the adjudicator, the institutional context, the type of the dispute, the specific rules under interpretation, the character of the rights involved, etc.

Although every single word in Article 31(3)(c) VCLT is open to distinct interpretations, the following section will focus on the interpretation of 'rules of international law' and the extent to which panels and the Appellate Body have looked at RTAs for the interpretation of the WTO covered agreements. In some respect, the interpretation of 'rules of international law' is inherently related to the interpretation of the 'parties' in Article 31(3)(c) VCLT; and whether the 'parties' means all WTO Members, merely the disputants, or the common intentions of the WTO membership.[17] Article 2.1(g) VCLT defines a 'party' as a 'State which has consented to be bound by the treaty and for which the treaty is in force', but this definition is not particularly instructive for the interpretation of the 'parties' in Article 31(3)(c) VCLT. The meaning of the 'parties' in Article 31(3)(c) VCLT remains unclear. The Appellate Body used Article 31(3)(c) VCLT in *US—Shrimp* to refer to treaties that were not even binding on all the disputants, but were arguably endorsed by WTO

---

[15] *See* Sir H. Waldock, Special Rapporteur, Sixth Report on the Law of Treaties, UN Doc. A/CN.4/186 and Add. 1–7, ILC Yb. 1966, v. II, 51, at 96 and ILC, Report of the International Law Commission on the Work of its 18th Session (1966), UN Doc. A/CN.4/191, at 222.

[16] *Case Concerning Oil Platforms (Iran v United States of America)*, Judgment 6 November 2003 [2003] ICJ Rep 161; *Esphahanian v Bank Tejarat*, 2 Iran-USCTR 157 (1983); *Dispute Concerning Access to Information under Article 9 of the OSPAR Convention (Ireland v United Kingdom)*, Order No 3 (2003) 42 ILM 1187 and *Golder v United Kingdom*, Judgment 21 February 1975 (1975) ECHR Ser. A., No 18, 17, at para. 35. For the reference to or application of Art. 31(3)(c) VCLT in WTO dispute settlement, *see* n 13.

[17] For a discussion of the interpretation of the 'parties' in the context of WTO dispute settlement, *see* G. Marceau, 'A Call for Coherence in International Law—Praises for the Prohibition Against "Clinical Isolation" in WTO Dispute Settlement' (1999) 33 JWT 87, at 124–26; D. Palmeter and P.C. Mavroidis, 'The WTO Legal System: Sources of Law' (1999) 92 AJIL 398, at 411; J. Meltzer, 'Interpreting the WTO Agreements—A Commentary on Professor Pauwelyn's Approach' (2004) 25 Mich J Int L 917, at 918; L. Bartels, 'Article XX of GATT and the Problem of Extraterritorial Jurisdiction: The Case of Trade Remedies for the Protection of Human Rights' (2002) 36 JWT 353, at 360–61; M. Lennard, 'Navigating by the Stars: Interpreting the WTO Agreements' (2002) 5 JIEL 17, at 38; G. Marceau, 'WTO Dispute Settlement and Human Rights' (2002) 13 EJIL 753, at 781; and W. Weiss, 'Security and Predictability under WTO Law' (2003) 2 WTR 183, at 196–97.

Members through the Committee on Trade and Environment ('CTE') work programme.[18] As a textbook example of the interpretation of an interpretation rule, a textual analysis of Article 31(3)(c) VCLT does not clarify the ordinary meaning with respect to the term 'parties' and does not clarify the intentions of the parties. Moreover, it seems that the drafters of the Vienna Convention did not pay too much attention to the implications of the various meanings of the term 'parties'.[19]

The principles of effective and good faith interpretation should guide the adjudicator to decide in a particular case what the 'relevant' rules of international law are in terms of the applicability *ratione personae* of these rules. The text of the WTO agreements should reflect the common intentions of all WTO Members,[20] but this does not imply that the means to interpret these agreements should be binding on all WTO Members or reflect the intentions of all WTO Members. The case law of various international and regional dispute settlement systems gives support to the argument that the 'parties' might have been read out of Article 31(3)(c) VCLT in the interpretation of this provision. Hereby, a principle of interpretation based on an effective re-interpretation of Article 31(3)(c) VCLT may be emerging, without implying that this is necessarily a customary principle or rule of treaty interpretation in international law. The interpretation of the 'parties' in Article 31(3)(c) VCLT is contextual. The context of the dispute as well as of the process of interpretation itself will determine the concrete result of the effective and good faith interpretation of the 'parties'. Interpretation is not only about the application of the customary principles and rules of interpretation, partially codified in the VCLT. The debate on the meaning of the 'parties' in the context of WTO dispute settlement has, so far, neglected the pertinence of the complexity of interpretation as a process, and not merely as a mechanical application of the VCLT. As long as the interpretation does not interfere with the rule of *pacta tertiis nec nocent nec prosunt* and with the rights and obligations of other WTO Members provided in the WTO covered agreements, panels and the Appellate Body should not exclude *ipso facto* from the interpretative framework relevant 'regional' international law because not all the disputants are bound by the 'regional' norm or not all WTO Members have implicitly supported that

---

[18] WTO Appellate Body Report, *US—Shrimp*, above at n 9, at paras 129–30.

[19] The Netherlands did express at some point concerns that the condition of 'understanding of all the parties' could potentially defeat the purpose of the article. The Netherlands further predicted that the increasing number of international organizations along with their ever-expanding membership would make it highly unlikely to find identity between the organization's membership and the membership of other treaties concluded under international law. Special Rapporteur Waldock merely responded that interpretation in good faith would easily prevent such difficulties. *See* Waldock, above at n 15, at 92.

[20] J. Pauwelyn, *Conflict of Norms in Public International Law—How WTO Law Relates to Other Rules of International Law* (Cambridge: CUP, 2003), 257 and 261; WTO Appellate Body Report, *EC—Computer Equipment*, WT/DS62/AB/R, WT/DS67/AB/R, WT/DS68/AB/R, adopted 22 June 1998, at para. 84.

rule.[21] The recent finding of the International Law Commission's Study Group on Fragmentation of International Law that 'systemic integration' is the underlying objective of Article 31(3)(c) VCLT supports this conclusion.[22] The Study Group emphasized that the nature of the treaty and the context of the dispute will influence the choice of the interpreter between the various possible interpretations of the 'parties', in support of the contextual nature of treaty interpretation.

A. The Challenge of the Specialization of International Law and Article 31(3)(c) VCLT

The ICJ's reliance on Article 31(3)(c) VCLT in the *Oil Platforms* case[23] and the recent interest of the International Law Commission in this interpretation rule has highlighted its potential to mitigate the current forces of fragmentation in international law and to promote a coherent view of international law.[24] The fragmentation of international law is currently at the forefront of the debate about the future direction of international law. The term 'fragmentation' is time and again re-invented in the context of polemics about the rationale of specialized sub-systems of international law, such as WTO law. Fragmentation—better described as specialization or multiplicity—of international law has, in theory, two meanings.[25] It covers both the proliferation of international institutional bodies and the propagation of international substantive and procedural norms. Both processes are not independent of each another. The increasing number of international institutions has undoubtedly contributed to the widening and deepening of international law. Over time, fragmentation has picked up a negative connotation. Typically, the term is

---

[21] This conclusion does not require recourse to arguments based on Art. 30 VCLT as suggested in Bartels, above at n 17, at 360–61.

[22] ILC, Report of the Study Group on Fragmentation of International Law: Difficulties arising from the Diversification and Expansion of International Law (29 July 2005), UN Doc. A/CN.4/L.676.

[23] Above at n 16. For commentaries on this case, *see* A. Laursen, 'The Judgment by the International Court of Justice in the Oil Platforms Case' (2004) 73 Nord J Int L, 135; A. Orakhelashvili, 'Current Developments: Oil Platforms (*Islamic Republic of Iran v United States of America*), Merits, Judgment of 6 November 2003' (2004) 53 ICLQ, 753; E. Jouannet, 'Le Juge International Face aux Problèmes d'Incohérence et d'Instabilité du Droit International—Quelques Réflexions à Propos de l'arrêt CIJ du 6 Novembre 2003, Affaire des Plates-formes Pétrolières' (2004) 108 Rev Gén Dr Int Publ 917; J. Kammerhofer, 'Oil's Well that Ends Well? Critical Comments on the Merits Judgement in the Oil Platforms Case' (2004) 17 Leiden J Int L 695; J.A. Green, 'The Oil Platforms Case: An Error in Judgment?' (2004) 9 J Confl & Sec L 357 and S.M. Young, 'Destruction of Property (on an International Scale): The Recent *Oil Platforms* Case and the International Court of Justice's Inconsistent Commentary on the Use of Force by the United States' (2004) 30 N C J Int L & Com Reg 335.

[24] ILC, Report of the International Law Commission, 56th Session (2004), UN Doc. A/59/10; *see also* ILC, Report of the International Law Commission on the Work of its 57th Session (2005), Official Records of the General Assembly, Fifty-seventh Session, Supplement No 10, UN Doc. A/60/10, Chapter XI.C.3; for an overview, *see also* B. Simma, 'The Work of the ILC at its Fifty-Fourth Session (2002)' (2003) 72 Nord J Int L 91, at 135–39.

[25] A third 'diagonal' meaning is explored below.

used to describe the foremost threat to international law in the polarized debate between those who claim to safeguard the unity of international law and those who advocate further specialization of international law. Undeniably, the international legal system has evolved in an unprecedented manner in the last sixty years, resulting in a plethora of treaties, international institutions, and dispute settlement systems. This evolution, rather than transformation, of the structure and substance of international law has prompted three distinct reactions. These different reactions are of a respectively progressive, precautionary, and conservative nature.

The progressive reaction applauds the emergence of innovative specialized rules, sources, and international institutions dealing with, for example, biodiversity, conflict diamonds, or child soldiers. The precautionary approach supports the further specialization of international law but pleads for built-in safeguards within the international legal system. Traces of this approach are visible in speeches by various presidents of the ICJ that call for the introduction of a procedure to allow other international and regional dispute settlement bodies to ask the ICJ for an advisory opinion.[26] The conservative approach recognizes and respects the evolution of international law in the last sixty years but entreats a return to classical concepts of general international law and to the predominance of the ICJ in this development.

In essence, the term 'fragmentation' is ill chosen. International law is not fragmented, nor is it in the process of fragmenting. Rather, international law has witnessed an irrevocable specialization (and multiplicity), and this is to be applauded. This specialization of international law has resulted in regulatory competition and diversity. It has made international law more inclusive and efficient, especially in terms of the enforcement of international rights and obligations of both states and individuals.[27] The emergence of specialized and semi-autonomous sub-systems of international law, such as WTO law, requires build-in guarantees for coherence between the various sub-systems. Article 31(3)(c) VCLT is one of the tools to achieve a certain degree of synchronization between these sub-systems of international law, through the interpretation of treaties in the context of other rules of international law. The

---

[26] For a recent example, *see* Speech by H.E. Judge Shi Jiuyong, President of the International Court of Justice, to the Sixth Committee of the General Assembly of the United Nations: The Advisory Function of the International Court of Justice, 5 November 2004, available at www.icj-cij.org (visited 30 December 2005). *See* G. Abi-Saab, 'Fragmentation or Unification: Some Concluding Remarks' (1999) 31 NYU J Int L & Pol 919, at 927–28. Note that Art. 96 of the Havana Charter, which never came into force, originally provided for this possibility of an advisory opinion.

[27] Klabbers has recently described fragmentation as the trend that '. . . breaks up the world of international law into smaller segments, and stimulates regulatory competition not within territorial units, but across regimes or issue areas': J. Klabbers, 'Constitutionalism Lite' (2004) 1 IOLR 31, at 49. Jackson has described the current state of international law as '. . . a struggle with international law concepts which seem no longer to work, in the face of non-governmental actors and frail international institutions': J.H. Jackson, 'The Changing Fundamentals of International Law and Ten Years of the WTO' (2005) 8 JIEL 3, at 10.

application of Article 31(3)(c) VCLT does not reduce specialization; instead it is a means to stabilize and structure the process of specialization.[28] Specialization and unification, or rather coherence, are not mutually exclusive processes. There is no choice between specialization and unification in international law because both legal processes are semi-autonomous and interacting features of the international legal system. Specialization is essential for the strength of international law. It is no longer an emerging trend or a process, but an irrevocable reality of the character and structure of the international legal system. Specialization offers the advantage of diversified and specialized legal rules, and potentially tailored monitoring and/or enforcement mechanisms.

However, the continuous institutional and normative expansion of international law has also led to substantial conflict of norms problems—such as the possible conflicts between the WTO covered agreements and MEAs—and divergent interpretations of international law. The specialization of international law should go hand in hand with parallel coherence-enforcing structures and tools,[29] and treaty interpretation is one means of synchronizing various rules of international law and institutional cooperation networks. These instruments contribute to a common international legal language, the legitimacy and consistency of the international legal system, and they remedy the flaws and limitations of specialization.

The proliferation of RTAs and other regional international law sources, institutions, and initiatives has, in effect, given a third meaning to the specialization of international law in addition to the institutional and normative meanings mentioned earlier. This third 'diagonal' meaning of specialization consists of co-existing—not necessarily hierarchical—multilateral, plurilateral, regional, and bilateral layers of both institutional and normative forms of specialization. Examples of this meaning range from the US–Chile Free Trade Agreement to the Lomé Convention and from NAFTA tribunals to the European Court of Human Rights. The diagonal meaning even leaves its traces in legal scholarship, where distinct regional conceptual legal (not political) schools of thought of international law exist, such as 'European international law' or Third World legal scholarship.[30] Although these regional conceptual schools of international law were and are still thought by some to potentially undermine the universality and unity of international law,[31] this has not

---

[28] *Contra* McLachlan, above at n 7, at 281.   [29] *See* Marceau, above at n 17, at 117.

[30] *See* M.N. Shaw, *International Law*, 5th ed. (Cambridge: CUP, 2003), at 34–41. *See* E. McWhinney, 'Comparative International Law: Regional or Sectorial, Inter-Systemic Approaches to Contemporary International Law', in R.J. Dupuy (ed), *The Future of International Law in a Multicultural World* (The Hague: Martinus Nijhoff Publishers, 1984), at 221; R.P. Anand, 'Role of the "New" Asian-African Countries in the Present International Legal Order' (1962) 56 AJIL 383; E.Y.J. Lee, 'Early Development of Modern International Law in East Asia' (2002) 4 J Hist Int L, 42 and B. Rajagopal, *International Law from Below—Development, Social Movements and Third World Resistance* (Cambridge: CUP, 2003).

[31] For example, S. Gonzáles Gálvez, 'The Future of Regionalism in an Asymmetrical International Society', in R.St.J. Macdonald and D.M. Johnston (eds), *The Structure and Process of*

proven to be the case. Lauterpacht has remarked that, despite conceptual differences in Anglo-American and Continental international law, these divergences do not, in practice, interfere with the outcome of international disputes or with international practice.[32] In fact, the debate on regional schools of international law is not a myth because any approach towards international law is inherently entrenched in regional interests and values.[33] For example, the particular American conceptual approach towards the law on the use of force has, contrary to Lauterpacht's assertions, significantly influenced the international legal response towards threats of terrorism. However, this primarily American view represents rather a functional than a regional approach towards a specific sub-system of international law. Functionality in this context refers to special interests that extend beyond cultural or regional interests, and claims of regionalism often disguise functional interests.[34] Such functional approaches are also noticeable in the WTO context, where functional groupings such as the G–20 put forward a particular non-regional concept of trade and development. Eventually these functional views may, in contrast to regional conceptual schools, undermine (the fiction of) the unity of international law because they are applied not only in relation to the heterogeneous members of the functional group (for example, between members of the G–20 alliances) but primarily in relation to non-members. This is a shift from the regional international law schools, such as Soviet international law, which essentially applied only to the members of the regional school.

1. 'Regional' International Law

The dynamic relationship between regionalism and international law is two-dimensional. Regional international law encapsulates a dialectic between the concept and the validity of regionalism.[35] In particular, regional international law describes trends or non-trends towards certain norms, principles, and

International Law (Dordrecht: Martinus Nijhoff, 1986), at 661; *see also* comments by P. Costa in W. Anders, 'Comparative Approaches to the Theory of International Law' (1986) 80 ASIL Proc, 152.

[32] H. Lauterpacht, 'The So-called Anglo-American and Continental Schools of Thought in International Law' (1931) 12 BYIL, 31. Almost 70 years later, Crawford came to similar conclusions in J. Crawford, 'Universalism and Regionalism from the Perspective of the Work of the International Law Commission', in J. Crawford, *International Law as an Open System: Selected Essays* (London: Cameron May, 2002), at 575; *see also* comments by I. Brownlie in Anders, *ibid.* and R. Jennings, 'Universal International Law in a Multicultural Word', in M. Bos and I. Brownlie (eds), *Liber Amicorum for the Right Honourable Lord Wilberforce* (Oxford: Clarendon, 1987), at 39–51.

[33] *See also* S.V. Scott, 'Universalism and Title to Territory in Antarctica' (1997) 66 Nord J Int L, 33.

[34] Comments by I. Brownlie in W. Anders, above at n 32; I. Brownlie, 'Problems Concerning the Unity of International Law', in P. Lamberti Zanardi et al. (eds), *International Law at the Time of its Codification: Essays in Honour of Roberto Ago*, Volume 1 (Milan: Giuffrè, 1987), at 153.

[35] For a detailed discussion of the meaning of 'regionalism' *see* M. Koskenniemi, 'Study on the Function and Scope of the *Lex Specialis* Rule and the Question of "Self-Contained Regimes"' (11 May 2005) UN Doc. ILC(LVII)/SG/FIL/CRD.1 (2005) and the ILC, Report of the International Law Commission on the Work of its 57th Session, above at n 24, at Ch XI.C.2.

doctrines of international law depending on regional interests. But regional international law also means specific sources of international law, such as RTAs or regional human rights treaties.

Regionalized sources of international law may be substantively distinct from general international law. As the International Law Commission's Study Group on the Fragmentation of International Law pointed out recently, in sub-systems of international law, such as international trade law, 'regionalism was influencing the general law in such great measure that it needed special highlighting'.[36] Although the first steps in European integration date from before the VCLT, there were few or no regional legal integration efforts at the time the VCLT was drafted, negotiated, and concluded. Consequently, there was no discussion of regional sources of international law in the various reports of the Special Rapporteurs and the International Law Commission. The VCLT applies to treaties defined as international agreements 'concluded between states in written form and governed by international law, where embodied in a single instrument or in two or more related instruments and whatever its particular designation'.[37] The VCLT does not distinguish between multilateral, plurilateral, regional, and bilateral treaties. Nor have the formal sources of international law, referred to in Article 38(1) of the ICJ Statute, been conceptualized as distinguishing between multilateral, plurilateral, regional, and bilateral sources. In 2002, for example, the International Law Commission refused to recognize the Calvo clause as a norm of regional international law; it was a regional practice at best.[38]

In contrast to general international law, several provisions in the WTO covered agreements do establish a hierarchy between the WTO covered agreements and bilateral and regional trade agreements, including Article XXIV GATT, Article 5 GATS, and Article IX:3 WTO Agreement. To the extent that these provisions set out the conditions that customs unions, free trade areas, and other preferential arrangements must meet, in order to be tolerated by the multilateral trading system, the multilateral WTO regime is superior to those preferential arrangements of various natures. It would be beyond the scope of this article to discuss the problematic interpretation of each of these provisions. It suffices to point out that a tension exists between the lack of a hierarchy in general international law and the hierarchy embedded in the WTO covered agreements. This tension is lowered on the one hand by way of Article 31(3)(c) VCLT according to which these bilateral and regional sources of international law should be interpreted in the light of other rules of international law, including general international law, WTO law, and other sub-systems of international law. Conversely, Article 31(3)(c) VCLT accommodates, where relevant, interpretative weight of RTAs and other preferential arrangements for establishing the meaning of the WTO covered

---

[36] ILC, *ibid.*, at para. 461.   [37] Art. 2(1)(a) VCLT.

[38] ILC, Report of the International Law Commission on the Work of its 54th Session (2002), Official Records Fifty-seventh Session, Supplement No 10, UN Doc. A/57/10.

agreements. This is distinct from the question of the application of RTAs to disputes arising in the context of the WTO dispute settlement system. In those cases, Articles 26, 30, 40, and 41 VCLT apply. A discussion of the complexity of applying those provisions to conflicting rights and obligations in RTAs and the WTO covered agreements, and of the (in)adequacy of the VCLT to deal with such problems, reaches beyond the scope of this article, which explores the potential interpretative weight of RTAs in WTO dispute settlement.

Recently, however, regionalism has manifested itself as both a catalyst for the further development of international law, and as a potential detriment for the coherence in international law. Shaw speaks of the development of 'regional–international law sub-systems within the universal framework' to describe the diagonal dimension of the specialization of international law.[39] Regional law in itself may contain several substantive sub-systems of law. For example, European human rights conventions co-exist with the wider body of international human rights law and European Union law, and European human rights law includes several categories of rights such as women's rights and children's rights. Another example is the precautionary principle. Approaches towards this principle differ in WTO law, European law, international environmental law, and general international law. The precautionary principle is recognized as a general principle of law or even as a customary norm in international environmental law (e.g. Principle 15 Rio Declaration), European law (Article 174.2 EC), and various national jurisdictions, including Australia and New Zealand.[40] The authority of this principle in international trade law and general international law is less clear. In *EC—Hormones*, the Appellate Body found that, although, the precautionary principle 'finds reflection in Article 5.7 of the *SPS Agreement*', '[w]hether it has been widely accepted by Members as a principle of *general* or *customary international law* appears less than clear'.[41] The question raised is whether, in interpreting Article 5.7 SPS Agreement in a dispute where all the parties have recognized and accepted the precautionary principle as a general principle of law or a customary principle of international law, panels and the Appellate Body should respect these regional or national views towards the precautionary principle, expressed in regional or bilateral sources such as treaties, court decisions, and possibly soft law. If a panel or the Appellate Body would come to this conclusion, it would, as a result, systemically integrate the 'regional' international law between the disputants with the multilateral WTO legal regime,[42] on the

[39] Shaw, above at n 30, at 46; *see also* J.H.F. van Panhuys, 'Regional or General International Law? A Misleading Dilemma' (1961) 8 Neth Int L Rev, 146.

[40] *See* P. Sands, *Principles of International Environmental Law*, 2nd ed. (Cambridge: CUP, 2003), at 266–79.

[41] WTO Appellate Body Report, *EC—Hormones*, WT/DS26/AB/R, WT/DS48/AB/R, adopted 13 February 1998, at paras 123–24.

[42] In its recent report, the ILC Study Group on the Fragmentation of International Law found that the underlying objective of Art. 31(3)(c) VCLT is 'systemic integration'. This objective is 'a

condition that this interpretation would not affect other WTO Members' rights and obligations.[43]

Article 31(3)(c) VCLT confronts the adjudicator with a plenitude of multi-lateral, regional, and bilateral sources of international law. It is not unlikely that normative tensions will arise between these various sources. There is no hierarchy as such between regionalism and universalism in international law, they co-exist rather than supersede each other.[44] The context of the dispute and the identity of the disputants might mitigate this argument and oblige panels and the Appellate Body to look at regional and bilateral rules.[45] The following section discusses the practice of panels and the Appellate Body, so far, in relying on 'regional' international law for the interpretation of the WTO covered agreements.

2. *Regional and Bilateral Agreements and the Interpretation of* WTO *Law*

I now turn to the discussion of panels' and the Appellate Body's reliance on bilateral and regional trade agreements[46] as distinct from the cases in which they have taken into consideration the jurisprudence of regional and bilateral dispute settlement systems established by those agreements. In some respect, inspiration from the case law of regional and bilateral dispute settlement systems implies acceptance of the relevance of the regional and bilateral agreements in question for the interpretation of WTO law.[47]

Courts and tribunals have relied on bilateral and regional agreements as 'rules of international law' for the interpretation of treaties. In some respect, panels and the Appellate Body are required to do so not only on the basis of Article 31(3)(c) VCLT, but also under Article 3.2 DSU. Panels and the Appellate Body need to provide 'security and predictability to the multilateral trading system'. The recent Report by the WTO Consultative Board to the Director-General has highlighted that the multilateral trading system is threatened by an upsurge of bilateral and regional trade agreements, though it should be noted that this might be more a problem than a prominent 'threat'.[48] As of 31 March 2006, 346 Agreements had been notified, of which 195 are

---

guideline according to which treaties should be interpreted against the background of all the rules and principles of international law—in other words, international law *understood as a system*': ILC, Report of the International Law Commission on the Work of its 57th Session, above at n 24, at Ch XI.C.3, para. 467.

[43] *See* Art. 34 VCLT, *pacta tertiis nec nocent nec prosunt*, Arts 3.2 and 19.2 DSU.

[44] C. Schreuer, 'Regionalism v. Universalism' (1995) 6 EJIL 477, at 498. Schreuer suggests applying principles of federalism to international law. *See also* E. Beyerly, *Eurocentric International Law? Contemporary Doctrinal Perspectives* (Buffalo: William S. Hein & Co. Inc, 1998).

[45] *See* Marceau, above at n 17, at 783.

[46] For the purpose of this analysis, I understand bilateral and regional trade agreements in a broader sense than the category of agreements that meet the requirements of Art. XXIV GATT.

[47] *See*, for example, WTO Panel Report, *US—Gambling*, above at n 13, at para. 6.473, fn 914.

[48] P. Sutherland et al., *The Future of the WTO: Addressing Institutional Challenges in the New Millennium* (Geneva: WTO, 2004), at 19–27.

currently in force.[49] The recognition by panels and the Appellate Body of the relevance of these regional agreements for the interpretation of WTO law is only one means to counter the problems arising from the proliferation of RTAs for the 'security and predictability of the multilateral trading system'. In *Turkey—Textiles*, the Panel remarked at the outset that 'regional trade agreements have greatly increased in number and importance since the establishment of GATT 1947 and today cover a signification proportion of world trade' and that 'the economic and political realities that prevailed when Article XXIV was drafted, have evolved and that the scope of regional trade agreements is now broader than it was in 1948'.[50] Therefore, panels and the Appellate Body should not ignore bilateral and regional trade agreements in the interpretation of the WTO Agreements.

The approach of panels and the Appellate Body towards regional and bilateral agreements might differ depending on the nature of the agreement, for example whether it deals with trade or human rights. Regional and bilateral trade agreements are often modelled identically on the text of the WTO Agreements, and in this respect they might be less interesting. To the extent that the dispute settlement body, provided for in the RTA, has clarified the meaning of the treaty language, this could be relevant for WTO dispute settlement. On the basis of 'competitive liberalization',[51] many of these agreements contain additional rights and obligations and they increasingly deal with non-trade values (e.g. labour and environmental provisions in US free trade agreements and the so-called human rights clause in EU trade agreements with third parties). On the one hand, such treaty language may help panels and the Appellate Body in determining the scope of WTO law, and in particular what the WTO Members did *not* negotiate within the WTO context. In other words, labour rights language in RTAs creates models for possible similar WTO language, but only if WTO Members would consent to such language. In absence of such consensus, labour rights provisions in RTAs help panels and the Appellate Body demarcate the scope of the WTO covered agreements.

---

[49] *See* Introduction, at n 2.

[50] WTO Panel Report, *Turkey—Textiles*, WT/DS34/R, adopted 19 November 1999, as modified by the Appellate Body Report, WT/DS34/AB/R, at para 9.97. The dispute raised the question of the application of non-WTO law to a WTO dispute. As for interpretation, the Panel found confirmation for its interpretation of Art. XXIV:8(a)(ii) GATT in Decision 1/95 of the EC–Turkey Association Council.

[51] 'Competitive liberalization' can be described as 'participation in preferential trade agreements provides a spur to liberalization on multiple fronts and contributes to innovative policies in such areas as investment and market regulations'. The WTO Consultative Board, nevertheless, concluded that 'while these so-called WTO-plus PTAs may act as testing grounds for new multilateral trade policy disciplines and regulations, the discretion enjoyed by PTA parties in designing such regulatory regimes can strike a serious WTO minus note for the multilateral trading system'. In particular with respect to the inclusion of non-trade provisions in regional and bilateral trade agreements, such as labour and environmental protection, the WTO Consultative Board found that 'if such requirements cannot be justified at the front door of the WTO they probably should not be encouraged to enter through the side door': Sutherland, above at n 48, at 84 and 87.

On the other hand, provisions on labour rights in, for example, the US–Chile FTA may reflect the intentions of particular members to broaden their WTO obligations with respect to each other, but not other WTO Members. Panels and the Appellate Body should not exclude the potential relevance of this language in the FTA in a dispute between Chile and the US concerning the interpretation of a particular WTO provision binding on all WTO Members. Despite the persuasive power of DSB reports, WTO provisions are binding on all WTO Members, interpretations by panels and the Appellate Body are not. The security and predictability of the multilateral trading system is not threatened by more diversification in the interpretation practices of panels and the Appellate Body, it might even need more of this kind of case-tailored *inter partes* interpretations. It does not follow from this conclusion that labour rights provisions in RTAs will become enforceable in WTO dispute settlement, and arguably the example used here of labour rights provision is exaggerated. Nevertheless, the WTO dispute settlement should not shy away from more composed and mutable interpretations on a case-by-case basis.

The argument could be made that this assumption of the relevance of RTAs for the interpretation of WTO law, as a *lex specialis*, potentially implies realizing a 'multi-speed' WTO through the dispute settlement system. This is neither realistic nor desirable. Panels and the Appellate Body will and should not resolve the trade linkages debate on their own initiative. These are in the first instance policy—not legal—issues and the political burden lies on the shoulders of negotiators to respond to these concerns appropriately and give the dispute settlement bodies clear and unambiguous guidance on how they should appreciate non-trade values. For example, the relationship between the WTO covered agreements and MEAs, which has been a contentious issue in WTO dispute settlement, is currently being discussed in the CTE. In the proposals submitted so far, a principle of 'mutual supportiveness' has been put forward by several WTO Members to describe the interface between trade and environment.[52] Depending on how members in the CTE further develop this principle, this example is a means of WTO Members to give practical guidance to panels and the Appellate Body on how to interpret and apply the WTO covered agreements, without having recourse to an authoritative interpretation under Article IX:2 WTO Agreement.

---

[52] Committee on Trade and Environment, The Relationship between WTO Rules and MEAs in the Context of the Global Governance System, Submission by the European Communities, WTO Doc. TN/TE/W/39, 24 March 2004 and Committee on Trade and Environment, The Relationship between Existing WTO Rules and Specific Trade Obligations (STOs) set out in Multilateral Environmental Agreements (MEAs): A Swiss Perspective on National Experiences and Criteria Used in the Negotiation and Implementation of MEAs, Submission by Switzerland, WTO Doc. TN/TE/W/58, 6 July 2005, at para. 16.

B. The Confusing Case Law of Panels and the Appellate Body

In *US—Tuna II*, the US had invoked a multitude of multilateral, plurilateral, regional, and bilateral trade and non-trade agreements as interpretative elements to justify its intermediary nation embargo under Article XX(g) GATT. However, the GATT Panel agreed with the EEC and the Netherlands that these agreements 'were bilateral or plurilateral agreements that were not concluded among the contracting parties' to the GATT and therefore were not relevant as primary means of interpretation.[53] The disputants had relied on Article 31(3)(c) VCLT in their submissions but the Panel only considered whether these agreements were relevant subsequent agreements or subsequent practice and seemed to overlook Article 31(3)(c) VCLT. The Panel found that 'practice under the bilateral and plurilateral treaties cited could not be taken as practice under the General Agreement, and therefore could not affect the interpretation of it'.[54]

In *Korea—Various Measures on Beef*, the Panel decided to look at various bilateral agreements between Korea and the disputants 'strictly for the purpose of interpreting an ambiguous WTO provision'.[55] The Panel justified its interpretation by reference to previous Appellate Body reports. The Panel did not rely on a specific interpretation rule, but it did consider the WTO provision at issue 'ambiguous'. Arguably, it considered these various bilateral agreements as supplementary means of interpretation.

When the Appellate Body in *US—FSC (Article 21.5—EC)* had to interpret 'foreign-source income' in footnote 59 to the SCM Agreement, it looked at a broad range of regional agreements, including the Andean Community Agreement, the Andean Community Model Tax Agreement, and the Caricom Agreement.[56] Similarly, the Appellate Body in *EC—Poultry* agreed with the Panel's consideration of the Oilseeds Agreement, concluded between the EC and Brazil to end their dispute in *EEC—Oilseeds*, as a *supplementary means* of interpretation pursuant to Article 32 of the Vienna Convention.[57] The Panel explicitly added that it looked at the Oilseeds Agreement 'to the extent relevant to the determination of the EC's obligations under the WTO Agreements *vis-à-vis* Brazil' and not in relation to other members.[58] Since adopted Panel and Appellate Body reports are only binding on the disputants, the Panel accepted that it should take the bilateral agreement into consideration in so far as it would clarify the obligations between the disputants, who were also the

[53] GATT Panel Report, *US—Tuna II*, 16 June 1994, unadopted, DS29/R, at para. 5.19.
[54] *Ibid.*
[55] WTO Panel Report, *Korea—Various Measures on Beef*, WT/DS161/R, adopted 10 January 2001, as modified by the Appellate Body Report, WT/DS161/AB/R, at para. 539.
[56] WTO Appellate Body Report, *US—FSC (Article 21.5—EC)*, WT/DS108/AB/RW, adopted 29 January 2002, at para. 144, fn 123.
[57] WTO Appellate Body Report, *EC—Poultry*, WT/DS69/AB/R, adopted 23 July 1998, at para. 83 (original emphasis).
[58] WTO Panel Report, *EC—Poultry*, WT/DS69/R, adopted 23 July 1998, as modified by the Appellate Body Report, WT/DS69/AB/R at para. 202.

signatories to the bilateral agreement. The Appellate Body went on to rely on the Oilseeds Agreement to interpret the EC's concession in Schedule LXXX. However, the weight it attributed to the Oilseeds Agreement was not of a supplementary or subsidiary nature. Rather, the Appellate Body valued the Oilseeds Agreement similarly as the elements in the general rule of interpretation of Article 31 VCLT. This is a representative example of how the formal treatment of certain rules of international law does not necessarily correspond with the substantive treatment of these rules in the interpretation by panels and the Appellate Body. Assuming there is an order between the various means of interpretation in Articles 31 and 32 VCLT, as the Appellate Body has, the place of a rule of international law in this order does not necessarily seem to correspond with the weight that a panel or the Appellate Body will attribute to that rule.

The Panel in *Chile—Price Band System* found that Article 24 of the Economic Complementarity Agreement No. 35 between Chile and Mercosur ('ECA 35') was not 'relevant' and could not influence the interpretation of Article 4.2 of the WTO Agreement on Agriculture.[59] The Panel came to this conclusion after a textual analysis of Article 24 of ECA 35:

> First, the Preamble [to ECA 35] states that the commercial policies and compromises of ECA 35 shall 'adjust to' the WTO framework of rights and obligations. A fortiori, Article 24 of ECA 35 cannot influence the interpretation of the WTO Agreement. Second, Chile's commitment regarding its PBS [Price Band System] in Article 24 of ECA 35 has been explicitly made 'within the framework of' ECA 35. Such language suggests that the parties to ECA 35 did not intend to exclude the possibility that different commitments regarding the Chile PBS may have been or will be made in the context of other international agreements.[60]

The Panel seemed to allude that the WTO Agreement on Agriculture might qualify as a 'relevant' rule for the interpretation of Article 24 of ECA 35 and the ECA 35 in general, but rejected the reverse reasoning. The Panel did not set out an abstract benchmark to assess the relevance of rules of international law for the purpose of the interpretation of the WTO covered agreements. The Panel in *Chile—Price Band System* gave the impression that Article 31(3)(c) VCLT is a residual category within Article 31(3) of the VCLT because it first tried to qualify ECA 35 as a subsequent agreement or subsequent practice.

Although the Panel in *Chile—Price Band System* did not exclude the possibility of using a regional agreement as an interpretative tool, its reasoning differs from that of the Appellate Body in *US—Shrimp*. In *US—Shrimp*, the Appellate Body relied on the Inter-American Convention for the Protection and Conservation of Sea Turtles ('Inter-American Convention') as both an element of evidence of the US' efforts to negotiate and conclude international agreements and an element of interpretation to assess the US' obligation

---

[59] WTO Panel Report, *Chile—Price Band System*, above at n 12, at para. 7.85.   [60] *Ibid.*

to contemplate alternative less restrictive measures under Article XX GATT.[61] The Appellate Body did not find that the text of Article XV of the Inter-American Convention, which obliges Contracting Parties to act in accordance with the WTO Agreements and especially the TBT Agreement and Article XI GATT, rendered the Inter-American Convention irrelevant; though it is necessary to add the proviso that this Convention is not a trade agreement. The Appellate Body was, however, reluctant to specify the weight it would attribute to the Inter-American Convention as an instrument of interpretation. The report seems to suggest that the Inter-American Convention was a supplementary means of interpretation to confirm its earlier interpretation of Article XX GATT on the basis of the general interpretation rule in Article 31 VCLT.

The reasoning in the previous cases differs from the Appellate Body's approach in *EC—Bananas III*. In that case, the Appellate Body did not rely on the Lomé Convention between the EC and the ACP countries to clarify the rights and obligations in the WTO Agreements. Instead, the Appellate Body agreed with the Panel that an interpretation of the Lomé Convention itself was required because through 'a reference to the Lomé Convention into the Lomé waiver, the meaning of the Lomé Convention became a GATT/WTO issue' and there was 'no alternative but to examine the provisions of the Lomé Convention [ourselves] in so far as it is necessary to interpret the Lomé waiver'.[62] It is not entirely clear what the Panel and the Appellate Body meant with a 'GATT/WTO issue'. The Appellate Body interpreted the Lomé Convention under the interpretation rules of the VCLT, like it would do for any other WTO agreement, and not 'in so far as it is necessary to interpret the Lomé waiver'. Although the Lomé waiver is, pursuant to Article IX, paragraphs 3 and 4 WTO Agreement and the Understanding in Respect of Waivers of Obligations under the General Agreement on Tariffs and Trade 1994, part of the WTO *acquis*, the Lomé Convention is not. This line of reasoning of the Appellate Body in *EC—Bananas III* could imply that it can interpret any international treaty that is referred to in any WTO instrument, without prejudice to the relevant competent international institutions or courts and tribunals. This would come close to the WTO dispute settlement acting as a 'global treaty interpreter'.

III. A HYPOTHESIS: THE INTERPRETATIVE WEIGHT OF THE US–CHILE FREE TRADE AGREEMENT

Assume that the US decides to impose an import quota on Chilean textile goods to protect public morals in the US and Chile, because it alleges that Chile does not enforce international labour standards, thereby violating

[61] WTO Appellate Body Report, *US—Shrimp*, above at n 9, at paras 167–71.

[62] WTO Appellate Body Report, *EC—Bananas III*, WT/DS27/AB/R, adopted 25 September 1997, at para. 167 (citing the Panel).

Articles I and XI GATT. This measure will likely also breach Articles 18.1 and 18.2 of the US–Chile Free Trade Agreement.[63] Under these provisions, the US and Chile confirmed their commitment as ILO Members to internationally recognized labour principles and rights. Under the Agreement, the US and Chile have taken on the commitment to protect and enforce these principles and rights under their domestic laws. The US–Chile FTA explicitly recognizes the right of each party to the Agreement to establish its own domestic labour standards but these should be consistent with the internationally recognized labour rights set out in Article 18(8). Assuming that Chile challenges the US's measure before the WTO dispute settlement system[64], the US could argue that its trade measure does not violate Articles I and XI GATT, and in the alternative, that the measure is justified by the public morals exception in Article XX(a) GATT.[65] According to the established case law on Article XX GATT, the Appellate Body will first examine, after finding a violation of Articles I and or XI GATT, whether the challenged measure falls within the scope of Article XX(a) GATT.[66] The Panel will have to examine whether the US measure addresses 'public morals' and whether there is a sufficient nexus or degree of connection between the challenged measure and the protection of 'public morals'. Once the Panel or Appellate Body has found that the measure falls within the scope of Article XX(a) GATT, they will then consider whether the requirements of the chapeau of Article XX GATT are met.

This US's defence raises the question of the interpretation of 'public morals' in the context of this dispute. The interpretation of 'public morals' in Article XIV(a) GATS, which allows members to adopt measures 'necessary to protect public morals or to maintain public order', was a critical issue in the recent *US—Gambling* case.[67] The US had invoked the 'public morals' exception to justify several GATS violations by state and federal laws that regulate online gambling services offered by foreign supplies to consumers in the US. The Panel recognized that, though the US had failed to meet the 'necessity' test of Article

[63] US–Chile FTA, signed 6 June 2003, in force 1 January 2004.

[64] Art. 22(3)(1) US-Chile FTA contains a choice of forum clause: 'Where a dispute regarding any matter arises under this Agreement and under another free trade agreement to which both Parties are party or the WTO Agreement, the complaining Party may select the forum in which to settle the dispute'. According to Art. 22(3)(2) this chosen forum will have exclusive jurisdiction over the dispute arising under both agreements.

[65] Art. XX(a) GATT: 'Subject to the requirement that such measures are not applied in a manner which would constitute a means of arbitrary or unjustifiable discrimination between countries where the same conditions prevail, or a disguised restriction on international trade, nothing in this Agreement shall be construed to prevent the adoption or enforcement by any contracting party of measures:

(a) necessary to protect public morals;

. . .

[66] This two-tiered test to examine whether measures are justified under Art. XX GATT was established by the WTO Appellate Body, *US—Shrimp*, above at n 9, at para. 147; WTO Appellate Body Report, *US—Gasoline*, above at n 8, at 20.

[67] WTO Appellate Body Report, *US—Gambling*, WT/DS285/AB/R, adopted 20 April 2005, at fn 351.

XIV(a) GATS, these federal and state laws were 'designed so as to protect public morals or maintain public order'.[68] According to the Panel, Article XIV(a) GATS gives Members 'some scope to define and apply for themselves the concepts of "public morals" and "public order" in their respective territories, according to their own systems and scales of values'.[69] This finding was not appealed.[70] In the appeal, the Appellate Body mainly focused on the Panel's findings on the 'necessity' test and the chapeau of Article XIV GATS. However, the Appellate Body did uphold the Panel's finding that concerns of money laundering, organized crime, fraud, underage gambling, and pathological gambling fall within the scope of Article XIV(a) GATS.[71]

Returning to the hypothetical example, in defending its import quota on Chilean textile products, the US could rely on *US—Gambling* to argue that the Panel should again give considerable deference to Members in defining 'public morals', especially in respect to the issue of whose and what morals a Member may protect. In this case, the Panel would have to deal with labour-related processes and production methods ('PPMs').[72] Also, the US could ask the Panel to interpret 'public morals' in the light of 'relevant rules of international law applicable between the parties', including the labour standard provisions in the US–Chile FTA. These labour standard provisions are relevant to the dispute and applicable between the disputants, though clearly not between all WTO Members. Arguably, the US could claim that 'public morals' can relate to the protection against forced labour, child labour, and inhumane work conditions.[73] Such a claim would also raise the question of whether the protection of 'public morals' in Article XX(a) GATT concerns the 'public morals' of the restricting Member or the targeted Member. The US could argue that its import quota was intended to protect both the 'public morals' of the US and of Chile because the protection and enforcement of regionally recognized labour standards is a global fundamental societal interest.[74] If the Panel were to accept this interpretation, this would not necessarily imply that the Panel has

---

[68] WTO Panel Report, *US—Gambling*, above at n 13, at para. 6.535.

[69] *Ibid.*, at paras 6.459–461.

[70] Antigua and Barbuda claimed that the Panel had failed to examine the US's concerns in light of footnote 5 of Art. XIV(a) GATS, but did not appeal the Panel's interpretation of 'public morals'. Art. XIV(a) GATS, fn 5: '[t]he public order exception may be invoked only where a genuine and sufficiently serious threat is posed to one of the fundamental interests of society'. Note that there is no similar footnote to Art. XX(a) GATT 1994.

[71] WTO Appellate Body Report, *US—Gambling*, above at n 67, at para. 299.

[72] The Appellate Body previously held that PPMs do not necessarily as such violate the GATT. *See* WTO Appellate Body Report, *US—Gasoline*, above at n 8, at 13–29; WTO Appellate Body Report, *US—Shrimp*, above at n 9, at paras 135–45; GATT Panel Report, *US—Section 337*, adopted 7 November 1989, BISD 36S/345 and S. Charnovitz, 'The Law of Environmental "PPMs" in the WTO: Debunking the Myth of Illegality' (2002) 27 Yale J Int L 59. *Contra* GATT Panel Report, *US—Tuna (EEC)*, DS29/R, 16 June 1994, unadopted (1994) 33 ILM 936.

[73] *See* R. Howse and M. Mutua, 'Protecting Human Rights in a Global Economy—Challenges for the World Trade Organization', Working Paper International Centre for Human Rights and Democratic Development (2000).

[74] *See* Bartels, above at n 17.

implicitly introduced a so-called 'social clause' in Article XX(a) GATT through treaty interpretation; rather, such interpretation could systemically integrate in this particular dispute the US–Chile FTA and both parties' obligations under the WTO covered agreement.[75] Reliance on the US–Chile FTA's labour standards would not authorize the Panel to rule on the enforcement and respect of labour standards by Chile, nor would its interpretation bind other WTO Members or influence the rights and obligations of other WTO Members than the disputants in succeeding cases. Neither could the Panel ignore the Singapore Ministerial Declaration in which the WTO Members recognized the ILO as 'the competent body to set and deal with [labour] standards'.[76] The legal status of this declaration in relation to the WTO covered agreements is not entirely clear and as such this declaration cannot prevent that the issue of labour rights emerges in WTO dispute settlement. The Panel could merely recognize these societal interests as meriting protection under the 'public morals' exception of Article XX(a) GATT. At the same time, the expansive body of (regional) case law from the European Court of Human Rights on the moral exception in Articles 8, 9, 10, and 11 of the European Convention and from the European Court of Justice on Article 30 of the EC Treaty could contribute to the Panel's interpretation of Article XX(a) GATT. This example illustrates the significance of regional and bilateral integration efforts in trade, human rights, environmental protection, etc. for the interpretation of the WTO Agreements, and especially of exception clauses such as Article XX GATT or Article XIV GATS. A similar analysis could, for example, be applied to use of the so-called 'human rights clause' in RTAs of the EU with third countries.

An added layer of complexity in the example discussed above arises when the disputants have expressed possibly conflicting notions of public morals in distinct regional agreements (with other Contracting Parties). It remains unclear whether a panel or the Appellate Body should consider these regional agreements between the disputants as the expression of a shared notion of public morals or whether they should consult the various regional agreements of each disputant to discern from those instruments the domestic public morals perception of each disputant and prioritize the latter. The question similarly arises in the case of regional agreements in which the disputant(s) have expressed various understandings of, say, 'proportionality' and how such different understandings should be prioritized or merged into a common understanding, to be used as a means of interpretation in the context of WTO dispute settlement.

The disadvantage of a regionally inspired interpretation is a decrease of the

[75] This is different from the argument that a mere 'expansive' interpretation of Art. XX(a) could introduce the effect of a social clause in the GATT. *See* C.T. Feddersen, 'Focusing on Substantive Law in International Economic Relations: The Public Morals of GATT'S Article XX(a) and "Conventional" Rules of Interpretation' (1998) 7 Minn J Global Trade, 75, at 97.

[76] Singapore Ministerial Declaration, WT/MIN(96)/DEC, adopted 13 December 1996, at para. 4.

precedent value of DSB reports. Other WTO Members would be less informed of the possible interpretation of, for example, exception clauses such as Article XX GATT. Arguably, this may have an impact on the 'security and predictability to the multilateral trading system' (Article 3.2 DSU). Members might claim that their sovereignty and their consent to the WTO multilateral trading system is threatened because their WTO commitments are interpreted in the light of regional international law, which they have not recognized or consented to. But despite the strong persuasive value of DSB reports, adopted panel and Appellate Body reports are only binding on the disputants, not on all WTO Members.[77] The interpretation of a specific WTO provision in the light of regional international law that is binding between all parties to the dispute would in theory not add or diminish the rights and obligations of other members. Where relevant, panels and the Appellate Body should recognize the potential interpretative weight of regional international law.[78]

IV. CONCLUSION

Generally, panels and the Appellate Body have been receptive to regional and bilateral agreements as means of interpretation. Ultimately the issue is not 'if' panels and the Appellate Body can rely on international law as a means of interpretation, but 'how', 'when', and 'how much' they look at international law to interpret the WTO Agreements. It is hard to draw conclusions from the available case law so far and to discern from the cases a certain practice of interpretation that can guide disputants and negotiators. This lack of clarity is partly due to the confusing and inconsistent reliance on Articles 31.1, 31(3)(b), 31(3)(c), and 32 VCLT to consider other rules of international law as means of interpretation. This is not merely a factual issue, but also a normative question and the response so far by panels and the Appellate Body has been unsatisfactory. Although they have recognized that WTO law is part of public international law, they have not specified to what extent they will allow the influence of international law in the interpretation of WTO law. The WTO dispute settlement is not unique in this lack of a consistent approach towards the use of international law for treaty interpretation. Most international and regional courts and tribunals have been reluctant to clarify their methodology or practice on this issue of interpretation. Nevertheless, panels and the Appellate Body should end the second-guessing by trade lawyers, diplomats, and scholars and gradually develop and clarify their approach to international law as a means of interpretation to provide 'security and predictability to the multilateral trading system'.

---

[77] WTO Appellate Body Report, *Japan—Alcoholic Beverages II*, WT/DS8/AB/R, WT/DS10/AB/R, WT/DS11/AB/R, adopted 1 November 1996, at para. 6.10. *See also* Arts XVI:1 and IX:2 WTO Agreement.

[78] *See also* Weiss, above at n 17, at 196–97.

General Agreement on Tariffs and Trade (GATT)

Article XXIV

(. . .) *Customs Unions and Free-trade Areas*

(. . .)

4. The contracting parties recognize the desirability of increasing freedom of trade by the development, through voluntary agreements, of closer integration between the economies of the countries parties to such agreements. They also recognize that the purpose of a customs union or of a free-trade area should be to facilitate trade between the constituent territories and not to raise barriers to the trade of other contracting parties with such territories.

5. Accordingly, the provisions of this Agreement shall not prevent, as between the territories of contracting parties, the formation of a customs union or of a free-trade area or the adoption of an interim agreement necessary for the formation of a customs union or of a free-trade area; *Provided* that:

(a) with respect to a customs union, or an interim agreement leading to a formation of a customs union, the duties and other regulations of commerce imposed at the institution of any such union or interim agreement in respect of trade with contracting parties not parties to such union or agreement shall not on the whole be higher or more restrictive than the general incidence of the duties and regulations of commerce applicable in the constituent territories prior to the formation of such union or the adoption of such interim agreement, as the case may be;

(b) with respect to a free-trade area, or an interim agreement leading to the formation of a free-trade area, the duties and other regulations of commerce maintained in each of the constituent territories and applicable at the formation of such free-trade area or the adoption of such interim agreement to the trade of contracting parties not included in such area or not parties to such agreement shall not be higher or more restrictive than the corresponding duties and other regulations of commerce existing in the same constituent territories prior to the formation of the free-trade area, or interim agreement as the case may be; and

(c) any interim agreement referred to in subparagraphs (a) and (b) shall include a plan and schedule for the formation of such a customs union or of such a free-trade area within a reasonable length of time.

6. If, in fulfilling the requirements of subparagraph 5 (a), a contracting party proposes to increase any rate of duty inconsistently with the provisions of Article II, the procedure set forth in Article XXVIII shall apply. In providing for compensatory adjustment, due account shall be taken of the compensation already afforded by the reduction brought about in the corresponding duty of the other constituents of the union.

7.

(*a*) Any contracting party deciding to enter into a customs union or free-trade area, or an interim agreement leading to the formation of such a union or area, shall promptly notify the CONTRACTING PARTIES and shall make available to them such information regarding the proposed union or area as will enable them to make such reports and recommendations to contracting parties as they may deem appropriate.

(*b*) If, after having studied the plan and schedule included in an interim agreement referred to in paragraph 5 in consultation with the parties to that agreement and taking due account of the information made available in accordance with the provisions of subparagraph (*a*), the CONTRACTING PARTIES find that such agreement is not likely to result in the formation of a customs union or of a free-trade area within the period contemplated by the parties to the agreement or that such period is not a reasonable one, the CONTRACTING PARTIES shall make recommendations to the parties to the agreement. The parties shall not maintain or put into force, as the case may be, such agreement if they are not prepared to modify it in accordance with these recommendations.

(*c*) Any substantial change in the plan or schedule referred to in paragraph 5 (*c*) shall be communicated to the CONTRACTING PARTIES, which may request the contracting parties concerned to consult with them if the change seems likely to jeopardize or delay unduly the formation of the customs union or of the free-trade area.

8. For the purposes of this Agreement:

(*a*) A customs union shall be understood to mean the substitution of a single customs territory for two or more customs territories, so that

  (i) duties and other restrictive regulations of commerce (except, where necessary, those permitted under Articles XI, XII, XIII, XIV, XV and XX) are eliminated with respect to substantially all the trade between the constituent territories of the union or at least with respect to substantially all the trade in products originating in such territories, and,

  (ii) subject to the provisions of paragraph 9, substantially the same duties and other regulations of commerce are applied by each of the members of the union to the trade of territories not included in the union;

(*b*) A free-trade area shall be understood to mean a group of two or more customs territories in which the duties and other restrictive regulations of commerce (except, where necessary, those permitted under Articles XI, XII, XIII, XIV, XV and XX) are eliminated on substantially all the trade between the constituent territories in products originating in such territories.

9. The preferences referred to in paragraph 2 of Article I shall not be affected by the formation of a customs union or of a free-trade area but may be eliminated or adjusted by means of negotiations with contracting parties affected.* This procedure of negotiations with affected contracting parties shall, in particular, apply to the elimination of preferences required to conform with the provisions of paragraph 8 (*a*)(i) and paragraph 8 (*b*).

10. The CONTRACTING PARTIES may by a two-thirds majority approve proposals

which do not fully comply with the requirements of paragraph 5 to 9 inclusive, provided that such proposals lead to the formation of a customs union or a free-trade area in the sense of this Article.

Understanding on the Interpretation of Article XXIV of the General Agreement on Tariffs and Trade 1994

Members,

Having regard to the provisions of Article XXIV of GATT 1994;

Recognizing that customs unions and free trade areas have greatly increased in number and importance since the establishment of GATT 1947 and today cover a significant proportion of world trade;

Recognizing the contribution to the expansion of world trade that may be made by closer integration between the economies of the parties to such agreements;

Recognizing also that such contribution is increased if the elimination between the constituent territories of duties and other restrictive regulations of commerce extends to all trade, and diminished if any major sector of trade is excluded;

Reaffirming that the purpose of such agreements should be to facilitate trade between the constituent territories and not to raise barriers to the trade of other Members with such territories; and that in their formation or enlargement the parties to them should to the greatest possible extent avoid creating adverse effects on the trade of other Members;

Convinced also of the need to reinforce the effectiveness of the role of the Council for Trade in Goods in reviewing agreements notified under Article XXIV, by clarifying the criteria and procedures for the assessment of new or enlarged agreements, and improving the transparency of all Article XXIV agreements;

Recognizing the need for a common understanding of the obligations of Members under paragraph 12 of Article XXIV;

Hereby *agree* as follows:

1. Customs unions, free-trade areas, and interim agreements leading to the formation of a customs union or free-trade area, to be consistent with Article XXIV, must satisfy, *inter alia*, the provisions of paragraphs 5, 6, 7 and 8 of that Article.

Article XXIV:5

2. The evaluation under paragraph 5(a) of Article XXIV of the general incidence of the duties and other regulations of commerce applicable before and after the formation of a customs union shall in respect of duties and charges be based upon an overall assessment of weighted average tariff rates and of customs duties collected. This assessment shall be based on import statistics for a previous representative period to be supplied by the customs union, on a tariff-line basis and in values and quantities, broken down by WTO country of origin. The Secretariat shall compute the weighted average tariff rates and customs duties collected in accordance with the methodology used in the assessment of tariff offers in the Uruguay Round of Multilateral Trade Negotiations. For this purpose, the duties and charges to be taken into consideration shall be the applied rates of duty. It is recognized that for the purpose of the overall assessment of the incidence of other regulations of commerce for which quantification and aggregation are

difficult, the examination of individual measures, regulations, products covered and trade flows affected may be required.

3. The "reasonable length of time" referred to in paragraph 5(c) of Article XXIV should exceed 10 years only in exceptional cases. In cases where Members parties to an interim agreement believe that 10 years would be insufficient they shall provide a full explanation to the Council for Trade in Goods of the need for a longer period.

Article XXIV:6

4. Paragraph 6 of Article XXIV establishes the procedure to be followed when a Member forming a customs union proposes to increase a bound rate of duty. In this regard Members reaffirm that the procedure set forth in Article XXVIII, as elaborated in the guidelines adopted on 10 November 1980 (BISD 27S/26–28) and in the Understanding on the Interpretation of Article XXVIII of GATT 1994, must be commenced before tariff concessions are modified or withdrawn upon the formation of a customs union or an interim agreement leading to the formation of a customs union.

5. These negotiations will be entered into in good faith with a view to achieving mutually satisfactory compensatory adjustment. In such negotiations, as required by paragraph 6 of Article XXIV, due account shall be taken of reductions of duties on the same tariff line made by other constituents of the customs union upon its formation. Should such reductions not be sufficient to provide the necessary compensatory adjustment, the customs union would offer compensation, which may take the form of reductions of duties on other tariff lines. Such an offer shall be taken into consideration by the Members having negotiating rights in the binding being modified or withdrawn. Should the compensatory adjustment remain unacceptable, negotiations should be continued. Where, despite such efforts, agreement in negotiations on compensatory adjustment under Article XXVIII as elaborated by the Understanding on the Interpretation of Article XXVIII of GATT 1994 cannot be reached within a reasonable period from the initiation of negotiations, the customs union shall, nevertheless, be free to modify or withdraw the concessions; affected Members shall then be free to withdraw substantially equivalent concessions in accordance with Article XXVIII.

6. GATT 1994 imposes no obligation on Members benefiting from a reduction of duties consequent upon the formation of a customs union, or an interim agreement leading to the formation of a customs union, to provide compensatory adjustment to its constituents.

Review of Customs Unions and Free-Trade Areas

7. All notifications made under paragraph 7(a) of Article XXIV shall be examined by a working party in the light of the relevant provisions of GATT 1994 and of paragraph 1 of this Understanding. The working party shall submit a report to the Council for Trade in Goods on its findings in this regard. The Council for Trade in Goods may make such recommendations to Members as it deems appropriate.

8. In regard to interim agreements, the working party may in its report make appropriate recommendations on the proposed time-frame and on measures required to complete the formation of the customs union or free-trade area. It may if necessary provide for further review of the agreement.

9. Members parties to an interim agreement shall notify substantial changes in the plan and schedule included in that agreement to the Council for Trade in Goods and, if so requested, the Council shall examine the changes.

10. Should an interim agreement notified under paragraph 7(a) of Article XXIV not include a plan and schedule, contrary to paragraph 5(c) of Article XXIV, the working party shall in its report recommend such a plan and schedule. The parties shall not maintain or put into force, as the case may be, such agreement if they are not prepared to modify it in accordance with these recommendations. Provision shall be made for subsequent review of the implementation of the recommendations.

11. Customs unions and constituents of free-trade areas shall report periodically to the Council for Trade in Goods, as envisaged by the CONTRACTING PARTIES to GATT 1947 in their instruction to the GATT 1947 Council concerning reports on regional agreements (BISD 18S/38), on the operation of the relevant agreement. Any significant changes and/or developments in the agreements should be reported as they occur.

Dispute Settlement

12. The provisions of Articles XXII and XXIII of GATT 1994 as elaborated and applied by the Dispute Settlement Understanding may be invoked with respect to any matters arising from the application of those provisions of Article XXIV relating to customs unions, free-trade areas or interim agreements leading to the formation of a customs union or free-trade area.

Article XXIV:12

13. Each Member is fully responsible under GATT 1994 for the observance of all provisions of GATT 1994, and shall take such reasonable measures as may be available to it to ensure such observance by regional and local governments and authorities within its territory.

14. The provisions of Articles XXII and XXIII of GATT 1994 as elaborated and applied by the Dispute Settlement Understanding may be invoked in respect of measures affecting its observance taken by regional or local governments or authorities within the territory of a Member. When the Dispute Settlement Body has ruled that a provision of GATT 1994 has not been observed, the responsible Member shall take such reasonable measures as may be available to it to ensure its observance. The provisions relating to compensation and suspension of concessions or other obligations apply in cases where it has not been possible to secure such observance.

15. Each Member undertakes to accord sympathetic consideration to and afford adequate opportunity for consultation regarding any representations made by another Member concerning measures affecting the operation of GATT 1994 taken within the territory of the former.

General Agreement on Trade in Services (GATS)

Article V

Economic Integration

1. This Agreement shall not prevent any of its Members from being a party to or entering into an agreement liberalizing trade in services between or among the parties to such an agreement, provided that such an agreement:

(a) has substantial sectoral coverage[1], and

(b) provides for the absence or elimination of substantially all discrimination, in the sense of Article XVII, between or among the parties, in the sectors covered under subparagraph (a), through:

(i)   elimination of existing discriminatory measures, and/or

(ii) prohibition of new or more discriminatory measures,

either at the entry into force of that agreement or on the basis of a reasonable time-frame, except for measures permitted under Articles XI, XII, XIV and XIV *bis*.

2. In evaluating whether the conditions under paragraph 1(b) are met, consideration may be given to the relationship of the agreement to a wider process of economic integration or trade liberalization among the countries concerned.

3.

(a) Where developing countries are parties to an agreement of the type referred to in paragraph 1, flexibility shall be provided for regarding the conditions set out in paragraph 1, particularly with reference to subparagraph (b) thereof, in accordance with the level of development of the countries concerned, both overall and in individual sectors and subsectors.

(b) Notwithstanding paragraph 6, in the case of an agreement of the type referred to in paragraph 1 involving only developing countries, more favourable treatment may be granted to juridical persons owned or controlled by natural persons of the parties to such an agreement.

4. Any agreement referred to in paragraph 1 shall be designed to facilitate trade between the parties to the agreement and shall not in respect of any Member outside the agreement raise the overall level of barriers to trade in services within the respective sectors or subsectors compared to the level applicable prior to such an agreement.

5. If, in the conclusion, enlargement or any significant modification of any agreement under paragraph 1, a Member intends to withdraw or modify a specific commitment inconsistently with the terms and conditions set out in its Schedule, it shall provide at least 90 days advance notice of such modification or withdrawal and the procedure set forth in paragraphs 2, 3 and 4 of Article XXI shall apply.

6. A service supplier of any other Member that is a juridical person constituted under the laws of a party to an agreement referred to in paragraph 1 shall be entitled to treatment granted under such agreement, provided that it engages in substantive business operations in the territory of the parties to such agreement.

7.

(a) Members which are parties to any agreement referred to in paragraph 1 shall promptly notify any such agreement and any enlargement or any significant modification of that agreement to the Council for Trade in Services. They shall also make available to the Council such relevant information as may be requested by it. The Council may establish a working party to examine such an agreement or enlargement or modification of that agreement and to report to the Council on its consistency with this Article.

---

[1] This condition is understood in terms of number of sectors, volume of trade affected and modes of supply. In order to meet this condition, agreements should not provide for the *a priori* exclusion of any mode of supply.

(b) Members which are parties to any agreement referred to in paragraph 1 which is implemented on the basis of a time-frame shall report periodically to the Council for Trade in Services on its implementation. The Council may establish a working party to examine such reports if it deems such a working party necessary.

(c) Based on the reports of the working parties referred to in subparagraphs (a) and (b), the Council may make recommendations to the parties as it deems appropriate.

8. A Member which is a party to any agreement referred to in paragraph 1 may not seek compensation for trade benefits that may accrue to any other Member from such agreement.

Article V bis

Labour Markets Integration Agreements

This Agreement shall not prevent any of its Members from being a party to an agreement establishing full integration[2] of the labour markets between or among the parties to such an agreement, provided that such an agreement:

(a) exempts citizens of parties to the agreement from requirements concerning residency and work permits;
(b) is notified to the Council for Trade in Services.

VIENNA CONVENTION ON THE LAW OF THE TREATIES

Article 31: General rule of interpretation

1. A treaty shall be interpreted in good faith in accordance with the ordinary meaning to be given to the terms of the treaty in their context and in the light of its object and purpose.

2. The context for the purpose of the interpretation of a treaty shall comprise, in addition to the text, including its preamble and annexes:

(a) any agreement relating to the treaty which was made between all the parties in connexion with the conclusion of the treaty;
(b) any instrument which was made by one or more parties in connexion with the conclusion of the treaty and accepted by the other parties as an instrument related to the treaty.

---

[2] Typically, such integration provides citizens of the parties concerned with a right of free entry to the employment markets of the parties and includes measures concerning conditions of pay, other conditions of employment and social benefits.

3. There shall be taken into account, together with the context:

(a) any subsequent agreement between the parties regarding the interpretation of the treaty or the application of its provisions;

(b) any subsequent practice in the application of the treaty which establishes the agreement of the parties regarding its interpretation;

(c) any relevant rules of international law applicable in the relations between the parties.

4. A special meaning shall be given to a term if it is established that the parties so intended.

Article 32: Supplementary means of interpretation

Recourse may be had to supplementary means of interpretation, including the preparatory work of the treaty and the circumstances of its conclusion, in order to confirm the meaning resulting from the application of article 31, or to determine the meaning when the interpretation according to article 31:

(a) leaves the meaning ambiguous or obscure; or

(b) leads to a result which is manifestly absurd or unreasonable.

Article 33: Interpretation of treaties authenticated in two or more languages

1. When a treaty has been authenticated in two or more languages, the text is equally authoritative in each language, unless the treaty provides or the parties agree that, in case of divergence, a particular text shall prevail.

2. A version of the treaty in a language other than one of those in which the text was authenticated shall be considered an authentic text only if the treaty so provides or the parties so agree.

3. The terms of the treaty are presumed to have the same meaning in each authentic text.

4. Except where a particular text prevails in accordance with paragraph 1, when a comparison of the authentic texts discloses a difference of meaning which the application of articles 31 and 32 does not remove, the meaning which best reconciles the texts, having regard to the object and purpose of the treaty, shall be adopted.

Select Bibliography

Abbott, F., *Law and Policy of Regional Integration: The NAFTA and Western Hemispheric Integration in the World Trade Organization System* (Dordrecht, London: Martinus Nijhoff, 1995)

—— 'The Doha Declaration on the TRIPS Agreement and Public Health and the Contradictory Trend in Bilateral and Regional Trade Agreements' (2004) QUNO Occasional Paper 14

—— 'Toward a New Era of Objective Assessment in the Field of TRIPS and Variable Geometry for the Preservation of Multilateralism' (2005) 8 JIEL 77

Acharya, A., 'How Ideas Spread: Whose Norms Matter? Norm Localization and Institutional Change in Asian Regionalism' (2004) 58 Int Org 239

—— 'Ideas, Identity, and Institution-building: From the "ASEAN Way" to the "Asia–Pacific Way"?' (1997) 10 Pac Rev 319

Afilalo, A., 'Towards a Common Law of International Investment: How NAFTA Chapter 11 Panels Should Solve Their Legitimacy Crisis' (2004) 17 Geo Int Envtl L Rev 51

Anand, R.P., 'Role of the "New" Asian–African Countries in the Present International Legal Order' (1962) 56 AJIL 383

ASEAN Secretariat, *Annual Report 2004–2005*, available at www.aseansec.org/AR05/TOC.pdf (visited 30 May 2006)

Ashiagbor, D., 'Soft Harmonisation: The Open Method of Co-ordination in the European Employment Strategy' (2004) 10 EPL 305

Atik, J., 'Repenser NAFTA Chapter 11: A Catalogue of Legitimacy Critiques' (2003) 3 Asper Rev Int Bus & Trade L 215

Banks, K. 'Civil Society and the North American Agreement on Labor Cooperation', in J. Kirton and V. Maclaren (eds), *Linking Trade, Environment and Social Cohesion: NAFTA Experiences, Global Challenges* (Aldershot: Ashgate, 2002)

Barr, J., 'Final Analytical Framework to Assess the Environmental Effects of NAFTA', in WWF and Fundación Futuro Latinoamericano, *The International Experts' Meeting on Sustainability Assessments of Trade Liberalisation—Quito, Ecuador 6–8 March 2000, Full Meeting Report* (Gland: WWF, 2000)

Bartels, L., *Human Rights Conditionality in the EU's International Agreements* (Oxford: OUP, 2005)

—— 'The Legality of the EC Mutual Recognition Clause under WTO Law' (2005) 8 JIEL 691

Baucus, M., 'A New Trade Strategy: The Case for Bilateral Agreements' (1989) 22 Cornell Int L J 1

Bhagwati, J., *The World Trading System at Risk* (Princeton, NJ: Princeton UP, 1991)

—— 'Reshaping the WTO' (2005) 168 FEER 25

—— and Krueger, A.O., *The Dangerous Drift to Preferential Trade Agreements* (Washington DC: AEI Press, 1995)

Blanco, H., 'Evaluación de la Sustentabilidad de los Acuerdos Comerciales y su Aplicación en el Contexto Latinoamericano y del ALCA', in H. Blanco, M. Araya, and C. Murillo, *ALCA y Medio Ambiente: Ideas desde Latinoamerica* (Santiago de Chile: CIPMA / GETS / CINPE, 2003)

Bøås, M. et al., 'The Political Economy of New Regionalisms' (1999) 20 TWQ 897

Brenton, P., 'Rules of Origin in Free Trade Agreements' (2003) Trade Note 4 (World Bank, 2000)

Breslin, S. et al. (eds), *New Regionalisms in the Global Political Economy* (London: Routledge, 2002)

Brownlie, I., 'Problems Concerning the Unity of International Law', in P. Lamberti Zanardi et al. (eds), *International Law at the Time of its Codification: Essays in Honour of Roberto Ago*, Volume 1 (Milan: Giuffrè, 1987)

Brusick, P. et al. (eds), 'Competition Provisions in Regional Trade Agreements: How to Assure Development Gains', UNCTAD Doc. UNCTAD/DITC/CLP/2005/1 (2005)

Burfisher, M.E. et al., *Regionalism: Old and New, Theory and Practice* (International Food Policy Research Institute, February 2004)

—— Robinson S. and Thierfelder K., 'The Impact of NAFTA on the United States' (2001) 15 J Econ Perspect 125

Byung-Woon, L., 'Building the Northeast Asian Community' (2004) 11 Ind J Global Legal Studies 257

Canada–Chile Agreement on Labour Cooperation, *First Annual Report (July 1997– June 1998)*, available at www110.hrdc-drhc.gc.ca/doc/ialc-cidt/eng/e/backen.htm (visited 30 May 2006)

Canada–Chile Agreement on Labour Cooperation, *Ministerial Council Report on the Three-Year Review of the Canada–Chile Agreement on Labour Cooperation (December 2002)*, available at www.hrsdc.gc.ca/en/lp/spila/ialc/2003_2004/ 02canada_chili_agreement.shtml (visited 30 May 2006)

Canadian Parliament, *Report of the Sub-Committee on International Trade Disputes and Investment and assigned it the responsibility of examining a Free Trade Area of the Americas (FTAA)*, available at www.parl.gc.ca/infocomdoc/36/2/fait/studies/ reports/faitrp01-e.htm (visited 30 May 2006)

Cardenas, E.J. and Tempesta G., 'Arbitral Awards under Mercosur's Dispute Settlement Mechanism' (2001) 4 JIEL 337

Carrillo-Tudela, C. and Li, C.A., 'Trade Blocks and the Gravity Model: Evidence from Latin American Countries' (2004) 19 J Econ Integration 667

Cavazos Villanueva, G. and Martinez Serna, L.F., 'Private Parties in the NAFTA Dispute Settlement Mechanisms: The Mexican Experience' (2003) 77 Tul L Rev 1017

Cernat, L., 'Assessing Regional Trade Arrangements: Are South–South RTAs More Trade Diverting?', UNCTAD Doc. UNCTAD/ITCD/TAB/17 (2001)

Charney, J., 'Is International Law Threatened by Multiple International Tribunals?' (1998) 271 Recueil des Cours 101

—— 'The Impact of the International Law System of the Growth of International Courts and Tribunals' (1999) 31 NYU J Int L & Pol 697

Charny, D., 'Competition among Jurisdictions in Formulating Corporate Law Rules: An American Perspective on the "Race to the Bottom" in the European Communities' (1991) 32 Harv Int L J 423

Chase, K., 'Multilateralism Compromised: The Mysterious Origins of GATT Article XXIV' (2006) 5 WTR 1

Chirathivat, S., 'ASEAN–China Free Trade Area: Background, Implications and Future Development' (2002) 13 J Asian Econ 671

Choi, W., 'Regional Economic Integration in East Asia: Prospect and Jurisprudence' (2003) 6 JIEL 49

Clarke, J., 'Mutual Recognition Agreements' (1996) 2 ITL Rev 31

Commission for Environmental Cooperation, *Analytic Framework for Assessing the Environmental Effects of the NAFTA* (Montreal: CEC, 1999)

—— *Assessing Environmental Effects of the North American Free Trade Agreement (NAFTA)—An Analytic Framework (Phase II) and Issue Studies* (Montreal: CEC 1999)

—— *Building a Framework for Assessing NAFTA Environmental Effects* (Montreal: CEC, 1996)

Cooper, J.M., (comment), 'NAFTA's Rules of Origin and Its Effects on the North American Automotive Industry' (1994) 14 NW J Int L & Bus 442

Corbin, H., 'The Proposed United States–Chile Free Trade Agreement: Reconciling Free Trade and Environmental Protection' (2003) 14 Colo J Int Envtl L & Policy 119

—— 'Enhancing Social and Environmental Cooperation in the Americas', in M.C. Cordonier Segger and M. Leichner Reynal (eds), *Beyond the Barricades: The Americas Trade and Sustainability Agenda* (Aldershot: Ashgate, 2005)

—— 'Sustainable Development in the Negotiation of the FTAA' (2004) 27 Fordham Int LJ 1118

Cordonier Segger, M.C. and Khalfan, A., *Sustainable Development Law: Principles, Practices and Prospects* (Oxford: OUP, 2004)

—— et al., *Ecological Rules and Sustainability in the Americas* (Winnipeg: IISD/UNEP, 2002)

—— et al., *Social Rules and Sustainability in the Americas* (Winnipeg: IISD/OAS, 2004)

—— et al., *Trade Rules and Sustainability in the Americas* (Winnipeg: IISD, 1999)

Cottier, T., 'The Challenge of Regionalization and Preferential Relations in World Trade Law and Policy' (1996) 2 EFA Rev 149

—— 'The Legal Framework for FTAs & CUs in WTO Law', in M. Godel and J. Gage (eds) *Multilateralism and Bilateralism after Cancun: Challenges and Opportunities of Regionalism* (Berne: Seco Publikation Welthandel No 2, 2004)

—— and Panizzon, M., 'Die sektoriellen Abkommen und das Recht der WTO: Grundlagen und Spannungsfelder', in D. Felder and C. Kaddous (eds), *Accords Bilatéraux Suisse-UE (commentaires); Bilaterale Abkommen Schweiz-EU (Erste Analysen)* (Basel: Helbing & Lichtenhahn, 2001)

—— and Schefer, K.N., 'The Relationship between World Trade Organization Law, National and Regional Law' (1998) 1 JIEL 83

Crawford, J. and Fiorentino, R.V., 'The Changing Landscape of Regional Trade Agreements', WTO Discussion Paper No 8 (2005)

—— and S. Laird, 'Regional Trade Agreements and the WTO' (2001) 12 N Amer J Econ Finance 193

Cremona, M., 'Regional Integration and the Rule of Law: Some Issues and Options', in Devlin, R. and A. Estevadeordal (eds), *Bridges for Development—Policies and Institutions for Trade and Integration* (Washington DC: Inter-American Development Bank, 2003)

Dakolias, M., 'The Second Bank Directive: The Issue of Reciprocity' (1991) 2 LIEI 69

Dam, K., 'Regional Economic Arrangements and the GATT, the Legacy of a Misconception' (1963) 30 U Chi L Rev 615

Dannenmaier, E., 'Inter American Perspective: Trade Democracy, and the FTAA: Public Access to the Process of Constructing a Free Trade Area of the Americas' (2004) 27 Fordham Int L J 1066

Davey, W.J., *Pine & Swine: Canada–United States Trade Dispute Settlement: The FTA Experience and NAFTA Prospects* (Ottawa: Centre for Trade Policy and Law, 1996)

——, 'Dispute Settlement in GATT' (1987) 11 Fordham Int L J 51

Davidson, P.J., 'The ASEAN Way and the Role of Law in ASEAN Economic Cooperation' (2004) 8 SYIL 165

Davies, G., *Nationality Discrimination in the European Internal Market* (The Hague, London: Kluwer, 2003)

De Melo, J. and Panagariya A., (eds), *New Dimensions in Regional Integration* (Cambridge: CUP, 1993)

De Mestral, A.L.C., 'The NAFTA Commission on Environmental Cooperation—Voice for the North American Environment?', in A. Kiss, D. Shelton and K. Ishibashi (eds), *Economic Globalization and Compliance with International Environmental Agreements* (The Hague, London: Kluwer, 2003)

——, 'The North American Free Trade Agreement: A Comparative Analysis' (1998) 275 Recueil des Cours 223

—— and J. Winter, 'Giving Direct Effect to NAFTA' in T.J. Courchene et al., *Thinking North America* (Institute for Research on Public Policy: Montreal, 2004)

Deere, C.L. and Esty, D.C. (eds), *Greening the Americas: NAFTA's Lessons for Hemispheric Trade* (Cambridge, MA: MIT Press, 2002)

Dehousse, R., 'Completing the Internal Market: Institutional Constraints and Challenges', in R. Bieber et al. (eds), *1992: One European Market?: A Critical Analysis of the Commission's Internal Market Strategy* (Baden-Baden: Nomos 1998)

Dent, C.M., 'Networking the Region? The Emergence and Impact of Asia-Pacific Bilateral Free Trade Agreement Projects' (2003) 16 Pac Rev 1

Desker, B., 'In Defence of FTAs: From Purity to Pragmatism in East Asia' (2004) 17 Pac Rev 3

Desta, M.G., 'OPEC, the WTO, Regionalism, and Unilateralism' (2003) 37 JWT 523

Devlin, R. and Ffrench-Davis, R., 'Towards an Evaluation of Regional Integration in Latin America in the 1990s' Inter-American Development Bank Integration and Regional Program Department, Working Paper No 2 (Buenos Aires: INTAL ITD, 1998)

Djordjevic, M., 'Domestic Regulation and Free Trade in Services—A Balancing Act' (2002) 29 LIEI 305

Dougan, M., 'Minimum Harmonization and the Internal Market' (2000) 37 CMLR 853

Drahos P. et al., 'Pharmaceuticals, Intellectual Property and Free Trade: The Case of the US-Australia Free Trade Agreement' (2004) 22 Prometheus 243

——, 'Bilateralism in Intellectual Property' (2001) 4 JWIP 6

Durbin, W., *A Comparison of the Environmental Provisions of the NAFTA, the Canada-Chile Trade Agreement and the Mexican-European Community Trade Agreement* (New Haven: Yale Centre for Environmental Law and Policy, 2000)

Eeckhout, P., *External Relations of the European Union: Legal and Constitutional Foundations* (Oxford: OUP, 2004)

Elliott, R.R. and Ikemoto, K., 'AFTA and the Asian Crisis: Help or Hindrance to ASEAN Intra-Regional Trade?' (2004) 18 Asian Econ J 1

El-Said, H. and El-Said, M., 'TRIPS, Bilateralism & Implications for Developing Countries: Jordan's Drug Sector' (2005) 2 MJIEL 59

Emmerson, D.K., 'What Do the Blind See? Reapproaching Regionalism in Southeast Asia' (2005) 18 Pac Rev 1

Ethier, W., 'Regionalism in a Multilateral World' (1998) 106 J Pol Econ 1214

Evtimov, E., 'East European Regionalism', in M. Godel and J. Gage (eds) *Multilateralism and Bilateralism after Cancun: Challenges and Opportunities of Regionalism* (Berne: Seco Publikation Welthandel No 2, 2004)

Falkenberg, K., 'EPAs and DDA—Parallelism or Crossroads?' (2004) 3(4) *Trade Negotiations Insights 1*

Fawcett, L. and Hurrell, A., *Regionalism in World Politics: Regional Organization and International Orders* (Oxford: OUP, 1995)

Felder, D., 'Appréciation juridique et politique du cadre institutionnel et des dispositions générales des accords sectoriels', in D. Felder and C. Kaddous (eds), *Accords bilatéraux Suisse-UE: Commentaires* (Basel: Helbing & Lichtenhahn, 2001)

Feng, C., 'Recent Developments in Singapore on International Law' (2004) 8 SYIL 207

Fink, C. and Reichenmiller, P., 'Tightening TRIPS: The Intellectual Property Provisions of Recent US Free Trade Agreements' Trade Note 20 (World Bank, 2005)

Fischer, T.C., 'A Commentary on Regional Institutions in the Pacific Rim: Do APEC and ASEAN Still Matter?' (2003) 13 Duke J Comp & Int L 337

Forrester, I., 'The End of Innocence', in J. Bourgeois, E. Vermulst and P. Waer (eds), *Rules Of Origin in International Trade: A Comparative Study* (Ann Arbor: U Michigan Press, 1993)

Frankel, J.A., *Regional Trading Blocs in the World Economic System* (Washington, DC: Institute for International Economics, 1997)

—— and S.J. Wei, 'Regionalization of World Trade and Currencies: Economics and Politics', in J.A. Frankel, (ed), *The Regionalization in the World Economy* (Chicago: U Chicago Press, 1998)

Freund, C., 'Reciprocity in Free Trade Agreements' World Bank Policy Research Paper 3061 (World Bank, 2003)

Gaja, G., 'The European Community's Rights and Obligations under Mixed Agreements', in D. O'Keeffe and H.G. Schermers (eds), *Mixed Agreements* (Deventer: Kluwer, 1983)

Galal, A. and Hoekman, B., *Regional Partners in Global Markets: Limits and Possibilities of the Euro-Med Agreements* (London: Centre for Economic Policy Research, 1997)

Gallagher, K.P. and Blanco, H., 'Sustainability Assessments: Tools for Effective Trade Policy in the Hemisphere' (IRC Paper, 9 April 2003)

Gantz, D.A., 'Government-to-Government Dispute Resolution under NAFTA's Chapter 20: A Commentary on the Process' (2000) 11 Am Rev Int Arb 481

——, 'Implementing the NAFTA Rules of Origin: Are the Parties Helping or Hurting Free Trade?' (1995) 12 Ariz J Int & Comp L 367

——, 'Potential Conflicts Between Investor Rights and Environmental Regulation under NAFTA's Chapter 11' (2001) 33 Geo Wash Int L Rev 651

——, 'The Evolution of FTA Investment Provisions: From NAFTA to the United States-Chile Free Trade Agreement' (2004) 19 Am U Int L Rev 679

Garcia, F.J., 'Integrating Trade and Human Rights in the Americas', in F. Abbott, C. Breining-Kaufmann and T. Cottier (eds), *International Trade and Human Rights* (Michigan: U Michigan Press, 2006)

Gitli, E. and Murillo, C., 'A Latin American Agenda for a Trade and Environment Link in the FTAA', in C.L. Deere, and D.C. Esty (eds), *Greening the Americas: NAFTA's Lessons for Hemispheric Trade* (Cambridge, MA: MIT Press, 2002)

Glick, L.A., *Understanding the North American Free Trade Agreement* (Deventer; Boston: Kluwer, 1993)

Gogo, J., 'East Asia & Oceanic Regionalism', in M. Godel and J. Gage (eds) *Multilateralism and Bilateralism after Cancun: Challenges and Opportunities of Regionalism* (Berne: Seco Publikation Welthandel No 2, April 2004)

Goldfarb, D., 'The Road to a Canada–US Customs Union: Step-by-Step or in a Single Bound?' (Toronto: C.D. Howe Institute Commentary, June 2003)

Gomula, J., 'Dispute Settlement under Association Agreements with Central and Eastern European States' (1995) 22 Polish YBIL 107

Gonzáles Gálvez, S., 'The Future of Regionalism in an Asymmetrical International Society', in R.St.J. Macdonald and D.M. Johnston (eds), *The Structure and Process of International Law* (Dordrecht: Martinus Nijhoff, 1986)

Griffin, P., 'The Delaware Effect: Keeping the Tiger in its Cage. The European Experience of Mutual Recognition in Financial Services' (2001) 7 Colum J Eur L 337

Groux, J. and Manin, P., *The European Communities in the International Order* (Brussels: European Commission, 1985)

Hart, M., *A Trading Nation: Canadian Trade Policy from Colonialism to Globalization* (Vancouver: UBC Press, 2002)

Hausman, W., Lee H.L., and Subramanian, U., 'Global Logistics Indicators, Supply Chain Metrics, and Bilateral Trade Patterns', World Bank Policy Research Working Paper 3773 (World Bank, 2005)

Hay, Q., 'Trans-Tasman Mutual Recognition: A New Dimension in Australia–New Zealand Legal Relations' (1997) 3 ITL Rev 6

Heiskanen, V., 'The Regulatory Philosophy of International Trade Law' (2004) 38 JWT 1

Hettne, B., Inotai, A., and Sunkel O. (eds), *Comparing Regionalism: Implications for Global Development* (Houndmills, Basingstoke: Palgrave, 2001)

Higgott, R., 'The International Political Economy of Regionalism', in W.D. Coleman and G.R.D. Underhill (eds), *Regionalism and Global Economic Integration: Europe, Asia and the Americas* (London: Routledge, 1998)

Hirst, M., 'Mercosur's Complex Political Agenda', in R. Roett (ed), *Mercosur: Regional Integration, World Markets* (Boulder, CO: Lynne Rienner, 1999)

Hoekman, B. and Sauvé, P., 'Regional and Multilateral Liberalisation of Service Markets: Complements or Substitutes?' (1994) 32 JCMS 283

Hsu, L., 'Non-Violation Complaints—World Trade Organization Issues and Recent Free Trade Agreements' (2005) 39 JWT 205

Hudec, R., 'A WTO Perspective on Private Anti-Competitive Behavior in World Markets' (1999) 34 New Eng L Rev 79

—— and Southwick, J.D., 'Regionalism and WTO Rules: Problems in the Fine Art of Discriminating Fairly', in M.P. Rodríguez Mendoza Low and B. Kotschwar (eds), *Trade Rules in the Making: Challenges in Regional and Multilateral Negotiations* (Washington, DC; OAS: Brookings, 1999)

Hund, M., 'ASEAN Plus Three: Towards a New Age of Pan-East Asian Regionalism? A Skeptic's Appraisal' (2003) 16 Pac Rev 383

James, E.W. and Umemoto, M., 'NAFTA Trade with East Asia: Rules of Origin and Market Access in Textiles, Apparel Footwear and Electrical Machinery' (2000) 17 ASEAN Econ Bull 293

—— , 'APEC Preferential Rules of Origin: Stumbling Blocks for Liberalization of Trade?' (1997) 31 JWT 113

Joerges, C. and Petersmann, E.-U. (eds), *Constitutionalism, Multilevel Trade Governance and Social Regulation* (Oxford: Hart, 2006)

Jones, R.C., 'NAFTA Chapter 11: Investor-to-State Dispute Resolution: A Shield to Be Embraced or a Sword to Be Feared?' (2002) BYU L Rev 527

Jorgensen, B.D., 'South Asia: An Anxious Journey towards Regionalization?', in M. Schulz, F. Söderbaum and J. Öjendal (eds), *Regionalization in a Globalizing World: A Comparative Perspective on Forms, Actors and Processes* (London: Zed Books, 2001)

Jouannet, E., 'Le Juge International Face aux Problèmes d'Incohérence et d'Instabilité du Droit International—Quelques Réflexions à Propos de l'arrêt CIJ du 6 Novembre 2003, Affaire des Plates-formes Pétrolières' (2004) 108 Rev Gén Dr Int Publ 917

Kahler, M., 'Legalization as Strategy: The Asia-Pacific Case' (2000) 54 Int Org 549

Kingston, E.I., 'The Economics of Rules of Origin', in J. Bourgeois et al (eds), *Rules Of Origin in International Trade: A Comparative Study* (Ann Arbor: U Michigan Press, 1993)

Kirton, J. and Maclaren, V.W. (eds), *Linking Trade, Environment and Social Cohesion: NAFTA Experiences, Global Challenges* (Aldershot: Ashgate, 2002)

Komuro, N., 'International Harmonization of Rules of Origin', in P. Ruttley et al., *The WTO and International Trade Regulation* (London: Cameron May, 1998)

Kong, Q., 'China's WTO Accession and the ASEAN-China Free Trade Area—The Perspective of a Chinese Lawyer' (2004) 7 JIEL 839

—— and M. Bronckers 'WTO Law in the European Court of Justice' (2005) 42 CMLR 1313

Koskenniemi, M., 'Study on the Function and Scope of the *Lex Specialis* Rule and the Question of "Self-Contained Regimes"' (11 May 2005) UN Doc. ILC(LVII)/SG/FIL/CRD.1 (2005)

Krajewski, M., *National Regulation and Liberalization of Trade in Services* (London and The Hague: Kluwer, 2003)

Kurcz, B., 'Harmonisation by Means of Directives—Never Ending Story?' (2001) 12 EBL Rev 287

Laanatza, M. et al, 'Regionalization in the Middle East?', in M. Schulz et al (eds), *Regionalization in a Globalizing World: A Comparative Perspective on Forms, Actors and Processes* (London: Zed Books, 2001)

Lawrence, R., 'Emerging Regional Arrangements: Building Blocks or Stumbling Blocks?', in R. O'Brien (ed), *Finance and the International Economy, The AMEX Bank Review Prize Essays* (Oxford: OUP, 1991)

Leathley, C., 'The Mercosur Dispute Resolution System', The Royal Institute of International Affairs (Chatham House), Mercosur Study Group, 27 September 2002

Lim, S.S., 'The US–Singapore Free Trade Agreement: Fostering Confidence and Commitment in Asia' (2004) 34 Cal W Int L J 301

Lockhart, N.J.S. and Mitchell, A.D., 'Regional Trade Agreements under GATT 1994: An Exception and its Limits', in A.D. Mitchell, *Challenges and Prospects for the WTO* (London: Cameron May, 2005)

Lowe, V., 'Overlapping Jurisdictions in International Tribunals' (2000) 20 Aust YIL 1

Lustig, N., Bosworth B.P., and Lawrence, R.Z., *North American Free Trade: Assessing the Impact* (Washington, DC: Brookings, 1992)

Marceau, G. and Reiman, C., 'When and How Is an RTA Compatible with the WTO?' (2001) 28 LIEI 297

Maskus, K., 'Implications of Regional and Multilateral Agreements for Intellectual Property Rights' (1997) 20 World Economy 681

Mathis, J.H., *Regional Trade Agreements in the GATT/WTO: Article XXIV and the Internal Trade Requirement* (The Hague: T.M.C. Asser, 2002)

——, 'Mutual Recognition Agreements: Transatlantic Parties and the Limits to Non-tariff Barrier Regionalism in the WTO' (1998) 32 JWT 5

——, 'WTO Core Principles and Prohibition: Obligations Relating to Private Practices, National Competition Laws, and Implications for a Competition Policy Framework', UNCTAD Doc. UNCTAD/DITC/CLP/2003/2 (2003)

Matsushita, M. and Ahn, D. (eds), *WTO and East Asia: New Perspectives* (London: Cameron May, 2004)

Matthies, J., 'EC Rules of Origin from an Official's Point of View', in J. Bourgeois, E. Vermulst, and P. Waer (eds), *Rules Of Origin in International Trade: A Comparative Study* (Ann Arbor: U Michigan Press, 1993)

Mattli, W., *The Logic of Regional Integration* (Cambridge: CUP, 1999)

Mattoo, A., 'MFN and the GATS', in T. Cottier et al. (eds) *Regulatory Barriers and the Principle of Non-Discrimination in World Trade Law* (Ann Arbor: U Michigan Press, 2000)

Mayne, R., 'Regionalism, Bilateralism, and "TRIP Plus" Agreements: The Threat to Developing Countries' UNDP Human Development Report Office Occasional Paper (UNDP, 2005)

McCall Smith, J., 'The Politics of Dispute Settlement Design: Explaining Legalism in Regional Trade Pacts' (2000) 54 Int Org 137

McGee, A. and Weatherill, S., 'The Evolution of the Single Market—Harmonisation or Liberalisation?' (1990) 53 MLR 578

McLachlan, C., 'The Principle of Systemic Integration and Article 31(3)(c) of the Vienna Convention', (2005) 54 ICLQ 279

McMillan, J., 'Does Regional Integration Foster Open Trade', in K. Anderson and R. Blackhurst (eds), *Regional Integration and the Global Trading System* (London: Harvester Wheatsheaf, 1993)

McWhinney, E., 'Comparative International Law: Regional or Sectorial, Inter-Systemic Approaches to Contemporary International Law', in R.J. Dupuy (ed), *The Future of International Law in a Multicultural World* (The Hague: Martinus Nijhoff, 1984)

Medaglia, J.C., 'The Central American Regional Protocol on Access to Genetic and Biochemical Resources', in C. Bellmann, G. Dutfield, and R. Meléndez-Ortiz (eds), *Trading in Knowledge: Development Perspectives on TRIPS, Trade and Sustainability* (London: Earthscan, 2003)

Mercurio, B., 'The Impact of the AUSFTA on the Provision of Health Services in Australia' (2005) 26 Whittier L Rev 1051

Milner, H., 'Regional Economic Co-operation, Global Markets and Domestics Politics: A Comparisons of NAFTA and the Maastricht Treaty', in W.D. Coleman and G.R.D. Underhill (eds), *Regionalism and Global Economic Integration: Europe, Asia and the Americas* (London: Routledge, 1998)

Mortelmans, K., 'The Common Market, the Internal Market and the Single Market: What's in a Market?' (1998) 35 CMLR 101

——, 'The Relationship between the Treaty Rules and Community Measures for the Establishment and Functioning of the Internal Market—Towards a Concordance Rule' (2002) 39 CMLR 1303

Nakagawa, J., 'Lessons from the Japan-China "Welsh Onion War" ' (2002) 36 JWT 1019

Nesadurai, H.E.S., *Globalization, Domestic Politics and Regionalism: The ASEAN Free Trade Area* (London: Routledge, 2003)

Nicolaïdis, K. and Schaffer, G., 'Transnational Mutual Recognition Regimes: Governance without Global Government' (2005) 68 LCP 263

—— and M. Egan, 'Regional Policy Externality and Market Governance: Why Recognise Foreign Standards?' (2001) 8 JEPP 454

Nye, J.S., *Peace in Parts: Integration and Conflict in Regional Organization* (Boston: Little, Brown & Co, 1971)

OECD, *Competition Provisions in Regional Trade Agreements*, OECD Doc. COM/DAF/TD(2005)3/FINAL (2005)

——, *Regional Integration Agreements* (Paris: OECD, 2001)

——, *Regional Integration: Observed Trade and Other Economic Effects*, OECD Doc. TD/TC/WP(2001)19/FINAL (2001)

Oesch, M., 'Commentary on Turkey—Restrictions on Imports of Textiles and Clothing Products' *International Trade Law Reports*, Vol 5 (London: Cameron May, 2001)

Okediji, R., 'Back to Bilateralism? Pendulum Swings in International Intellectual Property Protection' (2003) 1 U of Ottawa Law & Tech J 125

Ortino, F. and Petersmann, E.-U. (eds), *The WTO Dispute Settlement System 1995–2003* (London, Boston: Kluwer, 1994)

Ortiz Mena, A., 'Dispute Settlement under NAFTA', in E. Chambers and P. Smith (eds), *NAFTA in the New Millennium* (San Diego: Center for US–Mexican Studies, 2002)

Oxfam, *Undermining Access to Medicines: Comparison of Five US FTAs* (2004), available at www.oxfamamerica.org/newsandpublications/publications/briefing_papers/pdfs/fta_comparison.pdf (visited 30 May 2006)

Paez, L., 'Americas Regionalism', in M. Godel and J. Gage (eds) *Multilateralism and Bilateralism after Cancun: Challenges and Opportunities of Regionalism* (Berne: Seco Publikation Welthandel No 2, April 2004)

Panagariya, A., 'Preferential Trade Liberalization: The Traditional Theory and New Developments' (2000) 38 J Econ Lit 287

Pauwelyn, J., 'A Typology of Multilateral Treaty Obligations. Are WTO Obligations Bilateral or Collective in Nature?' (2003) 14 EJIL 907

——, 'The Puzzle of WTO Safeguards and Regional Trade Agreements' (2004) 7 JIEL 109

Peng, S., 'The WTO Legalistic Approach and East Asia: From the Legal Culture Perspective' (2000) Asian Pac L & Policy J 1

Petersmann, E.-U. (ed), *Developing Countries in the Doha Round*, (Florence: EUI, 2005)

——, (ed), *International Trade Law and the GATT/WTO Dispute Settlement System* (London, Boston: Kluwer, 1997)

——, (ed), *Reforming the World Trading System: Legitimacy, Efficiency and Democratic Governance* (Oxford: OUP, 2005)

——, *Constitutional Functions and Constitutional Problems of International Economic Law*, Vol 3 (Fribourg, Switzerland: University Press, 1991)

——, 'Constitutional Approaches to International Law: Interrelationships between National, International and Cosmopolitan Constitutional Rules', in J. Bröhmer et al (eds), *Internationale Gemeinschaft und Menschenrechte* (Berlin: Carl Heymanns Verlag, 2005)

——, 'Constitutionalism and WTO Law: From a State-Centered Approach towards a Human Rights Approach in International Economic Law', in D.L.M. Kennedy and J.D. Southwick (eds), *The Political Economy of International Trade Law* (Cambridge: CUP, 2002)

——, 'Justice as Conflict Resolution: Proliferation, Fragmentation and Decentralization of Dispute Settlement in International Trade', European University Institute, Working Paper No 2004/10, available at www.iue.it/PUB/law04–10.pdf (visited 30 May 2006)

——, 'Multilevel Trade Governance Requires Multilevel Constitutionalism', in C. Joerges, and E.-U. Petersmann (eds), *Constitutionalism, Multilevel Trade Governance and Social Regulation* (Oxford: Hart, 2006)

Productivity Commission (Australia), *Evaluation of the Mutual Recognition Schemes* (Canberra, 2003)

Rajkumar, R., 'The Central American Free Trade Agreement: An End Run Around The Doha Declaration on TRIPS and Public Health' (2005) 15 Alb L J Sci & Tech 433

Ramírez Robles, E., *Solución de Controversias en los Acuerdos Celebrados entre México y la Comunidad Europea* (Guadalajara: Universidad de Guadalajara, 2003)

Reich, N., 'Competition between Legal Orders: A New Paradigm of EC Law?' (1992) 29 CMLR 459

Reiter, J., 'The EU–Mexico Free Trade Agreement: Assessing the EU approach to Regulatory Issues in Regionalism, Multilateralism and Economic Integration, the Recent Experience', in G.P. Sampson and S. Woolcock (eds), *Regionalism, Multilateralism and Economic Integration, the Recent Experience* (Hong Kong: UN University, 2003)

Rezzouk, M., 'The Organization of Petroleum Exporting Countries, Competition and the World Trade Organization: Might a WTO Agreement on Competition Constitute a Threat to OPEC?', UNCTAD Doc. UNCTAD/DITC/CLP/2003/11 (2004)

Robert, M., *Negotiating NAFTA, Explaining the Outcome in Culture, Textiles, Autos and Pharmaceuticals* (Toronto: U Toronto Press, 2000)

Roessler, F., 'The Relationship between Regional Integration Agreements and the Multilateral Trade Order', in K. Anderson, and R. Blackhurst (eds) *Regional Integration and the Global Trading System* (London: Harvester Wheatsheaf and New York: St. Martin's Press, 1993)

Romano, C., 'The Proliferation of International Judicial Bodies: The Pieces of the Puzzle' (1999) 31 NYU J Int L & Pol 709

Rott, P., 'Minimum Harmonization for the Completion of the Internal Market? The Example of Consumer Sales Law' (2003) 40 CMLR 1107

Russett, B., *International Regions and the International System* (Chicago: Rand-McNally, 1967)

Sagar, J., 'The Labour and Environment Chapters of the United States-Chile Free Trade Agreement: An Improvement over the Weak Enforcement Provisions of the NAFTA Side Agreements on Labour and the Environment' (2004) 21 Ariz J Int & Comp L 913

Schiff, M., 'Will the Real "Natural Trading Partner" Please Stand Up?', World Bank Policy Research Working Paper 2161 (World Bank, 1999)

Schmidt, S.K., 'The Impact of Mutual Recognition—Inbuilt Limits and Domestic Responses to the Single Market' (2002) 9 JEPP 935

Schreuer, C., 'Regionalism v. Universalism' (1995) 6 EJIL 477

Schulz, M., Söderbaum, F. and Öjendal, J. (eds), *Regionalization in a Globalizing World: A Comparative Perspective on Forms, Actors and Processes* (London: Zed Books, 2001)

Shams, H., 'Regional Integration: Comparative Experience—Introduction' (2004) 10 Law & Bus Rev Am 457

Sharma, S.C. and Chua, S.Y., 'ASEAN: Economic Integration and Intra-regional Trade' (2000) 7 Appl Econ Lett 165

Sher, M., 'Chapter 20 Dispute Resolution under NAFTA: Fact or Fiction?' (2003) 35 Geo Wash Int L Rev 1001

Shibata, H., 'The Theory of Economic Unions: A Comparative Analysis of Customs Unions, Free Trade Areas and Tax Unions', in C.S. Shoup (ed) *Fiscal Harmonization In Common Markets*, Volume 1: Theory (New York: Columbia UP, 1967)

Silva, V., 'Cooperation on Commodity Policy in Latin America in Latin American and Caribbean Bilateral Trade Agreements' (UN Economic Commission for Latin America and the Caribbean (ECLAC), Santiago: 2004)

Slot, P.J., 'Harmonisation' (1996) 21 EL Rev 378

Smith, M., 'Regions and Regionalism', in B. White, R. Little, and M. Smith (eds), *Issues in World Politics*, 3rd ed. (Houndmills Basingstoke: Palgrave, 2005)

Snape, R.H. and Boswort, M., 'Advancing Services Negotiations', in J.J. Schott, (ed), *The World Trading System: Challenges Ahead* (Washington, DC: Institute for International Economics, 1996)

——, 'History and Economics of GATT's Article XXIV', in K. Anderson and R. Blackhurst (eds) *Regional Integration and the Global Trading System* (London: Harvester Wheatsheaf and New York: St. Martin's Press, 1993)

Söderbaum, F., and Shaw, T.M., *Theories of New Regionalism* (Houndmills, Basingstoke: Palgrave, 2003)

Soloaga, I. and Winters, A., 'Regionalism in the Nineties: What Effect on Trade' (2001) 12 N Amer J Econ Finance 1

Stephenson, S.M., 'GATS and Regional Integration', in P. Sauvé and R. Stern (eds), *GATS 2000: New Directions in Services Trade Liberalization* (Washington DC: Brookings, 2000)

——, 'Mutual Recognition and its Role in Trade Facilitation' (1999) 33 JWT 141

——, 'A comparison of existing services trade arrangements within APEC', in C. Findlay and T. Warren (eds), *Impediments to Trade in Services, Measurement and Policy Implications* (London: Routledge, 2000)

——, 'Regional versus Multilateral Liberalisation of Services' (2002) 1 WTR 187

Stubbs, R., 'Asia-Pacific Regionalism versus Globalization', in W.D. Coleman and

G.R.D. Underhill (eds), *Regionalism and Global Economic Integration: Europe, Asia and the Americas* (London: Routledge, 1998)

Sun, J.M. and J. Pelkmans, 'Regulatory Competition in the Single Market' (1995) 33 JCMS 67

Sutherland, P. et al., *The Future of the WTO: Addressing Institutional Challenges in the New Millennium* (Geneva: WTO, 2004)

Sykes, A., 'Constructive Unilateral Threats in International Commercial Relations: The Limited Case for Section 301' (1993) 23 Law & Policy Int Bus 263

Tan, L., 'Will ASEAN Economic Integration Progress Beyond a Free Trade Area?' (2004) 53 ICLQ 935

Tang, D., 'Effects of the Regional Trading Arrangements on Trade: Evidence from the NAFTA, ANZCER and ASEAN Countries, 1989–2000' (2005) 14 J Int Trade Econ Devel 241

Tavares de Araujo, J. and Tineo, L., 'Harmonization of Competition Policies among Mercosur Countries' (1998) 24 Brook J Int L 441

Terada, T., 'Constructing an "East Asian" Concept and Growing Regional Identity: From EAEC to ASEAN+3' (2003) 16 Pac Rev 251

Thomas, K.P. and Tetreault, M.A. (eds), *Racing to Regionalize, International Political Economy Yearbook*, Volume 11 (Boulder, CO: Lynne Reinner, 1999)

Thornton, J. and Goglio, A., 'Regional Bias and Intra-regional Trade in Southeast Asia' (2002) 9 Appl Econ Lett 205

Tongzon, J.L., *The Economics of Southeast Asia: Before and After the Crisis*, 2nd ed. (Cheltenham: Edward Elgar, 2002)

Trachtman, J.P., 'Towards Open Recognition? Standardization and Regional Integration under Article XXIV of GATT' (2003) 6 JIEL 459

Trubek, D. and Trubek, L., 'Hard and Soft Law in the Construction of Social Europe: The Role of the Open Method of Co-ordination' (2005) 11 ELJ 343

United Nations Development Programme, *Making Global Trade Work for People* (London: Earthscan, 2003)

United Nations Environment Programme, International Regime on Access and Benefit-Sharing: Proposals for an International Regime on Access and Benefit-sharing, adopted 7 January 2003, UN Doc. UNEP/CBD/MYPOW/6 (2003)

US Department of Labor, *A Review of the Likely Economic Impact of NAFTA on the US* (Washington DC, 1992)

US Department of State, *Suggested Charter for an International Trade Organization of the United Nations*, Washington DC, 1946

US International Trade Commission, *Economy-Wide Modeling of the Economic Implications of a FTA with Mexico and a NAFTA with Canada and Mexico* (Washington DC, 1992)

US Tariff Commission, *Report on the Havana Charter for an International Trade Organization, for the Committee on Ways and Means, House of Representatives* (Washington DC, 1949)

United States Trade Representative, *Final Environmental Review of the US-Chile FTA*, June 2003, available at www.ustr.gov (visited 30 May 2006)

——, *Interim Environmental Review of the US–Andean FTA*, February 2005, available at www.ustr.gov (visited 30 May 2006)

Van Panhuys, J.H.F., 'Regional or General International Law? A Misleading Dilemma' (1961) 8 Neth Int L Rev 146

Vega, G.C. and Winham, G.R., 'The Role of NAFTA Dispute Settlement in the Management of Canadian, Mexican and US Trade and Investment Relations' (2002) 28 ONLR, 651

Verhoosel, G., 'The Use of Investor-State Arbitration under Bilateral Investment Treaties to Seek Relief for Breaches of WTO Law' (2003) 6 JIEL 493

Vermulst, E. and Waer, P., 'European Community Rules of Origin as Commercial Policy Instruments?' (1990) 24 JWT 55

Viner, J., *The Customs Union Issue* (New York: Carnegie Endowment for International Peace, 1950)

Vivas-Eugui, D., 'Regional and Bilateral Agreements and a TRIPS plus world: the case of the FTAA' TRIPS Issues Paper No 1 (2003), available at www.qiap.ca/documents/ FTAASupptableA42.pdf (visited 30 May 2006)

Von Heydebrand u.d. Lasa, H.-C., 'Free Movement of Foodstuffs, Consumer Protection and Food Standards in the European Community: Has the Court of Justice got it Wrong?' (1991) 16 EL Rev 391

Walker, N., 'The EU and the WTO: Constitutionalism in a New Key', in: G. de Búrca and J. Scott (eds), *The EU and the WTO: Legal and Constitutional Issues* (Oxford: Hart, 2001)

Wang, J., 'China's Regional Trade Agreements: The Law, Geopolitics, and Impact on the Multilateral Trading System' (2004) 8 SYIL 119

Wang, W., 'CEPA: A Lawful Free Trade Agreement under "One Country, Two Customs Territories?" ' (2004) 10 Law & Bus Rev Am 647

Weatherill, S., 'Recent Case Law Concerning the Free Movement of Goods: Mapping the Frontiers of Market Deregulation' (1999) 36 CMLR 51

——, 'Why Object to the Harmonisation of Private Law?' (2004) 5 ERPL 633

Weissman, R., 'Dying for Drugs: How CAFTA Will Undermine Access to Essential Medicines' (2004), available at www.health-now.org/site/article.php?articleId= 75&menuId=13 (visited 30 May 2006)

Woolcock, S., 'A Framework for Assessing Regional Trade Agreements: WTO-plus', in G.P. Sampson, and S. Woolcock (eds), *Regionalism, Multilateralism and Economic Integration, the Recent Experience* (Hong Kong: UNU, 2003)

World Bank, *Global Economic Prospects 2005: Trade, Regionalism and Development* (Washington DC: World Bank, 2005)

World Commission on Environment and Development, *Our Common Future* (Oxford: OUP, 1987)

World Trade Organization, *Regionalism and the World Trading System* (Geneva: WTO, 1995)

——, *World Trade Report* (Geneva: WTO, 2003)

Wouters, J. and Coppens, D., 'Domestic Regulation Within the Framework of GATS', in K. Byttebier and K. Van den Borght (eds), *Issues of International Legal Trade Policy and Implementation: Challenges for the World Trade Organization* (London: Cameron May, 2006)

Yeung, M.T., Perdikis, N. and Kerr, W.A., *Regional Trading Blocs in the Global Economy: The EU and ASEAN* (Cheltenham UK, Northampton, MA: Edward Elgar, 1999)

Zahrnt, V., 'How Regionalization can be a Pillar of a More Effective World Trade Organization' (2005) 39 JWT 671

Index